Part 2
The Environment of Management   73

Chapter Three
The Organizational Environment   74

A Case in Contrast

Chapter Four
The Global Environment   108

A Case in Contrast

Chapter Five

Ethics, Social Responsibility,
and Diversity 144

A Case in Contrast

Part 3

Managing Decision Making
and Planning 191

Chapter Six

The Manager as a Decision Maker 192

A Case in Contrast

Contemporary Management

Gareth R. Jones

Texas A&M University

Jennifer M. George

Texas A&M University

Charles W. L. Hill

University of Washington

Boston   Burr Ridge, IL   Dubuque, IA   Madison, WI   New York   San Francisco   St. Louis
Bangkok   Bogatá   Carácas   Lisbon   London   Madrid   Mexico City   Milan
New Delhi   Seoul   Singapore   Sydney   Taipei   Toronto

For Nicholas and Julia
  G.R.J.   J.M.G.

For Alexandra, Elizabeth, Charlotte,
and Michelle Hill
  C.W.L.H.

McGraw-Hill Higher Education 🖉

*A Division of The **McGraw-Hill** Companies*

CONTEMPORARY MANAGEMENT
Copyright © 2000, 1998 by The McGraw-Hill Companies, Inc. All rights reserved. Printed in the United States of America. Except as permitted under the United States Copyright Act of 1976, no part of this publication may be reproduced or distributed in any form or by any means, or stored in a data base or retrieval system, without the prior written permission of the publisher.

This book is printed on acid-free paper.

domestic   1 2 3 4 5 6 7 8 9 0 VNH/VNH 9 0 9 8 7 6 5 4 3 2 1 0 9
international   1 2 3 4 5 6 7 8 9 0 VNH/VNH 9 0 9 8 7 6 5 4 3 2 1 0 9

ISBN 0-07-228147-2

Vice president/Editor-in-chief: *Michael W. Junior*
Publisher: *Craig S. Beytien*
Senior Sponsoring editor: *John E. Biernat*
Developmental editor: *Christine Scheid*
Marketing manager: *Ellen Cleary*
Senior project manager: *Mary Conzachi*
Production supervisor: *Kari Geltemeyer*
Designer: *Kiera Cunningham*
Cover and interior illustrations: © *Jose Ortega, Stock Illustration Source*
Senior photo research coordinator: *Keri Johnson*
Photo researcher: *Charlotte Goldman*
Supplement coordinator: *Cathy L. Tepper*
Compositor: *Precision Graphics*
Typeface: *10.5/12 Baskerville*
Printer: *Von Hoffmann Press, Inc.*

Library of Congress Cataloging-in-Publication Data

Jones, Gareth R.
    Contemporary management / Gareth R. Jones. Jennifer M. George, Charles W.L. Hill. -- 2nd ed.
        p.   cm.
    Accompanying student CD-ROM contains interactive quiz for exam prep, the complete PowerPoint Presentation, and Video Clips.
    Includes index.
    ISBN 0-07-228147-2
    1. Management.   I. George, Jennifer M.   II. Hill, Charles W.L.
III. Title. IV. Title: Management.
HD31.J597   2000
658--dc21   99-30271
                                                          CIP

INTERNATIONAL EDITION   ISBN 0-07117608-X
Copyright © 2000. Exclusive rights by The McGraw-Hill Companies, Inc. for manufacture and export.
This book cannot be re-exported from the country to which it is consigned by McGraw-Hill.
The International Edition is not available in North America.
http://www.mhhe.com

Brief Contents

Contents

Part 4

Managing Organizational
Architecture 267

Chapter Eight

Managing Organizational Structure 268

A Case in Contrast

Chapter Nine

Organizational Control and Culture 310

A Case in Contrast

Chapter Twelve
Motivation   424

Chapter Thirteen
Leadership   460

Chapter Sixteen
Organizational Conflict,
Negotiation, Politics, and Change 572

A Case in Contrast

Part 6
Managing Essential Operations
and Processes 609

Chapter Seventeen
Managing Information Systems
and Technologies 610

A Case in Contrast

Chapter Eighteen

Operations Management:
Managing Quality, Efficiency,
and Responsiveness to Customers 642

Chapter Nineteen

The Management of Innovation, Product Development, and Entrepreneurship 678

A Case in Contrast

Preface

Encouraged by the favorable reception and level of support that greeted the first edition of *Contemporary Management* we set out to revise and develop the second edition of our book in significant ways based on the reactions and suggestions of both users and reviewers. Both users and reviewers were very supportive of our attempts to integrate contemporary management theories and approaches into the analysis of management and organizations. Our goal has been to distill new and classic theorizing and research into a contemporary framework that is compatible with the traditional focus on management as planning, leading, organizing, and controlling, but which transcends this traditional approach.

Users and reviewers report that students appreciate and enjoy our presentation of management, a presentation which makes its relevance obvious even to those who lack exposure to "a real-life" management context. Students like both the book's content and the way we relate management theory to real-life examples to drive home the message that management matters both because it determines how well organizations perform, and because managers and organizations affect the lives of people who work inside them and people outside the organization, such as customers and shareholders.

The contemporary nature of our approach can be seen most clearly by examining our table of contents, and by perusing our treatment of management issues. The concepts and theories we discuss show how managers deal with the many new issues and challenges they face, such as promoting and sustaining a competitive advantage, managing new information technology, developing big global organizations, and managing a diverse workforce.

Unique Coverage

As you will see, we have some chapters that are not contained in any other management book. Chapter 11, for example, "The Manager as a Person," discusses managers as real people with their own personalities, strengths, weaknesses, opportunities, and problems. From this chapter, students will grasp that managers are people like themselves. Students will also appreciate the challenges managers face and how, as future managers, they can successfully meet them. Another unique chapter for a management book, Chapter 16, "Organizational Conflict, Politics, Negotiation, and Change," discusses how managers can successfully manage organizational politics, conflict, negotiation, and change. The chapter gives students a hands-on look at managing crucial organizational processes.

Emphasis on Applied Management

Our contemporary approach also is illustrated by the way we have chosen to organize and discuss contemporary management issues. We have gone to great lengths to bring the manager back into the subject matter of management. That is, we have written our chapters from the perspective of current or future managers to illustrate, in a hands-on way, the problems and opportunities they face and how they can effectively meet them. For example, in Chapter 5 we provide an integrated treatment of ethics, diversity, and sexual harassment that clearly explains their significance to practicing managers. In Chapter 7, on planning and strategy, we provide an integrated treatment of highlighting the choices managers face as they go about performing the planning role. We emphasize important issues managers face and how management theory, research, and practice can help them and their organizations be effective.

This applied approach can be most clearly seen in the last three chapters of the book in which we cover the topics of managing information systems, technology, and operations management, topics which have tended to be difficult to teach to new management students in an interesting and novel way. Our chapters provide a student-friendly, behavioral approach to understanding the management processes entailed in information systems, operations management, and innovation

and entrepreneurship. Our reviewers noted, while most books' treatment of these issues is dry and quantitative, ours comes alive with its focus on how managers can manage the people and processes necessary to give an organization a competitive advantage. In fact, the management of information to create a competitive advantage is a major theme of our book. Our communications chapter, information systems chapter, and internet exercises provide a state-of-the-art account of new developments in computer information systems that students will understand and enjoy.

Rich and Relevant Examples

An important feature of our book is the way we use real-world examples and stories about managers and companies to drive home the applied lessons to students. Our reviewers were unanimous in their praise of the sheer range and depth of the rich, interesting examples we use to illustrate the chapter material and make it come alive. Moreover, unlike other books, our boxes are seamlessly integrated in the text: They are an integral part of the learning experience, and not tacked on and unrelated to the text itself. This is central to our pedagogical approach.

Each chapter opens with a feature called "A Case in Contrast" which contrasts the behaviors and actions of two managers and organizations to help demonstrate the uncertainty and challenges surrounding the management process. The chapters then contain various kinds of boxes; the boxes entitled Management Insights illustrate the topics of the chapter, but the "Ethics in Action," "Managing Globally," and "Focus on Diversity" boxes examine the chapter topic from each of these perspectives. These are not "boxes" in the traditional sense, meaning they're not disembodied from the chapter narrative. These thematic applications are fully integrated into the reading. Students will no longer be forced to decide whether to read "boxed" material. It is also important to make these features interesting to students so that they engage students while illustrating the chapter material.

New to this edition is a new feature called "Tips for Managers" which distills the lessons that students can take from the chapter and use to develop their management skills.

Flexible Organization

Another factor of interest to instructors concerns the way we have designed the grouping of chapters to allow instructors to teach the chapter material in the order that best suits their needs. For example, the more micro-oriented instructor can follow Chapters 1 and 2 with 11 through 16 and then do the more macro chapters. The more macro-oriented professor can follow Chapters 1 and 2 with 3 through 7, jump to 17, 18, 19, and then do the micro Chapters 11–16. Our sequencing of parts and chapters gives the instructor considerable freedom to design the course that best suits him or her. Instructors are not tied to the planning, organizing, leading, controlling framework, even though our presentation remains consistent with this approach.

Experiential Learning Features

We have given considerable time and attention to developing state-of-the-art experiential end-of-chapter learning exercises that we hope will also drive home the meaning of management to students. Grouped together at the end of each chapter in the section called Management in Action, they include:

TOPICS FOR DISCUSSION AND ACTION A set of chapter-related questions and points for reflection some of which ask students to research actual management issues and learn first-hand from practicing managers.

BUILDING MANAGEMENT SKILLS A self-development exercise that asks students to apply what they have learned to their own experience of organizations and managers or to the experiences of others.

SMALL GROUP BREAKOUT EXERCISE This unique exercise is designed to allow instructors in large section classes to utilize interactive experiential exercises in groups of 3–4 students. The instructor calls on students to break up into small groups–simply by turning to people around them–and all students participate in the exercise in-class, and a mechanism is provided for the different groups to share what they have learned with each other.

EXPLORING THE WORLD WIDE WEB Two internet exercises designed to draw students into the web and give them experience of the new information systems, while applying what they have learned.

MANAGEMENT CASE A case for discussion, drawing on contemporary, real-world managers and organizations, which we have written to highlight chapter themes and issues.

MANAGEMENT CASE IN THE NEWS An actual article from a business publication like *The Wall Street Journal* or *Business Week* that shows students how practicing managers are facing the issues they have just learned about.

Our idea is that instructors can select from these exercises and vary them over the semester so that students can learn the meaning of management through many different avenues. These exercises complement the chapter material and have been class tested to add to the overall learning experience, and students report that they both learn from them and enjoy them.

Integrated Learning System

Great care was used in the creation of the supplemental materials to accompany *Contemporary Management*. The textbook authors were involved in the entire process to ensure quality and consistency with the textbook. Whether you are a seasoned faculty or a newly minted instructor, you'll find our support materials to be the most thorough and thoughtful ever created!

Student Resources

STUDENT STUDY GUIDE written by Ernest King of the University of Southern Mississippi. A printed choice for those students unavailable to access the CD-Rom or the website. It includes an outline of each of the chapters, multiple choice, true/false, and application questions, a "Student Journal," and Video exercises.

STUDENT CD-ROM With each new book, there will be included a CD-ROM containing an interactive quiz similar to the exam prep disk of the previous edition. Students can use these quizzes to prep for exams based on the content of each chapter. This CD will also include the complete PowerPoint Presentation, and Video Clips. Your students will value this special FREE CD with each new book.

WEBSITE AND ONLINE LEARNING CENTER at http://www.mhhe.com/jones2e with content by George Ruggiero of the Community College of Rhode Island. A resource for faculty and students, the CM website contains information for lecture and learning enhancement. Along with features of the text and author biographical information, you'll find Web exercises, outside research assignments, synopses of current articles relating to chapter material and related discussion questions, links to national and international news, a career area for student, and other course-enhancing materials.

Instructor Resources

INSTRUCTOR'S RESOURCE MANUAL
Updated by Ellyn Brecher and Susan Hilbert from Temple University contains:

- Detailed chapter outlines
- Detailed answers on all the Management in Action, or end-of-chapter, material
- Notes on using PowerPoint Presentation and Acetates
- Notes on Video Cases and Profiles in Management Videos
- Two lecture enhancers per chapter
- Transparency Master for all significant figures from the text

TEST BANK by Thomas Quirk of Webster University. This volume contains over 100 test items per chapter, including multiple choice, true/false, applied, and essay. Each question is ranked in terms of difficulty and page-referenced to the textbook.

COMPUTEST TEST GENERATION SYSTEM An easy-to-use computerized version of the test bank available in two versions: Windows and Macintosh.

POWERPOINT CLASSROOM PRE-SENTATION SOFTWARE created by Richard T. Christoph, James Madison University. Over 300 images for use in the classroom or as handouts are packaged ready-to-run with Windows installation program and a slide viewer. No additional software is required, but can be modified with Microsoft PowerPoint for Windows.

PROFILES IN MANAGEMENT VIDEO SERIES Ten segments profiling the management styles and practices of real managers on the job. Students will get real insight into the job of managers at various levels within an organization, and among very different types of businesses. Companies profiled include: Second City, Handy Andy, Specialized Bicycle, Tellabs, Washburn Guitars, Southwest Airlines, and 1st Chicago Bank.

VIDEO CASES AND NOTES For 17 of 19 chapters, a 7–12 minute video segment is provided that ties concepts from the text directly to a real company profile. Cases and additional instructional material is provided in the Instructor's Manual allowing for ultimate flexibility for faculty.

INSTRUCTOR PRESENTATION CD-ROM This is state-of-the-art technology that provides a single resource for faculty to customize in-class presentations. This CD-ROM contains:

- Instructor's Resource Manual
- Test Bank and Computest
- PowerPoint Classroom Presentation Software
- Student CD-Rom Quiz
- Video Clips
- Special Presentation Platform that allows faculty to build classroom presentations in sequence using the resources from the CD.

WEBSITE AND ONLINE LEARNING CENTER at http://www.mhhe.com/jones2e, as detailed above, the website contains an Instructor Online Learning Center with materials and resources to enhance classroom instruction.

Acknowledgments

Finding a way to integrate and present the rapidly growing literature on contemporary management and make it interesting and meaningful for students is not an easy task. In revising *Contemporary Management* we have been fortunate to have had the assistance of several people who have contributed greatly to the book's final form. First, we are grateful to John Biernat and Craig Beytien, our editor and publisher respectively, for their ongoing support and commitment to our project, and for always finding ways to provide the resources that we needed to improve and refine our book in its second edition. Second, we are grateful to Christine Scheid, our developmental editor, for her ongoing creative input into our project and for providing us with concise and timely feedback and information from professors and reviewers that have allowed us to shape the book to the needs of its intended market. Third, we are grateful to Ellen Cleary, our marketing manager for her unflagging support in helping us to articulate the meaning and message of our book. We also thank Joanne Tinsley, our external developmental editor, for her many useful suggestions and for helping us to present the material in the chapters in a way that ensures its integrated flow within and between the book's chapters and Pat Herbst, our copyeditor, for her work in improving the flow and readability of our manuscript. Finally, we thank Kiera Cunningham for executing an awe-inspiring design, Mary Conzachi for coordinating the production process, and Patsy Hartmangruber for providing us with excellent graphic support. We are also grateful to the many colleagues and reviewers who provided us with useful and detailed feedback, perceptive comments and valuable suggestions for improving the manuscript.

Producing any competitive work is a challenge. Producing a truly market-driven textbook requires tremendous effort beyond simply obtaining reviews on a draft manuscript. Our goal was simple with the development of *Contemporary Management,* to be the most customer-driven principles of management text and supplement package ever published! With the goal to exceed the expectations of both faculty and students, we executed one of the most aggressive product development plans ever undertaken in textbook publishing. Well over 200 faculty took part in developmental activities ranging from regional focus groups to manuscript reviews and surveys–and that was just for the first edition. For the second edition, we obtained 13 more full book reviews, and sent out more than 100 surveys. Consequently, we're confident in assuring you and your students, our customers, that every aspect of our text and support package reflects your advice and needs. As you review it we're confident that over and over your reaction will be "they listened!"

Our thanks to those professors who gave their comments and suggestions by reviewing the entire text:

Dianne Coleman, *Wichita State University*
Suzanne Crampton, *Grand Valley State University*
George DeLodzia, *University of Rhode Island*
Pat Dickson, *University of Louisville*
Bonnie Fremgen, *University of Notre Dame*
Ronald Gordon, *Florida Metropolitan State University*
John Hughes, *Texas Tech University*
Rick Lester, *University of North Alabama*
Thomas Lloyd, *Westmoreland County Community College*
Dan Sherman, *Rose-Hulman Institute of Technology*
Roy Shin, *Indiana University*
Gary Weaver, *University of Delaware*
Jonathan Young, *Thomas College*

We would also like to specially thank all of those who took the time to complete our survey:

Dave Arnott, *Dallas Baptist University*
Hal Babson, *Columbus State Community College*

Peggy D. Brewer, *Eastern Kentucky University*
David Burnis, *Pennsylvania State University*
Jacob Cohen, *Syracuse University*
Dianne Coleman, *Wichita State University*
Lyle Courtnage, *Rocky Mountain College*
Frederick J. DeCasperis, *Siena College*
Dick Devlin, *University of New Hampshire*
Ceasar Douglas, *Grand Valley State University*
Bill Dow, *University of St. Francis*
Vincent Dragone, *Buffalo State College*
Karen Eboch, *Bowling Green State University*
Joseph Flowers, *Indiana Wesleyan University*
Normandie Gaitley, *York College of Pennsylvania*
Eric Goodman, *Fort Hays State University*
Janet Gillespie, *Elmhurst College*
Gwendolyn Jones, *The University of Akron*
Nancy Landrum, *New Mexico State University*
Thomas R. Lerra, *Quinsigamond Community College*
James C. McElroy, *Iowa State University*
Paul Mochella, *University of Hartford*
Paula Morrow, *Iowa State University*
Bev Pray, *Union University*
Barbara Ribbens, *University of Evansville*
Irving E. Richards, *Cuyahoga Community College*
Roy Simerly, *East Carolina University*
John T. Snyder, *St. Charles County Community College*
James Terborg, *University of Oregon*
Linda Tibbetts, *Sinclair Community College*
Gary Weaver, *University of Delaware*
James A. Wolff, *Wichita State University*

Our thanks to these faculty who contributed greatly to the creation of the first edition of *Contemporary Management:*

Fred Anderson, *Indiana University of Pennsylvania*
Jacquelyn Appeldorn, *Dutchess Community College*
Barry Armandi, *SUNY–Old Westbury*
Douglas E. Ashby, *Lewis & Clark Community College*
Barry S. Axe, *Florida Atlantic University*
Jeff Bailey, *University of Idaho*
Robert M. Ballinger, *Siena College*
Donita Whitney-Bammerlin, *Kansas State University*
Sandy Jeanquart Barone, *Murray State University*

Lorraine P. Bassette, *Prince George's Community College*
Gene Baten, *Central Connecticut State University*
Josephine Bazan, *Holyoke Community College*
Hrach Bedrosian, *New York University*
Jack C. Blanton, *University of Kentucky*
David E. Blevins, *University of Arkansas at Little Rock*
Karen Boroff, *Seton Hall University*
Barbara Boyington, *Brookdale Community College*
Charles Braun, *Marshall University*
Gil Brookins, *Siena College*
Patricia M. Buhler, *Goldey-Beacom College*
David Cadden, *Quinnipiac College*
Thomas Campbell, *University of Texas–Austin*
Thomas Carey, *Western Michigan University*
Daniel P. Chamberlin, *Regents University–CRB*
Nicolette DeVille Christensen, *Guilford College*
Anthony A. Cioffi, *Lorain County Community College*
Sharon F. Clark, *Lebanon Valley College*
Sharon Clinebell, *University of Northern Colorado*
Dianne Coleman, *Wichita State University*
Elizabeth Cooper, *University of Rhode Island*
Thomas D. Craven, *York College of Pennsylvania*
Kent Curran, *University of North Carolina*
Arthur L. Darrow, *Bowling Green State University*
Ron DiBattista, *Bryant College*
Thomas Duening, *University of Houston*
Charles P. Duffy, *Iona College*
Subhash Durlabhji, *Northwestern State University*
Robert A. Eberle, *Iona College*
Robert R. Edwards, *Arkansas Tech University*
William Eldridge, *Kean College*
Pat Ellsberg, *Lower Columbia College*
Stan Elsea, *Kansas State University*
Dale Finn, *University of New Haven*
Charles Flaherty, *University of Minnesota*
Robert Flemming, *Delta State University*
P Jeanie M. Forray, *Eastern Connecticut State University*
Ellen Frank, *Southern Connecticut State University*
Joseph A. Gemma, *Providence College*
Neal Gersony, *University of New Haven*
Donna H. Giertz, *Parkland College*
Leo Giglio, *Dowling College*
David Glew, *Texas A&M University*

Carol R. Graham, *Western Kentucky University*
Matthew Gross, *Moraine Valley Community College*
John Hall, *University of Florida*
Eric L. Hansen, *California State University–Long Beach*
Justin U. Harris, *Strayer College*
Allison Harrison, *Mississippi State University*
Eileen Bartels Hewitt, *University of Scranton*
Stephen R. Hiatt, *Catawba College*
Tammy Bunn Hiller, *Bucknell University*
Jerry Horgesheiner, *Southern Utah State*
Gordon K. Huddleston, *South Carolina State University*
John Hughes, *Texas Tech University*
Charleen Jaeb, *Cuyahoga Community College*
Richard E. Johe, *Salem College*
Jehan G. Kavoosi, *Clarion University of Pennsylvania*
Ken Lehmenn, *Forsyth Technical Community College*
Lianlian Lin, *California State Polytechnic University*
Grand Lindstrom, *University of Wyoming*
Mary Lou Lockerby, *College of DuPage*
Esther Long, *University of Florida*
Bryan Malcolm, *University of Wisconsin*
Z. A. Malik, *Governors State University*
Mary J. Mallott, *George Washington University*
Reuben McDaniel, *University of Texas*
John A. Miller, *Bucknell University*
Thomas C. Neil, *Clark Atlanta University*
Brian Niehoff, *Kansas State University*
Judy Nixon, *University of Tennessee*
Cliff Olson, *Southern Adventists University*
Dane Partridge, *University of Southern Indiana*
Sheila J. Pechinski, *University of Maine*
Fred Pierce, *Northwood University*
Laynie Pizzolatto, *Nicholls State University*
Eleanor Polster, *Florida International University*
Paul Preston, *University of Texas–San Antonio*
Samuel Rabinowitz, *Rutgers University–Camden*
Gerald Ramsey, *Indiana University Southeast*
Charles Rarick, *Transylvania University*
Robert A. Reber, *Western Kentucky University*
Bob Redick, *Lincoln Land Community College*
Deborah Britt Roebuck, *Kennesaw State University*
Harvey Rothenberg, *Regis University*
George Ruggiero, *Community College of Rhode Island*

Cyndy Ruszkowski, *Illinois State University*
Michael Santoro, *Rutgers University*
Amit Shah, *Frostburg State University*
Richard Ray Shreve, *Indiana University Northwest*
Sidney Siegel, *Drexel University*
Raymond D. Smith, *Towson State University*
William Soukup, *University of San Diego*
H. T. Stanton, Jr., *Barton College*
Nestor St. Charles, *Dutchess Community College*
Lynda St. Clair, *Bryant College*
Gerald Schoenfeld, Jr., *James Madison University*
Michael Shapiro, *Dowling College*
Sharon Sloan, *Northwood University*
William A. Sodeman, *University of Southern Indiana*
Carl J. Sonntag, *Pikes Peak Community College*
Charles I. Stubbart, *Southern Illinois University*
James K. Swenson, *Moorhead State University*
Karen Ann Tarnoff, *East Tennessee State University*
Jerry L. Thomas, *Arapahoe Community College*
Kenneth Thompson, *DePaul University*
John Todd, *University of Arkansas*
Thomas Turk, *Chapman University*
Linn Van Dyne, *Michigan State University*
Jaen Vanhoegaerden, *Ashridge Management College*
Stuart H. Warnock, *University of Southern Colorado*
Toomy Lee Waterson, *Northwood University*
Philip A. Weatherford, *Embry-Riddle Aeronautical University*
Ben Weeks, *St. Xavier University*
W. J. Williams, *Chicago State University*
Robert Williams, *University of North Alabama*
Shirley A. Wilson, *Bryant College*
Michael A. Yahr, *Robert Morris College*
D. Kent Zimmerman, *James Madison University*

Finally, we are grateful to our families for supporting us, and providing us with much fun, joy, and affection as we went about the hard work of writing our book. It is to them that we dedicate this book.

G.R.J./J.M.G.
College Station, Texas

C.W.L.H.
Seattle, Washington

Authors

Gareth Jones

is a Professor of Management in the Lowry Mays College and Graduate School of Business and the Graduate School of Business at Texas A&M University. He received both his B.A. and Ph.D. from the University of Lancaster, U.K. He previously held teaching and research appointments at the University Warwick, Michigan State University, and the University of Illinois at Urbana–Champaign.

He specializes in both stategic management and organizational theory and is well known for his research that applies transaction cost analysis to explain many forms of strategic behavior. He is currently interested in strategy process and issues concerning the development of trust and the role of affect in the strategic decision making process. He has published many articles in leading journals of the field and his recent work has appeared in the *Academy of Management Review, Journal of International Business Studies, Human Relations,* and the *Journal of Management.* One of his articles won the *Academy of Management Journal* Best Paper Award, and he is one of the most prolific authors in the *Academy of Management Review.* He is serving or has served on the editorial boards of the *Academy of Management Review,* the *Journal of Management,* and *Management Inquiry.* In addition to his academic achievements, Gareth is co-author on three other major text books in the management discipline, including organizational behavior, organizational theory, and strategic management.

Jennifer George

is also a Professor of Management in the Lowry Mays College and Graduate School of Business at Texas A&M University. She received her B.A. in Psychology/Sociology from Wesleyan University, her M.B.A. in Finance from New York University, and her Ph.D. in Management and Organizational Behavior from New York University.

She specializes in Organizational Behavior and is well known for her research on affect and mood, their determinants, and their effects on various individual and group level work outcomes. She is the author of many articles in leading peer-reviewed journals, and her recent work has appeared in the *Academy of Management Review,* the *Journal of Management,* and *Human Relations.* One of her papers won the Academy of Management's Organizational Behavior Division Outstanding Competitive Paper Award. She is, or has been, on the editorial review boards of the *Journal of Applied Psychology, Academy of Management Journal, Journal of Management,* and *Journal of Managerial Issues* and was a consulting editor for the *Journal of Organizational Behavior.* She is a Fellow in the American Psychological Association, the American Psychological Society, and the Society for Industrial and Organizational Psychology.

With her husband, Gareth Jones, she has written a leading textbook in organizational behavior. They have also collaborated on two children, Nicholas, who is seven, and Julia, who is six.

Charles W. L. Hill

is the Hughes M. Blake Professor of International Business at the School of Business, University of Washington. Professor Hill received his Ph.D. in industrial organization economics in 1983 from the University of Manchester's Institute of Science and Technology (UMIST). In addition to the University of Washington, he has served on the faculties of UMIST, Texas A&M University, and Michigan State University. He has published many articles in peer-reviewed academic journals. He has also published two college textbooks, one on strategic management and the other on international business, both market leaders. Professor Hill is, or has served, on the editorial boards of several academic journals, such as the *Academy of Management Journal* and the *Strategic Management Journal* and was a consulting editor at the *Academy of Management Review.*

Professor Hill teaches in the undergraduate M.B.A. and executive M.B.A. programs at the University of Washington and has received awards for teaching excellence in these programs.

Part 1

MANAGEMENT

Chapter one

Managers and Managing

Learning Objectives

1. Describe what management is, what managers do, what organizations are for, and how managers utilize organizational resources efficiently and effectively to achieve organizational goals.

2. Distinguish among planning, organizing, leading, and controlling (the four principal managerial functions), and explain how managers' ability to handle each one can affect organizational performance.

3. Differentiate among three levels of management, and understand the responsibilities of managers at different levels in the organizational hierarchy.

4. Identify the roles managers perform and the skills they need to execute those roles effectively.

5. Discuss the principal challenges managers face in today's increasingly competitive global environment.

A Case in Contrast

Steve Jobs's Old and New Management Style at Apple Computer

In 1976, Steven P. Jobs sold his Volkswagen van, and invested the proceeds to produce a computer circuit board, which was built in his garage. So popular was the circuit board, which was eventually developed into the Apple II computer, that in 1977 the new business was incorporated as Apple Computer (www.apple.com). By 1985 company sales were almost $2 billion.[1] But in 1985 Jobs was forced out of the company he had founded. His approach to management was a big part of the reason he lost control of Apple.

After Apple was founded, Steve Jobs saw his role as leader of the development effort to create new computers, and he started many different project teams to develop several new and improved models. Although this was a good strategy, Jobs's management style caused many problems. Most important, he failed to establish a clear vision for employees to follow and often played favorites among various employees and teams—for example, championing his personal project, the Lisa computer team, against the Macintosh team.

Steve Jobs stands behind the original Apple Macintosh and the new Apple IMac that is turning around the fortunes of this pioneering company.

His actions led to fierce competition, many misunderstandings, and a great deal of distrust among members of competing teams.[2]

Moreover, Jobs's management style brought him into conflict with other managers, particularly Apple CEO John Sculley, and tension between them grew. Employees became unsure whether Jobs (the chairman) or Sculley (the CEO) was leading the company, and both were so busy competing for control of Apple that neither had the time or energy to ensure that Apple's resources were being used efficiently. For example, little attention was paid to evaluating the performance of the project teams; and there was not even a budget in place to control the teams' research and development spending. The result? Apple's costs started to soar, profits fell, and the whole organization began to disintegrate. Eventually, convinced that Jobs's management style was undermining company morale, Apple's board of directors asked Jobs to leave.

After leaving Apple, Jobs moved on to new ventures. He soon founded NEXT, which developed a new powerful computer, and then Pixar, a computer animation company that become a major success story after it made the Walt Disney movie *Toy Story*. In both of these companies he developed a clear vision for managers to follow and built strong management teams centered around the achievement of specific goals. However, both NEXT and Apple found it hard to compete with giants like Hewlett-Packard, Sun Microsystems, and IBM, so in 1996 Jobs suggested that Apple buy NEXT for $400 million and use NEXT's operating system for Apple's new generation of computers.[3] This deal went through, and Jobs was once again effectively back as part of Apple.

In 1997, after Apple's profit's continued to decline, the board of directors suggested to Jobs that he take full control of the company again and become its CEO. Jobs agreed to become interim CEO. In control of the company once again, he quickly put the new management skills he had developed over time to good use. Understanding more than he had ever before that what a company needs is clear leadership and a guiding mission to energize and motivate employees, the charismatic Jobs strove to create a new vision for Apple. He decided that to survive Apple had to replace the old Macintosh with a new, advanced model that would sell for under $2,000. To accomplish this, he began a comprehensive planning process with Apple managers, established clear objectives, and then created a structure of teams and team leadership to allow programmers and engineers to work together to develop the new computer. He delegated considerable authority to these team leaders, but he also established strict timetables and challenging "stretch" goals for these groups to achieve. Most important, he kept the teams focused on a single goal: bringing the new computer to market as quickly as possible.[4]

Jobs and Apple have been very successful in accomplishing their mission and meeting their goals. When Apple's sleek new iMac computer was launched in August 1998, it was an immediate success with back orders numbering over 150,000, and Apple expects to sell a million in the first year.[5] Jobs now has set new challenging goals for the company, which seems poised for an important comeback after years of declining sales and profits. Analysts believe that only Jobs could have accomplished this turnaround; they credit his success to the management skills that he was forced to develop after he was ousted from the company that he helped to found.

Overview

The history of Steve Jobs's ups and downs as both a founder and a manager at Apple Computer illustrates many of the challenges facing people who become managers: Managing a large company is a complex activity, and managers must learn the skills and acquire the knowledge necessary to become effective managers. Management is clearly an unpredictable process. Making the right decision is difficult. Even effective managers often make mistakes and, like Jobs, must learn from their mistakes if they are to help their organizations succeed.

In this chapter, we look at what managers do and what skills and abilities they must develop if they are to manage their organizations successfully over time. We also identify the different kinds of managers that organizations need and the skills and abilities they must develop if they are to be successful. Finally, we identify some of the challenges that managers must address if their organizations are to grow and prosper. ●

What Is Management?

When you think of a manager, what kind of person comes to mind? Do you see someone who, like Steve Jobs, can determine the future prosperity of a large for-profit company? Or do you see the administrator of a not-for-profit organization such as a school, library, or charity, or the person in charge of your local McDonald's restaurant or Wal-Mart store? What do all these managers have in common?

To answer this question, we first must consider a few key concepts. **Organizations** are collections of people who work together and coordinate their actions to achieve a wide variety of goals.[6] A **goal** is a desired future outcome that an organization strives to achieve. **Management** is the planning, organizing, leading, and controlling of resources to achieve organizational goals effectively and efficiently. **Resources** are assets such as people, machinery, raw materials, information, skills, and financial capital. Why are the individuals mentioned in the examples above managers? **Managers** are people responsible for supervising the use of an organization's resources to achieve its goals.

organization A collection of people who work together and coordinate their actions to achieve goals.

goal A desired future outcome that an organization strives to achieve.

management The planning, organizing, leading, and controlling of resources to achieve organizational goals effectively and efficiently.

resources Assets such as people, machinery, raw materials, information, skills, and financial capital.

manager A person who is responsible for supervising the use of an organization's resources to achieve its goals.

organizational performance A measure of how efficiently and effectively a manager uses resources to satisfy customers and achieve organizational goals.

Achieving High Performance: A Manager's Goal

One of the most important goals that organizations and their members try to achieve is to provide some kind of good or service that customers desire. The principal goal of interim CEO Steve Jobs is to manage Apple Computer so that it provides personal computers that customers are willing to buy; the principal goal of doctors, nurses, and hospital administrators is to increase their hospital's ability to make sick people well; the principal goal of each McDonald's restaurant manager is to produce burgers, fries, and shakes that people want to eat and pay for.

Organizational performance is a measure of how efficiently and effectively managers use resources to satisfy customers and achieve organizational goals. Organizational performance increases in direct proportion to increases in efficiency and effectiveness (see Figure 1.1).

EFFICIENCY

	LOW	**HIGH**
HIGH	Low efficiency/ High effectiveness Manager chooses the right goals to pursue, but does a poor job of using resources to achieve these goals. Result: A product that customers want, but that is too expensive for them to buy.	High efficiency/ High effectiveness Manager chooses the right goals to pursue and makes good use of resources to achieve these goals. Result: A product that customers want at a quality and price that they can afford.
LOW	Low efficiency/ Low effectiveness Manager chooses wrong goals to pursue and makes poor use of resources. Result: A low-quality product that customers do not want.	High efficiency/ Low effectiveness Manager chooses inapppropriate goals, but makes good use of resources to pursue these goals. Result: A high-quality product that customers do not want.

(The left side of the matrix is labeled vertically **EFFECTIVENESS**.)

High-performing organizations are efficient *and* effective.

efficiency A measure of how well or productively resources are used to achieve a goal.

Efficiency is a measure of how well or how productively resources are used to achieve a goal.[7] Organizations are efficient when managers minimize the amount of input resources (such as labor, raw materials, and component parts) or the amount of time needed to produce a given output of goods or services. For example, McDonald's recently developed a more efficient fat fryer that not only reduces (by 30 percent) the amount of oil used in cooking but also speeds up the cooking of french fries. A manager's responsibility is to ensure that an organization and its members perform, as efficiently as possible, all the activities that are needed to provide goods and services to customers.

effectiveness

A measure of the appropriateness of the goals an organization is pursuing and of the degree to which the organization achieves those goals.

Effectiveness is a measure of the appropriateness of the goals that managers have selected for the organization to pursue, and of the degree to which the organization achieves those goals. Organizations are effective when managers choose appropriate goals and then achieve them. Some years ago, for example, managers at McDonald's decided on the goal of providing breakfast service to attract more customers. The choice of this goal has proved very smart, for sales of breakfast food now account for over 30 percent of McDonald's revenues. High-performing organizations like Campbell Soup, McDonald's, Wal-Mart, Intel, Home Depot, Arthur Andersen, and the March of Dimes are simultaneously efficient and effective, as shown in Figure 1.1.

Managers who are effective are those who choose the right organizational goals to pursue and have the skills to utilize resources efficiently. Consider, for example, the way in which Deborah Kent, Ford Motor Company's only African-American plant manager, goes about her job of managing the production of Ford Econoline vans and Mercury Villager minivans.

Management Insight

How to Be an Effective Plant Manager

When Deborah Kent took control of Ford Motor Company's (www.ford. com) manufacturing plant in Avon Lake, Ohio, the first thing she did was walk the production line. She believed that the only way to know how goods are produced is to watch it happen and learn from the employees who actually perform the tasks necessary to get the job done and reach Ford's goals. Kent's hands-on approach to managing the organization's resources is the result of a 17-year career in the automobile industry, first with General Motors and then with Ford. The experience she gained in manufacturing, quality control, and customer relations during her career has allowed her to gain the know-how she needs to manage these crucial areas of the manufacturing process. Her ability to be an effective manager explains her rise up the ranks.

An industrial psychologist with a degree from Washington University in St. Louis, Kent is well known for her open, accessible management style and for her insistence that both managers and employees below her feel free to approach her with their opinions and suggestions about how to alter work procedures to improve quality in the car plant. She continually looks for feedback from her subordinates and is known for nurturing, developing, and energizing them so that they take responsibility for finding ways to increase efficiency and effectiveness.

Kent's hardworking, no-nonsense style also sits well with officials from the United Auto Workers (UAW) union. The UAW is cooperating with Ford's managers to increase quality in order to protect their members' jobs at a time of intense competition from other makers of minivans, especially from industry leader Chrysler. Since Mercury Villager minivans and Econoline vans are produced only at the Avon Lake plant, every time Kent sees one on the road she knows that its quality and reliability are the result of her managerial abilities and her plant's performance. She often asks owners what they think of their vehicles, and on the rare occasions when she sees one broken down, she stops to find out the cause and to offer assistance. Kent believes that this type of involvement is part of her responsibility.[8]

To perform her job effectively, Kent begins each workday with a walk through the plant to get a feel for the problems and issues at hand. Responsible for managing two shifts—including 3,746 employees and 420 robots—and for the quality and performance of the over 400,000 vehicles that her plant produces every year, she finds it hard to leave her responsibilities behind. Deborah Kent works long hours to make her plant one of Ford's highest-performing operations.

Managerial Functions

The job of management is to help an organization make the best use of its resources to achieve its goals. How do managers accomplish this objective? They do so by performing four essential managerial functions: *planning, organizing, leading,* and *controlling* (see Figure 1.2). French manager Henri Fayol first outlined the nature of these managerial activities around the turn of the twentieth century. Fayol trained as an industrial engineer and became the CEO of the huge Comambault coal-mining company in 1888; within two years he turned a losing proposition into one of the most successful in Europe. In 1916, he brought together his ideas about management in *General and Industrial Management,* a book that remains the classic statement of what managers must do to create a high-performing organization.[9]

Managers at all levels and in all departments—whether in small or large organizations, for-profit or not-for-profit organizations, or organizations that operate in one country or throughout the world—are responsible for performing these four functions, and we will look at each in turn. How well managers perform them determines how efficient and effective their organization is.

Planning

planning Identifying and selecting appropriate goals; one of the four principal functions of management.

Planning is a process that managers use to identify and select appropriate goals and courses of action. There are three steps in the planning process: (1) deciding which goals the organization will pursue, (2) deciding what courses of action to adopt to attain those goals, and (3) deciding how to allocate organizational resources to attain those goals. How well managers plan determines how effective and efficient their organization is—its performance level.[10]

Figure 1.2
Four Functions of Management

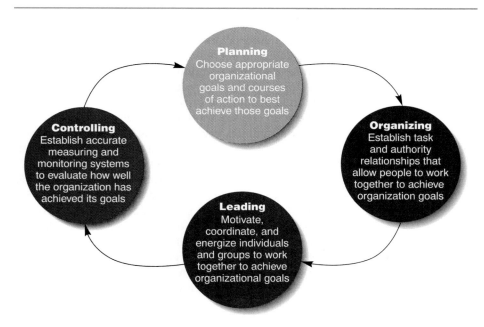

Planning
Choose appropriate organizational goals and courses of action to best achieve those goals

Organizing
Establish task and authority relationships that allow people to work together to achieve organization goals

Leading
Motivate, coordinate, and energize individuals and groups to work together to achieve organizational goals

Controlling
Establish accurate measuring and monitoring systems to evaluate how well the organization has achieved its goals

As an example of planning in action consider the situation confronting Michael Dell, CEO of Dell Computer.[11] In 1984, the 19-year-old Dell saw an opportunity to enter the personal computer market by making personal computers and then selling them directly to customers. Dell began to plan how to put this idea into practice. First, he decided that his goal was to sell an inexpensive personal computer, to undercut the prices of companies like IBM and Apple Computer. Second, he had to decide on a course of action to achieve this goal. He decided to sell directly to customers by telephone and to bypass expensive computer stores. He also had to decide how to obtain low-cost components and how to tell potential customers about his products. Third, he had to decide how to allocate his limited funds to buy labor and other resources. He chose to hire three people and work with them around a table to assemble his machines. Thus, to put his vision of making and selling personal computers into practice, Dell had to plan, and as his organization grew, his plans changed and became progressively more complex.

strategy A cluster of decisions about what goals to pursue, what actions to take, and how to use resources to achieve goals.

The outcome of planning is a **strategy,** a cluster of decisions concerning what organizational goals to pursue, what actions to take, and how to use resources to achieve goals. The decisions that were the outcome of Michael Dell's planning form a *low-cost strategy*. A low-cost strategy is a way of obtaining customers by making decisions that allow the organization to produce its goods or services cheaply so that prices can be kept low. This strategy worked spectacularly for Dell and resulted in his company becoming the second largest personal computer supplier in the United States.

Planning is a difficult activity because normally what goals an organization should pursue and how best to pursue them—which strategies to adopt—is not immediately clear. Managers take risks when they commit organizational resources to pursue a particular strategy. Either success or failure is a possible outcome of the planning process as we saw in the "Case in Contrast" at the beginning of the chapter. In Chapter 7 we focus on the planning process and on the strategies organizations can select to respond to opportunities or threats.

Organizing

organizing Structuring working relationships in a way that allows organizational members to work together to achieve organizational goals; one of the four principal functions of management.

organizational structure A formal system of task and reporting relationships that coordinates and motivates organizational members so that they work together to achieve organizational goals.

Organizing is a process that managers use to establish a structure of working relationships that allow organizational members to work together to achieve organizational goals. Organizing involves grouping people into departments according to the kinds of job-specific tasks they perform. In organizing, managers also lay out the lines of authority and responsibility between different individuals and groups, and they decide how best to coordinate organizational resources, particularly human resources.

The outcome of organizing is the creation of an **organizational structure,** a formal system of task and reporting relationships that coordinates and motivates organizational members so that they work together to achieve organizational goals. Organizational structure determines how an organization's resources can be best used to create goods and services. As Dell Computer grew, for example, Michael Dell faced the issue of how to structure the organization. At one point, he was hiring 100 new employees a week and had to decide how to design his managerial hierarchy to best motivate and coordinate their activities.

We examine the organizing process in Chapters 8 through 10. In Chapter 8 we consider the organizational structures that managers can use to coordinate and motivate people and other resources. In Chapter 9 we look at the important roles that an organization's culture, values, and norms play in binding people and departments together so that they work toward organizational goals. In Chapter 10 we discuss ways in which managers can develop and enhance the value of their employees through activities such as selection, training, and performance appraisal.

Leading

leading Articulating a clear vision and energizing and enabling organizational members so that they understand the part they play in achieving organizational goals; one of the four principal functions of management.

In **leading,** managers articulate a clear vision for organizational members to follow, and they energize and enable organizational members so that they understand the part they play in achieving organizational goals. Leadership depends on the use of power, influence, vision, persuasion, and communication skills to coordinate the behaviors of individuals and groups so that their activities and efforts are in harmony and to encourage employees to perform at a high level. The outcome of leadership is a high level of motivation and commitment among organizational members. Employees at Apple Computer, for example, responded well to Steve Jobs's new hands-on leadership style and team approach to developing Apple's iMac computer. His leadership style, like Michael Dell's, resulted in a hardworking, committed workforce.

We discuss the issues involved in managing and leading individuals and groups in Chapters 11 through 16. In Chapter 11 we consider what managers are like as people and the personal challenges managers face as they try to perform their jobs effectively. In Chapters 12 and 13 we examine theories about and models of the best ways to motivate and lead employees to encourage high motivation and commitment. In Chapter 14 we look at the way groups and teams can contribute to achieving organizational goals and the coordination problems that can arise when people work together in groups and teams. In Chapters 15 and 16 we consider how communication and coordination problems can arise between people and functions and how managers can try to manage these problems through bargaining and negotiation and by creating appropriate information networks.

Controlling

controlling Evaluating how well an organization is achieving its goals and taking action to maintain or improve performance; one of the four principal functions of management.

In **controlling,** managers evaluate how well an organization is achieving its goals and take action to maintain or improve performance. For example, managers monitor the performance of individuals, departments, and the organization as a whole to see whether they are meeting desired performance standards—Apple's Steve Jobs learned how important this is. If standards are not being met, managers take action to improve performance.

The outcome of the control process is the ability to measure performance accurately and regulate organizational efficiency and effectiveness. In order to exercise control, managers must decide which goals to measure—perhaps goals pertaining to productivity, quality, or responsiveness to customers—and then they must design information and control systems that will provide the data they need to assess performance. The controlling function also allows managers to evaluate how well they themselves are performing the other three functions of management—planning, organizing, and leading—and to take corrective action.

Michael Dell had difficulty establishing effective control systems, because his company was growing so rapidly and he lacked experienced managers. In 1988, Dell's costs soared because no controls were in place to monitor inventory, which had built up rapidly. In 1993, financial problems arose because of ill-advised foreign currency transactions. In 1994, Dell's new line of laptop computers crashed because poor quality control resulted in defective products, some of which caught fire. To solve these and other control problems, Dell hired experienced managers to put the right control systems in place. As a result, by 1998 Dell was able to make computers for about 10 percent less than its competitors, a major source of competitive advantage.

We cover the most important aspects of the control function in Chapter 9 and in Chapters 17 through 19. In Chapter 9 we outline the basic process of control and examine some control systems that managers can use to monitor and measure organizational performance. In Chapter 17 we look at how managers can develop information systems and technologies to enhance their ability to utilize resources efficiently and effectively. In Chapter 18 we discuss how managers can create specific control systems to improve quality, productivity, and responsiveness to customers. In Chapter 19 we consider ways in which managers can make their organizations more innovative so that they can create new and improved goods and services to better serve customers.

The four managerial functions—planning, organizing, leading, and controlling—are essential to a manager's job. At all levels in a managerial hierarchy, and across all departments in an organization, effective management means making decisions and managing these four activities successfully.

Types of Managers

To perform efficiently and effectively, organizations traditionally employ three types of managers—first-line managers, middle managers, and top managers—arranged in a hierarchy (see Figure 1.3). Typically, first-line managers report to middle managers, and middle managers report to top managers. Managers at each level have different but related types of responsibilities for utilizing organizational resources to increase efficiency and effectiveness. These three types of managers are grouped into departments according to their specific job responsibilities. A **department** such as manufacturing, accounting, or engineering is a group of people who work together and possess similar skills or use the same kind of knowledge, tools, or techniques to perform their jobs. Within each department are all three levels of management. Below, we examine the reasons why organizations use a hierarchy of managers and group them into departments. We then examine some recent changes that have been taking place in managerial hierarchies.

department A group of people who work together and possess similar skills or use the same knowledge, tools, or techniques to perform their jobs.

Levels of Management

As just discussed, organizations normally have three levels of management: first-line managers, middle managers, and top managers.

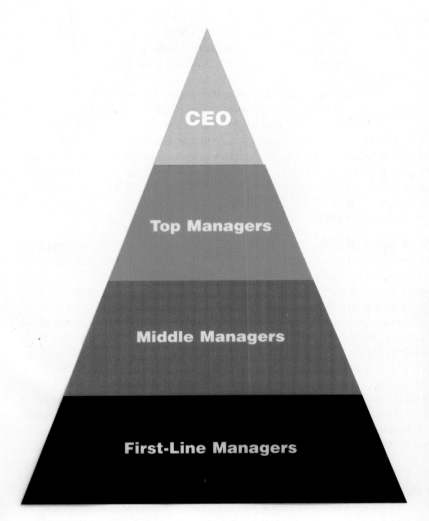

CEO

Top Managers

Middle Managers

First-Line Managers

FIRST-LINE MANAGERS   At the base of the managerial hierarchy are **first-line managers** (often called *supervisors*). They are responsible for the daily supervision of the nonmanagerial employees who perform many of the specific activities necessary to produce goods and services. First-line managers are found in all departments of an organization.

Examples of first-line managers include the supervisor of a work team in the manufacturing department of a car plant, the head nurse in the obstetrics department of a hospital, and the chief mechanic overseeing a crew of mechanics in the service department of a new car dealership. At Dell Computer, first-line managers include the supervisors responsible for controlling the quality of computers produced by Dell employees or the level of customer service provided by Dell's team of telephone salespeople. When Michael Dell started his company, he personally controlled the computer assembly process and thus performed as a first-line manager or supervisor.

MIDDLE MANAGERS   Supervising the first-line managers are **middle managers,** who have the responsibility to find the best way to organize human and other resources to achieve organizational goals. To increase efficiency, middle managers try to find ways to help first-line managers and nonmanagerial employees better utilize resources in order to reduce manufacturing costs or improve the way services are provided to customers. To increase effectiveness, middle managers are responsible for evaluating whether the goals that the organization is pursuing are appropriate and for suggesting to top managers ways in which goals should be changed. Very often, the suggestions that middle managers make to top managers can dramatically increase organizational performance, as we explain in Chapter 7. A major part of the middle manager's job is to develop and fine-tune skills and know-how, such as manufacturing or marketing expertise, that allow the organization to be efficient and effective. Middle managers make the thousands of specific decisions that go into the production of goods and services: Which first-line supervisors should be chosen for this particular project? Where can we find the highest-quality resources? How should employees be organized to allow them to make the best use of resources?

Behind a first-class sales force look for the middle managers responsible for training, motivating, and rewarding salespeople. Behind a committed staff of high school teachers look for the principal who energizes them to look for ways to obtain the resources they need to do an outstanding and innovative job in the classroom. Deborah Kent, the Ford plant manager discussed earlier, is a good example of a committed middle manager.

TOP MANAGERS   In contrast to middle managers, **top managers** are responsible for the performance of *all* departments.[12] They have *cross-departmental responsibility*. Top managers establish organizational goals, such as which goods and services the company should produce; they decide how the different departments should interact; and they monitor how well middle managers in each department utilize resources to achieve goals.[13] Top managers are ultimately responsible for the success or failure of an organization, and their performance (like that of Steve Jobs) is continually scrutinized by people inside and outside the organization, such as other employees and investors.[14]

Top managers report to a company's *chief executive officer*–such as General Electric CEO Jack Welsh, Warnaco CEO Linda Wachtner, and Chrysler CEO Robert Eaton–or to the *president* of the organization, who is second-

first-line manager A manager who is responsible for the daily supervision of nonmanagerial employees.

middle manager A manager who supervises first-line managers and is responsible for finding the best way to use resources to achieve organizational goals.

top manager A manager who establishes organizational goals, decides how departments should interact, and monitors the performance of middle managers.

top-management team A group composed of the CEO, the president, and the heads of the most important departments.

Pictured is Andrea Jung, the president and chief operating officer of Avon, the famous cosmetic products maker. She is next in line to be its first female chief executive officer.

in-command, such as Chrysler president Robert Lutz or Andrea Jung, president (and soon to be CEO) of Avon. The CEO and president are responsible for developing good working relationships among the top managers who head the various departments (manufacturing and marketing, for example), and who usually have the title *vice president.* A central concern of the CEO is the creation of a smoothly functioning **top-management team,** a group composed of the CEO, the president, and the department heads most responsible for helping achieve organizational goals.[15]

The relative importance of planning, organizing, leading, and controlling—the four managerial functions—to any particular manager depends on the manager's position in the managerial hierarchy.[16] The amount of time that managers spend planning and organizing resources to maintain and improve organizational performance increases the higher up they are in the hierarchy (see Figure 1.4). Top managers devote most of their time to planning and organizing, the functions that are so crucial to determining an organization's long-term performance. The lower a manager's position is in the hierarchy, the more time he or she spends leading and controlling first-line managers or nonmanagerial employees.

Areas of Managers

Because so much of a manager's responsibility is to acquire and develop critical resources, managers are typically a member of one of an organization's departments.[17] Managers inside a department possess *job-specific skills* and are known as, for example, marketing managers or manufacturing managers. As Figure 1.3 indicates, first-line, middle, and top managers, who differ from one another by virtue of their job-specific responsibilities, are found in each of an organization's major departments. Inside each department, the managerial hierarchy emerges.

At Dell Computer, for example, Michael Dell hired experts to take charge of the marketing, sales, and manufacturing departments and develop work procedures to help first-line managers control the company's explosive sales growth. The head of manufacturing quickly found that he had no time to supervise computer assembly, so he recruited manufacturing middle managers from other companies to assume this responsibility.

Recent Changes in Managerial Hierarchies

The tasks and responsibilities of managers at different levels have been changing dramatically in recent years. Increasingly, top managers are encouraging lower-level managers to look beyond the goals of their own departments and take a cross-departmental view to find new opportunities to improve organizational performance. Stiff competition for resources from organizations both at home and abroad has put increased pressure on all managers to improve efficiency, effectiveness, and organizational performance. To respond to these pressures, many organizations have been changing the managerial hierarchy.[18]

Figure 1.4
Relative Amount of Time That Managers Spend on the Four Managerial Functions

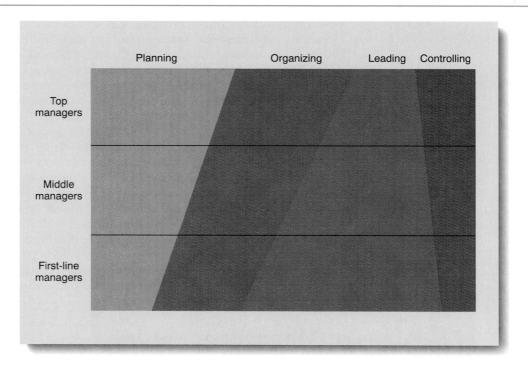

RESTRUCTURING   To decrease costs, CEOs and their top-management teams have been restructuring organizations to reduce the number of employees on the payroll. **Restructuring** involves downsizing an organization or shrinking its operations by eliminating the jobs of large numbers of top, middle, or first-line managers and nonmanagerial employees. Restructuring promotes efficiency by reducing costs and allowing the organization to make better use of its remaining resources. Both Gillette and Levi Strauss announced in 1998 that, due to declining global sales, they would close plants and lay off over 12 percent of their workforces worldwide, streamlining their global operations to cut costs.

Restructuring can produce some powerful negative outcomes. It can reduce the morale of the remaining employees, worried about their own job security. And top managers of many downsized organizations are realizing that they downsized too far, because customer complaints about poor-quality service are on the increase.[19]

Large for-profit organizations today typically employ 10 percent fewer managers than they did 10 years ago. General Motors, IBM, Digital Equipment Corporation, and many other organizations have eliminated several layers of middle management. The middle managers who still have jobs at these companies have had to assume additional responsibilities and are under increasing pressure to perform. Often, for example, middle managers who used to be responsible for coordinating and overseeing the work of first-line managers—but not for doing the work themselves—now have to perform specific job-related tasks while monitoring and coordinating the work of their subordinates.[20]

restructuring Downsizing an organization by eliminating the jobs of large numbers of top, middle, and first-line managers and nonmanagerial employees.

EMPOWERMENT AND SELF-MANAGED TEAMS   Another major change in management has taken place at the level of first-line managers, who typically supervise the employees engaged in producing goods and services. Many organizations have taken two steps to reduce costs and improve quality. One is the **empowerment** of the workforce, expanding employees' tasks and responsibilities. The other is the creation of **self-managed teams**–groups of employees who are given responsibility for supervising their own activities and for monitoring the quality of the goods and service they provide.

Members of self-managed teams assume many of the responsibilities and duties previously performed by first-line managers.[21] What is the role of the first-line manager in this new work context? First-line managers act as coaches or mentors whose job is not to tell employees what to do but to provide advice and guidance and help teams find new ways to perform their tasks more efficiently.[22]

As the story of John Deere suggests, the tasks and responsibilities of managers at different levels and in different departments may need to change rapidly as organizations try to improve their performance.

empowerment Expanding employees' tasks and responsibilities.

self-managed team A group of employees who supervise their own activities and monitor the quality of the goods and services they provide.

Management Insight

A New Approach at John Deere

John Deere (www.john-deere.com), a well-known agricultural equipment maker based in Moline, Illinois, has seen the farm market shrink in recent years. In addition, intense competition from Caterpillar and Komatsu, the other leading makers of agricultural equipment, has led to huge losses for Deere. Reacting to these problems, the company downsized steadily and laid off thousands of employees and managers to reduce costs, but these steps did not stem the losses. Seeing a bleak future if a new way to run the company could not be found, Deere CEO Hans W. Becherer decided to make some dramatic changes.

To build and develop the human and departmental skills and knowledge needed to give the company a new competitive advantage, Becherer gave his managers the responsibility to empower Deere's remaining employees and group them into self-managed teams. He started this process by trying to focus the attention of his managers and other employees on understanding what Deere's customers want. As part of the empowerment process Becherer decided that all factory workers periodically would be sent out from the factory to meet the company's customers. He empowered assembly-line workers to take limited leaves from their jobs so that they could interact with customers as marketing and sales people did and thus learn about customers' likes and dislikes. Employees bring their newfound knowledge back to the company, where it is passed on to the engineers whose job is to create improved products to satisfy customers' needs. Contact with customers also helps make employees more quality conscious.

Becherer also took steps to develop human resources. He established an extensive training program to enhance the skills of the workforce. Every employee is expected to attend classes to learn new manufacturing techniques. Pay is linked to skill development, and Deere's workforce has become one of the most skilled in the industry.

Self-managed work teams at Deere now are responsible for building the skills of the manufacturing department. Employees, having learned new skills, are expected to meet frequently as a group and find ways to continuously improve work procedures so that costs go down, quality increases, and products improve. Teams have suggested reorganizing the steps in the assembly process and reducing the number of brackets needed to hold tractor engines in place. The overall result of suggestions made by the self-managed teams has been a 10 percent cut in manufacturing costs and a significant reduction in customer complaints.[23]

As a result of empowerment and the use of self-managed teams, Deere is more efficient in its use of human and technical resources and once again is showing a profit–over $1 billion in 1998, a far cry from the losses of the early 1990s. In addition, managers and employees are enjoying the greater job security and higher wages that a high-performing organization can give its employees.

Tips for Managers

Managing Resources

1. Talk to customers to assess whether the goods or services that an organization provides adequately meets their needs and how they might be improved.

2. Analyze how an organization can better obtain or use resources to increase efficiency and effectiveness.

3. Critically assess how the skills and know-how of departments is helping an organization achieve a competitive advantage. Take steps to improve skills whenever possible.

4. Count the number of managers at each level in the organization and analyze how to increase efficiency and effectiveness of the workforce.

Managerial Roles and Skills

role The specific tasks that a person is expected to perform because of the position he or she holds in an organization.

In the midst of all this change, it is important to note that the roles managers need to play and the skills they need to utilize have changed little since the early 1970s, when Henry Mintzberg detailed 10 specific roles that effective managers undertake. Although the roles that Mintzberg described overlap with Fayol's model, they are useful because they focus on what managers do in a typical hour, day, or week in an organization, as they go about the business of managing.[24] A **role** is a set of specific tasks that a person is expected to perform because of the position he or she holds in an organization. Below, we discuss these roles and then examine the skills effective managers need to develop.

Managerial Roles Identified by Mintzberg

Mintzberg reduced to 10 roles the specific tasks that managers need to perform as they plan, organize, lead, and control organizational resources.[25] Managers assume each of these roles in order to influence the behavior of

Table 1.1

Managerial Roles Identified by Mintzberg

Type of Role	Specific Role	Examples of Role Activities
INTERPERSONAL	**Figurehead**	Outline future organizational goals to employees at company meetings; open a new corporate headquarters building; state the organization's ethical guidelines and the principles of behavior employees are to follow in their dealings with customers and suppliers.
	Leader	Provide an example for employees to follow; give direct commands and orders to subordinates; make decisions concerning the use of human and technical resources; mobilize employee support for specific organizational goals.
	Liaison	Coordinate the work of managers in different departments; establish alliances between different organizations to share resources to produce new goods and services.
INFORMATIONAL	**Monitor**	Evaluate the performance of managers in different functions and take corrective action to improve their performance; watch for changes occurring in the external and internal environment that may affect the organization in the future.
	Disseminator	Inform employees about changes taking place in the external and internal environment that will affect them and the organization; communicate to employees the organization's vision and purpose.
	Spokesperson	Launch a national advertising campaign to promote new goods and services; give a speech to inform the local community about the organization's future intentions.
DECISIONAL	**Entrepreneur**	Commit organizational resources to develop innovative goods and services; decide to expand internationally to obtain new customers for the organization's products.
	Disturbance Handler	Move quickly to take corrective action to deal with unexpected problems facing the organization from the external environment, such as a crisis like an oil spill, or from the internal environment, such as producing faulty goods or services.
	Resource Allocator	Allocate organizational resources among different functions and departments of the organization; set budgets and salaries of middle and first-level managers.
	Negotiator	Work with suppliers, distributors, and labor unions to reach agreements about the quality and price of input, technical, and human resources; work with other organizations to establish agreements to pool resources to work on joint projects.

individuals and groups inside and outside the organization. People inside the organization include other managers and employees. People outside the organization include shareholders, customers, suppliers, the local community in which an organization is located, and any local or government agency that has an interest in the organization and what it does.[26] Mintzberg grouped the 10 roles into three broad categories: *interpersonal, informational,* and *decisional* (see Table 1.1). Managers often perform several of these roles simultaneously.

INTERPERSONAL ROLES Managers assume interpersonal roles in order to coordinate and interact with organizational members and provide direction and supervision for both employees and the organization as a whole. A manager's first interpersonal role is to act as a *figurehead*—the person who symbolizes an organization or a department. Assuming the figurehead role, the chief executive officer determines the direction or mission of the organization and informs employees and other interested parties about what the organization is seeking to achieve. Managers at all levels act as figureheads and

Ken Chenault, pictured here, is the President and CEO of $19 billion American Express Company. Promoted in 1997, he climbed the rands from their Travel Related Services Company thanks to his "even temper and unrelenting drive." Respected by colleagues for his personality, most will say they can't remember him losing his temper or raising his voice. His open door policy for subordinates allows him to mentor AmEx managers and encourages all to enter and "speak their minds."

role models who establish the appropriate and inappropriate ways to behave in the organization. Steve Jobs, profiled earlier in the "Case in Contrast," is a manager who excels at performing the figurehead role at Apple Computer.

A manager's role as a *leader* is to encourage subordinates to perform at a high level and to take steps to train, counsel, and mentor subordinates to help them reach their full potential. A manager's power to lead comes both from formal authority due to his or her position in the organization's hierarchy and also from his or her personal qualities, including reputation, skills, or personality. The personal behavior of a leader affects employee attitudes and behavior; indeed, subordinates' desires to perform at a high level—and even whether they desire to arrive at work on time and not to be absent often—depend on how satisfied they are with working for the organization.

In performing as a *liaison,* managers link and coordinate the activities of people and groups both inside and outside the organization. Inside the organization, managers are responsible for coordinating the activities of people in different departments to improve their ability to cooperate. Outside the organization, managers are responsible for forming linkages with suppliers or customers or with the organization's local community in order to obtain scarce resources. People outside an organization often come to equate the organization with the manager they are dealing with, or with the person they see on television or read about in the newspaper. For example, Steve Jobs personifies Apple to business magazines like *Fortune* and *Business Week.*

INFORMATIONAL ROLES Informational roles are closely associated with the tasks necessary to obtain and transmit information. First, a manager acts as a *monitor* and analyzes information from inside and outside the organization. With this information, a manager can effectively organize and control people and other resources. Acting as a *disseminator,* the manager transmits information to other members of the organization to influence their work attitudes and behavior. In the role of *spokesperson,* a manager uses information to promote the organization so that people inside and outside the organization respond positively to it.

DECISIONAL ROLES Decisional roles are closely associated with the methods managers use to plan strategy and utilize resources. In the role of *entrepreneur,* a manager must decide which projects or programs to initiate and how to invest resources to increase organizational performance. As a *disturbance handler,* a manager assumes responsibility for handling an unexpected event or crisis that threatens the organization's access to resources. In this situation, a manager must also assume the roles of figurehead and leader to mobilize employees to help secure the resources needed to avert the problem.

Under typical conditions, an important role a manager plays is that of *resource allocator,* deciding how best to use people and other resources to increase organizational performance. While engaged in that role, the manager must also be a *negotiator,* reaching agreements with other managers or groups claiming the first right to resources, or with the organization and outside groups such as shareholders or customers. Terri Patsos Stanley, the manager of a small short-term rental business, performs many of these roles, as illustrated in the following "Management Insight."

Management Insight

Effective Small-Business Management

Terri Patsos Stanley is the president of Boston Short-Term Rentals, a small company that pioneered the concept of providing business travelers with high-quality apartments as an alternative to staying in more expensive and often less convenient hotels. Currently, she manages over 500 apartments, and her company, which employs 15 people, generates over $6 million in revenue yearly. With such a small staff, Patsos Stanley has a very hands-on approach to managing her company. She and her employees greet the new arrivals and perform the activities that porters, the concierge, and front-desk staff do in the typical hotel. In fact, in interpersonal terms, Patsos Stanley is the *figurehead* who provides the personal touch her guests expect and is the person they can contact if problems arise. With her small staff of carpenters, electricians, interior decorators, and maintenance staff, she acts like a *leader,* energizing them to provide the quick service that guests expect. She is also a *liaison,* able to link her guests to organizations that provide services they may need such as dry cleaning, catering, or hairdressing. She enjoys the variety of her work and relishes the pleasure of meeting the managers, actors, and overseas visitors who stay in the apartments.[27]

With over 500 apartments to oversee, Boston Short-Term Rentals' information management is a vital activity, and Patsos Stanley's role as *monitor* is important. A sophisticated computer system that she developed allows her to evaluate the performance of her business in terms of occupancy rates, customer complaints, and other indicators of the quality of service she is providing. The system facilitates her ability to respond quickly to problems as they arise. In her ongoing role as *disseminator,* she constantly gives her staff information about changes in visitor arrivals and departures, and as a *spokesperson* she is the main conduit of information to visitors who may be somewhat hesitant about staying in an apartment that they know nothing about as opposed to staying with a hotel chain that has a well-recognized name.

As the president of a rapidly growing company, Patsos Stanley is continually required to make decisions. In the role of *entrepreneur,* she searches for opportunities to increase revenues by increasing the number of apartments that she manages. As a *disturbance handler,* she deals with unexpected problems such as plumbing breakdowns in the middle of the night. As a *resource allocator,* she decides how much money to spend to refurbish and upgrade the apartments to maintain their luxury appeal and how much to pay her employees. As a *negotiator,* she contracts with other organizations such as cleaning or painting services to most economically obtain the services her business requires.

The owner/manager of a small business like Boston Short-Term Rentals continually performs all these managerial roles. Patsos Stanley, by all accounts, is performing them effectively, for her company's size and revenues are constantly increasing. Boston Short-Term Rentals serves as a model for other managers seeking to open similar businesses in other major U.S. cities.

Being a Manager

Our discussion of managerial roles may seem to suggest that a manager's job is highly orchestrated and that management is a logical, orderly process in which managers make a concerted effort to rationally calculate the best way to use resources to achieve organizational goals. In reality, being a manager often involves acting emotionally and relying on gut feelings. Quick, immediate reactions to situations rather than deliberate thought and reflection are an important aspect of managerial action.[28] Often, managers are overloaded with responsibilities, do not have time to spend in analyzing every nuance of a situation, and therefore make decisions in uncertain conditions without being sure which outcomes will be best.[29] Moreover, for top managers in particular, the current situation is constantly changing, and a decision that seems right today may prove to be wrong tomorrow.

The range of problems that managers face is enormous (*high variety*). Managers frequently must deal with many problems simultaneously (*fragmentation*), often must make snap decisions (*brevity*), and often must rely on experience gained throughout their careers to do the job to the best of their abilities.[30] It is no small wonder that many managers claim that they are performing their job well if they are right just half of the time, and it is understandable why many experienced managers accept failure by their subordinates as a normal part of the learning experience. Managers and their subordinates learn both from their successes and from their failures.

Managerial Skills

Both education and experience enable managers to recognize and develop the skills they need to put organizational resources to their best use. Michael Dell realized from the start that he lacked enough experience and technical expertise in marketing, finance, and planning to guide his company alone. Thus, he recruited experienced managers to help him build his company. Research has shown that education and experience help managers acquire three principal types of skills: *conceptual, human,* and *technical.*[31] As you might expect, the level of these skills that a manager needs depends on his or her level in the managerial hierarchy (see Figure 1.5).

conceptual skills The ability to analyze and diagnose a situation and to distinguish between cause and effect.

CONCEPTUAL SKILLS **Conceptual skills** are demonstrated in the ability to analyze and diagnose a situation and to distinguish between cause and effect. Planning and organizing require a high level of conceptual skill, as does performing the managerial roles discussed above. Top managers require the best conceptual skills, because their primary responsibilities are planning and organizing.[32]

Formal education and training are very important in helping managers develop conceptual skills. Business training at the undergraduate and graduate (MBA) levels provides many of the conceptual tools (theories and techniques in marketing, finance, and other areas) that managers need to perform their roles effectively. The study of management helps develop the skills that allow managers to understand the big picture confronting an organization. The ability to

Figure 1.5

Conceptual, Human, and Technical Skills Needed by Three Levels of Management

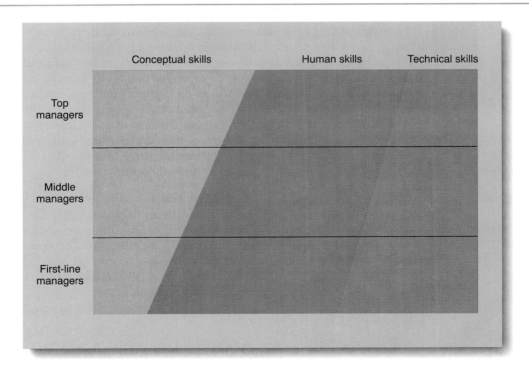

| | Conceptual skills | Human skills | Technical skills |

Top managers

Middle managers

First-line managers

focus on the big picture lets the manager see beyond the situation immediately at hand and consider choices while keeping in mind the organization's long-term goals.

Today, continuing management education and training are an integral step in building managerial skills, because new theories and techniques are constantly being promoted to improve organizational effectiveness. A quick scan through a magazine such as *Business Week* or *Fortune* reveals a host of seminars in topics such as advanced marketing, finance, leadership, managing human resources, and the global environment of business being offered to managers at many levels in the organization, from the most senior corporate executives to middle managers. In Xerox, IBM, Motorola, and many other organizations, a portion of each manager's personal budget is designated to be used at the manager's discretion to attend management development programs.

In addition, organizations may wish to develop a particular manager's skills in a specific skill area—perhaps to learn an advanced component of departmental skills, such as international bond trading, or to learn the skills necessary to implement a new program. The organization thus pays for managers to attend specialized programs to develop these skills. Indeed, one signal that an organization exhibits to show that a manager is performing well is to invest in that manager's skill development. Similarly, many nonmanagerial employees who are performing at a high level are sent to management training programs to develop their management skills and to prepare them for promotion to first-level management positions.

human skills The ability to understand, alter, lead, and control the behavior of other individuals and groups.

HUMAN SKILLS Human skills include the ability to understand, alter, lead, and control the behavior of other individuals and groups. The ability to communicate, to coordinate and motivate people, and to mold individuals into a cohesive team distinguishes effective from ineffective managers. By all accounts, Deborah Kent, Steve Jobs, and Terri Patsos Stanley all possess human skills.

Like conceptual skills, human skills can be learned through education and training, as well as developed through experience. Organizations increasingly utilize advanced programs in leadership skills and team leadership as they seek to capitalize on the advantages of self-managed teams. To manage interpersonal interactions effectively, each person in an organization needs to learn how to empathize with other people—to understand their viewpoints and the problems they face. One way to help managers understand their personal strengths and weaknesses is to have their superiors, peers, and subordinates provide feedback about their performance in the roles identified by Mintzberg. Thorough and direct feedback allows managers to develop their human skills.

technical skills Job-specific knowledge and techniques that are required to perform an organizational role.

TECHNICAL SKILLS Technical skills are the job-specific knowledge and techniques that are required to perform an organizational role. Examples include a manager's specific manufacturing, accounting, or marketing skills. Managers need a range of technical skills to be effective. The array of technical skills a person needs depends on his or her position in the organization. The manager of a restaurant, for example, may need cooking skills to fill in for an absent cook, accounting and bookkeeping skills to keep track of receipts and costs and to administer the payroll, and aesthetic skills to keep the restaurant looking attractive for customers.

Effective managers need all three kinds of skills—conceptual, human, and technical. The absence of even one type can lead to failure. One of the biggest problems that people who start small businesses confront is their lack of appropriate conceptual and human skills. Someone who has the technical skills to start a new business does not necessarily know what to do to manage the venture successfully. Similarly, one of the biggest problems that scientists or engineers who switch careers from research to management confront is their lack of effective human skills. Management skills, roles, and functions are closely related, and wise managers or prospective managers are constantly in search of the latest educational contributions to help them develop the conceptual, human, and technical skills they need to function in today's changing and increasingly competitive environment.

Tips for Managers

Tasks and Roles

1. Estimate how much time managers spend performing each of the four tasks of planning, organizing, leading, and controling. Decide if managers are spending the right amount of time on each task.

2. Decide which of Mintzberg's 10 managerial roles managers are performing well or poorly.

3. Based on this analysis, take steps to ensure managers possess the right levels of conceptual, technical, and human skills to perform their jobs effectively.

Challenges for Management in a Global Environment

global organization An organization that operates and competes in more than one country.

Because the world has been changing more rapidly than ever before, managers and other employees throughout an organization must perform at higher and higher levels. In the last 20 years, competition between organizations competing domestically (in the same country) and globally (in countries abroad) has increased dramatically. The rise of **global organizations,** organizations that operate and compete in more than one country, has put severe pressure on many organizations to improve their performance and to identify better ways to use their resources. The successes of German chemical companies Schering and Hoescht, Italian furniture manufacturer Natuzzi, Korean electronics companies Samsung and Lucky Goldstar, and Brazilian plane maker Embraer are putting pressure on organizations in other countries to raise their level of performance in order to compete successfully with these global companies.

Even in the not-for-profit sector, global competition is spurring change. Schools, universities, police forces, and government agencies are reexamining their operations as a result of looking at the way things are done in other countries. For example, many curriculum and teaching changes in the United States have resulted from the study of methods that Japanese and European school systems use. Similarly, European and Asian hospital systems have learned much from the U.S. system—which may be the most effective, though not the most efficient, in the world. Today, managers who make no attempt to learn and adapt to changes in the global environment find themselves reacting rather than innovating, and their organizations often become uncompetitive and fail.[33] Four major challenges stand out for managers in today's world: building a competitive advantage, maintaining ethical standards, managing a diverse workforce, and utilizing new kinds of information systems and technologies.

Building a Competitive Advantage

What are the most important lessons for managers and organizations to learn if they are to reach and remain at the top of the competitive environment of business? The answer relates to the use of organizational resources to build a competitive advantage. **Competitive advantage** is the ability of one organization to outperform other organizations because it produces desired goods or services more efficiently and effectively than its competitors. The four building blocks of competitive advantage are superior *efficiency, quality, innovation,* and *responsiveness to customers* (see Figure 1.6).

INCREASING EFFICIENCY   Organizations increase their efficiency when they reduce the quantity of resources (such as people and raw materials) they use to produce goods or services. In today's competitive environment, organizations constantly are seeking new ways to use their resources to improve efficiency. Many organizations are training their workforce in new skills and techniques that they need to operate heavily computerized assembly plants. Similarly, cross-training gives employees the range of skills they need to perform many different tasks, and organizing employees in new ways, such as in self-managed teams, allows them to make good use of their skills. These are important steps in the effort to improve productivity. Japanese and German companies invest far more in training employees than do American or Italian companies.

competitive advantage The ability of one organization to outperform other organizations because it produces desired goods or services more efficiently and effectively than they do.

Figure 1.6
Building Blocks of Competitive Advantage

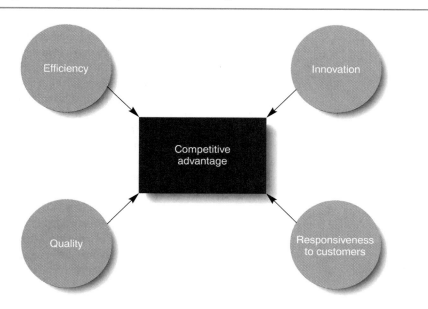

Today's steel rolling mills are almost all under the control of highly-skilled employees who use state of the art computer-controlled production systems to increase operating efficiency.

Managers must improve efficiency if their organizations are to compete successfully with companies operating in Mexico, Malaysia, and other countries where employees are paid comparatively low wages. New methods must be devised either to increase efficiency or to gain some other competitive advantage—higher-quality goods, for example—if the loss of jobs to low-cost countries is to be prevented.

INCREASING QUALITY The challenge from global organizations such as Korean electronics manufacturers, Mexican agricultural producers, and European marketing and financial firms has also increased pressure on companies to improve the skills and abilities of their workforce in order to improve the quality of goods and services. One major thrust to improve quality has been to introduce the quality-enhancing techniques known as *total quality management (TQM).* Employees involved in TQM are often organized into quality control teams and are given the responsibility to continually find new and better ways to perform their jobs; they also are given the responsibility for monitoring and evaluating the quality of the goods they produce. TQM is based on a significant new philosophy of managing behavior in organizations, and we thoroughly discuss this approach, and ways of managing TQM successfully, in Chapter 18.

innovation The process of creating new goods and services or developing better ways to produce or provide goods and services.

INCREASING INNOVATION **Innovation,** the process of creating new goods and services that customers want, or developing better ways to produce or provide goods and services, poses a special challenge. Managers must create an organizational setting in which people are encouraged to be innovative. Typically, innovation takes place in small groups or teams; management decentralizes control of work activities to team members and creates an organizational culture that rewards risk taking. Understanding and managing innovation and creating a work setting that encourages risk taking are among the most difficult managerial tasks. Innovation is discussed in depth in Chapter 19.

INCREASING RESPONSIVENESS TO CUSTOMERS Organizations compete for customers with their products and services, so training employees to be responsive to customers' needs is vital for all organizations, but particularly for service organizations. Retail stores, banks, and hospitals, for example, depend entirely on their employees to perform behaviors that result in high-quality service at a reasonable cost.[34] As many countries (the United States, Canada, and Great Britain are just a few) move toward a more service-based economy (in part because of the loss of manufacturing jobs to China, Malaysia, and other countries with low labor costs), managing behavior in service organizations is becoming increasingly important. Many organizations are empowering their customer service employees and giving them the authority to take the lead in providing high-quality customer service. As noted previously, the empowering of nonmanagerial employees changes the role of first-line managers and often leads to the more efficient use of organizational resources. The following "Managing Globally" feature discusses how Levi Strauss created self-managed teams to increase responsiveness to customers and increase efficiency, quality, and innovation.

Managing Globally

How Levi Strauss Built an International Competitive Advantage

Levi Strauss (www.levi.com), the world's largest clothing manufacturer, has over 60 production facilities in 20 countries around the world. Robert Hass, the great-nephew of Levi Strauss himself, took control of the company in 1985 and pioneered its international expansion. In 1985, the organization was struggling. Its classic blue jeans were under attack from designer labels, and the company had been slow to develop new styles or lines of clothing. Innovation at Levi Strauss was not much respected, and neither were efforts aimed at increasing efficiency and responding to the customer. As a result, the company's market share was falling, and its costs were rising because of competition from companies that made their jeans in countries such as Mexico, Thailand, and Malaysia, where labor costs were low.[35]

Hass realized that to fight back he needed to rebuild the company's competitive advantage. Levi Strauss had always enjoyed a reputation for high quality, and its jeans were known for their durability. So Hass decided to start by increasing efficiency and innovation. To increase efficiency, he decided to move most of the company's manufacturing operations to Malaysia, Indonesia, Costa Rica, and other countries with low labor costs. To make Levi Strauss more innovative, he implemented programs to design new styles of jeans and other lines of clothing.

First, Levi's loose-fitting "500" jeans and Levi's Silver Tab jeans were introduced. Then came a new line of casual clothing aimed at aging baby boomers: Dockers became a huge success. Finally, Hass realized that customers in different countries have different preferences regarding colors and sizes (for example, Asian customers typically wear smaller sizes than Australian and American customers). So he started a program to customize jeans to meet the needs of global customers. Levi Strauss now sells over 200 different styles of blue jeans alone. Sales have soared as increased efficiency has allowed Levi's to sell its new clothing at low prices that appeal to customers around the globe.

Having achieved higher levels of efficiency and innovation, Hass began to focus on improving the company's responsiveness to customers. The company had been offering standard lines of clothing, an approach that often did not provide the styles or even the brands that best fit customers. Studies show, however, that working men and women have less time than ever before to shop around for jeans. So in 1995 Levi's began to experiment in the United States with the selling of customized jeans at Original Levi Strauss stores.

In those stores, trained clerks measure customers and electronically transmit a customer's measurements to a Levi Strauss factory in Tennessee.[36] At that location, employees in self-managed teams with 20 or 30 members are responsible for completing individual orders by assembling each pair of jeans from waist to hem. Each worker is trained to perform all the tasks needed to assemble a pair of jeans (in the typical work system, each employee performed only one task). Within three weeks, the customer receives his or her jeans for about $10 a pair more than standard off-the-shelf jeans cost.

As the example of Levi Strauss suggests, achieving a competitive advantage requires managers to use all their skills and expertise to develop resources and improve efficiency, quality, innovation, and responsiveness to customers. We revisit this theme often as we examine the ways managers plan strategies, create an organizational setting, and lead and control people and groups to effectively use human and other resources to achieve organizational goals.

Maintaining Ethical Standards

While mobilizing organizational resources, managers at all levels are under considerable pressure to increase the level at which their organizations perform. For example, top managers receive pressure from shareholders to increase the performance of the entire organization in order to boost the stock price, improve profits, or raise dividends. In turn, top managers may then pressure middle managers to find new ways to use organizational resources to increase efficiency or quality in order to attract new customers and earn more revenues.

Pressure to increase performance can be healthy for an organization because it causes managers to question the organization's operations and it encourages them to find new and better ways to plan, organize, lead, and control.[37] However, too much pressure to perform can be harmful.[37] It may induce managers to behave unethically in dealings with individuals and groups both inside and outside the organization.[38] For example, a purchasing manager for a large retail chain might buy inferior clothing as a cost-cutting measure; or to secure a large foreign contract, a sales manager in a large defense company might offer bribes to foreign officials. In 1995, two former Honda officials were convicted of accepting bribes from several large U.S. auto dealers to increase the supply of cars to the dealers and thus increase the dealers' profits.[39] Another example illustrating unethical managerial behavior is described in the following "Ethics in Action" feature.

Ethics in Action

How to Destroy a Charity's Reputation

In 1995, William Aramony, former president of United Way of America, the largest charitable organization in the United States, was convicted of misappropriating the funds of the organization and was sentenced to seven years in prison. Aramony was found guilty of 25 counts of fraud, conspiracy, and money laundering of over $1 million of the agency's funds, which he is reported to have spent on lavish entertainment for himself and several girlfriends. At one point the United Way was paying for a New York penthouse and limousine service for Aramony's personal use. Other close associates of Aramony at United Way were found guilty of similar charges and sentenced to jail terms.

After the unethical and illegal behaviors of United Way top managers were discovered in 1992, the managers were fired and Elaine L. Chao, former head of the Peace Corps and an experienced investment banker, was appointed to head the United Way and restore its reputation, badly damaged as a result of the scandal. Chao's primary goal is to increase donations, which fell markedly after the scandal when people saw their money had not been used appropriately.

When managers act unethically, some individuals or groups may obtain short-term gains, but in the long run the organization and people inside and outside the organization will pay. In Chapter 5 we discuss the nature of ethics and the importance for managers and all members of an organization to behave ethically as they pursue organizational goals.

Managing a Diverse Workforce

Another challenge for managers is to recognize the need to treat human resources in a fair and equitable manner. In an era when the age, gender, race, ethnicity, religion, and socioeconomic background of the workforce are changing, managers must establish employment procedures and practices that are fair and do not discriminate against any organizational members.[40] In the past, white male employees dominated the ranks of management, but today increasing numbers of organizations are realizing that to motivate effectively and take advantage of the talents of a diverse workforce they must make promotion opportunities available to all employees, including women and minorities.[41] Managers must also recognize the performance-enhancing possibilities of a diverse workforce, such as the ability to take advantage of the skills and experiences of different kinds of people.[42] The following "Focus on Diversity" feature looks at how companies take advantage of diversity at home and abroad to enhance their competitive advantage.

Focus on Diversity

Making the Most of Difference

To better utilize resources, many organizations around the world are capitalizing on the country- and even continent-specific knowledge of their diverse managers and employees. For example, to increase domestic sales of its soft drinks, U.S.-based Coca-Cola (www.coca-cola.com) recruits African-American and Hispanic employees to create sales campaigns targeted to their respective ethnic groups. Abroad, Coca-Cola takes advantage of the knowledge of its diverse foreign workforce to develop marketing campaigns that will be effective in each of the major global markets in which it competes. At the top-management level too, Coca-Cola responds to the challenge that global diversity offers by employing a diverse group of top-level managers to lead the company. Former Coke chairman Roberto Goizueta originally came from Cuba; other top managers are from France, Brazil, and Spain.

Many other companies also rely on the talents of their diverse workforces. For example, Alex Trotman, the former chairman of Ford U.S., who pioneered Ford's global reorganization, is an Englishman. Trotman acquired extensive knowledge of the needs of European customers while he was in charge of Ford's European operations. Jac Nasser, Ford's new CEO, who took over in 1998, was born in Lebanon. He too has extensive international experience, having been the head of Ford's Australian operations.

Managers who value their diverse employees invest in developing these employees' skills and capabilities and link rewards to their performance. They are the managers who best succeed in promoting performance over the long run.[43] Today, more and more organizations are realizing that people are their

On the left is Alex Trotman, the Englishman who was responsible for transforming Ford Motors into a successful global company, and on the right is Lebanese-born Jac Nasser, Ford's current President and CEO who is now in control of Ford's global strategy. Between the two is William Clay Ford, Jr., the great-grandson of Ford Motor Company founder Henry Ford, who became Chairman of Ford on January 1, 1999.

most important resource and that developing and protecting human resources is an important challenge for management in a competitive global environment. We discuss many of the issues surrounding the management of a diverse workforce in Chapter 5.

Utilizing New Information Systems and Technologies

Another important challenge for managers facing pressure to increase performance is the utilization of new information systems and technologies.[44] New technologies such as computer-controlled manufacturing and automated inventory control are continually being developed and improved to increase efficiency and responsiveness to customers. New information systems are a vital component of TQM. In a setting that uses self-managed teams, for example, sophisticated computer information systems link the activities of team members so that each team member knows what the others are doing. This coordination helps to improve quality and increase the pace of innovation. Microsoft, Hitachi, Xerox, and other companies make extensive use of information systems such as e-mail, the Internet, and video teleconferencing, accessible by means of personal computers, to build a competitive advantage. The importance of information systems and technologies is discussed in great detail in Chapters 15 and 17, and throughout the text you will find icons that alert you to stories about how it is changing the way companies operate. Consider here how Hewlett-Packard uses new information technologies to improve its performance.

Management Insight

The Information Revolution at Hewlett-Packard

Hewlett-Packard (HP) (www.hp.com) is the second largest supplier of computers and computer-related products in the world. It produces over 40,000 products in hundreds of different locations. In the 1990s HP's major goals were to bring products faster to the market, to reduce costs, and to improve relationships with customers. To help achieve these goals, Hewlett-Packard made innovative use of new information systems and technologies.

Taking advantage of the possibilities of advanced new networking software, HP linked the 70,000 personal computers its employees use into an internal computer network and created several companywide information systems. Open Mail, a companywide e-mail system, has over 100,000 mailboxes and handles over 1.5 million messages a day. Electronic Sales Partner links all of Hewlett-Packard's operating units with their customers and allows managers to communicate with customers electronically and work with them to solve their problems. Personnel–Internal Policies, through which the human resource department continually updates and makes

Chapter Summary

available all of Hewlett-Packard's personnel policies, is accessible by managers throughout the organization and helps them solve personnel problems. These information systems give HP managers access to important information and allow them to communicate quickly and make decisions speedily, all of which help the company to achieve its goals. As a result of its innovative use of information systems, Hewlett-Packard is one of the highest-performing companies in the world.

Summary and Review

WHAT IS MANAGEMENT? A manager is a person responsible for supervising the use of an organization's resources to meet its goals. An organization is a collection of people who work together and coordinate their actions to achieve a wide variety of goals. Management is the process of using organizational resources to achieve organizational goals effectively and efficiently through planning, organizing, leading, and controlling. An efficient organization makes the most productive use of its resources. An effective organization pursues appropriate goals and achieves these goals by using its resources to create the goods or services that customers want.

MANAGERIAL FUNCTIONS According to Fayol, the four principal managerial functions are planning, organizing, leading, and controlling. Managers at all levels of the organization and in all departments perform these functions. Effective management means managing these activities successfully.

TYPES OF MANAGEMENT Organizations typically have three levels of management. First-line managers are responsible for the day-to-day supervision of nonmanagerial employees. Middle managers are responsible for developing and utilizing organizational resources efficiently and effectively. Top managers have cross-departmental responsibility. The top managers' job is to establish appropriate goals for the entire organization and to verify that department managers are utilizing resources to achieve those goals. To increase efficiency and effectiveness, some organizations have altered their managerial hierarchies by restructuring, by empowering their workforces, and by utilizing self-managed teams.

MANAGERIAL ROLES AND SKILLS According to Mintzberg, managers play 10 different roles: figurehead, leader, liaison, monitor, disseminator, spokesperson, entrepreneur, disturbance handler, resource allocator, and negotiator. Three types of skills help managers perform these roles effectively: conceptual, human, and technical skills.

CHALLENGES FOR MANAGEMENT IN A GLOBAL ENVIRONMENT Today's competitive global environment presents many interesting challenges to managers: to build a competitive advantage by increasing efficiency, quality, innovation, and responsiveness to customers; to behave ethically toward people inside and outside the organization; to manage a diverse workforce; and to utilize new information systems and technologies.

Management in Action

Topics for Discussion and Action

1. Describe the difference between efficiency and effectiveness, and identify real organizations that you think are, or are not, efficient and effective.

2. In what ways can managers at each of the three levels of management contribute to organizational efficiency and effectiveness?

3. Identify an organization that you believe is high performing and one that you believe is low performing. Give 10 reasons why you think the performance levels of the two organizations differ so much.

4. Choose an organization such as a school or a bank; visit it; then list the different kinds of organizational resources it uses.

5. Visit an organization, and talk to first-line, middle, and top managers about their respective management roles in the organization and what they do to help the organization be efficient and effective.

6. Ask a middle or top manager, perhaps someone you already know, to give examples of how he or she performs the managerial functions of planning, organizing, leading, and controlling. How much time

does he or she spend in performing each function?

7. Like Mintzberg, try to find a cooperative manager who will allow you to follow him or her around for a day. List the types of roles the manager plays, and indicate how much time he or she spends performing them.

8. What are the building blocks of competitive advantage? Why is obtaining a competitive advantage important to managers?

9. In what ways do you think managers' jobs have changed the most over the last 15 years? Why have these changes occurred?

Building Management Skills
Thinking About Managers and Management

Think of an organization that has provided you with a work experience and the manager to whom you reported (or talk to someone who has had extensive work experience); then answer these questions.

1. Think of your direct supervisor. Of what department is he or she a member, and at what level of management is this person?

2. How do you characterize your supervisor's approach to management? For example, which particular management functions and roles does this per-

son perform most often? What kinds of management skills does this manager have?

3. Do you think the functions, roles, and skills of your supervisor are appropriate for the particular job he or she performs? How could this manager improve his or her task performance?

4. How did your supervisor's approach to management affect your attitudes and behavior? For example, how well did you perform as a subordinate, and how motivated were you?

5. Think of the organization and its resources. Do its managers utilize organizational resources

Building Management Skills continued

effectively? Which resources contribute most to the organization's performance?

6. Describe the way the organization treats its human resources. How does this treatment affect the attitudes and behaviors of the workforce?

7. If you could give your manager one piece of advice or change one management practice in the organization, what would it be?

8. How attuned are the managers in the organization to the need to increase efficiency, quality, innovation, or responsiveness to customers? How well do you think the organization performs its prime goals of providing the goods or services that customers want or need the most?

Small Group Breakout Exercise
Opening a New Restaurant

Form groups of three or four people, and appoint one group member as the spokesperson who will communicate your findings to the entire class when called on by the instructor. Then discuss the following scenario.

You and your partners have decided to open in your local community a large, full-service restaurant that will be open from 7 A.M. to 10 P.M. to serve breakfast, lunch, and dinner. Each of you is investing $50,000 in the venture, and together you have secured a bank loan for $300,000 more to begin operations. You and your partners have little experience in managing a restaurant beyond serving meals or eating in restaurants, and you now face the task of deciding how you will manage the restaurant and what your respective roles will be.

1. Decide what your respective managerial roles in the restaurant will be. For example, who will be responsible for the necessary departments and specific activities? Describe your managerial hierarchy.

2. Which building blocks of competitive advantage do you need to establish to help your restaurant succeed? What criteria will you use to evaluate how successfully you are managing the restaurant?

3. Discuss the most important decisions that must be made about (a) planning, (b) organizing, (c) leading, and (d) controlling, to allow you and your partners to utilize organizational resources effectively and build a competitive advantage.

4. For each managerial function, list the issue that will contribute the most to your restaurant's success.

Exploring the World Wide Web

Specific Assignment

Enter Chrysler Corporation's website (www.Investor-rel. com.chrysler), and view chairman Robert Eaton's message about his company in the 1995 annual report (and later reports if available). Click on the annual report; click on "next"; then click on "To our shareholders." (Note: Sometimes the exact website address for a location changes. You may need to do some search to find the exact location in question.) Also, from its home page (www.chrysler.com) look at the message about its merger with Daimler-Benz.

1. What are the building blocks of Chrysler's competitive advantage? Explore other parts of Chrysler's website to identify other aspects of the company's approach to doing business.

2. Why do you think Chrysler agreed to a merger with Daimler-Benz in 1998?

General Assignment

Search for the website of a company in which a manager discusses his or her approach to planning, organizing, leading, or controlling. What is that manager's approach to managing? What effects has this approach had on the company's performance?

ManagementCase

Opposite Approaches to Management at Campbell Soup and Quaker Oats

The Campbell Soup (www.soup.com) and Quaker Oats (www.quakeroats.com) companies are two of the largest and best-known food manufacturers in the United States. In the 1990s, however, they performed very differently. While Campbell's performance and stock price boomed, Quaker's declined, largely analysts believe because of differences in the way the companies were managed and the characteristics of the people who managed them.

Campbell's chief executive officer (CEO), its top manager, is David W. Johnson, an easygoing, approachable Australian who enjoys dressing up and interacting with his employees. Once, for example, he donned a red cape and dubbed himself "Souperman" while leading a rally to energize his employees.[45] Johnson is a master at communicating his vision for Campbell's and for mobilizing the support of his managers and employees to achieve that vision.

First, Johnson sets ambitious "stretch" goals for his managers to achieve, such as finding new ways to reduce costs or to use the company's resources to introduce new products for customers. Then he

ManagementCase continued

delegates authority and makes his managers responsible for devising a plan of action to meet these challenging goals. He holds them strictly accountable for their actions and closely watches the numbers, because changes in sales and profits reflect how well the managers are doing. Over 1,200 of Campbell's managers receive large bonuses tied to the company's performance. The success of Johnson's carefully crafted management approach is reflected in the numbers: Campbell's earnings increased by 19 percent in each of the six years after he took over, and its stock price more than doubled.

Quaker Oats did not enjoy the same kind of success. Because of the company's poor performance, CEO William D. Smithburg had to fight to keep his job. The price of the company's stock did not increase for five years, and analysts think that a major reason for this sluggishness is Smithburg's approach to management. His management style is very different from Johnson's. Remote and distant from his employees, in the 1980s Smithburg used his powerful analytical skills to make brilliant tactical decisions. For example, Quaker Oats bought the company that made Gatorade, the sports drink, and Smithburg turned Gatorade into the best-selling brand. He tried to repeat this success by purchasing Snapple, the maker of exotic fruit drinks, for $1.7 billion in 1994, but disaster struck.[46] Snapple was at the peak of its popularity, and within months large companies like Coca-Cola and PepsiCo were introducing their own lines of exotic fruit drinks. Almost at once, Snapple started to lose money.

Like Johnson, Smithburg had always been a manager who made the big decisions and then left his managers to implement them. But when the problems facing Snapple became serious, he became increasingly involved in the day-to-day running of Snapple. He blamed his top executives for Snapple's problems and started to assume their responsibilities. When Snapple's problems got worse, he fired the Snapple management team and took full control over the management of the product.

Smithburg's actions on the people front totally demoralized Quaker Oats's managers, and outside analysts began to wonder whether he had the interpersonal skills needed to manage the troubled company. Analysts also began to question his analytical abilities. Why did Smithburg pay $1.7 billion for Snapple, when most other people thought it was worth only $700 million at most? Analysts think that he was much too confident about his ability to understand the beverage business and to duplicate the success of Gatorade. In 1997, Quaker Oats sold Snapple to Triarc Corporation for only $300 million, a huge loss.

Questions

1. What are the main differences between Johnson's and Smithburg's approaches to management?

2. How easy or difficult would it be to copy Johnson's management style?

ManagementCase

In the News

From the Pages of
Blockbuster's Fired-Up Mr. Fixit

When it comes to doing his homework, John F. Antioco is something of a fanatic. Take his job interview for the top post at Blockbuster Entertainment Group last spring. Viacom Chairman Sumner M. Redstone was quickly charmed by the former fast-food executive, who sounded as if he had been in the video-rental business for years. The lunch went on for hours. "He surprised me," recalls Redstone, who was quickly convinced that Antioco was "the guy who will turn Blockbuster around." . . .

Antioco spent his first months crisscrossing the country meeting with store employees, regional managers, and franchise operators. He's also schmoozing with Hollywood studio executives, trying to smoothe relations and hammer out deals that may allow Blockbuster to buy tapes more economically. Antioco, who lives in Scottsdale, Ariz., and commutes to Dallas every few days, keeps a low profile. He's not granting media interviews, nor has he met with analysts to articulate his strategy.

Already, though, the Brooklyn native is pumping some energy into a demoralized staff, employees say. At a meeting of 1,100 Blockbuster store managers in Dallas last fall, Antioco delivered a fiery speech, portraying Blockbuster as an underdog that would prove skeptics wrong by coming back stronger and more aggressive than ever. "Will this company fail?" a fired-up Antioco asked the managers. "Not on my watch. No way, nohow."

Current and former associates describe him as a charismatic, no-nonsense manager. "It's all about customer service with John," says Karl Eller, who preceded Antioco as CEO of the Circle K Corp. convenience chain. "Figure out what the customer wants and find a way to get it to him." Antioco also gets high marks for motivating employees. When Antioco was CEO at Circle K, he and a colleague closed a national sales meeting with their best Blues Brothers impression, down to the dark suits, glasses, and hats. "That kind of stuff struck a chord with employees," recalls Ann Vry, formerly Circle K's public-relations chief.

Energy and drive have always characterized Antioco, who as a boy would rise at 3 A.M. to help his father, a milkman. Antioco later did stints as a shoe salesman, gravedigger, and stock clerk.

Antioco took his first assignment in retailing with Dallas-based Southland Corp.'s 7-Eleven Stores chain. By age 30, he was one of the company's youngest division managers ever. That's where Antioco began showing a talent for troubleshooting. The New York-based unit was bleeding cash, so Antioco spruced up stores, created new marketing campaigns, and patched up rocky franchisee relationships. Within two years, Antioco's unit was the company's most profitable.

His biggest feat, however, came at Circle K. In his first two years as CEO of the troubled chain, he restructured debt and closed 2,000 stores. By 1993, Antioco and other top execs joined Bahrain-based Investcorp International Inc. in a $400 million buyout, taking Circle K out of Chapter 11.

With fresh capital, Antioco zeroed in on operations. He ditched parallel shelves and narrow aisles in favor of self-contained departments like "Beverage Depot." He scrapped the sky-high prices then typical of such stores. Recalls Mitchell E. Telson, then Circle K chief operating officer: "John reestablished the concept of what a convenience store was supposed to be."

Then, during his brief stint as CEO of Taco Bell Corp., owned at the time by PepsiCo Inc., Antioco presided over the chain's first same-store sales gain in more than two years. "John's a very smart, pragmatic guy who's very focused on the consumer," says PepsiCo CEO Roger A. Enrico. "Even in just a few months you could see his imprint on Taco Bell."

Can Antioco work his magic on Blockbuster? The new chief is keeping the focus tight on operations and customer satisfaction. He hopes new deals with Hollywood studios will give it access to more hit films at a lower price. In the past, many customers left Blockbuster stores empty-handed when hit releases were missing from the shelves. Antioco is also lowering prices and extending rental periods for new and older flicks.

Meantime, he has been cutting costs: He laid off about 180 employees, mostly at Dallas headquarters. Antioco also put the brakes on store expansions until later this year and shuttered all 17 stores in Germany, which were doing poorly.

There are early signs of improvement. Analysts estimate fourth-quarter, same-store sales of video rentals were up 2% from the year-earlier quarter, the first positive showing in more than a year. Still, even if Antioco works miracles, some investors question whether the unit, now in a slow-growth industry, will ever be a good fit for Viacom. Says Mario J. Gabelli, a large Viacom shareholder, with nearly 10%: "It was a mistake [for Viacom] to make the acquisition [in 1994], and it's [still] a mistake. The growth potential just isn't there."

But Redstone seems ready to declare a turnaround. "We don't need any more time to conclude that John is the right guy in the right job," he says. But of course, Redstone was just as publicly bullish on Antioco's short-lived predecessors. Viacom had hoped to spin off at least part of Blockbuster this year. Those plans are on hold—at least until Antioco delivers. Now, all Redstone has to do is hold on to him.

Source: Stephanie Anderson Forest, *Business Week*, February 9, 1998, 100–101.

Questions

1. What is John Antioco's approach to managing—that is, to planning, organizing, leading, and controlling?
2. How is Antioco trying to give Blockbuster a competitive advantage?

Chapter two

The Evolution of Management Theory

Learning Objectives

1. Describe how the need to increase organizational efficiency and effectiveness has guided the evolution of management theory.

2. Explain the principle of job specialization and division of labor, and tell why the study of person–task relationships is central to the pursuit of increased efficiency.

3. Identify the principles of administration and organization that underlie effective organizations.

4. Trace the changes that have occurred in theories about how managers should behave in order to motivate and control employees.

5. Explain the contributions of management science to the efficient use of organizational resources.

6. Explain why the study of the external environment and its impact on an organization has become a central issue in management thought.

A Case in Contrast

Changing Ways of Making Cars

Car production has changed dramatically over the years as managers have applied different views or philosophies of management to organize and control work activities. Prior to 1900, workers worked in small groups, cooperating to hand-build cars with parts that often had to be altered and modified to fit together. This system, a type of *small-batch production,* was very expensive; assembling just one car took considerable time and effort; and workers could produce only a few cars in a day. To reduce costs and sell more cars, managers of early car companies needed better techniques to increase efficiency.

Henry Ford revolutionized the car industry. In 1913, Ford opened the Highland Park car plant in Detroit to produce the Model T. Ford and his team of manufacturing managers pioneered the development of *mass-production manufacturing,* a system that made the small-batch system almost obsolete overnight. In mass production, moving conveyor belts bring the car to the workers.

In 1913, Henry Ford revolutionized the production process of a car by pioneering mass production manufacturing, a production system in which a conveyor belt brings each car to the workers, and each individual worker performs a single task along the production line. Even today cars are still built using this system, as evidenced in this photo of workers along a computerized automobile assembly line.

This photo taken in 1904 inside a Daimler Motor Co. is an examle of the use of small-batch production, a production system in which small groups of people work together and perform all the tasks needed to assemble a product.

Each individual worker performs a single assigned task along a production line, and the speed of the conveyor belt is the primary means of controlling their activities. Ford experimented to discover the most efficient way for each individual worker to perform an assigned task. The result was that each worker performed one specialized task, such as bolting on the door or attaching the door handle, and jobs in the Ford car plant became very repetitive.[1]

Ford's management approach increased efficiency and reduced costs by so much that by 1920 he was able to reduce the price of a car by two-thirds and sell over 2 million cars a year.[2] Ford Motor Company (www.ford.com) became the leading car company in the world, and many competitors rushed to adopt the new mass-production techniques. Two of these companies, General Motors (GM) (www.gm.com) and Chrysler (www.chryslercorp.com), eventually emerged as Ford's major competitors.

The CEOs of GM and Chrysler—Alfred Sloan and Walter Chrysler—went beyond simple imitation of the Ford approach by adopting a new strategy: offering customers a wide variety of cars to choose from. To keep costs low, Henry Ford had offered customers only one car—the Model T. The new strategy of offering a wide range of models was so popular that Ford was eventually forced to close his factory for seven months in order to reorganize his manufacturing system to widen his product range. Due to his limited vision of the changing car market, his company lost its competitive advantage. During the early 1930s, GM became the market leader.

The next revolution in car production took place not in the United States but in Japan. A change in management thinking occurred there when Ohno Taiichi, a Toyota production engineer, pioneered the development of *lean manufacturing* in the 1960s after touring the U.S. plants of the Big Three car companies. The management philosophy behind lean manufacturing is to continuously find methods to improve the efficiency of the production process in order to reduce costs, increase quality, and reduce car assembly time.

In lean manufacturing, workers work on a moving production line, but they are organized into small teams, each of which is responsible for a particular phase of car assembly, such as installing the car's transmission or electrical wiring system. Each team member is expected to learn all the tasks of all members of his or her team, and each work group is charged with the responsibility not only to assemble cars but also to continuously find ways to increase quality and reduce costs. By 1970, Japanese managers had applied the new lean production system so efficiently that they were producing higher-quality cars at lower prices than their U.S. counterparts, and by 1980 Japanese companies were dominating the global car market.

To compete with the Japanese, managers in the Big Three U.S. car makers visited Japan to learn lean production methods. Ford and Chrysler were the most successful in learning and utilizing the new manufacturing philosophy to increase quality and reduce costs. In fact, by 1995 their costs were almost as low as the costs of Japanese car companies. Ford, in particular, dramatically improved car quality. Still, although U.S. car makers have approached, they have not yet matched the high quality standards of Toyota (www.toyota.com). ●

Overview

As this sketch of the evolution of global car manufacturing suggests, changes in management practices occur as managers, theorists, researchers, and consultants seek new ways to increase organizational efficiency and effectiveness. The driving force behind the evolution of management theory is the search for better ways to utilize organizational resources. Advances in management theory typically occur as managers and researchers find better ways to perform the principal management tasks: planning, organizing, leading, and controlling human and other organizational resources.

In this chapter, we examine how management theory concerning appropriate management practices has evolved in modern times and the central concerns that have guided its development. First, we examine the so-called classical management theories that emerged around the turn of the twentieth century. These include scientific management, which focuses on matching people and tasks to maximize efficiency; and administrative management, which focuses on identifying the principles that will lead to the creation of the most efficient system of organization and management. Next, we consider behavioral management theories, developed both before and after the Second World War, which focus on how managers should lead and control their workforces to increase performance. Then we discuss management science theory, which developed during the Second World War and has become increasingly important as researchers have developed rigorous analytical and quantitative techniques to help managers measure and control organizational performance. Finally, we discuss business in the 1960s and 1970s and focus on the theories that were developed to help explain how the external environment affects the way organizations and managers operate.

By the end of this chapter you will understand the ways in which management theory has evolved over time. You will also understand how economic, political, and cultural forces have affected the development of these theories and the ways in which managers and their organizations behave. Figure 2.1 summarizes the chronology of the management theories that are discussed in this chapter. ●

Figure 2.1

The Evolution of Management Theory

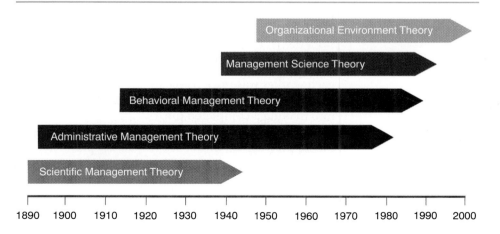

Scientific Management Theory

The evolution of modern management began in the closing decades of the nineteenth century, after the industrial revolution had swept through Europe and America. In the new economic climate, managers of all types of organizations–political, educational, and economic–were increasingly trying to find better ways to satisfy customers' needs. Many major economic, technical, and cultural changes were taking place at this time. The introduction of steam power and the development of sophisticated machinery and equipment changed the way goods were produced, particularly in the weaving and clothing industries. Small workshops run by skilled workers who produced hand-manufactured products (a system called *crafts production*) were being replaced by large factories in which sophisticated machines controlled by hundreds or even thousands of unskilled or semiskilled workers made products. For example, raw cotton and wool, which in the past families or whole villages working together had spun into yarn, were now shipped to factories where workers operated machines that spun and wove large quantities of yarn into cloth.

Owners and managers of the new factories found themselves unprepared for the challenges accompanying the change from small-scale crafts production to large-scale mechanized manufacturing. Moreover, many of the managers and supervisors in these workshops and factories were engineers who had only a technical orientation. They were unprepared for the social problems that occur when people work together in large groups (as in a factory or shop system). Managers began to search for new techniques to manage their organizations' resources, and soon they began to focus on ways to increase the efficiency of the worker–task mix.

Job Specialization and the Division of Labor

Initially, management theorists were interested in the subject of why the factory system and new machine shops were more efficient and produced greater quantities of goods and services than older, crafts-style production operations. Nearly 200 years before, Adam Smith had been one of the first writers to investigate the advantages associated with producing goods and services in factories. A famous economist, Smith journeyed around England in the 1700s studying the effects of the industrial revolution.[3] In a study of factories that produced different kinds of pins or nails, Smith identified two different manufacturing methods. The first was similar to crafts-style production, in which each worker was responsible for all of the 18 tasks involved in producing a pin. The other had each worker performing only 1 or a few of the 18 tasks that go into making a completed pin.

In a comparison of the relative performance of these different ways of organizing production, Smith found that the performance of the factories in which workers specialized in only 1 or a few tasks was much greater than the performance of the factory in which each worker performed all 18 pin-making tasks. In fact, Smith found that 10 workers specializing in a particular task could, between them, make 48,000 pins a day, whereas those workers who performed all the tasks could make only a few thousand at most.[4] Smith reasoned that this difference in performance was due to the fact that the workers who specialized became much more skilled at their specific tasks and as a group were thus able to produce a product faster than the group of workers who each had to perform many tasks. Smith concluded that increasing the level of **job specialization**—the process by which a division of labor occurs as different workers specialize in different tasks over time—increases efficiency and leads to higher organizational performance.[5]

Armed with the insights gained from Adam Smith's observations, other managers and researchers began to investigate how to improve job specialization to increase performance. Management practitioners and theorists focused on how managers should organize and control the work process to maximize the advantages of job specialization and the division of labor.

job specialization The process by which a division of labor occurs as different workers specialize in different tasks over time.

F. W. Taylor and Scientific Management

Frederick W. Taylor (1856–1915) is best known for defining the techniques of **scientific management**, the systematic study of relationships between people and tasks for the purpose of redesigning the work process to increase efficiency. Taylor was a manufacturing manager who eventually became a consultant and taught other managers how to apply his scientific management techniques. Taylor believed that if the amount of time and effort that each worker expends to produce a unit of output (a finished good or service) can be reduced by increasing specialization and the division of labor, the production process will become more efficient. Taylor believed the way to create the most efficient division of labor could best be determined by means of scientific management techniques, rather than intuitive or informal rule-of-thumb knowledge. Based on his experiments and observations as a manufacturing manager in a variety of settings, he developed four principles to increase efficiency in the workplace:[6]

scientific management The systematic study of relationships between people and tasks for the purpose of redesigning the work process to increase efficiency.

- Principle 1: *Study the way workers perform their tasks, gather all the informal job knowledge that workers possess, and experiment with ways of improving the way tasks are performed.*

To discover the most efficient method of performing specific tasks, Taylor studied in great detail and measured the ways different workers went about performing their tasks. One of the main tools he used was a time-and-motion study, which involves the careful timing and recording of the actions taken to perform a particular task. Once Taylor understood the existing method of performing a task, he then experimented to increase specialization. He tried different methods of dividing and coordinating the various tasks necessary to produce a finished product. Usually this meant simplifying jobs and having each worker perform fewer, more routine tasks, as at the pin factory or on Ford's car assembly line. Taylor also sought to find ways to improve each worker's ability to perform a particular task—for example, by reducing the number of motions workers made to complete the task, by changing the layout of the work area or the type of tool workers used, or by experimenting with tools of different sizes.

- Principle 2: *Codify the new methods of performing tasks into written rules and standard operating procedures.*

Once the best method of performing a particular task was determined, Taylor specified that it should be recorded so that the procedures could be taught to all workers performing the same task. These rules could be used to further standardize and simplify jobs—essentially, to make jobs even more routine. In this way efficiency could be increased throughout an organization.

- Principle 3: *Carefully select workers so that they possess skills and abilities that match the needs of the task, and train them to perform the task according to the established rules and procedures.*

To increase specialization, Taylor believed workers had to understand the tasks that were required and be thoroughly trained in order to perform the task at the required level. Workers who could not be trained to this level were to be transferred to a job where they were able to reach the minimum required level of proficiency.[7]

- Principle 4: *Establish a fair or acceptable level of performance for a task, and then develop a pay system that provides a reward for performance above the acceptable level.*

To encourage workers to perform at a high level of efficiency, and to provide them with an incentive to reveal the most efficient techniques for performing a task, Taylor advocated that workers benefit from any gains in performance. They should be paid a bonus and receive some percentage of the performance gains achieved through the more efficient work process.

By 1910, Taylor's system of scientific management had become nationally known and in many instances faithfully and fully practiced.[8] However, managers in many organizations chose to implement the new principles of scientific management selectively. This decision ultimately resulted in problems. For example, some managers using scientific management obtained increases in performance, but rather than sharing performance gains with workers through bonuses as Taylor had advocated, they simply increased the amount of work that each worker was expected to do. Many workers experiencing the reorganized work system found that as their performance increased, managers required them to do more work for the same pay. Workers also learned that increases in performance often meant fewer jobs and a greater threat of layoffs, because fewer workers were needed. In addition, the specialized, simplified jobs were often monotonous and repetitive, and many workers became dissatisfied with their jobs.

Scientific management brought many workers more hardship than gain and a distrust of managers who did not seem to care about their well-being.[9] These dissatisfied workers resisted attempts to use the new scientific management techniques and at times even withheld their job knowledge from managers to protect their jobs and pay. It is not all that difficult for workers to conceal the true potential efficiency of a work system in order to protect their interests. Experienced machine operators, for example, can slow their machines in undetectable ways by adjusting the tension in the belts or by misaligning the gears. Workers sometimes even develop informal work rules that discourage high performance and encourage shirking as work groups attempt to identify an acceptable or fair performance level (a tactic that is discussed in the next section).

Unable to inspire workers to accept the new scientific management techniques for performing tasks, some organizations increased the mechanization of the work process. For example, one reason why Henry Ford introduced moving conveyor belts in his factory was the realization that when a conveyor belt controls the pace of work (instead of workers setting their own pace), workers can be pushed to perform at higher levels—levels that they may have

Charlie Chaplin tries to extricate a fellow employee from the machinery of mass production in this clip from "Modern Times." The complex machinery is meant to represent the power that machinery has over the worker in the new work system.

thought were beyond their reach. Charlie Chaplin captured this aspect of mass production in one of the opening scenes of his famous movie *Modern Times* (1936). In the film, Chaplin caricatured a new factory employee fighting to work at the machine-imposed pace but losing the battle to the machine. Henry Ford also used the principles of scientific management to identify the tasks that each worker should perform on the production line and thus to determine the most effective way to create a division of labor to suit the needs of a mechanized production system.

From a performance perspective, the combination of the two management practices—(1) achieving the right mix of worker–task specialization and (2) linking people and tasks by the speed of the production line—makes sense. It produces the huge savings in cost and huge increases in output that occur in large, organized work settings. For example, in 1908, managers at the Franklin Motor Company using scientific management principles redesigned the work process, and the output of cars increased from 100 cars a *month* to 45 cars a *day;* workers' wages, however, increased by only 90 percent.[10] From other perspectives, however, scientific management practices raise many concerns. The definition of the workers' rights not by the workers themselves but by the owners or managers as a result of the introduction of the new management practices raised an ethical issue, which we examine in this "Ethics in Action."

Ethics in Action

Fordism in Practice

From 1908 to 1914, through trial and error, Henry Ford's talented team of production managers pioneered the development of the moving conveyor belt and thus changed manufacturing practices forever. Although the technical aspects of the move to mass production were a dramatic financial success for Ford and for the millions of Americans who could now afford cars, for the workers who actually produced the cars, many human and social problems resulted.

With simplification of the work process, workers grew to hate the monotony of the moving conveyor belt. By 1914, Ford's car plants were experiencing huge employee turnover—often reaching levels as high as 300 or 400 percent per year as workers left because they could not handle the work-induced stress.[11] Henry Ford recognized these problems and made an announcement: From that point on, to motivate his workforce, he would reduce the length of the workday from 9 hours to 8 hours, and the company would *double* the basic wage from $2.50 to $5.00 per day. This was a dramatic increase, similar to an announcement today of an overnight doubling of the minimum wage. Ford became an internationally famous figure, and the word *Fordism* was coined for his new approach.[12]

Ford's apparent generosity, however, was matched by an intense effort to control the resources—both human and material—with which his empire was built. He employed hundreds of inspectors to check up on employees, both inside and outside his factories. In the factory, supervision was close and confining. Employees were not allowed to leave their places at the production line, and they were not permitted to talk to one another. Their job was to concentrate fully on the task at hand. Few employees could adapt to this system, and they developed ways of talking out of the sides of their mouths, like ventriloquists, and invented a form of speech that became known as the "Ford Lisp."[13] Ford's obsession with control brought him into greater and greater conflict with managers, who were often fired when they disagreed with him. As a result, many talented people left Ford to join his growing rivals.

Outside the workplace, Ford went so far as to establish what he called the "Sociological Department" to check up on how his employees lived and the ways they spent their time. Inspectors from this department visited the homes of employees and investigated their habits and problems. Employees who exhibited behaviors contrary to Ford's standards (for instance, if they drank too much or were always in debt) were likely to be fired. Clearly, Ford's effort to control his employees led him and his managers to behave in ways that today would be considered unacceptable and unethical and in the long run would impair an organization's ability to prosper.

Despite the problems of worker turnover, absenteeism, and discontent at Ford Motor Company, managers of the other car companies watched Ford reap huge gains in efficiency from the application of the new management principles. They believed that their companies would have to imitate Ford if they were to survive. They followed Taylor and used many of his followers as consultants to teach them how to adopt the techniques of scientific management. In addition, Taylor elaborated his principles in several books, including

Shop Management (1903) and *The Principles of Scientific Management* (1911), which explain in detail how to apply the principles of scientific management to reorganize the work system.[14]

Taylor's work has had an enduring effect on the management of production systems. Managers in every organization, whether it produces goods or services, now carefully analyze the basic tasks that must be performed and try to devise the work systems that will allow their organizations to operate most efficiently.

The Gilbreths

Two prominent followers of Taylor were Frank Gilbreth (1868–1924) and Lillian Gilbreth (1878–1972), who refined Taylor's analysis of work movements and made many contributions to time-and-motion study.[15] Their aims were to (1) break up and analyze every individual action necessary to perform a particular task into each of its component actions, (2) find better ways to perform each component action, and (3) reorganize each of the component actions so that the action as a whole could be performed more efficiently—at less cost of time and effort.

The Gilbreths often filmed a worker performing a particular task and then separated the task actions, frame by frame, into their component movements. Their goal was to maximize the efficiency with which each individual task was performed so that gains across tasks would add up to enormous savings of time and effort. Their attempts to develop improved management principles were captured—at times quite humorously—in the movie *Cheaper by the Dozen,* which depicts how the Gilbreths (with their 12 children) tried to live their own lives according to these efficiency principles and apply them to daily actions such as shaving, cooking, and even raising a family.[16]

A scene from "Cheaper by the Dozen" illustrating how "efficient families," such as the Gilbreth's, use formal family courts to solve problems of assigning chores to different family members and to solve disputes when they arise.

Eventually, the Gilbreths became increasingly interested in the study of fatigue. They studied how the physical characteristics of the workplace contribute to job stress that often leads to fatigue and thus poor performance. They isolated factors, such as lighting, heating, the color of walls, and the design of tools and machines, that result in worker fatigue. Their pioneering studies paved the way for new advances in management theory.

In workshops and factories, the work of the Gilbreths, Taylor, and many others had a major effect on the practice of management. In comparison with the old crafts system, jobs in the new system were more repetitive, boring, and monotonous as a result of the application of scientific management principles, and workers became increasingly dissatisfied. Frequently, the management of work settings became a game between workers and managers: Managers tried to initiate work practices to increase performance, and workers tried to hide the true potential efficiency of the work setting in order to protect their own well-being.[17]

Administrative Management Theory

Side by side with scientific managers studying the person–task mix to increase efficiency, other researchers were focusing on **administrative management,** the study of how to create an organizational structure that leads to high efficiency and effectiveness. Organizational structure is the system of task and authority relationships that control how employees use resources to achieve the organization's goals. Two of the most influential views regarding the creation of efficient systems of organizational administration were developed in Europe: Max Weber, a German professor of sociology, developed one theory. Henri Fayol, the French manager who developed a model of management introduced in Chapter 1, developed the other.

administrative management The study of how to create an organizational structure that leads to high efficiency and effectiveness.

The Theory of Bureaucracy

Max Weber (1864–1920), wrote at the turn of the twentieth century, when Germany was undergoing its industrial revolution.[18] To help Germany manage its growing industrial enterprises at a time when it was striving to become a world power, Weber developed the principles of **bureaucracy**–a formal system of organization and administration designed to ensure efficiency and effectiveness. A bureaucratic system of administration is based on five principles (summarized in Figure 2.2).

bureaucracy A formal system of organization and administration designed to ensure efficiency and effectiveness.

• Principle 1: *In a bureaucracy, a manager's formal authority derives from the position he or she holds in the organization.*

Authority is the power to hold people accountable for their actions and to make decisions concerning the use of organizational resources. Authority gives managers the right to direct and control their subordinates' behavior to achieve organizational goals. In a bureaucratic system of administration, obedience is owed to a manager, not because of any personal qualities that he or she might possess–such as personality, wealth, or social status–but because the manager occupies a position that is associated with a certain level of authority and responsibility.[19]

authority The power to hold people accountable for their actions and to make decisions concerning the use of organizational resources.

• Principle 2: *In a bureaucracy, people should occupy positions because of their performance, not because of their social standing or personal contacts.*

This principle was not always followed in Weber's time and is often ignored today. Some organizations and industries are still affected by social networks in which personal contacts and relations, not job–related skills, influence hiring and promotional decisions.

• Principle 3: *The extent of each position's formal authority and task responsibilities, and its relationship to other positions in an organization, should be clearly specified.*

When the tasks and authority associated with various positions in the organization are clearly specified, managers and workers know what is expected of them and what to expect from each other. Moreover, an organization can hold

Figure 2.2
Weber's Principles of Bureaucracy

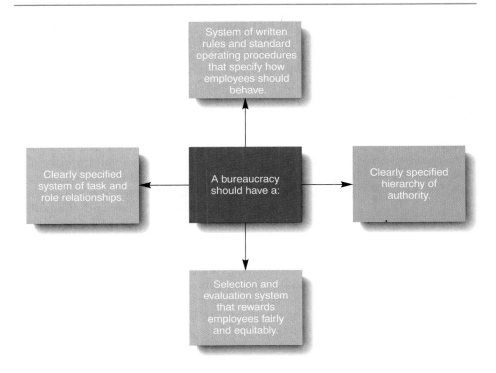

System of written rules and standard operating procedures that specify how employees should behave.

Clearly specified system of task and role relationships.

A bureaucracy should have a:

Clearly specified hierarchy of authority.

Selection and evaluation system that rewards employees fairly and equitably.

Pictured here is the daughter of Playboy founder Hugh Heffner, who now runs Playboy Enterprises. Do you think Ms. Heffner earned this position based on her performance or knowledge, or received it based on her relationship to Hugh Heffner? Do you consider her gender an opportunity or barrier for her success in the industry?

all its employees strictly accountable for their actions when each person knows exactly his or her responsibilities.

• Principle 4: *So that authority can be exercised effectively in an organization, positions should be arranged hierarchically, so employees know whom to report to and who reports to them.*[20]

Managers must create an organizational hierarchy of authority that makes it clear who reports to whom and to whom managers and workers should go if conflicts or problems arise. This principle is especially important in the armed forces, FBI, CIA, and other organizations that deal with sensitive issues involving possible major repercussions. It is vital that managers at high levels of the hierarchy be able to hold subordinates accountable for their actions.

• Principle 5: *Managers must create a well-defined system of rules, standard operating procedures, and norms so that they can effectively control behavior within an organization.*

Rules are formal written instructions that specify actions to be taken under different circumstances to achieve specific goals (for example, if A happens, do B). **Standard operating procedures (SOPs)** are specific sets of written instructions about how to perform a certain aspect of a task. A rule might state that at the end of the workday employees are to leave their machines in good order, and a set of SOPs then specifies exactly how they should do so, itemizing which machine parts

rules Formal written
instructions that specify
actions to be taken under
different circumstances to
achieve specific goals.

**standard operating
procedures** Specific sets
of written instructions
about how to perform a
certain aspect of a task.

norms Unwritten, informal
codes of conduct that prescribe how people should
act in particular situations.

must be oiled or replaced. **Norms** are unwritten, informal codes of conduct that prescribe how people should act in particular situations. For example, an organizational norm in a restaurant might be that waiters should help each other if time permits.

Rules, SOPs, and norms provide behavioral guidelines that increase the performance of a bureaucratic system because they specify the best ways to accomplish organizational tasks. Companies such as McDonald's and Wal-Mart have developed extensive rules and procedures to specify the types of behaviors that are required of their employees, such as "Always greet the customer with a smile."

Weber believed that organizations that implement all five principles will establish a bureaucratic system that will improve organizational performance. The specification of positions and the use of rules and SOPs to regulate how tasks are performed make it easier for managers to organize and control the work of subordinates. Similarly, fair and equitable selection and promotion systems improve managers' feelings of security, reduce stress, and encourage organizational members to act ethically and further promote the interests of the organization.[21]

If bureaucracies are not managed well, however, many problems can result. Sometimes, managers allow rules and SOPs—"bureaucratic red tape"—to become so cumbersome that decision making becomes slow and inefficient and organizations are unable to change. When managers rely too much on rules to solve problems and not enough on their own skills and judgment, their behavior becomes inflexible. A key challenge for managers is to use bureaucratic principles to benefit, rather than harm, an organization.

Fayol's Principles of Management

Working at the same time as, but independently from, Weber, Henri Fayol (1841–1925), the CEO of Comambault Mining, identified 14 principles (summarized in Table 2.1) that he believed to be essential to increasing the efficiency of the management process.[22] We discuss these principles in detail here because, although they were developed at the turn of the twentieth century, they remain the bedrock on which much of the recent management theory and research is based. In fact, as the "Management Insight" following this discussion suggests, modern writers such as well-known management guru Tom Peters continue to extol these principles.

DIVISION OF LABOR   A champion of job specialization and the division of labor for reasons already mentioned, Fayol was nevertheless among the first to point out the downside of too much specialization: boredom—a state of mind likely to cause a fall in product quality, worker initiative, and flexibility. As a result, Fayol advocated that workers be given more job duties to perform or be encouraged to assume more responsibility for work outcomes, a principle increasingly applied today in organizations that empower their workers.

AUTHORITY AND RESPONSIBILITY   Like Weber, Fayol emphasized the importance of authority and responsibility. Fayol, however, went beyond Weber's formal authority, which derives from a manager's position in the hierarchy, to recognize the informal authority that derives from personal

Table 2.1

Fayol's 14 Principles of Management

Division of Labor   Job specialization and the division of labor should increase efficiency, especially if managers take steps to lessen workers' boredom.

Authority and Responsibility   Managers have the right to give orders and the power to exhort subordinates for obedience.

Unity of Command   An employee should receive orders from only one superior.

Line of Authority   The length of the chain of command that extends from the top to the bottom of an organization should be limited.

Centralization   Authority should not be concentrated at the top of the chain of command.

Unity of Direction   The organization should have a single plan of action to guide managers and workers.

Equity   All organizational members are entitled to be treated with justice and respect.

Order   The arrangement of organizational positions should maximize organizational efficiency and provide employees with satisfying career opportunities.

Initiative   Managers should allow employees to be innovative and creative.

Discipline   Managers need to create a workforce that strives to achieve organizational goals.

Remuneration of Personnel   The system that managers use to reward employees should be equitable for both employees and the organization.

Stability of Tenure of Personnel   Long-term employees develop skills that can improve organizational efficiency.

Subordination of Individual Interests to the Common Interest   Employees should understand how their performance affects the performance of the whole organization.

Esprit de Corps   Managers should encourage the development of shared feelings of comradeship, enthusiasm, or devotion to a common cause.

expertise, technical knowledge, moral worth, and ability to lead and to generate commitment from subordinates. (The study of authority is the subject of recent research into leadership, discussed in Chapter 13.)

unity of command A reporting relationship in which an employee receives orders from, and reports to, only one superior.

UNITY OF COMMAND   The principle of **unity of command** specifies that an employee should receive orders from, and report to, only one superior. Fayol believed that *dual command,* the reporting relationship that exists when two supervisors give orders to the same subordinate, should be avoided except in exceptional circumstances. Dual command confuses the subordinate, undermines order and discipline, and creates havoc within the formal hierarchy of authority. Assessing any manager's authority and responsibility in a system of dual command is difficult, and the manager who is bypassed feels slighted and angry and may be uncooperative in the future.

line of authority The chain of command extending from the top to the bottom of an organization.

LINE OF AUTHORITY   The **line of authority** is the chain of command extending from the top to the bottom of an organization. Fayol was one of the first management theorists to point out the importance of limiting the length of the chain of command by controlling the number of levels in the managerial hierarchy. The greater the number of levels in the hierarchy, the longer communication between managers at the top and bottom takes and the slower is the pace of planning and organizing. Restricting the number of hierarchical levels to lessen these communication problems enables an organization to act quickly and flexibly and is one reason for the recent trend toward restructuring (discussed in Chapter 1).

Fayol also pointed out that when organizations are split into different departments, each with its own hierarchy, it is important to allow middle and first-line managers in each department to interact with managers at similar levels in other departments. This interaction helps to speed decision making, because managers know each other and know whom to go to when problems arise. For cross-departmental integration to work, Fayol noted the importance of keeping one's superiors informed about what is taking place so that lower-level decisions do not harm activities taking place in other parts of the organization. One alternative to cross-departmental integration is to create cross-departmental teams controlled by a team leader (see Chapter 1).

CENTRALIZATION

centralization The concentration of authority at the top of the managerial hierarchy.

Fayol also was one of the first management writers to focus on **centralization,** the concentration of authority at the top of the managerial hierarchy. Fayol believed that authority should not be concentrated at the top of the chain of command. One of the most significant issues that top managers face is how much authority to centralize at the top of the organization and what authority to decentralize to managers and workers at lower hierarchical levels. This is an important issue because it affects the behavior of people at all levels in the organization.

If authority is very centralized, only managers at the top make important decisions, and subordinates simply follow orders. This arrangement gives top managers great control over organizational activities and helps ensure that the organization is pursuing its strategy, but it makes it difficult for the people who are closest to problems and issues to respond to them in a timely manner. It also can lower the motivation of middle and first-line managers and make them less flexible and adaptable because they become reluctant to make decisions on their own, even when doing so is necessary. They get used to passing the buck. As we saw in Chapter 1, the pendulum is now swinging toward decentralization, as organizations seek to empower middle managers and create self-managed teams that monitor and control their own activities both to increase organizational flexibility and to reduce operating costs and increase efficiency.

UNITY OF DIRECTION

unity of direction The singleness of purpose that makes possible the creation of one plan of action to guide managers and workers as they use organizational resources.

Just as there is a need for unity of command, there is also a need for **unity of direction,** the singleness of purpose that makes possible the creation of one plan of action to guide managers and workers as they use organizational resources. An organization without a single guiding plan becomes inefficient and ineffective; its activities become unfocused, and individuals and groups work at cross-purposes. Successful planning starts with top managers working as a team to craft the organization's strategy, which they communicate to middle managers, who decide how to use organizational resources to implement the strategy.

EQUITY

equity The justice, impartiality, and fairness to which all organizational members are entitled.

As Fayol wrote: "For personnel to be encouraged to carry out their duties with all the devotion and loyalty of which they are capable, they must be treated with respect for their own sense of integrity, and equity results from the combination of respect and justice."[23] **Equity**—the justice, impartiality, and fairness to which all organizational members are entitled—is receiving much attention today; the desire to treat employees fairly is a primary concern for many managers (equity theory is discussed in Chapter 12).

ORDER   Like Taylor and the Gilbreths, Fayol was interested in analyzing jobs, positions, and individuals to ensure that the organization was using resources as efficiently as possible. To Fayol, **order** meant the methodical arrangement of positions to provide the organization with the greatest benefit and to provide employees with career opportunities to satisfy their needs. Thus, Fayol recommended the use of organizational charts to show the position and duties of each employee and to indicate which positions an employee might move to or be promoted into in the future. He also advocated that managers engage in extensive career planning to help ensure orderly career paths. Career planning is of primary interest today as organizations increase the resources they are willing to devote to training and developing their workforces.

order The methodical arrangement of positions to provide the organization with the greatest benefit and to provide employees with career opportunities.

INITIATIVE   Although order and equity are important means to fostering commitment and loyalty among employees, Fayol believed that managers must also encourage employees to exercise **initiative,** the ability to act on their own, without direction from a superior. Used properly, initiative can be a major source of strength for an organization because it leads to creativity and innovation. Managers need skill and tact to achieve the difficult balance between the organization's need for order and employees' desire for initiative. Fayol believed that the ability to strike this balance was a key indicator of a superior manager.

initiative The ability to act on one's own, without direction from a superior.

DISCIPLINE   In focusing on the importance of **discipline**—obedience, energy, application, and other outward marks of respect for a superior's authority—Fayol was addressing the concern of many early managers: How to create a workforce that was reliable and hardworking and would strive to achieve organizational goals. According to Fayol, discipline results in respectful relations between organizational members and reflects the quality of an organization's leadership and a manager's ability to act fairly and equitably.

discipline Obedience, energy, application, and other outward marks of respect for a superior's authority.

REMUNERATION OF PERSONNEL   Fayol proposed reward systems including bonuses and profit-sharing plans, which are increasingly utilized today as organizations seek improved ways to motivate employees. Convinced from his own experience that an organization's payment system has important implications for organizational success, Fayol believed that effective reward systems should be equitable for both employees and the organization, encourage productivity by rewarding well-directed effort, not be subject to abuse, and be uniformly applied to employees.

STABILITY OF TENURE OF PERSONNEL   Fayol also recognized the importance of long-term employment, and the idea has been echoed by contemporary management gurus such as Tom Peters, Jeff Pfeffer, and William Ouchi. When employees stay with an organization for extended periods of time, they develop skills that improve the organization's ability to utilize its resources. Long-term employment is one of the factors that may explain the success of many large Japanese companies.

SUBORDINATION OF INDIVIDUAL INTERESTS TO THE COMMON INTEREST   The interests of the organization as a whole must take precedence over the interests of any one individual or group if the organization is to survive. Equitable agreements must be established between the organization and its members to ensure that employees are treated fairly and rewarded for their performance and to maintain disciplined organizational relationships—vital to an efficient system of administration.

ESPRIT DE CORPS   As this discussion of Fayol's ideas suggests, the appropriate design of an organization's hierarchy of authority and the right mix of order and discipline foster cooperation and commitment. Likewise, a key element in a successful organization is the development of **esprit de corps,** a French expression that refers to shared feelings of comradeship, enthusiasm, or devotion to a common cause among members of a group. Esprit de corps can result when managers encourage personal, verbal contact between managers and workers and by encouraging communication to solve problems and implement solutions.

esprit de corps Shared feelings of comradeship, enthusiasm, or devotion to a common cause among members of a group.

Some of the principles that Fayol outlined have faded from contemporary management practices, but most have endured. The characteristics of organization that Tom Peters and Robert Waterman identified as being "excellently managed" in their best-selling book *In Search of Excellence* (1982) are discussed in this "Management Insight."[24]

Management Insight

How to Be an Excellent Company

In the early 1980s, Tom Peters and Robert Waterman identified 62 organizations that they considered to be the best performing organizations in the United States. They asked the question "Why do these companies perform better than their rivals?" and discovered that successful organizations have managers who manage according to three sets of related principles. Those principles have a great deal in common with Fayol's principles.

First, Peters and Waterman argued, top managers of successful companies create principles and guidelines that emphasize managerial autonomy and entrepreneurship and encourage risk taking and *initiative.* For example, they allow middle managers to develop new products, even though there is no assurance that these products will be winners. In high-performing organizations, top managers are closely involved in the day-to-day operations of the company, provide *unity of command* and *unity of direction,* and do not simply make decisions isolated in an "ivory tower." Top managers *decentralize authority* to lower-level managers and nonmanagerial employees and give them the freedom to get involved and the motivation to get things done.

The second approach that managers of excellent organizations use to increase performance is to create one central plan that puts organizational goals at center stage. In high-performing organizations, managers focus attention toward what the organization does best, and the emphasis is on continuously improving the goods and services the organization provides to its customers. Managers of top-performing companies resist the temptation to get sidetracked into pursuing ventures outside their area of expertise just because they seem to promise a quick return. They also focus on customers and establish close relationships with them to learn their needs, for responsiveness to customers increases competitive advantage.

The third set of management principles pertains to organizing and controlling the organization. Excellent companies establish a *division of work* and a *division of authority and responsibility* that will motivate employees to *subordinate their individual interests to the common interest.* Inherent in this approach is the belief that high performance derives from individual skills and abilities and that *equity, order, initiative,* and other indications of respect for the individual create the *esprit de corps* that fosters productive behavior. An emphasis on entrepreneurship and respect for every employee leads the best managers to create a structure that gives employees room to exercise *initiative* and motivates them to succeed. Because a simple, streamlined managerial hierarchy is best suited to achieve this outcome, top managers keep the *line of authority* as short as possible. They also *decentralize authority* to permit employee participation, but they keep enough control to maintain *unity of direction.*

As this insight into contemporary management suggests, the basic concerns that motivated Fayol continue to motivate management theorists.[25] The principles that Fayol and Weber set forth still provide a clear and appropriate set of guidelines that managers can use to create a work setting that makes efficient and effective use of organizational resources. These principles remain the bedrock of modern management theory; recent researchers have refined or developed them to suit modern conditions. For example, Weber's and Fayol's concerns for equity and for establishing appropriate links between performance and reward are central themes in contemporary theories of motivation and leadership.

Behavioral Management Theory

Because the writings of Weber and Fayol were not translated into English and published in the United States until the late 1940s, American management theorists in the first half of the twentieth century were unaware of the contributions of these European pioneers. American management theorists began where Taylor and his followers left off. Although their writings were all very different, the theorists all espoused a theme that focused on **behavioral management,** the study of how managers should personally behave in order to motivate employees and encourage them to perform at high levels and be committed to the achievement of organizational goals.

behavioral management The study of how managers should behave in order to motivate employees and encourage them to perform at high levels and be committed to the achievement of organizational goals.

The Work of Mary Parker Follett

If F. W. Taylor is considered the father of management thought, Mary Parker Follett (1868–1933) serves as its mother.[26] Much of her writing about management and about the way managers should behave toward workers was a response to her concern that Taylor was ignoring the human side of the organization. She pointed out that management often overlooks the multitude of ways in which employees can contribute to the organization when managers allow them to participate and exercise initiative in their everyday work lives.[27] Taylor, for example, never proposed that managers should involve workers in analyzing their jobs to identify better ways to perform tasks, or even ask workers how they felt about their jobs. Instead, he used time-and-motion experts to analyze workers' jobs for them. Follett, in contrast, argued that because workers know the most about their jobs, they should be involved in job analysis and managers should allow them to participate in the work development process.

Follett proposed that "Authority should go with knowledge . . . whether it is up the line or down." In other words, if workers have the relevant knowledge, then workers, rather than managers, should be in control of the work process itself, and managers should behave as coaches and facilitators—not as monitors and supervisors. In making this statement, Follett anticipated the current interest in self-managed teams and empowerment. She also recognized the importance of having managers in different departments communicate directly with each other to speed decision making. She advocated what she called "cross-functioning": members of different departments working together in cross-departmental teams to accomplish projects—an approach that is increasingly utilized today.[28]

Fayol also mentioned expertise and knowledge as important sources of managers' authority, but Follett went further. She proposed that knowledge and expertise, and not managers' formal authority deriving from their position in the hierarchy, should decide who would lead at any particular moment. She believed, as do many management theorists today, that power is fluid and should flow to the person who can best help the organization achieve its goals. Follett took a horizontal view of power and authority, in contrast to Fayol, who saw the formal line of authority and vertical chain of command as being most essential to effective management. Follett's behavioral approach to management was very radical for its time.

The Hawthorne Studies and Human Relations

Probably because of its radical nature, Follett's work was unappreciated by managers and researchers until quite recently. Most continued to follow in the footsteps of Taylor and the Gilbreths. To increase efficiency, they studied ways to improve various characteristics of the work setting, such as job specialization or the kinds of tools workers used. One series of studies was conducted from 1924 to 1932 at the Hawthorne Works of the Western Electric Company.[29] This research, now known as the Hawthorne studies, began as an attempt to investigate how characteristics of the work setting—specifically the level of lighting or illumination—affect worker fatigue and performance. The researchers conducted an experiment in which they systematically measured worker productivity at various levels of illumination.

The experiment produced some unexpected results. The researchers found that regardless of whether they raised or lowered the level of illumination, productivity increased. In fact, productivity began to fall only when the level of illumination dropped to the level of moonlight, a level at which presumably workers could no longer see well enough to do their work efficiently.

The researchers found these results puzzling and invited a noted Harvard psychologist, Elton Mayo, to help them. Mayo proposed another series of experiments to solve the mystery. These experiments, known as the relay assembly test experiments, were designed to investigate the effects of other aspects of the work context on job performance, such as the effect of the number and length of rest periods and hours of work on fatigue and monotony.[30] The goal was to raise productivity.

During a two-year study of a small group of female workers, the researchers again observed that productivity increased over time, but the increases could not be solely attributed to the effects of changes in the work setting. Gradually, the researchers discovered that, to some degree, the results they were obtaining were influenced by the fact that the researchers themselves had become part of the experiment. In other words, the presence of the researchers was affecting the results because the workers enjoyed receiving attention and being the subject of study and were willing to cooperate with the researchers to produce the results they believed the researchers desired.

Subsequently, it was found that many other factors also influence worker behavior, and it was not clear what was actually influencing the Hawthorne workers' behavior. However, this particular effect—which became known as the **Hawthorne effect**—seemed to suggest that workers' attitudes toward their managers affect the level of workers' performance. In particular, the significant finding was that a manager's behavior or leadership approach can affect performance. This finding led many researchers to turn their attention to managerial behavior and leadership. If supervisors could be trained to behave in ways that would elicit cooperative behavior from their subordinates, then productivity could be increased. From this view emerged the **human relations movement,** which advocates that supervisors be behaviorally trained to manage subordinates in ways that elicit their cooperation and increase their productivity.

The importance of behavioral or human relations training became even clearer to its supporters after another series of experiments—the bank wiring room experiments. In a study of workers making telephone switching equipment, researchers Elton Mayo and F. J. Roethlisberger discovered that the workers, as a group, had deliberately adopted a norm of output restriction to protect their jobs. Workers who violated this informal production norm were subjected to sanctions by other group members. Those who violated group performance norms and performed above the norm were called "ratebusters"; those who performed below the norm were called "chiselers."

The experimenters concluded that both types of workers threatened the group as a whole. Ratebusters threatened group members because they revealed to managers how fast the work could be done. Chiselers were looked down on because they were not doing their share of the work. Work-group members disciplined both ratebusters and chiselers in order to create a pace of work that the workers (not the managers) thought was fair. Thus, a work group's influence over output can be as great as the supervisors' influence. Since the work group can influence the behavior of its members, some management theorists argue that supervisors should be trained to behave in ways that gain the goodwill and cooperation of workers so that supervisors, not workers, control the level of work-group performance.

One of the main implications of the Hawthorne studies was that the behavior of managers and workers in the work setting is as important in explaining the level of performance as the technical aspects of the task. Managers must understand the workings of the **informal organization,** the system of behavioral rules and norms that emerge in a group, when they try to manage or change behavior in organizations. Many studies have found that, as time

Hawthorne effect The finding that a manager's behavior or leadership approach can affect workers' level of performance.

human relations movement Advocates of the idea that supervisors be behaviorally trained to manage subordinates in ways that elicit their cooperation and increase their productivity.

informal organization The system of behavioral rules and norms that emerge in a group.

passes, groups often develop elaborate procedures and norms that bond members together, allowing unified action either to cooperate with management in order to raise performance or to restrict output and thwart the attainment of organizational goals.[31] The Hawthorne studies demonstrated the importance of understanding how the feelings, thoughts, and behavior of work-group members and managers affect performance. It was becoming increasingly clear to researchers that understanding behavior in organizations is a complex process that is critical to increasing performance.[32] Indeed, the increasing interest in the area of management known as **organizational behavior,** the study of the factors that have an impact on how individuals and groups respond to and act in organizations, dates from these early studies.

organizational behavior The study of the factors that have an impact on how individuals and groups respond to and act in organizations.

Theory X and Theory Y

Several studies after the Second World War revealed how assumptions about workers' attitudes and behavior affect managers' behavior. Perhaps the most influential approach was developed by Douglas McGregor. He proposed that two different sets of assumptions about how work attitudes and behaviors dominate the way managers think and affect how they behave in organizations. McGregor named these two contrasting sets of assumptions *Theory X* and *Theory Y* (see Figure 2.3).[33]

THEORY X According to the assumptions of **Theory X,** the average worker is lazy, dislikes work, and will try to do as little as possible. Moreover, workers have little ambition and wish to avoid responsibility. Thus, the manager's task is to counteract workers' natural tendencies to avoid work. To keep workers' performance at a high level, the manager must supervise them closely and control their behavior by means of "the carrot and stick"—rewards and punishments.

Managers who accept the assumptions of Theory X design and shape the work setting to maximize their control over workers' behaviors and minimize workers' control over the pace of work. These managers believe that workers

Theory X Negative assumptions about workers that lead to the conclusion that a manager's task is to supervise them closely and control their behavior.

Figure 2.3
Theory X Versus Theory Y

THEORY X	THEORY Y
The average employee is lazy, dislikes work, and will try to do as little as possible.	Employees are not inherently lazy. Given the chance, employees will do what is good for the organization.
To ensure that employees work hard, managers should closely supervise employees.	To allow employees to work in the organization's interest, managers must create a work setting that provides opportunities for workers to exercise initiative and self-direction.
Managers should create strict work rules and implement a well-defined system of rewards and punishments to control employees.	Managers should decentralize authority to employees and make sure employees have the resources necessary to achieve organizational goals.

must be made to do what is necessary for the success of the organization, and they focus on developing rules, SOPs, and a well-defined system of rewards and punishments to control behavior. They see little point in giving workers autonomy to solve their own problems because they think that the workforce neither expects nor desires cooperation. Theory X managers see their role as to closely monitor workers to ensure that they contribute to the production process and do not threaten product quality. Henry Ford, who closely supervised and managed his workforce, fits McGregor's description of a manager who holds Theory X assumptions.

Theory Y Positive assumptions about workers that lead to the conclusion that a manager's task is to create a work setting that encourages commitment to organizational goals and provides opportunities for workers to be imaginative and to exercise initiative and self-direction.

THEORY Y   In contrast, **Theory Y** assumes that workers are not inherently lazy, do not naturally dislike work, and, if given the opportunity, will do what is good for the organization. According to Theory Y, the characteristics of the work setting determine whether workers consider work to be a source of satisfaction or punishment; and managers do not need to closely control workers' behavior in order to make them perform at a high level, because workers will exercise self-control when they are committed to organizational goals. The implication of Theory Y, according to McGregor, is that "the limits of collaboration in the organizational setting are not limits of human nature but of management's ingenuity in discovering how to realize the potential represented by its human resources."[34] It is the manager's task to create a work setting that encourages commitment to organizational goals and provides opportunities for workers to be imaginative and to exercise initiative and self-direction.

When managers design the organizational setting to reflect the assumptions about attitudes and behavior suggested by Theory Y, the characteristics of the organization are quite different from those of an organizational setting based on Theory X. Managers who believe that workers are motivated to help the organization reach its goals can decentralize authority and give more control over the job to workers, both as individuals and in groups. In this setting, individuals and groups are still accountable for their activities, but the manager's role is not to control employees but to provide support and advice, to make sure employees have the resources they need to perform their jobs, and to evaluate them on their ability to help the organization meet its goals. Henri Fayol's approach to administration more closely reflects the assumptions of Theory Y, rather than Theory X.

Theory Z

In the 1980s, William Ouchi, a professor interested in differences between work settings in Japan and the United States, took the management approach inherent in Theory Y one step further.[35] In the United States, national culture emphasizes the importance of the individual, and workers view their jobs from an individualist perspective and thus behave in ways that will benefit them personally. Perhaps because of this, Ouchi noted, many U.S. managers adopt Theory X rather than Theory Y assumptions. They expect workers to behave purely in their own self-interest and believe workers will leave an organization at a moment's notice if they see a better opportunity elsewhere. To counter this expectation, Ouchi speculated, managers simplify jobs and increase supervision to make it easy to replace workers and to minimize any problems that might result from high rates of turnover. In U.S. companies, control is frequently explicit and formalized: Job requirements are clearly specified, and most workers are evaluated on and rewarded for their individual level of performance.

In contrast, Japanese managers expect workers to be committed to their organizations, and therefore treat them differently. Some large Japanese companies guarantee workers lifetime employment and view the training and development of workers as a lifelong investment. Moreover, Japanese workers tend to have a collective or group orientation to their work, a result of the characteristics of Japan's national culture, which emphasizes the importance of groups and organizations rather than individuals. Consistent with the Japanese culture, Japanese managers create work settings that encourage a group-oriented approach to decision making, they give work groups responsibility for job performance, and they allow work groups to control their own behavior. As discussed in the "Case in Contrast" at the beginning of the chapter, lean production, pioneered by Toyota and other Japanese car manufacturers, is based on these principles.

Ouchi suggested that U.S. companies could capture many of the advantages that Japanese companies enjoy by combining various characteristics of the Japanese and U.S. management systems and following the approach to management that he called **Theory Z.** In what Ouchi calls a "Type Z organization," workers are guaranteed long-term (but not lifetime) employment, so that their fears of layoffs or unemployment are reduced. Type Z managers attempt to combine the Japanese emphasis on the work group with a recognition of individual contributions by setting objectives for individual workers so that individual performance achievements can be recognized within a group context. Thus, individuals are recognized and rewarded not only for individual performance but also for interpersonal skills that improve decision making or communication. As we discuss in later chapters, the implementation of Theory Z requires an organizational structure that allows the organization to be flexible and responsive to changes inside the organization and in the external

Theory Z An approach to management that recognizes and rewards individual achievements within a group context.

Japanese compainies excel in creating a group or team oriented approach to decision making that promotes efficiency and effectiveness. Here, using the metaphor of the fast Japanese bullet trains that can move at a speed of up to 160 miles an hour, members of a "bullet train" team at the Yokogawa company were responsible for finding ways to cut the cost of making industrial recorders by 45 percent.

environment. One company that operates with the type of management philosophy inherent in Theory Y and Theory Z is Hewlett-Packard, the subject of the next "Management Insight."

Management Insight

The Hewlett-Packard Way

Managers at the electronics company Hewlett-Packard (www.hp.com) consistently put into practice principles derived from Theory Y and Theory Z. Founders William Hewlett and David Packard–"Bill and Dave," as they are known throughout the organization–established a philosophy of management known as the "HP Way" that is people oriented, stresses the importance of treating every person with consideration and respect, and offers recognition for achievements.[36]

HP's philosophy rests on a few guiding principles. One is a policy of long-term employment. HP goes to great lengths not to lay off workers. At times when fewer people were needed, rather than lay off workers management cut pay and shortened the workday until demand for HP products picked up. This policy strengthened employees' loyalty to the organization.

The HP Way is based on several golden rules about how to treat members of the organization so that they feel free to be innovative and creative. HP managers believe that every employee of the company is a member of the HP team. They emphasize the need to increase the level of communication among employees, believing that horizontal communication between peers, not just vertical communication up and down the hierarchy, is essential for creating a positive climate for innovation.

To promote communication and cooperation between employees at different levels of the hierarchy, HP encourages informality. Managers and workers are on a first-name basis with each other and with the founders Bill and Dave. In addition, Bill and Dave pioneered the technique known as "managing by wandering around." People are expected to wander around learning what others are doing so that they can tap into opportunities to develop new products or find new avenues for cooperation. Bill and Dave also pioneered the principle that employees should spend 15 percent of their time working on projects of their own choosing, and they encouraged employees to take equipment and supplies home to experiment with them on their own time. HP's product design engineers leave their current work out in the open on their desks so that anybody can see what they are doing, can learn from it, or can suggest ways to improve it. Managers are selected and promoted because of their ability to engender excitement and enthusiasm for innovation in their subordinates. HP's offices have low walls and shared laboratories to facilitate communication and cooperation between managers and workers. In all these ways, HP managers seek to promote each employee's desire to be innovative and also to create a team and family atmosphere based on cooperation.[37]

The results of HP's practices have been very good. While electronics companies like IBM, Wang, and Digital Equipment suffered hard times in recent years, Hewlett-Packard continued to build on its strengths. In 1995, it made record profits. After its founders retired, their management philosophy and values continued to shape the company, and stories about Bill and Dave still circulate throughout the organization.

Management Science Theory

Management science theory is a contemporary approach to management that focuses on the use of rigorous quantitative techniques to help managers make maximum use of organizational resources to produce goods and services. In essence, management science theory is a contemporary extension of scientific management, which, as developed by Taylor, also took a quantitative approach to measuring the worker–task mix in order to raise efficiency. There are many branches of management science; each of them deals with a specific set of concerns:

- *Quantitative management* utilizes mathematical techniques, such as linear and nonlinear programming, modeling, simulation, queuing theory, and chaos theory, to help managers decide, for example, how much inventory to hold at different times of the year, where to locate a new factory, and how best to invest an organization's financial capital.

- *Operations management* (or *operations research*) provides managers with a set of techniques that they can use to analyze any aspect of an organization's production system to increase efficiency.

- *Total quality management (TQM)* focuses on analyzing an organization's input, conversion, and output activities to increase product quality.[38]

- *Management information systems (MIS)* help managers design information systems that provide information about events occurring inside the organization as well as in its external environment–information that is vital for effective decision making.

All these subfields of management science provide tools and techniques that managers can use to help improve the quality of their decision making and increase efficiency and effectiveness. We discuss many of the important developments in management science theory thoroughly in Part 6 of this book. In particular, Chapter 17, "Managing Information Systems and Technologies," describes the management of information systems and technologies, and Chapter 18, "Operations Management: Managing Quality, Efficiency, and Responsiveness to Customers," focuses on operations management and TQM.

Organizational Environment Theory

An important milestone in the history of management thought occurred when researchers went beyond the study of how managers can influence behavior within organizations to consider how managers control the organization's relationship with its external environment, or **organizational environment**–the set of forces and conditions that operate beyond an organization's boundaries but affect a manager's ability to acquire and utilize resources. Resources in the organizational environment include the raw materials and skilled people that an organization requires to produce goods and services, as well as the support of groups including customers who buy these goods and services and provide the organization with financial resources. One way of determining the relative success of an organization is to consider how effective its managers are at obtaining scarce and valuable resources.[39] The importance of studying the environment became clear after the development of open-systems theory and contingency theory during the 1960s.

The Open-Systems View

One of the most influential views of how an organization is affected by its external environment was developed by Daniel Katz, Robert Kahn, and James Thompson in the 1960s.[40] These theorists viewed the organization as an **open system**—a system that takes in resources from its external environment and converts or transforms them into goods and services that are then sent back to that environment, where they are bought by customers (see Figure 2.4).

At the *input stage* an organization acquires resources such as raw materials, money, and skilled workers to produce goods and services. Once the organization has gathered the necessary resources, conversion begins. At the *conversion stage* the organization's workforce, using appropriate tools, techniques, and machinery, transforms the inputs into outputs of finished goods and services such as cars, hamburgers, or flights to Hawaii. At the *output stage* the organization releases finished goods and services to its external environment, where customers purchase and use them to satisfy their needs. The money the organization obtains from the sales of its outputs allows the organization to acquire more resources so that the cycle can begin again.

The system just described is said to be "open" because the organization draws from and interacts with the external environment in order to survive; in other words, the organization is open to its environment. A **closed system,** in

open system A system that takes in resources from its external environment and converts them into goods and services that are then sent back to that environment for purchase by customers.

closed system A system that is self-contained and thus not affected by changes that occur in its external environment.

Figure 2.4

The Organization as an Open System

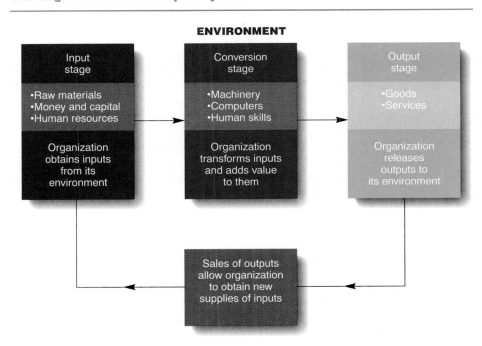

entropy The tendency of a system to lose its ability to control itself and thus to dissolve and disintegrate.

synergy Performance gains that result when individuals and departments coordinate their actions.

contingency theory The idea that managers' choice of organizational structures and control systems depends on—is contingent on—characteristics of the external environment in which the organization operates.

contrast, is a self-contained system that is not affected by changes that occur in its external environment. Organizations that operate as closed systems, that ignore the external environment, and that fail to acquire inputs are likely to experience **entropy,** the tendency of a system to lose its ability to control itself and thus to dissolve and disintegrate.

Management theorists can model the activities of most organizations by using the open-systems view. Manufacturing companies like Ford and General Electric, for example, buy inputs such as component parts, skilled and semi-skilled labor, and robots and computer-controlled manufacturing equipment; then at the conversion stage they use their manufacturing skills to assemble inputs into outputs of cars and computers. As we discuss in later chapters, competition between organizations for resources is one of several major challenges to managing the organizational environment.

Researchers using the open-systems view are also interested in how the various parts of a system work together to promote efficiency and effectiveness. Systems theorists like to argue that "the parts are more than the sum of the whole"; they mean that an organization performs at a higher level when its departments work together rather than separately. **Synergy,** the performance gains that result when individuals and departments coordinate their actions, is possible only in an organized system. The recent interest in using teams composed of people from different departments reflects systems theorists' interest in designing organizational systems to create synergy and thus increase efficiency and effectiveness.

Contingency Theory

Another milestone in management theory was the development of **contingency theory** in the 1960s by Tom Burns and G. M. Stalker in Britain and Paul Lawrence and Jay Lorsch in the United States.[41] The crucial message of contingency theory is that *there is no one best way to organize:* The organizational structures and the control systems that managers choose depend on—are contingent on—characteristics of the external environment in which the organization operates. According to contingency theory, the characteristics of the environment affect an organization's ability to obtain resources; and to maximize the likelihood of gaining access to resources, managers must allow an organization's departments to organize and control their activities in ways most likely to allow them to obtain resources, given the constraints of the particular environment they face. In other words, how managers design the organizational hierarchy, choose a control system, and lead and motivate their employees is contingent on the characteristics of the organizational environment (see Figure 2.5).

An important characteristic of the external environment that affects an organization's ability to obtain resources is the degree to which the environment is changing. Changes in the organizational environment include changes in technology, which can lead to the creation of new products (such as compact discs) and result in the obsolescence of existing products (eight-track tapes); the entry of new competitors (such as foreign organizations that compete for available resources); and unstable economic conditions. In general, the more quickly the organizational environment is changing, the greater are the problems associated with gaining access to resources and the greater is the manager's need to find ways to coordinate the activities of people in different departments in order to respond to the environment quickly and effectively.

Figure 2.5
Contingency Theory of Organizational Design

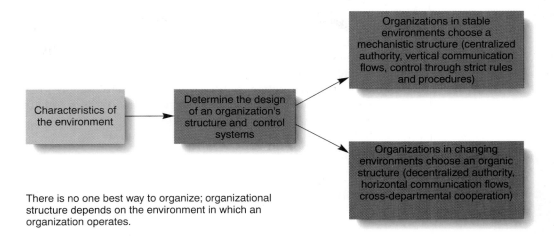

There is no one best way to organize; organizational structure depends on the environment in which an organization operates.

MECHANISTIC AND ORGANIC STRUCTURES Drawing on Weber's and Fayol's principles of organization and management, Burns and Stalker proposed two basic ways in which managers can organize and control an organization's activities to respond to characteristics of its external environment: They can use a *mechanistic structure* or an *organic structure*.[42] As you will see, a mechanistic structure typically rests on Theory X assumptions, and an organic structure typically rests on Theory Y or Theory Z assumptions.

When the environment surrounding an organization is stable, managers tend to choose a mechanistic structure to organize and control activities and make employee behavior predictable. In a **mechanistic structure,** authority is centralized at the top of the managerial hierarchy, and the vertical hierarchy of authority is the main means used to control subordinates' behavior. Tasks and roles are clearly specified, subordinates are closely supervised, and the emphasis is on strict discipline and order. Everyone knows his or her place, and there is a place for everyone. A mechanistic structure provides the most efficient way to operate in a stable environment because it allows managers to obtain inputs at the lowest cost, giving an organization the most control over its conversion processes and enabling the most efficient production of goods and services with the smallest expenditure of resources. McDonald's restaurants operate with a mechanistic structure. Supervisors make all important decisions; employees are closely supervised and follow well-defined rules and standard operating procedures.

In contrast, when the environment is changing rapidly, it is difficult to obtain access to resources, and managers need to organize their activities in a way that allows them to cooperate, to act quickly to acquire resources (such as new types of inputs to produce new kinds of products), and to respond effectively to the unexpected. In an **organic structure,** authority is decentralized to middle and first-line managers to encourage them to take responsibility and act quickly to pursue scarce resources. Departments are encouraged to take a cross-departmental or functional perspective, and, as in Mary Parker Follett's model, authority rests with the individuals and departments best positioned to

mechanistic structure An organizational structure in which authority is centralized, tasks and rules are clearly specified, and employees are closely supervised.

organic structure An organizational structure in which authority is decentralized to middle and first-line managers and tasks and roles are left ambiguous to encourage employees to cooperate and respond quickly to the unexpected.

control the current problems the organization is facing. In an organic structure, control is much looser than it is in a mechanistic structure, and reliance on shared norms to guide organizational activities is greater.

Managers in an organic structure can react more quickly to a changing environment than can managers in a mechanistic structure. However, an organic structure is generally more expensive to operate, so it is used only when needed—when the organizational environment is unstable and rapidly changing. To facilitate global expansion, managers at Philips, a Dutch electronics company, were forced to change from a mechanistic to an organic structure and their experience illustrates the different properties of these structures.

Managing Globally

Philips's Organic Structure Works

Established in 1891, the Dutch company Philips NV (www.philips.com) is one of the world's largest electronics companies, making products as diverse as light bulbs, computers, medical equipment, and semiconductors.[43] By 1990, Philips had over 700 divisions in over 60 countries and operated thousands of manufacturing plants employing more than 250,000 people worldwide. Despite its global reach, however, Philips was in deep trouble. In 1990, it lost $1.3 billion on sales of over $3 billion, and its very survival was threatened. What was the problem? The external environment was changing rapidly, and Philips's mechanistic structure was not allowing the company to adapt to the changes that were taking place.

Philips's environment was changing in several ways. First, the development of the European Union had increased competition from other European electronics companies, such as Britain's General Electric. Second, competition from Sony, Matsushita, and other low-cost Japanese companies had increased. Third, advances in technology in the form of new and more powerful computer chips and lasers had ushered in a new era of global competition. Philips's organizational structure was preventing managers from responding quickly to these challenges.

Over the years, decision making at Philips had become extremely centralized; all significant new product decisions were made in the Netherlands at its Eindhoven headquarters. At Eindhoven, 3,000 corporate managers supervised the 2,500 middle managers who were responsible for coordinating product development on a global scale. Decisions made by these 5,500 managers were communicated to managers in Philips's 700 divisions spread across 60 countries, who then made decisions for their respective countries. Philips's tall, centralized, mechanistic structure slowed communication and decision making and undermined the company's ability to respond to the global changes taking place. Moreover, very little communication was occurring between managers on the same hierarchical level but in different divisions (such horizontal communication is critical to speeding up the development of new products and reducing costs).

Top managers realized they had to change the organizational structure to allow the company to respond better to its environment. They began by dividing the organization into four product groups—lighting, consumer electronics, electronic components, and telecommunication. They gave each product group global responsibility for all aspects of its own activities—research, sales, and manufacturing.[44] In other words, they decentralized authority to the managers of the product groups. In this way, Philips tried to create a flatter, more flexible, organic structure at a global level—a structure in which managers close to the action, not top managers at distant corporate headquarters, made decisions. Throughout the 1990s, the change to an organic structure produced major success for Philips. Costs fell, the speed of new product development increased sharply, and Philips made record profits. Nevertheless, low-cost competition from countries such as China, Korea, and Malaysia is still forcing managers to search continuously for better, more efficient ways to meet the challenges of the global environment.

Because the managers of many global organizations have been facing problems similar to those of Philips, researchers' interest in managers' attempts to deal with the organizational environment both at home and abroad has increased rapidly. Part 3 of this book is devoted to *strategic management,* the study of the relationship between organizations and their external environment and of the strategies organizations adopt to manage that environment.[45]

Tips for Managers

Applying Management Principles

1. Analyze whether an organization's division of labor is meeting its current needs. Consider ways to change the level of job specialization to increase performance.

2. Examine the way an organization works in reference to Weber and Fayol's principles. Decide if the distribution of authority in the hierarchy best meets the organization's needs. Similarly, decide if the right system to discipline or remunerate employees is being used.

3. Examine organizational policies to see if managers are consistently behaving in an equitable manner and whether these policies lead to ethical employee behavior.

Summary and Review

In this chapter we examined the evolution of management theory and research over the last century. Much of the material in the rest of this book stems from developments and refinements of this work.

SCIENTIFIC MANAGEMENT THEORY The search for efficiency started with the study of how managers could improve person–task relationships to increase efficiency. The concept of job specialization and division of labor remains the basis for the design of work settings in modern organizations. New developments like lean production and total quality management are often viewed as advances on the early scientific management principles developed by Taylor and the Gilbreths.

Chapter Summary

ADMINISTRATIVE MANAGEMENT THEORY Max Weber and Henri Fayol outlined principles of bureaucracy and administration that are as relevant to managers today as when they were written at the turn of the twentieth century. Much of modern management research refines these principles to suit contemporary conditions. For example, the increasing interest in the use of cross-departmental teams and the empowerment of workers are issues that managers also faced a century ago.

BEHAVIORAL MANAGEMENT THEORY Researchers have described many different approaches to managerial behavior, including Theories X, Y, and Z. Often, the managerial behavior that researchers suggest reflects the context of their own historical era and culture. Mary Parker Follett advocated managerial behaviors that did not reflect accepted modes of managerial behavior at the time, but her work was largely ignored until conditions changed.

MANAGEMENT SCIENCE THEORY The various branches of management science theory provide rigorous quantitative techniques that give managers more control over their organization's use of resources to produce goods and services.

ORGANIZATIONAL ENVIRONMENT THEORY The importance of studying the organization's external environment became clear after the development of open-systems theory and contingency theory during the 1960s. A main focus of contemporary management research is to find methods to help managers improve the way they utilize organizational resources and compete successfully in the global environment. Strategic management and total quality management are two important approaches intended to help managers make better use of organizational resources.

Management in Action

Topics for Discussion and Action

1. Choose a fast-food restaurant, a department store, or some other organization with which you are familiar, and describe the division of labor and job specialization it uses to produce goods and services. How might this division of labor be improved?

2. Apply Taylor's principles of scientific management to improve the performance of the organization you chose in item 1.

3. In what ways are Weber's and Fayol's ideas about bureaucracy and administration similar? In what ways do they differ?

4. Question a manager about his or her views of the relative importance of Fayol's 14 principles of management.

5. Which of Weber's and Fayol's principles seem most relevant to the creation of an ethical organization?

6. Why was the work of Mary Parker Follett ahead of its time? To what degree do you think it is appropriate today?

7. Visit various organizations in your community, and identify those that seem to operate with a Theory X or a Theory Z approach to management.

8. What is contingency theory? What kinds of organizations familiar to you have been successful or unsuccessful in dealing with contingencies from the external environment?

9. Why are mechanistic and organic structures suited to different types of organizational environment?

Building Management Skills

Managing Your Own Business

Now that you understand the concerns addressed by management thinkers over the last century, use this exercise to apply your knowledge to develop your management skills.

Imagine that you are the founding entrepreneur of a software company that specializes in developing computer games for home computers. Customer demand for your games has increased so much that over the last year you have grown from a busy one-person operation to employ 16 people. In addition to yourself, you employ 6 software developers to produce the software, 3 graphic artists, 2 computer technicians, 2 marketing and sales personnel, and 2 secretaries. In the next year you expect to hire 30 new people, and you are wondering how best to manage your growing company.

Questions

1. Use the principles of Weber and Fayol to decide on the system of organization and management that you think will be most effective for your growing organization. How many levels will the managerial hierarchy of your organization have? How much authority will you decentralize to your subordinates? How will you establish the division of labor between subordinates? Will your subordinates work alone and report to you or work in teams?

2. What management approach (for example, Theory X, Y, or Z) do you propose to use to run your organization? In 50 words or less write a statement describing the management approach you propose to use to motivate and coordinate your subordinates, and tell why you think this style will be best.

Small Group Breakout Exercise

Modeling an Open System

Form groups of three to five people, and appoint one group member as the spokesperson who will communicate your findings to the class when called on by the instructor. Then discuss the following scenario.

Think of an organization with which you are all familiar, such as a local restaurant, store, or bank. After choosing an organization, model it from an open-systems perspective. Identify its input, conversion, and output processes; and identify forces in the external environment that help or hurt the organization's ability to obtain resources and dispose of its goods or services.

Exploring the World Wide Web

Specific Assignment

Investigate the history of Ford Motor Company by utilizing the extensive resources of Ford's historical library. Research Ford's website (www.ford.com), and locate and read the material on Ford's history and evolution over time.

1. What kinds of management concerns have occupied Ford's top managers from its beginnings to today?

2. Do these concerns seem to have changed over time?

General Assignment

Search for a website that contains the time line or a short history of a company, detailing the way the organization has developed over time. What are the significant stages in the company's development, and what problems and issues have confronted managers at these stages?

ManagementCase

A Shake-up at Eastman Kodak

Eastman Kodak Company was incorporated in New Jersey on October 24, 1901, as successor to Eastman Dry Plate Company, the business originally established by George Eastman in 1880. The Dry Plate Company had been formed to mass-produce the dry plates needed for early cameras. After George Eastman developed silver-halide paper-based photographic film and invented the first portable camera, he formed his new company to capitalize on his inventions.

From the beginning, Eastman was aware of the need to reduce costs to bring his products to the mass market, and he quickly adopted scientific management principles to improve production efficiency. Eastman also developed a people-oriented approach. Over the years Eastman Kodak became known as "Mother Kodak" because of the bonds that developed between the organization and its members. Until the 1980s, Kodak never had layoffs and turnover was very low. It was quite common for both managers and workers to spend their entire working careers with Kodak and for whole families or successive generations of families to be employed by the company at its Rochester, New York, headquarters and manufacturing plants.

With success, however, decision making became centralized at the top of the organization. A group of long-term managers made all significant operating decisions and then communicated the decisions down a very tall hierarchy to managers at

lower levels. When it came time to decide who would be promoted, seniority and loyalty to Mother Kodak were more important than a person's performance; fitting in and being a member of the "Kodak Team" were the keys to success.

This management approach worked well while Kodak had a virtual monopoly of the photographic products market, but it became a liability when Kodak faced stiff competition from foreign competitors like Germany's Agfa and Japan's Fuji Film. These companies, having found new ways to produce film and paper at costs lower than Kodak's, began to challenge Kodak's dominance. Managers at Kodak were slow to respond to the challenge. The organization's tall, centralized structure slowed decision making, and its conservative orientation made managers reluctant to change. In the 1980s things went from bad to worse for Kodak as its share of the market and profits fell. Top management had to address the problems.

After much soul searching, top managers decided they had to totally change Kodak's organizational structure to make the company more competitive. They divided the company into four separate product divisions and began a massive downsizing of the workforce. Kodak's policy of lifetime employment was discontinued as managers announced the first layoffs in its history. Top management's goal was to flatten the organization's hierarchy and push authority and responsibility to employees at

lower levels. Top management hoped that decentralized authority would help lower-level managers become more entrepreneurial and more inclined to search for new ways to cut costs.

These changes helped Kodak but were not enough to reverse its decline. In 1994, in a break with the past, Kodak appointed a CEO from outside the company to change the organization further. George Fisher, former CEO of Motorola, took charge. Fisher was renowned for creating a climate of innovation at Motorola and for helping that company become a market leader in the cellular telephone industry. To increase the rate of new product development and to help the company regain market share, he has been striving to change Kodak managers' conservative management style into an entrepreneurial approach. Fisher also has continued to restructure the company, laying off thousands more employees and managers and selling many of Kodak's divisions. The Kodak of today is very different from the Kodak of 10 years ago, and a new set of principles guides managers and workers.

Questions

1. What was the source of the problems facing Kodak in the 1980s?

2. Using the chapter material as a base, discuss the way Kodak altered its organization and management approach to deal with its problems.

ManagementCase

In the News

From the pages of *The Wall Street Journal*
Mr. Edens Profits from Watching His Workers' Every Move

Control is one of Ron Edens's favorite words. "This is a controlled environment," he says of the blank brick building that houses his company, Electronic Banking System Inc.

Inside, long lines of women sit at spartan desks, slitting envelopes, sorting contents and filling out "control cards" that record how many letters they have opened and how long it has taken them. Workers here, in "the cage," must process three envelopes a minute. Nearby, other women tap keyboards, keeping pace with a quota that demands 8,500 strokes an hour.

The room is silent. Talking is forbidden. The windows are covered. Coffee mugs, religious pictures and other adornments are barred from workers' desks.

In his office upstairs, Mr. Edens sits before a TV monitor that flashes images from eight cameras posted through the plant. "There's a little bit of Sneaky Pete to it," he says, using a remote control to zoom in on a document atop a worker's desk. "I can basically read that and figure out how someone's day is going."

This day, like most others, is going smoothly, and Mr. Edens's business has boomed as a result. "We maintain a lot of control," he says. "Order and control are everything in this business."

Mr. Edens's business belongs to a small but expanding financial service known as "lockbox processing." Many companies and charities that once did their paperwork in-house now "out-source" clerical tasks to firms like EBS, which processes donations to groups such as Mothers Against Drunk Driving, the Doris Day Animal League, Greenpeace and the National Organization for Women.

More broadly, EBS reflects the explosive growth of jobs in which workers perform low-wage and limited tasks in white-collar settings. This has transformed towns like Hagerstown—a blue-collar community hit hard by industrial layoffs in the 1970s—into sites for thousands of jobs in factory-sized offices.

Many of these jobs, though, are part-time and most pay far less than the manufacturing occupations they replaced. Some workers at EBS start at the minimum wage of $4.25 an hour and most earn about $6 an hour. The growth of such jobs—which often cluster outside major cities—also completes a curious historic circle. During the Industrial Revolution, farmers' daughters went to work in textile towns like Lowell, Mass. In post-industrial America, many women of modest means and skills are entering clerical mills where they process paper instead

of cloth (coincidentally, EBS occupies a former garment factory).

"The office of the future can look a lot like the factory of the past," says Barbara Garson, author of *The Electronic Sweatshop* and other books on the modern workplace. "Modern tools are being used to bring 19th-century working conditions into the white-collar world."

The time-motion philosophies of Frederick Taylor, for instance, have found a 1990s correlate in the phone, computer and camera, which can be used to monitor workers more closely than a foreman with a stopwatch ever could. Also, the nature of the work often justifies a vigilant eye. In EBS workers handle thousands of dollars in checks and cash, and Mr. Edens says cameras help deter would-be thieves. Tight security also reassures visiting clients. "If you're disorderly, they'll think we're out of control and that things could get lost," says Mr. Edens, who worked as a financial controller for the National Rifle Association before founding EBS in 1983.

But tight observation also helps EBS monitor productivity and weed out workers who don't keep up. "There's multiple uses," Mr. Edens says of surveillance. His desk is covered with computer printouts recording the precise toll of keystrokes tapped by each data-entry worker. He also keeps a day-to-day tally of errors. The work floor itself resembles an enormous classroom in the throes of exam period. Desks point toward the front, where a manager keeps watch from a raised platform that workers call "the pedestal" or "the birdhouse." Other supervisors are positioned toward the back of the room. "If you want to watch someone," Mr. Edens explains, "it's easier from behind because they don't know you're watching." There also is a black globe hanging from the ceiling, in which cameras are positioned.

Mr. Edens sees nothing Orwellian about this omniscience. "It's not a Big Brother attitude," he says. "It's more of a calming attitude."

But studies of workplace monitoring suggest otherwise. Experts say that surveillance can create a hostile environment in which workers feel pressured, paranoid and prone to stress-related illness. Surveillance also can be used punitively, to intimidate workers or to justify their firing.

Following a failed union drive at EBS, the National Labor Relations Board filed a series of complaints against the company, including charges that EBS threatened, interrogated and spied on workers. As part of an out-of-court settlement, EBS reinstated a fired worker and posted a notice that it would refrain from illegal practices during a second union vote, which also failed.

"It's all noise," Mr. Edens says of the unfair labor charges. As to the pressure that surveillance creates, Mr. Edens sees that simply as "the nature of the beast." He adds: "It's got to add stress when everyone knows their production is being monitored. I don't apologize for that."

Mr. Edens also is unapologetic about the Draconian work rules he maintains, including one that forbids all talk unrelated to the completion of each task. "I'm not paying people to chat. I'm paying them to open envelopes," he says. Of the blocked windows. Mr. Edens adds: "I don't want them looking out—it's distracting. They'll make mistakes."

This total focus boosts productivity but it makes many workers feel lonely and trapped. Some try to circumvent the silence rule, like kids in a school library. "If you don't turn your head and sort of mumble out of the side of your mouth, supervisors won't hear you most of the time," Cindy Kesselring explains during her lunch break. Even so, she feels isolated and often longs for her former job as a waitress. "Work is your social life, particularly if you've got kids," says the 27-year-old mother. "Here it's hard to get to know people because you can't talk."

During lunch, workers crowd in the parking lot outside, chatting nonstop. "Some of us don't eat much because the more you chew the less you can talk," Ms. Kesselring says. There aren't other breaks and workers aren't allowed to sip coffee or eat at their desks during the long stretches before and after lunch. Hard candy is the only permitted desk snack.

New technology, and the breaking down of labor into discrete, repetitive tasks, also have effectively stripped jobs such as those at EBS of whatever variety and skills clerical work once possessed. Workers in the cage (an antiquated banking term for a money-handling area) only open envelopes and sort contents: those in the audit department compute figures: and data-entry clerks punch in the information that the

others have collected. If they make a mistake, the computer buzzes and a message such as "check digit error" flashes on the screen.

"We don't ask these people to think—the machines think for them," Mr. Edens says. "They don't have to make any decisions." This makes the work simpler but also deepens its monotony. In the cage, Carol Smith says she looks forward to envelopes that contain anything out of the ordinary, such as letters reporting that the donor is deceased. Or she plays mental games. "I think to myself, A goes in this pile, B goes here and C goes there—sort of like Bingo." She says she sometimes feels "like a machine," particularly when she fills out the "control card" on which she lists "time in" and "time out" for each tray of envelopes. In a slot marked "cage operator" Ms. Smith writes her code number, 3173. "That's me," she says.

Barbara Ann Wiles, a keyboard operator, also plays mind games to break up the boredom. Tapping in the names and addresses of new donors, she tries to imagine the faces behind the names, particularly the odd ones. "Like this one, Mrs. Fittizzi," she chuckles. "I can picture her as a very stout lady with a strong accent, hollering on a street corner." She picks out another: "Doris Angelroth—she's very sophisticated, a monocle maybe, drinking tea on an overstuffed mohair couch."

It is a world remote from the one Ms. Wiles inhabits. Like most EBS employees, she must juggle her low-paying job with child care. On this Friday, for instance, Ms. Wiles will finish her eight-hour shift at about 4 P.M., go home for a few hours, then return for a second shift from midnight to 8 A.M. Otherwise, she would have to come in on Saturday to finish the week's work.

ManagementCase continued

This way I can be home on the weekend to look after my kids," she says.

Others find the work harder to leave behind at the end of the day. In the cage, Ms. Smith says her husband used to complain because she often woke him in the middle of the night. "I'd be shuffling my hands in my sleep," she says, mimicking the motion of opening envelopes.

Her cage colleague, Ms. Kesselring, says her fiancé has a different gripe. "He dodges me for a couple of hours after work because I don't shut up—I need to talk, talk, talk," she says. And there is one household task she can no longer abide.

"I won't pay bills because I can't stand to open another envelope," she says. "I'll leave letters sitting in the mailbox for days."

Source: Tony Horwitz, "Mr. Edens Profits from Watching His Workers' Every Move," The *Wall Street Journal*, December 1, 1994.

Questions

1. Which of the management theories described in the chapter does Ron Edens make most use of?

2. What is your view of Edens's management approach?

Part 2

Chapter three

The Organizational Environment

Learning Objectives

1. Explain why the ability to perceive, interpret, and respond appropriately to the organizational environment is crucial for managerial success.

2. Identify the main forces in an organization's task and general environments, and describe the challenges that each force presents to managers.

3. Discuss the main ways in which managers can manage the organizational environment.

4. Explain why boundary-spanning activities are important.

A Case in Contrast

What Kind of Personal Computers Do Customers Really Want?

One of the founders of Houston-based Compaq Computer Corporation (www.compaq.com) was Rod Canion, who served as CEO from 1982 until late 1991. Canion's vision for Compaq was shaped by his perception of the personal computer industry. He considered the company's highest priority was to meet the needs of the customers who used personal computers (PCs). In the 1980s, those customers were mostly large business organizations. Canion believed that business users wanted high-quality, powerful PCs and a high level of after-sales service. He believed that business users would pay a high price to a company that could deliver these character-istics, and he decided to create just such a company.

To attract customers and their resources, Canion positioned Compaq as a manufacturer of advanced PCs that incorporated leading-edge technology. To produce innovative PCs, he invested heavily in research and insisted that Compaq PCs feature unmatched quality even if significantly higher

Rod Canion, Compaq's original CEO was the technical mastermind who orchestrated Compaq's rise to fame as a supplier of state-of-the-art high powered computers.

Eckhard Pfeiffer, however, was the marketing genius who realized that the future of the personal computer industry lay in giving customers what they wanted—powerful low price computers.

costs were the result. So innovative did Compaq become that in 1985 it marketed a personal computer powered by Intel's 386 microprocessor, beating IBM by six months and everyone else by more. Canion also developed a network of 3,000 authorized dealers to sell Compaq PCs. However, they were priced so much higher than other IBM-compatible PCs that few nonbusiness customers could afford them.

Canion's reading of the personal computer industry worked well for several years. By 1990, Compaq sales had risen to $3.6 billion, and the company had become the third largest personal computer company in the world, behind IBM and Apple. But the industry was changing rapidly, and there were signs that Canion's perception of it was becoming outdated. For instance, new competitors, including AST, Gateway 2000, and Dell Computer, were producing low-priced IBM-compatible PCs. While Compaq continued to sell expensive PCs at full price through its dealers, Dell and Gateway began to sell directly to customers by means of direct telephone ordering. This distribution strategy minimized service but enabled Dell and Gateway to keep costs and prices down. Furthermore, AST, Dell, and Gateway used existing technology. They purchased most of their components from other companies and merely assembled them. So their cost for supplies was lower than Compaq's, because Compaq invested in expensive research to develop its own PC components. The combination of these factors allowed Compaq's competitors to undercut Compaq's prices by as much as 30 to 40 percent.

Customers' preferences also had changed. Small businesses, individuals, and large companies were buying large numbers of PCs and basing their purchasing decision on price rather than serviceability. Customers began to buy the least-expensive PCs from the new, low-cost computer companies, and Compaq's sales and profits dropped dramatically. Still, Canion clung to his original strategy. By November 1991, Compaq's board of directors, believing that Canion's vision of the computer industry was fundamentally flawed, removed him from office. His replacement as CEO was Eckhard Pfeiffer, one of Compaq's top managers.

Pfeiffer's view of the computer industry was very different from Canion's. He saw the principal users of PCs as small businesses and home users rather than big businesses. Pfeiffer believed that most of Compaq's new competitors could provide PCs that met customer demands for power, quality, and technology and that Compaq no longer had a competitive advantage to offer customers that justified its higher prices. In contrast to Canion, Pfeiffer viewed lower prices—not power and quality—as the main basis for competition. He also believed that consumers no longer needed nor could afford the level of dealer-provided after-sales service and support that Canion had insisted on.

Based on his view of the changing computer industry environment, Pfeiffer redirected Compaq's marketing efforts beyond large corporate customers to include all types of customers. Then he reduced costs by cutting expenditures on research, by buying components from low-cost suppliers, by opening up new low-cost channels of distribution such as mail order and discount stores, and by aiming for high but not unmatched product quality. Most important, to attract more customers, Pfeiffer cut Compaq's prices by as much as 50 percent between the end of 1991 and 1993. His vision of the new industry environment was rewarded quickly: Sales more than doubled from 1991 to 1993 and continued to climb, and Compaq became the number one seller of personal computers in the world.[1]

Overview

Because Rod Canion and Eckhard Pfeiffer viewed the computer industry environment very differently, they took different actions that had different outcomes. All managers face in the organizational environment a rich array of forces that they must recognize and respond to quickly and appropriately if their organizations are to survive and prosper. The external environment is uncertain and unpredictable because it is complex and constantly changing. Managers must position their organizations to deal efficiently and effectively with new developments. Canion saw no need to respond to the changes taking place in Compaq's environment and, as a result, lost his job. Pfeiffer interpreted the changes differently, took action, and remains Compaq's CEO—and Compaq's rapid growth has continued.

In this chapter, we examine the organizational environment in detail. We describe it and identify the principal forces—both task and general—that create pressure and influence managers and thus affect the way organizations operate. We conclude with a study of several methods that managers can use to help organizations adjust and respond to forces in the organizational environment. By the end of the chapter, you will understand the steps managers must take to ensure that organizations adequately address and appropriately respond to their external environment. ●

What Is the Organizational Environment?

organizational environment The set of forces and conditions that operate beyond an organization's boundaries but affect a manager's ability to acquire and utilize resources.

task environment The set of forces and conditions that originate with suppliers, distributors, customers, and competitors and affect an organization's ability to obtain inputs and dispose of its outputs, because they influence managers on a daily basis.

The **organizational environment** is a set of forces and conditions outside the organization's boundaries that have the potential to affect the way the organization operates.[2] These forces change over time and thus present managers with *opportunities* and *threats*. Changes in the environment, such as the introduction of new technology or the opening of foreign markets, create opportunities for managers to obtain resources or enter new markets and thereby strengthen their organizations. In contrast, the rise of new competitors, an economic recession, or an oil shortage poses a threat that can devastate an organization if managers are unable to obtain resources or sell the organization's goods and services. The quality of managers' understanding of forces in the organizational environment, and their ability to respond appropriately to those forces, are critical factors affecting organizational performance.

In this chapter we explore the nature of these forces and consider how managers can respond to them. A detailed discussion of the way the external environment affects the planning and organizing processes is presented in Parts 3 and 4. Our focus now is on understanding the organizational environment and its impact on managers and organizations.

To identify opportunities and threats caused by forces in the organizational environment, it is helpful for managers to distinguish between the *task environment* and the more encompassing *general environment* (see Figure 3.1).

The **task environment** is the set of forces and conditions that originate with suppliers, distributors, customers, and competitors and affect an organization's ability to obtain inputs and dispose of its outputs, because they pressure and influence managers on a daily basis. When managers turn on the radio or television, arrive at their offices in the morning, open their mail, or look at

Figure 3.1
Forces in the Organizational Environment

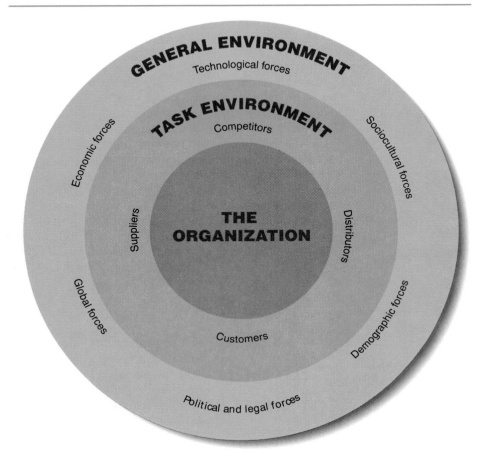

general environment

The wide-ranging economic, technological, sociocultural, demographic, political and legal, and global forces that affect an organization and its task environment.

their computer screens, they are likely to learn about problems facing them because of changing conditions in their organization's task environment.

The **general environment** is the wide-ranging economic, technological, sociocultural, demographic, political and legal, and global forces that affect the organization and its task environment. For the individual manager, opportunities and threats resulting from changes in the general environment are often more difficult to identify and respond to than are events in the task environment.

Some management theorists refer to another kind of environment, the *internal environment,* that managers must understand and control. The internal environment consists of forces operating within an organization and stemming from the organization's structure and culture. Although the task, general, and internal environments influence each other, we leave detailed discussion of how to manage structure and culture until Part 4, particularly, Chapter 9, "Organizational Control and Culture," and concentrate here on forces in the task and general environments and their effects on organizations.

The Task Environment

Forces in the task environment result from the actions of suppliers, distributors, customers, and competitors (see Figure 3.1). These four groups affect a manager's ability to obtain resources and dispose of outputs on a daily, weekly, and monthly basis and thus have a significant impact on short-term decision making.

Suppliers

suppliers Individuals and organizations that provide an organization with the input resources that it needs to produce goods and services.

Suppliers are the individuals and organizations that provide an organization with the input resources (such as raw materials, component parts, or employees) that it needs to produce goods and services. In return, the supplier receives compensation for those goods and services. An important aspect of a manager's job is to ensure a reliable supply of input resources.

Compaq, for example, has hundreds of suppliers. There are suppliers of component parts such as microprocessors (Intel and AMD) and disk drives (Quantum and Seagate Technologies). There are also suppliers of preinstalled software, including the operating system (Microsoft) and specific applications software (Lotus, Borland, and America Online). Compaq's providers of capital, such as banks and financial institutions, are also important suppliers.

There are several suppliers of labor to Compaq. One is the educational institutions that train future Compaq employees and therefore provide the company with skilled workers. Another is trade unions, organizations that represent employee interests and can control the supply of labor by exercising the right of unionized workers to strike. Unions also can influence the terms and conditions under which labor is employed. Compaq's workers were not unionized, and Pfeiffer experienced few problems when he laid off thousands of workers to reduce costs. In organizations and industries where unions are very strong, however, an important part of a manager's job is negotiating and administering agreements with unions and their representatives.

Changes in the nature, numbers, or types of any supplier result in forces that produce opportunities and threats to which managers must respond if their organizations are to prosper. As the "Case in Contrast" indicates, Rod Canion did not see the need to find low-cost suppliers, and this oversight clearly contributed to his downfall. Often, when managers do not respond to a threat—in Compaq's case, failing to utilize low-cost foreign suppliers—they put their organization at a competitive disadvantage.

Another major supplier-related threat that confronts managers arises when suppliers' bargaining position with an organization is so strong that they can raise the prices of the inputs they supply to the organization. A supplier's bargaining position is especially strong if (1) the supplier is the sole source of an input and (2) the input is vital to the organization.[3] For example, for 17 years G. D. Searle was the sole supplier of NutraSweet, the artificial sweetener used in most diet soft drinks. Not only was NutraSweet an important ingredient in diet soft drinks, it also was one for which there was no acceptable substitute (saccharin and other artificial sweeteners raised health concerns). Searle earned its privileged position because it invented and held the patent for NutraSweet. Patents prohibit other organizations from introducing competing products for 17 years. In 1992, Searle's patent expired, and many companies began to produce products similar to NutraSweet. Prior to 1992, Searle was able to demand a high price for NutraSweet, charging twice as much as the price of an equivalent amount of sugar. Paying that price raised the costs of soft-drink manufacturers, including Coca-Cola and PepsiCo, which had no alternative but to buy the product.[4] In contrast, when an organization has many suppliers for a particular input, it is in a relatively strong bargaining position with those suppliers and can demand low-cost, high-quality inputs from them.

In addition to raising prices, suppliers can make operations difficult for an organization by restricting its access to important inputs. For example, state governments supply financial resources to state universities and business schools and in recent years have often seriously hindered the operations of those institutions by reducing funding. This resource scarcity has forced business schools at state-run universities to eliminate perceived operating inefficiencies and actively pursue other sources of outside revenues—for instance, by increasing fees to students or by soliciting gifts from alumni.

Distributors

distributors Organizations that help other organizations sell their goods or services to customers.

Distributors are organizations that help other organizations sell their goods or services to customers. The decisions that managers make about how to distribute products to customers can have important effects on organizational performance. Rod Canion initially chose to use authorized distributors to sell and service Compaq computers. Later, to reduce costs and lower the price of a Compaq computer, Eckhard Pfeiffer decided to reverse Canion's strategy and allow discount stores and typical retail outlets to sell Compaq PCs. Compaq also began to sell computers by telephone and to ship packages directly to customers.

The changing nature of distributors and distribution methods can also bring opportunities and threats for managers. If distributors are so large and powerful that they can control customers' access to a particular organization's goods and services, they can threaten the organization by demanding that it reduce the prices of its goods and services.[5] For example, the huge retailer Wal-Mart controls suppliers' access to a great number of customers and thus often demands that its suppliers reduce their prices. If an organization such as Procter & Gamble refuses to reduce its prices, Wal-Mart might respond by buying products only from Procter & Gamble's competitors—companies such as Unilever and Dial.

In contrast, the power of a distributor may be weakened if there are many options. This has been the experience of the three broadcast television networks—ABC, NBC, and CBS. Their ability to demand lower prices from the producers of television programs has been weakened. The presence of hundreds of new cable television channels has reduced the three networks' clout by reducing their share of the viewing audience to 50 percent, down from over 90 percent a decade ago.

Customers

customers Individuals and groups that buy the goods and services that an organization produces.

Customers are the individuals and groups that buy the goods and services that an organization produces. Compaq's customers can be segmented into several distinct groups: (1) individuals who purchase PCs for home use, (2) small companies, (3) large companies, (4) government agencies, (5) educational institutions.

Changes in the number and types of customers or changes in customers' tastes and needs also result in opportunities and threats. An organization's success depends on its response to customers. Rod Canion lost his job at Compaq because he misjudged the changing types and needs of customers who were buying PCs. A school too must adapt to the changing needs of its customers. For example, if more Spanish-speaking students enroll, additional English as a second language classes may need to be scheduled. Managers' ability to identify an organization's main customers and produce the goods and services they want is a crucial factor affecting organizational and managerial success. The decision by Merck & Co. to give away a cure for a terrible parasitic disease, described in the following "Ethics in Action," is a dramatic example of how a company can respond to customer needs.

Ethics in Action

Merck & Co. Develops a Free Treatment for River Blindness

Merck & Co. (www.merck.com) is one of the largest producers of prescription drugs in the world. Much of Merck's success can be attributed to the company's ability to attract the very best research scientists. It is able to do this because of its reputation as an ethical company that puts people above profits.[6] Merck nurtures its scientists and places enormous value on their work. They are given great latitude to pursue intriguing ideas, even if a commercial payoff is uncertain. Moreover, they are inspired to think of their work as a quest to alleviate human disease and suffering worldwide. As George Merck, son of the company's founder and its former chairman, said: "We try never to forget that medicine is for the people . . . It is not for the profits. The profits follow . . . they have never failed to appear."

In 1978, Dr. Roy Vagelos, director of Merck's research labs, received a memo from a senior research scientist, Dr. William Campbell. Campbell thought that a compound that Merck was developing to treat parasites in cattle—Ivermectin—could be effective against river blindness, a

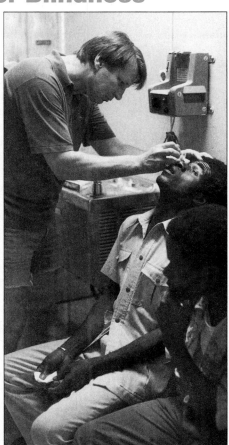

Dr. Sam D'Anna, one of Merck's research scientists, treats a patient with Ivermectin, now called Mectizan, free of charge to protect against the desease, river blindness.

parasitic disease that by 1978 was plaguing around 18 million people and had blinded more than 340,000, principally in Africa. Both Vagelos and Campbell knew that developing a treatment would be costly. Moreover, even if Merck succeeded, it seemed unlikely that the afflicted Third World populations would be able to afford the drug. Vagelos, however, felt that failure to investigate such a promising drug candidate was counter to Merck's ethical values and could demoralize Merck's scientists. So he authorized funds to support the development of a drug from Ivermectin.

Nearly 10 years and $50 million later, Merck received regulatory approval for the treatment, called Mectizan. Merck hoped that an agency such as the U.S. government or the World Health Organization would provide aid to help the company recoup its costs by paying the $3 per year dose fee for the drug treatment. However, no aid materialized, and in 1987 Merck announced that it would donate Mectizan free of charge to anyone who needed the drug.[7] In the 1990s, millions of people in the areas of the world most affected by river blindness were treated.

Competitors

competitors Organizations that produce goods and services that are similar to a particular organization's goods and services.

One of the most important forces that an organization confronts in its task environment is competitors. **Competitors** are organizations that produce goods and services that are similar to a particular organization's goods and services. In other words, competitors are organizations that are vying for the same customers. Compaq's competitors include other domestic manufacturers of PCs (such as Apple, AST, Dell Computer, Gateway 2000, and IBM) as well as foreign competitors (such as NEC and Toshiba in Japan and Group Bull in France).

Rivalry between competitors is potentially the most threatening force that managers must deal with. A high level of rivalry often results in price competition, and falling prices reduce access to resources and lower profits. Today, competition in the personal computer industry is intense as all the major players battle to increase their market share by offering customers better-equipped machines at lower prices.

potential competitors Organizations that presently are not in a task environment but could enter if they so chose.

Although the rivalry between existing competitors is a major threat, so is the potential for new competitors to enter the task environment. **Potential competitors** are organizations that are not presently in a task environment but could enter if they so chose. Hewlett-Packard, for example, is not currently in the wireless communication industry, but it could enter this industry if HP managers decided that doing so would be profitable. When new competitors enter an industry, competition increases and prices decrease.

barriers to entry Factors that make it difficult and costly for an organization to enter a particular task environment or industry.

In general, the potential for new competitors to enter a task environment (and thus boost the level of competition) is a function of barriers to entry.[8] **Barriers to entry** are factors that make it difficult and costly for an organization to enter a particular task environment or industry.[9] In other words, the more difficult and costly it is to enter the task environment, the higher are the barriers to entry. The higher the barriers to entry, the smaller is the number of competitors in an organization's task environment and thus the lower is the threat of competition. With fewer competitors, it is easier to obtain customers and keep prices high.

economies of scale Cost advantages associated with large operations.

Barriers to entry result from two main sources: *economies of scale* and *brand loyalty* (see Figure 3.2). **Economies of scale** are the cost advantages associated

Figure 3.2

Barriers to Entry and Competition

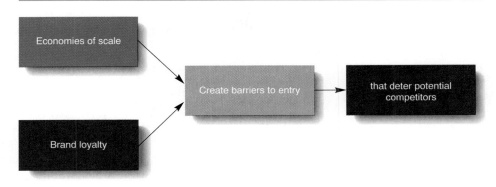

with large operations. Economies of scale result from factors such as being able to manufacture products in very large quantities, buy inputs in bulk, or make more effective use of organizational resources than competitors by fully utilizing employees' skills and knowledge. If organizations already in the task environment are large and enjoy significant economies of scale, then their costs are lower than the costs of potential entrants will be, and newcomers will find it very expensive to enter the industry.

brand loyalty

Customers' preference for the products of organizations currently existing in the task environment.

Brand loyalty is customers' preference for the products of organizations currently existing in the task environment. If established organizations enjoy significant brand loyalty, then a new entrant will find it extremely difficult and costly to obtain a share of the market. Newcomers must bear the huge advertising costs of building customer awareness of the good or service they intend to provide.[10]

In Britain, for example, retailer Marks & Spencer markets its own brand of clothing–St. Michael's brand–which accounts for 15 percent of all clothing sold in the country. The company buys clothing in huge volumes and thus is able to negotiate significant discounts from its suppliers, gaining an economy of scale in buying. Marks & Spencer has a well-developed reputation for selling high-quality clothing at moderate prices and thus enjoys considerable brand loyalty among British consumers. This loyalty to basic clothing items such as underwear and socks is particularly strong; the company's market share of these items exceeds 30 percent. Because Marks & Spencer enjoys barriers to entry from both economies of scale and brand loyalty, new retailing competitors have found it very difficult to break into the market for basic clothing.[11]

In some cases, government regulations function as a barrier to entry. For example, until 1995 government regulations prohibited regional telephone companies in the United States (the "Baby Bells") from offering long-distance service. This restriction prevented competition with the established long-distance companies–AT&T, MCI, and Sprint. When the regulation was amended to allow the Baby Bells to compete, the opportunities and threats facing companies in the telephone industry changed.

Another industry that has enjoyed high barriers to entry is the commercial jet aircraft industry, profiled in the following "Management Insight."

Management Insight

It's Hard to Get into the Jet Business

Because of high entry barriers, there are only three organizations in the large commercial jet aircraft industry—Airbus Industrie, Boeing (www.boeing.com), and McDonnell Douglas (www.dac.mdc.com). Developing a new jet airliner, such as Boeing's 777, can cost up to $5 billion. To recoup this investment, Boeing must sell nearly 300 Boeing 777s, a task that will probably take the company 8 to 10 years. As a result, it is estimated that Boeing will need at least 20 years to recoup its full investment in the 777.[12] Thus, to enter this task environment and compete with Boeing, a new company would have to bear enormous development costs and suffer years of heavy losses before a new product line became profitable—a very risky proposition. In addition, any new entrant would have to acquire quickly the high level of competency necessary to design and build aircraft that companies like Boeing and McDonnell Douglas have spent decades developing. Moreover, there are significant economies of scale in aircraft production; costs fall dramatically as large numbers of airplanes are manufactured. The risk that a new manufacturer would not attract enough customers and sell enough planes to enjoy these economies is sufficient to deter many potential entrants. Thus, barriers to entering the commercial aircraft industry are very high.[13]

In fact, there has been only one new entrant into this market in the last 20 years, Airbus Industrie. Airbus was founded as a consortium of four small European aircraft companies that had many years of experience in building small jet aircraft. Its costs were subsidized by the governments of Britain, France, Germany, and Spain, which effectively lowered the costs of entry for Airbus and reduced its risks.

In summary, intense rivalry among competitors creates a task environment that is highly threatening and causes difficulty for managers trying to gain access to the resources an organization needs. Conversely, low rivalry results in a task environment where competitive pressures are more moderate and managers have greater opportunities to acquire the resources they need for their organizations to be effective.

Not only for-profit organizations but also not-for-profit organizations have customers, suppliers, and competitors that influence and pressure managers because of the opportunities and threats they create. Consider a business school at a state-supported college or university. The customers of the business school are the organizations that hire its graduates, society at large (which benefits from an educated workforce), and the students themselves. Competitors of the business school include other business schools, both state and private, and in-house corporate education programs, such as Motorola's "Motorola U," which produces customized programs that satisfy many of Motorola's immediate business education needs. Suppliers include the university administration and the state government, both of which supply financial resources to the business school. The ultimate suppliers of these resources, of course, are taxpayers.

The Industry Life Cycle

An important determinant of the nature and strength of the forces in an organization's task environment (and thus of the nature of opportunities and threats) is the **industry life cycle**–the changes that take place in an industry as it goes through the stages of birth, growth, shakeout, maturity, and decline (see Figure 3.3). Each stage in the life cycle is associated with particular kinds of forces in the task environment. Managers need to understand which life-cycle stage their organization is in, if they are to accurately perceive the opportunities and threats that it faces.

BIRTH The birth stage of an industry is characterized by competition among companies to develop the winning technology–the one that will allow them to provide the goods or services that customers want. Early in an industry's evolution, managers of new organizations experiment with different ways of producing the product or delivering it to customers. In the early years of the videocassette recorder industry, for example, there were three competing technological standards: the Betamax standard produced by Sony, the VHS standard produced by Matsushita, and the V2000 standard produced by Philips NV. Today, in what is now a mature industry, just one technology is available: the VHS standard. In the birth stage, an organization's relationships with its suppliers, distributors, and customers are fluid and likely to change quickly, making the environment uncertain and difficult to predict and control.

Figure 3.3
Stages in the Industry Life Cycle

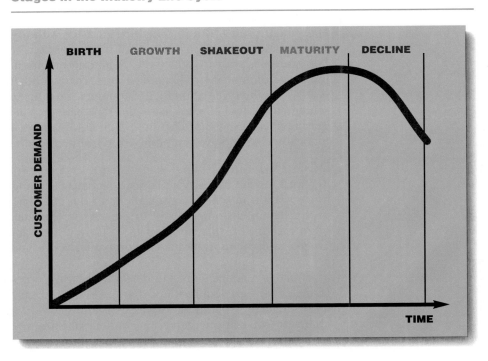

GROWTH   The growth stage begins at the point when a product gains customer acceptance and an influx of consumers enters the market. Rapid growth in customer demand attracts many new organizations into the industry, increasing the level of competition. The newcomers often pioneer new varieties of the industry's products and improved ways of producing and delivering those products to customers. This is occurring in the cellular phone and wireless communication industry today. These changes lead to a complex set of forces in the task environment as the relationships among suppliers, distributors, and competitors all change rapidly.

SHAKEOUT   Near the end of the growth stage there is a marked change in an industry's task environment because slowing customer demand for the industry's product raises the level of competition in the industry. In response, organizations often reduce their prices, and the result can be a price war, which causes prices to fall rapidly. In the shakeout stage, the least-efficient companies are driven out of the industry; consequently, there is significant uncertainty until the shakeout is complete.

MATURITY   By the time an industry reaches maturity, most customers have bought the product and demand is growing slowly or is constant. The task environment is more stable because relationships between suppliers, distributors, and competitors are more predictable. Customers have developed brand loyalty for the products of certain companies, and managers have developed good working relationships with suppliers and distributors. A few large companies usually dominate mature industries, so the level of competition is lower, or at least more predictable, because each company can predict how its competitors will behave. Finally, organizations that have survived into maturity are often protected from new competition by relatively high barriers to entry.

This stable situation may persist for a long time, allowing companies to enjoy high profits. But in a mature industry with low barriers to entry, competitors may enter the market, and if this happens, rapid change may occur. For example, prior to 1973 the U.S. automobile industry was a stable, mature industry dominated by General Motors, Ford, and Chrysler. However, a rapid increase in the price of oil in 1973 opened the door to Japanese producers. By selling small, fuel-efficient cars, the Japanese producers were able to capture market share from the Big Three U.S. auto makers. In the process, they dramatically changed the competitive environment in the auto industry.

DECLINE   In the final stage in the evolution of an industry, customer demand for the industry's product decreases. Falling demand typically leads to a situation in which organizations in the industry are making more of the product than customers want to buy. As in the shakeout period, companies often respond to this situation by cutting prices, and competition increases. Once again, the most inefficient companies are driven out of the industry.

Effective managers must understand the way forces in the task environment change over time as a result of changes in the industry environment. The quality of managers' planning, organizing, and decision making depends on their ability to correctly perceive and understand the forces operating in the task and general environments.

The General Environment

Economic, technological, sociocultural, demographic, political and legal, and global forces in an organization's general environment can have profound effects on the organization's task environment, effects that may not be evident to managers. For example, during the 1980s, advances in microprocessor technology increased the power of computers and ultimately affected the task environment in such a way that the cost of PCs fell and the purchase of a PC became within the reach of the average individual. Rod Canion's downfall resulted from his failure to anticipate (1) the effects that this technological change in the general environment would have on the types of customers who would want Compaq PCs and (2) the vastly increased size of the market for PCs.

Managers must constantly analyze forces in the general environment because these forces affect long-term decision making and planning. In Chapter 7 we examine one of the major tasks involved in planning—the careful and thorough analysis of forces in the general environment. Here, however, we next look in turn at each of the major forces in the general environment, exploring their impact on managers and on the organization's task environment and examining how managers can deal with them.

Economic Forces

economic forces
Interest rates, inflation, unemployment, economic growth, and other factors that affect the general health and well-being of a nation or the regional economy of an organization.

Economic forces affect the general health and well-being of a nation or the regional economy of an organization. They include interest rates, inflation, unemployment, and economic growth. Economic forces produce many opportunities and threats for managers. Low levels of unemployment and falling interest rates mean a change in the customer base: More people have more money to spend, and as a result organizations have an opportunity to sell more goods and services. Good economic times affect supplies: Resources become easier to acquire, and organizations have an opportunity to flourish, as Chrysler and GM did in the early 1990s when they made record profits as the economy recovered from a recession.

In contrast, worsening macroeconomic conditions pose a threat, because they limit managers' ability to gain access to the resources their organization needs. Profit-oriented organizations such as retail stores and hotels have fewer customers for their goods and services during economic downturns. Not-for-profit organizations such as charities and colleges receive fewer donations during economic downturns. Even a moderate deterioration in national or regional economic conditions can seriously affect performance. During the late 1980s, U.S. economic growth slowed to about 1 percent per year, price inflation rose to around 4 percent, and unemployment approached 8 percent. This mild recession reduced the demand for cars and light trucks from 16 million in 1988 to 12.4 million in 1992. Chrysler lost $538 million in 1991, Ford $2,258 million, and General Motors a staggering $4,992 million.[14] As a result of the drop in demand, hundreds of thousands of workers lost their jobs in the automobile and related industries, entire factories closed (General Motors closed 14 plants), and many managers at these enterprises faced momentous challenges. These organizations recovered only when the economy recovered in the 1990s.

General Motors' workers protest the plant closing and mass layoffs that occurred as the result of an increase in Japanese competition in the late 1980s and early 1990s.

technology The combination of skills and equipment that managers use in the design, production, and distribution of goods and services.

technological forces
Outcomes of changes in the technology that managers use to design, produce, or distribute goods and services.

Poor economic conditions make the environment more complex and managers' jobs more difficult and demanding. Managers may need to reduce the number of individuals in their departments and increase the motivation of remaining employees, and managers and workers alike may need to identify ways to acquire and utilize resources more efficiently. Successful managers, realize the important effects that economic forces have on their organizations and they pay close attention to what is occurring in the national and regional economy in order to respond appropriately.

Technological Forces

Technology is the combination of skills and equipment that managers use in the design, production, and distribution of goods and services. **Technological forces** are outcomes of changes in the technology that managers use to design, produce, or distribute goods and services. Technological forces have increased in magnitude since World War II because the overall pace of technological change has accelerated so greatly.[15]

Technological forces can have profound implications for managers and organizations. Technological change can make established products obsolete overnight—for example, eight-track tapes and black and white televisions—forcing managers to find new products to make. Although technological change can threaten an organization, it also can create a host of new opportunities for designing, making, or distributing new and better kinds of goods and services. More powerful microprocessors, primarily developed by Intel, caused a revolution in information technology that spurred demand for PCs, contributed to the success of companies such as Dell and Compaq, and led to the decline of others such as IBM.[16] IBM and other producers of mainframe computers have seen demand for their products decrease as organizationwide networks of PCs have replaced mainframes in many computing applications.[17] Managers must move quickly to respond to such changes if their organizations are to survive and prosper.

Changes in information technology also are changing the very nature of work itself within organizations and, in addition, the manager's job. Telecommuting along the information superhighway and teleconferencing are now everyday activities that provide opportunities for managers to supervise and coordinate geographically dispersed employees. Salespeople in many companies work from home offices and commute electronically to work. Salespeople communicate with other employees through companywide electronic mail networks and use video cameras attached to PCs for "face-to-face" meetings with fellow workers who may be many miles away. Managers at Boeing have utilized advances in information technology in a different way—to revolutionize the way the company designs and builds jet aircraft.

Management Insight

Computer-Aided Design Makes a Difference at Boeing

Boeing's (www.boeing.com) new wide-body twin engine jet, the 777, contains over 1 million individual parts. A change in the design of any one of these parts usually necessitates a change in dozens of other related parts. The challenge is to design each component so that everything fits together and works when the first plane is assembled. When building prototypes, Boeing found that if the alignment of an aircraft fuselage was off by as little as a foot, hundreds of components had to be reworked to fit together, an expensive and time-consuming proposition.

Boeing wanted to avoid such costly refitting when it launched a program in 1989 to build the new, fuel-efficient 777. Two hundred thirty-eight cross-functional teams were assigned to design the different component assemblies of the plane. To improve coordination among the teams, Boeing decided to use custom-made CAD (computer-aided design) software to design the aircraft. The custom system cost Boeing more than $1 billion and connected 2,200 engineering workstations in a network supported by eight mainframes.[18] Using the designers' specifications, the CAD system helped create a digitized mock-up of the aircraft and eliminated the need for paper drawings and a physical model. All teams were immediately notified when a design change made by any team would have an impact on their task. Thus, different components could be designed in a parallel rather than a sequential process, and problems could be spotted and resolved long before the assembly phase. The effort was well worth the cost. When the first 777 was assembled, it was not out of line by feet or even inches. The aircraft fit together perfectly, and there was no need for reworking that would have cost hundreds of millions of dollars.[19]

This system, which used advanced computing technology, changed both the customary organization of work at Boeing and the way managers' jobs were defined. First, interlocking parts were designed at the same time, rather than one at a time. Because design work could be parallel rather than sequential, designing and building the aircraft took much less time than usual. Second, because the computer network facilitated coordination among the 238 design teams, the managers of the 777 program did not need to concentrate on coordination. Instead, they devoted more attention to managing and leading the individual cross-functional teams, making sure that individual team members worked well together and that the teams consulted with customers and suppliers as they worked on their assigned components.

Sociocultural Forces

sociocultural forces

Pressures emanating from the social structure of a country or society or from the national culture.

Sociocultural forces are pressures emanating from the social structure of a country or society or from the national culture. Pressures from both sources can either constrain or facilitate the way organizations operate and managers behave. **Social structure** is the arrangement of relationships between individuals and groups in a society. Societies differ substantially in social structure. In societies that have a high degree of social stratification, there are

social structure
The arrangement of relationships between individuals and groups in a society.

many distinctions among individuals and groups. Caste systems in India and Tibet and the recognition of numerous social classes in Great Britain and France produce a multilayered social structure in each of those countries. In contrast, social stratification is lower in relatively egalitarian New Zealand and in the United States, and the social structure reveals few distinctions among people. Most top managers in France come from the upper classes of French society, but top managers in the United States come from all strata of American society.

Societies also differ in the extent to which they emphasize the individual over the group. For example, the United States emphasizes the primacy of the individual, and Japan emphasizes the primacy of the group. This difference may dictate the methods managers need to use to motivate and lead employees.

National culture is the set of values that a society considers important and the norms of behavior that are approved or sanctioned in that society. Societies differ substantially in the values and norms that they emphasize. For example, in the United States individualism is highly valued, and in Korea and Japan individuals are expected to conform to group expectations.[20] National culture also affects the way managers motivate and coordinate employees and the way organizations do business. Ethics, an important aspect of national culture, is discussed in detail in Chapter 5.

national culture The set of values that a society considers important and the norms of behavior that are approved or sanctioned in that society.

Social structure and national culture not only differ across societies but also change within societies over time. In the 1960s and 1970s in the United States, there were changes in attitudes about the roles of women, love, sex, and marriage. Many people in Asian countries such as Hong Kong, Singapore, Korea, and Japan think that the younger generation is far more individualistic and "American-like" than previous generations. Similarly, throughout much of eastern Europe, new values that emphasize individualism and entrepreneurship are replacing communist values based on collectivism and obedience to the state.

Individual managers and organizations must be responsive to changes in, and differences among, the social structures and national cultures of all the countries in which they operate. In today's increasingly integrated global economy, managers are likely to interact with people from several countries, and many live and work abroad. Effective managers are sensitive to differences between societies and adjust their behaviors accordingly.

Managers and organizations also must respond to social changes within a society. During the 1970s and 1980s, for example, Americans became more interested in their personal health and fitness. Managers who recognized this trend early and exploited the opportunities that resulted from it were able to reap significant gains for their organizations. Philip Morris's Miller Brewing subsidiary redefined competition in the beer industry with its introduction of low-calorie beer (Miller Lite) to appeal to "weight-conscious" beer drinkers. PepsiCo used the opportunity presented by the fitness trend and took market share from arch rival Coca-Cola by being the first to introduce diet colas and fruit-based soft drinks. The health trend, however, did not offer opportunities to all companies; to some it posed a threat. Tobacco companies are under pressure due to consumers' greater awareness of negative health impacts from smoking. Hershey Foods and other manufacturers of candy bars have been threatened by customers' desires for low-fat, healthy foods.

Demographic Forces

Demographic forces are outcomes of changes in, or changing attitudes toward, the characteristics of a population, such as age, gender, ethnic origin, race, sexual orientation, and social class. Like the other forces in the general environment, demographic forces present managers with opportunities and threats and can have major implications for organizations. Over the last 20 years, for example, women have entered the workforce in increasing numbers. Between 1973 and 1992, the percentage of working-age women in the workforce increased from 50 to 72 percent in the United States, from 48 to 68 percent in Canada, and from 51 to 68 percent in Britain.[21] The dramatic increase in the number of working women has brought to the forefront of public concern issues such as equal pay for equal work and sexual harassment at work. Managers must address these issues if they are to attract and make full use of the talents of female workers. We discuss the important issue of workforce diversity at length in Chapter 5.

Changes in the age distribution of a population are another example of a demographic force that affects managers and organizations. Currently, most industrialized nations are experiencing the aging of their populations as a consequence of falling birth and death rates and the aging of the baby-boom generation. In Germany, for example, the percentage of the population over age 65 is expected to rise from 15.4 percent in 1990 to 20.7 percent in 2010. Comparable figures for Canada are 11.4 and 14.4 percent; for Japan, 11.7 and 19.5 percent; and for the United States, 12.6 and 13.5 percent.[22] The aging of the population is increasing opportunities for organizations that cater to older people; the home health care and recreation industries, for example, are seeing an upswing in demand for their services.

Frieda Caplan, left, is the founder of Frieda's Inc., a produce distributor that specializes in exotic fruits and vegetables. She attributes the success of her company to the combined attempts of her employees and family to keep up to date with customers' changing needs.

The aging of the population also has several implications for the workplace. Most significant are a relative decline in the number of young people joining the workforce and an increase in active employees willing to postpone retirement past the traditional retirement age of 65. These changes suggest that organizations will need to find ways to motivate and utilize the skills and knowledge of older employees, an issue that many Western societies have yet to tackle.

Political and Legal Forces

political and legal forces Outcomes of changes in laws and regulations, such as the deregulation of industries, the privatization of organizations, and increased emphasis on environmental protection.

Political and legal forces are outcomes of changes in laws and regulations. They result from political and legal developments within society and significantly affect managers and organizations. Political processes shape a society's laws. Laws constrain the operations of organizations and managers and thus create both opportunities and threats.[23] For example, throughout much of the industrialized world there has been a strong trend toward deregulation of industries previously controlled by the state and privatization of organizations once owned by the state.

In the United States, deregulation of the airline industry in 1978 ushered into the task environment of commercial airlines major changes that are still working themselves out. Deregulation allowed 29 new airlines to enter the industry between 1978 and 1993. The increase in airline-passenger carrying capacity after deregulation led to excess capacity on many routes, intense competition, and fare wars. To respond to this more competitive task environment, airlines have had to look for ways to reduce operating costs. The development of hub-and-spoke systems, the rise of nonunion airlines, and the introduction of no-frills discount service are all responses to increased competition in the airlines' task environment. But despite these innovations, the airline industry still experiences intense fare wars, which have lowered profits and caused numerous airline company bankruptcies. Between 1990 and 1992, companies in the U.S. airline industry lost a total of $7.1 billion, more than the industry had made in the previous 50 years.[24]

Deregulation and privatization are just two examples of political and legal forces that can create challenges for organizations and managers. Others include increased emphasis on environmental protection and the preservation of endangered species, increased emphasis on safety in the workplace, and legal constraints against discrimination on the basis of race, gender, or age. Successful managers carefully monitor changes in laws and regulations in order to take advantage of the opportunities they create and counter the threats they pose in an organization's task environment.

Global Forces

global forces Outcomes of changes in international relationships, changes in nations' economic, political, and legal systems, and changes in technology, such as falling trade barriers, the growth of representative democracies, and reliable and instantaneous communication.

Global forces are outcomes of changes in international relationships, changes in nations' economic, political, and legal systems, and changes in technology. The global environment is the subject of Chapter 4, so here we are limiting our discussion to a few introductory comments. Perhaps the most important global force affecting managers and organizations is the increasing economic integration of countries around the world.[25] Free-trade agreements such as the General Agreement on Tariffs and Trade (GATT) and the North American Free Trade Agreement (NAFTA), and the growth of the European Union (EU), have led to a lowering of barriers to the free flow of goods and services between nations.[26]

Falling trade barriers have created enormous opportunities for organizations in one country to sell goods and services in other countries. But by allowing foreign companies to compete for an organization's domestic customers, falling trade barriers also pose a serious threat, because they increase competition in the task environment. Between 1973 and 1990, for example, U.S. car makers saw Japanese competitors increase their share of the U.S. car market from 3 to nearly 30 percent. This growth would not have been possible without relatively low trade barriers, which allowed producers in Japan to export cars to the United States. Competition from Toyota, Honda, and other Japanese companies forced managers of the U.S. car companies to find ways to improve their operations. To remain competitive, they had to transform the way their organizations designed and manufactured cars. Managers at Chrysler and Ford, for example, now use decentralized structures and cross-functional teams to design, manufacture, and market cars. As a result of these changes, U.S. companies seem to be gaining ground against their Japanese competitors; the share of the U.S. market held by Japanese companies fell from 30 percent to 27 percent between 1990 and 1993.[27] It is likely that none of the changes that U.S. managers introduced would have been made if global forces had not increased the intensity of competition in the task environment of U.S. car companies.

Tips for Managers

Forces in the Environment

1. List the forces in an organization's task environment that affect it the most. Analyze changes taking place that may result in opportunities or threats for the organization.

2. List the forces in the general environment that affect an organization the most. Analyze changes taking place that may result in opportunities or threats for the organization.

3. Devise a plan indicating how your managers propose to take advantage of opportunities or counter threats that arise from environmental forces and what kinds of resources they will need to do so.

Managing the Organizational Environment

As previously discussed, an important task for managers is to understand how forces in the task and general environments generate opportunities for, and threats to, their organizations. To analyze the importance of opportunities and threats in the organizational environment, managers must measure (1) the level of complexity in the environment and (2) the rate at which the environment is changing. With this information, they can plan appropriately and choose the best goals and courses of action.

The complexity of the organizational environment is a function of the number and potential impact of the forces to which managers must respond in both the task and the general environments. A force that seems likely to have a significant negative impact is a potential threat to which managers must devote a high level of organizational resources. A force likely to have a marginal impact poses little threat to an organization and requires only a minor commitment of managerial time and attention. A force likely to make a significant positive impact warrants a considerable commitment of managerial time and effort to take advantage of the opportunity.

In general, the larger an organization is, the greater is the number of environmental forces that managers must respond to. Compare, for example, the organizational environment facing the manager of a roadside diner with that facing top managers at Taco Bell's headquarters. At the local level, the main concern of a restaurant manager is to ensure an adequate supply of inputs, such as food supplies and restaurant employees, to provide customers with fast and efficient service. In contrast, top managers at Taco Bell must determine how to distribute food supplies to restaurants in the most efficient ways; how to ensure that the organization's practices do not discriminate against any ethnic groups or older workers; how to respond to customers' new preference for tacos made with low-fat cheese and sour cream; and how to deal with competition from McDonald's, which has reduced the cost of its hamburgers to compete with Taco Bell's low-cost tacos and burritos. Clearly, the more forces managers must deal with, the more complicated is the management process.

environmental change
The degree to which forces in the task and general environments change and evolve over time.

Environmental change is the degree to which forces in the task and general environments change and evolve over time. Change is problematic for an organization and its managers because the consequences of change can be difficult to predict.[28] For example, managers in the computer and telecommunications industries know that technological advances such as the increasing power and falling cost of microprocessors and the development of the information superhighway will produce dramatic changes in their task environments, but they do not know what the magnitude or effects of those changes will be. Managers can attempt to forecast or simply guess about future conditions in the task environment, such as where and how strong the new competition may be. But, confronted with a complex and changing task environment, managers cannot be sure that decisions and actions taken today will be appropriate in the future. This uncertainty makes their jobs especially challenging. It also makes it vitally important for managers to understand the forces that shape the organizational environment.

As a first step in managing the organizational environment, managers need to list the number and relative strength of the forces that affect their organization's task and general environments the most. Second, they need to analyze the way changes in these forces may result in opportunities or threats for their organizations. Third, they need to draw up a plan indicating how they propose to take advantage of those opportunities or counter those threats and what kinds of resources they will need to do so. An understanding of the organizational environment is necessary so that managers can anticipate how the task environment might look in the future and decide on the actions to pursue if the organization is to prosper.

Jill Barad, the CEO of Mattel, the toy maker, holds one of the thousands of models of Barbie dolls that have been produced over the years; the toy that remains the single most important product in Mattel's product line.

Reducing the Impact of Environmental Forces

Often, managers can counter threats in the task environment by reducing the potential impact of forces in that environment. In the 1980s, for example, managers at Xerox Corporation dealt with over 3,000 different suppliers and employed an army of managers to purchase inputs. To reduce costs and simplify dealings with suppliers, top managers at Xerox decided to reduce the number of the company's suppliers. Today, fewer than 300 suppliers provide Xerox with high-quality inputs at a much lower cost than in the past.

Finding ways to reduce the number and potential impact of forces in the organizational environment is the job of all managers in an organization. The principal task of the CEO and top-management team is to devise strategies that will allow an organization to take advantage of opportunities and counter threats in its general and task environments (see Part 3 for a discussion of this vital topic). Middle managers in an organization's departments collect relevant information about the task environment, such as (1) the future intentions of the organization's competitors, (2) the identity of new customers for the organization's products, and (3) the identity of new suppliers of crucial or low-cost inputs. First-line managers find ways to use resources more efficiently to hold down costs or to get close to customers and learn what they want.

Creating an Organizational Structure and Control Systems

Another way to respond to a complex and changing organizational environment is to increase the complexity of the organization's structure and its control systems. (We discuss organizational structure and control systems in detail in Part 4.) To do this, top managers assign various departments to deal with the various forces affecting the task and general environments (see Figure 3.4). For example, the sales and service departments develop the skills and knowledge necessary to handle relationships with customers. The research and development department is responsible for identifying changes in technology that will impact the organization and for using that technology to develop new goods and services to attract customers. The finance and accounting departments are responsible for scanning and monitoring economic forces and assessing their impact on the organization.

As discussed in Chapter 2, another important action that managers can take to organize and control an organization's activities in response to characteristics of the organizational environment is designing a mechanistic structure or an organic structure. In stable environments with low levels of complexity and competition, managers have relatively few problems in accessing resources and can effectively use a mechanistic structure to coordinate their activities. In a *mechanistic structure,* authority is centralized at the top of the hierarchy, and tasks and roles are clearly specified. Mechanistic structures help the organization to utilize its resources efficiently and effectively in a stable environment.

In contrast, when the environment is changing rapidly and there is a high level of complexity, an organic structure is more appropriate. In an *organic structure,*

Figure 3.4

How Managers Use Functions to Manage Forces in the Task and General Environments

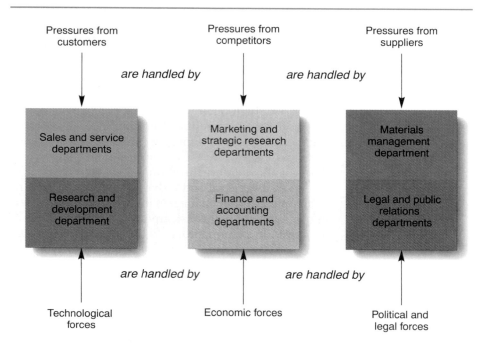

authority is decentralized to the middle and first-line managers close to the scene of the action. Roles and tasks are deliberately left ambiguous to encourage employees to cooperate and find creative responses to new and emerging situations that are continually arising. Organic structures allow managers to respond better to unpredictable and uncertain events or contingencies.

Middle managers within an organization's departments are responsible for identifying what is happening in the environment as it relates to their functional area and for forecasting how environmental forces are likely to affect their departments and the organization as a whole. The ability of department managers to (1) develop the skills they need to manage the segment of the environment they are responsible for and (2) work with other departments in an organic fashion determines organizational performance–the organization's ability to acquire and utilize resources efficiently and effectively. Effective organizations have departments that are able to respond quickly and appropriately to unforeseen situations and to take advantage of unexpected opportunities. Ineffective organizations lack the ability to respond to changes in the task and general environments and the skills needed to secure scarce and valuable resources.

Indeed, a recent influential book, *Competing on the Edge* argues that the most important challenge facing managers is not just the need to respond quickly to changing conditions in the environment, but to time their responses to the cycles or rhythms in their environments, such as the changing patterns of their customers' needs, so that they know when to change to respond to those needs. To accomplish this, the challenge facing managers is to adopt an organic structure that is partly structured so that they can get the organization to move quickly and change, but not so unstructured or loose that it can't get anywhere.[29] (Further details about this new approach can be found in an audio interview with the book's authors at www.computerworld.com/home/features.nsf/All/980511book).

In essence, managers must develop *internal* structure and control systems that allow them to respond appropriately to the specific forces and conditions in the *external* environment. Managing the match between the organization and its environment so that the organization's structure and control systems respond well to the forces in the task and general environments is a vital management task. In the long run, the ability of managers to perform this task is one key factor that separates high-performing from low-performing organizations.

Boundary-Spanning Roles

The ability of managers to gain access to the information they need to forecast the future and choose appropriate goals and courses of action is critical to successful management in times of uncertainty. This was evident in the "Case in Contrast" at the beginning of this chapter. Rod Canion's perception of Compaq's environment was inaccurate, and as a result the Compaq CEO did not take the actions necessary to reposition his organization in the increasingly price-competitive personal computer industry of the 1990s. Consequently, Compaq's performance deteriorated. In contrast, his successor, Eckhard Pfeiffer, more correctly perceived the changes taking place in Compaq's task environment and took appropriate actions to restore Compaq's performance.

The history of organizations is marked by numerous once-great organizations whose managers did not recognize and respond to significant changes taking place in the task and general environments. Examples include now-defunct Eastern Airlines and Pan Am, which were unable to reposition themselves to compete in the more competitive airline industry that came into being in the United States after the 1978 deregulation.

boundary spanning

Interacting with individuals and groups outside the organization to obtain valuable information from the task and general environments.

Managers can learn to perceive, interpret, and appreciate better their organizations' task and general environments by practicing **boundary spanning**–interacting with individuals and groups outside the organization to obtain valuable information from the task and general environments.[30] Managers who engage in boundary-spanning activities seek ways not only to respond to forces in the external environment but also to *directly influence and manage* the perceptions of stakeholders in that environment to increase their organizations' access to resources.

How does boundary spanning work (see Figure 3.5)? A manager in a boundary-spanning role in Organization X establishes a link with a manager in a boundary-spanning role in Organization Y. The two managers communicate and share information that helps both of them understand the changing forces and conditions in the industry environment. These managers then share this information with other managers in their respective organizations so that all managers become better informed about events outside their own organization's boundaries. As a result, the managers in both organizations can make more appropriate decisions.

For an example of a manager performing a boundary-spanning role, consider the situation of a purchasing manager for Taco Bell. The purchasing manager is charged with finding the lowest-cost supplier of low-fat cheese and sour cream. To perform this task, the manager could write to major food companies and ask for price quotes. Or the manager could phone food company

Figure 3.5
The Nature of Boundary-Spanning Roles

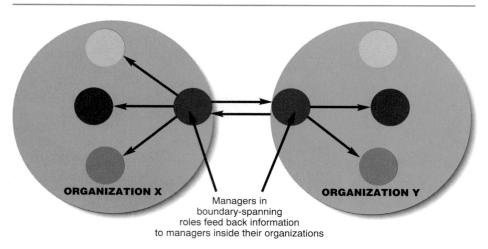

ORGANIZATION X   ORGANIZATION Y

Managers in
boundary-spanning
roles feed back information
to managers inside their organizations

managers personally, develop an informal yet professional relationship with them, and, over time, learn from them which food companies are active in the low-fat food area and what they envision for the future. By developing such a relationship, the purchasing manager will be able to provide Taco Bell with valuable information that will allow Taco Bell's purchasing department to make well-informed choices. This flow of information from the task environment may, in turn, allow marketing to develop more effective sales campaigns or product development to develop better-looking and better-tasting tacos.

What would happen if managers in *all* of an organization's departments performed boundary-spanning roles? The richness of the information available to managers throughout the organization probably would lead to an increase in the quality of managers' decision making and planning, enabling them to produce goods and services that customers prefer or to create advertising campaigns that attract new customers. Managers can engage in many kinds of boundary-spanning activities; some of them were identified by Henry Mintzberg (see Table 1.1). Four of the most important ones are discussed next.

REPRESENTING AND PROTECTING THE ORGANIZATION

Managers, by their actions alone, can shape the perceptions of outsiders—individuals, groups, and other organizations—to make them view an organization favorably.[31] For example, a manager who speaks in public is representing his or her organization, and the public often judges an organization by what its managers say. Organizations in many industries form and fund political action committees (PACs) and employ lobbyists to influence legislators to pass laws favoring their interests.

In time of crisis, managers can protect their organizations by acting quickly and appropriately across the organizational boundary to head off or respond to problems effectively. For example, the speed at which executives at Exxon or Shell respond to an oil spill affects the way the public views their companies, as Exxon found out to its cost when it was accused of being slow to react to the *Exxon Valdez* disaster in Alaska in 1989.

SCANNING AND MONITORING THE ENVIRONMENT Searching for and collecting information to understand how trends and forces in the task and general environments are changing is an important boundary-spanning activity. Many organizations employ researchers whose only job is to scan professional journals, trade association publications, and newspapers to identify changes in technology, government regulations, fashion trends, and so on, that will affect the way their organization operates. Managers regularly go to conferences, industry association meetings, and exhibitions to monitor and learn about changes taking place in the part of the task environment that they are responsible for.

GATEKEEPING AND INFORMATION PROCESSING Merely collecting information is not enough for the boundary-spanning manager. He or she must interpret what the information means and then practice **gatekeeping,** deciding what information to allow into the organization and what information to keep out. The nature of the information that the gatekeeper chooses to pass on to other managers will influence the decisions they make. Thus, accurate information processing is vital. Sometimes, however, managers pass on only the information that supports their interests or makes their job easier or the information that they think other managers want to hear. Such selectivity obscures rather than clarifies the situation and undermines the quality of decision making. Poor information processing delayed the responses of many once-dominant companies, such as IBM, General Motors, and Sears, to radical changes taking place in their organizational environments.[32]

gatekeeping Deciding what information to allow into the organization and what information to keep out.

ESTABLISHING INTERORGANIZATIONAL RELATIONSHIPS In today's integrated global environment it is more important than ever before for organizations to develop alliances and agreements with other organizations around the world to help themselves obtain and utilize resources. Alliances and agreements are developed when managers meet and develop personal relationships with one another, and establishing these *interorganizational relationships* is an increasingly important boundary-spanning task. An example of how a manager, by chance, started to engage in boundary-spanning activities with great success follows in this "Managing Globally" feature.

Managing Globally

T. Julie Berry Discovers China

T. Julie Berry is president of Johnston Tombigbee Furniture Manufacturing Company (www.jtbfurniture.com), a midsize furniture manufacturer based in Columbus, Mississippi, with annual sales of about $40 million and 1,000 employees. Columbus is not the kind of town that one imagines as being at the forefront of trading in the global economy. The most international things in town are Japanese cars and an occasional Chinese restaurant. But when Julie Berry, who charges like a halfback through his factories, first started trading in the global economy a decade ago, he began to import furniture from Brazil for sale in the United States. More recently he has found his horizons expanding to include China.

The contact began when a Chinese businessman dropped in unannounced to see Julie Berry. As Berry puts it, "So I go out and there's this guy standing there. I almost threw him out, but I said, O.K., I'll talk to him." Three months later, at the invitation of the Chinese businessman, Julie Berry traveled to Beijing to develop ways of involving Chinese manufacturers in his expansion plans. He returned from Beijing with a deal to have the Chinese make chairs for him. Julie Berry's new Chinese partner, Yang Yijian (who prefers to be called James), quoted prices for the chairs that were two-thirds lower than what Berry paid to his Brazilian supplier. "I said to myself, where is cheap labor and massive amounts of raw material?" remarked Mr. Berry. "I thought it was Brazil, but now it looks like it's China. James quoted me an outstanding price on it [the chairs]. This chair cost me $12.50 from Brazil. James gave me a quote of $4.50."[33]

As a result of a casual contact made while seeking information, Julie Berry is now considering the possibility of widening his imports from chairs to include selected bedroom furniture. He envisions low-cost Chinese furniture as a critical ingredient in his plans to grow Johnston Tombigbee into one of the top 100 furniture makers in the United States.

Managers as Agents of Change

It is important to note that, although much of the change that occurs in the organizational environment is independent of a particular organization (for example, basic advances in biotechnology or plastics), *a significant amount of environmental change is the direct consequence of actions taken by managers within organizations.*[34] As explained in Chapter 2 (see Figure 2.4), an organization is an open system: It takes in inputs from the environment and converts them into goods and services that are sent back to the environment. Thus, change in the environment is a two-way process (see Figure 3.6). Many times, however, the choices managers make about which products to produce, and even about how to compete with other organizations, affect the environment in many ways.

Consider how actions taken by managers at MCI Communications significantly changed the U.S. telecommunications industry. In 1974, managers at MCI (then a small company specializing in microwave communication) decided to launch a legal challenge to AT&T's monopoly of telephone services in the United States. MCI claimed that the AT&T monopoly was not in the best public interest and violated antitrust regulations. Ultimately, MCI won this

Figure 3.6
Change in the Environment as a Two-Way Process

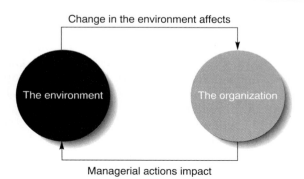

David versus Goliath battle, and in 1984 the U.S. Supreme Court ordered AT&T to separate into a long-distance company and seven regional telephone companies (the "Baby Bells"). The Court also opened the door for MCI to compete head-to-head with AT&T in the long-distance market. The result of MCI managers' actions was to usher in a new era of competition in the now-deregulated U.S. telecommunications industry. MCI has been a major beneficiary of this change, capturing more than 20 percent of the U.S. long-distance market. Occasionally the actions of just one manager can bring profound changes to an organization's external environment, as this "Management Insight" indicates.

Management Insight

Bill Lowe Changes the Rules of the Game

In 1980, Bill Lowe was a manager at IBM's (www.ibm.co.at) entry systems division in Boca Raton, Florida. Lowe had watched the growth of the personal computer industry—dominated by Apple, Atari, and Radio Shack—with growing interest and apprehension. He felt that IBM, the dominant force in the mainframe computer industry, should also be a leading player in the fast-growing PC segment. Thus, in mid-1980, acting on his own initiative, he assembled a team of managers to draft a proposal describing how IBM could build a viable personal computer within a year.

Lowe's plan called for IBM to adopt an open-system architecture for the new personal computer. This meant that Lowe proposed a departure from the company's normal practice of producing key components and software in-house; he recommended that IBM buy them "off-the-shelf" from other producers. The key components that Lowe proposed to buy included Intel's 8088 microprocessor and a software operating system known as MS-DOS from Microsoft, then a little-known Seattle company. The advantage of this approach was that it would enable IBM to get a personal computer to the market quickly. The disadvantage was that it would allow other companies to produce IBM-compatible PCs by simply buying the same Intel microprocessor and MS-DOS operating system. Such a strategy represented a radical departure for IBM, which in the past had tried to stop imitation of its products by producing all key components in-house.[35]

Lowe's team submitted the plan to IBM's powerful corporate management committee and in August 1980 received the authorization to go ahead. Just over a year later the first IBM PC was introduced into the marketplace. It was an overnight sensation and quickly grabbed the market lead from Apple. More important, however, Lowe's decision to go with an open system architecture enabled a flood of imitators to enter the market.

Within two years, the imitators were producing PCs that were compatible with the IBM standard. The first of these imitators was Compaq Computer. Compaq was soon followed by a myriad of other companies, including current industry stars such as AST, Dell Computer, and Gateway 2000. The result was the creation of today's highly competitive personal computer industry—an industry that IBM no longer dominates. Thus, Lowe's fateful decision to adopt open-system architecture forever changed the task environment in the personal computer industry.

Chapter Summary

Tips for Managers

Managing the Organizational Environment

1. To assess the level of uncertainty in the environment, analyze its level of complexity and rate of change.

2. Once the number and importance of the forces in the environment have been determined, decide how to build and develop departments to respond to them.

3. After analyzing your customers, competitors, and suppliers, decide which managers should be responsible for identifying and responding to their needs.

4. Once the rate of change in the task and general environment has been determined, decide whether a mechanistic or an organic structure is most appropriate for the organization.

Summary and Review

WHAT IS THE ORGANIZATIONAL ENVIRONMENT? The organizational environment is the set of forces and conditions that operate beyond an organization's boundaries but affect a manager's ability to acquire and utilize resources. The organizational environment has two components, the task environment and the general environment. The task environment is the set of forces and conditions that originate with suppliers, distributors, customers, and competitors and that influence managers on a daily basis. The general environment is wider-ranging economic, technological, sociocultural, demographic, political and legal, and global forces that affect an organization and its task environment.

MANAGING THE ORGANIZATIONAL ENVIRONMENT Two factors affect the nature of the opportunities and threats that organizations face: (1) the level of complexity in the environment and (2) the rate of change in the environment. Managers must learn how to analyze the forces in the environment in order to respond effectively to opportunities and threats.

ORGANIZATIONAL ENVIRONMENT RELATIONSHIPS The principal way in which managers increase their organization's ability to manage the environment is by creating an organizational structure and control systems to allow managers throughout the organization to deal with the specific parts of the environment for which they are responsible. Developing an organizational structure involves building departmental skills and resources, giving authority to managers at all levels to allow them to respond quickly, and choosing a mechanistic or an organic structure, depending on the complexity and rate of change in the task and general environments.

BOUNDARY-SPANNING ROLES Managers also can help their organization adapt to its general and task environments by engaging in boundary-spanning activities. Such activities include representing and protecting the organization, scanning and monitoring the environment, gatekeeping and information processing, and establishing interorganizational relationships.

Management in Action

Topics for Discussion and Action

1. Why is it important for managers to understand the nature of the environmental forces that are acting on them and their organization?

2. Choose an organization, and ask a manager in that organization to list the number and strengths of forces in the organization's task environment. Ask the manager to pay particular attention to identifying opportunities and threats that result from pressures and changes in customers, competitors, and suppliers.

3. Which organization is likely to face the most complex task environment: a biotechnology company trying to develop a new cure for cancer or a large retailer like the Gap or Macy's? Why?

4. The population is aging because of declining birth rates, declining death rates, and the aging of the baby-boom generation. What might some of the implications of this demographic trend be for (a) a pharmaceutical company, (b) the home construction industry, and (c) the agenda of political parties?

5. Currently, most households and businesses in Great Britain, the United States, and a number of other countries do not have a choice of electricity supplier. But as a result of deregulation, within a decade the average business and household will be able to choose from among several competing suppliers. How might this development alter the task environment facing a manager in an electric utility?

6. In what different ways can managers design an organization's structure to allow the organization to respond to its task environment?

7. Choose an organization, and ask its managers to describe the organizational structure and control systems that help the organization respond to its environment. Do you think managers in this organization are doing a good job of matching the organization to its task and general environments?

8. What is the purpose of boundary-spanning roles? List five ways in which managers in a biotechnology company can help their company by engaging in boundary-spanning activities.

Building Management Skills

Analyzing an Organization's Task and General Environments

Pick an organization with which you are familiar. It can be an organization in which you have worked or currently work, or it can be an organization that you interact with regularly as a customer (such as the college that you are currently attending). For this organization do the following.

1. Describe the main forces in the task environment that are affecting the organization.

2. Describe the main forces in the general environment that are affecting the organization.

3. Try to determine whether the organization's task and general environments are relatively stable or changing rapidly.

4. Explain how environmental forces affect the job of an individual manager within this organization. How do they determine the opportunities and threats that its managers must confront?

Small Group Breakout Exercise

How to Enter the Copying Business

Form groups of three to five people, and appoint one group member as the spokesperson who will communicate your findings to the whole class when called on by the instructor. Then discuss the following scenario.

You and your partners have decided to open a small printing and copying business in a college town of 100,000 people. Your business will compete with companies like Kinko's. You know that over 50 percent of small businesses fail in their first year, so to increase your chances of success, you have decided to do a detailed analysis of the task environment of the copying business in order to analyze the opportunities and threats you will encounter. As a group:

1. Decide what you must know about (a) your future customers, (b) your future competitors, and (c) other critical forces in the task environment, if you are to be successful.

2. Evaluate the main barriers to entry into the copying business.

3. Based on this analysis, list some of the steps you will take to help your new copying business succeed.

Exploring the World Wide Web

Specific Assignment

Examine the environment that the chemical company Du Pont faces as it pursues its activities around the globe. Explore Du Pont's website (www.dupont.com), and click on "About Du Pont" and "Du Pont Direction Statement." Explore these locations and other relevant ones for information about Du Pont's environment.

1. What major forces in the task and general environments present opportunities and threats for Du Pont?

2. How are Du Pont's managers managing these forces?

General Assignment

Search for the website of a company that has a complex, rapidly changing environment. What forces in its organizational environment are creating the strongest opportunities and threats? How are managers attempting to respond to these opportunities and threats?

ManagementCase
The Brewing Industry

In 1960, the brewing industry in the United States was made up of hundreds of small regional companies that produced beer for local markets such as Milwaukee, Detroit, and Dallas. Each of these companies had a loyal and stable customer base, typically used brewing techniques that had changed little over the century, and bought hops, barley, malt, and other raw materials that were readily available.

After 1960, a major change took place in the brewing industry. Large companies such as Anheuser-Busch (best known for its Budweiser brand), Miller Brewing (best known for Miller Lite), and Stroh, Coors, Heileman, and Pabst decided to increase their profits by developing larger markets for their beers. Anheuser-Busch, in particular, began an aggressive campaign to purchase small brewers, acquiring their names and resources and then closing their operations and selling the local beer under its original brand name as well as clearly associating it with Anheuser-Busch. Other large brewing companies followed Anheuser-Busch's example. By 1979 the six brewers mentioned above had gained 75 percent of the market (Anheuser-Busch alone had 27 percent), and the remaining small regional companies retained only 25 percent. By 1989, the six brewers together had over 95 percent of the market, Anheuser-Busch had emerged as "king" of the beer makers with over a 44 percent market share, and its Budweiser brand had become the largest selling beer in the United States.[36]

The success of the large brewers, and particularly Anheuser-Busch, resulted from two factors. First, by acquiring the small brewers, they established a local presence yet were able to produce beer for the entire U.S. market from just a few giant plants. Economies of scale allowed them to keep the costs of making beer low and to make higher profits as their market increased. At the same time, their national presence permitted them to engage in large-scale advertising campaigns and develop national brand names for their beers. The smaller brewers had higher costs and primarily regional customers and found themselves under increasing pressure, all of which made it easy for the large brewers to buy them out and close them down.[37]

Although the large brewers now dominate the U.S. brewing industry and have been enjoying record profits, they have continued to be impacted by a number of different forces. First, sales of beer are flat in the United States because many customers have switched to wine or wine coolers. Second, social attitudes toward drinking, and in particular toward drinking and driving, have changed. Concern over the health effects of drinking alcohol have increased, and organizations such as MADD (Mothers Against Drunk Driving) and SADD (Students Against Drinking Driving) have lobbied for tighter control over sales of alcohol to minors and for strengthening legal penalties for drunk driving. The minimum legal age for drinking alcohol is now 21 rather than 18 as it was in the past. To respond to these changes, the large brewers have developed major public relations campaigns to inform the public about their interest in encouraging responsible drinking (including the fact that they fund much of the advertising aimed at educating young people).[38]

Perhaps the most interesting force affecting the large brewers has been an increase in competition from small regional beer makers and import beer makers who are capitalizing on U.S. customers' demands for new tastes and higher beer quality. Beers such as Anchor Steam, made in San Francisco, and Samuel Adams, made in Boston and other locations, are attracting a growing customer base. Similarly, customer demand for Mexican and European beers is increasing. Many of the large brewers have been responding to these changes by introducing a new range of specialty beers of their own to attract former customers. They also have developed new technology to allow them to avoid the need to pasteurize their beer (which impairs flavor) and to keep it tasting fresh for a longer time. Competition among the big brewers remains fierce, as they all try to maintain or increase their share of customers in the U.S. beer market.

Questions

1. What are the principal forces in the organizational environment facing the major brewers?

2. How has the level of uncertainty changed over time in the brewing industry? What is the source of these changes?

ManagementCase

In the News

From the pages of **BusinessWeek**
Levi's Is Hiking Up Its Pants

Back in September, Levi Strauss & Co. was all set to ship to retailers its newest invention: a line of blue jeans called Special Reserve. Samples had been made. Stores had placed orders. Levi's had even handed out T-shirts with the Special Reserve logo at an August sales meeting in Palm Springs, Calif.

But weeks before the debut, an unprecedented thing occurred. Thomas A Fanoe—two months into his reign as president of Levi's USA—pulled the plug on the launch and sent nearly a year's worth of work into the circular file. Why? Because Special Reserve, which was likely to appeal to consumers 25 years and up, didn't solve Levi's core problem: teenage indifference.

That's quite a turnabout for a brand once synonymous with rebellious youth. While Levi retains its hold over the baby bommers who built the brand into mythic proportions, the company has neglected the whims of the latest crop of teens. "They missed all the kids, and those are your future buyers," says Bob Levy, owner of Dave's Army & Navy Store in New York, which devotes 50% of its shelves to Levi products.

The oversight has cost it dearly. With shrinking teen sales one of the key factors in the erosion of its once dominant market share, Levi Strauss was forced to announce on Nov. 3 that it would shutter 11 of its U.S. plants and lay off one-third of its North American workforce. The news followed a similar announcement in February in which Levi's said it would lay off 1,000 salaried U.S. employees.

Of course, increased competition added to Levi's tight fit. But the San Francisco clothing giant's biggest problem is plummeting market share: In 1990, Levi Strauss had 30.9% of the U.S. blue jeans market, but it has just 18.7% today, according to estimates by Tactical Retail Solutions Inc., a researcher in New York. Most troubling has been the drop among consumers aged 15 to 19. Levi says it enjoyed a 33% share of their jeans dollars in 1993, vs. about 26% now.

Missing those buyers can be a long term mistake. "It's very important that you attract this age group," says Gordon Harton, vice-president for the Lee brand at rival VF Corp. "By the time they're 24, they've adopted brands that they will use for the rest of their lives. Worse, since teens set fashion trends that influence even older shoppers, then defection to other brands affects sales all down the product line.

Caught with its pants down, the $7 billion company is scrambling to get back on track. Top management is giving virtually every aspect of the Levi's brand the once-over. Some products are being repositioned, while others are being scrapped altogether. Hiring policies are being reviewed to cultivate new talent and bring in fresh ideas. And marketing initiatives, including the company's 67-year-old relationship with ad agency Foote, Cone & Belding, are being completely revamped. "We are examining every element of the marketing, big M, of the Levi's brand," says Fanoe. "That means product, distribution, advertising, public relations, customer service. Everything."

How did the undisputed king of denim get into this hole? Levi Chairman and CEO Robert D. Haas says it was, in part, the classic corporate goof: taking your eyes off the ball. Projects during the last decade, such as expanding the casual clothing line Dockers and launching its upscale cousin Slates distracted executives from the threat to Levi's core jeans brand. "When you try to take on too many things, you are not as attentive to the warning signs," he concedes.

The warning signs became sirens at a July 31 meeting, when top U.S. managers learned the results of a yearlong research project into what the kids of baby boomers—called the Echo Boom generation—think of the world's largest branded-apparel maker. The news wasn't good.

For half a day, executive product managers, and marketers of the Levi's brand in the U.S. watched teen after teen on video talking about the blue-jeans king as if it were a has-been. Levi's they said, was uncool, more suitable for their parents or older siblings than for fashion-conscious kids. "That was scary," recalls Stephen Goldstein, vice-president for marketing and research for Levi's USA. "Kids say they love the Levi's brand. But if you ask them whether it's 'with it,' they'll say no."

Meanwhile, the competition had made inroads. Top-end designers such as Tommy Hilfiger and Ralph Lauren have squeezed Levi on one end, while private labels sold by low-priced retailers such as J.C. Penney Co. and Sears, Roebuck & Co. have come on strong from the other direction. Trends such as wide-legged and baggy jeans took hold without response from Levi. "Levi Strauss was zagging when the world was zigging," says retail consultant Alan Millstein. "The company totally missed the significance of the inner city and the huge impact it has on trends. It tells me they're sleepy in their marketing."

But Levi execs seem to be waking up. The decision to scrap Special Reserve came in tandem with a move to pump up Levi's Silver Tab brand, the eight-year-old jeans line that is considered more stylish among young consumers. Indeed, the median age of those who buy Silver Tab apparel is 18, compared with about 25 for other Levi's products. With its baggier fits and use of more than just denim fabrics, kids tag Silver Tab as Levi's hippest clothes. So the company plans to expand the line to include more tops, more trendy styles, and new khaki pants.

To catch teens' attention, Levi plans to spend five times as much in 1998 as it did this year on promoting Silver Tab. And for all its brands, it's also increasing marketing aimed specifically at teens. For instance, Levi is sponsoring concerts in New York and San Francisco for up-and-coming bands playing music know as Electronica. It's also outfitting characters on hot TV shows, such as *Friends* and *Beverly Hills 90210.* "As the Echo Boom generation goes, so goes Levi Strauss & Co.," says Goldstein. "We have to be relevant to this population.

The quest to jazz up Levi's image has also left the company searching for a new ad agency: A review, which includes longtime agency Foote, Cone & Belding, is under way. Although Levi has attempted to target teens in its latest ads, so far that hasn't translated into improved slaes. Levi says its most recent TV campaign—featuring images such as a young man driving through a car wash with the windows down—has logged positive response from young consumers on the company's Web site. But when kids hit the stores and found them stocked mostly with traditional styles, Goldstein concedes, they didn't buy.

Another way Levi hopes to overcome that problem is by working over its retail presentation and the packaging and labeling of all its goods. In 1998, the company says it will come out with jazzier, more colorful packaging aimed at giving its products a more exciting, youthful look. And Levi has ditched plans to open more than 100 new stores in malls around the country. Instead, it will follow Nike Inc.'s retail approach and open a handful of grand flagship stores in big cities. The first one is set to open in San Francisco in 1999.

But marketing and products aren't all that's getting a makeover.

The company is also shaking up management. Now, Levi is considering a plan calling for 30% of all new management jobs to be filled by outsiders. Critics argue that one reason Levi appears to be losing touch with what's happening in the marketplace is that it doesn't recruit enough outside executives or solicit enough independent opinions. "It has always been insular, paternalistic, and, quite frankly, a little smug," says Isaac Lagnado, president of Tactical Retail Solutions.

Will this work? Most industry experts believe that the 140-year-old apparel giant can right itself—given its vast resources and still formidable market presence. But it's likely to be a difficult, multiyear process. Retailer Levy says the wake-up call comes none too soon. "They are facing the problem," he says. "That's important because they weren't doing it before." No one is more confident than Haas. "From time to time, any brand is likely to have periods of great strength and relevancy and periods of regrouping and refocusing," he says. "We're going to restore the Levi's brand with consumers." The trick will be to keep the generation that grew up on Bob Dylan, while understanding the new age of Electronica.

Source: Linda Himelstein, "Levi's Is Hiking Up Its Pants," *Business Week,* December 1, 1997, 71, 75.

Questions

1. What factors in its environment are giving rise to opportunities and threats for Levi Strauss?

2. How are Levi's managers trying to manage these opportunities and threats?

Chapter four

The Global Environment

Learning Objectives

1. Explain why the global environment is becoming more open and competitive and why barriers to the global transfer of goods and services are falling, increasing the opportunities, complexities, and challenges that managers face.

2. Identify each of the forces in the global task environment, and explain why they create opportunities and threats for global managers.

3. Describe the way in which political and legal, economic, and socio-cultural forces in the general environment can affect managers and the way in which global organizations operate.

4. List the impediments to the development of a more open global environment.

A Case in Contrast

Why Expand Globally?

During the 1980s, The Limited emerged as one of the top women's clothing chains in the United States, and Toys 'R' Us (www.tru.com) became the largest toy retailer. Founded by entrepreneurial managers, The Limited by Leslie Wexner and Toys 'R' Us by Charles Lazarus, both companies grew at the expense of traditional retailers such as Sears, J. C. Penney, and Kmart. By charging low prices, and by pioneering new ways to retail goods to customers, such as The Limited's boutique-like stores and Toys 'R' Us's toy supermarkets, Wexner and Lazarus charged past their competitors. For most of the 1980s, sales at both companies grew at an annual rate of over 20 percent, and both companies opened hundreds of new stores around the country.

In the early 1990s, both Wexner and Lazarus realized that their companies were likely to grow more slowly because they already had captured as large a share of customers for their respective products as they could reasonably expect. However, CEOs Wexner and Lazarus wanted to grow their companies even more and searched for ways to expand sales and attract new customers. They chose very different routes: Lazarus decided that Toys 'R' Us should expand internationally and open toy stores around the globe; Wexner decided that The Limited should stay within the United States and open different kinds of retail stores.

Lazarus's idea was that Toys 'R' Us should transfer its retailing skills, which had served the company so well in the United States, to other countries and become a major competitor in foreign markets. By mid-1994, Toys 'R' Us had opened 234 stores internationally,

Pictured are a Toys R Us store in Japan crowded by customers who are drawn to its low prices and wide product line and The Limited store in an urban Chicago mall.

in addition to its 581 stores in the United States. The international expansion included 50 stores in Canada, 45 in Britain, 44 in Germany, 25 in France, 17 in Spain, and 16 in Japan.

Expansion into foreign markets has not been easy for Toys 'R' Us managers. They have had to work hard to respond to unfamiliar political, economic, and sociocultural forces present in foreign countries. The Japanese venture is an example of the difficulties the company has faced. Toys 'R' Us decided to enter the Japanese market in the mid-1980s but was unable to open a single store until late 1991. What caused the delay?

Quite simply, the delay was due to Japan's Large Scale Retail Store Law, which allowed small Japanese retailers to block the opening of new stores in their neighborhoods for 10 years or more. As a result of pressure from the U.S. government, the Japanese government changed the law in 1990 so that local store owners could delay a store opening for only 18 months. Shortly after that, Toys 'R' Us opened its first Japanese stores.

Another challenge facing Toys 'R' Us managers was Japan's system of distributing Japanese products. Traditionally, Japanese manufacturers sold their products only by means of wholesalers with which they had developed long-term business relationships. Because the wholesalers added their own price markup, the price Toys 'R' Us had to pay for Japanese toys increased and thus thwarted the U.S. company's attempt to establish a competitive advantage in Japan based on price discounting. As a result, to keep its costs low, Toys 'R' Us insisted on buying directly from Japanese manufacturers, but the manufacturers refused. This standoff was finally broken by Japan's deep recession in the early 1990s. Faced with slumping orders, computer-game maker Nintendo reversed its earlier decision and agreed to sell merchandise directly to Toys 'R' Us. Soon a host of other Japanese toy companies followed Nintendo's lead.

With those major problems solved, Toys 'R' Us's average sales in its Japanese stores were between $15 million and $20 million a year, roughly double the sales per store in the United States. The company plans to open 100 stores in Japan by 2002. However, because of the problems managers experienced in responding to the forces in the Japanese environment, the company did not break even on its Japan operations until 1995.

At The Limited, Leslie Wexner watched as many companies, including Toys 'R' Us, ventured into international expansion in the 1980s. Wexner decided against a global approach to increasing sales. Instead, he decided to broaden The Limited's presence in the United States. Believing that customer and shareholder interests would be served best by focusing on opportunities in the United States, Wexner initiated the opening of new kinds of stores, including Victoria's Secret (lingerie), The Bath & Body Works (toiletries), and Structure (men's clothing). Many of these new stores performed well enough to become market leaders and greatly contributed to sales and profits. However, by the mid-1990s, overall sales growth for The Limited's flagship clothing stores had stalled and earnings were declining.[1]

Facing the prospect of limited future expansion in the United States, Wexner and The Limited have been criticized by analysts for not seizing the opportunity for international expansion in the early 1990s.[2] Analysts pointed to the success of Toys 'R' Us and other companies that overcame many of the problems associated with managing the global environment and, as a result, benefited greatly from their foreign operations. In response to this criticism, Wexner decided to take The Limited global. In 1995, the company launched its first international retailing venture by opening 4 Bath & Body Works stores in Britain, with plans for as many as 100 international stores by 2001.[3] Then Wexner announced plans to open foreign stores for each of The Limited's different store chains. The Limited appears poised to become a major player in the global marketplace, a strategy that it hopes will allow it to grow and prosper well into the twenty-first century.[4] •

Overview

global organization An organization that operates and competes in more than one country.

Just a decade ago, many U.S. managers and organizations, not just Wexner and The Limited, decided against investing in the global environment because of the problems associated with expanding abroad. Instead, they chose to operate as if the United States were a closed system, detached from the rest of the world. Events of the last 10 years, however, have shown managers of organizations large and small, for-profit and not-for-profit, that they cannot afford to ignore the forces in the global environment. Many organizations and managers have concluded that in order to survive in the twenty-first century, they need to adopt a global perspective. Most organizations must become **global organizations,** organizations that operate and compete in more than one country.

If organizations are to adapt to the global environment, their managers must learn to understand the global forces that operate in it and how these forces give rise to opportunities and threats. In this chapter, we examine why the global environment is becoming more open, vibrant, and competitive. We examine how forces in the global task and general environments affect global organizations and their managers. We examine the different ways in which organizations can expand internationally. And we examine impediments to the creation of an even more open global environment. By the end of this chapter, you will appreciate the changes that have been taking place in the global environment and understand why it is important for managers to develop a global perspective as they strive to increase organizational efficiency and effectiveness. •

The Changing Global Environment

Until relatively recently, many managers did not regard the global environment as a significant source of opportunities and threats. Traditionally, managers regarded the global environment as *closed*—that is, as a set of distinct national markets and countries that were isolated physically, economically, and culturally from one another. As a result, they did not think much about global competition, exporting, obtaining inputs from foreign suppliers, or the challenges of managing in a foreign culture. These issues were simply outside the experience of the majority of managers, whose organizations remained firmly focused on competing at home, in the domestic marketplace.

Today, more and more managers regard the global environment as a source of important opportunities and threats that they must respond to (see Figure 4.1). Managers now view the global environment as *open*—that is, as an environment in which they and their organizations are free to buy goods and

Figure 4.1
The Global Environment

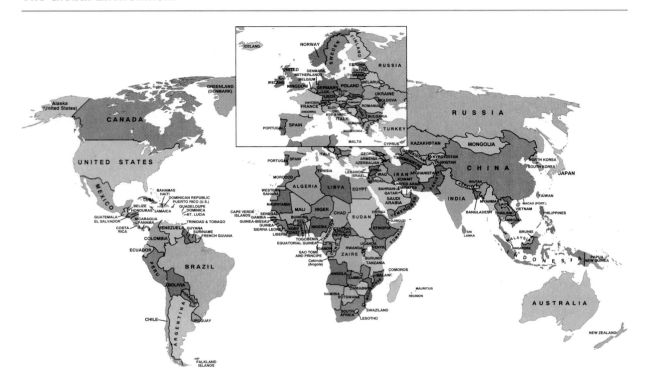

services from, and sell goods and services to, whichever countries they choose. An open environment is also one in which global organizations are free not only to compete against each other to attract customers but also to establish foreign subsidiaries to become the strongest competitors throughout the world. Coca-Cola and PepsiCo, for example, are currently competing to develop the strongest global soft-drinks empire. Table 4.1 lists the world's 100 largest global organizations in 1998.

In this section, we explain why the global environment is becoming more open and competitive and why this development is so significant for managers today. We examine how economic changes such as the lowering of barriers to trade and investment have led to greater interaction and exchanges between organizations and countries. We discuss how declines in barriers of distance and culture have increased the interdependencies between organizations and countries. And we consider the specific implications of these changes for managers and organizations.

Declining Barriers to Trade and Investment

tariff A tax that a government imposes on imported or, occasionally, exported goods.

During the 1920s and 1930s, many countries erected formidable barriers to international trade and investment in the belief that this was the best way to promote their economic well-being. Many of these barriers were high tariffs on imports of manufactured goods. A **tariff** is a tax that a government imposes

Table 4.1

The Top 100 Global Companies

Rank 1998	Rank 1997			Market Value Billions of U.S. dollars	Rank 1998	Rank 1997			Market Value Billions of U.S. dollars
1	1	General Electric	U.S.	271.64	51	27	PepsiCo	U.S.	60.85
2	5	Microsoft	U.S.	208.98	52	115	Credit Suisse Group	Switzerland	58.59
3	3	Royal Dutch/Shell	Neth./Britain	195.68	53	55	Chase Manhattan	U.S.	58.01
4	2	Coca-Cola	U.S.	193.53	54	79	Home Depot	U.S.	57.62
5	6	Exxon	U.S.	172.50	55	40	Abbot Laboratories	U.S.	57.26
6	9	Merck	U.S.	139.85	56	54	BankAmerica	U.S.	56.45
7	22	Pfizer	U.S.	133.03	57	57	ENI	Italy	56.42
8	4	NTT	Japan	130.91	58	52	GTE	U.S.	56.13
9	20	Wal-Mart Stores	U.S.	123.47	59	NR	France Telecom	France	56.01
10	7	Intel	U.S.	121.16	60	71	L.M. Ericsson	Sweden	55.62
11	11	Novartis	Switzerland	116.17	61	180	SAP	Germany	55.59
12	12	Procter & Gamble	U.S.	112.47	62	118	First Union	U.S.	53.33
13	13	IBM	U.S.	110.79	63	177	Dell Computer	U.S.	52.77
14	18	Bristol-Myers Squibb	U.S.	106.99	64	98	Warner-Lambert	U.S.	52.29
15	14	Roche Holding	Switzerland	98.90	65	44	Chevron	U.S.	52.24
16	26	AT&T	U.S.	98.87	66	58	Daimler Benz	Germany	52.11
17	19	Glaxo Wellcome	Britain	96.07	67	147	Telecom Italia	Italy	51.30
18	8	Toyota Motor	Japan	94.34	68	15	Bank of Tokyo-Mitsubishi	Japan	48.08
19	56	Lucent Technologies	U.S.	93.07	69	53	General Motors	U.S.	48.04
20	17	Johnson & Johnson	U.S.	92.87	70	73	American Express	U.S.	47.33
21	10	Philip Morris	U.S.	90.74	71	102	Worldcom	U.S.	46.96
22	32	Berkshire Hathaway	U.S.	87.74	72	255	Morgan Stanley Dean Witter	U.S.	46.90
23	24	Du Pont	U.S.	87.11	73	66	Ameritech	U.S.	46.56
24	33	Unilever	Neth/Britain	86.67	74	169	Aegon	Netherlands	46.50
25	23	AIG	U.S.	86.62	75	63	Boeing	U.S.	46.50
26	21	British Petroleum	Britain	85.28	76	105	Time Warner	U.S.	45.97
27	38	Nestlé	Switzerland	84.40	77	95	Deutsche Bank	Germany	45.92
28	30	Lloyds TSB Group	Britain	78.28	78	101	Telefonica	Spain	45.85
29	41	Allianz	Germany	77.41	79	69	McDonald's	U.S.	45.11
30	47	Cisco Systems	U.S.	77.36	80	135	TIM	Italy	44.94
31	28	Walt Disney	U.S.	77.21	81	92	UBS	Switzerland	43.19
32	25	Deutsche Telekom	Germany	73.64	82	83	Compaq Computer	U.S.	41.58
33	51	Nationsbank	U.S.	72.65	83	85	Barclays Bank	Britain	40.70
34	31	SBC Communications	U.S.	71.49	84	NR	Diageo	Britain	40.17
35	78	Bell Atlantic	U.S.	71.12	85	49	Amoco	U.S.	40.12
36	68	Travelers Group	U.S.	70.44	86	75	Allstate	U.S.	39.52
37	36	Eli Lilly	U.S.	67.97	87	166	Nokia	Finland	39.48
38	34	Citicorp	U.S.	67.39	88	84	Schlumberger	U.S.	38.90
39	16	HSBC Holdings	Britain	67.26	89	104	MCI Communications	U.S.	38.73
40	45	British Telecomms.	Britain	66.26	90	88	Zeneca Group	Britain	38.52
41	37	Gillette	U.S.	65.79	91	99	Elf Aquitaine	France	38.12
42	35	Hewlett-Packard	U.S.	64.31	92	230	Mannesmann	Germany	38.04
43	70	ING Groep	Netherlands	64.08	93	NR	Halifax	Britain	37.96
44	46	Bellsouth	U.S.	63.86	94	171	AXA-UAP	France	37.78
45	39	American Home Products	U.S.	63.42	95	61	Minnesota Mining & Mfg.	U.S.	37.47
46	48	Ford Motor	U.S.	62.92	96	153	Muenchener Ruck	Germany	37.31
47	43	Fannie Mae	U.S.	61.84	97	77	Siemens	Germany	37.06
48	72	Schering-Plough	U.S.	61.35	98	188	Banc One	U.S.	36.15
49	29	Mobil	U.S.	60.95	99	142	Chrysler	U.S.	35.91
50	42	Smithkline Beecham	Britain	60.89	100	91	Bayer	Germany	34.94

Source: *Business Week*, July 13, 1998, p. 53.

on imported or, occasionally, on exported goods. The U.S. government, for example, currently levies a 25 percent tariff on the price of four-wheel-drive vehicles imported to the United States. The aim of import tariffs is to protect domestic industries and jobs, such as those in the auto industry, from foreign competition by raising the price of goods from abroad.

Very often, however, when one country imposes an import tariff, others follow suit and the result is a series of retaliatory moves as countries progressively raise tariff barriers against each other. In the 1920s this behavior depressed world demand and helped usher in the Great Depression of the 1930s and massive unemployment. In short, rather than protecting jobs and promoting economic well-being, governments of countries that resort to raising high tariff barriers ultimately reduce employment and undermine economic growth.[5]

GATT AND THE RISE OF FREE TRADE   Having learned from the Great Depression, advanced Western industrial countries after the Second World War committed themselves to the goal of removing barriers to the free flow of resources between countries. This commitment was reinforced by acceptance of a principle that predicted that free trade, rather than tariff barriers, was the best way to foster a healthy domestic economy and low unemployment.[6]

free-trade doctrine
The idea that if each country specializes in the production of the goods and services that it can produce most efficiently, this will make the best use of global resources.

The **free-trade doctrine** predicts that if each country agrees to specialize in the production of the goods and services that it can produce most efficiently, this will make the best use of global resources and will result in lower prices. For example, if Indian companies are highly efficient in the production of textiles and U.S. companies are highly efficient in the production of computer software, then under a free-trade agreement production of textiles would shift to India and computer software to the United States. Under these conditions, prices of textiles and software should fall because both goods are being produced in the location where they can be made at the lowest cost, benefiting consumers and making the best use of scarce resources.

Countries that accepted this free-trade doctrine set as their goal the removal of barriers to the free flow of goods between countries. They attempted to achieve this through an international treaty known as the General Agreement on Tariffs and Trade (GATT). In the half-century since World War II, there have been eight rounds of GATT negotiations aimed at lowering tariff barriers. The last round, the Uruguay Round, involved 117 countries and was completed in December 1993. This round succeeded in lowering tariffs by over 30 percent from the previous level. The average decline in tariff barriers achieved among the governments of developed countries since 1947 is more than 94 percent (similar in theory to a 94 percent reduction in taxes on imports).

Declining Barriers of Distance and Culture

Barriers of distance and culture also "closed" the global environment and kept managers inward looking. The management problems Unilever, a large British soap and detergent maker, experienced at the turn of the twentieth century illustrate the effect of these barriers.

Founded in London during the 1880s by William Lever, Unilever had a worldwide reach by the early 1900s and operated subsidiaries in most major countries of the British Empire, including India, Canada, and Australia. Lever had a very hands-on, autocratic management style and found his far-flung business empire difficult to control. The reason for Lever's control problems was that communication over great distances was difficult. It took six weeks to reach India by ship from England, and international telephone and telegraph services were very unreliable.

Another problem that Unilever encountered was the difficulty of doing business in societies that were separated from Britain by barriers of language and culture. Different countries have different sets of national beliefs, values, and norms, and Lever found that a management approach that worked in Britain did not necessarily work in India or Persia (now Iran). As a result, management practices had to be tailored to suit each unique national culture. After Lever's death in 1925, top management at Unilever decentralized decision-making authority to the managers of the various national subsidiaries so that they could develop a management approach that suited the country in which they were operating. One result of this strategy was that the subsidiaries grew distant and remote from one another.[7]

Since the end of World War II, major advances in communications and transportation technology have been reducing the barriers of distance and culture that affected Unilever and other global organizations. Over the last 30 years, global communications have been revolutionized by developments in satellites, digital switching, and optical fiber telephone lines. Satellites and optical fibers can carry hundreds of thousands of messages simultaneously.[8] As a result of such developments, reliable and instantaneous communication is now possible with nearly any location in the world. Fax machines in Sri Lanka, cellular phones in the Brazilian rain forest, satellite dishes in Russia, video phones in Manhattan, and videoconferencing facilities in Japan are all part of the communications revolution that is changing the way the world works. This revolution has made it possible for a global organization—a tiny garment factory or a huge company such as Unilever—to do business anywhere, anytime, and to search out customers and suppliers from around the world.

In the middle of a maize field, villagers in Niger, Africa, gather to view worldwide news and events on their villages' communal television.

Several major innovations in transportation technology since World War II also have made the global environment more open. Most significant, the growth of commercial jet travel has reduced the time it takes to get from one location to another. Because of jet travel, New York is now closer to Tokyo than it was to Philadelphia in the days of the thirteen colonies—a fact that makes control of far-flung international businesses much easier today than in William Lever's era.

In addition to making travel faster, modern communications and transportation technologies have also helped reduce the cultural distance between countries. Global communications networks and global media are helping to create a *worldwide culture* above and beyond unique national cultures. U.S. television networks such as CNN, MTV, and HBO can now be received in many countries around the world, and Hollywood films are shown around the globe.

Effects of Free Trade on Managers

The lowering of barriers to trade and investment and the decline of distance and culture barriers have created enormous opportunities for organizations to expand the market for their goods and services through exports and investments in foreign countries. Although managers at some organizations, such as Leslie Wexner at The Limited, have shied away from trying to sell their goods and services overseas, the case of Toys 'R' Us is more typical. Not only has the shift toward a more open global economy created more opportunities to sell goods and services in foreign markets; it also has created the opportunity to buy more from foreign countries. Indeed, the success in the United States of both The Limited and Toys 'R' Us has been based in part on their managers' willingness to import low-cost clothes and toys from foreign manufacturers. The Limited, for example, purchases most of its clothing from Hong Kong, Taiwan, and China because, according to CEO Wexner, U.S. textile makers do not offer the same quality, styling, flexibility, or price.[9] So, despite Wexner's reluctance to expand his retail-store empire into foreign markets, his company is still a player in the global environment by virtue of its purchasing activities.

The manager's job is also more challenging in a dynamic global environment because of the increased intensity of competition that goes hand in hand with the lowering of barriers to trade and investment. Thus, the job of the average manager in a U.S. car company became a lot harder from the mid-1970s on as a result of the penetration of the U.S. market by efficient Japanese and German competitors and the increase in competition that resulted from it.

NAFTA   The growth of regional trade agreements such as the North American Free Trade Agreement (NAFTA) also presents opportunities and threats for managers and their organizations. NAFTA, which became effective on January 1, 1994, will abolish within 10 years the tariffs on 99 percent of the goods traded between Mexico, Canada, and the United States. NAFTA will also remove most barriers on the cross-border flow of resources, giving, for example, financial institutions and retail businesses in Canada and the United States unrestricted access to the Mexican marketplace by the year 2000. After NAFTA was signed, there was a flood of investment from the United States into Mexico. Wal-Mart, Kmart, Price Club, Radio Shack, and other major U.S. retail chains plan to expand their operations in Mexico.

The establishment of free-trade areas creates an opportunity for manufacturing organizations because it allows them to reduce their costs. They can do this either by shifting production to the lowest-cost location within the free-trade area (for example, U.S. textile companies shifting production to Mexico) or by serving the whole region from one location, rather than establishing separate operations in each country.

Some managers, however, might see regional free-trade agreements as a threat because they expose a company based in one member country to increased competition from companies based in the other member countries. Managers in Mexico, the United States, and Canada are experiencing this now that NAFTA is here. For the first time, Mexican managers find themselves facing a threat: head-to-head competition in some industries against efficient U.S. and Canadian organizations. But the opposite is true as well: U.S. and Canadian managers are experiencing threats in labor-intensive industries, such as the textile industry, where Mexican businesses have a cost advantage.

The three current NAFTA members have announced that they hope to expand the treaty in the future to include other countries in Central and South America to increase economic prosperity throughout the Americas. Chile, Brazil, and Argentina are likely to be future members. However the recent currency and economic problems that these countries have been experiencing has slowed down the attempt to expand NAFTA, as has political resistance within the United States.

In essence, the shift toward a more open, competitive global environment has increased both the opportunities that managers can take advantage of and the threats they must respond to in performing their jobs effectively. Next, we look in detail at the forces in the global task and general environments to see where these opportunities and threats are arising.

The Global Task Environment

As managers operate in the global environment, they confront forces that differ from country to country and from world region to world region.[10] In this section, we examine some of the forces in the global task environment that increase opportunities or threats for managers. The major forces in the global task environment are similar to those introduced in Chapter 3: suppliers, distributors, customers, and competitors (see Figure 4.2).

Suppliers

At a global level, managers have the opportunity to buy products from foreign suppliers or to become their own suppliers and manufacture their own products abroad. For example, as noted in the "Case in Contrast," to lower costs and increase product quality, The Limited and Toys 'R' Us, respectively, imported low-cost clothes and low-cost toys from foreign manufacturers. Organizations such as Levi Strauss and AT&T also have prospered by manufacturing their own low-cost products abroad, which has enabled them to charge their U.S. customers lower prices.

Figure 4.2
Forces in the Global Task Environment

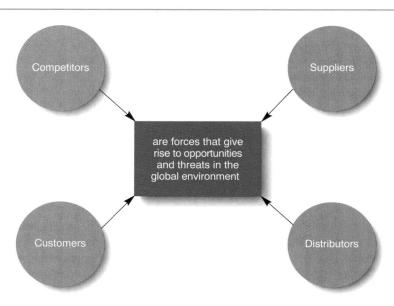

A common problem facing managers of large global organizations such as Ford, Procter & Gamble, and IBM is the development of a global network of suppliers that will allow their companies to keep costs down and quality high. For example, the building of Boeing's new commercial jet aircraft, the 777, requires 132,500 engineered parts that are produced around the world by 545 different suppliers.[11] Boeing makes the majority of these parts. But eight Japanese suppliers make parts for the 777's fuselage, doors, and wings; a Singapore supplier makes the doors for the plane's forward landing gear; and three Italian suppliers manufacture wing flaps. Boeing's rationale for buying so many inputs from foreign suppliers is that these suppliers are the best in the world at performing their particular activity, and doing business with them helps Boeing to produce a high-quality final product, a vital requirement given the need for aircraft safety and reliability.[12] Small organizations must also be alert to global opportunities to buy or manufacture low-cost products abroad in order to prosper, as the example of Swan Optical suggests.

Managing Globally

Swan Optical Spreads Its Wings

With annual sales of $30 million, Swan Optical is a small company that manufactures and distributes eyewear. Swan began its drive to become a global organization in the 1970s. At that time, the strong dollar made U.S.-based manufacturing expensive, and sales of low-priced imported eyewear were increasing rapidly in the U.S. eyewear market. Swan realized that it could not survive unless it also began to import inexpensive eyewear made abroad. At first, Swan bought from independent overseas manufacturers, primarily in Hong Kong. Swan's managers, however, were not satisfied with the quality of the eyewear or its slow delivery. Management decided that the best way to guarantee quality and on-time delivery was to set up its own foreign manufacturing operations and thus control quality and delivery schedules. Accordingly, in conjunction with a Chinese partner, Swan opened a manufacturing facility in Hong Kong to supply its own eyewear.

The choice of Hong Kong was influenced by the combination of low labor costs, a skilled workforce, and tax breaks given by the Hong Kong government.[13] The arrangement was successful for several years. By 1986, however, the increasing industrialization of Hong Kong and a growing labor shortage caused wage rates to increase, and Hong Kong could no longer be considered a low-cost location. In response, Swan's managers opened a manufacturing plant in China to take advantage of China's lower wage rates. The Chinese plant manufactures parts for eyewear frames, which are shipped to the Hong Kong factory for final assembly and then distributed to markets in both North and South America.

Obtaining and selling low-cost eyewear was not the managers' only goal; they were also interested in launching a line of high-quality "designer" eyewear but lacked the necessary in-house skills. Therefore, they looked for opportunities to invest in foreign eyewear companies that enjoyed reputations for fashionable design and high-quality products. They found such eyewear companies in Japan, France, and Italy and invested in a minority shareholding in each company.[14] These eyewear factories supply Swan's Status Eye division, which has successfully marketed high-priced designer eyewear to its U.S. customers.

global outsourcing
The purchase of inputs from foreign suppliers, or the production of inputs abroad, to lower production costs and improve product quality or design.

Global outsourcing is the process by which organizations purchase inputs from other companies or produce inputs themselves throughout the world, to lower their production costs and improve the quality or design of their products. To take advantage of national differences in the cost and quality of resources such as labor or raw materials, General Motors might build its own engines in one country, transmissions in another, brakes in a third, and buy other components from hundreds of global suppliers. Robert Reich, U.S. secretary of labor in the first Clinton administration, once calculated that of the $20,000 that customers pay GM for a Pontiac Le Mans, about $6,000 goes to South Korea, where the Le Mans is assembled; $3,500 to Japan for advanced components such as engines, transaxles, and electronics; $1,500 to Germany, where the Le Mans was designed; $800 to Taiwan, Singapore, and Japan for small components; $500 to Britain for advertising and marketing services; and about $100 to Ireland for data-processing services. The remaining $7,000 goes to GM—and to the lawyers, bankers, and insurance agents that GM retains in the United States.[15] Is the Le Mans a U.S. product? Yes, but it is also a Korean product, a Japanese product, and a German product.

Distributors

Another force that creates opportunities and threats for global managers is the nature of a country's distribution system. As Toys 'R' Us discovered in Japan, the traditional means by which goods and services are distributed and sold to customers can present challenges to managers of organizations pursuing international expansion. Managers must identify the hidden problems surrounding the distribution and sale of goods and services—such as anticompetitive government regulations—in order to discover hidden threats early and find ways to overcome them before significant resources are invested.

Customers

The most obvious opportunity associated with expanding into the global environment is the prospect of selling goods and services to new customers, as Toys 'R' Us CEO Lazarus realized. Similarly, Arthur Andersen and Price Waterhouse, two large accounting companies, have established foreign operations throughout the world and recruit and train thousands of foreign accountants to serve the needs of customers in a wide variety of countries.

Today, once-distinct national markets are merging into one huge global marketplace where the same basic product can be sold to customers worldwide. This consolidation is occurring both for consumer goods and for business products and has created enormous opportunities for managers. The global acceptance of Coca-Cola, Levi's blue jeans, Sony Walkmans, McDonald's hamburgers, and Motorola pagers and flip phones is a sign that the tastes and preferences of consumers in different countries are beginning to become more similar.[16] Similarly, large global markets currently exist for business products such as telecommunications equipment, electronic components, computer services, and financial services. Thus, Motorola sells its telecommunications equipment, Intel its microprocessors, and Computer Associates its business systems management software, to customers throughout the world.

Nevertheless, despite evidence that the same goods and services are receiving acceptance from customers worldwide, it is important not to place too much emphasis on this development. Because national cultures differ in many ways, significant differences between countries in consumer tastes and preferences still remain. These differences often require managers to customize goods and services to suit the preferences of local consumers. For example, despite McDonald's position as a leading global organization, its management has recognized a need for local customization. In Brazil, McDonald's sells a soft drink made from the guarana, an exotic berry that grows along the Amazon River (in 1996, Pepsi announced that it was test-marketing a drink made from this berry in the United States). In Malaysia, McDonald's sells milk shakes flavored with durian, a strong-smelling fruit that local people consider an aphrodisiac.[17] Similarly, when Mattel decided to begin selling Barbie Dolls in Japan, it had to redesign the doll's appearance (color of hair, facial features, and so on) to suit the tastes of its prospective customers.

Two newly affluent Chinese consumers enjoy a drink of Coca-Cola, a global brand, whose recipe has nevertheless been specially altered to satisfy the taste of Chinese consumers.

Competitors

Although finding less-expensive or higher-quality supplies and attracting new customers are global opportunities for managers, entry into the global environment also leads to major threats in the form of increases in competition both at home and abroad. U.S. managers in foreign markets, for example, face the problem of competing against local companies that are familiar with the local market and have generated considerable brand loyalty. As a result, U.S. managers might find it difficult to break into a foreign market and obtain new customers. Of course, foreign competitors trying to enter a U.S. company's domestic market face the same challenges. U.S. car companies faced strong global competition at home in the 1970s, when foreign competitors aggressively entered the U.S. market. In the global environment, the level of competition can increase rapidly, and managers must be alert to the changes taking place in order to respond appropriately.

The Global General Environment

Despite evidence that countries are becoming more similar to one another and that the world is on the verge of becoming a "global village," countries still differ across a range of political, legal, economic, and cultural dimensions. When an organization operates in the global environment, it confronts in the global general environment a series of forces that differ from country to country and world region to world region. In this section we consider how forces in the global general environment, such as political and legal, economic, and sociocultural forces, create opportunities and threats for managers of global organizations (see Figure 4.3).

Political and Legal Forces

Global political and legal forces result from the diverse and changing nature of various countries' political and legal systems. The global range of political systems includes everything from representative democracies to totalitarian regimes, and in order to manage global organizations effectively, managers must understand how these different political systems work.

In **representative democracies,** such as Britain, Canada, Germany, and the United States, citizens periodically elect individuals to represent their interests. These elected representatives form a government whose function is to make decisions on behalf of the electorate. To guarantee that voters can hold elected representatives legally accountable for their actions, an ideal representative democracy incorporates a number of safeguards into the law. These include (1) an individual's right to freedom of expression, opinion, and organization; (2) free media; (3) regular elections in which all eligible citizens are allowed to vote; (4) limited terms for elected representatives; (5) a fair court system that is independent from the political system; (6) a nonpolitical police force and armed service; and (7) relatively free access to state information.[18]

In contrast, in **totalitarian regimes** a single political party, individual, or group of individuals holds all political power. Typically, totalitarian regimes neither recognize nor permit opposition from individuals or groups. Most of the constitutional guarantees on which representative democracies are based are denied to the citizens of totalitarian states. In most totalitarian countries, political repression is widespread. Those who question the policies of the rulers and their right to rule find themselves imprisoned or worse. Totalitarian regimes are found in countries such as China, Iraq, and Iran.

representative democracy A political system in which representatives elected by citizens and legally accountable to the electorate form a government whose function is to make decisions on behalf of the electorate.

totalitarian regime A political system in which a single party, individual, or group holds all political power and neither recognizes nor permits opposition.

Figure 4.3
Forces in the Global General Environment

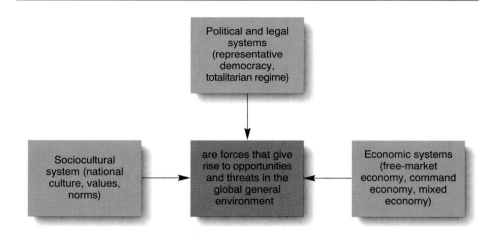

Why must managers be concerned about the political makeup of a foreign country in which they are doing business? First, stable democratic countries with a high degree of political freedom tend to be characterized by economic freedom and a well-defined legal system. In turn, economic freedom and a well-defined legal system protect the rights of individuals and corporations and are conducive to business.[19] Second, totalitarian regimes' lack of respect for human rights raises the question of whether it is ethical to trade with, or invest in, those countries (we examine the ethical issues of operating globally in Chapter 5).

Economic Forces

Economic forces are caused by the changing nature of countries' economic systems. Around the globe, economic systems range from free-market economies to command economies, and managers must learn how different economic systems work in order to understand the opportunities and threats associated with them.

In a **free-market economy,** the production of goods and services is left in the hands of *private* (as opposed to *government*) enterprise. The goods and services that are produced, and the quantities that are produced, are not specified by a central authority. Rather, production is determined by the interaction of the forces of supply and demand. If demand for a product exceeds supply, the price of the product will rise, prompting managers and organizations to produce more. If supply exceeds demand, prices will fall, causing managers and organizations to produce less. In a free-market economy the purchasing patterns of consumers, as signaled to managers by changes in demand, determine what and how much is produced.

In a **command economy,** the goods and services that a country produces, the quantity in which they are produced, and the prices at which they are sold are all planned by the government. In a pure command economy, all businesses are government owned and private enterprise is forbidden. As recently as 1989–1991, the communist countries of eastern Europe and the Soviet Union had command economies, as did other communist countries such as

free-market economy
An economic system in which private enterprise controls production and the interaction of supply and demand determines which and how many goods and services are produced and how much consumers pay for them.

command economy An economic system in which the government owns all businesses and specifies which and how many goods and services are produced and the prices at which they are sold.

China and Vietnam. The overall failure of these economies to perform as well as the free-market-oriented systems of western Europe, North America, and areas of the Pacific Rim helped precipitate the collapse of communism in many of these countries and the subsequent dismantlement of command economies. Even in China and Vietnam, which remain communist controlled, there has been a marked shift away from a command economy.

Between free-market economies, on the one hand, and command economies, on the other, are mixed economies. In a **mixed economy,** certain sectors of the economy are left to private ownership and free-market mechanisms, and other sectors are characterized by significant government ownership and government planning. Mixed economies are most commonly found in the democratic countries of western Europe, but they are disappearing as these countries shift toward the free-market model. For example, in Britain in the early 1980s the government owned a majority stake in many important industries, including airlines, health care, steel, and telecommunications. Since then, following a trend toward privatization, the British government has sold its airline, steel, and telecommunications interests to private investors, and a significant private health care sector has emerged to compete with government-provided health care. Similar privatization efforts have been undertaken in other western European countries.

mixed economy An economic system in which some sectors of the economy are left to private ownership and free-market mechanisms and others are owned by the government and subject to government planning.

The manager of a global organization generally prefers a free-market system, for two reasons. First, because much of the economy is in private hands, there tend to be few restrictions on organizations that decide to invest in countries with free-market economies. For example, U.S. companies face fewer impediments to investing in Britain, with its largely free-market system, than they do in China, where a free market is allowed in only certain sectors of the economy. Second, free-market economies tend to be more economically developed and have higher rates of economic growth than command or mixed economies, so their citizens tend to have higher per capita incomes and more spending power.[20] As a result, for companies attempting to export or to establish foreign subsidiaries, they are more attractive markets than are mixed economies or command economies, which are closely regulated by government.

Changes in Political and Legal and Economic Forces

In recent years, two large and related shifts in political and economic forces have occurred globally (see Figure 4.4).[21] One—the shift away from totalitarian dictatorships and toward more democratic regimes—has been most dramatic in eastern Europe and the former Soviet Union, where totalitarian communist regimes collapsed during the late 1980s and early 1990s. The other—the shift toward representative democracy—has occurred from Latin America to Africa. For the most part, the movement toward democracy has been precipitated by the failure of totalitarian regimes with command or mixed economies to improve the well-being of their citizens. This failure has been particularly noticeable in comparisons of these countries with democratic, free-market countries such as Germany, Japan, and the United States.

Accompanying this change in political forces has been a worldwide shift away from command and mixed economies and toward the free-market model, as noted previously.[22] This economic shift was triggered by the realization that

Figure 4.4
Changes in Political and Economic Forces

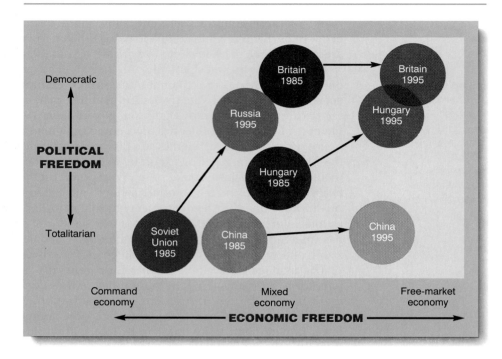

government involvement in economic activity often impedes economic growth. Thus, a wave of privatization and deregulation has swept throughout the world, from the former communist countries to Latin America, Asia, and western Europe. Governments have sold off government-owned organizations to private investors and have dismantled regulations that inhibit the operation of the free market.

These trends are good news for managers of global organizations because they result in the expansion of opportunities for exporting and investment abroad. A decade ago, few Western companies exported to or invested in eastern Europe because the combination of totalitarian political regimes and command economies created a hostile environment for Western businesses. Since 1990, however, the environment in eastern Europe has become far more favorable for Western businesses; and from 1990 to 1993, Western businesses invested $15 billion in eastern Europe.[23] A similar story is unfolding in China, where despite the continued presence of a totalitarian communist regime, a move toward greater economic freedom has occurred and has produced a surge of Western and Japanese business activity in this region of the world. From 1990 to 1993, foreign companies invested nearly $40 billion in China.[24]

The managers of many Western companies have experienced considerable difficulty in their attempts to establish business operations in eastern Europe and China, however. For example, when the Chiquita banana company entered the Czech Republic in 1990, the company was hoping to take advantage of that nation's rapid move toward a free-market economy. However, Chiquita found that the premium bananas it sold in the West could not be marketed in the Czech Republic. After decades of communism, Czech citizens apparently had difficulty understanding why something of better quality should cost more. Chiquita was forced to switch to lower-quality bananas after discovering that consumers were unwilling to pay higher prices for superior bananas.[25] The experience of General Electric's managers in Hungary provides another example of the problems that managers may encounter when doing business in eastern Europe.

Managing Globally

GE's U.S. Managers Stumble in Hungary

In 1989, General Electric (GE) (www.ge.com) agreed to acquire 51 percent of Tungsram, a maker of lighting products at a cost of $150 million. GE was attracted to Tungsram, widely regarded as one of Hungary's best companies, because of Hungary's low wage rates and the possibility of using the company as a base from which to export lighting products to western Europe. At the time, many analysts believed that GE would show other Western companies how to turn organizations once run by communist party officials into capitalist moneymakers. GE transferred some of its best managers to Tungsram and waited for the miracle to happen. Unfortunately, the company is still waiting!

One of the problems resulted from major misunderstandings between the American managers and the Hungarian workers. The Americans complained that the Hungarians were lazy; the Hungarians thought the Americans were pushy. GE's management system depends on extensive

These billboards in Moscow are a part of the explosion in product advertising by Western companies that has been sweeping through Russia since the fall of communism.

communication between workers and managers, a practice uncommon in the previous communist system. Changing behavior at Tungsram has proved to be difficult. The Americans wanted strong sales and marketing functions that would pamper customers. In the prior command economy, sales and marketing activities were unnecessary. In addition, Hungarians expected GE to deliver Western-style wages, but GE came to Hungary to take advantage of the country's low-wage structure.[26]

As Tungsram's losses mounted, GE learned what happens when grand expectations collide with the grim reality of inefficiency and indifference toward customers and quality. Looking back, GE managers admit that, because of differences in basic attitudes between countries, they underestimated the difficulties they would face in turning Tungsram around. GE now believes that it has turned the corner, but this progress has not come easily. General Electric laid off half of Tungsram's 20,000 employees, including two out of every three managers, and invested $400 million in a new plant and equipment and in retraining the remaining employees and managers to help them learn the work attitudes and behaviors that a company needs in order to survive in a competitive global environment.

As the example of GE and Tungsram illustrates, managers who want to take advantage of the opportunities created by changing global political and legal and economic forces face a major challenge.

Sociocultural Forces

What is interesting about the experiences of companies such as General Electric in Hungary and Chiquita in the Czech Republic is that many of their problems are the result of critical differences in the values, norms, and attitudes of Western cultures and of eastern European cultures conditioned by communism and a command economy. National culture is an important sociocultural force that global managers must take into account when they do business in foreign countries. **National culture** includes the values, norms, knowledge, beliefs, moral principles, laws, customs, and other practices that unite the citizens of a country.[27] National culture shapes individual behavior by specifying appropriate and inappropriate behavior and interaction with others. People learn national culture in their everyday lives by interacting with those around them. This learning starts at an early age and continues throughout a person's life.

national culture The set of values that a society considers important and the norms of behavior that are approved or sanctioned in that society.

VALUES AND NORMS   The basic building blocks of national culture are values and norms. **Values** are ideas about what a society believes to be good, right, desirable, or beautiful. They provide the basic underpinnings for notions of individual freedom, democracy, truth, justice, honesty, loyalty, social obligation, collective responsibility, the appropriate roles for men and women, love, sex, marriage, and so on. Values are more than merely abstract concepts; they are invested with considerable emotional significance. People argue, fight, and even die over values such as "freedom."

values Ideas about what a society believes to be good, right, desirable, or beautiful.

Though deeply embedded in society, values are not static—although change in a country's values is likely to be slow and painful. For example, the value systems of many formerly communist states, such as Russia, are undergoing significant changes as those countries move away from a value system that emphasizes the state and toward one that emphasizes individual freedom. Social turmoil often results when countries undergo major changes in their values.

norms Unwritten rules and codes of conduct that prescribe how people should act in particular situations.

folkways The routine social conventions of everyday life.

Norms are unwritten rules and codes of conduct that prescribe appropriate behavior in particular situations and shape the behavior of people toward one another. Two types of norms play a major role in national culture: folkways and mores. **Folkways** are the routine social conventions of everyday life. They concern customs and practices such as dressing appropriately for particular situations, good social manners, eating with the correct utensils, and neighborly behavior. Although folkways define the way people are expected to behave, violation of folkways is not a serious or moral matter. People who violate folkways are often thought to be eccentric or ill mannered, but they are not usually considered to be evil or bad. In many countries, foreigners may be excused initially for violating folkways because they are unaccustomed to local behavior, but repeated violations will not be excused because foreigners are expected to learn appropriate behavior.

mores Norms that are considered to be central to the functioning of society and to social life.

Mores are norms that are considered to be central to the functioning of society and to social life. They have much greater significance than folkways. Accordingly, the violation of mores can be expected to bring serious retribution. Mores include proscriptions against theft, adultery, and incest. In many societies mores have been enacted into law. Thus, all advanced societies have laws against theft and incest. However, there are many differences in mores from one society to another.[28] In the United States, for example, drinking alcohol is widely accepted; but in Saudi Arabia, the consumption of alcohol is viewed as a violation of social mores and is punishable by imprisonment (as many U.S. citizens working in Saudi Arabia have discovered).

HOFSTEDE'S MODEL OF NATIONAL CULTURE   Researchers have spent considerable time and effort identifying similarities and differences in the values and norms of different countries. One model of national culture was developed by Gert Hofstede.[29] As a psychologist for IBM, Hofstede collected data on employee values and norms from more than 100,000 IBM employees in 64 countries. Based on his research, Hofstede developed five dimensions along which national cultures can be placed (see Figure 4.5).

INDIVIDUALISM VERSUS COLLECTIVISM   The first dimension, which Hofstede labeled individualism versus collectivism, has a long history in human thought. **Individualism** is a worldview that values individual freedom and self-expression and adherence to the principle that people should be judged by their individual achievements rather than by their social background. In Western countries, individualism usually includes admiration for personal success, a strong belief in individual rights, and high regard for individual entrepreneurs.[30]

individualism A worldview that values individual freedom and self-expression and adherence to the principle that people should be judged by their individual achievements rather than by their social background.

collectivism A worldview that values subordination of the individual to the goals of the group and adherence to the principle that people should be judged by their contribution to the group.

In contrast, **collectivism** is a worldview that values subordination of the individual to the goals of the group and adherence to the principle that people should be judged by their contribution to the group. Collectivism was widespread in communist countries but has become less prevalent since the collapse of communism in those countries. Japan is a noncommunist country where collectivism is highly valued.

Collectivism in Japan traces its roots to the fusion of Confucian, Buddhist, and Shinto thought that occurred during the Tokugawa period in Japanese history (1600–1870s).[31] One of the central values that emerged during this period

Figure 4.5
Hofstede's Model of National Culture

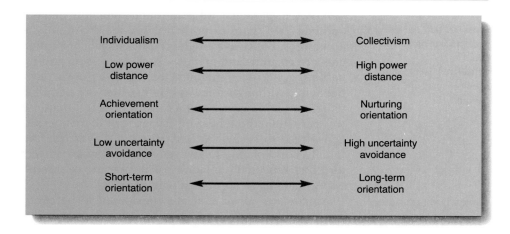

was strong attachment to the group—whether a village, a work group, or a company. Strong identification with the group is said to create pressures for collective action in Japan, as well as strong pressure for conformity to group norms and a relative lack of individualism.[32]

Managers must realize that organizations and organizational members reflect their national culture's emphasis on individualism or collectivism. Indeed, one of the major reasons why Japanese and American management practices differ is that Japanese culture values collectivism and U.S. culture values individualism.[33]

POWER DISTANCE   By **power distance** Hofstede meant the degree to which societies accept the idea that inequalities in the power and well-being of their citizens are due to differences in individuals' physical and intellectual capabilities and heritage. This concept also encompasses the degree to which societies accept the economic and social differences in wealth, status, and well-being that result from differences in individual capabilities.

Societies in which inequalities are allowed to persist or grow over time have *high power distance.* In high-power-distance societies, workers who are professionally successful amass wealth and pass it on to their children, and as a result, inequalities may grow over time. In such societies, the gap between rich and poor, with all the attendant political and social consequences, grows very large. In contrast, in societies with *low power distance,* large inequalities between citizens are not allowed to develop. In low-power-distance countries, the government uses taxation and social welfare programs to reduce inequality and improve the welfare of the least fortunate. These societies are more attuned to preventing a large gap between rich and poor and minimizing discord between different classes of citizens.

Advanced Western countries such as the United States, Germany, the Netherlands, and the United Kingdom have relatively low power distance and high individualism. Economically poor Latin American counties such as Guatemala and Panama, and Asian countries such as Malaysia and the Phil-

power distance The degree to which societies accept the idea that inequalities in the power and well-being of their citizens are due to differences in individuals' physical and intellectual capabilities and heritage.

ippines, have high power distance and low individualism.[34] These findings suggest that the cultural values of richer countries emphasize protecting the rights of individuals and, at the same time, provide a fair chance of success to every member of society.

ACHIEVEMENT VERSUS NURTURING ORIENTATION   Societies that have an **achievement orientation** value assertiveness, performance, success, competition, and results. Societies that have a **nurturing orientation** value the quality of life, warm personal relationships, and services and care for the weak. Japan and the United States tend to be achievement oriented; the Netherlands, Sweden, and Denmark are more nurturing oriented.

UNCERTAINTY AVOIDANCE   Societies as well as individuals differ in their tolerance for uncertainty and risk. Societies low on **uncertainty avoidance** (such as the United States and Hong Kong) are easygoing, value diversity, and tolerate differences in personal beliefs and actions. Societies high on uncertainty avoidance (such as Japan and France) are more rigid and skeptical about people whose behaviors or beliefs differ from the norm. In these societies, conformity to the values of the social and work groups to which a person belongs is the norm, and structured situations are preferred because they provide a sense of security.

LONG-TERM VERSUS SHORT-TERM ORIENTATION   The last dimension that Hofstede described is orientation toward life and work.[35] A national culture with a **long-term orientation** rests on values such as thrift (saving) and persistence in achieving goals. A national culture with a **short-term orientation** is concerned with maintaining personal stability or happiness and living for the present. Societies with a long-term orientation include Taiwan and Hong Kong, well known for their high rate of per capita savings. The United States and France have a short-term orientation, and their citizens tend to spend more and save less.

NATIONAL CULTURE AND GLOBAL MANAGEMENT   Differences among national cultures have important implications for managers. First, because of cultural differences, management practices that are effective in one country might be troublesome in another. GE managers learned this while trying to manage Tungsram, their Hungarian subsidiary. Often, management practices must be tailored to suit the cultural contexts within which an organization operates. An approach effective in the United States might not work in Japan, Hungary, or Mexico, because of differences in national culture. For example, American-style pay-for-performance systems that emphasize the performance of individuals alone might not work well in Japan, where individual performance in pursuit of group goals is the value that receives emphasis.

Managers doing business with individuals from another country must be sensitive to the value systems and norms of that country and behave accordingly. For example, Friday is the Islamic Sabbath. Thus, it would be impolite and inappropriate for a U.S. manager to schedule a busy day of activities for Saudi Arabian managers visiting on a Friday.

A culturally diverse management team can be a source of strength for an organization participating in the global marketplace. Organizations that employ managers from a variety of cultures appreciate better than do organizations with culturally homogeneous management teams how national cultures differ, and they tailor their management systems and behaviors to the

achievement orientation A worldview that values assertiveness, performance, success, and competition.

nurturing orientation A worldview that values the quality of life, warm personal friendships, and services and care for the weak.

uncertainty avoidance The degree to which societies are willing to tolerate uncertainty and risk.

long-term orientation A worldview that values thrift and persistence in achieving goals.

short-term orientation A worldview that values personal stability or happiness and living for the present.

differences. Indeed, one of the advantages that many Western companies have over their Japanese competitors is greater willingness to build an international team of senior managers.[36] For example, Compaq, one of America's most successful computer companies, is headed by a German-born CEO, and Ford Motor Company is headed by a British-born CEO. Japanese companies, in contrast, tend to be dominated by Japanese managers and consequently have a more culturally narrow view of doing business across borders.

Culture shock is a phrase that sums up the feelings of surprise and disorientation that people experience when they enter a foreign culture and do not understand the values, folkways, and mores that guide behavior in that culture. Many managers and their families experience culture shock when they move abroad. If they have received no training, they may not understand how to do business in a foreign country or how local stores and school systems operate. Learning a different culture takes time and effort, and global organizations must devote considerable resources to helping **expatriate managers** (managers who go abroad to work for a global organization) adapt to local conditions and learn the local culture.

culture shock The feelings of surprise and disorientation that people experience when they do not understand the values, folkways, and mores that guide behavior in a culture.

expatriate managers Managers who go abroad to work for a global organization.

Tips for Managers

Understanding the **Global Environment**

1. Carefully analyze forces in the global task environment to identify opportunities and threats, and then select the most appropriate way to operate in that task environment.

2. Find opportunities to take advantage of the global environment by, for example, finding new kinds of customers to export goods and services to, or new avenues to invest in foreign countries, or new ways to buy and make products overseas.

3. Identify the threats in the global environment, such as strong foreign companies poised to invade the home market or powerful suppliers who might withhold inputs.

4. Be sensitive to the differences between countries, and carefully analyze their political, economic, and sociocultural systems to find the best way to operate in those countries.

5. Recognize the need to become internationally and cross-culturally aware.

Choosing a Way to Expand Internationally

As we have discussed, the trend toward a more open, competitive global environment has proved to be both an opportunity and a threat for organizations and managers. The opportunity is that organizations that expand globally are able to open new markets and reach more customers and gain access to new sources of raw materials and to low-cost suppliers of inputs. The threat is that organizations that expand globally are likely to encounter new competitors in the foreign countries they enter and must respond to new political, economic, and cultural conditions.

Figure 4.6
Four Ways of Expanding Internationally

Before setting up foreign operations, managers of companies such as Toys 'R' Us, Boeing, and Swan Optical needed to analyze the forces in a particular country's environment (such as Korea or Brazil) in order to choose the right method to expand and respond to those forces in the most appropriate way. In general, there are four basic ways to operate in the global environment: importing and exporting, licensing and franchising, strategic alliances, and wholly owned foreign subsidiaries. We briefly discuss each one, moving from the lowest level of foreign involvement and investment required of a global organization and its managers, and the least amount of risk, to the high end of the spectrum (see Figure 4.6).[37]

Importing and Exporting

The least complex global operations are exporting and importing. A company engaged in **exporting** makes products at home and sells them abroad. An organization might sell its own products abroad or allow a local organization in the foreign country to distribute its products. Compaq and Microsoft, for example, control the distribution of their products to foreign computer retailers; makers of many luxury products, such as producers of French wine and spirits, allow local organizations to take responsibility for distribution activities. Few risks are associated with exporting because a company does not have to invest in developing manufacturing facilities abroad. It can further reduce its investment abroad if it allows a local company to distribute its products.

A company engaged in **importing** sells at home products that are made abroad (products it makes itself or buys from other companies). For example, most of the products that Pier 1 Imports, The Bombay Company, and The Limited sell to their customers are made abroad. In many cases the appeal of a product—such as Irish glass, French wine, Italian furniture, or Indian silk—is that it is made abroad.

Licensing and Franchising

In **licensing,** a company (the licenser) allows a foreign organization (the licensee) to take charge of both manufacturing and distributing one or more of its products in the licensee's country or world region in return for a negotiated fee. Chemical maker Du Pont might license a local factory in India to produce nylon or Teflon. The advantage of licensing is that the licenser does not have to bear the development costs associated with opening up in a foreign country;

exporting Making products at home and selling them abroad.

importing Selling at home products that are made abroad.

licensing Allowing a foreign organization to take charge of manufacturing and distributing a product in its country or world region in return for a negotiated fee.

the licensee bears the costs. The risks associated with this strategy are that the company granting the license has to give its foreign partner access to its technological know-how and so risks losing control over its secrets.

Whereas licensing is pursued primarily by manufacturing companies, franchising is pursued primarily by service organizations. In **franchising,** a company (the franchiser) sells to a foreign organization (the franchisee) the rights to use its brand name and operating know-how in return for a lump-sum payment and share of the franchiser's profits. Hilton Hotels might sell a franchise to a local company in Chile to operate hotels under the Hilton name in return for a franchise payment. The advantage of franchising is that the franchiser does not have to bear the development costs of overseas expansion and avoids the many problems associated with setting up foreign operations. The downside is that the organization that grants the franchise may lose control over the way in which the franchisee operates and product quality may fall. In this way, franchisers, such as Hilton, Avis, and McDonald's, risk losing their good names. American customers who buy McDonald's hamburgers in Korea may reasonably expect those burgers to be as good as the ones they get at home. If they are not, McDonald's reputation will suffer over time.

franchising Selling to a foreign organization the rights to use a brand name and operating know-how in return for a lump-sum payment and a share of the profits.

Strategic Alliances

One way to overcome the loss-of-control problems associated with exporting, licensing, and franchising is to expand globally by means of a strategic alliance. In a **strategic alliance,** managers pool or share their organization's resources and know-how with those of a foreign company, and the two organizations share the rewards or risks of starting a new venture in a foreign country. Sharing resources allows a U.S. company, for example, to take advantage of the high-quality skills of foreign manufacturers and the specialized knowledge of foreign managers about the needs of local customers, and to reduce the risks involved in a venture. At the same time, the terms of the alliance give the U.S. company more control over how the good or service is produced or sold in the foreign country than it would have as a franchiser or licenser.

strategic alliance An agreement in which managers pool or share their organization's resources and know-how with a foreign company, and the two organizations share the rewards and risks of starting a new venture.

A strategic alliance can take the form of a written contract between two or more companies to exchange resources, or it can result in the creation of a new organization. A **joint venture** is a strategic alliance among two or more companies that agree to jointly establish and share the ownership of a new business.[38] An organization's level of involvement abroad increases in a joint venture because it normally involves a capital investment in production facilities abroad in order to produce goods or services outside its home country. Risk, however, is reduced.

joint venture A strategic alliance among two or more companies that agree to jointly establish and share the ownership of a new business.

Wholly Owned Foreign Subsidiaries

When managers decide to establish a **wholly owned foreign subsidiary,** they invest in establishing production operations in a foreign country independent of any local direct involvement. Many Japanese car component companies, for example, have established their own operations in the United States to supply U.S.-based Japanese car makers such as Toyota with high-quality inputs.

Operating alone, without any direct involvement from foreign companies, an organization receives all of the rewards and bears all of the risks associated

wholly owned foreign subsidiary Production operations established in a foreign country independent of any local direct involvement.

with operating abroad.[39] This method of international expansion is much more expensive than the others because it requires a higher level of foreign investment and presents managers with many more threats. However, investment in a foreign subsidiary or division offers significant advantages: It gives an organization high potential returns because the organization does not have to share its profits with a foreign organization, and it reduces the level of risk because the organization's managers have full control over all aspects of their foreign subsidiary's operations. Moreover, this type of investment allows managers to protect their technology and know-how from foreign organizations. Large, well-known companies like Du Pont, General Motors, and Arthur Andersen, which have plenty of resources, make extensive use of wholly owned subsidiaries. However, they are not the only kind of organization that embarks on a global adventure, as the story of Harry Ramsden's fish and chips makes clear.

Managing Globally

How to Get the World Hooked on Fish and Chips

Deep-fried fish and chips is one of the most popular foods in England. Harry Ramsden's first fish and chips shop was located in Guiseley, Yorkshire, and the company has long been considered one of the premium fish and chips shops in England. In addition, it is one of the few shops to open in multiple locations. In 1995, the company had 12 branches in Britain, including one in Dublin. Its busiest British location, the beach resort town of Blackpool, generates annual sales of £1.5 million ($2.3 million).[40] Harry Ramsden managers, however, are not satisfied with their organization's success. They want to turn Harry Ramsden's into a global organization.

Thus, in 1992 in Hong Kong, the company opened its first wholly owned international operation, marketing its product as Britain's "fast food." Fish and chips, salted and doused with vinegar according to Ramsden's standard recipe, proved to be popular in Hong Kong, and in 1994 the Hong Kong location generated annual sales equivalent to those at the Blackpool operation. Moreover, although half of the initial customers at the Hong Kong location were British expatriates (British citizens who live and work in Hong Kong), by 1994 more than 80 percent of its customers were of Chinese origin.[41] Harry Ramsden's seemed to be well on the way to changing the tastes and preferences of Hong Kong's Chinese community.

Encouraged by their success, Harry Ramsden managers planned to open additional subsidiaries in Singapore and Melbourne, Australia. However, their biggest target market was Japan, whose citizens consume more fish per person than are eaten in any other country in the world. To establish a presence in Japan, Harry Ramsden's set up a temporary fish and chips shop in Tokyo's Yoyagi Park to serve fish and chips covered with the standard salt and vinegar. Despite Japanese consumers' traditional dislike of greasy food, Ramsden's fish and chips were accepted, and word spread that it was indeed a tasty treat.

Harry Ramsden managers decided that the best way to expand into Japan was to seek a Japanese partner and establish a joint venture. Their rationale was that they could take advantage of their joint-venture partner's in-depth knowledge of the market and local consumer tastes. The company found a venture partner and opened its first fish and chips shop in Japan in 1995.

No matter whether the business expands globally by establishing wholly owned subsidiaries or by establishing joint ventures, Harry Ramsden managers have recognized the need for some local product customization to suit local tastes. In each fish and chips shop, at least one dish caters to local tastes. In Glasgow, Scotland, the local item is haggis, a blended meat and grain product cooked in a sheep's stomach; in Hong Kong it is an exotic salad; and in Japan it is sushi.

Impediments to an Open Global Environment

To this point, we have emphasized the trend toward the creation of a more open, competitive global environment and the advantages that result from this, such as access to more customers or to higher-quality or cheaper inputs. However, as every manager of a global organization knows, we live in an imperfect world, and significant barriers to cross-border exchanges between countries continue to make global expansion risky and expensive.

Government-Imposed Impediments

One reason why barriers exist is that governments have ways of getting around free-trade agreements such as the GATT. GATT aims primarily to lower tariff barriers, but there are various nontariff barriers to trade that governments can erect. In other words, there are many loopholes in the GATT that countries can exploit. One class of nontariff impediments to international trade and investment is known as *administrative barriers*. Administrative barriers are government policies that in theory have nothing to do with international trade and investment but in practice have the intended effect of limiting imports of goods and inward investment by foreign corporations.

One example of an administrative trade barrier is mentioned in the "Case in Contrast." Japan's Large Scale Retail Store Law prior to 1991 allowed small retailers to block the establishment of a large retail establishment for up to 10 years and was used to slow the entry of Toys 'R' Us into the Japanese market. Another kind of administrative trade barrier prevents Dutch companies from exporting tulip bulbs to Japan. Why do Dutch companies export tulip bulbs to almost every country in the world except Japan? Japanese customs inspectors insist on checking every tulip bulb by cutting the stems vertically down the middle, and even Japanese ingenuity cannot put them back together.[42]

Of course, Japan is not the only country with administrative barriers to trade. Another example closer to home is apparent in Mexico's effort to slow the expansion of Wal-Mart in Mexico.

Managing Globally

Wal-Mart Runs into Red Tape

Wal-Mart (www.wal-mart.com), the largest U.S. discount retail chain, viewed the January 1, 1994, passage of the North American Free Trade Agreement (NAFTA) as an opportunity to expand operations into Mexico. Only five years before, Mexican regulations had severely limited any direct investment by foreign companies into Mexico. Wal-Mart's managers took the passage of NAFTA as a green light for investment. They launched an ambitious expansion program in Mexico and opened four Wal-Mart stores in 1994 and 10 warehouse-style Sam's Clubs in 1994 and had many more planned.

Reality struck in the early summer of 1994, however, when Mexican government inspectors made a surprise visit to Wal-Mart's new superstore in Mexico City. The inspectors found thousands of products that they claimed were improperly labeled. The inspectors charged that at least 11,700 pieces of merchandise lacked proper labels and that each product had to be labeled in Spanish to indicate the product's country of origin, content, and instructions for use—and also, in some cases, an import permit number.[43] Wal-Mart's managers pointed out that much of the merchandise—40 percent or more—was purchased from a local Mexican distributor. Nevertheless, the regulators insisted that Wal-Mart had the ultimate responsibility for labeling the products, and they closed the store for 72 hours until the problems were corrected.

This brush with administrative barriers and overzealous inspectors has sobered Wal-Mart managers. They view this kind of bureaucratic red tape as a deliberate attempt by government officials to raise Wal-Mart's costs of doing business in Mexico and thereby slowing the company's expansion plans.

Self-Imposed Ethical Impediments

Organizations impose on themselves other impediments to cross-border trade and investment. Why would managers choose to limit their own options for engaging in international trade and investment? In many countries, human rights, workers' rights, and environmental protection are of such low priority that managers decline to have their organizations trade with, or invest in, these countries on ethical grounds.

The human rights issue has recently been raised in the United States in connection with the importing of goods from China. China is not a democracy, and its human rights record is poor. Some of the goods imported into the United States from China are made by prison labor. Many prisoners in China are political prisoners, locked up because of their opposition to the communist-controlled state. Learning of this use of prisoners, many organizations broke off their ties with Chinese companies.

Similarly, U.S. investment in Mexico has fallen as a result of revelations about Mexico's poor environmental record and labor laws. Many critics argue that U.S. businesses investing in Mexico are doing so to take advantage of that nation's lax (by U.S. standards) environmental and labor laws.

There are arguments in favor of investing in countries that have poor records on human rights, environmental protection, and workers' rights. One goes like this: Rich countries tend to have better records in these areas than poor countries; economic growth increases a country's concern for human rights, environmental protection, and workers' rights; so trade or investment in a poor country eventually might improve its stance on human rights, environmental protection, and workers' rights.[44] One manager using trade and investment to improve conditions in poor countries is Anita Roddick, founder of The Body Shop International. As illustrated in the following "Ethics in Action," Roddick has long espoused a fair-trade philosophy that is designed to improve the welfare of people in less-developed countries while at the same time giving The Body Shop products for its stores.

Ethics in Action

Anita Roddick's Fair-Trade Philosophy

Anita Roddick started The Body Shop (www.the-body-shop.com) in 1976 with a store in the south of England. Today, the company is one of the largest retail chains in the skin and hair care market. From the beginning, Roddick has espoused a set of New Age business values that emphasize human, animal, and environmental rights. The Body Shop goes to great lengths to ensure that neither its products nor its ingredients have been tested on animals; the company includes natural, botanical ingredients in many of its preparations; and it actively encourages customers to refill or recycle its containers. One of Roddick's most interesting positions, however, is her "Trade Not Aid" policy.

Underlying this policy is the belief that by establishing sustainable trading relationships with communities in need, The Body Shop and other companies can help improve the welfare of poor people. Roddick does not deny the importance of humanitarian aid. She is simply making a statement that fair trade is the better option for long-term economic development in less-developed communities.

The "Trade Not Aid" policy works like this: A few years ago the Kayapo people living in the Brazilian rain forest received offers to permit logging and mining in their traditional area by both Brazilian and foreign companies. The Kayapo invited The Body Shop to identify an economic and sustainable alternative that would provide jobs and help preserve their homeland. Believing that Brazil nuts could be sustainably harvested and the oil used as a conditioner in a Body Shop hair care product, Roddick asked the Kayapo to gather Brazil nuts for The Body Shop. They, however, said that the price of Brazil nuts, $8 per kilo, was too low to make this option economically viable. In response, The Body Shop purchased some machinery for the Kayapo to use to grind and cook the nuts and then squash them to extract the oil. The pure, cold-pressed Brazil nut oil can be sold for $38 per kilo.[45] As a result, the Kayapo have been able to earn a living while preserving their culture and environment. Their relationship with The Body Shop has also helped them establish and maintain dental, cultural, and health care programs. The Body Shop's trade with the Kayapo and with other producers in less-developed countries seeks to ensure the people's right to control their own resources, land, and lives.

Tips for Managers

Managing the Global Environment

1. Identify the ways that the shift to a more open global environment has resulted in a more complex, competitive, and changing environment and how this affects a manager's job.

2. Analyze the changes taking place in relations between countries and world regions to forecast where new opportunities and threats may come from.

3. Try to foresee the way that impediments to trade and investment will make doing business in other countries difficult. Develop a plan to overcome these impediments.

Summary and Review

Chapter Summary

THE CHANGING GLOBAL ENVIRONMENT

- **Declining Barriers to Trade and Investment**

- **Declining Barriers of Distance and Culture**

- **Effects of Free Trade on Managers**

THE GLOBAL ENVIRONMENT In recent years there has been a marked shift away from a closed global environment, in which countries are cut off from each other by barriers to international trade and investment and by barriers of distance and culture, and toward a more open global environment. The emergence of an open global environment and the reduction of barriers to the free flow of goods, services, and investment owe much to the rise of global trade agreements such as GATT; to the growing global acceptance of a free-market philosophy; and to the poor performance of countries that protected their markets from international trade and investment.

THE GLOBAL TASK ENVIRONMENT Forces in the global task environment are more complex than those inside only one country and present managers with greater opportunities and threats. Managers must analyze forces in their global task environment to determine how best to operate abroad.

THE GLOBAL TASK ENVIRONMENT In the general environment, managers must recognize the substantial differences that exist among countries' political, legal, economic, and sociocultural systems. Political, legal, and

**THE GLOBAL TASK
ENVIRONMENT**

• Suppliers

• Distributors

• Customers

• Competitors

**THE GLOBAL
GENERAL
ENVIRONMENT**

• Political and Legal
Forces

• Economic Forces

• Changes in Political
and Legal and
Economic Forces

• Sociocultural
Forces

**CHOOSING A WAY
TO EXPAND
INTERNATIONALLY**

• Importing and
Exporting

• Licensing and
Franchising

• Strategic Alliances

• Wholly Owned
Foreign Subsidiaries

**IMPEDIMENTS TO
AN OPEN GLOBAL
ENVIRONMENT**

• Government-
Imposed
Impediments

• Self-Imposed
Ethical
Impediments

economic differences range from democratic states with free-market systems to totalitarian states with mixed or command economies. These differences impact on the attractiveness of a nation as a trading partner or as a target for foreign investment. Substantial differences in national culture can also be observed, such as those described in Hofstede's model of national culture. Management practices must be tailored to the particular culture in which they are to be applied. What works in the United States, for example, might not be appropriate in France, Peru, or Vietnam.

IMPEDIMENTS TO AN OPEN GLOBAL ENVIRONMENT

Despite the shift toward a more open, competitive global environment, many impediments to international trade and investment still remain. Some are imposed by governments. Others are self-imposed by organizations.

Management in Action

Topics for Discussion and Action

1. In what ways does a more open global environment increase opportunities and threats in the global task environment?

2. How do political, legal, and economic forces shape national culture? What characteristics of national culture do you think have the most important effect on how successful a country is in doing business abroad?

3. Ask an expatriate manager about the most important problems and challenges that he or she confronted during an assignment abroad.

4. The textile industry has a labor-intensive manufacturing process that utilizes unskilled and semiskilled workers. What are the implications of the shift to a more open global environment for textile companies whose manufacturing operations are based in high-wage countries such as Australia, Britain, and the United States?

5. "Over the next decade we will see the emergence of enormous global markets for standardized products such as cars, blue jeans, food products, and recorded music." In your view is this an accurate statement or an exaggeration?

6. After the passage of the North American Free Trade Agreement, many U.S. companies shifted production operations to Mexico to take advantage of lower labor costs and lower standards for environmental and worker protection. As a result, they cut their costs and were better able to survive in an increasingly competitive global environment. Was their behavior ethical—that is, did the ends justify the means?

7. Go to the library and gather information that allows you to compare and contrast the political, economic, and cultural systems of the United States, Mexico, and Canada. In what ways are the countries similar? How do they differ? How might the similarities and differences influence the activities of managers at an enterprise such as Wal-Mart, which does business in all three countries?

Building Management Skills
Studying a Global Organization

Pick one of the following companies—Ford Motor Company, Compaq Computer, Procter & Gamble, or Kellogg. Collect information about the company from its annual reports or from articles in business magazines such as *Fortune* or *Business Week;* then do the following.

1. Identify the three largest foreign markets in which the company operates.

2. List the forces in the global task environment that you think have most affected the company's organization, and try to determine how its managers have responded to those forces.

3. Identify the political, economic, and sociocultural forces that have the most effect on the company, paying particular attention to differences in national culture. What implications, if any, do such differences have for the way in which this company sells its product in different national markets?

4. Determine how the shift toward a more open global environment has affected the opportunities and threats facing managers in the company.

Small Group Breakout Exercise

How to Become Globally Aware

Form groups of three to five people, and appoint one group member as the spokesperson who will communicate your findings to the whole class when called on by the instructor. Then discuss the following scenario.

You are store managers who work for a large U.S. retailer that is planning to open a chain of new stores in France. Each of you has been given the responsibility to manage one of these stores, and you are meeting to develop a plan of action to help you and your families adjust to the conditions that you will encounter in France. As a group, do the following.

1. Decide which forces in the environment will most affect your ability and your family's ability to adjust to the French culture.

2. Identify the best ways to gather information about the French business and social environment to enable you to understand these forces.

3. Decide what steps you and your family can take before you leave for France to smooth your transition into the French culture and help you avoid culture shock.

Exploring the World Wide Web

Specific Assignment

This exercise deals with the global activities of Goodyear Tire and Rubber Company. Research Goodyear's website (www.goodyear.com), and click on "About Goodyear," then on "Inside Goodyear" and "Strategic Business Units" and "Worldwide Facilities" to access information about Goodyear's global presence. Also, look at the 1995–1997 annual reports, especially the section on strategic developments.

1. What is Goodyear's method of expanding into the global environment, and why do you think this approach was chosen?

2. How will declining barriers of distance and culture affect the way Goodyear operates?

General Assignment

Search for the website of a company with a strong global presence. What are the main forces in the task and general global environments that most affect the way this company operates?

ManagementCase

Managers Tackle Eastern Europe

After the collapse of totalitarian regimes in eastern Europe, many formerly communist-controlled companies were sold to foreign investors. In the car industry, for example, Skoda, the largest Czech car company, and FSM, Poland's largest car maker, were put up for sale. Managers of western European and U.S. car companies took very different approaches to taking advantage of the opportunities that such sales offered.

At the end of the Cold War, the managers of Volkswagen of Germany and Fiat of Italy rushed into eastern Europe and bought Skoda and FSM along with other car companies. The main reason why European managers took over the formerly communist car companies was the extremely low labor costs in eastern Europe. Managers at Volkswagen and Fiat hoped to quickly turn around the eastern European car plants to produce inexpensive cars for sale in western Europe. What they found when they took control, however, shocked them: outdated machinery and equipment operated by a demoralized workforce that lacked the skills necessary to produce cars meeting the high-quality standards expected by Western consumers. Volkswagen and Fiat had to pour billions of dollars into modernizing plants and equipment and retraining workers. They quickly learned how costly the strategy of large-scale foreign investment can be.

When managers at General Motors looked at eastern Europe, they saw not only the opportunities but also the threats. In the early 1990s, GM had established a major western European car division under the Vauxhall name in Britain and the Opel name in Germany. In the 1980s, GM's European car division was experiencing many of the same problems as its U.S. parent: Both were plagued by inefficient, high-cost car-making operations. Despite many attempts to restructure operations, GM's huge size and bureaucratic approach made change difficult and slow, especially in the United States. In Europe, GM had more success under the control of Jack Smith, head of European operations and a master of the art of Japanese-style lean production. In fact, Smith turned around GM's European operations, and his success as a global manager led to his appointment as CEO of General Motors in 1993. These experiences influenced GM managers' approach to expansion into eastern Europe—an approach very different from that of their European counterparts.

Unlike managers at Volkswagen and Fiat, GM managers anticipated the difficulty of restructuring eastern European car companies that had operated in totalitarian regimes and had been shaped by communistic political, economic, and sociocultural values. So, rather than simply taking over existing car-making operations and letting managers and workers continue to operate under the old communist values and norms, GM managers decided to start fresh ventures but do so in a small-scale way to test the waters. They established small factories in Warsaw, Poland; Szentgottard, Hungary; and Eisenach, Germany. Workers at these plants were trained to assemble cars from prefabricated parts made in the West.[46] GM hoped to get the benefit of low-cost eastern European labor with high-quality Western-made parts.

GM's ventures were successful and, unlike Volkswagen and Fiat, General Motors avoided the problems associated with changing outdated attitudes and behaviors. Having succeeded in this small way, GM managers then decided to make low-cost car parts in Poland and Hungary and ship them abroad for use in GM's worldwide assembly operations. This venture also succeeded, and GM is currently expanding both its assembly and its car parts manufacturing operations in Europe.

Questions

1. What problems did GM managers avoid by choosing a small-scale method of expansion into eastern Europe?

2. What kinds of problems do you think GM managers are likely to encounter as their eastern European operations grow?

ManagementCase

In the News

From the pages of **BusinessWeek**

The Next Ceo's Key Asset: A Worn Passport

In 1979, long before China was chic, Gillette Co.'s Michael C. Hawley flew into Shanghai. Hawley, then the Sydney-based head of Asia-Pacific operations, was on a mission to make Gillette one of the first Western companies to crack the Chinese market.

But his search for a joint venture to make razor blades was increasingly looking like Mission: Impossible. "We were flying blind," recalls Hawley. China didn't even have a law for joint ventures as yet. Worse, while Shanghai, home to China's largest razor-blade manufacturer was the natural site, the city was still under the sway of the Gang of Four.

Many American executives would have given up. But Hawley, an international veteran who had already broken ground in tough terrain from Teheran to Bogota, persevered. Eventually, he struck a deal in the northern city of Shenyang. It took over two dozen trips and nearly four years before the Shenyang Daily Use Metals Products Co., as Gillette's joint venture was called, began production. It was just a sliver of the market. But the payoff came in 1992 when Gillette beat the competition to buy 70% of the Shanghai operation, now the largest blade plant in Asia. As a result, Gillette controls over 80% of China's $51 million razor-blade market.

That achievement speaks volumes about why Hawley is being groomed as Gillette's next CEO. Foreign markets offer far more growth than the mature U.S., and Gillette is building an internationally seasoned management team to seize the opportunities.

While many American CEOs have done a brief stint abroad, Hawley, 59, built his career overseas. Although he joined Gillette in 1961 as an assistant to the controller in the Boston headquarters, by 1966 he was running Gillette's small import–export operation in Hong Kong. Promotions followed over the next two decades, taking him to five continents with a wife and three children in tow. Today, "he's the most skilled international manager in the company," says Chief Executive Alfred M. Zeien.

Hawley still spends much of his time traveling and garnering information—for example, on how Duracell batteries are moving in the open-air markets that ring Russian cities. Hawley isn't shy about shouting out overseas managers' errors: "Your name is right there, right across that really crappy display."

His years abroad have made Hawley opposed to any hint of a nationalistic approach to management. "I don't think you can be a global company and say you have to have Americans running it," he says. Two of Gillette's four executive vice presidents, the traditional stepping-stone to the top are Europeans. In some countries, Gillette management is beginning to rival the U.N. Its business in the former Soviet Union, for instance, is headed by Albert Richard, a Frenchman backed up by an Egyptian controller, an English sales director, and officers from Pakistan and Ireland.

But with Al Zeien still firmly at the helm, even insiders are uncertain how Hawley will evolve as CEO. He will have a different style" than Zeien, predicts Jacques Legarde, an executive vice-president who has worked with both men for years. "But I don't think we can see what his full style is until he is there." Zeien is known as a business theorist whose greatest contribution has been conceptualizing and then communicating Gillette's mission. The burly Hawley is more comfortable tackling nuts-and-bolts challenges. "He's a man who knows how to get things done," says Zeien. Gillette's board is betting that he is just the choice to see that the blueprint developed by Zeien is executed.

Source: William C. Symonds, "The Next CEO's Key Asset: A Worn Passport," *Business Week*, January 1, 1998, 76–77.

Questions

1. What is Michael Hawley's approach to global management?

2. What kind of skills does a global manager like Hawley need, and how can he use them to help Gillette manage the global environment?

Chapter five

Ethics, Social Responsibility, and Diversity

Learning Objectives

1. Explain how ethics help managers determine the right or proper way to behave when dealing with various organizational stakeholders.

2. Describe the concept of social responsibility, and detail the ways in which organizations can promote both ethical and socially responsible behavior by their employees.

3. Define *diversity*, and explain why the effective management of diverse employees is both an ethical issue and a means for an organization to improve its performance.

4. Identify instances of sexual harassment, and discuss how to prevent its occurrence.

A Case in Contrast

Ethical Stances at Johnson & Johnson and Dow Corning

In 1982, managers at Johnson & Johnson (www.jnj.com), the well-known maker of pharmaceutical and medical products, experienced a crisis. Seven people in the Chicago area had died after taking Tylenol capsules that had been laced with cyanide. Johnson & Johnson's top managers needed to decide what to do. The FBI advised them to take no action because the likelihood that supplies of Tylenol outside the Chicago area were contaminated was very low. Moreover, withdrawing the drug from the market would cost the company millions of dollars. Johnson & Johnson's managers were of a different mind, however. They immediately ordered that supplies of all Tylenol capsules in the U.S. market be withdrawn and sent back to the company, a move that eventually cost more than $150 million.

In 1992, managers at Dow Corning, a large pharmaceutical company that had pioneered the development of silicon breast implants, received disturbing news. An increasing number of reports from doctors throughout the United States indicated that many women whose Dow Corning silicon breast implants had ruptured were experiencing health problems ranging from fatigue to cancer and arthritis.[1] Dow Corning's managers believed that the available evidence did not prove that fluid leaking from the implants was the cause of these health problems. Nevertheless, a few

An employee removes Tylenol from a Chicago store's shelves on Johnson & Johnson's instructions after the discovery of contaminated supplies in 1982.

Protestors demonstrate against Dow Corning's slow handling of the silicone breast implant situation. Dow Corning has since declared bankruptcy and a settlement looks close in 1999.

months later, Dow Corning's chairman, Keith McKennon, announced that the company was discontinuing its breast implant business and closing the factories that produced the implants.

At first glance, it appears that the goal of managers at both companies was to protect customers and that both companies behaved responsibly. However, this was not the case. Soon after Dow Corning's withdrawal from the implant business, it became known that a Dow Corning engineer had questioned the safety of silicon breast implants as early as 1976. In 1977, the engineer had sent top managers a memo summarizing the results of a study by four doctors who reported that 52 out of 400 implant procedures had resulted in ruptures. In response to a court order, the company eventually released this memo, along with hundreds of other pages of internal documents. Women filed hundreds of lawsuits against Dow Corning for knowingly selling a product that may have been defective. Lawyers accused Dow Corning of deliberately misleading the public and of giving women whose implants had caused medical problems false information to protect the interests of the company.

The behavior of Dow Corning's managers seemed out of character to many people, for Dow Corning had widely publicized its well-developed ethics system, which monitored the behavior of its scientists and managers. Every one of Dow Corning's main divisions was supposed to be visited by six of its top managers every three years. Top managers were charged with the responsibility of questioning employees about wrongdoing at any level and of helping to reveal ethical lapses that could be corrected. The results of this ethics audit were then reported to the company's board of directors. Obviously, this ethics system did not prevent Dow Corning's managers from behaving unethically toward customers in regard to its breast implant product.[2]

Johnson & Johnson also had an ethics system in place. At its center was a credo describing in detail Johnson & Johnson's ethical stance toward customers, employees, and other groups (see Figure 5.1). Why did Johnson & Johnson's credo lead its managers to behave ethically while Dow Corning's ethics audit failed? One reason appears to be that Johnson & Johnson's managers had internalized the company's ethical position. Thus, to them, the credo clearly represented the company's values, and in 1982 they routinely followed the credo when they needed to make a decision that was likely to affect customers' health. At Dow Corning, in contrast, it appears that managers had been just going through the motions in their efforts to explore ethical issues and had not been taking appropriate steps to ensure that their own behavior was above reproach. Ethics experts agree that talking to large groups of employees every three years without an objective approach (the scientists' bosses were in the room listening to their subordinates' concerns or objections) was a poor way to uncover ethical lapses.[3]

Dow Corning's managers seem to have put what they erroneously thought were the interests of their company ahead of their customers' interests. Managers at Johnson & Johnson put the customers' interests first. Dow Corning's ethical stance eventually cost the company over $5 billion in costs and product liability claims (settled in 1998). Within months of its decision to pull Tylenol from store shelves, Johnson & Johnson regained its status as leader in the painkiller market and then increased its market share because of its enhanced reputation for socially responsible behavior.   ●

Figure 5.1
Johnson & Johnson's Credo

Our Credo

We believe our first responsibility is to the doctors, nurses and patients,
to mothers and fathers and all others who use our products and services.
In meeting their needs everything we do must be of high quality.
We must constantly strive to reduce our costs
in order to maintain reasonable prices.
Customers' orders must be serviced promptly and accurately.
Our suppliers and distributors must have an opportunity
to make a fair profit.

We are responsible to our employees,
the men and women who work with us throughout the world.
Everyone must be considered as an individual.
We must respect their dignity and recognize their merit.
They must have a sense of security in their jobs.
Compensation must be fair and adequate,
and working conditions clean, orderly and safe.
We must be mindful of ways to help our employees fulfill
their family responsibilities.
Employees must feel free to make suggestions and complaints.
There must be equal opportunity for employment, development
and advancement for those qualified.
We must provide competent management,
and their actions must be just and ethical.

We are responsible to the communities in which we live and work
and to the world community as well.
We must be good citizens—support good works and charities
and bear our fair share of taxes.
We must encourage civic improvements and better health and education.
We must maintain in good order
the property we are privileged to use,
protecting the environment and natural resources.

Our final responsibility is to our stockholders.
Business must make a sound profit.
We must experiment with new ideas.
Research must be carried on, innovative programs developed
and mistakes paid for
New equipment must be purchased, new facilities provided
and new products launched.
Reserves must be created to provide for adverse times.
When we operate according to these principles,
the stock holders should realize a fair return.

Johnson & Johnson

Source: Johnson & Johnson Annual Report.

Overview As the behavior of Johnson & Johnson's and Dow Corning's managers suggests, managers may interpret their responsibilities to their customers and to their organizations in very different ways. Johnson & Johnson moved immediately to protect the public even though there was little chance that any other supplies of Tylenol were contaminated. Dow Corning's managers postponed action and, to safeguard the profits of their company, did not confront the fact that their product was defective and dangerous. As a result, women continued to receive silicon breast implants, and the potential for harm increased.

The ways in which managers view their responsibilities to the individuals and groups that are affected by their actions are central to the discussion of ethics and social responsibility, and to the discussion of organizational performance as well. In this chapter we explore what it means to behave ethically. We describe how managers and organizations can behave in a socially responsible way toward the individuals and groups in their organizational environment.

We then focus on one particular dimension of ethical behavior that is receiving increasing attention today: how to manage diversity to ensure that all of the people whom an organization employs are fairly and equitably treated. In December 1996, Texaco agreed to pay $176.1 million to settle a race discrimination suit, including $35 million for diversity training. Managers' ability and desire to behave ethically and to manage diversity effectively are central concerns in today's complex business environment. Increasingly, if managers ignore or fail to act appropriately on these issues, their organizations are unlikely to prosper in the future.

We also discuss sexual harassment, a behavior that is both unethical and illegal and another critical issue that managers and organizations—military as well as civilian—must confront and respond to in a serious manner. In 1996 and 1997 the U.S Army was reeling from reports of widespread sexual harassment of female recruits by their male training officers. By the end of the chapter, you will appreciate why ethics, diversity, and sexual harassment are issues that make a manager's job both more challenging and more complex. ●

Ethics and Stakeholders

organizational stake-holders Shareholders, employees, customers, suppliers, and others who have an interest, claim, or stake in an organization and in what it does.

The individuals and groups that have an interest, claim, or stake in an organization and in what it does are known as **organizational stakeholders**.[4] Organizational stakeholders include shareholders, managers, nonmanagerial employees, customers, suppliers, the local community in which an organization operates, and even citizens of the country in which an organization operates. In order to survive and prosper, an organization must effectively satisfy its stakeholders.[5] Stockholders want dividends, managers and workers want salaries and stable employment, and customers want high-quality products at reasonable prices. If stakeholders do not receive these benefits, they may withdraw their support for the organization: Stockholders will sell their stock, managers and workers will seek jobs in other organizations, and customers will take their business elsewhere.

Managers are the stakeholder group that determines which goals an organization should pursue to most benefit stakeholders and how to make the most efficient use of resources to achieve those goals. In making such decisions, managers frequently have to juggle the interests of different stakeholders, including themselves.[6] The following examples describe managerial decisions that helped or harmed different stakeholders:

● In 1998, French pharmaceutical company Elf Atochem finally settled a lawsuit with thousands of claimants in Bryan, Texas, for over $100 million. The lawsuit resulted because managers at Elf Atochem's Bryan plant manufactured arsenic and for many years had allowed it to escape into the groundwater supply. The arsenic resulted in a large increase in the number of birth defects and cancer cases among people living near the plant.

• After a loss of over $1.5 billion in 1992, British Petroleum (BP) began a major restructuring to restore its profitability and benefit its stockholders. In two years, BP laid off almost half of its workforce, and employment fell from 112,000 in 1992 to 60,000 at the end of 1994 while profitability soared.[7]

• When Martin Putman, a lawyer employed by Pacific, Gas, and Electric (PG&E), experienced a period of severe depression, the quality of his work declined, and PG&E fired him for poor performance. Putman sued and won $1.2 million because he claimed (and the court agreed) that PG&E should have made an attempt to accommodate his illness to allow him to perform acceptably.[8]

• In 1995, managers at Levi Strauss, the jeans maker, announced that, because of declining jeans sales, the company would close two plants in San Antonio, Texas, and lay off over 1,200 workers to save over $600 million a year in salaries and other costs. Because Levi's was one of the largest employers in San Antonio, this decision had a serious impact on the prosperity of the local community.

In each of those examples, some stakeholders (managers and stockholders) benefited while others (individual workers and local communities) were harmed. Managerial decisions that may benefit some stakeholder groups and harm others involve questions of ethics.

ethics Moral principles or beliefs about what is right or wrong.

Ethics are moral principles or beliefs about what is right or wrong. These beliefs guide individuals in their dealings with other individuals and groups (stakeholders) and provide a basis for deciding whether behavior is right and proper.[9] Ethics help people determine moral responses to situations in which the best course of action is unclear. Ethics guide managers in their decisions about what to do in various situations. Ethics also help managers decide how best to respond to the interests of various organizational stakeholders.

Managers often experience an ethical dilemma when they confront a situation that requires them to choose between two courses of action, especially if each of them is likely to serve the interests of one particular stakeholder group to the detriment of the other.[10] To make an appropriate decision, managers must weigh the competing claims or rights of the various stakeholder groups. Sometimes, making a decision is easy because some obvious standard, value, or norm of behavior applies. In other cases, managers have trouble deciding what to do.

Philosophers have debated for centuries about the specific criteria that should be used to determine whether decisions are ethical or unethical. Three models of what determines whether a decision is ethical—the *utilitarian, moral rights,* and *justice* models—are summarized in Table 5.1.[11]

In theory, each model offers a different and complementary way of determining whether a decision or behavior is ethical, and all three models should be used to sort out the ethics of a particular course of action. Ethical issues, however, are seldom clear-cut, and the interests of different stakeholders often conflict, so frequently it is extremely difficult for a decision maker to use these models to ascertain the most ethical course of action. For this reason many experts on ethics propose this practical guide to determine whether a decision

Table 5.1

Utilitarian, Moral Rights, and Justice Models of Ethics

Utilitarian Model   An ethical decision is a decision that produces the greatest good for the greatest number of people.

Managerial Implication   Managers should compare and contrast alternative courses of action based on the benefits and costs of those alternatives for different organizational stakeholder groups. They should choose the course of action that provides the most benefits to stakeholders. For example, managers should locate a new manufacturing plant at the place that will most benefit its stakeholders.

Problems for Managers   How do managers decide on the relative importance of each stakeholder group? How are managers to precisely measure the benefits and harms to each stakeholder group? For example, how do managers choose between the interests of stockholders, workers, and customers?

Moral Rights Model   An ethical decision is a decision that best maintains and protects the fundamental rights and privileges of the people affected by it. For example, ethical decisions protect people's rights to freedom, life and safety, privacy, free speech, and freedom of conscience.

Managerial Implications   Managers should compare and contrast alternative courses of action based on the effect of those alternatives on stakeholders' rights. They should choose the course of action that best protects stakeholders' rights. For example, decisions that would involve significant harm to the safety or health of employees or customers are unethical.

Problems for Managers   If a decision will protect the rights of some stakeholders and hurt the rights of others, how do managers choose which stakeholder rights to protect? For example, in deciding whether it is ethical to snoop on an employee, does an employee's right to privacy outweigh an organization's right to protect its property or the safety of other employees?

Justice Model   An ethical decision is a decision that distributes benefits and harms among stakeholders in a fair, equitable, or impartial way.

Managerial Implications   Managers should compare and contrast alternative courses of action based on the degree to which the action will promote a fair distribution of outcomes. For example, employees who are similar in their level of skill, performance, or responsibility should receive the same kind of pay. The allocation of outcomes should not be based on arbitrary differences such as gender, race, or religion.

Problems for Managers   Managers must learn not to discriminate between people because of observable differences in their appearance or behavior. Managers must also learn how to use fair procedures to determine how to distribute outcomes to organizational members. For example, managers must not give people they like bigger raises than they give to people they do not like or bend the rules to help their favorites.

---

ethical decision A decision that reasonable or typical stakeholders would find acceptable because it aids stakeholders, the organization, or society.

unethical decision A decision that a manager would prefer to disguise or hide from other people because it enables a company or a particular individual to gain at the expense of society or other stakeholders.

or behavior is ethical.[12] A decision is probably acceptable on ethical grounds if a manager can answer "yes" to each of these questions:

1. Does my decision fall within the accepted values or standards that typically apply in the organizational environment?

2. Am I willing to see the decision communicated to all stakeholders affected by it—for example, by having it reported in newspapers or on television?

3. Would the people with whom I have a significant personal relationship, such as family members, friends, or even managers in other organizations, approve of the decision?

From a management perspective, an **ethical decision** is a decision that reasonable or typical stakeholders would find acceptable because it aids stakeholders, the organization, or society. By contrast, an **unethical decision** is a decision that a manager would prefer to disguise or hide from other people because it enables a company or a particular individual to gain at the expense of society or other stakeholders. How ethical problems arise, and how different companies respond to them, is profiled in this "Ethics in Action."

Ethics in Action

The Use of Animals in Cosmetics Testing

Along with other large cosmetics companies, Gillette, the well-known maker of razors and shaving-related products, has come under increasing attack for its use of animals in product testing to determine the safety and long-term effects of new product formulations. Gillette's managers receive hundreds of letters from angry adults and children who object to the use of animals in cosmetics testing because they regard such testing as cruel and unethical. Managers at several other companies try to avoid this ethical issue, but managers at Gillette approach the problem head-on. Gillette's ethical stance is that the health of people is more important than the health of animals and no other reliable method that would be accepted by a court of law exists to test the properties of new formulations. Thus, if the company is to protect the interests of its stockholders, employees, and customers and develop new, safe products that consumers want to buy, it must conduct animal testing.

Gillette's managers respond to each letter protesting this policy and often telephone children at home to explain their ethical position.[13] They emphasize that they use animals only when necessary, and they discuss their ethical position with their critics. As we saw in Chapter 4, however, other cosmetics companies, such as The Body Shop, do not test their products on animals; and managers such as Anita Roddick are equally willing to explain their ethical stance to the general public: They think animal testing is unethical. Roddick, however, has admitted that even though The Body Shop does not directly test its products on animals, some of the ingredients in its products have been tested on animals by Gillette and other companies to ensure their safety.

Clearly, the ethics of animal testing is a difficult issue, as are most other ethical questions. The view of the typical stakeholder at present seems to be that animal testing is an acceptable practice as long as it can be justified in terms of benefits to people. At the same time, most stakeholders believe such testing should minimize the harm done to animals and be used only when necessary.

Sources of an Organization's Code of Ethics

Codes of ethics are formal standards and rules, based on beliefs about right or wrong, that managers can use to help themselves make appropriate decisions with regard to the interests of their stakeholders.[14] Ethical standards embody views about abstractions such as justice, freedom, equity, and equality (see

Figure 5.2
Sources of an Organization's Code of Ethics

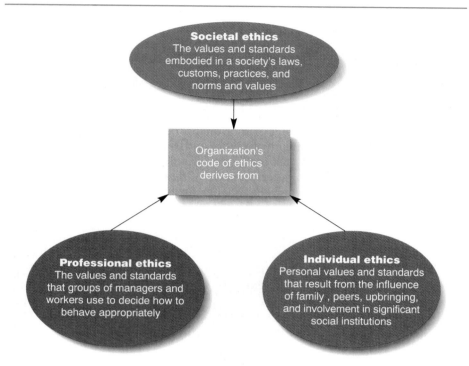

Societal ethics
The values and standards embodied in a society's laws, customs, practices, and norms and values

Organization's code of ethics derives from

Professional ethics
The values and standards that groups of managers and workers use to decide how to behave appropriately

Individual ethics
Personal values and standards that result from the influence of family , peers, upbringing, and involvement in significant social institutions

Table 5.1). An organization's code of ethics derives from three principal sources in the organizational environment: *societal* ethics, *professional* ethics, and the *individual* ethics of the organization's top managers (see Figure 5.2).

societal ethics

Standards that govern how members of a society are to deal with each other on issues such as fairness, justice, poverty, and the rights of the individual.

SOCIETAL ETHICS   Societal ethics are standards that govern how members of a society deal with each other in matters involving issues such as fairness, justice, poverty, and the rights of the individual. Societal ethics emanate from a society's laws, customs, and practices, and from the unwritten values and norms that influence how people interact with each other. People in a particular country may automatically behave ethically because they have internalized values and norms that specify how they should behave in certain situations. Not all values and norms are internalized, however. The typical ways of doing business in a society and laws governing the use of bribery and corruption are the result of decisions made and enforced by people with the power to determine what is appropriate.

Societal ethics vary among societies. For example, ethical standards accepted in the United States are not accepted in all other countries. In many economically poor countries bribery is standard practice to get things done—such as getting a telephone installed or a contract awarded. In the United States and many other Western countries, bribery is considered unethical and often illegal. IBM's quick action to fire three of its top Argentine managers accused of just such unethical behavior is profiled in the next "Ethics in Action."

Ethics in Action

How Not to Do Business in Argentina

In September 1995, IBM announced that it had fired the three top managers of its Argentine division because of their apparent involvement in an unethical scheme to secure a $250 million contract for IBM to provide and service the computers of one of Argentina's largest state-owned banks, Banco de la Nation Argentina.[15] The three executives reportedly paid $14 million of the contract money to a third company, CCR, which paid nearly $6 million to phantom companies. This $6 million was then used to bribe the bank executives who agreed to give IBM the contract.[16]

According to IBM managers, transactions like this, though unethical by IBM standards, are not necessarily illegal under Argentine law. The Argentine managers were fired, however, for failing to follow IBM's standard operating procedures, which preclude the payment of bribes to obtain contracts in foreign countries. Moreover, the payment of bribes violates the U.S. Foreign Corrupt Practices Act, which forbids payment of bribes by U.S. companies to secure contracts abroad, makes companies liable for the actions of their foreign managers, and allows companies found in violation to be prosecuted in the United States. By firing the managers, IBM signaled that it would not tolerate unethical behavior by any of its employees, and it continues today to take a rigorous stance toward ethical issues.

Societal ethics control self-interested behavior by individuals and organizations—behavior that threatens society's collective interests. Laws spelling out what is good or appropriate business practice provide benefits to everybody. Free and fair competition among organizations is possible only when laws and rules level the playing field and define what behavior is acceptable or unacceptable in certain situations. For example, it is ethical for a manager to compete with managers in other companies by producing a higher-quality or lower-priced product, but it is not ethical (or legal) to do so by spreading false claims about competitors' products, bribing stores to exclude competitors' products, or blowing up competitors' factories.

Several years ago, the owner of one country and western nightclub in College Station, Texas, decided that he did not like the competition offered by another local nightclub, so he hired someone to blow it up. The rival's club was completely destroyed and closed for several months to rebuild. But the other nightclub also had to close, because its owner ended up in prison. Clearly, societal ethics are the foundation of an organization's code of ethics.

professional ethics
Standards that govern how members of a profession are to make decisions when the way they should behave is not clear-cut.

PROFESSIONAL ETHICS Professional ethics are standards that govern how members of a profession, managers or workers, make decisions when the way in which they should behave is not clear-cut.[17] Medical ethics govern the way doctors and nurses are to treat patients. Doctors are expected to perform only necessary medical procedures and to act in a patient's interest and not in their own. The ethics of scientific research require scientists to conduct their experiments and present their findings in ways that ensure the validity of their conclusions. Like society at large, most professional groups can impose punishments for violations of ethical standards. Doctors and lawyers can be prevented from practicing their professions if they disregard professional ethics and put their own interests first, as managers at Dow Corning did.

Within an organization, professional rules and norms often govern how employees such as lawyers, researchers, and accountants make decisions and act in certain situations, and these rules and norms may become part of the organization's code of ethics. When they do, workers internalize the rules and norms of their profession (just as they do those of society) and often follow them automatically when deciding how to behave.[18] Because most people tend to follow established rules of behavior, people often take ethics for granted. However, when professional ethics are violated, such as when scientists fabricate data to disguise the harmful effects of products, ethical issues rise to the forefront of attention.

individual ethics

Personal standards that govern how individuals interact with other people.

INDIVIDUAL ETHICS   **Individual ethics** are personal standards and values that govern how individuals interact with other people.[19] Sources of individual ethics include the influence of one's family, peers, and upbringing in general. The experiences gained over a lifetime—through membership in significant social institutions such as schools and religions, for example—also contribute to the development of the personal standards and values that a person applies to decide what is right or wrong and whether to perform certain actions or make certain decisions.

Many decisions or behaviors that one person finds unethical, such as using animals for cosmetics testing, may be acceptable to another person. If decisions or behaviors are not illegal, individuals may agree to disagree about their ethical beliefs, or they may try to impose their beliefs on other people and make their own ethical beliefs the law.[20] Within an organization, the individual ethics of top managers are especially important in shaping the organization's code of ethics. Organizations whose founders had a vital role in creating a highly ethical code of organizational behavior include Merck, Hewlett-Packard, and Prudential Insurance Company.

Societal, professional, and individual ethics factor into the development of organizational codes of ethics—codes that influence how managers and workers make decisions affecting the interests of other organizational stakeholders. Johnson & Johnson's code of ethics—its credo—reflects a well-developed concern for all three sources of ethics (see Figure 5.1). To understand how an organization's code of ethics affects the choices of its managers, it is useful to examine some managers' behavior toward different stakeholder groups.

What Behaviors Are Ethical?

A key ethical decision facing managers is how to apportion harms and benefits among stakeholder groups.[21] Suppose a company has a few very good years and makes high profits. Who should receive these profits—managers, workers, or stockholders? In the early 1990s, Chrysler made record profits. Stakeholders at Chrysler—stockholders, managers, and workers—started to fight about how to divide them up. Chrysler had amassed $9 billion in cash. Its managers wanted to use this money to protect the company against future economic downturns, a tactic that would give the managers themselves security. Stockholders, however, and in particular billionaire Kirk Kekorian (who owned over 10 percent of Chrysler's stock), thought that this was the wrong choice. Kekorian saw that Chrysler's managers and workers were receiving record salaries and bonuses to reward them for their high performance, and he thought that stockholders (who had a strong claim on the organization's profits because they were the owners of the company) were being treated unethically because they were not receiving a larger share of the profits. Acting on his belief, Kekorian launched a takeover bid for the company to force out Chrysler's top managers so that stockholders could receive what he regarded as their proper share of the rewards. His takeover attempt failed, but he did succeed in forcing Chrysler's managers to substantially raise stockholder dividends.

The decision about how to divide profits among managers, workers, and stockholders might not seem to be an ethical issue, but it is—and in the same manner as how to apportion harms or costs among stakeholders when things go wrong.[22] Chrysler almost went bankrupt in the 1970s, and Lee Iacocca was appointed CEO to try to reverse the company's fortunes. Under Iacocca, Chrysler laid off over 65 percent of its workers and managers; many of them were unemployed for years in the hard-hit car industry of the 1970s. Similarly, we mentioned earlier in this chapter that both British Petroleum and Kellogg laid off large numbers of managers and workers when their performance declined.

Were these layoffs of managers and workers ethical? Managers at other companies did not take such drastic steps. AT&T, Kodak, and IBM, for example, laid off fewer workers or spread the layoffs over a much longer time period to reduce the harm done to their employees. Moreover, when layoffs became inevitable, managers of those companies made the layoffs as painless as possible by introducing generous early retirement programs that gave workers full pension rights if they retired early. To reduce harm to employees, they also paid workers a month's or several months' salary for each year of service to the company.

In the United States, severance payments are not required by law, so the decision to pay layoff benefits is typically an ethical choice made by a company's top managers in light of their organization's code of ethics. Many managers believe that employees who have worked for long periods of time for a company should receive layoff payments because they have made an investment in the company—providing their skills and loyalty—just as a stockholder invests in a company by providing capital. Workers, however, have a weaker claim on a company than do stockholders because they usually have no legally enforceable ownership rights in the company. Stockholders are the legal owners of a corporation. Moreover, when top managers decide to give layoff benefits to workers, the decision can harm stockholders, whose dividend payments may be reduced. Thus, deciding how to distribute organizational resources becomes an ethical issue. Top managers must choose the right or proper way to balance the interests of their different stakeholders, and their code of ethics helps them to do so.

Ethical issues loom large when a manager's decision is not governed by legal requirements and it is up to the manager to determine the appropriate actions to take. In western Europe, organizations are required by law to give employees layoff payments based on their years of service. Germany, France, and Britain specify how much managers and workers are entitled to receive if they are laid off. Managers in these organizations simply follow the rules in deciding how to behave. As noted above, there are no such laws in the United States. Although many organizations in the United States voluntarily provide layoff benefits, many do not. In general, the poorer a country is, the more likely are employees to be treated with little regard. One issue of particular ethical concern on a global level is whether it is ethical to use child labor.

Ethics in Action

Is It Right to Use Child Labor?

In recent years, the number of U.S. companies that buy their inputs from low-cost foreign suppliers has been growing, and concern about the ethics associated with employing young children in factories has been increasing. In Pakistan, children as young as age 6 work long hours in deplorable conditions to make rugs and carpets for export to Western countries. Children in poor countries throughout Africa, Asia, and South America work in similar conditions. Is it ethical to employ children in factories, and should U.S. companies buy and sell products made by these children?

Opinions about the ethics of child labor vary widely. Robert Reich, an economist and secretary of labor in the first Clinton administration, believes that the practice is totally reprehensible and should be outlawed on a global level. Another view, championed by *The Economist* magazine (www.economist.com), is that, although nobody wants to see children employed in factories, citizens of rich countries need to recognize that in poor countries children are often a family's only breadwinner. Thus, denying children employment would cause whole families to suffer, and one wrong (child labor) might produce a greater wrong (poverty). Instead, *The Economist* favors regulating the conditions under which children are employed and hopes that over time, as poor countries become richer, the need for child employment will disappear.

Many U.S. retailers typically buy their clothing from low-cost foreign suppliers, and managers in these companies have had to take their own ethical stance on child labor. Managers in Wal-Mart (www.wal-mart.com), Target (www.targetstores.com), J. C. Penney, and Kmart have followed U.S. standards and rules and have policies that dictate that their foreign suppliers not employ child labor; they also vow to sever ties with any foreign supplier found to be in violation of this standard.

Apparently, however, retailers differ widely in the way they choose to enforce this policy. Wal-Mart and some others take a tough stance and immediately sever links with suppliers who break this rule. But it has been estimated, for example, that more than 300,000 children under age 14 are being employed in garment factories in Guatemala, a popular low-cost location for clothing manufacturers that supply the U.S. market.[23] These children frequently work more than 60 hours a week and often are paid less than $2.80 a day, the minimum wage in Guatemala. Many U.S. retailers do not check up on their foreign suppliers. Clearly, if U.S. retailers are to be true to their ethical stance on this troubling issue, they cannot ignore the fact that they are buying clothing made by children, and they must do more to regulate the conditions under which these children work.

Managers also face ethical dilemmas when choosing how to deal with certain stakeholders. For example, suppliers provide an organization with its inputs and expect to be paid within a reasonable amount of time. Some managers, however, consistently delay payment to make the most use of their organization's money. This practice can hurt a supplier's cash flow and threaten its very survival.

An organization that is a powerful customer and buys large amounts of particular suppliers' products is in a position to demand that suppliers reduce their prices. If an organization does this, suppliers earn lower profits and the organization earns more. Is this behavior just "business as usual," or is it unethical?

In the early 1990s, Wal-Mart pressured suppliers to reduce prices, and for a short time suppliers were forced to do so in order to stay in business. However, the inequity of the arrangement upset the suppliers, and eventually they found new customers and reduced their dependence on Wal-Mart. The suppliers refused to spend their resources to develop the kinds of products that Wal-Mart wanted them to make. In addition, they slowed their deliveries to Wal-Mart's warehouses to keep their costs down. When Wal-Mart managers realized what was happening, they finally acknowledged they had to work with their suppliers to find ways to reduce costs for all parties involved.

Consider a different scenario. Suppose a supplier, to keep its costs down and profits high, secretly reduces the quality of the inputs it provides to an organization. This practice is obviously unethical because it is deceptive and dishonest. If suppliers do reduce the quality of their products, organizations are likely to stop buying from them when they discover the ruse, and the unethical suppliers ultimately will lose their customers. For this reason, many suppliers refrain from behaving unethically. Nevertheless, some companies do act unethically, especially if they expect to do little repeat business. One reason why McDonald's, for example, retains ownership of its restaurants along freeways is its fear that unscrupulous franchisees will provide poor-quality food because they think they are unlikely to see the same customers more than once. Were this to happen, McDonald's good name would be tarnished.

Customers are a critical stakeholder group because, as noted in Chapter 1, organizations depend on them for their very survival. Customers have the right to expect an organization to provide goods and services that will not harm them. A complex system of laws protects consumers in the United States, and they have legal rights for recourse if organizations provide unsafe products. As the "Case in Contrast" suggests, however, many issues are not under the direct control of legal rules and standards; in these instances, an organization's code of ethics, as formulated by its top managers, determines how the organization addresses such issues. Johnson & Johnson reacted quickly to protect its customers (Dow Corning did not) because its managers had internalized the ethical principles embedded in its credo. For Johnson & Johnson and other principled companies, the ultimate reward for ethical behavior is a long-term stream of revenue from customers. This benefit may translate into a variety of rewards for organizational stakeholders, including job security, bonuses, and good return on investment.

Local communities and the general public also have an interest or stake in whether the decisions that managers make are ethical. The quality of a city's school system or police department, the economic health of its downtown area, and its general level of prosperity all depend on choices made by managers of organizations. Kellogg, for example, is a major employer in Battle

Creek, Michigan, and the decision to lay off 800 of its workers caused major economic problems for the city as tax revenues, business sales, and house prices fell because fewer workers were employed. When Wal-Mart decides to open a store outside a small city, it frequently destroys the businesses in the downtown area because they cannot compete with Wal-Mart's low prices. Are these decisions just ordinary business decisions, or are they unethical?

Certainly, the owners of small businesses that go bankrupt might regard the Wal-Mart managers' decision to open a store as unethical, but Wal-Mart stockholders (who have become rich as a result of the organization's competitive advantage over small businesses) would regard the managers' decision as acceptable and in the realm of fair competition. Most people in the United States accept competition as a normal business practice. Nevertheless, some areas in the Northeast are trying to slow Wal-Mart's expansion into their communities, just as retailers in Japan tried to slow the entry of Toys 'R' Us into the Japanese market and government bureaucrats in Mexico took steps to stymie Wal-Mart's progress in the Mexican market (see Chapter 4).

In sum, managers face many ethical choices as they deal with the different and sometimes conflicting interests of organizational stakeholders. Deciding what behavior is ethical is often a difficult task requiring managers to make tough choices that will benefit some stakeholders and harm others.

Why Would Managers Behave Unethically Toward Other Stakeholders?

Typically, *unethical behavior*–behavior that falls outside the bounds of accepted standards or values–occurs because managers put their personal interests above the interests of other organizational stakeholders or choose to ignore the harm that they are inflicting on others.[24] Managers confront ethical dilemmas every time they have to balance the claims of one stakeholder group against the claims of another, and they might feel tempted to engage in unethical acts if the harm done to stakeholders is indirect or seems insignificant relative to the benefits that the managers themselves or their organization will receive from the unethical activity.[25]

In some countries but not in the United States, bribing foreign officials to get business is an acceptable practice. Suppose that bribery will ensure that an American expatriate manager can secure for her company a large contract that in turn will net her a huge bonus and promotion. Bribery is not illegal in the country in which she is doing business; her competitors are actively engaging in it, and nobody really gets hurt. Is such bribery really unethical behavior, and does the U.S. government really have the right to say that for American citizens living abroad it is illegal? Similarly, if all members of a company's sales force routinely pad their expense accounts, is this behavior really unethical, since it is the common practice in the company? As discussed previously, family, upbringing, and religion help teach people how to distinguish between right and wrong behavior and to be productive members of society. Managers who let self-interest take control of their decision making in such situations and ignore societal ethics as well are often those who have a poor or undeveloped code of individual ethics.[26]

Beyond the pursuit of ruthless self-interest, managers or workers may have other reasons to act unethically, such as feeling pressured by the situation they are in.[27] Sometimes the behavior of other managers (particularly superiors) may cause managers to behave unethically. Often, managers who find themselves under intense pressure to perform and to help their organization succeed encourage subordinates to act in dubious ways, such as bribing foreign officials, overcharging customers, or delivering substandard products. An example of this type of activity occurred in 1992 when the state of California accused Sears of consistently overcharging customers for car repairs.[28] Apparently, to improve a very weak financial position, Sears created a bonus system that encouraged its car repair employees to convince customers that they needed repairs that actually were unnecessary. Subsequently Sears changed its bonus system, but only after considerable harm had been done to the company's reputation.

Why Should Managers Behave Ethically?

Managers and other stakeholders must strongly resist pressures to behave unethically and to ignore widely accepted societal standards and values because of the harm that unethical behavior inflicts on others. Where is the source of this harm?

Perhaps the easiest way to illustrate how unethical behavior results in harm and ethical action brings universal benefits is to consider the "Tragedy of the Commons" scenario. Suppose that in an agricultural community there is common land that everybody has an equal right to use. Pursuing self-interest, each farmer acts to make the maximum use of the free resource to graze his or her own cattle and sheep. Collectively, the farmers overgraze the land, which quickly becomes worn-out. Then a strong wind blows away the exposed topsoil, so the common land is destroyed. The pursuit of individual self-interest with no consideration for societal interests leads to disaster for each individual and for the whole society because scarce resources are destroyed.[29]

As noted in Chapter 1, one of the major tasks of managers is to protect and nurture the resources under their control. Any organizational stakeholder—manager, worker, stockholder, supplier—who advances his or her own interests by behaving unethically toward other stakeholders, either by t king resources or by denying resources to others, wastes collective resources. If other individuals or groups copy the behavior of the unethical stakeholder ("if he can do it, we can do it too"), the rate at which collective resources are misused increases, and eventually there is little left to use to produce goods and services. Unethical behavior that goes unpunished creates incentives for people to put their unbridled self-interest above the rights of others. When this happens, the benefits that people reap from joining together in organizations disappear very quickly.

An important safeguard against unethical behavior is the potential for loss of reputation.[30] **Reputation,** the esteem or high repute that individuals or organizations gain when they behave ethically, is a valuable asset. Stakeholders have valuable reputations that they must protect because their ability to earn a living and obtain resources in the long run depends on the way they behave on a day-to-day, week-to-week, and month-to-month basis.

If a manager misuses resources, and other parties regard that behavior as at odds with acceptable standards, the manager's reputation will suffer. Behaving

reputation The esteem or high repute that individuals or organizations gain when they behave ethically.

unethically in the short run can have serious long-term consequences. A manager who has a poor reputation will have difficulty finding employment with other companies. Stockholders who see managers behaving unethically may refuse to invest in their companies, which will decrease the stock price, undermine the companies' reputations, and ultimately put the managers' jobs at risk.

All stakeholders have reputations to lose. Suppliers who provide shoddy inputs find that organizations learn over time not to deal with them, and eventually they go out of business. Powerful customers who demand ridiculously low prices find that their suppliers become less willing to deal with them, and resources ultimately become harder for them to obtain. Workers who shirk responsibilities on the job find it hard to get new jobs when they are fired.

In general, if a manager or company is known for being unethical, other stakeholders are likely to view that individual or organization with suspicion and hostility, and the reputation of each will be poor. But if a manager or company is known for ethical business practices, each will develop a good reputation. Beech-Nut, a maker of baby food, is a company that lost its reputation.[31] During the 1980s, Beech-Nut was in danger of going bankrupt; to cut costs, the company contracted with a low-cost supplier of apple juice concentrate. Shortly thereafter, one of Beech-Nut's quality control managers discovered that the apple juice, instead of being pure, contained large quantities of corn syrup. The manager quickly informed top managers. They, however, decided to ignore this information because of their need to keep costs down. Even when the quality control manager eventually went public, Beech-Nut's top managers conspired to mislead government investigators, distort information, and hide the truth. Eventually, the company was fined over $2 million, and its top managers were convicted of fraud. In addition, Beech-Nut's managers destroyed not only their own reputations but also the reputation of their organization. Customers lost confidence in Beech-Nut products, and, once again on the brink of bankruptcy, the company was sold off cheaply to Ralston Purina, a move that resulted in substantial losses for stockholders.

Often, unethical behavior comes back to haunt those who engage in it. If all stakeholders are alert to the need to stop it—because it reduces their own benefits in the long run—then the level of unethical behavior falls. Ethical standards and rules help to increase the value and wealth of people individually and countries collectively. As we saw in Chapter 4, countries tend to become more ethical as they become wealthier because people see how their behavior affects, and is affected by, the behavior of people around them.

Social Responsibility

social responsibility
A manager's duty or obligation to make decisions that promote the welfare and well-being of stakeholders and society as a whole.

There are many reasons why it is important for managers and organizations to act ethically and to do everything possible to avoid harming stakeholders. However, what about the other side of the coin? What responsibility do managers have to provide benefits to their stakeholders and to adopt courses of action that enhance the well-being of society at large? The term **social responsibility** refers to a manager's duty or obligation to make decisions that nurture, protect, enhance, and promote the welfare and well-being of stakeholders and society as a whole. Many kinds of decisions signal an organization's interest in being socially responsible (see Table 5.2).

Table 5.2

Forms of Socially Responsible Behavior

Managers are being socially responsible and showing their support for their stakeholders when they
- Provide severance payments to help laid-off workers make ends meet until they can find another job
- Provide workers with opportunities to enhance their skills and acquire additional education so they can remain productive and do not become obsolete because of changes in technology
- Allow employees to take time off when they need to and provide health care and pension benefits for employees
- Contribute to charities or support various civic-minded activities in the cities or towns in which they are located (Target and Levi Strauss both contribute 5 percent of their profits to support schools, charities, the arts, and other good works.)
- Decide to keep open a factory whose closure would devastate the local community
- Decide to keep a company's operations in the United States to protect the jobs of American workers rather than move abroad
- Decide to spend money to improve a new factory so that it will not pollute the environment
- Decline to invest in countries that have poor human rights records
- Choose to help poor countries develop an economic base to improve living standards

Approaches to Social Responsibility

obstructionist approach Disregard for social responsibility; willingness to engage in and cover up unethical and illegal behavior.

The strength of organizations' commitment to social responsibility ranges from low to high (see Figure 5.3).[32] At the low end of the range is an **obstructionist approach.** Obstructionist managers choose not to behave in a socially responsible way. Instead, they behave unethically and illegally and do all they can to prevent knowledge of their behavior from reaching other organizational stakeholders and society at large. Managers at the Mansville Corporation adopted this approach when evidence that asbestos causes lung damage was uncovered. Managers at Beech-Nut who sought to hide evidence about the use of corn syrup in their apple juice also adopted this approach. Managers at Dow Corning were slow to respond to the needs of their stakeholders. The managers of all these organizations chose an obstructionist approach. The result was not only a loss of reputation but devastation for their organizations and for all stakeholders involved.

Figure 5.3

Approaches to Social Responsibility

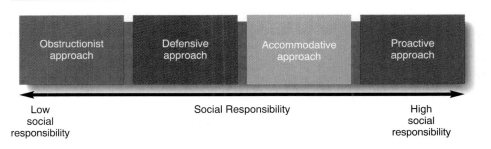

| Obstructionist approach | Defensive approach | Accommodative approach | Proactive approach |

Low social responsibility   Social Responsibility   High social responsibility

defensive approach
Minimal commitment to social responsibility; willingness to do what the law requires and no more.

A **defensive approach** indicates at least a commitment to ethical behavior. Defensive managers stay within the law and abide strictly with legal requirements but make no attempt to exercise social responsibility beyond what the law dictates. Managers adopting this approach do all they can to ensure that their employees behave legally and do not harm others. But when making ethical choices, these managers put the claims and interests of their shareholders first, at the expense of other stakeholders.

The very nature of a capitalist society—in which managers' primary responsibility is to the owners of the corporation, its shareholders—probably encourages the defensive response. Some economists believe that managers in a capitalist society should always put stockholders' claims first, and that if these choices are not acceptable to other members of society and are considered unethical, then society must pass laws and create rules and regulations to govern the choices managers make.[33] From a defensive perspective, it is not managers' responsibility to make socially responsible choices; their job is to abide by the rules that have been legally established. Thus, defensive managers have little active interest in social responsibility.

accommodative approach Moderate commitment to social responsibility; willingness to do more than the law requires if asked.

An **accommodative approach** is an acknowledgment of the need to support social responsibility. Accommodative managers agree that organizational members ought to behave legally and ethically, and they try to balance the interests of different stakeholders against one another so that the claims of stockholders are seen in relation to the claims of other stakeholders. Managers adopting this approach want to make choices that are reasonable in the eyes of society and want to do the right thing when called on to do so.

proactive approach
Strong commitment to social responsibility; eagerness to do more than the law requires and to use organizational resources to promote the interests of all organizational stakeholders.

Managers taking a **proactive approach** actively embrace the need to behave in socially responsible ways, go out of their way to learn about the needs of different stakeholder groups, and are willing to utilize organizational resources to promote the interests not only of stockholders but of the other stakeholders. Such companies—Hewlett-Packard, The Body Shop, McDonald's, Johnson & Johnson—are at the forefront of campaigns for causes such as a pollution-free environment, recycling and conservation of resources, minimizing or avoiding the use of animals in drug and cosmetic testing, and reducing crime, illiteracy, and poverty.

Why Be Socially Responsible?

Several advantages are argued to result when managers and organizations behave in a socially responsible manner. First, workers and society benefit directly because organizations (rather than the government) bear some of the costs of helping workers. Second, it has been said that if all organizations in a society were socially responsible, the quality of life as a whole would be higher. Indeed, several management experts have argued that the way organizations behave toward their employees determines many of a society's values and norms and the ethics of its citizens. It has been suggested that if all organizations adopted a caring approach and agreed that their responsibility is to promote the interests of their employees, a climate of caring would pervade the wider society.[34] Experts point to Japan, Sweden, Germany, the Netherlands, and Switzerland as countries where organizations are very socially responsible and where, as a result, crime and unemployment rates are relatively low, the literacy rate is relatively high, and sociocultural values promote harmony between different groups of people. Other reasons for being socially

McDonald's is one of the many global organizations that has declared its commitment to be socially responsible—it supports a proactive stance on the issues and wants its customers to support this stance too.

responsible are that it is the right thing to do and that companies that act responsibly toward their stakeholders benefit from increasing business and see their profits rise.[35]

Given these advantages, why would anyone quarrel over the pursuit of social responsibility by organizations and their managers? One issue that comes up is that although some stakeholders benefit from managers' commitment to social responsibility, other stakeholders, particularly shareholders, may think they are being harmed when organizational resources are used for socially responsible courses of action. Some people argue that business has only one kind of responsibility: to use its resources for activities that increase its profits and thus reward its stockholders.[36]

How should managers decide which social issues they will respond to and to what extent their organizations should trade profits for social gain? Obviously, illegal behavior should not be tolerated, and all managers and workers should be alert to its occurrence and report it promptly. The term **whistle-blower** is used to refer to a person who reports illegal or unethical behavior and takes a stand against unscrupulous managers or other stakeholders who are pursuing their own ends.[37] Laws now exist to protect the interests of whistle-blowers, who risk their jobs and careers to reveal unethical behavior.

In part, those laws were enacted because of the experiences of two engineers at Morton Thiokol who warned that the *Challenger* space shuttle's O-ring gaskets would be adversely affected by cold weather at launch.[38] Their warnings were ignored by everyone involved in the headlong rush to launch the

whistle-blower A person who reports illegal or unethical behavior.

shuttle. As a result, seven astronauts died when the *Challenger* exploded shortly after launch in January 1986. Although the actions of the engineers were applauded by the committee of inquiry, their subsequent careers suffered because managers at Morton Thiokol blamed them for damaging the company's reputation and harming its interests.

Beyond the need to behave legally, there are some criteria that managers may use to help themselves choose which social actions to undertake. A **social audit** allows managers to take into consideration both the private or organizational and the social effects of particular decisions. They rank various alternative courses of action according to both their profitability and their social benefits (see Figure 5.4). When the social audit framework is used, decisions showing both high profitability and high social benefits are the most likely to be adopted. Decisions with high profitability but negative social effects would worry a socially responsible organization and probably would not be implemented. And even the most socially responsible company would hesitate to make decisions with high social responsibility but negative or low profitability.

Another way in which managers can ascertain whether they are acting socially responsibly is to apply ethical standards and values. Managers' own ethics influence their behavior; and their own values strongly influence whether they will take a proactive approach to social responsibility. An organization's code of ethics, usually printed in its annual reports and mission statements, also influences how conscientiously managers seek to support the interests of all their stakeholders. Some organizations, like Johnson & Johnson, see the company's code of ethics as the only policy to follow when an ethical dilemma is evident, and they allow this code to govern their choices. Other organizations pay lip service to the organization's ethical code and, as a result, managers facing a moral dilemma seek to protect their own interests first and worry later about how other stakeholders will be affected.[39] When such managers talk about protecting the organization, what they are really talking about is protecting their own interests: their jobs, bonuses, careers, and abilities to use organizational resources for their own ends.

social audit A tool that allows managers to analyze the profitability and social returns of socially responsible actions.

Figure 5.4

Conducting a Social Audit: Comparing Profitability and Social Returns from Alternative Decisions

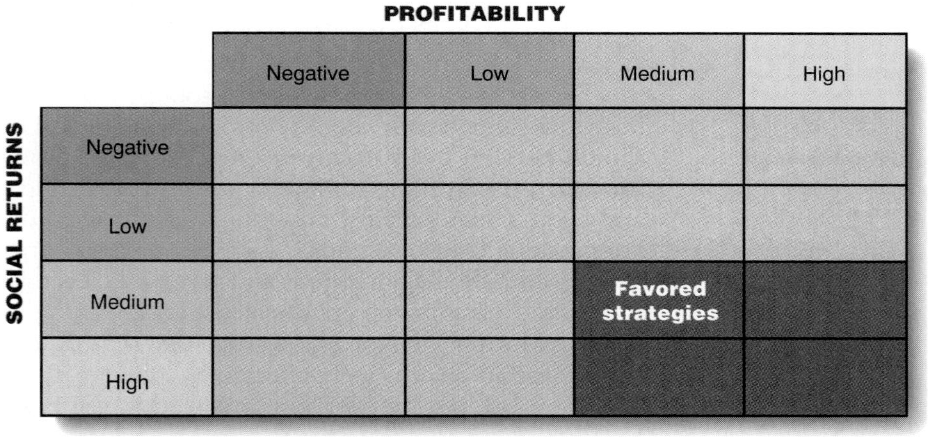

		PROFITABILITY		
		Negative	Low	Medium	High
SOCIAL RETURNS	Negative				
	Low				
	Medium			**Favored strategies**	
	High				

Evidence suggests that, in the long run, managers who behave socially responsibly will most benefit all organizational stakeholders (including stockholders). It appears that socially responsible companies, in comparison with less responsible competitors, are less risky investments, tend to be somewhat more profitable, have a more loyal and committed workforce, and have better reputations, which encourage stakeholders (including customers and suppliers) to establish long-term business relationships with them.[40] Socially responsible companies are also sought out by communities, which encourage such organizations to locate in their cities and offer them incentives such as property-tax reductions and the construction of new roads and free utilities for their plants. Thus, there are many reasons to believe that, over time, strong support of social responsibility confers the most benefits on organizational stakeholders (including stockholders) and on society at large.

Promoting Ethics and Social Responsibility

There are many ways in which managers can communicate their desire for employees at all levels to behave ethically and responsibly toward organizational stakeholders.

ESTABLISHING ETHICAL CONTROL SYSTEMS Perhaps the most important step to encourage ethical behavior is to develop a code of ethics that is given to every employee and published regularly in company newsletters and annual reports. Johnson & Johnson's credo is widely circulated, and all its employees know how they are expected to behave.[41]

ethics ombudsman An ethics officer who monitors an organization's practices and procedures to be sure they are ethical.

The next step is to provide a visible means of support for ethical behavior. Increasingly, organizations are creating the role of ethics officer, or **ethics ombudsman,** to monitor their ethical practices and procedures. The ethics ombudsman is responsible for communicating ethical standards to all employees, for designing systems to monitor employees' conformity to those standards, and for teaching managers and nonmanagerial employees at all levels of the organization how to respond to ethical dilemmas appropriately.[42] Because the ethics ombudsman has organizationwide authority, organizational members in any department can communicate instances of unethical behavior by their managers or coworkers without fear of retribution. This arrangement makes it easier for everyone to behave ethically. In addition, ethics ombudsmen can provide guidance when organizational members are uncertain about whether an action is ethical. Some organizations have an organizationwide ethics committee to provide guidance on ethical issues and help write and update the company code of ethics.

DEVELOPING AN ETHICAL CULTURE An organization can also communicate its position on ethics and social responsibility to employees by making ethical values and norms a central part of its organizational culture. Just as there are values, standards, and norms in a society, each organization has embedded in its code of ethics a set of values and norms that it teaches to its employees and expects them to abide by. We discuss organizational culture in depth in Chapter 9. Here it is important to note that when organizational members abide by the organization's values and norms, those values and norms become part of each individual's personal code of ethics, so an employee who faces an ethical dilemma automatically responds to the situation in a manner that reflects the ethical standards of the organization. High standards and strong values and norms help individuals resist self-interested action and recognize that they are part of something bigger than themselves.[43]

Managers' role in developing ethical values and standards in other employees is very important. Employees naturally look to those in authority to provide leadership, and managers become ethical role models whose behavior is scrutinized by their subordinates. If top managers are not ethical, their subordinates are not likely to behave in an ethical manner. They may think that if it's all right for a top manager to engage in dubious behavior, it's all right for them too. The actions of top managers such as CEOs and the president of the United States are scrutinized so closely for ethical improprieties because their actions represent the values of their organizations and, in the case of the president, the values of the nation.

Ethical control systems such as codes of ethics and regular training programs help employees learn an organization's ethical values. As the example of Dow Corning in the "Case in Contrast" suggests, it is important for all aspects of an organization's ethics control system to be in place. As long as those controls are in place and are taken seriously, organizations will do the right thing–behave ethically.

Tips for Managers

Championing **Ethical** Behavior

1.   Analyze the way stakeholders will be affected by managerial decisions and ensure managers make decisions in such a way that they can defend them to all those who will be affected by their actions.

2.   Develop a written code of ethics for an organization and encourage members of different functions to develop specific guidelines that will help them know how to behave when confronted by an ethical dilemma.

3.   Ensure all managers are responsible for helping their subordinates learn how to determine whether an action is unethical or not and to discover instances of unethical behavior.

4.   Ensure managers act as role models and always act ethically and with integrity.

Managing an Increasingly Diverse Workforce

One of the most important issues in management to emerge over the last 30 years has been the increasing diversity of the workforce. In Chapter 4, we addressed issues of diversity that result from organizations' expansion into the global environment. Here, we address diversity as it occurs closer to home–in an organization's workforce. **Diversity** is dissimilarities–differences–among people due to age, gender, race, ethnicity, religion, sexual orientation, socioeconomic background, and capabilities/disabilities

Figure 5.5

Sources of Diversity in the Workforce

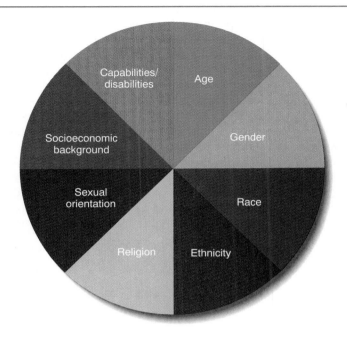

diversity Differences among people in age, gender, race, ethnicity, religion, sexual orientation, socioeconomic background, and capabilities/disabilities.

(see Figure 5.5). Diversity raises important ethical issues and social responsibility issues as well. It is also a critical issue for organizations, one that if not handled well can surely bring an organization to its knees, especially in our increasingly global environment.

Consider the following statistics: Thirty percent of the residents of New York City were born in foreign countries, 33 percent of the residents of San Francisco are Asian, 70 percent of the residents of Washington, D.C., are African-American, and approximately 70 percent of the people currently entering the workforce are either women or minorities.[44] Between 1979 and 1992, the number of women in the workforce increased at twice the rate of men, and currently 1 out of 10 U.S. workers is employed in a company owned by women. The U.S. Bureau of Labor Statistics reports that 58 percent of women 16 years of age and older are in the workforce (compared to 76 percent of men) and projects that by the year 2005 somewhere between 61 and 65 percent of women will be working.[45] There are many more women and minorities—including people with disabilities and gays and lesbians—in the workforce than ever before, and most experts agree that diversity is steadily increasing.

Why is diversity such a pressing concern and issue both in the popular press and for managers and organizations? There are several reasons:

• There is a strong ethical imperative in many societies that diverse people receive equal opportunities and be treated fairly and justly. Unfair treatment is also illegal.
• Effectively managing diversity can improve organizational effectiveness. When managers effectively manage diversity, they not only encourage other

managers to treat diverse members of an organization fairly and justly but also realize that diversity is an important organizational resource that can help an organization gain a competitive advantage.

• There is substantial evidence that diverse individuals continue to experience unfair treatment in the workplace as a result of biases, stereotypes, and overt discrimination. In one study, résumés of equally qualified men and women were sent to high-priced restaurants (where potential earnings are high) in Philadelphia. Though equally qualified, men were more than twice as likely as women to be called for a job interview and more than five times as likely to receive a job offer.[46] Ninety-seven percent of the top managers of the 1,500 largest companies in the United States are white men. The federal Glass Ceiling Commission Report (the term **glass ceiling** alludes to the invisible barriers that prevent minorities and women from being promoted to top corporate positions) indicated that African Americans have the hardest time being promoted and climbing the corporate ladder, that Asians are often stereotyped into technical jobs, and that Hispanics are assumed to be less well educated than other minority groups.[47]

In the rest of this section we examine each of these issues in detail. Then we look at the steps managers can take to effectively manage diversity in their organizations.

The Ethical Imperative to Manage Diversity Effectively

Effectively managing diversity not only makes good business sense but is an ethical imperative in U.S. society. Two moral principles provide managers with guidance in their efforts to meet this imperative: distributive justice and procedural justice.

DISTRIBUTIVE JUSTICE The principle of **distributive justice** dictates that the distribution of pay raises, promotions, job titles, interesting job assignments, office space, and other organizational resources among members of an organization be fair. The distribution of these outcomes should be based on the meaningful contributions that individuals have made to the organization (such as time, effort, education, skills, abilities, and performance levels) and not on irrelevant personal characteristics over which individuals have no control (such as gender, race, or age).[48] Managers have an obligation to ensure that distributive justice exists in their organizations. This does not mean that all members of an organization receive identical or similar outcomes; rather it means that members who receive more outcomes than others have made substantially higher or more significant contributions to the organization.

Is distributive justice common in organizations in corporate America? Probably the best way to answer this question is by saying that things are getting better. Fifty years ago, overt discrimination against women and minorities was not uncommon; today, organizations are inching closer toward the ideal of distributive justice. Statistics comparing the treatment of women and minorities with the treatment of white men suggest that most managers would need to take a proactive approach in order to achieve distributive justice in their organizations.

glass ceiling A metaphor alluding to the invisible barriers that prevent minorities and women from being promoted to top corporate positions.

distributive justice A moral principle calling for the distribution of pay raises, promotions, and other organizational resources to be based on meaningful contributions that individuals have made and not on personal characteristics over which they have no control.

Women, for example, hold practically 50 percent of all nonclerical white-collar jobs in corporate America but only about 31 percent of managerial positions. Here is another way to look at these statistics: Fifteen percent of all men in the workforce are managers, but only 7.5 percent of women are employed at that level. As Table 5.3 indicates, bias against female managers is a major obstacle to distributive justice, although it appears to be more prevalent in some industries than in others. In manufacturing, agriculture, construction, and mining, which typically have had an "old boys' club" culture, women (and minorities) seem to be having a particularly difficult time overcoming a managerial bias against them. Nevertheless, some organizations in these industries appear to be doing better than others. For example, only 4.4 percent of the managers at Ford Motor Company are women, but comparable figures for Chrysler and General Motors, respectively, are 7.8 and 11.7 percent.[49]

In many countries, managers have not only an ethical obligation to strive to achieve distributive justice in their organizations, but also a legal obligation to treat all employees fairly, and they risk being sued by employees who feel that they are not being fairly treated. That is precisely what six African-American employees at Texaco did. They contended that racial bias and discrimination were widespread at Texaco.

Pension analyst Bari-Ellen Roberts said that she was insulted, chastised, and ignored by her managers, who thought she was too "uppity." Sil Chambers, a top trader of Treasury notes at the Federal Reserve Bank of New York before joining Texaco, said that the company was reluctant to send African Americans to outside training seminars, that one of his white subordinates was allowed to report to Chambers's boss rather than to Chambers directly (presumably because the subordinate did not want to report to an African American), and that he was subject to insults from fellow managers, such as being told that he had been hired to improve Texaco's basketball team.

The six African Americans also included in their charges allegations that their pay levels and promotion rates had been negatively affected by the color

Table 5.3

Percentages of Male and Female Managers by Industry

Industry	Percentage of Managers who are women	Percentage of Managers who are men
Finance, insurance, and real estate	41.4%	58.6%
Services	38.9	61.1
Retail	38.5	61.5
Transportation and communication	25.6	74.4
Wholesale trade	20.9	79.1
Manufacturing	15.9	84.1
Agriculture	14.5	85.5
Construction	10.4	89.6
Mining	9.8	90.2

Source: R. Sharpe, "Women Make Strides, but Men Stay Firmly in Top Company Jobs," Wall Street Journal, March 29, 1994, A1, A8.

of their skin. The fact that only 3.97 percent of Texaco's corporate managers was African American and the fact that no minorities occupied the high-status three-window offices in Texaco's Harrison, New York, facility seemed to bear out their complaints of a lack of distributive justice.[50]

procedural justice

A moral principle calling for the use of fair procedures to determine how to distribute outcomes to organizational members.

PROCEDURAL JUSTICE   The principle of **procedural justice** requires managers to use fair procedures to determine how to distribute outcomes to organizational members.[51] This principle applies to typical procedures such as appraising subordinates' performance, deciding who should receive a raise or a promotion, and deciding whom to lay off when an organization is forced to downsize. Procedural justice exists, for example, when managers (1) carefully appraise a subordinate's performance, (2) take into account any environmental obstacles to high performance beyond the subordinate's control, such as lack of supplies, machine breakdowns, or dwindling customer demand for a product, and (3) ignore irrelevant personal characteristics such as the subordinate's age or ethnicity. Like distributive justice, procedural justice is necessary not only to ensure ethical conduct but also to avoid costly lawsuits, as illustrated in this "Focus on Diversity."

Focus on Diversity

Age Discrimination at Schering-Plough

A New Jersey court ordered Schering-Plough, a pharmaceutical maker based in Bordentown, New Jersey, to pay Fred Maiorino, a former salesman who was fired, $435,000 in punitive damages and $8 million in compensatory damages based on evidence that Maiorino's supervisors had engaged in age discrimination. Although Schering-Plough plans to appeal the decision, at the heart of the case is a series of actions and decisions that denied Maiorino procedural justice.

Maiorino worked for Schering-Plough for 35 years and had been commended for his sales performance. In his 60s, he repeatedly declined offers of early retirement. He reported that management's response to his decision was to institute a series of unfair procedures to make him look bad and to build a paper trail to justify his dismissal. Maiorino indicated that he was given very difficult sales goals to reach and was held to different and higher standards than other salespeople. He was accused of failing to meet work requirements without being informed of the requirements in advance, and Schering-Plough's managers spied on his house to see how early he left to start his sales rounds in the morning (while failing to take into account how late he worked in the evenings).

Even the procedures used to inform Maiorino, a 35-year company veteran, of his dismissal seem unjust. Maiorino's boss invited Maiorino to meet him one morning in a local diner for coffee. Maiorino assumed they were just going to chat prior to beginning their familiar routine of visiting doctors to discuss Schering-Plough's prescription drugs. Instead of having a pleasant conversation, however, the boss handed Maiorino a letter announcing his immediate termination. A few minutes later, Maiorino drove home and was followed by his boss and another Schering-Plough employee, who took all of Maiorino's sales materials and his company car. Maiorino was literally left standing in his driveway, unemployed—the last thing he had expected when he left home an hour earlier to start the workday.

Schering-Plough maintains that its treatment of Maiorino was appropriate and plans to appeal the court's decision. Several of Maiorino's former customers, however, agreed with the court and actually stopped prescribing Schering-Plough's drugs to protest the company's violation of procedural justice.[52]

Effectively Managing Diversity Makes Good Business Sense

The diversity of organizational members can be a source of competitive advantage, helping an organization provide customers with better goods and services.[53] The variety of points of view and approaches to problems and opportunities that diverse employees provide can improve managerial decision making. Suppose the Budget Gourmet frozen-food company is trying to come up with some creative ideas for new frozen dishes that will appeal to health-conscious time-conscious customers tired of the same old frozen-food fare. Which group do you think is likely to come up with the most creative ideas: a group of white women with master's degrees in marketing from Yale University who grew up in middle-class families in the Northeast or a racially mixed group of men and women who grew up in families with varying income levels in different parts of the country and attended a mix of business schools (New York University, Oklahoma State, University of Michigan, UCLA, Cornell University, Texas A&M University, and Iowa State)? Most people would agree that the diverse group is likely to come up with a wider range of creative ideas. Although this example is simplistic, it underscores one way in which diversity can lead to a competitive advantage.

Just as the workforce is becoming increasingly diverse, so too are the customers who buy an organization's goods or services. In an attempt to suit local customers' needs and tastes, managers of Target's chain of 623 discount stores vary the selection of products available in stores in different cities and regions. For example, the Target store in Phoenix, Arizona, stocks religious candles and Spanish-language diskettes and Disney videos to appeal to local Hispanic Catholics; the Target store in Scottsdale, Arizona, stocks in-line skates and bicycle baby trailers that appeal to well-to-do yuppies.[54]

Diverse members of an organization are likely to be attuned to what goods and services diverse segments of the market want and do not want. Major car companies, for example, are increasingly assigning women to their design teams to ensure that the needs and desires of female customers (a growing segment of the market) are taken into account in new car design.

Effectively managing diversity makes good business sense for another reason. More and more, managers and organizations concerned about diversity are insisting that their suppliers also support diversity. Managers of American Airlines, for example, recently announced that all the law firms they hire would need to submit quarterly reports indicating the extent to which diverse employees worked on the airline's account. Similarly, managers at Chrysler, Aetna Life & Casualty, and General Motors all consider information about the extent to which law firms support diversity when they are deciding which law firms will represent them.[55] Managers in the Teachers Insurance and Annuity Association–College Retirement Equities Fund (TIAA–CREF) are putting pressure on Nucor Corporation to add women and minorities to its board of directors, which currently consists entirely of white men. TIAA–CREF owns 912,900 shares in Nucor, and its managers feel that their heavy investment in Nucor gives them enough clout to bring diversity to the board of directors.[56]

Why Are Diverse Employees Sometimes Treated Unfairly?

Even though most people would agree that distributive justice and procedural justice are desirable goals, diverse organizational members are still sometimes treated unfairly, as previous examples illustrate. Why is this problem occurring? Three factors may induce some managers to act unethically, unfairly, or even illegally toward diverse organizational members: *biases,* stereotypes, and *overt discrimination.*

bias The systematic tendency to use information about others in ways that result in inaccurate perceptions.

BIASES Biases are systematic tendencies to use information about others in ways that result in inaccurate perceptions. Because of the way biases operate, people often are unaware that their perceptions of others are inaccurate. There are several types of biases.

The *similar-to-me effect* is the tendency to perceive others who are similar to ourselves more positively than we perceive people who are different.[57] The similar-to-me effect is summed up by the saying "Birds of a feather flock together." It can lead to unfair treatment of diverse employees simply because they are different from the managers who are perceiving them, evaluating them, and making decisions that will affect their future in the organization.

Managers (particularly top managers) are likely to be white men. Although these managers may endorse the principles of distributive and procedural justice, they may unintentionally fall into the trap of perceiving other white men more positively than they perceive women and minorities. This is the similar-to-me effect. Being aware of this bias and using objective information about employees' capabilities and performance as much as possible in decision making about job assignments, pay raises, promotions and other outcomes can help managers avoid the similar-to-me effect.

Social status, a person's real or perceived position in a society or an organization, can be the source of another bias. The *social status effect* is the tendency to perceive individuals with high social status more positively than we perceive those with low social status. A high-status person may be perceived as smarter and more believable, capable, knowledgeable, and responsible than a low-status person, even in the absence of objective information about either person.

Imagine being introduced to two people at a company Christmas party. Both are white men in their late 30s, and you learn that one is a member of the company's top-management team and the other is a supervisor in the mailroom. From this information alone, you are likely to assume that the top manager is smarter, more capable, more responsible, and even more interesting than the mailroom supervisor. Because women and minorities have traditionally had lower social status than white men, the social status effect may lead some people to perceive women and minorities less positively than they perceive white men.

Have you ever stood out in a crowd? Maybe you were the only man in a group of women, or maybe you were dressed differently from everyone else (you were dressed formally for a social gathering, and everyone else was in jeans). Salience—conspicuousness—is another source of bias. The *salience effect* is the tendency to focus attention on individuals who are conspicuously different from us. When people are salient, they often feel as though all eyes are watching them, and this perception is not too far off the mark. Salient individuals are more often the object of attention than are other members of a work group, for example. A manager who has six white subordinates and one Hispanic subordinate reporting to her may inadvertently pay more attention to the Hispanic in group meetings because of the salience effect.

Individuals who are salient are often perceived to be primarily responsible for outcomes and operations and are evaluated more extremely, in either a positive or a negative direction.[58] Thus, when the Hispanic subordinate does a good job on a project, she receives excessive praise, and when she misses a deadline, she is excessively chastised.

stereotype Simplistic and often inaccurate beliefs about the typical characteristics of particular groups of people.

STEREOTYPES **Stereotypes,** the second factor that can cause managers to treat diverse employees unfairly, are simplistic and often inaccurate beliefs about the typical characteristics of particular groups of people. Stereotypes are usually based on a highly visible characteristic such as a person's age, gender, or race.[59] Managers who allow stereotypes to influence their perceptions assume erroneously that a person possesses a whole host of characteristics simply because she or he happens to be an Asian woman, a white man, or a lesbian, for example. African-American men are often stereotyped as good athletes, Hispanic women as subservient.[60] Obviously, there is no reason to assume that every African-American man is a good athlete or that every Hispanic woman is subservient. Stereotypes, however, lead people to make such erroneous assumptions. A manager who accepts stereotypes might, for example, decide not to promote a highly capable Hispanic woman into a management position because the manager is certain that she will not be assertive enough to supervise others.

overt discrimination Knowingly and willingly denying diverse individuals access to opportunities and outcomes in an organization.

OVERT DISCRIMINATION **Overt discrimination** is the third factor that can cause managers to treat diverse employees unfairly. It occurs when managers knowingly and willingly deny diverse individuals access to opportunities and outcomes in an organization. Overt discrimination is not only unethical but also illegal. Unfortunately, just as some managers steal from their organizations, others engage in overt discrimination. Eight former male employees of Jenny Craig Inc., the Del Mar, California, weight-loss company with predominantly female employees and managers, for example, are suing the company for overt discrimination. The "Boston Eight," as they call themselves (all were employed by Jenny Craig in Boston), claim that they were subjected to insulting and derogatory comments because of their gender and also were denied access to pay raises and promotions. The case is still pending, but some women who were managers at Jenny Craig admit that men may have been less welcome in the company and if "management . . . could have gotten all of the men to quit, that would have interested them heavily."[61]

Harvard Pilgrim, a healthcare provider, uses role-playing training exercises to demonstrate to its employees the ways in which they may inadvertently stereotype their co-workers and customers. The workers all have cards on their caps that designate each of them with a certain attitude or personality. For example, the middle woman's card reads, "Agreeable."

Overt discrimination and decisions based on stereotypes are clear violations of the principles of distributive and procedural justice. But sometimes even managers who are committed to these principles treat diverse members of an organization unfairly because of the operation of biases. Simple awareness of these biases is the first step toward overcoming their effects. We next consider proactive steps that managers and organizations can take to ensure that the effects of biases and stereotypes are minimal and diverse members receive the respect and opportunities they deserve.

How to Manage Diversity Effectively

Effectively managing diversity ought to be a top priority for managers in all organizations, large and small, public and private, for-profit and not-for-profit. Managers need to ensure that they and their subordinates appreciate the value that diversity brings to an organization, understand why diversity should be celebrated rather than ignored, and have the ability to interact and work effectively with men and women who are physically challenged or are of a diverse race, age, gender, ethnicity, nationality, or sexual orientation. The effective management of diversity will help an organization gain a competitive advantage. In this section we describe how managers can increase diversity awareness and diversity skills in their organizations, and we explain the importance of top-management commitment to diversity.

Increasing Diversity Awareness

It is natural for you to view other people from your own perspective, because your feelings, thoughts, attitudes, and experiences guide how you perceive and interact with others. The ability to appreciate diversity, however, requires people to become aware of other perspectives and the various attitudes and experiences of others. Many diversity awareness programs in organizations strive to increase managers' and workers' awareness of (1) their own attitudes, biases, and stereotypes and (2) the differing perspectives of diverse managers, subordinates, coworkers, and customers. Diversity awareness programs often have these goals:[62]

- Providing organizational members with accurate information about diversity
- Uncovering personal biases and stereotypes
- Assessing personal beliefs, attitudes, and values and learning about other points of view
- Overturning inaccurate stereotypes and beliefs about different groups
- Developing an atmosphere in which people feel free to share their differing perspectives and points of view
- Improving understanding of others who are different from oneself

Increasing Diversity Skills

Efforts to increase diversity skills focus on improving the way managers and their subordinates interact with each other and on improving their ability to work with different kinds of people.[63]

UNDERSTANDING HOW CULTURAL DIFFERENCES AFFECT WORKING STYLES Educating managers and their subordinates about why and how people differ in the ways they think, communicate, and approach business and work can help all members of an organization develop a healthy respect for diversity and at the same time facilitate mutual understanding. When American and Japanese managers interact, for example, the Americans often feel frustrated by what they view as indecisiveness in the Japanese, and the Japanese are often frustrated by what they perceive as hasty, shortsighted decision making by the Americans. If Japanese managers and American managers realize that these different approaches to decision making are by-products of cultural differences and recognize the relative merits of each approach, they may be more likely to adopt a decision-making style that both are comfortable with, one that incorporates the advantages of each approach and minimizes the disadvantages.

BEING ABLE TO COMMUNICATE EFFECTIVELY WITH DIVERSE PEOPLE Diverse organizational members may have different styles of communication, may differ in their language fluency, may use words differently, may differ in the nonverbal signals they send through facial expression and body language, and may differ in the way they perceive and interpret information. Managers and their subordinates must learn to communicate effectively with one another if an organization is to take advantage of the skills and abilities of its diverse workforce. Educating organizational members about differences in ways of communicating is often a good starting point.

Organizational members should also feel comfortable enough to "clear the air" and solve communication difficulties and misunderstandings as they occur rather than letting problems grow and fester without acknowledgment. Take the case of Mary Cramer, a working mother with four children who is employed by a large airline company. Her newly hired manager, Alicia Fuller, who is single, recently commented that she did not know how Cramer managed to juggle her multiple responsibilities at work and at home. Cramer took offense at this comment. She felt that Fuller was questioning her ability to be a top performer at work and that Fuller was implying that Cramer could not possibly manage her home and work responsibilities effectively. For several weeks Cramer brooded about this apparent criticism and avoided interacting with Fuller as much as possible. Then one day one of her coworkers told her how impressed Fuller was with her work, and Cramer realized that she may have misinterpreted Fuller's remarks.

Diversity education can help managers and subordinates gain a better understanding of how people may interpret certain kinds of comments. Diversity education also can help employees learn how to resolve misunderstandings. For example, both Cramer and Fuller should have felt free to try to clear up their misunderstanding on the spot. If Cramer had immediately mentioned her concerns, Fuller could have explained that she intended her comments to be a compliment, not the implied criticism that Cramer misunderstood them to be. Cramer would have been spared all the stress this small incident caused her, and her relationship with Fuller would have gotten off to a better start.

BEING FLEXIBLE   Managers and their subordinates must learn how to be open to different approaches and ways of doing things. This does not mean that organizational members have to suppress their personal styles. Rather, it means that they must be open to, and not feel threatened by, different approaches and perspectives, and they must have the patience and flexibility needed to understand and appreciate diverse perspectives.

Techniques for Increasing Diversity Awareness and Skills

Many managers use a multipronged approach to increase diversity awareness and skills in their organizations: films and printed materials supplemented by experiential exercises to uncover hidden biases and stereotypes. Sometimes simply providing a forum for people to learn about and discuss their differing attitudes, values, and experiences can be a powerful means for increasing awareness. Also useful are role-plays that enact problems resulting from lack of awareness and indicate the increased understanding that comes from appreciating others' viewpoints. Accurate information and training experiences can debunk stereotypes. Group exercises, role-plays, and diversity-related experiences can help organizational members develop the skills they need to work effectively with a variety of people.

Managers sometimes hire outside consultants to provide diversity training. Some organizations have their own diversity experts in-house. Digital Equipment Corporation, for example, has a diversity management department, called "Valuing Differences," similar to other departments such as marketing or finance.[64]

United Parcel Service (UPS), a package delivery company, developed an innovative community internship program to increase the diversity awareness and skills of its managers and at the same time benefit the wider community. Upper and middle managers participating in the program take one month off the job to be community interns. They work in community organizations helping people who in many instances are very different from themselves—organizations such as a detention center in McAllen, Texas, for Mexican immigrants, homeless shelters, AIDS centers, Head Start programs, migrant farmworker assistance groups, and groups aiming to halt the spread of drug abuse in inner cities. Approximately 40 managers a year are community interns at an annual cost to UPS of $400,000.

Since the program began in 1968, 800 managers have been community interns. Interacting with and helping diverse people enhances the interns' awareness of diversity because they experience it firsthand. Bill Cox, a UPS division manager who spent a month in the McAllen detention center, summed up his experience of diversity: "You've got these [thousands of] migrant workers down in McAllen . . . and they don't want what you have. All they want is an

UPS managers, as a part of its "Community Internship Program," work in a soup kitchen for the homeless to learn about problems and opportunities in dealing with people who are different from themselves.

opportunity to *earn* what you have. That's a fundamental change in understanding that only comes from spending time with these people."[65]

Many managers who complete the UPS community internship program have superior diversity skills as a result of their experiences. During their internships, they learn about different cultures and approaches to work and life; they learn to interact effectively with people with whom they ordinarily do not come into contact; and they are forced to learn flexibility because of the dramatic difference between their role at the internship site and their role as manager at UPS.

The Importance of Top-Management Commitment to Diversity

When top management is truly committed to diversity, top managers embrace diversity through their actions and example, spread the message that diversity can be a source of competitive advantage, deal effectively with diverse employees, and are willing to commit organizational resources to managing diversity. That last step alone is not sufficient. If top managers commit resources to diversity (such as providing money for training programs) but as individuals do not value diversity, any initiatives they undertake are likely to fail.

Some organizations recruit and hire African Americans for first-level and middle-management positions, but after being promoted into middle management, some of these managers quit to start their own businesses. A major reason for their departure is their belief that they will not be promoted into top-management positions because of a lack of commitment to diversity among members of the top-management team. There are signs, however, that this situation may be changing. In 1995 four African Americans were appointed to prominent top-management positions: Kenneth Chenault, vice chairman of American Express; Warren E. Shaw, chief executive of Chancelor Capital Management, a money-management firm; Robert Holland, Jr., chief executive of Ben & Jerry's Homemade; and Richard D. Parsons, president of Time Warner.[66]

Many top managers need help in developing their own diversity awareness and related skills and in understanding what a commitment to diversity entails. Top managers at Ortho Pharmaceutical, a subsidiary of Johnson & Johnson, realized the importance of being actively committed to diversity themselves and took steps to translate their commitment into practice. The president of Ortho and the ten members of the board of directors were concerned about the relatively high turnover rates among women and minorities and the low numbers of minorities in top-management positions. They decided that before making any changes in their organization and its structure, they needed to make some personal changes. They hired a consultant to help them learn how to manage diversity effectively by making them aware of (1) their own feelings and beliefs about gender and race, (2) how their own attitudes influenced the decisions they made, and (3) how as individuals and as a group they could manage diversity at Ortho more effectively. Then they provided similar training to all Ortho managers, starting from the top and moving down—top managers first, then middle managers, and then first-line managers.

Today, managers at Ortho customize diversity training for the needs of their own work groups and subordinates, and company resources are available for films, printed materials, and advice on how to manage diversity effectively. Every employee at Ortho receives some kind of diversity training. As Ernie Urquhart, the director of human resources puts it, "Valuing diversity is seen not as a project but as a process: It's never 'done.'"[67] Ortho Pharmaceutical is not alone in its diversity initiatives. In 1994, 56 percent of organizations with 100 or more members provided diversity training to their employees.[68]

By now it should be clear that managers can take a variety of steps to manage diversity effectively. Many Fortune 500 companies and their managers continue to develop and experiment with new diversity initiatives to meet this ethical and business imperative. Although some initiatives prove to be unsuccessful, it is clear that managers must make a long-term commitment to diversity. Training sessions oriented toward the short term are doomed to failure: Participants quickly slip back into their old ways of doing things. The effective management of diversity, like the management of the organization as a whole, is an ongoing process: It never stops and never ends.

Tips for Managers

Managing an Increasingly Diverse Workforce

1. Make sure that managerial decision making conforms to the values of distributive and procedural justice.

2. Be careful managers do not treat subordinates who are similar to them more favorably than those who are different.

3. Help managers understand their stereotypes and why they are likely to be inaccurate.

4. Clearly communicate managerial commitment to effectively managing diversity to your subordinates.

5. Provide ongoing diversity training for subordinates.

Sexual Harassment

Sweeping changes will no doubt occur in the U.S. Army as a result of revelations about the harassment of female recruits in 1996. Sexual harassment seriously damages both the people who are harassed and the reputation of the organization in which it occurs. It also can cost organizations large amounts of money. In 1995, for example, Chevron Corporation agreed to pay $2.2 million to settle a sexual harassment lawsuit filed by four women who worked at Chevron Information Technology Company in San Ramon, California. One woman involved in the suit said that she had received violent pornographic material through the company mail. Another, an electrical engineer, said that she had been asked to bring pornographic videos to Chevron workers at an Alaska drill site.[69]

Unfortunately, what happened in the Army and at Chevron are not isolated incidents. Sixty percent of the 607 women surveyed by the National Association for Female Executives indicated that they had experienced some form of sexual harassment.[70] Although women are the most frequent victims of sexual harassment (particularly those in male-dominated occupations or those who occupy positions stereotypically associated with certain gender relationships such as a female secretary reporting to a male boss), men also can be victims of sexual harassment. Several male employees at Jenny Craig (who filed the lawsuit mentioned earlier) said that they were subject to lewd and inappropriate comments from female coworkers and managers.[71] Sexual harassment is not only unethical; it is also illegal. Managers have an ethical obligation to ensure that they, their coworkers, and their subordinates never engage in sexual harassment, even unintentionally.

Forms of Sexual Harassment

quid pro quo sexual harassment Asking for or forcing an employee to perform sexual favors in exchange for some reward or to avoid negative consequences.

There are two basic forms of sexual harassment: quid pro quo sexual harassment and hostile work environment sexual harassment. **Quid pro quo sexual harassment** occurs when a harasser asks or forces an employee to perform sexual favors to keep a job, receive a promotion, receive a raise, obtain some other work-related opportunity, or avoid receiving negative consequences such as demotion or dismissal.[72] This "Sleep with me, honey, or you're fired" form of harassment is the more extreme form of harassment and leaves no doubt in anyone's mind that sexual harassment has taken place.[73]

hostile work environment sexual harassment Telling lewd jokes, displaying pornography, making sexually oriented remarks about someone's personal appearance, and other sex-related actions that make the work environment unpleasant.

Hostile work environment sexual harassment is more subtle. **Hostile work environment sexual harassment** occurs when organizational members are faced with an intimidating, hostile, or offensive work environment because of their sex.[74] Lewd jokes, sexually oriented comments, displays of pornography, displays or distribution of sexually oriented objects, and sexually oriented remarks about one's physical appearance are examples of hostile work environment sexual harassment. A hostile work environment interferes with organizational members' ability to perform their jobs effectively and has been deemed illegal by the courts. Managers who engage in hostile work environment harassment or allow others to do so risk costly lawsuits for their organizations, as evidenced by the experience of Chevron.

Steps Managers Can Take to Eradicate Sexual Harassment

Managers have an ethical obligation to eradicate sexual harassment in their organizations. There are many ways to accomplish this objective. Here are four initial steps that managers can take to deal with the problem.[75]

• *Develop and clearly communicate a sexual harassment policy endorsed by top management.* This policy should include prohibitions against both quid pro quo and hostile work environment sexual harassment. It should contain (1) examples of types of behavior that are unacceptable, (2) a procedure for employees to use to report instances of harassment, (3) a discussion of the disciplinary actions that will be taken when harassment has taken place, and (4) a commitment to educate and train organizational members about sexual harassment.

• *Use a fair complaint procedure to investigate charges of sexual harassment.* Such a procedure should (1) be managed by a neutral third party, (2) ensure that complaints are dealt with promptly and thoroughly, (3) protect and fairly treat victims, and (4) ensure that alleged harassers are fairly treated.

• *When it has been determined that sexual harassment has taken place, take corrective actions as soon as possible.* These actions can vary depending on the severity of the harassment. When harassment is extensive, prolonged over a period of time, of a quid pro quo nature, or severely objectionable in some other manner, corrective action may include firing the harasser.

• *Provide sexual harassment education and training to organizational members, including managers.* The majority of Fortune 500 firms currently provide this kind of education and training for their employees. Managers at Du Pont, for example, developed Du Pont's "A Matter of Respect" program to help educate employees about sexual harassment and eliminate its occurrence. The program includes a four-hour workshop in which participants are given information that defines sexual harassment, sets forth the company's policy against it, and explains how to report complaints and access a 24-hour hotline. Participants watch video clips showing actual instances of harassment. One clip shows a saleswoman having dinner with a male client who, after much negotiating, seems about to give her company his business when he suddenly suggests that they continue their conversation in his hotel room. The saleswoman is confused about what to do. Will she be reprimanded if she says "no" and the deal is lost? After watching a video, participants discuss what they have seen, why the behavior is inappropriate, and what organizations can do to alleviate the problem.[76] Throughout the program, managers stress to employees that they do not have to tolerate sexual harassment or get involved in situations in which harassment is likely to occur.

The Navy is not alone in its fight against sexual harassment. Shown here is a U.S. Army antisexual harassment poster, introduced as a part of the Army's campaign to discourage and eliminate incidents of sexual harassment such as those that surfaced in 1996

Other organizations that are proactively addressing the sexual harassment problem are Corning, Digital Equipment, and the U.S. Navy. Digital Equipment Corporation offers a full-day training program that educates employees about the different forms of sexual harassment and makes extensive use of role playing.[77] In the wake of the much-publicized Tailhook scandal—Navy and Marine Corps pilots sexually harassed naval aviators at a convention in Las Vegas—the Navy is trying to eradicate sexual harassment and improve its managing of diversity (and its public image). All members of the Navy, regardless of rank, are educated about appropriate and inappropriate behavior. Men and women who have committed sexual harassment offenses have been discharged. Eighteen courses are offered on issues surrounding sexual harassment, and all members of the Navy are required to participate in continuous training. Evidence that these initiatives were sorely needed comes from the Navy's toll-free sexual harassment advice line. During its first four months of operation, 500 calls were received.[78]

In June 1998 the Supreme Court announced some important rulings concerning both an employee's and a company's responsibilities in trying to prevent sexual harassment. These guidelines are summarized in the following "Ethics in Action," reprinted from *Business Week*.

Ethics in Action

Finally, a Corporate Tip Sheet on Sexual Harassment by Susan B. Garland, *Business Week*[79]

A chill wind ran through corporate boardrooms on June 26 as the Supreme Court handed down two landmark rulings on sexual harassment. The justices ruled that companies can be held liable for a supervisor's sexually harassing behavior even if the offense was never reported to management. And the high court said an employer can be liable when a supervisor threatens to punish a worker for resisting sexual demands—even if such threats aren't carried out.

At first blush, the decisions sound like a prescription for a flood of new lawsuits. But take a deep breath, Corporate America. There's actually some good news for employers in the fine print of the justices' decisions. For the first time, the court is giving companies guidelines on how to protect themselves against sexual-harassment charges. There are no guarantees, of course. But, if companies get serious about stamping out harassment and sustain the efforts, they can be better protected in court—and their employees can feel safer at work.

The court's advice: Develop a zero-tolerance policy on harassment, communicate it to employees, and ensure that victims can report abuses without fear of retaliation. "Employers should feel safe as long as they are vigorous," says Susan R. Meisinger, senior vice president at the Society for Human Resource Management.

So even though the court has broadened the conditions under which suits can be brought, a company can deflect sexual-harassment charges with a two-pronged "affirmative defense," the justices said. First, it must take "reasonable care to prevent and correct promptly any sexually harassing behavior." Then, it must show that an employee failed to use internal procedures for reporting abusive behavior. This defense won't work when a supervisor retaliates against a worker for resisting sexual advances. But it will protect a company from charges that it tolerates a hostile work environment.

That means if a company has a strong antiharassment policy and a worker doesn't report an incident of sexual harassment and later sues, an employer can use that as part of a defense. Says Boston employment lawyer Marilyn D. Stempler: "The court places obligations on employers to set up policies, but it also places an obligation on the victim to come forward."

Not every nuance is spelled out. The court didn't describe, for example, what constitutes "reasonable care" for preventing or halting harassment. But employment consultants say companies should now publicize the policies as aggressively and regularly as possible—in handbooks, on posters, in training sessions, and in reminders in paychecks. Line supervisors and employees should be given real-life examples of what could constitute offensive conduct.

Companies also must ensure that workers won't face reprisals if they report offending behavior. Employment experts say companies should designate several managers to take these complaints, so that employees don't find themselves reporting to their immediate supervisor—very often the abuser. Managers should be trained in sexual-harassment issues. And, experts say, punishment against harassers should be swift and sure.

With legal costs for a jury trial running as high as $200,000, it's cheaper for most companies to put in place a basic sexual-harassment program. Still, none of this is simple. Small companies may not have the expertise to investigate complaints. And for all companies, once a complaint is filed, employers will face increased pressure to sort out who's telling the truth and to mete out serious punishments.

But by both expanding a company's potential liability and offering a valid defense, the Supreme Court noted that it was giving employers "an incentive to prevent and eliminate harassment." That means companies can protect themselves while doing right by their workers. That's an opportunity for Corporate America, not a threat.

Summary and Review

Chapter Summary

ETHICS AND STAKEHOLDERS

- Sources of an Organization's Code of Ethics
- What Behaviors Are Ethical?
- Why Would Managers Behave Unethically Toward Other Stakeholders?
- Why Should Managers Behave Ethically?

ETHICS AND STAKEHOLDERS Ethics are moral principles or beliefs about what is right or wrong. These beliefs guide people in their dealings with other individuals and groups (stakeholders) and provide a basis for deciding whether behavior is right and proper. Many organizations have a formal code of ethics derived primarily from societal ethics, professional ethics, and the individual ethics of the organization's top managers. Managers can apply ethical standards to help themselves decide on the proper way to behave toward organizational stakeholders.

SOCIAL RESPONSIBILITY Social responsibility refers to a manager's duty to make decisions that nurture, protect, enhance, and promote the welfare and well-being of stakeholders and society as a whole. Managers generally take one of four approaches to the issue of socially responsible behavior: obstructionist, defensive, accommodative, or proactive. Promoting ethical and socially responsible behavior is a major managerial challenge.

MANAGING AN INCREASINGLY DIVERSE WORKFORCE Diversity is differences among people due to age, gender, race, ethnicity, religion, sexual orientation, socioeconomic background, and capabilities/disabilities. Effectively managing diversity is an ethical imperative that makes good business sense. The effective management of diversity can be accomplished if top management is committed to principles of distributive and procedural justice, values diversity as a source of competitive advantage, and is willing to devote organizational resources to increasing employees' diversity awareness and diversity skills.

SEXUAL HARASSMENT Two forms of sexual harassment are quid pro quo sexual harassment and hostile work environment sexual harassment. Steps that managers can take to eradicate sexual harassment include development and communication of a sexual harassment policy endorsed by top management, use of fair complaint procedures, prompt corrective action when harassment occurs, and sexual harassment training and education for organizational members.

Management in Action

Topics for Discussion and Action

1. Why is it important for people and organizations to behave ethically?

2. Ask a manager to describe an instance of ethical behavior that she or he observed and an instance of unethical behavior. What caused these behaviors, and what were the outcomes?

3. Search business magazines such as *Fortune* or *Business Week* for an example of ethical or unethical behavior, and use the material in this chapter to analyze it.

4. Which stakeholder group should managers be most concerned about when they decide on their approach to social responsibility? Why?

5. Discuss why violations of the principles of distributive and procedural justice continue to occur in modern organizations. What can managers do to uphold these principles in their organizations?

6. Discuss an occasion when you may have been treated unfairly because of stereotypical thinking. What stereotypes were applied to you? How did they result in your being unfairly treated?

7. Choose a Fortune 500 company not mentioned in the chapter. Conduct library research to determine what steps this organization has taken to effectively manage diversity and eliminate sexual harassment.

Building Management Skills

Solving Diversity-Related Problems

Think about the last time that you (1) were treated unfairly because you differed from a decision maker on a particular dimension of diversity or (2) observed someone else being treated unfairly because that person differed from a decision maker on a particular dimension of diversity. Then answer these questions.

1. Why do you think the decision maker acted unfairly in this situation?

2. In what ways, if any, were biases, stereotypes, or overt discrimination involved in this situation?

3. Was the decision maker aware that he or she was acting unfairly?

4. What could you or the person who was treated unfairly have done to improve matters and rectify the injustice on the spot?

5. Was any sexual harassment involved in this situation? If so, what kind was it?

6. If you had authority over the decision maker (for example, if you were his or her manager or supervisor), what steps would you take to ensure that the decision maker no longer treated diverse individuals unfairly?

Small Group Breakout Exercise

What Is Ethical Behavior?

Form groups of three to five people, and appoint one group member as the spokesperson who will communicate your findings to the class when called on by the instructor. Then discuss the following scenario.

You are the managers of the functions of a large chain of for-profit hospitals, and you have been charged with the responsibility to develop a code of ethics to guide the members of your organization in their dealings with stakeholders. To guide you in creating the ethical code, do the following.

1. Discuss the various kinds of ethical dilemmas that hospital employees—doctors, nurses, pharmacists—may encounter in their dealings with stakeholders such as patients or suppliers.

2. Identify a specific behavior that the three kinds of hospital employees mentioned in item 1 might exhibit, and characterize the behavior as ethical or unethical.

3. Based on this discussion, identify three standards or values that you will incorporate into your personal ethical code to help yourself determine whether a behavior is ethical or unethical.

Exploring the World Wide Web

Specific Assignment

This exercise looks at how ice-cream maker Ben and Jerry's Homemade describes its stance on ethics and social responsibility. Explore Ben and Jerry's website (benjerry.com) and, in particular, its mission statement.

1. Which of the four approaches toward social responsibility has Ben and Jerry's adopted?

2. Why does the organization have this stance, and how appropriate do you think it is?

General Assignment

Search for a company website that has an explicit statement of the company's approach to ethics and social responsibility. What is its approach, and why does the company have this approach?

ManagementCase

Mentoring Diverse Employees Pays Off

Many successful managers today have had the help of a mentor at some point in their careers. A mentor is an experienced member of an organization who provides advice, guidance, and potential opportunities to a less-experienced member (the mentee) and helps the mentee learn the ropes and how to advance up the corporate ladder. Diverse employees often have a hard time finding mentors because experienced organizational members are different from them and, research studies indicate, managers are more likely to mentor people who are similar to them rather than those who are different.[80] The similar-to-me effect helps explain this phenomenon because it can lead managers to perceive employees who are similar to themselves more positively than they perceive those who are different. Managers may believe that employees who are similar to themselves are most deserving of their mentoring.

When managers do mentor diverse employees, however, both the mentee and the mentoring manager stand to benefit. Take the case of Wesley von Shack, chief executive of DQE Corporation, a small, conservative Pittsburgh utility managed predominantly by

white men, and Diana Green, a former vice president of Xerox Corporation and an African American. Von Shack recruited Green to DQE almost 10 years ago to manage DQE's human resources department. They seemed to have a similar approach to managing, and they had certain values in common (such as frankness, loyalty, devotion to career, and commitment to community service). He thought, too, that she would be able to help him make DQE more innovative and attractive to talented prospective employees and customers. In short, von Shack believed that Green could make a substantial contribution to his organization. Nevertheless, he realized the obstacles she might face in an organization in which (when she first joined the company) white men held practically all middle- and upper-management positions. How would first-line managers who had never reported to any woman feel about reporting to an African American woman?

Von Shack took an active role in mentoring Green so that she would have the opportunity to help his company change, improve, and gain a competitive advantage. He made sure that she had an understanding of DQE's conservative

corporate culture when she first started out. Von Shack took great pains to make sure that employees at DQE realized the contributions that Green was making to the company. He and his family even attended community affairs that Green was involved with to show his support of and admiration for her. He praised her capabilities to top managers outside DQE and thereby helped her gain positions on the boards of directors of other companies.

Von Shack was not content to keep Green in charge of human resources (a department that in many companies turns out to be limbo for many female and minority managers). He believed that she could make a more wide-ranging contribution to the organization, and he gave her the opportunities to do so. She now manages purchasing, transportation, customer service, real estate, materials management, and public affairs for DQE. Green is one of DQE's four top managers, and von Shack remains impressed with her ability to meet the challenges he presents her with.

While von Shack's mentoring has helped Green advance to her current top management position, it also has helped von Shack run his company. In Green he has a valuable top manager on whom he often tests out his ideas because he knows she will give him an honest reaction. Green is making major contributions to DQE and also helps von Shack in his grassroots efforts to diversify top management at other organizations. For example, when von Shack and top managers from other companies were scheduled to meet with Pennsylvania's governor, he sent Green in his place to deliberately try to diversify the group.

Green and von Shack acknowledge that they both have benefited greatly from the mentoring relationship they started practically 10 years ago. The fact that they were different from each other in race and gender never seemed to be an issue. Green says that von Shack is completely comfortable with women occupying powerful positions in organizations and with interacting with people of different races. What they both seem to focus on is what they have in common, such as their approach to management and their values, while at the same time valuing and respecting each other as individuals.[81]

Questions

1. Why are top and middle managers often reluctant to mentor diverse lower-level managers and nonmanagers even when such mentoring relationships can have tremendous payoffs as has been true for von Shack and Green?

2. What steps can managers take to mentor diverse organizational members?

3. What steps can a top manager take to encourage other top and middle managers to mentor diverse organizational members?

ManagementCase

In the News

From the Pages of **BusinessWeek**

How Executive Greed Cost Shareholders $675 Million

On July 22, Computer Associates International Inc.'s shares sank nearly 31%, to 391/2. Sure, the market was off that day. Yes, the company did warn that earnings and sales growth would be adversely affected for several quarters by the Asian meltdown. But really, the thrashing the stock took can be attributed to one item in its first-quarter report: a $675 million aftertax charge taken to pay three top executives, including Chairman and Chief Executive Officer Charles B. Wang, $1.1 billion in stock. Before the charge, the company earned $194.2 million; after the charge, it lost $480.8 million.

Even for Wall Street, the greedy excess was shocking. But what's more remarkable is how this could happen—and with shareholder approval.

The pay package, which received a nod from 78% of voting shareholders in their 1995 proxies, called for giving, not selling, CEO Wang, President Sanjay Kumar, and Executive Vice-President Russell M. Artzt more than 20 million shares if the company's stock closed above $53.33 for 60 days in a 12-month period. Wang was handed more than 12 million shares, then worth $670 million, while his two subordinates got the remainder, worth $447 million. The charge itself—the largest ever declared by a public company for executive pay—equaled 43% of Computer Associates entire net income for the three previous years.

Compensation plans that offer incentive rewards to executives based on hitting a stock price target are nothing new. In fact, they are generally thought to be shareholder-friendly, because at least they ensure that investors make money before executives do.

Clearly, Computer Associates' executive largesse is extraordinary. But it illustrates a fundamental flaw of incentives tied to stock prices when used in a bull market. When all boats are rising on the same powerful tide, a company's stock price is a flimsy measure of a company's actual strength and provides an equally bad yardstick with which to size up bonuses or pay. Almost uniformly, these plans do not take into account relative performance in either the overall market or in a company's industry group. In Computer Associates' case, some 44% of the companies in the Standard & Poor's 500-stock index racked up greater stock gains than CA since the plan won board approval in 1995.

A good deal of the blame for this should go to Computer Associates' compensation panel, which recommended the plan to shareholders. The three members of that committee are Richard A. Grasso, chairman and CEO of the New York Stock Exchange; William F. P. de Vogel, president of investment advisers Three Cities Research; and Irving Goldstein, CEO of Intelstat, a satellite-telecom company. None could be reached for comment. A spokesman defended the plan, saying it was designed to "enhance shareholder value for all CA shareholders."

But why would shareholders O.K. a plan that would severely hurt earnings? At the time, the company was doing extremely well—total shareholder return was a remarkable 93% the year before. "Whenever you perform like that, shareholders are likely to support just about anything," says Patrick S. McGurn, a vice-president at Institutional Shareholder Services, which urged a "no" vote on the plan.

Even in such flush times, however, shareholders might have thought twice had they fully appreciated the cost. Pay proposals are often written in language that's difficult even for pros to fathom. The way the Computer Associates options were presented was particularly opaque, says Graef "Bud" Crystal, the executive pay critic. "It was deliberately designed to be misleading and obfuscating," he says. Crystal says he would have had to do a day's worth of computer modeling to figure out the plan's impact.

That shouldn't be necessary. To help shareholders understand what they're voting on, the Securities & Exchange Commission should consider new rules forcing companies to spell out a resolution's implications and potential consequences. For instance, every new pay plan should have an impact statement detailing the potential cost to shareholders in dilution or charges to earnings. If Computer Associates' investors had understood that they were voting to erase hundreds of millions of dollars of net income, it's highly unlikely the billion-dollar pay pack would have passed. The SEC needs to act now to make sure that shareholders in other companies do not find out too late how much lush executive pay has cost them.

Source: John A. Byrne, "How Executive Greed Cost Shareholders $675 Million," *Business Week,* August 10, 1998, 29.

Questions

1. Which stakeholder groups were most affected by Computer Associates' new pay proposal?
2. What kinds of ethical issues does the new pay proposal raise?

Part 3

Chapter six

The Manager as a Decision Maker

Learning Objectives

1. Differentiate between programmed and nonprogrammed decisions, and explain why nonprogrammed decision making is a complex, uncertain process.

2. Describe the six steps that managers should take to make the best decisions.

3. Explain how cognitive biases can affect decision making and lead managers to make poor decisions.

4. Identify the advantages and disadvantages of group decision making, and describe techniques that can improve it.

5. Explain the role that organizational learning and creativity play in helping managers to improve their decisions.

A Case in Contrast

A Tale of Two Decisions at Calling Systems International

August 14, 1997, 9:30 AM Sharon Eastman glances one last time at her presentation slides. "This new product proposal looks unbeatable," she thinks. "I've covered every base and looked at the issue from every angle. I know the technology; I can handle any question that Redland throws at me. He has to approve this."

Sharon Eastman is the marketing manager at Calling Systems International (CSI), a 350-employee, Denver-based company that makes computer-controlled telephone calling and answering equipment. CSI was the creation of Alan Redland, an energetic man with a domineering personality and seemingly unlimited faith in his own vision. Redland had founded CSI five years earlier. Already the company had made the *Inc.* magazine list of the 100 fastest-growing small companies in America. Sharon was hired 12 months ago

Finding the right way to frame your arguments is an important part of the process of convincing others to take your ideas seriously and support your position. Managing the perceptions of individuals and groups is an important part of the decision making process.

as a newly minted MBA. Prior to getting her MBA, she had worked as a computer systems engineer for IBM.

Sharon's responsibilities as marketing manager at CSI include looking for new product opportunities. She has found what she thinks is a gem. Three months earlier, Sharon was visiting the credit collection department of a large bank to which CSI was trying to sell its equipment. The staff of this department tries to collect bad debts from delinquent loan customers over the phone. Sharon noticed that many of the employees spend an enormous amount of time dialing phone numbers, getting busy signals, or getting no answer at all. Little of their time is spent actually talking to delinquent customers.

"Wow," thought Sharon. "It should be possible to predict how often a telephone operator gets no answer, or a busy signal. We could also find out how long, on average, an operator talks to someone over the phone. We could write a computer program that takes this into account. This program could be used to control an automated dialing system. We could use a mathematical algorithm to predict when an operator will come free and how much time will be needed to get a 'live' person on the other end of the phone line. The dialing system, let's call it a *predictive dialing system,* would then know when to dial in order to match up a free telephone operator with a 'live' person. The result? Telephone operators would waste no time dialing, listening to busy signals, or getting no answer. Brilliant!"

Over the past three months Sharon worked on the idea with two engineers at CSI. She concluded that the idea not only was technically feasible but could be a commercial gold mine. Now she has to present her new product proposal to CSI's executive committee, which is composed of Redland and three other senior managers. They could OK the idea or kill it.

August 14, 1997, 11:00 AM   An angry and dejected Sharon bursts through her office and flings her presentation slides against the opposite wall. Her office mate Ron looks up and raises an eyebrow. "I gather things didn't go too well then?"

"It was awful, a complete disaster. Redland has just come back from some seminar at MIT on the information superhighway. He has decided that the company has to become involved in that area. He thinks he has seen the future, and we should be part of it. He wouldn't even let me explain my idea. He just kept asking me, 'How does this fit with our information superhighway strategy?' What information superhighway strategy? I didn't know we had one!"

"Didn't any of the other executive committee members speak up on your behalf?" asks Ron. "I know that Mike Kidder and John Matsuka were excited by the idea. They told me so."

"They just hung on every word Redland said and nodded in agreement," replies Sharon.

March 12, 1998, 9:30 AM   Sharon sits waiting for the summons from the executive team. "Here we go again, Predictive Dialing Systems Proposal Mark II," thinks Sharon. "It should be different this time."

Sharon's faith was not ill placed. Two months earlier, CSI was taken over by a large telecommunications company. Redland and the rest of the executive team left and were replaced by a team of managers from the acquiring company.

March 12, 1998, 3:30 PM An exhausted-looking Sharon stumbles into her office and slumps into her chair. "Where on earth have you been?" asks Ron.

"With the new executive team," replies Sharon. "They have been quizzing me for hours about the project. We didn't stop for lunch. They wanted to know absolutely everything. How big was the potential market? How much would the predictive dialing system sell for? What were my data sources? What were my assumptions? They challenged every single assumption I made! How did I know that this was technically feasible? How long would it take to get a predictive dialing system to market? And on and on and on!"

"And?" asks Ron.

Sharon takes a deep breath, "And, they liked the idea, but not enough to give me the go-ahead yet. They want some specific information on various topics. But they said that if things do check out, they will invest in the project. And if they do, I get to head it!"[1] ●

Overview

The "Case in Contrast" describes how two different management teams approached the same decision—namely, whether to pursue Sharon Eastman's new product idea. The first team dismissed Eastman's proposal without exploring it because it was not the brainchild of Alan Redland, the company's domineering CEO. The second management team not only listened to Sharon Eastman but bombarded her with questions, vigorously challenging the assumptions behind her proposal to determine its validity.

The purpose of this chapter is to examine how managers make decisions and to explore how individual, group, and organizational factors affect the quality of the decisions they make and thus determine organizational performance. We discuss the nature of managerial decision making and examine some models of the decision-making process that help reveal the complexities of successful decision making. Then we outline the main steps of the decision-making process; in addition, we explore the biases that may cause capable managers to make poor decisions both as individuals and as members of a group. Finally, we examine how managers can promote organizational learning and creativity and improve the quality of their decision making. By the end of this chapter you will understand the crucial role decision making plays in creating a high-performing organization. ●

The Nature of Managerial Decision Making

Every time a manager acts to plan, organize, direct, or control organizational activities, he or she makes a stream of decisions. In opening a new restaurant, for example, managers have to decide where to locate it, what kinds of food to provide to customers, what kinds of people to employ, and so on. Decision making is a basic part of every task in which a manager is involved, and in this chapter we study how decisions are made.

As we discussed in the previous three chapters, one of the main tasks facing a manager is to manage the organizational environment. Forces in the external environment give rise to many opportunities and threats for managers and their organizations. In addition, inside an organization managers must address many opportunities and threats that may arise during the course of utilizing organizational resources. To deal with these opportunities and threats, managers must make decisions—that is, they must select one solution from a set of alternatives. **Decision making** is the process by which managers respond to the opportunities and threats that confront them by analyzing the options and making determinations, or *decisions,* about specific organizational goals and courses of action. A good decision results in the selection of appropriate goals and courses of action that increase organizational performance; bad decisions result in lower performance.

Decision making is central to being a manager, and whenever managers engage in planning, organizing, leading, and controlling—their four principal functions—they are constantly making decisions. *Decision making in response to opportunities* occurs when managers search for ways to improve organizational performance to benefit customers, employees, and other stakeholder groups. In the "Case in Contrast," Sharon Eastman saw an opportunity to create a new product and develop a new telephone calling system that would appeal to customer-calling companies. *Decision making in response to threats* occurs when events inside or outside the organization are adversely affecting organizational performance and managers are searching for ways to increase performance.[2] For example, top managers must decide how to react to an aggressive foreign competitor with a new automated telephone calling system that outperforms their own and is taking away so many customers that salespeople have failed to meet their sales goals.

decision making

The process by which managers respond to opportunities and threats by analyzing options and making determinations about specific organizational goals and courses of action.

To regain market share from Coca-Cola when its sales dropped in many foreign markets, Pepsi's managers were forced to devise a wide range of innovative marketing approaches to attract consumers back. Shown is a promotion in Britain to launch Pepsi Max that involved the decision to give away 3.5 million cans of cola.

Managers are always searching for ways to improve their decision making in order to improve organizational performance. At the same time, they do their best to make sure that they make no costly mistakes that will hurt organizational performance. Examples of spectacularly good decisions include Liz Claiborne's decision in the 1980s to focus on producing clothes for the growing numbers of women entering the workforce—a decision that contributed to making her company one of the largest clothing manufacturers; and Bill Gates's decision to buy a computer operating system for $50,000 from a small company in Seattle and sell it to IBM for the new IBM personal computer—a decision that resulted in Gates and Microsoft, respectively, becoming the richest man and richest software company in the United States. Examples of spectacularly bad decisions include the decision by managers at NASA and Morton Thiokol to launch the *Challenger* space shuttle—a decision that resulted in the deaths of six astronauts in 1986; and the decision of Ken Olsen, founder of Digital Equipment Corporation, to stay with mainframe computers in the 1980s and not allow his engineers to spend the company's resources to create new kinds of personal computers because of his belief that "personal computers are just toys"—a decision that cost Olsen his job as CEO and almost ruined his company.

Programmed and Nonprogrammed Decision Making

Regardless of the specific decision that a manager is responsible for, the decision-making process is either programmed or nonprogrammed.[3]

PROGRAMMED DECISION MAKING   Programmed decision making is a *routine,* virtually automatic process. Programmed decisions are decisions that have been made so many times in the past that managers have been able to develop rules or guidelines to be applied when certain situations inevitably occur. Programmed decision making takes place when a school principal asks the school board to hire a new teacher whenever student enrollment increases by 40 students; when a manufacturing supervisor hires new workers whenever existing workers' overtime increases by more than 10 percent; and when an office manager orders basic office supplies, such as paper and pens, whenever the inventory of supplies on hand drops below a certain level. Furthermore, in the last example, the office manager probably orders the same amount of supplies each time. This decision making is called programmed because the office manager, for example, does not need to continually make judgments about what should be done. He or she can rely on long-established decision rules such as these:

- *Rule 1:* When the storage shelves are three-quarters empty, order more copy paper.
- *Rule 2:* When ordering paper, order enough to fill the shelves.

Managers can develop rules and guidelines to regulate all kinds of routine organizational activities. For example, rules can specify how a worker should perform a certain task, and rules can specify the quality standards that raw materials must meet to be acceptable. Most decision making that relates to the day-to-day running of an organization is programmed decision making. For example, decision making about how much inventory to hold, when to pay bills, when to bill customers, and when to take nonpaying customers to court is likely to fall into the programmed category. Programmed decision making is possible when managers have the information they need to create rules that will guide decision making. There is little ambiguity to overcome when assessing whether the stockroom is empty or when counting the number of new students in class.

NONPROGRAMMED DECISION MAKING   Suppose, however, managers are not certain that a course of action will lead to a desired outcome. Or, in a more ambiguous scenario, suppose managers are not even clear about what they are really trying to achieve. Obviously, rules cannot be developed to predict uncertain events. **Nonprogrammed decision making** is required for these *nonroutine* decisions. Nonprogrammed decisions are decisions that are made in response to unusual or novel opportunities and threats. Nonprogrammed decision making occurs when there are no ready-made decision rules that managers can apply to a situation. Why are there no rules? The situation is unexpected, and managers lack the information they would need to develop rules to cover it. Examples of nonprogrammed decision making include decisions to invest in a new kind of technology, to develop a new kind of product, to launch a new promotional campaign, to enter a new market, or to expand internationally.

How do managers make decisions in the absence of decision rules? First they must search for information about alternative courses of action; then they must rely on intuition and judgment to choose wisely among alternatives. **Intuition** is a person's ability to make sound decisions based on one's past experience and immediate feelings about the information at his or her disposal. **Judgment** is a person's ability to develop a sound opinion because of the way he or she evaluates the importance of the information available in a particular context. "Exercising" one's judgment is a more rational process than "going with" one's intuition. For reasons that we examine later in this chapter, both intuition and judgment are often flawed and can result in poor decision making. Thus, the likelihood of error is much greater in nonprogrammed decision making than in programmed decision making.[4] In the remainder of this chapter, when we talk about decision making, we are referring to *nonprogrammed* decision making because it is the type of decision making that causes the most problems for managers.

The classical and the administrative decision-making models reveal many of the assumptions, complexities, and pitfalls that affect decision making. These models help reveal the factors that managers and other decision makers must be aware of in order to improve the quality of their decision making. It is important to remember that the classical and administrative models are just that—guides that can help managers understand the decision-making process. In real life, the process is typically not cut-and-dried; these models, however, can help guide a manager through it.

The Classical Model

One of the earliest models of decision making, the **classical model,** is *prescriptive,* which means that it specifies how decisions *should* be made. Managers using the classical model make a series of simplifying assumptions about the nature of the decision-making process (see Figure 6.1). The premise of the

---

nonprogrammed decision making Nonroutine decision making that occurs in response to unusual, unpredictable opportunities and threats.

intuition Ability to make sound decisions based on one's past experience and immediate feelings about the information at hand. **judgment** Ability to develop a sound opinion based on one's evaluation of the importance of the information at hand.

classical decision-making model A prescriptive approach to decision making based on the assumption that the decision maker can identify and evaluate all possible alternatives and their consequences and rationally choose the most appropriate course of action.

Figure 6.1
The Classical Model of Decision Making

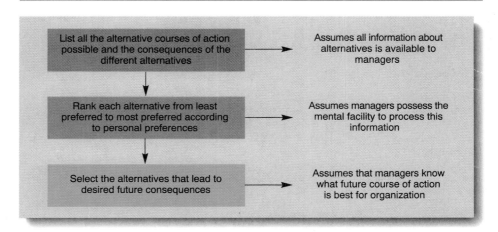

classical model is that once managers recognize the need to make a decision, they should be able to generate a complete list of *all* alternatives and consequences, from which they then can make the best choice. In other words, the classical model assumes that managers have access to *all* the information they need to make the **optimum decision,** which is the most appropriate decision possible in light of what they believe to be the most desirable future consequences for their organization. Furthermore, the classical model assumes that managers can easily list their own preferences for each alternative and rank them from least to most preferred in order to make the optimum decision.

The Administrative Model

James March and Herbert Simon disagreed with the underlying assumptions of the classical model of decision making. In contrast, they proposed that managers in the real world do *not* have access to all the information they need to make a decision. Moreover, they pointed out that even if all information were readily available, many managers would lack the mental or psychological ability to absorb and evaluate it correctly. As a result, March and Simon developed the **administrative model** of decision making to explain why decision making is always an inherently uncertain and risky process—and why managers can rarely make decisions in the manner prescribed by the classical model. The administrative model is based on three important concepts: *bounded rationality, incomplete information,* and *satisfying.*

BOUNDED RATIONALITY   March and Simon pointed out that human decision-making capabilities are bounded by people's cognitive limitations—that is, limitations in their ability to interpret, process, and act on information.[5] They argued that the limitations of human intelligence constrain the ability of decision makers to determine the optimum decision; and they coined the term **bounded rationality** to describe the situation in which the number of alternatives a manager must identify is so great and the amount of information so vast that it is difficult for the manager to even come close to evaluating it all before making a decision.[6]

optimum decision

The most appropriate decision in light of what managers believe to be the most desirable future consequences for their organization.

administrative model

An approach to decision making that explains why decision making is inherently uncertain and risky and why managers usually make satisfactory rather than optimum decisions.

bounded rationality

Cognitive limitations that constrain one's ability to interpret, process, and act on information.

Figure 6.2
Why Information Is Incomplete

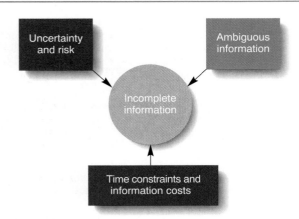

INCOMPLETE INFORMATION   Even if managers did have an unlimited ability to evaluate information, they still would not be able to arrive at the optimum decision because they would have incomplete information. Information is incomplete because the full range of decision-making alternatives is unknowable in most situations and the consequences associated with known alternatives are uncertain.[7] In other words, information is incomplete because of risk and uncertainty, ambiguity, and time constraints (see Figure 6.2).

RISK AND UNCERTAINTY   As we saw in Chapter 3, forces in the organizational environment are constantly changing. **Risk** is present when managers know the possible outcomes of a particular course of action and can assign probabilities to them. For example, managers in the biotechnology industry know that there is a 10 percent probability that a drug will successfully pass advanced clinical trials and a 90 percent probability that it will fail. These probabilities are known from the experiences of thousands of drugs that have gone through advanced clinical trials. Thus, when managers in the biotechnology industry decide whether to submit a drug for testing, they know that there is only a 10 percent chance that the drug will succeed, but at least they have some information on which to base their decision.

When **uncertainty** exists, the probabilities of alternative outcomes *cannot* be determined, and future outcomes are *unknown:* Managers are working blind, the probability of a given outcome occurring is *not* known, and managers have little information to use in making a decision. For example, in 1993, when Apple Computer introduced the Newton, its personal digital assistant (PDA), managers had no idea what the probability of a successful product launch for a PDA might be. Because Apple was the first to market this totally new type of product, there was no body of well-known data that Apple's managers could draw on to calculate the probability of a successful launch. Uncertainty plagues most managerial decision making.[8] Although Apple's initial launch of its PDA was a disaster due to technical problems, an improved version was more successful, and Apple has created a market for this product.

AMBIGUOUS INFORMATION   A second reason why information is incomplete is that much of the information that managers have at their dis-

risk The degree of probability that the possible outcomes of a particular course of action will occur.

uncertainty
Unpredictability.

Figure 6.3
Ambiguous Information: Young Woman or Old Woman?

ambiguous information

Information that can be interpreted in multiple and often conflicting ways.

posal is **ambiguous information.** Its meaning is not clear—it can be interpreted in multiple and often conflicting ways.[9] Take a look at Figure 6.3. Do you see a young woman or an old woman? In a similar fashion, different managers often interpret the same piece of information differently and make different decisions based on their own interpretations.

TIME CONSTRAINTS AND INFORMATION COSTS   The third reason why information is incomplete is that managers have neither the time nor the money to search for all possible alternative solutions and evaluate all the potential consequences of those alternatives. Consider the situation confronting a purchasing manager at Ford Motor Company who has one month to choose a supplier for a small engine part. There are thousands of potential suppliers for this part (there are 20,000 auto suppliers in the United States alone). Given the time available, there is no way for the purchasing manager to contact all potential suppliers and ask each for its terms (price, delivery schedules, and so on). Moreover, even if the time were available, the costs of obtaining the information, including the manager's own time, would be prohibitive.

satisficing Searching for and choosing an acceptable, or satisfactory, response to problems and opportunities, rather than trying to make the best decision.

SATISFICING   Faced with bounded rationality, an uncertain future, unquantifiable risks, considerable ambiguity, time constraints, and high information costs, March and Simon argue, managers do not attempt to discover every alternative. Rather, they use a strategy known as **satisficing,** exploring a limited sample of all potential alternatives.[10] When managers satisfice, they search for and choose acceptable, or satisfactory ways to respond to problems and opportunities rather than trying to make the optimum decision. In the case of the Ford purchasing manager, limited search involves asking a limited number of suppliers for their terms, trusting that they are representative of suppliers in general, and making a choice from that set. Although this course of action is reasonable from the perspective of the purchasing manager, it may mean that a potentially superior supplier is overlooked.

March and Simon pointed out that managerial decision making is often more art than science. In the real world, managers must rely on their intuition and judgment to make what seems to them to be the best decision in the face of uncertainty and ambiguity.[12] Consider, for example, the crucial decisions that Bill Jemas, a vice president of entertainment and business development at Fleet Corporation, a leading trading-card company, has to make.

Management Insight

Marketing Beavis and Butt-Head Trading Cards

As usual, Bill Jemas is under pressure. He must quickly make several crucial decisions about the marketing strategy for a new line of Beavis and Butt-Head trading cards to be launched by the Fleet Corporation (Beavis and Butt-Head are cartoon characters from a popular MTV show). At 10:00 AM two other managers, Lisa Weiner and Donna Johnson (production manager and assistant production manager respectively), enter Jemas's office to discuss the launch strategy. The trio begin a serious discussion about the cards' design and where the Fleet logo will appear. While two possible designs are being considered, the question of how to set the retail price for the cards is raised. The trio quickly arrive at a decision. Beavis and Butt-Head are extremely popular characters, they reason, so the cards should command a premium price—$1.79 per pack.[13] After agreeing on the price, they return to the design issue. By 10:15, it too has been settled.

Jemas and the others then turn their attention to advertising. A six-figure advertising budget has already been assigned to the project, and the trio have to decide where to spend the money. The target market group is primarily teenage boys, and the trio quickly decide to place advertisements in publications that serve this audience, including *Tough Stuff* and *Metal Edge*. Then a more involved discussion takes place about whether to advertise in *Rolling Stone* magazine, which covered Beavis and Butt-Head in a 1993 issue. *Rolling Stone* is considered an expensive alternative for the company, but the trio are leaning toward advertising with the magazine, particularly since the cards will be sold in record stores. "I heard that they [referring to the Beavis and Butt-Head cover issue] were *Rolling Stone*'s top selling issue last year," offers Lisa. Jemas likes the idea, but a final decision will have to wait a day or two. A larger advertising budget may be required.

It's now 10:30 AM and representatives from Daniel Edelman Inc., a New York public relations firm, enter the office. The conversation turns to the PR campaign that Edelman has planned for the Beavis and Butt-Head line. A decision has to be made about sampling (sampling involves sending out samples of the line—in this case to magazine writers). The group debates the pros and cons of sampling. "I think people just like to get stuff," says Jemas. It's agreed—a pack of cards will be sent to writers at all relevant magazines. At 11:50 AM the meeting ends with a swift discussion of Edelman's bill. Time for lunch.

Two things may surprise you about the previous example. First, the managers made a number of critical decisions very quickly. Two decisions, one about pricing and one about design, were made in 15 minutes. The pricing decision appeared to be almost an afterthought. A third decision, about advertising media, was made in the next 15 minutes. The final decision, about sampling, took longer to make, partly because the Edelman people required time to present examples of their work. Nevertheless, four crucial decisions were made in under two hours.

The second fact that stands out is that for each of their decisions, these managers were clearly satisficing. Knowing they had incomplete information, they did not try to discover all possible solutions and get involved in a detailed analysis of the pros and cons of different alternatives. Instead, they relied on their experience in this business and used their judgment to satisfice and reach an acceptable decision on crucial issues.

The Beavis and Butt-Head example illustrates that managerial decision making is often fast paced, as managers use their experience and judgment to make crucial decisions under conditions of incomplete information. Although there is nothing wrong with this approach, decision makers should be aware that human judgment is often flawed. As a result, even the best managers sometimes make poor decisions.[14] Later in this chapter we discuss cognitive and other factors that tend to skew decision making.

Steps in the Decision-Making Process

Using the work of March and Simon as a basis, researchers have developed a step-by-step model of the decision-making process and the issues and problems that managers confront at each step. Perhaps the best way to introduce this model is to examine the real-world nonprogrammed decision making that Scott McNealy, CEO of Sun Microsystems, (a computer workstation manufacturer based in Mountain View, California), had to engage in at a crucial point in his company's history.

In early August 1985, McNealy had to decide whether to go ahead with the launch of the company's new Carrera workstation computer, scheduled for September 10. Sun's managers had chosen the September 10 date nine months earlier when the development plan for the Carrera was first proposed. McNealy knew that it would take at least a month to prepare for the September 10 launch and that the decision could not be put off.

Customers were waiting for the new machine, and McNealy wanted to be the first to provide a workstation that took advantage of Motorola's powerful 16 megahertz 68020 microprocessor. Capitalizing on this opportunity would give Sun a significant edge over Apollo, its main competitor in the workstation market. McNealy knew, however, that committing to the September 10 launch date was risky. Motorola was having production problems with the 16 megahertz 68020 microprocessor and could not guarantee Sun a steady supply of these chips. Moreover, the operating system software was not completely free of bugs.

If Sun launched the Carrera on September 10, the company might have to ship some machines with software that was not fully operational and prone to crash the system and that utilized Motorola's less-powerful 12 megahertz 68020 microprocessor instead of the 16 megahertz version.[15] Of course, Sun could later upgrade the microprocessor and operating system software in any machines purchased by early customers, but the company's reputation would

Figure 6.4
Six Steps in Decision Making

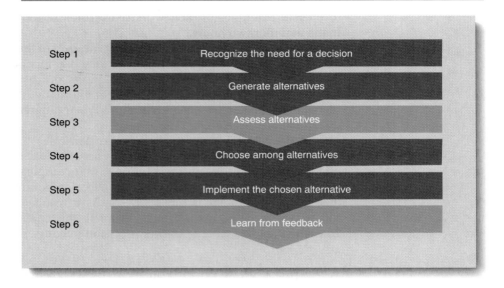

Step 1	Recognize the need for a decision
Step 2	Generate alternatives
Step 3	Assess alternatives
Step 4	Choose among alternatives
Step 5	Implement the chosen alternative
Step 6	Learn from feedback

suffer as a result. If Sun did not go ahead with the September launch, the company would miss an important opportunity.[16] Rumors were circulating in the industry that Apollo would be launching a new machine of its own in December. McNealy wondered what he should do. The microprocessor and operating system problems might be resolved by September 10, but then again they might not be.

Scott McNealy clearly had a difficult decision to make. He had to decide quickly whether to launch the Carrera, but he was not in full possession of the facts. He did not know, for example, whether the microprocessor or operating system problems could be resolved by September 10; nor did he know whether Apollo was indeed going to launch a competing machine in December. But he could not wait to find these things out—he had to make a decision. Later in the chapter we'll see what he decided.

A dilemma similar to McNealy's is faced by many managers who must make important decisions with incomplete information. There are six steps that managers should consciously follow to make a good decision (see Figure 6.4).[17] We review them in the remainder of this section.

Recognize the Need for a Decision

The first step in the decision-making process is to recognize the need for a decision. Scott McNealy recognized this need, and he realized that a decision had to be made quickly because it would take a month to get ready for the September 10 launch. McNealy also knew that the September 10 launch was a critical goal because Sun needed to beat Apollo to the market with a new machine to gain a competitive advantage over this strong challenger.

Some stimuli usually spark the realization that there is a need to make a decision. These stimuli often become apparent because changes in the organizational environment result in new kinds of opportunities and threats. This happened at Sun Microsystems. The September 10 launch date had been set when it seemed that Motorola chips would be readily available. Later, with the supply of chips in doubt and bugs remaining in the system software, Sun was in danger of failing to meet its launch date.

The stimuli that spark decision making are as likely to result from the actions of managers inside an organization as they are from changes in the external environment.[18] An organization possesses a set of skills, competencies, and resources in its employees and in departments such as marketing, manufacturing, and research and development. Managers who actively pursue opportunities to use these competencies create the need to make decisions. For example, Sharon Eastman, described in the "Case in Contrast," was on the lookout to find an opportunity to use Calling Systems International's competency to develop a new kind of telephone answering system, and she forced the company's managers to recognize that they needed to make a decision. Managers thus can be reactive or proactive in recognizing the need to make a decision, but the important issue is that they must recognize this need and respond in a timely and appropriate way.[19]

Generate Alternatives

Having recognized the need to make a decision, a manager must generate a set of feasible alternative courses of action to take in response to the opportunity or threat. Management experts cite failure to properly generate and consider different alternatives as one reason why managers sometimes make bad decisions.[20] In the Sun decision, the alternatives seem clear: to go ahead with the September 10 launch or to delay the launch until the Carrera was 100 percent ready for market introduction. Often, however, the alternatives are not so obvious or so clearly specified.

One major problem is that managers may find it difficult to come up with creative alternative solutions to specific problems. Perhaps some of them are used to seeing the world from a single perspective–they have a certain "managerial mind-set." In a manner similar to Digital's Olsen, many managers find it difficult to view problems from a fresh perspective. According to best-selling management author Peter Senge, we all are trapped within our personal mental models of the world–our ideas about what is important and how the world works.[21] Generating creative alternatives to solve problems and take advantage of opportunities may require that we abandon our existing mind-sets and develop new ones–something that usually is difficult to do.

The importance of getting managers to set aside their mental models of the world and generate creative alternatives is reflected in the growth of interest in the work of authors such as Peter Senge and Edward de Bono, who have popularized techniques for stimulating problem solving and creative thinking among managers.[22] Later in this chapter, we discuss the important issues of organizational learning and creativity in detail.

Assess Alternatives

Once managers have generated a set of alternatives, they must evaluate the advantages and disadvantages of each one.[23] The key to a good assessment of the alternatives is to define the opportunity or threat exactly and then specify the criteria that *should* influence the selection of alternatives for responding to

Figure 6.5
General Criteria for Evaluating Possible Courses of Action

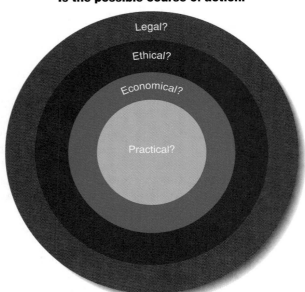

the problem or opportunity. One reason for bad decisions is that managers often fail to specify the criteria that are important in reaching a decision.[24] In general, successful managers use four criteria to evaluate the pros and cons of alternative courses of action (see Figure 6.5):

1. *Legality:* Managers must ensure that a possible course of action is legal and that they will not be in violation of any domestic and international laws or government regulations.

2. *Ethicalness:* Managers must ensure that a possible course of action is ethical and that it will not unnecessarily harm any stakeholder group. Many of the decisions that managers make may help some organizational stakeholders and harm others (see Chapter 5). When examining alternative courses of action, managers need to be very clear about the potential effects of their decisions.

3. *Economic feasibility:* Managers must decide whether the alternatives are economically feasible–that is, whether they can be accomplished, given the organization's performance goals. Typically, managers perform a cost–benefit analysis of the various alternatives to determine which one is likely to have the best net financial payoff.

4. *Practicality:* Managers must decide whether they have the capabilities and resources required to implement the alternative, and they must be sure that the alternative will not threaten the attainment of other organizational goals. At first glance, an alternative might seem to be economically superior to other alternatives, but if managers realize that it is likely to threaten other important projects, they might decide that it is not practical after all.

Very often, a manager must consider these four criteria simultaneously. Scott McNealy framed the problem at hand at Sun Microsystems quite well.

The key question was whether to go ahead with the September 10 launch date. Two main criteria were influencing McNealy's choice: the need to ship a machine that was as "complete" as possible (the *practicality* criterion) and the need to beat Apollo to market with a new workstation (the *economic feasibility* criterion). These two criteria conflicted. The first suggested that the launch should be delayed, the second that the launch should go ahead. McNealy's actual choice was based on the relative importance that he assigned to these two criteria. In fact, Sun Microsystems went ahead with the September 10 launch, which suggests that McNealy thought the need to beat Apollo to market was the more important criterion.

Some of the worst managerial decisions can be traced to poor assessment of the alternatives, such as the decision to launch the *Challenger* space shuttle discussed earlier. In that case, the desire of NASA and Morton Thiokol managers to demonstrate to the U.S. public the success of the U.S. space program in order to ensure future funding *(economic feasibility)* conflicted with the need to ensure the safety of the astronauts *(ethicalness)*. Managers deemed the economic criterion more important and decided to launch the space shuttle. At Digital Equipment, Olsen's remark that "personal computers are just toys" showed his lack of understanding of the economic considerations affecting competition in the computer industry. Selecting the right set of criteria by which to assess alternatives is never easy. Often it becomes necessary to collect additional information in order to make a satisfactory evaluation.

The disastrous launch of the Challenger space shuttle illustrates the importance of bringing all available information to bear on the decision-making process and making sure the alternative courses of action are evaluated using all relevant criteria.

Choose Among Alternatives

Once the set of alternative solutions has been carefully evaluated, the next task is to rank the various alternatives (using the criteria discussed in the previous section) and make a decision. When ranking alternatives, managers must be sure that *all* the information that is available is brought to bear on the problem or issue at hand. As the Sun case indicates, however, identifying all *relevant* information for a decision does not mean that the manager has *complete* information; in most instances, information is incomplete.

Perhaps more serious than the existence of incomplete information is the often-documented tendency of managers to ignore critical information even when it is available. We discuss this tendency in detail below when we examine the operation of cognitive biases and groupthink.

Implement the Chosen Alternative

Once a decision has been made and an alternative has been selected, the alternative must be implemented and many subsequent and related decisions must be made. Once a course of action has been decided (for example, to develop a new line of women's clothing), thousands of subsequent decisions are necessary to implement it (such as decisions to recruit dress designers, obtain fabrics, find high-quality manufacturers, and sign contracts with clothing stores to sell the new line).

Although the need to make subsequent decisions to implement the chosen course of action may seem obvious, many managers make a decision and then fail to act on it. This is the same as not making a decision at all. To ensure that a decision is implemented, top managers must assign to middle managers the responsibility for making the follow-up decisions necessary to achieve the goal. They must give middle managers sufficient resources to achieve the goal, and they must hold the middle managers accountable for their performance. If the middle managers are successful at implementing the decision, they should be rewarded; if they fail, they should be subject to sanctions.

Learn from Feedback

The final step in the decision-making process is learning from feedback. Effective managers always conduct a retrospective analysis to see what they can learn from past successes or failures. Managers who do not evaluate the results of their decisions do not learn from experience; instead, they stagnate and are likely to make the same mistakes again and again.[25] To avoid this problem, managers must establish a formal procedure with which they can learn from the results of past decisions. The procedure should include these steps:

1. Compare what actually happened to what was expected to happen as a result of the decision.

2. Explore why any expectations for the decision were not met.

3. Develop guidelines that will help in future decision making.

Managers who always strive to learn from past mistakes and successes are likely to continuously improve the decisions they make. The steps that managers at British Petroleum took to benefit from feedback are illustrated in this "Management Insight."

Management Insight

British Petroleum's Decision Auditing Unit

A few years ago, senior managers at British Petroleum (BP), one of the world's largest oil companies even before its 1998 merger with Amoco, realized that they had no procedure in place to help them learn from past decisions. To address this shortcoming, top managers created the Post-Project Appraisal Unit at BP's corporate headquarters in London. The objective of this unit was to conduct retrospective decision audits of important decisions to identify what could be learned from successes and failures, and to use this information to improve decision making at BP.

The unit was staffed with five managers who reported directly to BP's board of directors. It was charged with undertaking only six decision audits per year because, in the words of Frank Gulliver, one of the unit's founders, "The corporation can absorb only so much information at a time."[26] The unit was given complete freedom to select the decisions to be audited.

The decision auditing unit saved BP millions of dollars. As a result of one audit, for example, the unit discovered that BP was losing millions of dollars because it had been inadequately evaluating the capabilities of chemical and oil refinery contractors before hiring them. The unit suggested that the company create a separate team to evaluate contractors. Another audit of two separate decisions involving the construction of natural-gas conversion plants showed that a plant that had come in under budget and ahead of schedule, and therefore should have been highly profitable, subsequently produced poor returns. In contrast, another plant had been completed over budget and a year late yet turned out to be highly profitable. The unit's audit revealed that the timing of construction decisions, such as deciding in what year to begin construction, was the critical issue, rather than construction costs. For BP's managers, the vital component of the audit process was the development of much better techniques to forecast future demand patterns in individual markets in order to make more appropriate timing decisions.

The BP example illustrates that a significant amount of learning can take place when the outcomes of decisions are evaluated, and this assessment can produce enormous benefits. One great strength of BP's approach was that its decision auditing was performed by managers who worked in an independent unit that was not involved in the original decision and who, therefore, were more likely than the original decision makers to be objective in their assessment of the decision outcome. In contrast, when the original decision makers do the auditing, they are likely to try to present decisions in a favorable light—not necessarily for deceptive purposes but because the decisions were their "babies" and they are reluctant to second-guess themselves.

Tips for Managers

Managing the Decision Making Process

1. Recognize that it is impossible for managers to make the optimum decision and orient their actions to making the best decision possible.

2. To make the best decision possible, learn to use intuition and judgment to uncover acceptable alternatives and to choose between them.

3. Constantly monitor changes in organizational performance and in the environmental forces to discover if there are any opportunities or threats that need to be addressed.

4. Create a set of clearly defined criteria to frame opportunities and threats and apply these criteria consistently.

5. Encourage managers at all levels to make problem solving a major part of their jobs and to generate as many feasible alternatives as possible.

6. Be aware of the role people's preferences and interests play in generating alternative courses of action and learn how to manage coalitions to promote effective decision making.

7. Once an alternative course of action has been chosen, take steps to implement the decision. Request periodic updates on the situation from the managers responsible for implementing the chosen alternative.

8. Learn from your successes and mistakes and use this information to improve your next decision.

Cognitive Biases and Decision Making

heuristics Rules of thumb that simplify decision making.

systematic errors Errors that people make over and over and that result in poor decision making.

In the 1970s, two psychologists, Daniel Kahneman and Amos Tversky, suggested that because all decision makers are subject to bounded rationality, they tend to use **heuristics,** rules of thumb that simplify the process of making decisions.[27] Kahneman and Tversky argued that rules of thumb are often useful because they help decision makers make sense of complex, uncertain, and ambiguous information. Sometimes, however, the use of heuristics can lead to systematic errors in the way decision makers process information about alternatives and make decisions. **Systematic errors** are errors that people make over and over and that result in poor decision making. Because of cognitive biases, which are caused by systematic errors, otherwise capable managers may end up making bad decisions.[28] Four sources of bias that can adversely affect the way managers make decisions are prior hypotheses, representativeness, the illusion of control, and escalating commitment (see Figure 6.6).

Prior Hypothesis Bias

prior hypothesis bias A cognitive bias resulting from the tendency to base decisions on strong prior beliefs even if evidence shows that those beliefs are wrong.

Decision makers who have strong prior beliefs about the relationship between two variables tend to make decisions based on those beliefs *even when presented with evidence that their beliefs are wrong.* In doing so, they are falling victim to **prior hypothesis bias.** Moreover, decision makers tend to seek and use information that is consistent with their prior beliefs and to ignore information that contradicts those beliefs. At Calling Systems International (CSI), profiled in the "Case in Contrast," we saw CEO Alan Redland reject Sharon Eastman's new product proposal because it was not consistent with his prior beliefs about what CSI should be doing.

The prior hypothesis bias is also evident in the case of Bill Jemas and the Beavis and Butt-Head trading cards. Jemas and his associates quickly decided

Figure 6.6
Sources of Cognitive Bias at the Individual and Group Levels

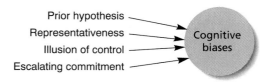

that the trading cards should be sold at a *premium* price. How could they make such an apparently important decision so quickly? One plausible answer is that a strong set of prior beliefs drove Jemas and his associates to this conclusion. They believed that Beavis and Butt-Head "were really hot right now, a sure winner."[29] Lisa Weiner's off-the-cuff comment that *Rolling Stone*'s top-selling issue featured Beavis and Butt-Head on the cover reinforced this belief. Notice, however, that they made no attempt to check the validity of their belief. There is no evidence that Jemas and his associates put their prior beliefs to even a minimal test such as by discussing the issue with retailers. Does this mean that the decision was incorrect? No, but it does suggest that the decision was the kind of intuitive decision that is prone to be affected by the prior hypothesis bias.

Representativeness Bias

representativeness bias A cognitive bias resulting from the tendency to generalize inappropriately from a small sample or from a single vivid event or episode.

Many decision makers inappropriately generalize from a small sample or even from a single vivid case or episode. An interesting example of the **representativeness bias** occurred after World War II, when Seawell Avery, CEO of Montgomery Ward, shelved plans for national expansion to meet competition from Sears because he believed there would be a depression after the war. The basis for Avery's belief was the occurrence of the Great Depression after World War I. However, there was no second Great Depression, and Avery's poor decision allowed Sears to establish itself as the number-one nationwide retailer. Avery's mistake was to generalize from the post–World War I experience and assume that "depressions always follow wars."

Illusion of Control

illusion of control A source of cognitive bias resulting from the tendency to overestimate one's own ability to control activities and events.

Other errors in decision making result from the **illusion of control,** the tendency of decision makers to overestimate their ability to control activities and events. Top-level managers seem to be particularly prone to this bias. Having worked their way to the top of an organization, they tend to have an exaggerated sense of their own worth and are overconfident about their ability to succeed and to control events.[30] The illusion of control causes managers to overestimate the odds of a favorable outcome and, consequently, to make inappropriate decisions. For example, in the 1980s, Nissan was run by Katsuji Kawamata, an autocratic manager who thought he had the skills to run the car company alone. He made all the decisions—decisions that resulted in a series of spectacular mistakes, including changing the company's name from Datsun to Nissan—and Nissan's share of the U.S. market fell dramatically.

Escalating Commitment

escalating commitment A source of cognitive bias resulting from the tendency to commit additional resources to a project even if evidence shows that the project is failing.

Having already committed significant resources to a course of action, some managers commit more resources to the project *even if they receive feedback that the project is failing.*[31] Feelings of personal responsibility for a project apparently bias the analysis of decision makers and lead to this **escalating commitment.** They decide to increase their investment of time and money in a course of action and ignore evidence that it is illegal, unethical, uneconomical, or impractical (see Figure 6.5). Often, the more appropriate decision would be to "cut and run."

A tragic example of where escalating commitment can lead is the *Challenger* disaster. Apparently, managers at both NASA and Morton Thiokol were so anxious to keep the shuttle program on schedule that they ignored or discounted any evidence that would slow the program down. Thus, the information offered by two engineers at Thiokol, who warned about O-ring failure in cold weather, was discounted, and the shuttle was launched on a chilly day in January 1986.

Another example of escalating commitment occurred during the 1960s and 1970s when large U.S. steelmakers responded to low-cost competition from minimills and foreign steelmakers by increasing their investments in the technologically obsolete steelmaking facilities they already possessed, rather than investing in new, cutting-edge technology.[32] This decision was irrational because investment in obsolete technology would never enable them to lower their costs and compete successfully.

Be Aware of Your Biases

How can managers avoid the negative effects of cognitive biases and improve their decision-making and problem-solving abilities? Managers must become aware of biases and their effects, and they must identify their own personal style of making decisions.[33] One useful way for managers to analyze their decision-making style is to review two decisions that they made recently—one decision that turned out well and one that turned out poorly. Problem-solving experts recommend that a manager start by determining how much time he or she spent on each of the decision-making steps, such as gathering information to identify the pros and cons of alternatives or ranking the alternatives, to make sure that sufficient time is being spent on each step.[34]

Another recommended technique for examining decision-making style is for managers to list the criteria they typically use to assess and evaluate alternatives—the heuristics (rules of thumb) they typically employ, their personal biases, and so on—and then critically evaluate the appropriateness of these different factors.

Many individual managers are likely to have difficulty identifying their own biases, so it is often advisable for managers to scrutinize their own assumptions by working with other managers to help expose weaknesses in their decision-making style. In this context, the issue of group decision making becomes important.

Group Decision Making

Many, perhaps most, important organizational decisions are made by groups of managers rather than by individuals. Group decision making is superior to individual decision making in several respects. When managers work as a team to make decisions and solve problems, their choices of alternatives are less likely to fall victim to the biases and errors discussed previously. They are able to draw on the combined skills, competencies, and accumulated knowledge of group members and thereby improve their ability to generate feasible alternatives and make good decisions. Group decision making also allows managers to process more information and to correct each other's errors. And in the implementation phase, all managers affected by the decisions agree to cooperate. When a group of managers makes a decision (as opposed to one top manager making a decision and imposing it on subordinate managers), the probability that the decision will be implemented successfully increases. (We discuss how to encourage employee participation in decision making in Chapter 15.)

Nevertheless, some disadvantages are associated with group decision making. Groups often take much longer than individuals to make decisions. Getting two or more managers to agree to the same solution can be difficult because managers' interests and preferences are often different. In addition, just like decision making by individual managers, group decision making can be undermined by biases. A major source of group bias is *groupthink*.

The Perils of Groupthink

groupthink A pattern of faulty and biased decision making that occurs in groups whose members strive for agreement among themselves at the expense of accurately assessing information relevant to a decision.

Groupthink is a pattern of faulty and biased decision making that occurs in groups whose members strive for agreement among themselves at the expense of accurately assessing information relevant to a decision.[35] When managers are subject to groupthink, they collectively embark on a course of action without developing appropriate criteria to evaluate alternatives. Typically, a group rallies around one central manager, such as the CEO, and the course of action that manager supports. Group members become blindly committed to that course of action without evaluating its merits. Commitment is often based on an emotional, rather than an objective, assessment of the optimal course of action.

In the "Case in Contrast," groupthink was probably at work when the first executive team at Calling Systems International, headed by Alan Redland, dismissed Sharon Eastman's new product proposal. Despite previously expressing support for Eastman's idea, two members of the executive team merely nodded their agreement with Redland when he criticized the proposal—a sure sign that pressures toward agreement were at work in this group. Pressures for agreement and harmony within a group have the unintended effect of discouraging individuals from raising issues that run counter to majority opinion. This same process preceded the *Challenger* disaster, as managers at NASA and Morton Thiokol fell victim to groupthink, convincing each other that all was well and that there was no need to delay the launch of the shuttle.

Devil's Advocacy and Dialectical Inquiry

The existence of cognitive biases and groupthink raises the question of how to improve the quality of group and individual decision making so that managers make decisions that are realistic and based on a thorough evaluation of alternatives. Two techniques known to counteract groupthink and cognitive biases are devil's advocacy and dialectical inquiry (see Figure 6.7).[36]

Figure 6.7
Devil's Advocacy and Dialectical Inquiry

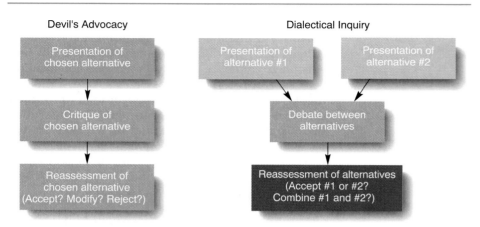

Devil's advocacy is a critical analysis of a preferred alternative to ascertain its strengths and weaknesses before it is implemented.[37] Typically, one member of the decision-making group plays the role of devil's advocate. The devil's advocate critiques and challenges the way the group evaluated alternatives and chose one over the others. The purpose of devil's advocacy is to identify all the reasons that might make the preferred alternative unacceptable after all. In this way, decision makers can be made aware of the possible perils of recommended courses of action.

Dialectical inquiry goes one step further. Two groups of managers are assigned to a problem, and each group is responsible for evaluating alternatives and selecting one of them.[38] Top managers hear each group present its preferred alternative, and then each group critiques the other's position. During this debate, top managers challenge both groups' positions to uncover potential problems and perils associated with their solutions. The goal is to find an even better alternative course of action for the organization to adopt.

Both devil's advocacy and dialectical inquiry can help counter the effects of cognitive biases and groupthink.[39] In practice, devil's advocacy is probably the easier method to implement because it involves less commitment of managerial time and effort than does dialectical inquiry.

Diversity Among Decision Makers

Another way to improve group decision making is to promote diversity in decision-making groups.[40] Bringing together managers of both genders and from various ethnic, national, and functional backgrounds, and so on, broadens the range of life experiences and opinions that group members can draw from as they generate, assess, and choose among alternatives. Moreover, diverse groups are sometimes less prone to groupthink because group members already differ from each other and thus are less subject to pressures for uniformity. The giant chemical company Hoechst Celanese, profiled in the following "Focus on Diversity," takes advantage of diversity to improve decision making.

Focus on Diversity

Diverse Employees Improve Decision Making at Hoechst Celanese

Ernest Drew, CEO of Hoechst Celanese, remembers the day in 1990 when it occurred to him that decisions produced by diverse groups of managers might be better than decisions produced by homogeneous groups of white males. He was attending a conference for Hoechst's top 125 managers (mostly white males), who were joined by 50 or so lower-level managers (mostly minorities or women). The managers were split into problem-solving teams; some were composed only of white men, others of men and women of various races. The main issue addressed by these teams was how the values and norms of Hoechst's culture affected the organization's performance and what could be done to improve the corporate culture. When the teams presented their results, Drew discovered that the most diverse teams had come up with the broadest and most creative solutions, solutions that had never occurred to him.[41]

At about the same time, Drew received another piece of evidence that convinced him of the value of diversity. Hoechst's polyester textile filament division had lost money for 18 straight years. Then, in the late 1980s, it launched a major effort to recruit women and minorities for its plant in Shelby, North Carolina. Under the leadership of Grover Smith, an African-American manager, and a diverse business team of managers, the division began to implement a strategy to turn around its performance. The team decided to stop producing commodity products and focus on producing products for niche markets such as automotive upholstery. The team also implemented a number of actions to drive down the division's costs and boost product quality. As a result of these initiatives, in 1992 the division made money for the first time in two decades, and in 1993 it made substantial profits. According to William Harris, head of worldwide fibers at Hoechst, the identification of the right course of action for improving the division's performance was the direct result of the diversity of its management team.

Organizational Learning and Creativity

The quality of managerial decision making ultimately depends on innovative responses to opportunities and threats. How can managers increase their ability to make nonprogrammed decisions, decisions that will allow them to adapt to, modify, and even drastically alter their task environments so that they can continually increase organizational performance? The answer is by encouraging organizational learning.[42]

Organizational learning is the process through which managers seek to improve employees' desire and ability to understand and manage the organization and its task environment so that employees can make decisions that continuously raise organizational effectiveness.[43] A **learning organization** is one

organizational learning The process through which managers seek to improve employees' desire and ability to understand and manage the organization and its task environment.

learning organization An organization in which managers try to maximize the ability of individuals and groups to think and behave creatively and thus maximize the potential for organizational learning to take place.

creativity A decision maker's ability to discover original and novel ideas that lead to feasible alternative courses of action.

in which managers do everything possible to maximize the ability of individuals and groups to think and behave creatively and thus maximize the potential for organizational learning to take place. At the heart of organizational learning is **creativity,** the ability of a decision maker to discover original and novel ideas that lead to feasible alternative courses of action. Encouraging creativity among managers is such a pressing organizational concern that many organizations hire outside experts to help them develop programs to train their managers in the art of creative thinking and problem solving.

Creating a Learning Organization

How do managers go about creating a learning organization? Learning theorist Peter Senge identified five principles for creating a learning organization (see Figure 6.8).[44]

1. For organizational learning to occur, top managers must allow every person in the organization to develop a sense of *personal mastery.* Managers must empower employees and allow them to experiment and create and explore what they want.

2. As part of attaining personal mastery, organizations need to encourage employees to develop and use *complex mental models*–sophisticated ways of thinking that challenge them to find new or better ways of performing a task– to deepen their understanding of what is involved in a particular activity. Senge argues that managers must encourage employees to develop a taste for experimenting and risk taking.[45]

3. Managers must do everything they can to promote group creativity. Senge thinks that *team learning* (learning that takes place in a group or team) is more important than individual learning in increasing organizational learning. He points out that most important decisions are made in subunits such as groups, functions, and divisions.

4. Managers must emphasize the importance of *building a shared vision*–a common mental model that all organizational members use to frame problems or opportunities.

5. Managers must encourage *systems thinking* (a concept drawn from systems theory, discussed in Chapter 2). Senge emphasizes that, in order to create a

Figure 6.8
Senge's Principles for Creating a Learning Organization

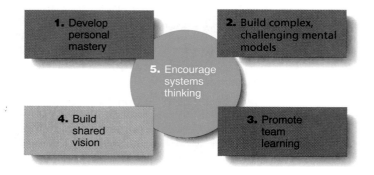

learning organization, managers must recognize the effects of one level of learning on another. Thus, for example, there is little point in creating teams to facilitate team learning if managers do not also take steps to give employees the freedom to develop a sense of personal mastery.

Building a learning organization requires managers to change their management assumptions radically. Developing a learning organization is neither a quick nor an easy process. Senge has been working with Ford Motor Company for the last 10 years to help Ford managers make theirs a learning organization. Why does Ford want this? Top management believes that to compete successfully in the twenty-first century Ford must improve its members' ability to be creative and make the right decisions. Next, we look at some specific ways in which managers can promote creativity at the individual, group, and global levels.[46]

Promoting Individual Creativity

Research suggests that managers are most likely to be creative when certain conditions are met. First, as just discussed, people must be given the opportunity and freedom to generate new ideas. Creativity declines when managers look over the shoulders of talented employees and try to "hurry up" a creative solution. How would you feel if your boss said you had one week to come up with a new product idea to beat the competition? Creativity results when managers have an opportunity to experiment, to take risks, and to make mistakes and learn from them. Highly innovative companies like 3M, Hewlett-Packard, and Rubbermaid are well known for the wide degree of freedom they give their managers. An informal norm at each of these companies is the expectation that managers will spend at least 10 percent of their time on projects of their own choosing, a policy that fosters creativity.

Once managers have generated alternatives, creativity can be fostered by providing them with constructive feedback so that they know how well they are doing. Ideas that seem to be going nowhere can be eliminated and creative energies refocused in other directions. Ideas that seem promising can be promoted, and help from other managers can be obtained as well.[47]

It is also important for top managers to stress the importance of looking for alternative solutions and to visibly reward employees who come up with creative ideas. Being creative can be demanding and stressful. Employees who believe that they are working on important, vital issues will be motivated to put forth the high levels of effort that creativity demands. Creative people like to receive the acclaim of others, and innovative organizations have many kinds of ceremonies and rewards to recognize creative employees. For example, 3M established the Carlton Hall of Fame to recognize successful innovators. They not only become members of the hall of fame but also receive financial rewards through the "Golden Step" program.

Promoting Group Creativity

To encourage creativity at the group level, organizations can make use of group problem-solving techniques that promote creative ideas and innovative solutions. These techniques can also be used to prevent groupthink and to help managers uncover biases. Here, we look at three group decision-making techniques: *brainstorming,* the *nominal group technique,* and the *Delphi technique.*

BRAINSTORMING   Brainstorming is a group problem-solving technique in which managers meet face-to-face to generate and debate a wide variety of alternatives from which to make a decision.[48] Generally, from 5 to 15 managers meet in a closed-door session and proceed like this:

- One manager describes in broad outline the problem the group is to address.
- Group members then share their ideas and generate alternative courses of action.
- As each alternative is described, group members are not allowed to criticize it, and everyone withholds judgment until all alternatives have been heard. One member of the group records the alternatives on a flip chart.
- Group members are encouraged to be as innovative and radical as possible. Anything goes; and the greater the number of ideas put forth, the better. Moreover, group members are encouraged to "piggy back"—that is, to build on each other's suggestions.
- When all alternatives have been generated, group members debate the pros and cons of each and develop a short list of the best alternatives.

Brainstorming is very useful in some problem-solving situations—for example, when managers are trying to find a new name for a perfume or for a model of car. But sometimes individuals working alone can generate more alternatives. The main reason for this loss of productivity appears to be **production blocking,** which occurs because group members cannot always simultaneously make sense of all the alternatives being generated, think up additional alternatives, and remember what they were thinking.[49]

NOMINAL GROUP TECHNIQUE   To avoid production blocking, the **nominal group technique** is often used. It provides a more structured way of generating alternatives in writing and gives each manager more time and opportunity to generate alternative solutions. The nominal group technique is especially useful when an issue is controversial and when different managers might be expected to champion different courses of action. Generally, a small group of managers meet in a closed-door session and adopt the following procedures:

- One manager outlines the problem to be addressed, and 30 or 40 minutes are allocated for each group member to write down ideas and solutions. Group members are encouraged to be innovative.
- Managers take turns reading their suggestions to the group. One manager writes the alternatives on a flip chart. No criticism or evaluation of alternatives is allowed until all alternatives have been read.
- The alternatives are then discussed, one by one, in the sequence in which they were first proposed. Group members can ask for clarifying information and critique each alternative to identify its pros and cons.

production blocking
A loss of productivity in brainstorming sessions due to the unstructured nature of brainstorming.

nominal group technique A decision-making technique in which group members write down ideas and solutions, read their suggestions to the whole group, and discuss and then rank the alternatives.

- When all alternatives have been discussed, each group member ranks all the alternatives from most preferred to least preferred, and the alternative that receives the highest ranking is chosen.[50]

DELPHI TECHNIQUE Both nominal group technique and brainstorming require managers to meet together to generate creative ideas and engage in joint problem solving. What happens if managers are in different cities or in different parts of the world and cannot meet face-to-face? Videoconferencing is one way to bring distant managers together to brainstorm. Another way is to use the **Delphi technique,** a written approach to creative problem solving.[51] The Delphi technique works like this:

- The group leader writes a statement of the problem and a series of questions to which participating managers are to respond.
- The questionnaire is sent to the managers and departmental experts who are most knowledgeable about the problem; they are asked to generate solutions and mail the questionnaire back to the group leader.
- A team of top managers records and summarizes the responses. The results are then sent back to the participants, with additional questions to be answered before a decision can be made.
- The process is repeated until a consensus is reached and the most suitable course of action is apparent.

Delphi technique A decision-making technique in which group members do not meet face to face but respond in writing to questions posed by the group leader.

Promoting Creativity at the Global Level

The Delphi technique is particularly useful when managers are separated by barriers of time and distance, a situation that is common in the global environment. Today, organizations are under increasing pressure to reduce costs and develop global products. To do so, they typically centralize their research and development (R&D) expertise by bringing R&D managers together at one location. Encouraging creativity among teams of R&D experts from different countries poses special problems, however. First, R&D experts often have difficulty communicating their ideas to one another because of language problems and because of cultural differences in their approaches to problem solving. Second, the decision-making process differs from country to country. In Japan, for example, decisions tend to be made in a very participative manner, and the group as a whole must agree on a course of action before a decision gets made. In contrast, decision making is very centralized in Mexico; top managers decide what to do with little input from subordinates.

Managers must take special steps to encourage creativity among people from different countries who are supposed to be working together. They must develop training programs that promote awareness and understanding so that diverse individuals can cooperate and brainstorm new ideas and approaches to problems, opportunities, and threats. The story of how IBM, Siemens, and Toshiba established a strategic alliance to design a new computer chip illustrates many of the issues involved in managing creativity on a global level.

Managing Globally

Building Cross-Cultural Creativity

In 1993, the U.S. computer giant IBM (www.pc.ibm.com) joined with two other global computer companies, Siemens AG of Germany and Toshiba of Japan (www.toshiba.com), to establish a joint venture to build the next generation of computer chips–chips capable of handling 16 times as much information as the most advanced computer chips available today. The joint venture was formed, and each company did not try to develop its own chip, because of the huge cost of developing a new chip–typically billions of dollars. Although each company has a world-class research and development program, top managers were hoping that pooling the talents of their best R&D scientists would enable all three organizations to reap the benefits of synergy and achieve major product breakthroughs quickly and efficiently.

The three companies brought together 100 of their best scientists at an IBM facility in East Fishkill, New York; there they worked together until 1998, developing the new chip. The companies have taken several steps to bridge the obvious cultural gaps among the scientists and to foster creativity. Various language training programs have been developed to help the Japanese and Germans speak colloquial English so that they and the Americans can better brainstorm with one another. Team-building programs have been designed to build cooperative relationships among the scientists assigned to each of the many different departments involved in various aspects of the project. For example, IBM established a buddy system whereby IBM scientists are responsible for introducing their Japanese and German counterparts to the intricacies of IBM's computer system.

Despite these efforts, fostering creativity and cooperation among the American, German, and Japanese scientists has proved to be difficult. The problem can be attributed in large part to cultural differences related to three different national approaches to problem solving and decision making. The North American scientists complain that the Japanese scientists like to spend so much time developing and assessing alternatives that decisions take a long time to make, and even when decisions are made, it often is not clear exactly what has been decided. The German scientists complain that the North American scientists will not accept advice and criticism. The Japanese scientists complain that they are not involved in the main decision-making process. Moreover, each group of scientists has complained that the other groups are hoarding information and ideas to protect their individual and their company's interests, thus undermining the joint creative process.[52]

Despite these problems, the project continues. However, the major breakthroughs that the three companies hope to achieve by bringing their scientists together have not yet occurred. Managers directing the joint venture have observed that, for the most part, cooperation and brainstorming are occurring not among the different groups of scientists but within each group. Managers believe that creativity will be further enhanced by increasing cooperation across the groups–the original goal of the project–and they are planning to develop more group training programs to break down cross-cultural barriers and encourage a truly cross-national approach to problem solving.

Tips for Managers

Improving Decision Making

1. Be aware of the operation of cognitive biases and test the assumptions managers use to frame problems, select alternatives, and make decisions.
2. Recognize the advantages of using diverse decision making groups.
3. Use devil's advocacy and dialectic inquiry to guard against groupthink.
4. Take all possible steps to promote creativity at the individual and group level and make a technique like brainstorming a routine part of the problem solving process.

Summary and Review

Chapter Summary

THE NATURE OF MANAGERIAL DECISION MAKING

- Programmed and Nonprogrammed Decision Making
- The Classical Model
- The Administrative Model

STEPS IN THE DECISION-MAKING PROCESS

- Recognize the Need for a Decision
- Generate Alternatives
- Assess Alternatives
- Choose Among Alternatives
- Implement the Chosen Alternative
- Learn from Feedback

THE NATURE OF MANAGERIAL DECISION MAKING Programmed decisions are routine decisions that are made so often that managers have developed decision rules to be followed automatically. Nonprogrammed decisions are made in response to situations that are unusual or novel; they are nonroutine decisions. The classical model of decision making assumes that decision makers have complete information, are able to process that information in an objective, rational manner, and make optimum decisions. March and Simon argue that managers are boundedly rational, rarely have access to all the information they need to make optimum decisions, and consequently satisfice and rely on their intuition and judgment when making decisions.

STEPS IN THE DECISION-MAKING PROCESS When making decisions, managers should take these six steps: recognizing the need for a decision, generating alternatives, assessing alternatives, choosing among alternatives, implementing the chosen alternative, and learning from feedback.

COGNITIVE BIASES AND DECISION MAKING Most of the time, managers are fairly good decision makers. On occasion, however, problems result because human judgment is adversely affected by the operation of cognitive biases that result in poor decisions. Cognitive biases are caused by systematic errors in the way decision makers process information and make decisions. Sources of these errors include prior hypotheses, representativeness, the illusion of control, and escalating commitment. Managers should undertake a personal decision audit to become aware of their biases in order to improve their decision making.

GROUP DECISION MAKING Many advantages are associated with group decision making, but there are also several disadvantages. One major source of poor decision making is groupthink. Afflicted decision makers collectively embark on a dubious course of action without questioning the assumptions that underlie their decision. Managers can improve the quality of group decision making by using techniques such as devil's advocacy and dialectical inquiry and by increasing diversity in the decision-making group.

ORGANIZATIONAL LEARNING AND CREATIVITY   Organizational learning is the process through which managers seek to improve employees' desire and ability to understand and manage the organization and its task environment so that employees can make decisions that continuously raise organizational effectiveness. Managers must take steps to promote organizational learning and creativity at the individual and group levels to improve the quality of decision making.

Management in Action

Topics for Discussion and Action

1. What are the main differences between programmed decision making and nonprogrammed decision making?

2. In what ways do the classical and administrative models of decision making help managers appreciate the complexities of real-world decision making?

3. Ask a manager to recall the best and the worst decisions he or she ever made. Try to determine why these decisions were so good or so bad.

4. Why do capable managers sometimes make bad decisions? What can individual managers do to improve their decision-making skills?

5. In what kinds of groups is groupthink most likely to be a problem? When is it least likely to be a problem? What steps can group members take to ward off groupthink?

6. What is organizational learning, and how can managers promote it?

Building Management Skills

How Do You Make Decisions?

Pick a decision that you made recently and that has had important consequences for you. This decision may be your decision about which college to attend, which major to select, whether to take a part-time job, which part-time job to take. Using the material in this chapter, analyze the way in which you made the decision.

1. Identify the criteria you used, either consciously or unconsciously, to guide your decision making.

2. List the alternatives you considered. Were these all possible alternatives? Did you unconsciously (or consciously) ignore some important alternatives?

3. How much information did you have about each alternative?

   Did you base the decision on complete or incomplete information?

4. Try to remember how you reached the decision. Did you sit down and consciously think through the implications of each alternative, or did you make the decision on the basis of intuition? Did you use any rules of thumb to help you make the decision?

5. In retrospect, do you think that your choice of alternative was shaped by any of the cognitive biases discussed in this chapter?

6. Having answered those five questions, do you think in retrospect that you made a reasonable decision? What, if anything, might you do to improve your ability to make good decisions in the future?

Small Group Breakout Exercise

Brainstorming

Form groups of three or four people, and appoint one member as the spokesperson who will communicate your findings to the whole class when called on by the instructor. Then discuss the following scenario.

You and your partners are trying to decide which kind of restaurant to open in a centrally located shopping center that has just been built in your city. The problem confronting you is that the city already has many restaurants that provide different kinds of food in all price ranges. You have the resources to open any type of restaurant. Your challenge is to decide which type is most likely to succeed.

Use the brainstorming technique to decide which type of restaurant to open. Follow these steps.

1. As a group, spend 5 or 10 minutes generating ideas about the alternative kinds of restaurants that you think will be most likely to succeed. Each group member should be as innovative and creative as possible, and no suggestions should be criticized.

2. Appoint one group member to write down the alternatives as they are identified.

3. Spend the next 10 or 15 minutes debating the pros and cons of the alternatives.

As a group try to reach a consensus on which alternative is most likely to succeed.

4. After making your decision, discuss the pros and cons of the brainstorming method, and decide whether any production blocking occurred.

When called on by the instructor, the spokesperson should be prepared to share your group's decision with the class, as well as the reasons you made your decision.

Exploring the World Wide Web

Specific Assignment

This exercise follows up on the activities of Scott McNealy and Sun Microsystems in the years since he made the vital decision to proceed with the launch of the new computer. Scan Sun's website (www.sun.com) to get a feel for this innovative company. In particular, from the home page click on "Corporate Information," then "News and Events," then "Sun in the Media," and read the stories about Sun CEO Scott McNealy.

1. What opportunities and threats do Scott McNealy and Sun currently face?

2. What kinds of decisions does McNealy need to make at the present time?

General Assignment

Search for a website that describes a company whose managers have just made a major decision. What was the decision? Why did they make it? How successful has it been?

ManagementCase

Tough Decisions at Rockwell International

In the 1990s, Rockwell International, like other big U.S. defense companies such as Lockheed Martin, TRW Systems, and McDonnell Douglas, was feeling the effect of drastic reductions in U.S. defense expenditures. With the breakup of the Soviet Union and the end of the Cold War, the Pentagon was buying only about 50 percent of the weaponry and equipment (such as missiles, tanks, and planes) that it had bought in the 1980s. Such an organizational environment was posing a significant threat to Rockwell's performance, and it was imperative for Rockwell's managers to find a new strategy to respond to these threats and improve organizational performance.

Under the leadership of CEO Donald Beall, Rockwell crafted a dramatic new strategy to lead the company into the twenty-first century. Beall, who joined Rockwell in the early 1960s and was running Rockwell's electronics division by age 30, became CEO in 1987. He has been the prime mover in deciding that Rockwell should lessen its dependence on defense spending by moving into the industrial and consumer products area. For example, Beall moved Rockwell into industrial automation by buying strong companies such as Allen Bradley and Reliance Electric. Once Rockwell buys a company, Beall provides it with Rockwell's considerable expertise in high technology and electronics so that the new acquisition becomes stronger and more skilled at what it does. Rockwell is the company that built the B-1 bomber, the Apollo spacecraft, and the space shuttle. The company has enormous skills and experience in innovating advanced new products and a highly creative team of engineers ready to apply their skills to new areas. Beall's goal is to use the skills that Rockwell has developed in the defense industry to develop advanced new products in many different areas.

Some analysts are critical of the kinds of acquisitions that Beall has been making, saying that he has no consistent goal or vision. They claim that at a time when many companies are deciding to focus on one core business, Beall seems to be building an empire of diverse businesses, including defense electronics, automotive products, printing presses, rockets for space shuttles, chips for fax machines, plastics, and telecommunications. They believe Beall may be overestimating his capacity to run such a diverse group of businesses, and they also question whether he is overestimating Rockwell's ability to compete successfully across so many businesses based on its success in just one—defense electronics.

Beall maintains that he and his management team use very clear criteria when they evaluate what kinds of businesses Rockwell should be in. First, they buy only businesses in industries where they can be the clear market leader. Second, they evaluate each business in terms of the opportunity for long-term returns (over as much as 10 years).[53] Critics reply that the environment is very uncertain and that it is impossible for Beall and his management team to predict with certainty whether the returns they project will be forthcoming.

Nevertheless, Rockwell's venture into industrial automation has been successful. After Rockwell transferred its high-tech skills and resources to Allen Bradley and Reliance, those companies gained a 30 percent share of the industrial automation market; currently they represent over 50 percent of Rockwell's profits. Is this just luck or the beginning of a series of successful ventures that will make Rockwell a leading high-tech company for years to come?

Questions

1. Evaluate Beall's actions in terms of the six-step decision-making process described in this chapter (see Figure 6.4).

2. Do you think Beall might be suffering from any of the cognitive biases described in the chapter? Which ones?

3. Do you think Beall has charted the right course for Rockwell? What new opportunities and threats might be on the horizon?

ManagementCase

In the News

From the Pages of *Fortune*
How Disney Keeps Ideas Coming

Starting with The Little Mermaid, *a string of animated blockbusters has earned the Walt Disney Co. some $5 billion since 1989. By any count, that's a tribute to how Disney not only sates its own notorious appetite for ever fatter profits but also gets the best out of that often-prickly-but-you-can't-live-without-'em bunch of folks, "the creatives." Most important, Disney sees to it that good ideas keep coming from all directions and that movies meet their deadlines. Peter Schneider, 45, president of feature animation, tells how a Gong Show for all his staffers—not to mention Ping-Pong with CEO Michael Eisner, who knows how to lose a game—helps the process.*

How does a Gong Show get you the best ideas? We have people thinking about what we should do next all the time. But lots of other people in the building, including secretaries, want to present their ideas too. So three times a year they get to do just that, pitching what they think would make a good animated film to me, Michael Eisner, Roy Disney, and my executive VP, Tom Schumacher.

Isn't that a pretty scary audience? Well, people with ideas get some help from their coworkers. Development helps them shape their pitch, for instance, so that it can be presented in three to five minutes, and coaches them on things such as the sort of visuals they could use. And if you're scared to death, someone else will hold your hand when you're up there. On the day of the Gong Show, it's very formal. The four of us all sit at a table and the room is full of people with ideas they want to

submit. That way everybody gets to hear all of the ideas. It's not as though you're pitching alone. There's a group supporting you. We usually have about 40 presenters. That morning we pick names at random, so there's no advance order, but each person knows when it's his or her turn.

Still, it must be tough for people to get up and say what they think to Michael Eisner. That's key, though. You have to create an environment where people feel safe about their ideas. And you do that by setting the example. Senior management has to take on the responsibility of saying, "Michael, you're wrong." When people see us saying that, it gives them permission to say it too.

Once all the ideas are presented, the four of us talk about which ones we liked and what aspects we liked about some of the others. Somebody may have a great concept, but the story may not be very good. Or somebody may have a great title. What we can't do is say, "Oh, that's fabulous. Great pitch, guys!" and when they leave, mumble, "What an idea! That was awful!" You must have immediate communication and not worry about people's egos and feelings and how to do it gently enough. You have to tell people why an idea didn't work. We don't pull our punches. If you do that enough, and people don't get fired or demoted, they begin to understand that no matter how good, bad, or indifferent the idea, it can be expressed, accepted, and thought about.

What films came out of the Gong Show? Most of Disney's animated features, in fact. In the case of *Hercules,* an animator came up with

the central idea that a man is judged by his inner strength and not his outer strength. The title was also his idea, but we didn't go for his story line. In the end that came from the two guys who became the directors of the film.

Did the guy with the original idea get paid for it? If we buy the pitch, the presenter usually gets what we'd pay for a first treatment. [Schneider would not give specifics, but a $20,000 payment, spread over the period between an accepted pitch and a movie's release, is not unusual.]

How does a good idea become a business? First we come up with a core value for each story. I hate calling anything a mission statement, but I suppose it could be called that. The core value puts process in creativity. It's written down, and we all talk about it. It's not mysterious or ethereal. It's a value that we hang on to in terms of judging whether we're doing a good job. Are we telling the story we agreed to tell? You can't manage anything that doesn't have agreed-upon goals and direction.

How do you reach an agreement? It's a very collective approach to our work. We spend a lot of time in meetings arguing, discussing, and trying to come to a consensus. For instance, there was a lot of initial debate about what story we were telling with *The Hunchback of Notre Dame.* People thought we could never make it work. So we went back to the book and asked questions. What was the fundamental value of the book? What could the story be? What should it be? We discussed what changes we were going to make to have it tell our tale. As everybody gave their input, the debate moved along a little bit and changed. We eventually decided that our story would be about discovering self-value.

But there's a time to talk and a time to start making the film. Yes, and that's the dilemma. As soon as you make the process concrete, it's wrong—but you have to lock things up or you can't go forward. You want to keep things in flux, in change, in chaos, until everybody says, "Gosh, that's exactly right." At the same time, there has to be a system and a certain amount of expectation. You have to say, "Within these boundaries, you will create. This is the budget. This is as big as it gets. These are your limitations. Make it work within this framework." And then be open to the judgment of, "My God, the framework's not right. Let's change it."

Do deadlines help you draw boundaries and do they play a role in managing creativity? They're a key ingredient to creativity. If you let people work on blank canvases with no rules, they tend to think too much. A deadline says, "By five o'clock tomorrow, you will have this up on storyboard, good, bad, or indifferent"—because we'll all come in and talk about it. We'll have something to react to. It'll spark the next idea.

Who sets the deadlines? Who's in charge? It's unclear who really is in charge of our process. Certainly the directors and the producers are the day-to-day point people. But there's a lot of give and take with Michael, Roy, Tom, and myself. The four of us are always asking if we're telling the story, if it's correct, if it's good. It's the dialogue that makes it work. At the end of the day, I think the idea of Disney animation is in charge. There's never really a possessiveness in terms of a particular person. I think you can assign it to a group of people.

But there must be some sort of hierarchy? I'm a very big believer in hierarchy, one that is not too structured. I don't think you can create things without it. When I first

came here ten years ago, it was very flat. There was no real acknowledgment in the animation ranks of who was good and who was not so good. Now it's very clear who the top five people in our business are. It gives people a sense of what they're progressing toward creatively.

The other kind of hierarchy is clearly that you have directors, an art director, a head of background. Each of these people is charged with leadership in terms of their troops. By and large we try to choose someone who is a great manager and a great artist. Those are very hard skills to find together. There has to be a certain sense of judgment, of quality, of speed, and the ability to say, "This is not good enough, not fast enough. You can do more. I expect more." Or to say, "Take your time. This is really important. Go slow." A real sense of judgment and an ability to communicate it.

How much autonomy do you give those who lead a Disney project? It's about putting the pieces together to allow people to do their job. It's about people clicking. So you want leadership to pick leadership. You want directors to pick their own art directors, the art directors to pick their head of background, heads of background to pick their own crew. You want people to have a sense of being chosen and wanted on a picture, not assigned, transferred, or exiled to it. You want people to say, "God, they want me."

How often can you do that? Seventy-five percent of the time. The other times we arrogantly say, even to directors, "Just do it." On one of our most successful projects, we told the director to shut up and do it. He was a very talented man but a bit indecisive in terms of where he wanted to go with his career. He didn't know if it was the right project. I said to him, "You've been offered to direct a major animated movie. Do it." He said, "But I don't think I like this and that." "Then change it," I said, "Get in there and start working." He did, and he became ecstatic about the work. But it was the

process of it, not that he came in saying, "I know what to do with this movie." It was the process: Going to work, drawing the drawing, talking about it, arguing about it, fighting about it, redoing it, being there.

But aren't you always going to have tension between the production side of the business and the creative side? Always is right. But it's very healthy. Production's job is to ask whether every decision is worth it. We recently discussed making a small change at the end of Hunchback. We were in our last weeks, and the final four shots didn't quite fire off. We were talking about 30 feet of film, which is a significant change. Production said, "Guys, it's 30 feet." And we said, "Yeah, but it doesn't work." They finally agreed, but we didn't go with our first choice, which was time-consuming and expensive, and figured out a way to make the change faster and for less money.

People are getting more comfortable with the idea that this is not about us and them. One of our managers organized a Ping-Pong tournament during lunch hours last year, and the winners played a final game with Michael Eisner and [President] Mike Ovitz. They said, "Oh, my God, Michael Eisner's playing Ping-Pong in our building. Wow, I'm important." I'm not sure they say that directly. But where else would the CEO be playing Ping-Pong with an hourly artist? The big guys lost the game, which goes to show people didn't feel they had to let Eisner win. The lines of hierarchy are so blurred that it makes no difference who you are to get access.

Source: Joe McGowan, "How Disney Keeps Ideas Coming," *Fortune,* April 1, 1996, 131–33.

Questions

1. How does the Walt Disney Company try to encourage its employees to be creative and innovative?

2. How would you describe Disney's approach to decision making?

Chapter seven

The Manager as a Planner and Strategist

Learning Objectives

1. Describe the three steps of the planning process.

2. Explain the relationship between planning and strategy.

3. Explain the role of planning in predicting the future and in mobilizing organizational resources to meet future contingencies.

4. Outline the main steps in SWOT analysis.

5. Differentiate among corporate-, business-, and functional-level strategies.

6. Describe the vital role that strategy implementation plays in determining managers' ability to achieve an organization's mission and goals.

A Case in Contrast

Gerald Pencer Starts a Cola War

Coca-Cola (www.coca-cola.com) and Pepsi-Cola (www.pepsi.com) are household names worldwide. In 1995, together they controlled over 70 percent of the global soft-drink market and over 75 percent of the U.S. soft-drink market. Their success can be attributed in part to the overall strategy that Coca-Cola and PepsiCo developed to produce and promote their products. Both companies decided to build global brands by manufacturing the soft-drink concentrate that gives cola its flavor and then selling the concentrate in syrup form to bottlers throughout the world. Coca-Cola and PepsiCo charge the bottlers a premium price for the syrup; they then invest part of the proceeds in advertising to build and maintain brand awareness. The bottlers are responsible for producing and distributing the actual cola. They add carbonated water to the syrup, package the resulting drink, and distribute it to vending machines, supermarkets, restaurants, and other retail outlets.

The bottlers leave all the advertising to Coca-Cola and PepsiCo. In addition, the bottlers must sign an exclusive agreement that prohibits them from distributing competing cola brands. A Coke or Pepsi bottler cannot bottle any other cola drink. This strategy has two major advantages for Coca-Cola and PepsiCo. First, it forces bottlers to enter

Which of these colas tastes the best? That depends on your personal preferences. However, there is no doubt which cola costs the least, that produced by the Cott corporation, which makes cola for organizations such as Albertson's and Wal-Mart, such as Sam's choice pictured here.

into exclusive agreements, which create a high barrier to entry into the industry; any potential competitors that might want to produce and distribute a new cola product must create their own distribution network rather than use the existing network. Second, the large amount of money spent on advertising (in 1990, Coca-Cola spent $190 million, and PepsiCo $170 million) to develop a global brand name has helped Coca-Cola and PepsiCo differentiate their products so that consumers are more likely to buy a Coke or a Pepsi rather than a lesser-known cola. Moreover, brand loyalty allows both companies to charge a premium or comparatively high price for what is, after all, merely colored water and flavoring. This differentiation strategy has made Coca-Cola and PepsiCo two of the most profitable companies in the world.

The global environment may be undergoing a change, however, because of Gerald Pencer, a Canadian entrepreneur who in the early 1990s came up with a new plan for competing in the cola market and created a new strategy to attract customers. Pencer's strategy was to produce a low-price cola, manufactured and bottled by his own company, the Cott Corporation, and sell directly to major retail establishments (such as supermarket chains) as a private-label "house brand," thus bypassing the bottlers. He implemented this plan first in Canada and then quickly expanded into the United States because of interest in his product. Retailers are attracted to Cott's cola because its low cost allows them to make 15 percent more profit than they receive from selling Coke or Pepsi.[1]

To implement his strategy, Pencer planned to do no advertising (so that he could charge a low price for his cola) and to take advantage of efficient national distribution systems that retailers such as Wal-Mart have created in recent years. This *low-cost strategy* enables Cott to circumvent the barrier to entry created by the exclusive distribution agreements that Coca-Cola and PepsiCo have signed with their bottlers. Cott delivers its products to Wal-Mart's regional distribution centers, and Wal-Mart handles distribution and advertising from that point on.

Pencer has gone on to supply an international network of bottlers by offering to sell cola concentrate for as little as one-sixth of the price that Coca-Cola and PepsiCo charge. In April 1994, for example, Cott launched a cola product in Britain for Sainsbury's, Britain's biggest food retailer. Sold as "Sainsbury's Classic Cola," the product was priced 30 percent below Coke and Pepsi. Within four weeks of the launch Cott's cola had won a 60 percent share of Sainsbury's cola sales, equal to a quarter of Britain's entire take-home cola market! Cott also scored big in its home province of Ontario, Canada, where Cott's private-label brands now account for 31 percent of the entire cola market. Building on this success, by mid-1994 Cott had signed supply agreements with 90 retail chains around the world, including major retailers in Britain, France, Spain, Japan, and the United States. ●

Overview

As the "Case in Contrast" suggests, there is more than one way to compete in an industry, and to find a viable way to enter and compete in an industry, managers must study the way other organizations behave and identify their strategies. By studying the strategies of Coca-Cola and PepsiCo, Gerald Pencer was able to devise a strategy that allowed him to enter the cola industry and take on these global giants. So far, he has had considerable success.

In an uncertain competitive environment, managers must engage in thorough planning to find a strategy that will allow them to compete effectively. This chapter explores the manager's role both as planner and as strategist. We discuss the different elements involved in the planning process, including its three major steps: (1) determining an organization's mission and major goals, (2) choosing strategies to realize the mission and goals, and (3) selecting the appropriate way of organizing resources to implement the strategies. We also discuss scenario planning and SWOT analysis, important techniques that managers use to analyze their current situation. By the end of this chapter, you will understand the role managers play in the planning and strategy-making process to create high-performing organizations. ●

An Overview of the Planning Process

planning Identifying and selecting appropriate goals and courses of action; one of the four principal functions of management.

strategy A cluster of decisions about what goals to pursue, what actions to take, and how to use resources to achieve goals.

mission statement A broad declaration of an organization's purpose that identifies the organization's products and customers and distinguishes the organization from its competitors.

Planning, as we noted in Chapter 1, is a process that managers use to identify and select appropriate goals and courses of action for an organization.[2] The organizational plan that results from the planning process details the goals of the organization and specifies how managers intend to attain those goals. The cluster of decisions and actions that managers take to help an organization attain its goals is its **strategy.** Thus, planning is both a goal-making and a strategy-making process.

In most organizations, planning is a three-step activity (see Figure 7.1). The first step is determining the organization's mission and goals. A **mission statement** is a broad declaration of an organization's overriding purpose; this statement is intended to identify an organization's products and customers as well as to distinguish the organization in some way from its competitors. The second step is formulating strategy. Managers analyze the organization's current situation and then conceive and develop the strategies necessary to attain the organization's mission and goals. The third step is implementing strategy. Managers decide how to allocate the resources and responsibilities required to

Figure 7.1
Three Steps in Planning

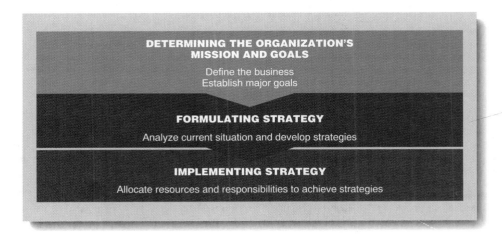

DETERMINING THE ORGANIZATION'S MISSION AND GOALS
Define the business
Establish major goals

FORMULATING STRATEGY
Analyze current situation and develop strategies

IMPLEMENTING STRATEGY
Allocate resources and responsibilities to achieve strategies

implement those strategies between people and groups within the organization.[3] In subsequent sections of this chapter we look in detail at the specifics of each of these steps. But first we examine the general nature and purpose of planning, one of the four managerial functions identified by Fayol.

Levels of Planning

In large organizations planning usually takes place at three levels of management: corporate, business or division, and department or functional. Figure 7.2 shows the link between the three steps in the planning process and these three levels. To understand this model, consider how General Electric (GE), a large organization that includes many businesses, operates.[4] GE has three main levels of management: corporate level, business level, and functional level (see Figure 7.3). At the corporate level are the CEO and chairman Jack Welch, three other top managers, and their corporate support staff. Below the corporate level is the business level. At the business level are the different divisions of the company. A **division** is a business unit that competes in a distinct industry; GE has over 150 divisions, including GE Aircraft Engines, GE Financial Services, GE Lighting, GE Motors, GE Plastics, and NBC. Each division has its own set of **divisional managers.** In turn, each division has its own set of functions or departments—manufacturing, marketing, human resource management, R&D, and so on. Thus, GE Aircraft has its own marketing function, as do GE Lighting, GE Motors, and NBC.

division A business unit that has its own set of managers and functions or departments and competes in a distinct industry.

divisional managers Managers who control the various divisions of an organization.

Figure 7.2
Levels and Types of Planning

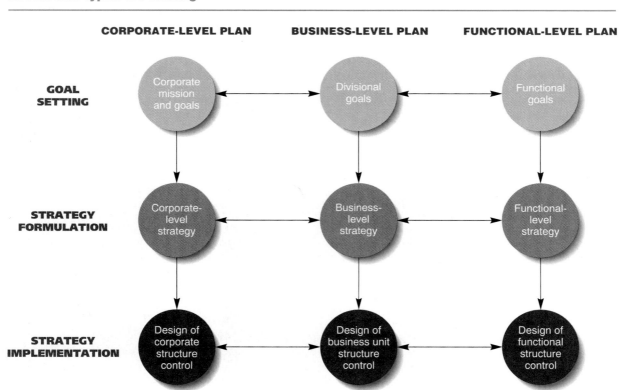

Figure 7.3
Levels of Planning at General Electric

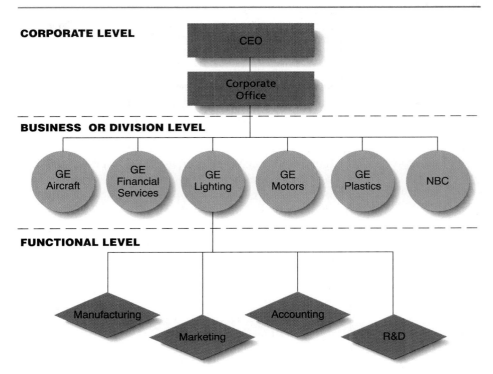

At General Electric, as at other large organizations, planning takes place at each level. The **corporate-level plan** contains top management's decisions pertaining to the organization's mission and goals, overall (corporate-level) strategy, and structure (see Figure 7.2). **Corporate-level strategy** indicates in which industries and national markets an organization intends to compete. One of the goals stated in GE's corporate-level plan is that GE should be first or second in market share in every industry in which it competes. A division that cannot attain this goal may be sold to another company. In the early 1990s, GE Medical Systems was sold to Thompson of France for this reason. Another GE goal is the acquisition of other companies to help build market share. Over the last decade, GE acquired several financial services companies and transformed the GE Financial Services Division into one of the largest financial service operations in the world.

The corporate-level plan provides the framework within which divisional managers create their business-level plans. At the business level, the managers of each division create a **business-level plan** that details (1) long-term goals that will allow the division to meet corporate goals and (2) the division's business-level strategy and structure. **Business-level strategy** states the methods a division or business intends to use to compete against its rivals in an industry. Managers at GE Lighting (currently number two in the global lighting industry behind the Dutch company Philips NV) develop strategies designed to help the division take over the number-one spot and better contribute to GE's corporate goals. The lighting division's competitive strategy might emphasize, for example, trying to reduce costs in all departments in order to lower prices and gain market share from Philips.

corporate-level plan Top management's decisions pertaining to the organization's mission, overall strategy, and structure.

corporate-level strategy A plan that indicates in which industries and national markets an organization intends to compete.

business-level plan Divisional managers' decisions pertaining to divisions' long-term goals, overall strategy, and structure.

business-level strategy A plan that indicates how a division intends to compete against its rivals in an industry.

function A unit or department in which people have the same skills or use the same resources to perform their jobs.

functional managers Managers who supervise the various functions, such as manufacturing, accounting, and sales, within a division.

functional-level plan Functional managers' decisions pertaining to the goals that functional managers propose to pursue to help the division attain its business-level goals.

functional-level strategy A plan that indicates how a function intends to achieve its goals.

A **function** is a unit or department in which people have the same skills or use the same resources to perform their jobs. Examples include manufacturing, accounting, and sales. The business-level plan provides the framework within which **functional managers** devise their plans. A **functional-level plan** states the goals that functional managers propose to pursue to help the division attain its business-level goals, which, in turn, will allow the organization to achieve its corporate goals. **Functional-level strategy** sets forth the actions that managers intend to take at the level of departments such as manufacturing, marketing, and R&D to allow the organization to attain its goals. Thus, for example, consistent with GE Lighting's strategy of driving down costs, the manufacturing function might adopt the goal "To reduce production costs by 20 percent over three years," and its functional strategy to achieve this goal might include (1) investing in state-of-the-art production facilities, (2) introducing improved inventory management procedures to reduce inventory-holding costs, and (3) adopting a total quality management program to improve quality and reduce costs.

An important issue in planning is ensuring *consistency* in planning across the three different levels. Functional goals and strategies should be consistent with divisional goals and strategies, which in turn should be consistent with corporate goals and strategies, and vice versa. Once complete, each function's plan is normally linked to its division's business-level plan, which, in turn, is linked to the corporate plan. Although few organizations are as large and complex as GE, most plan as GE does and have written plans to guide managerial decision making.

Who Plans?

In general, corporate-level planning is the primary responsibility of top managers.[5] At General Electric, the corporate-level goal that GE be first or second in every industry in which it competes was first articulated by the CEO, Jack Welch. Welch and his top-management team also decided which industries GE would compete in. Corporate-level managers are responsible for approving business- and functional-level plans to ensure that they are consistent with the corporate plan.

Corporate planning decisions are not made in a vacuum. Other managers have input to corporate-level planning. At General Electric and many other companies, divisional and functional managers are encouraged to submit proposals for new business ventures to the CEO and top managers, who evaluate the proposals and decide whether to fund them.[6] Thus, even though corporate-level planning is the responsibility of top managers, lower-level managers can be and usually are given the opportunity to become involved in the process.

This approach is common not only at the corporate level but also at the business and functional levels. At the business level, planning is the responsibility of divisional managers, who also review functional plans. Functional managers also typically participate in business-level planning. Similarly, although the functional managers bear primary responsibility for functional-level planning, they can and do involve their subordinates in this process. Thus, although ultimate responsibility for planning may lie with certain select managers within an organization, *all* managers and many nonmanagerial employees typically participate in the planning process.

Time Horizons of Plans

time horizon The intended duration of a plan.

Plans differ in their **time horizon,** or intended duration. Managers usually distinguish among *long-term plans* with a horizon of five years or more, *intermediate-term plans* with a horizon between one and five years, and *short-term plans* with a horizon of one year or less.[7] Typically, corporate- and business-level goals and strategies require long- and intermediate-term plans, and functional-level goals and strategies require intermediate- and short-term plans.

Although most organizations operate with planning horizons of five years or more, it would be inaccurate to infer from this that they undertake major planning exercises only once every five years and then "lock in" a specific set of goals and strategies for that time period. Most organizations have an annual planning cycle, which is usually linked to their annual financial budget (although a major planning effort may be undertaken only every few years).

Although a corporate- or business-level plan may extend over five years or more, it is typically treated as a *rolling plan,* a plan that is updated and amended every year to take account of changing conditions in the external environment. Thus, the time horizon for an organization's 1998 corporate-level plan might be 2003; for the 1999 plan it might be 2004; and so on. The use of rolling plans is essential because of the high rate of change in the environment and the difficulty of predicting competitive conditions five years in the future. Rolling plans allow managers to make midcourse corrections if environmental changes warrant, or to change the thrust of the plan altogether if it no longer seems appropriate. The use of rolling plans allows managers to plan flexibly, without losing sight of the need to plan for the long term.

Standing Plans and Single-Use Plans

Another distinction often made between plans is whether they are standing plans or single-use plans. Managers create standing and single-use plans to help achieve an organization's specific goals. *Standing plans* are used in situations in which programmed decision making is appropriate. When the same situations occur repeatedly, managers develop policies, rules, and standard operating procedures (SOPs) to control the way employees perform their tasks. A *policy* is a general guide to action; a *rule* is a formal, written guide to action; and a *standing operating procedure* is a written instruction describing the exact series of actions that should be followed in a specific situation. For example, an organization may have a standing plan about ethical behavior by employees. This plan includes a *policy* that all employees are expected to behave ethically in their dealings with suppliers and customers; a *rule* that requires any employee who receives from a supplier or customer a gift larger than $10 to report the gift; and an *SOP* that obliges the recipient of the gift to make the disclosure in writing within 30 days.

In contrast, *single-use plans* are developed to handle nonprogrammed decision making in unusual or one-of-a-kind situations. Examples of single-use plans include *programs,* which are integrated sets of plans for achieving certain goals, and *projects,* which are specific action plans created to complete various aspects of a program. One of NASA's major programs was to reach the moon, and one project in this program was to develop a lunar module capable of landing on the moon and returning to earth.

Why Planning Is Important

Essentially, planning is ascertaining where an organization is at the present time and deciding where it should be in the future and how to move it forward. When managers plan, they must consider the future and forecast what may happen in order to take action in the present and mobilize organizational resources to deal with future opportunities and threats. As we have discussed in previous chapters, however, the external environment is uncertain and complex, and managers typically must deal with incomplete information and bounded rationality. This is one reason why planning is so complex and difficult.

Almost all managers engage in planning, and all should participate because they must try to predict future opportunities and threats. The absence of a plan often results in hesitation, false steps, and mistaken changes of direction that can hurt an organization or even lead to disaster. Planning is important for four main reasons:

1. Planning is a useful way of getting managers to participate in decision making about the appropriate goals and strategies for an organization. Effective planning gives all managers the opportunity to participate in decision making. At Intel, for example, top managers, as part of their annual planning process, regularly request input from lower-level managers to determine what the organization's goals and strategies should be.

2. Planning is necessary to give the organization a sense of direction and purpose.[8] A plan states what goals an organization is trying to achieve and what strategies it intends to use to achieve them. Without the sense of direction and purpose that a formal plan provides, managers may interpret their own tasks and roles in ways that best suit themselves. The result will be an organization that is pursuing multiple and often conflicting goals and a set of managers who do not cooperate and work well together. By stating which organizational goals and strategies are important, a plan keeps managers on track so that they use the resources under their control effectively.

3. A plan helps coordinate managers of the different functions and divisions of an organization to ensure that they all pull in the same direction. Without a good plan, it is possible that the members of the manufacturing function will produce more products than the members of the sales function can sell, resulting in a mass of unsold inventory. Implausible as this might seem, according to Lee Iacocca, the former chairman of Chrysler Corporation, this situation prevailed at Chrysler in the late 1970s. Iacocca described how Chrysler's planning process had broken down because of power struggles and political infighting among managers. One result was that sales managers and manufacturing managers simply did not communicate with each other—each function acted alone without regard for the other.[9]

4. A plan can be used as a device for controlling managers within an organization. A good plan specifies not only which goals and strategies the organization is committed to but also who is responsible for putting the strategies into action to attain the goals. When managers know that they will be held accountable for attaining a goal, they are motivated to do their best to make sure the goal is achieved.

Henri Fayol, the originator of the model of management we discussed in Chapter 1, said that effective plans should have four qualities: unity, continuity, accuracy, and flexibility.[10] *Unity* means that at any one time only one central, guiding plan is put into operation to achieve an organizational goal; more than one plan to achieve a goal would cause confusion and disorder. *Continuity* means that planning is an ongoing process in which managers build and refine previous plans and continually modify plans at all levels—corporate, business, and functional—so that they fit together into one broad framework. *Accuracy* means that managers need to make every attempt to collect and utilize all available information at their disposal in the planning process. Of course, managers must recognize the fact that uncertainty exists and that information is almost always incomplete (for reasons we discussed in Chapter 6). Despite the need for continuity and accuracy, however, Fayol emphasized that the planning process should have enough *flexibility* so that plans can be altered and changed if the situation changes; managers must not be bound to a static plan.

Scenario Planning

scenario planning The generation of multiple forecasts of future conditions followed by an analysis of how to respond effectively to each of those conditions; also called *contingency planning.*

One way in which managers can try to create plans that have the four qualities that Fayol described is by utilizing scenario planning, one of the most widely used planning techniques. **Scenario planning** (also known as *contingency planning*) is the generation of multiple forecasts of future conditions followed by an analysis of how to respond effectively to each of those conditions.

As noted previously, planning is about trying to forecast and predict the future in order to be able to anticipate future opportunities and threats. The future, however, is inherently unpredictable. How can managers best deal with this unpredictability? This question preoccupied managers at Royal Dutch Shell in the 1970s. Managers at Shell, one of the largest global oil and gas producers, came to the conclusion that because the future is unpredictable the only reasonable approach to planning is first to generate "multiple futures"—or scenarios of the future—based on different assumptions about conditions in the world oil market that *might prevail* in the future, and then to develop different plans that detail what the company *should do* in the event that any of these scenarios actually occurs. Accordingly, Shell's managers used scenario planning to generate different future scenarios of conditions in the oil market, asked divisional managers how they would respond to these opportunities and threats if such a scenario occurred, and then developed a set of plans based on these responses.

Managers at Shell believe that the advantage of scenario planning was not only the plans that were generated but also the ability to educate managers at all levels about the dynamic and complex nature of Shell's environment and the breadth of strategies available to Shell. Indeed, Shell's top managers now see scenario planning as a learning tool that raises the quality of the planning process and brings real benefits to the organization.[11] The following "Management Insight" illustrates how scenario planning works for Shell.

Management Insight

Scenario Planning at Shell

In 1984, oil was $30 a barrel, and most analysts and managers, including Shell's (www.shellus.com), believed that it would hit $50 per barrel by 1990. Nevertheless, Shell conducted a scenario-planning exercise for its managers. They were asked to imagine a future scenario in which oil prices fell to $15 per barrel and to decide what they should do in such a case. Managers went to work with the goal of creating a plan consisting of a series of recommendations. The final plan included proposals to cut oil exploration costs by investing in new technologies, to accelerate investments in cost-efficient oil-refining facilities, and to weed out unprofitable gas stations.[12]

In reviewing these proposals, top management came to the conclusion that even if oil prices continued to rise, all of these actions would benefit Shell by widening the company's profit margin. They decided to put the plan into action. As it happened, in the mid-1980s oil prices did collapse to $15 a barrel, but Shell, unlike its competitors, had already taken steps to be profitable in a low-oil-price world. Consequently, by 1990, the company was twice as profitable as its major competitors.

Shell's success with scenario planning influenced many other companies to adopt similar systems. By 1990, over 50 percent of Fortune 500 companies were using some version of scenario planning (it is also called *contingency planning*), and the number has increased since then.[13] The great strength of scenario planning is its ability not only to anticipate the challenges of an uncertain future but also to educate managers to think about the future—to think *strategically*.

Tips for Managers

Planning

1. Think ahead by using exercises like scenario planning on a regular basis.

2. See plans as a guide to action. Don't feel straightjacketed by plans that may no longer be appropriate in a changing environment.

3. Make sure that the plans created at each of the three organizational levels are compatible with one another and that managers at all levels recognize how their actions fit into the overall corporate plan.

4. Give managers at all levels the opportunity to participate in the planning process to best analyze an organization's present situation and the future scenarios that may affect it.

Determining the Organization's Mission and Goals

Determining the organization's mission and goals is the first step of the planning process. Once the mission and goals are agreed upon and formally stated in the corporate plan, they guide the next steps by defining which strategies are appropriate and which are inappropriate.[14]

Defining the Business

To determine an organization's mission, managers must first define its business so that they can identify what kind of value they will provide to customers. To define the business, managers must ask three questions:[15] (1) Who are our customers? (2) What customer needs are being satisfied? (3) How are we satisfying customer needs? They ask these questions to identify the customer needs that the organization satisfies and the way the organization satisfies those needs. Answering these questions helps managers to identify not only what customer needs they are satisfying now but what needs they should try to satisfy in the future and who their true competitors are. All of this information helps managers plan and establish appropriate goals. The case of Seattle City Light shows the important role that defining the business has in the planning process.

Management Insight

Defining the Business of Seattle City Light

Seattle City Light (SCL) is one of the largest community-owned electric utilities in the United States. Traditionally, SCL had defined its business as "the generation and transmission of electricity." Because Seattle City Light is the only electric utility serving the city of Seattle, the organization had long seen itself as a regulated monopoly with no real competitors. In 1993, SCL's top-management team decided to embark on a comprehensive planning exercise to define SCL's business—something the utility had never done before.

Top management hired a consultant to design and facilitate the process.[16] The consultant's first recommendation was that the utility develop a new approach to defining its business, and the consultant took the managers through a planning exercise that involved identifying *who* the utility's customers were, *what* customer needs the utility was satisfying, and *how* those needs might be satisfied. This exercise revealed that the utility served three main customer groups—households, businesses, and other utilities (to which Seattle City Light sold surplus power). Focusing on households and business customers, the top-management team decided that the utility was *not* satisfying their need for electricity but was satisfying their need for energy. Having come to this conclusion, the top-management team realized that Seattle City Light was in the energy business, not the electricity business. This discovery led the managers to redefine their business as "the provision of energy and energy-related services" (such as energy conservation services).

Considering this new definition, SCL managers had to acknowledge that customer needs for energy and energy services could be, and were being, satisfied by a number of competing organizations. Managers realized that they had competitors after all and that they needed to change their strategies to compete effectively. Competitors included the local gas utility, independent energy conservation specialists, and several local operators of electricity generating facilities (including universities), which not only produced energy for their own needs but also sold surplus electric power. Thus, by going through a planning exercise to define their business, the top managers of SCL discovered that they were satisfying many more kinds of customer needs than they had originally thought and that they did have competitors.

Establishing Major Goals

Once the business is defined, managers must establish a set of primary goals to which the organization is committed. Developing these goals gives the organization a sense of direction or purpose. In most organizations, articulating major goals is the job of the CEO, although other managers have input into the process. Thus, as noted previously, under the leadership of Jack Welch, General Electric has operated with the primary goal that it be first or second in every business in which it competes.

The best statements of organizational goals are ambitious—that is, they stretch the organization and require managers to improve its performance capabilities.[17] For example, when Eckhard Pfeiffer took over as CEO of Compaq in 1992 (see the "Case in Contrast" in Chapter 3), his stated goal for the organization was that the company should become the number-one producer of personal computers in the world by 1995. Because Compaq was at that time the number-three company, behind Apple and IBM, this goal challenged managers within Compaq to look for ways to improve performance so that the company could gain market share and overtake Apple and IBM. Compaq's managers rose to the challenge, and Compaq achieved this primary goal in mid-1994. Compaq managers' vision of the mission and goals of their company, and those of AT&T and Wal-Mart, are presented in Figure 7.4.

In another example of setting a challenging goal, in 1994 Roberta Palm Bradley, CEO of Seattle City Light, stated that her primary goal for the utility was that it become the most customer-responsive, efficient, and innovative community-owned utility in the country by the year 2000. This goal represents a significant challenge for Seattle City Light because by the top-management team's own admission, the organization currently lacks a strong customer focus, is bureaucratic and inefficient, and has a history of resisting innovation.

Although goals should be challenging, they should be realistic. Challenging goals give managers an incentive to look for ways to improve an organization's operation, but a goal that is unrealistic and impossible to attain may prompt managers to give up.[18] For example, Boeing has set a challenging goal to reduce its costs by 30 percent, and managers will need to make many significant improvements in the efficiency of Boeing's operations to achieve this goal. Experience at other companies, however, has shown that it is possible to

Figure 7.4
Three Mission Statements

COMPANY	MISSION STATEMENT
Compaq	Compaq, along with our partners, will deliver compelling products and services of the highest quality that will transform computing into an intuitive experience that extends human capability on all planes—communication, education, work, and play.
Wal-Mart	We work for you. We think of ourselves as buyers for our customers, and we apply our considerable strengths to get the best value for you. We've built Wal-Mart by acting on behalf of our customers, and that concept continues to propel us. We're working hard to make our customers' shopping easy.
AT&T	We are dedicated to being the world's best at bringing people together–giving them easy access to each other and to the information and services they want and need–anytime, anywhere.

achieve 30 percent unit-cost reductions over a six-year period. Thus, the goal is challenging but not unrealistic.[19]

The time period in which a goal is expected to be achieved should be stated. Boeing's managers committed themselves to achieving the cost reduction goals by 1998. Time constraints are important because they emphasize that a goal must be attained within a reasonable period; they inject a sense of urgency into goal attainment and act as a motivator.

Formulating Strategy

Strategy formulation involves managers in analyzing an organization's current situation and then developing strategies to accomplish its mission and achieve its goals.[20] Strategy formulation begins with managers analyzing the factors within an organization and outside, in the task and general environments, that affect or may affect the organization's ability to meet its goals now and in the future. SWOT analysis and the five forces model are two techniques managers use to analyze these factors.

strategy formulation
Analysis of an organization's current situation followed by the development of strategies to accomplish its mission and achieve its goals.

SWOT analysis
A planning exercise in which managers identify organizational strengths (S) and weaknesses (W), and environmental opportunities (O) and threats (T).

SWOT Analysis

SWOT analysis is a planning exercise in which managers identify organizational strengths (S) and weaknesses (W), and environmental opportunities (O) and threats (T). Based on a SWOT analysis, managers at the different levels of the organization select the corporate-, business-, and functional-level strategies to best position the organization to achieve its mission and goals (see Figure 7.5). Because SWOT analysis is the first step in strategy formulation at any level, we consider it first, before turning specifically to corporate-, business-, and functional-level strategies.

Figure 7.5
Planning and Strategy Formulation

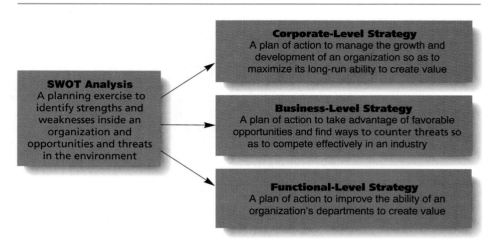

Table 7.1
Questions for SWOT Analysis

Potential Strengths	Potential Opportunities	Potential Weaknesses	Potential Threats
Well-developed strategy?	Expand core business(es)?	Poorly developed strategy?	Attacks on core business(es)?
Strong product lines?	Exploit new market segments?	Obsolete, narrow product lines?	Increase in domestic competition?
Broad market coverage?	Widen product range?	Rising manufacturing costs?	Increase in foreign competition?
Manufacturing competence?	Extend cost or differentiation advantage?	Decline in R&D innovations?	Change in consumer tastes?
Good marketing skills?	Diversify into new growth businesses?	Poor marketing plan?	Fall in barriers to entry?
Good materials management systems?	Expand into foreign markets?	Poor materials management systems?	Rise in new or substitute products?
R&D skills and leadership?	Apply R&D skills in new areas?	Loss of customer goodwill?	Increase in industry rivalry?
Human resource competencies?	Enter new related businesses?	Inadequate human resources?	New forms of industry competition?
Brand-name reputation?	Vertically integrate forward?	Loss of brand name?	Potential for takeover?
Cost of differentiation advantage?	Vertically integrate backward?	Growth without direction?	Changes in demographic factors?
Appropriate management style?	Overcome barriers to entry?	Loss of corporate direction?	Changes in economic factors?
Appropriate organizational structure?	Reduce rivalry among competitors?	Infighting among divisions?	Downturn in economy?
Appropriate control systems?	Apply brand-name capital in new areas?	Loss of corporate control?	Rising labor costs?
Ability to manage strategic change?	Seek fast market growth?	Inappropriate organizational structure and control systems?	Slower market growth?
Others?	Others?	High conflict and politics?	Others?
		Others?	

In Chapters 3 and 4 we discussed forces in the task and general environments that have the potential to affect an organization. We noted that changes in these forces can produce opportunities that an organization might take advantage of and threats that may harm its current situation. The first step in SWOT analysis is to identify an organization's strengths and weaknesses. Table 7.1 lists many important strengths (such as high-quality skills in marketing and in research and development) and weaknesses (such as rising manufacturing costs and outdated technology). The task facing managers is to identify the strengths and weaknesses that characterize the present state of their organization.

The second step in SWOT analysis begins when managers embark on a full-scale SWOT planning exercise to identify potential opportunities and threats in the environment that affect the organization at the present or may affect it in the future. Examples of possible opportunities and threats that must be anticipated (many of which were discussed in Chapter 3) are listed in Table 7.1.

With the SWOT analysis completed, and strengths, weaknesses, opportunities, and threats identified, managers can begin the planning process and determine strategies for achieving the organization's mission and goals. The resulting strategies should enable the organization to attain its goals by taking advantage of opportunities, countering threats, building strengths, and correcting organizational weaknesses. To appreciate how managers use SWOT analysis to formulate strategy, consider how James Unruh, CEO of Unisys, used it to select strategies to try to turn around this troubled manufacturer of mainframe computers.

Management Insight

James Unruh Transforms Unisys

Unisys (www.unisys.com) was formed by the 1986 merger of two manufacturers of mainframe computers—Burroughs and Sperry. Like other mainframe computer companies, Unisys in recent years has seen demand for its products plummet as customers have switched from large mainframe computers to organizationwide networks of personal computers to run many of their data-processing applications. After losing almost $2.5 billion between 1989 and 1991, however, Unisys is now making money again.

Much of the credit for this turnaround has been given to James Unruh, who became Unisys CEO in 1990. One of Unruh's first actions was to initiate a thorough SWOT planning exercise. An analysis of the environment identified the growth of the personal computer industry and companywide networks as a *threat* to Unisys's mainframe computer business (this was several years before other mainframe computer makers such as IBM (www.pc.ibm.com) and Digital Equipment (www.digital.com) recognized this threat). The analysis of the environment also revealed two growth *opportunities*.

One opportunity was in the software and computer services businesses. Many corporate computer users were looking for help in designing software to make better use of their existing mainframe computers and new networks of personal computers. They were also looking for help in identifying what information technologies to invest in. The other opportunity was in supercomputers—in particular, a new low-cost supercomputer utilizing large numbers of microprocessors linked together as a single unit, the so-called massively parallel processing machines (MPP). Experts envisage MPP machines as the hubs of organizationwide networks of thousands of personal computers.

With the analysis of the environment complete, Unruh turned his attention to his organization's resources and capabilities. His internal analysis of Unisys identified a number of major *weaknesses*. These included staffing levels that were too high given the projected decline in demand for mainframe computers and high costs associated with manufacturing many of the components that went into Unisys's computers, such as semiconductors. At the same time, the SWOT analysis identified an enormous *strength*. Unisys employed a collection

The giant network of personal computers for brokers at the Hong Kong Stock Exchange.

of highly skilled technical service and software employees who had extensive experience in helping customers with some of the most difficult existing computing applications systems, such as airline reservation systems and global banking systems.

Using the information gained from this SWOT analysis, Unruh and his managers decided to reinvent Unisys as a major force in the software and computer services business, and to dramatically downsize its mainframe and component-manufacturing operations. To allow the organization to survive with its new objectives, Unruh was forced to cut the number of Unisys employees from 120,000 to 50,000; most of the cuts were made in a single 12-month period. Unisys closed most of its component operations and saved $100 million a year in the process.[21] Managers also dramatically scaled down Unisys's traditional mainframe computer operations, so now Unisys primarily designs mainframes but contracts with other companies to manufacture them. At the same time, Unruh invested heavily in computer services and software, building on Unisys's existing skills in this area. Finally, to explore the promise of MPP supercomputers, Unisys entered into a joint venture with Intel to make an MPP supercomputer that uses hundreds of Intel's Pentium microprocessors. Estimates suggest that such a machine can be produced for under $100,000, compared with the more than $1 million price tag of a traditional large mainframe computer.

The Five Forces Model

A well-known model that helps managers isolate particular forces in the external environment that are potential threats is Michael Porter's five forces model. Porter identified five factors (the first four are also discussed in Chapter 3) that are major threats because they affect how much profit organizations competing within the same industry can expect to make:

- *The level of rivalry among organizations in an industry.* The more that companies compete against one another for customers—for example, by lowering the prices of their products or by increasing advertising—the lower is the level of industry profits (low prices mean less profit).
- *The potential for entry into an industry.* The easier it is for companies to enter an industry—because, for example, barriers to entry, such as brand loyalty, are low (see Chapter 3)—the more likely it is for industry prices and therefore industry profits to be low.
- *The power of suppliers.* If there are only a few suppliers of an important input, then (as discussed in Chapter 3) suppliers can drive up the price of that input, and expensive inputs result in lower profits for the producer.
- *The power of customers.* If only a few large customers are available to buy an industry's output, they can bargain to drive down the price of that output. As a result, producers make lower profits.
- *The threat of substitute products.* Often, the output of one industry is a substitute for the output of another industry (plastic may be a substitute for steel in some applications, for example). Companies that produce a product with a known substitute cannot demand high prices for their products, and this constraint keeps their profits low.

Porter argued that when managers analyze opportunities and threats they should pay particular attention to these five forces because they are the major threats that an organization will encounter. It is the job of managers at the corporate, business, and functional levels to formulate strategies to counter these threats so that an organization can respond to its tasks and general environments, perform at a high level, and generate high profits.

Formulating Corporate-Level Strategies

Corporate-level strategy is a plan of action concerning which industries and countries an organization should invest its resources in to achieve its mission and goals. In developing a corporate-level strategy, managers ask: How should the growth and development of the company be managed in order to increase its ability to create value for its customers (and thus increase performance) over the long run? Managers of most organizations have the goal to grow their companies and actively seek out new opportunities to use the organization's resources to create more goods and services for customers. An example of an organization growing rapidly is Microsoft; CEO Bill Gates pursues any feasible opportunity to use his company's skills to provide customers with new software products.

In addition, some managers must help their organizations respond to threats due to changing forces in the task or general environment. For example, customers may no longer be buying the kinds of goods and services a company is producing (manual typewriters, eight-track tapes, black and white televisions), or other organizations may have entered the market and attracted away customers (this happened to Xerox when its patents expired and many companies rushed into the market to sell photocopiers). Top managers aim to find the best strategies to help the organization respond to these changes and improve performance.

The principal corporate-level strategies that managers use to help a company grow, to keep it on top of its industry, and to help it retrench and reorganize in order to stop its decline are (1) concentration on a single business, (2) diversification, (3) international expansion, and (4) vertical integration. These four strategies are all based on one idea: An organization benefits from pursuing any one of them only when the strategy helps *further increase the value of the organization's goods and services for customers.* To increase the value of goods and services, a corporate-level strategy must help an organization, or one of its divisions, differentiate and add value to its products either by making them unique or special or by lowering the costs of value creation.

Concentration on a Single Business

Most organizations begin their growth and development with a corporate-level strategy aimed at concentrating resources in one business or industry in order to develop a strong competitive position within that industry. For example, McDonald's began as one restaurant in California, but its managers' long-term goal was to focus its resources in the fast-food business and use those resources to quickly expand across the United States.

Sometimes, concentration on a single business becomes an appropriate corporate-level strategy when managers see the need to reduce the size of their organizations in order to increase performance. Managers may decide to get out of certain industries, for example, when particular divisions lose their competitive advantage. Managers may sell off those divisions, lay off workers, and concentrate remaining organizational resources in another market or business to try to improve performance. This happened to the former agricultural equipment giant International Harvester, which was forced to get out of its primary business because of intense low-price competition. It liquidated or sold off all its divisions except one and then used the money to promote the one remaining business, producing trucks under the name Navistar. In contrast, when organizations are performing effectively, they often decide to enter new industries in which they can use their resources to create more value.

Diversification

diversification Expanding operations into a new business or industry and producing new goods or services.

related diversification Entering a new business or industry to create a competitive advantage in one or more of an organization's existing divisions or businesses.

Diversification is the strategy of expanding operations into a new business or industry and producing new goods or services.[22] Examples of diversification include PepsiCo's diversification into the snack-food business with the purchase of Frito-Lay, tobacco giant Philip Morris's diversification into the brewing industry with the acquisition of Miller Beer, and General Electric's move into broadcasting with its acquisition of NBC. There are two main kinds of diversification: related and unrelated.

RELATED DIVERSIFICATION   **Related diversification** is the strategy of entering a new business or industry to create a competitive advantage in one or more of an organization's existing divisions or businesses. Related diversification can add value to an organization's products if managers can

synergy Performance gains that result when individuals and departments coordinate their actions.

find ways for its various divisions or business units to share their valuable skills or resources so that synergy is created.[23] **Synergy** is obtained when the value created by two divisions cooperating is greater than the value that would be created if the two divisions operated separately. For example, suppose two or more divisions within a diversified company can utilize the same manufacturing facilities, distribution channels, advertising campaigns, and so on. Each division that shares resources has to invest less in the shared functions than it would have to invest if it had full responsibility for the activity. In this way, related diversification can be a major source of cost savings.[24] Similarly, if one division's R&D skills can be used to improve another division's products, the second division's products may receive a competitive advantage.

Procter & Gamble's disposable diaper and paper towel businesses offer one of the best examples of the successful production of synergies. These businesses share the costs of procuring inputs such as paper and developing new technology to reduce manufacturing costs. In addition, a joint sales force sells both products to supermarkets, and both products are shipped by means of the same distribution system. This resource sharing has enabled both divisions to reduce their costs, and as a result, they can charge lower prices than their competitors and thus attract more customers.[25]

In pursuing related diversification, managers often seek to find new businesses where they can use the existing skills and resources in their departments to create synergies, add value to the new business, and hence improve the competitive position of the company. Alternatively, managers may acquire a company in a new industry because they believe that some of the skills and resources of the *acquired* company might improve the efficiency of one or more of their existing divisions. If successful, such skill transfers can help an organization to lower its costs or better differentiate its products, because they create synergies between divisions.

unrelated diversification Entering a new industry or buying a company in a new industry that is not related in any way to an organization's current businesses or industries.

UNRELATED DIVERSIFICATION Managers pursue **unrelated diversification** when they enter new industries or buy companies in new industries that are not related in any way to their current businesses or industries. One main reason for pursuing unrelated diversification is that, sometimes, managers can buy a poorly performing company, transfer their management skills to that company, turn around its business, and increase its performance, all of which creates value.

Another reason for pursuing unrelated diversification is that purchasing businesses in different industries lets managers engage in *portfolio strategy,* which is apportioning financial resources among divisions to increase financial returns or spread risks among different businesses, much as individual investors do with their own portfolios. For example, managers may transfer funds from a rich division (a "cash cow") to a new and promising division (a "star") and, by appropriately allocating money between divisions, create value. Though used as a popular explanation in the 1980s for unrelated diversification, portfolio strategy ran into increasing criticism in the 1990s.[26]

Today, many companies and their managers are abandoning the strategy of unrelated diversification because there is evidence that too much diversification can cause managers to lose control of their organization's core business. Management experts suggest that although unrelated diversification might initially create value for a company, managers sometimes use portfolio strategy to expand the scope of their organization's businesses too much. When this happens, it becomes difficult for top managers to be knowledgeable about all of the organization's diverse businesses. Managers do not have the time to process all of the information that is required to assess adequately and objectively the strategy and performance of each division, and organizational performance often suffers.

This problem began to occur at General Electric in the 1970s. As then-CEO Reg Jones commented: "I tried to review each business unit plan in great detail. This effort took untold hours and placed a tremendous burden on the corporate executive office. After awhile I began to realize that no matter how hard we would work, we could not achieve the necessary in-depth understanding of the 40-odd business unit plans."[27] Unable to handle so much information, top managers are overwhelmed and eventually make important resource allocation decisions on the basis of only a superficial analysis of the competitive position of each division. This usually results in value being lost rather than created.[28]

Thus, although unrelated diversification can create value for a company, research evidence suggests that many diversification efforts have reduced value rather than created it.[29] As a consequence, during the 1990s there was a trend among many diversified companies to divest many of their unrelated divisions. Managers sold off divisions and concentrated organizational resources on their core business and focused more on related diversification.[30] Sears, for example, divested most of its stock brokerage and real-estate businesses, which were acquired during the 1980s, in order to concentrate on expanding its core retailing activities.

International Expansion

As if planning the appropriate level of diversification was not a difficult enough decision, corporate-level managers also must decide on the appropriate way to compete internationally. A basic question confronts the managers of any organization that competes in more than one national market: To what extent should the organization customize features of its products and marketing campaign to different national conditions?[31]

global strategy Selling the same standardized product and using the same basic marketing approach in each national market.

multidomestic strategy Customizing products and marketing strategies to specific national conditions.

If managers decide that their organization should sell the same standardized product in each national market in which it competes, and use the same basic marketing approach, they adopt a **global strategy.**[32] Such companies undertake very little, if any, customization to suit the specific needs of customers in different countries. But if managers decide to customize products and marketing strategies to specific national conditions, they adopt a **multidomestic strategy.** Matsushita has traditionally pursued a global strategy, selling the same basic TVs and VCRs in every market in which it does business and often using the same basic marketing approach. Unilever, the European food and household products company, has pursued a multidomestic strategy. Thus, to appeal to German customers, Unilever's German division sells a different range of food products and uses a different marketing approach than its North American division.

Both global and multidomestic strategies have advantages and disadvantages. The major advantage of a global strategy is the significant cost savings associated with not having to customize products and marketing approaches to different national conditions. For example, in the 1980s Levi Strauss paid an

M&M/Mars, the candy maker, previously used a *multidomestic strategy* and sold its candy under different brand names in the different countries in which it operates. Now it has changed to a *global strategy* to reduce costs and sells the candy under the same name throughout the world, as this billboard in Russia suggests.

advertising agency $500,000 to produce a series of TV commercials to promote its 501 jeans. By using the same series in many countries and simply changing the language, Levi was able to save a significant amount of money and keep its prices low.[33]

The major disadvantage of pursuing a global strategy is that, by ignoring national differences, managers may leave themselves vulnerable to local competitors that do differentiate their products to suit local tastes. This occurred in the British consumer electronics industry. Amstrad, a British computer and electronics company, got its start by recognizing and responding to local consumer needs. Amstrad captured a major share of the British audio market by ignoring the standardized inexpensive music centers marketed by companies pursuing a global strategy, such as Sony and Matsushita. Instead, Amstrad's product was encased in teak rather than metal and featured a control panel tailor-made to appeal to British consumers' preferences. To remain competitive in this market, Matsushita had to increase its emphasis on local customization.

The advantages and disadvantages of a multidomestic strategy are the opposite of those of a global strategy. The major advantage of a multidomestic strategy is that by customizing product offerings and marketing approaches to local conditions, managers may be able to gain market share or charge higher prices for their products. The major disadvantage is that customization raises production costs and puts the multidomestic company at a price disadvantage because it often has to charge prices higher than the prices charged by competitors pursuing a global strategy. Obviously, the choice between these two strategies calls for trade-offs. Managers at Caterpillar have created a strategy that combines the best features of both international strategies, as profiled in this "Management Insight."

Management Insight

Caterpillar's International Strategy

Caterpillar Tractor is the world's largest manufacturer of heavy earth-moving equipment. The need to compete with low-cost competitors such as Komatsu of Japan forced Caterpillar's managers to look for cost economies. At the same time, variations in construction practices and government regulations across countries required managers to be responsive to demands for local customization. Therefore, Caterpillar's managers were confronted with significant demands for cost reductions and for local customization.

To deal with these conflicting demands, Caterpillar's managers succeeded in combining elements of the global and the multidomestic strategies. Price pressures caused managers to redesign Caterpillar's many products to use many identical components. To keep costs down, they also invested in a few large-scale component-manufacturing facilities and located the facilities at favorable locations around the globe. At the same time, managers supplemented the centralized low-cost manufacturing of components with assembly plants in each of Caterpillar's major global markets. At these plants, Caterpillar tailors the finished product to local needs by adding features such as different colors of paint or steering wheels on the right or left side. Thus, Caterpillar is able to realize many of the benefits of global manufacturing while responding to pressures for local customization by differentiating its product among national markets.[34]

Vertical Integration

When an organization is doing well in its business, managers often see new opportunities to create value by either producing their own inputs or distributing their own outputs. Managers at E. & J. Gallo Winery, for example, realized that they could lower Gallo's costs if they produced their own wine bottles rather than buying them from a glass company. As a result, Gallo established a new division to produce glass bottles.

vertical integration

A strategy that allows an organization to create value by producing its own inputs or distributing and selling its own outputs.

Vertical integration is the corporate-level strategy through which an organization becomes involved in producing its own inputs (*backward* vertical integration) or distributing and selling its own outputs (*forward* vertical integration).[35] A steel company that supplies its iron ore needs from company-owned iron ore mines is engaging in backward vertical integration. A personal computer company that sells its computers through company-owned distribution outlets, as Tandy did through its Radio Shack stores, is engaging in forward vertical integration.

Figure 7.6 illustrates the four main stages in a typical raw-materials-to-consumer value chain; value is added at each stage. Typically, the primary operations of an organization take place in one of these stages. For a company based in the assembly stage, backward integration would involve establishing a new division in intermediate manufacturing or raw-material production, and forward integration would involve establishing a new division to distribute its products to wholesalers or to sell directly to customers. A division at one stage receives the product produced by the division in the previous stage, transforms

Figure 7.6
Stages in a Vertical Value Chain

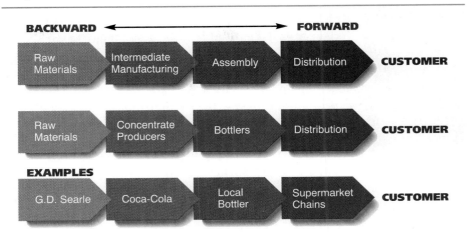

it in some way—adding value—and then transfers the output at a higher price to the division at the next stage in the chain.

As an example of how the value chain works, consider the cola segment of the soft-drink industry, discussed in the "Case in Contrast." Raw-materials suppliers include sugar companies and G. D. Searle, manufacturer of the artificial sweetener NutraSweet, which is used in diet colas. These companies sell their products to companies that make concentrate—such as Coca-Cola, PepsiCo, and Cott Corporation—which mix these inputs with others to produce the cola concentrate that they market. In the process, they add value to these inputs. The concentrate producers then sell the concentrate to bottlers, who add carbonated water to the concentrate and package the resulting drink—again adding value to the concentrate. Next, the bottlers sell the packaged product to various distributors, including retail stores such as Price Costco and Safeway, and fast-food chains such as McDonald's. These distributors add value by making the product accessible to customers. Thus, value is added by companies at each stage in the raw-materials-to-consumer chain.

A major reason why managers pursue vertical integration is that it allows them either to add value to their products by making them special or unique or to lower the costs of value creation. For example, Coca-Cola and PepsiCo, in a case of forward vertical integration to build brand loyalty and enhance the differentiated appeal of their colas, decided to buy up their major bottlers to increase control over marketing and promotion efforts—which the bottlers had been handling.[36] An example of using forward vertical integration to lower costs is Matsushita's decision to open company-owned stores to sell its own products and thus keep the profit that independent retailers otherwise would earn.[37] Another example of vertical integration is PepsiCo's decision to acquire three restaurant chains—Taco Bell, Pizza Hut, and Kentucky Fried Chicken—and sell only Pepsi products to their customers. The way in which McDonald's has used vertical integration to increase value is profiled in this "Managing Globally."

Managing Globally

McDonald's Vertically Integrates to Preserve Quality

McDonald's (www.mcdonalds.com) has been expanding into foreign markets ever since the mid-1970s, when managers became worried that a maturing market for fast food in the United States would limit growth opportunities. By the mid-1990s, McDonald's managers had operations in over 50 countries, and one-third of McDonald's revenues were generated by foreign sales.

When McDonald's enters a foreign market, managers try to apply the same basic approach to business that has proved successful in the United States. The main features of McDonald's restaurants, in other countries and in the United States, in particular the food, are essentially the same. To achieve this uniformity, McDonald's builds close relationships with the suppliers of key restaurant and food inputs—such as potatoes, hamburger meat, and hamburger buns.

McDonald's, however, has found that it cannot always get the supplies it needs in foreign countries. In the United States, suppliers are fiercely loyal to McDonald's because their fortunes are closely linked to McDonald's fortunes. McDonald's maintains rigorous specifications for all the inputs it uses, and these standards have been the key to its consistency and quality control. Outside the United States, however, McDonald's has found that suppliers are far less willing or able to meet McDonald's input specifications. As a result, managers in some countries have found it necessary to vertically integrate backward and produce their own inputs.

In Britain, McDonald's managers had problems persuading local bakeries to produce hamburger buns to the company's specifications. After quality problems were experienced with two local bakeries, McDonald's allocated resources to build a bakery in Britain to supply its own restaurants. In a more extreme case, when McDonald's managers decided to open their first store in Russia, they found that local suppliers simply lacked the capability to produce high-quality inputs. Managers were forced to vertically integrate through the local food industry on a heroic scale, importing potato seeds and indirectly managing dairy farms, cattle ranches, and vegetable plots. They ultimately ended up constructing the world's largest food-processing plant at a cost of $40 million. The restaurant itself cost only $4.5 million.[38] However, McDonald's managers expect a big payoff in the future.

Although vertical integration can help an organization to grow rapidly, it can be a problem when forces in the organizational environment counter the strategies of the organization and make it necessary for managers to reorganize or retrench. Vertical integration can reduce an organization's flexibility to respond to changing environmental conditions. For example, IBM used to produce most of its own components for mainframe computers. Doing this made sense in the 1960s, but it become a major handicap for the company in the fast-changing computer industry of the 1990s. The rise of organizationwide networks of personal computers has meant slumping demand for mainframes. As demand fell, IBM found itself with an excess-capacity problem, not only in its mainframe assembly operations but also in component operations. Closing down this capacity cost IBM over $5 billion in 1993 and clearly limited the company's ability to pursue other opportunities.[39] When considering vertical integration as a strategy to add value, managers must be careful because sometimes vertical integration actually reduces an organization's ability to create value when the environment changes.

Formulating Business-Level Strategies

Table 7.2
Porter's Business-Level Strategies

Strategy	Number of Market Segments Served	
	Many	**Few**
Low cost	✓	
Focused low cost		✓
Differentiation	✓	
Focused differentiation		✓

Michael Porter, the researcher who developed the five forces model discussed earlier, also formulated a theory of how managers can select a business-level strategy, a plan to gain a competitive advantage in a particular market or industry.[40] According to Porter, managers must choose between the two basic ways of increasing the value of an organization's products: differentiating the product to add value or lowering the costs of value creation. Porter also argues that managers must choose between serving the whole market or serving just one segment or part of a market. Given those choices, managers choose to pursue one of four business-level strategies: low cost, differentiation, focused low cost, or focused differentiation (see Table 7.2).

Low-Cost Strategy

low-cost strategy
Driving the organization's costs down below the costs of its rivals.

With a **low-cost strategy,** managers try to gain a competitive advantage by focusing the energy of all the organization's departments or functions on driving the organization's costs down below the costs of its rivals. This strategy would require manufacturing managers to search for new ways to reduce production costs, R&D managers to focus on developing new products that can be manufactured more cheaply, and marketing managers to find ways to lower the costs of attracting customers. According to Porter, organizations pursuing a low-cost strategy can sell a product for less than their rivals sell it and yet still make a profit because of their lower costs. Thus, organizations that pursue a low-cost strategy hope to enjoy a competitive advantage based on their low prices.

Differentiation Strategy

differentiation strategy Distinguishing an organization's products from the products of competitors in dimensions such as product design, quality, or after-sales service.

With a **differentiation strategy,** managers try to gain a competitive advantage by focusing all the energies of the organization's departments or functions on distinguishing the organization's products from those of competitors in one or more important dimensions, such as product design, quality, or after-sales service and support. Often, the process of making products unique and different is expensive. This strategy, for example, often requires managers to increase spending on product design or R&D to differentiate the product, and costs rise as a result. However, organizations that successfully pursue a differentiation strategy may be able to charge a *premium price* for their products, a price usually much higher than the price charged by a low-cost organization.

The premium price allows organizations pursuing a differentiation strategy to recoup their higher costs.

Coca-Cola and PepsiCo, profiled in the "Case in Contrast," are clearly pursuing a strategy of differentiation. Both companies spend enormous amounts of money on advertising to differentiate, and create a unique image for, their products. The Cott Corporation, in contrast, is pursuing a low-cost strategy. A major reason for Cott's low costs is the fact that the company does not advertise, which allows Cott to underprice both Coke and Pepsi.

"Stuck in the Middle"

According to Porter's theory, managers cannot simultaneously pursue both a low-cost strategy and a differentiation strategy. Porter identified a simple correlation: Differentiation raises costs and thus necessitates premium pricing to recoup those high costs. For example, if Cott Corporation suddenly began to advertise heavily to try to build a strong brand image for its products, Cott's costs would rise. Cott then could no longer make a profit simply by pricing its cola lower than Coca-Cola or Pepsi. According to Porter, managers must choose between a low-cost strategy and a differentiation strategy. He says that managers and organizations that have not made this choice are "stuck in the middle." According to Porter, organizations stuck in the middle tend to have lower levels of performance than do those that pursue a low-cost or a differentiation strategy. To avoid being stuck in the middle, top managers must instruct departmental managers to take actions that will result in either low cost or differentiation.

However, exceptions to this rule can be found. In many organizations managers have been able to drive costs down below those of rivals and simultaneously differentiate their products from those offered by rivals.[41] For example, Toyota's production system is reportedly the most efficient in the world. This efficiency gives Toyota a low-cost strategy vis à vis its rivals in the global car industry. At the same time, Toyota has differentiated its cars from those of rivals on the basis of superior design and quality. This superiority allows the company to charge a premium price for many of its popular models.[42] Thus, Toyota seems to be simultaneously pursuing both a low-cost and a differentiated business-level strategy. This example suggests that although Porter's ideas may be valid in most cases, very well managed companies such as Toyota, McDonald's, and Compaq may have both low costs and differentiated products.

Focused Low-Cost and Focused Differentiation Strategies

Both the differentiation strategy and the low-cost strategy are aimed at serving most or all segments of the market. Porter identified two other business-level strategies that aim to serve the needs of customers in only one or a few market segments.[43] A company pursuing a **focused low-cost strategy** serves one or a few segments of the overall market and aims to be the lowest-cost company serving that segment. This is the strategy that Cott Corporation adopted. Cott focuses on large retail chains and strives to be the lowest-cost company serving that segment of the market.

focused low-cost strategy Serving only one segment of the overall market and being the lowest-cost organization serving that segment.

focused differentiation strategy Serving only one segment of the overall market and trying to be the most differentiated organization serving that segment.

By contrast, a company pursuing a **focused differentiation strategy** serves just one or a few segments of the market and aims to be the most differentiated company serving that segment. BMW pursues a focused strategy, producing cars exclusively for higher-income customers. By contrast, Toyota pursues a differentiation strategy and produces cars that appeal to consumers in all segments of the car market, from basic transportation (Toyota Tercel), through the middle of the market (Toyota Camry), to the high-income end of the market (Lexus).

As these examples suggest, companies pursuing either of these focused strategies have chosen to *specialize* in some way—by directing their efforts at a particular kind of customer (such as serving the needs of babies or affluent customers) or even the needs of customers in a specific geographical region (customers on the east or west coast).

Formulating Functional-Level Strategies

functional-level strategy A plan that indicates how a function intends to achieve its goals.

Functional-level strategy is a plan of action to improve the ability of an organization's departments to create value. It is concerned with the actions that managers of individual departments (such as manufacturing or marketing) can take to add value to an organization's goods and services and thereby increase the value customers receive. The price that customers are prepared to pay for a product indicates how much they value an organization's products. The more customers value a product, the more they are willing to pay for it.

Companies often conduct market research to find ways in which they can improve their products or services over their competitors. Pictured here is a focus group—a representative sample of the market, or group of people that are customers, that are brought in and asked questions related to their peceptions of the product and/or competitor's products. The group members offer their views and insights, which, in turn, give companies the information to help improve their products or services.

There are two ways in which departments can add value to an organization's products:

1. Departmental managers can lower the costs of creating value so that an organization can attract customers by keeping its prices lower than its competitors' prices.

2. Departmental managers can add value to a product by finding ways to differentiate it from the products of other companies.

If customers see more value in one organization's products than in the products of its competitors, they may be willing to pay premium prices. Thus, there must be a fit between functional- and business-level strategies if an organization is to achieve its mission and goal of maximizing the amount of value it gives customers. The better the fit between functional- and business-level strategies, the greater will be the organization's competitive advantage—its ability to attract customers and the revenue they provide.

Each organizational function has an important role to play in lowering costs or adding value to a product (see Table 7.3). Manufacturing can find new ways to lower production costs or to build superior quality into the product to add value. Marketing, sales, and after-sales service and support can add value by, for example, building brand loyalty (as Coca-Cola and PepsiCo have done in the soft-drink industry) and finding more effective ways to attract customers. Human resource management can lower the costs of creating value by recruiting and training a highly productive workforce. The R&D function can lower the costs of creating value by developing more efficient production processes. Similarly, R&D can add value by developing new and improved products that customers value over established product offerings. Managers can lower the

Table 7.3

How Functions Can Lower Costs and Create Value or Add Value to Create a Competitive Advantage

Value-Creating Function	Ways to Lower the Cost of Creating Value (Low-Cost Advantage)	Ways to Add Value (Differentiation Advantage)
Sales and marketing Materials management Research and development Manufacturing Human resource management	• Find new customers • Find low-cost advertising methods • Use just-in-time inventory system/computerized warehousing • Develop long-term relationships with suppliers and customers • Improve efficiency of machinery and equipment • Design products that can be made more cheaply • Develop skills in low-cost manufacturing • Reduce turnover and absenteeism • Raise employee skills	• Promote brand-name awareness and loyalty • Tailor products to suit customers' needs • Develop long-term relationships with suppliers to provide high-quality inputs • Reduce shipping time to customers • Create new products • Improve existing products • Increase product quality and reliability • Hire highly skilled employees • Develop innovative training programs

costs of creating value and can add value through their effective leadership and coordination of the whole organization (see Chapter 13).

In trying to add value or lower the costs of creating value, all functional managers should attend to these four goals:[44]

1. *To attain superior efficiency.* Efficiency is a measure of the amount of inputs required to produce a given amount of outputs. The fewer the inputs required to produce a given output, the higher is the efficiency and the lower the cost of outputs. For example, a 1990 study of the automobile industry found that it took the average Japanese auto company 16.8 employee-hours to build a car, while the average American auto company took 25.1 employee-hours. These numbers suggest that Japanese companies at that time were more efficient and had lower costs than their American rivals.[45]

2. *To attain superior quality.* Here quality means producing goods and services that are reliable—they do the job they were designed for and do it well.[46] Providing high-quality products creates a brand-name reputation for an organization's products. In turn, this enhanced reputation allows the organization to charge a higher price. In the automobile industry, for example, not only does Toyota have an efficiency-based cost advantage over many American and European competitors, but the higher quality of Toyota's products has also enabled the company to earn more money because customers are willing to pay a premium price for its cars.

3. *To attain superior innovation.* Anything new or unusual about the way an organization operates or the goods and services it produces is the result of innovation. Innovation leads to advances in the kinds of products, production processes, management systems, organizational structures, and strategies that an organization develops. Successful innovation gives an organization something unique that its rivals lack. This uniqueness may enhance value added and thereby allow the organization to differentiate itself from its rivals and attract customers who will pay a premium price for its product. For example, Toyota is widely credited with pioneering a number of critical innovations in the way cars are built, and these innovations have helped Toyota achieve superior productivity and quality—the basis of Toyota's competitive advantage.

4. *To attain superior responsiveness to customers.* An organization that is responsive to customers tries to satisfy their needs and give them exactly what they want. An organization that treats customers better than its rivals treats them provides a valuable service for which customers may be willing to pay a higher price.

Attaining superior efficiency, quality, innovation, and responsiveness to customers requires the adoption of many state-of-the-art management techniques and practices, such as total quality management, flexible manufacturing systems, just-in-time inventory, self-managing teams, cross-functional teams, process reengineering, and employee empowerment. It is the responsibility of managers at the functional level to identify these techniques and develop a functional-level plan that contains the strategies necessary to develop them. We discuss these techniques at length in Part 6, where we focus on the management of operations and processes. The important issue to remember here is that all of these techniques can help an organization achieve a competitive advantage by lowering the costs of creating value or by adding value above and beyond that offered by rivals.

Planning and Implementing Strategy

After identifying appropriate strategies to attain an organization's mission and goals, managers confront the challenge of putting those strategies into action. Strategy implementation is a five-step process:

1. Allocating responsibility for implementation to the appropriate individuals or groups

2. Drafting detailed action plans that specify how a strategy is to be implemented

3. Establishing a timetable for implementation that includes precise, measurable goals linked to the attainment of the action plan

4. Allocating appropriate resources to the responsible individuals or groups

5. Holding specific individuals or groups responsible for the attainment of corporate, divisional, and functional goals

As an example of how strategy implementation works in practice, consider again the case of Seattle City Light. While analyzing the strengths and weaknesses of Seattle City Light (during a SWOT analysis), managers identified bureaucratic and clumsy management as a major weakness and a direct source of high costs, poor responsiveness to customers, and a lack of innovation within the organization. To correct this weakness, managers formulated and then adopted a plan they called "Operation Simplification."

The stated purpose of "Operation Simplification" was to reengineer or redesign the utility's management processes to reduce waste and inefficiencies and to speed decision making. Two individuals were identified as holding primary responsibility for the implementation of this initiative—one senior manager and one lower-level manager. Management drafted a plan that specified how this initiative would be implemented.

The plan called for the utility to train a small group of its own employees in reengineering techniques and to use this group as a reengineering team. The action plan also established a formal process for identifying reengineering opportunities within the organization and for deciding which opportunities the reengineering team should tackle first. A detailed timetable was established; it laid out deadlines for identifying and training the reengineering team, for identifying reengineering opportunities, for prioritizing opportunities, and for beginning the actual reengineering process. The individuals responsible were given a budget to provide them with the financial resources necessary to complete the project. They also were given the authority to recruit several employees from within the organization for their reengineering team. Finally, top management informed the individuals responsible that they would be held accountable for meeting the timetable associated with the plan and for the overall success of the strategic initiative.

As the case of Seattle City Light illustrates, the planning process goes beyond the mere identification of strategies; it also includes actions taken to ensure that the organization actually puts its strategies into action. It should be noted that the plan for implementing a strategy may require radical redesign of the structure of the organization, the development of new control systems, and the adoption of a program for changing the culture of the organization. We address these issues in the next three chapters.

Tips for Managers

1. Periodically define an organization's business to determine how well it is achieving its mission. Use this planning exercise to determine its future goals.

2. Make SWOT analysis an integral part of the planning process.

3. Always be alert for opportunities to increase the value of an organization's goods and services so it can better serve its customers' needs.

4. Ensure that functional managers focus on finding new ways in which to lower the costs of value creation or to add value to products so that an organization can pursue both a low-cost and a differentiation strategy.

5. Carefully assess the costs and benefits associated with using a corporate-level strategy and only enter a new business when it can clearly demonstrate that it will increase the value of a product(s).

Summary and Review

Chapter Summary

THE PLANNING PROCESS

• **Levels of Planning**

• **Who Plans?**

• **Time Horizons of Plans**

• **Standing Plans and Single-Use Plans**

• **Why Planning Is Important**

• **Scenario Planning**

DETERMINING MISSION AND GOALS

• **Defining the Business**

• **Establishing Major Goals**

PLANNING Planning is a three-step process: (1) determining an organization's mission and goals, (2) formulating strategy, and (3) implementing strategy. Managers use planning to identify and select appropriate goals and courses of action for an organization and to decide how to allocate the resources they need to attain those goals and carry out those actions. A good plan builds commitment for the organization's goals, gives the organization a sense of direction and purpose, coordinates the different functions and divisions of the organization, and controls managers by making them accountable for specific goals. In large organizations planning takes place at three levels: corporate, business or division, and department or functional. Although planning is typically the responsibility of a well-defined group of managers, the subordinates of those managers should be given every opportunity to have input into the process and to shape the outcome. Long-term plans have a time horizon of five years or more; intermediate-term plans, between one and five years; and short-term plans, one year or less.

DETERMINING MISSION AND GOALS AND FORMULATING STRATEGY Determining the organization's mission requires managers to define the business of the organization and establish major goals. Strategy formulation requires managers to perform a SWOT analysis and then choose appropriate strategies at the corporate, business, and functional levels. At the corporate level, organizations use strategies such as concentration on a single business, diversification, international expansion, and vertical integration to help increase the value of the goods and services provided to customers. At the business level, managers are responsible for developing a successful low-cost or differentiation strategy, either for the whole market or for a particular segment of it. At the functional level, departmental managers strive to develop and use their skills to help the organization either to add value to its products by differentiating them or to lower the costs of value creation.

IMPLEMENTING STRATEGY   Strategy implementation requires managers to allocate responsibilities to appropriate individuals or groups, draft detailed action plans that specify how a strategy is to be implemented, establish a timetable for implementation that includes precise, measurable goals linked to the attainment of the action plan, allocate appropriate resources to the responsible individuals or groups, and hold individuals or groups accountable for the attainment of goals.

Management in Action

Topics for Discussion and Action

1. Describe the three steps of planning. Explain how they are related.

2. How can scenario planning help managers predict the future?

3. Ask a manager about the kinds of planning exercises he or she regularly uses. What are the purposes of these exercises, and what are their advantages or disadvantages?

4. What is the role of divisional and functional managers in the formulation of strategy?

5. Why is it important for functional managers to have a clear grasp of the organization's mission when developing strategies within their departments?

6. What is the relationship among corporate-, business-, and functional-level strategies, and how do they create value for an organization?

7. Ask a manager to identify the corporate-, business-, and functional-level strategies used by his or her organization.

Building Management Skills

How to Analyze a Company's Strategy

Pick a well-known business organization that has received recent press coverage and for which you can get the annual reports or 10K filings from your school library for a number of years. For this organization do the following.

1. From the annual reports or 10K filings identify the main strategies pursued by the company over a 10-year period.

2. Try to identify why the company pursued these strategies. What reason was given in the annual reports, press reports, and elsewhere?

3. Document whether and when any major changes in the strategy of the organization occurred. If changes did occur, try to identify the reason for them.

4. If changes in strategy occurred, try to determine the extent to which they were the result of long-term plans and the extent to which they were responses to unforeseen changes in the company's task environment.

5. What is the main industry that the company competes in?

6. What business-level strategy does the company seem to be pursuing in this industry?

7. What is the company's reputation with regard to productivity, quality, innovation, and responsiveness to customers in this industry? If the company has attained an advantage in any of these areas, how has it done so?

8. What is the current corporate-level strategy of the company? What is the company's stated reason for pursuing this strategy?

9. Has the company expanded internationally? If it has, identify its largest international market. How did the company enter this market? Did its mode of entry change over time?

261

Small Group Breakout Exercise

Low Cost or Differentiation?

Form groups of three or four people, and appoint one member as spokesperson who will communicate your findings to the class when called on by the instructor. Then discuss the following scenario.

You are a team of managers of a major national clothing chain, and you have been charged with finding a way to restore your organization's competitive advantage. Recently, your organization has been experiencing increasing competition from two sources. First, discount stores such as Wal-Mart and Target have been undercutting your prices because they buy their clothes from low-cost foreign manufacturers while you buy most of yours from high-quality domestic suppliers. Discount stores have been attracting your customers who buy at the low end of the price range. Second, small boutiques opening in malls provide high-price designer clothing and are attracting away your customers at the high end of the market. Your company has become stuck in the middle, and you have to decide what to do: Should you start to buy abroad so that you can lower your prices and start to pursue a low-cost strategy? Should you focus on the high end of the market and become more of a differentiator?

Or should you try to do both and pursue both a low-cost and a differentiation strategy?

1. Using scenario planning, analyze the pros and cons of each alternative.

2. Think about the various clothing retailers in your local malls and city, and analyze the choices they have made about how to compete with one another along the low-cost and differentiation dimensions.

Exploring the World Wide Web

Specific Assignment

This exercise follows up on the activities of McDonald's Corporation (www.mcdonalds.com), which is vertically integrating on a global level. Research McDonald's website to get a feel for this global giant. In particular, focus on McDonald's most recent annual report and its descriptions of the company's goals and objectives.

1. What are the main elements of McDonald's strategy at the corporate, business, and functional levels?

2. How successful has the company been recently?

General Assignment

Search for a website that contains a good description of a company's strategy. What is the company's mission? Use the concepts and terminology of this chapter to describe the company's strategy to achieve its mission.

ManagementCase

In the News

From the Pages of BusinessWeek
Look Out Supermarkets— Wal-Mart Is Hungry

When Wal-Mart Stores Inc. recently announced plans for three "experimental" grocery stores in Arkansas, industry executives shuddered. After all, only a decade ago, Wal-Mart said it was merely testing giant "supercenters" that combined food and general merchandise. Today, its supercenters number nearly 500—and after ringing up grocery sales estimated at $12 billion this year, the Bentonville (Ark.) company will rank as the country's eighth-largest grocer.

With that kind of track record, it's no wonder that the new Wal-Mart Neighborhood Markets, to open in October, are drawing plenty of attention. The 40,000-square-foot stores, about the same size as traditional supermarkets, are one more sign of Wal-Mart's determination to dominate this highly fragmented $415 billion business, as it has the discount-store industry.

By leveraging its distribution and buying strengths, Wal-Mart is hoping the new markets will be able to beat grocery stores with lower everyday prices while offering more conveniences than its supercenters. That's why few are fooled by the small-scale start: If the test stores meet profit targets, Wal-Mart will likely roll the new format out nationwide. "Any supermarket

executive that looks at this latest development should be very concerned," says retail expert Philip St. Georges, managing director at KPMG Peat Marwick. "What it says is, one way or another, we're going to come and get your customer."

Already, Wal Mart's push into groceries is pressuring giants like Kroger Co. and Safeway Inc. to cut costs and boost service. And the pressures aren't coming just from the supercenters: Add food and other grocery items sold through the Wal-Mart discount and Sam's Clubs units, and retail consultant James M. Degen of J. M. Degen & Co. in Templeton, Calif., estimates that groceries now account for more than $30 billion of Wal-Mart's total $118 billion in sales. Wal-Mart "is totally flanking the grocery industry," warns Gary M. Stibel, principal of New England Consulting Group in Westport, Conn. "It is terribly threatening." He predicts that in 10 years, Wal-Mart and Safeway will be the two largest food retailers in the U.S., leaving such rivals as Kroger and Albertson's Inc. in the dust.

Certainly, the Neighborhood Markets look like an even more direct assault on traditional grocery chains. Wal-Mart executives insist the three stores—plus two on the drawing boards—are only a test. But many analysts already predict

the smaller stores will quickly prove a powerful complement to the giant supercenters, which average 182,000 square feet. Stibel thinks the new format alone, if it's rolled out nationally, could grab 5% to 10% of grocery volume in the U.S. within 10 to 12 years.

That's not to suggest that Wal-Mart is tapped out with its supercenters, where about one-third of the space is devoted to groceries. Indeed, Wal-Mart Executive Vice-President Nick White, who oversees the $26.5 billion operation, says that the company will add 120 to 130 supercenters a year in the U.S. "indefinitely." Most will replace smaller discount stores. Potentially, he adds, "every Wal-Mart store could be a supercenter." The retailer now operates about 1,900 conventional discount outlets in the U.S.

But even as it adds new prototypes to its portfolio of supercenters—the latest being a 200,000-square-foot model in Broken Arrow, Okla.—Wal-Mart is trying to bite into a new part of the market with the Neighborhood format. St. Georges notes that only 25% to 30% of grocery shoppers are motivated primarily by low prices, which is Wal-Mart's strong suit in the supercenters. Many other consumers put convenience at the top of their shopping list. With their huge size and reach—sometimes drawing customers from up to 60 miles away—the supercenters don't always hit the mark.

Consider the shoppers avoiding Wal-Mart's spanking new supercenter in Broken Arrow, a suburb of Tulsa, on a recent August day. Despite mouth-watering piles of fresh produce near the entrance, a display case filled with take-home meals such as calzones and tamales, and lots of grand-opening specials, Kristin Capeheart, 29, and her boyfriend Brian Garrett, 24, are shopping at their usual store—Albertson's, several miles down the road. "We don't like to go there if we don't have to," says Capeheart. "There's too many people."

Moreover, a Reasor's Food Warehouse store on the same street stocks a variety of fish and fancy breads that can't be found at the supercenter. Mary Brawley, 43, notes that four employees of this family-owned chain have offered to help her in the past hour. "Go find someone [to help you] in a super-store," she scoffs.

To lure in recalcitrant shoppers, Wal-Mart's new format is designed to look a lot more like a traditional supermarket. And the good news is that it's a low-risk proposition. By planting the new stores near existing supercenters, the company can use the same sophisticated food-distribution system that supports the big stores. Wal-Mart recently opened in Bedford, Pa., its eighth food-distribution center, with another to be added later this year. These mammoth 800,000-square-foot facilities boost efficiency by enabling Wal-Mart to deliver dry groceries and fresh products from the same location.

That alone should help Wal-Mart put the squeeze on competi-tiors in this traditionally tiny-margin business. And borrowing from the techniques that have allowed it to dominate in discounting, Wal-Mart also has many of its grocery items on "automatic replenishment," with computer systems helping to refill shelves as needed. The company now supplies virtually all of its own groceries, giving it a cost advantage over the many rival grocers that use third-party wholesalers.

As a result, most analysts expect the Neighborhood Markets to compete heavily on price when they open up. But it won't be their only selling point. The system also enables Wal-Mart to ensure fresher products and adequate supplies. "That puts us miles ahead of the bulk of the 35,000 grocery stores we compete with," says White.

It should also provide a juicy payoff. Wal-Mart believes its investment return on the small stores could be as good as it is on the supercenters. Burt P. Flickinger III, managing director of Reach Marketing in Westport, Conn., figures the supercenters achieve a high 25% return on investment, compared with 20% to 22% for grocery chains and about 22% for conventional discount stores.

Competitors, of course, are hardly waving the white flag. Noting that most major supermarket chans no longer open stores as small as the new Neighborhood Markets, one grocery industry rival points out that there's a reason why the median-size new grocery store is now about 52,400 square feet. Wal-Mart "cannot get the assortment that's necessary in the store," he says. White of Wal-Mart says the retailer hasn't yet decided how many products the new stores will carry, but that it will include fresh foods, health and beauty aids, and other traditional grocery categories.

Still, many in the industry aren't taking any chances. Wal-Mart's grocery expansion is one reason behind the flood of recent industry mergers, such as the marriage of Albertson's and American Stores or Safeway and Vons. These merg-ers are supposed to slash distribution and administrative costs while beefing up the combined chain's marketing and buying clout. That could pit Wal-Mart against much stronger grocery competition. The likely losers? The smaller chains and independent stores, which simply won't be able to spread their costs over enough volume to compete with the giants. "Most of the regionals will go away," warns consultant Stibel.

Already, those pressures are starting to play out. R. Randall Onstead, CEO of 116-store Randalls Food Markets Inc. in Texas, admits he's feeling heat from six Wal-Mart supercenters in his territory. And the new Neighborhood Market concept is clearly a threat. "Whatever they do, they've proven to me they can do it right," he says. These days, no one's underestimating the new grocery giant.

Source: Wendy Zellner, "Look Out Supermarkets—Wal-Mart Is Hungry;" *Business Week*, September 14, 1998, 98–100.

Questions

1. Use Porter's five forces model to analyze the nature of competition in the supermarket industry.

2. What business- and functional-level strategies is Wal-Mart pursuing to compete in this industry?

ManagementCase

In the News

From the Pages of BusinessWeek
Souping Up Campbell's

Dale F. Morrison has never lacked self-confidence. When he was growing up in Milton, N.D., pop. 200, there were so few kids around for sports and music programs that Morrison happily jumped into every after-school activity around: He played basketball, ran on the track team, even sang in the boys' quartet, despite what he discribes as a less-than-exceptional singing voice. "I left [Milton] thinking I could do everything and that anything was possible," Morrison says today.

That attitude has kept the 48-year-old Morrison on the corporate fast track, where he has distinguished himself as a marketing whiz for such all-American products as Doritos and Pepperidge Farm cookies. Now, as chief executive of Campbell Soup Co., Morrison needs to draw on every bit of that self-assurance as he tackles his toughest job yet.

Simply put, Morrison needs to stir up new ways to sell more soup—lots more. It sounds easy, but it isn't. Last July, Morrison took over the top spot at Campbell from the charismatic and financially astute David W. Johnson. Johnson did a great job boosting profits by raising prices and slashing costs. Wall Street rewarded Johnson with soaring share prices, up about 270% since January, 1990. But

persuading consumers to slurp up more chicken noodle and tomato soup was another matter. From 1990 through 1996, virtually all of Campbell's 4% annual gain in sales came from aggressive price increases.

Despite the strong performance —and Campbell's nearly 80% share of the U.S. canned soup market—the price hikes put the company at a critical juncture. Similar pricing strategies have come back to haunt leaders in such sectors as tobacco, diapers, and cereal; all have ended up with eroding market share, warns Steven M. Galbraith, an analyst with Sanford C. Bernstein & Co.

That's why Galbraith believes Campbell's earnings growth will likely slow from its recent torrid pace; from 1990 to 1996, profits grew at a 17% compounded annual rate. Morrison has already announced plans to spin off some slow-growing businesses. William Leach, a vice-president with Donaldson, Lufkin & Jenrette, figures net income for the remaining businesses, excluding an earlier charge, will be up about 12%, to $924 million, for the fiscal year ending July, 1998. Sales of the newly slimmed-down company should grow about 4.6%, to $6.8 billion.

That kind of middling sales growth, however, doesn't satisfy

Morrison. Indeed, he wants nothing less than for Campbell to enjoy the same global clout in soup that Coca-Cola Co. enjoys in the cola wars. And with Campbell holding just 10% of the soup market outside the U.S., Morrison sees a huge opportunity. To kick off his campaign, he has been rallying the troops. At a recent meeting for 1,200 employees, he revved up the crowd with his signature exhortation to set "big, hairy, audacious goals."

It's a role that comes naturally for the intensely likable and exuberant executive, who has been known to go out for beers with factory workers to win them over to his plans. Morrison wants to get Campbell's annual sales growth rate up around 8% to 10%, largely through increased marketing and acquisitions. "I have a healthy paranoia about pricing," he says.

The challenge seems tailor-made for Morrison. Through a series of posts at General Foods, PepsiCo, and most recently at Campbell's Pepperidge Farm unit, he has revealed a knack for clever marketing. When Morrison took over the snack and bakery unit in June, 1995, Pepperidge Farm was in sorry shape. Sales and earnings over the previous three years had been growing at an anemic annual rate of just 3% and 2%, respectively.

And though management had been pushing prices upward, it failed to support its products with solid advertising. As a result, market share and volumes were slipping.

Morrison improved manufacturing efficiency by reducing waste and focusing some plants on fewer products. The money saved was pumped into aggressive marketing targeted toward a few promising lines such as Goldfish crackers and Milano cookies. Morrison also met with hundreds of Pepperidge Farm's 2,500 independent distributors, even taking time out from his ski vacation in Colorado to meet with a Steamboat Springs distributor. "I don't want them to think of themselves as truck drivers but as business development people," he explains. And to appeal to the lucrative kid market, Morrison also introduced new kid-friendly packaging. . . .

Now, at Campbell, Morrison has much bigger battles on his agenda. In September, he announced plans to spin off slower-growth businesses accounting for $1.4 billion in sales, including Vlasic pickles and the Swanson frozen-food line. "We are driving the incredibly shrinking company," he recently warned employees.

To run the U.S. food unit, Morrison has brought in Mark M. Leckie, a veteran of the brutal price wars in the cereal business. And Morrison is taking a page out of the recipe book that worked so well for him at Pepperidge Farm. He plans to squeeze costs by more that $100 million annually over the next several years while launching an aggressive marketing blitz. To whet consumer appetites for Campbell's soups, Morrison ultimately wants to double advertising outlays from 4% of sales to 8%, including a homey, all American image campaign planned early next year.

Overseas markets are also attracting Morrison's energies. He has just struck a $170 million deal to buy Danone's Liebig soup business, one of the leading brands in France, and he is scouting more deals. Within two weeks of taking over at Campbell, Morrison sent one executive to Europe and another to Asia to head up the international push. Until then, senior managers in charge of international operations had been based in New Jersey.

Will the French and Japanese really run out and buy Campbell's products? Morrison hardly seems daunted by the challenge. "I feel great about the team we have and what we need to do," he says. Revitalizing a vintage brand like Campbell Soup may be tough, but Dale Morrison is just an older, wiser version of that North Dakota kid who knew he could do anything and everything.

Source: Amy Barrett, "Souping Up Campbell's," *Business Week,* November 5, 1997, 70–72.

Questions

1. What strategies did Dale Morrison use to increase the profitability of the Pepperidge Farm division?

2. What kinds of corporate- and business-level strategies is Morrison working on to help increase Campbell Soup's performance?

Part 4

Chapter eight

Managing Organizational Architecture

Learning Objectives

1. Identify the factors that influence managers' choice of an organizational structure.

2. Explain how managers group tasks into jobs that are motivating and satisfying for employees.

3. Describe the organizational structures managers can design, and explain why they choose one structure over another.

4. Explain why there is a need to both centralize and decentralize authority.

5. Explain why managers must coordinate and integrate jobs, functions, and divisions as an organization grows.

6. Explain why managers who seek new ways to increase efficiency and effectiveness are using strategic alliances and network structures.

A Case in Contrast

Kinko's Changes Its Organizational Structure

Kinko's Inc., the largest chain of 24-hour copying stores in the United States, holds an estimated 25 to 30 percent share of the $6 billion retail copying market and is the most well-known name. In 1996, however, founder Paul Orfalea realized that his company was facing major problems and that he had to change the way it operated if it was to remain successful.

First, Kinko's was under intense competitive pressures from two sources. Other rapidly growing copying chains like Sir Speedy Inc. and Kwik Kopy were opening outlets in Kinko's major markets and taking away Kinko's market share; and office supply chains such as OfficeMax and Office Depot had begun to offer low-priced copying, as well as other services, and also were taking away Kinko's customers. Second, the infor-

mal, decentralized way of managing Kinko's 850 stores that Orfalea had been using was not allowing the company to respond quickly enough to the moves of its competitors.[1] Third, Kinko's was having a difficult time managing its own growth and development—in particular, it was experiencing problems in deciding how to effectively service the needs of new kinds of customers like small and large businesses.

Orfalea had begun to feel that Kinko's was in danger of losing its leading industry position because of his, and his company's, inability to find a new way of operating in the changed industry environment. To help him find a solution to Kinko's problems, Orfalea called on the services of consultants from the New York investment firm Clayton, Dubilier & Rice, Inc. These consultants began to examine and

Managers and employees at Kinko's have been forced to adopt new, more efficient, work methods to compete in the fiercely competitive copying and office services industry as new competitors such as Sir Speedy and OfficeMax have entered.

analyze Kinko's method of operating. They soon realized that the root of Kinko's troubles was the kind of organizational structure—the task and authority relationships inside the company—Kinko's used to manage its far-flung store operations.[2]

Orfalea had grown his company by franchising. He had sold to investors the right to open stores using Kinko's name and copying expertise in a particular location, normally a city. Each Kinko's store was an independent operating unit, and the local investor, or franchisee, controlled how it grew in that location.[3] This method of operating let the company grow quickly but did little to help the company either control its costs or find better ways of meeting its customer's needs. The consultants decided that what Kinko's needed was a more centralized operating system, where, for example, purchasing and financing for the entire company were handled centrally by the head office to reduce costs.

Previously, Orfalea had not taken control of any operating activity; he had even refused to have an official title like "President." The consultants recommended that Kinko's recruit experienced top managers to provide the centralized control the company needed if it was going to develop a plan of action to respond to the challenges of its competitors and discover new and better ways of meeting the needs of its customers. Moreover, they recommend that Kinko's develop a clear set of internal authority relationships so that the new top managers would be able to orchestrate companywide changes to retain and attract new customers.

Given that Kinko's store managers had been in complete control of their operations, it was not clear how they would adapt to this new operating structure. However, they all agreed that they had to find a new way for the company to operate in a more competitive environment, and to make it work, if Kinko's was to survive and prosper.   ●

Overview

As the "Case in Contrast" suggests, the challenge facing Kinko's was to identify the best way to operate in the new, more competitive industry environment. With the help of consultants, Kinko's managers radically changed the way it organized its employees and other resources to meet that challenge, and the company has prospered.

In Part 4 we examine how managers can organize and control human and other resources to create high-performing organizations. To organize and control (two of the four functions of management identified in Chapter 1), managers must design an organizational architecture that makes the best use of resources to produce the goods and services customers want. **Organizational architecture** is the combination of the organizational structure, control systems, culture, and human resource management system that determines how efficiently and effectively organizational resources are used.

By the end of this chapter, you will be familiar not only with various organizational structures but also with various factors that determine the organizational design choices that managers make. Then in Chapters 9 and 10 we examine issues surrounding the design of an organization's control systems, culture, and human resource management systems.   ●

organizational architecture The organizational structure, control systems, culture, and human resource management system that together determine how efficiently and effectively organizational resources are used.

Designing Organizational Structure

organizational structure A formal system of task and reporting relationships that coordinates and motivates organizational members so that they work together to achieve organizational goals.

organizational design The process by which managers make specific organizing choices that result in a particular kind of organizational structure.

Organizing is the process by which managers establish the structure of working relationships among employees to allow them to achieve organizational goals efficiently and effectively. **Organizational structure** is the formal system of task and reporting relationships that determines how employees use resources to achieve organizational goals.[4] **Organizational design** is the process by which managers make specific organizing choices that result in the construction of a particular organizational structure.[5]

As noted in Chapter 2, according to contingency theory, managers design organizational structures to fit the factors or circumstances that are affecting the company the most and causing them the most uncertainty.[6] Thus, there is no "best" way to design an organization: Design reflects each organization's specific situation. Four factors are important determinants of organizational structure: the nature of the organizational environment, the type of strategy the organization pursues, the technology the organization uses, and the characteristics of the organization's human resources (see Figure 8.1).[7]

The Organizational Environment

In general, the more quickly the external environment is changing and the greater the uncertainty within it, the greater are the problems facing managers trying to gain access to scarce resources. In this situation, to speed decision making and communication and make it easier to obtain resources, managers typically make organizing choices that bring flexibility to the organizational structure.[8] They are likely to decentralize authority and empower lower-level employees to make important operating decisions. In contrast, if the external

Figure 8.1
Factors Affecting Organizational Structure

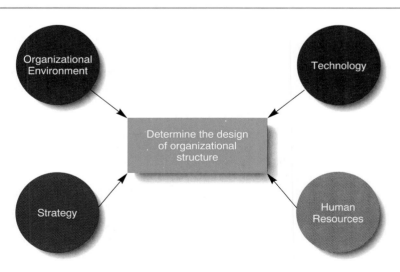

environment is stable, if resources are readily available, and if uncertainty is low, then less coordination and communication among people and functions is needed to obtain resources, and managers can make organizing choices that bring more formality to the organizational structure. Managers in this situation prefer to make decisions within a clearly defined hierarchy of authority and use extensive rules and standard operating procedures to govern activities.

As we discussed in Chapters 3 and 4, change is rapid in today's marketplace, and increasing competition both at home and abroad is putting greater pressure on managers to attract customers and increase efficiency and effectiveness. Consequently, interest in finding ways to structure organizations—such as through empowerment and self-managed teams—to allow people and departments to behave flexibly has been increasing.

Strategy

As discussed in Chapter 7, once managers decide on a strategy, they must choose the right means to implement it. Different strategies often call for the use of different organizational structures. For example, a differentiation strategy aimed at increasing the value customers perceive in an organization's goods and services usually succeeds best in a flexible structure. Flexibility facilitates a differentiation strategy because managers can develop new or innovative products quickly—an activity that requires extensive cooperation among functions or departments. In contrast, a low-cost strategy that is aimed at driving down costs in all functions usually fares best in a more formal structure, which gives managers greater control over the expenditures and actions of the organization's various departments.[9]

In addition, at the corporate level, when managers decide to expand the scope of organizational activities by, for example, vertical integration or diversification, they need to design a flexible structure to provide sufficient coordination among the different business divisions.[10] As discussed in Chapter 7, many companies have been divesting businesses because managers have been unable to create a competitive advantage to keep them up to speed in fast-changing industries. By moving to a more flexible structure, such as a product division structure, divisional managers gain more control over their different businesses, as suggested by the example of Amoco, profiled in the "Case in Contrast."

Finally, expanding internationally and operating in many different countries challenges managers to create organizational structures that allow organizations to be flexible on a global level.[11] As we discuss later, managers can group their departments or functions and divisions in several ways to allow them to effectively pursue an international strategy.

Technology

Technology is the combination of skills, knowledge, tools, machines, computers, and equipment that are used in the design, production, and distribution of goods and services. As a rule, the more complicated the technology that an organization uses, the more difficult it is for managers and workers to impose strict control on technology or to regulate it efficiently. Thus, the more complicated the technology, the greater is the need for a flexible structure to enhance managers' ability to respond to unexpected situations and give them the freedom to work out new solutions to the problems they encounter. In contrast, the more routine the technology, the more appropriate is a formal structure, because tasks are simple and the steps needed to produce goods and services have been worked out in advance.

What makes a technology routine or complicated? One researcher who investigated this issue, Charles Perrow, argued that two factors determine how complicated or nonroutine technology is: task variety and task analyzability.[12] *Task variety* is the number of new or unexpected problems or situations that a person or function encounters in performing tasks or jobs. *Task analyzability* is the degree to which programmed solutions are available to people or functions to solve the problems they encounter. Nonroutine or complicated technologies are characterized by high task variety and low task analyzability; this means that many varied problems occur and that solving these problems requires significant nonprogrammed decision making. In contrast, routine technologies are characterized by low task variety and high task analyzability; this means that the problems encountered do not vary much and are easily resolved through programmed decision making.

Examples of nonroutine technology are found in the work of scientists in a research and development laboratory who develop new products or discover new drugs, or in the planning exercises an organization's top-management team uses to chart the organization's future strategy. Examples of routine technology include typical mass-production or assembly operations, where workers perform the same task repeatedly and where managers have already identified the programmed solutions necessary to perform a task efficiently. Similarly, in service organizations such as fast-food restaurants, the tasks that crew members perform in making and serving fast food are very routine.

The extent to which the process of actually producing or creating goods and services depends on people or machines is another factor that determines how nonroutine a technology is. The more the technology used to produce goods and services is based on the skills, knowledge, and abilities of people working together on an ongoing basis and not on automated machines that can be programmed in advance, the more complex the technology is. Joan Woodward, a professor who investigated the relationship between technology and organizational structure, differentiated among three kinds of technology on the basis of the relative contribution made by people or machines.[13]

small-batch technology Technology that is used to produce small quantities of customized, one-of-a-kind products and is based on the skills of people who work together in small groups.

mass-production technology Technology that is based on the use of automated machines that are programmed to perform the same operations over and over.

Small-batch technology is used to produce small quantities of customized, one-of-a-kind products and is based on the skills of people who work together in small groups. Examples of goods and services produced by small-batch technology include custom-built cars, such as Ferraris and Rolls Royces, highly specialized metals and chemicals that are produced by the pound rather than by the ton, and the process of auditing in which a small team of auditors is sent to a company to evaluate and report on its accounts. Because small-batch goods or services are customized and unique, workers need to respond to each situation as required; thus, a structure that decentralizes authority to employees and allows them to respond flexibly is most appropriate with small-batch technology.

Woodward's second kind of technology, **mass-production technology,** is based primarily on the use of automated machines that are programmed to perform the same operations time and time again. Mass production works

Small teams of highly skilled workers assemble Ferraris, which cost in excess of $250,000. The hand-built nature of exclusive motorcars is a part of their appeal to wealthy customers.

continuous-process technology Technology that is almost totally mechanized and is based on the use of automated machines working in sequence and controlled through computers from a central monitoring station.

most efficiently when each person performs a repetitive task. There is little need for flexibility, and a formal organizational structure is the preferred choice because it gives managers the most control over the production process. Mass production results in an output of large quantities of standardized products such as tin cans, Ford Tauruses, washing machines, and light bulbs, or even services such as car washes or dry cleaning.

The third kind of technology that Woodward identified, **continuous-process technology,** is almost totally mechanized. Products are produced by automated machines working in sequence and controlled through computers from a central monitoring station. Examples of continuous-process technology include large steel mills, oil refineries, nuclear power stations, and large-scale brewing operations. The role of workers in continuous-process technology is to watch for problems that may occur unexpectedly and cause dangerous or even deadly situations. The possibility of a machinery or computer breakdown, for example, is a major source of uncertainty associated with this technology. If an unexpected situation does occur, employees must be able to respond quickly and appropriately to prevent a disaster from resulting (such as an explosion in a chemical complex), and the need for a flexible response makes a flexible organizational structure the preferred choice with this kind of technology.

In summary, the nature of an organization's technology is an important determinant of its structure. Today, with the increasing use of computer-controlled production, and the movement toward using self-managed teams (groups of workers who are given the responsibility for supervising their own activities and for monitoring the quality of the goods and service they provide) to promote innovation, increase quality, and reduce costs, many companies are trying to make their structures more flexible to take advantage of the value-creating benefits of complex technology.

Human Resources

A final important factor affecting an organization's choice of structure is the characteristics of the human resources it employs. In general, the more highly skilled an organization's workforce is and the more people are required to work together in groups or teams to perform their tasks, the more likely is the organization to use a flexible, decentralized structure. Highly skilled employees or employees who have internalized strong professional values and norms of behavior as part of their training usually desire freedom and autonomy and dislike close supervision. Accountants, for example, have learned the need to report company accounts honestly and impartially, and doctors and nurses have absorbed the obligation to give patients the best care possible.

Flexible structures, characterized by decentralized authority and empowered employees, are well suited to the needs of highly skilled people. Similarly, when people work in teams, they must be allowed to interact freely, which also is possible in a flexible organizational structure. Thus, when designing an organizational structure, managers must pay close attention to the workforce and to the work itself.

In summary, an organization's external environment, strategy, technology, and human resources are the factors to be considered by managers seeking to design the best structure for an organization. The greater the level of uncertainty in an organization's environment, the more complex its strategy and technology, and the more highly qualified and skilled its workforce, the more likely are managers to design a structure that is flexible. The more stable an organization's environment, the less complex and more well understood its strategy or technology, and the less skilled its workforce, the more likely are managers to design an organizational structure that is formal and controlling.

How do managers design a structure to be either flexible or formal? The way an organization's structure works depends on the organizing choices managers make about four issues:

- How to group tasks into individual jobs
- How to group jobs into functions and divisions
- How to allocate authority in the organization among jobs, functions, and divisions
- How to coordinate or integrate jobs, functions, and divisions

Grouping Tasks into Jobs: Job Design

job design The process by which managers decide how to divide tasks into specific jobs.

The first step in organizational design is **job design**, the process by which managers decide how to divide into specific jobs the tasks that have to be performed to provide customers with goods and services. Managers at McDonald's, for example, have decided how best to divide the tasks required to provide customers with fast, cheap food in each McDonald's restaurant. After experimenting with different job arrangements, McDonald's managers decided on a basic division of labor among chefs and food servers. Managers allocated all the tasks involved in actually cooking the food (putting oil in the fat fryers, opening packages of frozen french fries, putting beef patties on the grill, making salads, and so on) to the job of chef. They allocated all the tasks involved in giving the food to customers (such as greeting customers, taking orders, putting fries and burgers into bags, adding salt, pepper, and napkins, and taking money) to food servers. In addition, they created other jobs—the job of dealing with drive-in customers, the job of keeping the restaurant clean, and the job of shift manager responsible for overseeing employees and responding to unexpected events. The result of the job design process is a *division of labor* among employees, one that McDonald's and other managers have discovered through experience is most efficient.

Establishing an appropriate division of labor among employees is a critical part of the organizing process, one that is vital to increasing efficiency and effectiveness. At McDonald's, the tasks associated with chef and food server were split into different jobs because managers found that, for the kind of food McDonald's serves, this approach was most efficient. It is efficient because when each employee is given fewer tasks to perform (so that his or her job becomes more specialized), employees become more productive at performing the tasks that constitute their job.

At Subway sandwich shops, however, managers chose a different kind of job design. At Subway, there is no division of labor among the people who make the sandwiches, wrap the sandwiches, give them to customers, and take the money. The roles of chef and food server are combined into one role. This different division of tasks and jobs is efficient for Subway and not for McDonald's because Subway serves a limited menu of mostly submarine-style sandwiches that are prepared to order. Subway's production system is far simpler than McDonald's, because McDonald's menu is much more varied and its chefs must cook many different kinds of foods.

Workers at Subway Sandwich follow the carefully designed work procedures that allow the company to provide a large variety of sandwiches to customers quickly at peak times.

Managers of every organization must analyze the range of tasks to be performed and then create jobs that best allow the organization to give customers the goods and services they want. In deciding how to assign tasks to individual jobs, however, managers must be careful not to take **job simplification,** the process of reducing the number of tasks that each worker performs, too far.[14] Too much job simplification may reduce efficiency rather than increase it if workers find their simplified jobs boring and monotonous, become demotivated and unhappy, and as a result perform at a low level.

Job Enlargement and Job Enrichment

In an attempt to create a division of labor and design individual jobs to encourage workers to perform at a higher level and be more satisfied with their work, several researchers have proposed ways other than job simplification to group tasks into jobs: job enlargement and job enrichment.

Job enlargement is increasing the number of different tasks in a given job by changing the division of labor.[15] For example, because Subway food servers make the food as well as serve it, their jobs are "larger" than the jobs of McDonald's food servers. The idea behind job enlargement is that increasing the range of tasks performed by a worker will reduce boredom and fatigue and may increase motivation to perform at a high level—increasing both the quantity and the quality of goods and services provided.

Job enrichment is increasing the degree of responsibility a worker has over his or her job by, for example, (1) empowering workers to experiment to find new or better ways of doing the job, (2) encouraging workers to develop new skills, (3) allowing workers to decide how to do the work and giving them the responsibility for deciding how to respond to unexpected situations, and (4) allowing workers to monitor and measure their own performance.[16] The idea behind job enrichment is that increasing workers' responsibility increases their involvement in their jobs and thus increases their interest in the quality of the goods they make or the services they provide.

In general, managers who make design choices that increase job enrichment and job involvement are likely to increase the degree to which workers behave flexibly rather than rigidly or mechanically. Narrow, specialized jobs are likely to lead people to behave in predictable ways; workers who perform a variety of tasks and who are allowed and encouraged to discover new and better ways to perform their jobs are likely to act flexibly and creatively. Thus, managers who enlarge and enrich jobs create a flexible organizational structure, and those who simplify jobs create a more formal structure. If workers are also grouped into self-managed work teams, the organization is likely to be flexible because team members provide support for each other and can learn from one another.

The Job Characteristics Model

J. R. Hackman and G. R. Oldham's job characteristics model is an influential model of job design that explains in detail how managers can make jobs more interesting and motivating.[17] Hackman and Oldham's model (see Figure 8.2) also describes the likely personal and organizational outcomes that will result from enriched and enlarged jobs.

Figure 8.2
The Job Characteristics Model

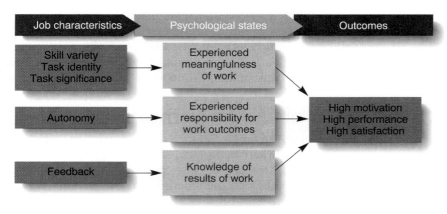

Source: Adapted from J. R. Hackman and G. R. Oldham, *Work Redesign* (Reading, MA: Addison-Wesley, 1980).

According to Hackman and Oldham, every job has five characteristics that determine how motivating the job is. These characteristics determine how employees react to their work and lead to outcomes such as high performance and satisfaction and low absenteeism and turnover:

• *Skill variety:* The extent to which a job requires an employee to use a wide range of different skills, abilities, or knowledge. *Example:* The skill variety required by the job of a research scientist is higher than that called for by the job of a McDonald's food server.

• *Task identity:* The extent to which a job requires a worker to perform all the tasks required to complete the job from the beginning to the end of the production process. *Example:* A craftworker who takes a piece of wood and transforms it into a custom-made piece of furniture such as a desk has higher task identity than does a worker who performs only one of the numerous operations required to assemble a television.

• *Task significance:* The degree to which a worker feels his or her job is meaningful because of its effect on people inside the organization such as coworkers or outside the organization such as customers. *Example:* A teacher who sees the effect of his or her efforts in a well-educated and well-adjusted student enjoys higher task significance than does a dishwasher who monotonously washes dishes as they come to the kitchen.

• *Autonomy:* The degree to which a job gives an employee the freedom and discretion needed to schedule different tasks and decide how to carry them out. *Example:* Salespeople who have to plan their schedules and decide how to allocate their time among different customers have relatively high autonomy compared to assembly-line workers whose actions are determined by the speed of the production line.

• *Feedback:* The extent to which actually doing a job provides a worker with clear and direct information about how well he or she has performed the job. *Example:* An air traffic controller whose mistakes may result in a midair collision receives immediate feedback on job performance; a person who compiles statistics for a business magazine often has little idea of when he or she makes a mistake or does a particularly good job.

Hackman and Oldham argue that those five job characteristics affect an employee's motivation because they affect three critical psychological states (see Figure 8.2). The more employees feel that their work is *meaningful* and that they are *responsible for work outcomes* and *responsible for knowing how those outcomes affect others,* the more motivating work becomes and the more likely employees are to be satisfied and to perform at a high level. Moreover, employees who have jobs that are highly motivating are called on to use their skills more and to perform more tasks, and they are given more responsibility for doing the job. All of the foregoing are characteristic of jobs and employees in flexible structures where authority is decentralized and where employees commonly work with others and must learn new skills to complete the range of tasks for which their group is responsible.

Grouping Jobs into Functions and Divisions

Once managers have decided which tasks to allocate to which jobs, they face the next organizing decision: how to group jobs together to best match the needs of the organization's environment, strategy, technology, and human resources. Most top-management teams decide to group jobs into departments and develop a functional structure to use organizational resources. As the organization grows, managers design a divisional structure or a more complex matrix or product team structure.

Choosing a structure and then designing it so that it works as intended is a significant challenge. As noted in Chapter 7, managers reap the rewards of a well-thought-out strategy only if they choose the right type of structure to implement and execute the strategy. The ability to make the right kinds of organizing choices is often what differentiates effective from ineffective managers.

Tips for Managers

Designing Structure and Jobs

1. Carefully analyze an organization's environment, strategy, technology, and human resources to decide which type of organizational structure to use.

2. To create a more formal structure, carefully define the limits of each worker's job, create clear job descriptions, and evaluate each worker on his or her individual job performance.

3. To create a more flexible structure, enlarge and enrich jobs and allow workers to expand their jobs over time. Also, encourage workers to work together and evaluate both individual and group performance.

4. Use the job characteristics model to guide job design and recognize that most jobs can be enriched to make them more motivating and satisfying.

Functional Structure

A *function* is a group of people, working together, who possess similar skills or use the same kind of knowledge, tools, or techniques to perform their jobs. Manufacturing, sales, and research and development are often organized into functional departments. A **functional structure** is an organizational structure composed of all the departments that an organization requires to produce its goods or services. Figure 8.3 shows the functional structure that Pier 1 Imports, a home furnishings company, uses to supply its customers with a range of goods from around the world to satisfy their desires for new and innovative products.

functional structure

An organizational structure composed of all the departments that an organization requires to produce its goods or services.

Figure 8.3

The Functional Structure of Pier 1 Imports

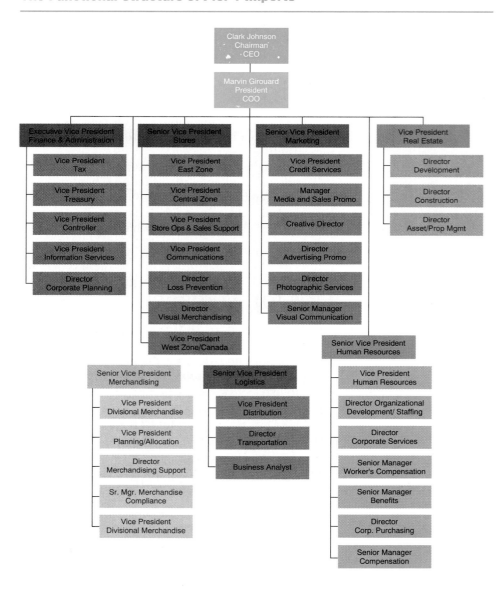

Pier 1's main functions are finance and administration, merchandising (purchasing the goods), stores (managing the retail outlets), logistics (managing product distribution), marketing, human resources, and real estate. Each job inside a function exists because it helps the function perform the activities necessary for high organizational performance. Thus, within the logistics department are all the jobs necessary to efficiently distribute and transport products to stores, and inside the marketing department are all the jobs (such as promotion, photography, and visual communication) that are necessary to increase the appeal of Pier 1's products to customers.

There are several advantages to grouping jobs according to function. First, when people who perform similar jobs are grouped together, they can learn from observing one another and thus become more specialized and can perform at a higher level. The tasks associated with one job often are related to the tasks associated to another job, which encourages cooperation within a function. In Pier 1's marketing department, for example, the person designing the photography program for an ad campaign works closely with the person responsible for designing store layouts and with visual communication experts. As a result, Pier 1 is able to develop a strong, focused marketing campaign to differentiate its products.

Second, when people who perform similar jobs are grouped together, it is easier for managers to monitor and evaluate their performance.[18] Imagine if marketing experts, logistics experts, and real-estate experts were grouped together in one function and supervised by a manager from merchandising. Obviously, the merchandising manager would not have the expertise to evaluate all these different people appropriately. A functional structure, however, allows coworkers to evaluate how well other coworkers are performing their jobs, and if some coworkers are performing poorly, more experienced coworkers can help them develop new skills.

Finally, as we saw in Chapter 3, managers appreciate functional structure because it allows them to create the set of functions they need in order to scan and monitor the task and general environments.[19] With the right set of functions in place, managers are in a good position to develop a strategy that allows the organization to respond to its particular situation. Employees in marketing can specialize in monitoring new marketing developments that will allow Pier 1 to better target its customers. Employees in merchandising can monitor all potential suppliers of home furnishings both at home and abroad to find the goods most likely to appeal to Pier 1's customers.

As an organization grows, and particularly as its task environment and strategy change because it is beginning to produce a wider range of goods and services for different kinds of customers, several problems can make a functional structure less efficient and effective.[20] First, managers in different functions may find it more difficult to communicate and coordinate with one another when they are responsible for several different kinds of products, especially as the organization grows both domestically and internationally. Second, functional managers may become so preoccupied with supervising their own specific departments and achieving their departmental goals that they lose sight of organizational goals. If that happens, organizational effectiveness will suffer because managers will be viewing issues and problems facing the organization only from their own, relatively narrow, departmental perspectives.[21] Both of these problems can reduce efficiency and effectiveness.

Divisional Structures: Product, Market, and Geographic

divisional structure

An organizational structure composed of separate business units within which are the functions that work together to produce a specific product for a specific customer.

As the problems associated with growth and diversification increase over time, managers must search for new ways to organize their activities to overcome the problems associated with a functional structure. Most managers of large organizations choose a **divisional structure** and create a series of business units to produce a specific kind of product for a specific kind of customer. Each *division* is a collection of functions or departments that work together to produce the product. The goal behind the change to a divisional structure is to create smaller, more manageable units within the organization. There are three forms of divisional structure (see Figure 8.4).[22] When managers organize divisions according to the type of good or service they provide, they adopt a *product* structure. When managers organize divisions according to the area of the country or world they operate in, they adopt a *geographic* structure. When managers organize divisions according to the types of customer they focus on, they adopt a *market* structure.

PRODUCT STRUCTURE Imagine the problems that managers at Pier 1 would encounter if they decided to diversify into producing and selling cars, fast food, and health insurance—in addition to home furnishings—and tried to use their existing set of functional managers to oversee the production of all four kinds of product. No manager would have the necessary skills or abilities to oversee those four products. No individual marketing manager, for example, could effectively market cars, fast food, health insurance, and home furnishings at the same time. To perform a functional activity successfully, managers must have experience in specific markets or industries. Consequently, if managers decide to diversify into new industries or to expand their range of products, they commonly design a product structure to organize their operations (see Figure 8.4A).

product structure An organizational structure in which each product line or business is handled by a self-contained division.

Using a **product structure,** managers place each distinct product line or business in its own self-contained division and give divisional managers the responsibility for devising an appropriate business-level strategy to allow the division to compete effectively in its industry or market.[23] Each division is self-contained because it has a complete set of all the functions—marketing, R&D, finance, and so on—that it needs to produce or provide goods or services efficiently and effectively. Functional managers report to divisional managers, and divisional managers report to top or corporate managers.

Grouping functions into divisions focused on particular products has several advantages for managers at all levels in the organization. First, a product structure allows functional managers to specialize in only one product area, so they are able to build expertise and fine-tune their skills in this particular area. Second, each division's managers can become experts in their industry; this expertise helps them choose and develop a business-level strategy to differentiate their products or lower their costs while meeting the needs of customers. Third, a product structure frees corporate managers from the need to supervise directly each division's day-to-day operations; this latitude allows corporate managers to create the best corporate-level strategy to maximize the organization's future growth and ability to create value. Corporate managers are likely to make fewer mistakes about which businesses to diversify into or

Figure 8.4
Product, Market, and Geographic Structures

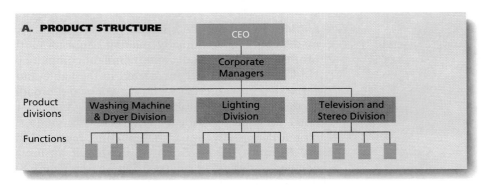

A. PRODUCT STRUCTURE

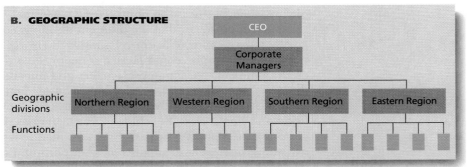

B. GEOGRAPHIC STRUCTURE

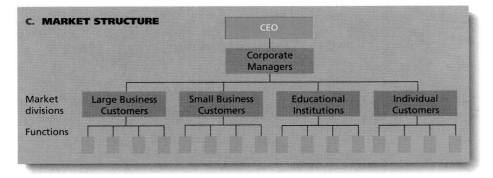

C. MARKET STRUCTURE

how to best expand internationally, for example, because they are able to take an organizationwide view.[24] Corporate managers also are likely to better evaluate how well divisional managers are doing, and they can intervene and take corrective action as needed.

The extra layer of management, the divisional management layer, can improve the use of organizational resources. Moreover, a product structure puts divisional managers close to their customers and lets them respond quickly and appropriately to the changing task environment. One reason why Amoco, profiled in the "Case in Contrast," moved to a product structure was to give the managers of its 17 new divisions more freedom. The way in which Viacom's managers created a product structure is profiled in this "Management Insight."

Management Insight

Viacom's Product Structure

Sumner Redstone, the billionaire chairman of Viacom (www.viacomnew-media.com), is continually making acquisitions that add to the range of products the huge media entertainment company provides to its customers. Under Redstone, Viacom started in the cable and television business and expanded into entertainment, networks and broadcasting, video music and theme parks, and publishing. In 1994, Viacom made two huge acquisitions—Blockbuster Video, the largest U.S. video store operator, and Paramount Pictures (www.paramount.com), maker of the movie *Forrest Gump*.

To manage Viacom's many different businesses effectively, Redstone decided to design a product structure (see Figure 8.5). He put each business in a separate division and gave managers in each division responsibility for making their business the number-one performer in its industry. Redstone recognized, however, that the different divisions could help each other and create synergies for Viacom by sharing their skills and resources. Blockbuster, for example, could launch a major advertising campaign to publicize the movies that Paramount makes and thus boost the visibility of both divisions' products, and Simon and Schuster could produce and publish specific books to tie in with the opening of a movie and thus boost both ticket and book sales. To achieve these synergies, Redstone created a team of corporate managers who are responsible for working with the different divisional managers to identify new opportunities to create value. So far, this method of organizing has served Viacom well, and analysts believe that it is positioned to become one of the leading entertainment companies in the twenty-first century.

GEOGRAPHIC STRUCTURE   When organizations expand rapidly both at home and abroad, functional structures can create special problems, because managers in one central location may find it increasingly difficult to deal with the different problems and issues that may arise in each region of a

Figure 8.5
The Product Structure of Viacom

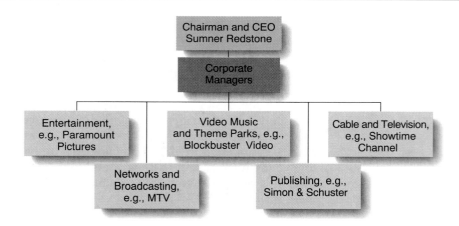

geographic structure

An organizational structure in which each region of a country or area of the world is served by a self-contained division.

country or area of the world. In these cases, a **geographic structure,** in which divisions are broken down by geographical location, is often chosen (see Figure 8.4B). To achieve the corporate mission of providing next-day mail service, Fred Smith, CEO of Federal Express, chose a geographic structure and divided up operations by creating a division in each region. Large retailers like Macy's, Neiman Marcus, and Brooks Brothers also use a geographic structure. Since the needs of retail customers differ by region—for example, surfboards in California and down parkas in the Midwest—a geographic structure gives retail regional managers the flexibility they need to choose products that best meet the needs of regional customers.

In adopting a *global geographic structure,* such as shown in Figure 8.6A, managers locate different divisions in each world region in which the organization operates. Managers are most likely to do this when they pursue a multidomestic strategy, because customer needs vary widely by country or world region. For example, if products that appeal to U.S. customers do not sell in Europe, the Pacific Rim, or South America, then managers must customize the products to meet the needs of customers in those different world regions; a global geographic structure with global divisions will allow them to do this.

In contrast, to the degree that customers abroad are willing to buy the same kind of product or slight variations thereof, managers are more likely to pursue a global strategy. In this case they are likely to use a *global product structure,*

Figure 8.6

Global Geographic and Global Product Structures

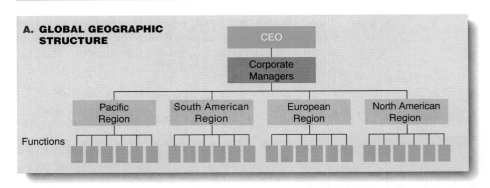

A. GLOBAL GEOGRAPHIC STRUCTURE

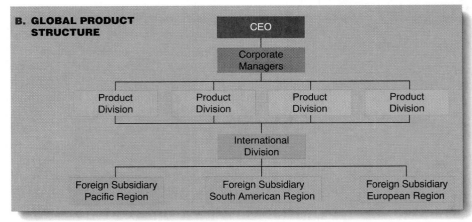

B. GLOBAL PRODUCT STRUCTURE

perform most important functional activities at home, and export the final product abroad. In a global product structure, managers create an international division, which takes responsibility for selling the different divisions' products in foreign countries (see Figure 8.6B). Often, managers in the international division create foreign subsidiaries to distribute and sell their products to customers in these foreign countries. Mercedes-Benz, for example, designs and manufactures most of its cars in Germany, and managers in Mercedes's international division take responsibility for shipping these cars to the company's foreign subsidiaries (such as Mercedes-Benz U.S.A.), which provide service to foreign customers. As we noted at the beginning of this chapter, an organization's strategy is a major determinant of its structure both at home and abroad.

MARKET STRUCTURE   Sometimes the pressing issue facing managers is to group functions according to the type of customer buying the product, in order to tailor the organization's products to each customer's unique demands. A computer company, for example, has several different kinds of customers, including large businesses (which might demand networks of computers linked to a mainframe computer), small companies (which may need just a few PCs linked together), educational users in schools and universities (which might want thousands of independent PCs for their students), and individual users (who may want high-quality multimedia PCs so that they can play the latest video games).

market structure

An organizational structure in which each kind of customer is served by a self-contained division; also called *customer structure.*

To satisfy the needs of diverse customers, a company might adopt a **market structure** (also called a *customer structure*), which groups divisions according to the particular kinds of customers they serve (see Figure 8.4C). A market structure allows managers to be responsive to the needs of their customers and allows them to act flexibly to make decisions in response to customers' changing needs. In organizations where the time factor is critical, a market structure is more effective than a geographic structure, as the experience of Eastman Kodak suggests.

Management Insight

From Geographic to Market Structure at Eastman Kodak

Eastman Kodak (www.kodak.com), based in Rochester, New York, produces and sells thousands of different imaging products. The consumer imaging division is charged with the responsibility to manage the distribution and sale of Kodak's well-known photographic products. Until 1995, the imaging division grouped its customers by region and used a geographic structure to distribute and sell its photographic products. For instance, all customers within a region—including mass merchandising outlets, photo specialty stores, drugstores, and supermarkets—were served by the same sales force.

Customers, however, began to complain that they were not getting the level of personalized service they required, and salespeople felt that their talents were being stretched thin because the needs of the different kinds of stores were quite different. As a result, the divisional managers decided to redesign the organization, changing from a geographic to a market structure to make it easier for the imaging division's sales force to serve its customers.[25]

In 1995, the sales force was reorganized into teams that serve the needs of specific kinds of customers—for example, teams service only drugstores or only supermarkets. The imaging division's managers hoped that each team, by being closer to a particular kind of customer, would be able to better understand the problems the customer faces and offer each a customized solution. This change to a market structure was so successful for the consumer imaging division that Kodak announced in 1996 that it also would reorganize its professional and printing imaging division by market rather than by region.

Matrix and Product Team Designs

Moving to a product, market, or geographic divisional structure allows managers to respond more quickly and flexibly to the particular set of circumstances they confront. However, when the environment is dynamic and is changing rapidly, and uncertainty is high, even a divisional structure may not provide managers with enough flexibility to respond to the environment quickly. When customer needs or technology is changing rapidly and the environment is very uncertain, managers must design the most flexible organizational structure available: a matrix structure or a product team structure (see Figure 8.7).

matrix structure

An organizational structure that simultaneously groups people and resources by function and by product.

MATRIX STRUCTURE In a **matrix structure,** managers group people and resources in two ways simultaneously: by function and by product.[26] Employees are grouped into *functions* to allow them to learn from one another and become more skilled and productive. In addition, employees are grouped into *product teams,* teams in which members of different functions work together to develop a specific product. The result is a complex network of reporting relationships among product teams and functions that makes the matrix structure very flexible (see Figure 8.7A). Each person in a product team reports to two bosses: (1) a functional boss, who assigns individuals to a team and evaluates their performance from a functional perspective, and (2) the boss of the product team, who evaluates their performance on the team. Thus, team members are known as *two-boss employees* because they report to two different managers.

The functional employees assigned to product teams change over time as the specific skills that the team needs change. At the beginning of the product development process, for example, engineers and R&D specialists are assigned to a product team because their skills are needed to develop new products. When a provisional design has been established, marketing experts are assigned to the team to gauge how customers will respond to the new product. Manufacturing personnel join when it is time to find the most efficient way to produce the product. As their specific jobs are completed, team members leave and are reassigned to new teams. In this way the matrix structure makes the most use of human resources.

To keep the matrix structure flexible, product teams are empowered and team members are responsible for making the most of the important decisions involved in product development.[27] The product team manager acts as a facilitator, controlling the financial resources and trying to keep the project on time and within budget. The functional managers try to ensure that the product is the best that it can be in order to maximize its differentiated appeal.

Figure 8.7
Matrix and Product Team Structures

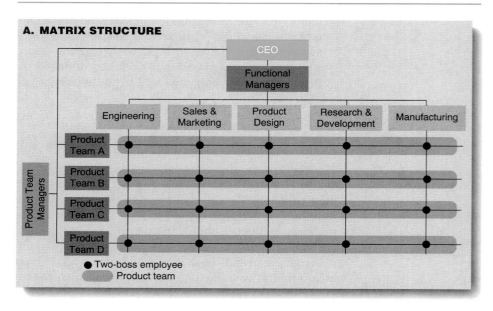

A. MATRIX STRUCTURE

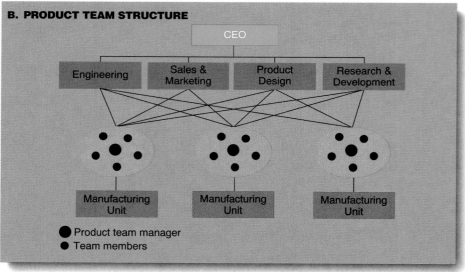

B. PRODUCT TEAM STRUCTURE

High-tech companies that operate in environments where new product developments take place monthly or yearly and the need to innovate quickly is vital to the organization's survival have been using matrix structures successfully for many years. The flexibility afforded by a matrix structure allows managers to keep pace with a changing and increasingly complex environment. For this reason, matrixes also have been designed by managers seeking to control international operations as they move abroad and face problems of coordinating their domestic and foreign divisions.[28] Motorola, for example, operates a global matrix structure because it hopes to obtain synergies from cooperation among its worldwide divisions, as does Caterpillar (profiled in "Managing Globally" in Chapter 7).

A global matrix structure allows an organization's domestic divisions to quickly supply its foreign divisions with knowledge about new R&D advances in order to help the foreign divisions gain a competitive advantage in their local markets. Likewise, the foreign divisions can transmit to domestic divisions new product marketing ideas that may give the domestic divisions an advantage in the domestic market. Many consumer products companies have used marketing campaigns developed for the European market with great success in the United States, such as Taster's Choice coffee and Kellogg's cereals. The expression "Think locally but act globally" describes the way managers in global matrix structures should behave.[29]

PRODUCT TEAM STRUCTURE The dual reporting relationships that are at the heart of a matrix structure have always been difficult for managers and employees to deal with. Often, the functional boss and the product boss make conflicting demands on team members, who do not know which boss to satisfy first. Also, functional and product team bosses may come into conflict over precisely who is in charge of which team members and for how long. To avoid these problems, managers have devised a way of organizing people and resources that still allows an organization to be flexible but makes its structure easier to operate: a product team structure.

The **product team structure** differs from a matrix structure in two ways: (1) It does away with dual reporting relationships and two-boss managers, and (2) functional employees are permanently assigned to a cross-functional team that is empowered to bring a new or redesigned product to market. A **cross-functional team** is a group of managers brought together from different departments to perform organizational tasks. When managers are grouped into cross-departmental teams, the artificial boundaries between departments disappear, and a narrow focus on departmental goals is replaced with a general interest in working together to achieve organizational goals. The results of such changes have been dramatic: Chrysler can introduce a new model of car in two years, down from five; Black & Decker can innovate new products in months, not years; and Hallmark Cards can respond to changing customer demands for types of cards in weeks, not months.

Members of a cross-functional team report only to the product team manager or to one of his or her direct subordinates. The heads of the functions have only an informal, advisory relationship with members of the product teams. The role of functional managers is only to counsel and help team members, share knowledge among teams, and provide new technological developments that can help improve each team's performance (see Figure 8.7B).[30]

Managers at Chrysler, Hallmark Cards, Rubbermaid, Hewlett-Packard, Microsoft, Lexmark, and other large companies have moved to product team structures in recent years to try to make their organizations work more flexibly. Many of these companies have had considerable success with this structure. Increasingly, organizations are making empowered cross-functional teams an essential part of their organizational architecture to help them gain a competitive advantage in fast-changing organizational environments.

product team structure An organizational structure in which employees are permanently assigned to a cross-functional team and report only to the product team manager or to one of his or her direct subordinates.

cross-functional team A group of managers from different departments brought together to perform organizational tasks.

Management Insight

Product Teams Produce Competitive Advantage

Based in Wellesley, Massachusetts, Sun Life is one of the largest insurance companies in North America. Like managers at most other insurance companies, managers at Sun Life became used to operating within a functional structure. When a potential customer requested information about insurance coverage, a member of the customer service department took the application and handed it over to the order fulfillment department for processing. Order fulfillment then sent the application to the actuarial department, which calculated insurance premiums, and only after several more steps was the customer finally informed about the outcome of his or her request. The process of handing the request over to many different departments took considerable time, and because most customers obtained multiple quotes from several insurance companies, this long time lag often resulted in lost business. So in 1995 Sun Life's managers dismantled the functional structure and reorganized 13 different functional groups into a series of cross-functional product teams.[31]

Employees from sales, customer service, order fulfillment, and so on, became members of "service teams," and each team performed all the steps necessary to process a customer's request for insurance. When all the exchanges among functions were eliminated, Sun Life's managers were astonished at the increase in efficiency and effectiveness that resulted from this new way of organizing the company's activities. The time needed to process a specific customer's request was reduced by as much as 75 percent, and the company found it much easier to attract new customers.

Rubbermaid (www.rubbermaid.com), the well-known maker of over 5,000 different household products, is another company that moved to a product team structure. Its managers wanted to speed up the rate of product innovation. Managers created 20 cross-functional teams composed of five to seven people from marketing, manufacturing, R&D, finance, and other functions.[32] Each team focuses its energies on a particular product line such as garden products, bathroom products, or kitchen products. The teams develop over 365 new products a year—a rate of one new product per day that is the envy of other organizations and has made Rubbermaid one of the most-admired companies in the United States.

Owens-Corning (www.owens-corning.com), the insulation maker, offers an extreme example of how to use teams in a factory setting. One hundred employees work in its Tennessee plant, and all 100 of them report directly to the plant manager![33] Owens-Corning has eliminated every level in the hierarchy between the plant manager and employees by putting all its employees in teams and making them jointly responsible for all operational decision making. The plant manager intervenes only when requested to do so by a team member, and even then only to act as a facilitator to help the empowered work teams solve their problems.

Hybrid Structure

A large organization that has many divisions and simultaneously uses many different structures has a **hybrid structure.** Most large organizations use product division structures and create self-contained divisions; then each division's managers select the structure that best meets the needs of the particular environment, strategy, and so on. Thus, one product division may choose to operate with a functional structure, another may choose a geographic structure, and a third may choose a product team structure because of the nature of the division's products or the desire to be more responsive to customers' needs.

Organizational structure may be likened to the layers of an onion. The outer layer provides the overarching organizational framework—most commonly a product division structure—and each inner layer is the structure that each division selects for itself in response to the contingencies it faces. The ability to break a large organization into smaller units or divisions makes it much easier for managers to change structure when the need arises—for example, when a change in technology or an increase in competition in the environment necessitates a change from a functional to a product team structure.

Coordinating Functions and Divisions

In organizing, managers' first task is to group functions and divisions and create the organizational structure best suited to the contingencies they face. Managers' next task is to ensure that there is sufficient coordination or integration among functions and divisions so that organizational resources are used efficiently and effectively. Having discussed how managers divide organizational activities into jobs, functions, and divisions to increase efficiency and effectiveness, we now look at how they put the parts back together.

We look first at the way in which managers design the hierarchy of authority to coordinate functions and divisions so that they work together effectively. Then we focus on integration and examine the many different integrating mechanisms that managers can use to coordinate functions and divisions.

Allocating Authority

As organizations grow and produce a wider range of goods and services, the size and number of their functions and divisions increase. To coordinate the activities of people, functions, and divisions and to allow them to work together effectively, managers must develop a clear hierarchy of authority.[34] **Authority** is the power vested in a manager to make decisions and use resources to achieve organizational goals by virtue of his or her position in an organization. The **hierarchy of authority** is an organization's chain of command—the relative authority that each manager has—extending from the CEO at the top, down through the middle managers and first-line managers, to the nonmanagerial employees who actually make goods or provide services.

span of control The number of subordinates who report directly to a manager.

Every manager, at every level of the hierarchy, supervises one or more subordinates. The term **span of control** refers to the number of subordinates who report directly to a manager.

Figure 8.8 shows a simplified picture of the hierarchy of authority and the span of control of managers in McDonald's. At the top of the hierarchy is Michael R. Quinlan, CEO and chairman of McDonald's board of directors. Quinlan is the manager who has ultimate responsibility for McDonald's performance, and he has the authority to decide how to use organizational resources to benefit McDonald's stakeholders. Both James R. Cantalupo and Edward Rensi report directly to Quinlan. Rensi is the president and CEO of McDonald's USA, Cantalupo is the head of McDonald's international operations, and they are next in the chain of command under Quinlan.

Figure 8.8
The Hierarchy of Authority and Span of Control at McDonald's Corporation

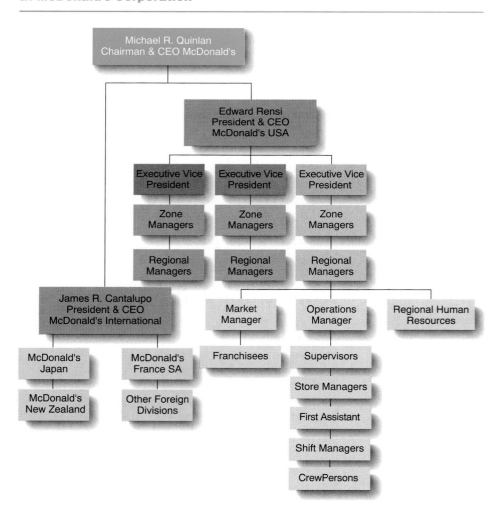

Managers at each level of the hierarchy confer on managers at the next level down the authority to make decisions about how to use organizational resources. Accepting this authority, those lower-level managers then become responsible for their decisions and are accountable for how well they make them. Managers who make the right decisions are typically promoted, and organizations motivate managers with the prospects of promotion and increased responsibility within the chain of command.

Below Rensi are the other main levels or layers in the McDonald's USA chain of command—executive vice presidents, zone managers, regional managers, and supervisors. A hierarchy is also evident in each company-owned McDonald's restaurant. At the top is the store manager; at lower levels are the first assistant, shift managers, and crew personnel. McDonald's managers have decided that this hierarchy of authority best allows the company to pursue its business-level strategy of providing fast food at reasonable prices.

TALL AND FLAT ORGANIZATIONS As an organization grows in size (normally measured by the number of its managers and employees), its hierarchy of authority normally lengthens, making the organizational structure taller. A *tall* organization has many levels of authority relative to company size; a *flat* organization has fewer levels relative to company size (see Figure 8.9).[35] As a hierarchy becomes taller, problems that make the organization's structure less flexible and slow managers' response to changes in the organizational environment may result.

Communication problems may arise. When an organization has many levels in the hierarchy, it can take a long time for the decisions and orders of upper-level managers to reach managers farther down in the hierarchy, and it can take a long time for top managers to learn how well their decisions worked out. Feeling out of touch, top managers may want to verify that lower-level managers are following orders and may require written confirmation from them. Middle managers, who know they will be held strictly accountable for their actions, start devoting more time to the process of making decisions in order to improve their chances of being right. They might even try to avoid responsibility by making top managers decide what actions to take.

Another communication problem that can result is the distortion of commands and orders being transmitted up and down the hierarchy, which causes managers at different levels to interpret what is happening differently. Distortion of orders and messages can be accidental, occurring because different managers interpret messages from their own narrow functional perspectives. Or it can be intentional, occurring because managers low in the hierarchy decide to interpret information to increase their own personal advantage.

Another problem with tall hierarchies is that they usually indicate that an organization is employing many managers, and managers are expensive. Managerial salaries, benefits, offices, and secretaries are a huge expense for organizations. Large companies such as IBM and General Motors pay their managers billions of dollars a year. Throughout the 1990s, hundreds of thousands of middle managers were laid off as companies attempted to reduce costs by restructuring and downsizing their workforces. The "Case in Contrast" noted that oil companies have laid off 500,000 middle managers in the last decades. But layoffs are not limited to the oil industry. In 1996, AT&T

Figure 8.9
Tall and Flat Organizations

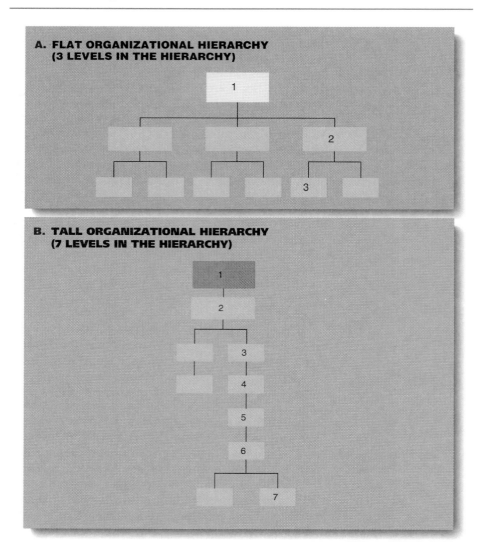

announced that it would encourage one-third of its top and middle managers—over 45,000 managers—to accept a generous early retirement program so that the company could reduce its workforce. AT&T had decided that it did not need as many managers to run its different businesses; furthermore, it had concluded that having too many managers was slowing its ability to respond to changes in the dynamic telecommunications industry.

THE MINIMUM CHAIN OF COMMAND   To ward off the problems that result when an organization becomes too tall and employs too many managers, top managers need to ascertain whether they are employing the right number of middle and first-line managers and see whether they can redesign their organizational architecture to reduce the number of managers. Top managers might well follow a basic organizing principle—the principle of the *mini-*

mum chain of command—which states that top managers should always construct a hierarchy with the fewest levels of authority necessary to efficiently and effectively use organizational resources.

Effective managers constantly scrutinize their hierarchies to see whether the number of levels can be reduced—for example, by eliminating one level and giving the responsibilities of managers at that level to managers above and empowering employees below. This practice has become increasingly common in the United States as companies that are battling low-cost foreign competitors search for new ways to reduce costs.

One manager who is constantly trying to empower employees and keep the hierarchy flat is Colleen C. Barrett, the number-two executive of Southwest Airlines.[36] Barrett is the highest-ranking woman in the airline industry. At Southwest, she is well known for continually reaffirming Southwest's message that employees should feel free to go above and beyond their prescribed roles to provide better customer service. Her central message is that Southwest values and trusts its employees, who are empowered to take responsibility. Southwest employees are encouraged not to look to their superiors for guidance but rather to take responsibility to find ways to do the job better themselves. As a result, Southwest keeps the number of its middle managers to a minimum.

CENTRALIZATION AND DECENTRALIZATION OF AUTHORITY

Another way in which managers can keep the organizational hierarchy flat is to decentralize authority to lower-level managers and nonmanagerial employees.[37] If managers at higher levels give lower-level employees the responsibility to make important decisions and only manage by exception, then the problems of slow and distorted communication noted previously are kept to a minimum. Moreover, fewer managers are needed because their role is not to make decisions but to act as coach and facilitator and to help other employees make the best decisions. In addition, when decision making is low in the organization and near the customer, employees are better able to recognize and respond to customer needs.

Decentralizing authority allows an organization and its employees to behave in a flexible way even as the organization grows and becomes taller. This is why managers are so interested in empowering employees, creating self-managed work teams, establishing cross-functional teams, and even moving to a product team structure. These design innovations help keep the organizational architecture flexible and responsive to complex task and general environments, complex technologies, and complex strategies.

Although more and more organizations are taking steps to decentralize authority, too much decentralization has certain disadvantages. If divisions, functions, or teams are given too much decision-making authority, they may begin to pursue their own goals at the expense of organizational goals. Managers in engineering design or R&D, for example, may become so focused on making the best possible product that they fail to realize that the best product may be so expensive that few people will be willing or able to buy it. Also with too much decentralization, lack of communication among functions or among divisions may prevent possible synergies among them from ever materializing, and organizational performance suffers.

Top managers must seek the balance between centralization and decentralization of authority that best meets the four major contingencies an organization faces (see Figure 8.1). If managers are in a stable environment, using well-understood technology, and producing staple kinds of products (such as cereal, canned soup, books, or televisions), then there is no pressing need to decentralize authority, and managers at the top can maintain control of much of the organizational decision making.[38] However, in uncertain, changing environments where high-tech companies are producing state-of-the-art products, top managers must empower employees and allow teams to make important strategic decisions so that the organization can keep up with the changes taking place. An interesting example of a company that has faced the issue of how best to distribute authority on a global level is Procter & Gamble, the U.S. consumer products company.

Managing Globally

Procter & Gamble's New World Hierarchy

In 1995, top managers at Procter & Gamble (P&G) took a long, hard look at the company's global operations and decided that they could make much better use of organizational resources if they altered the balance among centralized and decentralized decision making. Until 1995, managers in each P&G division, in each country in which the company operated, were more or less free to make their own decisions. Thus, managers in charge of the soap and detergent division in Britain operated independently from managers in the soap and detergent divisions in France and Germany. Moreover, even within Britain, the soap and detergent division operated independently from other British Procter & Gamble divisions such as the health care and beauty products divisions. Top managers saw that this highly decentralized global decision making was resulting in the loss of possible synergies to be obtained from cooperation both among managers of the same kind of division in the different countries (soap and detergent divisions throughout Europe) and among managers in different divisions operating in the same country or world region. So Procter & Gamble's top managers pioneered a new organizational structure.

They divided P&G's global operations into four main areas—North America, Europe, the Middle East and Africa, and Asia. In each area they created a new position, global executive vice president, and made the person in that position responsible for overseeing the operation of all the divisions within his or her world region. Procter & Gamble had never attempted this approach before.[39] Each global executive vice president is responsible for getting the various divisions within his or her area to cooperate and to share information and knowledge that will lead to synergies; thus, authority is centralized at the world area level. All of these new executive vice presidents report directly to the president of Procter & Gamble, further centralizing authority.

In another change to centralize authority, P&G's top managers grouped together divisions operating in the same area and put them under the control of one manager. For example, the manager of the British soap and detergent division took control over soap and detergent operations in Britain, Ireland, Spain, and Portugal and became responsible for obtaining synergies among them so the company could reduce costs and innovate products more quickly across Europe.

Procter & Gamble is delighted with its new balance between centralized and decentralized authority. Top managers believe they are making much better use of organizational resources to meet customers' needs, and they believe Procter & Gamble is poised to become the dominant consumer goods company in the world, not merely in the United States.

Types of Integrating Mechanisms

integrating mechanisms Organizing tools that managers can use to increase communication and coordination among functions and divisions.

Much coordination takes place through the hierarchy of authority. In addition, managers can use various **integrating mechanisms** to increase communication and coordination among functions and divisions. The greater the complexity of an organization's structure, the greater is the need for coordination among people, functions, and divisions to make the organizational structure work efficiently and effectively.[40] Thus, when managers choose to adopt a divisional, matrix, or product team structure, they must use complex kinds of integrating mechanisms to achieve organizational goals. Federal Express, for example, with its complex geographic structure, needs an enormous amount of coordination among regions to fulfill its promise of next-day package delivery. It achieves this coordination through an innovative use of integrating mechanisms, such as computer-controlled tracking equipment and customer-liaison personnel, to manage transactions quickly and efficiently.

Six integrating mechanisms are available to managers to increase communication and coordination.[41] These mechanisms—shown on a continuum ranging from simplest to most complex—are listed in Figure 8.10 together with examples of the individuals or groups that might use them. In the remainder of this section we examine each one, moving from least to most complex.

Figure 8.10
Types and Examples of Integrating Mechanisms

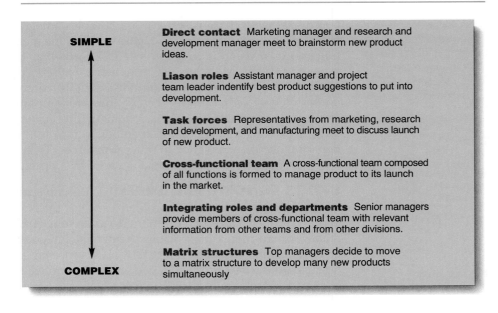

SIMPLE

Direct contact Marketing manager and research and development manager meet to brainstorm new product ideas.

Liason roles Assistant manager and project team leader indentify best product suggestions to put into development.

Task forces Representatives from marketing, research and development, and manufacturing meet to discuss launch of new product.

Cross-functional team A cross-functional team composed of all functions is formed to manage product to its launch in the market.

Integrating roles and departments Senior managers provide members of cross-functional team with relevant information from other teams and from other divisions.

Matrix structures Top managers decide to move to a matrix structure to develop many new products simultaneously

COMPLEX

DIRECT CONTACT   Direct contact among managers creates a context within which managers from different functions or divisions can work together to solve mutual problems. However, several problems are associated with establishing contact among managers in different functions or divisions. Managers from different functions may have different views about what must be done to achieve organizational goals. But if the managers have equal authority (as functional managers typically do), the only manager who can tell them what to do is the CEO. If functional and divisional managers cannot reach agreement, no mechanism exists to resolve the conflict apart from the authority of the boss. The need to solve everyday conflicts, however, wastes top-management time and effort and slows decision making. In fact, one sign of a poorly performing organizational structure is the number of problems sent up the hierarchy for top managers to solve. To increase coordination among functions and divisions and to prevent these problems from emerging, top managers can incorporate more complex integrating mechanisms into their organizational architecture.

LIAISON ROLES   Managers can increase coordination among functions and divisions by establishing liaison roles. When the volume of contacts between two functions increases, one way to improve coordination is to give one manager in each function or division the responsibility for coordinating with the other. These managers may meet daily, weekly, monthly, or as needed. Figure 8.11A depicts a liaison role; the small circles represent the individuals within each function who have responsibility for coordinating with another function. The responsibility for coordination is part of the liaison's full-time job, and usually an informal relationship forms between the people involved, greatly easing strains between functions. Furthermore, liaison roles provide a way of transmitting information across an organization, which is important in large organizations whose employees may know no one outside their immediate function or division.

TASK FORCES   When more than two functions or divisions share many common problems, direct contact and liaison roles may not provide sufficient coordination. In these cases, a more complex integrating mechanism, a **task force,** may be appropriate (see Figure 8.11B). One manager from each relevant function or division is assigned to a task force that meets to solve a specific, mutual problem. Members are responsible for reporting back to their departments on the issues addressed and the solutions recommended. Task forces are often called *ad hoc committees* because they are temporary; they may meet on a regular basis or only a few times. When the problem or issue is solved, the task force is no longer needed, and members return to their normal roles in their departments or are assigned to other task forces. Typically, task force members also perform many of their normal duties while serving on the task force.

CROSS-FUNCTIONAL TEAMS   In many cases, the issues addressed by a task force are recurring problems such as the need to develop new products or find new kinds of customers. To address recurring problems effectively, managers are increasingly using permanent integrating mechanisms such as cross-functional teams (see Figure 8.11C). An example of such a cross-functional team is a new product development committee that is responsible for the choice, design, manufacturing, and marketing of a new product. Such an activ-

task force A committee of managers from various functions or divisions who meet to solve a specific, mutual problem; also called an *ad hoc committee.*

Figure 8.11
Forms of Integrating Mechanisms

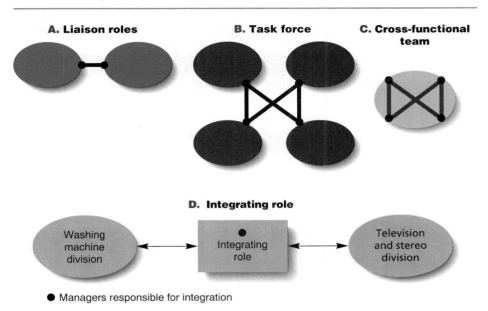

A. Liaison roles

B. Task force

C. Cross-functional team

D. Integrating role

Washing machine division ← → Integrating role ← → Television and stereo division

● Managers responsible for integration

ity obviously requires a great deal of integration among functions if new products are to be successfully introduced, and using a complex integrating mechanism such as a cross-functional team accomplishes this. Intel, for instance, emphasizes cross-functional teamwork. Its structure consists of over 90 cross-functional groups that meet regularly to set functional strategy in areas such as engineering and marketing and to develop business-level strategy.

The more complex an organization, the more important cross-functional teams become. Westinghouse, for example, has established a cross-functional team system to promote integration among divisions and improve organizational performance. As discussed previously, the product team structure is based on cross-functional teams to speed products to market. These teams assume responsibility for all aspects of product development.

INTEGRATING ROLES An integrating role is a role whose only function is to increase coordination and integration among functions or divisions to achieve performance gains from synergies (see Figure 8.11D). Usually, managers who perform integrating roles are experienced senior managers who can envisage how to use the resources of the functions or divisions to obtain new synergies. One study found that Du Pont, the giant chemical company, had created 160 integrating roles to provide coordination among the different divisions of the company and improve corporate performance.[42] Once again, the more complex an organization and the greater the number of its divisions, the more important integrating roles are.

MATRIX STRUCTURE When managers must be able to respond quickly to the task and general environments, they often use a matrix structure. The reason for choosing a matrix structure is clear. It contains many of the integrating mechanisms already discussed: Two-boss managers integrate functions and product teams; the matrix consists of temporary teams or task forces; and each member of a team performs a liaison role. The matrix structure is flexible precisely because it is formed from complex integrating mechanisms.

In summary, to keep an organization responsive to changes in its task and general environments, as the organization grows and becomes more complex, managers must increase coordination among functions and divisions by using complex integrating mechanisms. Managers must decide on the best way to organize their structures to create an organizational architecture that allows them to make the best use of organizational resources.

Strategic Alliances and Network Structure

Recently, innovations in organizational architecture pioneered by Japanese companies—strategic alliances and network structures—have been sweeping through U.S. and European business. A **strategic alliance** is a formal agreement that commits two or more companies to exchange or share their resources in order to produce and market a product.[43] A **network structure** is a series of strategic alliances that an organization creates with suppliers, manufacturers, and distributors to produce and market a product.

Japanese car companies such as Toyota and Honda have formed a series of strategic alliances with suppliers of inputs such as car axles, gearboxes, and air-conditioning systems. Network structures allow an organization to bring resources (workers especially) together on a long-term basis in order to find new ways to reduce costs and increase the quality of products—without incurring the high costs of operating a complex organizational structure (such as the costs of employing many managers). More and more U.S. and European organizations are relying on strategic alliances to gain access to low-cost foreign sources of inputs. This approach allows managers to keep costs low. The following "Managing Globally" describes the network structure that Nike uses to produce and market sports shoes.

strategic alliance An agreement in which managers pool or share their organization's resources and know-how with a foreign company, and the two organizations share the rewards and risks of starting a new venture.

network structure A series of strategic alliances that an organization creates with suppliers, manufacturers, and distributors to produce and market a product.

Managing Globally

Nike's Network Structure

Located in Beaverton, Oregon, Nike is the largest and most profitable sports shoe manufacturer in the world. The key to Nike's success is the network structure that Nike founder and CEO Philip Knight created to allow his company to produce and market shoes. As noted in Chapter 7, the most successful companies today are trying to pursue simultaneously a low-cost and a differentiation strategy. Knight decided early that to do this at Nike he needed organizational architecture that would allow his company to focus on some functions, such as design, and leave others, such as manufacturing, to other organizations.

Nike sees itself not just as a shoemaker but also as a trend or lifestyle setter through its innovative design, marketing, and retailing activities.

By far the largest function at Nike's headquarters in Beaverton is the design function, composed of talented designers who pioneered innovations in sports shoe design such as the air pump and "Air Jordans," which Nike introduced so successfully. Designers use computer-aided design (CAD) to design Nike shoes, and they electronically store all new product information, including manufacturing instructions. When the designers finish their work, they electronically transmit all the blueprints for the new products to a network of Southeast Asian suppliers and manufacturers with which Nike has formed strategic alliances.[44] Instructions for the design of a new sole may be sent to a supplier in Taiwan; instructions for the leather uppers, to a supplier in Malaysia. The suppliers produce the shoe parts and send them for final assembly to a manufacturer in China with which Nike has established another strategic alliance. From China the shoes are shipped to distributors throughout the world. Ninety-nine percent of the 99 million pairs of shoes that Nike makes each year are made in Southeast Asia.

This network structure gives Nike two important advantages. First, Nike's costs are very low because wages in Southeast Asia are a fraction of what they are in the United States, and this difference gives Nike a low-cost advantage. Second, Nike is able to respond to changes in sports shoe fashion very quickly. Using its global computer system, Nike literally can change the instructions it gives each of its suppliers overnight, so that within a few weeks its foreign manufacturers are producing new kinds of shoes.[45] If any of the alliance partners fail to perform up to Nike's standards, those partners are replaced with new partners. Obviously, Nike has a great deal of flexibility and control over its network structure.

outsource To use outside suppliers and manufacturers to produce goods and services.

Nike's ability to **outsource,** to use outside suppliers and manufacturers to produce all its shoes abroad, allows Knight to keep the organization's U.S. structure flat and flexible. Nike is able to use a simple functional structure to organize its activities. Knight decentralizes control of the design process to teams who are assigned to develop each new kind of sports shoes that Nike sells.

Some small companies go even further than Nike and create a network structure to perform almost all of their functional activities. Topsy Tail, a small company in Texas that sells hair-styling gadgets, has created strategic alliances with other companies that not only manufacture and distribute Topsy Tail products but also design, market, and package them. Apart from Topsy Tail's CEO, Tomima Edmark, who orchestrates these alliances and is at the hub of the network, the company has almost no permanent employees. Outside companies and individuals contract with Edmark to perform certain services in return for which they receive a set fee.[46]

The ability of managers to develop a network structure to produce or provide the goods and services customers want, rather than create a complex organizational structure to do so, has led many researchers and consultants to popularize the idea of a **boundaryless organization** composed of people who are linked by computers, faxes, computer-aided design systems, and video teleconferencing and who rarely, if ever, see one another face-to-face. People are utilized when their services are needed, much as in a matrix structure, but they are not formal members of an organization. They are functional experts who form an alliance with an organization, fulfill their contractual obligations, and then move on to the next project.

boundaryless organization An organization whose members are linked by computers, faxes, computer-aided design systems, and video teleconferencing and who rarely, if ever, see one another face-to-face.

The use of outsourcing and the development of network structures is increasing rapidly as organizations recognize the many opportunities the approaches offer to reduce costs and increase organizational flexibility. U.S. companies spent $100 billion on outsourcing in 1996. Companies that specialize in outsourced work, such as EDS, which manages the information systems of large organizations like Xerox and Eastman Kodak—are major beneficiaries of this new approach. Similarly, on a global level, the development of a global network of strategic alliances among companies is an alternative to the use of the complex global matrix structure. A global matrix is far more difficult to manage because an organization performs all the functional activities itself and thus must coordinate and integrate among them.

Designing organizational architecture is becoming an increasingly complex management function. To maximize efficiency and effectiveness, managers must assess carefully the relative benefits of having their own organization perform a functional activity versus forming an alliance with another organization to perform the activity.

Tips for Managers

Choosing a Structure

1. If an organization begins to produce a wider range of products, and especially if it enters new businesses or industries, evaluate whether a move to a product structure will keep the organization organic.

2. If your organization grows and expands regionally or nationally, evaluate whether a move to a geographic structure will keep the organization organic.

3. If an organization begins to serve different kinds of customers, evaluate whether or not a move to a market structure will keep the organization organic.

4. To increase efficiency, quality, innovation or responsiveness to customers, consider moving to a matrix or product team structure and find ways of decentralizing authority and empowering employees.

5. No matter what kind of structure an organization uses periodically analyze its hierarchy of authority and keep the number of levels in the hierarchy to a minimum.

6. Analyze if strategic alliances or a network structure are organizing choices that will help keep an organization flatter and more organic.

Summary and Review

Chapter Summary

ORGANIZATIONAL STRUCTURE

- **The Organizational Environment**
- **Strategy**
- **Technology**
- **Human Resources**

JOB DESIGN

- **Job Enlargement and Job Enrichment**
- **The Job Characteristics Model**

DESIGNING ORGANIZATIONAL STRUCTURE The four main determinants of organizational structure are the external environment, strategy, technology, and human resources. In general, the higher the level of uncertainty associated with these factors, the more appropriate is a flexible, adaptable structure as opposed to a formal, rigid one.

GROUPING TASKS INTO JOBS Job design is the process by which managers group tasks into jobs. To create more interesting jobs, and to get workers to act flexibly, managers can enlarge and enrich jobs. The job characteristics model provides a useful tool managers can use to measure how motivating or satisfying a particular job is.

GROUPING JOBS INTO FUNCTIONS AND DIVISIONS Managers can choose from many kinds of organizational structures to make the best use of organizational resources. Depending on the specific organizing problems they face, managers can choose from functional, product, geographic, market, matrix, and product team structures.

COORDINATING FUNCTIONS AND DIVISIONS No matter which structure managers choose, they must decide how to distribute authority in the organization, how many levels to have in the hierarchy of authority, and what balance to strike between centralization and decentralization to keep the number of levels in the hierarchy to a minimum. As organizations grow, managers must increase integration and coordination among functions and divisions. Six integrating mechanisms are available to facilitate this: direct contact, liaison roles, task forces, cross-functional teams, integrating roles, and the matrix structure.

STRATEGIC ALLIANCES AND NETWORK STRUCTURE To avoid many of the communications and coordination problems that emerge as organizations grow, managers are attempting to develop new ways of organizing. In a strategic alliance, managers enter into a contract with another organization to provide inputs or to perform a functional activity. If managers enter into a series of these contracts and a substantial number of activities are performed outside their organization, they have created a network structure.

Management in Action

Topics for Discussion and Action

1. Would a flexible or a more formal structure be appropriate for these organizations: (a) a large department store, (b) a Big Five accountancy firm, (c) a biotechnology company? Explain your reasoning.

2. Using the job characteristics model as a guide, discuss how a manager can enrich or enlarge subordinates' jobs.

3. How might a salesperson's job or a secretary's job be enlarged or enriched to make it more motivating?

4. When and under what conditions might managers change from a functional to (a) a product, (b) a geographic, or (c) a market structure?

5. How do matrix structure and product team structure differ? Why is product team structure more widely used?

6. Find a manager and identify the kind of organizational structure that his or her organization uses to coordinate its people and resources. Why is the organization using that structure? Do you think a different structure would be more appropriate? Which one?

7. With the same or another manager, discuss the distribution of authority in the organization. Does the manager think that decentralizing authority and empowering employees is appropriate?

8. Compare the pros and cons of using a network structure to perform organizational activities and performing all activities in-house or within one organizational hierarchy.

Building Management Skills

Understanding Organizing

Think of an organization with which you are familiar, perhaps one you have worked in—such as a store, restaurant, office, church, or school. Then answer the following questions.

1. Which contingencies are most important in explaining how the organization is organized? Do you think it is organized in the best way?

2. Using the job characteristics model, how motivating do you think the job of a typical employee in this organization is? Can you think of any ways in which a typical job could be enlarged or enriched?

3. What kind of organizational structure does the organization use? If it is part of a chain, what kind of structure does the entire organization use? What other structures discussed in the chapter might allow the organization to operate more effectively? For example, would the move to a product team structure lead to greater efficiency or effectiveness? Why or why not?

4. How many levels are there in the organization's hierarchy? Is authority centralized or decentralized? Describe the span of control of the top manager and of middle or first-line managers.

5. Is the distribution of authority appropriate for the organization and its activities? Would it be possible to flatten the hierarchy by decentralizing authority and empowering employees?

6. What are the principal integrating mechanisms used in the organization? Do they provide sufficient coordination among individuals and functions? How might they be improved?

7. Now that you have analyzed the way this organization is organized, what advice would you give its managers to help them improve the way it operates?

Small Group Breakout Exercise

Bob's Appliances

Form groups of three or four people, and appoint one member as the spokesperson who will communicate your findings to the whole class when called on by the instructor. Then discuss the following scenario.

Bob's Appliances sells and services household appliances such as washing machines, dishwashers, stoves, and refrigerators. Over the years, the company has developed a good reputation for the quality of its customer service, and many local builders patronize the store. Recently, some new appliance retailers, including Circuit City and REX, have opened stores that also provide numerous appliances. In addition to appliances, however, to attract more customers these stores carry a complete range of consumer electronics products like televisions, stereos, and computers. Bob Lange, the owner of Bob's Appliances, has decided that if he is to stay in business he must widen his product range and compete directly with the chains.

In 1996, he decided to build a new 20,000-square-foot store and service center, and he is now hiring new employees to sell and service the new line of consumer electronics. Because of his company's increased size, Lange is not sure of the best way to organize the employees. Currently, he uses a functional structure; employees are divided into sales, purchasing and accounting, and repair. Bob is wondering whether selling and servicing consumer electronics is so different from selling and servicing appliances that he should move to a product structure (see figure) and create separate sets of functions for each of his two lines of business.[47]

You are a team of local consultants that Bob has called in to advise him as he makes this crucial choice. Which structure do you recommend? Why?

FUNCTIONAL STRUCTURE

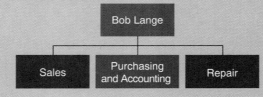

PRODUCT STRUCTURE

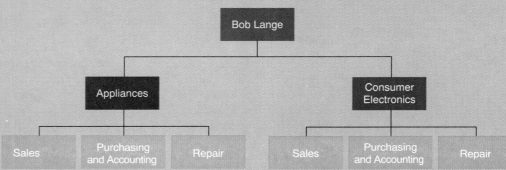

Exploring the World Wide Web

Specific Assignment

Enter the website of the German publishing company Bertelsmann (www.bertelsmann.com). Click on the English language version. Click on "Profile," then on "At a Glance" and "Activities" to examine the "Entrepreneurial Leadership and Organization" section.

1. What are Bertelsmann's mission and corporate goals?

2. What kind of organizational structure does Bertelsmann have?

3. What is Bertelsmann's approach to managing its structure (its approach to decentralization, delegation, and so on)?

General Assignment

Search for a website that tells the story of how an organization changed its structure in some way to increase its efficiency and effectiveness.

ManagementCase
How Bill Gates Organizes Microsoft

Microsoft, the biggest and most profitable software company in the world, has been called the best 15,000-person company in the country.[48] These 15,000 employees generated over $5 billion in revenues in 1996 alone. Perhaps even more impressive is the fact that since Bill Gates founded Microsoft in 1974, over 2,000 of these employees have become millionaires because of the stock options that Gates uses to attract and retain talented employees. Gates himself is the richest man in the United States, having a fortune estimated at over $60 billion. What is the secret of Microsoft's success?

At the level of individual employees, Gates's philosophy of managing his organization is evident in the sorts of people he recruits and selects. Microsoft goes to the best software departments in colleges and universities across the country and spends a lot of time recruiting people who like to work hard, be imaginative and creative, and take risks. These are work values that are Gates's own and that Microsoft prizes. Employees are expected to work long hours, often 60- or 80-hour workweeks. They are expected to become experts in the specific software projects they work on and to possess up-to-the-minute information and state-of-the-art knowledge about what Microsoft and its competitors are doing. Gates meets frequently with employees on different projects and is constantly probing their knowledge to make sure they are up-to-date. If they lack current information, they lose credibility with him because they are not doing their job.

Beyond stock options, Gates motivates his employees by providing them with the latest technology, flexible (though long) work hours, and even exercise rooms on the premises of a collegiate-type "campus." In addition, the way Gates motivates his employees is closely linked to the way Microsoft uses groups and teamwork as the basis of its organizing process.

At Microsoft, programmers work in teams that can be as small as five or six people, and different teams work on specific software applications. Often many small teams are working on different aspects of a larger project managed by a project manager. For example, over 300 people worked in small teams to develop Microsoft's Windows 98 operating system, a product that attempts to match the user-friendliness of Apple's operating system. The use of product teams allows people to cooperate and pool their skills and resources; it promotes among team members the intense interactions that often lead to the breakthroughs that help Microsoft pioneer new products so quickly. Moreover, team members can learn from one another and control one another's behavior.

At the organization level, Gates is careful to keep the distance between himself and the teams to a minimum by keeping his organization as flat as possible—that is, by keeping the number of levels in the organizational hierarchy to a minimum. Moreover, he designs Microsoft's structure around these teams and decentralizes authority and delegates important decisions to each team to give it maximum autonomy and freedom to be creative and to take risks. Gates is able to delegate so much authority because he pays so much attention to recruiting the right kinds of employees and because he appraises each team's performance regularly to ensure that all teams are on top of their projects.

Questions

1. What are the main elements in Bill Gates's organizing approach?

2. What organizing problems do you think might emerge in Microsoft as it continues to grow?

ManagementCase
Big Changes at Amoco

Amoco (www.amoco.com), like most other global oil companies, performs three major activities: (1) It explores for oil and pumps it out of the ground. (2) It refines the crude oil into gasoline and sells it through a nationwide system of gas stations. (3) It operates a chemicals company that uses the crude oil to manufacture plastics and other petroleum products that are sold to other companies. Throughout the 1970s, Amoco used a "three-legged structure" to manage their three activities: Independent operating subsidiaries managed each activity.

Each of the three subsidiaries had its own hierarchy of top managers who were responsible for overseeing the many business divisions of the subsidiary. The top managers of each subsidiary reported to Amoco's corporate-level managers, who oversaw their activities and made the final decision on what the subsidiaries should be doing. Under this setup, divisional managers within the subsidiaries were responsible for developing effective business-level strategies, but important decision making about whether to implement these strategies took place at the corporate level. As a result, strategy implementation often took a long time because of the many layers of managers separating Amoco's corporate managers from the managers of each division. The slow decision making hampered divisional managers' attempts to build a competitive advantage.

The three-legged structure worked well enough in the good economic times of the early 1970s when oil prices steadily increased. Then, in the late 1970s, global oil companies experienced a shock. Oil prices tumbled and 20 years later were still flat. Amoco and other global oil companies—such as Exxon, British Petroleum, Mobil, and Elf Aquitane—experienced increased pressure to reduce costs and boost sales because of flat gasoline prices. In the attempt to boost profits, most large global oil companies—including Amoco—laid off thousands of employees; indeed, some analysts estimate that 500,000 jobs were lost in the 1980s and early 1990s in the U.S. oil industry.[49]

Despite laying off over one-quarter of Amoco's workforce, however, managers were unable to boost profitability. As a result, in 1995, top management took a close look at Amoco's organizational structure to identify ways to increase both efficiency and effectiveness. H. Laurance Fuller, Amoco's new chairman and CEO, decided that

only a massive change in the way Amoco organized its activities would turn the company around and boost profits. Fuller decided that Amoco would completely eliminate the three-legged structure and remove the three top managers at the subsidiary level. The three subsidiaries would be divided into 17 independent business divisions, and decision-making authority would be decentralized to the managers of each division, who would be free to choose their own strategy for their division. Each division would be evaluated for its ability to reach certain growth targets set by corporate managers, but each division's managers would determine the approaches the division took to reach those targets.

When Fuller decentralized responsibility for the development and implementation of business-level strategy to the managers of each of the 17 new divisions, he also created a strong top-management team to oversee and manage corporate strategy. The three former heads of the subsidiaries became members of this team, and along with Fuller and four other top Amoco corporate managers, the group became

responsible for reviewing each division's performance and for trying to find ways to help divisional managers boost performance.

Fuller hopes that the new flatter, decentralized product division structure will lead managers to be more entrepreneurial—motivated both to increase efficiency and to innovate high-quality products. Fuller also hopes that because the 17 new product divisions are closer to their customers, they will be more responsive to customers' needs, and that if customers are satisfied, sales will be strong. Thus, Fuller hopes that changing the way Amoco organizes its human and other resources will allow the organization to build new sources of competitive advantage, which in turn will lead to the boost in profitability the company so badly needs.

Questions

1. What changes did Amoco make to its organizational structure?

2. Why did it make those changes?

Chapter nine

Organizational Control and Culture

Learning Objectives

1. Define *organizational control,* and describe the four steps of the control process.

2. Identify the main output controls, and discuss their advantages and disadvantages as means of coordinating and motivating employees.

3. Identify the main behavior controls, and discuss their advantages and disadvantages as means of coordinating and motivating employees.

4. Explain the role of organizational culture in creating effective organizational architecture.

A Case in Contrast

Different Approaches to Output Control Create Different Cultures

Giddings and Lewis, the well-known manufacturer of automated factory equipment for companies such as General Motors (www.gm.com), Boeing (www.boeing.com), and Ford (www.ford.com), was in trouble when CEO William J. Fife took control of the company. Fife had been given the responsibility to turn around the company's performance, which had been suffering because of rising costs and falling sales. Fife began the turnaround by embarking on a program to develop new products to widen the company's product range. Moreover, he coupled innovation with a focus on responsiveness to customers; indeed, he personally flew all over the United States to talk to customers to make sure the products that were being developed would suit their needs.[1]

To motivate Giddings and Lewis's managers to raise the company's performance, Fife established exacting performance targets and goals. For example, managers were told to achieve goals such as "a 20 percent increase in sales" or "a 20 percent reduction in costs," and their bonuses were closely tied to their ability to reach their goals. Periodically, Fife met with his managers and reviewed their progress toward meeting the goals. Measured by his managers' success in achieving their goals, Fife's turnaround program was successful. In five years, Giddings and Lewis was the most profitable firm in its industry.

Differing performance goals, and delivery of those performance goals, can often have successful effects on the outcomes, but different effects on managers and workers within the organizations. Both Fife and White were successful in turning their organizations around, but Fife destroyed the work values, norms, and culture of Giddings and Lewis in the process.

Informix, a high-tech company based in Menlo Park, California, specializes in creating software to link networks of workstations.[2] Informix's CEO, Philip White, also learned about the importance of establishing specific performance goals for managers when his company experienced deteriorating performance after its acquisition of another software company. After the acquisition, Informix was paying two different workforces, including two different sales forces and two sets of programmers; its soaring operating costs resulted in a loss of almost $50 million. White realized that he had to get costs back under control. Like Fife at Giddings and Lewis, White created an exacting set of performance goals that forced his managers to make some tough decisions.

To get manufacturing costs under control, White gave manufacturing managers a detailed budget that forced them to streamline their workforces to cut costs and find more efficient ways to make products. Within four years, manufacturing costs dropped from 13 percent of revenue to 5 percent. White developed tough performance goals in other functional areas as well and set revenue and profit targets that the managers of each product line were expected to achieve. As at Giddings and Lewis, the result of using tough performance goals at Informix was the launch of a large number of successful new products that made the company an industry leader.

Both CEOs seem to have had considerable success in using performance goals to turn their organizations around and control their managers, but the way each CEO implemented these goals had very different effects on managers and workers within the organizations. At Informix, White adopted a participatory approach to setting goals and measuring performance. White's managers felt involved in the goal-setting process, and they were challenged by the goals he set and were motivated to mobilize organizational resources to achieve them. Moreover, Informix's managers were told to create challenging goals for their subordinates, so, over time, Informix developed a goal-driven culture based on values and norms that reinforced managers' drive to make the company the best in its industry.

Fife's use of goals at Giddings and Lewis resulted in the emergence of a very different set of values and norms. Fife alone dictated the goals that his managers were expected to achieve. When the results did not please him (that is, when a manager did not meet his or her goals), Fife verbally abused the offending manager in front of other managers, who were forced to sit through the attacks in embarrassed silence. Managers began to claim that Fife's use of goals to control behavior was creating competitive rather than cooperative work values and norms and was destroying Giddings and Lewis's culture. Giddings and Lewis's board of directors took the managers' side and asked Fife to resign. In contrast, White is still securely entrenched as the leader at Informix. ●

Overview

As the "Case in Contrast" suggests, the different ways in which Fife and White decided to control the behavior of their managers had very different effects on the way those managers behaved. White adopted a participatory approach and involved his managers in setting goals and targets. Fife alone established the performance standards that managers at Giddings and Lewis were expected to achieve, and he closely monitored their progress. As a result of the different ways they controlled their employees, Fife and White created very different cultures in their organizations. When managers make choices about how to influence and regulate their subordinates' behavior and performance, they establish the second foundation of organizational architecture, organizational control; and a major source of control is culture.

As discussed in Chapter 8, the first task facing managers is to establish the structure of task and reporting relationships that will allow organizational members to use resources most efficiently and effectively. Structure alone, however, does not provide the incentive or motivation for people to behave in ways that help achieve organizational goals. The purpose of organizational control is to provide managers with a means to motivate subordinates to work toward achieving organizational goals and to provide managers with specific feedback on how well an organization and its members are performing. Organizational structure provides an organization with a skeleton; organizational control and culture provide the muscles, sinews, nerves, and sensations that allow managers to regulate and govern the organization's activities. The managerial functions of organizing and controlling are inseparable, and effective managers must learn to make them work together in a harmonious way.

In this chapter, we look in detail at the nature of organizational control and describe the steps in the control process. We discuss three types of control available to managers to control and influence organizational members—output control, behavior control, and clan control (which operates through the values and norms of an organization's culture).[3] By the end of this chapter, you will appreciate the rich variety of control systems available to managers and understand why developing an appropriate control system is vital to increasing the performance of an organization and its members. ●

This famous Leonardo da Vinci drawing illustrates the artist's concern for understanding how the human body controls its own movements and how the different parts of the body work together to maintain the body's integrity, similar to the way various departments operate in an organization.

What Is Organizational Control?

As noted in Chapter 1, *controlling* is the process whereby managers monitor and regulate how efficiently and effectively an organization and its members are performing the activities necessary to achieve organizational goals. As discussed in previous chapters, in *planning* and *organizing,* managers develop the organizational strategy and structure that they hope will allow the organization to use resources most effectively to create value for customers. In *controlling,* managers monitor and evaluate whether their organization's strategy and structure are working as managers intended, how they could be improved, and how they might be changed if they are not working.

Control, however, does not just mean reacting to events after they have occurred. It also means keeping an organization on track and anticipating events that might occur. Control is concerned with keeping employees motivated, focused on the important problems confronting the organization, and working together to take advantage of opportunities that will help an organization perform more highly over time.

The Importance of Organizational Control

To understand the importance of organizational control, consider how it helps managers obtain superior efficiency, quality, responsiveness to customers, and innovation—the four building blocks of competitive advantage.

To determine how *efficiently* they are using their resources, managers must be able to accurately measure how many units of inputs (raw materials, human resources, and so on) are being used to produce a unit of output. Managers also must be able to measure how many units of outputs (goods and services) are being produced. A control system contains the measures or yardsticks that allow managers to assess how efficiently the organization is producing goods and services. Moreover, if managers experiment with changing the way the organization produces goods and services to find a more efficient way of producing them, these measures tell managers how successful they have been. Thus, for example, when managers at Chrysler decided to change to a product team structure to design, engineer, and manufacture new cars, they used measures such as time taken to design a new car and cost savings per car produced to evaluate how well the new structure worked in comparison with the old structure. They found that the new one performed better. Without a control system in place, managers have no idea how well their organization is performing and how its performance can be improved—information that is becoming increasingly important in today's highly competitive environment.

Today, much of the competition among organizations revolves around increasing the *quality* of goods and services. In the car industry, for example, cars within each price range compete against one another in features, design, and reliability. Thus, whether a customer will buy a Ford Taurus, GM Cavalier, Chrysler Intrepid, Toyota Camry, or Honda Accord depends significantly on the quality of each product. Organizational control is important in determining the quality of goods and services because it gives managers feedback on product quality. If managers of an organization such as Chrysler consistently measure the number of customer complaints and the number of new cars returned for repairs, or if the principal of a school measures how many students drop out of school or how achievement scores on nationally based tests vary over time, they have a good indication of how much quality they have built into their product— be it an educated student or a car that does not break down. Effective managers create a control system that consistently monitors the quality of goods and services so that they can make continuous improvements to quality—an approach that can give them a competitive advantage.

Managers can also help make their organizations more *responsive to customers* if they develop a control system that allows them to evaluate how well customer-contact employees are performing their jobs. Monitoring employee behavior can help managers find ways to increase employees' performance levels, perhaps by revealing areas in which skill training can help employees or by finding new procedures that allow employees to perform their jobs better. When employees know that their behaviors are being monitored, they may also have more incentive to be helpful and consistent in their interaction with customers. To improve customer service, for example, Chrysler regularly surveys customers about their experiences with particular Chrysler dealers. If a dealership receives too many customer complaints, Chrysler's managers investigate the dealership to uncover the sources of the problems and suggest solutions. If necessary, they might even threaten to reduce the numbers of cars a dealership receives to force the dealer to improve the quality of its customer service.

Finally, controlling can raise the level of *innovation* in an organization. Successful innovation takes place when managers create an organizational setting in which employees feel empowered to be creative and in which authority is decentralized to employees so that they feel free to experiment and take risks. Deciding on the appropriate control systems to encourage risk taking is an important management challenge; organizational culture (discussed later in this chapter) becomes important in this regard. At Chrysler, to encourage each product team to perform highly, top managers monitored the performance of each team separately—by examining how each team reduced costs or increased quality, for example—and used a bonus system related to performance to pay each team. The product team manager then evaluated each team member's individual performance, and the most innovative employees received promotions and rewards based on their superior performance.

Control Systems

control systems

Formal target-setting, monitoring, evaluation, and feedback systems that provide managers with information about how well the organization's strategy and structure are working.

Control systems are formal target-setting, monitoring, evaluation, and feedback systems that provide managers with information about whether the organization's strategy and structure are working efficiently and effectively.[4] Effective control systems alert managers when something is going wrong and give them time to respond to opportunities and threats. An effective control system has three characteristics: (1) It is flexible enough to allow managers to respond as necessary to unexpected events. (2) It provides accurate information and gives managers a true picture of organizational performance. (3) It provides managers with the information in a timely manner because making decisions on the basis of outdated information is a recipe for failure.

feedforward control

Control that allows managers to anticipate problems before they arise.

Control systems are developed to measure performance at each stage in the conversion of inputs into finished goods and services (see Figure 9.1). At the *input* stage, managers use **feedforward control** to anticipate problems before they arise so that problems do not occur later, during the conversion process.[5] For example, by giving stringent product specifications to suppliers in advance (a form of performance target), an organization can control the quality of the inputs it receives from its suppliers and thus avoid potential problems at the conversion stage. Similarly, by screening job applicants and using several interviews to select the most highly skilled people, managers can lessen the chance that they will hire people who lack the necessary skills or experience to perform effectively. Another form of feedforward control is the development of management information systems that provide managers with timely information about changes in the task and general environments that may impact their organization later on. Effective managers always monitor trends and changes in the external environment to try to anticipate problems. (We discuss management information systems in detail in Chapter 17.)

concurrent control

Control that gives managers immediate feedback on how efficiently inputs are being transformed into outputs so that managers can correct problems as they arise.

At the *conversion* stage, **concurrent control** gives managers immediate feedback on how efficiently inputs are being transformed into outputs so that managers can correct problems as they arise. Concurrent control alerts managers to the need to react quickly to whatever is the source of the problem, be it a defective batch of inputs, a machine that is out of alignment, or a worker

Figure 9.1
Three Types of Control

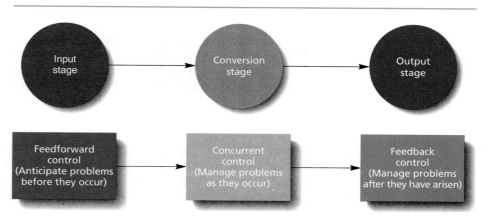

who lacks the skills necessary to perform a task efficiently. Concurrent control is at the heart of total quality management programs (discussed at length in Chapter 18), in which workers are expected to constantly monitor the quality of the goods or services they provide at every step of the production process and inform managers as soon as they discover problems. One of the strengths of Toyota's production system, for example, is that individual workers are given the authority to push a button to stop the assembly line whenever they discover a quality problem. When all problems have been corrected, the result is a finished product that is much more reliable.

At the *output* stage, managers use **feedback control** to provide information about customers' reactions to goods and services so that corrective action can be taken if necessary. For example, a feedback control system that monitors the number of customer returns alerts managers when defective products are being produced, and a system that measures increases or decreases in product sales alerts managers to changes in customer tastes so they can increase or reduce the production of specific products.

feedback control

Control that gives managers information about customers' reactions to goods and services so that corrective action can be taken if necessary.

The Control Process

The control process, whether at the input, conversion, or output stage, can be broken down into four steps: establishing standards of performance, then measuring, comparing, and evaluating actual performance (see Figure 9.2).[6]

● Step 1: *Establish the standards of performance, goals, or targets against which performance is to be evaluated.*

At Step 1 in the control process managers decide on the standards of performance, goals, or targets that they will use to evaluate the performance of the entire organization or some part of it, such as a division, a function, or an individual. The standards of performance that managers select measure efficiency, quality, responsiveness to customers, and innovation.[7] If managers decide to pursue a low-cost strategy, for example, then they need to measure efficiency at all levels in the organization.

At the corporate level, a standard of performance that measures efficiency is *operating costs,* the actual costs associated with producing goods and services,

Figure 9.2

Four Steps in Organizational Control

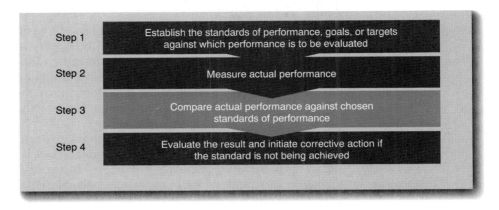

Step 1	Establish the standards of performance, goals, or targets against which performance is to be evaluated
Step 2	Measure actual performance
Step 3	Compare actual performance against chosen standards of performance
Step 4	Evaluate the result and initiate corrective action if the standard is not being achieved

including all employee-related costs. Top managers might set a corporate goal of "reducing operating costs by 10 percent for the next three years" to increase efficiency. Corporate managers might then evaluate divisional managers for their ability to reduce operating costs within their respective divisions, and divisional managers might set cost-savings targets for functional managers. Thus, performance standards selected at one level affect those at the other levels, and ultimately individual managers are evaluated for their ability to reduce costs. For example, S. I. Newhouse, the owner of Condé Nast, publisher of magazines such as *GQ, Vanity Fair,* and *Mademoiselle,* started an across-the-board attempt to reduce costs to reverse the company's losses and instructed all divisional managers to begin a cost-cutting program. When Newhouse decided to retire, he chose as the new CEO Steven T. Florio, the division head who had been most successful in reducing costs and increasing efficiency at *The New Yorker* magazine.

The number of standards of performance that an organization's managers use to evaluate efficiency, quality, and so on, can run into the thousands or hundreds of thousands. Managers at each level are responsible for selecting those standards that will best allow them to evaluate how well the part of the organization they are responsible for is performing.[8] Managers must be careful to choose the standards of performance that allow them to assess how well they are doing with *all four* of the building blocks of competitive advantage. If managers focus on just one (such as efficiency in the example above) and ignore others (such as determining what customers really want and developing a new line of products to satisfy them), managers may end up hurting their organization's performance. A classic case of this mistake involves the large U.S. car makers during the oil crisis of the 1970s. Although U.S. car companies were very efficient—they could produce large cars at low cost—they were not responsive to their customers, few of whom wanted to buy large, gas-guzzling cars. Establishing the appropriate standards for evaluating performance is an important aspect of controlling because these standards determine how managers at all levels will work to give an organization a competitive advantage.

- Step 2: *Measure actual performance.*
Once managers have decided which standards or targets they will use to evaluate performance, the next step in the control process is to measure

actual performance. In practice, managers can measure or evaluate two things: (1) the actual *outputs* that result from the behavior of their members and (2) the *behaviors* themselves (hence the terms *output control* and *behavior control* used below).[9]

Sometimes both outputs and behaviors can be easily measured. Measuring outputs and evaluating behavior are relatively easy in a fast-food restaurant, for example, because employees are performing routine tasks. Managers of a fast-food restaurant can quite easily measure outputs by counting how many customers their employees serve and how much money customers spend. Managers can easily observe each employee's behavior and quickly take action to solve any problems that may arise.

When an organization and its members perform complex, nonroutine activities that are intrinsically difficult to measure, it is much more difficult for managers to measure outputs or behavior.[10] It is very difficult, for example, for managers in charge of R&D departments at Merck or Microsoft to measure performance or to evaluate the performance of individual members because it can take 5 or 10 years to determine whether the new products that scientists are developing are going to be profitable. Moreover, it is impossible for a manager to measure how creative a research scientist is by watching his or her actions.

In general, the more nonroutine or complex organizational activities are, the harder it is for managers to measure outputs or behaviors.[11] Outputs, however, are usually easier to measure than behaviors because they are more tangible and objective. Therefore, the first kind of performance measures that managers tend to use are those that measure outputs. Then managers develop performance measures or standards that allow them to evaluate behaviors to determine whether employees at all levels are working toward organizational goals. Some simple behavior measures are, Do employees come to work on time? Do employees consistently follow the established rules for greeting and serving customers? Each type of output and behavior control and the way it is used at the different organizational levels—corporate, divisional, functional, and individual—is discussed in detail later in the chapter.

- Step 3: *Compare actual performance against chosen standards of performance.*

During Step 3, managers evaluate whether—and to what extent—performance deviates from the standards of performance chosen in Step 1. If performance is higher than expected, managers might decide that they set performance standards too low and may raise them for the next time period to challenge their subordinates.[12] Managers at Japanese companies are well known for the way they try to raise performance in manufacturing settings by constantly raising performance standards to motivate managers and workers to find new ways to reduce costs or increase quality.

However, if performance is too low and standards were not reached, or if standards were set so high that employees could not achieve them, managers must decide whether to take corrective action.[13] Taking corrective action is easy when the reasons for poor performance can be identified—for instance, high labor costs. To reduce costs, managers can search for low-cost foreign sources of supply or invest more in technology or implement cross-functional teams. More often, however, the reasons for poor performance are hard to identify. Changes in the environment such as the emergence of a new global competitor, a recession, or an increase in interest rates might be the source of the problem. Within an organization, perhaps the R&D function underestimated the problems it would encounter in developing the new product or the extra costs of doing unforeseen research. If managers are to take any form of corrective action, Step 4 is necessary.

• Step 4: *Evaluate the result and initiate corrective action if the standard is not being achieved.*

The final step in the control process is to evaluate the results. Whether performance standards have been met or not, managers can learn a great deal during this step. If managers decide that the level of performance is unacceptable, they must try to solve the problem. Sometimes, performance problems occur because the standard was too high—for example, a sales target was too optimistic and impossible to achieve. In this case, adopting more realistic standards can reduce the gap between actual performance and desired performance. However, if managers determine that something in the situation is causing the problem, then to raise performance they will need to change the way resources are being utilized.[14] Perhaps the latest technology is not being used; perhaps workers lack the advanced training they need to perform at a higher level; perhaps the organization needs to buy its inputs or assemble its products abroad to compete against low-cost rivals; perhaps it needs to restructure itself or reengineer its work processes to increase efficiency.

The simplest example of a control system is the thermostat in a home. By setting the thermostat, you establish the standard of performance with which actual temperature is to be compared. The thermostat contains a sensing or monitoring device, which measures the actual temperature against the desired temperature. Whenever there is a difference between them, the furnace or air-conditioning unit is activated to bring the temperature back to the standard: In other words, corrective action is initiated. This is a simple control system, for it is entirely self-contained and the target (temperature) is easy to measure.

Establishing targets and designing measurement systems is much more difficult for managers. Because of the high level of uncertainty in the organizational environment, managers rarely know what might happen. Thus, it is vital for managers to design control systems to alert them to problems so that they can be dealt with before they become threatening. Another issue is that managers are not just concerned to bring the organization's performance up to some predetermined standard; they want to push that standard forward, to encourage employees at all levels to find new ways to raise performance.

In the following sections, we consider the three most important types of control that managers use to coordinate and motivate employees to ensure they pursue superior efficiency, quality, innovation, and responsiveness to customers: *output control, behavior control,* and *organizational culture,* or clan control (see Figure 9.3). Managers use all three to govern and regulate organizational activities, no matter what specific organizational structure is in place.

Output Control

All managers, like William Fife and Philip White (profiled in the "Case in Contrast"), develop a system of output control for their organizations. First, they choose the goals or output performance standards or targets that they think will best measure efficiency, quality, innovation, and responsiveness to customers. Then they measure to

Figure 9.3
Three Organizational Control Systems

Type of control	Mechanisms of control
Output control	Financial measures of performance Organizational goals Operating budgets
Behavior control	Direct supervision Management by objectives Rules and standard operating procedures
Organizational culture/clan control	Values Norms Socialization

see whether the performance goals and standards are being achieved at the corporate, divisional or functional, and individual levels of the organization. The three main mechanisms that managers use to assess output or performance are financial measures, organizational goals, and operating budgets.

Financial Measures of Performance

Top managers are most concerned with overall organizational performance and use various financial measures to evaluate performance. The most common are profit ratios, liquidity ratios, leverage ratios, and activity ratios. They are discussed below and summarized in Table 9.1.[15]

• *Profit ratios* measure how efficiently managers are using the organization's resources to generate profits. *Return on investment (ROI),* an organization's net income before taxes divided by its total assets, is the most commonly used financial performance measure because it allows managers of one organization to compare performance with that of other organizations. ROI allows managers to assess an organization's competitive advantage. *Gross profit margin* is the difference between the amount of revenue generated by a product and the resources used to produce the product. This measure provides managers with information about how efficiently an organization is utilizing its resources and about how attractive customers find the product. It also provides managers with a way to assess how well an organization is building a competitive advantage.

• *Liquidity ratios* measure how well managers have protected organizational resources so as to be able to meet short-term obligations. The *current ratio* (current assets divided by current liabilities) tells managers whether they have the resources available to meet the claims of short-term creditors. The *quick ratio* tells whether they can pay these claims without selling inventory.

• *Leverage ratios* such as the *debt-to-assets ratio* and the *times-covered ratio* measure the degree to which managers use debt (borrow money) or equity (issue new shares) to finance ongoing operations. An organization is highly leveraged if it uses more debt than equity. Debt can be very risky when profits fail to cover the interest on the debt.

Table 9.1

Four Measures of Financial Performance

Profit Ratios			
Return on investment	=	$\dfrac{\text{Net profit before taxes}}{\text{Total assets}}$	Measures how well managers are using the organization's resources to generate profits.
Gross profit margin	=	$\dfrac{\text{Sales revenues} - \text{cost of goods sold}}{\text{Sales revenues}}$	The differences between the amount of revenue generated from the product and the resources used to produce the product.
Liquidity Ratios			
Current ratio	=	$\dfrac{\text{Current assets}}{\text{Current liabilities}}$	Do managers have resources available to meet claims of short-term creditors?
Quick ratio	=	$\dfrac{\text{Current assets} - \text{inventory}}{\text{Current liabilities}}$	Can managers pay off claims of short-term creditors without selling inventory?
Leverage Ratios			
Debt-to-assets ratio	=	$\dfrac{\text{Total debt}}{\text{Total assets}}$	To what extent have managers used borrowed funds to finance investments?
Times-covered ratio	=	$\dfrac{\text{Profit before interest and taxes}}{\text{Total interest charges}}$	Measures how far profits can decline before managers cannot meet interest charges. If ratio declines to less than 1, the organization is technically insolvent.
Activity Ratios			
Inventory turnover	=	$\dfrac{\text{Cost of goods sold}}{\text{Inventory}}$	Measures how efficiently managers are turning inventory over so excess inventory is not carried.
Days sales outstanding	=	$\dfrac{\dfrac{\text{Accounts receivable}}{\text{Total Sales}}}{300}$	Measures how efficiently managers are collecting revenues from customers to pay expenses.

- *Activity ratios* provide measures of how well managers are creating value from organizational assets. *Inventory turnover* measures how efficiently managers are turning inventory over so that excess inventory is not carried. *Days sales outstanding* provides information on how efficiently managers are collecting revenue from customers to pay expenses.

The objectivity of financial measures of performance is the reason why so many managers use them to assess the efficiency and effectiveness of their organizations. When an organization fails to meet performance standards such as ROI, revenue, or stock price targets, managers know that they must take corrective action. Thus, financial controls tell managers when a corporate reorganization might be necessary, when they should sell off divisions and exit from businesses, or when they should rethink their corporate-level strategies.[16]

Although financial information is an important output control, financial information by itself does not provide managers with all the information they need about the four building blocks of competitive advantage. Financial results inform managers about the results of decisions they have already made; they do not tell managers how to find new opportunities to build competitive advantage in the future. To encourage a future-oriented approach, top managers must establish organizational goals that encourage middle and first-line managers to achieve superior efficiency, quality, innovation, and responsiveness to customers.

Organizational Goals

Once top managers, after consultation with lower-level managers, have set the organization's overall goals, they then establish performance standards for the divisions and functions. These standards specify for divisional and functional managers the level at which their units must perform if the organization is to achieve its overall goals.[17] Each division is given a set of specific goals to achieve (see Figure 9.4). We saw in Chapter 7, for example, that General Electric CEO Jack Welch and his top-management team declared that the goal of each division was to be first or second in its industry in terms of profit. Divisional managers then develop a business-level strategy (based on achieving superior efficiency or innovation) that they hope will allow them to achieve that goal.[18] In consultation with functional managers, they specify the functional goals that the managers of different functions need to achieve to allow the division to achieve its goals. Sales managers might be evaluated for their ability to increase sales; materials management managers for their ability to increase the quality of inputs or lower their costs; R&D managers for the number of products they innovate or the number of patents they receive. In turn, functional managers establish goals that first-line managers and nonmanagerial employees need to achieve to allow the function to achieve its goals.

Output control is used at every level of the organization, and it is vital that the goals set at each level harmonize with the goals set at other levels so that managers and other employees throughout the organization work together to attain the corporate goals that top managers have set.[19] It is also important that goals be set appropriately so that managers are motivated to accomplish them. If goals are set at an impossibly high level, managers might work only half-heartedly to achieve them because they are certain they will fail. In contrast, if goals are set so low that they are too easy to achieve, managers will not be motivated to use all their resources as efficiently and effectively as possible. Research suggests that the best goals are *specific difficult goals*—goals that will challenge and stretch managers' ability but are not out of reach and will not require an impossibly high expenditure of managerial time and energy. Such goals are often called *stretch goals*.

Deciding what is a specific difficult goal and what is a goal that is too difficult or too easy is a skill that managers must develop. Based on their own judgment and work experience, managers at all levels must assess how difficult a certain task is, and they must assess the ability of a particular subordinate man-

Figure 9.4

Organizationwide Goal Setting

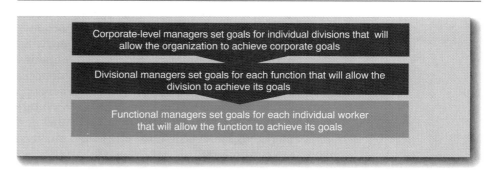

ager to achieve the goal. If they do so successfully, challenging interrelated goals–goals that reinforce one another and focus on achieving overall corporate objectives–will energize the organization (this is what Philip White achieved at Informix, profiled in the opening "Case in Contrast").

Operating Budgets

operating budget A budget that states how managers intend to use organizational resources to achieve organizational goals.

Once managers at each level have been given a goal or target to achieve, the next step in developing an output control system is to establish operating budgets that regulate how managers and workers attain those goals. An **operating budget** is a blueprint that states how managers intend to use organizational resources to achieve organizational goals efficiently. Typically, managers at one level allocate to subordinate managers a specific amount of resources to use to produce goods and services. Once they have been given a budget, these lower-level managers must decide how to allocate money for different organizational activities. They are then evaluated for their ability to stay within the budget and to make the best use of available resources. For example, managers at GE's washing machine division might have a budget of $50 million to spend to develop and sell a new line of washing machines. They must decide how much money to allocate to the various functions such as R&D, engineering, and sales so that the division generates the most customer revenue and makes the biggest profit.

Large organizations often treat each division as a singular or stand-alone responsibility center. Corporate managers then evaluate each division's contribution to corporate performance. Managers of a division may be given a fixed budget for resources and evaluated for the amount of goods or services they can produce using those resources (this is a *cost* or *expense* budget approach). Or managers may be asked to maximize the revenues from the sales of goods and services produced (a *revenue* budget approach). Or managers may be evaluated on the difference between the revenues generated by the sales of goods and services and the budgeted cost of making those goods and services (a *profit* budget approach). Japanese companies' use of operating budgets and challenging goals to increase efficiency is instructive in this context.

Managing Globally

Japan's New Concern for Output Control

In the 1990s, Japanese companies faced increasing problems competing in the global marketplace because the rising value of the yen made their products expensive abroad. In addition, the Japanese experienced problems because global competitors lowered their own costs by imitating many of the cost-saving innovations in manufacturing that Japanese companies had pioneered (total quality management, for example). With their competitive advantage eroding because foreign competitors' costs were as low as, or lower than, their own, Japanese companies searched for new ways to cut costs to increase efficiency.

At the top of their list of ways to reduce costs was making innovative use of output controls–such as goals and budgets–to increase efficiency but to do so in a way that did not destroy innovation. One of the techniques managers chose was to decentralize responsibility for meeting budgets and profit targets down to the level of the first-line supervisor and worker. At Kirin's brewery in Kyoto, for example, managers competed against one another to report the biggest profits. Information about costs was posted on the wall so all employees could see how their team's day-to-day performance was affecting progress toward meeting goals and budget targets.[20] To make it even more clear to employees how their performance directly impacts the bottom line, some companies divided their workforce into even smaller teams. The high-tech Kyocera company, for example, divided employees into over 800 small units (nicknamed "amoebas") that "traded" resources among each other and tried to get the most value for what they were doing.

In addition, recognizing that a large proportion of their costs was the costs they were paying for inputs such as component parts, Japanese companies worked with suppliers to help them reduce their own costs and raise product quality. Members of an organization's research and development, engineering, and manufacturing functions became temporary members of cross-company teams established to find new ways to reduce costs, not least of which was to teach suppliers how to use budgets and goals. Much of this new interest in output control paid off, and companies such as Toyota and Honda predicted that by the year 2000 they would be competitive in world markets regardless of the value of the yen.

In summary, three components—objective financial measures, challenging goals and performance standards, and appropriate operating budgets—are the essence of effective output control. Most organizations develop sophisticated output control systems to allow managers at all levels to keep accurate account of the organization so that they can move quickly to take corrective action as needed.[21] Output control is an essential part of management.

Problems with Output Control

When designing an output control system, managers must be careful to avoid some pitfalls. First, they must be sure that the output standards they create motivate managers at all levels and do not cause managers to behave in inappropriate ways to achieve organizational goals.

Suppose top managers give divisional managers the goal of doubling profits over a three-year period. This goal seems challenging and reachable when it is jointly agreed upon, and in the first two years profits go up by 70 percent. In the third year, however, an economic recession hits and sales plummet. Divisional managers think it is increasingly unlikely that they will meet their profit goal. Failure will mean losing the substantial monetary bonus tied to achieving the goal. How might managers behave to try to preserve their bonus?

One course of action they might take is to find ways to reduce costs, since profit can be increased either by raising revenues or by reducing costs. Thus, divisional managers might cut back on expensive research and development activities, delay maintenance on machinery, reduce marketing expenditures, and lay off middle managers and workers to reduce costs so that at the end of the year they will make their target of doubling profits and will receive their bonus. This tactic might help them achieve a short-run goal—doubling profits—but such actions could hurt long-term profitability or ROI (because a cutback

Marubishi Motor, the world's largest producer of electric motors, is one of the Japanese companies that has been making innovative use of output controls. By using output controls as targets, it is now able to satisfy over 70 percent of its customers' needs with just 20 different models, something that has significantly reduced its costs and raised quality to new levels. .

in R&D can reduce the rate of product innovation, a cutback in marketing will lead to the loss of customers, and so on).

The long term is what corporate managers should be most concerned about. Thus, top managers must consider carefully how flexible they should be when using output control. If conditions change (as they will because of uncertainty in the task and general environments), it is probably better for top managers to communicate to managers lower in the hierarchy that they are aware of the changes taking place and are willing to revise and lower goals and standards. Indeed, most organizations schedule yearly revisions of their five-year plan and goals.

Second, the inappropriate use of output control systems can lead lower-level managers and workers to behave unethically. If goals are too challenging, employees may be motivated to behave unethically toward customers, as happened in Sears's car repair shops.

Ethics in Action

Trouble at Sears

Sears, the huge U.S. retailer based in Chicago, found its performance dropping dramatically in the early 1990s because of intense competition; low-cost retailers such as Wal-Mart (www.wal-mart.com) and Target (www.target-stores.com) were taking away customers. Sears managers were forced to find ways to reduce costs and make employees more responsive to customers. One of the ways they tried to do this was to link the bonuses paid to the employees of their car repair workshops to the dollar volume of the car repairs each workshop generated—a form of output control. Therefore, in

1992 Sears cut the base salary of car repair personnel and linked pay to bonuses earned on the volume of sales. Managers hoped that using an output control system that linked pay to performance would motivate employees to be more efficient so that the number of cars going through a workshop each day would increase. Managers also hoped that linking pay to performance would make employees more responsive to customers, because satisfied customers would come back and also recommend Sears to their friends.[22]

Initial results of the new output control system seemed to suggest that it was working. Dollar volume of sales was up and so was employees' pay. Soon, however, a number of complaints were reported from disgruntled customers who believed that Sears employees were recommending expensive and unnecessary car repairs. California's Consumer Affairs Department was one of the first governmental agencies to investigate these claims. It concluded in late 1992 that on 34 of the 38 undercover runs that the department conducted, Sears personnel charged an average of $235 for unnecessary repairs. Sears employees, having difficulty keeping their take-home pay at previous base levels, apparently were deceiving customers about the dollar amount of repairs that were really necessary.[23]

In response to these findings, Sears management scrapped the new output control system and went back to paying employees a larger base salary. However, in 1995, to once again encourage higher performance, management reversed this stance and resumed bonuses based on dollar volume of sales. Whether the drive to increase efficiency will result in similar problems in the future, or Sears's new output control system will work as intended, remains to be seen.

As Sears's experience suggests, establishing an output control system that increases efficiency and avoids unethical behavior toward customers is hard to do. Managers must be aware of the problems surrounding the development of effective output control systems.

The message is clear: Although output control is a useful tool for keeping managers and employees at all levels motivated and the organization on track, it is only a guide to appropriate action. Managers must be sensitive to how they use output control and constantly monitor its effects at all levels in the organization.

Behavior Control

Organizational structure by itself does not provide any mechanism that motivates managers and nonmanagerial employees to behave in ways that make the structure work or even improve the way it works—hence the need for control. Put another way, managers can develop an elegant organizational structure with highly appropriate task and reporting relationships, but it will work as designed only if managers also establish control systems that allow them to motivate and shape employee behavior.[24] Output control is one method of motivating employees; behavior control is another method. In this section, we examine three mechanisms of behavior control that managers can use to keep subordinates on track and make organizational structures work as they are designed to work: direct supervision, management by objectives, and rules and standard operating procedures (see Figure 9.3).

Direct Supervision

The most immediate and potent form of behavior control is direct supervision by managers who actively monitor and observe the behavior of their subordinates, teach subordinates the behaviors that are appropriate and inappropriate, and intervene to take corrective action as needed. Moreover, when managers personally supervise subordinates, they lead by example and in this way can help subordinates develop and increase their own skill levels (leadership is the subject of Chapter 13). Thus, control through personal supervision can be a very effective way of motivating employees and promoting behaviors that increase efficiency and effectiveness.[25]

Nevertheless, certain problems are associated with direct supervision. First, it is very expensive because a manager can personally manage only a small number of subordinates effectively. Therefore, if direct supervision is the main kind of control being used in an organization, a lot of managers will be needed and costs will increase. For this reason, output control is usually preferred to behavior control; indeed, output control tends to be the first type of control that managers at all levels use to evaluate performance.

Second, direct supervision can demotivate subordinates if they feel that they are under such close scrutiny that they are not free to make their own decisions. Moreover, subordinates may start to pass the buck and avoid responsibility if they feel that their manager is waiting in the wings ready to reprimand anyone who makes the slightest error.

Third, as noted previously, for many jobs direct supervision is simply not feasible. The more complex a job is, the more difficult it is for a manager to evaluate how well a subordinate is performing. The performance of divisional and functional managers, for example, can be evaluated only over relatively long time periods (this is why an output control system is developed), so it makes little sense for top managers to continually monitor their performance.

Management by Objectives

management by objectives A goal-setting process in which a manager and his or her subordinates negotiate specific goals and objectives for the subordinate to achieve and then periodically evaluate the extent to which the subordinate is achieving those goals.

To provide a framework within which to evaluate subordinates' behavior and, in particular, to allow managers to monitor progress toward achieving goals, many organizations implement some version of management by objectives (MBO). **Management by objectives** is a system of evaluating subordinates for their ability to achieve specific organizational goals or performance standards and to meet operating budgets.[26] Most organizations make some use of management by objectives because it is pointless to establish goals and then fail to evaluate whether or not they are being achieved. Management by objectives involves three specific steps:

- Step 1: *Specific goals and objectives are established at each level of the organization.*

Management by objectives starts when top managers establish overall organizational objectives, such as specific financial performance targets. Then objective setting cascades down throughout the organization as managers at the divisional and functional levels set their objectives to achieve corporate objectives.[27] Finally, first-line managers and workers jointly set objectives that will contribute to achieving functional goals.

- Step 2: *Managers and their subordinates together determine the subordinates' goals.*

An important characteristic of management by objectives is its participatory nature. Managers at every level sit down with the subordinate managers who report directly to them, and together they determine appropriate and feasible goals for the subordinate and bargain over the budget that the subordinate will need so as to achieve his or her goals. The participation of subordinates in the objective-setting process is a way of strengthening their commitment to achieve their goals and meet their budgets.[28] Another reason why it is so important for subordinates (both individuals and teams) to participate in goal setting is so they can tell managers what they think they can realistically achieve.[29]

- Step 3: *Managers and their subordinates periodically review the subordinates' progress toward meeting goals.*

Once specific objectives have been agreed upon for managers at each level, managers are accountable for meeting those objectives. Periodically, they sit down with their subordinates to evaluate their progress. Normally, salary raises and promotions are linked to the goal-setting process, and managers who achieve their goals receive greater rewards than those who fall short. (The issue of how to design reward systems to motivate managers and other organizational employees is discussed in Chapter 10.)

In companies that decentralize responsibility for the production of goods and services to empowered teams and cross-functional teams, management by objectives works somewhat differently. Managers ask each team to develop a set of goals and performance targets that the team hopes to achieve—goals that are consistent with organizational objectives. Managers then negotiate with each team to establish its final goals and the budget the team will need to achieve them. The reward system is linked to team performance, not to the performance of any one team member.

One company that has spent considerable time developing a formal MBO system is Zytec Corporation, a leading manufacturer of power supplies for computers and other electronic equipment. Each of Zytec's managers and workers participates in goal setting. Top managers first establish cross-functional teams to create a five-year plan for the company and to set broad goals for each function.[30] Employees from all areas of the company review this plan. They evaluate the plan's feasibility and make suggestions about how to modify or improve it. Each function then uses the broad goals in the plan to set more specific goals for each manager and for each team in the organization; these goals are reviewed with top managers. The MBO system at Zytec is organizationwide and fully participatory, and performance is reviewed both from an annual and a five-year time horizon (compared to the goals in the company's rolling five-year plan). Zytec's MBO system has been very effective. Not only have organizational costs dropped dramatically but the company also won the Baldrige Award for quality.

Bureaucratic Control

When direct supervision is too expensive and management by objectives is inappropriate, managers might turn to another mechanism to shape and motivate employee behavior: bureaucratic control. **Bureaucratic control** is control by means of a comprehensive system of rules and standard operating procedures (SOPs) that shape and regulate the behavior of divisions, functions, and individuals. In Chapter 2, we discussed Max Weber's theory of bureaucracy and noted that all organizations use bureaucratic rules and procedures but some use them more than others.[31]

bureaucratic control
Control of behavior by means of a comprehensive system of rules and standard operating procedures.

Rules and SOPs guide behavior and specify what employees are to do when they confront a problem that needs a solution. It is the responsibility of a manager to develop rules that allow employees to perform their activities efficiently and effectively. When employees follow the rules that managers have developed, their behavior is *standardized*–actions are performed in the same way time and time again–and the outcomes of their work are predictable. And, to the degree that managers can make employees' behavior predictable, there is no need to monitor the outputs of behavior because standardized behavior leads to standardized outputs.

Suppose a worker at Toyota comes up with a way to attach exhaust pipes that reduces the number of steps in the assembly process and increases efficiency. Always on the lookout for ways to standardize procedures, managers make this idea the basis of a new rule: "From now on, the procedure for attaching the exhaust pipe to the car is as follows . . ." If all workers followed the rule to the letter, every car would come off the assembly line with its exhaust pipe attached in the new way, and there would be no need to check exhaust pipes at the end of the line. In practice, mistakes and lapses of attention do happen, so output control is used at the end of the line, and each car's exhaust system is given a routine inspection. However, the number of quality problems with the exhaust system is minimized because the rule (bureaucratic control) is being followed.

Service organizations such as retail stores and fast-food restaurants attempt to standardize the behavior of employees by instructing them on the correct way to greet customers or the appropriate way to serve and bag food. Employees are trained to follow the rules that have proved to be most effective in a particular situation. The better trained the employees are, the more standardized is their behavior, and the more trust managers can have that outputs (such as food quality) will be consistent. The experience of the China Coast restaurant is instructive in this regard.

Management Insight

Never Underestimate the Power of Rules

General Mills, the cereal maker best known for Cheerios cereal and Yoplait yogurt, is the creator of two of the best-known restaurant chains in the United States–Red Lobster and The Olive Garden. During the 1980s General Mills had great success with these restaurants, and by 1995 the company was operating over 1,200 restaurants in the United States, Canada, and Japan. Inspired by this success, top managers decided that they could use the skills and experience they had gained from operating restaurant chains to start a new chain specializing in Chinese food. Called China Coast, a prototype restaurant was opened in Orlando, Florida; customers were favorably impressed by the decor and by the food.

Excited by customers' positive response to the new restaurant, General Mills managers decided that they would rapidly expand the chain. Operating at breakneck speed, by 1995 managers had opened 38 restaurants in nine states.[32] With the restaurant chain in full swing, however, problems began to arise. Customers were no longer so enthusiastic about the quality of the food or the customer service, and sales volume fell off. What had gone wrong?

Apparently, in the attempt to open so many restaurants so quickly, managers lost control of quality. Chinese food is difficult to prepare properly, and employees require extensive training if they are to keep quality consistently high. Top managers had created a set of companywide food-quality standards for restaurant managers to follow, but the restaurant managers failed to ensure that these output standards were met consistently. Moreover, there were customer complaints about the quality of service that had not been reported to managers at the Orlando prototype. While searching for reasons for the failure of the new restaurants to meet company standards, top managers discovered that the primary problem was that they had not put the right set of bureaucratic controls in place.

Restaurant managers had not received enough restaurant operations training. Top managers had not created enough rules and standard operating procedures for restaurant managers either to follow or to teach to their employees–the cooks who actually prepared the food and the waiters who served it. Top managers thus decided that in the future each restaurant manager would attend a four-month intensive training course during which he or she would be taught the rules to be followed when preparing and serving the food. The rules would be written down and formalized in an operating manual that managers would take back to their restaurants for reference when training employees.

To make sure that restaurant managers did indeed follow the rules to ensure high-quality food and customer service, General Mills's top managers created a new layer of managers–regional managers whose responsibility was to supervise restaurant managers. Regional managers also were responsible for giving restaurant managers additional training as new dishes were introduced on the menu and for informing them of any changes in operating procedures that top managers had developed to improve the performance of individual restaurants. With the new set of bureaucratic controls in place to ensure that output standards were achieved, the managers responsible for China Coast were confident that the new chain would be able to expand successfully to serve customers throughout North America.

Problems with Bureaucratic Control

All organizations make extensive use of bureaucratic control because rules and SOPs effectively control routine organizational activities. With a bureaucratic control system in place, managers can manage by exception and intervene and take corrective action only when necessary. However, managers need to be aware of a number of problems associated with bureaucratic control, because they can reduce organizational effectiveness.[33]

First, establishing rules is always easier than discarding them. Organizations tend to become overly bureaucratic over time as managers do everything according to the rule book. If the amount of "red tape" becomes too great, decision making slows and managers react slowly to changing conditions. This sluggishness can imperil an organization's survival if agile new competitors emerge.

Second, because rules constrain and standardize behavior and lead people to behave in predictable ways, there is a danger that people become so used to automatically following rules that they stop thinking for themselves. Thus, too much standardization can actually reduce the level of learning taking place in an organization and get the organization off track if managers and workers focus on the wrong issues. An organization thrives when its members are constantly thinking of new ways to increase efficiency, quality, and customer responsiveness. By definition, new ideas do not come from blindly following standardized procedures. Similarly, the pursuit of innovation implies a commitment by managers to discover new ways of doing things; innovation, however, is incompatible with the use of extensive bureaucratic control.

Managers must therefore be sensitive about the way they use bureaucratic control. It is most useful when organizational activities are routine and well understood and when employees are making programmed decisions such as in mass-production settings or in a routine service setting such as restaurants and stores such as China Coast, Target, or Midas Muffler. Bureaucratic control is much less useful in situations where nonprogrammed decisions have to be made and managers have to react quickly to changes in the organizational environment.

To use output control and behavior control, managers must be able to identify the outcomes they want to achieve and the behaviors they want employees to perform to achieve these outcomes. For many of the most important and significant organizational activities, however, output control and behavior control are inappropriate for several reasons:

- A manager cannot evaluate the performance of workers such as doctors, research scientists, or engineers by observing their behavior on a day-to-day basis.
- Rules and SOPs are of little use in telling a doctor how to respond to an emergency situation or a scientist how to discover something new.
- Output controls such as the amount of time a surgeon takes for each operation or the costs of making a discovery are very crude measures of the quality of performance.

How can managers attempt to control and regulate the behavior of their subordinates when personal supervision is of little use, when rules cannot be developed to tell employees what to do, and when outputs and goals cannot be measured at all or can be measured usefully only over long periods? One source of control increasingly being used by organizations is a strong organizational culture.

Tips for Managers

Control

1. Identify the source(s) of an organization's competitive advantage (efficiency, quality, innovation, and customer responsiveness). Then design control systems that allow managers to evaluate how well they are building competitive advantage.

2. Involve employees in the goal setting process and make MBO an organizationwide activity.

3. Choose the right balance of direct supervision and bureaucratic controls to allow managers to monitor progress toward goals and to take corrective action as needed.

4. Periodically evaluate the output and behavior control system to keep it aligned with your current strategy and structure.

Organizational Culture and Clan Control

organizational culture
The set of values, norms, standards of behavior, and common expectations that control the ways in which individuals and groups in an organization interact with each other and work to achieve organizational goals.

clan control Control exerted on individuals and groups in an organization by shared values, norms, standards of behavior, and expectations.

Organizational culture is another control system that regulates and governs employee attitudes and behavior. **Organizational culture** is the set of values, norms, standards of behavior, and common expectations that control the ways in which individuals and groups in an organization interact with each other and work to achieve organizational goals. **Clan control** is the control exerted on individuals and groups in an organization by shared values, norms, standards of behavior, and expectations. Organizational culture is not an externally imposed system of constraints, such as direct supervision or rules and procedures. Rather, employees internalize organizational values and norms and then let those values and norms guide their decisions and actions. Just as people in society at large generally behave in accordance with socially acceptable values and norms, such as the norm that people should line up at the checkout counters in supermarkets, so are individuals in an organizational setting mindful of the force of organizational values and norms.

Organizational culture is an important source of control for two reasons. First, it makes control possible in situations where managers cannot use output or behavior control. Second and more important, when a strong and cohesive set of organizational values and norms is in place, employees focus on thinking about what is best for the organization in the long run—all their decisions and actions become oriented toward helping the organization perform well. For example, a teacher spends personal time after school coaching and counseling students; an R&D scientist works 80 hours a week, evenings and weekends, to help speed up a late project; a sales clerk at a department store runs after a customer who left a credit card at the cash register. Many researchers and managers believe that employees of some organizations go out of their way to help their organization because the organization has a strong and cohesive organizational culture—a culture that controls employee attitudes and behaviors.

Values and Norms: Creating a Strong Organizational Culture

In Chapter 4, we discussed values and norms in the context of national culture. *Values* are beliefs and ideas about the kinds of goals members of a society should pursue and about the kinds or modes of behavior people should use to achieve these goals.[34] *Norms* are unwritten rules or guidelines that prescribe appropriate behavior in particular situations. Norms emerge from values.[35] In an organization, values and norms inform organizational members about what goals they should pursue and how they should behave to reach those goals. Thus, values and norms perform the same function as formal goals, written rules, or direct supervision.

Managers can influence the kinds of values and norms that develop in an organization. Some managers might cultivate values and norms that let subordinates know that they are welcome to perform their roles in innovative, creative ways and to be innovative and entrepreneurial, willing to experiment and go out on a limb even if there is a significant chance of failure. Top managers at organizations such as Intel, Microsoft, and Sun Microsystems encourage employees to adopt such values to support their commitment to innovation as a source of competitive advantage.

Figure 9.5
Factors Creating a Strong Organizational Culture

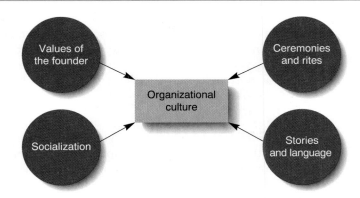

Other managers, however, might cultivate values and norms that let employees know that they should always be conservative and cautious in their dealings with others, should always consult with their superiors before making important decisions, and should always put their actions in writing so they can be held accountable for whatever happens. In any setting where caution is needed—nuclear power stations, large oil refineries, chemical plants, financial institutions, insurance companies—a conservative, cautious approach to making decisions might be highly appropriate.[36] In a nuclear power plant, for example, the catastrophic consequences of a mistake make a high level of supervision vital. Similarly, in a bank or mutual fund company the risk of losing investors' money also makes a cautious approach to investing highly appropriate.

The managers of different kinds of organizations may deliberately cultivate and develop the organizational values and norms that are best suited to their task and general environments, strategy, or technology. Organizational culture is transmitted to organizational members through the values of the founder, the process of socialization, ceremonies and rites, and stories and language (see Figure 9.5).

VALUES OF THE FOUNDER One manager who has a very important impact on the kind of organizational culture that emerges in an organization is the founder. An organization's founder and his or her personal values and beliefs have a substantial influence on the values, norms, and standards of behavior that develop over time within the organization.[37] Founders set the stage for the way cultural values and norms develop because they hire other managers to help them run their organizations. It is reasonable to assume that founders select managers who share their vision of the organization's goals and what it should be doing. In any case, new managers quickly learn from the founder what values and norms are appropriate in the organization and thus what is desired of them. Subordinates imitate the style of the founder and, in turn, transmit his or her values and norms to their subordinates. Gradually over time, the founder's values and norms permeate the organization.[38]

A founder who requires a great display of respect from subordinates and insists on proprieties such as formal job titles and formal modes of dress encourages subordinates to act in this way toward their subordinates. Often, a founder's personal values affect an organization's competitive advantage. For example, McDonald's founder Ray Kroc insisted from the beginning on high standards of customer service and cleanliness at McDonald's restaurants; these became core sources of McDonald's competitive advantage. Similarly, Bill Gates, the founder of Microsoft, pioneered certain cultural values in Microsoft. Employees are expected to be creative and to work hard, but they are encouraged to dress informally and to personalize their offices. Gates also established a host of company events such as cookouts, picnics, and sports events to emphasize to employees the importance of being both an individual and a team player.

SOCIALIZATION   Over time, organizational members learn from each other which values are important in an organization and the norms that specify appropriate and inappropriate behaviors. Eventually, organizational members behave in accordance with the organization's values and norms—often without realizing they are doing so. **Organizational socialization** is the process by which newcomers learn an organization's values and norms and acquire the work behaviors necessary to perform jobs effectively.[39] As a result of their socialization experiences, organizational members internalize an organization's values and norms and behave in accordance with them not only because they think they have to but because they think that these values and norms describe the right and proper way to behave.[40]

> **organizational socialization** The process by which newcomers learn an organization's values and norms and acquire the work behaviors necessary to perform jobs effectively.

At Texas A&M University, for example, all new students are encouraged to go to "Fish Camp" to learn how to be an "Aggie" (the traditional nickname of students at the university). They learn about the ceremonies that have developed over time to commemorate significant events or people in A&M's history. In addition, they learn the way to behave at football games and in class and what it means to be an "Aggie." As a result of this highly organized socialization program, by the time new students arrive on campus and start their first semester they have been socialized into what a Texas A&M student is supposed to do, and they have relatively few problems adjusting to the college environment.

Most organizations have some kind of socialization program to help new employees "learn the ropes"—the values, norms, and culture of their organization. The military, for example, is well known for the rigorous socialization process it uses to turn raw recruits into trained soldiers. Organizations such as Arthur Andersen also put new recruits through a rigorous training program to provide them with the knowledge they need not only to perform well in their jobs but also to represent the company to its clients. New recruits attend a six-week training program at Arthur Andersen's Chicago training center, where they learn from experienced organizational members how to behave and what they should be doing. Thus, through the organizational socialization program, the founder and top managers of an organization can transmit to employees the cultural values and norms that shape the behavior of organizational members.

CEREMONIES AND RITES   Another way in which managers can attempt to create or influence an organizational culture is by developing organizational ceremonies and rites—formal events that recognize incidents of importance to the organization as a whole and to specific employees.[41] The most common rites that organizations use to transmit cultural norms and values to their members are rites of passage, of integration, and of enhancement (see Table 9.2).[42]

Table 9.2
Organizational Rites

Type of Rite	Example of Rite	Purpose of Rite
Rite of passage	Induction and basic training	Learn and internalize norms and values
Rite of integration	Office Christmas party	Build common norms and values
Rite of enhancement	Presentation of annual award	Motivate commitment to norms and values

Rites of passage determine how individuals enter, advance within, or leave the organization. The socialization programs developed by military organizations (such as the U.S. Army) or by large accountancy firms (such as Arthur Andersen) described above are rites of passage. Likewise, the ways in which an organization prepares people for promotion or retirement are rites of passage.

Rites of integration, such as shared announcements of organizational successes, office parties, and company cookouts, build and reinforce common bonds among organizational members. Southwest Airlines is well known for its efforts to develop ceremonies and rituals to bond employees to the organization by showing them that they are valued members. Southwest holds cookouts in the parking lot of its Dallas headquarters, and CEO Herb Kelleher personally attends each employee Christmas party throughout the country. Because there are so many Christmas parties to attend, Kelleher often finds himself attending parties in July!

Flamboyant Southwest Airlines CEO Herb Kelleher, pictured here on a Harley-Davidson motorcycle given to him by his pilots, prepares to enjoy his company's annual Chili Cook-Off in Dallas. Such organizational rites and ceremonies help build his organization's culture.

A company's annual meeting also may be used as a ritual of integration, offering an opportunity to communicate organizational values to managers, other employees, and shareholders. Wal-Mart, for example, makes its annual stockholders' meeting an extravagant ceremony that celebrates the company's success. In 1994 the company flew 3,000 of its highest-performing employees to its annual meeting at headquarters, in Bentonville, Arkansas, for a huge entertainment festival that included performers such as exercise guru Richard Simmons and singers Reba McIntyre and Andy Williams. Wal-Mart believes that entertainment that rewards its supporters reinforces the company's high-performance values and culture. The proceedings are shown live over closed-circuit television in all Wal-Mart stores so that all employees can join in the rites celebrating the company's achievements.[43]

Rites of enhancement, such as awards dinners, newspaper releases, and employee promotions, let organizations publicly recognize and reward employees' contributions and thus strengthen their commitment to organizational values. By bonding members within the organization, rites of enhancement help promote clan control.

STORIES AND LANGUAGE   Stories and language also communicate organizational culture. Stories (whether fact or fiction) about organizational heroes and villains and their actions provide important clues about values and norms. Such stories can reveal the kinds of behaviors that are valued by the organization and the kinds of practices that are frowned on.[44] Stories about Ray Kroc, the person (hero) who made McDonald's the company it is today, shed light on many aspects of McDonald's corporate culture.

Management Insight

Ray Kroc: McDonald's Hero

McDonald's Corporation (www.mcdonalds.com) has a rich culture sustained by hundreds of stories that organizational members tell about founder Ray Kroc. Most of these stories have a common theme. They focus on how Kroc established the strict operating values and norms that are at the heart of McDonald's culture. Kroc was dedicated to achieving perfection in McDonald's quality, service, cleanliness, and value for money (QSC&V), and these four central values permeate McDonald's culture. The following story illustrates the way Kroc went about socializing McDonald's employees to these values.

One day Ray and a group of regional managers from the Houston region were touring various restaurants. One of the restaurants was having a bad day operationally. Ray was incensed about the long lines of customers, and he was furious when he realized that the product customers were receiving that day was not up to his high standards. To address the problem, he jumped up and stood on the front counter and got the attention of all customers and operating crew personnel. He introduced himself, apologized for the long wait and cold food, and told the customers that they could have freshly cooked food or their money back—whichever they wanted. As a result, the customers left happy, and when Kroc checked on the restaurant later, he found that his message had gotten through to its managers and crew—performance had improved.

Other stories describe Kroc scrubbing dirty toilets and picking up litter inside or outside a restaurant. These and similar stories are spread around the organization by McDonald's employees. They are the stories that have helped establish Kroc as McDonald's hero.

McDonald's employees are expected to be extremely dedicated to the central values of McCulture, to work hard, and to be loyal to McFamily. If they do accept its culture, McFamily will take care of them. McDonald's needs employees to be dedicated to QSC&V in order to maintain its high standards and keep its competitive advantage. Stories about heroes can help create a strong culture and increase employee dedication.

Because spoken language is a principal medium of communication in organizations, the characteristic slang or jargon—that is, organization-specific words or phrases—that people use to frame and describe events provides important clues about norms and values. "McLanguage," for example, is prevalent at all levels of McDonald's. A McDonald's employee described as having "ketchup in their blood" is someone who is truly dedicated to the McDonald's way—someone who has been completely socialized to its culture. McDonald's has an extensive training program teaching new employees "McDonald's speak," and new employees are welcomed into the family with a formal orientation that illustrates Kroc's dedication to QSC&V.

Motorola, the high-tech cellular phone and pager company, provides another example of the power of language to build organizational culture. The word *renewal* is continually spoken by managers. At Motorola it means continuous retraining, restructuring, and reengineering. Managers who embrace renewal are visionaries, they support open and free communication, they promote new learning and improvement, and they empower their subordinates so that they feel free to make significant contributions to the organization. At Motorola, one word conjures up the organization's central values—its commitment to innovation and entrepreneurship.

The concept of organizational language encompasses not only spoken language but how people dress, the offices they occupy, the cars they drive, and the degree of formality they use when they address one another. Casual dress reflects and reinforces Microsoft's entrepreneurial culture and values. Formal business attire supports Arthur Andersen's conservative culture, which emphasizes the importance of conforming to organizational norms such as respect for authority and staying within one's prescribed role. Traders in the Chicago Futures and Options trading pits frequently wear garish and flamboyant ties and jackets to make their presence known in a sea of faces. The demand for magenta, lime green, and silver lamé jackets featuring bold images such as the Power Rangers—anything that helps the traders stand out and attract customers—is enormous.[45] When employees "speak" and understand the language of their organization's culture, they know how to behave in the organization and what attitudes are expected of them.

Culture and Managerial Action

The way in which organizational culture shapes and controls employee behavior is evident in the way managers perform their four main functions: planning, organizing, leading, and controlling. As we consider these functions, we continue to distinguish between two kinds of top managers: those who create organizational values and norms that encourage creative, innovative behavior, and those who encourage a conservative, cautious approach by their subordinates. We noted earlier that both kinds of values and norms may be appropriate in different situations.

PLANNING Top managers in an organization with an *innovative* culture are likely to encourage lower-level managers to participate in the planning process and develop a flexible approach to planning. They are likely to be willing to listen to new ideas and to take risks involving the development of new products. In contrast, top managers in an organization with *conservative* values are likely to emphasize formal top-down planning. Suggestions from lower-level managers are likely to be subjected to a formal review, which can significantly slow decision making. Although this deliberate approach may improve the quality of decision making in a nuclear power plant, it can have unintended consequences. At conservative IBM, for example, the planning process became so formalized that managers spent most of their time assembling complex slide shows and overheads to defend their current positions rather than thinking about what they should be doing to keep IBM abreast of the changes taking place in the computer industry.

ORGANIZING   What kinds of organizing will managers in innovative and in conservative cultures encourage? Valuing creativity, managers in an *innovative* culture are likely to try to create an organic structure, one that is flat, with few levels in the hierarchy, and in which authority is decentralized so that employees are encouraged to work together to find solutions to ongoing problems. A product team structure may be very suitable for an organization with an innovative culture. In contrast, managers in a *conservative* culture are likely to create a well-defined hierarchy of authority and establish clear reporting relationships so that employees know exactly whom to report to and how to react to any problems that arise.

LEADING   In an *innovative* culture, managers are likely to lead by example, encouraging employees to take risks and experiment. They are supportive regardless of whether employees succeed or fail. In contrast, managers in a *conservative* culture are likely to develop a rigid management by objectives system and to constantly monitor subordinates' progress toward goals, overseeing their every move. We examine leadership in detail in Chapter 13 when we examine the leadership styles that managers can adopt to influence and shape employee behavior.

CONTROLLING   As this chapter makes clear, there are many control systems that managers can adopt to shape and influence employee behavior. The control systems they choose reflect a choice about how they want to motivate organizational members and keep them focused on organizational goals. Managers who want to encourage the development of *innovative* values and norms that encourage risk taking choose output and behavior controls that match this objective. They are likely to choose output controls that measure performance over the long run and develop a flexible MBO system suited to the long and uncertain process of innovation. In contrast, managers who want to encourage the development of *conservative* values choose the opposite combination of output and behavior controls. They develop specific, difficult goals for subordinates, frequently monitor progress toward these goals, and develop a clear set of rules that subordinates are expected to adhere to.

The values and norms of an organization's culture strongly affect the way managers perform their management functions. The extent to which managers buy into the values and norms of their organization shapes their view of the world and their actions and decisions in particular circumstances.[46] In turn, the actions that managers take can have an impact on the performance of the organization. Thus, organizational culture, managerial action, and organizational performance are linked together.

This linkage is apparent at Hewlett-Packard (HP), a leader in the electronic instrumentation and computer industries. Established in the 1940s, HP developed a culture that is an outgrowth of the strong personal beliefs of the company's founders, William Hewlett and David Packard. Bill and Dave, as they are known within the company, formalized HP's culture in 1957 in a statement of corporate objectives known as the "HP Way." The basic values informing the HP Way stress serving everyone who has a stake in the company with integrity and fairness, including customers, suppliers, employees, stockholders, and society in general. Bill and Dave helped build this culture within HP by hiring like-minded people and by letting the HP Way guide their own actions as managers. One outgrowth of their commitment to employees was a policy that HP would not be a "hire and fire company." This principle was severely tested on several occasions in the 1970s, when declines in business forced the company to institute a 10 percent pay cut and employees worked 10 percent fewer hours. Other companies had layoffs, but HP kept its full complement of staff, thereby underscoring the company's commitment to its employees.[47]

The values enshrined in the HP Way led directly to the policy of no layoffs. In turn, the commitment to employees that this policy signaled has fostered a productive workforce at HP that is willing to go to great lengths to help the company succeed. The result has been superior organizational performance over time.

The linkage among organizational culture, managerial actions, and organizational performance is also evident at Merck, whose managers decided to distribute Mectizan, a drug developed to treat river blindness, free to Third World nations whose citizens were too poor to pay for the drug (see Chapter 3). Merck is able to attract the best research scientists because its corporate culture nurtures scientists and places enormous value on innovation. Scientists are given great freedom to pursue intriguing ideas even if the commercial payoff is questionable. Moreover, researchers are inspired to think of their work as a quest to alleviate human disease and suffering worldwide. Thus, at the heart of Merck's corporate culture lies a set of values that stress the benefits to humanity of Merck's research. This culture is extremely attractive to Merck's scientists, who see themselves more as academics striving to improve the lot of humanity than as cogs in a corporate moneymaking machine. Thus, the culture at Merck motivates the scientists to perform well.

Although the Hewlett-Packard and Merck examples indicate that organizational culture can give rise to managerial actions that ultimately benefit the organization, this is not always the case. The cultures of some organizations become dysfunctional and encourage managerial actions that harm the organization and discourage actions that might lead to an improvement in performance.[48] For example, in 1987 the centralized and bureaucratic culture of Goodyear Tire & Rubber was identified by its CEO Robert Gault as a major reason for the company's disappointing performance. Gault proceeded systematically to change Goodyear's strategy and structure in order to change the way employees behaved. To speed product innovation, he decentralized control of new product development to product managers who were allowed to create their own teams. Each team received rewards based on its performance. Within five years Goodyear tires became the best-selling tires in the United States. Clearly, managers can influence the way their organizational culture develops over time.[49]

Summary and Review

Chapter Summary

WHAT IS ORGANIZATIONAL CONTROL? Controlling is the process whereby managers monitor and regulate how efficiently and effectively an organization and its members are performing the activities necessary to achieve organizational goals. Controlling is a four-step process: (1) establishing performance standards, (2) measuring actual performance, (3) comparing actual performance against performance standards, and (4) evaluating the results and taking corrective action if needed.

OUTPUT CONTROL To monitor output or performance, managers choose goals or performance standards that they think will best measure efficiency, quality, innovation, and responsiveness to customers at the corporate, divisional, departmental or functional, and individual levels. The main mechanisms that managers use to monitor output are financial measures of performance, organizational goals, and operating budgets.

BEHAVIOR CONTROL
In an attempt to shape behavior and induce employees to work toward achieving organizational goals, managers utilize direct supervision, management by objectives, and bureaucratic control by means of rules and standard operating procedures.

ORGANIZATIONAL CULTURE AND CLAN CONTROL Organizational culture is the set of values, norms, standards of behavior, and common expectations that control the ways individuals and groups in an organization interact with each other and work to achieve organizational goals. Clan control is the control exerted on individuals and groups by shared values, norms, standards of behavior, and expectations. Organizational culture is transmitted to employees through the values of the founder, the process of socialization, organizational ceremonies and rites, and stories and language. The way managers perform their management functions influences the kind of culture that develops in an organization.

Management in Action

Topics for Discussion and Action

1. What is the relationship between organizing and controlling?

2. How do output control and behavior control differ?

3. Ask a manager to list the main performance measures that he or she uses to evaluate how well the organization is achieving its goals.

4. Ask the same or a different manager to list the main forms of output control and behavior control that he or she uses to monitor and evaluate employee behavior.

5. Why is it important for managers to involve subordinates in the control process?

6. What is organizational culture, and how does it affect the way employees behave?

7. Interview some employees of an organization, and ask them about the organization's values, norms, socialization practices, ceremonies and rites, and special language and stories. Referring to this information, describe the organization's culture.

8. What kind of controls would you expect to find most used in (a) a hospital, (b) the Navy, (c) a city police force. Why?

Building Management Skills

Understanding Controlling

For this exercise you will analyze the control systems used by a real organization such as a department store, restaurant, hospital, police department, or small business. It can be the organization that you investigated in Chapter 8 or a different one. Your objective is to uncover all the different ways in which managers monitor and evaluate the performance of the organization and employees.

1. At what levels does control take place in this organization?

2. Which output performance standards (such as financial measures and organizational goals) do managers use most often to evaluate performance at each level?

3. Does the organization have a management by objectives system in place? If it does, describe it. If it does not, speculate about why not.

4. How important is behavior control in this organization? For example, how much of managers' time is spent directly supervising employees? How formal is the organization? Do employees receive a book of rules to instruct them about how to perform their jobs?

5. What kind of culture does the organization have? What are the values and norms? Do employees tell any particular stories that reveal the organization's norms and values? What effect does the organizational culture have on the way employees behave or treat customers?

6. Based on this analysis, do you think there is a fit between the organization's control systems and its culture? What is the nature of this fit? How could it be improved?

Small Group Breakout Exercise

How Best to Control the Sales Force?

Form groups of three or four people, and appoint one member as the spokesperson who will communicate your findings to the whole class when called on by the instructor. Then discuss the following scenario.

You are the regional sales managers of an organization that supplies high-quality windows and doors to building supply centers nationwide. Over the last three years, the rate of sales growth has slackened. There is increasing evidence that, to make their jobs easier, salespeople are primarily servicing large customer accounts and ignoring small accounts. In addition, the salespeople are not dealing promptly with customer questions and complaints, and this inattention has resulted in a drop in after-sales service. You have talked about these problems, and you are meeting to design a control system to increase both the amount of sales and the quality of customer service.

1. Design the control system that you think will best motivate salespeople to achieve these goals.

2. What relative importance do you put on (a) output control, (b) behavior control, and (c) organizational culture in this design?

Exploring the World Wide Web

Specific Assignment

Enter Hewlett-Packard's website (www.hp.com). Click on "Company Information"; then click on "About HP," "Corporate Objectives and the HP Way," and "The HP Way."

1. What are the main elements of the HP Way?

2. How does the HP Way lead to an organizational culture that helps Hewlett-Packard to achieve its strategies?

3. How easy would it be to institute the HP Way and culture in other companies?

General Assignment

Search for the website of a company that actively uses organizational culture (or one of the other types of control) to build competitive advantage. What kind of values and norms is the culture based on? How does it affect employee behavior?

ManagementCase

Marmon Runs Lean and Mean

The Marmon Group, Inc., is a privately owned company made up of over 60 different businesses that employ 28,000 employees and earn revenues of over $5.3 billion a year. Marmon CEO Robert Pritzker is a member of the Pritzker family, which owns the company; he believes in a "lean and mean" approach to organizing and controlling Marmon's businesses. The result has been a unique corporate culture.

Pritzker believes that corporate-level managers should play no direct role in actually running the company's different businesses; instead, their primary function should be to monitor and evaluate each division through a financial control system. Thus, Pritzker emphasizes output rather than behavior control. He has only 55 corporate managers at the Chicago headquarters to supervise the company's 60-plus businesses, and the jobs of 30 of these corporate managers are concerned purely with sorting out tax and other financial matters.[50]

Pritzker believes that his job is to select the best divisional managers he can find and then to step aside and let them develop a business-level strategy for the business they are in charge of. Each of the presidents of the 60-plus businesses reports to one of nine senior corporate executives. In addition, the financial controller of each business reports to one of three financial controllers in Chicago. This dual reporting relationship ensures that corporate managers receive accurate financial accounts for each division. At the same time, it frees them from the necessity of monitoring the day-to-day operations of all 60-plus businesses—hence the need for very few corporate executives.

The combination of a flat, decentralized structure and output control has another important advantage. Because the top managers of each of the business divisions are firmly in control, they assume "ownership" of their divisions and are motivated to be successful. Moreover, their pay is based on divisional performance. Decisions about the salaries of divisional managers and about the major capital expansion projects they want to fund to increase divisional performance are two of very few areas where Pritzker and his top-management team become involved in each division's activities.

So far, Pritzker's approach to organizing and controlling has proved to be successful. Marmon has achieved a 20 percent increase in return on equity for the last 10 years, and its profits are soaring. The main challenge now facing Pritzker is deciding what changes he may need to make to his organization's structure and control systems to allow Marmon to operate effectively as the company moves along the path of global expansion.

Questions

1. What kind of structure and control systems does Marmon use, and what are the advantages and disadvantages?

2. What kinds of challenges might Marmon encounter as it expands globally, and how might Pritzker have to change the organization's architecture?

ManagementCase

In the News

From the Pages of the *Boston Globe*
Fostering Corporate Culture

When Brown University buddies Tom First and Tom Scott launched their juice company, Nantucket Nectars, six years ago, they deliberately made things as informal as possible.

No hierarchy. No dress code. No stodgy corporate culture.

The free-spirited attitude of the blond beach boys is flaunted throughout their Brighton-based company from the dogs roaming the purple-toned offices to the naked man pictured jumping into the harbor on their juice labels.

But now, as juice sales approach $20 million, Nantucket Nectars is outgrowing its fraternity house culture, and "Tom and Tom" (as they're known) are grappling with how to manage that growth without destroying the entrepreneurial spirit that has made the company special.

"It's one of my biggest fears," admits First, 29, whose baby face belies his intensity. "Once you start departmentalizing, you lose that."

Whether identified by purple walls or conservative blue suits, a company's culture has everything to do with its success—or failure.

That's especially true within start-up companies, where hard-driving employees typically put in long hours for relatively low pay.

IBM's paternalistic culture—often identified by its propensity toward blue suits and red ties—fostered deep employee loyalty with promises of good benefits, good pay and, until recently, a lifetime job.

Too often, company cultures—especially at start-up firms—are measured by what people wear to work or how much time they spend playing games in the corridors. But while blue jeans and Nerf basketball games might inspire creativity or relieve tension, they are not what make the culture.

A company's culture has more to do with its employees' behavior, values and expectations. When employees understand and share a company's mission and values, specialists say, they are more productive, and the company is more prosperous.

So where does a company's culture come from?

Whether intentional or not, it's typically spawned by the founder early in the company's life.

First and Scott, 30, set the work ethic for Nantucket Nectars long before selling a single bottle of juice. During summers on Nantucket, they spent long hours selling supplies from a boat, shucking scallops, even walking dogs—anything to earn money and a reputation for service.

"Nantucket's a close-knit community. We needed to be respected as business people, and not just seen as college kids passing through," First says.

Today, Nantucket Nectars's employees put in equally long hours. The office is lit up well past 8 PM, and many staffers drop in on weekends to take care of business.

The founders didn't initially realize the example they were setting. About

two months ago, First called the staff together and encouraged them to leave at 6 PM each night.

The problem, says staffer Wink Mleczko, is that employees thought they were guilty of being inefficient.

"I'm like a tornado," First confesses. "I have tunnel vision. People look at their leaders and I have to be real careful about the tone I set."

Whether or not the founder of a company thinks much about cultural issues during its start-up phase, those issues become critical as a company matures, specialists and entrepreneurs agree.

"How you maintain a culture during explosive growth is probably the No. 1 thing that I worry about," says Frank Ingari, chief executive of Shiva Corp., a $118 million company that makes equipment and software for telecommuters.

In his view, a company's culture has to fit not only the employee, but the employee's family, too. Not surprisingly, then, Shiva encourages employees to work from home on flexible schedules, if it fits their lifestyle.

"I don't care whether people are working here or there, as long as they are self-starters, self-motivators and hard workers," Ingari says.

Pamela Reeve, president and chief executive of Lightbridge Inc., a Waltham-based provider of software for the cellular communications industry, shares Ingari's obsession with managing culture.

"You have to pay as much attention to cultural issues as you do to your financing or marketing. To me, it's one of the assets that has to be managed and fertilized and watered."

Without a clearly defined culture, employees may try to clone themselves in the image of the company's leader—by wearing similar clothes or adopting various personality traits—rather than embrace the leader's ideas and principles, says William Bygrave, director of the Center for Entrepreneurial Studies at Babson College.

Another problem as companies grow, adds Babson colleague Julian Lange, is that "people try to divine what's happening in the company by reading titles."

At Lightbridge, Reeve tried to head off that situation by giving her company a very flat organization. "We have very little structure," she says. "Sure, someone has to have spending responsibility and someone has to have responsibility for hiring and training. But that's all in the background. We're very team-oriented. I don't run the team. I'm just on it."

She compares the situation to her first whitewater rafting trip. The guide led the group through tumultuous waters, but he steered from the back of the boat.

To promote teamwork among the company's 300 employees, Lightbridge holds frequent brown bag lunches where goals are discussed, and ties performance incentives to companywide accomplishments, not individual ones.

When the company moved into larger office space at the end of a particularly stressful period of growth, Reeve invited art therapists in for a day to help employees design artwork that reflected the company's culture.

"We needed to put our soul in the building," she says.

In one exercise, each employee was assigned to paint a small area on a large canvas, which was their "home." The space between each area was their "neighborhood." Together, employees decided how to paint those common areas. The result is an "eclectic mix of colorful abstract paintings displayed throughout Lightbridge's offices.

The art helps tie employees together, something that becomes more difficult as companies grow beyond the start-up phase.

At Nantucket Nectars, weekly staff meetings include a guest speaker—an employee "who has to stand up and talk about their whole life, and what inspires them," First says. "We're so busy, sometimes we don't respect what other people do. I wanted everyone to understand who the people are and how they're helping this company."

"You have to respect the fact that your employees are smart," says David Blohm, president of software company Virtual Entertainment, who has used similar teambuilding tactics.

At his last company, Mathsoft Inc., which he founded in 1985 and took public in 1993, Blohm made sure every employee was plugged in by requiring them to demonstrate the company's software products to colleagues.

"We wanted them to talk about the product benefits, like they were demonstrating them to their in-laws. We wanted them to talk about it at that level. That raises the level of understanding and empathy for the customer," Blohm says.

To produce the cultural flavor of a small company, many entrepreneurs search for ways to bring employees together, whether for Halloween parties, pizza and beer blasts, or summer barbecues.

At Molten Metal Technology Inc. in Waltham, it's breakfast. Each Friday, two of the company's most recent hires are responsible for preparing breakfast for the rest of their colleagues.

In the beginning, when there were only a dozen or so employees, it was easy. "You just stopped and got a bag of bagels," says Ian Yates, vice president of sales and market development for the environmental technology company.

Now, however, Molten Metal has 300 employees, including 150 at its Waltham headquarters.

But the tradition continues, with some newcomers going all out, preparing everything from pancakes to such ethnic favorites as breakfast burritos. The company picks up the tab.

"It's a small price to pay for the benefit, which is bringing people together," says Yates. "We don't want the first chance for people to meet to be in a meeting or on a project. If you know someone first, you'd be surprised how much better you listen to them."

Another meeting place at Molten Metal is the fifth-floor atrium, where employees and executives talk over business issues, while shooting pool or playing table tennis or air hockey.

Having fun is actually part of the 7-year-old company's mission statement. But in the end, what makes any company's culture work is a shared sense of passion for the company's objectives.

"We're part of a team that is dedicated to changing the way the world deals with waste," Yates says. "We're pulling on the same end of the rope together. That's pretty powerful. It makes the time playing table tennis more fun."

Source: Joann Muller, "Fostering Corporate Culture," *Boston Globe,* February 4, 1996, 73.

Questions

1. What factors influence the values and norms of Nantucket Nectars's culture?

2. What factors make it easy or difficult to create or change an organization's culture?

Chapter ten

Human Resource Management

Learning Objectives

1. Explain why strategic human resource management can help an organization gain a competitive advantage.

2. Describe the steps managers take to recruit and select organizational members.

3. Discuss the training and development options that ensure that organizational members can effectively perform their jobs.

4. Explain why performance appraisal and feedback is such a crucial activity, and list the choices managers must make in designing effective performance appraisal and feedback procedures.

5. Explain the issues managers face in determining levels of pay and benefits.

A Case in Contrast

Training and Development at PepsiCo and Jet

PepsiCo (www.pepsi.com) is the global corporate giant that makes and sells drinks like Pepsi-Cola and snack foods like Frito-Lay chips (www.fritolay.com) around the world; it also owns the fast-food restaurants Pizza Hut (www.pizzahut.com), Taco Bell, and KFC.[1] Jet Products is a small aerospace-machine company based in Phoenix, Arizona.[2] In the early 1990s, Roger Enrico, now president of PepsiCo, decided that developing visionary top managers who would be able to lead employees in PepsiCo's various businesses was critical to PepsiCo's future success.[3] At about the same time, Jim Perlow, vice president of Jet Products, decided that Jet's future success depended on his ability to hire and retain skilled workers who could operate his company's complex machinery efficiently. Both Enrico and Perlow decided to invest in training and development programs to develop their employees and give their companies a competitive advantage, but they went about it in very different ways. PepsiCo's development program for top managers and Jet Products' apprenticeship program for high school juniors and seniors are as different as are these two companies.

PepsiCo's "Executive Leadership: Building the Business" development program for top managers starts with a five-day seminar at an off-site location. During the seminar, each of the nine or so managers in attendance is urged to take responsibility for the problems in his or her department or division. They are encouraged

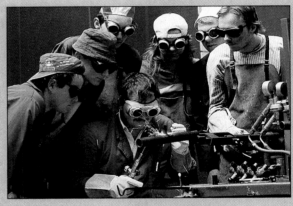

Both PepsiCo and Jet Products believe strongly in training and development. PepsiCo develops from within, having managers undergo a seminar and subsequent workshop. Jet Products reaches outside the company with an apprenticeship program, choosing high school juniors and seniors to receive classroom instruction and hands-on learning of machinery.

to focus on big ideas that will lead to a competitive advantage and to communicate their visions and goals to others in their departments or divisions. After the seminar, the managers go back to their regular jobs, apply what they have learned, and keep in close contact with Enrico for 90 days. When the 90 days are up, the development program culminates with a workshop lasting three days in which the managers share their insights about what they have learned.

Success stories from Enrico's program suggest that he is achieving his goal of developing visionary leaders and top managers. Peter Waller, Kentucky Fried Chicken's vice president for marketing, developed the KFC Mega Meals program as a result of the development he received; this program has contributed significantly to double-digit increases in sales and earnings. And, as a result of development training received in Enrico's program, Bill Nictakis, a marketing vice president at Frito-Lay, helped engineer a promising joint venture with Sara Lee to produce and distribute a new line of pastries.[4]

In contrast, Jim Perlow and other top managers at Jet Products developed an innovative apprenticeship program in conjunction with the local school district's cooperative education program. The apprenticeship program is geared toward high school juniors and seniors. Those chosen for the training receive instruction in a formal classroom setting from Jet's team leaders, and hands-on learning from operating machinery and from working on the shop floor. Apprentices who graduate from high school and want a full-time job with Jet must satisfactorily complete college courses at a local community college before they are hired. Jet fully covers the cost of their courses; indeed, Jet reimburses all its employees for the full cost of any higher education they pursue.

Jet's training program seems to be paying off. Jet has a highly skilled and loyal workforce, and 13 of Jet's valued employees are former apprentices. Practically all of Jet's employees have had some form of higher education, and over 70 percent of them have never worked for another company.[5]

Although their means are dramatically different, both Jet Products' training and PepsiCo's development programs are achieving similar goals: ensuring that the companies are building the human resources they need to be effective and gain a competitive advantage. Moreover, managers in both companies realize how valuable training and development are for employees at all hierarchical levels, from entry level to top management. ●

Overview

Managers are responsible for acquiring, developing, protecting, and utilizing the resources that an organization needs to be efficient and effective. One of the most important resources in all organizations is human resources–the people involved in the production and distribution of goods and services. Human resources include all members of an organization, ranging from top managers to entry-level employees. Effective managers like Roger Enrico and Jim Perlow in the "Case in Contrast" realize how valuable human resources are and take active steps to make sure that their organizations build and fully utilize their human resources to gain a competitive advantage.

This chapter examines how managers can tailor their human resource management system to their organization's strategy and structure. We discuss in particular the major components of human resource management: recruitment and selection, training and development, performance appraisal, pay and benefits, and labor relations. By the end of this chapter, you will understand the central role human resource management plays in creating a high-performing organization. ●

Strategic Human Resource Management

human resource management Activities that managers engage in to attract and retain employees and to ensure that they perform at a high level and contribute to the accomplishment of organizational goals.

strategic human resource management The process by which managers design the components of a human resource management system to be consistent with each other, with other elements of organizational architecture, and with the organization's strategy and goals.

Organizational architecture (see Chapter 8) is the combination of the organizational structure, control systems, culture, and human resource management system that managers develop to use resources efficiently and effectively. **Human resource management (HRM)** includes all the activities that managers engage in to attract and retain employees and to ensure that they perform at a high level and contribute to the accomplishment of organizational goals. These activities make up an organization's human resource management system, which has five major components: recruitment and selection, training and development, performance appraisal and feedback, pay and benefits, and labor relations (see Figure 10.1).

Strategic human resource management is the process by which managers design the components of an HRM system to be consistent with each other, with other elements of organizational architecture, and with the organization's strategy and goals.[6] The objective of strategic HRM is the development of an HRM system that enhances an organization's efficiency, quality, innovation, and responsiveness to customers—the four building blocks of competitive advantage.

Figure 10.1
Components of a Human Resource Management System

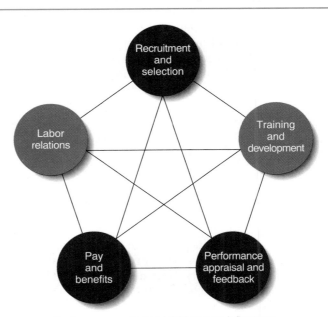

Each component of an HRM system influences
the others, and all five must fit together

Overview of the Components of HRM

Managers use *recruitment and selection,* the first component of an HRM system, to attract and hire new employees who have the abilities, skills, and experiences that will help an organization achieve its goals. Microsoft Corporation, for example, has the goal of remaining the premier computer software company in the world. To achieve this goal, Bill Gates realized the importance of hiring only the best software designers. When Microsoft hires new software designers, hundreds of highly qualified candidates with excellent recommendations are interviewed and rigorously tested; only the best are hired. This careful attention to selection has contributed to Microsoft's competitive advantage. Microsoft has little trouble recruiting top programmers because candidates know they will be at the forefront of the industry if they work for Microsoft, utilizing the latest technology and working with the best people.[7]

After recruiting and selecting employees, managers use the second component, *training and development,* to ensure that organizational members develop skills and abilities that will enable them to perform their jobs effectively in the present and the future. Training and development is an ongoing process; changes in technology and the environment, as well as in an organization's goals and strategies, often require organizational members to learn new techniques and ways of working. The "Case in Contrast" describes Roger Enrico and PepsiCo's heavy investment in the development of top managers to ensure that they acquire the visionary skills needed to find new ways to increase PepsiCo's revenues and profits. At Microsoft Corporation, newly hired program designers receive on-the-job training by joining small teams that include experienced employees who serve as mentors or advisers. New recruits learn firsthand from team members how to go about developing computer systems that are responsive to customers' programming needs.[8]

The third component, *performance appraisal and feedback,* serves two different purposes in HRM. First, performance appraisal can provide managers with the information they need to make good human resources decisions—decisions about how to train, motivate, and reward organizational members.[9] Thus, the performance appraisal and feedback component is a kind of *control system* that can be used with management by objectives (discussed in Chapter 9). Second, performance feedback from performance appraisal serves a developmental purpose for members of an organization. When managers regularly evaluate their subordinates' performance, they can provide subordinates with valuable information about their strengths and weaknesses and the areas in which they need to concentrate.

On the basis of performance appraisals, managers distribute *pay* to employees, part of the fourth component of an HRM system. By rewarding high-performing organizational members with pay raises, bonuses, and the like, managers increase the likelihood that an organization's most valued human resources are motivated to continue their high levels of contribution to the organization. Moreover, when pay is linked to performance, high-performing employees are more likely to stay with the organization, and managers are more likely to be able to fill positions that become open with highly talented individuals. *Benefits* are important outcomes, such as health insurance, that employees receive by virtue of their membership in an organization.

Jesus Corona instructs future union organizers at the United Farm Workers offices in Salinas, California, on how to conduct "home meetings," as the union prepares for a winter-long blitz with the goal of getting their message to more than 30,000 strawberry pickers. In the heart of the nation's most productive strawberry fields, growers, workers, and lawyers are preparing for another season of harvests and labor disputes.

Last but not least, *labor relations* encompasses the steps that managers take to develop and maintain good working relationships with the labor unions that may represent their employees' interests. For example, an organization's labor relations component can help managers establish safe working conditions and fair labor practices in their offices and plants.

Managers must ensure that all five of these components fit together and complement their company's structure and control systems.[10] For example, if managers decide to decentralize authority and empower employees, they need to invest in training and development to ensure that lower-level employees have the knowledge and expertise they need to make the decisions that top managers would make in a more centralized structure.

Each of the five components of HRM influences the others (see Figure 10.1).[11] The kinds of people that the organization attracts and hires through recruitment and selection, for example, determine (1) the training and development that are necessary, (2) the way performance is appraised, and (3) the appropriate levels of pay and benefits. Managers at Microsoft ensure that their organization has highly qualified program designers by (1) recruiting and selecting the best candidates, (2) providing new hires with the guidance of experienced team members so that they learn how to be responsive to customers' needs when designing programs and systems, (3) appraising program designers' performance in terms of their individual contributions and their team's performance, and (4) basing programmers' pay on individual and team performance.

The Legal Environment of HRM

In the rest of this chapter we focus in detail on the choices managers must make in strategically managing human resources to attain organizational goals and gain a competitive advantage. Effectively managing human resources is a complex undertaking for managers, and we provide an overview of some of the major issues they face. Before we do, however, we need to look at how the legal environment affects human resource management.

equal employment opportunity The equal right of all citizens to the opportunity to obtain employment regardless of their gender, age, race, country of origin, religion, color, age, or disabilities.

The local, state, and national laws and regulations that managers and organizations must abide by add to the complexity of HRM. For example, the U.S. government's commitment to **equal employment opportunity** (**EEO**) has resulted in the creation and enforcement of a number of laws that managers must abide by. The goal of EEO is to ensure that all citizens have an equal opportunity to obtain employment regardless of their gender, age, race, country of origin, religion, color, age, or disabilities. Table 10.1 summarizes some of the major EEO laws affecting HRM.

Table 10.1

Major Equal Employment Opportunity Laws Affecting HRM

Year	Law	Description
1963	Equal Pay Act	Requires men and women to be paid equally if they are performing equal work
1964	Title VII of the Civil Rights Act	Prohibits discrimination in employment decisions on the basis of race, religion, sex, color, or national origin; covers a wide range of employment decisions, including hiring, firing, pay, promotion, and working conditions
1967	Age Discrimination in Employment Act	Prohibits discrimination against workers over the age of 40 and restricts mandatory retirement
1978	Pregnancy Discrimination Act	Prohibits discrimination against women in employment decisions on the basis of pregnancy, childbirth, and related medical conditions
1990	Americans with Disabilities Act	Prohibits discrimination against disabled individuals in employment decisions and requires employers to make accommodations for disabled workers to enable them to perform their jobs
1991	Civil Rights Act	Prohibits discrimination (as does Title VII) and allows for the awarding of punitive and compensatory damages, in addition to back pay, in cases of intentional discrimination
1993	Family and Medical Leave Act	Requires employers to provide 12 weeks of unpaid leave for medical and family reasons including paternity and illness of a family member

In Chapter 5, we discussed why effectively managing diversity is an ethical and business imperative. EEO laws and their enforcement make the effective management of diversity a legal imperative as well. The Equal Employment Opportunity Commission (EEOC) is the division of the Department of Justice that enforces most of the EEO laws and handles discrimination complaints. In addition, the EEOC issues guidelines for managers to follow to ensure that they are abiding by EEO laws. For example, the Uniform Guidelines on Employee Selection Procedures issued by the EEOC (in conjunction with the Departments of Labor and Justice and the Civil Service Commission) provide managers with guidance about how to ensure that the recruitment and selection component of human resource management complies with Title VII of the Civil Rights Act (which prohibits discrimination based on gender, race, color, religion, and national origin).[12]

Contemporary challenges that managers face related to the legal environment include how to eliminate sexual harassment (see Chapter 5), how to make accommodations for disabled employees, how to deal with employees who have substance abuse problems, and how to manage HIV-positive employees and employees with AIDS.[13] HIV-positive employees are infected with the virus that causes AIDS, but they may show no AIDS symptoms and may not develop AIDS in the near future. Often, such employees are able to perform their jobs effectively, and managers must take steps to ensure that they are able to do so and are not discriminated against in the workplace.[14] Employees with AIDS may or may not be able to perform their jobs effectively, and, once again, managers need to ensure that they are not unfairly discriminated against.[15] Many organizations have instituted AIDS awareness training programs to educate organizational members about HIV and AIDS, dispel unfounded myths about how HIV is spread, and ensure that individuals infected with the virus are treated fairly and are able to be productive as long as they can be while not putting others at risk.[16]

Recruitment and Selection

recruitment Activities that managers engage in to develop a pool of qualified candidates for open positions.

selection The process that managers use to determine the relative qualifications of job applicants and their potential for performing well in a particular job.

human resource planning Activities that managers engage in to forecast their current and future needs for human resources.

Recruitment includes all the activities that managers engage in to develop a pool of qualified candidates for open positions.[17] **Selection** is the process by which managers determine the relative qualifications of job applicants and their potential for performing well in a particular job. Before actually recruiting and selecting employees, managers need to engage in two important activities: human resource planning and job analysis (see Figure 10.2).

Human Resource Planning

Human resource planning includes all the activities that managers engage in to forecast their current and future needs for human resources. Current human resources are the employees an organization needs today to provide high-quality goods and services to customers. Future human resources are the employees the organization will need at some later date to achieve its longer-term goals. As part of human resource planning, managers must make both demand forecasts and supply forecasts. *Demand forecasts* estimate the qualifications and numbers of employees an organization will need given its goals and strategies. *Supply forecasts* estimate the availability and qualifications of current employees now and in the future, and the supply of qualified workers in the external labor market. As indicated in this "Management Insight," the assessment of both current and future human resource needs helps managers determine whom they should be trying to recruit and select to achieve organizational goals now and in the future.

Figure 10.2
The Recruitment and Selection System

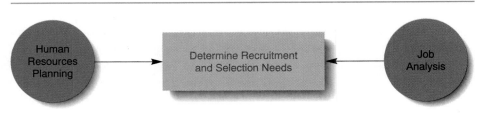

Management Insight

Human Resource Planning at Two Small Companies

Dennis and Ann Pence founded the catalog company Coldwater Creek in 1984, and since then its revenues have grown to an impressive $43 million. For the company's first six years, the husband and wife team managed all important functions—from marketing and advertising to finance. When their company was just starting out, they decided that they would not spend their scarce resources on paying salaries to managers, and they realized that, because of the inherent riskiness of the new venture, they would not be able to attract highly talented managers until Coldwater Creek had grown and developed a track record of high performance. The Pences' human resource planning led them to refrain from hiring top managers to oversee important functions until Coldwater Creek's size and 80-hour workweeks started to strain them and the company's existing employees.

The Pences' planning paid off. Between 1990 and 1995, they were able to hire a highly competent top-management team, including a director of human resources, a director of management information systems, a vice president of operations, a vice president of merchandising, and a chief financial officer who was a former top manager at Neiman Marcus. Dennis Pence indicates that "Because we're a little bigger, we were able to attract people of a much higher caliber."[18]

Results of Doug Mellinger's human resource planning led him to take a different route. Mellinger founded his company, PRT Corporation of America, a provider of computer software planning, training, and development, with $12,000 from his family. Mellinger's goal was to increase the revenues and profits of his company as quickly as possible. His strategy to attain this goal was to concentrate his own efforts on meeting with and being responsive to customers and to hire top managers right from the start to oversee important functions. In the first 18 months of PRT's existence, Mellinger hired a marketing vice president, a project management vice president, a human resources director, and a chief financial officer. PRT is now a successful company with revenues of $14 million, and Mellinger attributes his company's rapid growth at least partially to his own human resource planning for growth.[19]

outsource To use outside suppliers and manufacturers to produce goods and services.

As a result of their human resource planning, managers sometimes decide to **outsource** to fill some of their human resource needs. Instead of recruiting and selecting employees to produce goods and services, managers contract with people who are not members of their organization to produce goods and services. Managers in publishing companies, for example, frequently contract with freelance editors to copyedit new manuscripts that they intend to publish. Kelly Services is an organization that provides temporary typing, clerical, and secretarial workers to managers who want to use outsourcing to fill some of their human resource requirements in these areas. Outsourcing is increasingly being used on a global level. Managers in some U.S. computer software companies are outsourcing some of their programming work to Russian programmers who are highly skilled but cost the companies around 10 percent of what they would normally pay for the programming work to be done in-house.

There are at least two reasons why human resource planning sometimes leads managers to outsource: flexibility and cost. First, outsourcing can give managers increased flexibility, especially when accurately forecasting human resource needs is difficult, human resource needs fluctuate over time, or finding skilled workers in a particular area is difficult. Second, outsourcing can sometimes allow managers to make use of human resources at a lower cost. When work is outsourced, costs may be lower for a number of reasons: The organization does not have to provide benefits to workers; managers are able to contract for work only when the work is needed; and managers do not have to invest in training. Outsourcing can be used for functional activities such as after-sales service on appliances and equipment, legal work, and the management of information systems. Roy Richie, general counsel for Chrysler Corporation, uses temporary attorneys to write contracts and fill some of his department's human resource needs. As he says, "The math works . . . Savings can be tremendous."[20]

Outsourcing does have its disadvantages, however. When work is outsourced, managers may lose some control over the quality of goods and services. Also, individuals performing outsourced work may have less knowledge of organizational practices, procedures, and goals and less commitment to an organization than regular employees. In addition, unions resist outsourcing because it has the potential to eliminate the jobs of some of their members.

Job Analysis

job analysis Identifying the tasks, duties, and responsibilities that make up a job and the knowledge, skills, and abilities needed to perform the job.

Job analysis is a second important activity that managers need to undertake prior to recruitment and selection.[21] **Job analysis** is the process of identifying (1) the tasks, duties, and responsibilities that make up a job (the *job description*), and (2) the knowledge, skills, and abilities needed to perform the job (the job specifications).[22] For each job in an organization, a job analysis needs to be done.

A job analysis can be done in a number of ways, including observing current employees as they perform the job or interviewing them. Often, managers rely on questionnaires completed by jobholders and their managers. The questionnaires ask about the skills and abilities needed to perform the job, job tasks and the amount of time spent on them, responsibilities, supervisory activities, equipment used, reports prepared, and decisions made.[23]

The Position Analysis Questionnaire (PAQ) is a comprehensive standardized questionnaire that many managers rely on to conduct job analyses.[24] It focuses on behaviors jobholders perform, working conditions, and job characteristics, and it can be used for a variety of jobs.[25] The PAQ contains 194 items organized into six divisions: (1) information input (where and how the jobholder acquires information to perform the job), (2) mental processes (reasoning, decision-making, planning, and information-processing activities that are part of the job), (3) work output (physical activities performed on the job and machines and devices used), (4) relationships with others (interactions with other people that are necessary to perform the job), (5) job context (the physical and social environment of the job), and (6) other job characteristics (such as work pace).[26] A trend in some organizations is toward flexible jobs in which tasks and responsibilities change and cannot be clearly specified in advance. For these kinds of jobs, job analysis focuses more on determining the skills and knowledge workers need to be effective and less on specific duties.

When managers have completed human resource planning and job analyses for all jobs in an organization, they will know their human resource needs and the jobs they need to fill. They also will know what knowledge, skills, and abilities potential employees will need to perform those jobs. At this point, recruitment and selection can begin.

External and Internal Recruitment

As noted earlier, recruitment is what managers do to develop a pool of qualified candidates for open positions.[27] They generally use two types of recruiting: external and internal.

EXTERNAL RECRUITING   When managers recruit externally to fill open positions, they look outside the organization for people who have not worked for the organization previously. There are multiple means through which managers can recruit externally—advertisements in newspapers and magazines, open houses for students and career counselors at high schools and colleges or on site at the organization, career fairs at colleges, recruitment meetings with groups in the local community, and notices on the Internet and World Wide Web.

Kathy Santos, a manager at CLAM Associates, a small software company based in Cambridge, Massachusetts, posts open jobs at CLAM on the World Wide Web. Even though her company is small ($12 million in annual revenues), she receives about five responses per day to each open job listed on the Web. Santos has found that recruiting through computer networks such as the World Wide Web offers advantages in addition to helping her recruit applicants. For example, applicants recruited through the Web are much more knowledgeable about the company and its mission, products, goals, and customers than are applicants recruited through more conventional sources such as newspaper advertisements, because all this information is available on CLAM's home page on the Web.[28]

Many large organizations send teams of interviewers to college campuses to recruit new employees. External recruitment can also take place through informal networks such as when current employees inform friends about open positions in their companies or recommend people they know to fill vacant spots. Some organizations use employment agencies for external recruitment, and some external recruitment takes place simply through walk-ins—jobhunters coming to an organization and inquiring about employment possibilities.

With all the downsizings and corporate layoffs that have taken place in recent years, you might think that external recruiting would be a relatively easy task for managers. However, it often is not, because even though many people may be looking for jobs, many of the jobs that are opening up require skills and abilities that these jobhunters do not have. For example, managers at Lincoln Electric, a manufacturer of motors and welding products based in Euclid, Ohio, are having a very hard time filling about 200 positions on the factory floor even though Lincoln receives around 20,000 applications in an 18-month period.[29] Most applicants do not have the skills Lincoln needs. Managers at Lincoln say that they have spent more money on recruiting in the past few years to find the right people than they have spent in all the other years of the company's 99-year existence. As is typical for many companies, managers at Lincoln Electric have adopted a multipronged recruiting approach to develop a large pool of applicants. Lincoln Electric uses sources ranging from newspaper advertisements, to open houses for career counselors and students, to meetings with area ROTC units and church groups. Many other companies are facing external recruitment challenges similar to those of Lincoln Electric.

External recruiting has both advantages and disadvantages for managers. Advantages include having access to a potentially large applicant pool, being able to attract people to an organization who have the skills, knowledge, and abilities the organization needs to achieve its goals, and being able to bring in newcomers who may have a fresh approach to problems and be up-to-date on the latest technology. These advantages have to be weighed against the disadvantages, including the relatively high costs of external recruitment. Employees recruited externally also lack knowledge about the inner workings of the organization and may need to receive more training than those recruited internally. Finally, when employees are recruited externally, there always is uncertainty about whether they actually will be good performers.

INTERNAL RECRUITING   When recruiting is internal, managers turn to existing employees to fill open positions. Employees recruited internally are either seeking **lateral moves** (job changes that entail no major changes in responsibility or authority levels) or promotions. Internal recruiting has several advantages. First, internal applicants are already familiar with the organization (including its goals, structure, culture, rules, and norms). Second, managers already know internal candidates; they have considerable information about their skills and abilities and actual behavior on the job. Third, internal recruiting can help boost levels of employee motivation and morale, both for the employee who gets the job and for other workers. Those who are not seeking a promotion or who may not be ready for a promotion can see that it is a possibility for the future; or a lateral move can alleviate boredom once a job has been fully mastered and also provide a useful way to learn new skills. Finally, internal recruiting is normally less time-consuming and expensive.

Given the advantages of internal recruiting, why do managers rely on external recruiting as much as they do? The answer is because there are disadvantages to internal recruiting—among them, a limited pool of candidates and a tendency among those candidates to be "set" in the organization's ways. Often, the organization simply does not have suitable internal candidates. Sometimes, even when suitable internal applicants are available, managers may rely on external recruiting to find the very best candidate or to help bring new ideas and approaches into the organization. When organizations are in trouble and performing poorly, external recruiting is often relied on to bring in managerial talent with a fresh approach. For example, when IBM's performance was suffering in the 1990s and the board of directors was looking to recruit a new CEO, rather than consider any of IBM's existing top managers for this position, the board recruited Louis Gerstner, an outsider who had no previous experience in the computer industry.

HONESTY IN RECRUITING   At times, when trying to recruit the most qualified applicants, managers may be tempted to paint overly rosy pictures of both the open positions and the organization as a whole. They may worry that if they are totally honest about advantages and disadvantages, they either will not be able to fill positions or will have fewer or less well qualified applicants. A manager trying to fill a secretarial position, for example, may emphasize the

lateral move A job change that entails no major changes in responsibility or authority levels.

high level of pay and benefits the job offers and fail to mention the fact that the position is usually a dead-end job offering few opportunities for promotion.

Research suggests that painting an overly rosy picture of a job and organization is not a wise recruiting strategy. Recruitment is most likely to be effective when managers provide potential applicants with an honest assessment of both the advantages and the disadvantages of a job and organization. Such an assessment is called a **realistic job preview (RJP).**[30] RJPs can be effective because they reduce the number of new hires who quit because their jobs and organizations fail to meet their unrealistic expectations and they help applicants decide for themselves whether a job is right for them.

realistic job preview

An honest assessment of the advantages and disadvantages of a job and organization.

Take the earlier example of the manager trying to recruit a secretary. The manager who paints a rosy picture of the job might have an easy time filling it but might end up hiring a secretary who expects to be promoted quickly to an administrative assistant position. After a few weeks on the job, the secretary may realize that a promotion is highly unlikely no matter how good his or her performance, become dissatisfied, and look for and accept another job. The manager then would have to recruit, select, and train another new secretary. The manager could have avoided this waste of valuable organizational resources by using a realistic job preview. An RJP would have increased the likelihood that a secretary comfortable with low promotional opportunities was hired and subsequently remained on the job and was satisfied.

The Selection Process

Once managers develop a pool of applicants for open positions through the recruitment process, they need to find out whether each applicant is qualified for the position and whether he or she is likely to be a good performer. If more than one applicant meets these two conditions, managers must further determine which applicants are likely to be better performers than others. They have several selection tools to help them sort out the relative qualifications of job applicants and appraise their potential for being good performers in a particular job. Those tools include background information, interviews, paper-and-pencil tests, physical ability tests, performance tests, and references (see Figure 10.3).[31]

BACKGROUND INFORMATION   To aid in the selection process, managers obtain background information from job applications and from résumés. Such information might include highest levels of education obtained, college majors and minors, type of college or university attended, years and type of work experience, and mastery of foreign languages. Background information can be helpful both to screen out applicants who are lacking key qualifications (such as a college degree) and to determine which qualified applicants are more promising than others (for example, applicants with a BS may be acceptable, but those who also have an MBA are preferable).

INTERVIEWS   Virtually all organizations use interviews during the selection process. Two general types of interview are structured and unstructured. In a *structured interview,* managers ask each applicant the same standard questions (such as "What are your unique qualifications for this position?" and "What characteristics of a job are most important for you?"). Particularly infor-

Figure 10.3
Selection Tools

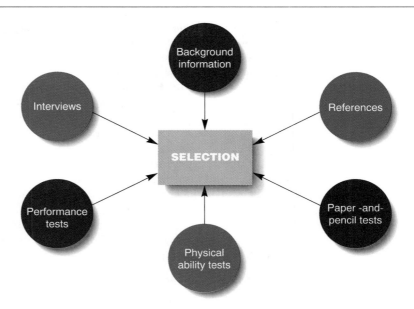

mative questions may be those that prompt an interviewee to demonstrate skills and abilities needed for the job by answering the question. Sometimes called *situational interview questions,* these questions present interviewees with a scenario that they would likely encounter on the job and ask them to indicate how they would handle it.[32] For example, applicants for a sales job may be asked to indicate how they would respond to a customer who complains about waiting too long for service, a customer who is indecisive, and a customer whose order is lost.

An *unstructured interview* proceeds more like an ordinary conversation. The interviewer feels free to ask probing questions to discover what the applicant is like and does not ask a fixed set of questions prepared in advance. In general, structured interviews are superior to unstructured interviews because they are more likely to yield information that will help identify qualified candidates and they are less subjective. Also, evaluations based on structured interviews may be less likely to be influenced by the biases of the interviewer than evaluations based on unstructured interviews.

Even when structured interviews are used, however, there is always the potential for the biases of the interviewer to influence his or her judgments. Recall from Chapter 5 how the similar-to-me effect can cause people to perceive others who are similar to themselves more positively than they perceive those who are different and how stereotypes can result in inaccurate perceptions. It is important for interviewers to be trained to avoid these biases and sources of inaccurate perceptions as much as possible. Many of the approaches to increasing diversity awareness and diversity skills described in Chapter 5 can be used to train interviewers to avoid the effects of biases and stereotypes. In addition, using multiple interviewers can be advantageous, for their individual biases and idiosyncrasies may cancel one another out.[33]

When conducting interviews, managers have to be careful not to ask questions that are irrelevant to the job in question; otherwise their organizations run the risk of costly lawsuits. It is inappropriate and illegal, for example, to inquire about an interviewee's spouse or to ask questions about whether an interviewee plans to have children. Questions such as these, which are irrelevant to job performance, may be viewed as discriminatory and as violating EEO laws (see Table 10.1). Thus, interviewers also need to be instructed in EEO laws and informed about questions that may be seen as violating those laws.

Managers can use interviews at various stages in the selection process. Some use interviews as initial screening devices; others use them as a final hurdle that applicants must pass. Regardless of when they are used, managers typically use other selection tools in conjunction with interviews because of the potential for bias and for interviewers forming inaccurate assessments of interviewees. Even though training and using structured rather than unstructured interviews can eliminate the effects of some of these biases, interviewers can still come to erroneous conclusions about interviewees' qualifications. Interviewees, for example, who make a bad initial impression or are overly nervous in the first minute or two of an interview tend to be judged more harshly than less nervous candidates, even if the rest of the interview goes well.

PAPER-AND-PENCIL TESTS   Two main kinds of paper-and-pencil tests are used for selection purposes: ability tests and personality tests. *Ability tests* assess the extent to which applicants possess skills necessary for job performance, such as verbal comprehension or numerical skills. Autoworkers hired by General Motors, Chrysler, and Ford, for example, are typically tested for their ability to read and to do mathematics.[34]

Personality tests measure personality traits and characteristics relevant to job performance. Some retail organizations, for example, give job applicants honesty tests to determine how trustworthy they are. The use of personality tests (including honesty tests) for hiring purposes is controversial. Some critics maintain that honesty tests do not really measure honesty (that is, they are not valid) and can be subject to faking by job applicants. Before using any paper-and-pencil tests for selection purposes, managers should have sound evidence that the tests are actually good predictors of performance on the job in question. Managers who use tests without such evidence may be subject to costly discrimination lawsuits.

PHYSICAL ABILITY TESTS   For jobs that require physical abilities, such as firefighting, garbage collecting, and package delivery, managers use, as selection tools, physical ability tests that measure physical strength and stamina. Autoworkers are typically tested for mechanical dexterity because this physical ability is an important skill for high job performance in many auto plants.[35]

PERFORMANCE TESTS   Performance tests measure job applicants' performance on actual job tasks. Applicants for secretarial positions, for example, are typically required to complete a typing test that measures how quickly and accurately they are able to type. Applicants for middle- and top-management positions are sometimes given short-term projects to complete—projects that mirror the kinds of situations that arise in the job being filled—to assess their knowledge and problem-solving capabilities.[36]

Lisa Cedars grimaces as she hauls a 165-lb. dummy to the finish line during a physical fitness test for firefighting applicants at the fire department in Alexandria, Louisiana. The physical test is just one of many used to determine the top candidates.

Assessment centers, first used by AT&T, take performance tests one step further. In a typical assessment center, between 10 and 15 candidates for managerial positions participate in a variety of activities over a few days. During this time they are assessed for the skills that an effective manager needs—problem-solving skills, organization skills, communication skills, and conflict resolution skills. Some of the activities are performed individually; others are performed in groups. Throughout the process, current managers observe the candidates' behavior and measure performance. Summary evaluations are then used as a selection tool.

REFERENCES Applicants for many jobs are required to provide references from former employers or other knowledgeable sources (such as a college instructor or adviser) who know the applicants' skills, abilities, and other personal characteristics. These individuals are asked to provide candid information about the applicant. References are often used at the end of the selection process to confirm a decision to hire. Yet the fact that many former employers are reluctant to provide negative information in references sometimes makes it difficult to interpret what a reference is really saying about an applicant.

In fact, several recent lawsuits filed by applicants who felt that they were unfairly denigrated or had their privacy invaded by unfavorable references from former employers have caused managers to be increasingly wary of providing any kind of negative information in a reference, even if it is accurate. For jobs in which the jobholder is responsible for the safety and lives of other people, however, failing to provide accurate, negative information in a reference does not just mean that the wrong person might get hired; it also may mean that other people's lives will be at stake, as indicated in this "Ethics in Action."

Ethics in Action

The Costs of Withholding Negative Information in References

In late 1994, an American Airlines (www.americanair.com) commuter plane crashed near Raleigh, North Carolina, because the pilot mistakenly thought there was engine failure. Subsequent inquiries indicated that the same pilot had been found unfit to fly on his previous job. Managers at American Airlines, however, did not have access to this information when they hired him. Why? Airlines that in the past provided negative references and documented poor performance have been sued by former employees for invasion of privacy. The former employer of this particular pilot was unwilling to risk getting sued and thus failed to provide an accurate (and negative) reference.[37]

Is it ethical to withhold negative information when lives are at stake? This question haunts many managers, including Stephen Sayler of Kansas City, who did not mention in a reference that a former employee and truck driver for his company had been fired for drinking; and Donna Salinas of Salt Lake City, who did not report that a health care worker she supervised had been fired for stealing from an elderly patient. Salinas indicated that "It absolutely made me sick that I couldn't tell."[38] Managers like Sayler and Salinas who withhold negative information from references often do so because they fear that their companies may be subject to costly lawsuits if they give a negative reference for a former employee, even if it is accurate.

Realizing the ethical dilemma faced by these managers and the potential risks to human life and well-being, legislators have taken steps to protect former employers who give accurate, negative information in references for former employees. In Utah, former employees can win defamation suits only if they can prove that information in the reference was false or disregarded the truth. Georgia, too, provides protection to former employers against lawsuits arising from references for health care workers and bank employees.[39] Similar initiatives at the national level are taking place, particularly to provide airlines with liability protection so that accurate information can be provided in references for former pilots seeking new positions.[40] Clearly, rights to privacy and protection against defamation are important societal values, but when human lives and well-being are at stake, former employers need to be able to provide accurate information in references, even if it is negative and prevents an applicant from obtaining a job.

THE IMPORTANCE OF RELIABILITY AND VALIDITY Whatever selection tools a manager uses, they need to be both reliable and valid. **Reliability** is the degree to which a tool or test measures the same thing each time it is administered. Scores on a selection test should be very similar if the same person is assessed with the same test on two different days; if there is quite a bit of variability, the test is unreliable. For interviews, determining reliability is more complex because the dynamic is more one of personal interpretation. Suffice it to say here that the reliability of interviews can be increased if two or more different qualified interviewers interview the same candidate. If the interviews are reliable, the interviewers should come to similar conclusions about the interviewee's qualifications.

Validity is the degree to which a tool or test measures what it purports to measure—in the case of selection tests, that is the degree to which the test predicts performance on the tasks or job in question. Does a physical ability test used to select firefighters, for example, actually predict on-the-job performance? Do assessment center ratings actually predict managerial performance? Do typing tests predict secretarial performance? These are all questions of validity. Honesty tests, for example, are controversial because it is not clear that they are valid predictors of honesty in jobs such as retailing and banking.

Managers have an ethical and legal obligation to use reliable and valid selection tools. Yet reliability and validity are a matter of degree rather than all-or-nothing characteristics. Thus, managers should strive to use selection

reliability The degree to which a tool or test measures the same thing each time it is used.

validity The degree to which a tool or test measures what it purports to measure.

tools in such a way that they can achieve the greatest degree of reliability and validity. In the case of ability tests for a particular skill, for example, managers should keep up-to-date on the latest advances in the development of valid paper-and-pencil tests and use the test with the highest reliability and validity ratings possible for their purposes. In the case of interviews, managers can improve reliability by having more than one person interview job candidates.

Tips for Managers

Recruitment and Selection

1. Prior to recruiting and selecting new employees, use human resource planning and job analysis to determine your human resource needs now and in the future.

2. Provide job applicants with an honest assessment of the advantages and disadvantages of a job.

3. Use other selection tools in addition to interviews to decide which applicants to hire.

4. Make sure that the selection tools you use are reliable and valid.

Training and Development

training Teaching organizational members how to perform their current jobs and helping them acquire the knowledge and skills they need to be effective performers.

development Building the knowledge and skills of organizational members so that they will be prepared to take on new responsibilities and challenges.

needs assessment An assessment of which employees need training or development and what type of skills or knowledge they need to acquire.

Training and development helps to ensure that organizational members have the knowledge and skills they need to perform their jobs effectively, take on new responsibilities, and adapt to changing conditions. **Training** primarily focuses on teaching organizational members how to perform their current jobs and helping them acquire the knowledge and skills they need to be effective performers. **Development** focuses on building the knowledge and skills of organizational members so that they will be prepared to take on new responsibilities and challenges. Training tends to be used more frequently at lower levels of an organization; development tends to be used more frequently with professionals and managers. Jet Products' apprenticeship program, described in the "Case in Contrast," focuses in large part on ensuring that entry-level workers have the skills they need to perform their jobs effectively. The program aims to ensure that when workers start their first jobs at Jet, they have the knowledge and skills needed for good performance. PepsiCo's development program for top managers focuses on helping top managers formulate a vision for their respective units and successfully implement the vision to obtain a competitive advantage.

Before creating training and development programs, managers should perform a **needs assessment** in which they determine which employees need training or development and what type of skills or knowledge they need to acquire (see Figure 10.4).[41] Results of Jim Perlow's needs assessment at Jet Products indicated that entry-level employees needed training to ensure that they could effectively perform their jobs on the shop floor. Results of Roger Enrico's needs assessment at PepsiCo indicated that top managers needed development to become truly visionary leaders.

Figure 10.4
Training and Development

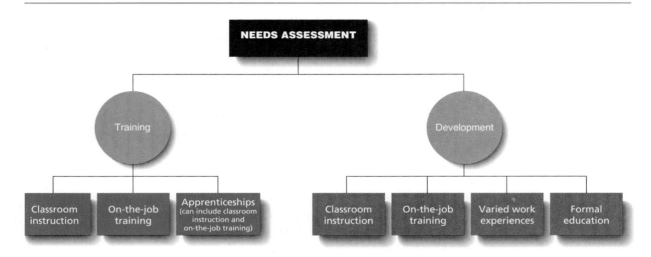

Types of Training

The apprenticeship program at Jet Products represents a mix of two types of training: classroom instruction and on-the-job training.

CLASSROOM INSTRUCTION   Through classroom instruction, employees acquire knowledge and skills in a classroom setting. The instruction itself may take place within the organization or outside it, such as when employees are encouraged to take courses at local colleges and universities. Many organizations actually establish their own formal instructional divisions—some are even called "colleges"—to provide needed classroom instruction.

At Ethan Allen Interiors Inc., for example, employees from stores around the country attend Ethan Allen College at company headquarters in Danbury, Connecticut. During classes, employees acquire in-depth knowledge about the company's products and learn how to listen to customers and accurately assess their needs. In addition, the college provides instruction on diverse topics such as floor plans and window treatments. Training at Ethan Allen is an ongoing process. Veteran employees attend two- or three-day sessions at the college to brush up on their skills and keep abreast of the latest developments. M. Farooq Kathwari, chairman and CEO of Ethan Allen, believes that the classroom instruction that employees receive at Ethan Allen College has contributed significantly to his company's competitive advantage.[42]

Classroom instruction frequently includes the use of videos and role-plays in addition to traditional written materials, lectures, and group discussions. *Videos* can be used to demonstrate appropriate and inappropriate job behaviors. For example, by watching an experienced salesperson effectively deal with a loud and angry customer in a video clip, inexperienced salespeople can develop skills in handling similar situations. During a *role-play,* trainees either directly participate in or watch others perform actual job activities in a simulated setting. At McDonald's Hamburger University, for example, role playing is used to help franchisees acquire the knowledge and skills they need to manage their restaurants.

Simulations also can be used as part of classroom instruction, particularly on complicated jobs that require an extensive amount of learning and in which errors carry a high cost. In a simulation, key aspects of the work situation and job tasks are duplicated as closely as possible in an artificial setting. For example, air traffic controllers are trained by means of simulations because of the complicated nature of the work, the extensive amount of learning involved, and the very high costs of air traffic control errors.

on-the-job training

Training that takes place in the work setting as employees perform their job tasks.

ON-THE-JOB TRAINING In **on-the-job training,** learning occurs in the work setting as employees perform their job tasks. On-the-job training can be provided by coworkers or supervisors or occur simply as jobholders gain experience and knowledge from doing the work. Newly hired waiters and waitresses in chains such as Red Lobster or The Olive Garden often receive on-the-job training from experienced employees. The supervisor of a new bus driver for a campus bus system may ride with the bus driver for a week to ensure that he or she learns the routes and follows safety procedures. Chefs learn to create new and innovative dishes by experimenting with different combinations of ingredients and cooking techniques. What these different kinds of on-the-job training have in common is that employees learn by doing.

Managers often use on-the-job training on a continuing basis to ensure that their subordinates keep up-to-date with changes in goals, technology, products, or customer needs and desires. For example, sales representatives in Mary Kay Cosmetics Inc. receive ongoing training so that they are knowledgeable about new cosmetic products and currently popular colors and are reminded of Mary Kay's guiding principles. Mary Kay's expansion into Russia has been very successful, in part because of the ongoing training that Mary Kay's Russian salespeople receive.[43]

Types of Development

Although both classroom instruction and on-the-job training can be used for development purposes as well as for training, development often includes additional activities such as varied work experiences and formal education.

VARIED WORK EXPERIENCES Top managers need to develop an understanding of, and expertise in, a variety of functions, products and services, and markets. In order to develop executives who will have this expertise, managers frequently make sure that employees with high potential have a wide variety of job experiences, some in line positions and some in staff positions. Varied work experiences broaden employees' horizons and help them think in terms of the big picture. For example, a one- to three-year stint overseas is being used increasingly to provide managers with international work experiences. With organizations becoming more global, managers need to develop an understanding of the different values, beliefs, cultures, regions, and ways of doing business in different countries.

FORMAL EDUCATION Many large corporations reimburse employees for tuition expenses they incur for taking college courses and obtaining advanced degrees. This is not just benevolence on the part of the employer or even a simple reward given to the employee; it is an effective way to develop employees who will be able to take on new responsibilities and more challenging positions. For similar reasons, corporations spend thousands of dollars sending managers to executive development programs such as executive MBA programs. In these programs, managers learn from experts the latest in business and management techniques and practices.

To save time and travel costs, managers are increasingly relying on *long-distance learning* to formally educate and develop employees. Using videoconferencing technologies, business schools such as Harvard Business School, the University of Michigan, and Babson College are teaching courses on video screens in corporate conference rooms. Business schools also are customizing courses and degrees to fit the development needs of employees in a particular company. The University of Michigan uses long-distance learning, for example, to provide instruction for customized MBA degrees for employees of the Daewoo Corporation in Korea and Cathay Pacific Airways Ltd. in Hong Kong. In conjunction with Westcott Communications Inc., eight business schools have actually formed a new venture, Executive Education Network, to create and operate satellite classrooms in major corporations; almost 100 companies have already signed on, including Eastman Kodak, Walt Disney, and Texas Instruments.[44]

Transfer of Training and Development

Whenever training and development take place off the job or in a classroom setting, it is vital for managers to promote the transfer of the knowledge and skills acquired *to the actual work situation*. Trainees should be encouraged and expected to use their new-found expertise on the job. Recall how Roger Enrico in the "Case in Contrast" ensures that transfer of development activities takes place in the "Executive Leadership" program at PepsiCo. Managers participating in the program attend a five-day session in a classroom setting. They then go back to their jobs with the charge to apply what they have learned and keep in close contact with Enrico to ensure that transfer of training takes place. After applying their new knowledge on the job for three months, the managers return for a three-day classroom session during which they share insights with each other and Enrico.

Performance Appraisal and Feedback

performance appraisal The evaluation of employees' job performance and contributions to their organization.

The recruitment and selection and the training and development components of a human resource management system ensure that employees have the knowledge and skills they need to be effective now and in the future. **Performance appraisal** and feedback complement recruitment, selection, training, and development. Performance appraisal is the evaluation of employees' job performance and contributions to their organization. **Performance feedback** is the process through which managers share performance appraisal information with their subordinates, give subordinates an opportunity to reflect on their own performance, and develop, with subordinates, plans for the future. In order for there to be performance feedback, performance appraisal must take place. Performance appraisal could take place without providing performance feedback, but wise managers are careful to provide feedback because it can contribute to employee motivation and performance.

Performance appraisal and feedback contribute to the effective management of human resources in two ways. Performance appraisal gives managers important information on which to base human resources decisions.[45] Decisions about pay raises, bonuses, promotions, and job moves all hinge on the accurate appraisal of performance. Performance appraisal also can help managers determine which workers are candidates for training and development, and in what areas. Performance feedback encourages high levels of employee motivation and performance. It lets good performers know that their efforts are valued and appreciated and lets poor performers know that their lackluster performance needs improvement. Performance feedback can provide both good and poor performers with insight into their strengths and weaknesses and ways in which they can improve their performance in the future.

Types of Performance Appraisal

Performance appraisal focuses on the evaluation of traits, behaviors, or results.[46]

TRAIT APPRAISALS When trait appraisals are used, managers assess subordinates on personal characteristics that are relevant to job performance, such as skills, abilities, or personality. A factory worker, for example, may be evaluated for her ability to use computerized equipment and perform numerical calculations. A social worker may be evaluated for his empathy and communication skills.

Three disadvantages of trait appraisals often lead managers to rely on other appraisal methods. First, possessing a certain personal characteristic does not ensure that the personal characteristic will actually be used on the job and result in high performance. For example, a factory worker may possess superior computer and numerical skills but be a poor performer because of a low level of motivation. The second disadvantage of trait appraisals is linked to the first. Because traits do not always show a direct association with performance, workers and courts of law may view them as unfair and potentially discriminatory.

The third disadvantage of trait appraisals is that they often do not enable managers to provide employees with feedback that they can use to improve performance. Because trait appraisals focus on relatively enduring human characteristics that change only over the long term, employees can do little to change their behavior in response to performance feedback from a trait appraisal. Telling the social worker that he lacks empathy provides him with little guidance about how to improve his interactions with clients, for example. The disadvantages of trait appraisals suggest that managers should use them only when they can demonstrate that the traits assessed are accurate and important indicators of job performance.

BEHAVIOR APPRAISALS Through behavior appraisals, managers assess how workers perform their jobs—the actual actions and behaviors that workers exhibit on the job. Whereas trait appraisals assess what workers *are like,* behavior appraisals assess what workers *do.* For example, with a behavior appraisal a manager might evaluate a social worker on the extent to which he looks clients in the eye when talking with them, expresses sympathy when they are upset, and refers them to community counseling and support groups geared toward the specific problem they are encountering. Behavior appraisals are especially useful when *how* workers perform their jobs is important. In educational organizations such as high schools, for example, it is important not just how many classes and students are taught but also how they are taught or the methods teachers use to ensure that learning takes place.

Behavior appraisals have the advantage of providing employees with clear information about what they are doing right and wrong and how they can improve their performance. And, because behaviors are much easier than traits for employees to change, performance feedback from behavior appraisals is more likely to lead to performance improvements.

RESULTS APPRAISALS   For some jobs, *how* people perform the job is not as important as *what* they accomplish or the results they obtain. With results appraisals, managers appraise performance in terms of results or the actual outcomes of work behaviors.

Take the case of two new-car salesmen. One salesman strives to develop personal relationships with his customers. He spends hours talking to them and frequently calls them up to see how their decision-making process is going. The other salesman has a much more hands-off approach. He is very knowledgeable, answers customers' questions, and then waits for them to come to him. Both salesmen sell, on average, the same number of cars, and the customers of both are satisfied with the customer service they receive (customers respond to postcards that the dealership mails to them asking them to assess their satisfaction). The manager of the dealership appropriately uses results appraisals (sales and customer satisfaction) to evaluate the salespeople's performance because it does not matter which behavior salespeople use to sell cars as long as they sell the desired number and satisfy customers. If one salesperson sells too few cars, however, the manager can give that salesperson performance feedback that he is not selling enough.

OBJECTIVE AND SUBJECTIVE APPRAISALS   Whether managers appraise performance in terms of traits, behaviors, or results, the information they assess is either *objective* or *subjective*. **Objective appraisals** are based on facts and are likely to be numerical—the number of cars sold, the number of meals prepared, the number of times late, the number of audits completed. Managers often use objective appraisals when results are being appraised, because results tend to be easier to quantify than traits or behaviors. However, when *how* workers perform their jobs is important, more subjective behavior appraisals are more appropriate than results appraisals.

Subjective appraisals are based on managers' perceptions of traits, behaviors, or results. Because subjective appraisals rest on managers' perceptions, there is always the chance that they are inaccurate (we discuss managerial perception in more detail in the next chapter). It is for this reason that both researchers and managers have spent considerable time and effort to develop reliable and valid subjective measures of performance.

Some popular subjective measures, such as the graphic rating scale, the behaviorally anchored rating scale (BARS), and the behavior observation scale (BOS), are illustrated in Figure 10.5.[47] When graphic rating scales are used, performance is assessed along a continuum with specified intervals. With a BARS,

objective appraisal
An appraisal that is based on facts and is likely to be numerical.

subjective appraisal
An appraisal that is based on perceptions of traits, behaviors, or results.

Figure 10.5
Subjective Measures of Performance

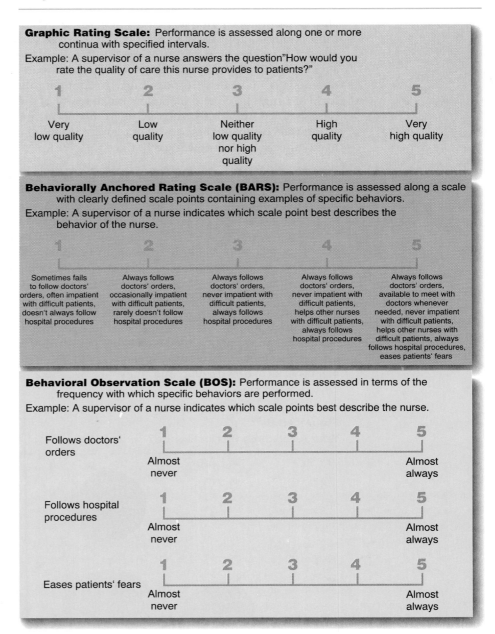

Graphic Rating Scale: Performance is assessed along one or more continua with specified intervals.

Example: A supervisor of a nurse answers the question"How would you rate the quality of care this nurse provides to patients?"

1	2	3	4	5
Very low quality	Low quality	Neither low quality nor high quality	High quality	Very high quality

Behaviorally Anchored Rating Scale (BARS): Performance is assessed along a scale with clearly defined scale points containing examples of specific behaviors.

Example: A supervisor of a nurse indicates which scale point best describes the behavior of the nurse.

1	2	3	4	5
Sometimes fails to follow doctors' orders, often impatient with difficult patients, doesn't always follow hospital procedures	Always follows doctors' orders, occasionally impatient with difficult patients, rarely doesn't follow hospital procedures	Always follows doctors' orders, never impatient with difficult patients, always follows hospital procedures	Always follows doctors' orders, never impatient with difficult patients, helps other nurses with difficult patients, always follows hospital procedures	Always follows doctors' orders, available to meet with doctors whenever needed, never impatient with difficult patients, helps other nurses with difficult patients, always follows hospital procedures, eases patients' fears

Behavioral Observation Scale (BOS): Performance is assessed in terms of the frequency with which specific behaviors are performed.

Example: A supervisor of a nurse indicates which scale points best describe the nurse.

Follows doctors' orders

1	2	3	4	5
Almost never				Almost always

Follows hospital procedures

1	2	3	4	5
Almost never				Almost always

Eases patients' fears

1	2	3	4	5
Almost never				Almost always

performance is assessed along a scale with clearly defined scale points containing examples of specific behaviors. A BOS assesses performance in terms of how often specific behaviors are performed. Many managers use both objective and subjective appraisals. For example, a salesperson may be appraised in terms of the dollar value of sales (objective) and the quality of customer service (subjective).

Who Appraises Performance?

We have been assuming that managers or the supervisors of employees evaluate performance. This is a pretty fair assumption, for supervisors are the most common appraisers of performance; indeed, each year 70 million U.S. citizens have their job performance appraised by their managers or supervisors.[48] Performance appraisal is an important part of most managers' job duties. It is managers' responsibility to motivate their subordinates to perform at a high level, and managers make many of the decisions that hinge on performance appraisals, such as decisions about pay raises or promotions. Appraisals by managers, however, can be usefully augmented by appraisals from other sources (see Figure 10.6).

SELF, PEERS, SUBORDINATES, AND CLIENTS When self-appraisals are used, managers supplement their evaluations with an employee's assessment of his or her own performance. Peer appraisals are provided by an employee's coworkers. Especially when subordinates work in groups or teams, feedback from peer appraisals can motivate team members while providing managers with important information for decision making. A growing number of companies are having subordinates appraise their own managers' performance and leadership as well. And sometimes customers or clients provide assessments of employee performance in terms of responsiveness to customers and quality of service.

Although appraisals from each of these sources can be useful, managers need to be aware of potential issues that may arise when they are used. Subordinates sometimes may be inclined to inflate self-appraisals, especially if organizations are downsizing and they are worried about their job security.

Figure 10.6
Who Appraises Performance?

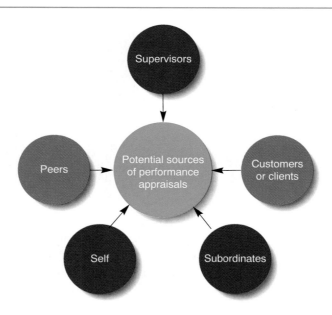

Managers who are appraised by their subordinates may fail to take needed but unpopular actions out of fear that their subordinates will appraise them negatively.

360-DEGREE PERFORMANCE APPRAISALS
To improve motivation and performance, some organizations include 360-degree appraisals and feedback in their performance appraisal systems, especially for managers. In a **360-degree appraisal,** a manager's performance is appraised by a variety of people, such as the manager himself or herself and the manager's peers or coworkers, subordinates, superiors, and sometimes even customers or clients. The manager receives feedback based on evaluations from these multiple sources.

360-degree appraisal

A performance appraisal by peers, subordinates, superiors, and sometimes clients who are in a position to evaluate a manager's performance.

The growing number of companies using 360-degree appraisals and feedback includes AT&T Corp., Allied Signal Inc., Eastman Chemical Co., and Baxter International Inc.[49] At AT&T, the performance of chairman and chief executive Robert E. Allen is appraised by his subordinates (members of his top-management team), and Allen acts on the performance feedback he receives. For example, after members of his team reported that they did not like the passive manner in which he ran executive committee meetings, Allen took a more proactive approach to leading the meetings.[50] A 360-degree appraisal and feedback is not always as clear-cut as it might seem. On the one hand, some subordinates try to get back at their bosses by giving managers negative evaluations, especially when evaluations are anonymous (to encourage honesty and openness). A top manager at Citicorp indicated that he received from a subordinate a highly negative appraisal that tried to smear him personally. The manager was pretty sure that the evaluation came from a very poor performer.[51] On the other hand, some managers coach subordinates to give, or even threaten sanctions if they fail to give, positive evaluations.

Peers often are very knowledgeable about performance but may be reluctant to provide an accurate and negative appraisal of someone they like or a positive appraisal of someone they dislike. At Baxter International, when peer appraisals were used in the information technology unit, workers tended to provide each other with uniformly positive evaluations because they knew the evaluations were going to be used for pay raise decisions and they were not able to provide negative feedback anonymously. Managers at Baxter then decided to continue conducting the peer appraisals but to use them primarily for self-development activities and not for pay decisions.[52]

In addition, whenever peers, subordinates, or anyone else evaluates a worker's performance, managers must be sure that the evaluators are actually knowledgeable about the performance dimensions being assessed. For example, subordinates should not evaluate their supervisor's decision making if they have little opportunity to observe this dimension of his or her performance.

These potential problems with 360-degree appraisals and feedback do not mean that they are not useful. Rather they suggest that in order for 360-degree appraisals and feedback to be effective, there has to be trust throughout an organization. More generally, trust is a critical ingredient in any performance appraisal and feedback procedure. In addition, managers using 360-degree appraisals and feedback have to carefully consider the pros and cons of using anonymous evaluations and of using the results of the appraisals for decision making about important issues such as pay raises.

Effective Performance Feedback

In order for the performance appraisal and feedback component of a human resource management system to encourage and motivate high performance, managers must provide their subordinates with performance feedback. To generate useful information to feed back to subordinates, managers can use both formal and informal appraisals. **Formal appraisals** are conducted at set times during the year and are based on performance dimensions and measures that have been specified in advance. A salesperson, for example, may be evaluated by his or her manager twice a year on the performance dimensions of sales and customer service, sales being objectively measured from sales reports and customer service being measured with a BARS (see Figure 10.5).

Managers in most large organizations use formal performance appraisals on a fixed schedule such as every six months or every year, as dictated by company policy. An integral part of a formal appraisal is a meeting between the manager and the subordinate in which the subordinate is given feedback on his or her performance. Performance feedback lets subordinates know areas in which they are excelling and areas in which they are in need of improvement; it also should provide them with guidance for improving performance.

Realizing the value of formal appraisals, managers in many large corporations have committed substantial resources to updating performance appraisal procedures and training lower-level managers in how to use them and provide accurate feedback to employees. Top managers at the pharmaceutical company Hoffmann–La Roche Inc., for example, recently spent $1.5 million updating and improving their performance appraisal procedures. Alan Rubino, vice president of human resources for Hoffmann–La Roche, believes that this was money well spent because "people need to know exactly where they stand and what's required of them." Before Hoffmann–La Roche's new system was implemented, managers attended a three-day training and development session to improve their performance appraisal skills. The new procedures call for every manager and subordinate to develop a performance plan for the subordinate for the coming year—a plan that is linked to the company's strategy and goals and approved by the manager's own superiors. Formal performance appraisals are conducted every six months, during which actual performance is compared to planned performance.[53]

Formal performance appraisals supply both managers and subordinates with valuable information, but subordinates often want feedback on a more frequent basis, and managers often want to motivate subordinates as the need arises. It is for these reasons that many companies, including Hoffman–La Roche, supplement formal performance appraisal with frequent **informal appraisals,** for which managers and their subordinates meet informally as the need arises to discuss ongoing progress and areas for improvement. Moreover, when job duties, assignments, or goals change, informal appraisals can be used to provide workers with timely feedback about how they are handling their new responsibilities.

Managers often dislike providing performance feedback, especially when the feedback is negative, but doing so is an important managerial activity. Here are some guidelines for effectively giving performance feedback that will contribute to employee motivation and performance:

• Be specific and focus on behaviors or outcomes that are correctable and within a worker's ability to improve. *Example:* Telling a salesperson that he is too shy when interacting with customers is likely to do nothing more than lower the person's self-confidence and prompt him to become defensive. A more effective approach is to give the salesperson feedback about specific behaviors to engage in—greeting customers as soon as they enter the department; asking customers whether they need help; volunteering to help customers find items if they seem to be having trouble.

• Approach performance appraisal as an exercise in problem solving and solution finding, not criticizing. *Example:* Rather than criticize a financial analyst for turning in reports late, the manager helps the analyst determine why the reports are late and identify ways to better manage his time.

• Express confidence in a subordinate's ability to improve. *Example:* Instead of being skeptical, a first-level manager tells a subordinate that she is confident that the subordinate can increase quality levels.

• Provide performance feedback both formally and informally. *Example:* The staff of a preschool receives feedback from formal performance appraisals twice a year. The director of the school also provides frequent informal feedback, such as complimenting staff members on creative ideas for special projects, noticing when they do a particularly good job handling a difficult child, and pointing out when they provide inadequate supervision.

• Praise instances of high performance and areas of a job in which a worker excels. *Example:* Rather than focusing on just the negative, a manager discusses the areas the subordinate excels in as well as areas in need of improvement.

• Avoid personal criticisms, and treat subordinates with respect. *Example:* An engineering manager acknowledges subordinates' expertise and treats them as professionals. Even when the manager points out performance problems to subordinates, she refrains from criticizing them personally.

• Agree to a timetable for performance improvements. *Example:* A first-level manager and her subordinate decide to meet again in one month to determine whether quality has improved.

In following these guidelines, managers need to keep in mind *why* they are giving performance feedback: to encourage high levels of motivation and performance. Moreover, the information that managers gather through performance appraisal and feedback helps them determine how to distribute pay raises and bonuses.

Tips for Managers

Performance **Appraisal**

1. Supplement periodic formal performance appraisals with more frequent informal appraisals and give performance feedback often.

2. When high performance can be reached by different kinds of behaviors and how employees perform their jobs is not important, use results appraisals to evaluate performance and give feedback.

3. When providing performance feedback, focus on specific behaviors or outcomes, adopt a problem-solving mode, express confidence in employees, praise instances of high performance, and agree to a timetable for improvements.

4. Avoid personal criticisms and treat employees with respect when providing feedback.

5. Provide performance feedback from both formal and informal performance appraisals.

Pay and Benefits

Pay includes employees' base salaries, pay raises, and bonuses and is determined by a number of factors, including characteristics of the organization and of the job and levels of performance. Employee benefits are based on membership in an organization (and not necessarily on the particular job held) and include sick days, vacation days, and medical and life insurance. In Chapter 12, we discuss the ways in which pay can be used to motivate organizational members to perform at a high level, as well as pay plans managers can use to help an organization achieve its goals and gain a competitive advantage. Here we focus on establishing an organization's pay level and pay structure.

Pay Level

pay level The relative position of an organization's pay incentives in comparison with those of other organizations in the same industry employing similar kinds of workers.

Pay level is a broad comparative concept that refers to how an organization's pay incentives compare, in general, to those of other organizations in the same industry employing similar kinds of workers. Managers must decide whether they want to offer relatively high wages, average wages, or relatively low wages. High wages help ensure that an organization is going to be able to recruit, select, and retain high performers, but high wages also raise costs. Low wages give an organization a cost advantage but may undermine the organization's ability to select and recruit high performers and motivate current employees to perform at a high level. Either of these situations may lead to inferior quality or inferior customer service.

In determining pay levels, managers should take into account their organization's strategy. A high pay level may prohibit managers from effectively pursuing a low-cost strategy. But a high pay level may be well worth the added costs in an organization whose competitive advantage lies in superior quality and excellent customer service. As one might expect, hotel and motel chains with a low-cost strategy such as Days Inn and Hampton Inns have lower pay levels than chains striving to provide high-quality rooms and services such as Four Seasons and Hyatt Regency.

Pay Structure

pay structure The arrangement of jobs into categories reflecting their relative importance to the organization and its goals, levels of skill required, and other characteristics.

After deciding on a pay level, managers have to establish a pay structure for the different jobs in the organization. A **pay structure** clusters jobs into categories reflecting their relative importance to the organization and its goals, levels of skill required, and other characteristics that managers consider to be important. Pay ranges are established for each job category. Individual jobholders' pay within job categories is then determined by factors such as performance, seniority, and skill levels.

There are some interesting global differences in pay structures. Large corporations based in the United States tend to pay their CEOs and top managers higher salaries than do their European or Japanese counterparts. There also is a much greater pay differential between employees at the bottom of the corporate hierarchy and employees high up the hierarchy in U.S. companies than in European or Japanese companies. In 1994, for example, European CEOs' average annual salary was $389,711, and U.S. CEOs' average annual salary was $819,428.[54]

Concerns have been raised over whether it is equitable or fair for CEOs of large companies in the United States to be making hundreds of thousands or even millions of dollars in years when their companies are restructuring and laying off a good portion of their workforces. In 1995, CEO pay levels in the United States rose an average of 30 percent while massive layoffs were also taking place.[55] Robert Allen, for example, CEO of AT&T, came under intense scrutiny in 1996 because he was earning $5 million a year when AT&T announced plans to lay off thousands of employees.

Stride-Rite, the children's shoe maker, has established an intergenerational day care center for its employees in which the families of employees are encouraged to take an active interest in the care of its employee's children.

Benefits

Organizations are legally required to provide certain benefits to their employees, including workers' compensation, Social Security, and unemployment insurance. Workers' compensation provides employees with financial assistance if they become unable to work because of a work-related injury or illness. Social Security provides financial assistance to retirees and disabled former employees. Unemployment insurance provides financial assistance to workers who lose their jobs through no fault of their own. The legal system in the United States views these three benefits as ethical requirements for organizations and thus mandates that they be provided.

Other benefits such as health insurance, dental insurance, vacation time, pension plans, life insurance, flexible working hours, company-provided day care, and employee assistance and wellness programs are provided at the option of employers. Benefits mandated by public policy and benefits provided at the option of employers cost organizations a substantial amount of money. For example, in 1990, the cost of benefits to employers was an average of 38.4 percent of their payroll costs.[56]

In some organizations, top managers decide which benefits might best suit the organization and employees and offer the same benefit package to all employees. Other organizations, realizing that employees' needs and desires for benefits might differ, offer **cafeteria-style benefit plans** that let employees themselves choose the benefits they want. Some organizations have success with cafeteria-style plans; others find them difficult to manage. As indicated in this "Management Insight," benefits that give employees more control over their time are growing in popularity.

cafeteria-style benefit plan A plan from which employees can choose the benefits that they want.

Management Insight

Managing Time with Benefits

Traditional benefits such as health insurance, pension plans, and vacation days are likely to continue to be high-priority items for most workers, but nontraditional benefits are also gaining in importance. Many nontraditional benefits aim to increase workers' flexibility in their use of time. Given the multiple demands on workers' time both on and off the job, it is not surprising that the popularity of benefits that provide workers with more control over their time is growing.

One such benefit is the time-off bank. Time-off banks allow employees to group their vacation days, holidays, and sick days into a single pool that they can dip into at their own discretion, with no questions asked by their supervisors. For an individual who wants to extend a holiday vacation, the time may be there for the taking. Time banks also can help parents of young children better control their time, especially when they need to take a day or two off to accommodate a child's school schedule.

Universal Health Services Inc., a hospital management company based in King of Prussia, Pennsylvania, has been using time-off banks since 1991. Eileen Bove, director of human resources, indicates that the time-off bank is a popular benefit because "Employees get control of their own destiny, and we get cost savings and productivity." Some of the cost savings and productivity gains apparently come from employees scheduling time off in advance and making arrangements for their absence rather than just calling in sick when they need or want to take a day off.[57]

Time-off banks also give employees increased privacy because they no longer have to tell their supervisors why they need to take a day off and justify not coming to work.[58] Moreover, time-off banks help ensure that the distribution of days off is fair or equitable in an organization because all employees are able to use all of their days with no questions asked (and without having to be sick).

Labor Relations

labor relations The activities that managers engage in to ensure that they have effective working relationships with the labor unions that represent their employees' interests.

Labor relations are the activities that managers engage in to ensure that they have effective working relationships with the labor unions that represent their employees' interests. Although the U.S. government has responded to the potential for unethical organizations and managers to treat workers unfairly—by creating and enforcing laws regulating employment (including the EEO laws listed in Table 10.1)—some workers believe that a union will help ensure that their interests are fairly represented in their organizations.

Before we describe unions in more detail, let's take a look at some examples of important employment legislation. In 1938, the government passed the Fair Labor Standards Act, which prohibited child labor and made provisions for minimum wages, overtime pay, and maximum working hours to protect workers' rights. In 1963, the Equal Pay Act mandated that men and women performing equal work (work requiring the same levels of skill, responsibility, and effort performed in the same kind of working conditions) receive equal pay (see Table 10.1). In 1970, the Occupational Safety and Health Act mandated procedures for managers to follow to ensure workplace safety. These are just a few of the U.S. government's efforts to protect workers' rights. State legislatures also have been active in promoting safe, ethical, and fair workplaces.

Unions

Unions exist to represent workers' interests in organizations. Given that managers have more power than rank-and-file workers and that organizations have multiple stakeholders, there is always the potential that managers might take steps that will benefit one set of stakeholders such as shareholders while hurting another such as employees. For example, managers might decide to speed up a production line to lower costs and increase production in the hopes of increasing returns to shareholders. This action, however, could hurt employees who are forced to work at a rapid pace, who may have increased risk of injuries as a result of the line speedup, and who receive no additional pay for the extra work they are performing. Unions represent workers' interests in scenarios such as this one.

The U.S. Congress acknowledged the role that unions could play in ensuring safe and fair workplaces when it passed the National Labor Relations Act of 1935. This act made it legal for workers to organize into unions to protect their rights and interests, and it declared certain unfair or unethical organizational practices to be illegal. The National Labor Relations Act also established the National Labor Relations Board (NLRB) to oversee union activity. Currently, the NLRB conducts certification elections, which are held among the employees of an organization to determine whether a union will be used to represent the employees' interests. The NLRB also makes judgments concerning unfair labor practices and specifies practices that managers must refrain from.

Employees might vote to have a union represent them for any number of reasons.[59] They may feel that their wages and working conditions are in need of improvement. They may feel that managers are not treating them with respect. They may think that their working hours are unfair or that they need more job security or a safer work environment. Or they may be dissatisfied with management and find it difficult to communicate their concerns with their bosses. Regardless of the specific reason, one overriding reason is power: A united group inevitably wields more power than an individual, and this type of power may be especially helpful to employees in some organizations.

Although these would seem to be potent forces for unionization, some workers are reluctant to join unions. Sometimes this reluctance is due to the perception that union leaders are corrupt. Some workers may simply feel that belonging to a union might not do them much good or might actually cause more harm than good while costing them money in membership dues. Employees also might not want to be "forced" into doing something they do not want to do (such as striking) because the union thinks it is in their best interest. Moreover, although unions can be a positive force in organizations, they sometimes can be a negative force, impairing organizational effectiveness. For example, when union leaders resist needed changes in an organization or are corrupt, organizational performance can suffer.

The percentage of U.S. workers represented by unions today is less than half of the percentage in the 1950s, an era when unions were especially strong. Approximately 15.5 percent of the workforce were members of the AFL-CIO (a national federation of 78 unions) in the 1990s, compared to 35 percent of the workforce in the 1950s.[60] Union influence in manufacturing and heavy industry has been on the decline, presumably because these workers no longer see the need to be represented by unions. Unions have recently made inroads in other segments of the workforce, however, particularly the low-wage end. Garbage collectors in New Jersey, poultry plant workers in North Carolina, and janitors in Baltimore are among the growing numbers of low-paid workers who are currently finding union membership attractive. North Carolina poultry workers voted in a union in part because they thought it was unfair that they had to buy their own gloves and hairnets used on the job and had to ask their supervisors' permission to go to the restroom.[61]

Union membership and leadership, traditionally dominated by white men, is also becoming increasingly diverse. Meet Linda Chavez-Thompson, the first woman and Hispanic to hold a top-management position in the AFL-CIO.

Focus on Diversity

Linda Chavez-Thompson and the AFL-CIO

When Linda Chavez-Thompson, daughter of a sharecropper, was 10 years old, she began picking cotton for 30 cents an hour in Lubbock, Texas. When she was 16, she negotiated with her father to let her mother stay home from work to get some needed rest. No wonder, then, that Mexican-American Chavez-Thompson went on to become a union organizer and leader. In 1995, she was appointed first executive vice president of the AFL-CIO (www.aflcio.com).

Chavez-Thompson's appointment reflects the AFL-CIO's current goals. Although union members traditionally have been white men earning salaries above the minimum wage, unions have become less popular with this group of workers, and union membership has been declining. AFL-CIO management, including Chavez-Thompson, feels that now and in the future unions may become more attractive to minorities, women, and workers at the bottom of the pay scale. Workers in these categories may be dissatisfied with their current work arrangements and may believe that belonging to a union will help improve their working conditions, pay, benefits, or job security. Currently, 40 percent of AFL-CIO members are women, compared to 33 percent in the 1980s.

In her position as executive vice president, Chavez-Thompson represents the interests of 13 million U.S. workers, and her goal is to increase union membership and power. Key to attaining that goal is attracting new kinds of union members—women, African Americans, Hispanics, and other minority groups. As Chavez-Thompson puts it, "I represent the America that organized labor has tended to overlook."[62]

Collective Bargaining

collective bargaining

Negotiation between labor unions and managers to resolve conflicts and disputes about issues such as working hours, wages, benefits, working conditions, and job security.

Collective bargaining is negotiation between labor unions and managers to resolve conflicts and disputes about important issues such as working hours, wages, benefits, working conditions, and job security. Before sitting down with management to negotiate, union members sometimes go on strike to drive home their concerns to managers. Once an agreement that union members support has been reached (sometimes with the help of a neutral third party called a *mediator*), union leaders and managers sign a contract spelling out the terms of the collective bargaining agreement. We discuss conflict and negotiation in depth in Chapter 16, but some brief observations are in order here because collective bargaining is an ongoing consideration in labor relations.

The signing of a contract, for example, does not bring collective bargaining to a halt. Disagreement and conflicts can arise over the interpretation of the contract. In these cases, a neutral third party called an *arbitrator* is usually called in to resolve the conflict. An important component of a collective bargaining agreement is a *grievance procedure* through which workers who feel they are not being fairly treated are allowed to voice their concerns and have their interests represented by the union. Workers who feel they were unjustly fired in violation of a union contract, for example, may file a grievance, have the union represent them, and get their jobs back if an arbitrator agrees with them.

Union members sometimes go on strike when managers make decisions that they feel will hurt them and are not in their best interests. This is precisely what happened in 1996 when General Motors' North American assembly plants employing 177,000 workers were idled for 18 days. The strike, which originated in GM's Dayton, Ohio, brake assembly plants, was due to management's decision to buy some parts from other companies rather than make them in GM's own plants.[63] The United Auto Workers called a strike because outsourcing threatens union members' jobs. The agreement that the union and management, bargaining collectively, reached allowed the outsourcing to continue but contained provisions for the creation of hundreds of new jobs as well as for improvements in working conditions.[64]

Summary and Review

Chapter Summary

STRATEGIC HUMAN RESOURCE MANAGEMENT

- **Overview of the Components of HRM**

- **The Legal Environment of HRM**

RECRUITMENT AND SELECTION

- **Human Resource Planning**

- **Job Analysis**

- **External and Internal Recruitment**

- **The Selection Process**

STRATEGIC HUMAN RESOURCE MANAGEMENT Human resource management (HRM) includes all the activities that managers engage in to ensure that their organizations are able to attract, retain, and effectively utilize human resources. Strategic HRM is the process by which managers design the components of a human resource management system to be consistent with each other, with other elements of organizational architecture, and with the organization's strategies and goals.

RECRUITMENT AND SELECTION Before recruiting and selecting employees, managers must engage in human resource planning and job analysis. Human resource planning includes all the activities managers engage in to forecast their current and future needs for human resources. Job analysis is the process of identifying (1) the tasks, duties, and responsibilities that make up a job and (2) the knowledge, skills, and abilities needed to perform the job. Recruitment includes all the activities that managers engage in to develop a pool of qualified applicants for open positions. Selection is the process by which managers determine the relative qualifications of job applicants and their potential for performing well in a particular job.

TRAINING AND DEVELOPMENT Training focuses on teaching organizational members how to perform effectively in their current jobs. Development focuses on broadening organizational members' knowledge and skills so that employees will be prepared to take on new responsibilities and challenges.

PERFORMANCE APPRAISAL AND FEEDBACK Performance appraisal is the evaluation of employees' job performance and contributions to their organization. Performance feedback is the process through which managers share performance appraisal information with their subordinates, give subordinates an opportunity to reflect on their own performance, and develop, with subordinates, plans for the future. Performance appraisal provides managers with useful information for decision making. Performance feedback can encourage high levels of motivation and performance.

PAY AND BENEFITS   Pay level is the relative position of an organization's pay incentives in comparison with those of other organizations in the same industry employing similar kinds of workers. A pay structure clusters jobs into categories reflecting their relative importance to the organization and its goals, levels of skill required, and other characteristics. Pay ranges are established for each job category. Organizations are legally required to provide certain benefits to their employees; other benefits are provided at the discretion of employers.

LABOR RELATIONS   Labor relations are the activities that managers engage in to ensure that they have effective working relationships with the labor unions that may represent their employees' interests. The National Labor Relations Board oversees union activity. Collective bargaining is the process through which labor unions and managers resolve conflicts and disputes and negotiate agreements.

Management in Action

Topics for Discussion and Action

1. Discuss why it is important for human resource management systems to be in sync with an organization's strategy and goals and with each other.

2. Interview a manager in a local organization to determine how that organization recruits and selects employees.

3. Discuss why training and development is an ongoing activity for all organizations.

4. Describe the type of development activities that you think middle managers are most in need of.

5. Evaluate the pros and cons of 360-degree performance appraisals and feedback.

Would you like your performance to be appraised in this manner? Why or why not?

6. Discuss why two restaurants in the same community might have different pay levels.

7. Explain why union membership is becoming more diverse.

Building Management Skills

Analyzing Human Resource Systems

Think about your current job or a job that you had in the past. If you have never had a job, then interview a friend or family member who is currently working. Answer the following questions about the job you have chosen.

1. How are people recruited and selected for this job? Are the recruitment and selection procedures that the organization uses effective or ineffective? Why?

2. What training and development do people who hold this job receive? Is it appropriate? Why or why not?

3. How is performance of this job appraised? Does performance feedback contribute to motivation and high performance on this job?

4. What levels of pay and benefits are provided for this job? Are these levels of pay and benefits appropriate? Why or why not?

Small Group Breakout Exercise

Building a Human Resource Management System

Form groups of three or four people, and appoint one group member as the spokesperson who will communicate your findings to the whole class when called on by the instructor. Then discuss the following scenario.

You and your two or three partners are engineers with a business minor who have decided to start a consulting business. Your goal is to provide manufacturing-process engineering and other engineering services to large and small organizations. You forecast that there will be an increased use of outsourcing for these activities. You discussed with managers in several large organizations the services you plan to offer, and they expressed considerable interest. You have secured funding to start the business and now are building the HRM system. Your human resource planning suggests that you need to hire between 5 and 8 experienced engineers with good communication skills, 2 clerical/secretarial workers, and 2 MBAs who between them will have financial, accounting, and human resource skills. You are striving to develop an approach to building your human resources that will enable your new business to prosper.

1. Describe the steps you will take to recruit and select (a) the engineers, (b) the clerical/secretarial workers, and (c) the MBAs.

2. Describe the training and development the engineers, the clerical/secretarial workers, and the MBAs will receive.

3. Describe how you will appraise the performance of each group of employees and how you will provide feedback.

4. Describe the pay level and pay structure of your consulting firm.

Exploring the World Wide Web

Specific Assignment

Many companies take active steps to recruit and retain valuable employees. One such company is Alltel Information Services. Scan Alltel's website to learn more about this company (http://www.alltel.com/). Click on "Career Opportunities," and explore the pages at this location.

1. What steps is Alltel taking to recruit and retain employees?

2. Do you think that its approach is effective? Why or why not?

General Assignment

Find websites of two companies that try to recruit new employees by means of the World Wide Web. Are their approaches to recruitment on the World Wide Web similar or different? What are the potential advantages of the approaches of each? What are the potential disadvantages?

ManagementCase

Human Resource Management in an Era of Downsizing

In an era of downsizing and massive corporate layoffs, human resource management becomes increasingly complex. Managers must make layoff decisions carefully and fairly, communicate accurate information about upcoming layoffs to organizational members, and treat employees being laid off with dignity and respect. Managers also must maintain the trust and motivation of those remaining employees who may feel guilty, resentful, angry, or fearful that they will be the next to lose their jobs. Negative reactions among employees are much more likely when managers fail to communicate accurate and complete information about the layoff, do not manage the layoff in a fair manner, and show a lack of concern for those laid off.

For organizations considering layoffs, outplacement services appear to be an important component to effectively manage the process, both for ethical and for performance considerations. Outplacement services not only help former employees find new employment but also help maintain the loyalty and trust of remaining employees when they realize that managers are doing everything they can to ease the pain of laid-off employees. Outplacement services can range from career counseling, help with résumé writing, providing listings of open jobs in other companies, social support, and clinical counseling, to providing former employees with additional training to update or expand their knowledge and skills.

For example, outplacement services were a big priority for managers at AT&T when it broke up into three separate companies in 1996. The breakup led to 40,000 jobs being eliminated, including thousands of managerial positions. During a one-week period in 1996, 2,000 AT&T employees were told that they would not have a job when the breakup was complete. In one month, 7,400 managers agreed to accept buyout packages (incentives to quit).[65] Stress levels were at an all-time high in AT&T as middle managers tried to keep their subordinates focused on performing their jobs while at the same time they decided whom to lay off and wondered whether they would lose their own jobs as well.

As part of outplacement services, AT&T provided employees with seminars on topics ranging from how to find a new job to how to plan for and adjust to retirement. Managers set up a $15 million database that listed open positions both within AT&T and in other companies; all employees had access to the database. Resource Link, AT&T's own temporary employment agency, helped laid-off employees find new jobs.[66]

Top managers at AT&T also set up regional outplacement facilities. The largest of these, in Murray Hill, New Jersey, is managed by Janice Cooley. Cooley was working 70-hour weeks as the outplacement resource center expanded to meet the needs of the growing number of laid-off employees. The center offers counseling services, secretarial services, workshops, courses, use of computerized job banks, a reference library, access to job postings from other companies, and office space for use by jobhunters. Robert Stawicki, a 39-year-old research engineer who came to AT&T in 1978 fresh out of college, recently attended an all-day seminar on self-employment at the center.[67]

Employees at Boeing Corporation have also been hard hit by layoffs. In response to some of their needs, Boeing managers have teamed up with the state of Washington and a local organization called the Private Industry Council to train laid-off workers who want to start their own businesses. Former employees who want to take the training program have to complete a 13-page application in which they discuss their idea for a new business, describe who their customers and competitors will be, and provide a budget detailing how they will support themselves until they start earning a profit. Applicants who are accepted into the program take 4 weeks of management classes, spend 2 weeks having their business plans reviewed, and receive 13 weeks of private consultation as they start their businesses. The program also helps participants obtain loans and financing.

After completing the training program, Chris Contreras, a laid-off aircraft toolmaker at Boeing, started his own business, Top Auto Repair, with a $25,000 federal loan. When Boeing offered to rehire Contreras, he declined even though he now works 10-hour days and earns two-thirds of what he made at Boeing. Contreras does not want to give up being his own boss and also likes not having to worry about losing his job in another round of layoffs.[68]

Questions

1. How can managers determine which outplacement services are most appropriate for laid-off employees of their companies?

2. How might appropriate outplacement services differ for the following groups of employees: (a) entry-level employees, (b) nonmanagerial employees who have been with the company 15 years or more, (c) first-line managers, (d) middle managers, (e) top managers?

3. How might failure to provide adequate outplacement services negatively affect employees who remain after a layoff?

ManagementCase

In the News

From the Pages of BusinessWeek
Stock Options: Lou Takes a Cue from Silicon Valley

Louis V. Gerstner Jr. is not yet in the same league as high-tech billionaires such as William H. Gates III and Lawrence J. Ellison. But the IBM CEO doesn't lack for incentive pay. His 1997 salary and bonus was $6 million, up 26% from a year ago. What's more, he stands to make a bundle on the 2.2 million shares he received as part of his annual compensation. According to IBM's proxy statement, Gerstner's stock could have a value of $130 million if the share price appreciates at 5% annually for the 10-year option period. At a 10% annual increase, Gerstner's windfall swells to a cool $330 million.

Now, Gerstner wants more IBMers to get Silicon Valley–style rewards. In a break from Big Blue tradition, he's opening stock-option programs to a wider group of employees—namely nonexecutives. Even though stock options for the rank and file have long been standard at other high-tech companies, IBM has typically granted options only to a small executive group. That makes IBMers an easy mark for other high-tech companies that come wooing. "They have lost a lot of people over the years," says Andrew W. West, whose San Francisco consulting firm, WardWest Pay Strategies, designs stock plans for high-tech companies. "They seeded the companies in the valley."

To halt the brain drain, Gerstner in 1998 is sweetening the pot for performance-related bonuses by 30%, to $1.3 billion. Meanwhile, the merit-pay pool is getting an extra $2 billion.

The big motivator, though, is stock. This year, IBM will more than triple the number of employees who get stock options. That's on top of a 100% increase in 1997. "This is a great way to help bring the best people to IBM, says Josephine Tsao, the company's head of executive compensation.

IBM is starting to catch up, but it is still lagging behind most high-tech companies. The average tech concern distributes about 3.3% of its stock in the form of employee options each year, according to Mark Edwards, a consultant with compensation specialist iQuantic Inc. This year, IBM is planning to set aside 2.5% of its outstanding shares for employees, up from 1.8% in 1997.

Gerstner's inner circle is also receiving more generous packages. In addition to salary and bonus raises of up to 31%, Gerstner is giving out hefty incentives in the form of restricted stock—essentially shares executives can cash in after a certain period for the full value. It's a much better deal than options, which increase in value only when they exceed a preset price. According to the proxy, IBM's top three executives received $2 million worth of restricted stock each in 1997. "That's great for retention, but it doesn't do much for performance," says West.

So far, it's too early to tell if Gerstner's compensation scheme is working. But, says recruiter Jeffrey E. Christian of Christian & Timbers Inc., IBM isn't the recruiting paradise "it once was." And it won't be as long as Big Blue's stock keeps heading north.

Source: Ira Sager, *Business Week,* March 30, 1998, 34.

Questions

1. What is Lou Gerstner's new approach to pay at IBM?

2. How many of IBM's managers and employees should receive stock options in your opinion?

Part 5

Chapter eleven

The Manager as a Person

Learning Objectives

1. Describe the various personality traits that affect how managers think, feel, and behave.

2. Explain what values, attitudes, and moods are, and describe their impact on managerial action.

3. Explain why managers' perceptions are central to decision making, why they are inherently subjective, and how they are formed.

4. Identify the career stages that managers typically go through and the challenges they face at each stage.

5. Describe the consequences and sources of the stress that managers experience.

A Case in Contrast

Low-Key Determination versus Flamboyant Outspokenness

Orit Gadiesh and Anne Sweeney are two successful top managers who in some ways could not be more different from each other but in other ways think and act quite similarly. Attesting to their successful careers, both Gadiesh and Sweeney were included in *Fortune* magazine's 1998 listing of the "Fifty Most Powerful Women in American Business."[1] Gadiesh was born in Israel and is chair of Bain & Company, a prominent consulting firm.[2] Sweeney was born in New York and has held a number of positions in cable TV. In August 1998, Sweeney became the president of Disney/ABC Cable Networks, including the Disney Channel and Toon Disney (www.disney.com).[3] Her prior positions include president of the Disney Channel and executive vice president of Disney/ABC Cable Networks and chair of FX Networks (www.fxnetworks.com), a somewhat unconventional cable network owned by TV mogul and billionaire Rupert Murdoch, which airs programs ranging from news shows to situation comedies.[4]

Gadiesh and Sweeney share a number of personal characteristics. Both are intelligent, widely respected by their peers, self-confident, achievement oriented, and self-disciplined. Both have satisfying careers and personal lives and are take-charge, determined individuals.

Once you get past these basic similarities, however, Gadiesh and Sweeney differ in interesting and important ways. Gadiesh is very outspoken and blunt, dresses flamboyantly, and often takes center stage at business meetings. She is very outgoing, sometimes even shocking, and has a powerful influence

Although Orit Gadiesh and Anne Sweeney are two successful top managers, their personalities and stories of how they reached the top differ greatly. In this chapter, you will see the many variables that can affect managers and their styles.

on those around her. Sweeney, in contrast, is unassuming, low-key, quiet, and restrained. She keeps her cool and always seems composed. During executive meetings, she often does more listening than talking; when interrupted, she sometimes lets lower-ranking managers have the floor. She has an accommodating, laid-back style that at times masks her determination, assertiveness, strength, good ideas, and ability to make things happen.[5]

Gadiesh and Sweeney also differ in how long they have been a member of their current organizations. Gadiesh has worked at Bain & Company for over 20 years; Sweeney has been working at Disney since 1996. When Bain was experiencing financial difficulties in the early 1990s and some of its top-performing consultants were tempted to jump ship, Gadiesh (a senior partner at the time) and the 12 other senior partners in the firm declared their commitment to Bain and pledged to stay. Bain partner Keith Aspinall noted that "Everyone looked to her to see what she would do." In 1992, after the company was well on the road to recovery, Gadiesh made a stirring 40-minute speech to the firm's 600 consultants at the annual meeting on the need to restore pride and confidence to Bain & Company. As she put it: "We've turned around financially, we've turned around the business—and even our competitors are beginning to acknowledge that . . . Now it's time to turn around what they really fear . . . It's time to turn around our collective pride in what we do." Gadiesh's speech was met with cheers; Aspinall summed up the audience's reaction by saying, "It was electric."[6]

During Sweeney's tenure as president of the Disney Channel, Disney more than doubled the number of its subscribers (from 15 million to 42 million).[7] She also was a successful top manager at FX Networks; and, prior to joining FX, Sweeney was an enterprising top manager at Nickelodeon, in charge of acquisitions. One of her coups at Nickelodeon was the purchase of the MTM library, which includes such old-time favorites as the *Dick Van Dyke Show, Mary Tyler Moore,* and other programs shown during Nickelodeon's evening programming ("Nick at Nite"). Sweeney had been at Nickelodeon for 12 years when she was offered the top position at FX and was chair of FX Networks for three years before joining Disney.[8]

The differences between Gadiesh and Sweeney are also evident in how their careers started and unfolded. As a child, Gadiesh wanted to be a singer and actress. In high school in Israel, she played the role of Eliza Doolittle in a production of the play *My Fair Lady.* After high school, she served two years in the Israeli army, earned a bachelor's degree in psychology from Hebrew University, and went on to graduate in the top 5 percent of her class from Harvard Business School. As a child, Sweeney dreamed of being a teacher. After observing a class of children all day as part of a requirement for a teaching course at the College of New Rochelle in New York, however, Sweeney decided that a career in children's television might be more to her liking.[9] She enrolled in Harvard's School of Education and received a master's degree in education in 1980.

Even the stresses Gadiesh and Sweeney experience differ. Although they experience similar kinds of stress from being in top-management positions with high levels of responsibility, other sources of stress are quite different for these two managers. Sweeney is married, has two young children, and sometimes experiences stress from trying to meet her family's needs while at the same time being responsible for the success of Disney/ABC Cable Networks. Gadiesh is married to an adventurer who in the late 1980s sailed around the world by himself for three years; she has no children. Given her husband's love of sailing, Gadiesh sometimes puts up with seasickness to share in his pastime; indeed, in the midst of helping with the turnaround at Bain, Gadiesh sometimes flew off to meet up with her husband at various locations around the world.[10]

All in all, Gadiesh and Sweeney illustrate how two very successful managers can differ from each other in many ways. ●

Overview

In previous chapters, we discussed many of the challenges managers face as they seek to achieve organizational goals through planning, organizing, and controlling. Considering the multiple challenges managers face, one might almost start to think that effective managers must be superhuman. Managers are people, however, and like people everywhere they have their own distinctive personalities, ways of viewing things, personal challenges and disappointments, shortcomings, and the like.

In this chapter, we focus on the manager as a feeling, thinking human being; we look at what managers like Gadiesh and Sweeney, featured in the "Case in Contrast," are like, what makes them tick, and what makes them act the way they do as managers. We start by describing enduring characteristics that seem to influence how managers "manage," as well as how they view other people, their organizations, and the world around them. We discuss as well how managers' values, attitudes, and moods may play out in organizations. We describe how all managerial action is based on managers' perceptions and the need for their perceptions to be as accurate as possible. We complete the picture of a manager as a feeling, thinking human being by discussing managerial careers and the stress managers experience in their daily lives. By the end of this chapter, you will have a good appreciation of how the personal characteristics of managers influence the process of management. ●

Enduring Characteristics: Personality Traits

personality traits
Enduring tendencies to feel, think, and act in certain ways.

All people, including managers, have certain enduring characteristics that influence how they think, feel, and behave both on and off the job. These characteristics are **personality traits,** particular tendencies to feel, think, and act in certain ways that can be used to describe the personalities of all individuals—tendencies, for example, to be enthusiastic and flamboyant like Gadiesh or low-key like Sweeney, demanding or easygoing, excited or mellow, nervous or relaxed, risk seeking or risk-averse, outgoing or shy. It is important to understand the personalities of managers because their personalities influence their behavior and their approach to management.

Some managers, like Procter & Gamble's former chair Edwin Artzt, are demanding, difficult to get along with, and highly critical of other people.[11] Other managers, like Southwest Airlines' CEO Herb Kelleher, may be as concerned about effectiveness and efficiency as highly critical managers but are easier to get along with and likable and frequently praise the people around them. Both styles of management may produce excellent results, but their effects on employees are quite different. Do managers deliberately decide to adopt one or the other of these approaches to management? Although they may do so part of the time, in all likelihood their personalities also account for their different approaches.

The Big Five Personality Traits

We can think of an individual's personality as being composed of five general traits or characteristics: extroversion, negative affectivity, agreeableness, conscientiousness, and openness to experience.[12] Researchers often consider these the "Big Five" personality traits.[13] Each of them can be viewed as a continuum along which every individual or, more specifically, every manager falls (see Figure 11.1).

Some managers may be at the high end of one trait continuum, others at the low end, and still others somewhere in between. An easy way to understand how these traits can affect a person's approach to management is to describe what people are like at the high and low ends of each trait continuum. As will become evident as you read about each trait, there is no single "right" or "wrong" trait for being an effective manager; rather, effectiveness is determined by a complex interaction between characteristics of managers (including personality traits) and the nature of the job and organization in which they are working. Moreover, personality traits that enhance managerial effectiveness in one situation may impair it in another.

Figure 11.1
The Big Five Personality Traits

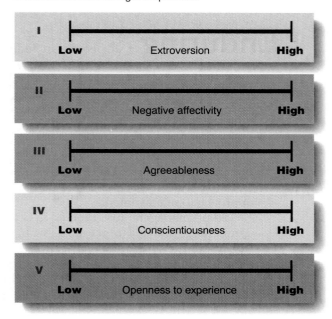

Manager's personalities can be described by determining which point on each of the following dimensions best characterizes the manager in question:

I	Low	Extroversion	High
II	Low	Negative affectivity	High
III	Low	Agreeableness	High
IV	Low	Conscientiousness	High
V	Low	Openness to experience	High

extroversion The tendency to experience positive emotions and moods and to feel good about oneself and the rest of the world.

EXTROVERSION Extroversion is the tendency to experience positive emotions and moods and to feel good about oneself and the rest of the world. Managers who are at the high end of the extroversion continuum (often called *extroverts*) tend to be sociable, affectionate, outgoing, and friendly. Managers who are low on extroversion (often called *introverts*) tend to be less inclined toward social interaction and to have a less positive outlook. Being high on extroversion may be an asset for managers whose jobs entail especially high levels of social interaction. Managers who are low on extroversion may nevertheless be very effective and efficient, especially when their jobs do not require excessive social interaction. Their more "quiet" approach may enable them to accomplish quite a bit of work in a limited time. Orit Gadiesh, from the "Case in Contrast," might be higher on extroversion than Anne Sweeney; Sweeney, however, is a successful manager whose low-key approach has worked well.

negative affectivity The tendency to experience negative emotions and moods, to feel distressed, and to be critical of oneself and others.

NEGATIVE AFFECTIVITY Negative affectivity is the tendency to experience negative emotions and moods, feel distressed, and be critical of oneself and others. Managers who are high on this trait continuum may often feel angry and dissatisfied and complain about their own and others' lack of progress. Managers who are low on negative affectivity do not tend to experience many negative emotions and moods and are less pessimistic and critical of themselves and others. On the plus side, the "critical" approach of a manager high on negative affectivity may sometimes be effective if this trait spurs both the manager and others around him or her to improve their performance. Nevertheless, it is probably more pleasant to work with a manager who is low on negative affectivity; the better working relationships that such a manager is likely to cultivate also can be an important asset. Figure 11.2 is an example of a scale developed to measure a person's level of negative affectivity.

agreeableness The tendency to get along well with other people.

AGREEABLENESS Agreeableness is the tendency to get along well with others. Managers who are high on the agreeableness continuum are likeable, tend to be affectionate, and care about other people. Managers who are low on agreeableness may be somewhat distrustful of others, unsympathetic, uncooperative, and even at times antagonistic. Being high on agreeableness may be especially important for managers whose responsibilities require them to develop good, close relationships with others. Rochelle Lazarus, president of the North American unit of the advertising agency Ogilvy & Mather, is known for her agreeableness and ability to develop close, warm, and lasting relationships. In fact, her close friendships with Louis Gerstner (IBM's CEO) and Abby Kohnstamm (IBM's vice president of corporate marketing) helped her win IBM's worldwide advertising account in a closely contested battle with rival ad agencies.[14] Nevertheless, a low level of agreeableness may be an asset in managerial jobs that actually require managers to be antagonistic, such as drill sergeants and some other kinds of military managers.

conscientiousness The tendency to be careful, scrupulous, and persevering.

CONSCIENTIOUSNESS Conscientiousness is the tendency to be careful, scrupulous, and persevering. Managers who are high on the conscientiousness continuum are organized and self-disciplined; those who are low on this trait might sometimes appear to lack direction and self-discipline. Conscientiousness has been found to be a good predictor of performance in many kinds of jobs, including managerial jobs in a variety of organizations.[15] CEOs

Figure 11.2
A Measure of Negative Affectivity

Instructions: Listed below are a series of statements a person might use to describe her/his attitudes, opinions, interests, and other characteristics. If a statement is true or largely true, put a "T" in the space next to the item. Or , if the statement is false or largely false, mark an "F" in the space.

Please answer every statement, even if you are not completely sure of the answer. Read each statement carefully, but don't spend too much time deciding on the answer.

_____ **1.** I often find myself worrying about something.

_____ **2.** My feelings are hurt rather easily.

_____ **3.** Often I get irritated at little annoyances.

_____ **4.** I suffer from nervousness.

_____ **5.** My mood often goes up and down.

_____ **6.** I sometimes feel "just miserable" for no good reason.

_____ **7.** Often I experience strong emotions—anxiety, anger— without really knowing what causes them.

_____ **8.** I am easily startled by things that happen unexpectedly.

_____ **9.** I sometimes get myself into a state of tension and turmoil as I think of the day's events.

_____ **10.** Minor setbacks sometimes irritate me too much.

_____ **11.** I often lose sleep over my worries.

_____ **12.** There are days when I'm "on edge" all of the time.

_____ **13.** I am too sensitive for my own good.

_____ **14.** I sometimes change from happy to sad, or vice versa, without good reason.

Scoring: Level of negative affectivity is equal to the number of items answered "True."

Source: A. Tellegen, *Brief Manual for the Differential Personality Questionnaire* (unpublished manuscript, University of Minnesota, 1982).

of major companies, such as Lou Gerstner of IBM, often show signs of being high on conscientiousness—the long hours they work, their attention to detail, and their ability to handle their multiple responsibilities in an organized manner. The self-determination of both Gadiesh and Sweeney attests to their conscientiousness.

openness to experience The tendency to be original, have broad interests, be open to a wide range of stimuli, be daring, and take risks.

OPENNESS TO EXPERIENCE   **Openness to experience** is the tendency to be original, have broad interests, be open to a wide range of stimuli, be daring, and take risks.[16] Managers who are high on this trait continuum may be especially likely to take risks and be innovative in their planning and decision making. Entrepreneurs who start their own businesses—like Bill Gates of Microsoft and Anita Roddick of The Body Shop—are, in all likelihood, high on openness to experience, which has contributed to their success as entrepreneurs and managers. The two managers featured in the "Case in Contrast" are also likely to be high on openness to experience. Sweeney started out her career wanting to be a teacher, went to school to learn about children's television broadcasting, and had a series of responsible positions with Nickelodeon, FX Networks, and Disney before taking on her current challenge as president of Disney/ABC Cable Networks. Gadiesh worked in the Israeli army for two years and applied to and was accepted by Harvard Business School before starting to work for Bain.[17]

Managers who are low on openness to experience may be less prone to take risks and more conservative in their planning and decision making. In certain kinds of organizations and positions, this tendency might be an asset.

The manager of the fiscal office in a public university, for example, must ensure that all university departments and units follow the university's rules and regulations pertaining to budgets, spending accounts, and reimbursements of expenses.

Age stereotypes might lead one to think that as workers get older they may be less open to new experiences and taking risks. But that is not necessarily the case, as this "Focus on Diversity" indicates.

Focus on Diversity

Openness to Experience Reigns at Any Age

Joan and David Helpern founded, own, and manage the elegant and hip Joan & David specialty chain of shoe and clothing stores catering to a posh 30-something crowd. The youthful, modern appeal of their sophisticated stores and merchandise belies the fact that both Helperns are in their 70s (and David recently had quintuple bypass surgery), their press agent Eleanor Lambert is in her 90s, and even their poodle Bijou has bald spots.

Throughout their careers, the Helperns have demonstrated their openness to experience. When Joan met David in 1961, she was managing the New York City Board of Education's child psychology programs, and he was managing a chain of New England shoe stores. In 1962, Joan attended a meeting of shoe manufacturers and talked about how the shoes they were designing and producing for women were uncomfortable and painful for any active person to wear. She started to design high-quality soft leather shoes with low heels that were both comfortable and attractive, and both Helperns decided to make a radical change in their careers and lives. David sold his shoe business, and he and Joan went to Europe in 1964 seeking shoe manufacturers with high quality and creativity. They found what they were looking for in Italy, and the Joan & David legacy began.

Looking for a way to sell their shoes, Joan and David happened upon the Ann Taylor chain of clothing stores, which seemed to be appealing to the customer base that they had in mind for their shoes. The Helperns leased space in Ann Taylor stores throughout the country and by 1989 were managing shoe departments in 127 Ann Taylor stores. At this time, they also were selling their shoes to upscale department stores like Bloomingdale's and Neiman Marcus. Just when they seemed to be doing well, however, the Ann Taylor chain started having troubles (it was part of a leveraged buyout). The Helperns stopped selling shoes in Ann Taylor stores, cutting their revenues by 66 percent in the early 1990s. Then some of the department stores selling their shoes reduced their stock of expensive shoes and cost the Helperns $25 million in lost sales.

At this point, Joan and David might have decided to retire. After all, they had enough money to live the rest of their lives in the style to which they had become accustomed. But their high level of openness to experience propelled them to new heights. The couple decided to open stand-alone boutiques in a number of U.S. cities such as Boston, Los Angeles, Dallas, and Houston. David concentrated his efforts on finding prime locations and managing day-to-day operations. Joan focused on designing clothes and accessories to complement the mainstay of the boutiques: the famous Joan & David shoes. Are they content just to manage the 43 boutiques now operating throughout the United States and in Paris, London, and Hong Kong? No. Once again demonstrating their high levels of openness to experience, each Helpern is focusing on a new challenge. David wants to risk opening boutiques in Germany and Switzerland, and Joan wants to risk opening more boutiques in the competitive New York market. True to his high level of openness to experience, and without regard to his advancing years, David suggests, "We'll do both."[18]

By now it should be clear that successful managers occupy a variety of positions on the "Big Five" personality-trait continua. One highly effective manager may be high on extroversion and negative affectivity, another equally effective manager low on both these traits, and still another somewhere in between. It is important for members of an organization to understand these differences across managers because they can shed light on how managers behave and on their approach to planning, leading, organizing, and controlling. If subordinates realize, for example, that their manager is low on extroversion, they will not feel slighted when their manager seems to be aloof because they will realize that by nature he or she is simply not outgoing.

Managers themselves also need to be aware of their own personality traits and the traits of others, including their subordinates and fellow managers. A manager who knows that he has a tendency to be highly critical of other people might try to tone down his negative approach. Similarly, a manager who realizes that her chronically complaining subordinate tends to be so negative because of his personality may take all his complaints with a grain of salt and realize that things probably are not as bad as this subordinate says they are.

In order for all members of an organization to work well together and with people outside the organization, such as customers and suppliers, it is important for them to understand each other. Such understanding comes, in part, from an appreciation of some of the fundamental ways in which people differ from one another—that is, from an appreciation of personality traits.

Other Personality Traits That Affect Managerial Behavior

Many other specific traits, in addition to the Big Five, can be used to describe people's personalities. Here we look at some that are particularly important for understanding managerial effectiveness: locus of control, self-esteem, and the needs for achievement, affiliation, and power.

LOCUS OF CONTROL   People differ in their views about how much control they have over what happens to and around them. The locus of control trait captures these beliefs.[19] People with an **internal locus of control** believe that they themselves are responsible for their own fate; they see their own actions and behaviors as being important and decisive determinants of important outcomes such as levels of job performance, promotion, or being turned down for a choice job assignment. Some managers with an internal locus of control see the success of a whole organization resting on their shoulders, as do Gadiesh and Sweeney in the "Case in Contrast." People with an

internal locus of control The tendency to locate responsibility for one's fate within oneself.

external locus of control The tendency to locate responsibility for one's fate within outside forces and to believe that one's own behavior has little impact on outcomes.

external locus of control believe that outside forces are responsible for what happens to and around them; they do not think that their own actions make much difference.

Managers need to have an internal locus of control because they *are* responsible for what happens in organizations; they need to believe that they can and do make a difference. George Fisher's internal locus of control predisposed him to believe that he could solve Eastman Kodak's problems and turn around this troubled organization. Thus, he left his job as CEO of highly successful Motorola to become CEO of Eastman Kodak.[20] CEOs like Fisher believe so strongly in their ability to influence what happens around them that they are confident they can improve the performance of organizations that are in deep trouble and in which other capable managers and CEOs have been ineffective.

self-esteem The degree to which individuals feel good about themselves and their capabilities.

SELF-ESTEEM **Self-esteem** is the degree to which individuals feel good about themselves and their capabilities. People with high self-esteem feel that they are competent, deserving, and capable of handling most situations, as do Gadiesh and Sweeney. People with low self-esteem have poor opinions of themselves, are unsure about their capabilities, and question their ability to succeed at different endeavors.[21] Research suggests that people tend to choose activities and goals that are consistent with their levels of self-esteem. High self-esteem is desirable for managers because it is likely to facilitate their setting and keeping high standards for themselves, to push them ahead on difficult projects, and to give them the confidence they need to make and carry out important decisions.

need for achievement The extent to which an individual has a strong desire to perform challenging tasks well and to meet personal standards for excellence.

NEEDS FOR ACHIEVEMENT, AFFILIATION, AND POWER Psychologist David McClelland has extensively researched the needs for achievement, affiliation, and power.[22] The **need for achievement** is the extent to which an individual has a strong desire to perform challenging tasks well and to meet personal standards for excellence. People with a high need for achievement often set clear goals for themselves and like to receive performance feedback. The **need for affiliation** is the extent to which an individual is concerned about establishing and maintaining good interpersonal relations, being liked, and having other people get along with each other. The **need for power** is the extent to which an individual desires to control or influence others.[23]

Research suggests that high needs for achievement and for power are assets for first-line and middle managers and that a high need for power is especially important for upper managers.[24] One study found that U.S. presidents with a relatively high need for power tended to be especially effective during their terms of office.[25] A high need for affiliation may not always be desirable in managers because it might lead them to try too hard to be liked by others (including subordinates) rather than

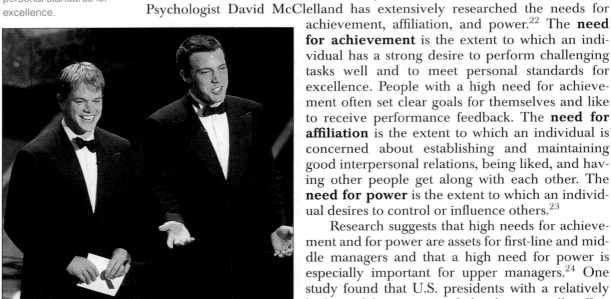

The quintessential achievement award for the movie industry is the "Oscar" or Academy Award, and is often a catalyst for the recipient and their career. Time will tell if Ben Affleck's and Matt Damon's win for Best Screenwriting of "Good Will Hunting" will help them get more movie roles.

need for affiliation The extent to which an individual is concerned about establishing and maintaining good interpersonal relations, being liked, and having other people get along.

need for power The extent to which an individual desires to control or influence others.

doing all they can to ensure that performance is as high as it can and should be. Although most research on these needs has been done in the United States, some studies suggest that the findings may also be applicable to people in other countries as well, such as India and New Zealand.[26]

Taken together, the personality traits desirable in managers—an internal locus of control, high self-esteem, and high needs for achievement and power—suggest that managers need to be take-charge individuals who believe that their own actions are decisive in determining their own and their organization's fate, believe in their own capabilities, and have a personal desire for accomplishment and influence over others.

Values, Attitudes, and Moods

What are managers striving to achieve, how do they think they should behave, what do they think about their jobs and organizations, and how do they actually feel at work? Some answers to these questions can be found by exploring managers' values, attitudes, and moods.

Values, attitudes, and moods capture how managers experience their jobs as individuals. *Values* describe what managers are trying to achieve through work and how they think they should behave. *Attitudes* capture their thoughts and feelings about their specific jobs and organizations. *Moods* encompass how managers actually feel when they are managing. Although these three aspects of managers' work experience are highly personal, they also have important implications for understanding how managers behave, how they treat and respond to others, and how, through their efforts, they help contribute to organizational effectiveness through planning, leading, organizing, and controlling.

Values: Terminal and Instrumental

terminal value
A personal conviction about lifelong goals or objectives that an individual seeks to achieve.

instrumental value
A personal conviction about modes of conduct or ways of behaving that an individual seeks to follow.

value system The terminal and instrumental values that are guiding principles in an individual's life.

There are two kinds of personal values—*terminal* and *instrumental*. A **terminal value** is a personal conviction about lifelong goals or objectives; an **instrumental value** is a personal conviction about desired modes of conduct or ways of behaving.[27] Milton Rokeach, one of the leading researchers in the area of human values, identified 18 terminal values and 18 instrumental values that describe each person's value system (see Figure 11.3).[28] By rank ordering the terminal values from 1 (most important as a guiding principle in one's life) to 18 (least important as a guiding principle in one's life) and then rank ordering the instrumental values from 1 to 18, a person gives a good picture of his or her **value system**—what he or she is striving to achieve in life and how he or she wants to behave.[29] (You can gain a good understanding of your own values by rank ordering first the terminal values and then the instrumental values listed in Figure 11.3.)

Several of the terminal values listed in Figure 11.3 seem to be especially important for managers—such as *a sense of accomplishment (a lasting contribution)*, *equality (brotherhood, equal opportunity for all)*, and *self-respect (or self-esteem)*. A manager who thinks a sense of accomplishment is of paramount importance might focus on making a lasting contribution to an organization by developing

Figure 11.3

Terminal and Instrumental Values

Terminal Values	Instrumental Values
A comfortable life (a prosperous life)	Ambitious (hard-working, aspiring)
An exciting life (a stimulating, active life)	Broad-minded (open-minded)
A sense of accomplishment (lasting contribution)	Capable (competent, effective)
A world at peace (free of war and conflict)	Cheerful (lighthearted, joyful)
A world of beauty (beauty of nature and the arts)	Clean (neat, tidy)
Equality (brotherhood, equal opportunity for all)	Courageous (standing up for your beliefs)
Family security (taking care of loved ones)	Forgiving (willing to pardon others)
Freedom (independence, free choice)	Helpful (working for the welfare of others)
Happiness (contentedness)	Honest (sincere, truthful)
Inner harmony (freedom from inner conflict)	Imaginative (daring, creative)
Mature love (sexual and spiritual intimacy)	Independent (self-reliant, self-sufficient)
National security (protection from attack)	Intellectual (intelligent, reflective)
Pleasure (an enjoyable, leisurely life)	Logical (consistent, rational)
Salvation (saved, eternal life)	Loving (affectionate, tender)
Self-respect (self-esteem)	Obedient (dutiful, respectful)
Social recognition (respect, admiration)	Polite (courteous, well-mannered)
True friendship (close companionship)	Responsible (dependable, reliable)
Wisdom (a mature understanding of life)	Self-controlled (restrained, self-disciplined)

Source: M. Rokeach, *The Nature of Human Values* (New York: Free Press, 1973).

a new product line or opening a new foreign subsidiary. A manager who places equality at the top of his or her list of terminal values may be at the forefront of an organization's efforts to support, provide equal opportunities to, and capitalize on the many talents of an increasingly diverse workforce.

Other values are likely to be considered important by many managers, such as *a comfortable life (a prosperous life), an exciting life (a stimulating, active life), freedom (independence, free choice),* and *social recognition (respect, admiration).* The relative importance that managers place on each terminal value helps explain what they are striving to achieve in their organizations and what they will focus their efforts on.

Several of the instrumental values listed in Figure 11.3 seem to be important modes of conduct for managers, such as being *ambitious (hard-working, aspiring), broad-minded (open-minded), capable (competent, effective), responsible (dependable, reliable),* and *self-controlled (restrained, self-disciplined).* Moreover, the relative importance a manager places on these and other instrumental values may be a significant determinant of his or her actual behaviors on the job. A manager who considers being *imaginative (daring, creative)* to be highly important, for example, is more likely to be innovative and take risks than is a manager who considers this to be less important (all else being equal). A manager who considers being *honest (sincere, truthful)* to be of paramount importance may be a driving force for taking steps to ensure that all members of a unit or organization behave ethically.

Although much of Rokeach's research was based in the United States, the terminal and instrumental values he identified can be used to describe the values of people from other cultures as well, as indicated in this "Managing Globally."

Managing Globally

Values of the Overseas Chinese

Over 55 million Chinese people work outside China, manage much of the trade and investment in all East Asia (except for Korea and Japan), and now are expanding beyond Asia to Europe and the United States. Often referred to as the "Overseas Chinese," they are prominent in businesses such as real estate and investment in countries like Singapore and Malaysia.[30] They tend to be successful at what they do, so successful that some of them are now running multi-billion-dollar companies.

Y. C. Wang is the founder and chairman of the Taiwan-based Formosa Plastics Group, which established a $2.1 billion plastics manufacturing and petrochemical plant in Point Comfort, Texas, in 1994. Cheng Yu-tong, a Hong Kong–based real-estate manager, owns the Stouffer and Renaissance United States hotel chains and has taken control of some of Donald Trump's New York City real-estate ventures. President Enterprises, a Taiwanese food company, produces Girl Scout cookies in eight of its United States bakeries and also owns the bakery that makes Famous Amos chocolate chip cookies.

One distinguishing characteristic of some Overseas Chinese, whether they are managing a bank in Hong Kong or a truly global organization, is their values. Above all else, they seem to value hard work, ambition, strong family ties, family security, responsibility, self-control, and competence. Billionaire Y. C. Wang has never taken a day off, and Kao Chin-yen, vice chairman of President Enterprises, says that he would feel sick if he had no work to do. Many of the businesses managed and owned by Overseas Chinese are family businesses, and parents work hard to ensure that their children have both the education and the experience they will need to assume responsible positions in their companies. That many Overseas Chinese are very disciplined and responsible managers who are highly competent is evident from their successes around the world.

Given these values, you might think that the Overseas Chinese are somewhat risk-averse, but they are not. They also consider being daring and being creative to be important guiding principles, as evidenced by their multi-million-dollar investments around the world. Y. C. Wang is building one of the largest manufacturing facilities in the world in Taiwan at an estimated cost of $9 billion.

Respect, admiration, and social recognition also are important for these entrepreneurial managers. Many of the business deals between organizations owned and managed by Overseas Chinese are conducted through networks of managers who have developed close relationships of mutual trust and respect over decades. Personal relationships and connections built on respect and admiration are called *guanxi* and are the modus operandi for many Overseas Chinese. Similarly, *xinyong,* having a good reputation and a good credit rating, is a most valued asset for many Overseas Chinese managers.[31]

All in all, managers' value systems signify what managers as individuals are trying to accomplish and be like in their personal lives and at work. Thus, a manager's value system is a fundamental guide to his or her behavior and efforts at planning, leading, organizing, and controlling.

Attitudes

attitude A collection of feelings and beliefs.

An **attitude** is a collection of feelings and beliefs. Like everyone else, managers have attitudes about their jobs and organizations, and these attitudes affect how they approach their jobs. Two of the most important attitudes in this context are job satisfaction and organizational commitment.

job satisfaction The collection of feelings and beliefs that managers have about their current jobs.

JOB SATISFACTION Job **satisfaction** is the collection of feelings and beliefs that managers have about their current jobs. Managers who are high in job satisfaction generally like their jobs, feel that they are being fairly treated, and believe that their jobs have many desirable features or characteristics (such as interesting work, good pay and job security, autonomy, or nice coworkers). Figure 11.4 shows sample items from two scales that managers can use to measure job satisfaction. Levels of job satisfaction tend to increase as one moves up the hierarchy in an organization. Upper managers, in general, tend to be more satisfied with their jobs than entry-level employees. Managers' levels of job satisfaction can range from very low to very high and anywhere in between.

In general, it is desirable for managers to be satisfied with their jobs, for at least two reasons. First, satisfied managers may be more likely to go the extra mile for their organization or perform **organizational citizenship behaviors (OCBs),** behaviors that are not required of organizational members but that contribute to and are necessary for organizational efficiency, effectiveness, and gaining a competitive advantage.[32] Managers who are satisfied with their jobs are more likely to perform these "above and beyond the call of duty" behaviors, which can range from putting in extra-long hours when needed, to coming up with truly creative ideas and overcoming obstacles to implement them (even when doing so is not part of the manager's job), to going out of one's way to help a coworker, subordinate, or superior (even when doing so entails considerable personal sacrifice).[33]

organizational citizenship behaviors Behaviors that are not required of organizational members but that contribute to and are necessary for organizational efficiency, effectiveness, and gaining a competitive advantage.

A second reason why it is desirable for managers to be satisfied with their jobs is that satisfied managers may be less likely to quit.[34] A manager who is highly satisfied may never even think about looking for another position; a dissatisfied manager may always be on the lookout for new opportunities. Turnover can hurt an organization because it results in the loss of the experience and knowledge that managers have gained about the company, industry, and the environment.

Figure 11.4
Sample Items from Two Measures of Job Satisfaction

Sample items from the Minnesota Satisfaction Questionnaire:
People respond to each of the items in the scale by checking whether they are:

[ ] Very dissatisfied   [ ] Satisfied
[ ] Dissatisfied   [ ] Very satisfied
[ ] Can't decide whether satisfied or not

On my present job, this is how I feel about . . .

_____ **1.** Being able to do things that don't go against my conscience.

_____ **2.** The way my job provides for steady employment.

_____ **3.** The chance to do things for other people.

_____ **4.** The chance to do something that makes use of my abilities.

_____ **5.** The way company policies are put into practice.

_____ **6.** My pay and the amount of work I do.

_____ **7.** The chances for advancement on this job.

_____ **8.** The freedom to use my own judgment.

_____ **9.** The working conditions.

_____ **10.** The way my co-workers get along with each other.

_____ **11.** The praise I get for doing a good job.

_____ **12.** The feeling of accomplishment I get from the job.

Source: D. J. Weiss, R. V. Dawis, G. W. England, and L. H. Lofquist, Manual for the Minnesota Satisfaction Questionnaire, 1967, Minnesota Studies in Vocational Rehabilitation: XXII University of Minnesota

The Faces Scale
Workers select the face which best expresses how they feel about their job in general.

11   10   9   8   7   6   5   4   3   2   1

Source: R.B. Dunham and J.B. Herman, "Development of a Female Faces Scale for Measuring Job Satisfaction," Journal of Applied Psychology 60 (1975): 629–31.

A growing source of dissatisfaction for many lower-level and middle managers, as well as for nonmanagerial employees, is the threat of unemployment and increased workloads from organizational downsizings. A recent study of 4,300 workers conducted by Wyatt Co. found that 76 percent of the employees of expanding companies are satisfied with their jobs but only 57 percent of the employees of companies that have downsized are satisfied.[35] Organizations that try to improve their efficiency through restructuring often eliminate a sizable number of first-line and middle management positions. This decision obviously hurts the managers who are laid off, and it also can reduce the job satisfaction of managers who remain, who might fear that they will be the next to be let go. In addition, the workloads of remaining managers often are dramatically increased as a result of restructuring, which also can contribute to dissatisfaction.

organizational commitment The collection of feelings and beliefs that managers have about their organization as a whole.

ORGANIZATIONAL COMMITMENT Organizational commitment is the collection of feelings and beliefs that managers have about their organization as a whole. Managers who are committed to their organization believe in what their organization is doing, are proud of what the organization stands for, and feel a high degree of loyalty toward the organization. Committed managers are more likely to go above and beyond the call of duty to help their company and are less likely to quit.[36] The commitment of the senior partners at Bain & Company in the "Case in Contrast" resulted in their sticking with their organization through hard times, as did some IBM-lifers, who now are in CEO Lou Gerstner's inner circle.

Management Insight

Managerial Commitment at IBM

Despite all the turmoil, shake-ups, and layoffs at IBM (www.ibm.com), some managers remain committed to this organization and are seen by Lou Gerstner, IBM's chairman, as crucial for its future success. Although Gerstner has certainly brought in his share of outsiders to help turn around IBM, he also appears to realize what these committed managers who have been with IBM around 20 years can do for the company. Four such committed managers are Nicholas Donofrio, Ned Lautenbach, John Thompson, and Dennie Welsh, whom Gerstner recently promoted to more responsible positions.

Donofrio is the senior vice president of the server group, which focuses on large computer systems and mainframes. After receiving a bachelor's degree in electrical engineering and a master's in engineering, Donofrio joined IBM in 1967 as a technologist and chip designer. His accomplishments include cutting costs by millions of dollars and championing the use of new technology. However, his commitment to IBM includes a commitment to IBM's employees. When he had to tell the employees of IBM's mainframe facility in Kingston, New York, that the plant would close in a year, he got all choked up.

Lautenbach is the senior vice president for IBM's worldwide sales and has held many different jobs in marketing since his start as an IBM salesman in 1968. Thompson, senior vice president for the software division, first started at IBM as a systems engineer in 1966. Welsh, a corporate vice president in charge of IBM's consulting company, Integrated Systems Solutions Corp., began his IBM career as an engineer in 1966 working on the Apollo space program.[37]

In an era of reengineering and downsizing and in an era when managers sometimes seem to change organizations as much as they change jobs (through promotions or lateral moves), these committed managers almost seem too much of an anomaly. However, as Gerstner seems to think, they may be a necessary and crucial ingredient for IBM's future success, and their high levels of commitment may give IBM and its employees a needed bit of continuity in its time of rapid change.[38]

Organizational commitment also is likely to help managers perform some of their figurehead and spokesperson roles (see Chapter 1). It is likely to be

Figure 11.5

A Measure of Organizational Commitment

People respond to each of the items in the scale by checking whether they:
[ ] Strongly disagree   [ ] Slightly disagree   [ ] Slightly agree
[ ] Moderately disagree   [ ] Neither disagree nor agree [ ] Moderately agree
                                                               [ ] Strongly agree

____ 1. I am willing to put in a great deal of effort beyond that normally expected in order to help this organization be successful.

____ 2. I talk up this organization to my friends as a great organization to work for.

____ 3. I feel very little loyalty to this organization.*

____ 4. I would accept almost any type of job assignment in order to keep working for this organization.

____ 5. I find that my values and the organization's values are very similar.

____ 6. I am proud to tell others that I am part of this organization.

____ 7. I could just as well be working for a different organization as long as the type of work were similar.*

____ 8. This organization really inspires the very best in me in the way of job performance.

____ 9. It would take very little change in my present circumstances to cause me to leave this organization.*

____ 10. I am extremely glad that I chose this organization to work for over others I was considering at the time I joined.

____ 11. There's not too much to be gained by sticking with this organization indefinitely.*

____ 12. Often, I find it difficult to agree with this organization's policies on important matters relating to its employees.*

____ 13. I really care about the fate of this organization.

____ 14. For me this is the best of all possible organizations for which to work.

____ 15. Deciding to work for this organization was a definite mistake on my part.*

Scoring: Responses to items 1, 2, 4, 5, 6, 8, 10, 13, and 14 are scored such that 1 = strongly disagree; 2 = moderately disagree; 3 = slightly disagree; 4 = neither disagree nor agree; 5 = slightly agree; 6 = moderately agree; and 7 = strongly agree. Responses to "*" items 3, 7, 9, 11, 12, and 15 are scored 7 = strongly disagree; 6 = moderately disagree; 5 = slightly disagree; 4 = neither disagree nor agree; 3 = slightly agree; 2 = moderately agree; and 1 = strongly agree. Responses to the 15 items are averaged for an overall score from 1 to 7; the higher the score, the higher the level of organizational commitment.

Source: L. W. Porter and F. J. Smith, "Organizational Commitment Questionnaire," in J. D. Cook, S. J. Hepworth, T. D. Wall, and P. B. Warr, eds., *The Experience of Work: A Compendium and Review of 249 Measures and Their Use* (New York: Academic Press, 1981), 84–86.

much easier for a manager to persuade others both inside and outside the organization of the merits of what the organization has done and is seeking to accomplish if the manager truly believes in and is committed to the organization. Figure 11.5 is an example of a scale that managers can use to measure a person's level of organizational commitment.

Do managers in different countries have similar or different attitudes? Differences in levels of job satisfaction and organizational commitment among managers in different countries are likely because these managers have different kinds of opportunities and rewards and because they face different economic, political, or sociocultural forces in their organizations' general environments. In countries with relatively high unemployment rates, such as France, levels of job satisfaction may be higher among employed managers because they may be happy simply to have a job.

Levels of organizational commitment from one country to another may depend on the extent to which countries have legislation affecting firings and layoffs and the extent to which citizens of a country are geographically mobile. In both France and Germany legislation protects workers (including managers) from being fired or laid off. U.S. workers, in contrast, have very little protection. In addition, managers in the United States are more willing to relocate than managers in France and Germany. French citizens have relatively stronger family and community ties, and housing is expensive and difficult to find in Germany. For those reasons citizens in both countries tend to be less geographically mobile than Americans.[39] Managers who know that their jobs are secure and who are reluctant to relocate (such as those in Germany and France) may be more committed to their organizations than managers who know that their organizations could lay them off any day and who would not mind geographic relocations.

Moods

mood A feeling or state of mind.

Just as you sometimes are in a bad mood and at other times in a good mood, so too are managers. A **mood** is a feeling or state of mind. When people are in a positive mood, they feel excited, enthusiastic, active, or elated.[40] When people are in a negative mood, they feel distressed, fearful, scornful, hostile, jittery, or nervous.[41] People who are high on extroversion are especially likely to experience positive moods; people who are high on negative affectivity are especially likely to experience negative moods. Moods, however, are also determined by the situation or circumstances a person is in; receiving a raise is likely to put most people in a good mood regardless of their personality traits. People who are high on negative affectivity are not always in a bad mood, and people who are low on extroversion still experience positive moods.[42]

Research on the effects of mood on the behavior of managers and other members of an organization has just begun. Preliminary studies suggest that the subordinates of managers who experience positive moods at work may perform at somewhat higher levels and be less likely to resign and leave the organization than the subordinates of managers who do not tend to be in a positive mood at work.[43] Other research suggests that creativity might be enhanced by positive moods.[44]

Recognizing the benefits of positive moods, the Northbrook, Illinois, accounting firm of Lipschultz, Levin, & Gray goes to great lengths to promote positive feelings among its employees. Chief executive Steven Siegel claims that positive feelings promote relaxation and alleviate stress, increase revenues and attract clients, and reduce turnover. Positive moods are promoted in a variety of ways at Lipschultz, Levin, & Gray. Siegel has been known to put on a gorilla mask at especially busy times; clerks sometimes don chicken costumes; a foghorn announces the signing of a new client; employees can take a break and play miniature golf in the office, play darts, or exercise with a Hula-Hoop (even during tax time). A casual dress code also lightens things up at the firm. By all counts, positive moods seem to be paying off for this group of accountants, whose good feelings seem to be attracting new clients.

Patrick Corboy, president and chief executive of Austin Chemical, switched his account from a bigger firm to Lipschultz, Levin, & Gray because he found the people at the bigger firm to be "too stuffy and dour for us." Of the accountant William Finestone, who manages the Austin Chemical account, Corboy says the following: "[he] is a barrel of laughs . . . Bill not only solves our problems more quickly but he puts us at ease, too."[45]

Nevertheless, sometimes negative moods can have their advantages. Some studies suggest that critical thinking and devil's advocacy may be promoted by a negative mood, and sometimes especially accurate judgments may be made by managers in negative moods.[46]

Figure 11.6
A Measure of Positive and Negative Mood at Work

People respond to each item by indicating the extent to which the item descibes how they felt at work during the past week on the following scale:

1 = Very slightly or not at all   4 = Quite a bit
2 = A little   5 = Very much
3 = Moderately

_____ **1.** Active   _____ **7.** Enthusiastic

_____ **2.** Distressed   _____ **8.** Fearful

_____ **3.** Strong   _____ **9.** Peppy

_____ **4.** Excited   _____ **10.** Nervous

_____ **5.** Scornful   _____ **11.** Elated

_____ **6.** Hostile   _____ **12.** Jittery

Scoring: Responses to items 1, 3, 4, 7, 9, and 11 are summed for a positive mood score; the higher the score, the more positive mood is experienced at work. Responses to items 2, 5, 6, 8, 10, and 12 are summed for a negative mood score; the higher the score, the more negative mood is experienced at work.

Source: A. P. Brief, M. J. Burke, J. M. George, B. Robinson, and J. Webster, "Should Negative Affectivity Remain an Unmeasured Variable in the Study of Job Stress?" *Journal of Applied Psychology* 73 (1988): 193–98; M. J. Burke, A. P. Brief, J. M. George, L. Roberson, and J. Webster, "Measuring Affect at Work: Confirmatory Analyses of Competing Mood Structures with Conceptual Linkage to Cortical Regulatory Systems," *Journal of Personality and Social Psychology* 57 (1989): 1091–1102.

Managers and other members of an organization need to realize that how they feel affects how they treat others and how others respond to them, including their subordinates. For example, a subordinate may be more likely to approach a manager with a somewhat far-out but potentially useful idea if the subordinate thinks the manager is in a good mood. Likewise, when managers are in very bad moods, their subordinates might try to avoid them at all costs. Figure 11.6 is an example of a scale that managers can use to measure the extent to which a person experiences positive and negative moods at work.

Perceptions
Most people tend to think that the decisions managers make in organizations and the actions they take are the result of some "objective" determination of the issues involved and the surrounding situation. However, each manager's interpretation of a situation or even of another person is precisely that—an interpretation. For example, different managers may see the same nonconformist subordinate in different ways: One may see a creative maverick while another may see a troublemaker. Different managers may even view what appears to be an "objectively" negative event—such as declining sales of a major product line—in different ways: One may see it as a looming threat to the profitability of the division while another may view it as an important opportunity to revamp and reorient the product line to increase revenues and market share.

perception The process through which people select, organize, and interpret what they see, hear, touch, smell, and taste, to give meaning and order to the world around them.

Perception is the process through which people select, organize, and interpret sensory input—what they see, hear, touch, smell, and taste—to give meaning and order to the world around them.[47] All decisions and actions that managers take are based on their subjective perceptions. When these perceptions are relatively accurate—close to the true nature of what is actually being perceived—good decisions are likely to be made and appropriate actions taken. Managers of fast-food restaurant chains such as McDonald's, Pizza Hut, and Wendy's accurately perceived that their customers were becoming more health conscious in the 1980s and 1990s and added salad bars and low-fat entries to their menus. Managers at Kentucky Fried Chicken, Jack-in-the-Box, and Burger King took much longer to perceive this change in what customers wanted.

One reason why McDonald's is so successful is that its managers go to great lengths to make sure that their perceptions of what customers want are accurate. McDonald's has 4,700 restaurants outside the United States (including 1,070 in Japan, 694 in Canada, 550 in Britain, 535 in Germany, 411 in Australia, 314 in France, 23 in China, and 3 in Russia), which generate approximately $3.4 billion in annual revenues. Key to McDonald's success in these diverse markets are managers' efforts to perceive accurately a country's culture and taste in food and then to act on these perceptions. For instance, McDonald's serves veggie burgers in Holland and black currant shakes in Poland.[48]

When managers' perceptions are relatively inaccurate, managers are likely to make bad decisions and take inappropriate actions, which hurt organizational effectiveness. Bad decisions may range from providing products or services that customers do not want, to hiring unqualified people, to failing to promote top-performing subordinates, who subsequently decide to take their skills to competing organizations.

Factors that Influence Managerial Perception

Different managers' perceptions of the same person, event, or situation are likely to differ because the managers are different from each other. They differ in personality, values, attitudes, and moods. Each of these factors can influence the way someone perceives a situation. A manager who is high on openness to experience is likely to perceive a risky new venture as a positive opportunity; a manager who is low on openness to experience may perceive the same venture as a threat. A manager who has high levels of job satisfaction and organizational commitment may perceive a job transfer to another geographic location as an opportunity to learn and develop new skills; a dissatisfied, uncommitted manager may perceive the same transfer as a demotion and unwanted extra work.

Managers' perceptions also are affected by their past experience and acquired knowledge about or biases toward people, events, and situations. Suppose a manager's past experience of computer experts suggests that they are intelligent, quiet, shy, not very athletic, and somewhat eccentric. When introduced to a computer software developer at a party, this manager uses this information to form a perception of the developer. The information causes the manager to notice that the developer is dressed casually while other party goers are dressed up, to ignore the fact that the developer told a funny joke, to sense that the developer often seems to be at a loss for words, and to ignore the fact that the developer used to be a quarterback on his college's football team even though this accomplishment came up in conversation.

Although this example is a bit extreme, it does show how people tend to perceive other people and events and situations in ways that are consistent with their past knowledge and experience. Managers are as likely as any other member of an organization to do this. A manager who has had a bad experience launching new products might perceive a proposal for a new product more negatively than he should, because his past experience suggests that new product launches are risky and often doomed to failure. Similarly, a manager who has always been successful in her efforts to sell a domestically popular product in foreign countries might perceive that the product has great potential in India even though most of the available evidence suggests the opposite.

Ways to Ensure Accurate Perceptions

What can managers (and other organizational members) do to ensure that they perceive people and situations as they truly are? First, managers should try to be open to other points of view and perspectives.[49] Managers who are open to other perspectives put their own beliefs and knowledge to an important reality test and will be more inclined to modify or change them when necessary. Second, managers should not be afraid to change their views about a person, issue, or event. In the previous case of the manager who had negative experiences with new product launches, if other managers present convincing information that suggests a product looks like a winner, then the manager should not be afraid to reverse his position. In fact, reversing position and supporting a new product that turns out to be a best-seller will help the manager develop a more balanced and accurate perception of the potential for success in new product launches.

Tips for Managers

Perception

1. Be open to points of view and perspectives different from your own.
2. Seek out opinions from others who have had different kinds of experiences than yourself.
3. Do not be afraid to change your views about a person, issue, or event.
4. When you have made what turns out to be a bad decision or have not performed up to expectations, try to determine if your perceptions were faulty.

Career Development

Any discussion of managers as real people with their own thoughts and feelings, challenges and disappointments, requires a consideration of careers. Managers face several challenges both in the course of their own careers and in facilitating effective career management for their subordinates. A **career** is the sum total of work-related experiences throughout a person's

career The sum total of work-related experiences throughout a person's life.

life.[50] Careers encompass all of the different jobs people hold throughout their lives and the different organizations they work for. Careers are important to most people for at least two reasons. First, a career is a means to support one-self and one's loved ones, providing basic necessities and opportunities to pursue outside interests. Second, a career can be a source of personal fulfillment and meaning. Many managers find making a difference in an organization and helping improve organizational efficiency and effectiveness to be personally as well as financially rewarding.

linear career A career consisting of a sequence of jobs in which each new job entails additional responsibility, a greater impact on an organization, new skills, and upward movement in an organization's hierarchy.

The careers of some managers are called **linear careers.** A person whose career is linear moves through a sequence of jobs in which each new job entails additional responsibility, a greater impact on an organization, new skills, and upward movement in an organization's hierarchy.[51] Whether a manager stays with the same company or frequently switches organizations, a linear career traces a line of upward progress in the positions held.

The careers of Orit Gadiesh and Anne Sweeney, described in the "Case in Contrast," have been linear. Top managers in large corporations like Lou Gerstner, CEO of IBM, and George Fisher, CEO of Eastman Kodak, moved through a series of low-level positions in a variety of organizations before they became CEOs. Similarly, the assistant manager at the Red Lobster in College Station, Texas, started out in an entry-level position as a cashier. A linear career at Dillard's Department Stores may include the following sequencing of positions: executive trainee, area sales manager, assistant buyer, buyer, assistant store manager of merchandising, store manager, and divisional merchandise manager.[52] Managers' subordinates also may have linear careers, although some subordinates may have other types of careers.

steady-state career A career consisting of the same kind of job during a large part of an individual's work life.

Some managers choose to keep the same kind of job during a large part of their work life, often becoming highly skilled and expert in what they do. Such a career is called a **steady-state career.**[53] A talented and creative graphic artist at a magazine publishing company, for example, may turn down promotions into supervisory positions and other "opportunities" so that he can continue to design attractive magazine spreads and covers, which he really likes to do. Similarly, some managers at Dillard's have steady-state careers as area sales managers because they enjoy the direct supervision of salespeople and the opportunity to "stay close to" customers.

spiral career A career consisting of a series of jobs that build on each other but tend to be fundamentally different.

A third type of career is called a **spiral career** because the jobholder has a series of jobs that build on each other but tend to be fundamentally different.[54] A marketing manager in a large corporation who transfers to a job in public relations and then, after several years in that position, takes a job in an advertising firm has a spiral career. Those three jobs tend to be quite different from each other and do not necessarily entail increases in responsibility.

Stages in a Linear Career

Because linear careers are sequenced or progress toward more responsible or demanding kinds of jobs, it is not surprising that a number of stages commonly occur in many linear careers (see Figure 11.7).[55] In the remainder of this section we examine these stages and see what issues managers and non-managers face at each one.

PREPARATION FOR WORK During this stage, people decide what kind of career they desire and learn what qualifications and experiences they

Figure 11.7

Stages in a Linear Career

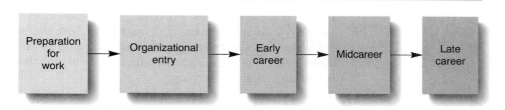

will need in order to pursue their chosen career.[56] Deciding on a career is no easy task and requires self-awareness and reflection. Sometimes people turn to professionals to help them discover the kinds of careers in which they are most likely to be happy. A person's personality, values, attitudes, and moods impact the initial choice of a career.[57]

After choosing a career area, a person must gain the knowledge, skills, and education necessary to get a good starting position. A person may need an undergraduate or graduate degree or may be able to acquire on-the-job training through an apprenticeship program (common in Germany and some other countries). Both Gadiesh and Sweeney, described in the "Case in Contrast," obtained master's degrees during the preparation-for-work stage of their careers. Gadiesh's was in business administration, Sweeney's in education.

ORGANIZATIONAL ENTRY   At this stage, people are trying to find a good first job. The effort requires the job seeker to identify potential opportunities in a variety of ways (such as reading advertisements, attending career/job fairs, and mining personal contacts), find out as much as possible about alternative positions, and make himself or herself an attractive candidate for prospective employers. Organizational entry is a more challenging stage for some kinds of careers than for others. An accounting major who knows she wants to work for a Big Five accounting firm already has a good idea of her opportunities and of how to make herself attractive to such firms. An English major who wants a career as an editor for a book publisher may find entry-level positions that seem a "good" start to such a career few and far between and may decide his best bet is to take a position as a sales representative for a well-respected publisher. More often than not, managers do not start out in management positions but rather begin their careers in an entry-level position in a department such as finance, marketing, or engineering.

EARLY CAREER   The early-career stage begins after a person obtains a first job in his or her chosen career. At this stage there are two important steps: establishment and achievement. *Establishment* means learning the ropes of one's new job and organization–learning, for example, specific job responsibilities and duties, expected and desired behaviors, and important values of other organizational members such as the boss.[58] A person who has acquired the basic know-how to perform a job and function in the wider organization is ready to take the second step. *Achievement* means making one's mark, accomplishing something noteworthy, or making an important contribution to the job or organization.[59]

The achievement step can be crucial for future career progression. It is a means of demonstrating one's potential and standing out from others who are aspiring to become managers and are competing for desired positions. Downsizing and restructuring have reduced the number of management positions at many large companies, making it very important for individuals to manage the early-career stage effectively and thus increase their chances of advancement. By identifying where and how you can make a truly significant contribution to an organization, you can enhance your career prospects both inside and outside the organization.

Increasing numbers of Americans at this stage are working abroad to make their significant achievements—in regions as diverse as eastern Europe, Southeast Asia, and Latin America and in cities such as Budapest and Hong Kong. And their bold decisions seem to be paying off. When Daniel Arbess was an associate at the prestigious New York law firm White & Case, he worked in the late 1980s and early 1990s in Czechoslovakia, trying to gain the legal account of Skoda Auto Company for his firm, and eventually he succeeded. Volkswagen subsequently invested $6.4 billion in Skoda, greatly increasing the volume of Skoda's legal work, which White & Case was asked to perform. Arbess's work overseas not only enabled him to make a significant achievement at the early-career stage but also earned him the position of partner at White & Case. At the age of 33, he was the youngest partner in the history of the firm.[60]

mentor An experienced member of an organization who provides advice and guidance to a less-experienced worker.

Some people find that the assistance of a mentor can be a valuable asset at the early-career and subsequent stages. A **mentor** is an experienced member of an organization who provides advice and guidance to a less-experienced worker (the protégé, or mentee). The help that a mentor provides can range from advice about handling a tricky job assignment, dealing with a disagreement with a supervisor, and what kind of subsequent positions to strive for, to information about appropriate behavior and what to wear in various situations. Mentors often seek out protégés, but individuals also can be proactive and try to enlist the help of a potential mentor. Generally, especially good potential mentors are successful managers who have had a variety of experiences, genuinely desire to help junior colleagues, and are interpersonally compatible with the would-be-protégé. Research has found that receiving help from a mentor is associated with an increase in pay, pay satisfaction, promotion, and feeling good about one's accomplishments.[61]

Michael Eisner, chairman of Walt Disney Co., is a manager who throughout his career has consistently made job and organizational contributions that have singled him out as a person who would rise to the top. Here he is pictured at the dedication ceremonies of DisneyWorld's new theme park, Animal Kingdom.

MIDCAREER   The midcareer stage generally occurs when people have been in the workforce between 20 and 35 years. Different managers experience this stage in quite different ways. For Anita Roddick, CEO of The Body Shop, Michael Eisner, CEO of Walt Disney Company, and Jack Smith, CEO of General Motors, the midcareer stage is a high point—a time of major accomplishment and success. The midcareer is also a time of success and major achievement for Gadiesh and Sweeney. Sweeney arrived at this stage quite early, being just 36 when she accepted the chief executive position at FX.

For other managers, the midcareer stage is a letdown because their career plateaus. Managers reach a **career**

career plateau
A position from which the chances of being promoted or obtaining a more responsible job are slight.

plateau when their chances of being promoted into a higher position in their current organizations or of obtaining a more responsible position in another organization dwindle.[62] Some managers inevitably will experience a career plateau because fewer and fewer managerial positions are available as one moves up an organization's hierarchy. In some organizations upper-level positions are especially scarce because of downsizing and restructuring.

Plateaued managers who are able to come to terms with their situation can continue to enjoy their work and make important contributions to their organization. Some plateaued managers, for example, welcome lateral moves, which give them the chance to learn new things and contribute in different ways to the organization. Some find being a mentor especially appealing and a chance to share their wisdom and make a difference for someone just starting out in their field.

LATE CAREER   This stage lasts as long as a person continues to work and has an active career. Many managers remain productive at this stage and show no signs of slowing down. William Dillard, the founder of Dillard's Department Stores, and Gwen Mellon, a major fund-raiser and supporter of the Albert Schweitzer Hospital in Haiti, are well into their 80s, and Joan and David Helpern, the founders of Joan & David shoe stores, are in their 70s.[63]

Effective Career Management

Managers face the challenge of ensuring not only that they have the kind of career they personally desire but also that effective career management exists for all employees in their organization. **Effective career management** means that at all levels in the organization there are well-qualified workers who can assume more responsible positions as needed and that as many members of the organization as possible are highly motivated and satisfied with their jobs and careers. As you might imagine, effectively managing careers in a whole organization is no easy task, and in subsequent chapters we focus on many of the issues involved in managing a highly motivated workforce. At this point, however, it is useful to discuss two important foundations of effective career management in any organization: a commitment to ethical career practices and accommodations for workers' multidimensional lives.

effective career management Ensuring that at all levels in the organization there are well-qualified workers who can assume more responsible positions as needed.

COMMITMENT TO ETHICAL CAREER PRACTICES   In Chapter 5 we discussed the importance of managers behaving ethically and of an organization's commitment to ethics, social responsibility, and diversity. It bears repeating here. Ethical career practices are one of the most important ingredients to effective career management and, at a basic level, rest on honesty, trust, and open communication among organizational members. Ethical career practices include basing promotions on performance, not on irrelevant considerations such as personal friendships and ties, and ensuring that diverse members of an organization receive the career opportunities they deserve. Supervisors must never abuse their power to make career decisions affecting others and must never behave unethically to advance their own careers. Managers at all levels must abide by and be committed to ethical career practices and actively demonstrate this commitment; they must communicate that violation of these practices will not be tolerated; and they must make sure that organizational members who feel that they were not ethically treated can communicate their concerns without fear of retaliation.

ACCOMMODATIONS FOR WORKERS' MULTIDIMENSIONAL LIVES   Effectively managing careers also means being sensitive to and providing accommodations for the multiple demands that many organizational members face. The dual-career couple is now the norm rather than the exception, the number of single parents is at an all-time high, and more and more midcareer workers are needing to care for their elderly and infirm parents. By, for example, limiting unnecessary moves and travel, adopting flexible work arrangements and schedules, providing on-site day care, and allowing workers to take time off to care for children or elderly parents, managers make it possible for workers to have satisfying and productive careers while fulfilling their other commitments.

Ernst & Young, for example, gives workers the choice of part-time work or flex-time work (full-time work scheduled to be convenient for a worker's personal life). Workers who have taken advantage of these options at Ernst & Young include Keeca, who switched to a flexible schedule (flex-time work) after adopting three children ranging in age from 4 to 9; Nancy, who has a new daughter and works three days in the office and is available on an as-needed basis at home the other two days; and Al, whose flex-time work allows him to help out at his son's cooperative preschool.[64] By making accommodations for workers' multidimensional lives, managers not only help organizational members to have satisfying and productive careers but also help the organization to achieve its goals.

Careers are as important for managers' subordinates as they are for managers themselves. Understanding the many issues involved in effectively managing careers helps ensure that both managers and their subordinates will have the kinds of careers they want while helping an organization achieve its goals.

stress A condition that individuals experience when they face important opportunities or threats and are uncertain about their ability to handle or deal with them effectively.

Stress
To round out the picture of managers as feeling and thinking human beings, we turn now to a challenge that both managers and nonmanagers face throughout their careers and lives–stress. People experience **stress** when they face important opportunities or threats and are uncertain about their ability to handle or deal with them effectively.[65] The nature of managerial jobs almost ensures that managers experience stress. Many opportunities in an organization and in the task and general environments give managers a chance to improve their organization's efficiency and effectiveness, and many threats jeopardize an organization's success and even survival. Whether a manager can successfully take advantage of opportunities and overcome threats is often uncertain. This uncertainty makes management a stressful business.

Consequences of Stress
High levels of stress can take a toll on managers. Stress can be especially damaging when it lasts for a long time. Although reactions to stress differ across individuals, one way to understand the effect that incessant stress can have on managers is by considering the physiological, psychological, and behavioral consequences of stress.

PHYSIOLOGICAL CONSEQUENCES Physiological consequences of stress range from mild to severe. Sleep disturbances, sweaty palms, feeling flushed, headaches, stomachaches, backaches, and nausea are some physical reactions to stress, as are high blood pressure, heart attacks, and impaired functioning of the immune system. The relationship between levels of stress and these physiological consequences is complicated.[66] Some people tend to experience more of these physiological consequences than others, and different people experience different kinds of consequences. What does seem to be clear is that the most severe consequences of stress, such as high blood pressure and heart attacks, are likely to occur only when excessive levels of stress are experienced over an extended period of time.

PSYCHOLOGICAL CONSEQUENCES You are probably quite familiar with some of the psychological consequences of stress—being in a bad mood, feeling nervous, angry, or upset, or feeling scornful, bitter, or hostile.[67] These negative feelings carry over into work attitudes such as lower levels of job satisfaction and organizational commitment. At some point all workers are likely to experience these psychological consequences. When stress levels become too high for too long a time, however, these negative feelings can become overwhelming.

BEHAVIORAL CONSEQUENCES How can managers perform their many and varied duties when they are experiencing stress, especially given the stressful nature of their jobs? Stress does not necessarily impair job performance and in some cases actually enhances it. Just as the stress you may experience before an exam energizes you to study, or the stress a worker experiences trying to meet a tight deadline pushes him or her to make more efficient use of time, so too can the stress managers experience push them to do a good job. Facing an important opportunity to increase sales often propels marketing managers to develop innovative marketing campaigns that appeal to different segments of the customer base. The threat posed by the opening of a new Mexican restaurant a block away from what had been the only Mexican restaurant in a small college town may encourage the manager of the older restaurant to make some needed changes in the menu and run some advertised specials in the local newspaper, and those steps may result in the restaurant being busier than it ever was before the new restaurant appeared on the scene. In these cases, stress has positive effects on performance.

Nevertheless, stress sometimes impairs performance. A student who experiences test anxiety draws a blank on material that she knew well the day before the exam. The manager of a dry cleaning store who forgets to turn off the presses one day before closing the shop because he is consumed with worry over dwindling profits is not functioning up to his usual level because of too much stress.

One way to understand the seemingly contradictory effects that stress can and does have on people's functioning and performance is to picture the relationship between stress and performance as an inverted U (see Figure 11.8). Stress up to a certain point (point A in the figure) is positive in that it propels people to do their best. Once this point is reached, however, stress becomes negative; increases in stress detract from performance and are dysfunctional. When stress impairs performance, many people also experience some of the physiological and psychological consequences of stress.

Figure 11.8
The Inverted-U Relationship Between Stress and Performance

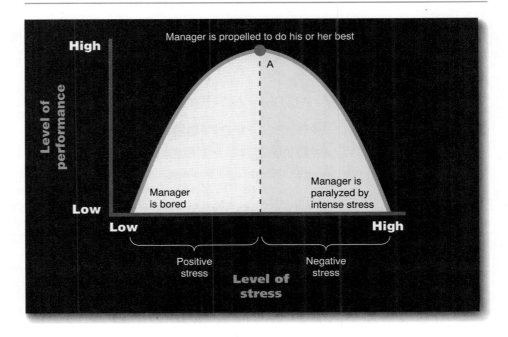

Manager is propelled to do his or her best

High

A

Level of performance

Manager is bored

Low

Manager is paralyzed by intense stress

Low   High

Positive stress   Negative stress

Level of stress

Sources of Managerial Stress

role conflict The conflict or friction that occurs when expected behaviors are at odds with each other.

There are many sources of managerial stress—individuals' jobs, organizations, and personal lives. Two particularly common sources within the workplace are *role conflict* and *role overload*. In Chapter 1 we described the multiple roles that managers play, such as spokesperson and figurehead (see Table 1.1). In performing these roles, managers are expected to demonstrate certain behaviors. **Role conflict** occurs when there is conflict or friction between expected behaviors.[68] In performing the roles of spokesperson and information disseminator, managers may find their responsibility to transmit accurate information to be at odds with their responsibility to promote a positive image for the organization in the eyes of the public. In performing the roles of leader and resource allocator, managers may experience conflict between their responsibility to motivate organizational members and reward high performance and their responsibility to allocate scarce resources (including money for raises and bonuses).

Managers also may experience conflict between their role responsibilities at work and in their personal lives. Edward G. Harshfield, chief executive of California Federal Bank, and his wife, Terry Savage, a financial columnist, author, and television commentator, both have successful and satisfying careers (Harshfield has been known to wear a T-shirt that says "Male Underachiever Married to Female Overachiever").[69] However, their multiple responsibilities at work necessitate that Savage live in Chicago and Harshfield in Los Angeles, and the conflict between work responsibilities and their desire to live together is sometimes a source of stress for them. Similarly, in the "Case in Contrast," Anne Sweeney experiences stress from her sometimes conflicting responsibilities as a top-level manager and a parent.

role overload The condition of having too many responsibilities and activities to perform.

Role overload occurs when managers have too many responsibilities and activities to perform.[70] At this point you might be thinking that role overload is part and parcel of most managers' jobs. Managers do have multiple responsibilities, and at times these can become excessive, resulting in high levels of stress. The next "Management Insight" describes the effect of role overload on Neil Rudenstine, president of Harvard University.

Management Insight

Role Overload Downs Harvard President

The academic and business communities were surprised when Neil Rudenstine, Harvard University's (www.harvard.com) highly esteemed president, took a medical leave of absence due to extreme exhaustion and fatigue in November 1994.[71] Other university administrators, however, were not really surprised. Judith Rodin, president of the University of Pennsylvania, sympathized with Rudenstine, knowing full well the rigors of the job: Rodin's daily schedule is completely booked six months in advance (14 hours a day). In addition to running a large university, she also attends committee and staff meetings, goes to football games, receptions, and alumni activities, and serves on the boards of the Philadelphia area Chamber of Commerce and association of top executives.

Prior to his leave, Rudenstine had a very heavy schedule. A typical day might include a meeting with deans and university development staff, lunch with Russian dignitaries, additional meetings with deans, faculty meetings, student and alumni receptions, and dinner with a student group. According to Rudenstine, Harvard's $2.1 billion, five-year fund-raising drive required him to raise practically $1 million per day. Dr. Robert Rosenzweig, who is writing a book about university presidents, suggests that overload is the norm rather than the exception for these top-ranking administrators. Moreover, they face considerable role conflict, for the multiple stakeholders in a university—faculty, students, alumni, benefactors, administrators—often disagree about what is best for the university. Presidents often have to make decisions that will alienate one or more of these groups. Rudenstine, for example, was very troubled when Harvard's faculty was in an uproar over health care and pension reductions that he made to cut costs; he feared that the professors no longer had confidence in him.

Although overload and role conflict are inherent in jobs such as Rudenstine's, insiders at Harvard suggest that his attention to detail and reluctance to delegate work to others may have contributed to his high stress level. He personally chaired the tenure process for practically every professor at Harvard, a responsibility that took a full day per week of his time. Robert Clark, dean of Harvard's Law School, suggested that Rudenstine had a tough time saying "no" to requests for his input and time and often did not get enough sleep at night.[72]

Stress appears to have taken its toll on Rudenstine, but there are steps that managers can take to effectively deal with high stress levels.

Coping with Stress

problem-focused coping The actions people take to deal directly with the source of their stress.

emotion-focused coping The actions people take to deal with their stressful feelings and emotions.

People manage or deal with stress in two basic ways: problem-focused coping and emotion-focused coping. **Problem-focused coping** is the actions people take to deal directly with the source of their stress.[73] If Rudenstine had turned down some of the invitations he had received for student receptions or had agreed to a provost's suggestion to share the chairing of tenure proceedings, he would have been engaging in problem-focused coping by reducing his role overload. **Emotion-focused coping** is the actions people take to deal with their stressful feelings and emotions.[74] If Rudenstine had regularly meditated at the end of each day to relieve some of his built-up tension, he would have been engaging in emotion-focused coping.

Although individuals may cope with stress somewhat differently, here we look at two problem-focused strategies (time management and getting help from a mentor) and three emotion-focused strategies (exercise, meditation, and social support) that managers can use. We also look at how emotional intelligence may help managers cope with stress as well as be more effective.

PROBLEM-FOCUSED COPING

TIME MANAGEMENT   Time management can be an especially useful strategy for managers trying to cope with numerous and sometimes conflicting demands. Time management includes various techniques that help people to make better use of, and accomplish more with, their time: making lists of what needs to be accomplished in a certain relatively short time period (such as a day or week), prioritizing tasks to clarify which ones are most important and which ones could be delegated or put off, and estimating how long it will take to accomplish tasks and dividing one's day(s) accordingly.[75]

GETTING HELP FROM A MENTOR   Seeking the advice and guidance of a mentor can be an effective problem-focused strategy for managers at all levels. A mentor is likely to have faced a problem (threat or opportunity) similar to the problem the manager is currently facing and thus will be in a good position to comment on what are especially effective or ineffective ways of dealing with it. In any case, receiving advice from someone who has had more experience and also is less personally involved in the issue at hand can be helpful.

EMOTION-FOCUSED COPING

EXERCISE   Many managers jog, swim, or use exercise machines such as Nordic Tracks, rowing machines, or treadmills in their homes or offices. Physical exercise is among the most effective ways to deal with stressful feelings and emotions. Regular exercise also can improve cardiovascular functioning and contribute to a general sense of well-being and relaxation.

MEDITATION   Temporarily putting everyday cares aside by being in a quiet environment and focusing on some soothing mental or visual image or verbal phrase also can be an effective means of emotion-focused coping.[76] Akin to meditation are special breathing techniques that can be used to combat stressful feelings. In Japan, many managers practice special breathing techniques (such as breathing slowly and shallowly) in a variety of positions (such as standing, bending, and squatting) to improve their *Ki,* or life force and energy. They believe that doing this improves their health and stamina, alleviates stress, and allows them to remain in control and even to stay youthful.[77]

Employees at Netscape, the internet software company, play rollerblade hockey to help them relax after an intense day keeping Netscape on track in its ongoing battle with Microsoft to be the dominant internet browser provider.

social support

Emotional support provided by other people such as friends, relatives, and coworkers.

SOCIAL SUPPORT   There is more than a grain of truth in the old saying that sometimes all you need is a shoulder to cry on. **Social support,** the availability of other people (such as friends, relatives, coworkers, or supervisors) to talk to, discuss problems with, or receive advice from, can alleviate stressful feelings and emotions.[78] Managers often seek social support from their families or from coworkers in similar kinds of positions. Mentors also can be a good source of social support as well as practical advice for dealing with actual sources of stress.

When coping is successful, opportunities and threats responsible for stress are dealt with directly and stressful feelings and emotions do not get out of hand. Sometimes when people are unable to cope effectively with the stress they are experiencing, help from a trained expert such as a psychologist can be beneficial.

emotional intelligence The ability to understand and manage one's own moods and emotions and the moods and emotions of other people.

EMOTIONAL INTELLIGENCE   In addition to problem-focused and emotion-focused coping, emotional intelligence also helps managers cope with stress. **Emotional intelligence** is the ability to understand and manage one's own moods and emotions and the moods and emotions of other people.[79] Managers with a high level of emotional intelligence are more likely to understand how they are feeling and why, and are more able to effectively manage their feelings. When managers are experiencing stressful feelings and emotions such as fear or anxiety, emotional intelligence enables them to understand why and manage these feelings so that they do not get in the way of effective decision making.[80]

Emotional intelligence also can help managers perform their interpersonal roles (figurehead, leader, and liaison) and many of their other important roles. Understanding how subordinates feel, why they feel that way, and how to manage these feelings is central to developing strong interpersonal bonds with them. Daniel Goleman, a psychologist and former reporter for the *New York Times,* suggests that emotional intelligence is often an important ingredient for managerial success at all levels in an organization.[81]

Tips for Managers

Career **Issues and Stress**

1. Make sure that promotions in your organization are based on performance levels.

2. Take active steps to accommodate workers' multidimensional lives whenever possible.

3. If you are experiencing especially high levels of stress, try to make better use of your time, ask for advice from others who have been in similar situations, and consider trying to cut back on or delegating some of your less important responsibilities.

4. If you often feel anxious, nervous, worried, upset, or angry, consider exercising more regularly or try to find some alternative way to cope with your stressful feelings such as meditation or involvement in a hobby or leisure activity.

Summary and Review

Chapter Summary

ENDURING CHARACTERISTICS: PERSONALITY TRAITS

- **The Big Five Personality Traits**

- **Other Personality Traits that Affect Managerial Behavior**

PERSONALITY TRAITS Personality traits are enduring tendencies to feel, think, and act in certain ways. The Big Five general traits are extroversion, negative affectivity, agreeableness, conscientiousness, and openness to experience. Other personality traits that affect managerial behavior are locus of control, self-esteem, and the needs for achievement, affiliation, and power.

VALUES, ATTITUDES, AND MOODS A terminal value is a personal conviction about lifelong goals or objectives; an instrumental value is a personal conviction about modes of conduct. Terminal and instrumental values have an impact on what managers try to achieve in their organization and the kinds of behaviors they engage in. An attitude is a collection of feelings and beliefs. Two attitudes important for understanding managerial behaviors include job satisfaction (the collection of feelings and beliefs that managers have about their jobs) and organizational commitment (the collection of feelings and beliefs that managers have about their organization). A mood is a feeling or state of mind. Managers' moods, or how they feel at work on a day-to-day basis, have the potential to impact their own behavior and effectiveness as well as their subordinates'.

PERCEPTIONS   Perception, the process through which managers select, organize, and interpret sensory input to give meaning and order to the world around them, is inherently subjective. Managers' personalities, values, attitudes, moods, knowledge, and past experience all have the potential to influence their perceptions. Accurate perceptions are a necessary ingredient for making good decisions.

CAREER DEVELOPMENT   A career is the sum total of work-related experiences throughout a person's life. The stages in a linear career are preparation for work, organizational entry, early career, midcareer, and late career. Managers face different tasks and challenges at each stage. Managers not only have to manage their own careers but also have to ensure that effective career management exists in their organizations. Effective career management means that at all levels in the organization there are well-qualified workers who can assume more responsible positions and that as many members of an organization as possible are highly motivated and satisfied with their jobs and careers. Important foundations for effective career management are a commitment to ethical career practices and accommodations for workers' multidimensional lives.

STRESS   People experience stress when they face important opportunities or threats and are uncertain about their ability to handle or deal with them effectively. Stress has physiological, psychological, and behavioral consequences. Two common sources of managerial stress are role conflict and role overload. People manage or deal with stress in two basic ways. Problem-focused coping strategies for managers include time management and getting help from a mentor. Emotion-focused coping strategies for managers include exercise, meditation, and social support. Emotional intelligence helps managers cope with stress as well as perform their roles effectively.

Management in Action

Topics for Discussion and Action

1. Discuss why managers who have different types of personalities can be equally effective and successful.

2. Interview a manager in a local organization. Ask the manager to describe situations in which he or she is especially likely to act in accordance with his or her values. Ask the manager to describe situations in which he or she is less likely to act in accordance with his or her values.

3. Can managers be too satisfied with their jobs? Can they be too committed to their organizations? Why or why not?

4. Assume that you are a manager of a restaurant. Describe what it is like to work for you when you are in a negative mood.

5. Develop guidelines for managers to use to ensure that their perceptions are as accurate as possible.

6. Discuss why a successful middle manager might turn down a promotion to an upper-level management position.

7. Describe the steps that organizations can take to help managers and nonmanagers alike effectively cope with stress.

Building Management Skills

Diagnosing Stress

Everybody experiences stress in their daily lives. Think about your own life and the extent to which you are currently experiencing stress. Then answer the following questions.

1. What are the sources of the stress that you are currently experiencing?

2. Are you experiencing any physiological, psychological, or behavioral consequences of stress? If so, describe these consequences.

3. In what problem-focused ways are you coping with stress? Are these helping you deal with the sources of your stress?

4. In what emotion-focused ways are you coping with stress? Are these helping you deal with your stressful feelings and emotions?

5. Can you think of any other problem-focused and emotion-focused coping techniques that may help you deal with the stress that you are currently experiencing?

Small Group Breakout Exercise

Coping with Managerial Stress in Hard Times

Form groups of three or four people, and appoint one member as the spokesperson who will communicate your findings to the whole class when called on by the instructor. Then discuss the following scenario.

You are the top-management team of a medium-size company that manufactures cardboard boxes, containers, and other kinds of cardboard packaging materials. Your company is facing increasing levels of competition for major corporate customer accounts. In an effort to cut costs and remain competitive, your company recently downsized. Approximately 25 percent of the production workers were laid off, 30 percent of the first-line managers, and 40 percent of the middle managers. You anticipated how stressful the downsizing would be for the production workers and took the appropriate steps to help both those who were laid off and those who kept their jobs cope effectively with the stress they were experiencing. However, you did not anticipate the high levels of stress that the first-line managers and the middle managers appear to be experiencing. The workloads of these managers have increased substantially, they are facing many changes in their and their subordinates' jobs, some have reported feeling guilty that coworkers were laid off, and their own sense of job security has been shattered. You are meeting today to address this problem.

1. Describe the likely sources of stress for the first-line managers.

2. Describe the likely sources of stress for the middle managers.

3. Develop a plan of action to help the first-line managers effectively cope with the stress they are experiencing.

4. Develop a plan of action to help the middle managers effectively cope with the stress they are experiencing.

Exploring the World Wide Web

Specific Assignment

Many companies take active steps to ensure that their employees behave in an ethical manner. One such company is Lockheed Martin. Scan Lockheed Martin's website to learn more about this company (http://www.lmco.com/). Click on "About Lockheed Martin" and then on "Ethics." Read the various documents available

1. Which values does Lockheed Martin encourage its employees to abide by?

2. How might the availability of ethics officers and ethics helplines influence employees' work attitudes and moods?

General Assignment

Find the website of a company that is undertaking initiatives to enhance levels of job satisfaction or organizational commitment among employees. What are those initiatives? Do you think they will be successful in promoting job satisfaction or organizational commitment? Why or why not?

ManagementCase

Stamina: Who Has It, Why It's Important, and How to Get It

Top managers put in longer hours and sleep less than most of us. For example, Ray Smith, CEO of Bell Atlantic, works 70 hours a week and averages $6^1/_2$ hours of sleep per night; Herb Kelleher, CEO of Southwest Airlines, works 90 and sleeps 5, Bill Gates, CEO of Microsoft, works 60 and sleeps 6, and Tony O'Reilly, CEO of H. J. Heinz, works 80 and sleeps 5. How do they do it? They have stamina—a seemingly endless amount of energy that enables them to do more with less sleep than most people can do each day.[82]

Stamina is not important just for managers at the top of an organization. Managers at all levels are under increasing pressure to take on more responsibility. Corporate downsizing and restructuring often double the workload of those remaining. An increasingly global economy is increasing the need to travel and communicate with associates around the world. And developments such as electronic communication and voice mail are keeping managers constantly informed and in touch. On a typical day, public relations manager Pam Alexander may rush from a press conference in California to the airport to travel to London for another press conference.

People with high levels of stamina seem to be especially optimistic about the future. William Morgan, who is director of the Sport Psychology Laboratory at the University of Wisconsin, suggests that people who are high on the personality trait of extroversion may be at somewhat of

an advantage when it comes to stamina. He has found that when people are asked to perform stressful exercises in his laboratory, extroverts often describe the exercises as easier and less painful than introverts. Extroverts also may be more likely to derive support from those around them because of their outgoing nature.

Nevertheless, many extroverts might not have the stamina of some highly successful managers. How can people in general boost their stamina so that they too can gain an extra day for work or leisure per week by getting more done each day? You might not actually want to cut back too much on your sleep. Although some people are probably born with the ability to function on little sleep, sleep experiments have found that people generally tend to sleep eight hours a day, even when they are kept away from radio and TVs, clocks, windows, and anything else that would let them know whether it is night or day and what time it is. Timothy Monk, sleep researcher and professor at the University of Pittsburgh Medical Center, suggests that some people probably can comfortably cut back to around six hours a night (preferably with a 20-minute nap during the day).[83] Further cuts in sleep time might actually hurt a manager's ability to perform because lack of sleep can impair memory and short-term judgment, often without people being aware of what is happening.

Diet seems to have a considerable impact on stamina. Fatty foods are hard to digest and rob

blood from the brain, causing sleepiness. Alcohol also robs one of stamina by dehydrating the body of important fluids and disturbing sleep. Ideally, two-thirds of one's diet should be composed of complex carbohydrates (grains, fruits, and vegetables). Carbohydrates increase levels of serotonin (nature's own tranquilizer) in the brain. If you are nervous during the day, a high-carbohydrate lunch can help calm you, but if you are already relaxed, you might want to indulge in 4 ounces of protein at lunchtime to be at your peak energy level the rest of the day.

Exercise is also a key contributor to stamina. Sports psychologist James Loehr suggests a routine of 100 stomach crunches (a variant of the sit-up entailing lying on the floor with your knees bent and lifting your shoulders a few inches from the floor). Loehr says that stomach crunches help one's posture and respiratory functioning, which contribute to stamina (and confidence as well). Interval training in which you raise and lower your heartbeat by, for example, running or cycling at different speeds also contributes to stamina. Loehr has helped speed skater Dan Jansen, tennis stars Jim Courier and Arantxa Sanchez Vicario, and boxer Ray Mancini increase their stamina and lower their levels of debilitating stress.

With all this advice, what about managers like Herb Kelleher, who, at age 63, smokes cigarettes, eats chicken-fried steak, and has been known to indulge in Wild Turkey and the likes? Kelleher's energy and long working hours and the fact that he often has time left over for socializing are truly phenomenal.[84] Maybe he and others like him were just born with an exceptional amount of stamina. For the rest of us, diet and exercise might help.

Questions

1. Why might being high on the extroversion continuum contribute to stamina?

2. Might a manager with a lot of stamina nevertheless succumb to some of the negative consequences of too much stress? Why or why not?

3. What can organizations do to help their members increase their stamina?

4. What are some of the potential personal costs of working 60 or more hours per week?

ManagementCase

In the News

From the Pages of BusinessWeek
Mr. House Finds His Fixer-Upper

When David L. House left Intel Corp. in 1996 to head struggling Bay Networks Inc., it looked like career suicide. But after 22 years as a rising star at Intel, including 12 years as head of its core microprocessor business, House hankered to run his own show. And Intel CEO Andrew S. Grove had already made it plain that House would not succeed him. "It was time for Dave to go out and lead," says Marty Ruberry, a long-time friend and racquetball partner.

If any company ever needed a leader, it was Bay Networks. Formed from the uneasy 1994 merger of two smaller companies, the $2 billion maker of computer networking gear was deeply troubled when House took charge. While industry leader Cisco Systems Inc. grew fivefold, Bay missed product launches and lost market share. Employees defected in droves while the leadership vacuum, says House, "spiraled down" to "almost chaos and anarchy." Worse

yet, customers were losing faith. When DreamWorks SKG networking director Petrus Wilson suggested buying Bay gear last year, his boss just "looked at me cross-eyed," he recalls.

No longer. In 15 months at the helm, House, 54, has thoroughly revived Bay with a series of savvy acquisitions and the strict imposition of Intel-like management discipline. These days, investors and customers alike—including DreamWorks—are elated with the hard-charging exec, who is so full of energy that his Intel colleagues once gave him a T-shirt reading "Captain Adrenaline." Says Prudential Securities analyst Luke T. Szymczak: "People thought this company was on its deathbed a year ago, and just look at what he's done."

A driven manager, House trained at the knee of Grove and survived years of Intel's rough-and-tumble culture. He's proud of his endurance and self-control, boasting that on a recent business trip he held seven meetings

in nine hours, did more business on his car phone, and then attended a dinner. "He's a very disciplined guy and very orderly in the way he goes about things," Grove says.

Tall and fit, House also exudes a confidence honed from years as Intel's smoothest front man at countless public events. Yet those who have worked with him describe House as unpretentious and down-to-earth. He regularly eats lunch in the company cafeteria and even led the staff in the macarena at Bay's recent holiday party in San Francisco. Last July, he ran around Bay's summer barbecue in a raincoat, dousing employees with a squirt gun, says sales and marketing Vice-President Dave Shrigley.

More than mere antics, these gestures have gone miles to revitalize Bay's once dispirited staff. Indeed, the company is off to a sizzling start in fiscal 1998: Earnings rose to $89 million for the first half, up from a $167 million loss last year. For the full year ending June 30, Wall Street expects profits to hit $243 million, on 28% sales growth, to $2.7 billion. Optimism about 1998 helped double Bay's stock from 20, when House took over, to 42 last October, though it has since fallen, along with other technology stocks, to around 30 on fears of an Asia-led industry slowdown.

To get those kinds of results, the hyperkinetic House dug down to the roots of Bay's malaise, sending out teams of execs to interview customers and employees. To boost morale for nonexecutive employees, he reset the price of Bay's stock options to $19.50—well below the elevated level many were stuck with before Bay's stock tanked. And he taught his own classes in management skills to 120 top executives. The result: Turnover has dropped by nearly half, from 27% annually a year ago to a more typical Silicon Valley rate of about 16% now.

Next, House broadened Bay's product line. Last June, he nabbed Rapid City, one of a dozen startups pioneering ultrafast "gigabit" switches. Meantime, Bay's 1996 acquisition of Netics has paid huge dividends with a hot-selling network switch that is handily beating out Cisco and 3Com Corp. "It was a grand slam," says analyst Noel P. Lindsay of Deutsch Morgan Grenfell.

House is just as intense at play as he is at work. A fastidious dresser known for his tailored suits, House schedules his life down to the minute. He exercises five mornings a week at 6 A.M. sharp—three days of weight lifting with a personal trainer and two days of racquetball. He plays so rough that he has sent five opponents to the doctor for stitches, says friend and Intel Vice-President Michael Aymar. A helicopter skiing fanatic, House prides himself on battling the mountain from dawn until dusk: "I've never quit before the chopper did." Grove, a skiing buddy with whom he remains on friendly terms, quips that House is "a wild skier—far more guts than skill."

That may be true on the slopes. But in life, House has always had plenty of both. "Dave always seemed to know what he was doing," says his father, Norman. One of four children in a working-class family in Muskegon, Mich., House hustled for extra cash—shoveling snow in the winter or reading utility meters in the summer. He contemplated a career in mechanical engineering until a high school teacher convinced him that the future lay in electronics.

After earning degrees in engineering he went to work for Honeywell Inc. as a computer designer. Then in 1971, his boss posted a clipping about a new microprocessor from a small California chipmaker. House understood immediately that the chip, called the Intel 8008, would transform computers by radically reducing their cost and size.

House eventually joined the scrappy upstart in 1974 as a technical marketing manager. As Intel's fortunes soared, so did House's career. With a knack for translating technical jargon into snappy phrases even nontechies could understand, by 1976 he was named marketing manager for microprocessors. During his tenure, Intel grew from $68 million to $20 billion in revenue and House presided over the launch of every major chip from the 286 to the Pentium. One of his greatest successes came when he devised the slogan "Intel Inside" in 1991, helping to establish it as one of the world's best-known brands.

For all his achievements, though, House was passed over for the top job when Grove decided the same year to give the nod to operations guru Craig E. Barrett. Intel had become a manufacturing powerhouse, and that wasn't House's forte. Always the trooper, he stayed on as a top corporate strategist until he left to run Bay.

In part because of his grueling schedule, House says, his two marriages have ended in divorce. With two grown children and a stepson, he likes to indulge in grand gestures, like splurging on a two-week Mediterranean cruise for 11 family members and pals. Once, he even took both his ex-wife and future wife shopping together and wound up buying each a piano. "He does things 120%," says Ruberry.

Cruises aren't likely to be on House's 1998 calendar. He'll be working harder than ever to fend off expected price-cutting by Cisco and others. But the looming battle is dismissed with characteristic bravado: "Cisco is a bit arrogant." House argues that buyers are eager for a choice. He has been right so far. Now, Captain Adrenalin just has to keep leading with as much skill as guts.

Source: Andy Reinhardt, "Mr. House Finds His Fixer-Upper," February 2, 1998, 66–68.

Questions

1. How would you describe David House's personality?

2. How would you describe House's values, attitudes, and moods?

3. What kind of career has House had?

4. How does House cope with stress?

Chapter twelve

Motivation

Learning Objectives

1. Explain what motivation is and why managers need to be concerned about it.

2. Describe from the perspectives of expectancy theory and equity theory what managers should do to have a highly motivated workforce.

3. Explain how goals and needs motivate people and what kinds of goals are especially likely to result in high performance.

4. Identify the motivation lessons that managers can learn from operant conditioning theory and social learning theory.

5. Explain why and how managers can use pay as a major motivation tool.

A Case in Contrast

Motivating Employees at Eastman Kodak and Mars

George Fisher, CEO of Eastman Kodak (www.kodak.com), the well-known photographic products company, and John and Forrest Mars, the brothers who run the privately owned candy company Mars Inc., could not have more different ways of motivating their employees.[1]

George Fisher's approach to motivation includes raising levels of responsibility at Kodak and encouraging employees to make decisions in a timely manner and to take risks in order to meet quality, customer satisfaction, and product development goals. Fisher sets specific, difficult goals for his employees to attain but gives them the responsibility to figure out how to meet them. In contrast, the Mars brothers like to call the shots and are reluctant to share responsibility, even with top managers. As one former manager at Mars put it, "Senior managers are scared of the Mars boys. They are like Russian czars, dictatorial in spirit and manner. There's a court around them. You don't pick a fight with John or Forrest."[2] The Mars brothers are so autocratic that not even high-level managers are motivated to take risks and come up with creative new ideas, because they are likely to get shot down by Forrest or John.

Fisher expresses confidence in his subordinates' ability to succeed.

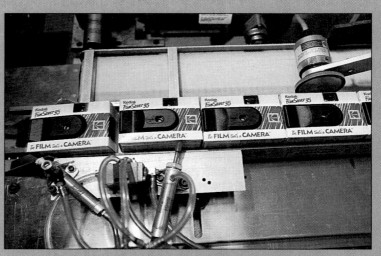

George Fisher, CEO of Kodak and John and Forrest Mars, the brothers who run the candy company Mars Inc., have very different ways of motivating their employees. Fisher likes to give employees the responsibility of making decisions and to take risks. The Mars brothers like to call the shots and are reluctant to share responsibility, even with top managers.

He expects high performance, has made it clear that shortfalls will not go unnoticed, and holds employees accountable for reaching their difficult goals. Forrest and John Mars not only do not express confidence in their subordinates but frequently criticize them and their capabilities and are prone to angry outbursts when things displease them. Former Mars managers suggest that Forrest and John are such difficult people to work for that they make other hard-hitting CEOs look like Barney, PBS's purple dinosaur character for young children. Some Mars employees feel that the Mars brothers have little faith in employees' competence and capabilities, given their tendencies to be so critical.

Fisher has an informal, approachable style; he practically never raises his voice or shows anger or displeasure. He treats employees so well that they want to do a good job to help him turn around Kodak. As Carl Kohrt, general manager of the $1.6 billion health sciences unit, says, "It's like talking to your father . . . You don't want to disappoint him." The Mars brothers are anything but approachable. Their frequent angry outbursts and tirades motivate employees to avoid them whenever possible.

Positive feedback for a job well done is an integral part of Fisher's approach to motivation. He takes great pains to make sure that he is accessible to Kodak employees so that he can help spur them on and provide positive feedback and praise. For example, Fisher often visits with Kodak researchers for updates on their projects, and he praises their efforts. The only feedback the Mars brothers seem to provide is negative. They are impatient and punish employees who disappoint them in a variety of ways, including criticizing and berating them in front of their coworkers.

Consistent with his approachable style, Fisher is always available to talk to employees and has breakfast in the company cafeteria for this purpose. He encourages all employees to send him e-mail messages and some days receives as many as 30. His secretary prints out the messages, and Fisher personally responds to each one with a handwritten note on the printout, typically within a day. Fisher shows that he cares about what his employees think, gives them input on their ideas, and commends them for good suggestions. The Mars brothers do not welcome input from their employees. Managers and workers at all levels are afraid of them, are reluctant to stand up for what they believe in if it might not be what the brothers want to hear, and are reluctant to interact with them. "Fear of Forrest" causes many Mars employees to keep their opinions to themselves so as to avoid Forrest Mars's angry outbursts.

How are the Mars brothers able to attract employees despite what some former Mars executives claim is a very negative approach to motivation? They do it by paying salaries that are twice as large as the salaries paid by other companies in their industry. George Fisher also uses pay to motivate; he does it, however, by linking pay to performance levels. Even researchers in Kodak's labs are being held accountable for progress on their projects, including ensuring that projects are completed in a timely fashion.

How does the difference in Fisher's and the Mars brothers' styles of motivating employees affect their companies' performance? Currently, Kodak, under Fisher, is performing better than it has for decades, while Mars is losing market share in the candy industry both in the United States and in western Europe. ●

Overview

Even with the best strategy in place and an appropriate organizational architecture, an organization will be effective only if its members are motivated to perform at a high level. George Fisher clearly realizes this. One reason why leading is such an important managerial activity is that it entails ensuring that each member of an organization is motivated to perform highly and help the organization achieve its goals. When managers are effective, the outcome of the leading process is a highly motivated workforce. A key challenge for managers of organizations both large and small is to encourage employees to perform at a high level.

In this chapter we describe what motivation is, where it comes from, and why managers need to promote high levels of it for an organization to be effective and achieve its goals. We examine important theories of motivation: expectancy theory, need theories, equity theory, goal-setting theory, and learning theories. Each provides managers with important insights about how to motivate organizational members. The theories are complementary in that each focuses on a somewhat different aspect of motivation. Considering all of the theories together will give managers a rich understanding of the many issues and problems involved in encouraging high levels of motivation throughout an organization. Last, we consider the use of pay as a motivation tool. By the end of this chapter, you will understand what it takes to have a highly motivated workforce. ●

The Nature of Motivation

motivation Psychological forces that determine the direction of a person's behavior in an organization, a person's level of effort, and a person's level of persistence.

Motivation may be defined as psychological forces that determine the direction of a person's behavior in an organization, a person's level of effort, and a person's level of persistence in the face of obstacles.[3] The *direction of a person's behavior* refers to which of the many possible behaviors that people could engage in. For example, employees at Kodak have frequent interactions with their CEO, George Fisher; they even send him e-mail messages. In contrast, employees at Mars try to avoid John and Forrest Mars and often hold their tongues out of fear of displeasing them. *Effort* refers to how hard people work. Employees at Kodak exert high levels of effort to attain their difficult goals and help George Fisher get Kodak back on the right track. *Persistence* refers to whether, when faced with roadblocks and obstacles, people keep trying or give up. Researchers in Kodak's labs sometimes face what seem to be insurmountable problems, yet they persist in their efforts to complete their projects on a timely basis and meet their goals.

Motivation is so central to management because it explains *why* people behave the way they do in organizations—why employees at Kodak are striving to reach difficult goals and do not want to let George Fisher down and why employees at Mars are afraid to stand up for what they believe in. Motivation also explains why a waiter is polite or rude, why a kindergarten teacher really tries to get children to enjoy learning or just goes through the motions, and why some workers put forth twice the effort of others.

intrinsically motivated behavior
Behavior that is performed for its own sake.

Motivation can come from *intrinsic* or *extrinsic* sources. **Intrinsically motivated behavior** is behavior that is performed for its own sake; the source of motivation is actually performing the behavior, and motivation comes from doing the work itself. Many managers are intrinsically motivated; they derive a sense of accomplishment and achievement from helping their organizations to achieve their goals and gain a competitive advantage. Jobs that are interesting and challenging or high on the five characteristics described by the job characteristics model (see Chapter 8) are more likely to lead to intrinsic motivation than are jobs that are boring or do not make use of a person's skills and abilities. An elementary school teacher who enjoys teaching children, a computer programmer who loves solving programming problems, and a commercial photographer who relishes taking creative photographs are all intrinsically motivated. For these individuals, motivation comes from performing their jobs whether they be teaching children, finding bugs in computer programs, or taking pictures.

extrinsically motivated behavior
Behavior that is performed to acquire material or social rewards or to avoid punishment.

Extrinsically motivated behavior is behavior that is performed to acquire material or social rewards or to avoid punishment; the source of motivation is the consequences of the behavior, not the behavior itself. Employees at Mars who keep their ideas to themselves and agree with whatever the Mars brothers tell them are extrinsically motivated; fear of punishment motivates them to behave in this manner. Similarly, a car salesperson who is motivated by receiving a commission on all cars sold, a lawyer who is motivated by the high salary and status that go along with the job, and a factory worker who is motivated by the opportunity to earn a secure income are all extrinsically motivated. Their motivation comes from the consequences they receive as a result of their work behaviors.

People can be intrinsically motivated, extrinsically motivated, or both intrinsically and extrinsically motivated. A top manager who derives a sense of accomplishment and achievement from managing a large corporation and strives to reach year-end targets to obtain a hefty bonus is both intrinsically and extrinsically motivated. Similarly, a nurse who enjoys helping and taking care of patients and is motivated by having a secure job with good benefits is both intrinsically and extrinsically motivated. Whether workers are intrinsically motivated, extrinsically motivated, or both depends on a wide variety of factors: workers' own personal characteristics (such as their personalities, abilities, values, attitudes, and needs), the nature of their jobs (such as whether they have been enriched or whether they are high or low on the five core characteristics of the job characteristics model), and the nature of the organization (such as its structure, its culture, its control systems, its human resource management system, and the ways in which rewards such as pay are distributed to employees).

outcome Anything a person gets from a job or organization.

Regardless of whether people are intrinsically or extrinsically motivated, they join and are motivated to work in organizations to obtain certain outcomes. An **outcome** is anything a person gets from a job or organization. Some outcomes, such as autonomy, responsibility, a feeling of accomplishment, and the pleasure of doing interesting or enjoyable work, result in intrinsically motivated behavior. Other outcomes, such as pay, job security, benefits, and vacation time, result in extrinsically motivated behavior.

input Anything a person contributes to his or her job or organization.

Organizations hire people to obtain important inputs. An **input** is anything a person contributes to his or her job or organization, such as time, effort, education, experience, skills, knowledge, and actual work behaviors. Inputs such as these are necessary for an organization to achieve its goals. Managers strive

Figure 12.1
The Motivation Equation

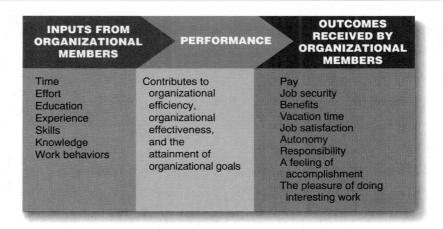

INPUTS FROM ORGANIZATIONAL MEMBERS	PERFORMANCE	OUTCOMES RECEIVED BY ORGANIZATIONAL MEMBERS
Time Effort Education Experience Skills Knowledge Work behaviors	Contributes to organizational efficiency, organizational effectiveness, and the attainment of organizational goals	Pay Job security Benefits Vacation time Job satisfaction Autonomy Responsibility A feeling of accomplishment The pleasure of doing interesting work

to motivate members of an organization to contribute inputs–through their behavior, effort, and persistence–that help the organization achieve its goals. How do managers do this? They ensure that members of an organization obtain the outcomes they desire when they make valuable contributions to the organization. Managers use outcomes to motivate people to contribute their inputs to the organization. Giving people outcomes when they contribute inputs and perform well aligns the interests of employees with the goals of the organization as a whole because when employees do what is good for the organization, they personally benefit.

This alignment between employees and organizational goals as a whole can be described by the motivation equation depicted in Figure 12.1. Managers seek to ensure that people are motivated to contribute important inputs to the organization, that these inputs are put to good use or focused in the direction of high performance, and that high performance results in workers obtaining the outcomes they desire.

Each of the theories of motivation discussed in this chapter focuses on one or more aspects of this equation. Each theory focuses on a different set of issues that managers need to address to have a highly motivated workforce. Together, the theories provide a comprehensive set of guidelines for managers to follow to promote high levels of employee motivation. Effective managers such as George Fisher in the "Case in Contrast" tend to follow many of these guidelines, whereas ineffective managers often fail to follow them and seem to have trouble motivating organizational members.

Expectancy Theory

Expectancy theory, formulated by Victor H. Vroom in the 1960s, posits that motivation will be high when workers believe that high levels of effort will lead to high performance and high performance will lead to the attainment of desired outcomes. Expectancy theory is one of the most popular theories of work motivation because it focuses on all three parts of the

Figure 12.2
Expectancy, Instrumentality, and Valence

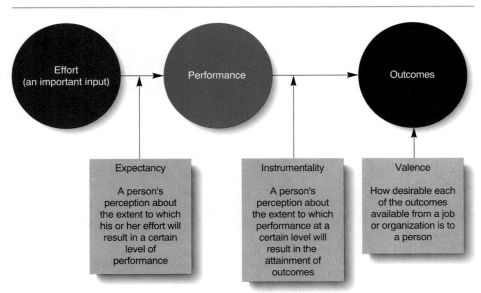

motivation equation: inputs, performance, and outcomes. Expectancy theory identifies three major factors that determine a person's motivation: *expectancy, instrumentality,* and *valence* (see Figure 12.2).[4]

Expectancy

Expectancy is a person's perception about the extent to which effort (an input) will result in a certain level of performance. A person's level of expectancy determines whether he or she believes that a high level of effort will result in a high level of performance. People are motivated to put forth a lot of effort on their jobs only if they think that their effort will pay off in high performance—that is, if they have a high expectancy. Think about how motivated you would be to study for a test if you thought that no matter how hard you tried you would get a D. Think about how motivated a marketing manager would be who thought that no matter how hard he or she worked there was no way to increase sales of an unpopular product. In these cases, expectancy is low, so overall motivation is also low.

Members of an organization will be motivated to put forth a high level of effort only if they think that doing so will lead to high performance. In other words, in order for people's motivation to be high, expectancy must be high. Thus, in attempting to influence motivation, managers need to make sure that their subordinates believe that if they do try hard they actually can succeed. George Fisher actively encourages high levels of expectancy among Kodak employees by expressing confidence in their ability to perform at a high level, holding them to high standards, and giving them the responsibility to determine the best ways of achieving goals. As the "Case in Contrast" indicates, the Mars brothers' excessive criticism leads to relatively low levels of expectancy among Mars employees, who do not believe in their own ability to succeed and consequently have low motivation.

In addition to expressing confidence in subordinates, another way for managers to boost subordinates' expectancy levels and motivation is by providing training so that people have all the expertise they need for high performance. Managers at Julius Blum GmbH, a manufacturing company that produces hinges in Hoechst, Austria, boost their employees' expectancy and motivation through a four-year apprenticeship program combining classroom-type and on-the-job instruction that costs practically $5 million a year. The program is well worth its cost, however. Blum has some of the best-trained employees in Austria, and the combination of their training and high expectancy and motivation has resulted in the company being very successful.[5]

Instrumentality

instrumentality In expectancy theory, a perception about the extent to which performance will result in the attainment of outcomes.

Expectancy captures a person's perceptions about the relationship between effort and performance. **Instrumentality,** the second major concept in expectancy theory, is a person's perception about the extent to which performance at a certain level will result in the attainment of outcomes (see Figure 12.2). According to expectancy theory, employees will be motivated to perform at a high level only if they think that high performance will lead to (or is *instrumental* for attaining) outcomes such as pay, job security, interesting job assignments, bonuses, or a feeling of accomplishment. In other words, instrumentalities must be high for motivation to be high—people must perceive that if they do perform highly they will receive outcomes.

Managers promote high levels of instrumentality when they clearly link performance to desired outcomes. In addition, managers must clearly communicate this linkage to subordinates. By making sure that outcomes available in an organization are distributed to organizational members on the basis of their performance, managers promote high instrumentality and motivation. When outcomes are linked to performance in this way, high performers receive more outcomes than low performers. In the "Case in Contrast," George Fisher raised levels of instrumentality for Kodak employees by closely linking their pay to their performance.

Another example of high instrumentality contributing to high motivation can be found in the Cambodian immigrants who own, manage, and work in more than 80 percent of the doughnut shops in California.[6] These immigrants see high performance as leading to many important outcomes such as income, a comfortable existence, family security, and the autonomy provided by working in a small business. Their high instrumentality contributes to their high motivation to succeed.

Valence

valence In expectancy theory, how desirable each of the outcomes available from a job or organization is to a person.

Although it is important for all members of an organization to have high expectancies and instrumentalities, expectancy theory acknowledges that people differ in their preferences for outcomes. For many people, pay is the most important outcome of working. For others, a feeling of accomplishment or enjoying one's work is more important than pay. The term **valence** refers to how desirable each of the outcomes available from a job or organization is to a person. To motivate organizational members, managers need to determine which outcomes have high valence for them—are highly desired—and make sure that those outcomes are provided when members perform at a high level. From the "Case in Contrast," it appears that for many employees at Mars the pay that is twice the industry average has such high valence that it keeps them working for the demanding Mars brothers in spite of the presence of few other desirable outcomes.

Desi DiSimone, CEO of 3M, suggests that overseas assignments—despite the stress they can bring—can have particularly high valence for managers because of the high levels of autonomy and the opportunities for learning that such assignments often provide. DiSimone himself speaks five languages and worked in Brazil and Australia prior to heading up 3M. He thinks overseas assignments are attractive to managers because they enable them to learn about different cultures and tastes and different ways of doing things and accomplishing goals—skills that often help them perform well in managerial roles. Consistent with DiSimone's observations, 75 percent of the 135 top managers at 3M have worked abroad for a minimum of three years.[7]

Bringing It All Together

According to expectancy theory, high motivation results from high levels of expectancy, instrumentality, and valence (see Figure 12.3). If any one of these factors is low, motivation is likely to be low. No matter how tightly desired outcomes are linked to performance, if a person thinks that it is practically impossible for him or her to perform at a high level, then motivation to perform at a high level will be exceedingly low. Similarly, if a person does not think that outcomes are linked to high performance, or if a person does not desire the outcomes that are linked to high performance, then motivation to perform at a high level will be low.

Managers of successful companies often strive to ensure that employees' levels of expectancy, instrumentality, and valence are high so that they will be highly motivated, as is illustrated by Motorola's efforts at managing globally.

Figure 12.3
Expectancy Theory

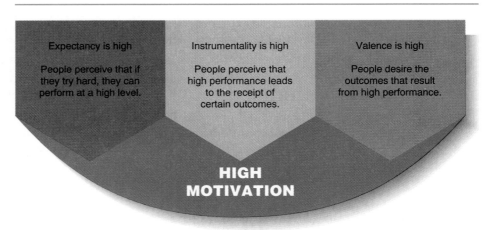

| Expectancy is high | Instrumentality is high | Valence is high |
| People perceive that if they try hard, they can perform at a high level. | People perceive that high performance leads to the receipt of certain outcomes. | People desire the outcomes that result from high performance. |

HIGH MOTIVATION

Managing Globally

Motorola Promotes High Motivation in Malaysia

Motorola (www.motorola.com) is a truly global organization with major operations in countries such as India and China.[8] At Motorola's plant in Penang, Malaysia, which produces walkie-talkies and cordless phones, workers have such high levels of motivation that managers are trying to transplant what goes on there to some of Motorola's U.S. operations. Key to Motorola's success in Malaysia is the fact that employees in the Penang plant have high levels of expectancy, instrumentality, and valence and are highly motivated.

What did managers do to motivate workers in Malaysia, a developing country in which managers in most organizations typically treat workers not as important contributors to the organization but as easily replaceable units of labor? First, Motorola's managers made a major commitment to boosting expectancy levels so that workers are confident that they can perform highly and make valuable contributions to the organization, not only in their actual job performance but also in the form of suggestions for ways to cut costs and boost quality. New employees have two days of classroom instruction in which they are taught about quality control, how to use statistical procedures, and how to work together in teams to come up with ideas to improve quality and cut costs. Employees then have, on average, 48 hours of classroom training per year to further hone their skills. The training boosts not only workers' skills and capabilities but also their confidence and expectancy levels. New employees are also assigned a mentor who is a skilled worker who helps them and provides them with encouragement. Motorola pays for engineers in the plant to receive a master's degree, and the best production workers are selected for a two-year training program to become technicians.

Penang managers also took steps to boost instrumentality by making sure that employees' efforts lead to outcomes they desire. Workers who win quality competitions are given trophies and other forms of recognition. Workers who make at least 100 cost-saving ideas in a year and have at least 60 percent of them implemented become members of the prestigious "100 Club." Belonging to the club does not bring many material rewards, but the recognition alone is a highly valent outcome for workers.

Mariana Osman is a member of the 100 Club. She is responsible for reworking cordless phones that have quality defects and has made over 150 suggestions for cutting costs and reducing defects in one year. Valent outcomes (in addition to the recognition) that Motorola provides to Osman for her high performance and valuable contributions are a salary that is relatively high in Malaysia ($185 per month), job security, promotional opportunities (which someday may lead to her being a manager or engineer), and the feeling that she is a valued member of Motorola. As Osman puts it, "I'm one of the family here . . . I want to do what is best for the company."[9]

Employees like Osman are the norm rather than the exception at the Penang plant. So it is no wonder that Motorola is taking steps to boost expectancy, instrumentality, valence, and ultimately motivation at its U.S. plants by using some of the initiatives that Penang managers put into place, such as training to boost expectancy and linking valent outcomes to high performance.[10]

Need Theories

A **need** is a requirement or necessity for survival and well-being. The basic premise of **need theories** is that people are motivated to obtain outcomes at work that will satisfy their needs. Need theory complements expectancy theory by exploring in depth which outcomes motivate people to perform at a high level. Need theories suggest that in order to motivate a person to contribute valuable inputs to a job and perform at a high level, a manager must determine what needs the person is trying to satisfy at work and ensure that the person receives outcomes that help to satisfy those needs when the person performs at a high level and helps the organization achieve its goals.

There are several different need theories. In Chapter 11 we discussed David McClelland's ideas about managers' needs for achievement, affiliation, and power. Here we discuss Abraham Maslow's hierarchy of needs, Clayton Alderfer's ERG theory, and Frederick Herzberg's motivator–hygiene theory. These theories describe needs that people try to satisfy at work. In doing so, they provide managers with insights about what outcomes will motivate members of an organization to perform at a high level and contribute inputs to help the organization achieve its goals.

Maslow's Hierarchy of Needs

Psychologist Abraham Maslow proposed that all people seek to satisfy five basic kinds of needs: physiological needs, safety needs, belongingness needs, esteem needs, and self-actualization needs (see Table 12.1).[11] He suggested that these needs constitute a **hierarchy of needs,** with the most basic or compelling needs–physiological and safety needs–at the bottom. Maslow argued that these lowest-level needs must be met before a person will strive to satisfy needs higher up in the hierarchy, such as self-esteem needs. Once a need is satisfied, he proposed, it ceases to operate as a source of motivation. The lowest level of *unmet* needs in the hierarchy is the prime motivator of behavior; if and when this level is satisfied, needs at the next highest level in the hierarchy motivate behavior.

Although this theory identifies needs that are likely to be important sources of motivation for many people, research does not support Maslow's contention that there is a need hierarchy or his notion that only one level of needs is motivational at a time.[12] Nevertheless, a key conclusion can be drawn from Maslow's theory: People differ in what needs they are trying to satisfy at work. To have a motivated workforce, managers must determine which needs employees are trying to satisfy in organizations and then make sure that individuals receive outcomes that will satisfy their needs when they perform at a high level and contribute to organizational effectiveness. By doing this, managers align the interests of individual members with the interests of the organization as a whole. By doing what is good for the organization (that is, performing at a high level), employees receive outcomes that satisfy their needs.

In addition, in an increasingly global economy it is important for managers to realize that citizens of different countries might differ in the needs they seek to satisfy through work.[13] Some research suggests, for example, that people in Greece and Japan are especially motivated by safety needs and that people in Sweden, Norway, and Denmark are motivated by belongingness needs.[14] In poor countries with low standards of living, physiological and safety needs

Table 12.1

Maslow's Hierarchy of Needs

	Needs	Description	Examples of How Managers Can Help People Satisfy These Needs at Work
Highest-level needs	**Self-actualization needs**	The needs to realize one's full potential as a human being	By giving people the opportunity to use their skills and abilities to the fullest extent possible
	Esteem needs	The needs to feel good about oneself and one's capabilities, to be respected by others, and to receive recognition and appreciation	By granting promotions and recognizing accomplishments
	Belongingness needs	Needs for social interaction, friendship, affection, and love	By promoting good interpersonal relations and organizing social functions such as company picnics and holiday parties
	Safety needs	Needs for security, stability, and a safe environment	By providing job security, adequate medical benefits, and safe working conditions
Lowest-level needs (most basic or compelling)	**Physiological needs**	Basic needs for things such as food, water, and shelter that must be met in order for a person to survive	By providing a level of pay that enables a person to buy food and clothing and have adequate housing

The lowest level of unsatisfied needs motivates behavior; once this level of needs is satisfied, a person tries to satisfy the needs at the next level.

are likely to be the prime motivators of behavior. As countries become wealthier and have higher standards of living, it is likely that needs related to personal growth and accomplishment (such as esteem and self-actualization) become important as motivators of behavior.

Alderfer's ERG Theory

Alderfer's ERG theory
The theory that three universal needs—for existence, relatedness, and growth—constitute a hierarchy of needs and motivate behavior. Alderfer proposed that needs at more than one level can be motivational at the same time.

Clayton Alderfer's **ERG theory** collapses the five categories of needs in Maslow's hierarchy into three universal categories–existence, relatedness, and growth–also arranged in a hierarchy (see Table 12.2). Alderfer agrees with Maslow that as lower-level needs become satisfied, a person seeks to satisfy higher-level needs. Unlike Maslow, however, Alderfer believes that a person can be motivated by needs at more than one level at the same time. A cashier in a supermarket, for example, may be motivated both by existence needs and by relatedness needs. The existence needs motivate the cashier to come to work regularly and not make mistakes so that his job will be secure and he will be able to pay his rent and buy food. The relatedness needs motivate the cashier to become friends with some of the other cashiers and have a good relationship with the store manager. Alderfer also suggests that when people experience *need frustration* or are unable to satisfy needs at a certain level, they will focus all the more on satisfying the needs at the next lowest level in the hierarchy.[15]

As with Maslow's theory, research does not tend to support some of the specific ideas outlined in ERG theory, such as the existence of the three-level need hierarchy that Alderfer proposed.[16] However, for managers, the important

Table 12.2

Alderfer's ERG Theory

	Needs	Description	Examples of How Managers Can Help People Satisfy These Needs at Work
Highest-level needs	Growth needs	The needs for self-development and creative and productive work	By allowing people to continually improve their skills and abilities and engage in meaningful work
↕	Relatedness needs	The needs to have good interpersonal relations, to share thoughts and feelings, and to have open two-way communication	By promoting good interpersonal relations and by providing accurate feedback
Lowest-level needs	Existence needs	Basic needs for food, water, clothing, shelter, and a secure and safe environment	By promoting enough pay to provide for the basic necessities of life and safe working conditions

As lower-level needs are satisfied, a person is motivated to satisfy higher-level needs. When a person is unable to satisfy higher-level needs (or is frustrated), motivation to satisfy lower-level needs increases

message from ERG theory is the same as that from Maslow's theory: Determine what needs your subordinates are trying to satisfy at work, and make sure that they receive outcomes that will satisfy those needs when they perform at a high level and help the organization achieve its goals.

Herzberg's Motivator–Hygiene Theory

Adopting an approach different from Maslow's and Alderfer's, Frederick Herzberg focuses on two factors: (1) outcomes that can lead to high levels of motivation and job satisfaction and (2) outcomes that can prevent people from being dissatisfied. According to **Herzberg's motivator–hygiene theory,** people have two sets of needs or requirements: motivator needs and hygiene needs.[17] *Motivator needs* are related to the nature of the work itself and how challenging it is. Outcomes such as interesting work, autonomy, responsibility, being able to grow and develop on the job, and a sense of accomplishment and achievement help to satisfy motivator needs. In order to have a highly motivated and satisfied workforce, Herzberg suggested, managers should take steps to ensure that employees' motivator needs are being met.

Hygiene needs are related to the physical and psychological context in which the work is performed. Hygiene needs are satisfied by outcomes such as pleasant and comfortable working conditions, pay, job security, good relationships with coworkers, and effective supervision. According to Herzberg, when hygiene needs are not met, workers will be dissatisfied, and when hygiene needs are met, workers will not be dissatisfied. Satisfying hygiene needs, however, will not result in high levels of motivation or even high levels of job satisfaction. For motivation and job satisfaction to be high, motivator needs must be met.

Many research studies have tested Herzberg's propositions, and, by and large, the theory fails to receive support.[18] Nevertheless, Herzberg's formulations have contributed to our understanding of motivation in at least two

Herzberg's motivator–hygiene theory A need theory that distinguishes between motivator needs (related to the nature of the work itself) and hygiene needs (related to the physical and psychological context in which the work is performed). Herzberg proposed that motivator needs must be met in order for motivation and job satisfaction to be high.

ways. First, Herzberg helped to focus researchers' and managers' attention on the important distinction between intrinsic motivation (related to motivator needs) and extrinsic motivation (related to hygiene needs), covered earlier in the chapter. Second, his theory helped to prompt researchers and managers to study how jobs can be designed or redesigned so that they are intrinsically motivating.

Equity Theory

equity theory A theory of motivation that focuses on people's perceptions of the fairness of their work outcomes relative to their work inputs.

Equity theory is a theory of motivation that concentrates on people's perceptions of the fairness of their work *outcomes* relative to, or in proportion to, their work *inputs*. Equity theory complements expectancy and need theories by focusing on how people perceive the relationship between the outcomes they receive from their jobs and organizations and the inputs they contribute. Equity theory was formulated in the 1960s by J. Stacy Adams, who stressed that what is important in determining motivation is the *relative* rather than the *absolute* level of outcomes a person receives and inputs a person contributes. Specifically, motivation is influenced by the comparison of one's own outcome/input ratio with the outcome/input ratio of a referent.[19] The *referent* could be another person or a group of people who are perceived to be similar to oneself; the referent also could be oneself in a previous job or one's expectations about what outcome/input ratios should be. In a comparison of one's own outcome/input ratio to a referent's outcome/input ratio, one's *perceptions* of outcomes and inputs (not any objective indicator of them) are key.

Equity

equity The justice, impartiality, and fairness to which all organizational members are entitled.

Equity exists when a person perceives his or her own outcome/input ratio to be equal to a referent's outcome/input ratio. Under conditions of equity (see Table 12.3), if a referent receives more outcomes than you receive, the referent contributes proportionally more inputs to the organization, so his or her outcome/input ratio still equals your outcome/input ratio. Maria Sanchez and Claudia King, for example, both work in a shoe store in a large mall. Sanchez is paid more per hour than King but also contributes more inputs, including being responsible for some of the store's bookkeeping, closing the store, and periodically depositing cash in the bank. When King compares her outcome/input ratio to Sanchez's (her referent's), she perceives the ratios to be equitable because Sanchez's higher level of pay (an outcome) is proportional to her higher level of inputs (bookkeeping, closing the store, and going to the bank).

Similarly, under conditions of equity, if you receive more outcomes than a referent, then your inputs are perceived to be proportionally higher. Continuing with our example, when Sanchez compares her outcome/input ratio to King's (her referent's) outcome/input ratio, she perceives them to be equitable because her higher level of pay is proportional to her higher level of inputs.

When equity exists, people are motivated to continue contributing their current levels of inputs to their organizations in order to receive their current levels of outcomes. Under conditions of equity, if people wish to increase their outcomes, they are motivated to increase their inputs.

Table 12.3

Equity Theory

Condition	Person		Referent	Example
Equity	$\dfrac{\text{Outcomes}}{\text{Inputs}}$	$=$	$\dfrac{\text{Outcomes}}{\text{Inputs}}$	An engineer perceives that he contributes more inputs (time and effort), and receives proportionally more outcomes (a higher salary and choice job assignments), than his referent.
Underpayment inequity	$\dfrac{\text{Outcomes}}{\text{Inputs}}$	$<$ (less than)	$\dfrac{\text{Outcomes}}{\text{Inputs}}$	An engineer perceives that he contributes more inputs but receives the same outcomes as his referent.
Overpayment inequity	$\dfrac{\text{Outcomes}}{\text{Inputs}}$	$>$ (greater than)	$\dfrac{\text{Outcomes}}{\text{Inputs}}$	An engineer perceives that he contributes the same inputs but receives more outcomes than his referent.

Inequity

inequity Lack of fairness.

Inequity, lack of fairness, exists when a person's outcome/input ratio is not perceived to be equal to a referent's. Inequity creates pressure or tension inside people and motivates them to restore equity by bringing the two ratios back into balance.

There are two types of inequity: underpayment inequity and overpayment inequity (see Table 12.3). **Underpayment inequity** exists when a person's own outcome/input ratio is perceived to be *less* than that of a referent: In comparing yourself to a referent, you think that you are *not* receiving the outcomes you should be, given your inputs. **Overpayment inequity** exists when a person perceives that his or her own outcome/input ratio is *greater* than that of a referent: In comparing yourself to a referent, you think that the referent is receiving fewer outcomes than he or she should be, given his or her inputs.

underpayment inequity Inequity that exists when a person perceives that his or her own outcome/input ratio is less than the ratio of a referent.

overpayment inequity Inequity that exists when a person perceives that his or her own outcome/input ratio is greater than the ratio of a referent.

Ways to Restore Equity

According to equity theory, both underpayment inequity and overpayment inequity create tension that motivates most people to restore equity by bringing the ratios back into balance.[20] When people experience *underpayment* inequity, they may be motivated to lower their inputs by reducing their working hours, putting forth less effort on the job, or being absent, or they may be motivated to increase their outcomes by asking for a raise or a promotion. Susan Richie, a financial analyst at a large corporation, noticed that she was working longer hours and getting more work accomplished than a coworker who had the same position, yet they both received the exact same pay and other outcomes. To restore equity, Richie decided to stop coming in early and staying late. Alternatively, she could have tried to restore equity by trying to increase her outcomes by, for example, asking her boss for a raise.

When people experience *overpayment* inequity, they may try to restore equity by changing their perceptions of their own or their referents' inputs or outcomes. Equity can be restored when people "realize" that they are contributing more inputs than they originally thought. Equity also can be restored by perceiving the referent's inputs to be lower or the referent's outcomes to be higher than one originally thought. When equity is restored in this way, actual inputs and outcomes are unchanged. What is changed is how people think about or view their or the referent's inputs and outcomes. Mary McMann experienced overpayment inequity when she realized that she was being paid $2 an hour more than a coworker who had the same job as she did in a record store and who contributed the same amount of inputs. McMann restored equity by changing her perceptions of her inputs. She "realized" that she worked harder than her coworker and solved more problems that came up in the store.

Experiencing either overpayment or underpayment inequity, you might decide that your referent is not appropriate because, for example, the referent is too different from yourself. Choosing a more appropriate referent may bring the ratios back into balance. Angela Martinez, a middle manager in the engineering department of a chemical company, experienced *overpayment* inequity when she realized that she was being paid quite a bit more than her friend who was a middle manager in the marketing department of the same company. After thinking about the discrepancy for a while, Martinez decided that engineering and marketing were so different that she should not be comparing her job to her friend's job even though they were both middle managers. Martinez restored equity by changing her referent; she picked a fellow middle manager in the engineering department as a new referent.

When people experience *underpayment* inequity and other means of equity restoration fail, they may leave the organization. John Steinberg, an assistant principal in a high school, experienced underpayment inequity when he realized that all of the other assistant principals of high schools in his school district had received promotions to the position of principal even though they had been in their jobs for a shorter period of time than he had been. Steinberg's performance had always been appraised as being high, so after his repeated requests for a promotion went unheeded, he found a job as a principal in a different school district.

Motivation is highest when as many people as possible in an organization perceive that they are being equitably treated—their outcomes and inputs are in balance. Top contributors and performers are motivated to continue contributing a high level of inputs because they are receiving the outcomes they deserve. Mediocre contributors and performers realize that if they want to increase their outcomes, they have to increase their inputs. Managers of effective organizations, like George Fisher at Eastman Kodak, realize the importance of equity for motivation and performance and continually strive to ensure that employees feel they are being equitably treated.

Goal-Setting Theory

Goal-setting theory focuses on motivating workers to contribute their inputs to their jobs and organizations; in this way it is similar to expectancy theory and equity theory. But goal-setting theory takes this focus a step further by considering as well how managers can ensure that organizational members focus their inputs in the direction of high performance and the achievement of organizational goals.

goal-setting theory
A theory that focuses on identifying the types of goals that are most effective in producing high levels of motivation and performance and explaining why goals have these effects.

Ed Locke and Gary Latham, the leading researchers on goal-setting theory, suggest that the goals that organizational members strive to attain are prime determinants of their motivation and subsequent performance. A *goal* is what a person is trying to accomplish through his or her efforts and behaviors.[21] Just as you may have a goal to get a good grade in this course, so do members of an organization have goals that they strive to meet. In the "Case in Contrast," we mentioned that researchers in Kodak's labs have goals for finishing their projects in a timely fashion. Similarly, salespeople at Neiman Marcus strive to meet sales goals, and top managers have market share and profitability goals.

Goal-setting theory suggests that in order to result in high motivation and performance, goals must be *specific* and *difficult*.[22] Specific goals are often quantitative—a salesperson's goal to sell $200 worth of merchandise per day, a scientist's goal to finish a project in one year, a CEO's goal to reduce debt by 40 percent and increase revenues by 20 percent, a restaurant manager's goal to serve 150 customers per evening. In contrast to specific goals, vague goals such as "doing your best" or "selling as much as you can" do not have much motivational force.

Difficult goals are hard but not impossible to attain. In contrast to difficult goals, easy goals are goals that practically everyone can attain, and moderate goals are goals that about one-half of the people can attain. Both easy and moderate goals have less motivational power than difficult goals.

Regardless of whether specific, difficult goals are set by managers, workers, or managers and workers together, they lead to high levels of motivation and performance. At Kodak, George Fisher sets specific, difficult goals for his employees but then leaves decisions about how to meet the goals up to them. When managers set goals for their subordinates, it is important that their subordinates accept the goals or agree to work toward them and also that they are committed to them or really want to attain them. Some managers find having subordinates participate in the actual setting of goals boosts their acceptance of and commitment to the goals. In addition, it is important for organizational members to receive *feedback* about how they are doing; feedback can often be provided by the performance appraisal and feedback component of an organization's human resource management system (see Chapter 10).

Specific, difficult goals affect motivation in two ways. First, they motivate people to contribute more inputs to their jobs. Specific, difficult goals cause people to put forth high levels of effort, for example. Just as you would study harder if you were trying to get an A in a course instead of a C, so too will a salesperson work harder to reach a $200 sales goal instead of a $100 goal. Specific, difficult goals also cause people to be more persistent than easy, moderate, or vague goals when they run into difficulties. A salesperson who is told to sell as much as possible might stop trying on a slow day, whereas having a specific, difficult goal to reach causes him or her to keep trying.

As a part of George Fisher's attempt to *motivate* his workforce, he created teams of workers who were given the responsibility of developing innovative new products quickly and cost effectively. Pictured is Kodak's Zebra Team, so named because it is responsible for Kodak's black-and-white photographic products, and which has achieved major gains in productivity and profitability over the last two years.

A second way in which specific, difficult goals affect motivation is by helping people focus their inputs in the right direction. These goals let people know what they should be focusing their attention on, be it increasing the quality of customer service or sales or lowering new product development times. The fact that the goals are specific and difficult also frequently causes people to develop *action plans* for reaching them.[23] Action plans can include the strategies that will be used to attain the goals and timetables or schedules for the completion of different activities crucial to goal attainment. Like the goals themselves, action plans also help ensure that efforts are focused in the right direction and that people do not get sidetracked along the way.

Although specific, difficult goals have been found to increase motivation and performance in a wide variety of jobs and organizations both in the United States and abroad, recent research suggests that they may detract from performance under certain conditions. When people are performing complicated and very challenging tasks that require a considerable amount of learning, specific, difficult goals may actually impair performance.[24] All of a person's attention needs to be focused on learning complicated and difficult tasks. Striving to reach a specific, difficult goal may detract from performance on complex tasks because some of a person's attention is directed away from learning about the task and toward trying to figure out how to achieve the goal. Once a person has learned the task and it no longer seems complicated or difficult, then the assignment of specific, difficult goals is likely to have its usual effects.

Tips for Managers

Expectancy and Equity Theories

1. Express sincere confidence in your subordinates' capabilities and let them know that you expect them to succeed.
2. Distribute outcomes based on important inputs and performance levels and clearly communicate that this is the case to your subordinates.
3. Determine which outcomes your subordinates desire and try to gain control over as many of these as possible (i.e., have the authority to distribute or withhold outcomes).
4. Provide clear information to your subordinates about which inputs are most valuable for them to contribute to their jobs and the organization to receive desired outcomes.

Learning Theories

The basic premise of **learning theories** as applied to organizations is that managers can increase employee motivation and performance by the ways in which they link the outcomes that employees receive to the performance of desired behaviors in an organization and the attainment of goals. Thus, learning theory focuses on the linkage between performance and outcomes in the motivation equation (see Figure 12.1).

learning theories
Theories that focus on increasing employee motivation and performance by linking the outcomes that employees receive to the performance of desired behaviors and the attainment of goals.

learning A relatively permanent change in knowledge or behavior that results from practice or experience.

operant conditioning theory The theory that people learn to perform behaviors that lead to desired consequences and learn not to perform behaviors that lead to undesired consequences.

Learning can be defined as a relatively permanent change in a person's knowledge or behavior that results from practice or experience.[25] Learning takes place in organizations when people learn to perform certain behaviors to receive certain outcomes. For example, a person learns to perform at a higher level than in the past or to come to work earlier because he or she is motivated to obtain the outcomes that will result from these behaviors, such as a pay raise or praise from a supervisor. There are several different learning theories. The two that provide the most guidance to managers in their efforts to have a highly motivated workforce are operant conditioning theory and social learning theory.

Operant Conditioning Theory

According to **operant conditioning theory,** developed by psychologist B. F. Skinner, people learn to perform behaviors that lead to desired consequences and learn not to perform behaviors that lead to undesired consequences.[26] Translated into motivation terms, Skinner's theory means that people will be motivated to perform at a high level and attain their work goals to the extent that high performance and goal attainment allow them to obtain outcomes they desire. Similarly, people will avoid performing behaviors that lead to outcomes they do not desire. By linking the performance of *specific behaviors* to the attainment of *specific outcomes,* managers can motivate organizational members to perform in ways that help an organization achieve its goals.

Operant conditioning theory provides four tools that managers can use to motivate high performance and prevent workers from engaging in absenteeism and other behaviors that detract from organizational effectiveness. These tools are positive reinforcement, negative reinforcement, punishment, and extinction.[27]

positive reinforcement Giving people outcomes they desire when they perform organizationally functional behaviors.

POSITIVE REINFORCEMENT Positive Reinforcement gives people outcomes they desire when they perform organizationally functional behaviors. These desired outcomes, called *positive reinforcers,* include any outcomes that a person desires, such as pay, praise, or a promotion. Organizationally functional behaviors are behaviors that contribute to organizational effectiveness; they can include producing high-quality goods and services, providing high-quality customer service, and meeting deadlines. By linking positive reinforcers to the performance of functional behaviors, managers motivate people to perform the desired behaviors. In the "Case in Contrast," for example, George Fisher motivates Kodak employees to perform desired behaviors by giving them positive feedback and praise and by linking pay to performance levels.

negative reinforcement Eliminating or removing undesired outcomes when people perform organizationally functional behaviors.

NEGATIVE REINFORCEMENT Negative reinforcement also can be used to encourage members of an organization to perform desired or organizationally functional behaviors. Managers using negative reinforcement actually eliminate or remove undesired outcomes once the functional behavior is performed. These undesired outcomes, called *negative reinforcers,* can range from a manager's constant nagging or criticism, to unpleasant assignments, to the ever-present threat of losing one's job. When negative reinforcement is used, people are motivated to perform behaviors because they want to stop receiving or avoid undesired outcomes. Managers who try to encourage

Workers at a Lincoln Electric plant assemble electric generators. Lincoln Electric is well known for its policy of *positively reinforcing* work behaviors that promote safety and productivity.

salespeople to sell more by threatening them with being fired are using negative reinforcement. In this case, the negative reinforcer is the threat of job loss, which is removed once the functional behaviors are performed.

Whenever possible, managers should try to use positive reinforcement. Negative reinforcement can make for a very unpleasant work environment and even a negative culture in an organization. No one likes to be nagged, threatened, or exposed to other kinds of negative outcomes. The use of negative reinforcement sometimes causes subordinates to resent managers and try to get back at them.

IDENTIFYING THE RIGHT BEHAVIORS FOR REINFORCEMENT Even managers who use positive reinforcement (and refrain from using negative reinforcement) can get into trouble if they are not careful to identify the right behaviors to reinforce—behaviors that are truly functional for the organization. Doing this is not always as straightforward as it might seem. First, it is crucial for managers to choose behaviors over which subordinates have control; in other words, subordinates must have the freedom and opportunity to perform the behaviors that are being reinforced. Second, it is crucial that these behaviors contribute to organizational effectiveness. Recall from Chapter 5 that Sears suffered a major blow to its reputation when it inadvertently encouraged car repair employees to overcharge customers. This problem arose because managers at Sears did not follow these two guidelines for using reinforcement.

In an effort to increase revenues from Sears Tire & Auto Centers, managers instituted a system of positive and negative reinforcement: Workers in the centers were positively reinforced (with sales commissions and other rewards) for making different kinds of repairs on customers' cars, and they were negatively reinforced (with the constant threat of being fired) if they did not meet sales quotas for different kinds of repairs.[28] Instead of motivating workers to provide good service to customers, managers were motivating them to make unnecessary repairs on customers' cars so as to receive commissions and other rewards and avoid being fired. The workers did not have control over the volume of repairs at the centers or the kinds of repairs that might be needed—because customer traffic determined both—and thus the workers did not always have the opportunity to perform the behaviors necessary to receive positive reinforcement. Reinforcement should not have been based on factors that were beyond their control. In addition, as many retailing organizations are realizing, reinforcing simply on a sales basis might not be functional for an organization because employees become focused on making the "quick" sale and not on satisfying repeat-business customers.

Although identifying the right behaviors to reinforce can be difficult, many managers find that the effort is well worthwhile, as indicated in this "Management Insight."

Management Insight

Positive Reinforcement in Luling, Louisiana

Managers at Monsanto's chemical plant at Luling, Louisiana, realized several years ago that positively reinforcing high performance and safety would improve the overall effectiveness of the plant. They also realized that pay was a powerful positive reinforcer for their employees. What they had difficulty determining, however, were the right behaviors to reinforce.

For example, in an effort to boost plant safety and reduce accidents, they decided to positively reinforce workers for having no or relatively few accidents. However, after some careful thinking, managers realized that rather than motivating workers to follow safety procedures, this strategy might actually motivate them to cover up accidents. Managers then decided to reinforce workers by basing their pay on the plant's performance. This strategy backfired because workers complained that although they had control over their own performance, which did contribute to plant performance, they had no control over the performance of other people. Workers hated having their pay based on things beyond their control, and managers abandoned the strategy.

After eight years of trying these and other unsuccessful reinforcement strategies, managers in the Luling plant finally think that they have discovered the right behaviors to positively reinforce. Even though individual performance is hard to assess and reinforce, managers realized that the performance of work units (50 or 60 people who work together) can be assessed and reinforced. In addition, individual employees have considerable control over their unit's performance—not only through their own personal levels of job performance but also by helping each other out, cooperating with each other, pointing out problems, and coming up with good ideas to cut costs, improve unit performance, and increase safety. Managers at the plant positively reinforce these functional behaviors by providing workers with a 5 to 10 percent bonus based on unit performance.

With this strategy in place, managers still struggled to develop a strategy to positively reinforce safe work practices that would not have the unintended side effect of motivating workers to hide accidents to improve their safety records. Managers finally decided that the most appropriate behaviors to reinforce were proactive steps that employees take to improve safety levels before potential accidents have a chance to occur. Workers are now positively reinforced, for example, when they attend safety training programs to reduce the likelihood of accidents occurring.

Managers in the plant indicate that positive reinforcement is having its intended effects of promoting high performance and safety. Key to the success of their current reinforcement strategies is a focus on tying rewards to behaviors and results over which workers have control. Gina Maney, a traffic manager at the plant, suggests that "Once you feel some sort of ownership, it works well."[29]

EXTINCTION   Sometimes members of an organization are motivated to perform behaviors that actually detract from organizational effectiveness. Because (according to operant conditioning theory) all behavior is controlled

extinction Curtailing the performance of dysfunctional behaviors by eliminating whatever is reinforcing them.

or determined by its consequences, one way for managers to curtail the performance of dysfunctional behaviors is to eliminate whatever is reinforcing the behaviors. This process is called **extinction.**

Suppose a manager has a subordinate who frequently stops by his office to chat—sometimes about work-related matters but at other times about various topics ranging from politics to last night's football game. The manager and the subordinate share certain interests and views, so these conversations can get quite involved, and both seem to enjoy them. The manager, however, realizes that these frequent and sometimes lengthy conversations are actually causing him to stay at work later in the evenings to make up for the time he loses during the day. The manager realizes that he is actually reinforcing his subordinate's behavior by acting interested in the topics the subordinate brings up and responding at length to them. To extinguish this behavior, the manager stops acting interested in these non-work-related conversations and keeps his responses polite and friendly but brief. No longer being reinforced with a pleasurable conversation, the subordinate eventually ceases to be motivated to interrupt the manager during working hours to discuss non-work-related issues.

punishment Administering an undesired or negative consequence when dysfunctional behavior occurs.

PUNISHMENT Sometimes managers cannot rely on extinction to eliminate dysfunctional behaviors because they do not have control over whatever is reinforcing the behavior or because they cannot afford the time needed for extinction to work. When employees are performing dangerous behaviors or behaviors that are illegal or unethical, the behavior needs to be eliminated immediately. Sexual harassment, for example, is an organizationally dysfunctional behavior that cannot be tolerated. In cases such as these, managers often rely on **punishment,** administering an undesired or negative consequence to subordinates when they perform the dysfunctional behavior. Punishments used by organizations range from verbal reprimands to pay cuts, temporary suspensions, demotions, and firings. Punishment, however, can have some unintended side effects—resentment, loss of self-respect, a desire for retaliation—and should be used only when necessary. The "Case in Contrast" relates how the Mars brothers' excessive use of punishment is dysfunctional for their company.

To avoid the unintended side effects of punishment, managers should keep in mind these guidelines:

- Downplay the emotional element involved in punishment. Make it clear that you are punishing a person's performance of a dysfunctional behavior, not the person himself or herself.
- Try to punish dysfunctional behaviors as soon after they occur as possible, and make sure the negative consequence is a source of punishment for the individuals involved. Make sure organizational members know exactly why they are being punished.
- Try to avoid punishing in front of others,[30] for this can hurt a person's self-respect and lower his or her esteem in the eyes of coworkers as well as make coworkers feel uncomfortable. However, keep in mind that making organizational members aware of the fact that an individual who has committed a serious infraction has been punished can sometimes be effective in preventing future infractions and teaching all members of the organization that certain behaviors are unacceptable. For example, when organizational members are informed that a manager who has sexually harassed subordinates has been punished, they learn or are reminded of the fact that sexual harassment will not be tolerated in the organization.

Managers and students alike often confuse negative reinforcement and punishment. To avoid such confusion, it is important to keep in mind the two major differences between them. First, negative reinforcement is used to promote the performance of functional behaviors in organizations; punishment is used to stop the performance of dysfunctional behaviors. Second, negative reinforcement entails the *removal* of a negative consequence when functional behaviors are performed; punishment entails the *administration* of negative consequences when dysfunctional behaviors are performed.

organizational behavior modification The systematic application of operant conditioning techniques to promote the performance of organizationally functional behaviors and discourage the performance of dysfunctional behaviors.

ORGANIZATIONAL BEHAVIOR MODIFICATION   When managers systematically apply operant conditioning techniques to promote the performance of organizationally functional behaviors and discourage the performance of dysfunctional behaviors, they are engaging in **organizational behavior modification (OB MOD)**.[31] OB MOD has been successfully used to improve productivity, efficiency, attendance, punctuality, compliance with safety procedures, and other important behaviors in a wide variety of organizations such as Michigan Bell, Connecticut General Life Insurance, Emery Air Freight, General Electric, Standard Oil of Ohio, B. F. Goodrich, and Weyerhaeuser. The five basic steps in OB MOD are described in Figure 12.4.

OB MOD works best for behaviors that are specific, objective, and countable, such as attendance and punctuality, making sales, or putting telephones together, which lend themselves to careful scrutiny and control. OB MOD may be questioned because of its lack of relevance to certain kinds of work behaviors (for example, the many work behaviors that are not specific, objective, and countable). Some people also have questioned it on ethical grounds. Critics of OB MOD suggest that it is overly controlling and robs workers of their dignity, individuality, freedom of choice, and even their creativity. Supporters counter that OB MOD is a highly effective means of promoting organizational efficiency. There is some merit to both sides of this argument. What is clear, however, is that when used appropriately, OB MOD provides managers with a technique to motivate the performance of at least some organizationally functional behaviors.

Social Learning Theory

social learning theory A theory that takes into account how learning and motivation are influenced by people's thoughts and beliefs and their observations of other people's behavior.

Social learning theory proposes that motivation results not only from direct experience of rewards and punishments but also from a person's thoughts and beliefs. Social learning theory extends operant conditioning's contribution to managers' understanding of motivation by explaining (1) how people can be motivated by observing other people perform a behavior and be reinforced for doing so *(vicarious learning)*, (2) how people can be motivated to control their behavior themselves *(self-reinforcement)*, and (3) how people's beliefs about their ability to successfully perform a behavior affect motivation *(self-efficacy)*.[32] We look briefly at each of these motivators.

vicarious learning Learning that occurs when the learner becomes motivated to perform a behavior by watching another person perform it; also called *observational learning*.

VICARIOUS LEARNING   Vicarious learning, often called *observational learning,* occurs when a person (the learner) becomes motivated to perform a behavior by watching another person (the model) perform the behavior and be positively reinforced for doing so. Vicarious learning is a powerful source of motivation on many jobs in which people learn to perform functional behaviors by watching others. Salespeople learn how to be helpful to customers, medical school students learn how to treat patients, law clerks learn how to

Figure 12.4
Five Steps in OB MOD

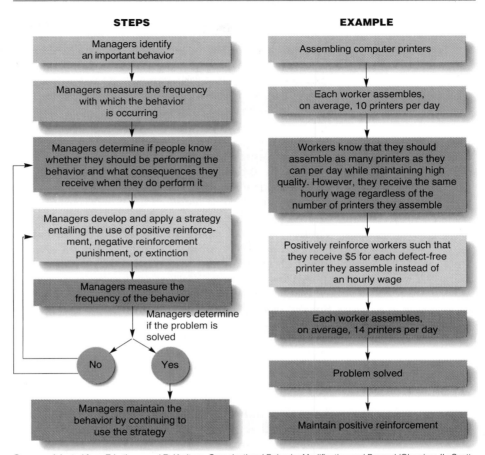

STEPS

Managers identify an important behavior

↓

Managers measure the frequency with which the behavior is occurring

↓

Managers determine if people know whether they should be performing the behavior and what consequences they receive when they do perform it

↓

Managers develop and apply a strategy entailing the use of positive reinforcement, negative reinforcement punishment, or extinction

↓

Managers measure the frequency of the behavior

Managers determine if the problem is solved

No   Yes

Managers maintain the behavior by continuing to use the strategy

EXAMPLE

Assembling computer printers

↓

Each worker assembles, on average, 10 printers per day

↓

Workers know that they should assemble as many printers as they can per day while maintaining high quality. However, they receive the same hourly wage regardless of the number of printers they assemble

↓

Positively reinforce workers such that they receive $5 for each defect-free printer they assemble instead of an hourly wage

↓

Each worker assembles, on average, 14 printers per day

↓

Problem solved

↓

Maintain positive reinforcement

Source: Adapted from F. Luthans and R. Kreitner, *Organizational Behavior Modification and Beyond* (Glenview, IL: Scott, Foresman, 1985).

practice law, and nonmanagers learn how to be a manager, in part, by observing experienced members of an organization perform these behaviors properly and being reinforced for them. In general, people are more likely to be motivated to imitate the behavior of models who are highly competent, are (to some extent) experts in the behavior, have high status, receive attractive reinforcers, and are friendly or approachable.[33]

To promote vicarious learning, managers should strive to have the learner meet the following conditions:[34]

- The learner observes the model performing the behavior.
- The learner accurately perceives the model's behavior.
- The learner remembers the behavior.
- The learner has the skills and abilities needed to perform the behavior.
- The learner sees or knows that the model is positively reinforced for the behavior.

SELF-REINFORCEMENT   Although managers are often the providers of reinforcement in organizations, sometimes people motivate themselves through self-reinforcement. People can control their own behavior by setting goals for themselves and then reinforcing themselves when they achieve the goals.[35] **Self-reinforcers** are any desired or attractive outcomes or rewards that people can give to themselves for good performance, such as a feeling of accomplishment, going to a movie, having dinner out, buying a new CD, or taking time out for a golf game. When members of an organization control their own behavior through self-reinforcement, managers do not need to spend as much time as they ordinarily would trying to motivate and control behavior through the administration of consequences because subordinates are controlling and motivating themselves. In fact, this self-control is often referred to as the self-management of behavior.

Chinese students at the prestigious Jiaotong University in Shanghai exemplify how strong motivation through self-control can be. These students, many of whom are aspiring engineers, live in Spartan conditions (a barely lit small room is home for seven students) and take exceptionally heavy course loads. They spend their spare time reading up on subjects not covered in their classes, and many ultimately hope to obtain engineering jobs overseas with high-tech companies. Illustrating high self-control, 22-year-old Yan Kangrong spends his spare time reading computer textbooks and designing software for local companies. As Kangrong puts it, "We learn the basics from teachers . . . But we need to expand on this knowledge by ourselves."[36]

SELF-EFFICACY   **Self-efficacy** is a person's belief about his or her ability to perform a behavior successfully. Even with all the most attractive consequences or reinforcers hinging on high performance, people are not going to be motivated if they do not think that they actually can perform at a high level. Similarly, when people control their own behavior, they are likely to set for themselves difficult goals that will lead to outstanding accomplishments only if they think that they have the capability to reach those goals. Thus, self-efficacy influences motivation both when managers provide reinforcement and when workers themselves provide it.[37] The greater the self-efficacy, the greater is the motivation and performance. In the "Case in Contrast," George Fisher boosts self-efficacy at Kodak by expressing confidence in his employees' abilities to reach their challenging goals; in contrast, the harsh and critical manner of the Mars brothers serves to dampen levels of self-efficacy at Mars Inc. Verbal persuasion such as that provided by George Fisher, a person's own past performance and accomplishments, and the accomplishments of other people play a role in determining a person's self-efficacy.

self-reinforcer Any desired or attractive outcome or reward that a person gives to himself or herself for good performance.

self-efficacy A person's belief about his or her ability to perform a behavior successfully.

Pay and Motivation

In Chapter 10, we discussed how managers establish a pay level and structure for an organization as a whole. Here we focus on how, once a pay level and structure is in place, managers can use pay to motivate employees to perform at a high level and attain their work goals. Pay is used to motivate entry-level workers, first-line and middle managers, and even top managers such as CEOs. Pay can be used to motivate people to perform behaviors that will help an organization achieve its goals (as at Kodak in the "Case in Contrast"), and it can be used to motivate people to join and remain with an organization (as at Mars Inc.).

Each of the theories described in this chapter alludes to the importance of pay and suggests that pay should be based on performance:

- *Expectancy theory:* Instrumentality, the association between performance and outcomes such as pay, must be high for motivation to be high. In addition, pay is an outcome that has high valence for many people.
- *Need theories:* People should be able to satisfy their needs by performing at a high level; pay can be used to satisfy several different kinds of needs.
- *Equity theory:* Outcomes such as pay should be distributed in proportion to inputs (including performance levels).
- *Goal-setting theory:* Outcomes such as pay should be linked to the attainment of goals.
- *Learning theories:* The distribution of outcomes such as pay should be contingent on the performance of organizationally functional behaviors.

As these theories suggest, to promote high motivation, managers should base the distribution of pay to organizational members on performance levels so that high performers receive more pay than low performers (other things being equal).[38] At General Mills, for example, the pay of all employees ranging from mailroom clerks to senior managers is based, at least in part, on performance.[39] A compensation plan basing pay on performance is often called a **merit pay plan.** Once managers have decided to use a merit pay plan, they face two important choices: whether to base pay on individual, group, or organizational performance and whether to use salary increases or bonuses.

merit pay plan A compensation plan that bases pay on performance.

Basing Merit Pay on Individual, Group, or Organizational Performance

Managers can base merit pay on individual, group, or organizational performance. When individual performance (such as the dollar value of merchandise a salesperson sells, the number of loudspeakers a factory worker assembles, and a lawyer's billable hours) can be accurately determined, individual motivation is likely to be highest when pay is based on individual performance.[40] When members of an organization work closely together and individual performance cannot be accurately determined (as in a team of computer programmers developing a single software package), pay cannot be based on individual performance, and a group- or organization-based plan must be used. When the attainment of organizational goals hinges on members working closely together and cooperating with each other (as in a small construction company that builds custom homes), group- or organization-based plans may be more appropriate than individual-based plans.[41]

It is possible to combine elements of an individual-based plan with a group- or organization-based plan to motivate each individual to perform highly while at the same time motivating all individuals to work well together, cooperate with each other, and help each other as needed. Lincoln Electric, a very successful company and a leading manufacturer of welding machines, uses a combination individual- and organization-based plan.[42] Pay is based on individual performance, but in addition, each year there is a bonus fund, the size of which depends on organizational performance. Money from the bonus fund is distributed to people on the basis of their contributions to the organization, attendance, levels of cooperation, and other indications of performance. Employees of Lincoln Electric are motivated to cooperate and help each other because when the firm as a whole performs well, everybody benefits by having a larger bonus fund. Employees also are motivated to contribute their inputs to the organization because their contributions determine their share of the bonus fund.

Salary Increase or Bonus?

Managers can distribute merit pay to people in the form of a salary increase or a bonus on top of regular salaries. Although the dollar amount of a salary increase or bonus might be identical, bonuses tend to have more motivational impact for at least three reasons. First, salary levels are typically based on performance levels, cost-of-living increases, and so forth from the day people start working in an organization, which means that the absolute level of the salary is based largely on factors unrelated to *current* performance. A 5 percent merit increase in salary, for example, may seem relatively small in comparison to one's total salary. Second, a current salary increase may be affected by other factors in addition to performance, such as cost-of-living increases or across-the-board market adjustments. Third, because organizations rarely reduce salaries, salary levels tend to vary less than performance levels do. Related to this point is the fact that bonuses give managers more flexibility in distributing outcomes. If an organization is doing well, bonuses can be relatively high to reward employees for their contributions. However, unlike salary increases, bonus levels can be reduced when an organization's performance lags. All in all, bonus plans have more motivational impact than salary increases because the amount of the bonus can be directly and exclusively based on performance.[43]

Consistent with the lessons from motivation theories, bonuses can be linked directly to performance and vary from year to year and employee to employee, as is the case at Gradient Corporation, a Cambridge, Massachusetts, environmental consulting firm named "Small Business of the Year" by the Greater Boston Chamber of Commerce in 1994.[44] Another example of an organization that successfully uses bonuses is Nucor Corporation. Steelworkers at Nucor tend to be much more productive than steelworkers in other companies—probably because they can receive bonuses tied to performance and quality that are from 130 to 150 percent of their regular or base pay.[45]

To motivate middle managers, many organizations are returning to pay-for-performance incentive pay systems. Here, a team of middle managers at Yoplait, the yougurt maker, celebrate the results of their high performance—bonuses that will average more than $50,000 for each person.

Examples of Merit Pay Plans

Managers can choose among several merit pay plans, depending on the work that employees perform and other considerations. Using *piece-rate pay,* an individual-based merit plan, managers base employees' pay on the number of units each employee produces, whether televisions, computer components, or welded auto parts. Managers at Lincoln Electric use piece-rate pay to determine individual pay levels. Advances in technology are currently simplifying the administration of piece-rate pay in the farming industry, as indicated in this "Management Insight."

Management Insight

Semiconductors Simplify the Administration of Piece-Rate Pay

Agricultural workers have long been paid on a piece-rate basis—by the number of boxes of fruit or vegetables they pick. However, the traditional means of administering piece-rate pay for farmworkers is time-consuming and tedious. For example, workers are often given a token or have a card punched for each box of produce they packed during the day. Then, at the end of the day, a manager counts the tokens or the punches on the cards and writes the number down. Figures for all workers are entered into a computer, and pay rates for the day are determined. Gary Parke, a manager and partner at Parkesdale Farms in Plant City, Florida, calls this type of system a "big payroll monster" because of the large amount of counting, record keeping, and computer entries required.

New metal buttons the size of a dime that farmworkers clip to their shirts or put in their pockets have tamed the payroll monster while providing managers with important information for planning such as how quickly a harvest is proceeding and which fields have the highest yields. The buttons are made by Dallas Semiconductor Corp.[46] and customized for use in farming by Agricultural Data Systems based in Laguna Niguel, California. Each button contains a semiconductor linked to payroll computers by use of a wandlike probe in the field.[47] The wand relays the number of boxes of fruit or vegetables that each worker picks as well as the type and quality of the produce picked, the location where it was picked in, and the time and the date. The buttons are activated by touching them with the probe; hence, they are called Touch Memory Buttons.

Farmworkers who pick strawberries at the Bob Jones Ranch in Oxnard, California, were originally opposed to using the buttons and after a trial period were able to go back to the old punch card system. The workers' primary complaint was that the buttons were too controlling of their behavior. However, according to Ann Woods, office manager at the ranch, being back on the old punch card system for just one day convinced the workers that the buttons were effective and actually saved them time as well.

Managers generally find that the buttons save time, improve accuracy, and provide valuable information about their crops and yields. Some workers have resisted the buttons because they are afraid that they give managers too much information about a worker's behavior (detailed histories of work performance can be stored on computers). Nevertheless, the buttons have certainly helped managers to more accurately and efficiently administer piece-rate pay to farmworkers while gathering useful information for planning and decision making.[48]

Using *commission pay,* another individual-based merit pay plan, managers base pay on a percentage of sales. Managers at the successful real-estate company Re/Max International Inc. use commission pay for their agents, who are paid a percentage of their sales. Some department stores, such as Neiman Marcus, use commission pay for their salespeople.

Examples of organization-based merit pay plans include the Scanlon plan and profit sharing. The *Scanlon plan* (developed by Joseph Scanlon, a union leader in a steel and tin plant in the 1920s) focuses on reducing expenses or cutting costs; members of an organization are motivated to come up with and implement cost-cutting strategies because a percentage of the cost savings achieved during a specified period of time is distributed back to employees.[49] Under *profit sharing,* employees receive a share of an organization's profits. Approximately 16 percent of the employees in firms that are medium or large in size receive profit sharing, and about 25 percent of small firms give their employees a share of the profits.[50] Regardless of the specific kind of plan that is used, managers should always strive to link pay to the performance of behaviors that help an organization achieve its goals.

Tips for Managers

Learning **Theory**

1. Distribute outcomes (reinforcers) to workers based on their performance of organizationally functional behaviors.

2. Use positive reinforcement instead of negative reinforcement whenever possible.

3. When feasible, use extinction rather than punishment to curtail dysfunctional behaviors. When punishment is necessary, focus on the behavior, not the person, and downplay the emotional element.

4. Make sure that good performer models are available for others to imitate, especially when someone is new to a job or organization.

5. Make sure that members of an organization see top performers being positively reinforced for their contributions.

6. Have high expectations for your subordinates and express confidence in their ability to succeed.

7. For subordinates who have low self-efficacy, encourage small successes by assigning them tasks they are likely to succeed at. Progressively increase the difficulty level of the tasks so success builds on itself.

Summary and Review

Chapter Summary

THE NATURE OF MOTIVATION

EXPECTANCY THEORY

- **Expectancy**
- **Instrumentality**
- **Valence**
- **Bringing It All Together**

NEED THEORIES

- **Maslow's Hierarchy of Needs**
- **Alderfer's ERG Theory**
- **Herzberg's Motivator–Hygiene Theory**

EQUITY THEORY

- **Equity**
- **Inequity**
- **Ways to Restore Equity**

GOAL-SETTING THEORY

THE NATURE OF MOTIVATION Motivation encompasses the psychological forces within a person that determine the direction of a person's behavior in an organization, a person's level of effort, and a person's level of persistence in the face of obstacles. Managers strive to motivate people to contribute their inputs to an organization, to focus these inputs in the direction of high performance, and to ensure that people receive the outcomes they desire when they perform at a high level.

EXPECTANCY THEORY According to expectancy theory, managers can promote high levels of motivation in their organizations by taking steps to ensure that expectancy is high (people think that if they try, they can perform at a high level), instrumentality is high (people think that if they perform at a high level, they will receive certain outcomes), and valence is high (people desire these outcomes).

NEED THEORIES Need theories suggest that in order to have a motivated workforce, managers should determine what needs people are trying to satisfy in organizations and then ensure that people receive outcomes that will satisfy these needs when they perform at a high level and contribute to organizational effectiveness.

EQUITY THEORY According to equity theory, managers can promote high levels of motivation by ensuring that people perceive that there is equity in the organization or that outcomes are distributed in proportion to inputs. Equity exists when a person perceives that his or her own outcome/input ratio equals the outcome/input ratio of a referent. Inequity motivates people to try to restore equity.

GOAL-SETTING THEORY Goal-setting theory suggests that managers can promote high motivation and performance by ensuring that people are striving to achieve specific, difficult goals. It also is important for people to accept the goals, be committed to them, and receive feedback about how they are doing.

LEARNING THEORIES Operant conditioning theory suggests that managers can motivate people to perform highly by using positive reinforcement or negative reinforcement (positive reinforcement being the preferred strategy). Managers can motivate people to avoid performing dysfunctional behaviors by using extinction or punishment. Social learning theory suggests that people can also be motivated by observing how others perform behaviors and receive rewards, by engaging in self-reinforcement, and by having high levels of self-efficacy.

PAY AND MOTIVATION   Each of the motivation theories discussed in this chapter alludes to the importance of pay and suggests that pay should be based on performance. Merit pay plans can be based on individual, group, or organizational performance and can entail the use of salary increases or bonuses.

Management in Action

Topics for Discussion and Action

1. Discuss why two people with similar abilities may have very different expectancies for performing at a high level.

2. Describe why some people have low instrumentalities even when their managers distribute outcomes based on performance.

3. Interview four people who have the same kind of job (such as salesperson, waiter/waitress, or teacher), and determine what kinds of needs they are trying to satisfy at work.

4. Analyze how professors try to promote equity to motivate students.

5. Describe three techniques or procedures that managers can use to determine whether a goal is difficult.

6. Discuss why managers should always try to use positive reinforcement instead of negative reinforcement.

7. Interview a manager in an organization in your community to determine the extent to which the manager takes advantage of vicarious learning to promote high motivation among his or her subordinates.

Building Management Skills

Diagnosing Motivation

Think about the ideal job that you would like to obtain upon graduation. Describe this job, the kind of manager you would like to report to, and the kind of organization you would be working in. Then answer the following questions.

1. What would be your levels of expectancy and instrumentality on this job? Which outcomes would have high valence for you on this job? What steps would your manager take to influence your levels of expectancy, instrumentality, and valence?

2. Whom would you choose as a referent on this job? What steps would your manager take to make you feel that you were being equitably treated? What would you do if, after a year on the job, you experienced underpayment inequity?

3. What goals would you strive to achieve on this job? Why? What role would your manager play in determining your goals?

4. What needs would you strive to satisfy on this job? Why? What role would your manager play in helping you satisfy these needs?

5. What behaviors would your manager positively reinforce you for on this job? Why? What positive reinforcers would your manager use?

6. Would there be any vicarious learning on this job? Why or why not?

7. To what extent would you be motivated by self-control on this job? Why?

8. What would be your level of self-efficacy on this job? Why would your self-efficacy be at this level? Should your manager take steps to boost your self-efficacy? If not, why not? If so, what would these steps be?

Small Group Breakout Exercise

Increasing Motivation

Form groups of three or four people, and appoint one member as the spokesperson who will communicate your findings to the whole class when called on by the instructor. Then discuss the following scenario.

You are a group of partners who own a chain of 15 dry-cleaning stores in a medium-size town. You are meeting today to discuss a problem in customer service that surfaced recently. When any one of you is spending the day or even part of the day in a particular store, clerks seem to be providing excellent customer service, spotters are making sure all stains are removed from garments, and pressers are doing a good job of pressing difficult items such as silk blouses. Yet during those same visits customers complain to you about such things as stains not being removed and items being poorly pressed in some of their previous orders; indeed, several customers have brought garments in to be redone. Customers also sometimes comment on having waited too long for service on previous visits. You are meeting today to address this problem.

1. Discuss the extent to which you believe that you have a motivation problem in your stores.

2. Given what you have learned in this chapter, design a plan to increase the motivation of clerks to provide prompt service to customers even when they are not being watched by a partner.

3. Design a plan to increase the motivation of spotters to remove as many stains as possible even when they are not being watched by a partner.

4. Design a plan to increase the motivation of pressers to do a top-notch job on all clothes they press, no matter how difficult.

Exploring the World Wide Web

Specific Assignment

Many companies take active steps to ensure that their employees are highly motivated. One such company is Nucor. Scan Nucor's website to learn more about this company (http://www.fwi.com/nucor/). Then click on "About Nucor Corp."

1. What steps is Nucor taking to motivate its employees to perform at a high level?

2. How are teamwork and cooperation encouraged at Nucor?

General Assignment

Find a website of a company that bases pay on performance for some or all of its employees. Describe the merit pay plan in use at this company. Which employees are covered by the plan? Do you think this pay plan will foster high levels of motivation? Why or why not?

ManagementCase
Motivating with Stretch Targets

Top managers of many organizations have discovered a powerful tool to increase motivation and performance: stretch targets. Stretch targets are goals that call for dramatic improvements in key aspects of organizational performance and effectiveness, such as extraordinary increases in revenues, reductions in costs, or increases in the rate at which new products are developed and brought to market.[51] Typically, organizational goals or objectives are incremental, involving changes such as a 10 percent reduction in inventory costs or a 5 percent increase in revenues. These goals seem to motivate members of an organization to achieve the specified increments in performance but often little more. Top managers who use stretch targets instead of incremental goals have a vision of how much better an organization could be performing and then choose a target to motivate members of the organization to achieve this high level of performance. Much careful planning goes into the establishment of stretch targets.

At 3M, for example, Desi DeSimone was concerned about a depressed market for some of the goods 3M produced and especially concerned about a lack of increase in revenues from new products. He decided to set a stretch target for employees to increase by 30 percent 3M's revenues from products that had been introduced within the last four years. Along with this

stretch target came some changes in 3M's strategies. Rather than spending time developing products with modest potential that were akin to existing products on the market, 3M employees were encouraged to focus on developing major new products with high sales potential. In addition, employees were urged to bring these potential best-sellers to market quickly. As a result of the specific, difficult goal DeSimone set, the newly introduced Scotch-Brite Never Rust soap pad gained 22 percent of the soap pad market from Brillo and SOS in its first 18 months on the market.

At Boeing, CEO Frank Shrontz was concerned about the slow and inefficient ways in which airplanes were produced. He decided to motivate his employees with an ambitious stretch target that would cut costs to such a great extent that Boeing would be able to lower its prices and sell more planes. After considerable planning and strategic analysis, the stretch target he decided on was a 25 percent reduction in the cost of producing a plane, while maintaining Boeing's high-quality standards. At the same time, he implemented a second stretch target: reducing the amount of time it took to build a plane from 18 months to 8 months—again, while maintaining high quality. If achieved, this second stretch target would result in lower costs (due to less inventory expense) and more sales (due to decreased risk for airlines). Progress toward

these stretch targets has been good: New, more efficient, and less costly methods of production are being implemented in practically all phases of airplane production at Boeing, and the time needed to complete a plane has already dropped to between 10 and 12 months.[52]

Stretch targets seem to be powerful motivators that result in organizations and their members achieving the unthinkable in performance and effectiveness improvements. Five key aspects of stretch targets and the ways that managers implement them in organizations can account for their stunning success. First, stretch targets are specific, difficult goals, as illustrated by the examples above. Second, managers who implement stretch targets do whatever they can to boost expectancy so employees believe they actually can reach the target. CEO Steven Mason, who has implemented stretch targets at Mead, a large paper manufacturer, suggests that one way to make sure that employees are confident that the targets are reachable is by concentrating "on things . . . [they] can control."

Third, managers boost self-efficacy by demonstrating to employees that other organizations have been able to reach the standards set by the stretch targets. Mason, for example, had his employees visit General Electric's successful light bulb and appliance divisions to boost their self-efficacy. Like Mead, those divisions operate in mature industries with stable prices, yet they have been more profitable than many of Mead's operations because of their constant drive to increase productivity. If those divisions of GE could increase productivity in a mature industry with stable prices, why, Mason asked, couldn't Mead?

Fourth, managers take advantage of opportunities for vicarious learning. At Boeing, for example, Shrontz sent teams of employees to top-performing manufacturing companies in diverse industries ranging from shipbuilding to computer manufacturing so that they could learn from and become motivated by these exemplary organizations. Fifth, once managers set the stretch target and employees believe they can reach it, employees are given considerable autonomy in working to achieve it, setting intermediary goals, and so forth— that is, the employees control how they go about meeting the goal. For example, at CSX, a shipping and railroad company, CEO John Snow indicates that once stretch targets are set, "It's people in the field who find the right path."[53] Stretch targets certainly seem to be the right path for at least some top managers to take to motivate employees to achieve dramatic improvements in organizational performance.

Questions

1. Why do stretch targets result in high levels of motivation and performance?

2. How can or should managers respond to employees who complain that a stretch target is impossible to achieve?

3. In what kinds of situations might it be particularly appropriate for managers to implement stretch targets?

4. In what kinds of situations might stretch targets not be such a good idea?

ManagementCase

In the News

From the Pages of BusinessWeek
A Nice Business Built on Being Nice

A lot of experts tell Andrew Wilson he doesn't understand business: His prices are too low, his pay scale too high. But the 41-year-old founder of Boston Duck Tours, which offers land/water sightseeing trips in World War II–era amphibious vehicles known as DUKWs, or "Ducks," has built a flourishing company in just four years by swimming against the current. "Other businesspeople don't get it," he says. "Why argue with success?"

Why indeed? Buoyed by Boston's recent tourism boom, Wilson has made his entertaining tours stand out—even in a market so cut-throat that tour-ticket vendors have been known to fight over customers on Boston Common. His colorful flock of 16 Ducks, bearing proud local names such as Kenmore Carla and Fenway Fanny, take visitors on a fun yet fact-packed trip that cruises along the Charles River as well as around the city's fabled sights.

The 80-minute excursion costs adults $20. Boston Duck Tours carried 300,000 passengers from April to October, 1997, when the Small Business Administration named Wilson Massachusetts Entrepreneur of the Year. That traffic produced revenues of $4.4 million—and profits of $900,000—even though school groups get discounts and Wilson gives away thousands of free tickets. Revenues are expected to pass $5 million in 1998.

But what makes this former investment bank vice-president a rare bird is the way he operates.

Wilson won't raise prices, even though he turned away 250,000 customers last year because of limited capacity. (The city gave him permits for 4 more Ducks this year, up from 12. He has asked for 8 more.) "It'd be greedy," says Wilson, who relies on word-of-mouth and customer satisfaction to generate business. "People remember when you've gouged them." The situation has made Boston Duck Tours a B-school case study. At Harvard University, the professors thought he should expand outside Boston. But Wilson thinks the city's calm river and compact historical district are uniquely suited to the business.

Then there's his attitude toward profits. Last year, he donated 10% of pretax profits, or about $90,000, to community projects such as cleaning up the Charles. He also paid out about $1.1 million in bonuses—to everyone but himself. His own salary is "significantly under six figures," he says. Managers get 1.5%–3% equity in the business after five years, and after three months, all 50 or so employees enjoy benefits almost unknown in seasonal work: year-round medical, dental, and life insurance, plus a 401(k). Such largesse is practical, Wilson argues, citing the success of employee-oriented Southwest Airlines Co.: "Ultimately, this business is about people. If they're enthusiastic, it works."

Enthusiasm is definitely on display aboard the Ducks. Each driver/guide "conducktor" develops a theatrical identity, costume, and spiel—Brad Rigby, for example, calls himself "Ace Bandage" and dresses like a New England Patriots football player. But besides encouraging wackiness—the crew carry kazoos to quack at passersby, who often reply in kind—the company insists employees know what they're talking about. Guides study with the local historical society, for example.

And they're well-paid. The highest-earning conducktor made more than $50,000 last year—for eight months' work. Even the part-time, mostly student, ticket-takers earn a $1-an-hour bonus on top of their $9-an-hour wages if they stay through their contracts.

Wilson says the generosity reduces labor costs by cutting down on turnover. (All four of the original conducktors are still aboard.) Recruiting is also easier. Brad Rigby came from a rival tour company that runs trolleys year-round but offers no benefits. "I'm not gonna leave here unless they make me," he says.

Wilson hatched the idea for the company in 1992 when he saw tourist-bearing Ducks lumbering around Memphis. He had recently bailed out of "100-hour workweeks" as a vice-president for operations at investment-banking firm Boston Co., feeling, among other things, underpaid for his contributions. "I just hit a wall one day," recalls the Chicago native, who put himself through college working nights as a deputy sheriff. He thought Ducks would do well in Boston, where visiting friends loved to be taken out on the Charles in his sailboat.

At the time, there were only two other Duck tours in the country: in Branson, Mo.—a waterfront tourist destination, like Boston—and in the scenic Wisconsin Dells, where a returning serviceman launched the original Duck tour right after World War II. Wilson started tracking down collectors of the vintage military vehicles and met Cambridge (Mass.) funeral-home owner Manuel Rogers Jr., who loved the idea and took a $90,000 stake in the business. That kept Wilson afloat until he could raise $1.2 million more from 35 limited partners rounded up by a small Boston investment bank. (As general partner, Wilson owns about 25%.) Wilson bought four Ducks, available for as little as $500, and then came the hard part—a two-year odyssey through "100 halls of government" to get the 30 permits he needed to launch in late summer '94.

Then Boston Duck Tours hit rough water. Wilson, $270,000 in debt, lost $80,000 the first year. But his whole crew pitched in to keep the startup going—painting, wiring, and laying the carpets in the office themselves. He spent nothing on advertising, figuring, correctly, that he didn't need it; local media gave lots of play to the diverting newcomers. Revenues rose to $1.9 million in '95, and the business has been making money ever since. "The investors are very pleased," says Jeffrey S. McCormick of Saturn Asset Management, though he adds that Wilson's "passionate commitment" to his city, employees, and investors creates a "healthy tension over where to dedicate resources and, frankly, profits."

These days, the Ducks are local icons, featured in ads for the Bank of Boston. Yet Wilson is thinking about moving on to other things. With nearly 600,000 tourists a year coming to his door, he can see expanding his "entertainment business"—the business he says he ultimately is in—into profitable new directions involving tours and merchandise for tourists. On the other hand, success has meant more seven-day weeks, and he hasn't taken a vacation in 18 months. "I'm at a crossroads in my life," he says. "You need balance. You've got to have time to watch the clouds roll by."

Although a number of buyers have made offers, he says, they tend to melt away when he insists they continue his profit distribution and benefits. Now, he's considering a sale to his staff through an employee stock-ownership program. "I believe in employee ownership," he says. "I'm not anticapitalism, but the human element isn't taken into account enough." By making the most of his human assets, this engagingly odd duck has made his business swim.

Source: Edith Hill Updike, "A Nice Business Built on Being Nice," *Business Week,* September 14, 1998, ENT10, ENT11.

Questions

1. What steps has Andrew Wilson, founder of Boston Duck Tours, taken to ensure that he has a highly motivated workforce?

2. What steps has Wilson taken to ensure that Boston Duck Tours' employees perform at a high level?

Chapter thirteen

Leadership

Learning Objectives

1. Describe what leadership is, when leaders are effective and ineffective, and the sources of power that enables managers to be effective leaders.

2. Identify the traits that show the strongest relationship to leadership, the behaviors leaders engage in, and the limitations of the trait and behavior models of leadership.

3. Explain how contingency models of leadership enhance our understanding of effective leadership and management in organizations.

4. Describe what transformational leadership is, and explain how managers can engage in it.

5. Characterize the relationship between gender and leadership.

A Case in Contrast

Welch Fosters Prosperity While Agee Fosters Decline

Jack Welch, CEO of General Electric (GE) (www.ge.com) since 1981, has been credited with leading this generator of $60 billion of annual sales to domination of the global markets in which it operates.[1] In fact, in 1998, GE was rated the "World's Most Admired Company" by *Fortune* magazine's panel of business experts.[2] In contrast, Bill Agee, CEO of the construction company Morrison Knudsen (www.mk.com) from 1988 until the board of directors fired him in 1995, has been credited with contributing to the problems this company experienced in the early to mid 1990s. It lost $310 million on $2.5 billion in sales in 1995.[3]

Many industry analysts attribute the differences in the companies' performance to their CEOs' different leadership styles. Welch has a hands-off approach to managing his company and acknowledges that he does not know all the inner workings of GE's various businesses. His approach to leadership is to empower his subordinates. He encourages and motivates managers who do know the ins and outs of, for example, appliance manufacturing to figure out for themselves how to achieve huge gains in efficiency and effectiveness. By contrast, Agee presided over the making of decisions for many of Morrison Knudsen's businesses even though his background did not always suggest he

had the expertise to do so. Nor did Agee take the appropriate steps to acquire the information needed to make good decisions.[4] In the early 1990s, for example, he decided that Morrison should expand beyond the

Leadership styles, such as the contrasting ones presented by Jack Welch of GE, and Bill Agee of Morrison Knudsen, are often the difference between an effective organization and managerial misfortune.

construction industry and focus on manufacturing passenger railcars and loco-motives.[5] However, neither Agee nor Morrison Knudsen had the needed exper-tise to compete in this industry. Agee committed major resources to this endeavor, which turned out to be a fiasco.

Welch has realized all along that much of his effectiveness as a leader hinges on recruiting and developing talented managers, helping them to have a vision of what needs to be done in their respective units, motivating them, and rewarding them for a job well done. He respects his managers, wants them to stand up to him, and truly wants them to enjoy what they do. GE's managers, in turn, tend to respect, like, and feel loyalty toward Welch. Nevertheless, while fostering good relations with his managers, Welch never loses sight of his top priority: continually increasing GE's bottom line.

Agee, in contrast, tended to surround himself with relatively inexperienced managers who would simply agree with what he proposed. One member of Morrison's board of directors suggested that "He [Agee] was afraid to have tal-ent around."[6] Some hard facts seem to back up this assertion. In 1989, the aver-age age of top managers at Morrison was 53. In 1993, the average age was 40, some vice presidents were in their early 30s, and the company's treasurer was 28. These relatively young top managers lacked experience in running a large company and standing up to someone like Agee. As Morrison's fortunes started to decline, Agee blamed his managers and even fired some of them. The remaining managers started to believe that if they wanted to keep their jobs, they had to give Agee overly optimistic performance projections for their divi-sions and projects (which would make it appear as if the company's ongoing operations were in good shape). Agee also appeared not to care how his employees felt and was insensitive to how his own actions might alienate oth-ers, particularly loyal and committed Morrison employees. For example, he took down a portrait of the company's founder, Harry Morrison, which had long been a fixture in Morrison Knudsen's headquarters, and replaced it with a large por-trait of himself and his wife, Mary Cunningham.

Bill Agee seemed overly concerned that the numbers reflecting short-run performance look good at Morrison Knudsen; and to make them so, he occa-sionally sold off parts of the company or its assets and reported the proceeds as operating income. Jack Welch has the opposite approach. He strives to max-imize long-run performance and is not overly concerned that things look good in the short run as long as employees are performing their jobs as efficiently and effectively as possible.

For example, one year GE's plastics unit had increased earnings of around 10 percent. Many managers would applaud such a short-run increase, but Welch was not pleased; he believed the unit could have done much better (an increase of 30 or 40 percent), building a solid base for long-run success. In con-trast, GE's aircraft engine unit had lower earnings than in the previous year, but Welch believed this unit had done much better than its global competitors, so he was not concerned about this short-run decline. True to his commitment to moti-vating subordinates to perform their best, Welch rewarded managers in the air-craft unit with a hefty bonus while those in the plastics unit saw their bonuses decline.

Jack Welch appears to be such an effective leader at GE that there is actually some concern about whether anyone could possibly fill his shoes when he eventually retires. However, Welch's cultivation and development of his subordinates practically ensures that, when the time comes, a suitable candidate will be found among the ranks of GE's top managers. And fortunately, Morrison Knudsen's fortunes have changed under its current CEO, Robert Tintstman; in 1997, Morrison Knudsen's net income was $32 million on $1.7 billion in revenues.[7] ●

Overview

Jack Welch exemplifies how effective leadership results in a high-performing organization just as Bill Agee illustrates how ineffective leadership can cripple an organization. In Chapter 1 we explained that one of the four principal tasks of managers is leading. Thus, it should come as no surprise that leadership is a key ingredient in effective management. When leaders are effective, their subordinates or followers are highly motivated, committed, and high performing. When leaders are ineffective, chances are good that their subordinates do not perform up to their capabilities, are demotivated, and may be dissatisfied as well. CEOs Welch and Agee are leaders at the very top of an organization, but leadership is an important ingredient for managerial success at all levels of an organization: top management, middle management, and first-line management. Moreover, leadership is a key ingredient for managerial success for organizations large and small.

In this chapter we describe what leadership is and examine the major leadership models that shed light on the factors that contribute to a manager being an effective leader: trait and behavior models, which focus on what leaders are like and what they do, and contingency models–Fiedler's contingency model, path–goal theory, and the leader substitutes model. Each of them takes into account the complexity surrounding leadership and the role of the situation in leader effectiveness. We describe how managers can have dramatic effects in their organizations by means of transformational leadership. We also examine the relationship between gender and leadership. By the end of this chapter, you will have a good appreciation of the many factors and issues that managers face in their quest to be effective leaders. ●

The Nature of Leadership

leadership The process by which an individual exerts influence over other people and inspires, motivates, and directs their activities to help achieve group or organizational goals.

Leadership is the process by which a person exerts influence over other people and inspires, motivates, and directs their activities to help achieve group or organizational goals.[8] The person who exerts such influence is a **leader.** When leaders are effective, the influence they exert over others helps a group or organization achieve its performance goals. When leaders are ineffective, their influence does not contribute to, and often detracts from, goal attainment. As the "Case in Contrast" makes clear, Jack Welch is an effective leader: He exerts strong influence over his managers, and the way he motivates and rewards them has helped GE achieve its goals. By contrast, Bill Agee was an ineffective leader: He influenced employees at Morrison Knudsen, but the kind of influence he exerted hindered organizational goal attainment as overly optimistic performance projections led to poor decision making.

leader An individual who is able to exert influence over other people to help achieve group or organizational goals.

Beyond performance goals, effective leadership increases an organization's ability to meet all the contemporary challenges discussed throughout this book, including the need to obtain a competitive advantage, the need to foster ethical behavior, and the need to manage a diverse workforce fairly and equitably. Leaders who exert influence over organizational members to help meet these goals increase their organization's chances of success.

In considering the nature of leadership, we first look at leadership styles and how they affect managerial tasks and at the influence of culture on leadership styles. We then focus on the key to leadership, *power,* which can come from a variety of sources. Finally, we consider the contemporary dynamic of empowerment and how it relates to effective leadership.

Personal Leadership Style and Managerial Tasks

A manager's *personal leadership style*–that is, the specific ways in which a manager chooses to influence other people–shapes the way that manager approaches planning, organizing, and controlling (the other principal tasks of managing). Consider how Jack Welch's and Bill Agee's personal leadership styles affect the way they perform these other important management tasks. Jack Welch's personal style is to support and encourage other managers to assume responsibility for the performance of their divisions. He delegates authority (an organizing task), allows his subordinates to develop their own strategies for their divisions (a planning task), and periodically reviews their performance to evaluate their success (a control task). By contrast, Agee's personal leadership style was to make decisions himself even when he lacked expertise and to surround himself with subordinates who would agree with him. Agee therefore centralized authority and decision making at Morrison Knudsen (an organizing task), took major responsibility for strategy development (a planning task), and threatened subordinates with job loss when they did not support him or give him overly optimistic performance projections (a control task).

Managers at all levels and in all kinds of organizations have their own personal leadership styles, which determine not only how they lead their subordinates but also how they perform the other management tasks. Michael Kraus, owner and manager of a dry-cleaning store in the northeastern United States, for example, takes a very hands-on approach to leadership. He has the sole authority for determining work schedules and job assignments for the 15 employees in his store (an organizing task), makes all important decisions by himself (a planning task), and closely monitors his employees' performance and rewards top performers with pay increases (a control task). Kraus's personal leadership style is effective in his organization. His employees are generally motivated, perform highly, and are satisfied, and his store is highly profitable. Though on the surface Kraus's personal leadership style might seem similar to Agee's, important differences can account for Kraus's effectiveness and Agee's ineffectiveness. In contrast to Agee, Kraus makes sure he has all the information he needs to make good decisions, respects his subordinates and looks out for their well-being, and encourages them to be open and honest with him.

Samsung's Japanese managers have had to spend considerable time learning new leadership skills to influence and motivate U. S. employees. In the United States, leaders need to be more *directive* as well as *participative* as compared to Japan.

Leadership Styles Across Cultures

Some evidence suggests that leadership styles vary not only among individuals but also among countries or cultures. Some research suggests that European managers tend to be more humanistic or people oriented than both Japanese and American managers. The collectivistic culture in Japan places prime emphasis on the group rather than the individual, so the importance of individuals' own personalities, needs, and desires is minimized. Organizations in the United States tend to be very profit oriented and thus tend to downplay the importance of individual employees' needs and desires. Many countries in Europe have a more individualistic perspective than Japan and a more humanistic perspective than the United States, which may result in some European managers being more people oriented than their Japanese or American counterparts. European managers, for example, tend to be reluctant to lay off employees, and when a layoff is absolutely necessary, they take careful steps to make it as painless as possible.[9]

Another cross-cultural difference that has been noted is in time horizons. Managers in any one country often differ in their time horizons (recall that Jack Welch focuses on long-run performance and Bill Agee focused on making things look good in the short run), but there also may be cultural differences. U.S. organizations tend to have a short-run profit orientation, which results in U.S. managers' personal leadership styles emphasizing short-run performance. Japanese organizations tend to have a long-run growth orientation, which results in Japanese managers' personal leadership styles emphasizing long-run performance. Justus Mische, a personnel manager at the European organization Hoechst suggests that "Europe, at least the big international firms in Europe, have a philosophy between the Japanese, long term, and the United States, short term."[10] Research on these and other global aspects of leadership is in its infancy, but as it continues, more cultural differences in managers' personal leadership styles may be discovered.

Power: The Key to Leadership

No matter what one's leadership style, a key component of effective leadership is found in the *power* the leader has to affect other people's behavior and get them to act in certain ways.[11] There are several types of power: legitimate, reward, coercive, expert, and referent power (see Figure 13.1).[12] Effective leaders take steps to ensure that they have sufficient levels of each type and that they use the power they have in beneficial ways.

legitimate power
The authority that a manager has by virtue of his or her position in an organization's hierarchy.

LEGITIMATE POWER Legitimate power is the authority a manager has by virtue of his or her position in an organization's hierarchy. Personal leadership style often influences how a manager exercises legitimate power. Take the case of Carol Loray, who is a first-line manager in a greeting card

Figure 13.1
Sources of Managerial Power

company and leads a group of 15 artists and designers. Loray has the legitimate power to hire new employees, assign projects to the artists and designers, monitor their work, and appraise their performance. She uses this power effectively. She always makes sure that her project assignments match the interests of her subordinates as much as possible so they will enjoy their work. She monitors their work to make sure they are on track but does not engage in close supervision, which can hamper creativity. She makes sure her performance appraisals are developmental, providing concrete advice for areas where improvements could be made. Recently, Loray negotiated with her manager to increase her legitimate power, so now she can initiate and develop proposals for new card lines.

REWARD POWER **Reward power** is the ability of a manager to give or withhold tangible rewards (pay raises, bonuses, choice job assignments) and intangible rewards (verbal praise, a pat on the back, respect). As you learned in Chapter 12, members of an organization are motivated to perform at a high level by a variety of rewards. Being able to give or withhold rewards based on performance is a major source of power that allows managers to have a highly motivated workforce. Managers of salespeople in retail organizations like Neiman Marcus and Dillard's Department Stores, in car dealerships like Chrysler's and Ford's, and in travel agencies like Liberty Travel and the Travel Company often use their reward power to motivate their subordinates. Subordinates in organizations such as these often receive a commission on whatever they sell and rewards for the quality of their customer service, which motivate them to do the best they can.

Effective managers use their reward power in such a way that subordinates feel that their rewards signal that they are doing a good job and their efforts are appreciated. Ineffective managers use rewards in a more controlling manner (wielding the "stick" instead of offering the "carrot"), which signals to subordinates that the manager has the upper hand. Managers also can take steps to increase their reward power. Carol Loray had the legitimate power to appraise her subordinates' performance, but she lacked the reward power to distribute raises and end-of-year bonuses until she discussed with her own manager why this would be a valuable motivational tool for her to use. Loray now receives a pool of money each year for salary increases and bonuses and has the reward power to distribute them as she sees fit.

COERCIVE POWER **Coercive power** is the ability of a manager to punish others. Punishment can range from verbal reprimands, to reductions in pay or working hours, to actual dismissal. In the last chapter, we discussed

reward power The ability of a manager to give or withhold tangible and intangible rewards.

coercive power The ability of a manager to punish others.

"Corporate America's most feared female activist."—Darla Moore, President of Rainwater, Inc. Here she stands with Sen. John McGill of South Carolina waiting to speak to the South Carolina Senate chamber about the problems with the state education system and recommendations for improving it.

how punishment can have negative side effects such as resentment and retaliation and should be used only when necessary (for example, to curtail a dangerous behavior). Managers who rely heavily on coercive power tend to be ineffective as leaders and sometimes even get fired themselves. William J. Fife is one example; he was fired from his position as CEO of Giddings and Lewis Inc., a manufacturer of factory equipment, because of his overreliance on coercive power. In meetings, Fife often verbally criticized, attacked, and embarrassed top managers. Realizing how destructive Fife's use of punishment was for them and the company, these managers complained to the board of directors, who, after a careful consideration of the issues, asked Fife to resign.[13]

Excessive use of coercive power seldom produces high performance and is questionable ethically. Sometimes it amounts to a form of mental abuse, robbing workers of their dignity and causing excessive levels of stress. Overuse of coercive power can even result in dangerous working conditions. Better results can be obtained with reward power, as indicated in this "Ethics in Action."

Ethics in Action

Curtailing Coercive Power Makes Good Business Sense

Ricardo Semler was only 21 in 1979 when he took control of his family business, Semco, a Brazilian manufacturer of industrial products such as pumps, mixers, and propellers.[14] Use of coercive power had been the norm rather than the exception at Semco. Fear was rampant. Guards policed the factory, workers were frisked when they left for the day, their visits to the restroom were timed, and anyone who broke a piece of equipment had to pay for it. Though some other traditional Brazilian companies were and still are managed in a similar fashion, Semler found managing Semco in this manner to be so stressful that after collapsing one day on a business trip, he vowed to make Semco "a true democracy, a place run on trust and freedom, not fear."[15] His goal was to create an ethical workplace in which all employees were treated with respect and dignity. By all reports, he has achieved his goal.

How did Semler achieve this feat? After careful planning and analysis, he decided to use reward power instead of coercive power to get things done. Workers are no longer closely monitored and actually can come and go when they want. Workers are allowed to choose their own bosses. A record 23 percent of Semco's profits are given back to employees for a job well done. Semler even rewards top managers by sharing his title as CEO. Semler rotates the CEO position among himself and six other managers every six months.[16]

Aside from creating more ethical working conditions that have lowered levels of fear, distrust, and stress for Semco employees, what have been the consequences of Semler's radical changes? When Semler took over the business in 1979, Semco had sales of $10,800 per employee (about half of the amount of its competitors in Brazil). In recent years, Semco's sales averaged around $135,000 per employee (four times the figures for its competitors). Nonmanagers and managers alike realize that Semler must be on the right track. The company receives 1,000 job applications per open position, and managers from global organizations such as Mobil (www.mobil.com) and IBM (www.ibm.com) have traveled to Brazil to see firsthand what is happening at Semco.[17]

expert power Power that is based in the special knowledge, skills, and expertise that a leader possesses.

EXPERT POWER

Expert power is based in the special knowledge, skills, and expertise that a leader possesses. The nature of expert power varies, depending on the leader's level in the hierarchy. First-line and middle managers often have technical expertise relevant to the tasks that their subordinates perform. Their expert power gives them considerable influence over subordinates. Carol Loray has expert power: She is an artist herself and has drawn and designed some of her company's top-selling greeting cards.

Some top managers derive expert power from their technical expertise. Andrew Grove, CEO of Intel, has a PhD in chemical engineering and is very knowledgeable about the ins and outs of producing semiconductors and microprocessors (what Intel does).[18] Similarly, Bill Gates, chairman of Microsoft, has expertise in software design; and Roy Vagelos, former CEO of Merck, a major pharmaceutical company, was an outstanding research scientist in his own right. Many top-level managers, however, lack technical expertise and derive their expert power from their abilities as decision makers, planners, and strategists. Jack Welch, described in the "Case in Contrast," is one of these. He puts it this way: "The basic thing that we at the top of the company know is that we don't know the business. What we have, I hope, is the ability to allocate resources, people, and dollars."[19]

Effective leaders take steps to ensure that they do have an adequate amount of expert power to perform their leadership roles. They may obtain additional training or education in their fields, make sure they keep up-to-date with the latest developments and changes in technology, stay abreast of changes in their fields through involvement in professional associations, and read widely to be aware of momentous changes in the organization's task and general environments. Expert power tends to be best used in a guiding or coaching manner rather than in an arrogant, high-handed manner.

referent power Power that comes from subordinates' and coworkers' respect, admiration, and loyalty.

REFERENT POWER

Referent power is more informal than the other kinds of power. Referent power is a function of the personal characteristics of a leader; it is the power that comes from subordinates' and coworkers' respect, admiration, and loyalty. Leaders who are likeable and whom subordinates wish to use as a role model are especially likely to possess referent power. Rochelle Lazarus, a top manager at the advertising agency Ogilvy & Mather, won IBM's worldwide advertising account in part because of her referent power.[20]

In addition to being a valuable asset for top managers like Lazarus, referent power can help first-line and middle managers be effective leaders as well. Sally Carruthers, for example, is the first-line manager of a group of secretaries in the finance department of a large state university. Carruthers's secretaries are known to be among the best in the university. Much of their willingness to go above and beyond the call of duty has been attributed to Carruthers's warm and caring nature, which makes each of them feel important and valued. Managers can take steps to increase their referent power, such as taking time to get to know their subordinates and showing interest in and concern for them.

Empowerment: An Ingredient in Modern Management

empowerment Expanding employees' tasks and responsibilities.

More and more managers today are incorporating in their personal leadership styles an aspect that at first glance seems to be the opposite of being a leader. In Chapter 1, we described how **empowerment,** the process of giving employees at all levels in the organization the authority to make decisions, be responsible for their outcomes, improve quality, and cut costs, is becoming increasingly popular in organizations. When leaders empower their subordinates, the subordinates typically take over some of the responsibilities and authority that used to reside with the leader or manager, such as the right to reject parts that do not meet quality standards, the right to check one's own work, and the right to schedule work activities. Empowered subordinates are given the power to make some of the decisions that their leaders or supervisors used to make.

At first glance, empowerment might seem to be the opposite of effective leadership because managers are allowing subordinates to take a more active role in leading themselves. In actuality, however, empowerment can contribute to effective leadership for several reasons:

- Empowerment increases a manager's ability to get things done because the manager has the support and help of subordinates who may have special knowledge of work tasks.

- Empowerment often increases workers' involvement, motivation, and commitment, which helps ensure that they will be working toward organizational goals.

- Empowerment gives managers more time to concentrate on their pressing concerns because they spend less time on day-to-day supervisory activities.

Effective managers like Jack Welch realize the benefits of empowerment; ineffective managers like Bill Agee try to keep control over all decision making and force agreement from subordinates. The personal leadership style of managers who empower subordinates often entails developing subordinates so that they can make good decisions and being subordinates' guide, coach, and source of inspiration. Empowerment is a popular trend in the United States at companies as diverse as United Parcel Service (a package delivery company) and Coram Healthcare Corporation (a provider of medical equipment and services), and it is also taking off around the world.[21] Even companies in South Korea (such as Samsung, Hyundai, and Daewoo), in which decision making typically was centralized with the founding families, are empowering managers at lower levels to make decisions.[22]

Trait and Behavior Models of Leadership

Leading is such an important process in all organizations—nonprofit organizations, government agencies, and schools as well as for-profit corporations—that it has been researched for decades. Early approaches to leadership, called the *trait model* and the *behavior model,* sought to determine what effective leaders are like as people and what they do that makes them so effective.

The Trait Model

The trait model of leadership focused on identifying the personal characteristics that are responsible for effective leadership. Researchers thought that effective leaders must have certain personal qualities that set them apart from ineffective leaders and from people who never become leaders. Decades of research (beginning in the 1930s) and hundreds of studies indicate that certain personal characteristics do appear to be associated with effective leadership (see Table 13.1 for a list of these).[23] Notice that although this model is called the "trait" model, some of the personal characteristics that it identifies are not personality traits per se but rather are concerned with a leader's skills, abilities, knowledge, and expertise. As the "Case in Contrast" shows, Jack Welch certainly appears to possess many of these characteristics (such as intelligence, self-confidence, and integrity and honesty). Leaders who do not possess these traits may be ineffective.

Traits alone, however, are not the key to understanding leader effectiveness. Some effective leaders do not possess all of these traits, and some leaders who do possess them are not effective in their leadership roles. This lack of a consistent relationship between leader traits and leader effectiveness led researchers to shift their attention away from traits and to search for new explanations for effective leadership. Rather than focusing on what leaders are

Table 13.1

Traits and Personal Characteristics Related to Effective Leadership

TRAIT	DESCRIPTION
Intelligence	Helps managers understand complex issues and solve problems
Knowledge and expertise	Helps managers make good decisions and discover ways to increase efficiency and effectiveness
Dominance	Helps managers influence their subordinates to achieve organizational goals
Self-confidence	Contributes to managers' effectively influencing subordinates and persisting when faced with obstacles or difficulties
High energy	Helps managers deal with the many demands they face
Tolerance for stress	Helps managers deal with uncertainty and make difficult decisions
Integrity and honesty	Helps managers behave ethically and earn their subordinates' trust and confidence
Maturity	Helps managers avoid acting selfishly, control their feelings, and admit when they have made a mistake

like (the traits they possess), researchers began to turn their attention to what effective leaders actually do—in other words, to the behaviors that allow effective leaders to influence their subordinates to achieve group and organizational goals.

The Behavior Model

After extensive study, researchers at Ohio State University in the 1940s and 1950s identified two basic kinds of leader behaviors that many leaders in the United States, Germany, and other countries engaged in to influence their subordinates: *consideration* and *initiating structure.*[24]

consideration Behavior indicating that a manager trusts, respects, and cares about subordinates.

CONSIDERATION   Leaders engage in **consideration** when they show their subordinates that they trust, respect, and care about them. Managers who truly look out for the well-being of their subordinates and do what they can to help subordinates feel good and enjoy their work perform consideration behaviors. In the "Case in Contrast," Jack Welch engages in consideration when he treats his subordinates with respect; Bill Agee's insensitive treatment of subordinates at Morrison Knudsen exemplifies a lack of consideration. Louis Hughes, CEO of General Motors Europe, learned German so that he could communicate with employees in Germany and show them that he truly cared.[25] With the increasing focus on the importance of high-quality customer service, many managers are realizing that when they are considerate to subordinates, subordinates are more likely to be considerate to customers and vice versa. The experiences of Staples, a discount office supply retailer, and the advertising agency Chiat/Day are consistent with this observation, as indicated in this "Management Insight."

Management Insight

Consideration and Customer Service at Staples and Chiat/Day

Staples (www.staples.com) is a top-performing retailer with annual percentage increases in sales and profits as high as 50 percent. Tom Stemberg, founder and CEO of Staples, has raised customer service to an art form. He is constantly on the lookout for new ways to please customers, and salespeople at Staples go out of their way to help customers no matter how large or small their orders are. Salespeople develop close, long-term relationships with customers and strive to provide innovative solutions to their office supply problems.

Other retailers also realize the value of high-quality customer service but have tended not to be as successful as Staples in actually providing it. One of Stemberg's guiding principles is that managers should treat subordinates in the way that they would like subordinates to treat customers. Stemberg goes out of his way to be considerate to the managers who report to him, and he encourages them to do likewise with their own subordinates. Rod Sargent, one of Stemberg's subordinates, recalls that when his newborn son was sick and in intensive care for a week, Stemberg called him every night to see how the baby was doing and provide support.[26]

Things could not have been more different at the Chiat/Day advertising agency (www.chiatday.com). Jay Chiat founded this unconventional company, responsible for innovative ad campaigns such as the Energizer bunny and Reebok's "U.B.U." campaign. Chiat, however, was not considerate to his employees, and they in turn were not considerate to the firm's customers. Former Chiat/Day vice chair Jane Newman said that Jay Chiat "would terrorize people."[27] Chiat took away his employees' offices and gave them lockers, laptop computers, and cellular phones, claiming that they did not need offices to get their work done and should not be focused on their own egos. Even when things were going well in the agency, Chiat rarely offered a kind word to his subordinates, let alone showing any concern for their well-being.

In turn, Chiat/Day employees tended to be rude and inconsiderate to the agency's major corporate customers. Nike (www.nike.com), once one of Chiat/Day's clients, left the agency for this very reason. Nike creative director Peter Moore recalled, "They were arrogant. Our people were miserable having to deal with them."[28] The lack of consideration that Jay Chiat showed his employees and the lack of consideration that they showed Chiat/Day's clients played a major role in the decline of the agency. Key clients ultimately took their accounts elsewhere, Chiat/Day lost talented employees tired of not being treated well, and eventually the company was sold to Omnicom Group Inc., an advertising agency holding company.[29]

initiating structure

Behavior that managers engage in to ensure that work gets done, subordinates perform their jobs acceptably, and the organization is efficient and effective.

INITIATING STRUCTURE   Leaders engage in **initiating structure** when they take steps to make sure that work gets done, subordinates perform their jobs acceptably, and the organization is efficient and effective. Assigning tasks to individuals or work groups, letting subordinates know what is expected of them, deciding how work should be done, making schedules, encouraging adherence to rules and regulations, and motivating subordinates to do a good job are all examples of initiating structure.[30] Michael Teckel, the manager of an upscale imported men's and women's shoe store in a midwestern U.S. city, engages in initiating structure when he establishes weekly work, lunch, and break schedules to ensure that the store has enough salespeople on the floor, when he discusses the latest shoe designs with his subordinates so that they are knowledgeable with customers, when he encourages adherence to the store's refund and exchange policies, and when he encourages his subordinates to provide high-quality customer service and to avoid a hard-sell approach.

Initiating structure and consideration are independent leader behaviors. Leaders can be high on both, low on both, or high on one and low on the other.

Leadership researchers have identified leader behaviors similar to consideration and initiating structure. Researchers at the University of Michigan, for example, identified two categories of leadership behaviors, *employee-centered behaviors* and *job-oriented behaviors,* that correspond roughly to consideration and initiating structure, respectively.[31] Models of leadership popular with consultants also tend to zero in on these two kinds of behaviors. For example, Robert Blake and Jane Mouton's Managerial Grid® focuses on *concern for people* (similar to consideration) and *concern for production* (similar to initiating structure). Blake and Mouton advise that effective leadership often requires both a high level of concern for people and a high level of concern for production.[32] As another example, Paul Hersey and Kenneth Blanchard's model focuses on *supportive behaviors* (similar to consideration) and *task-oriented behaviors* (similar to initiating structure). According to Hersey and Blanchard, leaders need to consider the nature of their subordinates when trying to determine the extent to which they should perform these two types of behavior.[33]

You might expect that effective leaders and managers would perform both kinds of behaviors, but research has found that this is not necessarily the case. The relationship between performance of consideration and initiating structure behaviors and leader effectiveness is not clear-cut. Some leaders are effective even when they do not perform consideration behaviors or initiating structure behaviors, and some leaders are ineffective even when they do perform both kinds of behaviors. Like the trait model of leadership, the behavior model alone cannot explain leader effectiveness. Realizing this, researchers began building more complicated models of leadership, models that focused not only on the leader and what he or she does but also on the situation or context in which leadership occurs.

Contingency Models of Leadership

Simply possessing certain traits or performing certain behaviors does not ensure that a manager will be an effective leader in all situations calling for leadership. Some managers who seem to possess the "right" traits and perform the "right" behaviors turn out to be ineffective leaders. Managers lead in a wide variety of situations and organizations and have various kinds of subordinates performing diverse tasks in many environmental contexts. Given the wide variety of situations in which leadership occurs, what makes a manager an effective leader in one situation (such as certain traits or certain behaviors) is not necessarily what that manager needs in order to be equally effective in a different situation. An effective army general might not be an effective university president, an effective manager of a restaurant might not be an effective manager of a clothing store, an effective coach of a football team might not be an effective manager of a fitness center, and an effective first-line manager in a manufacturing company might not be an effective middle manager. The traits or behaviors that may contribute to a manager being an effective leader in one situation might actually result in the same manager being an ineffective leader in another situation.

Contingency models of leadership take into account the situation or context within which leadership occurs. According to contingency models, whether or not a manager is an effective leader is the result of the interplay between what the manager is like, what he or she does, and the situation in which leadership takes place. Contingency models propose that whether a leader who possesses certain traits or performs certain behaviors is effective depends on, or is contingent on, the situation or context. In this section, we discuss three prominent contingency models developed to shed light on what makes managers effective leaders: Fred Fiedler's contingency model, Robert House's path–goal theory, and the leader substitutes model. As you will see, these leadership models are complementary; each focuses on a somewhat different aspect of effective leadership in organizations.

Fiedler's Contingency Model

Fred E. Fiedler was among the first leadership researchers to acknowledge that effective leadership is contingent on, or depends on, the characteristics of the leader *and* of the situation. Fiedler's contingency model helps explain why a manager may be an effective leader in one situation and ineffective in another; it also suggests which kinds of managers are likely to be most effective in which situations.[34]

LEADER STYLE   Like the trait approach, Fiedler hypothesized that personal characteristics can influence leader effectiveness. He used the term *leader style* to refer to a manager's characteristic approach to leadership, and he identified two basic leader styles: *relationship oriented* and *task oriented*. All managers can be described as having one style or the other.

relationship-oriented leaders Leaders whose primary concern is to develop good relationships with their subordinates and to be liked by them.

Relationship-oriented leaders are primarily concerned with developing good relationships with their subordinates and being liked by them. Relationship-oriented managers focus on having high-quality interpersonal relationships with subordinates. This does not mean, however, that the job does not get done when relationship-oriented leaders are at the helm. But it does mean that the quality of interpersonal relationships with subordinates is a prime concern for relationship-oriented leaders. Lawrence Fish, for example, is chairman of Citizens Financial Group Inc. of Providence, Rhode Island, which tripled its assets in three years. As the top manager who helped to engineer this rapid growth, Fish never loses sight of the importance of good relationships and personally writes a thank you note to at least one of his subordinates each day.[35]

task-oriented leaders
Leaders whose primary concern is to ensure that subordinates perform at a high level.

Task-oriented leaders are primarily concerned with ensuring that subordinates perform at a high level. Task-oriented managers focus on task accomplishment and making sure the job gets done. Some task-oriented leaders like the top managers of the family-owned C. R. England refrigerated trucking company based in Salt Lake City, Utah, go so far as to closely measure and evaluate performance on a weekly basis to ensure subordinates are performing as well as they can.[36]

In his research, Fiedler measured leader style by asking leaders to rate the coworker with whom they have had the most difficulty working (called the *least-preferred coworker* or LPC) on a number of dimensions such as whether the person is boring or interesting, gloomy or cheerful, enthusiastic or unenthusiastic, cooperative or uncooperative. Relationship-oriented leaders tend to describe the LPC in relatively positive terms; their concern for good relationships leads them to think about others in positive terms. Task-oriented leaders tend to describe the LPC in negative terms; their concern for task accomplishment causes them to think badly about others who make getting the job done difficult. Thus, relationship-oriented and task-oriented leaders are sometimes referred to, respectfully, as *high* LPC and *low* LPC leaders. Figure 13.2 shows the least-preferred coworker scale that Fiedler developed and used in some of his research.

SITUATIONAL CHARACTERISTICS   According to Fiedler, leadership style is an enduring characteristic; managers cannot change their style, nor can they adopt different styles in different kinds of situations. With this is mind, Fiedler identified three situational characteristics that are important

Figure 13.2
Fiedler's Least-Preferred Coworker Scale: A Measure of Leader Style

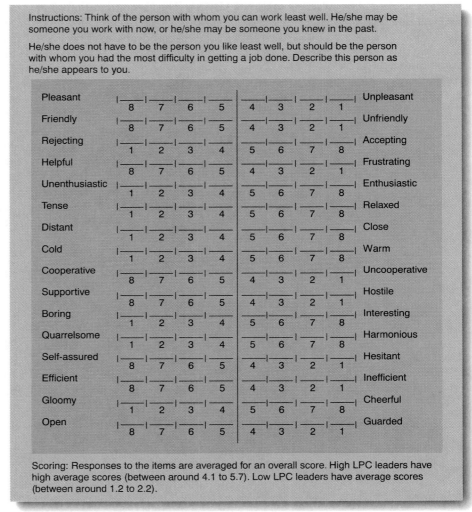

Instructions: Think of the person with whom you can work least well. He/she may be someone you work with now, or he/she may be someone you knew in the past.

He/she does not have to be the person you like least well, but should be the person with whom you had the most difficulty in getting a job done. Describe this person as he/she appears to you.

	8	7	6	5	4	3	2	1	
Pleasant	8	7	6	5	4	3	2	1	Unpleasant
Friendly	8	7	6	5	4	3	2	1	Unfriendly
Rejecting	1	2	3	4	5	6	7	8	Accepting
Helpful	8	7	6	5	4	3	2	1	Frustrating
Unenthusiastic	1	2	3	4	5	6	7	8	Enthusiastic
Tense	1	2	3	4	5	6	7	8	Relaxed
Distant	1	2	3	4	5	6	7	8	Close
Cold	1	2	3	4	5	6	7	8	Warm
Cooperative	8	7	6	5	4	3	2	1	Uncooperative
Supportive	8	7	6	5	4	3	2	1	Hostile
Boring	1	2	3	4	5	6	7	8	Interesting
Quarrelsome	1	2	3	4	5	6	7	8	Harmonious
Self-assured	8	7	6	5	4	3	2	1	Hesitant
Efficient	8	7	6	5	4	3	2	1	Inefficient
Gloomy	1	2	3	4	5	6	7	8	Cheerful
Open	8	7	6	5	4	3	2	1	Guarded

Scoring: Responses to the items are averaged for an overall score. High LPC leaders have high average scores (between around 4.1 to 5.7). Low LPC leaders have average scores (between around 1.2 to 2.2).

Source: F. E. Fiedler, *A Theory of Leadership Effectiveness* (New York: McGraw-Hill, 1967).

determinants of how favorable a situation is for leading: leader–member relations, task structure, and position power. When a situation is favorable for leading, it is relatively easy for a manager to influence subordinates so that they perform at a high level and contribute to organizational efficiency and effectiveness. In a situation unfavorable for leading, it is much more difficult for a manager to exert influence.

LEADER–MEMBER RELATIONS The first situational characteristic that Fiedler described, **leader–member relations,** is the extent to which followers like, trust, and are loyal to their leader. Situations are more favorable for leading when leader–member relations are good. From the "Case in Contrast," it is clear that Jack Welch's leadership situation is characterized by

leader–member relations The extent to which followers like, trust, and are loyal to their leader; a determinant of how favorable a situation is for leading.

good leader–member relations and Bill Agee's leadership situation had such poor leader–member relations that his subordinates actually cheered when he was fired.

task structure The extent to which the work to be performed is clear-cut so that a leader's subordinates know what needs to be accomplished and how to go about doing it; a determinant of how favorable a situation is for leading.

TASK STRUCTURE   The second situational characteristic that Fiedler described, **task structure,** is the extent to which the work to be performed is clear-cut so that a leader's subordinates know what needs to be accomplished and how to go about doing it. When task structure is high, situations are favorable for leading. When task structure is low, goals may be vague, subordinates may be unsure of what they should be doing or how they should do it, and the situation is unfavorable for leading.

Task structure was low for Geraldine Laybourne when she was a top manager at Nickelodeon, the children's television network. It was never precisely clear what would appeal to her young viewers, whose tastes can change dramatically, or how to motivate her subordinates to come up with creative and novel ideas.[37] In contrast, Herman Mashaba, founder and owner of Black Like Me, a hair care products company based in South Africa, seems to have relatively high task structure in his leadership situation. His company's goals are to produce and sell inexpensive hair care products to native Africans, and managers accomplish these goals by using simple yet appealing packaging and distributing the products through neighborhood beauty salons.[38]

position power The amount of legitimate, reward, and coercive power that a leader has by virtue of his or her position in an organization; a determinant of how favorable a situation is for leading.

POSITION POWER   The third situational characteristic that Fiedler described, **position power,** is the amount of legitimate, reward, and coercive power a leader has by virtue of his or her position in an organization. Leadership situations are more favorable for leading when position power is strong.

COMBINING LEADER STYLE AND THE SITUATION   By

taking all possible combinations of good and poor leader–member relations, high and low task structure, and strong and weak position power, Fiedler identified eight leadership situations, which vary in their favorability for leading (see Figure 13.3). After extensive research, he determined that relationship-oriented leaders are most effective in moderately favorable situations (situations IV, V, VI, and VII in Figure 13.3) and task-oriented leaders are most effective in very favorable (situations I, II, and III) or very unfavorable situations (situation VIII).

Can Fiedler's model help explain why Jack Welch appears to be an effective leader and manager and Bill Agee was ineffective? Both leaders appear to be task oriented. As top managers, their major concern is (was, in Agee's case) to improve the performance of their companies. What about their leadership situations? Both faced relatively low task structure. As CEOs of major corporations they faced considerable uncertainty about what their organizations' strategies should be and the best way to implement those strategies. Both also had relatively strong position power stemming from their position as the top managers in their organizations. However, their leadership situations differed in leader–member relations. Welch has good relations with his subordinates; Agee's leader–member relations were poor. According to Fiedler's model, Welch's leadership situation (situation III in Figure 13.3) is very favorable for leading, which suits his task-oriented style; and Agee's leadership situation is moderately favorable for leading (situation VII). According to the contingency model, in moderately favorable situations, relationship-oriented leaders are more effective than task-oriented leaders.

Figure 13.3
Fiedler's Contingency Theory of Leadership

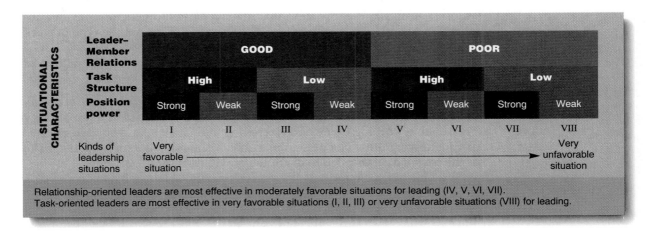

Relationship-oriented leaders are most effective in moderately favorable situations for leading (IV, V, VI, VII).
Task-oriented leaders are most effective in very favorable situations (I, II, III) or very unfavorable situations (VIII) for leading.

PUTTING THE CONTINGENCY MODEL INTO PRACTICE

According to Fiedler, leader style is an enduring characteristic that managers cannot change. This suggests that, in order to be effective, managers need to be placed in leadership situations that fit their style or situations need to be changed to suit the manager. Situations can be changed, for example, by giving a manager more position power or taking steps to increase task structure such as by clarifying goals.

Take the case of Mark Compton, a relationship-oriented leader employed by a small construction company who was in a very unfavorable situation for leading his construction crew and was having a rough time. His subordinates did not trust him to look out for their well-being (poor leader–member relations), the construction jobs he supervised tended to be novel and complex (low task structure), and he had no control over the rewards and disciplinary actions his subordinates received (weak position power). Recognizing the need to improve matters, Compton's supervisor gave him the power to reward crew members with bonuses and overtime work as he saw fit and to discipline crew members for poor-quality work and unsafe on-the-job behavior. As his leadership situation improved to be moderately favorable, so too did Compton's effectiveness as a leader and the performance of his crew.

Research studies tend to support Fiedler's model but also suggest that, like most theories, it is in need of some modifications.[39] Some researchers have questioned what the LPC scale really measures. Others find fault with the model's premise that leaders cannot alter their styles.

House's Path–Goal Theory

In what he called **path–goal theory,** leadership researcher Robert House focused on what leaders can do to motivate their subordinates to achieve group and organizational goals.[40] The premise of path–goal theory is that effective leaders motivate subordinates to achieve goals by (1) clearly identifying the outcomes that subordinates are trying to obtain from the workplace,

path–goal theory
A contingency model of
leadership proposing that
leaders can motivate sub-
ordinates by identifying
their desired outcomes,
rewarding them for high
performance and the
attainment of work goals
with these desired
outcomes, and clarifying
for them the paths leading
to the attainment of work
goals.

(2) rewarding subordinates with these outcomes for high performance and the attainment of work goals, and (3) clarifying for subordinates the *paths* leading to the attainment of work *goals*. Path–goal theory is a contingency model because it proposes that the steps that managers should take to motivate subordinates depend on both the nature of the subordinates and the type of work they do.

Based on the expectancy theory of motivation (see Chapter 12), path–goal theory provides managers with three guidelines to follow to be effective leaders:

1. *Find out what outcomes your subordinates are trying to obtain from their jobs and the organization.* These outcomes can range from satisfactory pay and job security to reasonable working hours and interesting and challenging job assignments. After identifying these outcomes, the manager should make sure that he or she has the *reward power* needed to distribute or withhold these outcomes.

Mark Crane, for example, is the vice principal of a large elementary school. Crane determined that the teachers he leads are trying to obtain the following outcomes from their jobs: pay raises, autonomy in the classroom, and the choice of what grades they teach. Crane had reward power for the latter two outcomes, but the school's principal determined how the pool of money for raises was to be distributed each year. Because Crane was the first-line manager who led the teachers and was most familiar with their performance, he asked the principal (his boss) to give him some say in determining pay raises. Realizing that this made a lot of sense, his principal gave Crane full power to distribute raises and requested only that Crane review his decisions with him prior to informing the teachers about them.

2. *Reward subordinates for high performance and goal attainment with the outcomes they desire.* The teachers and administrators at Crane's school considered several dimensions of teacher performance critical to achieving their goal of providing high-quality education—high-quality in-class instruction, special programs to enhance student interest and learning (such as science and computer projects), and availability for meetings with parents to discuss their children's progress and special needs. Crane distributed pay raises to the teachers based on the extent to which they performed highly on each of these dimensions. The top-performing teachers were given first choice of grade assignments and also had nearly complete autonomy in their classrooms.

3. *Clarify the paths to goal attainment for subordinates, remove any obstacles to high performance, and express confidence in subordinates' capabilities.* This does not mean that a manager needs to tell his or her subordinates what to do. Rather, it means that a manager needs to make sure that subordinates are clear about what they should be trying to accomplish and have the capabilities, resources, and confidence levels they need to be successful.

Crane made sure that all the teachers understood the importance of the three targeted goals and asked them whether, to reach them, they needed any special resources or supplies for their classes. Crane also gave additional coaching and guidance to teachers who seemed to be struggling. For example, Patrick Conolly, in his first year of teaching after graduate school, was unsure about how to use special projects in a third-grade class and how to react to parents who he thought were being critical. Conolly's actual teaching was excellent, but he

Malden Mills, the makers of Polartec fabrics was going bankrupt when Aaron Feuerstein took over the leadership of the organization. However, by *empowering* his workers, telling them exactly what needed to be done to keep the factory afloat, and giving them the resources they needed to get the job done, he created a committed workforce that has allowed the company to make record profits.

even felt insecure about how he was doing on this dimension. To help build Conolly's confidence, Crane told Conolly that he truly thought he could be one of the school's top teachers (which was true). He gave Conolly some ideas about special projects that worked particularly well with the third grade, such as a writing project. Crane also role-played teacher–parent interactions with Conolly. Conolly played the role of a particularly dissatisfied or troubled parent while Crane played the role of a teacher who is trying to solve the underlying problem while making the parent feel that his or her child's needs are being met. Crane's efforts to clarify the paths to goal attainment for Conolly paid off: Within two years the local PTA voted Conolly teacher of the year.

Path–goal theory identifies four kinds of behaviors that leaders can engage in to motivate subordinates:

- *Directive behaviors* are similar to initiating structure and include setting goals, assigning tasks, showing subordinates how to complete tasks, and taking concrete steps to improve performance.
- *Supportive behaviors* are similar to consideration and include expressing concern for subordinates and looking out for their best interests.
- *Participative behaviors* give subordinates a say in matters and decisions that affect them.
- *Achievement-oriented behaviors* motivate subordinates to perform at the highest level possible by, for example, setting very challenging goals, expecting that they be met, and believing in subordinates' capabilities.

Which of these behaviors should managers use to lead effectively? The answer to this question depends, or is contingent, on the nature of the subordinates and the kind of work they do.

Directive behaviors may be beneficial when subordinates are having difficulty completing assigned tasks, but they might be detrimental when subordinates are independent thinkers who work best when left alone. *Supportive* behaviors are often advisable when subordinates are experiencing high levels of stress. *Participative* behaviors can be particularly effective when subordinates' support of a decision is required. *Achievement-oriented* behaviors may increase motivation levels of highly capable subordinates who are bored from having too few challenges, but they might backfire if used with subordinates who are already pushed to their limit.

Effective managers seem to have a knack for determining the kinds of leader behaviors that are likely to work in different situations and result in increased efficiency and effectiveness, as indicated in this "Management Insight."

Management Insight

Turnarounds in the Steel Industry

Tom Graham, a steel industry executive in his late 60s, has a reputation for being blunt and callous, which has led some to call him the "Smiling Barracuda."[41] This nickname notwithstanding, Graham has turned around the fortunes of one failing steel company after another by engaging in behaviors needed to improve motivation, efficiency, and effectiveness.

In the early 1980s, Graham became president of U.S. Steel (www.ussteel.com), which at that time was losing $100 million per month. Graham began by using directive behaviors to cut costs. He took the unpopular step of eliminating 55,000 jobs—a cut he decided was necessary to save the company from bankruptcy. He used achievement-oriented behaviors to encourage up-and-coming managers to suggest changes and make improvements to increase efficiency. Graham must have done something right, for by 1988 U.S. Steel was making rather than losing money.

Graham moved on to head up a very small, unionized steel company, Washington Steel, located in Washington, Pennsylvania. Washington Steel was losing millions per month, and Washington Steel's creditors brought Graham in, in a last-ditch attempt to save the company from bankruptcy. Graham realized that he needed the union's support to cut costs and increase efficiency. Thus, in addition to using directive and achievement-oriented behaviors, he also engaged in participative behaviors with union leaders and got them to agree to steps to operate the mill more efficiently, including changing from a six-day workweek to a seven-day workweek.

Graham is currently vice president of research and engineering of AK Steel (www.aksteel.com), a joint venture between the U.S. company Armco (www.armco.com) and the Japanese company Kawasaki (www.kawasaki.com). His directive and achievement-oriented behaviors seem to have paid off in improving motivation and performance in this now very successful and profitable company, which at one point was losing both money and customers at a rapid pace.[42]

The Leader Substitutes Model

The leader substitutes model suggests that leadership is sometimes unnecessary because substitutes for leadership are present. A **leadership substitute** is something that acts in place of the influence of a leader and makes leadership unnecessary. This model suggests that under certain conditions managers do not have to play a leadership role—that members of an organization sometimes can perform highly without a manager exerting influence over them.[43] The leader substitutes model is a contingency model because it suggests that in some situations leadership is unnecessary.

leadership substitute
Characteristics of subordinates or characteristics of a situation or context that act in place of the influence of a leader and make leadership unnecessary.

Take the case of David Cotsonas, who teaches English at a foreign language school in Cypress, an island in the Mediterranean Sea. Cotsonas is fluent in Greek, English, and French, an excellent teacher, and highly motivated. Many of his students are businesspeople who have some rudimentary English skills and wish to increase their fluency to be able to conduct more of their business in English. He enjoys not only teaching them English but learning about the work they do, and he often keeps in touch with his students after they have finished his classes. Cotsonas meets with the director of the school twice a year to discuss semiannual class schedules and enrollments.

With practically no influence from a leader, Cotsonas is a highly motivated top performer at the school. In his situation, leadership is unnecessary because substitutes for leadership are present. Cotsonas's teaching expertise, his motivation, and his enjoyment of his work all are substitutes for the influence of a leader—in this case, the school's director. If the school's director were to try to exert influence over the way Cotsonas goes about performing his job, Cotsonas would probably resent this infringement on his autonomy, and it is unlikely that his performance would increase because he is already one of the school's best teachers.

As in Cotsonas's case, *characteristics of subordinates*—such as their skills, abilities, experience, knowledge, and motivation—can be substitutes for leadership.[44] *Characteristics of the situation or context*—such as the extent to which the work is interesting and enjoyable—also can be substitutes. When work is interesting and enjoyable, as it is for Cotsonas, jobholders do not need to be coaxed into performing because performing is rewarding in its own right. Similarly, when managers *empower* their subordinates or use *self-managed work teams* (discussed in detail in Chapter 14), the need for leadership influence from a manager is decreased because team members manage themselves.

Substitutes for leadership can increase organizational efficiency and effectiveness because they free up some of managers' valuable time and allow managers to focus their efforts on discovering new ways to improve organizational effectiveness. The director of the language school, for example, was able to spend much of his time making arrangements to open a second school in Rhodes, an island in the Aegean Sea, because of the presence of leadership substitutes not only in the case of Cotsonas but for most of the other teachers at the school as well.

Bringing It All Together

Effective leadership in organizations occurs when managers take steps to lead in a way that is appropriate for the situation or context in which leadership occurs and for the subordinates who are being led. The three contingency models of leadership discussed above help managers home in on the necessary ingredients for effective leadership. They are complementary in that each one looks at the leadership question from a different angle. Fiedler's contingency model explores how a manager's leadership style needs to be matched to the leadership situation that the manager is in for maximum effectiveness. House's path–goal theory focuses on how managers should motivate subordinates and describes the specific kinds of behaviors that managers can engage in to have a highly motivated workforce. The leadership substitutes model alerts managers to the fact that sometimes they do not need to exert influence over subordinates and thus can free up their time for other important activities. Table 13.2 recaps these three contingency models of leadership.

Table 13.2

Contingency Models of Leadership

MODEL	FOCUS	KEY CONTINGENCIES
Fiedler's contingency model	Describes two leader styles, relationship-oriented and task-oriented, and the kinds of situations in which each kind of leader will be most effective	Whether or not a relationship-oriented or a task-oriented leader is effective is contingent on the situation
House's path–goal theory	Describes how effective leaders motivate their followers	The behaviors that managers should engage in to be effective leaders are contingent on the nature of the subordinates and the work they do
Leader substitutes model	Describes when leadership is unnecessary	Whether or not leadership is necessary for subordinates to perform highly is contingent on characteristics of the subordinates and the situation

Tips for Managers

Contingency Models of Leadership

1. If you or one of your subordinates is relationship-oriented and in a very unfavorable situation for leading, try to increase the favorability of the situation by increasing task structure or position power or improving leader–member relations.

2. Determine what outcomes your subordinates are trying to obtain from their jobs, make sure you have reward power for these outcomes, and distribute the outcomes based on performance levels.

3. Express confidence in your subordinates' capabilities and do whatever you can to help them believe in their ability to succeed. Remove any obstacles to success.

4. Explore how you can take advantage of leadership substitutes to free up some of the time you spend supervising your subordinates.

Transformational Leadership

transformational leadership Leadership that makes subordinates aware of the importance of their jobs and performance to the organization and aware of their own needs for personal growth and that motivates subordinates to work for the good of the organization.

An exciting new kind of leadership is sweeping the globe. The dramatic changes that Heinrich von Pierer, chief executive of the German electronics company Siemens, has made in his company exemplify what this new leadership is all about. When von Pierer took over in 1992, Siemens had a rigid hierarchy, was suffering from increased global competition, and was saddled with a conservative, perfectionist culture that stifled creativity and innovation and slowed decision making. Von Pierer's changes have been nothing short of revolutionary.[45] At the new Siemens, subordinates critique their managers, who receive training in how to be more democratic and participative and how to spur creativity. Employees are no longer afraid to speak their minds, and the quest for innovation is a driving force throughout the company.

Von Pierer is literally transforming Siemens and its thousands of employees to be more innovative and take the steps needed to gain a competitive advantage. When managers have such dramatic effects on their subordinates and on an organization as a whole, they are engaging in transformational leadership. **Transformational leadership** occurs when managers change (or transform) their subordinates in three important ways:[46]

1. *Transformational managers make subordinates aware of how important their jobs are for the organization and how necessary it is for them to perform those jobs as best they can so that the organization can attain its goals.* Von Pierer sent the message throughout Siemens that innovation, cost cutting, and increasing customer service and satisfaction were everyone's responsibilities and that improvements could be and needed to be made in these areas. For example, when

von Pierer realized that managers in charge of microprocessor sales were not realizing the importance of their jobs and of performing them in a top-notch fashion, he had managers from Siemens's top microprocessor customers give the Siemens's microprocessor managers feedback about their poor service and unreliable delivery schedules. The microprocessor managers quickly realized how important it was for them to take steps to improve customer service.

2. *Transformational managers make their subordinates aware of the subordinates' own needs for personal growth, development, and accomplishment.* Von Pierer has made Siemens's employees aware of their own needs in this regard through numerous workshops and training sessions, through empowering employees throughout the company, through the development of fast-track career programs, and through increased reliance on self-managed work teams.[47]

3. *Transformational managers motivate their subordinates to work for the good of the organization as a whole, not just for their own personal gain or benefit.* Von Pierer's message to Siemens's employees has been clear: Dramatic changes in the way they perform their jobs are crucial for the future viability and success of Siemens. As von Pierer puts it, "We have to keep asking ourselves: Are we flexible enough? Are we changing enough?"[48] One way von Pierer has tried to get all employees thinking in these terms is by inserting in the company magazine distributed to all employees self-addressed postcards urging them to send to him directly their ideas for making improvements.

When managers transform their subordinates in these three ways, subordinates trust the manager, are highly motivated, and help the organization achieve its goals. As a result of von Pierer's transformational leadership, for example, a team of Siemens's engineers working in blue jeans in a rented house developed a tool control system in one-third the time and at one-third the cost of other similar systems developed at Siemens.[49] How do managers like von Pierer transform subordinates and produce dramatic effects in their organizations? There are at least three ways in which managers and other transformational leaders can influence their followers: by being a charismatic leader, by intellectually stimulating subordinates, and by engaging in developmental consideration (see Table 13.3).

Table 13.3

Transformational Leadership

Transformational Managers
- Are charismatic
- Intellectually stimulate subordinates
- Engage in developmental consideration

Subordinates of Transformational Managers
- Have increased awareness of the importance of their jobs and high performance
- Are aware of their own needs for growth, development, and accomplishment
- Work for the good of the organization and not just their own personal benefit

Being a Charismatic Leader

Transformational managers are **charismatic leaders.** They have a vision of how good things could be in their work groups and organizations that is in contrast with the status quo. Their vision usually entails dramatic improvements in group and organizational performance as a result of changes in the organization's structure, culture, strategy, decision making, and other critical processes and factors. This vision paves the way for gaining a competitive advantage.

Charismatic leaders are excited and enthusiastic about their vision and clearly communicate it to their subordinates. The excitement, enthusiasm, and self-confidence of a charismatic leader contribute to the leader's being able to inspire followers to enthusiastically support his or her vision.[50] As Mal Ransom, vice president of marketing at Packard Bell Computers, puts it, "we all buy into the dream; we all buy into the vision."[51] People often think of charismatic leaders or managers as being "larger than life." The essence of charisma, however, is having a vision and enthusiastically communicating it to others. Thus, managers who appear to be quiet and earnest can also be charismatic.

Stimulating Subordinates Intellectually

Transformational managers openly share information with their subordinates so that subordinates are aware of problems and the need for change. The manager causes subordinates to view problems in their groups and throughout the organization from a different perspective, consistent with the manager's vision. Whereas in the past subordinates may not have been aware of some problems, may have viewed problems as a "management issue" beyond their concern, or may have viewed problems as insurmountable, the transformational manager leads subordinates to view problems as challenges that they can and will meet and conquer. The manager engages and empowers subordinates to take personal responsibility for helping to solve problems.[52]

From the "Case in Contrast," it is clear that part of Jack Welch's vision for General Electric is that the company achieve huge gains in profitability in as many of its businesses as possible. When managers in the plastics unit reported increased earnings of around 10 percent, they probably saw this gain not as a problem but rather as a considerable achievement. Welch, however, caused them to realize that it was a problem that they were responsible for fixing, because the unit could have achieved a much bigger—30 or 40 percent—increase.

Engaging in Developmental Consideration

When managers engage in developmental consideration, they not only perform the consideration behaviors described earlier, such as demonstrating true concern for the well-being of subordinates, but go one step further. The manager goes out of his or her way to support and encourage subordinates, giving them opportunities to enhance their skills and capabilities and to grow and excel on the job.[53] Heinrich von Pierer engages in developmental consideration in numerous ways, such as providing counseling sessions with a psychologist for managers who are having a hard time adapting to the changes at Siemens and sponsoring hiking trips to stimulate employees to think and work in new ways.[54]

All organizations, no matter how large or small, successful or unsuccessful, can benefit when their managers engage in transformational leadership. The benefits of transformational leadership, however, are often most apparent when an organization is in trouble, as indicated in this "Managing Globally."

Managing Globally

Transformational Leadership in South Korea

In 1989, when Lee Hun-Jo became chief executive of the once-successful Korean electrical appliance and electronics company Goldstar, the company was headed for ruin. Global and domestic market share was slipping, quality was declining, and even rank-and-file employees realized that bankruptcy was imminent if things did not change. Less than 10 years after Hun-Jo took over, Goldstar (renamed LG Electronics Co. in 1994) recovered its spot as the top producer of washing machines, refrigerators, and color TVs in South Korea. LG Electronics also is gaining ground globally in the areas of liquid-crystal displays and semiconductors.[55]

Hun-Jo realized from the start that nothing short of a major transformation would turn around LG Electronics' fortunes. As he put it, "You have to transform human beings . . . If you can't change your people, you can't change your organization. If you can't do that, you can't reach your goal."[56]

Hun-Jo's vision for LG Electronics included its being a top performer domestically and globally. He also envisioned dramatic changes for the organization's structure and culture. Like many Korean companies, LG Electronics had a relatively rigid hierarchy with decision making centralized at the top and a culture that respected authority and tradition. Hun-Jo's vision included decentralization of decision making and a culture supportive of efficiency, effectiveness, and innovation. In numerous face-to-face meetings, Hun-Jo enthusiastically communicated his vision throughout LG Electronics, made many changes to support it, and even has taken symbolic steps to communicate that things are changing. Rather than wearing the conservative neckties favored by Korean top managers, Hun-Jo wears radiantly colored ties and refuses to sit in the traditionally honored spots reserved for the chief executive in meetings with managers.

Hun-Jo intellectually stimulates his subordinates in multiple ways. He has opened new paths of communication between nonmanagerial employees and managers and has openly shared the company's problems with employees and made them feel responsible for helping to solve them. Decision making has been decentralized, and all employees are encouraged to feel responsible for coming up with improvements, ideas for new products, and ways to increase quality. LG Electronics traditionally took products developed by foreign competitors, such as the Japanese, and tried to copy and customize them for the Korean marketplace. Part of Hun-Jo's vision is for LG Electronics to come up with its own innovative products. He made product development engineers feel responsible for doing this and sent them out to talk to LG Electronics's customers to see what they really wanted. As a result of this intellectual stimulation, LG Electronics now has an innovative and best-selling product on its hands—a refrigerator specially designed to keep *kimchi* (Korea's national dish of pickled and fermented cabbage and radishes) fresh tasting and smelling for much longer than is possible in a conventional refrigerator.

Hun-Jo also engages in developmental consideration. He has taken dramatic steps to improve management relations with the union and not only has shared information with union leaders but also has encouraged them to meet with him whenever they want to determine how to improve things at LG Electronics.[57] He wants his employees to reach their full potential and is doing whatever he can think of to help them do that. Hun-Jo also reads extensively about the latest advances in management thought and practice in the United States and other countries, to help himself be an effective manager and leader. All in all, Hun-Jo seems to be just the kind of leader LG Electronics needed to regain its position as a top-performing global organization—a transformational leader.

Transformational managers in large corporations are often highly visible because their dramatic changes are reported in the popular press, as is the case with Lee Hun-Jo. But transformational leadership can occur in all kinds of organizations, big or small, profit or nonprofit. Sally Graceton, for example, the manager of a small health food restaurant on the U.S. west coast, engaged in transformational leadership when she envisioned dramatic improvements in the quality of the restaurant's food, customer traffic, and profitability; made all employees responsible for helping to achieve this vision; and provided her employees with benefit packages unheard of in the restaurant industry while at the same time sending them to seminars on nutrition and healthy cooking and eating. As a result of Graceton's transformational leadership, the restaurant is expanding to accommodate growing numbers of loyal patrons. Similarly, John Rivero, the principal of an inner-city high school notorious for high crime rates and low scholastic achievement, engaged in transformational leadership when he enthusiastically communicated his vision of a crime-free model urban high school to teachers and students, challenged teachers to more proactively motivate their students, challenged students to take back control of their lives and education, and showed everyone that he really cared.

Tips for Managers

Transformational Leadership

1. Let subordinates know how their own jobs contribute to organizational effectiveness and stress the importance of high performance.
2. Help subordinates learn new skills and develop on the job.
3. Have a vision of how much better things can be in your organization and enthusiastically communicate your vision throughout the organization.
4. Share organizational problems and challenges with subordinates and engage them to help solve the problems and meet the challenges.
5. Take a personal interest in your subordinates and inspire them to accomplish as much as they can.

The Distinction Between Transformational and Transactional Leadership

transactional leadership Leadership that motivates subordinates by rewarding high performance and reprimanding low performance.

Transformational leadership is often contrasted with transactional leadership. **Transactional leadership** involves managers using their reward and coercive power to encourage high performance. When managers reward high performers, reprimand or otherwise punish low performers, and motivate subordinates by reinforcing desired behaviors and extinguishing or punishing undesired ones, they are engaging in transactional leadership.[58] Managers who effectively influence their subordinates to achieve goals yet do not seem to be making the kind of dramatic changes that are part of transformational leadership are engaging in transactional leadership.

Many transformational leaders engage in transactional leadership. They reward subordinates for a job well done and notice and respond to substandard performance. But they also have their eyes on the bigger picture of how much better things could be in their organizations, how much more their subordinates are capable of achieving, and how important it is to treat their subordinates with respect and to help them reach their full potential.

Gender and Leadership

The increasing number of women entering the ranks of management as well as the problems some women face in their efforts to be hired as managers or promoted into management positions has prompted researchers to explore the relationship between gender and leadership. Although relatively more women are in management positions today than there were ten years ago, relatively few women are in top management and, in some organizations, even in middle management.

When women do advance to top-management positions, special attention often is focused on the fact that they are women. In 1992, Ellen M. Knapp was appointed to a top-management position, vice chair of technology, at Coopers & Lybrand, a Big Six accounting firm. She was the only woman to reach this level in the hierarchy of any of the Big Six firms at that time. Coopers & Lybrand was thought to have a "men's club atmosphere," and the vast majority of the partners in the firm were men.[59] When Knapp first assumed her position, some observers likened her appointment to anarchy. However, her superior capabilities and determination have earned her the respect of her predominantly male coworkers. Her transformational leadership over the past several years has dramatically upgraded Cooper & Lybrand's technology base—an upgrade that was sorely needed and late in coming prior to Knapp's assuming her top-management position.[60] Nevertheless, when she was appointed to this position, much attention was focused on the simple fact that she was a woman. If she had been a man, gender never would have entered the picture.

A widespread stereotype of women is that they are nurturing, supportive, and concerned with interpersonal relations. Men are stereotypically viewed as being directive and focused on task accomplishment. Such stereotypes suggest that women tend to be more relationship oriented as managers and engage in more consideration behaviors, whereas men are more task oriented and engage in more initiating structure behaviors. Does the behavior of actual male and female managers bear out these stereotypes? Do women managers lead in different ways than men? Are male or female managers more effective as leaders?

Research suggests that male managers and female managers who have leadership positions in organizations behave in similar ways.[61] Women do not engage in more consideration than men, and men do not engage in more initiating structure than women. Research does suggest, however, that leadership style may vary between women and men. Women tend to be somewhat more participative as leaders than men, involving subordinates in decision making and seeking their input.[62] Male managers tend to be less participative than female managers, making more decisions on their own and wanting to do things their own way.

There are at least two reasons why female managers may be more participative as leaders than male managers.[63] First, subordinates may try to resist the influence of female managers more than they do the influence of male managers. Some subordinates may never have reported to a woman before, some may inappropriately see management roles as being more appropriate for men than for women, and some may just resist being led by a woman. To overcome this resistance and encourage subordinates' trust and respect, women managers may adopt a participative approach.

A second reason why female managers may be more participative is that they sometimes have better interpersonal skills than male managers.[64] A participative approach to leadership requires high levels of interaction and involvement between a manager and his or her subordinates, sensitivity to subordinates' feelings, and the ability to make decisions that may be unpopular with subordinates but necessary for goal attainment. Good interpersonal skills may help female managers have the effective interactions with their subordinates that are crucial to a participative approach.[65] To the extent that male managers have more difficulty managing interpersonal relationships, they may shy away from the high levels of interaction with subordinates necessary for true participation.

The key finding from research on leader behaviors, however, is that male and female managers do *not* differ significantly in their propensities to perform different leader behaviors. Even though they may be more participative, female managers do not engage in more consideration or less initiating structure than male managers.

Perhaps a question even more important than whether male and female managers differ in the leadership behaviors they perform is whether they differ in effectiveness. Consistent with the findings for leader behaviors, research suggests that across different kinds of organizational settings, male and female managers tend to be *equally* effective as leaders.[66] Thus, there is no logical basis for stereotypes favoring male managers and leaders or for the existence of the glass ceiling (an invisible barrier that seems to prevent women from advancing as far as they should in some organizations). Because women and men are equally effective as leaders, the increasing number of women in the workforce should result in a larger pool of highly qualified candidates for management positions in organizations, ultimately enhancing organizational effectiveness.[67]

Summary and Review

Chapter Summary

THE NATURE OF LEADERSHIP

- Personal Leadership Style and Managerial Tasks

- Leadership Styles Across Cultures

- Power: The Key to Leadership

- Empowerment: An Ingredient in Modern Management

TRAIT AND BEHAVIOR MODELS OF LEADERSHIP

- The Trait Model

- The Behavior Model

CONTINGENCY MODELS OF LEADERSHIP

- Fiedler's Contingency Model

- House's Path–Goal Theory

- The Leader Substitutes Model

- Bringing It All Together

THE NATURE OF LEADERSHIP Leadership is the process by which a person exerts influence over other people and inspires, motivates, and directs their activities to help achieve group or organizational goals. Leaders are able to influence others because they possess power. The five types of power available to managers are legitimate power, reward power, coercive power, expert power, and referent power. Many managers are using empowerment as a tool to increase their effectiveness as leaders.

TRAIT AND BEHAVIOR MODELS OF LEADERSHIP The trait model of leadership describes personal characteristics or traits that contribute to effective leadership. However, some managers who possess these traits are not effective leaders, and some managers who do not possess all the traits are nevertheless effective leaders. The behavior model of leadership describes two kinds of behavior that most leaders engage in: consideration and initiating structure.

CONTINGENCY MODELS OF LEADERSHIP Contingency models take into account the complexity surrounding leadership and the role of the situation in determining whether a manager is an effective or ineffective leader. Fiedler's contingency model explains why managers may be effective leaders in one situation and ineffective in another. According to Fiedler's model, relationship-oriented leaders are most effective in situations that are moderately favorable for leading, and task-oriented leaders are most effective in situations that are very favorable or very unfavorable for leading. House's path–goal theory describes how effective managers motivate their subordinates by determining what outcomes their subordinates want, rewarding subordinates with these outcomes when they achieve their goals and perform at a high level, and clarifying the paths to goal attainment. Managers can engage in four different kinds of behaviors to motivate subordinates: directive behaviors, supportive behaviors, participative behaviors, or achievement-oriented behaviors. The leader substitutes model suggests that sometimes managers do not have to play a leadership role because their subordinates perform highly without the manager having to exert influence over them.

TRANSFORMATIONAL LEADERSHIP Transformational leadership occurs when managers have dramatic effects on their subordinates and on the organization as a whole and inspire and energize subordinates to solve problems and improve performance. These effects include making subordinates aware of the importance of their own jobs and high performance, making subordinates aware of their own needs for personal growth, development, and accomplishment, and motivating subordinates to work for the good of the organization and not just their own personal gain. Managers can engage in transformational leadership by being charismatic leaders, by intellectually stimulating subordinates, and by engaging in developmental consideration. Transformational managers also often engage in transactional leadership by using their reward and coercive powers to encourage high performance.

GENDER AND LEADERSHIP   Female and male managers do not dif-fer in the leadership behaviors that they perform, contrary to stereotypes sug-gesting that women are more relationship oriented and men more task oriented. Female managers sometimes are more participative than male man-agers, however. Research has found that women and men are equally effective as managers and leaders.

Management in Action

Topics for Discussion and Action

1. Describe the steps managers can take to increase their power and ability to be effective leaders.

2. Think of specific situations in which it might be especially important for a manager to engage in consideration and in initiating structure.

3. Interview an actual manager to find out how the three situational characteristics that Fiedler identified are affecting the manager's ability to provide leadership.

4. For your current job or for a future job that you expect to hold, describe what your supervisor could do to strongly motivate you to be a top performer.

5. Discuss why managers might want to change the behaviors they engage in, given their situation, their subordinates, and the nature of the work being done. Do you think managers are able to readily change their leadership behaviors? Why or why not?

6. Discuss why substitutes for leadership can contribute to organizational effectiveness.

7. Describe what transformational leadership is, and explain how managers can engage in it.

8. Find an example of a company that has dramatically turned around its fortunes and improved its performance. Determine whether a transformational manager was behind the turnaround and, if one was, what this manager did.

9. Discuss why some people still think that men make better managers than women even though research indicates that men and women are equally effective as managers and leaders.

Building Management Skills

Analyzing Failures of Leadership

Think about a situation you are familiar with in which a leader was very ineffective. Then answer the following questions.

1. What sources of power did this leader have? Did the leader have enough power to influence his or her followers?

2. What kinds of behaviors did this leader engage in? Were they appropriate for the situation? Why or why not?

3. From what you know, do you think this leader was a task-oriented leader or a relationship-oriented leader? How favorable was this leader's situation for leading?

4. What steps did this leader take to motivate his or her followers? Were these steps appropriate or inappropriate? Why?

5. What signs, if any, did this leader show of being a transformational leader?

Small Group Breakout Exercise

Improving Leadership Effectiveness

Form groups of three to five people, and appoint one member as the spokesperson who will communicate your findings and conclusions to the whole class when called on by the instructor. Then discuss the following scenario.

You are a team of human resource consultants who have been hired by Carla Caruso, an entrepreneur who started her own interior decorating business. A highly competent and creative interior decorator, Caruso established a working relationship with most of the major home builders in her community. At first, she worked on her own as an independent contractor. Then, because of a dramatic increase in the number of new homes being built, she became swamped with requests for her services and decided to form her own company.

She hired a secretary/bookkeeper and four interior decorators, all of whom are highly competent. Caruso still does decorating jobs herself and has adopted a hands-off approach to leading the four decorators because she feels that interior design is a very personal, creative endeavor. Rather than pay the decorators on some kind of commission basis (such as a percentage of their customers' total billings), she pays them a premium salary higher than average so that they are motivated to do what's best for their customers, not what will result in higher billings and commissions.

Caruso thought everything was going smoothly until customer complaints started coming in. These complaints were about the decorators' being hard to get hold of, promising unrealistic delivery times, being late for or failing to keep appointments, and being impatient and rude when customers had trouble making up their minds. Caruso knows that her decorators are competent people and is concerned that she is not effectively leading and managing them. She wonders, in particular, if her hands-off approach is to blame and if she should change the manner in which she rewards or pays her decorators. She has asked for your advice.

1. Analyze the sources of power that Caruso has available to her to influence the decorators. What advice can you give her to either increase her power or use her existing power more effectively?

2. Given what you have learned in this chapter (for example, from the behavior model and path–goal theory), does Caruso seem to be performing appropriate leader behaviors in this situation? What advice can you give her about the kinds of behaviors she should perform?

3. What steps would you advise Caruso to take to increase the decorators' motivation to deliver high-quality customer service?

4. Would you advise Caruso to try to engage in transformational leadership in this situation? If not, why not? If so, what steps would you advise her to take?

Exploring the World Wide Web

Specific Assignment

Many CEOs are highly visible leaders in their companies and industries. One such CEO is Scott McNealy of Sun Microsystems. Scan the Sun Microsystems website to learn more about this company (http://www.sun.com/). Click on "Corporate Information," then on "News & Events," and then on "Sun in the Media." Click on "Continue" to read the rest of the article.

1. How would you characterize Scott McNealy's personal leadership style?

2. In what ways is McNealy a transformational leader?

General Assignment

Find the website of a company that provides information on the company's missions, goals, and values. Also, scan the website for information about this company's top managers and their personal leadership styles. How do you think the company's missions, goals, and values may impact the process of leadership in this company?

ManagementCase

Leading the Farming Revolution in Mexico

Farming in Mexico is undergoing dramatic changes that not only are necessary for the continued viability of the industry but also are improving the fortunes of farmers. Traditionally, farming in Mexico has been organized around small family farms with only a few acres apiece to plant. Such small-scale farming makes it virtually impossible for farmers to purchase sophisticated equipment and engage in any kind of modern mechanized farming. This constraint in turn makes it hard for farmers to compete in the global marketplace. And the fact that Mexico is engaging in more free trade with other countries means that produce prices fluctuate more than they did in the past. When prices fluctuate, small farmers who typically make only enough money to barely support their families are placed at great risk, because even a modest price drop can imperil their livelihood. Mexico's economic problems and the devaluation of the peso have added to the need to make major changes to improve farm efficiency and effectiveness.

Luckily for the farmers, an innovative manager is on hand to lead the farming revolution: Alfonso Romo Garza.[68]

Garza's vision for the farm industry and for farmers is one of modernization, utilization of the latest technology, efficiency, and effectiveness. He has motivated farmers to work together to improve their fortunes. Garza's company, Empresas La Moderna SA, has entered into agreements with farmers to join their small farms into 150- to 200-acre tracts that are farmed by modern, mechanized methods.[69] Garza and other managers at Moderna provide farmers with information on the latest technology, advice on all kinds of farming issues, seeds, irrigation and harvesting machinery, and interest-free loans to update their farms. In return, Moderna receives one-half of the profits from the crops. Moderna and the farmers gain the advantages of modern, large-scale farming, and the farmers continue to own and operate their individual farms, something they highly value. There is a strong cultural belief in Mexico that farmers have the right to own and harvest their own land. Garza's knowledge of and respect for this tradition has earned him the respect and trust of farmers who nevertheless realize the need for change.

Garza has made sure that the farmers themselves are personally benefiting from this innovative arrangement. As he puts it, "If you reward the farmer and give him [her] what he [she] deserves, you will have a good return."[70] Crop yields have increased dramatically under Moderna's system while costs have fallen. Farmers are working hard, but they always have worked hard. Now, however, they are reaping the rewards of their effort; in the past they were barely getting by. Their knowledge, skills, and expertise also are increasing as they learn more about modern farming techniques.

Always on the lookout for new ways to improve his company's effectiveness, and consistent with his vision of utilizing high technology to the greatest extent possible, Garza is currently expanding Moderna into the seed genetics business. He also has established in the Chiapan jungle a laboratory in which scientists and biologists are working to develop disease-resistant varieties of fruits including mango, papaya, guayaba, and mamey, while at the same time producing insects that are beneficial for produce because they eat other damaging pests.[71]

Garza seems to understand that in their leadership roles managers need to be constantly on the lookout for ways to make dramatic improvements consistent with their vision while at the same time motivating others to work hard to achieve this vision.

Questions

1. In what ways has Garza exerted influence over farmers in Mexico? Why has he been able to exert this influence?

2. How has Garza engaged in transformational leadership?

ManagementCase

In the News

From the Pages of BusinessWeek

Bill's Co-Pilot

It was vintage Steve Ballmer, Microsoft Corp.'s self-appointed cheerleader bounded onstage at the company's annual sales meeting in New Orleans on July 27 and shouted at the top of his lungs: "I love this company! I love this company! I love this company!" The 6,000-person sales team responded with a five-minute standing ovation. Then Ballmer whizzed through a 90-minute pep talk on the virtues of customer obsession, bringing the audience to its feet once more when he finished by playing a recording he listens to before every major milestone in his life: Dionne Warwick's *I Say a Little Prayer.*"

Ballmer might need their prayers. After six years of running sales and support for the software giant, he has been elevated by CEO William H. Gates III to the position of president—in charge of both sales and product development—allowing Gates to focus more on technology and mapping out the company's future.

With this move, Steven A. Ballmer finally gets public recognition for the role he has long played at Microsoft: Bill Gates's co-pilot. Together, the two college chums have spent 18 years forging a fiercely competitive company unmatched in computerdom. Gates has been the company's big brain and Ballmer its wildly thumping

494

heart, inspiring the troops as no one else can. Now, while Gates remains CEO and point man in the company's antitrust battle with the Justice Dept., it's up to Ballmer to run day-to-day operations at a juncture that's as crucial as any in the company's history.

Microsoft is under fire from all sides—not just from Justice but from tough competitors such as IBM and Sun Microsystems, Inc. To sustain a blistering 28% yearly growth rate, Microsoft must succeed in markets far afield from its dominance in desktop computing. That means persuading corporate customers that Microsoft's software can be trusted to run their most vital operations. At the same time, Microsoft is pushing its Windows software into everything from cars to building alarms to telephones. And the company must transform its Web sites, which lost $300 million last year, into moneymakers.

In many ways, the 42-year-old Detroit native is tailor-made for the job. While Gates is the company's technology visionary, Ballmer is its top business strategist. He earned his stripes by building Microsoft's sales operation into a major-league force in corporate computing. He has had every major management job at Microsoft, and he has the kind of gimlet-eyed financial discipline necessary to pick apart the flaws in any ailing business plan.

Already, Ballmer is sending hundreds of product engineers out to learn from corporate customers what Microsoft needs to do to help solve their computing problems. He is doing sit-downs with some 100 employees to ferret out what's happening with product development. And he is boning up on what makes a Web site a hit. Look for him to whip into shape the company's E-commerce operations

by boosting revenues and pruning unnecessary costs.

Ballmer's omnipresent intensity should help. He's larger and louder than life—6 feet tall, built like a linebacker, with a huge, balding head and a booming voice. Despite his stock options worth some $6 billion, he's not easing off one bit, and responds with bug-eyed indignity to rumors he was considering retirement before getting his promotion. "That's just not true," he says. He's the kind of guy who, while jogging, charges up hills—gutting out the pain.

At home, too, Ballmer's devotion is boundless. He tries to be there to put his two young sons to bed every night. And when his parents became ill with cancer last summer, he moved them to Seattle and took 12 weeks off from work to care for them. "Not too many senior executives will just drop out like that for their family," says Mike Maples, a former Microsoft executive vice-president who is now retired.

But Ballmer's intensity has a dark side. He can sometimes be a hothead whose emotions get the better of him. He can be rough on people who work for him, bawling them out so violently that his voice can be heard through the vents at Microsoft's Redmond (Wash.) headquarters. And sometimes, Ballmer blurts out public comments that simply do not become a company president.

Gates—no diplomat himself—doesn't hold Ballmer's shortcomings against him. The two have been close friends since they met as undergraduates at Harvard University. Later, in 1980, Gates persuaded Ballmer to drop out of Stanford University's business school to help run a fledgling Microsoft that was growing so fast it was nearly out of control. Ballmer

was the company's first nonengineer, and Gates valued his management experience at Procter & Gamble Co., where he helped market cake mixes.

Even today, they spend hours together talking over their frustrations and dreams. "He's my best friend," says Gates. "We love working together on very hard problems. We trust each other and understand how the other one thinks." Ballmer's affection for Gates runs just as deep. "Our friendship has grown much stronger as a result of working together. It's like a marriage," says Ballmer. In an interview last fall he said Microsoft's vaunted long-term approach to business emerged partly because he and Gates "wanted to prove our commitment to one another."

But where Gates calculates his moves, Ballmer simply makes them. "Steve's invention is: Don't have an elegant plan. Do the smart, obvious thing. Then fix it as you go," says Peter Neupert, a former Microsoft executive who is now CEO of Drugstore.com.

As president, Ballmer will have to be more judicious—and diplomatic. "He's proven he can be General Patton," says Paul A. Maritz, Microsoft's group vice-president for products. "Now, he has to be more like Eisenhower."

Source: S. Hamm, "Bill's Co-Pilot," *Business Week*, September 14, 1998, 76–77.

Questions

1. How would you describe Steve Ballmer's personal leadership style?
2. What leadership behaviors does Ballmer engage in?
3. Is Ballmer a transformational leader? Why or why not?

Chapter fourteen

Groups and Teams

A Case in Contrast

Teams Work Wonders at Hallmark Cards

Hallmark Cards Inc. (www.hallmark.com), based in Kansas City, is the leading U.S. greeting card company. In the 1980s, Robert L. Stark, president of Hallmark's Personal Communications Group, which includes the Hallmark and Ambassador lines of cards and the Binney & Smith subsidiary (which manufactures Crayola crayons) (www.crayola.com), realized that Hallmark was facing a crisis. Dramatic changes taking place in the greeting card industry meant that Hallmark had to create and produce new cards more quickly.[1]

Customers were becoming increasingly diverse and were demanding more and different kinds of cards than in the past. Retailers needed to sell more cards to pay higher rents, and large retailers, such as Wal-Mart (www.wal-mart.com) and Kmart, wanted new customized cards for their stores from the Ambassador line. Stark realized that taking two or three years to develop a new line of cards would not provide customers with the variety they wanted, small retailers with the volume they needed, or large retailers with the customized lines they demanded.

Stark faced a daunting task: How could he improve on a process that Hallmark had been perfecting for the past 85 years of its existence and cut new product development time by 50 or 75 percent? His answer was to examine the way Hallmark went about producing new cards.

In the 1980s, the President of Hallmark's Personal Communications group, Robert Stark, realized that the greeting card industry was changing rapidly and he needed to find a way to broaden the types of greeting cards for consumers, and to make them more quickly. Stark decided to use cross-functional teams (one of them pictured here) to work intensively together to develop a new line of coordinated products.

About two-thirds of the two or three years it took to bring new cards to market in the 1980s was spent on creative activity, planning the concept, and developing marketing approaches. The idea for a new line of cards put into motion a lengthy sequential process—artists drawing the designs, writers putting together the words, marketing experts ensuring that the new cards would appeal to customers, and so on. While each department worked separately on its contribution to the new cards, numerous interdepartmental meetings and discussions took place, frequent changes were made, and departmental managers all along the way had to approve the progress of the new cards. Before a new line of cards was actually released to production for printing, 25 different managers might sign off on it at various stages.

Rather than producing new cards the old way—having the cards pass from department to department and each department contribute its own part—Stark decided to bring all the different departments together in a cross-functional team (a team composed of members from different departments; see Chapter 8). According to Stark's plan, artists, writers, designers, and marketing experts, who in the past were in different departments and sometimes in different buildings, would all work together as members of a team to develop new cards. Instead of managers passing ideas and criticisms back and forth from one department to another as in the past, team members would communicate directly with each other, creative discussions would ensue, and problems would be solved on the spot. Also, instead of managers signing off on new cards as they progressed from department to department, the team would have the responsibility for approving its own work, making changes if need be, and putting the new line of cards into production.

The use of cross-functional teams to develop new cards is in sharp contrast to the traditional sequential process that Hallmark relied on for so many years. Although Stark and his top-management team are still ironing out the bugs in the new system, it certainly seems to be helping Hallmark achieve its goal of producing many more different kinds of cards in a timely fashion. Cross-functional teams are developing new lines of cards in less than a year. Not only is the new process quicker and more efficient but the quality of the cards made by the teams often is superior. Moreover, artists and writers on the teams are more motivated and satisfied because they work on a card from start to finish and see the fruits of their labor in a much more timely fashion than in the past. As Robert Stark puts it, "All you have to do is talk to our people . . . about the things they are doing, the teams they are affiliated with . . . They tell you it is much more fulfilling to come to work."[2] ●

Overview

Robert Stark and Hallmark Cards are not alone in the shift toward using groups and teams to produce goods and services that better meet customers' needs. Managers in large companies such as Du Pont, Digital Equipment Corporation, Tandem Computers, and Data General and in small companies such as Web Industries, Perdue Farms, and Risk International Services are all relying on teams to help them gain a competitive advantage.[3] In this chapter we look in detail at how groups and teams can contribute to organizational effectiveness and the types of groups and teams used in organizations. We discuss how different elements of group dynamics influence the functioning and effectiveness of groups, and we describe how managers can motivate group members to achieve organizational goals and reduce social loafing in groups and teams. By the end of this chapter, you will appreciate why the effective management of groups and teams is a key ingredient for organizational performance and a source of competitive advantage. ●

Groups, Teams, and Organizational Effectiveness

A **group** may be defined as two or more people who interact with each other to accomplish certain goals or meet certain needs.[4] A **team** is a group whose members work *intensely* with each other to achieve a specific common goal or objective. As these definitions imply, all teams are groups but not all groups are teams. The two characteristics that distinguish teams from groups are the *intensity* with which team members work together and the presence of a *specific, overriding team goal or objective*.

group Two or more people who interact with each other to accomplish certain goals or meet certain needs.

team A group whose members work intensely with each other to achieve a specific, common goal or objective.

As described in the "Case in Contrast," members of the cross-functional teams at Hallmark Cards work intensely together to achieve the specific objective of developing new cards and successfully bringing them to market. In contrast, the accountants who work in a small CPA firm are a group: They may interact with each other to achieve goals such as keeping up-to-date on the latest changes in accounting rules and regulations, maintaining a smoothly functioning office, satisfying clients, and attracting new clients. But they are not a team because they do not work intensely with each other. Each accountant concentrates on serving the needs of his or her own clients.

Because all teams are also groups, whenever we use the term *group* in this chapter, we are referring to both groups and teams. As you might imagine, because members of teams do work intensely together, teams can sometimes be difficult to form, and it may take time for members to learn how to work together effectively. Groups and teams can help an organization gain a competitive advantage because they can (1) enhance its performance, (2) increase its responsiveness to customers, (3) increase innovation, and (4) increase employees' motivation and satisfaction (see Figure 14.1). In this section, we look at each of these contributions.

Groups and Teams as Performance Enhancers

synergy Performance gains that result when individuals and departments coordinate their actions.

One of the main advantages of using groups is the opportunity to obtain a type of **synergy:** People working in a group are able to produce more or higher-quality outputs than would have been produced if each person had worked separately and all their individual efforts were combined. The essence of synergy is captured in the saying "The whole is more than the sum of its parts." Factors that can contribute to synergy in groups include the ability of group members to bounce ideas off one another, to correct each other's mistakes, to solve problems immediately as they arise, and to bring a diverse knowledge base to bear on a problem or goal. At Hallmark Cards, cross-functional teams

Figure 14.1

Groups' and Teams' Contributions to Organizational Effectiveness

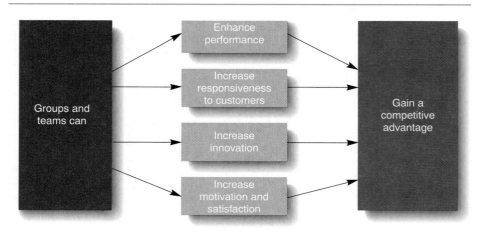

created a synergy that promoted the generation of higher-quality greeting cards in less than half of the time it used to take when members of different departments worked individually and separately on the cards.

To take advantage of the potential for synergy in groups, managers need to make sure that groups are composed of members who have complementary skills and knowledge relevant to the group's work. At Hallmark, for example, the skills and expertise of the artists complement the contributions of the writers and vice versa. Managers also need to give groups enough autonomy so that the groups, rather than the manager, are solving problems and determining how to achieve goals and objectives, as is true in the cross-functional teams at Hallmark. To promote synergy, managers need to empower their subordinates and be coaches, guides, and resources for groups, while refraining from playing a more directive or supervisory role. The potential for synergy in groups may be the reason why more and more managers are incorporating empowerment in their personal leadership styles (see Chapter 13).

Groups, Teams, and Responsiveness to Customers

Being responsive to customers is not always easy. In manufacturing organizations, for example, customers' needs and desires for new and improved products have to be balanced against engineering constraints, production costs and feasibilities, government safety regulations, and marketing challenges. In service organizations such as HMOs (health maintenance organizations), being responsive to patients' needs and desires for prompt, high-quality medical care and treatment has to be balanced against meeting physicians' needs and desires and keeping health care costs under control. Being responsive to customers often requires the wide variety of skills and expertise found in different departments and at different levels in an organization's hierarchy. Sometimes employees at lower levels in the hierarchy, such as sales representatives for a computer company, are closest to customers and most attuned to their needs.

However, lower-level employees like salespeople often lack the technical expertise needed to come up with new product ideas; such expertise is found in the research and development department. Bringing salespeople, research and development experts, and members of other departments together in a group or cross-functional team can enhance responsiveness to customers. Consequently, when managers form a team, they need to make sure that the diversity of expertise and knowledge needed to be responsive to customers exists within the team; this is why cross-functional teams are so popular.

In a cross-functional team, the expertise and knowledge that are housed in different organizational departments are brought together in the skills and knowledge of the team members. Managers of high-performing organizations are careful to determine which types of expertise and knowledge are required for teams to be responsive to customers, and they use this information in forming teams, as illustrated in this "Management Insight."

Management Insight

Teams Foster Responsiveness to Customers at Rubbermaid

Rubbermaid Corporation (www.rubbermaid.com), one of the most-admired companies in the United States, and Wolfgang Schmitt, its German-born CEO, are masters at being responsive to customers. Rubbermaid produces over 400 new products each year, ranging from plastic toys, buckets, baskets, and housewares to office supplies. Approximately one-third of Rubbermaid's annual revenues of $2 billion are generated by products that are five years old or younger. Schmitt strives to discard products that have passed their prime and to introduce, at a rapid pace, new products that customers want or will want when they are available.

Managers in other companies might have similar goals, but Schmitt seems especially successful at reaching them. Part of Schmitt's knack for being responsive to customers comes from his use of cross-functional teams to generate new product ideas and then to produce and market the new products. Each of Rubbermaid's teams has five members, one from each of the key departments in the company: sales, marketing, finance, manufacturing, and R&D. Each team is charged with creating, improving, and marketing a new or existing line of products. If Schmitt decides to create a whole new series of products, a team is formed to handle the products. When a line of products ceases to meet customers' needs, the team that handled it is dissolved, and its members are transferred to new teams in need of their expertise.

Although the teams can always seek advice from managers and other Rubbermaid employees, Schmitt empowers the teams and gives them the autonomy to develop their own strategies, do their own planning, and make their own decisions. Each team's ultimate goal is to make a profit, and the teams are evaluated on, and held accountable for, this goal. Empowering members of the cross-functional teams increases their motivation. Team members feel like entrepreneurs working on "their" products, and they have a real sense of ownership of, and responsibility for, the success of their lines.[5]

Teams and Innovation

Innovation, the creative development of new products, new technologies, new services, or even new organizational structures, is a topic we discuss in detail in Chapter 18. Often, an individual working alone does not possess the extensive and diverse set of skills, knowledge, and expertise frequently required for successful innovation. Managers can better encourage innovation by creating teams of diverse individuals who together have the knowledge relevant to a particular type of innovation rather than by relying on individuals working alone.

Using teams to innovate has other advantages as well. First, team members can often uncover each other's errors or false assumptions; an individual acting alone would not be able to do this. Second, team members can critique each other's approaches when need be and build off each other's strengths while compensating for weaknesses, one of the advantages of devil's advocacy and dialectical inquiry discussed in Chapter 6.

To further promote innovation, managers are well advised to empower teams and make their members fully responsible and accountable for the innovation process. The manager's role is to provide guidance, assistance, coaching, and the resources team members need, and *not* to direct or supervise their activities closely. To speed innovation, managers also need to form teams in which each member brings some unique resource to the team, such as engineering prowess, knowledge of production, marketing expertise, or financial savvy. Successful innovation sometimes requires that managers form teams with members from different countries and cultures, as indicated in this "Managing Globally."

Managing Globally

Cross-Cultural Team's Innovation Yields the 1996 Honda Civic

Ron Shriver, a manager and engineer at Honda's East Liberty, Ohio, factory, played a prominent role in the development of Honda's 1992 Civic model (www.honda.com). When the model first came out, rather than basking in glory, Shriver was concerned. Many of the Civic's features, including heat vents for the rear seats and a more powerful engine, had raised its price at a time when car sales were falling in both the United States and Japan. Shriver realized that innovation was needed for the 1996 model and that costs had to be cut to keep the price low, but without sacrificing quality.

Shriver formed a 12-person team composed of members from Honda's most significant departments to determine how to reduce costs for the 1996 model. Unbeknownst to Shriver, Honda's president in Japan, Nobuhiko Kawamoto, had come to a similar conclusion: The strong yen and slumping demand meant that Honda had to lower costs. Hiroyuki Itoh, the manager and chief engineer for the Civic in Japan, formed his own team to determine how to innovate for the 1996 Civic.

Within a few months, Shriver's and Itoh's teams were merged to form a cross-cultural team to identify innovative changes to the Civic that would cut costs but not turn off customers. In search of ways to reduce costs, the new team of both Japanese and American managers took a hands-on approach and talked to all people and groups who affected costs, such as engineers, factory workers, and suppliers. Jodie Kavanagh, a Honda employee working in the paint shop in Liberty, Ohio, for example, suggested a change that resulted in $1.2 million in savings. Suppliers also had a major input into the process, and agreements on specifications were reached with low-cost U.S. suppliers, who replaced their more expensive Japanese counterparts. As a result of the team's efforts, the price of the 1996 Civic was only marginally higher than the price of the 1992 model even though it was bigger, peppier, and had many new features.[6] Shriver, Itoh, and their cross-cultural team at Honda are now working on innovations to be included in the Civic's year 2000 model.

Groups and Teams as Motivators

Managers often decide to form groups and teams to accomplish organizational goals, then find that using groups and teams brings additional benefits. Members of groups, and especially members of teams (because of the higher intensity of interaction in teams), are likely to be more highly motivated and satisfied than they would have been if they were working on their own. The experience of working alongside other highly charged and motivated people can be very stimulating. In addition, working on a team can be very motivating: Team members more readily see how their efforts and expertise directly contribute to the achievement of team and organizational goals, and they feel personally responsible for the outcomes or results of their work. This has been the case at Hallmark Cards and Rubbermaid.

The increased motivation and satisfaction that can accompany the use of teams can also lead to other outcomes, such as lower turnover. This has been Frank B. Day's experience as founder and CEO of Rock Bottom Restaurants Inc. To provide high-quality customer service, Day has organized the restaurants' employees into wait staff teams, whose members work together to refill beers, take orders, bring hot chicken enchiladas to the table, or clear off the table. Team members share the burden of undesirable activities and unpopular shift times, and customers no longer have to wait until a particular waitress or waiter is available. Motivation and satisfaction levels in the Rock Bottom restaurants seem to be higher than in other restaurants, and turnover is about one-half of that experienced in other U.S. restaurant chains.[7]

Working in a group or team can also satisfy organizational members' needs for social interaction and feeling connected to other people. For workers who perform highly stressful jobs, such as hospital emergency and operating room staff, group membership can be an important source of social support and motivation. Family members or friends may not be able to fully understand or appreciate some sources of work stress that these group members experience firsthand. Moreover, group members may cope better with work stressors when they are able to share them with other members of their group. In addition, groups often devise techniques to relieve stress, such as the telling of jokes among hospital operating room staff.

Why do managers in all kinds of organizations rely so heavily on groups and teams? Effectively managed groups and teams can help managers in their quest for high performance, responsiveness to customers, and employee motivation. Before explaining how managers can effectively manage groups, however, we will describe the types of groups that are formed in organizations.

Types of Groups and Teams

formal group A group that managers establish to achieve organizational goals.

To achieve their goals of high performance, responsiveness to customers, innovation, and employee motivation, managers can form various types of groups and teams (see Figure 14.2). **Formal groups** are groups that managers establish to achieve organizational goals. We just described two types of formal work groups: cross-functional teams, used at Hallmark Cards and Rubbermaid, and cross-cultural teams, used at Honda. (Recall that *cross-functional* teams are teams composed of members from different departments and *cross-cultural* teams are teams composed of members from different cultures or countries.) As you will see, some of the groups discussed in this section also can be considered cross-functional (if they are composed of members from different departments) or cross-cultural (if they are composed of members from different countries or cultures).

informal group A group that managers or nonmanagerial employees form to help achieve their own goals or meet their own needs.

Sometimes organizational members, managers or nonmanagers, form groups because they feel that groups will help them achieve their own goals or meet their own needs (for example, the need for social interaction). Groups formed in this way are **informal groups.** Four nurses who work in a hospital and have lunch together twice a week constitute an informal group.

Below, we describe important types of formal and informal groups that can affect organizational performance.

The Top-Management Team

top-management team A group composed of the CEO, the president, and the heads of the most important departments.

A central concern of the CEO and president of a company is to form a **top-management team** to help the organization achieve its mission and goals. Top-management teams are responsible for developing the strategies that produce an organization's competitive advantage; most have between five and seven members. In forming their top-management teams, CEOs are well advised to stress diversity—diversity in expertise, skills, knowledge, and experience. Thus, many top-management teams are cross-functional teams: They are composed of members from different departments such as finance, marketing, production, and engineering. Diversity helps ensure that the top-

Figure 14.2
Types of Groups and Teams in Organizations

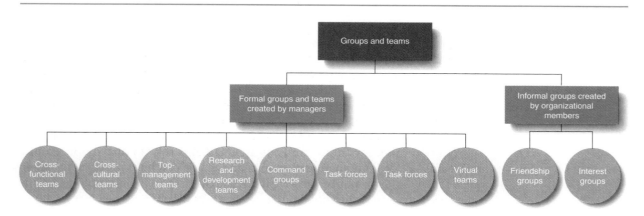

Rock star turned Lionel trains part-owner, Neil Young, wants to take model trains to the Nintendo generation. His top-management team consists of such diverse talent as that which graced Atari, Silicon Valley, and Lionel itself.

management team will have all the backgrounds and resources it needs to make good decisions. Diversity also helps guard against *groupthink,* faulty group decision making that results when group members strive for agreement at the expense of an accurate assessment of the situation (see Chapter 6).

Better known as a rock star than as a top manager, Neil Young stressed diversity in the top-management team he recently formed. A long-time model train enthusiast, Young bought Lionel Trains with partner Martin Davis (former CEO of Paramount Pictures and now president of the New York Investment firm Wellspring Associates). Young's ultimate goal is to update the technology and appeal of model trains so that they are attractive to young customers accustomed to the dazzle of Nintendo games and video arcades. Young's top-management team consists of Davis (who brings financial expertise in turnaround situations), former Lionel CEO Richard Kughn (who has a wealth of experience in the industry), Nolan Bushnell (founder of Atari and Chuck E. Cheese's Pizza Time Theatre), and Rick Davis and Ron Milner (well-known Silicon Valley engineers). This diverse team has innovated a high-tech wireless remote control called CAB-1, which uses a computer chip to move trains and accessories and control sound effects (recorded from real steam engines).[8] Only time will tell whether the trains will be big hits with young customers, but the diversity present in Young's top-management team has already contributed to the development of a new technology.

Research and Development Teams

research and development team

A team whose members have the expertise and experience needed to develop new products.

Managers in pharmaceuticals, computers, electronics, electronic imaging, and other high-tech industries often create **research and development teams** to develop new products. Eric Fossum, a researcher and manager with NASA's Jet Propulsion Laboratory at the California Institute of Technology, for example, formed and heads up a three-member R&D team that is developing a camera that is so small that its basic operational parts can fit on a single computer chip.[9] Managers select R&D team members on the basis of their expertise and experience in a certain area. Sometimes R&D teams are cross-functional teams with members from departments such as engineering, marketing, and production in addition to members from the research and development department.

Command Groups

command group

A group composed of subordinates who report to the same supervisor; also called a *department* or *unit.*

Subordinates who report to the same supervisor compose a **command group.** When top managers design an organization's structure and establish reporting relationships and a chain of command, they are essentially creating command groups. Command groups, often called *departments* or *units,* perform a significant amount of the work in many organizations. In order to have command groups that help an organization gain a competitive advantage, managers need to motivate group members to perform at a high level, and managers need to be effective leaders. Examples of command groups include the salespeople in a large department store in New York who report to the same supervisor, the employees of a small swimming pool sales and maintenance company in

Florida who report to a general manager, the telephone operators at the MetLife insurance company who report to the same supervisor, and workers on an automobile assembly line in the Ford Motor Company who report to the same first-line manager.

Task Forces

task force A committee of managers or nonmanagerial employees from various departments or divisions who meet to solve a specific, mutual problem; also called an *ad hoc committee.*

Managers form **task forces** to accomplish specific goals or solve problems in a certain time period; task forces are sometimes called *ad hoc committees.* For example, Michael Rider, owner and top manager of a chain of six gyms and fitness centers in the Midwest, created a task force composed of the general managers of each of the six gyms to determine whether the fitness centers should institute a separate fee schedule for customers who wanted to use the centers only for aerobics classes (and not use other facilities such as weights, steps, tracks, and swimming pools). The task force was given three months to prepare a report summarizing the pros and cons of the proposed change in fee schedules. Once the task force completed its report and reached the conclusion that the change in fee structure probably would reduce revenues rather than increase them and thus should not be implemented, it was disbanded. As in Rider's case, task forces can be a valuable tool for busy managers who do not have the time to explore an important issue in depth on their own.

Sometimes managers need to form task forces whose work, so to speak, is never done. The task force may be addressing a long-term or enduring problem or issue facing an organization, such as how to most usefully contribute to the local community or how to make sure that the organization provides opportunities for potential employees with disabilities. Task forces that are relatively permanent are often referred to as *standing committees.* Membership in standing committees changes over time. Members may have, for example, a two- or three-year term on the committee, and memberships expire at varying times so that there are always some members with experience on the committee. Managers often form and maintain standing committees to make sure that important issues continue to be addressed.

Self-Managed Work Teams

self-managed work team A group of employees who supervise their own activities and monitor the quality of the goods and services they provide.

Self-managed work teams are teams in which team members are empowered and have the responsibility and autonomy to complete identifiable pieces of work. On a day-to-day basis, team members decide what the team will do, how it will do it, and which team members will perform which specific tasks.[10] Managers provide self-managed work teams with their overall goals (such as assembling defect-free computer keyboards) but let team members decide how to meet those goals. Managers usually form self-managed work teams to improve quality, increase motivation and satisfaction, and lower costs. Often, by creating self-managed work teams, they combine tasks that individuals working separately used to perform, so the team is responsible for the whole set of tasks that yield an identifiable output or end product.

In response to increasing competition, William George, chief executive of Johnson Wax, maker of household products such as Pledge furniture polish, Glade air freshener, and Windex window cleaner, formed self-managed work teams to find ways to cut costs. Traditionally, Johnson Wax used assembly-line production, and workers were not encouraged or required to do much real thinking on the job, let alone determine how to cut costs. Things could not be more different at Johnson Wax now. Consider, for example, the nine-member self-managed work team that is responsible for molding plastic containers. Team members choose their own leader, train new members, have their own budget to manage, and are responsible for figuring out how to cut costs of molding plastic containers. Kim Litrenta, a 17-year veteran of Johnson's Waxdale, Wisconsin, plant sums up the effects of the change from assembly-line production to self-managed work teams this way: "In the past you'd have no idea how much things cost because you weren't involved in decisions. Now it's amazing how many different ways people try to save money."[11]

Managers can take a number of steps to ensure that self-managed work teams are effective and help an organization gain a competitive advantage:[12]

- Give teams enough responsibility and autonomy to be truly self-managing. Refrain from telling team members what to do or solving problems for them even if you (as a manager) know what should be done.

- Make sure that a team's work is sufficiently complex so that it entails a number of different steps or procedures that must be performed and results in some kind of finished end product.

- Carefully select members of self-managed work teams. Team members should have the diversity of skills needed to complete the team's work, have the ability to work with others, and want to be part of a team.

- As a manager, realize that your role vis-à-vis self-managed work teams calls for guidance, coaching, and supporting, not supervising. You are a resource for teams to turn to when needed.

- Analyze what type of training team members need, and provide it. Working in a self-managed work team often requires that employees have more extensive technical and interpersonal skills.

Managers in a wide variety of organizations have found that self-managed work teams help the organization achieve its goals.[13] However, self-managed work teams can run into trouble. Members are often reluctant to discipline one another by withholding bonuses from members who are not performing up to par or by firing members.[14] Buster Jarrell, a manager who oversees self-managed work teams in AES Corporation's Houston plant, has found that although self-managed work teams are highly effective, they have a very difficult time firing team members who are performing poorly.[15]

The Dallas office of the New York Life Insurance Co. recently experimented with having members of self-managed teams evaluate each other's performance and determine pay levels. Team members did not feel comfortable assuming this role, however, and managers ended up evaluating performance and determining pay levels.[16] One reason for team members' discomfort may be the close personal relationships they sometimes develop with each other. In addition, sometimes members of self-managed work teams actually do take longer to accomplish tasks, such as when team members have difficulties coordinating their efforts.

Virtual Teams

Virtual teams are teams whose members rarely or never meet face to face and interact by using various forms of information technology such as e-mail, computer networks, telephones, faxes, and video conferences. As organizations become increasingly global and have operations in far-flung regions of the world, and as the need for specialized knowledge increases due to advances in technology, virtual teams allow managers to create teams to solve problems or explore opportunities without being limited by the need for team members to be working in the same geographic location.[17]

Take the case of an organization that has manufacturing facilities in Australia, Canada, the United States, and Mexico and is encountering a quality problem in a complex manufacturing process. Each of its manufacturing facilities has a quality control team headed by a quality control manager. The vice president for production does not try to solve the problem by forming and leading a team at one of the four manufacturing facilities; instead, she forms and leads a virtual team composed of the quality control managers of the four plants and the plants' general managers. Team members communicate via e-mail and videoconferencing, and a wide array of knowledge and experience is brought to bear to solve the problem.

The principal advantage of virtual teams is that they enable managers to disregard geographic distances and form teams whose members have the knowledge, expertise, and experience to tackle a particular problem or take advantage of a specific opportunity.[18] Virtual teams can include members who are not employees of the organization itself; a virtual team might include members of an organization that is used for outsourcing. More and more companies, including Hewlett-Packard, Price-Waterhouse, Lotus Development, Eastman Kodak, Whirlpool, and VeriFone, are either using or exploring the use of virtual teams.[19]

Friendship Groups

The groups described so far are formal groups created by managers. **Friendship groups** are informal groups composed of employees who enjoy each other's company and socialize with each other. Members of friendship groups may have lunch together, take breaks together, or meet after work for meals, sports, or other activities. Friendship groups help satisfy employees' needs for interpersonal interaction, can provide needed social support in times of stress, and can contribute to people feeling good at work and satisfied with their jobs. Managers themselves often form friendship groups. The informal relationships that managers build in friendship groups can often help them solve work-related problems because members of these groups typically discuss work-related matters and offer advice.

Interest Groups

Employees form informal **interest groups** when they seek to achieve a common goal related to their membership in an organization. Employees may form interest groups to encourage managers to consider instituting flexible working hours, providing on-site child care, improving working conditions, or more proactively supporting environmental protection. Interest groups can provide managers with valuable insights into the issues and concerns that are foremost in employees' minds. They also can signal the need for change.

Group Dynamics
The ways in which groups function and, ultimately, group effectiveness hinge on a number of group characteristics and processes known collectively as *group dynamics*. In this section, we discuss five key elements of group dynamics: group size, tasks, and roles; group leadership; group development; group norms; and group cohesiveness.

Group Size, Tasks, and Roles

Managers need to take group size, group tasks, and group roles into account as they create and maintain high-performing groups and teams.

GROUP SIZE The number of members in a group can be an important determinant of members' motivation and commitment and of group performance. There are several advantages to keeping a group relatively small— between two and nine members. Compared with members of large groups, members of small groups tend to (1) interact more with each other and find it easier to coordinate their efforts, (2) be more motivated, satisfied, and committed, (3) find it easier to share information, and (4) be better able to see the importance of their personal contributions for group success. Recognizing these advantages, Nathan Myhrvold, senior vice president for advanced technology in Microsoft Corporation, has found that eight is the ideal size for the type of R&D teams he forms to develop new software.[20] A disadvantage of small rather than large groups is that members of small groups have fewer resources available to accomplish their goals.

Large groups—with 10 or more members—also offer some advantages. They have at their disposal more resources to achieve group goals than do small groups. These resources include the knowledge, experience, skills, and abilities of group members as well as their actual time and effort. Large groups also enable managers to obtain the advantages stemming from the **division of labor**—splitting the work to be performed into particular tasks and assigning tasks to individual workers. Workers who specialize in particular tasks are likely to become skilled at performing those tasks and contribute significantly to high group performance.

division of labor

Splitting the work to be performed into particular tasks and assigning tasks to individual workers.

The disadvantages of large groups include the problems of communication and coordination and the lower levels of motivation, satisfaction, and commitment that members of large groups sometimes experience. It is clearly more difficult to share information with, and coordinate the activities of, 16 people rather than 8 people. Moreover, members of large groups might not feel that their efforts are really needed and sometimes might not even feel a part of the group.

In deciding on the appropriate size for any group, managers attempt to gain the advantages of small group size while at the same time forming groups with sufficient resources to accomplish their goals and have a well-developed division of labor. As a general rule of thumb, groups should have no more members than necessary to achieve a division of labor and provide the resources needed to achieve group goals. In R&D teams, for example, group size is too large when (1) members spend more time communicating what they know to others rather than applying what they know to solve problems and create new products, (2) individual productivity decreases, and (3) group performance suffers.[21]

GROUP TASKS   The appropriate size of a high-performing group is affected by the kind of tasks the group is to perform. An important characteristic of group tasks that affects performance is **task interdependence,** the degree to which the work performed by one member of a group influences the work performed by other members.[22] As task interdependence increases, group members need to interact more frequently and intensely with each other, and their efforts have to be more closely coordinated if they are to perform at a high level. Management expert James D. Thompson identified three types of task interdependence: pooled, sequential, and reciprocal (see Figure 14.3).[23]

POOLED TASK INTERDEPENDENCE   **Pooled task interdependence** exists when group members make separate and independent contributions to group performance; overall group performance is the sum of the performance of the individual members (see Figure 14.3A). Examples of groups that have pooled task interdependence include a group of teachers in an elementary school, a group of salespeople in a department store, a group of secretaries in an office, and a group of custodians in an office building. In these examples, group performance, whether it be the number of children who are taught and the quality of their education, the dollar value of sales, the amount of secretarial work completed, or the number of offices that are cleaned, is determined by summing the individual contributions of group members.

For groups with pooled interdependence, managers should determine the appropriate group size primarily from the amount of work to be accomplished. Large groups can be effective because group members work independently and do not have to interact frequently with each other. Motivation in groups with pooled interdependence will be highest when managers reward group members for their *individual* performance.

SEQUENTIAL TASK INTERDEPENDENCE   **Sequential task interdependence** exists when group members must perform specific tasks in a predetermined order; certain tasks have to be performed before others, and what one worker does affects the work of others (see Figure 14.3B). Assembly lines and mass-production processes are characterized by sequential task interdependence.

When group members are sequentially interdependent, group size is usually dictated by the needs of the production process—for example, the number of steps needed in an assembly line to efficiently produce a CD player. With sequential interdependence, it is difficult to identify individual performance because one group member's performance depends on how well others perform their tasks. A slow worker at the start of an assembly line, for example, causes all workers farther down the line to work slowly. Thus, managers are often advised to reward group members for *group* performance. Group mem-

task interdependence
The degree to which the work performed by one member of a group influences the work performed by other members.

pooled task interdependence The task interdependence that exists when group members make separate and independent contributions to group performance.

sequential task interdependence The task interdependence that exists when group members must perform specific tasks in a predetermined order.

Figure 14.3
Types of Task Interdependence

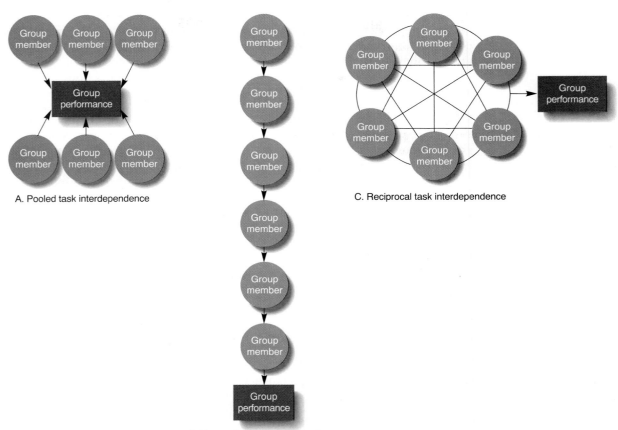

A. Pooled task interdependence

B. Sequential task interdependence

C. Reciprocal task interdependence

bers will be motivated to perform highly because each member will benefit if the group performs well. In addition, group members may put pressure on poor performers to improve so that group performance and rewards do not suffer.

reciprocal task inter-dependence The task interdependence that exists when the work performed by each group member is fully dependent on the work performed by other group members.

RECIPROCAL TASK INTERDEPENDENCE **Reciprocal task interdependence** exists when the work performed by each group member is fully dependent on the work performed by other group members; group members have to share information, intensely interact with each other, and coordinate their efforts in order for the group to achieve its goals (see Figure 14.3C). In general, reciprocal task interdependence characterizes the operation of teams, rather than other kinds of groups. The task interdependence of R&D teams, top-management teams, and many self-managed work teams is reciprocal.

When group members are reciprocally interdependent, managers are advised to keep group size relatively small because of the necessity to coordinate team members' activities. Communication difficulties can arise in teams with reciprocally interdependent tasks, because team members need to interact frequently with one another and be available when needed. As group size increases, communication difficulties increase and can impair team performance.

When a group's members are reciprocally interdependent, managers also are advised to reward group members on the basis of group performance. Individual levels of performance are often difficult for managers to identify, and group-based rewards help ensure that group members will be motivated to perform at a high level and make valuable contributions to the group. Of course, if a manager can identify instances of individual performance in such groups, they too can be rewarded to maintain high levels of motivation. Microsoft and many other companies reward group members both for their individual performance and for the performance of their group.

group role A set of behaviors and tasks that a member of a group is expected to perform because of his or her position in the group.

GROUP ROLES   A **group role** is a set of behaviors and tasks that a member of a group is expected to perform because of his or her position in the group. Members of cross-functional teams, for example, are expected to perform roles relevant to their special areas of expertise. At Hallmark Cards, discussed in the "Case in Contrast," the role of writers on the cross-functional teams is to create verses for new cards, the role of artists is to draw illustrations, and the role of designers is to bring verse and artwork together to create an attractive and appealing card. The roles of members of top-management teams are shaped primarily by their areas of expertise—production, marketing, finance, research and development—but members of top-management teams also typically draw on their broad expertise as planners and strategists.

In forming groups and teams, managers need to clearly communicate to group members the expectations for their roles in the group, what is required of them, and how the different roles in the group fit together to accomplish group goals. Managers also need to realize that group roles change and evolve as a group's tasks and goals change and as group members gain experience and knowledge. Thus, to get the performance gains that come from experience or "learning by doing," managers should encourage group members to take the initiative to assume additional responsibilities as they see fit and modify their assigned roles. This process, called **role making,** can enhance individual and group performance.

role making Taking the initiative to modify an assigned role by assuming additional responsibilities.

In self-managed work teams and some other groups, group members themselves are responsible for creating and assigning roles. Many self-managed work teams also pick their own team leaders. When group members create their own roles, managers should be available in an advisory capacity, helping group members effectively settle conflicts and disagreements. At Johnsonville Foods, for example, the position titles of first-line managers were changed to "advisory coach" to reflect the managers' new role vis-à-vis the self-managed work teams they oversee.[24]

Group Leadership

All groups and teams need leadership. Indeed, as we discussed in detail in Chapter 13, effective leadership is a key ingredient for high-performing groups, teams, and organizations. Sometimes managers assume the leadership role, as is the case in many command groups and top-management teams. Or a manager may appoint a member of a group who is not a manager to be group leader or chairperson, as is the case in a task force or standing committee. In other cases, group or team members may choose their own leaders, or a leader may emerge naturally as group members work together to achieve group goals.

When managers empower members of self-managed work teams, they often let group members choose their own leaders. Some self-managed work teams find it effective to rotate the leadership role among their members. Whether leaders of groups and teams are managers or not, and whether they are appointed by managers or emerge naturally in a group, they play an important role in ensuring that groups and teams perform up to their potential.

Group Development over Time

Richard (Skip) LeFauve, president of Saturn Corporation, which uses self-managed work teams, learned that it sometimes takes a self-managed work team two or three years to perform up to its true capabilities.[25] As LeFauve's experience suggests, what a group is capable of achieving depends in part on its stage of development. Knowing that it takes considerable time for self-managed work teams to get up and running helped LeFauve have realistic expectations for new teams at Saturn. He also knows that he has to provide new team members with considerable training and guidance.

Although every group's development over time is somewhat unique, researchers have identified five stages of group development that many groups seem to pass through (see Figure 14.4).[26] In the first stage, *forming*, members try to get to know each other and reach a common understanding of what the group is trying to accomplish and how group members should behave. During this stage, managers should strive to make each member feel a valued part of the group.

In the second stage, *storming*, group members experience conflict and disagreements because some members do not wish to submit to the demands of other group members. Disputes may arise over who should lead the group. Self-managed work teams can be particularly vulnerable during the storming stage. Managers need to keep an eye on groups at this stage to make sure that conflict does not get out of hand.

During the third stage, *norming*, close ties between group members develop, and feelings of friendship and camaraderie emerge. Group members arrive at a consensus about what goals they should be seeking to achieve and how group members should behave toward one another. In the fourth stage, *performing*, the real work of the group gets accomplished. Depending on the type of group in question, managers need to take different steps at this stage to help ensure that groups are effective. Managers of command groups need to make sure that group members are motivated and that they are effectively leading group members. Managers overseeing self-managed work teams have to empower team members and make sure that teams are given enough responsibility and autonomy at the performing stage.

Figure 14.4

Five Stages of Group Development

The last stage, *adjourning,* applies only to groups that eventually are disbanded, such as task forces. During adjourning a group is dispersed. Sometimes, adjourning takes place when a group completes a finished product, such as when a task force evaluating the pros and cons of providing on-site child care produces a report supporting its recommendation.

Managers need a flexible approach to group development and need to keep attuned to the different needs and requirements of groups at the various stages.[27] Above all else, and regardless of the stage of development, managers need to think of themselves as *resources* for groups. Thus, managers always should be striving to find ways to help groups and teams function more effectively.

Group Norms

All groups, whether top-management teams, self-managed work teams, or command groups, need to control their members' behavior to ensure that the group performs well and meets its goals. Assigning roles to each group member is one way to control behavior in groups. Another important way in which groups influence members' behavior is through the development and enforcement of group norms.[28] **Group norms** are shared guidelines or rules for behavior that most group members follow. Groups develop norms for a wide variety of behaviors, including working hours, the sharing of information among group members, how certain group tasks should be performed, and even how members of a group should dress.

Managers should encourage members of a group to develop norms that contribute to group performance and the attainment of group goals. For example, group norms that dictate that each member of a cross-functional team should always be available for the rest of the team when his or her input is needed, return phone calls as soon as possible, inform other team members of travel plans, and give team members a phone number at which he or she can

group norms Shared guidelines or rules for behavior that most group members follow.

The Armed Forces are an example of groups who must perform highly and have established group norms. The movie "G.I. Jane" starring Demi Moore portrayed her as a female trying to join the ranks of the elite Navy Seals, who have strict rules of behavior and assigned roles.

be reached when traveling on business, help to ensure that the team is efficient, performs highly, and achieves its goals. A norm in a command group of secretaries that dictates that secretaries who have a light workload in any given week should assist secretaries with heavier workloads helps to ensure that the group completes all assignments in a timely and efficient manner. And a norm in a top-management team that dictates that team members should always consult with each other before making major decisions helps to ensure that good decisions are made with a minimum of errors.

CONFORMITY AND DEVIANCE Group members conform to norms for three reasons: (1) They want to obtain rewards and avoid punishments. (2) They want to imitate group members whom they like and admire. (3) They have internalized the norm and believe it is the right and proper way to behave.[29] Consider the case of Robert King, who conformed to his department's norm of attending a fund-raiser for a community food bank. King's conformity could be due to (1) his desire to be a member of the group in good standing and to have friendly relationships with other group members (rewards), (2) his copying the behavior of other members of the department whom he respects and who always attend the fund-raiser (imitating other group members), or (3) his belief in the merits of supporting the activities of the food bank (believing that is the right and proper way to behave).

Failure to conform, or deviance, occurs when a member of a group violates a group norm. Deviance signals that a group is not controlling one of its members' behaviors. Groups generally respond to members who behave defiantly in one of three ways:[30]

1. The group might try to get the member to change his or her deviant ways and conform to the norm. Group members might try to convince the member of the need to conform, or they might ignore or even punish the deviant. For example, Liz Senkbiel, a member of a self-managed work team in a Johnsonville Foods plant responsible for weighing sausages, failed to conform to a group norm dictating that group members should periodically clean up an untidy room used to interview prospective employees. Senkbiel refused to take part in the team's cleanup efforts, and team members reduced her monthly bonus by about $225 for a two-month period.[31] Senkbiel clearly learned the costs of deviant behavior in her team.

2. The group might expel the member.

3. The group might change the norm to be consistent with the member's behavior.

That last alternative suggests that some deviant behavior can be functional for groups. Deviance is functional for a group when it causes group members to stop and evaluate norms that may be dysfunctional but are taken for granted by the group. Often, group members do not think about why they behave in a certain way or why they follow certain norms. Deviance can cause group members to reflect on their norms and change them when appropriate.

Take the case of a group of receptionists in a beauty salon who followed the norm that all appointments would be handwritten in an appointment book and at the end of each day the receptionist on duty would enter the appointments into the salon's computer system, which was used to print out the hairdressers' daily schedules. One day, a receptionist decided to enter appointments directly into the computer system at the time they were being made, bypassing the appointment book. This deviant behavior caused the other receptionists to think about why they were using the appointment book at all since appointments always could be entered into the computer directly. After consulting with the owner of the salon, the group changed its norm. Now appointments are entered directly into the computer, which saves time and cuts down on scheduling errors.

ENCOURAGING A BALANCE OF CONFORMITY AND DEVIANCE

In order for groups and teams to be effective and help an organization gain a competitive advantage, they need to have the right balance of conformity and deviance (see Figure 14.5). A group needs a certain level of conformity to ensure that it can control members' behavior and channel it in the direction of high performance and group goal accomplishment. A group also needs a certain level of deviance to ensure that dysfunctional norms are discarded and replaced with functional ones. Balancing conformity and deviance is a pressing concern for all groups, whether they are top-management teams, R&D teams, command groups, or self-managed work teams.

Figure 14.5
Balancing Conformity and Deviance in Groups

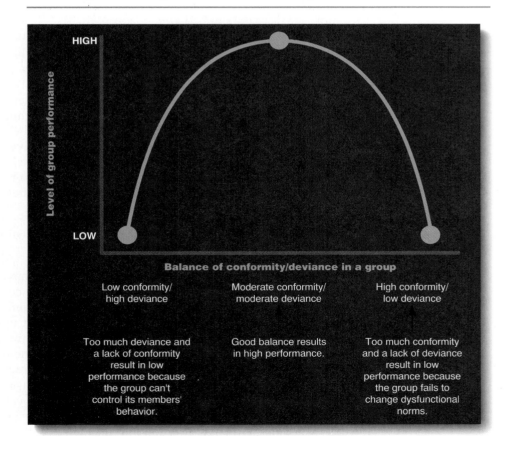

In the top-management team composed of the four co-presidents who manage the Nordstrom chain of department stores, for example, it is important for team members to conform to group norms stressing open and frequent communication, lively debate, and attendance at the team's weekly meetings.[32] It is equally important, however, for team members to deviate from norms dictating the kinds of merchandise that the co-presidents routinely select for sale in Nordstrom stores when they discover new and innovative merchandise lines that may increase customer satisfaction.

The extent of conformity and reactions to deviance within groups are determined by group members themselves. The three bases for conformity described above are powerful forces that more often than not result in group members' conforming to norms. Sometimes these forces are so strong that deviance rarely occurs in groups, and when it does, it is stamped out.

Managers can take several steps to ensure that there is enough tolerance of deviance in groups so that group members are willing to deviate from dysfunctional norms and, when deviance occurs in their group, reflect on the appropriateness of the violated norm and change the norm if necessary. First, managers can be role models for the groups and teams they oversee. When managers encourage and accept employees' suggestions for changes in procedures, do not rigidly insist that tasks be accomplished in a certain way, and admit when a norm that they once supported is no longer functional, they signal to group members that conformity should not come at the expense of needed changes and improvements. Second, managers should let employees know that there are always ways to improve group processes and performance levels and thus opportunities to replace existing norms with norms that will better enable a group to achieve its goals and perform at a high level. Third, managers should encourage members of groups and teams to periodically assess the appropriateness of their existing norms.

Group Cohesiveness

group cohesiveness
The degree to which members are attracted or loyal to a group.

Another important element of group dynamics that affects group performance and effectiveness is **group cohesiveness,** the degree to which members are attracted or loyal to their group or team.[33] When group cohesiveness is high, individuals strongly value their group membership, find the group very appealing, and have strong desires to remain part of the group. When group cohesiveness is low, group members do not find their group particularly appealing and have little desire to retain their group membership. Research suggests that managers should strive to have a moderate level of cohesiveness in the groups and teams they manage because that is most likely to contribute to an organization's competitive advantage.

CONSEQUENCES OF GROUP COHESIVENESS There are three major consequences of group cohesiveness: level of participation within a group, level of conformity to group norms, and emphasis on group goal accomplishment (see Figure 14.6).[34]

LEVEL OF PARTICIPATION WITHIN A GROUP As group cohesiveness increases, the extent of group members' participation within the group increases. Participation contributes to group effectiveness because group members are actively involved in the group, ensure that group tasks get accomplished, readily

Figure 14.6
Sources and Consequences of Group Cohesiveness

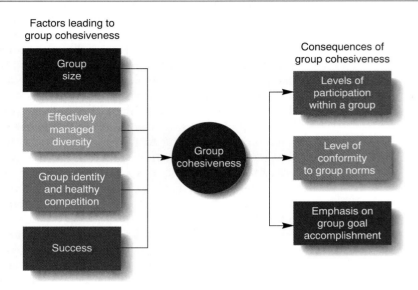

Factors leading to
group cohesiveness

Group size

Effectively managed diversity

Group identity and healthy competition

Success

Group cohesiveness

Consequences of
group cohesiveness

Levels of participation within a group

Level of conformity to group norms

Emphasis on group goal accomplishment

share information with each other, and have frequent and open communication (the important topic of communication is covered in depth in Chapter 15).

A moderate level of group cohesiveness helps to ensure that group members actively participate in the group and communicate effectively with each other. The reason why managers may not want to encourage high levels of cohesiveness is illustrated by the example of two cross-functional teams responsible for developing new toys. Members of the highly cohesive Team Alpha have lengthy meetings that usually start with non-work-related conversations and jokes, meet more often than most of the other cross-functional teams in the company, and spend a good portion of their time communicating the ins and outs of their department's contribution to toy development to other team members. Members of the moderately cohesive Team Beta generally have efficient meetings in which ideas are communicated and discussed as needed, do not meet more often than necessary, and share the ins and outs of their expertise with each other to the extent that it is needed for the development process. Teams Alpha and Beta have both developed some top-selling toys. However, it generally takes Team Alpha 30 percent longer than Team Beta to do so. This is why too much cohesiveness can be too much of a good thing.

LEVEL OF CONFORMITY TO GROUP NORMS Increasing levels of group cohesiveness result in increasing levels of conformity to group norms, and, when cohesiveness becomes high, there may be so little deviance in groups that group members conform to norms even when they are dysfunctional. In contrast, low cohesiveness can result in too much deviance and can undermine the ability of a group to control its members' behaviors to get things done.

Teams Alpha and Beta both had the same norm for toy development. It dictated that members of each team would discuss potential ideas for new toys, decide on a line of toys to pursue, and then have the team member from R&D design a prototype. Recently, a new animated movie featuring a family of rabbits produced by a small film company was an unexpected hit, and major toy companies were scrambling to reach licensing agreements to produce toy lines featuring the rabbits. The top-management team in the toy company assigned Teams Alpha and Beta to develop the new toy lines and to do so quickly to beat out the competition.

Members of Team Alpha followed their usual toy development norm even though the marketing expert on the team felt that the process could have been streamlined to save time. The marketing expert on Team Beta urged the team to deviate from its toy development norm. She suggested that the team not have R&D develop prototypes but instead modify top-selling toys the company already made to feature rabbits and then reach a licensing agreement with the film company based on the high sales potential (given the company's prior success). Once the licensing agreement was signed, the company could take the time needed to develop innovative and unique rabbit toys with more input from R&D.

As a result of the willingness of the marketing expert on Team Beta to deviate from the norm for toy development, the toy company obtained an exclusive licensing agreement with the film company and had its first rabbit toys on store shelves in a record three months. Groups need a balance of conformity and deviance, so a moderate level of cohesiveness often yields the best outcome, as it did in the case of Team Beta.

EMPHASIS ON GROUP GOAL ACCOMPLISHMENT As group cohesiveness increases, emphasis on group goal accomplishment also increases within a group. Very strong emphasis on group goal accomplishment, however, does not always lead to organizational effectiveness. For an organization to be effective and gain a competitive advantage, it is important for the different groups and teams in the organization to cooperate with each other and to be motivated to achieve *organizational* goals, even if doing so sometimes comes at the expense of the achievement of group goals. A moderate level of cohesiveness motivates group members to accomplish both group and organizational goals. High levels of cohesiveness can cause group members to focus so strongly on group goal accomplishment that they strive to achieve group goals no matter what—even when doing so jeopardizes organizational performance.

At the toy company, the major goal of the cross-functional teams was to develop toy lines that were truly innovative, utilized the latest in technology, and in some way were fundamentally distinct from other toys on the market. Team Alpha's high level of cohesiveness contributed to its emphasis of the *group* goal to develop an innovative line of toys; thus, Team Alpha followed its usual design process. Team Beta, in contrast, realized that, at least in the short run, to develop the new line of toys quickly was an important *organizational* goal that should take precedence over the group goal to develop pathbreaking new toys. Team Beta's moderate level of cohesiveness contributed to team members doing what was best for the toy company in this instance.

FACTORS LEADING TO GROUP COHESIVENESS Four factors affect group cohesiveness (see Figure 14.6).[35] By influencing these *determinants of group cohesiveness,* managers can raise or lower the level of cohesiveness to promote moderate levels of cohesiveness in groups and teams.

GROUP SIZE   As we mentioned earlier, members of small groups tend to be more motivated and committed than members of large groups. Thus, to promote cohesiveness in groups, when feasible, managers should form groups that are small to medium in size (between around 2 and 15 members). If a group is low in cohesiveness and large in size, managers might want to consider the feasibility of dividing the group in two and assigning different tasks and goals to the two newly formed groups.

EFFECTIVELY MANAGED DIVERSITY   In general, people tend to like and get along with others who are similar to themselves. It is easier to communicate with someone, for example, who shares your values, has a similar background, and has had similar experiences. However, as discussed in Chapter 5, diversity in groups, teams, and organizations can help an organization gain a competitive advantage. Diverse groups often come up with more innovative and creative ideas. One reason why cross-functional teams are so popular in organizations like Hallmark Cards is that the diversity in expertise represented in the teams results in higher levels of team performance.

In forming groups and teams, managers need to make sure that the diversity in knowledge, experience, expertise, and other characteristics necessary for group goal accomplishment is represented in the new groups. Managers then have to make sure that this diversity in group membership is effectively managed so that groups will be cohesive. We discussed the effective management of diversity in detail in Chapter 5, and the following "Focus on Diversity" provides additional insight into the steps managers can take to ensure that diverse groups and teams are cohesive.

Focus on Diversity

Promoting Cohesiveness in a Diverse Team at Mercedes-Benz

Andreas Renschler is president of Mercedes-Benz U.S. International Inc. (www.mercedes-benz.com), which in 1997 produced Mercedes's first sport-utility vehicle (the M-Class sport-utility vehicle) at a plant in Vance, Alabama. Mercedes-Benz CEO Helmut Werner committed more than $1 billion to the project, which he hopes will move Mercedes to the front of the global market for utility vehicles. The new car plant is Mercedes's first major foreign manufacturing facility outside Germany and embodies Werner's global cost-cutting strategy for Mercedes-Benz.

Renschler had a daunting task–to develop the new vehicle, design the factory and manufacturing process, and recruit and motivate the workforce. His goal was to find and use the most efficient manufacturing processes, and he assembled a diverse top-management team to help him meet this challenge. The team is made up of managers from various countries, including the United States, Germany, and Canada, who gained their experience in companies such as Ford, Nissan, General Motors, and Toyota.[36] Together, German and American team members debate issues such as the best way to design the factory and which manufacturing processes to use.

Given the diverse nature of team members, Renschler recognized early on the need to take steps to build group cohesiveness. To foster trust and camaraderie, he had team members, including himself, participate in three-day wilderness adventures in the Austrian Alps, where they climbed cliffs and rafted down icy rivers. He encourages the development of personal bonds and cohesiveness in his team through his own informal and gregarious style and by socializing with team members. He openly communicates with team members and expects the same from them and is never one to stand on ceremony or adopt Mercedes's traditional formalities.

Signs that Renschler's efforts to build cohesiveness in his top-management team are working come from the productive way in which team members debate ideas. They often disagree with each other but end up making a decision that all team members can support.[37] And Renschler's approach seems to be paying off; in 1998, the plant increased its capacity to meet the high demand for the M-Class sport-utility vehicle.[38]

GROUP IDENTITY AND HEALTHY COMPETITION When group cohesiveness is low, managers often can increase it by encouraging groups to develop their own identities or personalities and to engage in healthy competition. This is precisely what managers at Eaton Corporation based in Lincoln, Illinois, did. Eaton's employees manufacture products such as engine valves, gears, truck axles, and circuit breakers. Managers at Eaton created self-managed work teams to cut costs and improve performance. They realized, however, that the teams would have to be cohesive to ensure that they would strive to achieve their goals. Managers promoted group identity by having the teams give themselves names such as "The Hoods," "The Worms," and "Scrap Attack" (a team striving to reduce costly scrap metal waste by 50 percent). Healthy competition among groups is promoted by displaying on a large TV screen in the cafeteria measures of each team's performance and the extent to which teams have met their goals and by rewarding team members for team performance.[39]

If groups are too cohesive, managers can try to decrease cohesiveness by promoting organizational (rather than group) identity and making the organization as a whole the focus of groups' efforts. Organizational identity can be promoted by making group members feel that they are valued members of the organization as a whole and by stressing cooperation across groups to promote the achievement of organizational goals. Excessive levels of cohesiveness also can be reduced by reducing or eliminating competition between groups and rewarding cooperation.

SUCCESS When it comes to promoting group cohesiveness, there is more than a grain of truth to the saying that "Nothing succeeds like success." As groups become more successful, they become increasingly attractive to their members, and their cohesiveness tends to increase. When cohesiveness is low, managers can increase cohesiveness by making sure that a group can achieve some noticeable and visible successes.

Take the case of a group of salespeople in the housewares department of a medium-size department store. The housewares department was recently moved to a corner of the basement of the store. Its remote location resulted in low sales because of infrequent customer traffic in that part of the store. The salespeople, who were generally evaluated favorably by their supervisors and were valued members of the store, tried various initiatives to boost sales, but to no avail. As a result of this lack of success and the poor performance of their department, their cohesiveness plummeted. To increase and preserve the cohesiveness of the group, the store manager implemented a group-based incentive program across the store. In any month, members of the group with the best attendance and

Managers at Ortho Biotech have developed a vision statement for their organization that is shared with all employees and is constantly referred to as a way of enhancing commitment and *group cohesiveness* in its teams of research scientists.

punctuality records saw their names and pictures posted on a bulletin board in the cafeteria, and each member received a $50 gift certificate. The housewares group frequently had the best records, and success on this dimension helped to build and maintain its cohesiveness. Moreover, this initiative boosted attendance and discouraged lateness throughout the store.

Managing Groups and Teams for High Performance

Now that you have a good understanding of why groups and teams are so important for organizations, the types of groups that managers create, and group dynamics, we consider additional steps that managers can take to make sure groups and teams perform highly and contribute to organizational effectiveness. Managers striving to have top-performing groups and teams need to (1) motivate group members to work toward the achievement of organizational goals, (2) reduce social loafing, and (3) help groups to manage conflict effectively.

Motivating Group Members to Achieve Organizational Goals

When work is difficult or tedious or requires a high level of commitment and energy, managers cannot assume that group members will always be motivated to work toward the achievement of organizational goals. Consider the case of a group of house painters who paint the interiors and exteriors of new homes for a construction company and are paid on an hourly basis. Why should they strive to complete painting jobs quickly and efficiently if doing so will just make them feel more tired at the end of the day and they will not receive any tangible benefits? It would make more sense for the painters to adopt a relaxed approach, to take frequent breaks, and to work at a leisurely pace. This relaxed approach, however, would impair the construction company's ability to gain a competitive advantage because it would raise costs and increase the time needed to complete a new home.

Managers can motivate members of groups and teams to achieve organizational goals and create a competitive advantage by making sure that the members themselves benefit when the group or team performs highly. If members of a self-managed work team know that they will receive a percentage of any cost savings discovered and implemented in the team, they probably will strive to cut costs. Recall the example of Eric Fossum and the other members of the R&D team at NASA's Jet Propulsion Laboratory: Each member will receive a share of any royalties resulting from the innovation the team is working on (a tiny camera that fits on a computer chip); knowing this contributes to team members' high levels of motivation.[40] If the house painters' pay reflected the amount of surface area they actually painted, or if they received a bonus for each house completed in a timely, efficient manner, it is likely that they would not adopt a leisurely approach to their work.

Managers often rely on some combination of individual and group-based incentives to motivate members of groups and teams to work toward the achievement of organizational goals and a competitive advantage. When individual performance within a group can be assessed, pay is often determined by individual performance or by both individual and group performance. When individual performance within a group cannot be accurately assessed, then group performance should be the key determinant of pay levels. Approximately 75 percent of companies that use self-managed work teams base team members' pay in part on team performance.[41] A major challenge for managers is to develop a fair pay system that will lead to both high individual motivation and high group or team performance, as indicated in this "Management Insight."

Management Insight

Rewarding Team Members

Chester Labetz, vice president of Textron Inc.'s Defense Systems subsidiary (www.textron.com), and his fellow managers have experimented with many different pay plans to motivate members of self-managed work teams. To motivate team members to cooperate and to encourage high performance, Textron managers implemented a pay plan that awarded teams annual bonuses based on team performance; the bonus was split equally among team members. The managers realized, however, that this pay plan did not provide any extra rewards for individual employees who made outstanding contributions. Labetz and his managers wanted to reward these contributions in order to motivate team members to make them. Thus, they revised their pay system. Teams are still awarded bonuses that are divided equally among the members, but now team members can also receive individual bonuses, between 3 and 10 percent of their regular salaries, for individual accomplishments such as coming up with a new patent or taking a well-thought-out risk. Over 100 team members (from a total of 900 in the subsidiary) receive these individual rewards in a typical year.[42]

At Johnsonville Foods (www.johnsonville.com), a sausage maker with sales over $150 million, CEO Ralph Stayer implemented self-managed work teams in the 1980s to improve employee motivation, commitment, and concern for quality. To reward high performance, Stayer created a profit-sharing system; whether employees received profit-sharing bonuses depended on their individual performance. Although the teams themselves were performing many of the activities that first-line managers typically perform, such as hiring and firing, team members did not want to apportion bonuses among themselves; they preferred that the supervisors make the bonus decisions, and Stayer went along with their wishes.

This all changed in the 1990s, when Stayer implemented a new pay system to increase motivation. Now, 28 percent of Johnsonville's pretax profits each month are given to work teams to reward accomplishments. Whether a team receives its monthly profit-sharing bonus, called "Great Performance Shares," depends on the team's meeting previously agreed-upon goals. When a team does meet its goals, team members decide how to distribute the money among themselves, again based on performance.[43] Team members try to be objective when assessing each member's performance so that they will not feel bad about withholding a low performer's bonus.

Stayer indicates that he would like to see all team members get their bonuses each month because that would signal that everyone was performing highly. This has not happened yet (and probably never will), but Johnsonville's performance improved significantly after this pay system was implemented. Tim Lenz, a member and leader of a maintenance team at a smoked-sausage plant in Sheboygan Falls, Wisconsin, sums up the effects of the pay plan this way, "If my peers are judging me, I will try that much harder . . . Just pleasing one guy on a pedestal? Forget it. Pleasing the people I work with—that's where the pride comes in."[44]

Other benefits that managers can make available to group members when a group performs highly, in addition to monetary rewards, include extra resources such as equipment and computer software, awards and other forms of recognition, and choice future work assignments. For example, members of self-managed work teams that develop new software at companies like Microsoft often value working on interesting and important projects; members of teams that perform highly are rewarded with interesting and important new projects.

Reducing Social Loafing in Groups

We have been focusing on the steps that managers can take to encourage high levels of performance in groups. Managers, however, need to be aware of an important downside to group and team work: the potential for social loafing, which reduces group performance. **Social loafing** is the tendency of individuals to put forth less effort when they work in groups than when they work alone.[45] Have you ever worked on a group project in which one or two group members never seemed to be pulling their weight? Have you ever

social loafing The tendency of individuals to put forth less effort when they work in groups than when they work alone.

Figure 14.7
Three Ways to Reduce Social Loafing

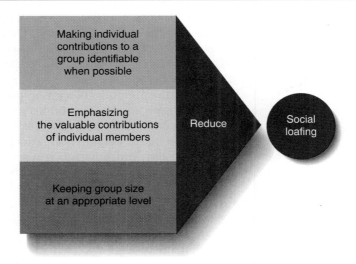

worked on a student club or committee in which some members always seemed to be missing meetings and never volunteered for activities? Have you ever had a job in which one or two of your coworkers seemed to be slacking off because they knew that you or other members of your work group would make up for their low levels of effort? If you have, you have witnessed social loafing.

Social loafing can occur in all kinds of groups and teams and in all kinds of organizations. It can result in lower group performance and may even prevent a group from attaining its goals. Fortunately, managers can take steps to reduce social loafing and sometimes completely eliminate it; we will look at three (see Figure 14.7).

1. *Make individual contributions to a group identifiable.*

Some people may engage in social loafing when they work in groups because they think that they can hide in the crowd—that no one will notice if they put forth less effort than they should. Other people may think that if they put forth high levels of effort and make substantial contributions to the group, their contribution will not be noticed and they will receive no rewards for their work—so why should they bother.[46]

One way in which managers can effectively eliminate social loafing is by making individual contributions to a group identifiable so that group members perceive that low and high levels of effort will be noticed and individual contributions evaluated.[47] Managers can accomplish this by assigning specific tasks to group members and holding them accountable for their completion. Take the case of a group of eight employees responsible for reshelving returned books in a large public library in New York. The head librarian was concerned that there was always a backlog of seven or eight carts of books to be reshelved even though the employees never seemed to be particularly busy and some even found time to sit down in the current periodicals section to read newspapers and magazines. The librarian decided to try to eliminate the apparent social loafing by assigning each employee a particular section of the library that he or she would always be responsible for reshelving on his or her shift. Because the library's front-desk employees sorted the books by section on the carts as they were returned, holding the shelvers responsible for particular sections was easily accomplished. Once the shelvers knew that the librarian could identify their effort or lack of effort, there were rarely any backlogs of books to be reshelved.

Sometimes the members of a group can cooperate to eliminate social loafing by making individual contributions identifiable. For example, members of a self-managed work team in a small security company who assemble control boxes for home alarm systems start each day by deciding who will perform what tasks that day and how much work each member and the group as a whole should strive to accomplish. Each team member knows that, at the end of the day, the other team members will know exactly how much he or she has accomplished. With this system in place, social loafing never occurs in the team. It is important to realize, however, that in some teams, individual contributions cannot be made identifiable, as in teams whose members are reciprocally interdependent.

2. *Emphasize the valuable contributions of individual members.*

Another reason why social loafing may occur is that people sometimes think that their efforts are unnecessary or unimportant when they work in a group. They feel the group will accomplish its goals and perform at an acceptable level whether or not they personally perform at a high level. To counteract this belief, when managers form groups, they should assign individuals to groups on the basis of the valuable contributions that *each* person can make to the group as a whole. Clearly communicating to group members why each of their contributions is valuable to the group is an effective means by which managers and group members themselves can reduce or eliminate social loafing.[48] This is most clearly illustrated in the case of cross-functional teams where each member's valuable contribution to the team derives from his or her area of expertise. By emphasizing why each member's skills are important, managers can reduce social loafing in such teams.

3. *Keep group size at an appropriate level.*

Group size is related to the causes of social loafing we just described. As size increases, identifying individual contributions becomes increasingly difficult, and members are increasingly likely to think that their individual contributions are not very important. To overcome this, managers should form groups with no more members than are needed to accomplish group goals and perform highly.[49]

Helping Groups to Manage Conflict Effectively

At some point or other, practically all groups experience conflict either within the group (intragroup conflict) or with other groups (intergroup conflict). In Chapter 16 we discuss conflict in depth and explore ways to manage it effectively. As you will learn there, managers can take several steps to help groups manage conflict and disagreements.

Tips for Managers

Group Dynamics and Managing Groups and Teams for High Performance

1. Make sure that members of groups and teams personally benefit when the group or team performs highly.

2. Form groups and teams with no more members than are necessary to achieve group and team goals.

3. Reward members of groups whose tasks are characterized by pooled task interdependence based upon individual performance.

4. Reward members of groups or teams whose tasks are characterized by sequential task interdependence based upon group performance.

5. Reward team members whose tasks are characterized by reciprocal task interdependence based upon team performance or a combination of individual and team performance (if individual performance can be identified).

6. Clearly communicate to members of groups and teams the expectations for their roles and how the different roles in the group fit together.

7. Encourage group and team members to periodically assess the appropriateness of existing norms.

Summary and Review

Chapter Summary

GROUPS, TEAMS, AND ORGANIZATIONAL EFFECTIVENESS

- Groups and Teams as Performance Enhancers

- Groups, Teams, and Responsiveness to Customers

GROUPS, TEAMS, AND ORGANIZATIONAL EFFECTIVENESS A group is two or more people who interact with each other to accomplish certain goals or meet certain needs. A team is a group whose members work intensely with each other to achieve a specific common goal or objective. Groups and teams can contribute to organizational effectiveness by enhancing performance, increasing responsiveness to customers, increasing innovation, and being a source of motivation for their members.

TYPES OF GROUPS AND TEAMS Formal groups are groups that managers establish to achieve organizational goals; they include cross-functional teams, cross-cultural teams, top-management teams, research and development teams, command groups, task forces, self-managed work teams, and virtual teams. Informal groups are groups that employees form because they feel that the groups will help them achieve their own goals or meet their needs; they include friendship groups and interest groups.

GROUP DYNAMICS Key elements of group dynamics are group size, tasks, and roles; group leadership; group development; group norms; and group cohesiveness. The advantages and disadvantages of large and small groups suggest that managers should form groups with no more members than are needed to provide the group with the human resources it needs to achieve its goals and use a division of labor. The type of task interdependence that characterizes a group's work gives managers a clue about the appropriate size of the group. A group role is a set of behaviors and tasks that a member of a group is expected to perform because of his or her position in the group. All groups and teams need leadership.

Five stages of development that many groups pass through are forming, storming, norming, performing, and adjourning. Group norms are shared rules for behavior that most group members follow. To be effective, groups need a balance of conformity and deviance. Conformity allows a group to control its members' behavior in order to achieve group goals; deviance provides the impetus for needed change.

Group cohesiveness is the attractiveness of a group or team to its members. As group cohesiveness increases, so, too, do the level of participation and communication within a group, the level of conformity to group norms, and the emphasis on group goal accomplishment. Managers should strive to achieve a moderate level of group cohesiveness in the groups and teams they manage.

MANAGING GROUPS AND TEAMS FOR HIGH PERFORMANCE   To make sure that groups and teams perform highly, managers need to motivate group members to work toward the achievement of organizational goals, reduce social loafing, and help groups to effectively manage conflict. Managers can motivate members of groups and teams to work toward the achievement of organizational goals by making sure that members personally benefit when their group or team performs highly.

Management in Action

Topics for Discussion and Action

1. Why do all organizations need to rely on groups and teams to achieve their goals and gain a competitive advantage?

2. Interview one or more managers in an organization in your local community to identify the types of groups and teams that the organization uses to achieve its goals.

3. Think about a group that you are a member of, and describe the stage of development that your group is currently in.

Does the development of this group seem to be following the forming-storming-norming-performing-adjourning stages described in the chapter?

4. Think about a group of employees who work in a McDonald's restaurant. What type of task interdependence characterizes this group? What potential problems in the group should the restaurant manager be aware of and take steps to avoid?

5. Discuss the reasons why too much conformity can hurt groups and their organizations.

6. Why do some groups have very low levels of cohesiveness?

7. Imagine that you are the manager of a hotel. What steps will you take to reduce social loafing by members of the cleaning staff who are responsible for keeping all common areas and guest rooms spotless?

Building Management Skills

Diagnosing Group Failures

Think about the last dissatisfying or discouraging experience you had as a member of a group or team. Perhaps the group did not accomplish its goals, perhaps group members could agree about nothing, or perhaps there was too much social loafing. Now answer the following questions.

1. What type of group was this?

2. Were group members motivated to achieve group goals? Why or why not?

3. How large was the group, what type of task interdependence existed in the group, and what group roles did members play?

4. What were the group's norms? How much conformity and deviance existed in the group?

5. How cohesive was the group? Why do you think the group's cohesiveness was at this level? What consequences did this level of group cohesiveness have for the group and its members?

6. Was social loafing a problem in this group? Why or why not?

7. What could the group's leader or manager have done differently to increase group effectiveness?

8. What could group members have done differently to increase group effectiveness?

Small Group Breakout Exercise

Creating a Cross-Functional Team

Form groups of three or four people, and appoint one member as the spokesperson who will communicate your findings to the whole class when called on by the instructor. Then discuss the following scenario.

You are a group of managers in charge of food services for a large state university in the Midwest. Recently a survey of students, faculty, and staff was conducted to evaluate customer satisfaction with the food services provided by the university's eight cafeterias. The results were disappointing, to put it mildly. Complaints ranged from dissatisfaction with the type and range of meals and snacks provided, operating hours, and food temperature, to unresponsiveness to current concerns about the importance of low-fat/high-fiber diets and the preferences of vegetarians. You have decided to form a cross-functional team to further evaluate reactions to the food services and to develop a proposal for changes to be made to increase customer satisfaction.

1. Indicate who should be on this important cross-functional team and why.

2. Describe the goals the team should be striving to achieve.

3. Describe the different roles team members will need to perform.

4. Describe the steps you will take to help ensure that the team has a good balance between conformity and deviance and a moderate level of cohesiveness.

Exploring the World Wide Web

Specific Assignment

Many companies are committed to the use of teams, including Chevron Corporation. Scan Chevron's website to learn more about this company (http://www.chevron.com/). Then click on "Newsroom" and then on "Speeches." Go to the speech that Chevron CEO and chairman Kenneth T. Derr made to the American Productivity and Quality Center's Knowledge Symposium on September 9, 1995.

1. What principles or values underlie Chevron's use of teams?

2. How does Chevron use teams to build employee commitment?

General Assignment

Find the website of a company that relies heavily on teams to accomplish its goals. What kinds of teams does this company use? What steps do managers take to ensure that team members are motivated to perform at a high level?

ManagementCase

Teams Manage AES (with the Help of a Few Managers)

In the late 1970s, Dennis W. Bakke and R. W. Sant founded AES Corporation, a power company that sells electricity to public utilities and steam to industrial corporations. Since the early days, AES's revenues have been increasing, on average, about 23 percent per year, annual profits have reached the $100 million mark, and the company has grown to 1,500 employees. AES has only four levels in its corporate hierarchy: workers, plant managers, division managers, and corporate managers. There are no corporate departments or managers in charge of areas such as purchasing, finance, human resources, or operations. Who oversees such activities? They are all handled by volunteer teams formed by plant managers and composed of rank-and-file workers. In a nutshell, AES appears to be a well-managed company with a minimum of managers and many teams.[50]

Do workers in an electric power plant make million-dollar investment decisions or negotiate major contracts with suppliers? This is exactly what is done at AES. Jeff Hatch, an employee in the Montville, Connecticut, plant who performs activities such as unloading coal from barges, and Joe Oddo, a maintenance technician at the plant, are both part of a voluntary team that manages the plant's $33 million investment fund. Other teams of technicians handle the purchasing of materials ranging

from mops to turbines, and teams of engineers arrange financing for new plants. Multi-million-dollar contracts normally negotiated by CEOs are handled by teams of engineers as well. New employees are hired by teams with diverse members ranging from pipe fitters to accountants.

Why does AES manage with teams (and without many managers)? According to Bakke and Sant, four core values underlie this unique approach to management—integrity, social responsibility, fairness, and fun. Observes Sant, "Fun is when you're intellectually excited and you are interacting with others . . . It's the struggle, and even the failures that go with it, that makes work fun."[51]

AES has experienced its share of failures as well as successes. In 1992, seven workers falsified emission-control reports at the Shady Point, Oklahoma, plant. When managers discovered and reported this violation to the authorities, the result was a $125,000 fine. Why did the violation occur? Sometimes team members feel so responsible for what happens at AES that they are afraid to admit when they make a mistake. The Shady Point workers who falsified the reports had been afraid they would be fired when managers realized emissions were high.

When problems like this occur, managers interpret them as a signal that AES's values are not coming through. Bakke and Sant felt so

personally responsible for not getting AES's values across to the plant's employees that they reduced their own bonuses by over 50 percent in 1992. To avoid a recurrence of this kind of problem, they also made it clear to employees in the plant that they can trust managers to stand by them even when they make a mistake.

True to the spirit of social responsibility, a team of employees in the Montville, Connecticut, plant determined how much carbon dioxide the plant would release into the environment in the foreseeable future. The team then had thousands of trees planted in Guatemala to offset the omissions, to the tune of $2 million.

Making high-powered decisions can be stressful for AES employees. Paul Burdick, for example, described how he felt when, after being on the job as a mechanical engineer at AES for only a few months, he had major responsibility in a team to complete a $1 billion purchase of coal: "I'd never negotiated anything before, save for a used car . . . I was afraid to make some of the decisions." He found the experience very motivating, challenging, and energizing, however, while also feeling intense pressure to do "right" by other AES employees. As Burdick suggests, such intellectual stimulation has "a flip side . . . You're given a lot of leeway and a lot of rope. You can use it to climb or you can hang yourself."[52]

Evidence that most employees might actually enjoy the stimulation of making important decisions and being responsible for them (and not overly stressful) is provided by the fact that AES's turnover rate is less than 1 percent. Nevertheless, suppliers, financiers, and company presidents often balk at having to negotiate and deal with rank-and-file workers in order to do business with AES. As Sant puts it, "Outside parties clearly are frustrated at having to deal with people who have more authority than top management. So many people want to come to the CEO, but we generally back off and say, 'It's up to these guys. You've just got to work these relationships.'"

What does coal handler Jeff Hatch think about this innovative use of teams at AES? "Who would have thought I'd be reading the *Wall Street Journal* every day and second-guessing Alan Greenspan? . . . It definitely makes it a lot more fun to show up for work every day."[53]

Questions

1. What are the advantages of AES's innovative use of teams?

2. What are the potential disadvantages of having teams of workers rather than managers make most of the important decisions?

3. Do you think Sant and Bakke's approach to managing AES would work in other companies? Why or why not?

ManagementCase

In the News

From the Pages of BusinessWeek
Getting Iridium off the Ground

It was a crucial meeting. So, last April, Iridium CEO Edward F. Staiano boarded a 12-hour flight to Beijing despite a terrible cold and sore throat. Once in China, his condition was so bad he could barely speak. Still, Staiano wasn't about to miss his one chance for a powwow with China's powerful Minister of Information Industry, Wu Jichuan. And when Wu offered him an odd-looking Chinese cold remedy, Staiano gamely downed the dark, steaming brew without flinching. The meeting was a success, and Iridium got its coveted Chinese license.

Doing whatever it takes to advance the ball has long been standard operating procedure for the 62-year-old former Motorola Inc. hotshot. But these days, with the debut of Washington-based Iridium's hugely ambitious global wireless-phone system falling behind schedule and its stock price plummeting by nearly half since May, Staiano is even more driven than usual. Indeed, he has staked his reputation on the monumentally complex system, which relies on 66 satellites, reams of software code, and scores of sensitive agreements with foreign governments.

In recent months, Staiano has been under especially intense pressure as the Sept. 23 deadline, set five years ago, for the system's inception has come and gone. Over the summer, two satellites failed and had to be replaced. Then a rocket explosion, hurricanes, and even a lightning strike delayed launching the last set of Iridium satellites. Even more troubling, a spate of computer glitches on the ground has postponed offering service until Nov. 1 at the earliest.

Staiano insists he isn't fazed. Known as "Fast Eddie" during his Motorola days, he built the electronic giant's huge cellular-phone business from zip to $11 billion during a frenzy of growth in the late '80s and '90s. Still, Iridium's $5.7 billion satellite network is an enormous technological and marketing challenge. If all goes as planned, it will provide a reliable dial tone anywhere on the globe. But, even assuming its numerous technical snags can be worked out, Iridium's $3,000 handsets and up to $7-a-minute airtime charges make commercial success far from certain.

What is certain is that Staiano has been pushing his team of 500 engineers and sales staffers with a ferocity that borders on obsession. At recent board meetings—which consist of 28 telecom executives and investors from around the world—Staiano has taken to egging on members in front of their peers for falling behind schedule, says one executive present at the meetings. At one recent board meeting, members were ranked with little green, yellow, or red race cars—green cars for those who were ahead of schedule and yellow and red ones for those who had fallen behind.

If there is one thing Staiano hates, it's being behind schedule. As it became clear Iridium might miss its deadline, he canceled all employee vacations in August and September. But for many staffers, a missed vacation is the least of their worries. Late last year, for instance, Staiano gave Vice-President Craig W. Bond four weeks to identify every wireless-phone number now in use around the globe to ensure that Iridium doesn't assign those numbers to its customers. "We pulled out all the stops to do as much as physically possible," recalls Bond. At the end of four weeks, Bond's team had rounded up 60% of the planet's phone numbers, but Staiano said the results were " 'totally unacceptable.' " Says Bond: "He gives absolutely no leeway. He shows no mercy."

Staiano insists he has little choice. With a $1 billion bank loan due at the end of the year, and Globalstar Limited Partnership, a Loral Space & Communications Ltd.–backed competitor, set to offer a competing yet more affordable satellite service late next year, Staiano needs paying customers. The Globalstar system, which makes more extensive use of ground networks than Iridium's, cost just $2.6 billion, and its handsets are likely to retail at a third the price of Iridium sets. Staiano maintains Iridium's one-year lead and better technology will still give it the edge over Globalstar.

To maintain his own edge and boost morale among the ranks, the 6-foot, 4-inch Staiano starts each day with a three-mile run at 6:30 A.M., eats a turkey sandwich at his desk for lunch, and works seven days a week. The longest vacation he has ever taken is five days. "You have to be prepared to walk the same mile that the technical people in the trenches do every day," he says. "I pride myself on equal pressure on everyone."

The son of an Italian immigrant father and a Canadian-born mother, Staiano grew up in a working-class neighborhood where few kids ever considered going to college, let alone running a multibillion-dollar business. His father, Dominick, ran a produce business on Long Island, N.Y., where Ed, the middle child, grew up with his two sisters. More interested in hanging out than in pursuing an education, Staiano was "very happy driving a truck for my dad for $200 a week," he says. But papa had loftier ambitions for his only son. To persuade Ed to go to college, Dominick Staiano even offered to buy him a car. That clinched the deal.

Once at Bucknell University, Staiano seemed to excel only at partying with his fraternity pals and working on the huge wooden floats for the homecoming parade. As a result, he wound up on academic probation. "I didn't buy any books the first year," he says. "I was there because I wanted my car." Some teachers, though, were impressed with Staiano's potential despite his poor showing. "He had a lot on the ball beyond some of the other kids who were getting better grades," says retired professor Charles H. Coder. A summer school course in engineering proved Coder right. "It was like a switch" going on, says Staiano, who developed an instant passion for the field. Staiano went on to earn a doctorate and was teaching at Bucknell before he went to work for Motorola in 1973.

In 1984, Staiano became head of the then tiny cellular-phone unit. By 1996, the division he ran was generating $11 billion, 40% of the company's total revenues. And Staiano had long since established his reputation as an unyielding boss. Former Motorola engineer Chris Jenner, now an executive at Sphere Communications, recalls a series of monthly quality review meetings in the spring of 1990. They tended to last four hours and proceeded along predictable lines. "One day, Ed sticks his head in," says Jenner. "He went

on a tirade: 'You call this a quality review?' " For the next 18 months, Staiano presided over each meeting. Starting at 6:30 A.M., they lasted 12 hours. Stragglers arriving just two minutes late were met with a cold stare from Staiano. "It was definitely effective," says Jenner, who adds that he admires Staiano's work ethic.

By 1996, Staiano had hit a wall. Motorola was stumbling, and Staiano, now in charge of 30,000 workers, "wasn't having fun anymore," he says. Meantime, Motorola had spun off its Iridium venture and was looking for a CEO. As a member of the search committee, Staiano threw his hat into the ring and got the job.

At Iridium, Staiano's first stop was Wall Street, to raise $2.8 billion needed to complete the system. But many investors balked. Staiano appeased skeptics by agreeing to make Iridium handsets compatible with ground-based cellular systems. Calls can now bypass Iridium satellites when within range of existing networks, making them more affordable but less lucrative for Iridium.

Now, after blitzing the media with a $180 million ad campaign, Iridium has yet to commence service. Staiano insists he's not disappointed. "To pick a date five years ago and be within a month of it is phenomenal," he says. Still, for the man who hates to miss a deadline, these are anxious times indeed.

Source: Catherine Yang and Roger O. Crockett, "Getting Iridium off the Ground," *Business Week,* October 5, 1998, 76, 80.

Questions

1. How does CEO Edward Staiano motivate team members in Iridium?

2. How does Staiano help to ensure that team members remain committed to helping Iridium achieve its goals?

Chapter
fifteen

Communication

Learning Objectives

1. Explain why effective communication helps an organization gain a competitive advantage.

2. Describe the communication process, and explain the role of perception in communication.

3. Define information richness, and describe the information richness of communication media available to managers.

4. Describe the communication networks that exist in groups and teams.

5. Explain how advances in technology have given managers new options for managing communication.

6. Describe important communication skills that managers need as senders and as receivers of messages.

A Case in Contrast

The Importance of Good Communication Skills

Effectively managing a health maintenance organization (HMO) would seem to be an undertaking vastly different from managing a small company that maintains private planes for clients, makes charter flights, and provides other kinds of small aircraft services. However, just as Dave Hurley, founder and CEO of Flight Services Group, based in Connecticut, learned that the future success of his business depended on good communication and improving his own communication skills, so too have many HMOs recognized that their effectiveness hinges on the communication skills of their doctors.

Hurley started Flight Services to help well-to-do individuals and corporations manage their private planes. The company provides crews, maintenance work, and charter flights. A pilot himself, Hurley focused on efficient,

high-quality service with an abiding emphasis on safety and had no trouble attracting clients and expanding the business. He adopted a hands-off management approach by default: He became so busy making flights and maintaining aircraft that he left his managers pretty much on their own to invest in new, sometimes high-stakes ventures, such as expanding into helicopter services.[1]

As the company grew, Hurley recognized the need for some financial oversight and

Just as doctors have realized that good communication is key to satisfying patients, so too has Dave Hurley, founder and CEO of Flight Services Group, realized that good communication is necessary for the survival and prosperity of his private plane managing company.

hired Hugh Regan to manage the firm's finances. Surprised and dismayed by the lack of financial planning and control at Flight Services, Regan repeatedly tried to communicate his concerns to Hurley, but they fell on deaf ears; Hurley did not listen or pay attention to his warnings. Regan became so concerned about the future of the company and his inability to make Hurley understand the seriousness of the situation that he turned to Hurley's wife, Johanna Hurley, for help in communicating the firm's problems to Dave. Luckily, Johanna was able to get through to her husband and effectively convey Flight Services' dire financial straits. Dave then agreed to a number of steps to safeguard the company's future—moving into less expensive offices, laying off unnecessary personnel, and cutting back on tangential services, and actually planning for the future.[2]

Providing medical services in an HMO may not seem to have much in common with managing a small business like Flight Services. But just as Dave Hurley recognized the need to listen to Regan's warnings and communicate with him more effectively, so too are many HMOs realizing how important it is for doctors to have good communication skills and listen to their patients. HMOs are increasingly learning that patients are dissatisfied with the abrupt manner of many doctors. Some doctors fail not only to explain important information adequately but also to listen to patients and try to understand their needs and concerns.[3] In the competitive market for organized medical care, HMOs and some doctors recognize the need to improve communication skills or else lose patients like Julie Robertson of Woodland Hills, California, who changed obstetricians late in her pregnancy because of communication problems. Some evidence suggests that poor communication skills can even increase the risk of malpractice lawsuits.[4]

Not surprisingly, many HMOs are requiring doctors to learn how to be better communicators. More than 70 medical organizations, including Kaiser Permanente and PacifiCare Health Systems, rely on the Bayer Institute for Health Care Communication in West Haven, Connecticut, to provide communication classes for doctors. Dr. Bone, a surgeon with the Scripps Clinic in La Jolla, California, recognized the need for good communication when he encountered a disconcerting problem with one of his own patients and realized that he often did not understand his patients' needs and problems. After learning better communication skills himself, he began teaching other doctors in the Scripps Clinic important communication tips such as letting patients talk and really listening to them. As Bone puts it, "The secret [for doctors] is to bite your lip for two minutes . . . First let the patient tell a narrative story. Then follow it up with questions."[5] In addition to learning how to listen, doctors are learning how to be empathetic, instill trust, develop rapport, and engage in two-way communication with their patients so that common understandings are reached.

Just as doctors like Bone realize that good communication is key to satisfying patients, so too does Dave Hurley realize that good communication is necessary for the survival and prosperity of his business. Effectively communicating with his managers enables Hurley not only to save his business but also to turn things around so much that the company is expanding once again and has annual revenues over $15 million.[6]

Overview

As should be clear from the "Case in Contrast," ineffective communication is detrimental for managers, workers, and organizations; it can lead to poor performance, strained interpersonal relations, poor service, and dissatisfied customers. Managers at all levels need to be good communicators in order for an organization to be effective and gain a competitive advantage.

In this chapter, we describe the nature of communication and the communication process and explain why it is so important for all managers and their subordinates to be effective communicators. We describe the communication media available to managers and the factors they need to consider in selecting a communication medium for each message they send. We consider the communication networks that organizational members rely on, and we explore how advances in information technology are expanding managers' communication options. We describe the communication skills that help managers be effective senders and receivers of messages. By the end of this chapter, you will have a good appreciation of the nature of communication and the steps that managers can take to ensure that they are effective communicators. •

Communication and Management

communication The sharing of information between two or more individuals or groups to reach a common understanding.

Communication is the sharing of information between two or more individuals or groups to reach a common understanding.[7] From the "Case in Contrast," it is clear that this is often not as easy as it might seem. Dave Hurley hired Hugh Regan to oversee Flight Services Group's finances, but Regan could not communicate his concerns about the firm's finances and current operations and take corrective action because Hurley would not pay attention and listen to what he was trying to tell him. Similarly, many doctors have problems sharing information with patients and reaching a common understanding, and their patients become dissatisfied and frustrated with the care they are receiving.

The Importance of Good Communication

In Chapter 1, we explained that in order for an organization to gain a competitive advantage, managers must strive to increase efficiency, quality, responsiveness to customers, and innovation. Good communication is essential for reaching each of these four goals and thus is a necessity for gaining a competitive advantage.

Managers can *increase efficiency* by updating the production process to take advantage of new and more efficient technologies and by training workers to operate the new technologies and expand their skills. Good communication is necessary for managers to learn about new technologies, implement them in their organizations, and train workers in how to use them. Similarly, *improving quality* hinges on effective communication. Managers need to communicate to all members of an organization the meaning and importance of high quality and the routes to attaining it. Subordinates need to communicate quality problems and suggestions for increasing quality to their superiors, and members of self-managed work teams need to share their ideas for improving quality with each other.

Good communication can also help to increase *responsiveness to customers.* When the organizational members who are closest to customers, such as salespeople in department stores and tellers in banks, are empowered to communicate customers' needs and desires to managers, managers are better able to respond to these needs. Managers, in turn, must communicate with other organizational members to determine how best to respond to changing customer preferences.

Innovation, which often takes place in cross-functional teams, also requires effective communication. Members of a cross-functional team developing a new kind of compact disc player, for example, must effectively communicate with each other to develop a disc player that customers will want, that will be of high quality, and that can be produced efficiently. Members of the team also must communicate with managers to secure the resources they need to develop the disc player and must keep managers informed of progress on the project.

Effective communication is necessary for managers and all other members of an organization to increase efficiency, quality, responsiveness to customers, and innovation and thus gain a competitive advantage for their organization. Managers therefore must have a good understanding of the communication process if they are to perform effectively.

The Communication Process

The communication process consists of two phases. In the *transmission phase,* information is shared between two or more individuals or groups. In the *feedback phase,* a common understanding is reached. In both phases, a number of distinct stages must occur for communication to take place (see Figure 15.1).[8]

Starting the transmission phase, the **sender,** the person or group wishing to share information with some other person or group, decides on the **message,** what information to communicate. Then the sender translates the message into symbols or language, a process called **encoding;** often messages are encoded into words. **Noise** is a general term that refers to anything that hampers any stage of the communication process. In the "Case in Contrast," Hurley's failure to pay attention and listen to Regan's messages about Flight Services' financial problems was a source of noise.

Once encoded, a message is transmitted through a medium to the **receiver,** the person or group for which the message is intended. A **medium** is simply the pathway, such as a phone call, a letter, a memo, or face-to-face communication in a meeting, through which an encoded message is transmitted to a receiver. At the next stage, the receiver interprets and tries to make sense of the message, a process called **decoding.** This is a critical point in communication.

The feedback phase is begun by the receiver (who becomes a sender). The receiver decides what message to send to the original sender (who becomes a receiver), encodes it, and transmits it through a chosen medium (see Figure 15.1). The message might contain a confirmation that the original message was received and understood, a restatement of the original message to make sure that it was correctly interpreted, or a request for more information. The original sender decodes the message and makes sure that a common understanding

sender The person or group wishing to share information.

message The information that a sender wants to share.

encoding Translating a message into understandable symbols or language.

noise Anything that hampers any stage of the communication process.

receiver The person or group for which a message is intended.

medium The pathway through which an encoded message is transmitted to a receiver.

decoding Interpreting and trying to make sense of a message.

Figure 15.1
The Communication Process

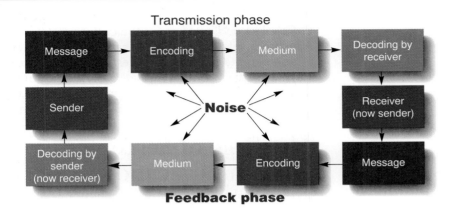

has been reached. If the original sender determines that a common under-standing has not been reached, sender and receiver cycle through the whole process as many times as are needed to reach a common understanding. As the "Case in Contrast" indicates, an abrupt manner and failure to listen to patients prevent many doctors from receiving feedback and reaching a common understanding with their patients. Feedback eliminates misunderstand-ings, ensures that messages are correctly interpreted, and enables senders and receivers to reach a common understanding.

The encoding of messages into words, written or spoken, is **verbal communication.** We also encode messages without using written or spoken language. **Nonverbal communication** shares information by means of facial expressions (smiling, raising an eyebrow, frowning, dropping one's jaw), body language (posture, gestures, nods, shrugs), and even style of dress (casual, for-mal, conservative, trendy). J. T. Battenberg, executive vice president of General Motors, says that when he and CEO Jack Smith walk around GM's plants, they wear slacks and sport jackets rather than suits to communicate or signal that GM's old bureaucracy has been dismantled and that the company is decentralized and more informal than it used to be.[9] The trend toward increas-ing empowerment of the workforce also has led managers such as Battenberg and Smith to dress informally to communicate that all employees of an organi-zation are team members, working together to create value for customers.

As Battenberg and Smith realize, nonverbal communication can back up or reinforce verbal communication. Just as a warm and genuine smile can back up words of appreciation for a job well done, a concerned facial expression can back up words of sympathy for a personal problem. In such cases, the con-gruence between verbal and nonverbal communication helps to ensure that a common understanding is reached.

Sometimes when members of an organization decide not to express a mes-sage verbally, they inadvertently express it nonverbally. People tend to have less control over nonverbal communication, and often a verbal message that is withheld gets expressed through body language or facial expressions. A man-ager who agrees to a proposal that she or he actually is not in favor of may unintentionally communicate disfavor by grimacing.

verbal communication The encoding of messages into words, either written or spoken.

nonverbal communication The encoding of messages by means of facial expressions, body language, and styles of dress.

Sometimes nonverbal communication is used to convey messages that cannot be sent through verbal channels. Many lawyers are well aware of this communication tactic. Lawyers are often schooled in techniques of nonverbal communication such as choosing where to stand in the courtroom for maximum effect and using eye contact during different stages of a trial. Lawyers sometimes get into trouble for using inappropriate nonverbal communication in an attempt to influence juries. In a Louisiana court, prosecuting attorney Thomas Pirtle was admonished and fined $2,500 by Judge Yada Magee for shaking his head in an expression of doubt, waving his arms indicating disfavor, and chuckling when attorneys for the defense were stating their case.[10]

The Role of Perception in Communication

Perception plays a central role in communication and affects both transmission and feedback. In Chapter 11, we defined *perception* as the process through which people select, organize, and interpret sensory input to give meaning and order to the world around them. We mentioned that perception is inherently subjective and influenced by people's personalities, values, attitudes, and moods as well as by their experience and knowledge. When senders and receivers communicate with each other, they are doing so based on their own subjective perceptions. The encoding and decoding of messages and even the choice of a medium hinge on the perceptions of senders and receivers.

In addition, perceptual biases can hamper effective communication. Recall from Chapter 5 that *biases* are systematic tendencies to use information about others in ways that result in inaccurate perceptions. In Chapter 5, we described a number of biases that can result in diverse members of an organization being treated unfairly. These same biases also can lead to ineffective communication. For example, *stereotypes,* simplified and often inaccurate beliefs about the characteristics of particular groups of people, can interfere with the encoding and decoding of messages.

Suppose a manager stereotypes older workers as being fearful of change. When this manager encodes a message to an older worker about an upcoming change in the organization, she may downplay the extent of the change so as not to make the older worker feel stressed. The older worker, however, fears change no more than his younger colleagues fear it and decodes the message to mean that hardly any changes are going to be made. The older worker fails to adequately prepare for the change, and his performance subsequently suffers because of his lack of preparation for the change. Clearly, the ineffective communication was due to the manager's inaccurate assumptions about older workers. Instead of relying on stereotypes, effective managers strive to perceive other people accurately by focusing on their actual behaviors, knowledge, skills, and abilities. Accurate perceptions, in turn, contribute to effective communication.

The Dangers of Ineffective Communication

Because managers must communicate with others to perform their various roles and tasks, managers spend most of their time communicating, whether in meetings, in telephone conversations, through e-mail, or in face-to-face interactions. Indeed, some experts estimate that managers spend approximately 85 percent of their time engaged in some form of communication.[11] So important is effective communication that managers cannot just be concerned that they themselves are effective communicators; they also have to help their subordinates be effective communicators. When all members of an organization are able to communicate effectively with each other and with people outside the organization, the organization is much more likely to perform highly and gain a competitive advantage.

When managers and other members of an organization are ineffective communicators, organizational performance suffers, and any competitive advantage the organization might have is likely to be lost. Moreover, poor communication sometimes can be downright dangerous and even lead to tragic and unnecessary loss of human life. For example, researchers from Harvard University recently studied the causes of mistakes, such as a patient receiving the wrong medication, in two large hospitals in the Boston area. They discovered that some mistakes in hospitals occur because of communication problems–physicians not having the information they need to correctly order medications for their patients or nurses not having the information they need to correctly administer medications. The researchers concluded that some of the responsibility for these mistakes lies with hospital management, which has not taken active steps to improve communication.[12]

Communication problems in the cockpit of airplanes and between flying crews and air traffic controllers are unfortunately all too common, sometimes with deadly consequences. In the late 1970s, two jets collided in Tenerife (one of the Canary Islands) because of miscommunication between a pilot and the control tower, and 600 people were killed. The tower radioed to the pilot, "Clipper 1736 report clear of runway." The pilot mistakenly interpreted this message to mean that he was cleared for takeoff. Unfortunately, errors like this one are not a thing of the past. A safety group at NASA tracked over 6,000 unsafe flying incidents and found that communication difficulties caused approximately 529 of them.[14]

Information Richness and Communication Media

To be effective communicators, managers (and other members of an organization) need to select an appropriate communication medium for *each* message they send. Should a change in procedures be communicated to subordinates in a memo sent as e-mail? Should a congratulatory message about a major accomplishment be communicated in a letter, in a phone call, or over lunch? Should a layoff announcement be made in a memo or at a plant meeting? Should the members of a purchasing team travel to Europe to cement a major agreement with a new supplier, or should they do so through faxes? Managers deal with these questions day in and day out.

There is no one best communication medium for managers to rely on. In choosing a communication medium for any message, managers need to consider three factors. The first and most important is the level of information richness that is needed. **Information richness** is the amount of information a communication medium can carry and the extent to which the medium

Figure 15.2

The Information Richness of Communication Media

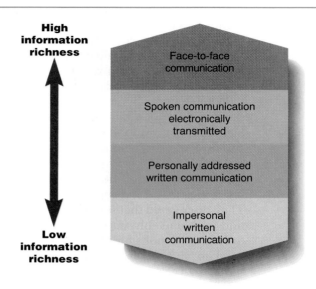

information richness

The amount of information that a communication medium can carry and the extent to which the medium enables sender and receiver to reach a common understanding.

enables sender and receiver to reach a common understanding.[15] The communication media that managers use vary in their information richness (see Figure 15.2).[16] Media high in information richness are able to carry a lot of information and generally enable receivers and senders to come to a common understanding.

The second factor that managers need to take into account in selecting a communication medium is the *time* needed for communication, because managers' and other organizational members' time is valuable. Managers at United Parcel Service, for example, dramatically reduced the amount of time they spent communicating with colleagues in Germany and England by using video conferences instead of face-to-face communication, which required travel overseas.[17]

The third factor that affects the choice of a communication medium is the *need for a paper or electronic trail,* or some kind of written documentation that a message was sent and received. A manager may wish to document in writing, for example, that a subordinate was given a formal warning about excessive lateness.

In the remainder of this section we examine four types of communication media that vary along these three dimensions: information richness, time, and need for a paper or electronic trail.[18]

Face-to-Face Communication

Face-to-face communication is the medium that is highest in information richness. When managers communicate face-to-face, they not only can take advantage of verbal communication but also can interpret each other's nonverbal signals such as facial expressions and body language. A look of concern or puzzlement can sometimes tell more than a thousand words, and managers can respond to these nonverbal signals on the spot. Face-to-face communication also enables managers to receive instant feedback. Points of confusion, ambiguity, or misunderstanding can be resolved, and managers can cycle through the communication process as many times as they need to, to reach a common understanding.

Management by wandering around is a face-to-face communication technique that for many managers at all levels in an organization find effective.[19] Rather than scheduling formal meetings with subordinates, managers walk around work areas and talk informally with employees about issues and concerns that both employees and managers may have. These informal conversations provide managers and subordinates with important information and at the same time foster the development of positive relationships. William Hewlett and David Packard, founders and former top managers of Hewlett-Packard, found management by wandering around a highly effective way to communicate with their employees.

Because face-to-face communication is highest in information richness, you might think that it should always be the medium of choice for managers. This is not the case, however, because of the amount of time it takes and the lack of a paper or electronic trail resulting from it. For messages that are important, personal, or likely to be misunderstood, it is often well worth managers' time to use face-to-face communication and, if need be, supplement it with some form of written communication documenting the message.

Advances in information technology are providing managers with new and close alternative communication media for face-to-face communication. Many organizations such as American Greetings Corp. and Hewlett-Packard are using *video conferences* to capture some of the advantages of face-to-face communication (such as access to facial expressions) while saving time and money because managers in different locations do not have to travel to meet with one another. During a video conference, managers in two or more locations communicate with each other over large TV or video screens; they not only hear each other but also see each other throughout the meeting.

In addition to saving travel costs, video conferences sometimes have other advantages. Managers at American Greetings have found that decisions get made more quickly when video conferences are used, because more managers can be involved in the decision-making process and therefore fewer managers

have to be consulted outside the meeting itself. Managers at Hewlett-Packard have found that video conferences shorten new product development time by 30 percent for similar reasons. Video conferences also seem to lead to more efficient meetings. Some managers have found that meetings are 20 to 30 percent shorter when they use video conferences instead of face-to-face meetings.[20]

Taking video conferences one step further, IBM and TelePort Corporation have joined forces to build virtual dining rooms in which top managers can actually have power meals with other managers in another location. Managers in one location sit around a large, round table bisected by a huge video screen on which they are able to see (life-size) their dining partners in

Video conferencing allows for face-to-face communication between 2 or more people. It also saves on travel costs and the time involved to fly to other locations.

another location sitting around the same kind of table and having the same kind of meal. Even though these managers are hundreds or thousands of miles apart, they eat together as they discuss pressing concerns. The cameras enabling the transmission of the video images are hidden in flower arrangements so as not to unnerve the diners. The tables start at $150,000, and major hotel chains such as Hilton, Hyatt, and Doubletree are interested in purchasing them for use by their business customers.[21]

Spoken Communication Electronically Transmitted

After face-to-face communication, spoken communication electronically transmitted over phone lines is second highest in information richness (see Figure 15.2). Although managers communicating over the telephone do not have access to body language and facial expressions, they do have access to the tone of voice in which a message is delivered, the parts of the message the sender emphasizes, and the general manner in which the message is spoken, in addition to the actual words themselves. Thus, telephone conversations have the capacity to convey extensive amounts of information. Managers also can ensure that mutual understanding is reached because they can get quick feedback over the phone and answer questions.

Voice mail systems and answering machines also allow managers to send and receive verbal electronic messages over telephone lines. Voice mail systems are companywide systems that enable senders to record messages for members of an organization who are away from their desks and allow receivers to access their messages when hundreds of miles away from the office. Such systems are obviously a necessity when managers are frequently out of the office, and managers on the road are well advised to periodically check their voice mail. The increasing use of voice mail in companies large and small has led to some ethical concerns, as depicted in the following "Ethics in Action."

Ethics in Action

Eavesdropping on Voice Mail

Should managers listen to their subordinates' voice mail messages? Many employees who currently use voice mail would probably answer this question with an emphatic "No!" Just as workers do not expect their bosses to eavesdrop on their telephone conversations, intercepting voice mail messages without the consent of the receiver seems unethical and an invasion of privacy. Some managers, however, evidently feel differently. Over 20 percent of managers contacted for a recent survey indicated that they monitored their subordinates' voice mail, e-mail, or computer files. Some of these managers contend that because the systems the employees are using are company owned or are paid for with company funds, managers should have access to the information contained on them.

Michael Huffcut, who was fired from his job as a manager at a McDonald's (www.mcdonalds.com) restaurant in Elmira, New York, after his boss listened to Huffcut's voice mail, thinks otherwise. Huffcut was having an affair with a coworker, and the two of them got into the habit of leaving romantic voice mail messages for each other. One of Huffcut's other coworkers listened to the messages and then played them for Huffcut's boss and Huffcut's wife. Upon learning of this, Huffcut complained to his boss that he thought his privacy had been invaded. The boss's response was to fire Huffcut. Huffcut and his wife filed a lawsuit against McDonald's, the franchisee who owns the Elmira restaurant, and the coworker who accessed the messages, accusing them of violating federal legislation against wiretapping and state legislation against eavesdropping.

Related lawsuits dealing with managers' surveillance of employees' e-mail messages have tended to be decided in favor of the employer. Recently in California, for example, two former Nissan employees who had been fired after their boss read e-mail messages critical of him that they had written to each other lost their lawsuit. In that case, the judge ruled that the boss (as a representative of Nissan) had the right to read the messages because Nissan owned the system on which they were sent.[22] The ethics of listening to other people's voice mail or reading their e-mail is likely to be a growing concern for many managers.

Personally Addressed Written Communication

Lower than electronically transmitted verbal communication in information richness is personally addressed written communication (see Figure 15.2). One of the advantages of face-to-face communication and verbal communication electronically transmitted is that they both tend to demand attention, which helps ensure that receivers pay attention. Personally addressed written communication such as memos and letters also has this advantage. Because it is addressed to a particular person, the chances are good that the person will actually pay attention to (and read) it. Moreover, the sender can write the message in a way that the receiver is most likely to understand. Like voice mail, written communication does not enable a receiver to have his or her questions answered immediately, but when messages are clearly written and feedback is provided, common understandings can still be reached.

Even if managers use face-to-face communication, a follow-up in writing is often needed for messages that are important or complicated and need to be referred to later on. This is precisely what Karen Stracker, a hospital administrator, did when she needed to tell one of her subordinates about an important change in the way the hospital would be handling denials of insurance benefits. Stracker met with the subordinate and described the changes face-to-face. Once she was sure that the subordinate understood them, she handed her a sheet of instructions to follow, which essentially summarized the information they had discussed.

E-mail also fits into this category of communication media because senders and receivers are communicating through personally addressed written words. The words, however, are appearing on their personal computer screens rather than on pieces of paper. E-mail is becoming so widespread in the business world that managers are even developing their own e-mail etiquette. To save time, Andrew Giangola, a manager at Simon & Schuster, a book publisher, used to type all his e-mail messages in capital letters. He was surprised when a receiver of one of his messages responded, "Why are you screaming at me?" Messages in capital letters are often perceived as being shouted or screamed, and thus Giangola's routine use of capital letters was bad e-mail etiquette. Here are some other guidelines from polite e-mailers: Always punctuate messages; do not ramble on or say more than you need to; do not act as though you do not understand something when in fact you do understand it; and pay attention to spelling and format (put a memo in memo form). To avoid embarrassments like Giangola's, managers at Simon & Schuster created a task force to develop guidelines for e-mail etiquette.[23]

Although e-mail is extensively used in many large organizations, small companies are less likely to rely on e-mail, and if they do use it, they use it primarily for internal communication. A recent survey of small and medium-size businesses conducted by *Inc.* magazine found that 56 percent of the businesses surveyed use e-mail within the company, 41 percent use e-mail to communicate with employees who are not on the premises, 23 percent use e-mail to communicate with suppliers, and 18 percent use e-mail with business advisers.[24]

The growing popularity of e-mail has enabled many workers and managers to become *telecommuters,* people who are employed by organizations and work out of offices in their own homes. There are approximately 8.4 million telecommuters in the United States. Many telecommuters indicate that the flexibility of working at home enables them to be more productive while giving them a chance to be closer to their families and not waste time traveling to and from the office.[25] A recent study conducted by Georgetown University found that 75 percent of the telecommuters surveyed said their productivity increased and 83 percent said their home life improved once they started telecommuting.[26]

Unfortunately, the growing use of e-mail has been accompanied by the growing abuse of e-mail. Some employees sexually harass coworkers through e-mail, and divorcing spouses who work together sometimes sign their spouse's name to e-mail and send insulting or derogatory messages to the spouse's boss. Robert Mirguet, information systems manager at Eastman Kodak, has indicated that some Kodak employees have used Kodak's e-mail system to try to start their own businesses during working hours. Kodak managers monitor employees' e-mail messages when they suspect some form of abuse. Top managers also complain that sometimes their e-mail is clogged with junk mail. In a recent survey over half of the organizations surveyed acknowledged some problems with their e-mail systems.[27]

To avoid these and other costly forms of e-mail abuse, managers need to develop a clear policy specifying what company e-mail can and should be used for and what is out of bounds. Managers also should clearly communicate this policy to all members of an organization, as well as the procedures that will be used when e-mail abuse is suspected and the consequences that will result when e-mail abuse is confirmed.

Impersonal Written Communication

Impersonal written communication is lowest in information richness and is well suited for messages that need to reach a large number of receivers. Because such messages are not addressed to particular receivers, feedback is unlikely, so managers must make sure that messages sent by this medium are written clearly in language that all receivers will understand.

Managers often find company newsletters useful vehicles for reaching large numbers of employees. Many managers give their newsletters catchy names to spark employee interest and also to inject a bit of humor into the workplace. Managers at the pork-sausage maker Bob Evans Farms Inc. called their newsletter "The Squealer" for many years but recently changed the title to "The Homesteader" to reflect the company's broadened line of products. Managers at American Greetings Corp., at Yokohama Tire Corp., and at Eastman Kodak call their newsletters "Expressions," "TreadLines," and "Kodakery," respectively. Managers at Quaker State Corp. held a contest in 1994 to rename their newsletter. Among the 1,000 submitted names were "The Big Q Review," "The Pipeline," and "Q.S. Oil Press"; the winner was "On Q."[28]

Managers can use impersonal written communication for various types of messages, including rules, regulations, policies, newsworthy information, and announcements of changes in procedures or the arrival of new organizational members. Impersonal written communication also can be used to communicate instructions about how to use machinery or how to process work orders or customer requests. For these kinds of messages, the paper trail left by this communication medium can be invaluable for employees.

Communication Networks

Although various communication media are utilized, communication in organizations tends to flow in certain patterns. The pathways along which information flows in groups and teams and throughout an organization are called **communication networks.** The type of communication network that exists in a group depends on the nature of the group's tasks and the extent to which group members need to communicate with each other in order to achieve group goals.

communication networks The pathways along which information flows in groups and teams and throughout the organization.

Communication Networks in Groups and Teams

As you learned in Chapter 14, groups and teams—cross-functional teams, top-management teams, command groups, self-managed work teams, task forces—are the building blocks of organizations. Four kinds of communication networks can develop in groups and teams: the wheel, the chain, the circle, and the all-channel network (see Figure 15.3).

WHEEL NETWORK In a wheel network, information flows to and from one central member of the group. Other group members do not need to communicate with each other to perform highly, and the group can accomplish its goals by directing all communication to and from the central member. Wheel networks are often found in command groups with pooled task interdependence. Picture a group of taxi cab drivers who report to the same dispatcher, who is also their supervisor. Each driver needs to communicate with the dispatcher, but the drivers do not need to communicate with each other. In groups such as this, the wheel network results in efficient communication, saving time without compromising performance. Though found in groups, wheel networks are not found in teams because they do not allow for the intense interactions characteristic of teamwork.

Figure 15.3
Communication Networks in Groups and Teams

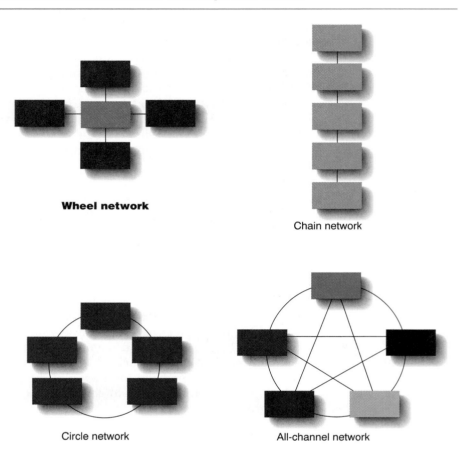

Wheel network

Chain network

Circle network

All-channel network

CHAIN NETWORK   In a chain network, members communicate with each other in a predetermined sequence. Chain networks are found in groups with sequential task interdependence, such as in assembly-line groups. When group work has to be performed in a predetermined order, the chain network is often found because group members need to communicate with those whose work directly precedes and follows their own. Like wheel networks, chain networks tend not to exist in teams because of the limited amount of interaction among team members.

CIRCLE NETWORK   In a circle network, group members communicate with others who are similar to them in experiences, beliefs, areas of expertise, background, office location, or even where they sit when the group meets. Members of task forces and standing committees, for example, tend to communicate with others who have similar experiences or backgrounds. People also tend to communicate with people whose offices are next to their own. Like wheel and chain networks, circle networks are most often found in groups that are not teams.

ALL-CHANNEL NETWORK   An all-channel network is found in teams. It is characterized by high levels of communication: Every team member communicates with every other team member. Top-management teams, cross-functional teams, and self-managed work teams frequently have all-channel networks. The reciprocal task interdependence often present in such teams requires information flows in all directions. Computer software specially designed for use by work groups can help maintain effective communication in teams with all-channel networks because it provides team members with an efficient way to share information with each other.

Organizational Communication Networks

An organization chart may seem to be a good summary of an organization's communication network, but often it is not. An organization chart summarizes *formal* reporting relationships in an organization and the formal pathways along which communication takes place. Often, however, communication is *informal* and flows around issues, goals, projects, and ideas instead of moving up and down the organizational hierarchy in an orderly fashion. Thus, an organization's communication network includes not only the formal communication pathways summarized in an organizational chart but also informal communication pathways along which a great deal of communication takes place (see Figure 15.4)

Figure 15.4

Formal and Informal Communication Networks in an Organization

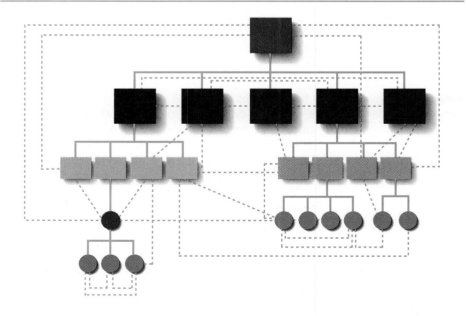

——— Formal pathways of communication summarized in an organizational chart

- - - - - Informal pathways along which a great deal of communication takes place

Communication can and should occur across departments and groups as well as within them and up and down and sideways in the corporate hierarchy. Communication up and down the corporate hierarchy is often called *vertical* communication. Communication among employees at the same level in the hierarchy or sideways is called *horizontal* communication. Managers obviously cannot determine in advance what an organization's communication network will be, nor should they try to. Instead, to accomplish goals and perform at a high level, organizational members should be free to communicate with whomever they need to contact. Because organizational goals change over time, so too do organizational communication networks. Informal communication networks can contribute to an organization's competitive advantage because they help ensure that organizational members have the information they need when they need it to accomplish their goals.

One informal organizational communication network along which information flows quickly if not always accurately is the grapevine. The **grapevine** is an informal network along which unofficial information flows.[29] People in an organization who seem to know everything about everyone are prominent in the grapevine. Information spread over the grapevine can be on issues of either a business nature (an impending takeover) or a personal nature (the CEO's separation from his wife).

grapevine An informal communication network along which unofficial information flows.

Technical Advances in Communication

Exciting advances in information technology are dramatically increasing managers' abilities to communicate with others as well as to quickly access information to make decisions. Three advances that are having major impacts on managerial communication are the Internet, intranets, and groupware.

The Internet

Internet A global system of computer networks.

The **Internet** is a global system of computer networks that is easy to join and is used by employees of organizations around the world to communicate inside and outside their companies. Approximately 44 million people in the United States alone use the Internet on a regular basis.[30] Managers in over 21,000 companies use the Internet to communicate, and over 75 percent of new users are hooked up by means of their companies' Internet links.[31]

Managers and companies use the Internet for a variety of communication purposes: to communicate with suppliers and contractors in order to maintain appropriate inventory levels and keep them informed of progress on projects and changes in schedules; to communicate within a company, primarily to and from distant offices to corporate headquarters by e-mail; to advertise to potential customers; to sell goods and services to customers; to obtain information about other companies including competitors; to provide the general public with information about the company; to recruit new employees.[32]

The World Wide Web is the fast-growing business district on the Internet with multimedia capabilities. Companies on the World Wide Web have home pages that are like offices that potential customers can visit. In attractive graphic displays on home pages, managers communicate information about

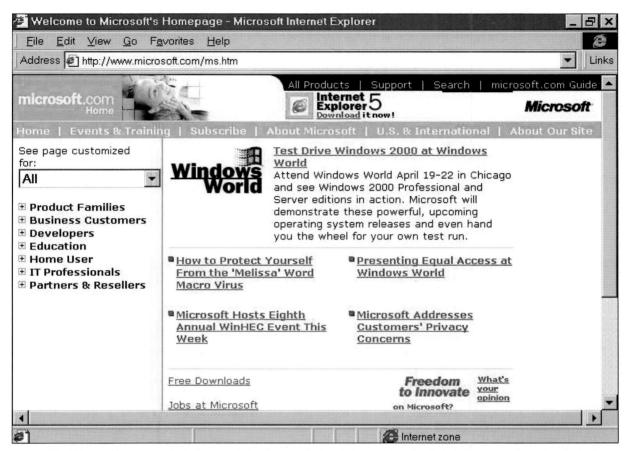

The Microsoft home page includes everything from product updates and downloads, to job postings, to a place to post your opinion. It even has an "About Our Site" link that details how it updates and maintains one of the world's largest Web sites.

the goods and services they offer, why customers should want to purchase them, how to purchase them, and where to purchase them. By "surfing" the Web and visiting competitors' home pages, managers can see what their competitors are doing.[33] Each day, hundreds of new companies add themselves to the growing numbers of organizations on the World Wide Web.[34] Approximately 18 million people in the United States have used the World Wide Web within the last twenty-four hours.[35]

By all counts, use of the Internet for communication is burgeoning. Nevertheless, some managers and organizations do not conduct certain business transactions over the Internet because of security concerns. Ironically, the very reason why the Internet was created and why it is so popular—it allows millions of senders and receivers of messages to share vast amounts of information with each other—hampers its use for certain business transactions because of a lack of security. Just as managers do not want to freely distribute information about their accounts to the public, customers want to hide rather than share their credit card numbers. Experts suggest, however, that the Internet can be made reasonably secure so that accounts, credit cards, and business documents are relatively safe.

Only time will tell whether the Internet will be secure enough and people will believe that it is secure enough for it to be used for many business transactions. Gene Spafford, a professor who is working on Purdue University's computer-security research project called COAST, suggests that although perfect security can never be obtained with any form of communication, good security on the Internet is certainly possible.[36] In addition, when considering security on the Internet, managers need to consider the security of alternative communication media. Scott McNealy, chairman and CEO of Sun Microsystems, for example, says that his e-mail is much more secure and harder for unwanted intruders to access than is his regular mail, which is just dropped into an unlocked box.[37]

In addition to the challenge of securing communication over the Internet, managers are facing another Internet dilemma. As profiled in the next "Management Insight," when employees surf the net on company time for fun, costs mount.

Management Insight

Surfing the Net

Managers at companies such as Pepsico, MCI, IBM, AT&T Bell Laboratories, Martin Marietta, and Intel are spotting a worrisome trend. Some of their subordinates, busy typing into their personal computer screens, are not working but rather are surfing the net. They may be playing games or visiting sports, news, or entertainment websites such as the *USA Today* website, the Sportszone website, or even the Playboy website. Some workers visit chat rooms on the Internet and have on-line conversations with other users about a wide variety of non-work-related issues.

Some net surfing is on the order of deliberate goofing off, but other workers inadvertently get sucked into surfing the net. Ron Barfield, a sales manager from Arlington, Texas, said that when he hooked up to the Internet, "I kept heading out on tangents and the next thing I knew I was miles from where I started." John Hallman, a salesman from Charlotte, North Carolina, indicated that the Internet "got in the way of my job . . . The chat rooms are the equivalent of old CB radio, where you just sit and gab."

Is surfing the net any more costly to organizations than the other kinds of breaks that employees take, such as chats in the coffee room or telephone conversations with friends? A recent study conducted by Webster Network Strategies (www.webster.com), a company that sells software that managers can buy to prevent subordinates from having access to certain websites, found that the average employee in a large corporation wastes approximately 1.5 hours per day surfing the net. For a company with 1,000 employees, that adds up to 1,500 lost hours per day; at $20 an hour, this represents a daily cost of $30,000 and a yearly cost of $7.8 million!

In addition to buying software to block certain websites, managers can take other steps to stop cyber goof-offs. At Pepsico (www.pepsi.com), flashing warnings that appear when workers log on to their computers state that computers should be used only for business purposes. Managers also communicate this message through memos stating that using the Internet for personal business or entertainment on company time is prohibited and could be grounds for termination. In addition to taking steps such as these, managers also can purchase software that prints out a listing of all the websites that each employee visits during the week.[38] One might wonder, however, how many managers themselves are secret surfers. And, for managers and other employees who are working increasingly long hours, a little net surfing may provide a needed respite and may not always be cause for concern.

Intranets

intranet A companywide system of computer networks.

Growing numbers of managers are finding that the technology on which the World Wide Web and the Internet are based enables them to improve communication within their own companies by creating a new type of communication medium. These managers are using the technology that allows for information sharing over the Internet to share information within their own companies through company networks called **intranets.** Intranets are being used not just in high-tech companies such as Sun Microsystems and Digital Equipment but also in companies such as Chevron, Goodyear, Levi Strauss, Pfizer, DaimlerChrysler, Motorola, and Ford.[39]

Intranets allow employees to have many kinds of information at their fingertips (or keyboards). Directories, phone books, manuals, inventory figures, product specifications, information about customers, biographies of top managers and the board of directors, global sales figures, minutes from meetings, annual reports, delivery schedules, and up-to-the minute revenue, cost, and profit figures are just a few examples of the kinds of information that can be shared through intranets. Intranets can be accessed with different kinds of computers so that all members of an organization can be linked together. Intranets are protected from unwanted intrusions by hackers or by competitors with firewall security systems that request users to provide passwords and other pieces of identification before being able to access the intranet.[40] How managers can develop, implement, and benefit from intranets is illustrated in the following "Management Insight," which profiles USWest's intranet, the Global Village.

Management Insight

The Global Village

USWest (www.uswest.com), one of the Baby Bells, has 15,000 employees who communicate all day long over USWest's own intranet called the Global Village. The Global Village was the brainchild of Sherman Woo, USWest's director of information tools and technologies. In 1994, Margaret Tumey, a top financial manager at USWest, asked Woo to develop a way to show company employees how new technology would change the services USWest provides to customers. Woo decided that the best way to teach employees about new technology was to allow them to experience it firsthand. In a conference room he built a basic intranet system, which established communication lines between a number of computers and also had access to the Internet. He also created a computerized demonstration of the kinds of services that an intranet might enable USWest to provide to customers.

USWest has a total of 60,000 employees, and Woo devised a clever strategy to communicate the virtue of his newly developed intranet to them all.

Any computer user at USWest could be connected to the intranet on request and would be given "browser" software, which allows the user to scan the types of information available on the intranet. The only catch was that the user had to show two other employees how the intranet worked. More often than not, seeing turned into believing, and most employees wanted to be connected after they were shown the workings of the intranet.

Thus, the Global Village was born and continues to grow and prosper. Currently the Village connects 15,000 employees and managers in 14 states. They communicate in a variety of ways. Some employees meet in chat rooms to discuss projects and share information, salespeople keep their managers up-to-date at headquarters in Denver, and all employees can use the "rumor mill" to quiz top managers anonymously about their pressing concerns.

Managers at USWest are now using the Global Village to provide better service to customers. For example, they are currently developing ways to use the Village to allow service representatives to immediately fill customers' requests for services such as call waiting rather than having customers wait hours or days.[41]

The advantage of intranets lies in their versatility· as a communication medium. They can be used for different purposes by people who may have little expertise in computer software and programming. While some managers complain that the Internet is too crowded and the World Wide Web too glitzy, informed managers are realizing that the use of Internet technology to create their own computer networks may be one of the Internet's biggest contributions to organizational effectiveness.

Groupware

groupware Computer software that enables members of groups and teams to share information with each other.

Groupware is computer software such as Lotus Notes and Digital Equipment's Linkworks that enables members of groups and teams to share information with each other to improve their communication and performance. Managers in the Bank of Montreal and other organizations have had success in introducing groupware into their organizations; managers in the advertising agency Young & Rubicam and other organizations have encountered considerable resistance to groupware.[42] Even in companies where the introduction of groupware has been successful, some employees resist using it. Some clerical and secretarial workers at the Bank of Montreal, for example, were dismayed to find that their neat and accurate files were being consolidated into computer files that would be accessible to many of their coworkers.

Managers are most likely to be able to successfully use groupware in their organizations as a communication medium when certain conditions are met:[43]

1. The work is group or team based, and members are rewarded, at least in part, for group performance.

2. Groupware has the full support of top management.

3. The culture of the organization stresses flexibility and knowledge sharing, and the organization does not have a rigid hierarchy of authority.

4. Groupware is being used for a specific purpose and is viewed as a tool for group or team members to use to work more effectively together, not as a personal source of power or advantage.

5. Employees receive adequate training in the use of computers and groupware.[44]

Employees are likely to resist using groupware and managers are likely to have a difficult time implementing it when people are working primarily on their own and are rewarded for their own individual performance.[45] Under these circumstances, information is often viewed as a source of power, and people are reluctant to share information with others by means of groupware.

Take the case of three salespeople who sell insurance policies in the same geographic area and are paid individually based on the number of policies each of them sells and the retention of their customers. The supervisor of the salespeople invested in some groupware and encouraged the salespeople to use it to share information about their sales, sales tactics, customers, insurance providers, and claim histories. The supervisor told the salespeople that having all this information at their fingertips would allow them to be more efficient as well as sell more policies and provide better service to customers.

Even though they received extensive training in how to use the groupware, the salespeople never got around to using it. Why? They all were afraid that they would be giving away their secrets to their coworkers and might reduce their own commissions. In this situation, the salespeople were essentially competing with each other and thus had no incentive to share information. Under such circumstances, a groupware system may not be a wise choice of communication medium. Conversely, had the salespeople been working as a team and had they received bonuses based on team performance, groupware might have been an effective communication medium.

In order for an organization to gain a competitive advantage, managers need to keep up-to-date on advances in information technology such as groupware, intranets, and the Internet. But managers should not adopt these or other advances without first considering carefully how the advance in question might improve communication and performance in their particular groups, teams, or whole organization.

Tips for Managers

Information Richness and Communication Media

1. For messages that are important, personal, or likely to be misunderstood, consider using face-to-face communication or video conferences.

2. Consider using video conferences instead of face-to-face meetings to save time and travel costs.

3. Frequently check voice mail when out of the office.

4. For messages that are complex and need to be referred to later on, use written communication either alone or in conjunction with face-to-face communication, verbal communication electronically transmitted, or video conferences.

5. Develop a clear policy specifying what company e-mail can and cannot be used for and communicate this policy to all organizational members.

Communication Skills for Managers

There are various kinds of barriers to effective communication in organizations. Some barriers have their origins in senders. When messages are unclear, incomplete, or difficult to understand, when they are sent over an inappropriate medium, or when no provision for feedback is made, communication suffers. Other communication barriers have their origins in receivers. When receivers pay no attention to or do not listen to messages or when they make no effort to understand the meaning of a message, communication is likely to be ineffective.

To overcome these barriers and effectively communicate with others, managers (as well as other organizational members) must possess or develop certain communication skills. Some of these skills are particularly important when managers send messages; others are critical when managers receive messages. These skills help ensure that managers will be able to share information, will have the information they need to make good decisions and take action, and will be able to reach a common understanding with others.

Communication Skills for Managers as Senders

Organizational effectiveness depends on managers (as well as other organizational members) being able to effectively send messages to people both inside and outside an organization. Table 15.1 summarizes seven communication skills that help ensure that when managers send messages, they are properly understood and the transmission phase of the communication process is effective. Let's see what each skill entails.

SEND CLEAR AND COMPLETE MESSAGES   Managers need to learn how to send a message that is clear and complete. A message is clear when it is easy for the receiver to understand and interpret, and it is complete when it contains all the information that the sender and receiver need to reach a common understanding. In striving to send messages that are both clear and complete, managers must learn to anticipate how receivers will interpret messages and adjust messages to eliminate sources of misunderstanding or confusion.

Table 15.1

Seven Communication Skills for Managers as Senders of Messages

- Send messages that are clear and complete.
- Encode messages in symbols that the receiver understands.
- Select a medium that is appropriate for the message.
- Select a medium that the receiver monitors.
- Avoid filtering and information distortion.
- Ensure that a feedback mechanism is built into messages.
- Provide accurate information to ensure that misleading rumors are not spread.

ENCODE MESSAGES IN SYMBOLS THE RECEIVER UNDER-STANDS

Managers need to appreciate that when they encode messages, they should use symbols or language that the receiver understands. When sending messages in English to receivers whose native language is not English, for example, it is important to use commonplace vocabulary and to avoid clichés that, when translated, may make little sense and in some cases are either comical or insulting.

jargon Specialized language that members of an occupation, group, or organization develop to facilitate communication among themselves.

Jargon, specialized language that members of an occupation, group, or organization develop to facilitate communication among themselves, should never be used to communicate with people outside the occupation, group, or organization. For example, truck drivers refer to senior-citizen drivers as "double-knits," compact cars as "rollerskates," highway dividing lines as "paints," double or triple freight trailers as "pups," and orange barrels around road construction areas as "Schneider eggs." Using this jargon among themselves results in effective communication because they know precisely what is being referred to. But if a truck driver used this language to send a message to a receiver who did not drive trucks (such as "That rollerskate can't stay off the paint"), the receiver would be without a clue about what the message meant.[46]

SELECT A MEDIUM APPROPRIATE FOR THE MESSAGE

As you have learned, when relying on verbal communication, managers can choose from a variety of communication media, including face-to-face communication in person, written letters, memos, newsletters, phone conversations, e-mail, voice mail, faxes, and video conferences. When choosing among these media, managers need to take into account the level of information richness required, time constraints, and the need for a paper or electronic trail. A primary concern in choosing an appropriate medium is the nature of the message. Is it personal, important, nonroutine, and likely to be misunderstood and in need of further clarification? If it is, face-to-face communication is likely to be in order.

SELECT A MEDIUM THAT THE RECEIVER MONITORS

Another factor that managers need to take into account when selecting a communication medium is whether the medium is one that the receiver monitors. Managers differ in the communication media they pay attention to. Many managers simply select the medium that they themselves use the most and are most comfortable with, but doing this can often lead to ineffective communication. Managers who dislike telephone conversations and face-to-face interactions may prefer to use e-mail, send many e-mail messages every day, and check their own e-mail every few hours. Managers who prefer to communicate with people in person or over the phone may have e-mail addresses but rarely use e-mail and forget to check for e-mail messages. No matter how much a manager likes e-mail, sending an e-mail message to someone else who never checks his or her e-mail is futile. Learning which managers like things in writing and which prefer face-to-face interactions and then using the appropriate medium enhances the chance that receivers will actually receive and pay attention to messages.

A related consideration is whether receivers have disabilities that limit their ability to decode certain kinds of messages. A blind receiver, for example, cannot read a written message. Managers should ensure that their employees with disabilities have resources available to communicate effectively with others, as the following "Focus on Diversity" highlights.

Focus on Diversity

Options in Communication Media for the Deaf

In the past, certain kinds of jobs were off limits for deaf people. Seven years ago William Hughes was in precisely this situation; he was denied a position as an auditor because he could not use the telephone. Now, however, Hughes is an auditor at the Pension Benefit Guaranty Corporation (a federal agency) because managers in that organization made sure that he has access to advanced communication technology that enables him to use the telephone, faxes, and e-mail to communicate with company auditors, insurers, and lawyers. He uses the telephone lines to communicate by means of a text-typewriter that has a screen and a keyboard on which senders can type messages. The message travels along the phone lines to special operators called communications assistants, who translate the typed message into a text that receivers can listen to. Receivers' spoken replies are translated into typewritten text by the communication assistants and appear on the sender's screen. The communication assistant relays messages back and forth to each sender and receiver.

Danny Delcambre, owner, manager, and head chef of Delcambre's Ragin' Cajun Restaurant in Seattle, is hearing impaired and uses a text-typewriter to make reservations, to take catering orders for gumbo and blackened fish, and to order special foods from K Paul's, a famous New Orleans restaurant. The majority of Ragin' Cajun's employees are also deaf, but they too are able to communicate effectively with each other and with customers because of Delcambre's responsiveness to their special needs.

These advances in media not only enable the deaf to communicate effectively but also let them be more independent and less stigmatized by their disability. As Sue Decker, who is AT&T's (www.att.com) marketing and outreach programs manager and is hearing impaired, indicated, e-mail "levels the playing field for me . . . When I communicate through e-mail, there is no reference to my hearing impairment. I look and act no differently from any other e-mailer."[47] To fully utilize the talents of hearing-impaired employees and employees with other kinds of disabilities, managers must ensure that they take advantage of advances in communication media such as the text-typewriter and e-mail.

filtering Withholding part of a message out of the mistaken belief that the receiver does not need or will not want the information.

AVOID FILTERING AND INFORMATION DISTORTION   **Filtering** occurs when senders withhold part of a message because they (mistakenly) think that the receiver does not need the information or will not want to receive it. Filtering can occur at all levels in an organization and in both vertical and horizontal communication. As described in Chapter 8, rank-and-file workers may filter messages they send to first-line managers, first-line managers may filter messages to middle managers, and middle managers may filter messages to top managers. Such filtering is most likely to take place when messages contain bad news or problems that subordinates are afraid they will be blamed for. Recall from the "Management Case" at the end of Chapter 14 that workers at AES Corporation's Shady Point, Oklahoma, plant not only failed to tell managers that emissions were high but even falsified emission-control reports so that managers would not find out.

information distortion
Changes in the meaning of a message as the message passes through a series of senders and receivers.

Information distortion occurs when the meaning of a message changes as the message passes through a series of senders and receivers. Some information distortion is accidental–due to faulty encoding and decoding or to a lack of feedback. Other information distortion is deliberate. Senders may alter a message to make themselves or their groups look good and to receive special treatment.

Managers themselves should avoid filtering and distorting information. But how can they eliminate these barriers to effective communication throughout their organization? They need to establish trust throughout the organization. Subordinates who trust their managers believe that they will not be blamed for things beyond their control and will be treated fairly. Managers who trust their subordinates provide them with clear and complete information and do not hold things back.

INCLUDE A FEEDBACK MECHANISM IN MESSAGES Because feedback is essential for effective communication, managers should build a feedback mechanism into the messages they send. They either should include a request for feedback or indicate when and how they will follow up on the message to make sure that it was received and understood. When managers write letters and memos or send faxes, they can request that the receiver respond with comments and suggestions in a letter, memo, or fax; schedule a meeting to discuss the issue; or follow up with a phone call. By building feedback mechanisms such as these into their messages, managers ensure that they get heard and are understood.

rumors Unofficial pieces of information of interest to organizational members but with no identifiable source.

PROVIDE ACCURATE INFORMATION **Rumors** are unofficial pieces of information of interest to organizational members but with no identifiable source. Rumors spread quickly once they are started, and usually they concern topics that organizational members think are important, interesting, or amusing. Rumors, however, can be misleading and can cause harm to individual employees and to an organization when they are false, malicious, or unfounded. Managers can halt the spread of misleading rumors by providing organizational members with accurate information on matters that concern them. This is precisely what CEO Louis Gerstner has done at IBM, as described in this "Management Insight."

Management Insight

Communicating Accurate Information to Minimize Rumors

Since becoming CEO of IBM (www.ibm.com) in 1993, Louis Gerstner has regularly communicated with IBM employees in the United States and around the world through the company's own TV system. IBM was in deep trouble when Gerstner took over, and he engineered massive layoffs affecting over 30,000 employees. He also made major changes in IBM's goals, strategies, structure, and even the way managers are compensated. An uncertain situation such as this, with many changes that will affect employees' jobs taking place and planned for the future, was ripe for the spread of rumors. To help ensure that inaccurate rumors do not spread throughout IBM and to provide employees with clear and accurate information, Gerstner has put IBM's television system to good use.

In early 1995, to prevent the spread of rumors that IBM would be implementing another major round of layoffs, Gerstner spoke for 15 minutes over the company television system. He was upbeat about IBM's future prospects and announced that most of the layoffs were over. IBM employees around the world listened to Gerstner in IBM conference rooms and offices, some while lunching on pizza. After making his initial remarks, Gerstner was able to answer live questions from IBMers located in five studio offices.[48] This question-and-answer session, which lasted an additional 45 minutes, provided Gerstner with feedback that his message was understood and enabled him to clarify points of confusion and provide additional information to reduce misunderstanding.

Gerstner's hour on the TV system helped to halt the spread of damaging rumors and took a weight off the shoulders of many IBM employees. Having survived the massive layoffs thus far, they could breathe a bit easier knowing that their jobs were more secure than they had been in the past.

Communication Skills for Managers as Receivers

Managers receive as many messages as they send. Thus, managers must possess or develop communication skills that allow them to be effective receivers of messages. Table 15.2 summarizes three of these important skills, which we examine in greater detail.

Table 15.2

Three Communication Skills for Managers as Receivers of Messages

- Pay attention.
- Be a good listener.
- Be empathetic.

PAY ATTENTION   Because of their multiple roles and tasks, managers often are overloaded and forced to think about several things at once. Pulled in many different directions, they sometimes do not pay sufficient attention to the messages they receive, as was true of Dave Hurley in the "Case in Contrast." To be effective, however, managers should always pay attention to messages they receive, no matter how busy they are. When discussing a project with a subordinate, an effective manager focuses on the project and not on an upcoming meeting with his or her own boss. Similarly, when managers are reading written forms of communication, they should focus their attention on understanding what they are reading; they should not be sidetracked into thinking about other issues.

BE A GOOD LISTENER   Managers (and all other members of an organization) can do several things to be good listeners. First, managers should refrain from interrupting senders in the middle of a message so that senders do not lose their train of thought and managers do not jump to erroneous conclusions based on incomplete information. Second, managers should maintain good eye contact with senders so that senders feel their listeners are paying attention; doing this also helps managers focus on what they are hearing. Third, after receiving a message, managers should ask questions to clarify points of ambiguity or confusion. Fourth, managers should paraphrase, or restate in their own words, points senders make that are important, complex, or open to alternative interpretations; this is the feedback component so critical to successful communication.

Managers, like most people, often like to hear themselves talk rather than listen to others. Part of being a good communicator, however, is being a good listener, an essential communication skill for managers as receivers of messages transmitted face-to-face and over the telephone. As the "Case in Contrast" makes clear, being a good listener is an essential communication skill in many different kinds of organizations, from small businesses such as Flight Services Group to HMOs.

BE EMPATHETIC   Receivers are empathetic when they try to understand how the sender feels and try to interpret a message from the sender's perspective, rather than view a message from only their own point of view. Marcia Mazulo, chief psychologist in a public school system in the Northwest, recently learned this lesson after interacting with Karen Sanchez, a new psychologist on her staff. Sanchez was distraught after meeting with the parent of a child she had been working with extensively. The parent was difficult to talk to and argumentative and was not supportive of her own child. Sanchez told Mazulo how upset she was, and Mazulo responded by reminding Sanchez that she was a professional and that dealing with such a situation was part of her job. This feedback upset Sanchez further and caused her to storm out of the room.

In hindsight, Mazulo realized that her response had been inappropriate. She had failed to empathize with Sanchez, who had spent so much time with the child and was deeply concerned about the child's well-being. Instead of dismissing Sanchez's concerns, Mazulo realized, she should have tried to understand how Sanchez felt and given her some support and advice for dealing positively with the situation. Similarly, as indicated in the "Case in Contrast," more and more doctors are realizing the need to be empathetic when communicating with patients.

Understanding Linguistic Styles

Consider the following scenarios:

• A manager from New York is having a conversation with a manager from Iowa City. The Iowa City manager never seems to get a chance to talk. He keeps waiting for a pause to signal his turn to talk, but the New York manager never pauses long enough. The New York manager wonders why the Iowa City manager does not say much. He feels uncomfortable when he pauses and the Iowa City manager says nothing, so he starts talking again.

• Elizabeth compliments Bob on his presentation to upper management and asks Bob what he thought of her presentation. Bob launches into a lengthy critique of Elizabeth's presentation and describes how he would have handled it differently. This is hardly the response Elizabeth expected.

• Catherine shares with fellow members of a self-managed work team a new way to cut costs. Michael, another team member, thinks her idea is a good one and encourages the rest of the team to support it. Catherine is quietly pleased by Michael's support. The group implements "Michael's" suggestion, and it is written up as such in the company newsletter.

• Robert was recently promoted and transferred from his company's Oklahoma office to its headquarters in New Jersey. Robert is perplexed because he never seems to get a chance to talk in management meetings; someone else always seems to get the floor. Robert's new boss wonders whether Robert's new responsibilities are too much for him, although Robert's supervisor in Oklahoma rated him highly and said he is a real "go-getter." Robert is timid in management meetings and rarely says a word.

What do these scenarios have in common? Essentially, they all describe situations in which a misunderstanding of linguistic styles leads to a breakdown in communication. The scenarios are based on the research of linguist Deborah Tannen, who describes **linguistic style** as a person's characteristic way of speaking. Elements of linguistic style include tone of voice, speed, volume, use of pauses, directness or indirectness, choice of words, credit-taking, and use of questions, jokes, and other manners of speech. When people's linguistic styles differ and these differences are not understood, ineffective communication is likely.

linguistic style A person's characteristic way of speaking.

The first and last scenarios illustrate regional differences in linguistic style.[50] The Iowa City manager and Robert from Oklahoma expect the pauses that signal turn-taking in conversations to be longer than the pauses made by their colleagues in New York and New Jersey. This difference causes communication problems. The Iowan and transplanted Oklahoman think that their eastern colleagues never let them get a word in edgewise, and the easterners cannot figure out why their colleagues from the Midwest and Southwest do not get more actively involved in conversations.

Differences in linguistic style can be a particularly insidious source of communication problems because linguistic style is often taken for granted. People rarely think about their own linguistic styles and often are unaware of how linguistic styles can differ. In the example above, Robert never realized that when dealing with his New Jersey colleagues he could and should jump into conversations more quickly than he used to do in Oklahoma, and Robert's boss in New Jersey never realized that Robert felt that he was not being given a chance to speak in meetings.

The aspect of linguistic style just described, length of pauses, differs by region in the United States. Much more dramatic differences in linguistic style occur cross-culturally.

CROSS-CULTURAL DIFFERENCES   Managers from Japan tend to be more formal in their conversations and more deferential toward upper-level managers and people with high status than are managers from the United States. Japanese managers do not mind extensive pauses in conversations when they are thinking things through or when they think that further conversation might be detrimental. U.S. managers, in contrast (even managers from regions of the United States where pauses tend to be long), find very lengthy pauses disconcerting and feel obligated to talk to fill the silence.[51]

Another cross-cultural difference in linguistic style concerns the appropriate physical distance separating speakers and listeners in business-oriented conversations.[52] The distance between speakers and listeners is greater in the United States, for example, than it is in Brazil or Saudi Arabia. Citizens of different countries also vary in how direct or indirect they are in conversations and in the extent to which they take individual credit for accomplishments. Japanese culture, with its collectivist or group orientation, tends to encourage linguistic styles in which group rather than individual accomplishments are emphasized. The opposite tends to be true in the United States.

These and other cross-cultural differences in linguistic style can and often do lead to misunderstandings. For example, when a team of American managers presented a proposal for a joint venture to Japanese managers, the Japanese managers were silent as they thought about the implications of what they had just heard. The American managers took this silence as a sign that the Japanese managers wanted more information, so they went into more detail about the proposal. When they finished, the Japanese were silent again, not only frustrating the Americans but also making them wonder whether the Japanese were at all interested in the project. The American managers suggested that if the Japanese already had decided that they did not want to pursue the project, there was no reason for the meeting to continue. The Japanese were truly bewildered. They were trying to carefully think out the proposal, but the Americans thought they were not interested!

Communication misunderstandings and problems like this can be overcome if managers make themselves familiar with cross-cultural differences in linguistic styles. If the American managers and the Japanese managers had realized that periods of silence are viewed differently in Japan and in the United States, their different linguistic styles might have been less troublesome barriers to communication. Before managers communicate with people from abroad, they should try to find out as much as they can about the aspects of linguistic style that are specific to the country or culture in question. Expatriate managers who have lived in the country in question for an extended period of time can be good sources of information about linguistic styles because they are likely to have experienced firsthand some of the differences that citizens of a country are not aware of. Finding out as much as possible about cultural differences also can help managers learn about differences in linguistic styles, for the two are often closely linked.

GENDER DIFFERENCES Thinking back on the four scenarios that open this section, you may be wondering why Bob launched into a lengthy critique of Elizabeth's presentation after she paid him a routine compliment on his presentation, or you may be wondering why Michael got the credit for Catherine's idea in the self-managed work team. Research conducted by Tannen and other linguists indicates that the linguistic styles of men and women

Differences in linguistic style may come from early childhood, when girls and boys are inclined to play with their own gender. Girls tend to play in small groups trying to be, and noting how they are similar to each other. Boys tend to emphasize status differences, challenging each other and relying on a leader to emerge.

differ in practically every culture or language.[53] Men and women take their own linguistic styles for granted and thus do not realize when they are talking with someone of a different gender that differences in style may lead to ineffective communication.

In the United States, women tend to downplay differences between people, are not overly concerned about receiving credit for their own accomplishments, and want to make everyone feel more or less on an equal footing so that even poor performers or low-status individuals feel valued. Men, in contrast, tend to emphasize their own superiority and are not reluctant to acknowledge differences in status. These differences in linguistic style led Elizabeth to routinely compliment Bob on his presentation even though she thought that he had not done a particularly good job. She asked him how her presentation was so that he could reciprocate and give her a routine compliment, putting them on an equal footing. Bob took Elizabeth's compliment and question about her own presentation as an opportunity to confirm his superiority, never realizing that all she was expecting was a routine compliment. Similarly, Michael's enthusiastic support for Catherine's cost-cutting idea and her apparent surrender of ownership of the idea after she described it led team members to assume incorrectly that the idea was Michael's.[54]

Do some women try to prove that they are better than everyone else, and are some men unconcerned about taking credit for ideas and accomplishments? Of course. The gender differences in linguistic style that Tannen and other linguists have uncovered are general tendencies evident in many women and men but not in all women and men.

Where do gender differences in linguistic style come from? Tannen suggests that they develop from early childhood on. Girls and boys tend to play with children of their own gender, and the ways in which girls and boys play are quite different. Girls play in small groups, engage in a lot of close conversation, emphasize how similar they are to each other, and view boastfulness negatively. Boys play in large groups, emphasize status differences, expect leaders to emerge who boss others around, and give each other challenges to try to meet. These differences in styles of play and interaction result in differences in linguistic styles when boys and girls grow up and communicate as adults. The ways in which men communicate emphasize status differences and play up relative strengths; the ways in which women communicate emphasize similarities and downplay individual strengths.[55]

MANAGING DIFFERENCES IN LINGUISTIC STYLES Managers should not expect to change people's linguistic styles and should not try to. Instead, to be effective, managers need to understand differences in linguistic styles. Knowing, for example, that some women are reluctant to speak up in meetings not because they have nothing to contribute but because of their linguistic style should lead managers to ensure that these women have a chance to talk. And a manager who knows that certain people are reluctant to take credit for ideas can be extra careful to give credit where it is deserved. As Tannen points out, "Talk is the lifeblood of managerial work, and understanding that different people have different ways of saying what they mean will make it possible to take advantage of the talents of people with a broad range of linguistic styles."[56]

Tips for Managers

Sending and Receiving **Messages**

1. Make sure that the messages you send are clear, complete, encoded in symbols the receiver will understand, and sent over a medium the receiver monitors.

2. Establish a sense of trust in your organization to discourage filtering and information distortion.

3. Send your messages in a way that will ensure that you receive feedback.

4. Pay attention to the messages you receive, be a good listener, and try to understand the sender's perspective.

5. Be attuned to differences in linguistic style and try to understand the ways they affect communication in your organization.

Summary and Review

Chapter Summary

COMMUNICATION AND MANAGEMENT

- **The Importance of Good Communication**

- **The Communication Process**

- **The Role of Perception in Communication**

- **The Dangers of Ineffective Communication**

INFORMATION RICHNESS AND COMMUNICATION MEDIA

- **Face-to-Face Communication**

COMMUNICATION AND MANAGEMENT Communication is the sharing of information between two or more individuals or groups to reach a common understanding. Good communication is necessary for an organization to gain a competitive advantage. Communication occurs in a cyclical process that entails two phases, transmission and feedback.

INFORMATION RICHNESS AND COMMUNICATION MEDIA Information richness is the amount of information a communication medium can carry and the extent to which the medium enables the sender and receiver to reach a common understanding. Four categories of communication media in descending order of information richness are face-to-face communication (includes video conferences), spoken communication electronically transmitted (includes voice mail), personally addressed written communication (includes e-mail), and impersonal written communication.

COMMUNICATION NETWORKS Communication networks are the pathways along which information flows in an organization. Four communication networks found in groups and teams are the wheel, the chain, the circle, and the all-channel network. An organizational chart summarizes formal pathways of communication, but communication in organizations is often informal, as is true of communication by means of the grapevine.

TECHNOLOGICAL ADVANCES IN COMMUNICATION The Internet is a global system of computer networks that managers around the world use to communicate within and outside their companies. The World Wide Web is the multimedia business district on the Internet. Intranets are internal communication networks that managers can create to improve communication, performance, and customer service. Intranets use the technology that the Internet and World Wide Web are based on. Groupware is computer software that enables members of groups and teams to share information with each other to improve their communication and performance.

COMMUNICATION SKILLS FOR MANAGERS   There are various barriers to effective communication in organizations. To overcome these barriers and effectively communicate with others, managers must possess or develop certain communication skills. As senders of messages, managers should send messages that are clear and complete, encode messages in symbols the receiver understands, choose a medium appropriate for the message and monitored by the receiver, avoid filtering and information distortion, include a feedback mechanism in the message, and provide accurate information to ensure that misleading rumors are not spread. Communication skills for managers as receivers of messages include paying attention, being a good listener, and being empathetic. Understanding linguistic styles is also an essential communication skill for managers. Linguistic styles can vary by geographic region, gender, and country or culture. When these differences are not understood, ineffective communication can occur.

Management in Action

Topics for Discussion and Action

1. Interview a manager in an organization in your community to determine with whom he or she communicates on a typical day and what communication media he or she uses.

2. Which medium (or media) do you think would be appropriate for each of the following kinds of messages that a subordinate could receive from his or her boss: (a) a raise, (b) not receiving a promotion, (c) an error in a report prepared by the subordinate, (d) additional job responsibilities, and (e) the schedule for company holidays for the upcoming year? Explain your choices.

3. Discuss the pros and cons of using the Internet and World Wide Web to conduct business transactions such as purchasing goods and services.

4. Why do some organizational members resist using groupware?

5. Why do some managers find it difficult to be good listeners?

6. Explain why subordinates might filter and distort information about problems and performance shortfalls when communicating with their bosses.

7. Explain why differences in linguistic style, when not understood by senders and receivers of messages, can lead to ineffective communication.

Building Management Skills

Diagnosing Ineffective Communication

Think about the last time you experienced very ineffective communication with another person—someone you work with, a classmate, a friend, a member of your family. Describe the incident. Then answer the following questions.

1. Why was your communication ineffective in this incident?

2. What stages of the communication process were particularly problematic and why?

3. Describe any filtering or information distortion that occurred.

4. Do you think differences in linguistic styles adversely affected the communication that took place? Why or why not?

5. How could you have handled this situation differently so that communication would have been effective?

Small Group Breakout Exercise

Reducing Resistance to Advances in Information Technology

Form groups of three or four people, and appoint one member as the spokesperson who will communicate your findings to the whole class when called on by the instructor. Then discuss the following scenario.

You are a team of managers in charge of information and communications in a large consumer products corporation. Your company has already implemented many advances in information technology. Managers and workers have access to voice mail, e-mail, the Internet, your company's own intranet, and groupware.

Many employees use the new technology, but the resistance of some is causing communication problems. For example, all managers have e-mail addresses and computers in their offices, but some refuse to turn on their computers, let alone send and receive e-mail. These managers feel that they should be able to communicate as they always have done—in person, over the phone, or in writing. Consequently, when managers who are unaware of their preferences send them e-mail messages, those messages are never retrieved. Moreover, the resistant managers never read company

news sent over e-mail. Another example of the resistance that your company is encountering concerns the use of groupware. Members of some work groups do not want to share information with each other electronically.

Although you do not want to force people to use the technology, you want them to at least try it and give it a chance. You are meeting today to develop strategies for reducing resistance to the new technologies.

1. One resistant group of employees is made up of top managers. Some of them seem computer-phobic. They never have used, and do not want to start using, personal computers for any purpose, including communication. What steps will you take to get these managers to give their PCs a chance?

2. A second group of resistant employees consists of middle

managers. Some middle managers resist using your company's intranet. Although these middle managers do not resist the technology per se and use their PCs for multiple purposes, including communication, they seem to distrust the intranet as a viable way to communicate and get things done. What steps will you take to get these middle managers to take advantage of the intranet?

3. A third group of resistant employees is made up of members of groups and teams who do not want to use the groupware that has been provided to them. You think that the groupware could improve their communication and performance, but they seem to think otherwise. What steps will you take to get these members of groups and teams to start using groupware?

Exploring the World Wide Web

Specific Assignment

Many companies use the World Wide Web to communicate with prospective employees, including the Ford Motor Company. Scan Ford's website (http://www2.ford.com) to learn more about this company and the kinds of information it communicates to prospective employees through its website. Then click on "site map" and then "human resources" (under "career center"). Click on the various selections in this location of the website, such as "ideal candidate," "job search," "recent college graduates," "opportunities," and "lifestyle."

1. What kinds of information does Ford communicate to prospective employees through its website?

2. How might providing this information on the World Wide Web help Ford attract new employees?

General Assignment

Find the website of a company that you know very little about. Scan the website of this company. Do you think it effectively communicates important information about the company? Why or why not? Can you think of anything that customers or prospective employees might want to see on the website that is not currently there? Is there anything on the website that you think should not be there?

ManagementCase

Communicating with Electronic Secretaries

Managers who frequently rely on human secretaries to take messages, make calls, and keep them in touch when they are out of the office are finding that electronic secretaries can perform many of these tasks. Moreover, electronic secretaries are available 24 hours a day, do not get sick or take time off, and can even dial numbers for managers who may be thousands of miles away from their offices.

If this sounds too good to be true, listen to what some true believers say about their electronic secretaries. George M. Vetter, a manager and investment banker at Montgomery Securities in San Francisco, says that his electronic secretary enables him to be more productive, especially when he is out of the office. His secretary can make a series of telephone calls for him without his ever having to hang up the phone. Once he finishes with one call, the electronic secretary comes on again to ask for further instructions. Paul Saffo, a manager and consultant at the Institute for the Future in Palo Alto, California, says that his electronic secretary has dramatically increased his efficiency. Before he had an electronic secretary, Saffo used to be 40 or 50 calls behind in the messages that he needed to respond to from callers. Now, he rarely has a backlog of calls at the end of the day, even when he is out of town.[57]

Electronic secretaries are made possible by a combination of computer, voice-recognition, and telephone technologies.[58] A leading maker of electronic secretaries is Wildfire Communications Inc., based in Lexington, Massachusetts; its electronic secretaries are called "Wildfire." Managers can call Wildfire on a cellular phone in their car and listen to their messages. After hearing a message, if they want to call the person back, they simply

569

say "Wildfire, call," and Wildfire calls the person—the manager does not even have to hang up the phone. Wildfire can forward important calls to wherever a manager is. If a manager is taking one call and another call comes in, Wildfire can whisper the name of the other caller so that only the manager can hear, enabling the manager to decide whether to take the call or let Wildfire take a message. Managers also can instruct Wildfire to forward important calls to them while taking messages from other callers.

Because computers are unable to recognize random speech, Wildfire understands only words and phrases that have been preprogrammed. Managers have pocket reference cards and on-line help (provided by asking Wildfire, "What are my options?") to help them make requests in a form that Wildfire can understand. Wildfire also helps out by telling managers how to phrase their requests. For example, upon receiving a call, Wildfire might say, "Would you like me to put you through or take a message? Please say, 'put my call through' or 'take a message.' "[59] After Wildfire and a manager get to know one another, they can have conversations such as this: "Call." "Call whom?" "Susan Watson." "Which Place?" "Car." "Dialing."[60]

There are some up-front costs to using an electronic secretary like Wildfire. Managers have to input a list of contacts and their phone numbers through a somewhat laborious process. A company system that provides Wildfire capabilities to 25 managers costs an organization about $50,000.[61] Some small companies provide Wildfire services for a monthly fee ranging from around $40 a month for 15 minutes a day to $400 a month for an unlimited, round-the-clock Wildfire.[62]

Wildfire can be an indispensable communication tool for managers who, like Paul Saffo, make and receive many calls and are often out of the office. In fact, Wildfire can make it so easy for managers to keep in touch when they are out of the office that they may never be able to really get away, even when they are on vacation. One wonders, however, if somehow these managers may miss working with a human secretary. Or perhaps managers will start interacting with Wildfire as if "he or she" is a person. Steven Wildstrom, a writer for *Business Week*, found that he started to call Wildfire "she" after interacting with "her" a while.[63]

Questions

1. In what ways might the use of electronic secretaries like Wildfire improve managerial communication?

2. What might be some disadvantages of using Wildfire as a communication tool for managers?

3. With the increasingly sophisticated developments in information technology currently taking place, do you think virtual secretaries could make human secretaries obsolete? Why or why not?

ManagementCase

In the News

From the Pages of BusinessWeek

Saying Adios to the Office

Now that her commute to the office lasts all of 10 seconds, Vicki Hall has lots of time on her hands. A senior communications analyst for Visa International, Hall used to drive some 2½ hours each day to and from Visa's San Francisco headquarters. After moving to Pensacola, Fla., Hall, a single mother, is still taking care of business. With the blessing of her California bosses and armed with a company-paid PC, fax, ISDN phone line, and storage shelves, Hall has turned a spare bedroom into an office. "Telecommuting gave me my life back," she says.

As professional men and women attempt to do justice to their careers while attending to family and personal needs, more and more are working without visiting the office more than once in a blue moon. The appeal is enormous. At home, you can spend more time with the kids, work in casual clothes, and tailor a schedule that lets you tackle your job at odd hours. Some 9.9 million people work outside their main corporate offices at least three days a month, up from 9.1 million in 1997 and 5.4 million in 1993, according to Raymond Boggs, director of home-office research for International Data Corp. in Framingham, Mass.

Telecommuting has gotten an added boost from a strong economy in which employers must make accommodations to attract the best and brightest workers. There are also environmental and political pressures as companies respond to Clean Air Act provisions that aim to cut traffic. And businesses want to pare real estate costs by creating "hoteling" arrangements in which, say, 10 people share a single cubicle on an as-needed basis. Companies are finding that telecommuting can boost productivity 5% to 20%, according to Jack M. Nilles, author of *Managing Telework*.

Technology is helping people break free of the office. With laptops, speedy modems, the Internet, and the emergence of corporate intranets, jobs are becoming portable. Employers and employees can easily swap E-mail and share PC documents from afar. This cuts down on faxing and overnight-courier costs.

Is telecommuting for you? Nearly 75% of teleworkers responding to an AT&T survey last year said they were more satisfied with their personal and family lives than before they started working at home. But telecommuting is not for every person or job, and you'll need a massive dose of self-discipline to pull it off. Ask yourself if you can perform your duties without the boss breathing down your neck. On the other hand, would you go stir-crazy without being able to schmooze with officemates?

Many companies insist that you iron out a schedule with your supervisor before you begin. You may prefer to work at 6 A.M. and hit the links at 3 P.M.—just be sure you're available for those 9 A.M. meetings. Not every company will require formal training before you set up a remote office, but it's a good idea to sound out your boss about his or her concerns.

It's equally smart to assuage the fears of co-workers. Your colleagues may become resentful if they think you're on paid vacation or suspect they'll get saddled with extra work in your absence. As a result, you may want to trade favors with your cohorts—by covering for them if they leave early one day, for example. And make sure they know they can call you at home. Appearances count: If you choose to work two days a week at home, you may not want to make them Monday and Friday, advises telecommuting consultant Gil Gordon in Monmouth Junction, N.J. Peers might think you're taking long weekends.

It's also imperative to set up ground rules with your family. The good news about telecommuting is that you can be close to your loved ones. That's also the bad news. Spouses and small children have to understand that even though you're in the house, you are busy earning a living. It's fine to throw in a few loads of laundry or answer the door when the plumber comes. It's another thing to take the kids to the mall or let them play games on your office PC.

Clearly demarcate your workspace by using a separate room with a door you can shut. Let your family know that, emergencies excepted, the space is off-limits during working hours. Some employees wear corporate badges or business attire at home to alert the family that they do not want to be disturbed.

If you have infants or toddlers, arrange for child care. "Telecommuting is not a substitute for dependent care," says Barbara M. Reeves, a virtual-office program manager for Boeing. "With a young child, you're really trying to hold down two jobs—and probably not doing very well with either one."

Once you get down to business, you may have to work hard to remain in the loop. That's why so many telecommuters stay at home only a couple of days a week. Aside from rubbing elbows with bosses and cohorts, there are meetings and other situations where face time is essential. Just one in five telecommuters responding to the AT&T study indicated that they felt more isolated working at home. But some teleworkers worry that being out of sight means being out of mind, and that that will hurt their chances for a promotion or a bonus. Moreover, you may be concerned that if bad times hit, you'll be the first to get sacked.

The best way to eliminate such concerns is to produce. "You need to establish your credibility," says Betty Sun, who works from her house in Bethesda, Md., as an acquisitions editor for publisher John Wiley & Sons in New York. Of course, while it's important to put in a full day of work while telecommuting, also remember that there's a time to leave the office. When the lines between your home and office blur, it can be hard to pull yourself away.

Maintaining the balance has not been a problem for Sun. She has been promoted since she began telecommuting and now manages two New York employees from a distance. But there may come a time when you'll have to ponder a difficult question: Would your rather climb the corporate ladder or the stairs to your home office? The higher up you move in your organization, the more likely it is that your presence at headquarters may be required at all times. Telecommuting can be terrific at certain stages of your life and career. But when the kids are older, you may be ready to return to the office full-time.

Even though the telecommuting phenomenon continues to mushroom, you may still encounter old-fashioned employers who are resisting the trend. But if you're a star performer, lots of companies will let you telecommute if that's the way to hook you. "The whole drift of the '90s is to introduce flexibility into work flow," says Thomas E. Miller, a vice-president for Cyber Dialogue, a New York–based research and consulting firm. That's good to know if you find the back-and-forth pull of train or car commuting is pulling you apart at the seams.

Source: E. C. Baig, "Saying Adios to the Office," *Business Week,* October 12, 1998, 152–53.

Questions

1. What are the advantages of telecommuting?

2. What are the disadvantages of telecommuting? What can telecommuters do to try to overcome these disadvantages?

Chapter sixteen

Organizational Conflict, Negotiation, Politics, and Change

Learning Objectives

1. Explain why conflict arises, and identify the types and sources of conflict in organizations.

2. Describe conflict management strategies that managers can use to resolve conflict effectively.

3. Describe negotiation strategies that managers can use to resolve conflict through integrative bargaining.

4. Explain why managers need to be attuned to organizational politics, and describe the political strategies that managers can use to become politically skilled.

5. Identify the main steps in the organizational change process.

A Case in Contrast

The Power of Political Skills

Paul Cappuccio and Yanira Merino could not be more different. Cappuccio, born in Massachusetts, is one of the hottest lawyers in Washington, D.C., and a partner in a prestigious law firm, Kirkland & Ellis (www.kirkland.com).[1] Merino, an immigrant from El Salvador, is a former production worker turned union organizer.[2] What Cappuccio and Merino do have in common, however, are superior political skills, which have enabled them to obtain the power they need to change situations so that they can achieve their goals.

Cappuccio, in his late 30's, is already handling cases usually reserved for lawyers with 20-plus years of experience. When Harry Pearce, general counsel for General Motors (www.gm.com), needed an attorney to represent GM in a product liability suit involving 5 million pickup trucks, he called on Cappuccio. When John Thorne, Bell Atlantic's (www.ba.com) associate general counsel, needed help with an antitrust suit against AT&T (www.att.com), he called on Cappuccio.[3] Among other major clients that Cappuccio has represented in court is Hughes Aircraft.[4]

When she was only 29, Merino effectively managed and led a union-organizing campaign at Ore-Cal Corporation's shrimp-packaging plant. Two years earlier, when Merino took a $5 an hour job at the plant, she had no experience with unions or union organizing.

The cards were stacked against Merino from the start. Men dominate union leadership and management. Low-wage workers often do not perceive how unions can help them, and both men and women are unlikely to rally behind a woman—as Merino learned the hard way when she scheduled a meeting of Ore-Cal workers to discuss complaints and no one showed up. Nevertheless, when a vote was taken at the Ore-Cal plant, 89 of the plant's 103 workers voted in favor of unionization.[5]

Most people would not see the parallels of a lawyer from D.C., and immigrant from El Salvador turned union activist in a shrimp-packaging plant, but both Paul Cappuccio and Yanira Merino both have one quality that has enabled them to "get what they want"—superior political skills. They've used their power to influence others and to bring about changes that allow them to achieve their goals.

Although Cappuccio and Merino are very talented, at least one reason for their success is their superior political skills—skills that enable them to influence others and receive the support they need to achieve their goals. As managers and leaders, they both realize that they need to work actively to gain the support and allegiance of their colleagues. Cappuccio has a large network of friends, is pleasant to be around and work with, and makes sure his friends and subordinates benefit from helping him achieve his goals.

Early in her organizing efforts, Merino realized that she needed to enlist the support of skilled male workers whom other workers at the Ore-Cal plant would respect and listen to and who also would give workers the courage to stand up to their bosses. She met individually with five male workers and described her goal to eliminate injustices in the plant (such as managers insulting workers and calling them "stupid dogs," calling Mexican workers "turkeys," rewarding workers for reporting how their coworkers could be doing a better job, and making sexually oriented jokes). Merino told the men how she was striving to change the situation to restore a sense of dignity to the workers and encouraged them to enlist the support of seven other male workers. These supporters then recruited men and women alike.

Cappuccio and Merino also are particularly skilled in the ways they unobtrusively influence others and change their beliefs and attitudes. As Cappuccio points out, "You're persuading people to do what you want them to do, but without them realizing that you're persuading them."[6] Ricardo Ramos, one of the men Merino initially enlisted to help her with the unionizing effort, says, "When she speaks, you feel she means it . . . She . . . automatically makes you trust her." Merino's influence in the plant was so unobtrusive that the company's owner, William Shinbane, was shocked when the union was voted in and especially shocked to learn that Merino had managed the campaign. He remarked, "I never thought she'd be able to do this."[7] Even when her organizing efforts do not yield significant wage increases, Merino feels that she has accomplished her goals. As she puts it, "Just so he can't crack his fingers anymore—that is a triumph."[8] ●

Overview

Successful leaders like Cappuccio and Merino are able to effectively use their power to influence others and to bring about changes that allow them to achieve their goals. In Chapter 13 we described how managers, as leaders, exert influence over other people to achieve group and organizational goals and how managers' sources of power enable them to exert such influence. In this chapter we describe why managers need to develop the skills necessary to manage organizational conflict, politics, and change if they are going to be effective and achieve their goals.

First, we describe conflict and the strategies that managers can use to resolve it effectively. We discuss one major conflict resolution technique, negotiation, in detail, outlining the steps managers can take to be good negotiators. Second, we describe organizational politics and the political strategies that managers can use to expand their power and use it effectively. Third, we examine the skills that managers must develop to analyze and change organizations to increase their efficiency and effectiveness. By the end of this chapter, you will appreciate why managers must develop the skills necessary to manage these important organizational processes if they are to be effective and achieve organizational goals. ●

Organizational
Conflict

organizational conflict The discord that arises when the goals, interests, or values of different individuals or groups are incompatible and those individuals or groups block or thwart each other's attempts to achieve their objectives.

Organizational conflict is the discord that arises when the goals, interests, or values of different individuals or groups are incompatible and those individuals or groups block or thwart each other's attempts to achieve their objectives.[9] The "Case in Contrast" describes the conflict that existed between workers and managers at Ore-Cal Corporation's shrimp-packaging plant because of the incompatible interests and goals of managers and workers. Conflict is an inevitable part of organizational life because the goals of different stakeholders such as managers and workers are often incompatible. Organizational conflict also can exist between departments and divisions that compete for resources or even between managers who may be competing for promotion to the next level in the organizational hierarchy. An extreme example of conflict between brothers who inherited what is now the second largest private company in the United States is profiled in this "Management Insight."

Management Insight

Conflict at Koch Industries

Koch Industries, based in Witchita, Kansas, has annual revenues of over $35 billion from its oil and chemical, finance, and agricultural businesses. Koch was founded and run by Fred Koch until his death in 1967. Koch had four sons: Charles, Fred, and the twins David and Bill. The empire their father built ensured that the sons would be financially well-off for the rest of their lives. Unfortunately, it also has given rise to conflicts spanning more than a decade and generating bitter lawsuits.

Charles has been CEO of Koch Industries since his father's death, and David is executive vice president. In a lawsuit settled in June 1998, Bill and Fred sued Charles and David for allegedly swindling them out of $1 billion. Bill and Fred claimed that in 1983 they were misled into selling their shares of the company for $1.1 billion even though the shares were worth much more than that.[10] Bill and Fred lost the case in court, but Bill plans to appeal the judge's ruling.[11]

Unfortunately, the Koch brothers have been at war for over 15 years, trading nasty allegations. No amount of money seems likely to help the brothers resolve their conflicts and live happy, peaceful lives. When their father chose Charles to succeed him, he may have stirred up some of the bitter rivalries among the brothers. Charles is a driven, hardworking man who Bill feels has "cheated me all my life."[12] Bill and Charles haven't spoken to each other in over a decade, and a pall comes over Charles and his wife, Liz, when Bill's name is mentioned.[13] Charles tends not to discuss his ongoing conflicts with his brothers, but Bill is driven to portray Charles as a dishonest man, and is pursuing a new case against Charles and Koch Industries, claiming that they took advantage of independent oil companies and Indian tribes.[14] If only the Koch brothers had found a way to resolve their differences years ago, they might have avoided having their lives and work disrupted by ongoing bitter conflicts.

As the Koch case illustrates, it is important for managers to develop the skills necessary to manage conflict effectively. In addition, the level of conflict present in an organization has important implications for organizational performance. Figure 16.1 illustrates the relationship between organizational conflict and performance. At point A, there is little or no conflict and organizational performance suffers. Lack of conflict in an organization often signals that managers emphasize conformity at the expense of new ideas, are resistant to change, and strive for agreement rather than effective decision making. As the level of conflict increases from point A to point B, organizational effectiveness is likely to increase. When an organization has an optimum level of conflict (point B), managers are likely to be open to, and encourage, a variety of perspectives, look for ways to improve organizational functioning and effectiveness, and view debates and disagreements as a necessary ingredient for effective decision making. As the level of conflict increases from point B to point C, conflict escalates to the point where organizational performance suffers. When an organization has a dysfunctionally high level of conflict, managers are likely to waste organizational resources to

Figure 16.1
The Effect of Conflict on Organizational Performance

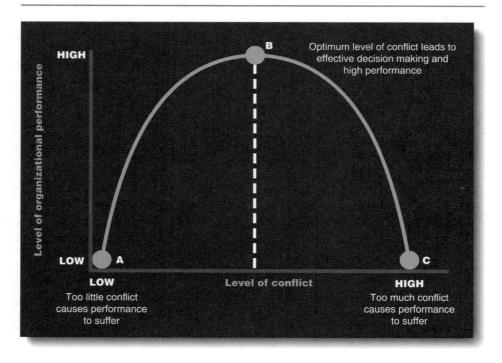

Figure 16.2
Types of Conflict in Organizations

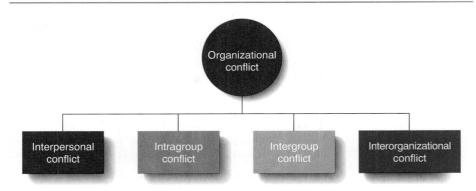

achieve their own ends, to be more concerned about winning political battles than about doing what will lead to a competitive advantage for their organization, and to try to get even with their opponents rather than make good decisions.

Conflict is a force that needs to be managed rather than eliminated.[15] Managers should never try to eliminate all conflict but rather should try to keep conflict at a moderate and functional level to promote change efforts that benefit the organization. To manage conflict, it is important for managers to understand the types and sources of conflict and to be familiar with certain strategies that can be effective in dealing with it.

On July 17, 1998, 18,000 ticket agents at United Airlines voted to join The International Association of Machinists and Aerospace Workers (IAM) union. This decision set-off a series of internal conflicts, or *intergroup conflicts,* between the IAM, the pilot's union, and the carrier. The top issues include demands by the IAM for pay gains from 20–30% for the new union members, mechanics concern that there will not be anything left for their own wage increases, and what is going to happen to the ESOP, or Employee Stock Ownership Plan, since United is 55% owned by employees.

Types of Conflict

There are several types of conflict in organizations: interpersonal, intragroup, intergroup, and interorganizational (see Figure 16.2).[16] Understanding how these types differ can help managers to deal with conflict.

INTERPERSONAL CONFLICT Interpersonal conflict is conflict between individual members of an organization, occurring because of differences in their goals or values. Two managers may experience interpersonal conflict when their values concerning protection of the environment, differ. One manager may argue that the organization should do only what is required by law. The other manager may counter that the organization should invest in equipment to reduce emissions even though the organization's current level of emissions is below the legal limit.

INTRAGROUP CONFLICT Intragroup conflict is conflict that arises within a group, team, or department. When members of the marketing department in a clothing company disagree about how they should spend budgeted advertising dollars for a new line of men's designer jeans, they are experiencing intragroup conflict. Some of the members want to spend all the money on advertisements in magazines. Others want to devote half of the money to billboards and ads in city buses and subways.

INTERGROUP CONFLICT Intergroup conflict is conflict that occurs between groups, teams, or departments. R&D departments, for example, sometimes experience intergroup conflict with production departments. Members of the R&D department may develop a new product that they think production can make inexpensively by using existing manufacturing capabilities. Members of the production department, however, may disagree and believe that the costs of making the product will be high. Managers of departments usually play a key role in managing intergroup conflicts such as this.

INTERORGANIZATIONAL CONFLICT Interorganizational conflict is conflict that arises across organizations. Sometimes interorganizational conflict arises when managers in one organization feel that another organization is not behaving ethically and is threatening the well-being of certain stakeholder groups, as illustrated in this "Ethics in Action."

Ethics in Action

Iacocca's Gamble

Lee Iacocca's latest endeavor is pretty far afield from his days as chairman of Chrysler Corporation (www.chryslercorp.com). Iacocca is part owner and a top manager of Full House Resorts Inc., a small company that aims to build a casino in the Coos Bay area of western Oregon. Iacocca plans to build the casino on land owned by the Coquille Indians, providing them with thousands of jobs and the area with a dramatic increase in income. In return, Full House will receive 30 percent of the casino's profits for financing the casino.

The Coquille tribe and Bruce Anderson, the tribal economic development chief and manager, embrace Iacocca's plan, but Iacocca and Full House are embroiled in a series of interorganizational conflicts with other area organizations opposed to bringing gambling to Oregon's backwoods. Dorothy Christianson, a manager in the local organization Citizens for Responsible Economic and Environmental Development, opposes the casino because she fears it will take business away from area stores and restaurants. She cites research indicating that casino patrons tend to spend money and eat food in casinos, not in local restaurants and shops. Her organization is in conflict with Iacocca's, and she believes that the former Chrysler executive is trying to do not what is best for the well-being of the community (an ethical concern) but rather what will earn him a hefty return.

Leaders of religious organizations in the area also oppose the casino; they fear gambling will bring an increase in crime and bankruptcy. A new anticasino organization has been founded to oppose the casino and purportedly has signatures of 540 anti-casino citizens. Some of these citizens believe the casino will bring to Coos Bay the very thing they are trying to escape by living there—crime.

Adding to the conflict with Iacocca and Full House on ethical grounds are the Coos Indians. The Coos have long been in conflict with the Coquilles, who bought the land for the proposed casino from them. The Coos think it would be unethical to build a casino on their ancestral grounds, even though the Coquilles purchased the land. Moreover, the Coos think that the Coquilles are a branch of the Coos rather than a separate tribe (many historians concur on this point).[17] If Iacocca's latest gamble is to pay off, he has considerable interorganizational conflict to manage and ethical issues to resolve before he can proceed toward his goal.

Sources of Conflict

Conflict in organizations springs from a variety of sources. The ones that we examine here are incompatible goals and time horizons, overlapping authority, task interdependencies, incompatible evaluation or reward systems, scarce resources, and status inconsistencies (see Figure 16.3).[18]

INCOMPATIBLE GOALS AND TIME HORIZONS Recall from Chapter 8 that an important managerial activity is organizing people and tasks into departments and divisions to accomplish an organization's goals. Almost inevitably, this grouping results in the creation of departments and divisions that have incompatible goals and time horizons, and the result can be conflict. Production and production managers, for example, usually concentrate on efficiency and cost cutting; they have a relatively short time horizon and focus on producing quality goods or services in a timely and efficient manner. In contrast, marketing and marketing managers focus on sales and responsiveness to customers. Their time horizon is longer than that of production because they are trying to be responsive not only to customers' needs today but also to their changing needs in the future in order to build long-term customer loyalty.

Figure 16.3
Sources of Conflict in Organizations

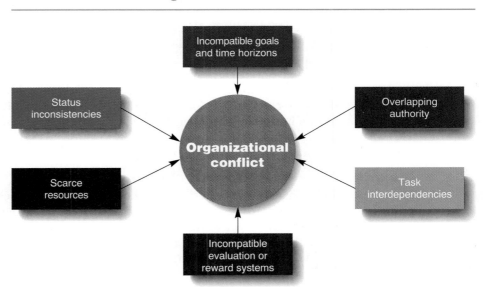

These fundamental differences between marketing and production are often breeding grounds for conflict.

Suppose production is behind schedule in its plan to produce a specialized product for a key customer. The marketing manager believes that the delay will reduce sales of the product and therefore insists that the product must be delivered on time even if saving the production schedule means increasing costs by paying production workers overtime. The production manager says that she will happily schedule overtime if marketing will pay for it. Both managers' positions are reasonable from the perspective of their own departments, and conflict is likely.

OVERLAPPING AUTHORITY   When two or more managers, departments, or functions claim authority for the same activities or tasks, conflict is likely.[19] This is precisely what happened when heirs of the Forman liquor distribution company based in Washington, D.C., inherited the company from their parents. One of the heirs, Barry Forman, wanted to control the company and was reluctant to share power with the other heirs. Several of the heirs felt that they had authority over certain tasks crucial to Forman's success (such as maintaining good relationships with the top managers of liquor companies). What emerged was a battle of wills and considerable conflict, which escalated to the point where it became dysfunctional, requiring the family to hire a consulting firm to help resolve it.[20]

TASK INTERDEPENDENCIES   Have you ever been assigned a group project for one of your classes and one group member consistently failed to get things done on time? This probably created some conflict in your group because other group members were dependent on the late member's contributions to complete the project. Whenever individuals, groups, teams, or departments are interdependent, the potential for conflict exists.[21] Managers of marketing and production with differing goals and time horizons come into conflict precisely because the departments are interdependent. Marketing is dependent on production for the goods it markets and sells, and production is dependent on marketing for creating demand for the things it makes.

INCOMPATIBLE EVALUATION OR REWARD SYSTEMS   The way in which interdependent groups, teams, or departments are evaluated and rewarded can be another source of conflict.[22] Production managers are evaluated and rewarded for their success in staying within budget or lowering costs while maintaining quality. So they are reluctant to take any steps that will increase costs, such as paying workers high overtime rates to finish a late order for an important customer. Marketing managers, in contrast, are evaluated and rewarded for their success in generating sales and customer satisfaction. So they often think that overtime pay is a small price to pay for responsiveness to customers. Thus, conflict between production and marketing is rarely unexpected.

SCARCE RESOURCES   Management is the process of acquiring, developing, protecting, and utilizing the resources that allow an organization to be efficient and effective (see Chapter 1). When resources are scarce, management is all the more difficult and conflict is likely.[23] When resources are scarce, divisional managers, for example, may be in conflict over who has access to financial capital, and organizational members at all levels may be in conflict over who gets raises and promotions.

STATUS INCONSISTENCIES   The fact that some individuals, groups, teams, or departments within an organization are more highly regarded than others in the organization can also create conflict. In some restaurants, for example, the chefs have relatively higher status than the people who wait on tables. Nevertheless, the chefs receive customer orders from the wait staff, and the wait staff can return to the chefs food that their customers or they think is not acceptable. This status inconsistency—high-status chefs taking orders from low-status wait staff—can be the source of considerable conflict between chefs and wait staff. It is for this reason that in some restaurants the wait staff puts orders on a spindle, thereby reducing the amount of direct order-giving from the wait staff to the chefs.[24]

Conflict Management Strategies

If an organization is to achieve its goals, managers must be able to resolve conflicts in a functional manner. *Functional conflict resolution* means that the conflict is settled by compromise or by collaboration between the parties in conflict. *Compromise* is possible when each party is concerned about its own goal accomplishment and the goal accomplishment of the other party and is willing to engage in a give-and-take exchange and to make concessions until a reasonable resolution of the conflict is reached. *Collaboration* is a way of handling conflict in which the parties to a conflict try to satisfy their goals without making any concessions and instead come up with a way to resolve their differences that leaves them both better off.[25]

When the parties to a conflict are willing to cooperate with each other and devise a solution that each finds acceptable (through compromise or collaboration), an organization is more likely to achieve its goals. Conflict management strategies that managers can use to ensure that conflicts are resolved in a functional manner focus on individuals and on the organization as a whole. Below, we describe four strategies that focus on individuals: increasing awareness of the sources of conflict, increasing diversity awareness and skills, practicing job rotation or temporary assignments, and using permanent transfers or dismissals when necessary. We also describe two strategies that focus on the organization as a whole: changing an organization's structure or culture and directly altering the source of conflict.

STRATEGIES FOCUSED ON INDIVIDUALS

INCREASING AWARENESS OF THE SOURCES OF CONFLICT   Sometimes conflict arises because of communication problems and interpersonal misunderstandings. For example, differences in linguistic styles (see Chapter 15) may lead some men in work teams to talk more, and take more credit for ideas, than women in those teams. These communication differences can result in conflict when the men incorrectly assume that the women are uninterested or less capable because they participate less and the women incorrectly assume that the men are being bossy and are not interested in their ideas because they seem to do all the talking. By increasing people's awareness of this source of conflict, managers can help to resolve conflict functionally. And once men and women realize that the source of their conflict is differences in linguistic styles, they can take steps to interact with each other more effectively. The men can give the women more of a chance to provide input, and the women can be more proactive in providing this input.

Sometimes personalities clash in an organization. In these situations, too, managers can help resolve conflicts functionally by increasing organizational members' awareness of the source of their difficulties. For example, some people who are not inclined to take risks may come in conflict with those who are prone to taking risks. The non-risk-takers might complain that those who welcome risk propose outlandish ideas without justification, while the risk-takers complain that their innovative ideas are always getting shot down. When both types of people are made aware that their conflicts are due to fundamental differences in their ways of approaching problems, they will likely be better able to cooperate to come up with innovative ideas that entail only moderate levels of risk.

INCREASING DIVERSITY AWARENESS AND SKILLS Interpersonal conflicts also can arise because of diversity. Older workers may feel uncomfortable or resentful about reporting to a younger supervisor, a Hispanic may feel singled out in a group of white workers, or a female top manager may feel that members of her predominantly male top-management team band together whenever one of them disagrees with one of her proposals. Whether these feelings are justified, they are likely to cause recurring conflicts. Many of the techniques we described in Chapter 5 to increase diversity awareness and skills can help managers effectively manage diversity and resolve conflicts that have their origins in differences between organizational members.

PRACTICING JOB ROTATION OR TEMPORARY ASSIGNMENTS Sometimes conflicts arise because individual organizational members simply do not have a good understanding of the work activities and demands that others in an organization face. A financial analyst, for example, may be required to submit monthly reports to a member of the accounting department. These reports have a low priority for the analyst, and she typically turns them in a couple of days late. On the due date, the accountant always calls up the financial analyst, and conflict ensues as the accountant describes in detail why she must have the reports on time and the financial analyst describes everything else she needs to do. In situations such as this, job rotation or temporary assignments, which expand organizational members' knowledge base and appreciation of other departments, can be a useful way of resolving the conflict. If the financial analyst spends some time working in the accounting department, she may appreciate better the need for timely reports. Similarly, a temporary assignment in the finance department may help the accountant realize the demands a financial analyst faces and the need to streamline unnecessary aspects of reporting.

USING PERMANENT TRANSFERS OR DISMISSALS WHEN NECESSARY Sometimes when other conflict resolution strategies do not work, managers may need to take more drastic steps, including permanent transfers or dismissals.

Suppose two first-line managers who work in the same department are always at each other's throats; frequent bitter conflicts arise between them even though they both seem to get along well with the other people they work with. No matter what their supervisor does to increase their understanding of each other, these conflicts keep occurring. In this case, the supervisor may want to transfer one or both managers so that they do not have to interact as frequently.

When dysfunctionally high levels of conflict occur among top managers who cannot resolve their differences and understand each other, it may be necessary for one of them to leave the company. This is how Gerald Levin, chairman of Time Warner, managed dysfunctionally high levels of conflict among top managers in his company. Robert Daly and Terry Semel, one of the most respected management teams in Hollywood and top managers in the Warner Brothers film company, had been in conflict with Michael Fuchs, a long-time veteran of Time Warner and head of the music division, for two years. As Semel described it, the company "was running like a dysfunctional family, and it needed one management team to run it."[26] Levin realized that Time Warner's future success rested on resolving this conflict, that it was unlikely that Fuchs would ever be able to work effectively with Daly and Semel, and that he risked losing Daly and Semel to another company if he did not resolve the conflict. Faced with that scenario, Levin asked Fuchs to resign.[27]

STRATEGIES FOCUSED ON THE WHOLE ORGANIZATION

CHANGING AN ORGANIZATION'S STRUCTURE OR CULTURE Conflict can signal the need for changes in an organization's structure or culture. Sometimes, managers can effectively resolve conflict by changing the organizational structure they use to group people and tasks.[28] As an organization grows, for example, the *functional structure* (composed of departments such as marketing, finance, and production) that was effective when the organization was small may cease to be effective, and a shift to a *product structure* might effectively resolve conflicts (see Chapter 8).

Managers also can effectively resolve conflicts by increasing levels of integration in an organization. Recall from the "Case in Contrast" in Chapter 14 that Robert Stark, president of Hallmark Cards' Personal Communications Group, increased integration by using cross-functional teams to produce new cards. The use of cross-functional teams speeded new card development and helped to resolve conflicts between different departments. When a writer and an artist have a conflict over the appropriateness of the artist's illustrations, they do not pass criticisms back and forth from one department to another, because now they are on the same team and can directly resolve the issue on the spot.

Sometimes managers may need to take steps to change an organization's culture to resolve conflict (see Chapter 9). Norms and values in an organizational culture might inadvertently promote dysfunctionally high levels of conflict that are difficult to resolve. For instance, norms that stress respect for formal authority may create conflict that is difficult to resolve when an organization creates self-managed work teams and managers' roles and the structure of authority in the organization change. Values stressing individual competition may make it difficult to resolve conflicts when organizational members need to put others' interests ahead of their own. In circumstances such as these, taking steps to change norms and values can be an effective conflict resolution strategy.

Allstate Insurance appears to be plagued by conflicts between workers and managers due to a culture in need of change. In a recent survey, two-thirds of Allstate employees indicated that they did not trust the company and its managers. Employees claim that they have been tailed by private investigators after making complaints or even if a manager thought they were being paid too much.[29] Top managers deny many of these charges, and the "true" story may never be revealed. But what is clear is that Allstate's culture of mistrust is dysfunctional. A strong top-management commitment to the values of trust and open communication might help resolve some of the dysfunctionally high levels of conflict that this company has experienced.

ALTERING THE SOURCE OF CONFLICT   When conflict is due to over-lapping authority, incompatible evaluation or reward systems, and status inconsistencies, managers can sometimes effectively resolve the conflict by directly altering the source of conflict–the overlapping authority, the evaluation or reward system, or the status inconsistency. For example, managers can clarify the chain of command and reassign tasks and responsibilities to resolve conflicts due to overlapping authority.

Tips for Managers

Conflict

1. Try to handle conflicts by compromise or collaboration.

2. Analyze how the ways in which parties to a conflict differ from each other (such as linguistic styles, personality, age, or gender) may be contributing to misunderstandings and conflict.

3. Consider using job rotation or temporary assignments to help your subordinates understand the work activities and demands of other organizational members.

4. Analyze the extent to which conflict in your organization is due to a faulty organizational structure or a dysfunctional culture.

Negotiation Strategies for Integrative Bargaining

negotiation A method of conflict resolution in which the parties in conflict consider various alternative ways to allocate resources to each other in order to come up with a solution acceptable to them all.

A particularly important conflict resolution technique for managers and other organizational members to use in situations in which the parties to a conflict have approximately equal levels of power is negotiation. During **negotiation,** the parties to a conflict try to come up with a solution acceptable to themselves by considering various alternative ways to allocate resources to each other.[30]

There are two major types of negotiation–distributive negotiation and integrative bargaining.[31] In **distributive negotiation,** the parties perceive that they have a "fixed pie" of resources that they need to divide up.[32] They take a competitive, adversarial stance. Each party realizes that he or she must concede something but is out to get the lion's share of resources.[33] The parties see no need to interact with each other in the future and do not care if their interpersonal relationship is damaged or destroyed by their competitive negotiations.[34]

In **integrative bargaining,** the parties perceive that they might be able to increase the resource pie by trying to come up with a creative solution to the conflict. They do not view the conflict competitively, as a win-or-lose situation;

Table 16.1

Negotiation Strategies for Integrative Bargaining

- Emphasize superordinate goals.
- Focus on the problem, not the people.
- Focus on interests, not demands.
- Create new options for joint gain.
- Focus on what is fair.

distributive negotiation Adversarial negotiation in which the parties in conflict compete to win the most resources while conceding as little as possible.

integrative bargaining Cooperative negotiation in which the parties in conflict work together to achieve a resolution that is good for them all.

instead, they view it cooperatively, as a win–win situation in which all parties can gain. Integrative bargaining is characterized by trust, information sharing, and the desire of all parties to achieve a good resolution of the conflict.[35]

Consider how Adrian Hofbeck and Joseph Steinberg, partners in a successful German restaurant in the Midwest, resolved their conflict. Hofbeck and Steinberg founded the restaurant over 15 years ago, share management responsibilities, and share equally in the restaurant's profits. Hofbeck recently decided that he wanted to retire and sell the restaurant, but retirement was the last thing Steinberg had in mind; he wanted to continue to own and manage the restaurant. Distributive negotiation was out of the question, for Hofbeck and Steinberg were close friends and valued their friendship; neither wanted to do something that would hurt the other or their continuing relationship. So they opted for integrative bargaining, which they thought would help them resolve their conflict and help both of them achieve their goals and maintain their friendship.

There are five strategies that managers in all kinds of organizations can rely on to facilitate integrative bargaining and avoid distributive negotiation: emphasizing superordinate goals; focusing on the problem, not the people; focusing on interests, not demands; creating new options for joint gain; and focusing on what is fair (see Table 16.1).[36] Hofbeck and Steinberg used each of these strategies to resolve their conflict.

Emphasizing Superordinate Goals

superordinate goals Goals that all parties in conflict agree to regardless of the source of their conflicts.

Superordinate goals are goals that all parties agree to regardless of the source of their conflict. Increasing organizational effectiveness, increasing responsiveness to customers, and gaining a competitive advantage are just a few of the many superordinate goals that members of an organization can emphasize during integrative bargaining. Superordinate goals help parties in conflict to keep in mind the big picture and the fact that they are working together for a larger purpose or goal despite their disagreements. Hofbeck and Steinberg emphasized three superordinate goals during their bargaining: ensuring that the restaurant continued to survive and prosper, allowing Hofbeck to retire, and allowing Steinberg to remain an owner and manager as long as he wished.

Focusing on the Problem, Not the People

People who are in conflict may not be able to resist the temptation to focus on the shortcomings and weaknesses of the other party or parties, thereby personalizing the conflict. Instead of attacking the problem, the parties to the conflict attack each other. This approach is inconsistent with integrative bargaining and can easily lead the parties into distributive negotiation. All parties to a conflict need to keep focused on the problem or on the source of the conflict and avoid the temptation to discredit each other.

Given their strong friendship, this was not much of an issue for Hofbeck and Steinberg, but they still had to be on their guard to avoid personalizing the conflict. Steinberg recalls that once when they were having a hard time coming up with a solution, he started thinking how lazy Hofbeck, a healthy 57-year-old, was to want to retire so young: "If only he wasn't so lazy, we would never be in the mess we're in right now." Steinberg never mentioned these thoughts to Hofbeck (who later admitted that sometimes he was annoyed with Steinberg for being such a workaholic), because he realized that they would hurt their chances for reaching an integrative solution.

Focusing on Interests, Not Demands

Demands are *what* a person wants; interests are *why* the person wants them. When two people are in conflict, it is unlikely that the demands of both can be met. Their underlying interests, however, can be met, and meeting them is what integrative bargaining is all about.

Hofbeck's demand was that they sell the restaurant and split the proceeds. Steinberg's demand was that they keep the restaurant and maintain the status quo. Obviously, both demands could not be met, but perhaps the interests of both men could be. Hofbeck wanted to be able to retire, invest his share of the money from the restaurant, and live off the returns on the investment. Steinberg wanted to continue managing, owning, and deriving income from the restaurant.

Creating New Options for Joint Gain

Once the parties to a conflict focus on their interests, they are on the road toward achieving creative solutions that will benefit them all. This win–win scenario means that rather than having a fixed set of alternatives from which to choose, the parties can come up with new alternatives that might even expand the resource pie.

Hofbeck and Steinberg came up with three such alternatives. First, even though Steinberg did not have the capital, he could "buy out" Hofbeck's share of the restaurant. Hofbeck would provide the financing for the purchase, and in return Steinberg would pay him a reasonable return on his investment (the same kind of return he could have obtained had he taken his money out of the restaurant and invested it). Second, the partners could seek to sell Hofbeck's share of the restaurant to a third party under the stipulation that Steinberg would continue to manage the restaurant and receive income for his services. Third, the partners could continue to jointly own the restaurant. Steinberg would manage it and receive a proportionally greater share of its profits than Hofbeck, who would be an absentee owner not involved in day-to-day operations but would still receive a return on his investment in the restaurant.

Focusing on What is Fair

Focusing on what is fair is consistent with the principle of distributive justice, which emphasizes the fair distribution of outcomes based on the meaningful contributions that people make to organizations (see Chapter 5). It is likely that parties in conflict will disagree on certain points and prefer different alternatives that each party feels may better serve his or her own interests or maximize his or her own outcomes. Emphasizing fairness and distributive justice will help the parties come to a mutual agreement about what is the best solution to the problem.

Steinberg and Hofbeck agreed that Hofbeck should be able to cut his ties with the restaurant if he chose to do so. They thus decided to pursue the second alternative described above and seek a suitable buyer for Hofbeck's share. They were successful in finding an investor who was willing to buy out Hofbeck's share and continue to let Steinberg manage the restaurant. And they remained good friends.

When managers pursue those five strategies and encourage other organizational members to do so, they are more likely to resolve their conflicts effectively, through integrative bargaining. In addition, throughout the negotiation process, managers and other organizational members need to be aware of, and on their guard against, the biases that can lead to faulty decision making (see Chapter 6).[37]

Tips for Future Managers

Negotiation

1. Whenever feasible, use integrative bargaining rather than distributive negotiation.

2. To help ensure that conflicts are effectively resolved through integrative bargaining, emphasize superordinate goals, focus on the problem not the people, focus on interests not demands, create new options for joint gain, and focus on what is fair.

Organizational Politics

organizational politics
Activities that managers engage in to increase their power and to use power effectively to achieve their goals and overcome resistance or opposition.

political strategies
Tactics that managers use to increase their power and to use power effectively to influence and gain the support of other people while overcoming resistance or opposition.

Managers must develop the skills necessary to manage organizational conflict in order for an organization to be effective. Suppose, however, that top managers are in conflict over the best strategy for an organization to pursue or the best structure to adopt to utilize organizational resources efficiently. In such situations, resolving conflict is often difficult, and the parties to the conflict resort to organizational politics and political strategies to try to resolve the conflict in their favor.

Organizational politics are the activities that managers (and other members of an organization) engage in to increase their power and to use power effectively to achieve their goals and overcome resistance or opposition.[38] Managers often engage in organizational politics to resolve conflicts in their favor.

Political strategies are the specific tactics that managers (and other members of an organization) use to increase their power and to use power effectively to influence and gain the support of other people while overcoming resistance or opposition. Political strategies are especially important when managers are

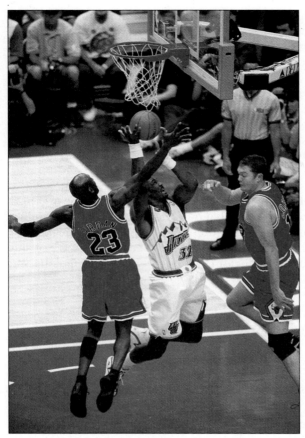

As this book is going into production, the NBA players are in the midst of a strike which threatens the entire '98–'99 season. What sort of problems do you feel plague the players and the owners in their *focus on what is fair?* What could be some of the *interests* involved for both parties? What do you think are some of the *solutions?* What are the implications of this conflict on the customers—the fans?

planning and implementing major changes in an organization: Managers not only need to gain support for their change initiatives and influence organizational members to behave in new ways but also must overcome often strong opposition from people who feel threatened by the change and prefer the status quo. By increasing their power, managers are better able to make needed changes. In addition to moving to increase their power, managers also must make sure that they use their power in a way that actually does enable them to influence others.

The Importance of Organizational Politics

The term *politics* has a negative connotation for many people. Some may think that managers who are "political" are individuals who have risen to the top not because of their own merit and capabilities but because of "who they know." Or they may think that "political" managers are self-interested and wield power to benefit themselves, not their organization. There is a grain of truth to this negative connotation. Some managers do appear to misuse their power for personal benefit at the expense of their organization's effectiveness. Recall, for example, from the "Case in Contrast" in Chapter 13 how Bill Agee misused his power as CEO of Morrison Knudsen by hiring inexperienced top managers who would agree with his decisions and by changing his company's strategy in inappropriate ways.

Nevertheless, organizational politics are often a positive force. Managers striving to make needed changes are likely to encounter resistance from individuals and groups who feel threatened and wish to preserve the status quo. Effective managers engage in politics to gain support for and implement needed changes. Similarly, managers often face resistance from other managers who disagree with their goals for a group or for the organization and also disagree with what they are trying to accomplish. Engaging in organizational politics can help managers overcome this resistance and achieve their goals.

Indeed, managers cannot afford to ignore organizational politics. Everyone engages in politics to a degree–other managers, coworkers, and subordinates, as well as people outside an organization such as suppliers. Those who try to ignore politics might as well bury their heads in the sand because in all likelihood they will be unable to gain support for their initiatives and goals.

Political Strategies for Increasing Power

Managers who use political strategies to increase their power are better able to influence others to work toward the achievement of group and organizational goals. By controlling uncertainty, making themselves irreplaceable,

Figure 16.4
Political Strategies for Increasing Power

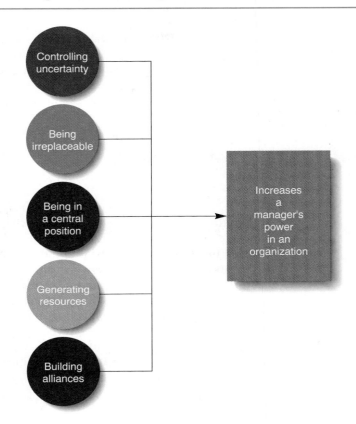

being in a central position, generating resources, and building alliances, managers can increase their power (see Figure 16.4).[38] We next look at each of these strategies.

CONTROLLING UNCERTAINTY   Uncertainty is a threat for individuals, groups, and whole organizations and can interfere with effective performance and goal attainment. For example, uncertainty about job security is threatening for many workers and may cause top performers (who have the best chance of finding another job) to quit and take a more secure position with another organization. When an R&D department faces uncertainty about customer preferences, its members may waste valuable resources to develop a product, such as smokeless cigarettes, which customers do not want. When top managers face uncertainty about global demand, they may fail to export products to countries that want them and thus lose a source of competitive advantage.

Managers who are able to control and reduce uncertainty for other managers, teams, departments, and the organization as a whole are likely to see their power increase.[40] Managers of labor unions gain power when they can eliminate uncertainty over job security for workers. Marketing and sales managers gain power when they can eliminate uncertainty for other departments such as R&D by accurately forecasting customers' changing preferences. Top managers gain power when they are knowledgeable about global demand for

In this still from the movie *Disclosure,* a top manager attempts to play politics with Michael Douglas by threatening him with a sexual harassment charge brought by Demi Moore's character.

an organization's products. Managers who are able to control uncertainty are likely to be in demand and sought after by other organizations.

MAKING ONESELF IRREPLACEABLE
Managers gain power when they have valuable knowledge and expertise that allow them to perform activities that no one else can handle. This is the essence of being irreplaceable.[41] The more central these activities are to organizational effectiveness, the more power managers gain from being irreplaceable.

Managers at 7th Level Inc., for example, learned how important being irreplaceable is when they formed cross-functional managerial teams composed of Hollywood writers and directors and computer programmers. 7th Level is one of a growing number of companies striving to develop computer games that are of movie quality and thus combine state-of-the-art computer game programming capabilities with movie-quality story plots and visuals that stir players' emotions. The writers and directors have had numerous clashes with the programmers because of their different backgrounds and working styles (the programmers tend to be logical and exact; the writers and directors, freewheeling and spontaneous). Ultimately, however, the programmers have more power than the writers and directors because they are irreplaceable.[42] Without their expertise, entertainment-quality computer games cannot be created; the activities of expert programmers cannot be duplicated by others.

BEING IN A CENTRAL POSITION Managers in central positions are responsible for activities that are directly connected to an organization's goals and sources of competitive advantage and often are located in central positions in important communication networks in an organization.[43] Managers in central positions have control over crucial organizational activities and initiatives and have access to important information. Other organizational members are dependent on them for their knowledge, expertise, advice, and support, and the success of the organization as a whole is seen as riding on these managers. These consequences of being in a central position are likely to increase managers' power.

Managers who are outstanding performers, have a wide knowledge base, and have made important and visible contributions to their organizations are likely to be offered central positions that will increase their power. For example, in a recent reorganization General Motors CEO Jack Smith and his top-management team created 17 or so new managerial positions with very high levels of power due to their centrality.[44] Some of the managers are vehicle line executives responsible for planning, organizing, leading, and controlling the activities of designers, engineers, manufacturing managers, and marketing managers to design and produce new cars and trucks. Other managers are brand managers responsible for pricing new cars and trucks and determining how to position them with customers.

Both the vehicle line executives and the branch managers are responsible for earning profits on the cars and trucks they manage, and both are likely to have unprecedented power in GM. The activities these executives will manage are central to GM's effectiveness and are potential sources of competitive advantage—developing, manufacturing, and selling new cars and trucks. Moreover, the executives are at the center of communication networks linking managers of key functions—manufacturing, engineering, research and development, and sales—who need to share information to enable GM to gain a competitive advantage. It is likely that the managers chosen for these positions were outstanding performers in their previous jobs, have a wide knowledge base, and have had some visible successes in their careers.

GENERATING RESOURCES Organizations need three kinds of resources to be effective: (1) input resources such as raw materials, skilled workers, and financial capital, (2) technical resources such as machinery and computers, and (3) knowledge resources such as marketing or engineering expertise. To the extent that a manager is able to generate one or more of these kinds of resources for an organization, that manager's power is likely to increase.[45] In universities, for example, professors who are able to win large research grants from associations such as the National Science Foundation and the Army Research Institute gain power because of the financial resources they are generating for their departments and for the university as a whole.

Andrew C. Sigler, chairman of the board of the paper producer Champion International Corporation, gained so much power from generating resources that he remained at the top of a Fortune 500 company for 20 years despite Champion's poor returns to shareholders. A sudden rise in paper prices turned Champion's fortunes around, but insiders attribute at least part of Sigler's staying power at the top to his close relationships with major investors such as billionaires Warren Buffett and Laurence Tisch, which enabled him to generate capital for Champion.[46]

BUILDING ALLIANCES When managers build alliances, they develop mutually beneficial relationships with people both inside and outside the organization. The two parties to an alliance support one another because doing so is in their best interests, and both parties benefit from the alliance. Alliances provide a manager with power because they provide the manager with support for his or her initiatives. The partner to the alliance provides support because he or she knows that the manager will reciprocate when the partner needs support. Alliances can help managers achieve their goals and implement needed changes in organizations because they increase managers' levels of power.

Recall from the "Case in Contrast" that Merino and Cappuccio took great pains to gain the support of other members of their organizations. This is the essence of building alliances. Merino and Cappuccio were able to build alliances with organizational members who would support them because the organizational members saw their support as being in their own best interests. Both Merino and Cappuccio made sure that people who supported them benefited; Cappuccio even enlisted the support of subordinates by providing them with choice assignments in return for their allegiance.

Many powerful top managers focus on building alliances not only inside their organizations but also with individuals, groups, and organizations in the task and general environments on which their organizations are dependent for resources. These individuals, groups, and organizations enter into alliances with managers because doing so is in their best interests and they know that they can count on the managers' support when they need it.

Political Strategies for Exercising Power

Politically skilled managers not only have a good understanding of, and ability to use, those five strategies to increase their power; they also have a good appreciation of strategies for exercising their power. These strategies generally focus on how managers can use their power *unobtrusively,* as did Merino and Cappuccio in the "Case in Contrast."[47] When a manager exercises power unobtrusively, other members of the organization may not be aware that the manager is using his or her power to influence them. They may think that they support the manager for a variety of reasons: because they believe that doing so is a rational or logical thing to do, because they believe that doing so is in their own best interests, or because they believe that the position or decision that the manager is advocating is legitimate or appropriate.

The unobtrusive use of power may seem devious, but managers typically use this strategy to bring about change and achieve organizational goals. Political strategies for exercising power to gain the support and concurrence of others include relying on objective information, bringing in an outside expert, controlling the agenda, and making everyone a winner (see Figure 16.5).[48]

RELYING ON OBJECTIVE INFORMATION   Managers require the support of others to achieve their goals, implement changes, and overcome opposition. One way for a manager to gain this support and overcome opposition is to rely on objective information that supports the manager's initiatives. Reliance on objective information leads others to support the manager because of the facts; objective information causes others to believe that what the manager is proposing is the proper course of action. By relying on objec-

Figure 16.5
Political Strategies for Exercising Power

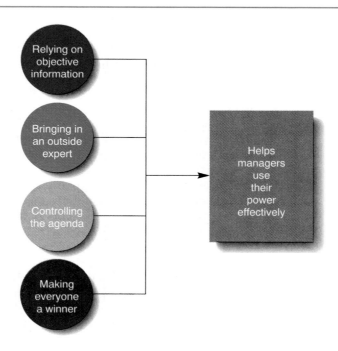

tive information, politically skilled managers unobtrusively exercise their power to influence others.

Take the case of Mary Callahan, vice president of Better Built Cabinets, a small cabinet company in the Southeast. Callahan is extremely influential in the company; practically every new initiative that she proposes to the president and owner of the company is implemented. Why is Callahan able to use her power in the company so effectively? Whenever she has an idea for a new initiative that she thinks the company might pursue, she and her subordinates collect objective information supporting the initiative.

Recently, Callahan decided that Better Built should develop a line of high-priced European-style kitchen cabinets. Before presenting her proposal to Better Built's president, she compiled objective information showing that (1) there was strong unmet demand for these kinds of cabinets, (2) Better Built could manufacture them in its existing production facilities, and (3) the new line had the potential to increase Better Built's sales by 20 percent while not detracting from sales of the company's other cabinets. Presented with this information, the president agreed to Callahan's proposal. Moreover, the president and other members of Better Built whose cooperation was needed to implement the proposal supported it because they thought it would help Better Built gain a competitive advantage. Using objective information to support her position enabled Callahan to unobtrusively exercise her power and influence others to support her proposal.

BRINGING IN AN OUTSIDE EXPERT Bringing in an outside expert to support a proposal or decision can, at times, provide managers with some of the same benefits that the use of objective information does. It lends credibility to a manager's initiatives and causes others to believe that what the manager is proposing is the appropriate or rational thing to do. Suppose Callahan had hired a consultant to evaluate whether her idea was a good one. The consultant reports back to the president that the new European-style cabinets are likely to fulfill Callahan's promises and increase Better Built's sales and profits. This information provided by an "objective" expert can lend a sense of legitimacy to Callahan's proposal and allow her to unobtrusively exercise power to influence others.

Although you might think that consultants and other outside experts are "neutral" or "objective," they sometimes are hired by managers who want them to support a certain position or decision in an organization. Particularly when managers are facing strong opposition from others who fear that a decision will harm their or their departments' interests, they may bring in an outside expert who they hope will be perceived as a neutral observer to lend credibility and objectivity to the managers' point of view. The support of an outside expert may cause others to believe that a decision is indeed the right one. Of course, sometimes consultants and other outside experts really are brought into organizations to be objective and provide managers with guidance on the appropriate course of action to take.

CONTROLLING THE AGENDA Managers also can exercise power unobtrusively by controlling the agenda—influencing what alternatives are considered or even whether a decision is made.[49] When managers influence the alternatives that are considered, they can make sure that each considered alternative is acceptable to them and that undesirable alternatives are not in the feasible set. In a hiring context, for example, managers can exert their power unobtrusively by ensuring that job candidates whom they do not find acceptable do not make their way onto the list of finalists for an open position. They do this by, for example, making sure that these candidates' drawbacks or deficiencies are communicated to everyone involved in making the hiring decision. When three finalists for an open position are discussed and evaluated in a hiring meeting, a manager may seem to exert little power or influence and just go along with what the rest of the group wants. However, the manager may have exerted power in the hiring process unobtrusively, by controlling which candidates made it to the final stage.

Sometimes managers can prevent a decision from being made. A manager in charge of a community relations committee, for example, may not favor a proposal for the organization to become more involved in local youth groups such as the Boy Scouts and the Girl Scouts. The manager can exert influence in this situation by not including the proposal on the agenda for the committee's next meeting. Alternatively, the manager could place the proposal at the end of the agenda for the meeting and feel confident that the committee will run out of time and not get to the last items on the agenda because that is what always happens. Either not including the proposal or putting it at the end of the agenda enables the manager to unobtrusively exercise power. Committee members do not perceive this manager as trying to influence them to turn down the proposal. Rather, he or she has made the proposal into a nonissue that is not even considered.

MAKING EVERYONE A WINNER   Often, politically skilled managers are able to exercise their power unobtrusively because they make sure that everyone whose support they need benefits personally from providing that support. By making everyone a winner, a manager is able to influence other organizational members because these members see supporting the manager to be in their best interest. Recall how both Paul Cappuccio and Yanira Merino in the "Case in Contrast" made sure that organizational members who supported them personally benefited.

Tips for Managers

Political Strategies

1. Determine the major sources of uncertainty for your work group and organization and take steps to help control these sources of uncertainty.

2. Try to develop skills or expertise that are crucial to your organization and not possessed by other organizational members.

3. Determine which resources are crucial for your organization and try to help generate these resources.

4. Build alliances with powerful organizational members to gain support for your ideas.

5. Whenever possible, use objective information to support positions that you advocate.

Managing Organizational Change

Both politics and conflict can signal to managers that the way an organization operates needs to change. For example, poor communication and a lack of cooperation between manufacturing and marketing may signal a need to increase the integration of these departments or even change the managers involved. However, organizational conflict and politics often arise because changes in the way an organization operates, particularly changes in strategy or structure, inevitably favor some individuals or groups over others (see Figure 16.6).

Because organizational conflict, politics, and change are intertwined, it is important for managers to develop the skills necessary to manage change effectively. Several experts have proposed a model that managers can follow to implement change successfully while effectively managing conflict and politics.[50] Figure 16.7 outlines the steps that managers must take to manage change effectively. In the rest of this section we examine each one.

Assessing the Need for Change

Organizational change can affect practically all aspects of organizational functioning, including organizational structure, culture, strategies, control systems, groups and teams, and the human resource management system, as well as critical organizational processes such as communication, motivation, and leadership. Organizational change can bring alterations in the ways managers carry out the critical tasks of planning, organizing, leading, and controlling and the ways they perform their managerial roles.

Deciding how to change an organization is a complex matter, not least because change disrupts the status quo and poses a threat, prompting employees to resist attempts to alter work relationships and procedures. Organizational

Figure 16.6

The Relationship Between Organizational Conflict, Politics, and Change

Figure 16.7

Four Steps in the Organizational Change Process

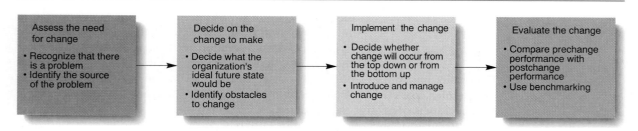

learning, the process through which managers try to increase organizational members' abilities to understand and appropriately respond to changing conditions (see Chapter 6), can be an important impetus for change and help all members of an organization, including managers, effectively make decisions about needed changes.

Assessing the need for change calls for two important activities: recognizing that there is a problem and identifying its source. Sometimes the need for change is obvious, such as when an organization's performance is suffering. Often, however, managers have trouble determining that something is going wrong because problems develop gradually; organizational performance may slip for a number of years before it becomes obvious. Thus, during the first step in the change process, managers need to recognize that there is a problem that requires change.

Often the problems that managers detect have produced a gap between desired performance and actual performance. To detect such a gap, managers need to look at performance measures, such as falling market share or profits, rising costs, or employees' failure to meet their established goals or stay within budgets, which indicate whether change is needed. These measures are provided by organizational control systems (discussed in Chapter 9).

To discover the source of the problem, managers need to look both inside and outside the organization. Outside the organization, they must examine how changes in environmental forces may be creating opportunities and threats that are affecting internal work relationships. Perhaps the emergence of low-cost foreign competitors has led to conflict among different departments that are trying to find new ways to gain a competitive advantage. Managers also need to look within the organization to see whether its structure and culture are causing problems between departments. Perhaps a company does not have the integrating mechanisms in place to allow different departments to respond to low-cost competition (see Chapter 8).

Deciding on the Change to Make

Once managers have identified the source of the problem, they must decide what they think the organization's ideal future state would be. In other words, they must decide where they would like their organization to be in the future—what kinds of goods and services it should be making, what its business-level strategy should be, how the organizational structure should be changed, and so on. During this step, managers also must engage in planning how they are going to attain the organization's ideal future state.

This step in the change process also includes identifying obstacles or sources of resistance to change. Managers must analyze the factors that may prevent the company from reaching its ideal future state. Obstacles to change are found at the corporate, divisional, departmental, and individual levels of the organization.

Corporate-level changes in an organization's strategy or structure, even seemingly trivial changes, may significantly affect how divisional and departmental managers behave. Suppose that to compete with low-cost foreign competitors, top managers decide to increase the resources spent on state-of-the-art machinery and reduce the resources spent on marketing or R&D. The power of manufacturing managers would increase, and the power of marketing and R&D managers would fall. This decision would alter the balance of power among departments and might lead to increased politics and conflict as departments start fighting to retain their status in the organization. An organization's present strategy and structure are powerful obstacles to change.

Organizational culture also can facilitate or obstruct change. Organizations with entrepreneurial, flexible cultures, such as high-tech companies, are much easier to change than are organizations with more rigid cultures such as those sometimes found in large bureaucratic organizations like the military or General Motors.

The same obstacles to change exist at the divisional and departmental levels as well. Division managers may differ in their attitudes toward the changes that top managers propose and will resist those changes if their interests and power seem threatened. Managers at all levels usually fight to protect their power and control over resources. Given that departments have different goals and time horizons, they may also react differently to the changes that other managers propose. When top managers are trying to reduce costs, for example, sales managers may resist attempts to cut back on sales expenditures if they believe that problems stem from manufacturing managers' inefficiencies.

At the individual level, too, people are often resistant to change because change brings uncertainty and uncertainty brings stress (see Chapter 11). For example, individuals may resist the introduction of a new technology because they are uncertain about their abilities to learn it and effectively use it.

These obstacles make organizational change a slow process. Managers must recognize these potential obstacles to change and take them into consideration. Some obstacles can be overcome by improving communication so all organizational members are aware of the need for change and of the nature of the changes being made. Empowering employees and inviting them to participate in the planning for change also can help overcome resistance and allay employees' fears. In addition, managers can sometimes overcome resistance by using the integrative bargaining strategies discussed earlier in this chapter. For example, emphasizing superordinate goals such as organizational effectiveness and gaining a competitive advantage can make organizational members who resist a change realize that the change is ultimately in everyone's best interests because it will increase organizational performance. The larger and more complex an organization is, the more complex is the change process.

Implementing the Change

top-down change

Change that is implemented quickly throughout an organization by upper-level managers.

Generally, managers implement—that is, introduce and manage—change from the top down or from the bottom up.[51] **Top-down change** is implemented quickly: Top managers identify the need for change, decide what to do, and then move quickly to implement the changes throughout the organization. For example, top managers may decide to restructure and downsize the organization and then give divisional and departmental managers specific goals to achieve. With top-down change, the emphasis is on making the changes quickly and dealing with problems as they arise.

bottom-up change

Change that is implemented gradually and involves managers and employees at all levels of an organization.

Bottom-up change is typically more gradual. Top managers consult with middle and first-line managers about the need for change. Then, over time, these low-level managers work with nonmanagerial employees to develop a detailed plan for change. A major advantage of bottom-up change is that it can co-opt resistance to change. Because the emphasis in bottom-up change is on participation and on keeping people informed about what is going on, uncertainty and resistance are minimized.

Evaluating the Change

The last step in the change process is to evaluate how successful the change effort has been in improving organizational performance.[52] Using measures such as changes in market share, in profits, or in the ability of managers to meet their goals, managers compare how well an organization is performing after the change with how well it was performing before. Managers also can use **benchmarking,** comparing their performance on specific dimensions with the performance of high-performing organizations to decide how successful a change effort has been. For example, when Xerox was doing poorly in the 1980s, it benchmarked the efficiency of its distribution operations against those of L. L. Bean, the efficiency of its central computer operations against those of John Deere, and its marketing abilities against those of Procter & Gamble. Those companies are renowned for their skills in those different areas, and by studying how they performed, Xerox was able to dramatically increase its own performance. Benchmarking is a key tool in total quality management, an important change program discussed at length in Chapter 18.

benchmarking

Comparing performance on specific dimensions with the performance of high-performing organizations.

The kinds of issues that managers must deal with as they go about changing organizations are illustrated in the following "Management Insight" by the actions Michael Walsh took to bring about change at Tenneco.

Management Insight

Big Changes at Tenneco

Tenneco Inc., based in Houston, Texas, operates in businesses such as natural gas, shipbuilding, auto parts, chemicals, and farm equipment. With sales of over $14 billion, it is one of the biggest Fortune 500 companies. However, when Michael H. Walsh became president of Tenneco in 1991, he entered a company that had experienced falling earnings for years. Walsh's job was to change the way the company operated and turn around its performance.

Walsh was accustomed to the problems of changing a large company. He had successfully turned around Union Pacific (www.up.com), a large railroad company, and Tenneco hired him because of his reputation as a "change agent." On taking over the change effort, Walsh's first step was to analyze the problems facing the company. What he found were problems in organizational structure and culture that were undermining performance in Tenneco's various operating divisions. For example, Case, the company's maker of agricultural equipment, was in poor financial shape and was a major contributor to the organization's poor performance. To keep Case afloat, top managers had been siphoning off the profits of the chemicals and auto parts divisions, which were doing well. This practice, however, gave managers in those two divisions little incentive to cooperate with one another and caused a lot of conflict between divisional managers. Moreover, over the years, divisional managers had been allowed to run their divisions with little oversight from corporate managers and had been spending organizational resources to support their divisions' interests but not necessarily Tenneco's interests.

Walsh recognized that Tenneco's structure and culture were powerful obstacles to change. He realized that to change the way divisional managers behaved, he would have to change the corporate-divisional relationship. He started from the top down by changing managers' attitudes and behaviors. First, he instituted a strict set of financial goals for divisional managers and made it clear that he would rigorously monitor their performance toward achieving those goals. Then he created a system of teams consisting of managers from the different divisions, who met together to critique one another's performance. In addition, he flattened Tenneco's hierarchy, wiping out three layers of corporate managers to bring himself closer to the divisions. After this change in structure, divisional managers had more incentive to improve corporate performance. Moreover, these changes effectively destroyed Tenneco's old organizational structure and changed managers' emphasis from being concerned primarily with the achievement of divisional goals to being concerned about the achievement of corporate or organizational goals.

Walsh continued these change efforts at all levels of the company. To change attitudes and behavior at the departmental level, he instituted a system of quality teams in every division in the company. Employees in these cross-functional teams searched for new ways to improve quality and reduce costs, and Walsh regularly videotaped messages to Tenneco employees encouraging them to find new ways to improve performance. Walsh also tried to destroy Tenneco's old culture of apathy, which had been permitting managers and nonmanagerial employees to preserve the status quo and ignore the problems facing the company.

Walsh's efforts to change Tenneco have been spectacularly successful when measured by the increase in profits the company has achieved. Tenneco is now very profitable, and analysts expect the gains from Walsh's restructuring efforts to increase steadily over the years. Overcoming obstacles to change in a company may be a difficult process, but it can reap big dividends, as Tenneco's experience suggests.

Summary and Review

Chapter Summary

ORGANIZATIONAL CONFLICT Organizational conflict is the discord that arises when the goals, interests, or values of different individuals or groups are incompatible and those individuals or groups block or thwart each other's attempts to achieve their objectives. Four types of conflict arising in organizations are interpersonal conflict, intragroup conflict, intergroup conflict, and interorganizational conflict. Sources of conflict in organizations include incompatible goals and time horizons, overlapping authority, task interdependencies, incompatible evaluation or reward systems, scarce resources, and status inconsistencies. Conflict management strategies focused on individuals include increasing awareness of the sources of conflict, increasing diversity awareness and skills, practicing job rotation or temporary assignments, and using permanent transfers or dismissals when necessary. Strategies focused on the whole organization include changing an organization's structure or culture and altering the source of conflict.

NEGOTIATION STRATEGIES FOR INTEGRATIVE BARGAINING Negotiation is a conflict resolution technique used when parties to a conflict have approximately equal levels of power and try to come up with an acceptable way to allocate resources to each other. In distributive negotiation, the parties perceive that there is a fixed level of resources for them to allocate, and each competes to receive as much as possible at the expense of the others, not caring about their relationship in the future. In integrative bargaining, the parties perceive that they may be able to increase the resource pie by coming up with a creative solution to the conflict, trusting each other, and cooperating with each other to achieve a win–win resolution. Five strategies that managers can use to facilitate integrative bargaining are to emphasize superordinate goals; focus on the problem, not the people; focus on interests, not demands; create new options for joint gain; and focus on what is fair.

ORGANIZATIONAL POLITICS Organizational politics are the activities that managers (and other members of an organization) engage in to increase their power and to use power effectively to achieve their goals and overcome resistance or opposition. Effective managers realize that politics can be a positive force that enables them to make needed changes in an organization. Five important political strategies for increasing power are controlling uncertainty, making oneself irreplaceable, being in a central position, generating resources, and building alliances. Political strategies for effectively exercising power focus on how to use power unobtrusively and include relying on objective information, bringing in an outside expert, controlling the agenda, and making everyone a winner.

MANAGING ORGANIZATIONAL CHANGE Managing organizational change is one of managers' most important and difficult tasks. Four steps in the organizational change process are assessing the need for change, deciding on the change to make, implementing the change, and evaluating how successful the change effort has been.

Management in Action

Topics for Discussion and Action

1. Discuss why too little conflict in an organization can be just as detrimental as too much conflict.

2. Interview a manager in a local organization to determine the kinds of conflicts that occur in that manager's organization and the strategies that are used to manage them.

3. Why is integrative bargaining a more effective way of resolving conflicts than distributive negotiation?

4. Why do organizational politics affect practically every organization? Why do effective managers need good political skills?

5. What steps can managers take to ensure that organizational politics are a positive force leading to a competitive advantage, not a negative force leading to personal advantage at the expense of organizational goal attainment?

6. Think of a member of an organization whom you know and who is particularly powerful. What political strategies does this person use to increase his or her power?

7. Why is it best to use power unobtrusively? How are people likely to react to power that is exercised obtrusively?

8. What are the main obstacles to change?

9. Interview a manager about a change effort that he or she was involved in. What issues were involved? What problems were encountered? What was the outcome of the change process?

Building Management Skills

Effective and Ineffective Conflict Resolution

Think about two recent conflicts that you had with other people, one conflict that you felt was effectively resolved (C1) and one that you felt was ineffectively resolved (C2). The other people involved could be coworkers, students, family members, friends, or members of an organization that you are a member of. Answer the following questions.

1. Briefly describe C1 and C2. What type of conflict was involved in each of these incidents?

2. What was the source of the conflict in C1 and in C2?

3. What conflict management strategies were used in C1 and in C2?

4. What could you have done differently to more effectively manage conflict in C2?

5. How was conflict resolved in C1 and in C2?

Small Group Breakout Exercise

Negotiating a Solution

Form groups of three or four people. One member of your group will play the role of Jane Rister, one member will play the role of Michael Schwartz, and one or two members will be observer(s) and spokesperson(s) for your group.

Jane Rister and Michael Schwartz are assistant managers in a large department store. They report directly to the store manager. Today they are meeting to discuss some important problems that they need to solve but about which they disagree.

The first problem hinges on the fact that either Rister or Schwartz needs to be on duty whenever the store is open. For the last six months, Rister has taken most of the least desirable hours (nights and weekends). They are planning their schedules for the next six months. Rister hoped Schwartz would take more of the undesirable times, but Schwartz has informed Rister that his wife has just gotten a nursing job that requires her to work weekends, so he needs to stay home weekends to take care of their infant daughter.

The second problem concerns a department manager who has had a hard time retaining salespeople in his department. The turnover rate in his department is twice that of the other departments in the store. Rister thinks the manager is ineffective and wants to fire him. Schwartz thinks the high turnover is a fluke and the manager is effective.

The last problem concerns Rister's and Schwartz's vacation schedules. Both managers want to take off the week of July 4, but one of them needs to be in the store whenever it is open.

1. The group members playing Rister and Schwartz assume their roles and negotiate a solution to these three problems.

2. Observers take notes on how Rister and Schwartz negotiate solutions to their problems.

3. Observers determine the extent to which Rister and Schwartz use distributive negotiation or integrative bargaining to resolve their conflicts.

4. When called on by the instructor, observers communicate to the rest of the class how Rister and Schwartz resolved their conflicts, whether they used distributive negotiation or integrative bargaining, and their actual solutions.

Exploring the World Wide Web

Specific Assignment

Many companies are making major changes in their organizations to increase their effectiveness and gain a competitive advantage. One such company is IBM. Scan IBM's website to familiarize yourself with IBM's current initiatives (http://www.ibm.com/IBM). Click on "Employment" and read the material provided, click on "IBM Workplace" and read the material provided, and then click on "Pay Dirt" and read the material provided.

1. How would you characterize IBM's approach to change?

2. How does IBM encourage change?

General Assignment

Find the website of a company that is making major organizational changes. What are those changes? How are they being implemented? What kinds of obstacles to change do you think managers in this company may be encountering?

ManagementCase

In the News

From the Pages of BusinessWeek

Half a Loaf at Blimpie

Shortly after dawn on St. Patrick's Day, 1,000 corned-beef sandwiches were trucked from Blimpie on Long Island to the American Stock Exchange in Lower Manhattan, passing dozens of Blimpie shops that were much closer. To the bleat of bagpipes, Chief Executive Anthony P. Conza rang the opening bell to herald his switch from the New York Stock Exchange. The traders devoured the subs, unaware of a strange truth: Conza was on the turf of "the other" Blimpie.

Long before Blimpie became America's No. 2 submarine-sandwich chain, Conza and co-founder Peter DeCarlo sliced the company in half. State by state, city by city, they divvied the nation in 1976 to resolve warring business philosophies. "It was like Monopoly," Conza says.

Starting with 50 stores each, they began a grueling race. "I said I could do it better, and he said he could do it better," DeCarlo explains. If size matters, Conza won: With 2,000 stores and $39 million in revenues, his publicly traded Blimpie International Inc. is about 10 times as big as DeCarlo's privately held Blimpie Associates.

But it's a hollow victory. Blimpie remains a bifurcated anomaly in a business that thrives on uniformity. Its divided status has throttled growth at the larger company and given it one of the more convoluted histories in the annals of Corporate America. And that's only the start of the problems caused by mishandling the Blimpie name. Investors in Blimpie International, too, have been left holding crumbs. Amid free-falling profits, they have questioned the multimillion-dollar payouts the company makes to its executives for rights to use the name overseas. The result: Shares have slid to around $3, down from $16 two years ago. "I've never heard of such a ludicrous arrangement in all my life," says Wendy Liebmann, a New York retail consultant.

Indeed, even as Conza tries to bail his chain out by expanding abroad and developing new restaurants featuring tacos and pasta, he is hampered by the other Blimpie's control of Manhattan—a showcase serving everyone from Wall Streeters to tourists. "It's like I've invited people over for dinner," Conza says, "and they arrive at somebody else's house and eat their cooking."

For all the problems the name has caused, it was born innocently enough. In 1964, Conza and DeCarlo were 24—the best of friends, the most naive of businessmen. At a Halloween Party in Hoboken, N.J., Conza, DeCarlo, and a third friend talked about starting a business. The product: the sub sandwich they had tried on the Jersey Shore. Thinking the name "sub" sounded like a greasy spoon, they rifled through the dictionary and stopped at "blimp."

They borrowed $2,000 from a friend of DeCarlo's in the textile business. DeCarlo, with a perpetual smile and a crushing handshake, sweet-talked suppliers. Conza, the shy son of a New York Stock Exchange runner, quit his clerking job at E.F. Hutton to handle the books. "He was the pencil man with patience," says David Pierro, whose three stores in Manhattan and New Jersey overlap both Blimpies. "Peter was the limo guy with $1,000 suits and checks bouncing all over the place."

Customers flooded in. And within a year, Blimpie sold its first franchise. While Conza sought to control Blimpie's fate, DeCarlo pushed to open anywhere a franchisee was interested. DeCarlo won, and both say that unbridled expansion ate up all their cash, forcing them to sell the stores they owned. They cashed in their cars and life-insurance policies. Both recall the last straw: Approaching the bridge from New Jersey to Manhattan, neither could come up with the 50¢ toll. Soon after that, they sliced Blimpie in half. Conza took Chicago. DeCarlo grabbed parts of California, Maryland, and Virginia. On it went. "I woke up one day to a call saying, 'Three of your stores are under Peter. Three are under Tony,'" recalls New York franchisee Joe Martignano. "It was like my parents split up."

Both soon floundered, and DeCarlo gave Conza his rights outside the Northeast in exchange for a cut of profits in those regions. Conza took Blimpie International public in 1983 but pumped money into a Southwestern-style chain that almost pulled him under. In 1987, he began selling huge subfranchises. Since 1994, the strategy more than doubled sales.

But like divorced parents bickering over the kids, the two never stopped arguing. Conza has criticized the occasional sanitary violations of the New York stores. DeCarlo, who blames New York's aging real estate, demanded that Conza stop undercutting quality by selling prepackaged sandwiches at Southern gas stations. Conza ordered thousands of baseballs with the Blimpie logo for a promotion, but DeCarlo refused to buy any. Confusing customers further, they even have competing ad campaigns.

Amid the squabbling, archrival Subway closed in on Manhattan, forcing Conza and DeCarlo to unify. Conza's offer to buy the smaller Blimpie for $40 million— about 10 times sales—was rebuffed. "The money wasn't right," DeCarlo says. But he sent emissaries to Conza's test kitchen to nibble on turkey, ham, and beef. They agreed on standardizing cold cuts but still diverge on cheese and bread. Nor can they settle on a menu. "They didn't have the chicken fajita I eat at home," gripes a Florida tourist, leaving a New York store.

The arrangement was tolerable until the mid-1990s, when Blimpie International ran out of territory in the U.S. With revenues limited to franchise fees and equipment sales, Conza looked overseas. But unlike most trademarks, which are registered to a corporation, "Blimpie" is owned by Conza, DeCarlo, and Chief Operating Officer David L. Siegel. Without control of the name, Blimpie couldn't raise money to go abroad.

To solve the problem in advance of a $10 million offering in 1995, the company agreed to pay DeCarlo, who refused to give up his rights, 30% of the international profits. Conza and Siegel were advised to fork over the name for free by Miami investment banker Steven N. Bronson. His firm, Barber & Bronson, a major Blimpie shareholder, sponsored the offering. But instead, the pair leased the name to Blimpie for 99 years. Last year, the chain paid them $4.5 million to use the name abroad—a good deal more than the $3.28 million it earned in profits. By 2002, they are to get $3 million more for its use. "They wanted to maximize their personal wealth," Bronson says. "We had a problem with it. But it was better than leaving ownership with management."

Conza and Siegel, who own 31% and 15% of the stock, respectively, insist the arrangement is fair. "We've compromised our salaries and benefits to build the company," Siegel says. "Why should we give away our rights?" But the deal is a big reason Wall Street soured on the stock. "When management is taking money out the backdoor so a company can use its own name, something's rotten in Denmark," says analyst Michael D. Smith of brokerage Fahnestock & Co.

Worse, despite the hefty payments, Blimpie has made little dent abroad: So far, Conza has opened just 37 stores overseas. And profits, which sank 19% for the fiscal year ended June, 1997, were off a further 20% for the first three quarters of fiscal 1998. Blimpie's problems may have started with its name—but they surely don't end there.

Source: I. Jeanne Dugan, "Half a Loaf at Blimpie," *Business Week, August 10, 1998,* 43–44.

Questions

1. What are the sources of conflict between Anthony P. Conza and Peter DeCarlo?

2. How have Conza and DeCarlo tried to manage the conflict between them?

3. Have they been successful at managing conflict? Why or why not?

ManagementCase

In the News

From the Pages of BusinessWeek
The Corporation of the Future

The once unthinkable decline of many of the world's largest corporations has become all too common in recent years. Strategic blunders and oversights by management have pulled down such powerful and might giants as AT&T, Eastman Kodak, and General Motors.

Yet there is a less visible but even more critical danger: the inability to adapt to the speed and turbulence of technological change. After massive high-tech investments, management is only beginning to make the organizational changes needed to transform information technology into the potent competitive weapon that it will need to be in the 21st century.

Few companies have grasped the far-reaching importance of the new technology for management better than Cisco Systems Inc. The San Jose (Calif.) company has become the global leader in networking for the Internet, with annual revenues of more than $8 billion. It's also a Wall Street darling, with a market cap approaching $100 billion.

Cisco could well provide one of the best road maps to a new model of management. Partly because it makes the tools to build the powerful networks that link businesses to their customers and suppliers, Cisco itself has been at the forefront of using technology to transform management practices.

But it's not only the company's innovative use of technology that wins favorable reviews. It's also the company's mind-set and culture, its willingness to team up with outsiders to acquire and retain intellectual assets, its near-religious focus on the customer, and its progressive human resource policies. "Cisco is the quintessential outside-in company" says James F. Moore, chairman of consultants GeoPartners Research Inc. "They have mastered how to source talent, products, and momentum from outside their own walls. That's a powerful advantage."

This corporate adolescent—founded in 1984 by a group of computer scientists from Stanford University—is headed by a leader, John T. Chambers, who cut his teeth at successful companies that stumbled. At both IBM and Wang Laboratories Inc., the soft-spoken West Virginian got a firsthand glimpse of how arrogance and reluctance to change caused severe pain and dislocation.

Those experiences, including a traumatic time when he survived five layoffs in 15 months at Wang—before resigning in 1990—colored his view of what a healthy organization should be. "It taught me how a company should be built in the first place and how to do things dramatically different the next time," says Chambers, 48, who joined Cisco in 1991 and became CEO in 1995. "Laying off people was the toughest thing I ever did. I'll move

heaven and earth to avoid doing that again."

To hear Chambers tell it, his people and his organization are "in the sweet spot"—where technology and the future meet to transform not only business but all of life. His vision is simple: "We can change the way people live and work, play and learn." It is an idealistic phrase that falls out of his mouth repeatedly and unabashedly. It is also an inspiring and motivating declaration for each of Cisco's 13,000-plus employees.

Chambers aims to be the Jack Welch of the new millenium. Like General Electric Co.'s Chairman Welch, he has decided he wants to be No. 1 or No. 2 in every market, a condition that already exists in 14 of the 15 markets in which Cisco competes. Beyond that strategic goal, Chambers believes that the new rules of competition demand organizations built on change, not stability; organized around networks, not a rigid hierarchy; based on interdependencies of partners, not self-sufficiency; and constructed on technological advantage, not old-fashioned bricks and mortar.

The network structure has vast implications for managing in the next century. GM's Saturn Div. and Dell Computer Corp. have shown how the network can eliminate inventory, by connecting with partners that deliver goods only when they are needed. In the new model that Chambers is creating at Cisco, however, the network is pervasive, central to nearly everything.

It seamlessly links Cisco to its customers, prospects, business partners, suppliers, and employees. This year, Cisco will sell more than $5 billion worth of

goods—more than half its total—over the Internet, nearly three times the Internet sales booked by pioneer Dell. So successful has Cisco been in selling complex, expensive equipment over the Net that last year Cisco alone accounted for one-third of all electronic commerce.

Seven out of 10 customer requests for technical support are filled electronically—at satisfaction rates that eclipse those involving human interaction. Using the network for tech support allows Cisco to save more money than its nearest competitor spends on research and development. "It has saved me 1,000 engineers," gushes Chambers. "I take those 1,000 engineers, and instead of putting them into support, I put them into building new products. That gives you a gigantic competitive advantage."

The network also is the glue for the internal workings of the company. It swiftly connects Cisco with its web of partners, making the constellation of suppliers, contract manufacturers, and assemblers look like one company—Cisco—to the outside world. Via the company's intranet, outside contractors directly monitor orders from Cisco customers and ship the assembled hardware to buyers later in the day—often without Cisco even touching the box. By outsourcing production of 70% of its products, Cisco has quadrupled output without building new plants and has cut the time it takes to get a new product to market by two-thirds, to just six months.

The network also is Cisco's primary tool for recruiting talent, with half of all applications for jobs coming over the Net. When an employee wants information about a company event or health benefits, or needs to track an expense report, the network is the place to go at Cisco. The upshot: More than 1.7 million pages of information are accessible by employees who use the Cisco network thousands of times every day. "We are," says Chambers, "the best example of how the Internet is going to change everything."

Technology aids and abets this business model, but it does not completely displace human interaction. "The network works better when you've already had a personal touch," insists Chambers. That's why he does quarterly meetings with employees at a nearby convention center, why all employees in the month of their birth are invited to one of his $1\frac{1}{2}$-hour "birthday breakfasts," and why he works harder than most to encourage open and direct communication with all of Cisco's leaders.

Chambers also believes in partnering with other businesses. Plenty of companies forge links with others, but Cisco has a track record of making them work. "Partnerships are key to the new world strategies of the 21st century," says Donald J. Listwin, a Cisco senior vice-president. "Partners collapse time because they allow you to take on more things and bring them together quicker."

A good example is Cisco's partnership with Microsoft Corp., which last year resulted in a new technology to make networks more intelligent. The software lets networks know immediately a user's identity and location and to respond differently to each one. The partnership allows both companies to expand this market together more rapidly.

"From initial discussion to technology, it took 18 months to get the product out," says Listwin. "It would have taken us four years to get to where we are [without such a partnership], and it's not clear we had the competence to get there alone."

Another theme—often heard but seldom exercised by corporate leaders—is the central importance of the customer. Nothing causes Chambers more restless nights than worry over how to serve customers better. That's why he spends as much as 55% of his time with customers and why he receives every night, 365 nights a year, voice mail updates on as many as 15 key clients.

In this new model, strategic direction is not formed by an insular group of top executives, but by the company's leading customers. It's an outside-in approach, as opposed to an inside-out. The customer is the strategy. "There is nothing more arrogant than telling the customer: 'Here is what you need to know,'" says Chambers. "Most of the time, you are not going to be right." Rather, Cisco's leading-edge customers are seen as partners in forming the company strategy. Example: After Boeing Co. and Ford Motor Co. informed Chambers that their future network needs were unlikely to be satisfied by Cisco, Chambers went out to make his first acquisition to solve the problem. That deal, to acquire local-area-network switchmaker Crescendo Communications in 1993, put the company into a sector of the industry that now accounts for $2.8 billion in annual revenue.

Even such tactical moves as acquisitions and mergers are seen differently by a new-world

company. Rather than acquire merely to speed growth or swell market share, Cisco routinely employs acquisitions to capture intellectual assets and next-generation products. "Most people forget that in a high-tech acquisition, you really are acquiring only people," says Chambers. "That's why so many of them fail. At what we pay, at $500,000 to $2 million an employee, we are not acquiring current market share. We are acquiring futures."

While most companies immediately cut costs and people from newly acquired outfits, Cisco adheres to what it calls the "Mario rule"—named after Senior Vice-President Mario Mazzola, who had been CEO of Crescendo when it was bought by Cisco. Before any employee in a newly acquired company can be terminated, both Chambers and the former CEO must give their consent. "It tells new employees that Cisco wants them, that Cisco cares about them, and that we're not just another big company," says Daniel Scheinman, vice-president for legal and government affairs. "It buys the trust of the people … and their passion is worth a lot more than any of the downside legal protection."

In talent-hungry Silicon Valley, Cisco measures the success of every acquisition first by employee retention, then by new product development, and finally return on investment. The company has been phenomenally successful at holding on to the intellectual assets it buys: Overall turnover among acquired employees is just 6% a year, two percentage points lower than Cisco's overall employee churn. The company works hard to embrace employees acquired in deals, often giving top talent key jobs in the new organization. Three of Cisco's main businesses are led by former CEOs of acquired companies.

Every acquisition, moreover, must meet Cisco guidelines. For years, Chambers watched IBM and other high-tech outfits acquire and then slowly smother any number of entrepreneurial companies. What he learned was that you never buy a company whose values and culture are much different from your own. Nor do you buy a company that is too far away from your central base of operations. The latter makes a cultural fit less likely and severely limits the speed a company needs to compete in the new economy.

Chambers also believes that each deal must boast both short-term and long-term wins for customers, shareholders, and employees. "If there are no results in three to six months, people begin to question the acquisition," says Charles H. Giancarlo, vice-president for global alliances. "If you have good short-term wins, it's a virtuous cycle."

Through it all, the emphasis is on doing it faster, cheaper, and better—an integral part of success in the new economy. At Cisco, wages are less important than ownership. Some 40% of the stock options at the company are held by "individual contributors" who on average boast more than $150,000 in option gains. Egalitarianism is critical to successful teamwork and to morale. "You never ask your team to do something you wouldn't do yourself," says Chambers, who flies coach and has no reserved parking space at headquarters.

There are other leaders, of course, besides Chambers, who hope to create an organization that may very well revolutionize the fundamental business models of major global companies. But he's surely in the "sweet spot," helping to write the new rules for managing.

Source: John A. Byrne, "The Corporation of the Future," *Business Week,* August 31, 1998, 102, 104, 106.

Questions

1. What is Cisco Systems' approach to change?

2. How does Cisco Systems use technology to facilitate and promote change?

3. How does Cisco Systems ensure that it will have talented employees who will be able to keep up with and capitalize on the latest developments in the field?

Part 6

Chapter seventeen

Managing Information Systems and Technologies

Learning Objectives

1. Differentiate between data and information, and list the attributes of useful information.

2. Describe three reasons why managers must have access to information to perform their tasks and roles effectively.

3. Describe the computer hardware and software innovations that have created the information technology revolution.

4. Differentiate among five kinds of management information systems.

5. Explain how advances in information systems can give an organization a competitive advantage.

A Case in Contrast

Information Flows at Tel Co. and Soft Co.

Tel Co. (www.telco.com) is a division of a large telecommunications company. Despite being involved in the telecommunications industry, managers at Tel Co. have been slow to adopt an internal electronic mail system (e-mail) to facilitate communication throughout the company. Soft Co. (www.softco.com), in contrast, is a major software company in which managers virtually "live on line"; most communication between them takes place by means of e-mail. Commenting on how the two companies differ, a manager who moved from Tel Co. to Soft Co. said:

At Tel Co. I would take two boxes of memos and company reports home with me each weekend to read. Then I had to go through all this stuff, most of which was irrelevant to my job, to find those pieces of paper that mattered to me. It was very time-consuming, very unproductive. At Soft Co. there is no paper to take home; most communication takes place via the company's e-mail system. I use a software agent to scan all my incoming e-mail and prioritize it (a software agent is a computer program that can be used to perform certain tasks–such as sorting through and prioritizing incoming e-mail). This saves a massive amount of time. The system alerts me instantly to e-mail that is relevant to my job.[1]

This manager also noted that the use of an e-mail system led to other communications differences between the two companies. At Tel Co. communication is primarily vertical; middle managers send information up the organizational hierarchy, and top managers send their responses back down. At Soft Co., however, communication between managers at different levels has become far less structured, and because of the e-mail system there is much less emphasis on formal channels of communication. E-mail allows managers at any level to communicate easily with each other, so managers at Soft Co. communicate directly with whomever they need to contact in order to get the job done. Also, e-mail has resulted in much more cross-functional, horizontal communication because it is so easy for managers in different functions to communicate.

The observations of this manager about communication flows at Tel Co. and Soft Co. were confirmed in a study undertaken by Alta Analytics, a management consulting company.[2] Figure 17.1 shows maps of the communication flows between managers based in different departments at Tel Co. and Soft Co. The boxes in these two maps are employees grouped by function. To make these maps, Alta asked employees to name every manager with whom they had communication in any form—phone, meeting, memo, e-mail—in the past week. If two people agreed that they had three or more important contacts, the mapmakers drew a line between their boxes, indicating a significant link.

The differences between the two companies are immediately apparent. At Tel Co., the general manager communicated only with four senior functional managers, all of

Figure 17.1
Communication Flows at Tel Co. and Soft Co.

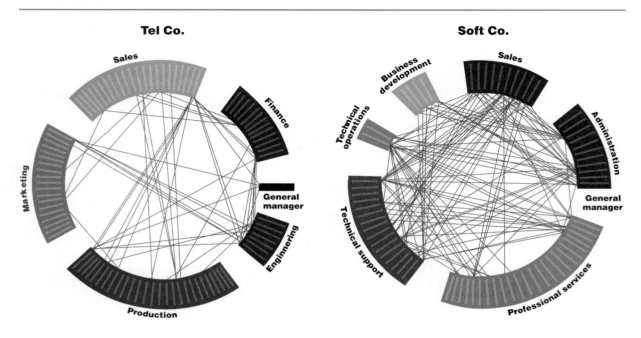

whom had a direct reporting relationship to him; there were hardly any links between the marketing and production departments; and a handful of functional managers accounted for most of the interfunctional communication. At Soft Co., there was a much richer flow of communication between managers in the different functions, as indicated by the number of lines connecting the different boxes. Clearly, boundaries between functions mean little at Soft Co., and so do differences in rank. Almost everybody talks to everybody else because of Soft Co.'s e-mail system.

Overview

The "Case in Contrast" describes differences in communication and coordination within two organizations—differences resulting from the information technology that each organization uses. Because of an e-mail system, the volume of cross-functional communication is much greater in Soft Co. than in Tel Co., and this difference has resulted in a higher level of innovation in Soft Co. than in Tel Co. Thus, the adoption of new information technology can help give an organization a competitive advantage and lead to high performance.

In this chapter we begin by surveying information systems and information technology in general, looking at the relationship between information and the manager's job and the nature of the current information technology revolution. Then we discuss several types of information systems that managers can use to help themselves perform their jobs, and we examine the impact that rapidly evolving information systems and technologies may have on managers' jobs and on an organization's competitive advantage. By the end of this chapter, you will understand the profound ways in which new developments in information systems and technology are shaping managers' functions and roles.

Information and the Manager's Job

data Raw, unsummarized, and unanalyzed facts.

information Data that is organized in a meaningful fashion.

Managers cannot plan, organize, lead, and control effectively unless they have access to information. Information is the source of the knowledge and intelligence that they need to make the right decisions. Information, however, is not the same as data.[3] **Data** is raw, unsummarized, and unanalyzed facts such as volume of sales, level of costs, or number of customers. **Information** is data that is organized in a meaningful fashion, such as in a graph showing the change in sales volume or costs over time. By itself, data does not tell managers anything; information, in contrast, can communicate a great deal of useful knowledge to the person who receives it—such as a manager who sees sales falling or costs rising. The distinction between data and information is important because one of the uses of information technology is to help managers transform data into information in order to make better managerial decisions.

To further clarify the difference between data and information, consider the case of a manager in a supermarket who must decide how much shelf space to allocate to two breakfast cereal brands for children: Dentist's Delight and Sugar Supreme. Most supermarkets use checkout scanners to record individual sales and store the data on a computer. Accessing this computer, the manager might find that Dentist's Delight sells 50 boxes per day and Sugar Supreme sells 25 boxes per day. This raw data, however, is of little help in assisting the manager to reach a decision about how to allocate shelf space. The manager also needs to know how much shelf space each cereal currently occupies and how much profit each cereal generates for the supermarket.

Suppose the manager discovers that Dentist's Delight occupies 10 feet of shelf space and Sugar Supreme occupies 4 feet and that Dentist's Delight generates 20 cents of profit a box while Sugar Supreme generates 40 cents of profit a box. By putting these three bits of *data* together (number of boxes sold, amount of shelf space, and profit per box), the manager gets some useful *information* on which to base a decision: Dentist's Delight generates $1 of profit per foot of shelf space per day [(50 boxes @ $.20)/10 feet], and Sugar Supreme generates $2.50 of profit per foot of shelf space per day [(25 boxes @ $.40)/4 feet]. Armed with this information, the manager might decide to allocate less shelf space to Dentist's Delight and more to Sugar Supreme.

Attributes of Useful Information

Four factors determine the usefulness of information to a manager: quality, timeliness, completeness, and relevance (see Figure 17.2).

QUALITY   Accuracy and reliability determine the quality of information.[4] The greater accuracy and reliability are, the higher is the quality of information. For an information system to work well, the information that it provides

Figure 17.2
Factors Affecting the Usefulness of Information

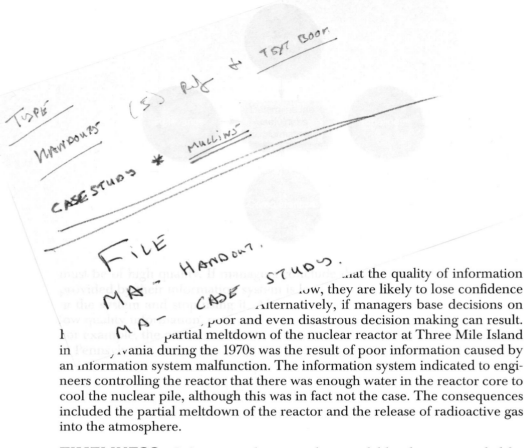

...that the quality of information provided by their information system is low, they are likely to lose confidence in the system and stop using it. Alternatively, if managers base decisions on low-quality information, poor and even disastrous decision making can result. For example, the partial meltdown of the nuclear reactor at Three Mile Island in Pennsylvania during the 1970s was the result of poor information caused by an information system malfunction. The information system indicated to engineers controlling the reactor that there was enough water in the reactor core to cool the nuclear pile, although this was in fact not the case. The consequences included the partial meltdown of the reactor and the release of radioactive gas into the atmosphere.

TIMELINESS   Information that is timely is available when it is needed for managerial action, not after the decision has been made. In today's rapidly changing world, the need for timely information often means that information must be available on a real-time basis.[5] **Real-time information** is information that reflects current conditions. In an industry that experiences rapid changes, real-time information may need to be updated frequently.

Airlines use real-time information on the number of flight bookings and competitors' prices to adjust their prices on an hour-to-hour basis to maximize their revenues. Thus, for example, the fare for flights from New York to Seattle might change from one hour to the next as fares are reduced to fill empty seats and raised when most seats have been sold. Airlines use real-time information on reservations to adjust fares at the last possible moment to fill planes and maximize revenues. In 1996 airlines in the United States made more than 80,000 fare changes each day.[6] Obviously, the managers who make such pricing decisions need real-time information about the current state of demand in the marketplace.

COMPLETENESS   Information that is complete gives managers all the information they need to exercise control, achieve coordination, or make an

real-time information
Frequently updated information that reflects current conditions.

effective decision. Recall from Chapter 6, however, that managers rarely have access to complete information. Instead, because of uncertainty, ambiguity, and bounded rationality, they have to make do with incomplete information.[7] One of the functions of information systems is to increase the completeness of the information that managers have at their disposal.

RELEVANCE Information that is relevant is useful and suits a manager's particular needs and circumstances. Irrelevant information is useless and may actually hurt the performance of a busy manager who has to spend valuable time determining whether information is relevant. Given the massive amounts of information that managers are now exposed to and humans' limited information-processing capabilities, the people who design information systems need to make sure that managers receive only relevant information.

The manager quoted in the "Case in Contrast" mentioned that Soft Co. uses a "software agent" to scan incoming e-mail and prioritize it. A *software agent* is a software program that can be used to perform simple tasks such as scanning incoming information for relevance, taking some of the burden away from managers. Moreover, by recording and analyzing a manager's own efforts to prioritize incoming information, the software agent can "learn" about the manager's preferences and thus perform such tasks more effectively. For example, the software agent can automatically reprogram itself to place incoming e-mail from the manager's boss at the top of the pile.[8]

Information Systems and Technology

information system A system for acquiring, organizing, storing, manipulating, and transmitting information.

An **information system** is a system for acquiring, organizing, storing, manipulating, and transmitting information.[9] A **management information system** (**MIS**) is an information system that managers plan and design to provide themselves with the specific information they need to perform their roles effectively. Information systems have existed for as long as there have been organizations—a long time indeed. Before the computer age, most information systems were paper based: Clerks recorded important information on documents (often in duplicate or triplicate) in the form of words and numbers, sent a copy of the document to superiors, customers, or suppliers, as the case might be, and stored other copies in files for future reference.

management information system An information system that managers plan and design to provide themselves with the specific information they need.

information technology The means by which information is acquired, organized, stored, manipulated, and transmitted.

Information technology is the means by which information is acquired, organized, stored, manipulated, and transmitted. Rapid advances in the power of information technology—specifically, through the use of computers—are having a fundamental impact on information systems and on managers and their organizations.[10] So important are these advances in information technology that many experts argue that organizations that, like Tel Co., do not adopt new information technology will become uncompetitive with those that do.[11] Managers need information for three reasons: to make effective decisions; to control the activities of the organization; and to coordinate the activities of the organization.

Information and Decisions

Much of management (planning, organizing, leading, and controlling) is about making decisions. For example, the marketing manager must decide what price to charge for a product, what distribution channels to use, and what promotional messages to emphasize. The manufacturing manager must decide how much of a product to make and how to make it. The purchasing manager must decide from whom to purchase inputs and what inventory of inputs to hold. The human relations manager must decide how much employees should be paid, how they should be trained, and what benefits they should be given. The engineering manager must make decisions about new product design. Top managers must decide how to allocate scarce financial resources among competing projects, how best to structure and control the organization, and what business-level strategy the organization should be pursuing. And, regardless of their functional orientation, all managers have to make decisions about matters such as what performance evaluation to give to a subordinate.

Decision making cannot be effective in an information vacuum. To make effective decisions, managers need information, both from inside the organization and from external stakeholders. When deciding how to price a product, for example, the marketing manager needs information about how consumers will react to different prices. She needs information about unit costs because she does not want to set the price below the costs of production. And she needs information about competitive strategy, since pricing strategy should be consistent with an organization's competitive strategy. Some of this information will come from outside the organization (for example, from consumer surveys) and some from inside the organization (information about unit production costs comes from manufacturing). As this example suggests, managers' ability to make effective decisions rests on their ability to acquire and process information.

Information and Control

As discussed in Chapter 9, *controlling* is the process whereby managers regulate how efficiently and effectively an organization and its members are performing the activities necessary to achieve organizational goals.[12] Managers achieve control over organizational activities by taking four steps (see Figure 9.2): (1) They establish measurable standards of performance or goals. (2) They measure actual performance. (3) They compare actual performance against established goals. (4) They evaluate the result and take corrective action if necessary.[13] Airborne Express, for example, has a delivery goal: to deliver 95 percent of the packages it picks up by noon the next day. Throughout the United States, Airborne has thousands of ground stations (branch offices that coordinate the pickup and delivery of packages in a particular area) that are responsible for the physical pickup and delivery of packages. Airborne managers monitor the delivery performance of these stations on a regular basis; if they find that the 95 percent goal is not being attained, they determine why and take corrective action if necessary.[14]

To achieve control over any organizational activity, managers must have information. To control a ground station, a manager at Airborne needs to know how many of that station's packages are being delivered by noon.

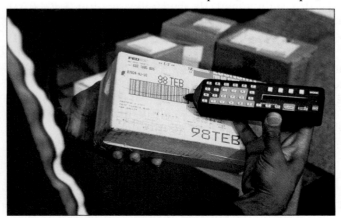

This photo shows an example of a FedEx employee scanning a bar code on a package using a portable tracking computer.

To get this information, the manager needs to make sure that an information system is in place. Packages to be shipped by Airborne are scanned with a hand-held scanner by the Airborne Express driver who first picks them up. The pickup information is sent by a wireless link to a central computer at Airborne's Seattle headquarters. The packages are scanned again by the truck driver when they are delivered. The delivery information is also transmitted to Airborne's central computer. By accessing the central computer, a manager can quickly find out not only what percentage of packages are delivered by noon of the day after they were picked up but also how this information breaks down on a station-by-station basis.

Management information systems are used to control a variety of operations within organizations. In accounting, for example, information systems can be used to monitor expenditures and compare them against budgets.[15] To track expenditures against budgets, managers need information on current expenditures, broken down by relevant organizational units. Accounting information systems are designed to provide managers with such information. Another example of an information system, one that is used to monitor and control the daily activities of employees, is discussed in this "Management Insight."

Management Insight

Information Systems and Control at Cypress Semiconductor

In the fast-moving semiconductor business a premium is placed on organizational adaptability. At Cypress Semiconductor (www.cypress.com), CEO T. J. Rodgers was facing a problem. How could he control his growing, 1,500-employee organization without developing a bureaucratic management hierarchy? Rodgers believed that a tall hierarchy hinders the ability of an organization to adapt to changing conditions. He was committed to maintaining a flat and decentralized organizational structure with a minimum of management layers. At the same time, he needed to control his employees to ensure that they perform in a manner that is consistent with the goals of the company. How could he achieve this without resorting to direct supervision and the management hierarchy that it implies?

The solution that Rodgers adopted was to implement a computer-based information system through which he can manage what every employee and team is doing in his fast-moving and decentralized organization. Each employee maintains a list of 10 to 15 goals, such as "Meet with marketing for new product launch" or "Make sure to check with customer X." Noted next to each goal is when it was agreed upon, when it is due to be finished, and whether it has been finished. All of this information is stored on a central computer. Rodgers claims that he can review the goals of all 1,500 employees in about four hours, and he does so each week.[16] How is this possible? He manages by exception and looks only for employees who are falling behind. He then calls them, not to scold but to ask whether there is anything he can do to help them get the job done. It takes only about half an hour each week for employees to review and update their lists. This system allows Rodgers to exercise control over his organization without resorting to the expensive layers of a management hierarchy.

Information and Coordination

Coordinating department and divisional activities to achieve organizational goals is another basic task of management. As an extreme example of the size of the coordination task that managers face, consider the coordination effort involved in building Boeing's new commercial jet aircraft, the 777. The 777 is composed of 3 million individual parts and thousands of major components. Managers at Boeing have to coordinate the production and delivery of all of these parts so that they all arrive at Boeing's Everett, Washington, facility exactly when they are needed (for example, they want the wings to arrive before the engines). Boeing managers jokingly refer to this task as "coordinating 3 million parts in flying formation." To achieve this high level of coordination, managers need information about which supplier is producing what, when it is to be produced, and when it is to be delivered. Managers also need this information so that they are able to track the delivery performance of suppliers against expectations and receive advance warning of any likely problems. To meet these needs, managers at Boeing established a computer-based information system that links Boeing to all its suppliers and can track the flow of 3 million component parts through the production process—an immense task.

Nowadays the coordination problems that managers face are complicated by organizations' expansion of operations abroad to take advantage of national differences in the costs of production. To deal with global coordination problems, managers have been adopting sophisticated computer-based information systems that help them coordinate the flow of materials, semifinished goods, and finished products around the world. The computer-based information system used by Bose Corporation, profiled in this "Managing Globally," illustrates the nature of the global coordination problem.

Managing Globally

Coordinating Global Production Flows at Bose Corporation

Bose Corporation (www.bose.com) of Boston, Massachusetts, manufactures some of the world's best-known high-fidelity speakers. Bose purchases most of the electronic and nonelectronic components for its speakers from independent suppliers. About 50 percent of its purchases are from foreign suppliers, the majority of which are in the Far East. The challenge for managers is to coordinate this globally dispersed supply chain to minimize Bose's inventory and transportation costs. Minimizing these costs requires that component parts arrive at Bose's assembly plant just in time to enter the production process and not before. Bose also has to remain responsive to customer demands. This requirement means that the company has to respond quickly to increases in demand for certain kinds of speakers, such as outdoor speakers in the summer. Failure to respond quickly can cause the loss of a big order to competitors. Since Bose does not want to hold extensive inventories at its Massachusetts plant, the need to remain responsive to customer demands requires that Bose's suppliers be able to respond rapidly to increased demand for component parts.

The responsibility for coordinating the supply chain to simultaneously minimize inventory and transportation costs and respond quickly to customer demands belongs to Bose's logistics managers, who have contracted with W. N. Procter, a Boston-based freight forwarder and customs broker, to develop a sophisticated logistics information system. Procter offers Bose up-to-the-minute electronic data interchange (EDI) capabilities, which give Bose the real-time information it needs to track parts as they move through the global supply chain. The EDI system is known as ProcterLink. When a shipment leaves a supplier, it is logged into ProcterLink.[17] From that point on, Bose can track the supplies as they move across the globe toward Massachusetts. This system allows Bose to fine-tune its production scheduling so that supplies enter the production process exactly when they are needed.

How well this system can work was illustrated recently when one Japanese customer doubled its order for Bose speakers. Bose had to gear up its manufacturing in a hurry, but many of its components were stretched out across long distances. By using ProcterLink, Bose was able to locate the needed parts in its supply chain. It then broke them out of the normal delivery chain and moved them by air freight to get them to the assembly line in time for the accelerated schedule. As a result, Bose was able to meet the request of its customer.

An interesting aspect of the Bose example concerns not only how Bose uses information systems to achieve coordination but also how these same systems allow the company to improve its responsiveness to customers, minimize its costs, and thus improve its competitive position. The link between information systems and competitive position is an important one that may determine the success or failure of organizations in an increasingly competitive global environment.

The Information Technology Revolution

Computer-based information technology is an enabling technology. It has allowed managers to develop computer-based management information systems that provide timely, complete, relevant, and high-quality information. To better understand the current revolution in information technology, in this section we examine several key aspects of computer-based information technology.

The Tumbling Price of Information

The information technology revolution began with the development of the first computers—the hardware of computer-based information technology—in the 1950s. The language of computers is a *digital language* of zeros and ones. Words, numbers, images, and sound can all be expressed in zeros and ones. Each letter in the alphabet has its own unique code of zeros and ones, as does each number, each color, and each sound. For example, the digital code for the number 20 is 10100. In the language of computers it takes a lot of zeros and ones to express even a simple sentence, to say nothing of complex color graphics or

Figure 17.3
The Price–Performance Ratio of Computers

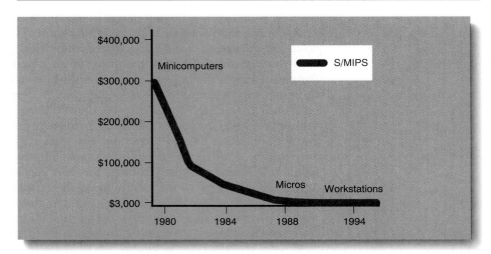

Source: Adapted from J. J. Donovan, *Business Re-engineering with Information Technology* (Englewood Cliffs, NJ: Prentice-Hall, 1994), 24.

moving video images. Nevertheless, modern computers can read, process, and store millions of instructions per second (an instruction is a line of software code) and thus vast amounts of zeros and ones. It is this awesome power that forms the foundation of the current information technology revolution.

The brains of modern computers are microprocessors (Intel's 386, 486, and Pentium chips are microprocessors). Over the last 25 years the power of microprocessors has doubled every 18 months, and the cost of producing them has been cut in half every 2 years or so. The result has been a rapid fall in the price and a rapid rise in the performance of computers (see Figure 17.3). The costs of acquiring, organizing, storing, and transmitting information have tumbled. If prices continue to fall, computers soon will become as common as wristwatches–everyone who wants one will be able to afford one.[18] In addition, advances in microprocessor technology have led to dramatic reductions in the cost of communication *between* computers, which also have contributed to the falling price of information and information systems.[19]

Wireless Communications

Another trend of considerable significance for information systems has been the rapid growth of wireless communication technologies, particularly cellular communications. Cellular service was first offered in the United States in 1983. Initially, growth was slow, but since 1990 cellular service has spread rapidly. In 1984 there were 100,000 cellular subscribers in the United States; by 1993 this figure had mushroomed to 19 million. Some projections suggest that the number of cellular subscribers in the United States will triple by the year 2000 to more than 21 percent of the population, or 60 million people; a similar explosion in demand is expected in other countries.[20]

Wireless communication is significant for the information technology revolution because it facilitates the linking together of computers, which greatly increases their power and adaptability. It is already possible to purchase a battery-operated laptop computer that has a wireless modem built in to facilitate communication with a "home" computer. An engineer or salesperson working in the field can send information to, and receive information from, the home office by using the wireless capabilities built into his or her computer. Because a computer no longer has to be plugged into a hard-wired telephone line, accessing a large computer-based information system is much easier than it used to be.

Computer Networks

networking The exchange of information through a group or network of interlinked computers.

The tumbling price of computing power and information and the use of wireless communication channels has facilitated **networking,** the exchange of information through a group or network of interlinked computers. The most common arrangement now emerging is a three-tier network consisting of clients, servers, and a mainframe (see Figure 17.4). At the outer nodes of a typical three-tier network are the *personal computers (PCs)* that sit on the desks of individual users. These personal computers, referred to as *clients,* are linked to a local *server,* a high-powered midrange computer that "serves" the client personal computers. Servers often store power-hungry software programs that can be run more effectively on the server than on an individual's personal computer. Servers may also manage several printers that can be used by hundreds of clients, store data files, and handle e-mail communications between

Figure 17.4
A Typical Three-Tier Information System

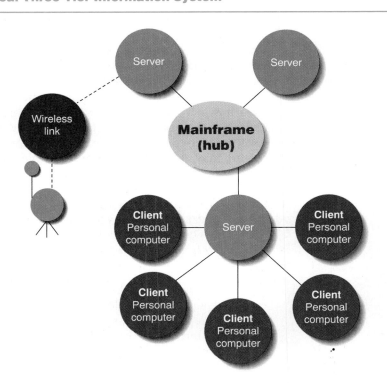

clients. The client computers linked directly to a server constitute a *local area network (LAN)*. Within any organization there may be several LANs–for example, one in every division and function.

At the hub of a three-tier system are mainframe computers. *Mainframes* are large and powerful computers that can be used to store and process vast amounts of information. The mainframe can also be used to handle electronic communications between personal computers situated in different LANs. In addition, the mainframe may be connected to mainframes in other organizations and, through them, to LANs in other organizations. Increasingly, the Internet, a worldwide network of interlinked computers, is used as the conduit for connecting the computer systems of different organizations (see Chapter 15).

A manager with a personal computer hooked into a three-tier system can access data and software stored in the local server, in the mainframe, or, through the Internet, in computers based in another organization. A manager can therefore communicate electronically with other individuals hooked into the system, whether they are in the manager's LAN, in another LAN within the manager's organization, or in another organization altogether. Moreover, because of the growth of wireless communications, an individual with the proper equipment can hook into the system from any location–at home, on a boat, on the beach, in the air–anywhere a wireless communications link can be established.

Software Developments

If computer hardware has been developing rapidly, so has computer software. **Operating system software** tells the computer hardware how to run. **Applications software,** such as programs for word processing, spreadsheets, graphics, and database management, is software developed for a specific task or use. The increase in the power of computer hardware has allowed software developers to write increasingly powerful programs that are, at the same time, increasingly user-friendly. By harnessing the rapidly growing power of microprocessors, this applications software has vastly increased the ability of managers to acquire, organize, manipulate, and transmit information. In doing so, it also has increased the ability of managers to coordinate and control the activities of their organization and to make decisions. The way in which IBM uses computer-controlled information systems and wireless communications to coordinate and control the flow of production in an automated factory illustrates how profound the change taking place in information technology is.

operating system software Software that tells computer hardware how to run.

applications software Software designed for a specific task or use.

Management Insight

IBM's Digital Factory

At IBM's personal computer factory (www.ibm.com) in Triangle Park, North Carolina, rows of sales reps answer about 5,000 customer calls a day and take customized orders for various models of IBM's PCs. As they talk, the sales reps enter the specific details of a customer's order on their own computer terminals. For example, a customer may order a PC that contains a Pentium 200 microprocessor, 32 megabytes of memory, a 250-megabyte hard drive, a built-in fax modem, and so on. Each sales rep's computer is linked to an inventory control computer system through a local area network, so the rep can relay immediately to the customer information about whether the parts needed to assemble the customized computer are in stock. Completed orders are sent through the LAN to the computer that controls assembly-line operations.

The assembly-line computer checks for new incoming orders every 10 minutes. Every time it receives a new order, the computer sends a radio signal over a wireless link to employees, called "kitters," on the assembly floor. A kitter receives data on a handheld bar-code reader (which is a miniature computer) and moves from one bar-code location to the next to pick up the various parts that a particular customer requires. When a complete kit has been gathered, the kitter takes it to an assembly station.[21]

As the PC is assembled, an assembly-line worker scans the bar code on each part to tell the inventory control computer that the part has been used. Soon the new PC travels down the line to be automatically tested and packaged for delivery to the customer—next day service by Airborne Express is available if the customer has requested it. Explaining this system, Barry Eveland, vice president for order fulfillment, says, "In plants like this we may be seeing the merger of a manufacturing plant with a retail store."

artificial intelligence

Behavior performed by a machine that, if performed by a human being, would be called intelligent.

Artificial intelligence is another interesting and potentially fruitful software development. **Artificial intelligence** has been defined as behavior by a machine that, if performed by a human being, would be called intelligent.[22] Artificial intelligence has already made it possible to write programs that can solve problems and perform simple tasks. For example, software programs variously called "software agents," "softbots," or "knowbots" can be used to perform simple managerial tasks such as sorting through reams of data or incoming e-mail messages to look for important data and messages. The interesting feature of these programs is that from "watching" a manager sort through such data they can "learn" what his or her preferences are. Having done this, they then can take over some of this work from the manager, freeing up more time to work on other tasks. Most of these programs are still in the development stage, but they may be commonplace within a decade.[23]

Another software development that is starting to have an impact on the manager's job is speech recognition software. Currently speech recognition software must be "trained" to recognize and understand each individual's voice, and it requires the speaker to pause after each word. The increasing power of microprocessors, however, is allowing for the development of faster speech recognition programs that can handle more variables and much greater complexity. It is not inconceivable that the time will come soon when a manager driving down the road may be able to communicate with his or her computer through a wireless link and give that computer voice instructions.[24]

In conclusion, as an example of the possibilities created by the combination of ever-more-powerful hardware and software, consider the following vision of a manager's life in the year 2000 offered by researchers at MIT's Center for Information Systems Research:

It's a Monday morning in the year 2000. Executive Joanne Smith gets into her car and voice activates her remote telecommunications access workstation. She requests all voice and mail messages, open and pending, as well as her schedule for the day. Her workstation consolidates the items from home and office databases, and her message ordering knowbot, a program she has instructed, delivers the accumulated messages in the order she prefers. By the time Joanne gets to the office she has sent the necessary messages, revised her day's schedule, and completed a to-do list for the week, all of which have been filed in her virtual database by her personal organizer knowbot.[25]

Is this vision of modern management information systems science fiction? Right now it is, but within a decade it easily could be science fact.

Types of Management Information Systems

Four types of computer-based management information systems can be particularly helpful in providing managers with the information they need to make decisions and to coordinate and control organizational resources: transaction-processing systems, operations information systems, decision support systems, and expert systems (see Figure 17.5). These systems are arranged along a continuum according to their increasing usefulness in providing managers with the information they need to make nonprogrammed decisions. (Recall from Chapter 6 that *nonprogrammed* decision making occurs in response to unusual, unpredictable opportunities and threats.) We examine each of these below. But first it is useful to focus on the management information system that preceded them all: the organizational hierarchy.

The Organizational Hierarchy: The Traditional Information System

Traditionally, managers have used the organizational hierarchy as a system for gathering the information they need to achieve coordination and control and make decisions (see Chapter 8 for a detailed discussion of organizational structure and hierarchy). According to business historian Alfred Chandler, the use of the hierarchy as an information network was perfected by railroad companies in the United States during the 1850s.[26] At that time, the railroads were the largest industrial organizations in the United States. By virtue of their size and geographical spread they faced unique problems of coordination and control. In the 1850s, railroad companies started to solve these problems by designing hierarchical management structures that provided senior managers

Figure 17.5

Four Computer-Based Management Information Systems

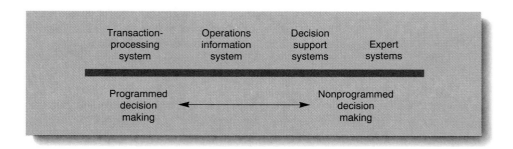

with the information they needed to achieve coordination and control and to make decisions about the running of the railroads.

Daniel McCallum, superintendent of the Erie Railroad in the 1850s, realized that the lines of authority and responsibility defining the Erie's management hierarchy also represented channels of communication along which information traveled. McCallum established what was perhaps the first modern management information system. Regular daily and monthly reports were fed up the management chain so that top managers could make decisions about, for example, controlling costs and setting freight rates. Decisions were then relayed back down the hierarchy so they could be carried out. Imitating the railroads, most other organizations used their hierarchies as systems for collecting and channeling information. This practice began to change only when electronic information technologies became more reasonably priced in the 1960s.

Although hierarchy is a useful information system, several drawbacks are associated with it. First, in organizations with many layers of managers, it can take a long time for information to travel up the hierarchy and for decisions to travel back down. This slow pace can reduce the *timeliness* and usefulness of that information and prevent an organization from responding quickly to changing market conditions.[27] Second, information can be distorted as it moves from one layer of management to another, and information distortion reduces the *quality* of information.[28] Third, because managers have only a limited span of control, as an organization grows larger its hierarchy lengthens and this tall structure can make the hierarchy a very expensive information system. The popular idea that companies with tall management hierarchies are bureaucratic and unresponsive to the needs of their customers arises from the inability of tall hierarchies to effectively process data and provide managers with timely, complete, relevant, and high-quality information. Until modern computer-based information systems came along, however, the management hierarchy was the best information system available.

Transaction-Processing Systems

A **transaction-processing system** is a system designed to handle large volumes of routine, recurring transactions (see Figure 17.5). Transaction-processing systems began to appear in the early 1960s with the advent of commercially available mainframe computers. They were the first type of computer-based management information system adopted by many organizations, and today they are commonplace. Bank managers use a transaction-processing system to record deposits into, and payments out of, bank accounts. Supermarket managers use a transaction-processing system to record the sale of items and to track inventory levels. More generally, most managers in large organizations use a transaction-processing system to handle tasks such as payroll preparation and payment, customer billing, and payment of suppliers.

Operations Information Systems

Many types of management information systems followed hard on the heels of transaction-processing systems in the 1960s. An **operations information system** is a system that gathers comprehensive data, organizes it, and summarizes it

operations information system

A management information system that gathers, organizes, and summarizes comprehensive data in a form that managers can use in their nonroutine coordinating, controlling, and decision-making tasks.

in a form that is of value to managers. Whereas a transaction-processing system processes *routine* transactions, an operations information system provides managers with information that they can use in their *nonroutine* coordinating, controlling, and decision-making tasks. Most operations information systems are coupled with a transaction-processing system. An operations information system typically accesses the data that is gathered by a transaction-processing system, processes that data into useful information, and organizes that information into a form that is accessible to managers. Managers often use an operations information system to get sales, inventory, accounting, and other performance-related information. For example, the information that T. J. Rodgers at Cypress Semiconductors gets on individual employee goals and performance is provided by an operations information system.

Airborne Express uses an operations information system to track the performance of its 500 or so ground stations. Each ground station is evaluated according to four criteria: delivery (the goal is to deliver 95 percent of all packages by noon the day after they were picked up), productivity (measured by the number of packages shipped per employee hour), controllable cost, and station profitability. Each ground station also has specific delivery, efficiency, cost, and profitability targets that it must attain. Every month Airborne's operations information system is used to gather information on these four criteria and summarize it for top managers, who are then able to compare the performance of each station against its previously established targets. The system quickly alerts senior managers to underperforming ground stations, so they can intervene selectively to help solve any problems that may have given rise to the poor performance.[29]

Decision Support Systems

decision support system An interactive computer-based management information system that managers can use to make nonroutine decisions.

A **decision support system** is an interactive computer-based system that provides models that help managers make better nonprogrammed decisions.[30] Recall from Chapter 6 that *nonprogrammed decisions* are decisions that are relatively unusual or novel, such as decisions to invest in new productive capacity, develop a new product, launch a new promotional campaign, enter a new market, or expand internationally. Although an operations information system organizes important information for managers, a decision support system gives managers a model-building capability and so provides them with the ability to manipulate information in a variety of ways. Managers might use a decision support system to help them decide whether to cut prices for a product. The decision support system might contain models of how customers and competitors would respond to a price cut. Managers could run these models and use the results as an *aid* to decision making.

The stress on the word *aid* is important, for in the final analysis a decision support system is not meant to make decisions for managers. Rather, its function is to provide managers with valuable information that they can use to improve the quality of their decisions. A good example of a sophisticated decision support system, developed by Judy Lewent, chief financial officer of the U.S. pharmaceutical company Merck, is given in the next "Management Insight."

Management Insight

How Judy Lewent Became One of the Most Powerful Women in Corporate America

With annual sales of over $30 billion, Merck (www.merck.com) is one of the world's largest developers and marketers of advanced pharmaceuticals. In 1994, the company spent over $2 billion on R&D to develop new drugs—an expensive and difficult process that is fraught with risks. Most new drug ideas fail to make it through the development process. It takes an average of $300 million and 10 years to bring a new drug to market, and 7 out of 10 new drugs fail to make a profit for the developing company.

Given the costs, risks, and uncertainties involved in the new drug development process, 10 years ago Judy Lewent, then director of capital analysis at Merck, decided to develop a decision support system that could be used to help managers make more effective R&D investment decisions. Her aim was to give Merck's top managers the information they needed to evaluate proposed R&D projects on a case-by-case basis. The system that Lewent and her staff developed is referred to in Merck as the "Research Planning Model."[31] At the heart of this decision support system is a sophisticated model. The input variables to the model include data on R&D spending, manufacturing costs, selling costs, and demand conditions. The relationships between the input variables are modeled by means of several equations that factor in the probability of a drug's making it through the development process and to market. The outputs of this modeling process are the revenues, cash flows, and profits that a project might generate.

The Merck model does not use a single value for an input variable, nor does it compute a single value for each output. Rather, a range is specified for each input variable (such as high, medium, and low R&D spending). The computer repeatedly samples at random from the range of values for each input variable and produces a probability distribution of values for each output. So, for example, instead of stating categorically that a proposed R&D project will yield a profit of $500 million, the decision support system produces a probability distribution that might state that although $500 million is the most likely profit, there is a 25 percent chance that the profit will be less than $300 million and a 25 percent chance that it will be greater than $700 million.

Merck now uses Lewent's decision support system to evaluate all proposed R&D investment decisions. In addition, Lewent has developed other decision support system models that Merck's managers can use to help them decide, for example, whether to enter into joint ventures with other companies or how best to hedge foreign exchange risk. As for Lewent, her reward was promotion to the position of chief financial officer of Merck. The 45-year-old Lewent, now the only woman to hold the title *chief financial officer* at a major corporation, is one of the most powerful women in corporate America.

executive support system A sophisticated version of a decision support system that is designed to meet the needs of top managers.

group decision support system An executive support system that links top managers so that they can function as a team.

Most decision support systems are geared toward aiding middle managers in the decision-making process. For example, a loan manager at a bank might use a decision support system to evaluate the credit risk involved in lending money to a particular client. Very rarely does a top manager use a decision support system. One reason for this may be that most electronic management information systems are not yet sophisticated enough to handle effectively the ambiguous types of problems facing top managers. To improve this situation, information systems professionals have been developing a variant of the decision support system: an executive support system.

An **executive support system** is a sophisticated version of a decision support system that is designed to meet the needs of top managers. Lewent's "Research Planning Model" is actually an executive support system. One of the defining characteristics of executive support systems is user-friendliness. Many of them include simple pull-down menus to take a manager through a decision analysis problem. Moreover, they may contain stunning graphics and other visual features to encourage top managers to use them.[32] Increasingly, executive support systems are being used to link top managers so that they can function as a team, and this type of executive support system is called a **group decision support system.**

Expert Systems and Artificial Intelligence

Expert systems are the most advanced management information systems available. An **expert system** is a system that employs human knowledge captured in a computer to solve problems that ordinarily require human expertise.[33] Expert systems are a variant of artificial intelligence.[34] Mimicking human expertise (and intelligence) requires a computer that can at a minimum (1) recognize, formulate, and solve a problem, (2) explain the solution, and (3) learn from experience.

expert system A management information system that employs human knowledge captured in a computer to solve problems that ordinarily require human expertise.

Recent developments in artificial intelligence that go by names such as "fuzzy logic" and "neural networks" have resulted in computer programs that, in a primitive way, try to mimic human thought processes. Although artificial intelligence is still at a fairly early stage of development, an increasing number of business applications are beginning to emerge in the form of expert systems. General Electric, for example, has developed an expert system to help troubleshoot problems in the diesel locomotive engines it manufactures. The expert system was originally based on knowledge collected from David Smith, GE's top locomotive troubleshooter, who retired in the 1980s after 40 years of service at GE. A novice engineer or technician can use the system to uncover a fault by spending only a few minutes at a computer terminal. The system also can explain to the user the logic of its advice, thereby serving as a teacher as well as a problem solver. The system is based on a flexible, humanlike thought process, and it can be updated to incorporate new knowledge as it becomes available. GE has installed the system in every railroad repair shop that it serves, thus eliminating delays and boosting maintenance productivity.[35]

The Impact and Limitations of Information Systems and Technology

The advances in management information systems and technology described in this chapter are having important effects on managers and organizations. By improving the ability of managers to coordinate and control the activities of the organization, and by helping managers make more effective decisions, modern computer-based information systems have become a central component of any organization's structure. And evidence that information systems can be a source of competitive advantage is growing; organizations that do not adopt leading-edge information systems are likely to be at a competitive disadvantage. In this section we examine how the rapid growth of computerized information systems is affecting organizational structure and competitive advantage. We also examine problems associated with implementing management information systems effectively, as well as their limitations.

Information Systems and Organizational Structure

Until the development of modern computer-based information systems, there was no viable alternative to the organizational hierarchy, despite the information problems associated with it. The rapid rise of computer-based information systems has been associated with a "delayering" (flattening) of the organizational hierarchy and a move toward greater decentralization and horizontal information flows within organizations (see Figure 17.6).[36]

Figure 17.6
How Computer-Based Information Systems Affect
the Organizational Hierarchy

Before

Tall structure
primarily up-down
communication

After

Flat structure
both up-down
and lateral
communication

FLATTENING ORGANIZATIONS   By electronically providing managers with high-quality, timely, relevant, and relatively complete information, modern management information systems have reduced the need for tall management hierarchies. Consider again the computer-based operations information system that T. J. Rodgers uses at Cypress Semiconductor to review the performance of his 1,500 employees. Ten years ago, Rodgers might have needed 100 managers to conduct such performance reviews; now he can do them himself in four hours a week. Modern information systems have reduced the need for a hierarchy to function as a means to control the activities of the organization. In addition, they have reduced the need for a management hierarchy to coordinate organizational activities. At both Bose and IBM, for example, information systems have reduced the need for managers to coordinate the flow of production.

HORIZONTAL INFORMATION FLOWS   Fired by the growth of three-tier mainframe–server–client computing architecture (see Figure 17.4), expansion of organizationwide computer networks has been rapid in recent years. E-mail systems, the development of software programs for sharing documents electronically, and the development of intranets (see Chapter 15) have accelerated this trend. An important consequence has been to increase horizontal information flows within organizations. The "Case in Contrast" contrasts the horizontal and vertical information flows in Soft Co. (which has an e-mail system) with the vertical flows in Tel Co. (which relies on the organizational hierarchy).

The inference that is often drawn from the comparison of companies such as Tel Co. and Soft Co. is that the development of organizationwide computer networks is breaking down the barriers that have traditionally separated departments.[37] If this is the case, the result should be improved performance, for achieving superior efficiency, quality, innovation, and customer responsiveness that requires managers to break down the barriers between departments. Organizationwide computer networks are a tool for doing this.

Information Systems and Competitive Advantage

State-of-the-art information technology can improve the competitiveness of an organization. Indeed, the search for competitive advantage is driving much of the rapid development and adoption of such systems. By improving the decision-making capability of managers, for example, management information systems like executive support systems and decision support systems should help an organization enhance its competitive position. Similarly, by reducing the need for hierarchy, modern information systems can directly increase an organization's efficiency. One reason for an increase in efficiency is that the use of advanced information systems can reduce the number of employees required to perform organizational activities. At one time, for example, 13 layers of management separated Eastman Kodak's general manager of manufacturing and factory workers. Now, with the help of information systems, the number of layers is 4. Similarly, Intel found that by increasing the sophistication of its information systems it could cut the number of hierarchical layers in the organization from 10 to 5.[38]

Moreover, by increasing horizontal information flows, and helping to break down the barriers that separate departments, computer networks are allowing managers to boost quality, innovation, and responsiveness to customers. The experience of Lotus Development Corporation, the company that developed Lotus Notes, illustrates how information systems can speed product development. Using their own Notes technology, Lotus's managers found that software writers in Asia and Europe can work almost in parallel with their U.S. counterparts, sharing documentation and messages among themselves on a real-time basis. As a result, a Japanese version of a new product can be introduced within three or four weeks of its English-language release, instead of the three or four months that were necessary before the adoption of Notes.[39]

William Davidow and Michael Malone, co-authors of *The Virtual Corporation,* coined the term *virtual products* to describe another way in which information systems can be used to improve an organization's responsiveness to customers. They argue that information systems and technology are allowing companies to customize their product offerings without incurring any extra cost penalty. IBM's digital factory illustrates their argument. IBM managers have developed an information system that is able to customize personal computers to the needs of individual customers, and to do so at no extra cost. Levi Strauss & Co.'s use of advanced information systems to produce made-to-order jeans, thereby boosting its responsiveness to customers, is another example of how information systems can help to build a competitive advantage.

Management Insight

Levi's® Personal Pair™ Made-to-Order Jeans

In November 1994, Levi Strauss & Co. (www.levi.com) began the introduction of a system that could change the face of apparel retailing. Levi Strauss & Co. had long been aware that women often complained about the difficulty of finding off-the-rack jeans that fit properly. Now advances in information technology may be allowing Levi Strauss & Co. to do something about it. Using the new technology, a fit specialist at an Original Levi's® Store can use a personal computer to input the customer's vital statistics and create what amounts to a digital blue-jeans blueprint. A touch-screen software system leads a fit specialist through the fitting process and requires no special computer skills. The software allows for 20,000 possible combinations of four basic measurements: hips, waist, inseam, and rise. The fit specialist gets these measurements with a tape measure and enters them into the personal computer, along with other desired features (such as color and style).

Once completed, a customer's order is sent electronically to the company's factory in Mountain City, Tennessee, where denim for the jeans is cut to specifications by a computer-driven cutting machine. The pieces are then tagged with bar codes and sent through the regular mass-production washing and sewing processes. At the end of the assembly process, scanning equipment separates out the jeans, which are then sent to the store where they were ordered or, if the customer prefers, are shipped by Federal Express to the customer's home.

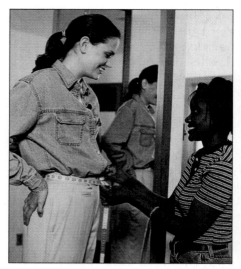

Here, a Fit Specialist measures a customer for a pair of Levi's Personal Pair Jeans. The customer's information is then loaded into the computer and transmitted to Levi's factory where the jeans are made and sent directly to the customer.

The total additional cost to the customer is $10—a bargain, according to one satisfied customer, Beth Gilmore, who paid $65 for a pair of digitally tailored Levi's from a store in Cincinnati. "I'm tall," she said, "In the past, there's always been a compromise—they're either too big or too little somewhere." Her digital jeans, in contrast, "fit like a glove."[40]

Levi Strauss & Co. will not disclose how many jeans it has sold this way, but the company notes that sales of women's jeans at the Cincinnati store where the system was being tested rose by 300 percent over the prior year. By 1999 the company was offering the service at over 100 Original Levi's® Stores.

Barriers to Implementing New Management Information Systems

Implementing advanced computer-based management information systems in organizations is no easy matter, despite their many advantages.[41] Technological problems, resistance from individual users, and political opposition within the organization are among the factors that make implementation difficult.

TECHNOLOGICAL PROBLEMS A major technological barrier to the successful implementation of information systems is the lack of consistent technological standards. Different manufacturers of computer and communications equipment may use different technical standards. For example, an IBM mainframe may be manufactured according to technical standards different from those of a Compaq server or an Apple personal computer. These different standards make it difficult to integrate various machines into a seamless computer network, and machines designed according to different standards may find it difficult to "talk" to one another.

An example of this problem is the difficulty of transferring files from an Apple personal computer to a personal computer based on the Intel/Microsoft standard. Because these machines use different technical standards, transferring files from one to the other without, for example, losing the formatting of a word-processed document is not always easy. This kind of connectivity problem can occur on a much larger scale within organizationwide computer networks; and when it does, it holds back their development.

RESISTANCE FROM INDIVIDUAL USERS   Resistance from individual users shows itself in a failure to fully exploit an organization's information systems. One study found that many managers failed to use the decision and executive support systems at their disposal.[42] Their primary reasons included fear of the technology (technophobia), failure to appreciate the power of the technology, and lack of in-house staff support. Resistance can be reduced by making the technology user-friendly and accessible to managers who have no prior computer experience. User-friendliness is enhanced by, for example, attractive graphical user interfaces and easy-to-negotiate pull-down menus to help users navigate through and use a system. Adequate training, when coupled with the availability of competent in-house support staff, can help enormously in educating managers about the value of the systems at their disposal, thereby encouraging their use.

POLITICAL OPPOSITION   Information systems can change the way in which an organization is managed by flattening its hierarchy and encouraging horizontal, cross-functional information flows. Many managers find these changes threatening, particularly if they suspect that such changes may negatively impact their power and authority, or even their job security.[43] Middle managers may worry (often with good reason) that the adoption of computer-based management information systems will be followed by widespread management layoffs. Thus, they may try to resist the implementation of such systems. Similarly, the head of a functional department may worry that the adoption of a computer network that encourages cross-functional information flows may limit his or her ability to control the flow of information into and out of the department. If the resulting lack of control over information flow negatively affects the manager's power (as well it might, for, as noted in Chapter 16, control over information is a major source of power), the manager may be tempted to try to block the implementation of an information system.[44]

One study found that managers who opposed the implementation of an information system for political reasons adopted a number of "counter implementation" tactics: (1) diverting resources from the project, (2) deflecting the goals of the project, (3) dissipating the energies of the project, and (4) neglecting the project in the hope that it would go away.[45]

Limitations of Information Systems

For all of their usefulness, information systems have some limitations. A serious potential problem is that in all of the enthusiasm for management information systems, electronic communication by means of a computer network, and the like, a vital *human* element of communication might be lost. Some kinds of information cannot be aggregated and summarized on an MIS report. Henry

Mintzberg noted that *thick information* is often required to coordinate and control an enterprise and to make informed decisions; Mintzberg means information rich in meaning and significance, far beyond that which can be quantified and aggregated.[46] According to Mintzberg, such information must be dug out, on site, by people closely involved in the events they wish to influence.

The importance of thick information is a strong argument in favor of using electronic communication to support face-to-face communication, not to replace it. For example, it would be wrong to make a judgment about an individual's performance merely by "reading the numbers" provided by a management information system. Instead, the numbers should be used to alert managers to individuals who may have a performance problem. The nature of this performance problem should then be explored in a face-to-face meeting, during which thick information can be gathered. As a top Boeing manager has noted, "In our company, the use of e-mail and videoconferencing has not reduced the need to visit people at other sites; it has increased it. E-mail has facilitated the establishment of communications channels between people who previously would not communicate, which is good, but direct visits are still required to cement any working relationships that evolve out of these electronic meetings."[47]

At Soft Co., profiled in the "Case in Contrast," managers have been heard to complain that one drawback of their internal e-mail system is that people spend a lot of time behind closed doors looking at computer screens and communicating electronically and very little time interacting directly with other managers.[48] When this is the case in an organization, management decisions may suffer because of a lack of thick information.

Managing Information Systems

Managers can take several steps to ease the implementation of information systems. First, they need to develop a list of the organization's principal goals and then decide on the major types of information they need to collect in order to measure how well they are achieving those goals. After making this analysis, managers audit their current management information systems to determine the degree to which the information they are currently collecting is accurate, reliable, timely, and relevant. Then managers need to investigate what other sources of information might be available to measure and improve efficiency, quality, innovation, and responsiveness to customers. For example, are organizational members using state-of-the-art information systems like e-mail, computer-assisted design, and three-tier designs? It is useful to benchmark competitors to determine what kinds of systems they are using.

When this analysis is complete, managers need to build support for the introduction of new information systems and convince employees that these systems will help raise job and organizational performance. Managers then should create formal training programs, with appropriate backup support, to help train employees to use the new information systems and technology, making sure that these systems are as user-friendly as possible. Finally, managers should emphasize that information systems are not a substitute for face-to-face communication and that employees at all levels should be involved in a continuing discussion about how best to exploit information technology to create a competitive advantage.

Tips for Managers

Managing Information

1. For effective decision making, design management information systems to ensure they provide high quality, timely, complete, and relevant information.

2. Train mangers how to use advanced information systems to ensure that they make best use of the information they receive to improve their planning and decision making.

3. Recognize that implementing an advanced MIS is a difficult process and that problems managers may encounter include technical problems, resistance from individual users, and political resistance in the organization.

4. Make the improvement of information technology a priority at all levels in the organization and in all functions.

Summary and Review

Chapter Summary

INFORMATION AND THE MANAGER'S JOB

- Attributes of Useful Information
- Information Systems and Technology
- Information and Decisions
- Information and Control
- Information and Coordination

INFORMATION AND THE MANAGER'S JOB Computer-based information systems are central to the operation of most organizations. By providing managers with high-quality, timely, relevant, and relatively complete information, properly implemented information systems can improve managers' ability to coordinate and control the operations of an organization and to make effective decisions. Moreover, information systems can help the organization to attain a competitive advantage through their beneficial impact on productivity, quality, innovation, and responsiveness to customers. Thus, modern information systems are becoming an indispensable management tool.

THE INFORMATION TECHNOLOGY REVOLUTION In recent years there have been rapid advances in the power, and rapid declines in the cost, of information technology. Falling prices, wireless communication, computer networks, and software developments have all increased the potential for information technology to radically improve the power and efficacy of computer-based information systems.

TYPES OF MANAGEMENT INFORMATION SYSTEMS Traditionally managers have used the organizational hierarchy as a system for gathering the information they needed to coordinate and control the organization and to make effective decisions. Today, managers use four main types of computer-based information systems. Listed in ascending order of sophistication, they are transaction-processing systems, operations information systems, decision support systems, and expert systems.

THE IMPACT AND LIMITATIONS OF INFORMATION SYSTEMS AND TECHNOLOGY Modern information systems and technology have changed organizational structure by making it flatter and by encouraging more cross-functional communication. In turn, this has helped organizations achieve a competitive advantage. Problems in implementing information systems can arise for technological reasons and because of resistance from employees who seek to protect their jobs and power.

Management in Action

Topics for Discussion and Action

1. To be useful, information must be of high quality, timely, relevant, and as complete as possible. Describe the negative impact that a tall management hierarchy, when used as an information system, can have on these desirable attributes.

2. What is the relationship between information systems and competitive advantage?

3. Ask a manager to describe the main kinds of information systems that he or she uses on a routine basis at work.

4. Because of the growth of high-powered low-cost computing, wireless communications, and technologies such as video-conferencing, many managers soon may not need to come into the office to do their jobs. They will be able to work at home. What are the pros and cons of such an arrangement?

5. Many companies have reported that it is difficult to implement advanced management information and decision support systems. Why do you think this is so? How might the roadblocks to implementation be removed?

6. How can information systems help in the new product development process?

7. Why is face-to-face communication between managers still important in an organization?

Building Management Skills

Analyzing Information Systems

Pick an organization about which you have some direct knowledge. It may be an organization that you worked for in the past or are in contact with now (such as the college or school that you attend). For this organization, do the following.

1. Describe the information systems that managers use to coordinate and control organizational activities and to help make decisions. Are these information systems computer based or based on paper and hierarchy? Does the organization use a transaction-processing system, operations information system, decision support system, or expert system?

2. Do you think that the organization's existing information systems provide managers with high-quality, timely, relevant, and relatively complete information? Explain your answer.

3. What, if anything, might be done to improve the information systems in this organization?

4. How might advanced information systems be used to improve the competitive position of this organization? In particular, try to identify the impact the information systems might have on the organization's productivity, quality, innovation, and responsiveness to customers.

Small Group Breakout Exercise
Using New Information Systems

Form groups of three or four people, and appoint one member as the spokesperson who will communicate your findings to the whole class when called on by the instructor. Then discuss the following scenario.

You are a team of managing partners of a large firm of accountants. You have been charged with the responsibility to audit your firm's information systems to determine whether they are appropriate and up-to-date. To your surprise, you find that although your organization does have an e-mail system in place and accountants are connected into a powerful local area network (LAN), most of the accountants (including partners) are not using this technology. You also find that the organizational hierarchy is still the preferred information system of the managing partners.

Given this situation, you are concerned that your organization is not exploiting the opportunities offered by new information systems to obtain a competitive advantage. You have discussed this issue and are meeting to develop an action plan to get accountants to appreciate the need to learn, and to take advantage of, the potential of the new information technology.

1. What advantages can you tell accountants they will obtain when they use the new information technology?

2. What problems do you think you may encounter in convincing accountants to use the new information technology?

3. Discuss how you might make it easy for accountants to learn to use the new technology.

Exploring the World Wide Web
Specific Assignment

Enter the website of United Parcel Service (UPS) (www.ups.com). Click on "services" to obtain a list of customer services that the company provides.

1. Describe the kinds of information systems and technologies that UPS uses to improve services to customers.

2. In what ways does the use of these information systems and technologies provide UPS with a competitive advantage?

General Assignment

Search for the website of a company that makes extensive use of information systems to deliver its goods or services to customers. What systems does it use, and how do they give the company a competitive advantage?

ManagementCase

Woolworth's New Information System

F. W. Woolworth Co. operates over 8,000 stores, including hundreds of stores—such as Foot Locker, Kinney Shoes, Afterthoughts, Accessory Lady, Northern Reflections, and Champs Sports—that operate under separate divisions.[49] In the 1990s, experiencing deteriorating performance because of intense competition from low-price competitors such as Wal-Mart, Woolworth's top managers began to search for new and better ways to manage the information that they needed to run the company efficiently. They wanted an information system that could accomplish two things.

First, top managers wanted an information system that could link each of Woolworth's individual stores with the managers in charge of each of the respective store divisions and link each of the divisions with Woolworth's top managers so that top managers would have easy access to in-store information. Second, top managers wanted an information system that could deliver large amounts of information in a user-friendly manner, both to allow them to intervene quickly to change a division's strategy and to transmit information down to the individual store managers to help them to respond to changes in the task and general environments.

Needing specialized help to develop a new computer-based information system, Woolworth turned to IBM's consulting division. A team of IBM consultants met with a team of Woolworth managers to discuss the nature of the information system that they should jointly develop.

Questions

1. What kind of computer network do Woolworth's managers need to help them manage the company?
2. Given the nature of Woolworth's information needs, what kind of computer-based management information system would you recommend?

ManagementCase

In the News

From the Pages of BusinessWeek

The Many Virtues of "Virtual Services"

The young founders of Manhattan's StockObjects don't need a pep talk on the power of the Internet. That's where they make their living, marketing a Web-based library of animated pictures, 3-D models, and other multimedia elements for companies' Web sites. And when they need to custom-produce projects for their library, they hire programmers from around the world—again, over the Internet. So when StockObjects wanted some Net-savvy financial help, Chairman and President Mark Tribe turned to a Net-focused accounting firm for help: Virtual Growth Inc.

The firm, also in Manhattan, offers clients such as StockObjects the services of a chief financial officer, controller, and accountant over the Net. For example, as part of the "Virtual CFO" service, StockObjects Chief Operating Officer Jeff Phillips plugs quarterly financial data into an Excel software template set up by Virtual Growth, and the program generates a balance sheet and cash-flow projections. Phillips E-mails those spreadsheets to the firm, where an assigned CPA interprets the data and advises the company on strategy. Besides acting as CFO, Virtual Growth does traditional accounting work, files tax forms, takes care of payroll, and pays the bills. The total cost: $1,700 a month. Granted, it's not quite the same as having a full-time financial staff. Business communications are handled mostly by E-mail and telephone, along with periodic face-to-face meetings. But hiring a full-time CFO could cost $100,000 or more. StockObjects President Tribe says the arrangement works well for now. "They're not a substitute for a CFO—they're allowing us to go longer without one."

It's the latest twist on outsourcing: Small businesses are starting to get help from virtual services camped out on the cyber-frontier. Do a little surfing and you'll find "virtual assistants" who word-process, plan events, and handle other office chores over the Net; online consultants who dispense advice by E-mail; a computerized transcription service; and human-resource management companies that let you tap into expensive software for managing employee benefits. These virtual service providers will probably never shake your

hand. The bulk of their work will be done by E-mail, electronic file transfers, password-protected Web sites, and Web-based software.

While the move to "virtual services" is in its infancy, small-business consultants say these services are worth considering. Outsourcing, in general, can cost 50% less than hiring a full-time employee, according to Hackett Group, a Hudson (Ohio) consultancy. And Bill Ebeling, a partner at Boston's Braxton Strategy practice of Deloitte & Touche Consulting Group, predicts that more services will be migrating to the Web soon—particularly those that rely on databases—because of its greater speed, convenience, and lower cost. "If you can program something, and it fits 75% of business situations, it's got to be cheaper than a human being," says Ebeling.

Such thinking propelled Stephen King to start Virtual Growth in December, 1995, figuring he could focus on financial strategies for his clients while letting software handle the donkey work. "Clients don't want to pay for bank reconciliations and sales-tax calculations, they want to pay for consulting advice," says King, whose 17-person firm serves about 50 small businesses, most of them new media startups in New York, Boston, and Phoenix.

Another new service that hopes to capitalize on savings from technology is Falls Church (Va.)–based V.com LLC, which was launched in mid-August. The firm has created a database of federal Occupational Safety & Health Administration regulations that will let clients design their own compliance program rather than pay a consultant. At

V.com's Web site, you fill out a questionnaire, and the database spits back both a compliance checklist, tailored to your business profile, and a schedule to follow to stay within the law. Fees are expected to range from $550 to $1,000 a year, depending on the number of users at a company.

While the system won't alert you automatically when regulatory changes take place, V.com's attorneys will update the database frequently, and clients can check in to get updates on changes. "We could do this thing by hand, but we'd have to charge about 10 to 20 times what we're charging," says Managing Partner David C. Frankil.

Need some secretarial or administrative help? Thanks to the Internet, virtual assistants, who often work from their homes for customers they never meet, might make your business run more smoothly. For fees ranging from $15 an hour for more sophisticated services, such as event planning or publicity, virtual assistants handle business by E-mail, file transfers, and Web sites. For example, at the Web site of virtual assistant Chris Durst, owner of My Staff in Woodstock, Conn., clients can check virtual calendars, where Durst has scheduled their appointments, or get reminders on their "to do" list, which she keeps current.

Meanwhile, Branch Office, owned by Amy Sarai in Bridgewater, N.J., and her sister Julie Hewett in Huntington, W. Va., works with about 30 clients, some as far away as Japan. Client Robert Horowitz, a Stamford (Conn.) investment adviser, uses Sarai to supplement his part-time office help. "Amy is doing things for me that someone who's not in the virtual world can't do, like searching the Web and managing E-mail," he says.

Another new service hardly depends on human contact at all, thanks to voice-recognition technology. Cyber-Transcriber lets clients such as Tom Thees, owner of the Pinnacle, a 120-employee company that owns three meeting and banquet facilities in Toledo, dictate letters and memos from his cellular telephone anywhere, anytime. Operated by Speech Machines of Menlo Park, Calif., the service's computers translate speech into text at 120 words per minute. After proofreaders check for misspellings, the text is E-mailed back to the client. In addition to a monthly subscription fee, Thees pays about $3.50 a page—the same as a local transcription service—but gets it back much faster.

Smaller companies are just starting to go online for access to the type of sophisticated human-resources software big companies use. Employease Inc. in Atlanta is marketing a new service for small and medium-size companies that manages benefits information on its computers. Company employees can log on to a password-protected Web site to change or update benefits information, and a company can analyze data to see how it is utilizing benefits. At $1 to $4 per employee per month, plus setup fees, it's cheaper than buying your own software system, which can run upwards of $100,000. And you don't have to install, maintain, or upgrade it.

In some cases, traditional outsourcers are starting to offer a new Internet option as a convenience. Roseland (N.J.)–based Automatic Data Processing Inc., a big-payroll processor, plans to bring its service online in the coming months. Clients will be able to log on to ADP's Web site and enter all the relevant information on employees' hours right into ADP's payroll database. Now, the majority of ADP's 40,000 customers call in their payroll information.

If you're interested in finding virtual services, be prepared for a little homework. Try using an Internet search engine to browse under specific topics, such as accounting, or inquire about virtual services with the relevant trade groups. Checking references becomes particularly important when you can't meet your virtual providers in the flesh and have only their Web site to go by. And, as with any outsourcing, there's no free ride. "Remember," warns Heather Ashton, an analyst with Hurwitz Group, a Framingham (Mass.) consulting firm, "the function still requires management." Or, should we say, virtual management?

Source: Anne Zieger, "The Many Virtues of 'Virtual Services,'" *Business Week,* September 14, 1998, 18, 20.

Questions

1. In what ways can virtual outsourcing help managers?

2. How will virtual outsourcing affect a company's information systems in the future?

Chapter eighteen

Operations Management: Managing Quality, Efficiency, and Responsiveness to Customers

Learning Objectives

1. Explain the role of operations management in achieving superior quality, efficiency, and responsiveness to customers.

2. Describe what customers want, and explain why it is so important for managers to be responsive to their needs.

3. Explain why achieving superior quality is so important.

4. Describe the main features of total quality management.

5. Describe the challenges facing managers and organizations that seek to implement total quality management.

6. Explain why achieving superior efficiency is so important.

7. Differentiate among flexible manufacturing, just-in-time inventory, *kaizen,* and process reengineering.

A Case in Contrast

Two Production Systems at Federal-Mogul

In the mid-1980s when Federal-Mogul (www. federal-mogul.com), an auto-parts manufacturer in Lancaster, Pennsylvania, was getting hammered by low-cost Japanese competitors, managers resolved to reduce operating costs. Brief visits to a few Japanese plants led Federal-Mogul managers to suspect that the major source of their Japanese competitors' cost advantage was the sophisticated computers, robots, and other automated equipment they used. Accordingly, in 1987 the company reorganized its auto-parts plant with state-of-the art automation, including robots, overhead conveyer belts to carry semifinished parts along the production line, and automated guided vehicles (carts that are guided by signals from underground wires and haul parts from one workstation to another). Several sophisticated production-line computers controlled this automated system.

The results of this reorganization were not what Federal-Mogul's managers hoped for.[1] The automated plant turned out parts faster than before, but managers found that the plant could not switch quickly from producing one type of part to another. To switch from making a small clutch bearing to a large one, for example, required many time-consuming changes, ranging from readjusting the parts' "feeding system" to realigning the mechanisms that held the parts in place while they were being machined.

In a business where a plant that is not running is losing money, this lack of flexibility made it difficult for Federal-Mogul to produce

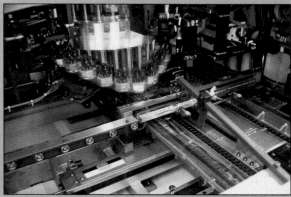

These two photos contrast the different types of production lines: the conveyor belt type, and the fully automated type. One would think there are a lot of advantages to a fully-automated site, but Federal-Mogul, an auto parts manufacturer, found out differently.

a wide range of parts at a reasonable cost. Indeed, to cover the fixed costs of setting up the equipment for a production run, managers found that they had to produce parts in batches ranging from 5,000 to 10,000 units, even if a customer wanted only 250. Surplus parts then had to be stored in a warehouse until a customer desired them, and this storage was extremely costly. To make matters worse, automobile companies were increasing the number of car models they made and consequently were demanding from suppliers such as Federal-Mogul a wider range of parts in smaller quantities.

Managers at Federal-Mogul found that the plant could not respond quickly and cost-effectively to customer demands; it lacked the required flexibility. Thus, instead of gaining on Japanese competitors, Federal-Mogul fell farther behind.

Faced with a deteriorating situation, in 1993 Federal-Mogul once more reorganized its Lancaster auto-parts plant. This time, manufacturing flexibility was the goal uppermost in the minds of the company's managers. Out went the robots, most production-line computers, the overhead conveyer belts, and the automated guided vehicles. In their place, managers created a modular production assembly line that could be changed or retooled quickly to produce different parts. Now, when a switch is made from assembling, for example, a washer ring for the steering column of a car to a ring for a pickup truck, workers simply wheel away sections of the modular assembly line and replace them with sections geared for the next product. The parts needed to alter the production line are kept in bins within easy reach of workers.

The reengineered plant, which assembles 1,800 different parts, produces three times as many different varieties as before in the same amount of time. And because it can switch from producing one part to another very quickly, it produces only what customers immediately want and eliminated the need for a warehouse to store excess inventory. It now can make cost-effective parts in batches ranging from 250 to 500 units instead of the 5,000 to 10,000 previously needed to break even. Federal-Mogul managers have found that the change from a high-tech automated factory to a low-tech factory has simultaneously increased their organization's flexibility and lowered its costs. •

Overview

The "Case in Contrast" describes the response of auto-parts maker Federal-Mogul to low-cost Japanese competition. Federal-Mogul first built a state-of-the-art automated factory. However, setting up the computer-controlled machinery for a production run took so long that Federal-Mogul was unable to provide its customers with the products they wanted at a reasonable cost. Seeing high equipment setup times translate into low responsiveness to customers and low efficiency, Federal-Mogul reorganized again, bringing in a low-tech, modular production assembly line that allowed the organization to improve performance and achieve its goals.

To achieve superior quality, efficiency, responsiveness to customers, and innovation—the four building blocks of competitive advantage—managers at all levels in an organization must adopt state-of-the-art management techniques and practices that give them more control over the organization's activities. In this chapter we focus on the operations management techniques that managers can use to control and increase the quality of an organization's products, the efficiency of production, and the organization's responsiveness to customers. By the end of this chapter, you will understand the vital role operations management plays in building competitive advantage and creating a high-performing organization. In the next chapter we examine techniques that managers can use to enhance innovation and manage the product development process. ●

Operations Management and Competitive Advantage

operations management The management of any aspect of the production system that transforms inputs into finished goods and services.

production system The system that an organization uses to acquire inputs, convert the inputs into outputs, and dispose of the outputs.

operations manager A manager who is responsible for managing an organization's production system and for determining where operating improvements might be made.

Operations management is the management of any aspect of the production system that transforms inputs into finished goods and services. A **production system** is the system that an organization uses to acquire inputs, convert the inputs into outputs, and dispose of the outputs (goods or services). **Operations managers** are managers who are responsible for managing an organization's production system. They do whatever it takes to transform inputs into outputs. Their job is to manage the three stages of production—acquisition of inputs, control of conversion processes, and disposal of goods and services—and to determine where operating improvements might be made in order to increase quality, efficiency, and responsiveness to customers and so give an organization a competitive advantage (see Figure 18.1).

Quality refers to goods and services that are reliable, dependable, and satisfying: They do the job they were designed for, and do it well, so that they give customers what they want.[2] *Efficiency* refers to the amount of inputs required to produce a given output. *Responsiveness to customers* refers to actions taken to meet the demands and needs of customers. Operations managers are responsible for ensuring that an organization has sufficient supplies of high-quality, low-cost inputs, and they are responsible for designing a production system that creates high-quality, low-cost products that customers are willing to buy.

Notice that achieving superior efficiency and quality is part of attaining superior responsiveness to customers. Customers want value for money, and an organization whose efficient production system creates high-quality, low-cost products is best able to deliver this value. For this reason, we first discuss how operations managers can design the production system to increase responsiveness to customers.

Improving Responsiveness to Customers

Organizations produce outputs—goods or services—that are consumed by customers. All organizations, profit seeking or not-for-profit, have customers. Without customers, most organizations would cease to exist. If Federal-Mogul lost the business of its customers Chrysler, Ford, and General Motors, it would go bankrupt. The customers of a business school are students, the businesses that hire the school's graduates, and society at large, which benefits from an educated and informed population. If a business school failed to attract student applicants—perhaps because employers were no longer hiring the school's graduates—it too could no longer function and would have to close its doors.

Figure 18.1
The Purpose of Operations Management

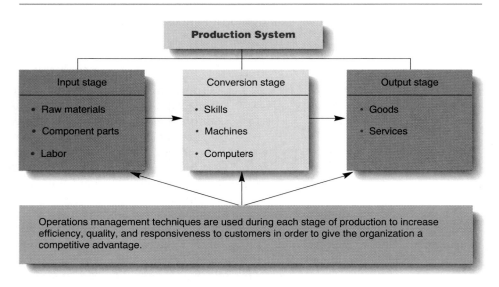

Because customers are vital to the survival of most organizations, it is important for managers to correctly identify customers and promote organizational strategies that respond to their needs. This is why management writers recommend that organizations define their business in terms of the customer needs they are satisfying, not the type of products they are producing.[3] The credo of pharmaceutical company Johnson & Johnson, for example, begins, "We believe our first responsibility is to the doctors, nurses and patients, to mothers and fathers and all others who use our products and services."[4] Through the credo Johnson & Johnson's managers emphasize their commitment to exemplary customer service (the credo is reproduced in full in Figure 5.1).

In contrast, in the 1980s, Digital Equipment Corporation (DEC) defined its business as producing high-powered mainframe computers. When the dramatic shift away from mainframe computers to personal computers occurred in the 1980s, DEC found itself unprepared and almost went bankrupt after suffering over $2.5 billion in losses. Had DEC's managers defined its business as "satisfying customer needs for computing solutions" (a customer-oriented definition) as opposed to "producing powerful computers" (a product-oriented definition), they might have recognized the shift in consumer demand and begun producing personal computers earlier.

What Do Customers Want?

Given that satisfying customer demands is central to the survival of an organization, an important question is, What do customers want? To specify exactly what they want is not possible because their wants vary from industry to industry. However, it is possible to identify some universal product attributes that most customers in most industries want. Generally, other things being equal, most customers prefer

1. A lower price to a higher price

2. Higher-quality products to low-quality products

3. Quick service to slow service (They will always prefer good after-sales service and support to poor after-sales support.)

4. Products with many features to products with few features (They will prefer a personal computer with a CD-ROM drive, lots of memory, and a powerful microprocessor to one without these features.)

5. Products that are, as far as possible, customized or tailored to their unique needs

Of course, the problem is that other things are not equal. For example, providing higher quality, quick service, and after-sales service and support, products with many features, and products that are customized raises costs and thus the price that must be charged to cover costs.[5] So customers' demands for these attributes typically conflict with their demands for lower price. Accordingly, customers must make a trade-off between price and preferred attributes, and so must managers. This price/attribute trade-off is illustrated in Figure 18.2.

Desired attributes of a product—such as high quality, service, speed, after-sales support, features, and customization—are plotted on the horizontal axis; price is plotted on the vertical axis; and the solid line shows the price/attribute relationship—that is, the combination of price and attributes an organization can offer and still make a profit. As the figure illustrates, the higher the price the customer is willing to pay for a product, the more desired attributes the customer is able to get. Or, in other words, the more desired attributes that an organization builds into its products, the higher is the price that the organization has to charge to cover its costs. At price P1 managers can offer a product with A1 attributes. If managers offer a product with A2 attributes at price P1, they will lose money because the price is too low to cover costs. A product with A2 attributes needs a price of P2 to be profitable for the organization. Thus, the nature of the organization's production system limits how responsive managers can be to customers.

Figure 18.2
The Price/Attribute Relationship

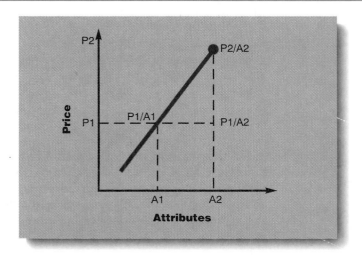

Figure 18.3
Federal-Mogul's Price/Attribute Relationship in 1987 and 1993

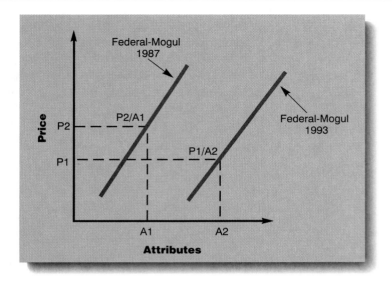

Given the limits imposed on managers by their existing production system, what do the managers of a customer-responsive organization try to do? They try to push the price/attribute curve to the right (toward the vertical dotted line in Figure 18.2) by developing new or improved production systems that are able to deliver either more desired product attributes for the same price or the same product attributes for a lower price.[6]

Figure 18.3 shows the price/attribute curves for Federal-Mogul in 1987, when the automated production system was put in place, and in 1993, when the low-tech modular system was installed. By accommodating customer demands for greater product customization and speedy delivery, the flexible modular system lowered operating costs so much that it allowed Federal-Mogul to offer more product attributes than previously—at a *lower* price to customers. The shift from an automated to a flexible production system increased Federal-Mogul's responsiveness to customers on two fronts—lower cost and more attributes—and did so without imposing higher costs on Federal-Mogul.

Designing Production Systems That Are Responsive to Customers

Because satisfying customers is so important, managers try to design production systems that can produce the outputs that have the attributes customers desire. The attributes of an organization's outputs—their quality, cost, and features—are determined by the organization's production system.[7] As we saw in the "Case in Contrast," for example, the need to respond to customer demands for competitively priced small batches of different products drove Federal-Mogul managers to dismantle the automated system of production and replace it with a more flexible modular layout. The imperative of satisfying customer needs shaped Federal-Mogul's production system. When managers focus on being responsive to their customers, and not just on producing a product, they see new ways to reduce costs and increase quality.

Since the ability of an organization to satisfy the demands of its customers derives from its production system, managers need to devote considerable attention to constantly improving production systems. Managers' desire to attract customers by shifting the price/attribute line to the right explains their adoption of many new operations management techniques in recent years— such as total quality management, flexible manufacturing systems, and just-in-time inventory, discussed in detail later in this chapter.

The total quality management movement, for example, is concerned with designing production systems that produce high-quality outputs, thereby satisfying customer demands for product quality. The redesign of Motorola's semiconductor production system resulted in a sharp increase in product quality; the production of defective semiconductor chips fell from 6,000 per million to 40 per million.[8] This quality improvement made Motorola's output more attractive to its customers. By redesigning the production system, Motorola managers increased the organization's ability to respond to customer demands for quality products; Motorola became more responsive to customers. As another example of the link between responsiveness to customers and an organization's production system, this time in a service organization, consider the case of Southwest Airlines.

Management Insight

How Southwest Airlines Keeps Its Customers Happy

Southwest Airlines (www.iflyswa.com) is one of the most successful airlines in the United States. During the early 1990s, it was one of the few airlines in the world to remain profitable in the face of a serious slump in airline travel. One reason for Southwest's success is that CEO Herb Kelleher created a production system uniquely tailored to satisfying the demands of its customers: people who want low-priced, reliable (on-time), and convenient air travel. Southwest is able to command high customer loyalty precisely because its production system delivers products, such as flights from Houston to Dallas, that have desired attributes: reliability, convenience, and low price.

Southwest's low-cost production system focuses not only on improving the maintenance of aircraft but also on the company's ticket reservation system, route structure, flight frequency, baggage-handling system, and in-flight services. Each of these elements of Southwest's production system is geared toward satisfying customer demands for low-priced, reliable, and convenient air travel. For example, Southwest offers a no-frills approach to in-flight customer service. No meals are served on board, and there are no first-class seats. Southwest does not subscribe to the big reservation computers used by travel agents because it believes the booking fees are too costly. Also, the airline flies only one type of aircraft, the fuel-efficient Boeing 737, which keeps training and maintenance costs down. All this translates into low prices to the customer.

This employee of Southwest Airlines continues to perform the magic that helped make their airline number one in customer satisfaction in 1998 and highly profitable.

Southwest's reliability derives from the fact that it has the quickest aircraft turnaround time in the industry. A Southwest ground crew needs only 15 minutes to turn around an incoming aircraft and prepare it for departure. This speedy operation helps to keep flights on time. Southwest has such quick turnaround because it has a flexible workforce that has been cross-trained to perform multiple tasks. Thus, the person who checks tickets might also help with baggage loading if time is short.

Southwest's convenience comes from its scheduling multiple flights every day between its popular locations, such as Dallas and Houston, and its use of airports that are close to downtown (Hobby at Houston and Love Field at Dallas) instead of more distant major airports.[9]

Although managers must seek to improve the responsiveness to customers of their organization by improving its production system, they should *not* offer a level of responsiveness to customers that is more than that production system can profitably sustain. The company that customizes every product to the unique demands of individual customers is likely to see its cost structure become so high that unit costs exceed unit revenues.

Something like this appears to have occurred at Toyota (www.toyota.com) in the early 1990s. Toyota's flexible production system allows the company to produce a wide range of variations on a basic automobile model (for example, different colors and options). Extreme customization at first attracted many new customers and raised revenues. Toyota managers, however, pushed customization to the point where it increased costs faster than it generated additional revenues. At one point, literally thousands of different variations of Toyota's basic models, such as the Camry and Corolla, were being produced by Toyota factories. When a recession hit in Japan in the early 1990s, Toyota reexamined its approach to customization, and managers decided to reduce the number of model specifications by 20 percent and the options offered with models by 30 percent. Managers at Toyota apparently concluded that the costs of extreme customization were exceeding the benefits.[10]

Improving Quality

As noted earlier, high-quality products are reliable, dependable, and satisfying; they do the job they were designed for and meet customer requirements.[11] Quality is a concept that can be applied to the products of both manufacturing and service organizations—goods such as a Toyota car or a McDonald's hamburger or services such as Southwest Airlines flight service or customer service in a bank. Why do managers seek to control and improve the quality of their organization's products?[12] There are two reasons (see Figure 18.4).

Figure 18.4

The Impact of Increased Quality on Organizational Performance

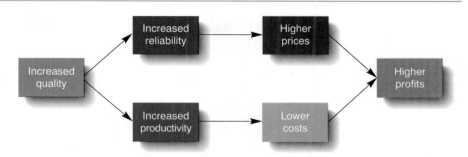

First, customers usually prefer a higher-quality product to a lower-quality product. So an organization able to provide, *for the same price,* a product of higher quality than a competitor's product is serving its customers better—it is being more responsive to its customers. Often, providing high-quality products creates a brand-name reputation for an organization's products. In turn, this enhanced reputation may allow the organization to charge more for its products than its competitors are able to charge for theirs and thus make even greater profits. In 1993, 6 of the top 10 places in the J. D. Power list of the 10 most reliable cars sold in the U.S. market were captured by Toyota vehicles.[13] The high quality of Toyota vehicles has enabled Toyota to charge higher prices for its cars than the prices charged by rival automakers.

The second reason for trying to boost product quality is that higher product quality can increase efficiency and thereby lower operating costs and boost profits. Many managers in Western companies did not appreciate this relationship until the mid-to-late 1980s. They were operating with the belief, now known to be incorrect, that improving product quality raised operating costs. This belief was based on the (mistaken) assumption that building quality into a product is expensive. By contrast, managers in many Japanese companies had long operated on the assumption that achieving high product quality lowered operating costs because of the effect of quality on employee productivity: Higher product quality means that less employee time is wasted in making defective products that must be discarded or in providing substandard services, and less time has to be spent in fixing mistakes. This translates into higher employee productivity, which means lower costs.

Total Quality Management

total quality management A management technique that focuses on improving the quality of an organization's products and services.

At the forefront of the drive to improve product quality is a technique known as total quality management.[14] **Total quality management (TQM)** focuses on improving the quality of an organization's products and services and stresses that all of an organization's functional activities should be directed toward this goal. Conceived as an organizationwide management program, TQM requires the cooperation of managers in every function of an organization if it is to succeed. The TQM concept was first developed by a number of American consultants, including the late W. Edwards Deming, Joseph Juran, and A. V. Feigenbaum.[15]

Table 18.1

Deming's 14 Steps to Quality

1. Create constancy of purpose toward improvement of product and service, with the aim to become competitive, to stay in business, and to provide jobs.
2. Adopt the new philosophy. We are in a new economic age. Western management must awaken to the challenge, must learn its responsibilities, and must take on leadership for change.
3. Cease dependence on inspection to achieve quality. Eliminate the need for inspection on a mass basis by building quality into the product from the start.
4. End the practice of awarding business on the basis of price tag. Instead, minimize total cost.
5. Improve constantly and forever the system of production and service, to improve quality and productivity and thus constantly decrease costs.
6. Institute training on the job.
7. Institute leadership. The aim of leadership should be to help people and machines and gadgets do a better job. Leadership of management is in need of an overhaul, as well as leadership of production workers.
8. Drive out fear, so that everyone may work effectively for the company.
9. Break down barriers between departments. People in research, design, sales, and production must work as a team, to foresee problems of production and in use that may be encountered with the product or service.
10. Eliminate slogans, exhortations, and targets for the workforce asking for zero defects and new levels of productivity. Such exhortations only create adversarial relationships. The bulk of the causes of low quality and low productivity belongs to the system and thus lies beyond the power of the workforce.
11. (a) Eliminate work standards on the factory floor. Substitute leadership. (b) Eliminate management by objectives. Eliminate management by numbers, numerical goals. Substitute leadership.
12. (a) Remove barriers that rob the hourly worker of his or her right to pride of workmanship. The responsibility of supervisors must be changed from sheer numbers to quality. (b) Remove barriers that rob people in management and in engineering of their right to pride of workmanship.
13. Institute a vigorous program of education and self-improvement.
14. Put everybody in the company to work to accomplish the transformation. The transformation is everybody's job.

Originally, these consultants won few converts in the United States but were enthusiastically embraced by the Japanese, who named their premier annual prize for manufacturing excellence after Deming. Deming identified 14 steps that should be part of any TQM program (see Table 18.1).[16]

In essence, to increase quality, Deming urged managers to develop strategic plans that state goals exactly and spell out how they will be achieved. He argued that managers should embrace the philosophy that mistakes, defects, and poor-quality materials are not acceptable and should be eliminated. He suggested that first-line managers be allowed to spend more time working with employees and providing them with the tools they need to do the job. He recommended that management create an environment in which employees will not be afraid to report problems or recommend improvements. He believed that output goals and targets needed to include not only numbers or quotas but also some notion of quality to promote the production of defect-free output. Deming also argued that management has the responsibility to train employees in new skills to keep pace with changes in the workplace. Furthermore, he believed that achieving better quality requires managers to develop organizational values and norms centered on improving quality and that every manager and worker in an organization must commit to the goal of quality.

From the early 1980s, as word of the remarkable production successes resulting from TQM practices spread, many Western managers began implementing TQM within their organizations. In some organizations the results have been nothing short of spectacular. For example, when managers at Xerox first introduced a TQM program in conjunction with suppliers in 1983, the suppliers were producing about 25,000 defective parts per million. By 1992 the defect rate on parts from suppliers was under 300 per million.[17] Ford Motor Company claims that its companywide implementation of a TQM program reduced the company's operating budget by over $40 billion over a ten-year period.[18] Partly as a consequence, in 1994 Ford emerged from a period of financial turmoil as the most profitable car company in the world. The positive effect that a TQM program can have on an organization can also be seen in the example of McDevitt Street Bovis, a construction services company whose adoption of TQM led to a major improvement in the company's competitive position.

Management Insight

McDevitt Street Bovis Applies TQM

In November 1987, managers at McDevitt Street Bovis, a construction services company based in Charlotte, North Carolina, received a shock. One of their largest clients, Hospital Corporation of America, informed McDevitt that its managers were going to award all future construction contracts on the basis of construction companies' commitment to total quality management. Managers at McDevitt were floored. They had no idea what TQM was or how it could be applied to a construction services company. Despite their ignorance, at 3:30 in the afternoon of November 13, 1987, top management of McDevitt decided to embrace TQM.

Top managers soon discovered that a principal objective of TQM was to eliminate costly mistakes, which are very common in the construction industry. Cost and time overruns, poor-quality work, and legal disputes among construction companies, subcontractors, and architects and their clients are commonplace in the industry. As they embarked on a TQM program, managers at McDevitt came to realize that many wasteful and costly mistakes resulted from misunderstandings caused by a lack of communication among the parties involved in a construction project. To improve communication, McDevitt's managers decided to develop a total quality plan for each contract that they worked on; they called their plan "Jobsite Quality Planning" (JQP).

JQP brings together clients, architects, the construction company, and subcontractors to agree on a written mission statement for a job and on tangible performance measures that will allow them to evaluate the success of a project. Performance measures typically include the frequency with which architects and engineers have to visit the job to correct mistakes; the manner of resolving disputes among subcontractors; coordination among mechanical, electrical, and plumbing contractors; and the cost method for measuring progress. As of 1995, managers at McDevitt had used Jobsite Quality Planning on over 400 projects. Seven years down the total quality management road, they found that TQM had produced some interesting results:

- Virtually every company with which JQP was used awarded McDevitt additional business.
- Not a single construction-related lawsuit arose from a JQP project. By 1993, McDevitt's legal expenses were down 50 percent, and the number of legal disputes had declined more than 60 percent since their peak in 1989.[19]
- McDevitt has made money each year since 1987, despite turmoil in the industry and widespread financial troubles among competing companies.
- Clients, subcontractors, architects, and engineers all informed McDevitt that the JQP process truly improves the quality of a job.

It would be wrong to think that these achievements have been easy or inexpensive to attain. McDevitt continues to invest $500,000 per year in JQP training efforts. Moreover, it took years to get people at all levels of the company to buy into total quality management. Initial resistance ranged from middle managers who saw huge expenditures associated with JQP with no immediate payback, to job-site workers who did not understand the concept. Indeed, getting JQP widely accepted within McDevitt necessitated major changes in the culture of the organization. To this end, Luther Cochran, CEO of McDevitt, really supported early adopters of JQP in the company, making them heroes for their successes. The result? Over time, most of the doubters were converted to JQP, and an obsession with quality has become a central value of McDevitt's culture.

Despite the many TQM success stories such as those of Xerox, Motorola, and McDevitt Street Bovis, evidence is mounting that there is still a long way to go before Western managers widely accept TQM practices. A 1992 study by the American Quality Foundation found that only 20 percent of U.S. companies regularly review the consequences of quality performance, compared with 70 percent of Japanese companies.[20] A study by Arthur D. Little of 500 American companies that use TQM found that only 36 percent believed that TQM was increasing their competitiveness.[21] The main reason for this finding, according to the study, was that many managers failed to fully understand or embrace the TQM concept. A survey of European companies by the European Foundation for Quality Management revealed that only 30 percent of European companies claimed to have adopted TQM practices, and a mere 5 or 10 percent said they were still actively pursuing TQM programs.[22] The European Foundation study also found that many TQM programs fail because of a lack of commitment by managers, who frequently talk up the importance of TQM but do not act on it.

Putting TQM into Action: The Management Challenge

Given the mixed track record of TQM, what actions can managers take to increase the probability of successful implementation of a TQM program? Studies of companies that have successfully implemented TQM programs suggest that the following 10 steps are necessary to make a TQM control system work.

1. *Build organizational commitment to quality.* TQM will do little to improve the performance of an organization unless all employees embrace it, and this often requires a change in an organization's culture.[23] Getting TQM thinking to become part of everyday thinking took a change in McDevitt's culture. The need to engineer a cultural change was also at the forefront of management thinking at Xerox when its managers first introduced TQM. When Xerox launched its total quality program, managers' first actions were to educate the entire workforce, from top management down, about the importance and operation of TQM. Managers formed groups. The first was a group of top managers, including the CEO. Outside consultants were hired to give this group basic TQM training. Each member of the top-management group was then given the responsibility to train a group at the next level in the hierarchy, and so on down throughout the organization until all 100,000 employees had received basic TQM training.

It is important to emphasize the ongoing nature of the effort to build commitment to TQM. The TQM philosophy needs to be continually emphasized, applied, and reinforced, for changing the culture of a company can take years. If TQM is treated as the hot management technique of the moment, pursued for a year, and then forgotten, it will fail to deliver on its promise to improve organizational performance.

2. *Focus on the customer.* TQM practitioners see a focus on the customer as the starting point.[24] According to TQM philosophy, the *customer,* not managers in quality control or engineering, "defines" what quality is. The challenge is fourfold: (1) to identify what customers want from the good or service that the company provides; (2) to identify what the company actually provides to customers; (3) to identify the gap that exists between what customers want and what they actually get (the *quality gap*); and (4) to formulate a plan for closing the quality gap.

3. *Find ways to measure quality.* Another crucial element of any TQM program is the creation of a measuring system that managers can consistently use to evaluate quality. Devising appropriate measures is relatively easy in manufacturing companies where quality can be measured by criteria such as defects per million parts. It is more difficult in service companies where outputs are less tangible. But with a little creativity, suitable measures can be devised. For example, one of the measures that managers at Florida Power & Light use to evaluate quality is the number of meter-reading errors per month; another is the frequency and duration of power outages. At L. L. Bean, the Freeport, Maine, mail-order retailer of outdoor gear, managers use the percentage of orders that are correctly filled as one of their quality measures. Some banks use measures such as the number of customer defections per year or the number of statement errors per thousand customers to evaluate quality. The common theme running through all of these examples is that managers must identify what quality means from a customer's perspective and devise some measure that captures this.

4. *Set goals and create incentives.* Once a measure has been devised, managers' next step is to set a challenging quality goal and to create incentives for reaching that goal. At Xerox, the CEO set an initial goal of reducing defective parts from 25,000 per million to 1,000 per million. One way of creating incentives to attain a goal is to link rewards, such as bonus pay and promotional opportunities, to the goal.

5. *Solicit input from employees.* Employees can be a major source of information about the sources of poor quality. Therefore, it is important for managers to establish a framework for soliciting employee suggestions about improvements that can be made. **Quality circles**–groups of employees who meet regularly to discuss ways to increase quality–are often created to achieve this goal. Other companies create self-managed teams to further quality improvement efforts. Whatever the means chosen to solicit input from lower-level employees, managers must be open to receiving, and acting on, bad news and criticism from employees. According to Deming, however, Western managers have grown used to "killing the bearer of bad tidings."[25] Deming argued that managers who are committed to the quality concept must be open to bad news, for as he put it, bad news is a gold mine of information.

6. *Identify defects and trace them to their source.* A major source of product defects is the production system. TQM preaches the need for managers to identify defects in the work process, trace those defects back to their source, find out why they occurred, and make corrections so that they do not occur again. To identify defects, Deming advocated the use of statistical procedures to spot variations in the quality of goods or services. Deming considered variation to be the enemy of quality.[26] Once variations have been identified, he said, they need to be traced back to their source and eliminated.

One technique that helps greatly in finding the source of defects is reducing the lot sizes of manufactured products (*lot size* is the number of units of a product produced in a particular run). When lot sizes are small, defects show up immediately, they can be quickly traced to their source, and the problem can be fixed. Also, reducing lot sizes means that when defective products are produced, their number will be small, thereby reducing waste. Flexible manufacturing techniques (discussed later in this chapter) can be used to reduce lot sizes without raising costs. Thus the adoption of flexible manufacturing techniques may be an important aspect of a TQM program.

7. *Introduce just-in-time inventory systems.* **Inventory** is the stock of raw materials, inputs, and component parts that an organization has on hand at a particular time. Just-in-time (JIT) inventory systems play a major role in the process of identifying and finding the source of defects in inputs. When an organization has a **just-in-time inventory system,** parts or supplies arrive at the organization when they are needed, not before. This system can be contrasted with a *just-in-case* view of inventory, which leads an organization to stockpile excess inputs in a warehouse just in case it needs them to meet sudden upturns in demand. Under a JIT inventory system, defective parts enter an organization's production system immediately; they are not warehoused for months before

quality circles Groups of employees who meet regularly to discuss ways to increase quality.

inventory The stock of raw materials, inputs, and component parts that an organization has on hand at a particular time.

just-in-time inventory system A system in which parts or supplies arrive at an organization when they are needed, not before.

use. This means that defective inputs can be quickly spotted. Managers can then trace the problem to the supply source and fix it before more defective parts are produced.

Just-in-time systems were originally developed in Japan during the 1950s and 1960s. As this "Managing Globally" explains, they were developed in an attempt to improve product quality.

Managing Globally

The *Kanban* System in Japan

The Japanese *kanban* system of just-in-time inventory was originally developed at the Toyota Motor Company (www.toyota.com) during the 1950s by a mechanical engineer, Ohno Taiichi. At the time Taiichi was a middle manager in charge of a Toyota machine shop that produced component parts for Toyota's automobile assembly lines. In developing the *kanban* system, Taiichi was trying to achieve two goals. First, he wanted to reduce the costs associated with stockpiling inventory before it was used in an automobile assembly line. Second, and more important from his perspective, he wanted to improve the quality of Toyota's cars. Taiichi reasoned that achieving these goals required an improvement in the quality of component parts.

At the time, vast numbers of component parts were produced at once and stored in a warehouse until they were needed. Taiichi saw a major problem with this approach: A defective part might not be discovered for weeks or months, when the part was needed in the assembly process. But by that time, it might be too late to determine why the defect had occurred, and correcting the problem that had produced the defect would be difficult. Moreover, if the defect was due to the initial machine settings, the outcome was likely to be the production of large volumes of defective individual parts and enormous waste.

Taiichi decided to experiment with a new production system. Starting in his small machine shop, he developed a simple system of levers and pulleys that allowed him to reduce the time required to set up production machinery from hours to minutes and made the production of small lots of component parts economical. He then produced and sent component parts to the assembly line just as they were needed. The parts traveled from his machine shop to the assembly line in a small wheeled container known as a *kanban*. The assembly-line workers emptied the *kanban* and then sent the container back to Taiichi's machine shop. The return of the *kanban* container was the signal to produce another small batch of component parts, and so the process repeated itself.

The system worked beautifully, and Taiichi was able to get rid of most of the warehouse space needed to store inventory. Moreover, the short production runs meant that defects in parts showed up

Kanban boxes stacked at a Toyota plant ready to be taken to the production line for final assembly.

at the assembly line almost immediately, which helped enormously in the process of identifying and eliminating the source of a defect. As a result, Taiichi's machine shop quickly gained a reputation for quality within Toyota.

Over the years, Taiichi was repeatedly promoted for his efforts (when he ended his career in the mid-1980s, he was Toyota's chief engineer) and given the authority to spread his *kanban* innovation, first within Toyota and then to Toyota's suppliers. During the 1970s other companies in Japan copied Toyota's revolutionary *kanban* system. Much of the subsequent success of Japanese companies globally during the 1980s can be attributed to improvements in product quality brought about by the wide-scale adoption of the *kanban* system in Japan, a full decade before managers in Western companies imitated the idea.[27]

8. *Work closely with suppliers.* As the "Managing Globally" makes clear, a major cause of poor-quality finished goods is poor-quality component parts. To decrease product defects, managers must work closely with suppliers to improve the quality of the parts they supply. Managers at Xerox worked closely with suppliers to get them to adopt TQM programs, and the result was a huge reduction in the defect rate of component parts. Managers also need to work closely with suppliers to get them to adopt a JIT inventory system, also required for high quality.

To implement JIT systems with suppliers, and to get suppliers to set up their own TQM programs, two steps are necessary. First, managers must reduce the number of suppliers with which their organization does business. Managers at Xerox, for example, reduced the number of suppliers from 5,000 to 325, greatly streamlining their interactions with suppliers. Second, managers need to develop cooperative long-term relationships with remaining suppliers. Asking suppliers to invest in JIT and TQM systems means asking them to make major investments that tie them to the company. For example, to fully implement a JIT system, a company may ask a supplier to relocate its manufacturing plant so that it is next door to the company's assembly plant. Suppliers will be hesitant about making such investments unless they feel that the company is committed to an enduring long-term relationship with them.

9. *Design for ease of manufacture.* The more steps that are required to assemble a product, the more opportunities there are for making a mistake. It follows that designing products that have fewer parts and thus making their assembly easier should be linked to fewer defects. For example, after Texas Instruments redesigned an infrared sighting mechanism that it supplies to the Pentagon, the company found that it had reduced the number of parts from 47 to 12 and the number of assembly steps from 56 to 13. The consequence of this redesign was a fall in assembly costs and marked improvement in product quality.

10. *Break down barriers between functions.* Successful implementation of TQM requires organizationwide commitment from managers to quality and substantial cooperation between the different functions of an organization. R&D managers have to cooperate with manufacturing managers to design products that are easy to manufacture; marketing managers have to cooperate with manufacturing and R&D managers so that customer problems identified by marketing can be acted on; human resource managers have to cooperate with all of the other functions of the company in order to devise suitable quality training programs, and so on.

The Role of Top and Functional-Level Managers in TQM

All managers have critical roles to play in the TQM process. Normally, top managers initiate a TQM program, and a continuing emphasis on TQM requires their long-term commitment and willingness to make TQM an organizationwide priority. What cannot be stressed strongly enough, however, is that it is functional-level managers who carry prime responsibility for implementing most of the steps outlined above. Although top managers may be the ones who establish the initial TQM program, much of the actual work required to make a TQM program succeed is done by functional-level managers. It is functional-level managers who

- Identify defects, trace them back to their source, and fix quality problems
- Design products that are easy to assemble
- Identify customer needs, translate those needs into quality requirements, and see that these quality requirements shape the production system of the organization
- Work to break down the barriers between functional departments
- Solicit suggestions from lower-level employees about how to improve the quality of the organization's output

If the TQM philosophy is to become part of an organization's culture, functional-level managers must learn how to live and breathe the TQM philosophy. In those organizations where TQM has failed to deliver on its promise to improve product quality, lack of commitment by functional-level managers may be the reason. To develop a successful TQM program, managers must first involve employees at all levels in the organization. They then must clearly assign responsibility for improving quality to each employee and create a goal-setting system that allows them to evaluate how well each employee has achieved these goals. Finally, they must try to develop cultural values and norms that make quality an important goal and create organizational ceremonies to reward employees when quality targets are met.

Improving Efficiency

The third goal of operations management is to increase the efficiency of an organization's production system. The fewer the inputs required to produce a given output, the higher will be the efficiency of the production system. Managers can measure efficiency at the organization level in two ways. The measure known as *total factor productivity* looks at how well an organization utilizes all of its resources—such as labor, capital, materials, energy—to produce its outputs. It is expressed in the following equation:

$$\text{Total factor productivity} = \frac{\text{outputs}}{\text{all inputs}}$$

The problem with total factor productivity is that each input is typically measured in different units: Labor's contribution to producing an output is measured by hours worked; the contribution of materials is measured by the amount consumed (for example, tons of iron ore required to make a ton of steel); the contribution of energy is measured by the units of energy consumed (for example, kilowatt-hours), and so on. To compute total factor productivity, managers must convert all the inputs to a common unit, such as dollars, before they can work the equation.

Though sometimes a useful measure of efficiency overall, total factor productivity obscures the exact contribution of an individual input—such as labor—to the production of a given output. Consequently, most organizations focus on specific measures of efficiency, known as *partial productivity*, that measure the efficiency of an individual unit. For example, the efficiency of labor inputs is expressed as

$$\text{Labor productivity} = \frac{\text{outputs}}{\text{direct labor}}$$

Labor productivity is most commonly used to draw efficiency comparisons between different organizations. For example, a 1994 study found that it took the average Japanese company in the automobile components industry half as many labor hours to produce a component part such as a car seat or exhaust system as the average British company.[28] Thus, the study concluded, Japanese companies use labor more efficiently than British companies.

The management of efficiency is an extremely important issue in most organizations, because increased efficiency lowers production costs, thereby allowing the organization to make a greater profit or to attract more customers by lowering its price. For example, in 1990 the price of the average personal computer sold in the United States was $3,000; by 1995 the price was around $1,800. This decrease occurred despite the fact that the features of the average personal computer increased during this time period (microprocessors became more powerful; memory increased; communication facilities such as built-in modems were added). Why was the decrease in price possible? The manufacturers of personal computers took several steps to boost their efficiency, which allowed them to lower their costs and prices yet still make a profit. At Compaq Computer, for example, managers redesigned personal computers so that they were easier to assemble; this reduced the time it took to assemble a ProLine desktop computer from 20.85 minutes in 1991 to 10.49 minutes by 1994, a significant increase in efficiency.[29]

Managers can boost efficiency in their organizations by focusing on TQM and a number of other factors.

Total Quality Management and Efficiency

Increased product quality, obtained through the adoption of a TQM program, can have a major positive impact on labor productivity: When quality rises, less employee time is wasted in making defective products that have to be discarded or in fixing defective products. Moreover, a major source of quality improvement can come from designing products that have fewer parts and are therefore relatively easy to assemble. Designing products with fewer parts also cuts down on total assembly time and increases efficiency.[30] When managers at Texas Instruments redesigned the infrared sighting mechanism for the Pentagon, for example, they achieved a significant increase in efficiency.

Facilities Layout, Flexible Manufacturing, and Efficiency

Another factor that influences efficiency is the way managers decide to lay out or design an organization's physical work facilities. This is important for two reasons. First, the way in which machines and workers are organized or grouped together into workstations affects the efficiency of the production system. Second, a major determinant of efficiency is the cost associated with setting up the equipment needed to make a particular product. **Facilities layout** is the operations management technique whose goal is to design the machine–worker interface to increase production system efficiency. **Flexible manufacturing** is the set of operations management techniques that attempt to reduce the setup costs associated with a production system.

facilities layout The operations management technique whose goal is to design the machine–worker interface to increase production system efficiency.

flexible manufacturing Operations management techniques that attempt to reduce the setup costs associated with a production system.

FACILITIES LAYOUT The way in which machines, robots, and people are grouped together affects how productive they can be. Figure 18.5 shows three basic ways of arranging workstations: product layout, process layout, and fixed-position layout.

In a *product layout,* machines are organized so that each operation needed to manufacture a product is performed at workstations arranged in a fixed sequence.

Figure 18.5
Three Facilities Layouts

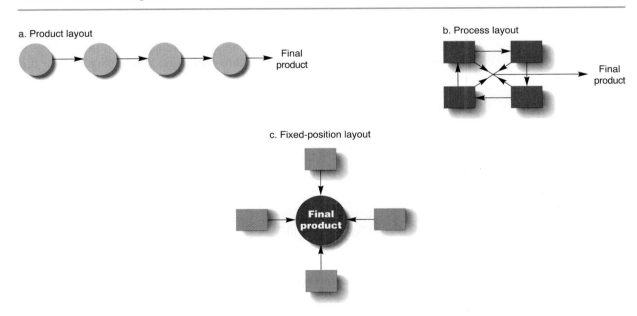

a. Product layout

Final product

b. Process layout

Final product

c. Fixed-position layout

Final product

Typically, workers are stationary in this arrangement, and a moving conveyor belt takes the product being worked on to the next workstation so that it is progressively assembled. *Mass production* is the familiar name for this layout; car assembly lines are probably the best-known example. It used to be that product layout was efficient only when products were made in large quantities; however, as the "Case in Contrast" indicates, the introduction of modular assembly lines controlled by computers is making it efficient to make products in small batches.

In a *process layout,* workstations are not organized in a fixed sequence. Rather, each workstation is relatively self-contained, and a product goes to whichever workstation is needed to perform the next operation to complete the product. Process layout is often suited to manufacturing settings that produce a variety of custom-made products, each tailored to the needs of a different kind of customer. For example, a custom furniture manufacturer might use a process layout so that different teams of workers can produce different styles of chairs or tables made from different kinds of woods and finishes. A process layout provides the flexibility needed to change the product. Such flexibility, however, often reduces efficiency because it is expensive.

In a *fixed-position layout,* the product stays in a fixed position. Its component parts are produced in remote workstations and brought to the production area for final assembly. Increasingly, self-managed teams are being used in fixed-position layouts. Different teams assemble each component part and then send these parts to the final assembly team, which makes the final product. A fixed-position layout is commonly used for products such as jet airlines, mainframe computers, and gas turbines—products that are complex and difficult to assemble or so large that moving them from one workstation to another would be difficult.

FLEXIBLE MANUFACTURING In a manufacturing company, a major source of costs is the costs associated with setting up the equipment needed to make a particular product. One of these costs is the cost of production that is forgone because nothing is being produced while the equipment is being set up. Federal-Mogul employees, discussed in the "Case in Contrast," needed as much as half a day to set up the automated production equipment when switching from production of one auto part (such as a washer ring for the steering column of a car) to another (such as a washer ring for the steering column of a truck). During this half-day, the plant was not producing anything, but employees were paid for this "nonproductive" time.

It follows that if setup times for complex production equipment can be reduced, so can setup costs, and efficiency will rise. In other words, if setup times can be reduced, the time that plant and employees spend in actually producing something will increase. This simple insight has been the driving force behind the development of flexible manufacturing techniques.

Flexible manufacturing aims to reduce the time required to set up production equipment.[31] The positive effects of flexible manufacturing techniques are evident in the case of Federal-Mogul. By redesigning its production system so that equipment geared for manufacturing one product could be quickly wheeled away and replaced with equipment geared to make another product, Federal-Mogul was able to reduce setup times from as much as half a day in 1987 to 10 minutes in 1993. One result was a dramatic improvement in efficiency because of the reduction in "nonproductive" time. Another favorable result was that Federal-Mogul was able to produce three times as many different product varieties as before, in the same amount of time. In other words, flexible manufacturing increased Federal-Mogul's ability to be responsive to its customers.

Increasingly, organizations are experimenting with new designs for production systems that not only allow workers to be more productive but also make the work process more flexible, thus reducing setup costs. Some Japanese companies are experimenting with facilities layouts arranged as a spiral, as the letter Y, and as the number 6, to see how these various configurations affect setup costs and worker productivity. At a camcorder plant in Kohda, Japan, for example, Sony changed from a fixed-position layout in which 50 workers sequentially built a camcorder to a spiral process design in which 4 workers perform all the operations necessary to produce the camcorder. This new layout allows the most efficient workers to work at the highest pace, and it reduces setup costs because workers can easily switch from one model to another, increasing efficiency by 10 percent.[32]

Just-in-Time Inventory and Efficiency

Although JIT systems, such as Toyota's *kanban* system, were originally developed as part of the effort to improve product quality, they have major implications for efficiency. Major cost savings can result from increasing inventory turnover and reducing inventory holding costs, such as warehousing and storage costs and the cost of capital tied up in inventory. Ford's switch to JIT systems in the 1980s, for example, reportedly bought the company a huge one-time saving of $3 billion, and inventory-holding costs have been reduced by one-third.

More recently, several service companies have adopted the JIT concept, often with great success. Wal-Mart, the fastest-growing general retailer in the United States, uses JIT systems to replenish the stock in its stores at least twice a week. Many Wal-Mart stores receive daily deliveries. Wal-Mart's main competitors, Kmart and Sears, typically replenish their stock every two weeks. Wal-Mart can maintain the same service levels as these competitors but at one-fourth the inventory-holding cost, a major source of cost saving. Faster inventory turnover has helped Wal-Mart achieve an efficiency-based competitive advantage in the retailing industry.[33]

One drawback of JIT systems is that they leave an organization without a buffer stock of inventory.[34] Although buffer stocks of inventory can be expensive to store, they can help an organization when it is affected by shortages of inputs brought about by a disruption among suppliers (such as a labor dispute in a key supplier). Moreover, buffer stocks can help an organization respond quickly to increases in customer demand—that is, they can increase an organization's responsiveness to customers.

Because holding a buffer stock of inventory does have advantages, some early adopters of JIT systems have recently pulled back from a complete commitment to JIT. An example is GE Appliances, profiled in this "Management Insight."

Management Insight

Problems with JIT at GE Appliances

GE (www.ge.com) Appliances' managers first became interested in Japan's *kanban* system of just-in-time inventory in the early 1980s when General Electric CEO Jack Welsh was urging GE's various divisions to boost their efficiency by adopting Japanese-style manufacturing techniques. At first the system seemed to work well. The appliances division realized a one-time saving of over $50 million from inventory reductions as inventory-holding costs fell by close to one-half. Moreover, managers found that JIT systems helped them identify defective inputs from suppliers, trace problems back to their source, and fix problems that caused defects so that they would not occur again.

By the early 1990s, however, managers at GE were becoming disillusioned with some aspects of their JIT system. One problem was that low inventories of some critical parts prevented GE from responding quickly to customer demands. GE gets 475 parts from 75 suppliers–some of which are located several thousand miles from GE's assembly plant. Getting critical parts from some of these suppliers often took so long that GE was unable to promptly fill orders from important customers, who then turned to GE's competitors.

In 1993 managers decided to increase by 24 percent their inventory of critical parts that had long delivery times. This change helped the company to respond more rapidly to customer orders. By 1994 GE was filling orders in 3.6 weeks, down from 18 weeks in 1990.[35] According to managers, the benefits of a faster order-to-delivery cycle more than offset the cost of stocking additional parts.

Self-Managed Work Teams and Efficiency

Another efficiency-boosting innovation that is gaining wide acceptance in the workplace is the use of self-managed work teams (see Chapter 14).[36] The typical team consists of from 5 to 15 employees who produce an entire product instead of just parts of it.[37] Team members learn all team tasks and move from job to job. The result is a flexible workforce, because team members can fill in for absent coworkers. The members of each team also assume responsibility for work and vacation scheduling, ordering materials, and hiring new members–previous responsibilities of first-line managers. Because people often respond well to being given greater autonomy and responsibility, the use of empowered self-managed teams can increase productivity and efficiency. Moreover, cost savings arise from eliminating supervisors and creating a flatter organizational hierarchy, which further increases efficiency.

The effect of introducing self-managed teams is often an increase in efficiency of 30 percent or more, sometimes much more. After the introduction of flexible manufacturing technology and self-managed teams, a GE plant in Salisbury, North Carolina, increased efficiency by 250 percent compared with other GE plants producing the same products.[38]

Kaizen (Continuous Improvement) and Efficiency

kaizen An all-embracing operations management philosophy that emphasizes the need for continuous improvement in the efficiency of an organization's production system.

Kaizen is the Japanese term for an all-embracing operations management philosophy that emphasizes the need for continuous improvement in the efficiency of an organization's production system.[39] Unlike TQM or JIT, *kaizen* is not a specific operations management technique; rather, *kaizen* stresses the contribution to improving efficiency and quality that can come from numerous small, incremental improvements in production processes.

The central principle of *kaizen* is the elimination of waste: wasted materials, piles of excess inventory, time wasted when a production employee makes more moves than are necessary to complete a task because, for example, his or her machine is poorly positioned, and time wasted in activities that do not add value, such as moving parts from one machine to another. (See the discussion of scientific management theory in Chapter 2 for some historical background on these issues.) According to representatives from the Kaizen Institute, a European management consultancy, in the average factory for every second spent adding value by, for example, assembling a product, another 1,000 seconds are spent not adding value.[40]

The *kaizen* philosophy emphasizes that managers and other employees should be taught to critically analyze all aspects of their organization's production system, to identify any sources of waste, and to suggest ways to eliminate waste. Often, self-managed work teams perform this analysis. They take time out once a week or once a month to analyze the design of their jobs and to suggest potential improvements to functional managers.[41]

Increasingly, as part of the *kaizen* process, managers are experimenting with changing facilities layouts to try to increase efficiency. In Paddy Hopkirk's car accessory factory, located in Bedfordshire, England, and profiled in the next "Managing Globally," the application of *kaizen* resulted in a change in facilities layout that reduced the time wasted in moving parts from one workstation to another.

Managing Globally

Applying *Kaizen* to Improve Facilities Layout

Paddy Hopkirk established his car accessories business in the 1960s, shortly after he had shot to motor car racing fame by winning the Monte Carlo Rally. Sales of Hopkirk's accessories, such as bicycle racks and axle stands, were always brisk, and by 1993 his company was doing over $6 million worth of business. Hopkirk, however, was the first to admit that his production system left a lot to be desired. So in 1993, after hearing about *kaizen* from a customer, he invited consultants from the Kaizen Institute to help him reorganize his production system.

After analyzing his factory's production system, the consultants realized that the source of the problem was the facilities layout Hopkirk had established. Over time, as sales grew, Hopkirk simply added new workstations to

Figure 18.6

The Application of *Kaizen* to Facilities Layout

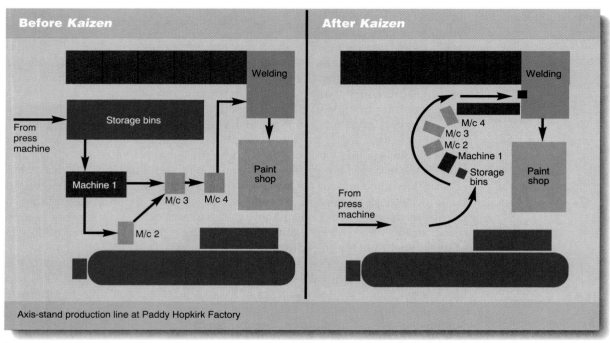

Axis-stand production line at Paddy Hopkirk Factory

Source: Reprinted from *Financial Times* of January 4, 1994, by permission of Financial Times Syndication, London.

the production system as they were needed. The result was a process layout in which the product being assembled moved in the irregular sequences shown in the "Before *Kaizen*" half of Figure 18.6. The consultants suggested that to save time and effort, the workstations should be reorganized into the sequential product layout shown in the "After *Kaizen*" illustration.

Once this change was made, the results were dramatic. One morning the factory was an untidy sprawl of workstations surrounded by piles of crates holding semifinished components. Two days later, when the 170-person workforce came back to work, the machines had been brought together into tightly grouped workstations arranged in the fixed sequence shown in the illustration. The piles of components had disappeared, and the newly cleared floor space was neatly marked with color-coded lines mapping out the new flow of materials between workstations.

In the first full day of production, efficiency increased by as much as 30 percent. The space needed for some operations had been cut in half, and work-in-progress had been cut considerably. Moreover, the improved layout allowed for some jobs to be combined, freeing operators for deployment elsewhere in the factory. An amazed Hopkirk exclaimed, "I was expecting a change but nothing as dramatic as this . . . it is fantastic."[42]

The implementation of self-managed teams, flexible manufacturing systems and facilities layouts, TQM, and JIT are all consistent with the *kaizen* approach: All seek to reduce wasted materials and time. Indeed, these techniques were originally developed by Toyota and other Japanese companies that had adopted the *kaizen* philosophy and were looking for specific ways to improve their production processes.

Process Reengineering and Efficiency

process reengineering
The fundamental rethinking and radical redesign of business processes to achieve dramatic improvements in critical measures of performance such as cost, quality, service, and speed.

Think of the major activities of businesses as processes that take one or more kinds of inputs and create an output that is of value to the customer.[43] **Process reengineering** is the fundamental rethinking and radical redesign of business processes to achieve dramatic improvements in critical measures of performance such as cost, quality, service, and speed.[44] Order fulfillment, for example, can be thought of as a business process: Once a customer's order is received (the input), all the activities necessary to process the order are performed, and the ordered goods are delivered to the customer (the output).

Like *kaizen,* process reengineering can boost efficiency because it eliminates the time devoted to activities that do not add value. Unlike *kaizen,* with its emphasis on continuous incremental improvements, process reengineering is about re-designing business processes from scratch. It is concerned with the radical redesign of business processes, not incremental changes in those processes. Because process reengineering burst on the management scene in 1993, it is too early to evaluate its effectiveness as a management tool. But some interesting examples of reengineering suggest that if properly implemented it can have a major impact on efficiency. Consider the case of Ford Motor Company, profiled in this "Management Insight."

Management Insight

Reengineering of Procurement at Ford

Ford (www.ford.com) has a strategic alliance with Mazda (www.mazda.com). One day a Ford manager discovered, quite by accident, that the Japanese car company had only five people in its accounts payable department. The Ford manager was shocked, for Ford's U.S. operation alone had 500 employees in accounts payable. He reported his discovery to Ford's U.S. managers, who decided to form a task force to analyze Ford's procurement process and to see whether it could be reengineered.

Ford managers discovered that procurement began when the purchasing department sent a purchase order to a supplier and sent a copy of the purchase order to Ford's accounts payable department. When the supplier shipped the goods and they arrived at Ford, a clerk at the receiving dock completed a form describing the goods and sent the form to accounts payable. The supplier, meanwhile, sent accounts payable an invoice. Thus, accounts payable received three documents relating to these goods: a copy

A team of operating workers at a Union Carbide plant in Taft, Louisiana, hold up a new process map of plant operations that they created as a part of a major *reengineering* effort. They found savings worth over $20 million.

of the original purchase order, the receiving document, and the invoice. If the information in all three was in agreement (most of the time it was), a clerk in accounts payable issued payment. Occasionally, however, all three documents did not agree. And Ford discovered that accounts payable clerks spent most of their time straightening out the 1 percent of instances in which the purchase order, receiving document, and invoice contained conflicting information.[45]

Ford managers decided to reengineer the procurement process to simplify it. Now when a buyer in the purchasing department issues a purchase order to a supplier, that buyer also enters the order into an on-line database. As before, suppliers send goods to the receiving dock. When the goods arrive, the clerk at the receiving dock checks a computer terminal to see whether the received shipment matches the description on the purchase order. If it does, the clerk accepts the goods and pushes a button on the terminal keyboard that tells the database that the goods have arrived. Receipt of the goods is recorded in the database, and a computer automatically issues and sends a check to the supplier. If the goods do not correspond to the description on the purchase order in the database, the clerk at the dock refuses the shipment and sends it back to the supplier.

Payment authorization, which used to be performed by accounts payable, is now accomplished at the receiving dock. The new process has come close to eliminating the need for an accounts payable department. In some parts of Ford, the size of the accounts payable department has been cut by 95 percent. By reducing the head count in accounts payable, the reengineering effort reduced the amount of time wasted on unproductive activities, thereby increasing the efficiency of the total organization.

The Role of Top and Functional-Level Managers in Efficiency

As with TQM, managers at all levels have important roles to play in the effort to boost efficiency. Top management's role is to encourage efficiency improvements by, for example, emphasizing the need for continuous improvement (*kaizen*) or reengineering. Top management also must ensure that managers from different functional departments work together to find ways to increase efficiency. Achieving functional cooperation is important because many of the steps that must be taken to raise efficiency involve actions that cut across functional boundaries. Reengineering, for example, may require personnel from different departments to cooperate on the design of a new process.

As with TQM, however, it is middle managers who bear the prime responsibility for identifying and implementing many of the efficiency-enhancing improvements to a production system. It is typically functional-level managers who identify opportunities for continuous improvement or reengineering. Top managers might recognize the need for such actions, but functional-level managers are in the best position to identify opportunities for making efficiency-enhancing improvements (especially *kaizen* ones) to an organization's production systems. They are the managers who are involved in an organization's production system on a day-to-day basis.

Operations Management: Some Remaining Issues

Achieving superior responsiveness to customers through quality and efficiency often requires a profound shift in management operations and in the culture of an organization. The message of both TQM and *kaizen* for improving operations management in the future is that all employees need to constantly evaluate an organization's production system in an ongoing and never-ending search for improvements. Many reports are appearing in the popular press about widespread disillusionment with TQM, JIT, flexible manufacturing, *kaizen,* and reengineering. It is possible that many of the disillusioned organizations are those that failed to understand that implementing these systems requires a marked shift in organizational culture.[46] None of these systems is a panacea that can be taken once like a pill to cure industrial ills. Making these techniques work within an organization can pose a significant challenge that calls for hard work and years of persistence by the sponsoring managers.

Managers also need to understand the ethical implications of the adoption of many of the production techniques discussed here. TQM, JIT, flexible manufacturing, *kaizen,* and reengineering can all increase quality, efficiency, and responsiveness to customers, but they may do so at great cost to employees. Employees may see the demands of their job increase as the result of TQM or *kaizen,* or, worse, they may see themselves reengineered out of a job. Consider, for example, the incidents described in this "Ethics in Action."

Ethics in Action

The Human Cost of Improving Productivity

Toyota (www.toyota.com) may be the most productive automobile company in the world, but some of its gains have been achieved at a significant cost to its employees. Take Hisashi Tomiki, the leader of a four-man self-managed team in Toyota's huge Toyota City production plant, 200 miles south of Tokyo, Japan. Tomiki and his team work at a grueling pace to build cowls (steel chambers onto which windshields and steering columns are attached). Consider this description of Tomiki at work:

> *In two minutes Tomiki fits 24 metal pieces into designated slots on three welding machines; runs two large metal sheets through each of the machines, which weld on*

the parts; and fuses the two sheets together with two spot welds. There is little room for error. Once or twice an hour a mistake is made or a machine sticks, causing the next machine in line to stop. A yellow light flashes. Tomiki runs over. The squad must fix the part and work faster to catch up. A red button halts the production line if the problems are severe, but there is an unspoken rule against pushing it. Only once this day does Tomiki call in a special maintenance worker.[47]

The experience of workers like Tomiki makes many Western workers nervous about the spread of Japanese management techniques. Workers are heard to complain that constant improvement really means continuous speedup and added job stress. Consider this comment on *kaizen* from one employee at Mazda's auto plant in Flat Rock, Michigan. "Under *kaizen* management constantly reduces the parts, the resources, the manpower, to do the job. We are building 1,000 good cars a day, an incredible effort. But if we learn to do it with 90 percent [of the time and resources], they go to 80 percent. They take away another person, they take away another part."[48] The implication, of course, is that there is no end to the search for continuous improvement (which, in essence, is what the *kaizen* philosophy recommends) and therefore no end to the steady increase in the pressure put on employees to perform. Although some pressure is good, past a certain point it can seriously harm employees.

Nor is it just Japanese techniques that have such an impact. Process reengineering, first developed in America, is also taking its toll. Consider the following quote from Jerry Miller, a former employee of US West, whose team of billing clerks reengineered themselves out of a job in 1994: "When we first formed our teams, the company came in talking teams and empowerment and promised that we wouldn't lose any jobs. It turns out all this was a big cover. The company had us all set up for reengineering. We showed them how to streamline the work, and now 9,000 people are gone. It was cut-your-own-throat. It makes you feel used."[49]

The problems highlighted in that "Ethics in Action" raise serious questions about the introduction of *kaizen* and reengineering: They may constitute a violation of basic ethics, principally because they may require some deception. With regard to *kaizen,* one must ask whether it is ethical to continually increase the demands placed on employees, regardless of the human cost in terms of job stress. It is obvious that the answer is no. Employees are important stakeholders in an organization, and their support is vital if the organization is to function effectively. What are the limits to *kaizen;* what kind of work pressures are legitimate, and what pressures are excessive? There is no clear answer to this question. Ultimately the issue comes down to the judgment of responsible managers acting ethically toward all their stakeholders.

Tips for Managers

Operations Management

1. Be mindful of the links between superior customer responsiveness and the production system of an organization.

2. While managers must seek to improve the customer responsiveness of their organization by improving its production system, they must not offer a product whose cost becomes so high profits suffer.

3. Achieving superior quality and productivity requires the adoption of organizationwide philosophies such as *kaizen* and TQM.

4. Making these techniques work within an organization requires hard work and years of persistence from the managers, and a recognition of the ethical implications of these techniques for affected employees.

Summary and Review

Chapter Summary

OPERATIONS MANAGEMENT AND COMPETITIVE ADVANTAGE

IMPROVING RESPON- SIVENESS TO CUSTOMERS

• What Do Customers Want?

• Designing Produc- tion Systems That Are Responsive to Customers

OPERATIONS MANAGEMENT AND COM- PETITIVE ADVANTAGE To achieve high perfor- mance, managers try to improve their responsiveness to customers, the quality of their products, and the efficiency of their organization. To achieve these goals, managers can use a number of operations management techniques to improve the way an organization's pro- duction system operates.

IMPROVING RESPONSIVENESS TO CUSTOMERS To achieve high performance in a competitive environment, it is imperative that the pro- duction system of an organization respond to customer demands. Managers try to design production systems that produce outputs that have the attributes that customers desire. One of the central tasks of operations management is to develop new and improved production systems that enhance the ability of the organization to economically deliver more of the product attributes that cus- tomers desire for the same price. Techniques such as TQM, JIT, flexible man- ufacturing, *kaizen,* and process reengineering are popular because they promise to do this. Managers should carefully analyze the links between responsiveness to customers and the production system of an organization. The ability of an organization to satisfy the demands of its customers for lower prices, acceptable quality, better features, and so on, depends critically on the nature of the organization's production system. As important as responsive- ness to customers is, however, managers need to recognize that there are limits to how responsive an organization can be and still cover its costs.

IMPROVING QUALITY Managers seek to improve the quality of their organization's output because doing so enables them to better serve cus- tomers, to raise prices, and to lower production costs. Total quality manage- ment focuses on improving the quality of an organization's products and services and stresses that all of an organization's operations should be directed toward this goal. Putting TQM into practice requires an organizationwide commitment to TQM, a strong customer focus, finding ways to measure quality, setting quality improvement goals, soliciting input from employees about how to improve product quality, identifying defects and tracing them to their source, introducing just-in-time inventory systems, getting suppliers to adopt TQM practices, designing products for ease of manufacture, and breaking down barriers between functional departments.

IMPROVING EFFICIENCY Improving efficiency requires one or more of the following: the introduction of a TQM program, the adoption of flexible manufacturing technologies, the introduction of just-in-time inventory systems, the establishment of self-managed work teams, the institutionalization of a _kaizen_ philosophy of continuous improvement within the organization, and process reengineering. Top management is responsible for setting the context within which efficiency improvements can take place by, for example, emphasizing the need for a _kaizen_ philosophy. Functional-level managers bear prime responsibility for identifying and implementing efficiency-enhancing improvements in production systems.

Management in Action

Topics for Discussion and Action

1. What are the main challenges to be overcome in implementing a successful total quality management program?

2. Ask a manager how quality, efficiency, and responsiveness to customers are defined and measured in his or her organization.

3. Go into a local store, restaurant, or supermarket and list the ways in which you think the organization is being responsive or unresponsive to the needs of its customers. How could this business's responsiveness to customers be improved?

4. Widespread dissatisfaction with the results of TQM programs has been reported in the popular press. Why do you think TQM programs frequently fail to deliver their promised benefits?

5. What is efficiency, and what are some of the techniques that managers can use to increase it?

6. Why is it important for managers to pay close attention to their organization's production system if they wish to be responsive to their customers?

7. What, if any, are the ethical limitations to the aggressive implementation of the *kaizen* philosophy of continuous improvement?

8. "Total customer service is the goal toward which most organizations should strive." To what degree is this statement correct?

Building Management Skills

Managing a Production System

Choose an organization with which you are familiar—one that you have worked in or patronized or one that has received extensive coverage in the popular press. The organization should be involved in only one industry or business. Answer these questions about the organization.

1. What is the output of the organization?

2. Describe the production system that the organization uses to produce this output.

3. What product attributes do customers of the organization desire?

4. Does its production system allow the organization to deliver the desired product attributes?

5. Try to identify improvements that might be made to the organization's production system to boost the organization's responsiveness to customers, quality, and efficiency.

Small Group Breakout Exercise

How to Compete in the Sandwich Business

Form groups of three or four people, and appoint one member as the spokesperson who will communicate your findings to the whole class when called on by the instructor. Then discuss the following scenario.

You and your partners are thinking about opening a new kind of sandwich shop that will compete head-to-head with Subway and Thundercloud Subs. Because these chains have good brand-name recognition, it is vital that you find some source of competitive advantage for your new sandwich shop, and you are meeting to brainstorm ways of obtaining one.

1. Identify the product attributes that a typical sandwich shop customer wants the most.

2. In what ways do you think you will be able to improve on the operations and processes of existing sandwich shops and achieve a competitive advantage through better (a) product quality, (b) efficiency, or (c) responsiveness to customers?

Exploring the World Wide Web

Specific Assignment

Enter the website of the Kaizen Institute (www.kaizen-institute.com), and click on the "jewellry room" for an introduction to *kaizen* concepts; then explore some *kaizen* stories at the "classics room."

1. How does the *kaizen* technique help give a company a competitive advantage?

2. What must a company do to apply *kaizen* techniques successfully?

General Assignment

Search for the website of a company that outlines the way it tries to improve responsiveness to customers, quality, or efficiency. What specific techniques does the company use to improve the way it operates? How have those techniques helped the company improve its performance?

ManagementCase

Kaizen at Frigidaire

Until 1990, the Frigidaire Company (www.frigidaire.com) plant in Jefferson, Iowa, used a traditional mass-production assembly system to produce transmissions. One hundred sixty employees, working in shifts, stood along a straight conveyor belt assembling transmissions, and supervisors were responsible for monitoring their performance and making all production-related decisions. According to managers, the management approach was like Theory X (see Chapter 2), and although productivity was acceptable, quality was poor.

This situation changed rapidly in 1991 when a new plant manager took control of the Jefferson plant. The newcomer had experience with *kaizen* and the use of teams, or "cells," as the basis of the production system, rather than a conveyor belt. The production man-

ager moved quickly to implement a new team-based approach in the factory based on *kaizen* principles.

He instructed his managers to examine the current production system and machinery layout and figure out how to divide the workforce into teams to produce the transmissions. Managers went to work and found that the most efficient way to group machines and workers into teams would be to divide the workforce into 28 teams.[50] The 28 teams were positioned so that they could efficiently exchange the component parts necessary to produce the final transmission.

The supervisors' role was totally changed. Responsibility for all assembly-related decision making was passed down the line to team members. Supervisors were renamed "primary facilitators," and their new role was to support a team and to provide it with the

resources it needed. Each team and its facilitator were instructed to meet once a week to set production goals and to discuss ways to increase productivity and quality. Facilitators also were responsible for meeting together as a team once a week to share their knowledge and information and so spread the new learning among teams across the organization. By 1996, the new work system had succeeded dramatically. The performance of some teams had increased by 50 percent, and quality was up sharply too.

Questions

1. What changes did managers at Frigidaire make to the work system?

2. Why do you think the new work system was successful?

ManagementCase

Selling a Bright Idea—
Along with the Kilowatts

By the time Florida Power & Light (FPL) Co. (www.fpl.com) became the first U.S. company to capture Japan's prestigious W. E. Deming Prize in 1989, the Miami-based utility had become a kind of mecca for corporate America's quality mavens. Visitors marveled at FPL's quality department, numbering 80 staffers. And they were awestruck by the utility's 1,800 quality-improvement teams. "We had checkers checking checkers in everything we did," says J. Thomas Petillo, then an executive in the quality office.

In the end, however, FPL kept better tabs on quality than it did on its basic business. The utility's managers, preoccupied with such quality issues as timely billing and preventing downed power lines, woke up too late to the population explosion in southern Florida and the sudden surge in demand for power. FPL had to buy electricity from nearby utilities. It even had to initiate rolling brownouts to conserve power. The year it won the Deming, FPL's profits fell 8%, to $412 million, even though its revenues climbed 13% to $5.3 billion.

With results like that, many companies would have turned out the lights on quality programs. Not FPL. Instead, the utility revamped its entire quality approach—this time with an emphasis on cost reduction. Nowadays, FPL's bottom line is much brighter. Its profits rose 23% last year, to $572.4 million. And building on its reputation as a Deming winner, FPL has launched a thriving return-on-quality consulting business. FPL's Qualtec Quality Services Inc. unit has 52 consultants, annual billings of more than $13 million, and a list of 100 clients worldwide, from US West Inc. to Britain's Nuclear Electric PLC.

Qualtec's approach is straightforward. First, it tries to persuade managers to throw out their old views of quality. The consultants break up management—from top executives through middle managers—into groups to talk about quality and how it should be used only as a means to produce healthier results. The message is spread through teams made up of managers and blue-collar workers. Then, with everyone in agreement on how to define quality, Qualtec does a top-to-bottom review of the way a company operates, identifying potential quality improvements that could yield financial benefits.

At American President Co., a shipping company based in Oakland, Calif., Qualtec consultant Joe L. Webb made three transpacific voyages before singling out 45 processes that were key to keeping American President's ships running smoothly. Of those, Webb figured that 25, including loading cargo and meeting schedules, were critical to customers—and therefore likely candidates for quality improvements. Since then, Webb has recommended a number of measures, such as streamlining paperwork to reduce the time it takes customs officials to clear cargo.

Not all of Qualtec's consultants have time for cruises. As more companies look for tangible payoffs from quality, they are also demanding speedier results. "Twelve to 18 months? Surely you can do better than that" is the common refrain from clients, says Petillo, now Qualtec's president. In response, Qualtec has formed "turbo teams" of consultants and managers to develop quality programs in a matter of weeks, not months. Gauging the financial impact of quality improvements is still a challenge. To help its clients, Qualtec is developing new computer software to measure the cost of quality against projected financial results, such as sales and return on capital.

As for the old Deming process that FPL once championed, Petillo thinks it still has merits. But even the Japanese quality devotees he sees these days are no longer blind to cost. Japan's weakened economy has seen to that. "Before, the Japanese wouldn't talk about cost," says Petillo. "Now they understand." It's a revelation that Qualtec is helping to spread.

Source: D. Greising, "Selling a Bright Idea—Along with the Kilowatts," *Business Week,* August 8, 1994, 59.

Questions

1. What were the positive outcomes of Florida Power & Light's obsession with total quality management? What were the negative outcomes?

2. The Florida Power & Light case highlights a potential flaw in the TQM philosophy. What is this flaw?

3. Given the information in this case, how do you think the TQM philosophy needs to be modified in order to improve its effectiveness as a management tool?

Chapter nineteen

The Management of Innovation, Product Development, and Entrepreneurship

Learning Objectives

1. Explain managers' role in facilitating product development.

2. Identify the factors that shorten the product life cycle, and explain why reducing product development time increases the level of industry competition.

3. Identify the goals of product development, and explain the relationships among them.

4. Explain the principles of product development, and describe the way in which managers can encourage and promote innovation.

5. Describe how managers can encourage and promote entrepreneurship to help create a learning organization.

A Case in Contrast

Two Product Development Teams at Quantum Corporation

The hard disk drive industry, which makes hard disks for personal computers, is buffeted by rapid technological change. The sales life of a hard disk is short. After about 18 months, most hard disk models are considered technologically obsolete because a better model has been developed. Thus, the key to competitive success in this industry is managers' ability to develop improved disk drives rapidly. The organization that is first to market with a disk drive that incorporates state-of-the-art technology is able to command a high price for its products. When other companies introduce comparable products, however, prices tumble and making a profit becomes increasingly difficult.

With 1994 revenues of $2.5 billion, Quantum Corporation (www.quantum.com) is one of the world's largest manufacturers of hard disk drives for personal computers. Given the need to reduce product development time, Quantum reorganized the company and grouped its engineers into several product development teams. Each team was composed of six "core members" from different functions, such as engineering, manufacturing, marketing, and quality assurance, who were physically located together in the same office space. Under the control of a team leader, each team was responsible for developing a particular model of hard disk.

An effective product team like the one pictured above, will often have strong, committed leadership, coordination, and cohesiveness. The successful Wolverine team at Quantum was able to create and deliver a 2.5-inch, 80-megabyte hard disk drive for notebook computers under budget and ahead of schedule, making Quantum the first company to market this size disk for notebook computers.

One product development team was given the responsibility to develop a technologically sophisticated 3.5-inch hard disk drive known as the Aerostar. With 150 megabytes of memory, the Aerostar was poised to be the largest computer disk drive that Quantum had ever made and also the fastest. The team began with high hopes but ultimately performed poorly. The Aerostar was several months late to market, it overran its budget, and it failed to obtain the market share, prices, and profit margins that top managers were hoping for.

In analyzing why the Aerostar team performed poorly, top managers determined that at least some of the problem lay in the way they had selected the team leader. The team's first leader had been the engineering manager in charge of the Aerostar's design. A dedicated engineer, he resented the management responsibilities that team management required, and he accepted his team leadership assignment reluctantly. In his view, his job was to resolve product engineering design crises, not to spend time managing the relationships among engineering, manufacturing, marketing, and quality assurance. As a consequence, the team functioned poorly, characterized by a lack of coordination and cohesiveness among its members.[1]

Without strong and committed leadership, the team drifted along and soon slipped behind schedule. Senior managers replaced the team leader, trying to find a combination of team members who could work effectively together. But the effort was to no avail: The Aerostar team went through four leaders and 16 core members in its first 18 months. Despite attempts to get the right mix of personnel, or perhaps because of them, the team continued to suffer from low morale and a lack of interfunctional respect.[2]

Quantum had a more successful outcome with the team charged with developing the Wolverine, a 2.5-inch, 80-megabyte hard disk drive for notebook computers. Like the Aerostar team, the Wolverine team was composed of six core members from different functions. However, here all comparisons ended. The Wolverine team leader, Larry Peterson, was not a technical specialist but an experienced product development manager who knew how to coordinate the efforts of members from different functions. Even though his team members lacked prior cross-functional experience, he knew how to build them into a team, and he motivated them.

As one of his first actions, Peterson had team members agree to some objectives, prioritize those objectives, and develop procedures for resolving disagreements. He also required all his team members to attend a regular Monday morning meeting at which all key decisions were made. Peterson also insisted that team members work closely together to ensure that the Wolverine was easy to manufacture after it had been designed. He took all possible steps to promote cooperation between members so that, over time, his team became a highly cohesive group. Ultimately, the Wolverine disk drive project came in under budget and ahead of schedule, making Quantum the first company to market a 2.5-inch disk drive targeted specifically at notebook computers.[3] ●

Overview

The Aerostar team's product development effort ended up behind schedule and over budget. The Wolverine team came in ahead of schedule and under budget. Why this difference? The "Case in Contrast" suggests that the way in which product development teams are organized and managed is one crucial factor that helps explain why some product development efforts are more successful than others.

In Chapter 18 we examined the actions managers can take at the operational level to improve responsiveness to customers, quality, and efficiency. There we discussed one aspect of innovation—developing new and better ways to make goods and services by means of operations management techniques such as total quality management, just-in-time inventory systems, and process reengineering. In this chapter we examine the actions managers can take to improve the ability of their organization to be innovative by developing new goods and services, another building block of competitive advantage. We discuss the relationship between technological change, product innovation, and competition. We examine the goals of product development efforts. We explain several principles for structuring an organization's product development effort to attain these goals, and we examine the nature of entrepreneurship and discuss steps managers can take to promote entrepreneurship inside organizations. By the end of this chapter, you will understand why, in today's rapidly changing environment, managers' ability to effectively manage innovation, product development, and entrepreneurship is often the key to an organization's success and even survival. ●

Innovation, Technological Change, and Competition

As discussed in Chapter 3, *technology* is the skills, knowledge, experience, body of scientific knowledge, tools, machines, computers, and equipment that are used in the design, production, and distribution of goods and services. Technology is involved in all organizational activities, and the rapid rate of technological change makes technological change a significant factor in almost every organizational innovation.[4]

There are two main types of technological change: quantum and incremental. **Quantum technological change** is a fundamental shift in technology that results in the innovation of new kinds of goods and services. Two recent examples are the development of the Internet, which has revolutionized the computer industry, and the development of genetic engineering (biotechnology), which is promising to revolutionize the treatment of illness with the development of genetically engineered medicines. McDonald's development of the principles behind the provision of fast food also qualifies as a quantum technological change.

Incremental technological change is change that refines existing technology and leads to gradual improvements or refinements in products over time. Since 1971, for example, Intel has made a series of incremental improvements to its original 4004 microprocessor, leading to the introduction of its 8088, 8086, 286, 386, 486, and Pentium chips.

quantum technological change A fundamental shift in technology that results in the innovation of new kinds of goods and services.

incremental technological change Change that refines existing technology and leads to gradual improvements or refinements in products over time.

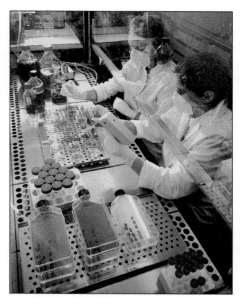

Biotechnicians working on cell culture in a sterile environment to create a new generation of drug products—an example of *quantum technological change.*

quantum product innovations Products that result from quantum technological changes.

incremental product innovations Products that result from incremental technological changes.

Products that result from quantum technological changes are called **quantum product innovations** and are relatively rare. Managers in most organizations spend most of their time managing products that result from incremental technological changes, called **incremental product innovations.** The new disk drives that Quantum's product development teams are trying to develop, for example, are incremental product innovations. Similarly, every time engineers in an automobile company redesign a car model, and every time McDonald's managers try to improve the flavor and texture of burgers and fries, they are engaged in product development efforts designed to lead to incremental product innovations. Just because incremental change is less dramatic than quantum change does not imply that incremental product innovations are unimportant. In fact, as discussed below, it is often managers' ability to successfully manage incremental product development that results in success or failure in an industry.

The Effects of Technological Change

The consequences of quantum and incremental technological change are all around us. Microprocessors, personal computers, cellular phones, pagers, personal digital assistants, word-processing software, computer networks, camcorders, compact disc players, videocassette players, genetically engineered medicines, fast food, on-line information services, superstores, and mass travel either did not exist a generation ago or were considered to be exotic and expensive products. Now these products are commonplace, and they are being improved all the time. Many of the organizations whose managers helped develop and exploit new technologies have reaped enormous gains. They include many of the most successful and rapidly growing organizations of our times, such as Dell Computer and Compaq Computer (personal computers), Microsoft (computer software), Intel (microprocessors), Motorola (microprocessors, cellular phones, and pagers), McCaw Cellular (cellular phone service), Sony (camcorders and compact discs), Matsushita (videocassette recorders), Amgen (biotechnology), America Online (on-line information services), McDonald's (fast food), Wal-Mart (superstores), and Carnival Cruises (cruise ships).

While some organizations have benefited from technological change, others have seen their markets threatened and their future in doubt. The decline of mainframe and midrange computer companies such as IBM and Digital Equipment Corporation is a direct reflection of the rise of the personal computer technology. Traditional telephone companies the world over have seen their market dominance threatened by new companies offering cellular telephone technology (in Britain the dominance of British Telecom is being challenged by Mercury, a cellular telephone company). The decline of once-dominant consumer electronics companies such as RCA can be directly linked to their failure to innovate products such as videocassette recorders and compact disc players.

Technological change offers both an opportunity and a threat.[5] On the one hand, it helps create new product opportunities that managers and their organizations can exploit. On the other hand, new and improved products can harm or even destroy demand for older, established products. Wal-Mart has put thousands of small stores out of business, and McDonald's has caused thousands of small diners to close, in part because both organizations have been so innovative in their production systems that they can give customers lower-priced products. Similarly, the development of the microprocessor by Intel has helped create a host of new product opportunities for entrepreneurs who have created thousands of companies that provide innovative computer software and hardware. At the same time, these microprocessors have destroyed demand for older products and have ruined organizations whose managers who did not see the changes in time and act on them. Managers of typewriter companies, for example, might have noticed that the new technology would compete directly with their products and moved to acquire or merge with new computer companies. Most did not, however, and once-famous companies like Smith Corona are out of business. The nature of entrepreneurship is discussed in detail later in this chapter.

Product Life Cycles and Product Development

When technology is changing, organizational survival requires that managers quickly adopt and apply new technologies to innovate products. Managers who do not do so soon find that they have no market for their products—and destroy their organizations. The rate of technological change in an industry—and particularly the length of the product life cycle—determines how important it is for managers to innovate.

product life cycle

Changes in demand for a product that occur from its introduction through its growth and maturity to its decline.

The **product life cycle** is the changes in demand for a product that occur over time.[6] Demand for most successful products passes through four stages: the embryonic stage, growth, maturity, and decline (see Figure 19.1). In the *embryonic stage* a product has yet to gain widespread acceptance; customers are unsure what the product has to offer, and demand for it is minimal. This is the stage that personal digital assistants, such as Apple's Newton, are currently in. If a product does become accepted by customers (and many do not), demand takes off, and the product enters its growth stage. In the *growth stage* many consumers are entering the market and buying the product for the first time; demand increases rapidly. Products such as cellular telephones, personal computers for home use, and on-line information services are currently in this stage.

The growth stage ends and the *mature stage* begins when market demand peaks because most customers have already bought the product (there are relatively few first-time buyers left). At this stage demand is typically replacement demand. In the car market, for example, most cars are bought by people who already have a car and are either trading up or replacing an old model. The *decline stage* follows the mature stage if and when demand for a product falls. Falling demand often occurs because a product has become technologically obsolescent and superseded by a more advanced product. For example, demand for Intel's 486 microprocessor fell as it was superseded by the company's more powerful Pentium chips.

Figure 19.1
A Product Life Cycle

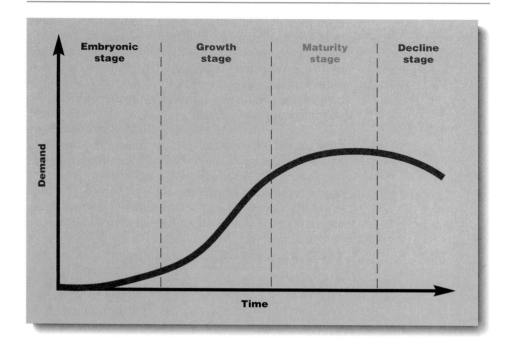

THE RATE OF TECHNOLOGICAL CHANGE One of the main determinants of the length of a product's life cycle is the rate of technological change.[7] Figure 19.2 illustrates the relationship between the rate of technological change and the length of product life cycles. In some industries—such as personal computers, semiconductors, and disk drives—technological change is rapid and product life cycles are very short. The "Case in Contrast" mentions that technological change is so rapid in the disk drive industry that a disk drive model becomes technologically obsolete about 18 months after introduction. The same is true in the personal computer industry, where product life cycles have shrunk from three years during the late 1980s to 18 months today.

In other industries the product life cycle is somewhat longer. In the car industry, for example, the average product life cycle is about five years. The life cycle of a car is so short because fairly rapid technological change is producing a continual stream of incremental innovations in car design, such as the introduction of door airbags, advanced electronic microcontrollers, plastic body parts, and more fuel-efficient engines. In contrast, in many basic industries where the pace of technological change is slower, product life cycles tend to be much longer. In steel or electricity, for example, change in product technology is very limited, and products such as steel girders and electric cable can remain in the mature stage indefinitely.

THE ROLE OF FADS AND FASHIONS Fads and fashion are important determinants of the length of product life cycles.[8] A five-year-old car design is likely to be technologically outmoded and to look out-of-date and thus lose its attractiveness to customers. Similarly, in the restaurant business, the demand for certain kinds of food changes rapidly. The Cajun or Southwest

Figure 19.2

The Relationship Between Technological Change and Length
of the Product Life Cycle

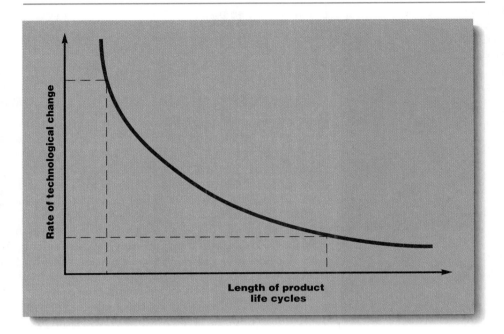

cuisine popular one year may be history the next as Caribbean fare becomes the food of choice. Fashion considerations are even more important in the high-fashion end of the clothing industry, where last season's clothing line is usually out-of-date by the next season, and product life cycles may last no more than three months. Thus, fads and fashions are another reason why product life cycles may be short.

MANAGERIAL IMPLICATIONS Whether short product life cycles are caused by rapid technological change, changing fads and fashions, or some combination of the two, the message for managers is clear: The shorter the length of your product's life cycle, the more important it is to innovate products quickly and on a continuing basis. In industries where product life cycles are very short, managers must continually develop new products; otherwise, their organizations may go out of business. The personal computer company that cannot develop a new and improved product line every 18 months will soon find itself in trouble, as will the fashion house that fails to develop a new line of clothing for every season, or the small restaurant, club, or bar that is not alert to current fads and fashions. Car and phone companies have a little more time, but even here it is important for managers to develop new and improved models every five years or so.

Increasingly, there is evidence that in a wide range of industries product life cycles are becoming more compressed as managers focus their organization's resources on innovation to increase responsiveness to customers. To attract new customers, managers are trying to outdo each other by being the first to market with a product that incorporates a new technology or that plays to a new fashion trend.[9] In the automobile industry a typical five-year product life cycle is being reduced to three years as managers are increasingly competing with one another to attract new customers and encourage existing customers to upgrade and buy the newest product.[10] The way in which Intel has managed the shrinking product life cycles for microprocessors is considered in this "Management Insight."

Management Insight

Shrinking Product Life Cycles at Intel

Intel's (www.intel.com) microprocessors are the brains of 85 percent of the personal computers sold worldwide today. Intel's dominance in this business can be traced back to IBM's 1980 decision to use Intel's 8086 microprocessor in its first PC. Since then Intel has produced a series of ever-more-powerful microprocessors, including the 286, the 386, the 486, and the Pentium chips. But Intel has not had things all its own way.

Two companies, AMD (www.amd.com) and Cyrix (www.cyrix.com), have been producing clones of Intel microprocessors that can manipulate computer software in the same way as an Intel chip. Once a clone is introduced, prices fall, and so do Intel's market share and profit margins. Shortly after AMD and Cyrix introduced a clone of Intel's 486 microprocessor, prices for the 486 fell by more than 30 percent.

The source of Intel's competitive advantage over AMD and Cyrix is that these companies cannot start to design a clone of Intel's next microprocessor until they actually obtain it. So, for each new microprocessor, Intel normally has several years of lead time before AMD and Cyrix develop a

This is a shot of Intel Corp.'s latest—the faster-yet Pentium II chip. The chip will be in the 350–400 megahertz range, considerably faster than older chips. This photo was taken in April 1998—let's see how long it takes for clones of the latest Intel offerings to appear.

clone. The time it takes AMD and Cyrix to clone an Intel microprocessor has been shrinking, however. It took AMD five years to come up with a compatible processor after Intel released its 386 chip in 1985. Matching Intel's next generation, the 486, took three years. Intel began volume production of the Pentium in early 1993. AMD introduced its clone, the P5, just two years later. This increasingly rapid rate of imitation is shrinking the time Intel has the market to itself and can reap its highest profit.[11]

In an attempt to stay ahead of the competition, Intel has responded by increasing the speed of its own product development process—effectively shrinking the length of its own product life cycles. Intel released its successor to the Pentium, the Pentium Pro, in 1995—twice as fast as it replaced the 486 with the Pentium—to keep the pressure on its rivals, which have been experiencing problems keeping up.

Tips for Managers

Innovation

1. New product development is about trying to satisfy the future needs of customers with products that incorporate new, untried features.

2. Because the future is so unpredictable managers must try to increase their success rate by following the four principles of product development outlined in this chapter.

3. Managers must also encourage employees to take risks and be innovative, and they need to develop a structure and culture that supports intrapreneurship.

4. Recognize that only those organizations that are successful at new product development will be those that prosper in the new century.

Product Development

In this section we examine the steps that managers can take to promote innovation and encourage product development. Product development is the process or procedure that managers use to bring new or improved kinds of goods and services to the market. First, we discuss the goals of product development; second, we describe some principles for guiding and speeding the product development process; and third, we discuss some problems associated with managing product development successfully.

Goals of Product Development

When managers and organizations face the choice of innovating products or going out of business, what product development goals should they pursue? Most researchers and consultants recommend that managers aim to reduce development time, maximize a product's fit with customer needs, maximize product quality, and maximize manufacturability—the efficiency and ease of production (see Figure 19.3).[12]

Figure 19.3
Four Goals of New Product Development

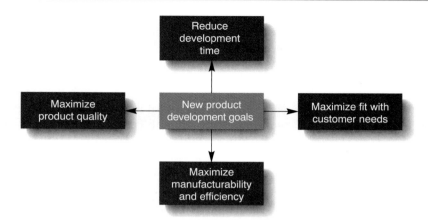

REDUCING DEVELOPMENT TIME Product development time is the time from the initial conception of a product to its introduction into the market. Reducing development time offers three important advantages.[13] First, the management team that reduces development time may be the first to market a product that incorporates new, state-of-the-art features.[14] Those managers will be able to charge a high price for the product and earn high profits. Moreover, the earlier managers are able to bring a new product to the market, relative to competitors, the longer is the period in which they will be able to charge high prices and obtain high profits.

This advantage is the reason why Intel's managers make such efforts to reduce the time required to develop a new microprocessor. It is also why Quantum Corporation puts so much emphasis on development time, as we saw in the "Case in Contrast." Quantum's top managers know that if they can get a new model disk drive to market before competitors such as Seagate Technologies, they can charge a higher price until competitors introduce their new models. In contrast, managers who are slow to introduce new products will have to charge lower prices to attract customers away from fast-track managers (as AMD and Cyrix have to do in the microprocessor market to lure customers away from Intel).

A second advantage of reducing product development time is that managers who can shorten times can upgrade their products relatively quickly and incorporate state-of-the-art technology as soon as it becomes available. Managers with more advanced products are better able to serve customer needs, build brand loyalty, and stay one step ahead of slower competitors.

A third advantage of reducing development time is that managers find it easier to experiment with new products and replace them with a superior product if they fail to meet customer needs. For example, Toyota's first minivan was a disaster. Recognizing this, Toyota's engineers were able to redesign the minivan within 18 months—instead of the three to five years typical at other car companies. The result was the Previa, one of the most successful minivans ever made.

For all these reasons, reducing product development time has become a key competitive priority of managers. An example of how important the competitive advantage obtained from faster product development can be is illustrated by the battle for market share in the computer workstation market between Sun Microsystems and Apollo Computer.

Management Insight

How Sun Captured the Lead from Apollo

In 1980, managers at Apollo Computer (www.apollo.com) created the market for engineering computer workstations (computer workstations are high-powered free-standing minicomputers). Apollo was rewarded with rapid growth and a virtual monopoly position. Its first competitor, Sun Microsystems (www.sun.com), did not introduce a competing product until 1982. However, by 1988 Apollo had lost its lead in the workstation market to Sun. Although Apollo was generating revenues of $600 million in 1988, Sun's revenues were over $1 billion. Between 1984 and 1988 Sun's revenues from workstations grew 100 percent per year. Apollo's growth rate was 35 percent per year.[15]

The cause of Apollo's slower growth was slow product development. To stay abreast of new microprocessor technology, computer company managers must continually update their products. Sun's managers had succeeded in introducing a new product every 12 months and in doubling the power of Sun workstations every 18 months on average. Apollo's product development cycle had stretched out to over 24 months. As a result, Apollo's products were regularly superseded by the more technologically advanced products introduced by Sun, and Apollo was falling farther and farther behind. Consequently, Sun increased its market share from 21 to 33 percent between 1985 and 1988, and Apollo's market share fell from 41 to under 20 percent. Unable to compete, in 1989 Apollo was acquired by Hewlett-Packard, a company whose managers are well known for their ability to reduce development time and effectively manage product development.

MAXIMIZING THE FIT WITH CUSTOMER NEEDS Many new products fail when they reach the marketplace because they were not designed with customer needs in mind.[16] In a survey of 77 companies that introduced nearly 11,000 new products and services from 1988 to 1992, Kuczmarski & Associates, a Chicago management consultancy, found that the most common reason why new products flopped when they got to the marketplace was that managers did not understand or care about the needs of their customers.[17] It follows that maximizing the fit between a product's attributes and customers' needs is one of the main elements of successful product development.

Strange as it may seem, one reason why many managers fail to investigate whether a new technology can actually satisfy a customer need is that managers are dazzled by the technology itself. Take Steve Jobs, one of the two cofounders of Apple Computer. After Jobs left Apple in 1985, he started a company called NeXT to manufacture high-powered personal computers. Captivated by the most advanced technology, Jobs made sure that the NeXT machines incorporated innovative features such as optical disk drives and hi-fidelity sound. However, the NeXT system failed to gain market share because customers simply did not want many of these features. The optical disk drives turned customers off because they made it difficult to switch work from a personal computer using a regular disk drive to a NeXT machine. Moreover, the microprocessor for the NeXT machine could not run Microsoft's popular software. NeXT failed because Jobs was so dazzled by leading-edge technology that he lost sight of customer needs.[18]

MAXIMIZING PRODUCT QUALITY   If managers introduce into the marketplace new products that have not been properly engineered and that suffer from substandard quality, their company's efforts to attract customers are doomed.[19] Poor quality is often the result of managers' rushing a product to market in an attempt to reduce development time. Development time is important, but so is product quality. Meeting development time goals with a poor-quality product can be self-defeating.

Consider the Newton personal digital assistant (PDA), introduced by Apple in 1993. The Newton is a small, handheld device that combines some computer functions with some functions of a cellular phone. In theory, a user writes a message on the screen of the Newton, and handwriting recognition software in the Newton reads the message, converts it into a digital form, and stores it in its memory. If the user so desires, the message can be sent to a fax machine by means of the Newton's cellular phone feature. When Apple introduced the product, Apple managers claimed that it would revolutionize business communication because it would enable a manager with a Newton to send a message to anyone at any time. The Newton, however, turned out to be a market flop because its handwriting recognition software was not reliable and could not read handwritten messages accurately. The quality of the product was poor, and, despite its promise, the Newton soon became the butt of jokes.

MAXIMIZING MANUFACTURABILITY AND EFFICIENCY   The production process used to manufacture a product can either shorten or lengthen development times and result in either low or high manufacturing costs—affecting efficiency.[20] Consider what happens when product engineers design a product but fail to keep manufacturing requirements in mind. After examining specifications for the product, the manufacturing managers tell the product engineers that the product cannot be manufactured efficiently and cost-effectively because of the way it is designed. The engineers then must redesign the product, thereby lengthening development times.

Poor design may raise manufacturing costs because, for example, the product has numerous components and is costly to assemble. Consultants recommend that ensuring that products can be made as efficiently as possible should be a key goal of managers' product development efforts.[21]

Principles of Product Development

How can managers increase their organizations' ability to innovate new goods and services and so increase competitive advantage? Here, we examine several ways in which managers can organize and control the product development process to reduce development time, maximize the product's fit with customer needs, maximize quality, and maximize both manufacturability and efficiency. Consider the steps that Thermos took to develop a barbecue grill.

Management Insight

How Thermos Developed a New Barbecue Grill

In late 1990, Monte Peterson, CEO of Thermos, decided it was time to energize his sluggish company by emphasizing new product development. Best known for its vacuum bottles and barbecue grills, Thermos has annual sales of $250 million. Peterson assembled a cross-functional product development team of six middle managers from functions such as marketing, engineering, manufacturing, and finance. He told them to develop a new barbecue grill and to do it by August 1992. To ensure that managers were not spread too thin, he assigned these managers to this product development team only. Peterson also arranged for leadership of the team to rotate. Initially, to focus on what customers wanted, the marketing manager would take the lead; then, when technical developments became the main consideration, leadership would switch to engineering, and so on.

Team members christened the group the "Lifestyle team." In 1990, to find out what people really wanted in a grill, the marketing manager and nine subordinates spent a month on the road visiting customers. While in the field the Lifestyle team set up focus groups, visited people's homes, and even videotaped barbecues. What team members found surprised them. The stereotype of Dad with apron and chef's hat slaving over a smoky barbecue grill was wrong. More women were barbecuing, and many cooks were tired of messy charcoal. Many homeowners were spending big money building decks, and they did not like rusty grills that spoiled the appearance of their deck. Moreover, environmental and safety issues were also increasing in importance. In California charcoal starter fluid is considered a pollutant and is banned; in New Jersey the use of charcoal and gas grills on the balconies of condos and apartments has been prohibited to avoid fires.

When the marketing group returned to Thermos headquarters and discussed their findings, they decided that Thermos had to produce a new kind of product. What they needed was a barbecue grill that looked like a handsome piece of furniture, required no pollutants such as charcoal lighter, and made the food taste good. The grill also had to be safe for use by apartment and condo dwellers—which meant it had to be electric.

By late 1991, the basic attributes of the product were defined, and leadership of the team moved to engineering. The product engineers had been working on electric grill technology for about six months—ever since marketing had alerted them that an electric grill was a likely possibility. The critical task for engineering was to design a grill that gave food the cookout taste that conventional electric grills could not provide because they do

The Thermos team with their new outdoor grill. The team concept proved so successful that Thermos now uses teams in all its divisions.

not get hot enough. To raise the cooking temperature, Thermos drew on its vacuum technology to design a domed vacuum top that trapped heat inside the grill. They also built electric heat rods directly into the surface of the grill. These, along with the vacuum top, made the grill hot enough to sear meat and give it brown barbecue lines and a barbecue taste.[22]

Manufacturing had also been active from the early days of the development process, making sure that any proposed design could be produced economically. Because manufacturing was involved from the beginning, the team avoided some costly mistakes. At one critical team meeting the engineers said they wanted tapered legs on the grill. Manufacturing explained that tapered legs would have to be custom-made—and would raise manufacturing costs—and persuaded the team to go with straight legs.

The product was introduced on schedule in August 1992 and has been a big success for Thermos. Most of the company's sales growth has come from its new line of electric grills.

The study of product development successes such as those of Thermos's Lifestyle team and Quantum's Wolverine team suggests four principles that managers can follow to increase the likelihood of success for their product development efforts.[23]

PRINCIPLE 1: ESTABLISH A STAGE–GATE DEVELOPMENT FUNNEL

One of the most common mistakes that managers make in product development is trying to fund too many new projects at any one time.[24] The result is to spread limited financial, technical, and human resources too thinly over too many different projects. As a consequence, no single project is given the resources that are required to make it succeed.

Given this potential problem, managers need to develop a structured process for evaluating product development proposals and deciding which to support and which to reject. A common solution is to establish a **stage–gate development funnel,** a planning model that forces managers to make choices among competing projects so that organizational resources are not spread thinly over too many projects.[25] The funnel gives managers control over product development and allows them to intervene and take corrective action quickly and appropriately (see Figure 19.4).

At Stage 1, the development funnel has a wide mouth, so top managers initially can encourage employees to come up with as many new product ideas as possible. Managers can create incentives for employees to come up with ideas. Many organizations run "bright idea programs" that reward employees whose ideas eventually make it through the development process. Other organizations allow research scientists to devote a certain amount of work time to their own projects. Top managers at Hewlett-Packard and 3M, for example, have a 15 percent rule: They expect a research scientist to spend 15 percent of the workweek working on a project of his or her own choosing. Ideas may be submitted by individuals or by groups. Brainstorming (see Chapter 6) is a technique that managers frequently use to encourage new ideas.

New product ideas are written up as brief proposals. The proposals are submitted to a cross-functional team of managers, who evaluate the proposal at Gate 1. The cross-functional team considers the proposal's fit with the organization's strategy and its technical feasibility. Proposals that are consistent with the

stage–gate development funnel A planning model that forces managers to make choices among competing projects so that organizational resources are not spread thinly over too many projects.

Figure 19.4
A Stage–Gate Development Funnel

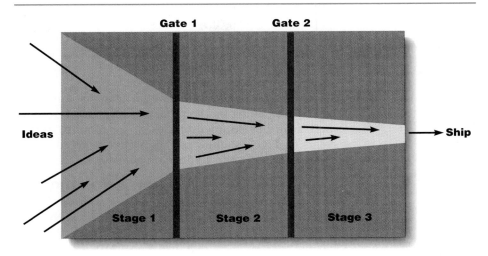

strategy of the organization and are judged technically feasible pass through Gate 1 and into Stage 2. Other proposals are turned down (although the door is often left open for reconsidering a proposal at a later date).

The primary goal in Stage 2 is to draft a detailed product development plan. The **product development plan** specifies all of the relevant information that managers need to make a decision about whether to go ahead with a full-blown product development effort. The product development plan should include strategic and financial objectives, an analysis of the product's market potential, a list of desired product features, a list of technological requirements, a list of financial and human resource requirements, a detailed development budget, and a time line that contains specific milestones (for example, dates for prototype completion and final launch).

This plan is normally drafted by a cross-functional team of managers. Good planning requires a good strategic analysis (see Chapter 7), and team members must be prepared to spend considerable time out in the field with customers trying to understand their needs. Drafting a product development plan generally takes about three months. Once completed, the plan is reviewed by a senior management committee at Gate 2 (see Figure 19.4). These managers focus on the details of the plan to see whether the proposal is attractive (given its market potential) and viable (given the technological, financial, and human resources that would be needed to develop the product). Senior managers making this review keep in mind all other product development efforts currently being undertaken by the organization. One goal at this point is to ensure that limited organizational resources are used to their maximum effect.

At Gate 2 projects are rejected, sent back for revision, or allowed to pass through into Stage 3, the development phase. Product development starts with the formation of a cross-functional team that is given primary responsibility for developing the product (Quantum Corporation's Aerostar and Wolverine teams were Stage 3 product development teams). In some companies, at the beginning of Stage 3 top managers and cross-functional team members sign a

product development plan A plan that specifies all of the relevant information that managers need in order to decide whether to proceed with a full-blown product development effort.

contract book A written
agreement that details
product development fac-
tors such as responsibilities, resource
commitments, budgets,
time lines, and
development milestones.

contract book, a written agreement that details factors such as responsibilities, resource commitments, budgets, time lines, and development milestones.[26] Signing the contract book is viewed as the symbolic launch of a product development effort. The contract book is also a document against which actual development progress can be measured. At Motorola, for example, team members and top management negotiate a contract and sign a contract book at the launch of a development effort, thereby signaling their commitment to the objectives contained in the contract.[27]

The Stage 3 development effort can last anywhere from six months to ten years, depending on the industry and type of product. Some electronics products have development cycles of six months, but it takes from three to five years to develop a new car, about five years to develop a new jet aircraft, and as much as ten years to develop a new medical drug.

PRINCIPLE 2: ESTABLISH CROSS-FUNCTIONAL TEAMS   A smooth-running cross-functional team seems to be a critical component of successful product development, as suggested by the experiences of Thermos and Quantum.[28] In both these companies marketing, engineering, and manufacturing personnel were **core members** of successful product development teams—the people who bear primary responsibility for the product development effort. Other people besides core members work on the project as and when the need arises, but the core members (generally from three to six individuals) stay with the project from inception to completion of the development effort (see Figure 19.5).

core members The
members of a team who
bear primary responsibility
for the success of a project
and who stay with a
project from inception to
completion.

The reason for using a cross-functional team is to ensure a high level of coordination and communication among managers in different functions, which increases group cohesiveness and performance, as we saw in Chapter 14. Input from both marketing and manufacturing members of Thermos's Lifestyle team determined the characteristics of the barbecue that the engineers on the team ended up designing.

If a cross-functional team is to succeed, it must have the right kind of leadership, and it must be managed in an effective manner.[29] The "Case in Contrast" makes clear that the differentiating factor leading to the success of the Wolverine team and the failure of the Aerostar team was the way in which the teams were led and managed. The Aerostar team suffered from poor leadership, an absence of structured team management, and a lack of functional cooperation; it was a cross-functional team in name only. The Wolverine team benefited from a strong leader who managed the team in a structured way and emphasized the importance of cross-functional cooperation. To be successful, a product development team needs a team leader who can rise above his or her functional background and take a cross-functional view.[30]

In addition to effective leadership, successful cross-functional product development teams have several other key characteristics.[31] Often, core members of successful teams are located close to each other in the same office space to foster a sense of shared mission and commitment to a development program. Successful teams develop a clear sense of their objectives and how to achieve them, the purpose again being to create a sense of shared mission. A clear, explicit statement of objectives allows the team to measure its actual performance against its plan.

Figure 19.5
Members of a Cross-Functional Product Development Team

PRINCIPLE 3: USE CONCURRENT ENGINEERING   Traditional product development is a sequential process consisting of five steps: opportunity identification, concept development, product design, process design, and commercial production (see Figure 19.6a). Opportunity development occurs at Stage 1 of the stage–gate funnel (see Figure 19.4), commercial production occurs at Stage 3, and the other three steps occur at Stage 2. The problem with sequential product development is that long product development times, poor product quality, and high manufacturing costs are likely if there is no direct communication among the marketing managers who develop the concept, the engineering or R&D managers who design the product, and the manufacturing managers. In many organizations engineers in R&D design a product and then "throw it over the wall" to manufacturing. The result can be a design that is too costly to manufacture. If solving this problem requires redesign, manufacturing sends the product back to the design engineers, thereby lengthening development time.

Cross-functional teams can help solve this problem, and it is also helpful to alter the process so that it is partly parallel rather than sequential. In partly parallel product development, one step begins before the prior step is finished, and managers from one function are familiar with what is going on in other functions (see Figure 19.6b). The goal is to facilitate **concurrent engineering,** the simultaneous design of the product and of the process for manufacturing the product.[32] Recall that in the interests of reducing manufacturing costs,

concurrent engineering The simultaneous design of the product and of the process for manufacturing the product.

Figure 19.6
Sequential and Partly Parallel Development Processes

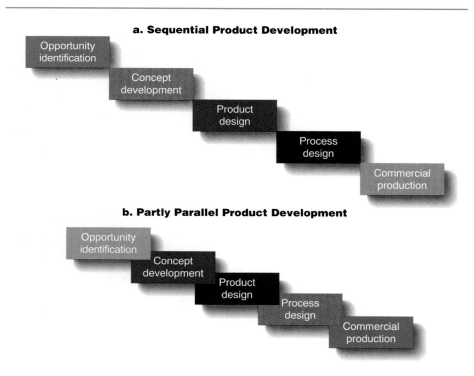

a. Sequential Product Development

Opportunity identification

Concept development

Product design

Process design

Commercial production

b. Partly Parallel Product Development

Opportunity identification

Concept development

Product design

Process design

Commercial production

manufacturing members of the Lifestyle team at Thermos persuaded their colleagues in engineering to design an electric grill with straight legs. That is an example of concurrent engineering. The usual outcome of concurrent engineering is a product that is easy to manufacture. Concurrent engineering thus helps to reduce manufacturing costs and to increase product quality. The other benefit of a partly parallel process is that it reduces development time, for two reasons. The whole development process is compressed, and concurrent engineering reduces the probability that costly and time-consuming product redesigns will be needed.

PRINCIPLE 4: INVOLVE BOTH CUSTOMERS AND SUPPLIERS

Many new products fail when they reach the marketplace because they were designed with scant attention to customer needs. Successful product development requires inputs from more than just an organization's members; also needed are inputs from customers and suppliers.[33] At Thermos, team members spent a month on the road visiting customers to identify their needs. The revolutionary electric barbecue grill was a direct result of this process. In other cases, companies have found it worthwhile to include customer representatives as peripheral members of their product development team. Boeing's approach to designing its latest commercial jet aircraft, the 400-seat 777, provides an example of this.

Management Insight

Developing the 777 at Boeing

In October 1990, Boeing Corporation (www.boeing.com) decided to build an all-new wide-body 400-seat commercial jet aircraft, the Boeing 777. Less than four years later the first 777 took off from Boeing's production facility in Everett, Washington. The relatively short development time for the 777 was a triumph for Boeing; the typical development time for jet aircraft is six years. Moreover, on the day the 777 took off, Boeing already had 150 firm orders for the plane, and airlines had taken out options on another 150. This kind of advance ordering is a sure sign that Boeing had developed an aircraft that customers wanted.

To build a plane that was designed with customer needs in mind, Boeing invited eight U.S. and foreign airlines to help its engineers design the aircraft. The group included United, which launched the program with orders for 32 planes, American (www.americanair.com), Delta, British Airways, Japan Air Lines, All Nippon Airlines, Quantas, and Cathay Pacific (www.cathay-usa.com). For almost a year, technical representatives from these airlines took up residence in Boeing's Everett facility and met with the engineering staff assigned to the 777 project. This was a dramatic shift for Boeing, which in the past had been very secretive about its design work.

Input from the eight carriers clearly determined the shape of the 777. They wanted a fuselage that was wider than rival McDonnell Douglas (www.dac.mdc.com) and Airbus models so that they could pack another 30 or so seats onto the aircraft. The result is an aircraft that is 5 inches wider than the McDonnell Douglas MD-11 and 25 inches wider than the Airbus A-330. They wanted a plane in which the galleys and lavatories could be relocated almost anywhere within the plane within hours. Boeing therefore designed a plane whose interior can be completely changed in three or four hours, configured with one, two, or three classes to fit whatever a carrier's market of the moment demands. And they wanted better overhead bins for carry-on baggage, so Boeing designed new overhead bins to meet their requirements.[34]

Besides customers, Boeing also brought 18 of its major suppliers into the 777 program and told them exactly what it wanted from them. Suppliers consulted with Boeing's project engineers. As a result, many potential production problems were solved ahead of time, thereby reducing the need for costly design changes late in the development process.

Including suppliers in the product development process is clearly another important factor in successful product development. When suppliers are responsible for major components of a product (such as the tail section of the 777), it is important to extend the principle of concurrent engineering to embrace them so that they too can manufacture quality components in a timely, cost-effective way.

Many of the information technologies discussed in Chapter 17 are becoming an increasingly important part of concurrent engineering. The way in which Boeing used computer-aided design (CAD) to design the 777, the first airliner to be designed entirely by computer, provides a graphic illustration of the advantages of CAD. Each of the thousands of components of the 777 was first engineered and tested in virtual space by means of three-dimensional CAD technology to make sure that everything fit together. If parts did not fit, they were redesigned on the computer until they did. Only then were real parts and subassemblies manufactured. By using CAD, Boeing dramatically reduced the need for expensive mockups and design changes and shortened development time.[35] The use of CAD technology in product development has exploded in recent years as design engineers employed by car makers, furniture makers, and architects have found that CAD allows them to cut down on design time and improve the accuracy of their engineering drawings.[36]

In sum, managers need to recognize that successful product development cuts across roles and functions and requires a high level of integration. They should recognize the importance of common values and norms in promoting the high levels of cooperation and cohesiveness necessary to build a culture for innovation. They also should be careful to reward successful innovators and make heroes of the employees and teams that develop successful new products. Finally, managers should fully utilize the four principles of product development to guide the process.

Problems with Product Development

Given today's rapid rate of technological change and its impact on the length of product life cycles, successful product development has become a major source of competitive advantage in many industries. To survive and compete successfully, managers must look for ways to reduce development time, achieve a close fit between new product attributes and customer demands, and maximize the quality and ease of production of new products. The four principles for effective product development described above indicate some of the actions that managers are taking to increase the effectiveness of product development efforts.

These principles, however, have not been universally adopted. The track record for product development is actually quite poor. Several studies have concluded that most product development projects either are terminated before completion or result in the production of new products that flop when they reach the marketplace.[37] Although many managers know the theory underlying successful product development, making that theory work within an organization can be very difficult. Consider the attempts of Ford Motor Company to streamline its global product development effort, profiled in this "Managing Globally."

Managing Globally

Ford's Attempt at Global Product Development

Ford (www.ford.com), a company with substantial operations in both North America and Europe, has long championed the concept of a global car that would be developed with the cooperation and input of design managers in Europe and the United States and sold as the same model worldwide. In the late 1980s Ford decided to try to bring together managers in its European and North American operations to produce a new line of compact cars and engines to be sold in Europe as the Mondeo and in the United States as the Ford Contour and Mercury Mystique.

The new car was to be designed by an international product development team located at three centers—one in Dearborn, Michigan, one in Britain, and one in Germany. Cross-functional teams were established at each center and linked together by advanced information systems, including a computer-aided design network. The idea was to eliminate duplication of effort by developing a vehicle that, with minor modifications, could be sold worldwide. The plan called for the development centers in Britain and Germany to take the lead in developing the car and for the center in Dearborn to have an important advisory function.[38]

The results were less than Ford had hoped for. The car cost $6 billion to develop—four times as much as it cost Chrysler Corporation (www.chrysler.corp.com) to develop a competing vehicle, the Neon. The cost was partly due to an expensive and time-consuming coordination effort needed to link managers at the three design centers. Moreover, the U.S. model was not introduced until 1994, one year after the European model. The reason? Ford's U.S. marketing managers decided that the European-designed car would not appeal to U.S. consumers, so they insisted late in the development process that the styling of the U.S. model be changed. This redesign stretched out development time and produced a U.S. model that looked significantly different from its European cousin. According to industry observers, managers at Ford's U.S. design center resented the loss of power that was implied by the development effort, so they worked to regain control over the project by constantly challenging the work of the European designers—hence the cost and time overruns. Nevertheless, despite these problems, the new model has been selling well throughout the world, and Ford's efforts paid off.

The problems that Ford encountered illustrate how problems of power and conflict can arise when managers try to implement effective product development within their organization. Revolutionizing product development requires a break with traditional ways of thinking and managing. The establishment of cross-functional teams can help top managers redirect power and responsibility away from functional managers and toward the leaders and core members of product development teams. Not surprisingly, functional managers often resent such challenges to their authority and resist attempts to limit their power and influence within the organization. However, by assessing the need for change, deciding on the change to make, implementing the change, and evaluating the change (see Figure 16.7), top managers will be well positioned to overcome resistance and move the organization toward its desired future state.

Entrepreneurship

At the heart of innovation and product development are **entrepreneurs,** individuals who notice opportunities and take responsibility for mobilizing the resources necessary to produce new and improved goods and services. Entrepreneurs start new business ventures and do all of the planning, organizing, leading, and controlling necessary to meet organizational goals. Most commonly entrepreneurs assume all the risk and receive all the returns associated with the new business venture. These people

entrepreneur An individual who notices opportunities and takes responsibility for mobilizing the resources necessary to produce new and improved goods and services.

intrapreneur A manager, scientist, or researcher who works inside an existing organization and notices opportunities for product improvements and is responsible for managing the product development process.

entrepreneurship The mobilization of resources to take advantage of an opportunity to provide customers with new or improved goods and services.

are the Bill Gates or Liz Claibornes of the world who make vast fortunes if their business succeeds, or they are among the millions of people who start new business ventures only to lose their money when they fail. Despite the fact that an estimated 80 percent of small businesses fail in the first three to five years, by some recent estimates more than 38 percent of men and nearly 50 percent of women in today's workforce want to start their own companies.[39]

Some managers, scientists, or researchers employed by existing companies engage in entrepreneurial activity. They are involved in the innovation and product development process described in this chapter. To distinguish these individuals from entrepreneurs who found their own businesses, employees of existing organizations who notice opportunities for either quantum or incremental product improvements and are responsible for managing the product development process are known as **intrapreneurs.** In general, then, **entrepreneurship** is the mobilization of resources to take advantage of an opportunity to provide customers with new or improved goods and services.

There is an interesting relationship between entrepreneurs and intrapreneurs. Many intrapreneurs become dissatisfied when their superiors decide neither to support nor to fund new product ideas and development efforts that the intrapreneurs think will succeed. What do intrapreneurs who feel that they are getting nowhere do? Very often they decide to leave an organization and start their own organization to take advantage of their new product ideas. In other words, intrapreneurs become entrepreneurs and found companies that may compete with the companies they left.

Many of the world's most successful organizations have been started by frustrated intrapreneurs who became entrepreneurs. William Hewlett and David Packard left Fairchild Semiconductor, an early industry leader, when managers of that company would not support their ideas; their company soon

Stacy Munic Mintz, pictured with her brother Kenny Munic, are the entrepreneurs who developed the highly successful Little Miss Muffin, a new low-fat, low-cholesterol muffin for coffee houses and other clients in the Chicago area.

outperformed Fairchild. Compaq Computer was founded by Rod Canion and some of his colleagues, who left Texas Instruments (TI) when managers there would not support Canion's idea that TI should develop its own personal computer. To prevent the departure of talented people, organizations need to take steps to promote internal entrepreneurship. In the remainder of this section we consider issues involved in promoting successful entrepreneurship in both new and existing organizations.

Entrepreneurship and New Ventures

The fact that a significant number of entrepreneurs were frustrated intrapreneurs provides a clue about the personal characteristics of people who are likely to start a new venture and bear all the uncertainty and risk associated with being an entrepreneur.

CHARACTERISTICS OF ENTREPRENEURS Entrepreneurs are likely to be high on the personality trait of *openness to experience,* meaning that they are predisposed to be original, to be open to a wide range of stimuli, to be daring, and to take risks (see Chapter 11 for a discussion of this and the other traits of entrepreneurs mentioned here). Entrepreneurs also are likely to have an *internal locus of control* and believe that they are responsible for what happens to themselves and that their own actions determine important outcomes such as the success or failure of a new business. People with an external locus of control, in contrast, would be very unlikely to leave a secure job in an organization and assume the risk associated with a new venture.

Entrepreneurs are likely to have a high level of *self-esteem* and feel competent and capable of handling most situations—including the stress and uncertainty surrounding a plunge into a risky new venture. Entrepreneurs are likely to have a high *need for achievement* and have a strong desire to perform challenging tasks and meet high personal standards of excellence.

ENTREPRENEURSHIP AND MANAGEMENT Given that entrepreneurs are predisposed to activities that are somewhat adventurous and risky, in what ways can people become involved in entrepreneurial ventures? One way is to start a business from scratch. Taking advantage of computer-based information systems, many people are starting solo ventures and going it alone. The total number of small office/home office workers is more than 40 million, and each year more than a million new solo entrepreneurs join the ranks of the more than 29 million self-employed.

When people who go it alone succeed, they frequently need to hire other people to help them run the business. Michael Dell, for example, began his computer business as a college student and within weeks had hired several people to help him to assemble computers from the component parts he bought from suppliers. From his solo venture grew Dell Computer, the third largest computer company in the United States today.

Entrepreneurs who found a new business often have difficulty managing the organization as it grows; entrepreneurship is *not* the same as management. Management encompasses all the decisions involved in planning, organizing, leading, and controlling resources. Entrepreneurship is noticing an opportunity to satisfy a customer need and then mobilizing resources to make a product that satisfies that need. When an entrepreneur finds that he or she has produced something that customers want, entrepreneurship gives way to management as the pressing need becomes to provide the product both efficiently and effectively.

Frequently, a founding entrepreneur lacks the skills, patience, and experience to engage in the difficult and challenging work of management. Some entrepreneurs find it very hard to delegate authority because they are afraid to risk their company by letting others manage it. As a result, they become overloaded, and the quality of their decision making declines. Other entrepreneurs lack the detailed knowledge necessary to establish state-of-the-art information systems and technology or to create the operations management procedures that are vital to increase the efficiency of their organization's production system. Thus, to succeed, it is necessary to do more than create a new product; an entrepreneur must hire managers who can create an operating system that will let a new venture survive and prosper.

DEVELOPING A PLAN FOR A NEW BUSINESS One crucial factor that can help promote the success of a new venture is a clear business plan. The purpose of a business plan is to guide the development of the new business, just as the stage–gate development funnel guides the product development effort. The steps in the development of a business plan are listed in Table 19.1.

Planning for a new business begins when an entrepreneur notices an opportunity to develop a new or improved good or service for the whole market or for a specific market niche. For example, an entrepreneur might notice an opportunity in the fast-food market to provide customers with healthy fast food such as rotisserie chicken served with fresh vegetables. This is what the founders of the Boston Market restaurant chain did.

The next step is to test the feasibility of the new product idea. The entrepreneur conducts as thorough a strategic planning exercise as possible, using the SWOT analysis technique discussed in Chapter 7. First, the entrepreneur ana-

Table 19.1

Developing a Business Plan

1. Notice a product opportunity, and develop a basic business idea • Goods/services • Customers/markets
2. Conduct a strategic (SWOT) analysis • Identify opportunities • Identify threats • Identify strengths • Identify weaknesses
3. Decide whether the business opportunity is feasible
4. Prepare a detailed business plan • Statement of mission, goals, and financial objectives • Statement of strategic objectives • List of necessary resources • Organizational time line of events

lyzes opportunities and threats. For example, a potential threat might be that KFC will decide to imitate the idea and offer its customers rotisserie chicken (KFC actually did this after Boston Market identified the new market niche). The entrepreneur should conduct a thorough analysis of the external environment (see Chapter 3) to test the potential of a new product idea and must be willing to abandon an idea if it seems likely that the threats and risks may overwhelm the opportunities and returns. Entrepreneurship is always a very risky process, and many entrepreneurs become so committed to their new ideas that they ignore or discount the potential threats and forge ahead—only to lose their shirts.

If the environmental analysis suggests that the product idea is feasible, the next step is to examine the strengths and weaknesses of the idea. At this stage the main strength is the resources possessed by the entrepreneur. Does the entrepreneur have access to an adequate source of funds? Does the entrepreneur have any experience in the fast-food industry such as managing a restaurant? To identify weaknesses, the entrepreneur needs to assess how many and what kind of resources will be necessary to establish a viable new venture—such as a chain of chicken restaurants. Analysis might reveal that the new product idea will not generate an adequate return on investment. Or it might reveal that the entrepreneur needs to find partners to help provide the resources needed to open a chain on a sufficient scale to generate a high enough return on investment.

After conducting a thorough SWOT analysis, if the entrepreneur decides that the new product idea is feasible, the hard work begins of developing the actual business plan that will be used to attract investors or funds from banks. Included in the business plan should be the same basic elements as in the product development plan: (1) a statement of the organization's mission, goals, and financial objectives; (2) a statement of the organization's strategic objectives, including an analysis of the product's market potential, based on the SWOT analysis that has already been conducted; (3) a list of all the functional and organizational resources that will be required to successfully implement the new product idea, including a list of technological, financial, and human resource requirements; and (4) a time line that contains specific milestones for the entrepreneur and others to use to measure the progress of the venture, such as target dates for the final design and the opening of the first restaurant.

Many entrepreneurs do not have the luxury of having a team of cross-functional managers to help develop a detailed business plan. This is obviously true of solo ventures. One reason why franchising has become so popular in the United States is that an entrepreneur can purchase and draw on the business plan and experience of an already existing company, thereby reducing the risks associated with opening a new business. Entrepreneurs today can purchase the right to open a Boston Market restaurant. The founders of that chain, however, had to develop the business plan that made the franchise possible.

In sum, entrepreneurs have a number of significant challenges to confront and conquer if they are to be successful. It is not uncommon for an entrepreneur to fail repeatedly before he or she finds a venture that proves successful. It also is not uncommon for an entrepreneur who establishes a successful new company to sell it in order to move on to new ventures that promise new risks and returns. An example of such an entrepreneur is Wayne Huizenga, who bought many small waste disposal companies to create the giant WMX waste disposal company, which he eventually sold. A few years later Huizenga took control of Blockbuster Video and, by opening and buying other video store chains, turned Blockbuster Video into the biggest video chain in the United States, only to sell it in 1994. Over a billion dollars richer, recently he has been attempting to develop a national chain of used-car superstores, and investors have been snapping up stock in this successful entrepreneur's new company.

Intrapreneurship and Organizational Learning

The intensity of competition today, particularly from agile, small companies, has made it increasingly important for large established organizations to promote and encourage intrapreneurship so as to raise the level of innovation and organizational learning. A learning organization (see Chapter 6) encourages all employees to identify opportunities and solve problems, thus enabling the organization to continuously experiment, improve, and increase its ability to provide customers with new and improved goods and services. The higher the level of intrapreneurship is, the higher will be the levels of learning and innovation. How can organizations promote organizational learning and intrapreneurship?

product champion
A manager who takes "ownership" of a project and provides the leadership and vision that take a product from the idea stage to the final customer.

PRODUCT CHAMPIONS   One way to promote intrapreneurship is to encourage individuals to assume the role of **product champion,** a manager who takes "ownership" of a project and provides the leadership and vision that take a product from the idea stage to the final customer. 3M, a company well known for its attempts to promote intrapreneurship, encourages all its managers to become product champions and identify new product ideas. Product champions become responsible for developing a business plan for the product. Armed with this business plan, they appear before 3M's product development committee, a team of senior 3M managers who probe the strengths and weaknesses of the plan to decide whether it should be funded. If the plan is accepted, the production champion assumes responsibility for product development.

skunkworks A group of intrapreneurs who are deliberately separated from the normal operation of an organization to encourage them to devote all their attention to developing new products.

SKUNKWORKS AND NEW VENTURE DIVISIONS   The idea behind the product champion role is that employees who feel ownership for a project will be inclined to act like outside entrepreneurs and go to great lengths to make the project succeed. This feeling of ownership can also be strengthened by using skunkworks and new venture divisions. A **skunkworks** is a group of intrapreneurs who are deliberately separated from the normal operation of an organization—for example, from the normal chain of command—to encourage them to devote all their attention to developing new products. The idea is that if these people are isolated they will become so intensely involved in a project that development time will be relatively brief and the quality of the final product will be enhanced. The term *skunkworks* was coined at the Lockheed Corporation, which formed a team of design engineers to develop special aircraft such as the U2 spy plane. The secrecy with which this unit functioned and speculation about its goals led others to refer to it as the "skunkworks."

Large organizations can become tall, inflexible, and bureaucratic, and these characteristics are not ideal for encouraging learning and experimentation. Recognizing this problem, many organizations create new venture divisions, separate from the parent organization and free from close scrutiny, to take charge of product development. A **new venture division** is an autonomous division that is given all the resources it needs to develop and market a new product. In essence, a new venture division functions in the same way that a new venture would; the division's managers become intrapreneurs in charge of product development. The hope is that this new setting will encourage a high level of organizational learning and entrepreneurship.

REWARDS FOR INNOVATION To encourage managers to bear the uncertainty and risk associated with the hard work of entrepreneurship, it is necessary to link performance to rewards. Increasingly, companies are rewarding intrapreneurs on the basis of the outcome of the product development process. Intrapreneurs are granted large bonuses if their projects succeed, or they are granted stock options that can make them millionaires if the product sells well. Both Microsoft and Cisco Systems, for example, have made hundreds of their employees multimillionaires as a result of the stock options they were granted as part of their reward package. In addition to money, successful intrapreneurs can expect to receive promotion to the ranks of top management. Most of 3M's top managers reached the executive suite because they had a track record of successful entrepreneurship. Organizations must reward intrapreneurs equitably if they wish to prevent them from leaving and becoming outside entrepreneurs who might form a new venture that competes directly against them. Nevertheless, they frequently do so.

Summary and Review

Chapter Summary

INNOVATION, TECHNOLOGICAL CHANGE, AND COMPETITION The high level of technological change in today's world creates new opportunities for managers to market new products but can destroy the market for older products. Rapid technological change and changing fads and fashions can shorten product life cycles. The shorter a product life cycle is, the greater is the importance of product development as a competitive weapon.

PRODUCT DEVELOPMENT Successful product development requires managers to pursue four goals: reducing development time and maximizing the product's fit with customer needs, its quality, and its manufacturability. To meet these goals, managers should follow four principles of product development: (1) Establish a structured stage–gate development funnel for evaluating and controlling different product development efforts. (2) Establish cross-functional teams composed of individuals from different functional departments, and give each team a leader who can rise above his or her functional background. (3) Use concurrent engineering, the simultaneous design of the product and of the process for manufacturing the product, to reduce development time and increase manufacturability and product quality. (4) Involve both customers and suppliers in the development process.

**PRODUCT
DEVELOPMENT**

- **Goals of Product
  Development**

- **Principles of Prod-
  uct Development**

- **Problems with Prod-
  uct Development**

ENTREPRENEURSHIP

- **Entrepreneurship
  and New Ventures**

- **Intrapreneurship
  and Organizational
  Learning**

ENTREPRENEURSHIP Entrepreneurship is the mobilization of resources to take advantage of an opportunity to provide customers with new or improved goods and services. Entrepreneurs find new ventures of their own. Intrapreneurs work inside organizations and manage the product development process. Organizations need to encourage intrapreneurship because it leads to organizational learning and innovation.

Management in Action

Topics for Discussion and Action

1. Identify two industries where product life cycles are short and product development is an important competitive imperative. Identify two industries where product life cycles are long. What factors make the length of the product life cycle different in these industries?

2. When product life cycles are long, is product development *not* an important consideration for a company? Explain your answer.

3. The microprocessor that Intel developed can be classified as a quantum product innovation. Identify two other quantum product innovations, and explore their implications for product development.

4. What do you think are the greatest impediments to successful product development within an organization?

5. Why is it so important for managers to shorten the duration of product development? What steps can managers take to reduce development time? What risks are associated with compressing development time?

6. Ask a manager to describe an example of incremental product improvement in which he or she was involved. What was it? What were the problems surrounding it? Did it succeed?

7. What are the four principles of successful product development? How do they affect one another?

Building Management Skills

Promoting Successful Product Development

Pick a well-known company that is operating in an industry characterized by technological change (such as Apple Computer in the personal computer industry, Amgen in biotechnology, America Online in information services, Microsoft in computer software). Then answer the following questions.

1. What is the source of technological change in the company's task and general environments?

2. What is the average length of the product life cycle in the company's industry?

3. Approximately how many new products has the company introduced over the last five years?

4. How successful have the company's product development efforts been?

5. What accounts for the company's product successes? What accounts for its failures?

6. From what you have been able to find out, do you think there is potential for improving the company's product development efforts? If so, how?

Small Group Breakout Exercise

Keeping Up with Your Customers

Form groups of three or four people, and appoint one member as the spokesperson who will communicate your findings to the whole class when called on by the instructor. Then discuss the following scenario.

You are the top managers in charge of a chain of stores selling high-quality, high-priced men's and women's clothing. Store sales are flat, and you are increasingly concerned that the clothing that your stores offer to customers is failing to satisfy changing customer needs. You think that the purchasing managers are failing to spot changing fads and fashions in time, and you believe that store management is not doing enough to communicate to purchasing managers what customers are demanding. You want to revitalize your organization's product development process, which, in the case of your stores, means stocking the products that customers want.

1. Clearly state how and why each of the four goals of product development (development time, customer needs, quality, and manufacturability) is relevant to your organization.

2. Develop a program based on the four principles of product development that you intend to implement in your stores to achieve these goals. For example, how will you encourage input from employees and customers, and who will be responsible for managing the program?

Exploring the World Wide Web

Specific Assignment

Enter the website of the Italian company Pirelli (www.pirelli.com), and locate its cable division. Click on the "products" and "research and development" buttons, and then explore these locations.

1. What is Pirelli's approach to innovation and product development?

General Assignment

Search for the website of a company that describes the company's approach to innovation or product development. What kind of activities does this company engage in, and how does it manage the product development process?

ManagementCase

In the News

From the Pages of **BusinessWeek**

P&G's Hottest New Product: P&G

At Washington State's Clark County Fair last month, coffee lovers got a front-row seat at a corporate revolution in the making. The local sales force for Procter & Gamble Co. was out in force at the Pancake Feed, distributing samples of P&G's Millstone Coffee. To the amazement of the Fred Meyer supermarket employees running the pancake breakfast, the Procter reps worked the crowd, chatting with customers, even taking turns in the full-size coffee-maker costume with the cup-and-saucer hat. "You don't generally see them out there doing that kind of grassroots work with customers," says Jeanne Lawson, a Fred Meyer buyer. Procter is better known for serving up advertising dollars and display-design tips, she says. "I'd never seen anything like it."

But then, P&G has never needed ordinary customers quite so badly. Battered by disappointing revenue growth and demanding retail customers, Procter & Gamble is a company in a bind. Two years ago, its executive boldly declared that the consumer-products giant would double its net sales by 2006, to $70 billion. P&G has consistently missed its growth targets ever since. Olestra, the company's high-profile fat substitute, more than a decade in development, is showing weak sales. And global economic turmoil is crimping overseas operations. Shares have dropped from $94 apiece in July to $70. The behemoth so used to leading the pack is looking lost.

So P&G, a company notorious for secrecy, has set itself on a remarkably outward-looking self-improvement plan. Breaking from decades of tradition, it has sought external advice. It is undergoing a structural shift prompted at least in part by outsiders—namely, its big chain-store customers. And it is already rolling out an aggressive global marketing blitz, from working the fairgrounds to marshaling the Internet.

Chief Executive John E. Pepper will step down about two years early to make way for President and Chief Operating Officer Durk I. Jager, who will drive the changes. It's a shift away from internal themes of recent years in which Procter focused heavily on such tasks as cost-cutting and shedding underperforming brands. But even as the giant revs its engines to push for faster sales growth, critics wonder if it can overcome both economic turmoil around the world and what will surely be cultural turmoil within its own ranks. "This is a very big deal, for Procter and for all the companies that watch Procter's moves," says Watts Wacker, chairman of consulting firm FirstMatter in Westport, Conn. "But great plans often come with great obstacles."

In preparation for the task, Pepper and other top execs have been traversing the country, visiting the CEOs of a dozen major companies, including Kellogg Co. and 3M, in search of advice. Pepper went to Jack Welch at General Electric Co. to learn how the company streamlined global marketing. He persuaded Hewlett-Packard Co. CEO Lewis E. Platt to share enough secrets about new-product development to make a 30-minute instructional video for P&G staffers. The message from all was clear, says Pepper: "What thousands of people have been telling us is that we need to be simpler and move faster."

The result of this unprecedented road trip is Organization 2005, a shuffling of the P&G hierarchy and a new product-development process designed to speed innovative offerings to the global market. The old bureaucracy, based on geography, will be reshaped into seven global business units organized by category, such as baby care, beauty care, and fabric-and-home care. The global business units will develop and sell products on a worldwide basis, erasing the old system that let Procter's country managers rule as colonial governors, setting prices and handling products as they saw fit.

This new global vision has already had an accidental test run.

Last year, P&G introduced an extension of its Pantene shampoo line. The ad campaign for the product was almost entirely visual, with images of beautiful women and their lustrous hair, and had a very limited script. That meant the campaign was easily translated and shipped to P&G markets around the world without the usual months of testing and tinkering. The result: P&G was able to introduce the brand extension in 14 countries in six months, vs. the two years it took to get the original shampoo into stores abroad. "It's a success story that gets quite a bit of talk internally," says Chris T. Allen, a marketing professor at the University of Cincinnati, who spent his sabbatical year working in the P&G new-products department. "I see the reorganization as an attempt to do more Pantenes on a regular basis."

P&G didn't come to this global focus entirely on its own. Its biggest chain-store customers, such as Wal-Mart Stores Inc. and French-owned Carrefour, have been agitating for just such a program to mirror their own global expansion. It has been Topic A at retail conventions for months, says Robin Lanier, senior vice-president for industry affairs at the International Mass Retail Assn. While P&G craves an international image for its products, retailers want something more tangible: a global price. As it stands, prices are negotiable on a country or regional basis. What an international retailer pays for Crest in the U.S. could be considerably less than what it costs the chain in Europe or Latin America. A consistent global price gives big chains more power to plan efficiently and save money. Wal-Mart Chief Executive David D. Glass describes his company's goal as "global sourcing," which includes worldwide relationships on pricing and distribution. Moving P&G

products from regional to global management is "pointing somewhat in that direction," Glass says.

In addition to marketing and pricing, global business units will supervise new-product development. P&G will move away from its long-used "sequential" method, which tested products first in midsize U.S. cities and then gradually rolled them out to the world. An example: Swiffer, a new disposable mop designed by P&G, is being tested simultaneously in Cedar Rapids, Iowa; Pittsfield, Mass.; and Sens, France, in hopes of sculpting a globally popular product right out of the box.

Jager concedes that it won't be a quick fix. The new regime won't start until January and won't really be functioning for about 18 to 24 months. He expects to see some top-line growth improvement within 12 to 16 months, with obviously better results two years out. Many observers doubt that will be fast enough to make the 2006 deadline. "[The plan] seems to work on paper, but it requires an accelerated sales growth in the final four years," says Constance M. Maneaty, an analyst at Bear, Stearns & Co. "We haven't seen that kind of sales growth from them in a while."

Even if P&G could implement its strategy more quickly, it would still run into the ugly realities of global economic markets. For its extra $35 billion in revenues through 2006, Procter is counting on about $8 billion from emerging markets in Eastern Europe, China, and Latin America, says Clayton C. Daley Jr., P&G's treasurer, who becomes chief financial officer in October. Yet Asian emerging markets are likely to remain mired in deep economic slumps for at least two more years. Recent turmoil in Russia, which was a bright prospect for Procter just a

year ago, has gotten so bad that the company has temporarily halted shipments there. "Growing in underdeveloped geographies is clearly questionable," says Jay Freedman, an analyst at Lincoln Capital, a big institutional holder of Procter & Gamble stock. "Whatever they thought purchasing power of those new customers was going to be is less now."

Procter has additional obstacles closer to home. How, for example, will tradition-bound P&G managers react to the new hierarchy? "You're going from 144 chiefs to 8. That's a lot of ex-chiefs," says consultant Wacker. And everyone will be affected by the change in tone that is sure to come from the corner office. Gentlemanly Pepper, 60, will be succeeded by Jager, a Dutch-born P&G lifer with a reputation for aggressive moves and abrasiveness. In the 1980s, he turned around Procter's failing Japanese business with such a fury that his Japanese managers called him "Crazy Man Durk" behind his back.

Crazy or no, Jager is sticking to the 2006 target date. He's wasting no time stepping into his new role as champion of the global focus: Already, even before taking on the official title of CEO, he has started preaching the new structure to P&G managers. After all, the clock is ticking.

Source: Peter Galuszka and Ellen Newborne, "P&G's Hottest New Product: P&G," *Business Week,* October 5, 1998, 92, 96.

Questions

1. How is Procter & Gamble trying to speed up the development of new products?

2. How is P&G trying to change itself in the process?

ManagementCase

In the News

From the Pages of *The Wall Street Journal*
How a "Skunk Works" Kept Mustang Alive on a Tight Budget

Although the Ford Mustang is an American icon, it was almost killed because a projected $1 billion cost to overhaul the model seemed too much to Ford planners in 1989. However, a special 400-member group known inside Ford as "Team Mustang" worked for three years, instead of the usual four, and spent only $700 million to redesign the car, 25% to 30% less than any comparable new car program in Ford's recent history. The new model went on sale on December 9, 1993.

The Mustang team broke many of the rules that govern product development in the rigidly disciplined corporation. As the Mustang team fleshed out the plan in mid-1990, it agreed that the Mustang effort would need unprecedented freedom to make decisions without waiting for approval from headquarters or other departments. Team members wanted to think of themselves as independent stockholders of a "Mustang Car Co.," which happened to be financed by Ford.

The plan called for putting everyone involved under one roof—drafters sitting next to "bean counters," engineers one room away from stylists. That meant breaching the budgetary walls that divided departments and persuading department managers to cede some control over their subordinates. One of the boldest decisions was that Mr. Hothi, the program's manufacturing chief, would get veto power over changes to the body that threatened to derail his efforts to build the car with many of the factory tools used for the old

one. All this cut sharply against the grain of Ford's corporate culture.

They set up Mustang Car Co. in a converted furniture warehouse in Allen Park, Mich., a few miles south of Dearborn. They got approval to move engineers from various departments into their cramped offices, then grouped them into "chunk teams" with responsibility for every aspect of a particular piece, or "chunk" of the car.

They also did away with the arduous bidding process most Ford programs endure when selecting suppliers. With no time for that "rain dance" the Mustang team leaders agreed to pick the best available suppliers and simply ask them to join the Mustang process, from the start.

To save time and money, most of the convertible's designs were tested first on computer images, not on actual cars. Unfortunately, what happened on the screen didn't match what happened on the road. In July 1991, Mr. Zevalkink test-drove the first convertible prototype and discovered that it shimmied and shook. With Mr. Boddie's approval, he ordered a crash program to fix it. About a year later, in August 1992, Mr. Zevalkink took another test drive in another prototype convertible. To his dismay, it still shook.

Mr. Zevalkink felt queasy. Without a convertible, the Mustang line would lack its "image car" and miss out on sales. It had to be fixed. But that would mean ordering new reinforcement parts, new tooling. It might also require redesigning wiring and hoses under the hood. All that could make

the car miss its September 1993 start-of-production target and overshoot the budget. The team went into a crisis drill. Mr. Boddie assembled a special team of about 50 people to attack the convertible's problems. Suppliers were called in, and round-the-clock work began.

For eight weeks, the team ran a blitz of re-engineering work, computer manipulations and tough budget sessions. Engineers slept on the floors at the Allen Park warehouse. Mr. Boddie was even emboldened to go further. After seeing a new Mercedes-Benz convertible parked in front of a restaurant, he instructed his engineers to get one and take it apart to find the secrets of its smooth ride. The result: Mustang engineers bolted a 25-pound steel cylinder to a spot behind the front fender. On the Mercedes, a similar "damper" muffled vibrations like a finger on a tuning fork. Mustang team leaders say the new convertibles and coupes are ready today.

Source: Joseph B. White and Oscar Suris, "How a 'Skunk Works' Kept Mustang Alive on a Tight Budget," *Wall Street Journal,* September 21, 1993, A1.

Questions

1. What factors account for the success of the Mustang new product development project at Ford?

2. Which of the principles of new product development outlined in this chapter did Ford use in the Mustang project?

Glossary

A

ACCOMMODATIVE APPROACH
Moderate commitment to social responsibility; willingness to do more than the law requires if asked.

ACHIEVEMENT ORIENTATION
A worldview that values assertiveness, performance, success, and competition.

ADMINISTRATIVE MANAGEMENT The study of how to create an organizational structure that leads to high efficiency and effectiveness.

ADMINISTRATIVE MODEL An approach to decision making that explains why decision making is inherently uncertain and risky and why managers usually make satisfactory rather than optimum decisions.

AGREEABLENESS The tendency to get along well with other people.

ALDERFER'S ERG THEORY The theory that three universal needs—for existence, relatedness, and growth—constitute a hierarchy of needs and motivate behavior. Alderfer proposed that needs at more than one level can be motivational at the same time.

AMBIGUOUS INFORMATION
Information that can be interpreted in multiple and often conflicting ways.

APPLICATIONS SOFTWARE
Software designed for a specific task or use.

ARTIFICIAL INTELLIGENCE
Behavior performed by a machine that, if performed by a human being, would be called intelligent.

ATTITUDE A collection of feelings and beliefs.

AUTHORITY The power to hold people accountable for their actions and to make decisions concerning the use of organizational resources.

B

BARRIERS TO ENTRY Factors that make it difficult and costly for an organization to enter a particular task environment or industry.

BEHAVIORAL MANAGEMENT
The study of how managers should behave in order to motivate employees and encourage them to perform at high levels and be committed to the achievement of organizational goals.

BENCHMARKING Comparing performance on specific dimensions with the performance of high-performing organizations.

BIAS The systematic tendency to use information about others in ways that result in inaccurate perceptions.

BOTTOM-UP CHANGE Change that is implemented gradually and involves managers and employees at all levels of an organization.

BOUNDARY SPANNING
Interacting with individuals and groups outside the organization to obtain valuable information from the task and general environments.

BOUNDARYLESS ORGANIZATION An organization whose members are linked by computers, faxes, computer-aided design systems, and video teleconferencing and who rarely, if ever, see one another face-to-face.

BOUNDED RATIONALITY
Cognitive limitations that constrain one's ability to interpret, process, and act on information.

BRAND LOYALTY Customers' preference for the products of organizations currently existing in the task environment.

BUREAUCRACY A formal system of organization and administration designed to ensure efficiency and effectiveness.

BUREAUCRATIC CONTROL
Control of behavior by means of a comprehensive system of rules and standard operating procedures.

BUSINESS-LEVEL PLAN
Divisional managers' decisions pertaining to divisions' long-term goals, overall strategy, and structure.

BUSINESS-LEVEL STRATEGY
A plan that indicates how a division intends to compete against its rivals in an industry.

C

CAFETERIA-STYLE BENEFIT PLAN A plan from which employees can choose the benefits that they want.

CAREER The sum total of work-related experiences throughout a person's life.

CAREER PLATEAU A position from which the chances of being promoted or obtaining a more responsible job are slight.

CENTRALIZATION The concentration of authority at the top of the managerial hierarchy.

CHARISMATIC LEADER An enthusiastic, self-confident leader able to clearly communicate his or her vision of how good things could be.

CLAN CONTROL Control exerted on individuals and groups in an organization by shared values, norms, standards of behavior, and expectations.

CLASSICAL DECISION-MAKING MODEL A prescriptive approach to decision making based on the assumption that the decision maker can identify and evaluate all possible alternatives and their consequences and rationally choose the most appropriate course of action.

CLOSED SYSTEM A system that is self-contained and thus not affected by changes that occur in its external environment.

COERCIVE POWER The ability of a manager to punish others.

COLLECTIVE BARGAINING Negotiation between labor unions and managers to resolve conflicts and disputes about issues such as working hours, wages, benefits, working conditions, and job security.

COLLECTIVISM A worldview that values subordination of the individual to the goals of the group and adherence to the principle that people should be judged by their contribution to the group.

COMMAND ECONOMY An economic system in which the government owns all businesses and specifies which and how many goods and services are produced and the prices at which they are sold.

COMMAND GROUP A group composed of subordinates who report to the same supervisor; also called a department or unit.

COMMUNICATION The sharing of information between two or more individuals or groups to reach a common understanding.

COMMUNICATION NETWORKS The pathways along which information flows in groups and teams and throughout the organization.

COMPETITIVE ADVANTAGE The ability of one organization to outperform other organizations because it produces desired goods or services more efficiently and effectively than they do.

COMPETITORS Organizations that produce goods and services that are similar to a particular organization's goods and services.

CONCEPTUAL SKILLS The ability to analyze and diagnose a situation and to distinguish between cause and effect.

CONCURRENT CONTROL Control that gives managers immediate feedback on how efficiently inputs are being transformed into outputs so that managers can correct problems as they arise.

CONCURRENT ENGINEERING The simultaneous design of the product and of the process for manufacturing the product.

CONSCIENTIOUSNESS The tendency to be careful, scrupulous, and persevering.

CONSIDERATION Behavior indicating that a manager trusts, respects, and cares about subordinates.

CONTINGENCY THEORY The idea that managers' choice of organizational structures and control systems depends on—is contingent on—characteristics of the external environment in which the organization operates.

CONTINUOUS-PROCESS TECHNOLOGY Technology that is almost totally mechanized and is based on the use of automated machines working in sequence and controlled through computers from a central monitoring station.

CONTRACT BOOK A written agreement that details product development factors such as responsibilities, resource commitments, budgets, time lines, and development milestones.

CONTROL SYSTEMS Formal target-setting, monitoring, evaluation, and feedback systems that provide managers with information about how well the organization's strategy and structure are working.

CONTROLLING Evaluating how well an organization is achieving its goals and taking action to maintain or improve performance; one of the four principal functions of management.

CORE MEMBERS The members of a team who bear primary responsibility for the success of a project and who stay with a project from inception to completion.

CORPORATE-LEVEL PLAN Top management's decisions pertaining to the organization's mission, overall strategy, and structure.

CORPORATE-LEVEL STRATEGY A plan that indicates in which industries and national markets an organization intends to compete.

CREATIVITY A decision maker's ability to discover original and novel ideas that lead to feasible alternative courses of action.

CROSS-FUNCTIONAL TEAM A group of managers from different departments brought together to perform organizational tasks.

CULTURE SHOCK The feelings of surprise and disorientation that people experience when they do not understand the values, folkways, and mores that guide behavior in a culture.

CUSTOMERS Individuals and groups that buy the goods and services that an organization produces.

D

DATA Raw, unsummarized, and unanalyzed facts.

DECISION MAKING The process by which managers respond to opportunities and threats by analyzing options and making determinations about specific organizational goals and courses of action.

DECISION SUPPORT SYSTEM An interactive computer-based management information system that managers can use to make nonroutine decisions.

DECODING Interpreting and trying to make sense of a message.

DEFENSIVE APPROACH Minimal commitment to social responsibility; willingness to do what the law requires and no more.

DELPHI TECHNIQUE A decision-making technique in which group members do not meet face to face, but respond in writing to questions posed by the group leader.

DEMOGRAPHIC FORCES The outcomes of changes in, or changing attitudes toward, the characteristics of a population, such as age, gender, ethnic origin, race, sexual orientation, and social class.

DEVELOPMENT Building the knowledge and skills of organizational members so that they will be prepared to take on new responsibilities and challenges.

DEVIL'S ADVOCACY Critical analysis of a preferred alternative, made in response to challenges raised by a group member who, playing the role of devil's advocate, defends unpopular or opposing alternatives for the sake of argument.

DIALECTICAL INQUIRY Critical analysis of two preferred alternatives in order to find an even better alternative for the organization to adopt.

DIFFERENTIATION STRATEGY Distinguishing an organization's products from the products of competitors in dimensions such as product design, quality, or after-sales service.

DISCIPLINE Obedience, energy, application, and other outward marks of respect for a superior's authority.

DISTRIBUTIVE JUSTICE A moral principle calling for the distribution of pay raises, promotions, and other organizational resources to be based on meaningful contributions that individuals have made and not on personal characteristics over which they have no control.

DISTRIBUTIVE NEGOTIATION Adversarial negotiation in which the parties in conflict compete to win the most resources while conceding as little as possible.

DISTRIBUTORS Organizations that help other organizations sell their goods or services to customers.

DIVERSIFICATION Expanding operations into a new business or industry and producing new goods or services.

DIVERSITY Differences among people in age, gender, race, ethnicity, religion, sexual orientation, socioeconomic background, and capabilities/disabilities.

DIVISION A business unit that has its own set of managers and functions or departments and competes in a distinct industry.

DIVISION OF LABOR Splitting the work to be performed into particular tasks and assigning tasks to individual workers.

DIVISIONAL MANAGERS Managers who control the various divisions of an organization.

DIVISIONAL STRUCTURE An organizational structure composed of separate business units within which are the functions that work together to produce a specific product for a specific customer.

E

ECONOMIC FORCES Interest rates, inflation, unemployment, economic growth, and other factors that affect the general health and well-being of a nation or the regional economy of an organization.

ECONOMIES OF SCALE Cost advantages associated with large operations.

EFFECTIVE CAREER MANAGEMENT Ensuring that at all levels in the organization there are well-qualified workers who can assume more responsible positions as needed.

EFFECTIVENESS A measure of the appropriateness of the goals an organization is pursuing and of the degree to which the organization achieves those goals.

EFFICIENCY A measure of how well or productively resources are used to achieve a goal.

EMOTION-FOCUSED COPING The actions people take to deal with their stressful feelings and emotions.

EMOTIONAL INTELLIGENCE The ability to understand and manage one's own moods and emotions and the moods and emotions of other people.

EMPOWERMENT Expanding employees' tasks and responsibilities.

ENCODING Translating a message into understandable symbols or language.

ENTREPRENEUR An individual who notices opportunities and takes responsibility for mobilizing the resources necessary to produce new and improved goods and services.

ENTREPRENEURSHIP The mobilization of resources to take advantage of an opportunity to provide customers with new or improved goods and services.

ENTROPY The tendency of a system to lose its ability to control itself and thus to dissolve and disintegrate.

ENVIRONMENTAL CHANGE The degree to which forces in the task and general environments change and evolve over time.

EQUAL EMPLOYMENT OPPORTUNITY The equal right of all citizens to the opportunity to obtain employment regardless of their gender, age, race, country of origin, religion, color, age, or disabilities.

EQUITY The justice, impartiality, and fairness to which all organizational members are entitled.

EQUITY THEORY A theory of motivation that focuses on people's perceptions of the fairness of their work outcomes relative to their work inputs.

ESCALATING COMMITMENT A source of cognitive bias resulting from the tendency to commit additional resources to a project even if evidence shows that the project is failing.

ESPRIT DE CORPS Shared feelings of comradeship, enthusiasm, or devotion to a common cause among members of a group.

ETHICAL DECISION A decision that reasonable or typical stakeholders would find acceptable because it aids stakeholders, the organization, or society.

ETHICS Moral principles or beliefs about what is right or wrong.

ETHICS OMBUDSMAN An ethics officer who monitors an organization's practices and procedures to be sure they are ethical.

EXECUTIVE SUPPORT SYSTEM A sophisticated version of a decision support system that is designed to meet the needs of top managers.

EXPATRIATE MANAGERS Managers who go abroad to work for a global organization.

EXPECTANCY In expectancy theory, a perception about the extent to which effort will result in a certain level of performance.

EXPECTANCY THEORY The theory that motivation will be high when workers believe that high levels of effort will lead to high performance and high performance will lead to the attainment of desired outcomes.

EXPERT POWER Power that is based in the special knowledge, skills, and expertise that a leader possesses.

EXPERT SYSTEM A management information system that employs human knowledge captured in a computer to solve problems that ordinarily require human expertise.

EXPORTING Making products at home and selling them abroad.

EXTERNAL LOCUS OF CONTROL The tendency to locate responsibility for one's fate within outside forces and to believe that one's own behavior has little impact on outcomes.

EXTINCTION Curtailing the performance of dysfunctional behaviors by eliminating whatever is reinforcing them.

EXTRINSICALLY MOTIVATED BEHAVIOR Behavior that is performed to acquire material or social rewards or to avoid punishment.

EXTROVERSION The tendency to experience positive emotions and moods and to feel good about oneself and the rest of the world.

F

FACILITIES LAYOUT The operations management technique whose goal is to design the machine–worker interface to increase production system efficiency.

FEEDBACK CONTROL Control that gives managers information about customers' reactions to goods and services so that corrective action can be taken if necessary.

FEEDFORWARD CONTROL Control that allows managers to anticipate problems before they arise.

FILTERING Withholding part of a message out of the mistaken belief that the receiver does not need or will not want the information.

FIRST-LINE MANAGER A manager who is responsible for the daily supervision of nonmanagerial employees.

FLEXIBLE MANUFACTURING Operations management techniques that attempt to reduce the setup costs associated with a production system.

FOCUSED DIFFERENTIATION STRATEGY Serving only one segment of the overall market and trying to be the most differentiated organization serving that segment.

FOCUSED LOW-COST STRATEGY Serving only one segment of the overall market and being the lowest-cost organization serving that segment.

FOLKWAYS The routine social conventions of everyday life.

FORMAL APPRAISAL An appraisal conducted at a set time during the year and based on performance dimensions and measures that were specified in advance.

FORMAL GROUP A group that managers establish to achieve organizational goals.

FRANCHISING Selling to a foreign organization the rights to use a brand name and operating know-how in return for a lump-sum payment and a share of the profits.

FREE-MARKET ECONOMY An economic system in which private enterprise controls production and the interaction of supply and demand determines which and how many goods and services are produced and how much consumers pay for them.

FREE-TRADE DOCTRINE The idea that if each country specializes in the production of the goods and services that it can produce most efficiently, this will make the best use of global resources.

FRIENDSHIP GROUP An informal group composed of employees who enjoy each other's company and socialize with each other.

FUNCTION A unit or department in which people have the same skills or use the same resources to perform their jobs.

FUNCTIONAL MANAGERS Managers who supervise the various functions, such as manufacturing, accounting, and sales, within a division.

FUNCTIONAL STRUCTURE An organizational structure composed of all the departments that an organization requires to produce its goods or services.

FUNCTIONAL-LEVEL STRATEGY A plan that indicates how a function intends to achieve its goals.

FUNCTIONAL-LEVEL PLAN Functional managers' decisions pertaining to the goals that functional managers propose to pursue to help the division attain its business-level goals.

G

GATEKEEPING Deciding what information to allow into the organization and what information to keep out.

GENERAL ENVIRONMENT The wide-ranging economic, technological, sociocultural, demographic, political and legal, and global forces that affect an organization and its task environment.

GEOGRAPHIC STRUCTURE An organizational structure in which each region of a country or area of the world is served by a self-contained division.

GLASS CEILING A metaphor alluding to the invisible barriers that prevent minorities and women from being promoted to top corporate positions.

GLOBAL FORCES Outcomes of changes in international relationships, changes in nations' economic, political, and legal systems, and changes in technology, such as falling trade barriers, the growth of representative democracies, and reliable and instantaneous communication.

GLOBAL ORGANIZATION An organization that operates and competes in more than one country.

GLOBAL OUTSOURCING The purchase of inputs from foreign suppliers, or the production of inputs abroad, to lower production costs and improve product quality or design.

GLOBAL STRATEGY Selling the same standardized product and using the same basic marketing approach in each national market.

GOAL A desired future outcome that an organization strives to achieve.

GOAL-SETTING THEORY A theory that focuses on identifying the types of goals that are most effective in producing high levels of motivation and performance and explaining why goals have these effects.

GRAPEVINE An informal communication network along which unofficial information flows.

GROUP Two or more people who interact with each other to accomplish certain goals or meet certain needs.

GROUP COHESIVENESS The degree to which members are attracted or loyal to a group.

GROUP DECISION SUPPORT SYSTEM An executive support system that links top managers so that they can function as a team.

GROUP NORMS Shared guidelines or rules for behavior that most group members follow.

GROUP ROLE A set of behaviors and tasks that a member of a group is expected to perform because of his or her position in the group.

GROUPTHINK A pattern of faulty and biased decision making that occurs in groups whose members strive for agreement among themselves at the expense of accurately assessing information relevant to a decision.

GROUPWARE Computer software that enables members of groups and teams to share information with each other.

H

HAWTHORNE EFFECT The finding that a manager's behavior or leadership approach can affect workers' level of performance.

HERZBERG'S MOTIVATOR–HYGIENE THEORY A need theory that distinguishes between motivator needs (related to the nature of the work itself) and hygiene needs (related to the physical and psychological context in which the work is performed). Herzberg proposes that motivator needs must be met in

order for motivation and job satisfaction to be high.

HEURISTICS Rules of thumb that simplify decision making.

HIERARCHY OF AUTHORITY An organization's chain of command, specifying the relative authority of each manager.

HOSTILE WORK ENVIRONMENT SEXUAL HARASSMENT Telling lewd jokes, displaying pornography, making sexually oriented remarks about someone's personal appearance, and other sex-related actions that make the work environment unpleasant.

HUMAN RELATIONS MOVEMENT Advocates of the idea that supervisors be behaviorally trained to manage subordinates in ways that elicit their cooperation and increase their productivity.

HUMAN RESOURCE MANAGEMENT Activities that managers engage in to attract and retain employees and to ensure that they perform at a high level and contribute to the accomplishment of organizational goals.

HUMAN RESOURCE PLANNING Activities that managers engage in to forecast their current and future needs for human resources.

HUMAN SKILLS The ability to understand, alter, lead, and control the behavior of other individuals and groups.

HYBRID STRUCTURE The structure of a large organization that has many divisions and simultaneously uses many different organizational structures.

I

ILLUSION OF CONTROL A source of cognitive bias resulting from the tendency to overestimate one's own ability to control activities and events.

IMPORTING Selling at home products that are made abroad.

INCREMENTAL PRODUCT INNOVATIONS Products that result from incremental technological changes.

INCREMENTAL TECHNOLOGICAL CHANGE Change that refines existing technology and leads to gradual improvements or refinements in products over time.

INDIVIDUAL ETHICS Personal standards that govern how individuals interact with other people.

INDIVIDUALISM A worldview that values individual freedom and self-expression and adherence to the principle that people should be judged by their individual achievements rather than by their social background.

INDUSTRY LIFE CYCLE The changes that take place in an industry as it goes through the stages of birth, growth, shakeout, maturity, and decline.

INEQUITY Lack of fairness.

INFORMAL APPRAISAL An unscheduled appraisal of ongoing progress and areas for improvement.

INFORMAL GROUP A group that managers or nonmanagerial employees form to help achieve their own goals or meet their own needs.

INFORMAL ORGANIZATION The system of behavioral rules and norms that emerge in a group.

INFORMATION Data that is organized in a meaningful fashion.

INFORMATION DISTORTION Changes in the meaning of a message as the message passes through a series of senders and receivers.

INFORMATION RICHNESS The amount of information that a communication medium can carry and the extent to which the medium enables sender and receiver to reach a common understanding.

INFORMATION SYSTEM A system for acquiring, organizing, storing, manipulating, and transmitting information.

INFORMATION TECHNOLOGY The means by which information is acquired, organized, stored, manipulated, and transmitted.

INITIATING STRUCTURE Behavior that managers engage in to ensure that work gets done, subordinates perform their jobs acceptably, and the organization is efficient and effective.

INITIATIVE The ability to act on one's own, without direction from a superior.

INNOVATION The process of creating new goods and services or developing better ways to produce or provide goods and services.

INPUT Anything a person contributes to his or her job or organization.

INSTRUMENTAL VALUE A personal conviction about modes of conduct or ways of behaving that an individual seeks to follow.

INSTRUMENTALITY In expectancy theory, a perception about the extent to which performance will result in the attainment of outcomes.

INTEGRATING MECHANISMS Organizing tools that managers can use to increase communication and coordination among functions and divisions.

INTEGRATIVE BARGAINING Cooperative negotiation in which the parties in conflict work together to achieve a resolution that is good for them all.

INTEREST GROUP An informal group composed of employees seeking to achieve a common goal related to their membership in an organization.

INTERNAL LOCUS OF CONTROL The tendency to locate responsibility for one's fate within oneself.

INTERNET A global system of computer networks.

INTRANET A companywide system of computer networks.

INTRAPRENEUR A manager, scientist, or researcher who works inside an existing organization and notices opportunities for product improvements and is responsible for managing the product development process.

INTRINSICALLY MOTIVATED BEHAVIOR Behavior that is performed for its own sake.

INTUITION Ability to make sound decisions based on one's past experience and immediate feelings about the information at hand.

INVENTORY The stock of raw materials, inputs, and component parts that an organization has on hand at a particular time.

J

JARGON Specialized language that members of an occupation, group, or organization develop to facilitate communication among themselves.

JOB ANALYSIS Identifying the tasks, duties, and responsibilities that make up a job and the knowledge, skills, and abilities needed to perform the job.

JOB DESIGN The process by which managers decide how to divide tasks into specific jobs.

JOB ENLARGEMENT Increasing the number of different tasks in a given job by changing the division of labor.

JOB ENRICHMENT Increasing the degree of responsibility a worker has over his or her job.

JOB SATISFACTION The collection of feelings and beliefs that managers have about their current jobs.

JOB SIMPLIFICATION Reducing the number of tasks that each worker performs.

JOB SPECIALIZATION The process by which a division of labor occurs as different workers specialize in different tasks over time.

JOINT VENTURE A strategic alliance among two or more companies that agree to jointly establish and share the ownership of a new business.

JUDGMENT Ability to develop a sound opinion based on one's evaluation of the importance of the information at hand.

JUST-IN-TIME INVENTORY SYSTEM A system in which parts or supplies arrive at an organization when they are needed, not before.

K

KAIZEN An all-embracing operations management philosophy that emphasizes the need for continuous improvement in the efficiency of an organization's production system.

L

LABOR RELATIONS The activities that managers engage in to ensure that they have effective working relationships with the labor unions that represent their employees' interests.

LATERAL MOVE A job change that entails no major changes in responsibility or authority levels.

LEADER An individual who is able to exert influence over other people to help achieve group or organizational goals.

LEADER–MEMBER RELATIONS The extent to which followers like, trust, and are loyal to their leader; a determinant of how favorable a situation is for leading.

LEADERSHIP SUBSTITUTE Characteristics of subordinates or characteristics of a situation or context that act in place of the influence of a leader and make leadership unnecessary.

LEADERSHIP The process by which an individual exerts influence over other people and inspires, motivates, and directs their activities to help achieve group or organizational goals.

LEADING Articulating a clear vision and energizing and enabling organizational members so that they understand the part they play in achieving organizational goals; one of the four principal functions of management.

LEARNING A relatively permanent change in knowledge or behavior that results from practice or experience.

LEARNING ORGANIZATION An organization in which managers try to maximize the ability of individuals and groups to think and behave creatively and thus maximize the potential for organizational learning to take place.

LEARNING THEORIES Theories that focus on increasing employee motivation and performance by linking the outcomes that employees receive to the performance of desired behaviors and the attainment of goals.

LEGITIMATE POWER The authority that a manager has by virtue of his or her position in an organization's hierarchy.

LICENSING Allowing a foreign organization to take charge of manufacturing and distributing a product in its country or world region in return for a negotiated fee.

LINE OF AUTHORITY The chain of command extending from the top to the bottom of an organization.

LINEAR CAREER A career consisting of a sequence of jobs in which each new job entails additional responsibility, a greater impact on an organization, new skills, and upward movement in an organization's hierarchy.

LINGUISTIC STYLE A person's characteristic way of speaking.

LONG-TERM ORIENTATION A worldview that values thrift and persistence in achieving goals.

LOW-COST STRATEGY Driving the organization's costs down below the costs of its rivals.

M

MANAGEMENT The planning, organizing, leading, and controlling of resources to achieve organizational goals effectively and efficiently.

MANAGEMENT BY OBJECTIVES A goal-setting process in which a manager and his or her subordinates negotiate specific goals and objectives for the subordinate to achieve and then periodically evaluate the extent to which the subordinate is achieving those goals.

MANAGEMENT BY WANDERING AROUND A face-to-face communication technique in which a manager walks around a work area and talks informally with employees about issues and concerns.

MANAGEMENT INFORMATION SYSTEM An information system that managers plan and design to provide themselves with the specific information they need.

MANAGEMENT SCIENCE THEORY An approach to management that uses rigorous quantitative techniques to help managers make maximum use of organizational resources.

MANAGER A person who is responsible for supervising the use of an organization's resources to achieve its goals.

MARKET STRUCTURE An organizational structure in which each kind of customer is served by a self-contained division; also called customer structure.

MASLOW'S HIERARCHY OF NEEDS An arrangement of five basic needs that, according to Maslow, motivate behavior. Maslow proposed that the lowest level of unmet needs is the prime motivator and that only one level of needs is motivational at a time.

MASS-PRODUCTION TECHNOLOGY Technology that is based on the use of automated machines that are programmed to perform the same operations over and over.

MATRIX STRUCTURE An organizational structure that simultaneously groups people and resources by function and by product.

MECHANISTIC STRUCTURE An organizational structure in which authority is centralized, tasks and rules are clearly specified, and employees are closely supervised.

MEDIUM The pathway through which an encoded message is transmitted to a receiver.

MENTOR An experienced member of an organization who provides advice and guidance to a less-experienced worker.

MERIT PAY PLAN A compensation plan that bases pay on performance.

MESSAGE The information that a sender wants to share.

MISSION STATEMENT A broad declaration of an organization's purpose that identifies the organization's products and customers and distinguishes the organization from its competitors.

MIXED ECONOMY An economic system in which some sectors of the economy are left to private ownership and free-market mechanisms and others are owned by the government and subject to government planning.

MOOD A feeling or state of mind.

MORES Norms that are considered to be central to the functioning of society and to social life.

MOTIVATION Psychological forces that determine the direction of a person's behavior in an organization, a person's level of effort, and a person's level of persistence.

MULTIDOMESTIC STRATEGY Customizing products and marketing strategies to specific national conditions.

N

NATIONAL CULTURE The set of values that a society considers important and the norms of behavior that are approved or sanctioned in that society.

NEED A requirement or necessity for survival and well-being.

NEED FOR ACHIEVEMENT The extent to which an individual has a strong desire to perform challenging tasks well and to meet personal standards for excellence.

NEED FOR AFFILIATION The extent to which an individual is concerned about establishing and maintaining good interpersonal relations, being liked, and having other people get along.

NEED FOR POWER The extent to which an individual desires to control or influence others.

NEED THEORIES Theories of motivation that focus on what needs people are trying to satisfy at work and what outcomes will satisfy those needs.

NEEDS ASSESSMENT An assessment of which employees need training or development and what type of skills or knowledge they need to acquire.

NEGATIVE AFFECTIVITY The tendency to experience negative emotions and moods, to feel distressed, and to be critical of oneself and others.

NEGATIVE REINFORCEMENT Eliminating or removing undesired outcomes when people perform organizationally functional behaviors.

NEGOTIATION A method of conflict resolution in which the parties in conflict consider various alternative ways to allocate resources to each other in order to come up with a solution acceptable to them all.

NETWORK STRUCTURE A series of strategic alliances that an organization creates with suppliers, manufacturers, and distributors to produce and market a product.

NETWORKING The exchange of information through a group or network of interlinked computers.

NEW VENTURE DIVISION An autonomous division that is given all the resources it needs to develop and market a new product.

NOISE Anything that hampers any stage of the communication process.

NOMINAL GROUP TECHNIQUE A decision-making technique in which group members write down ideas and solutions, read their suggestions to the whole group, and discuss and then rank the alternatives.

NONPROGRAMMED DECISION MAKING Nonroutine decision making that occurs in response to unusual, unpredictable opportunities and threats.

NONVERBAL COMMUNICATION The encoding of messages by means of facial expressions, body language, and styles of dress.

NORMS Unwritten rules and codes of conduct that prescribe how people should act in particular situations.

NURTURING ORIENTATION A worldview that values the quality of life, warm personal friendships, and services and care for the weak.

O

OBJECTIVE APPRAISAL An appraisal that is based on facts and is likely to be numerical.

OBSTRUCTIONIST APPROACH Disregard for social responsibility; willingness to engage in and cover up unethical and illegal behavior.

ON-THE-JOB TRAINING Training that takes place in the work setting as employees perform their job tasks.

OPEN SYSTEM A system that takes in resources from its external environment and converts them into goods and services that are then sent back to that environment for purchase by customers.

OPENNESS TO EXPERIENCE The tendency to be original, have broad interests, be open to a wide range of stimuli, be daring, and take risks.

OPERANT CONDITIONING THEORY The theory that people learn to perform behaviors that lead to desired consequences and learn not to perform behaviors that lead to undesired consequences.

OPERATING BUDGET A budget that states how managers intend to use organizational resources to achieve organizational goals.

OPERATING SYSTEM SOFTWARE Software that tells computer hardware how to run.

OPERATIONS INFORMATION SYSTEM A management information system that gathers, organizes, and summarizes comprehensive data in a form that managers can use in their nonroutine coordinating, controlling, and decision-making tasks.

OPERATIONS MANAGEMENT The management of any aspect of the production system that transforms inputs into finished goods and services.

OPERATIONS MANAGER A manager who is responsible for managing an organization's production system and for determining where operating improvements might be made.

OPTIMUM DECISION The most appropriate decision in light of what managers believe to be the most desirable future consequences for their organization.

ORDER The methodical arrangement of positions to provide the organization with the greatest benefit and to provide employees with career opportunities.

ORGANIC STRUCTURE An organizational structure in which authority is decentralized to middle and first-line managers and tasks and roles are left ambiguous to encourage employees to cooperate and respond quickly to the unexpected.

ORGANIZATION A collection of people who work together and coordinate their actions to achieve goals.

ORGANIZATIONAL ARCHITEC- TURE The organizational structure, control systems, culture, and human resource management system that together determine how efficiently and effectively organizational resources are used.

ORGANIZATIONAL BEHAVIOR The study of the factors that have an impact on how individuals and groups respond to and act in organizations.

ORGANIZATIONAL BEHAVIOR MODIFICATION The systematic application of operant conditioning techniques to promote the performance of organizationally functional behaviors and discourage the performance of dysfunctional behaviors.

ORGANIZATIONAL CITIZENSHIP BEHAVIORS Behaviors that are not required of organizational members but that contribute to and are necessary for organizational efficiency, effectiveness, and gaining a competitive advantage.

ORGANIZATIONAL COMMITMENT The collection of feelings and beliefs that managers have about their organization as a whole.

ORGANIZATIONAL CONFLICT The discord that arises when the goals, interests, or values of different individuals or groups are incompatible and those individuals or groups block or thwart each other's attempts to achieve their objectives.

ORGANIZATIONAL CULTURE The set of values, norms, standards of behavior, and common expectations that control the ways in which individuals and groups in an organization interact with each other and work to achieve organizational goals.

ORGANIZATIONAL DESIGN The process by which managers make specific organizing choices that result in a particular kind of organizational structure.

ORGANIZATIONAL ENVIRONMENT The set of forces and conditions that operate beyond an organization's boundaries but affect a manager's ability to acquire and utilize resources.

ORGANIZATIONAL LEARNING The process through which managers seek to improve employees' desire and ability to understand and manage the organization and its task environment.

ORGANIZATIONAL PERFORMANCE A measure of how efficiently and effectively a manager uses resources to satisfy customers and achieve organizational goals.

ORGANIZATIONAL POLITICS Activities that managers engage in to increase their power and to use power effectively to achieve their goals and overcome resistance or opposition.

ORGANIZATIONAL SOCIALIZA- TION The process by which newcomers learn an organization's values and norms and acquire the work behaviors necessary to perform jobs effectively.

ORGANIZATIONAL STAKEHOLDERS Shareholders, employees, customers, suppliers, and others who have an interest, claim, or stake in an organization and in what it does.

ORGANIZATIONAL STRUCTURE A formal system of task and reporting relationships that coordinates and motivates organizational members so that they work together to achieve organizational goals.

ORGANIZING Structuring working relationships in a way that allows organizational members to work together to achieve organizational goals; one of the four principal functions of management.

OUTCOME Anything a person gets from a job or organization.

OUTSOURCE To use outside suppliers and manufacturers to produce goods and services.

OVERPAYMENT INEQUITY Inequity that exists when a person perceives that his or her own outcome/input ratio is greater than the ratio of a referent.

OVERT DISCRIMINATION Knowingly and willingly denying diverse individuals access to opportunities and outcomes in an organization.

P

PATH–GOAL THEORY A contingency model of leadership proposing that leaders can motivate subordinates by identifying their desired outcomes, rewarding them for high performance and the attainment of work goals with these desired outcomes, and clarifying for them the paths leading to attainment of work goals.

PAY LEVEL The relative position of an organization's pay incentives in comparison with those of other organizations in the same industry employing similar kinds of workers.

PAY STRUCTURE The arrangement of jobs into categories reflecting their relative importance to the organization and its goals, levels of skill required, and other characteristics.

PERCEPTION The process through which people select, organize, and interpret what they see, hear, touch, smell, and taste, to give meaning and order to the world around them.

PERFORMANCE APPRAISAL The evaluation of employees' job performance and contributions to their organization.

PERFORMANCE FEEDBACK The process through which managers share performance appraisal information with subordinates, give subordinates an opportunity to reflect on their own performance, and develop, with subordinates, plans for the future.

PERSONALITY TRAITS Enduring tendencies to feel, think, and act in certain ways.

PLANNING Identifying and selecting appropriate goals and courses of action; one of the four principal functions of management.

POLITICAL AND LEGAL FORCES Outcomes of changes in laws and regulations, such as the deregulation of industries, the privatization of organizations, and increased emphasis on environmental protection.

POLITICAL STRATEGIES Tactics that managers use to increase their power and to use power effectively to influence and gain the support of other people while overcoming resistance or opposition.

POOLED TASK INTERDEPENDENCE The task interdependence that exists when group members make separate and independent contributions to group performance.

POSITION POWER The amount of legitimate, reward, and coercive power that a leader has by virtue of his or her position in an organization; a determinant of how favorable a situation is for leading.

POSITIVE REINFORCEMENT Giving people outcomes they desire when they perform organizationally functional behaviors.

POTENTIAL COMPETITORS Organizations that presently are not in a task environment but could enter if they so chose.

POWER DISTANCE The degree to which societies accept the idea that inequalities in the power and well-being of their citizens are due to differences in individuals' physical and intellectual capabilities and heritage.

PRIOR HYPOTHESIS BIAS A cognitive bias resulting from the tendency to base decisions on strong prior beliefs even if evidence shows that those beliefs are wrong.

PROACTIVE APPROACH Strong commitment to social responsibility; eagerness to do more than the law requires and to use organizational resources to promote the interests of all organizational stakeholders.

PROBLEM-FOCUSED COPING The actions people take to deal directly with the source of their stress.

PROCEDURAL JUSTICE A moral principle calling for the use of fair procedures to determine how to distribute outcomes to organizational members.

PROCESS REENGINEERING The fundamental rethinking and radical redesign of business processes to achieve dramatic improvements in critical measures of performance such as cost, quality, service, and speed.

PRODUCT CHAMPION A manager who takes "ownership" of a project and provides the leadership and vision that take a product from the idea stage to the final customer.

PRODUCT DEVELOPMENT PLAN A plan that specifies all of the relevant information that managers need in order to decide whether to proceed with a full-blown product development effort.

PRODUCT LIFE CYCLE Changes in demand for a product that occur from its introduction through its growth and maturity to its decline.

PRODUCT STRUCTURE An organizational structure in which each product line or business is handled by a self-contained division.

PRODUCT TEAM STRUCTURE An organizational structure in which employees are permanently assigned to a cross-functional team and report only to the product team manager or to one of his or her direct subordinates.

PRODUCTION BLOCKING A loss of productivity in brainstorming sessions due to the unstructured nature of brainstorming.

PRODUCTION SYSTEM The system that an organization uses to acquire inputs, convert the inputs into outputs, and dispose of the outputs.

PROFESSIONAL ETHICS Standards that govern how members of a profession are to make decisions when the way they should behave is not clear-cut.

PROGRAMMED DECISION MAKING Routine, virtually automatic decision making that follows established rules or guidelines.

PUNISHMENT Administering an undesired or negative consequence when dysfunctional behavior occurs.

Q

QUALITY CIRCLES Groups of employees who meet regularly to discuss ways to increase quality.

QUANTUM PRODUCT INNOVATIONS Products that result from quantum technological changes.

QUANTUM TECHNOLOGICAL CHANGE A fundamental shift in technology that results in the innovation of new kinds of goods and services.

QUID PRO QUO SEXUAL HARASSMENT Asking for or forcing an employee to perform sexual favors in exchange for some reward or to avoid negative consequences.

R

REAL-TIME INFORMATION Frequently updated information that reflects current conditions.

REALISTIC JOB PREVIEW An honest assessment of the advantages and disadvantages of a job and organization.

RECEIVER The person or group for which a message is intended.

RECIPROCAL TASK INTERDEPENDENCE The task interdependence that exists when the work performed by each group member is fully dependent on the work performed by other group members.

RECRUITMENT Activities that managers engage in to develop a pool of qualified candidates for open positions.

REFERENT POWER Power that comes from subordinates' and co-workers' respect, admiration, and loyalty.

RELATED DIVERSIFICATION Entering a new business or industry to create a competitive advantage in one or more of an organization's existing divisions or businesses.

RELATIONSHIP-ORIENTED LEADERS Leaders whose primary concern is to develop good relationships with their subordinates and to be liked by them.

RELIABILITY The degree to which a tool or test measures the same thing each time it is used.

REPRESENTATIVE DEMOCRACY A political system in which representatives elected by citizens and legally accountable to the electorate form a government whose function is to make decisions on behalf of the electorate.

REPRESENTATIVENESS BIAS A cognitive bias resulting from the tendency to generalize inappropriately from a small sample or from a single vivid event or episode.

REPUTATION The esteem or high repute that individuals or organizations gain when they behave ethically.

RESEARCH AND DEVELOPMENT TEAM A team whose members have the expertise and experience needed to develop new products.

RESOURCES Assets such as people, machinery, raw materials, information, skills, and financial capital.

RESTRUCTURING Downsizing an organization by eliminating the jobs of large numbers of top, middle, and first-line managers and nonmanagerial employees.

REWARD POWER The ability of a manager to give or withhold tangible and intangible rewards.

RISK The degree of probability that the possible outcomes of a particular course of action will occur.

ROLE The specific tasks that a person is expected to perform because of the position he or she holds in an organization.

ROLE CONFLICT The conflict or friction that occurs when expected behaviors are at odds with each other.

ROLE MAKING Taking the initiative to modify an assigned role by assuming additional responsibilities.

ROLE OVERLOAD The condition of having too many responsibilities and activities to perform.

RULES Formal written instructions that specify actions to be taken under different circumstances to achieve specific goals.

RUMORS Unofficial pieces of information of interest to organizational members but with no identifiable source.

S

SATISFICING Searching for and choosing an acceptable, or satisfactory, response to problems and opportunities, rather than trying to make the best decision.

SCENARIO PLANNING The generation of multiple forecasts of future conditions followed by an analysis of how to respond effectively to each of those conditions; also called contingency planning.

SCIENTIFIC MANAGEMENT The systematic study of relationships between people and tasks for the purpose of redesigning the work process to increase efficiency.

SELECTION The process that managers use to determine the relative qualifications of job applicants and their potential for performing well in a particular job.

SELF-EFFICACY A person's belief about his or her ability to perform a behavior successfully.

SELF-ESTEEM The degree to which individuals feel good about themselves and their capabilities.

SELF-MANAGED WORK TEAM A group of employees who supervise their own activities and monitor the quality of the goods and services they provide.

SELF-REINFORCER Any desired or attractive outcome or reward that a person gives to himself or herself for good performance.

SENDER The person or group wishing to share information.

SEQUENTIAL TASK INTERDEPENDENCE The task interdependence that exists when group members must perform specific tasks in a predetermined order.

SHORT-TERM ORIENTATION A worldview that values personal stability or happiness and living for the present.

SKUNKWORKS A group of intrapreneurs who are deliberately separated from the normal operation of an organization to encourage them to devote all their attention to developing new products.

SMALL-BATCH TECHNOLOGY Technology that is used to produce small quantities of customized, one-of-a-kind products and is based on the skills of people who work together in small groups.

SOCIAL AUDIT A tool that allows managers to analyze the profitability and social returns of socially responsible actions.

SOCIAL LEARNING THEORY A theory that takes into account how learning and motivation are influenced by people's thoughts and beliefs and their observations of other people's behavior.

SOCIAL LOAFING The tendency of individuals to put forth less effort when they work in groups than when they work alone.

SOCIAL RESPONSIBILITY A manager's duty or obligation to make decisions that promote the welfare and well-being of stakeholders and society as a whole.

SOCIAL STRUCTURE The arrangement of relationships between individuals and groups in a society.

SOCIAL SUPPORT Emotional support provided by other people such as friends, relatives, and co-workers.

SOCIETAL ETHICS Standards that govern how members of a society are to deal with each other on issues such as fairness, justice, poverty, and the rights of the individual.

SOCIOCULTURAL FORCES Pressures emanating from the social structure of a country or society or from the national culture.

SPAN OF CONTROL The number of subordinates who report directly to a manager.

SPIRAL CAREER A career consisting of a series of jobs that build on each other but tend to be fundamentally different.

STAGE–GATE DEVELOPMENT FUNNEL A planning model that forces managers to make choices among competing projects so that organizational resources are not spread thinly over too many projects.

STANDARD OPERATING PROCEDURES Specific sets of written instructions about how to perform a certain aspect of a task.

STEADY-STATE CAREER A career consisting of the same kind of job during a large part of an individual's work life.

STEREOTYPE Simplistic and often inaccurate beliefs about the typical characteristics of particular groups of people.

STRATEGIC ALLIANCE An agreement in which managers pool or share their organization's resources and know-how with a foreign company, and the two organizations share the rewards and risks of starting a new venture.

STRATEGIC HUMAN RESOURCE MANAGEMENT The process by which managers design the components of a human resource management system to be consistent with each other, with other elements of organizational architecture, and with the organization's strategy and goals.

STRATEGY A cluster of decisions about what goals to pursue, what actions to take, and how to use resources to achieve goals.

STRATEGY FORMULATION Analysis of an organization's current situation followed by the development of strategies to accomplish its mission and achieve its goals.

STRESS A condition that individuals experience when they face important opportunities or threats and are uncertain about their ability to handle or deal with them effectively.

SUBJECTIVE APPRAISAL An appraisal that is based on perceptions of traits, behaviors, or results.

SUPERORDINATE GOALS Goals that all parties in conflict agree to regardless of the source of their conflicts.

SUPPLIERS Individuals and organizations that provide an organization with the input resources that it needs to produce goods and services.

SWOT ANALYSIS A planning exercise in which managers identify organizational strengths (S) and weaknesses (W), and environmental opportunities (O) and threats (T).

SYNERGY Performance gains that result when individuals and departments coordinate their actions.

SYSTEMATIC ERRORS Errors that people make over and over and that result in poor decision making.

T

TARIFF A tax that a government imposes on imported or, occasionally, exported goods.

TASK ENVIRONMENT The set of forces and conditions that originate with suppliers, distributors, customers, and competitors and affect an organization's ability to obtain inputs and dispose of its outputs, because they influence managers on a daily basis.

TASK FORCE A committee of managers from various functions or divisions who meet to solve a specific, mutual problem; also called an ad hoc committee.

TASK INTERDEPENDENCE The degree to which the work performed by one member of a group influences the work performed by other members.

TASK STRUCTURE The extent to which the work to be performed is clear-cut so that a leader's subordinates know what needs to be accomplished and how to go about doing it; a determinant of how favorable a situation is for leading.

TASK-ORIENTED LEADERS Leaders whose primary concern is to ensure that subordinates perform at a high level.

TEAM A group whose members work intensely with each other to achieve a specific, common goal or objective.

TECHNICAL SKILLS Job-specific knowledge and techniques that are required to perform an organizational role.

TECHNOLOGICAL FORCES Outcomes of changes in the technology that managers use to design, produce, or distribute goods and services.

TECHNOLOGY The combination of skills and equipment that managers use in the design, production, and distribution of goods and services.

TERMINAL VALUE A personal conviction about lifelong goals or objectives that an individual seeks to achieve.

THEORY X Negative assumptions about workers that lead to the conclusion that a manager's task is to supervise them closely and control their behavior.

THEORY Y Positive assumptions about workers that lead to the conclusion that a manager's task is to create a work setting that encourages commitment to organizational goals and provides opportunities for workers to be imaginative and to exercise initiative and self-direction.

THEORY Z An approach to management that recognizes and rewards individual achievements within a group context.

360-DEGREE APPRAISAL A performance appraisal by peers, subordinates, superiors, and sometimes clients who are in a position to evaluate a manager's performance.

TIME HORIZON The intended duration of a plan.

TOP-DOWN CHANGE Change that is implemented quickly throughout an organization by upper-level managers.

TOP-MANAGEMENT TEAM A group composed of the CEO, the president, and the heads of the most important departments.

TOP MANAGER A manager who establishes organizational goals, decides how departments should interact, and monitors the performance of middle managers.

TOTAL QUALITY MANAGEMENT A management technique that focuses on improving the quality of an organization's products and services.

TOTALITARIAN REGIME A political system in which a single party, individual, or group holds all political power and neither recognizes nor permits opposition.

TRAINING Teaching organizational members how to perform their current jobs and helping them acquire the knowledge and skills they need to be effective performers.

TRANSACTIONAL LEADERSHIP Leadership that motivates subordinates by rewarding high performance and reprimanding them for low performance.

TRANSACTION-PROCESSING SYSTEM A management information system designed to handle large volumes of routine, recurring transactions.

TRANSFORMATIONAL LEADERSHIP Leadership that makes subordinates aware of the importance of their jobs and performance to the organization and aware of their own needs for personal growth and that motivates subordinates to work for the good of the organization.

U

UNCERTAINTY Unpredictability.

UNCERTAINTY AVOIDANCE The degree to which societies are willing to tolerate uncertainty and risk.

UNDERPAYMENT INEQUITY Inequity that exists when a person perceives that his or her own outcome/input ratio is less than the ratio of a referent.

UNETHICAL DECISION A decision that a manager would prefer to disguise or hide from other people because it enables a company or a particular individual to gain at the expense of society or other stakeholders.

UNITY OF COMMAND A reporting relationship in which an employee receives orders from, and reports to, only one superior.

UNITY OF DIRECTION The singleness of purpose that makes possible the creation of one plan of action to guide managers and workers as they use organizational resources.

UNRELATED DIVERSIFICATION Entering a new industry or buying a company in a new industry that is not related in any way to an organization's current businesses or industries.

V

VALENCE In expectancy theory, how desirable each of the outcomes available from a job or organization is to a person.

VALIDITY The degree to which a tool or test measures what it purports to measure.

VALUE SYSTEM The terminal and instrumental values that are guiding principles in an individual's life.

VALUES Ideas about what a society believes to be good, right, desirable, or beautiful.

VERBAL COMMUNICATION The encoding of messages into words, either written or spoken.

VERTICAL INTEGRATION A strategy that allows an organization to create value by producing its own inputs or distributing and selling its own outputs.

VICARIOUS LEARNING Learning that occurs when the learner becomes motivated to perform a behavior by watching another person perform it; also called observational learning.

VIRTUAL TEAM A team whose members rarely or never meet face-to-face and interact by using various forms of information technology such as e-mail, computer networks, telephones, faxes, and video conferences.

W

WHISTLE-BLOWER A person who reports illegal or unethical behavior.

WHOLLY OWNED FOREIGN SUBSIDIARY Production operations established in a foreign country independent of any local direct involvement.

Credits

Endnotes

Chapter 1

1. M. Moritz, *The Little Kingdom: The Private Story of Apple Computer* (New York: Morrow, 1984).

2. R. Cringely, *Accidental Empires* (New York: Harper Business, 1994); B. Dumaine, "America's Toughest Bosses," *Fortune,* October 18, 1993, 38–50.

3. S. Alsop, "Just call Me The Seer: I Was Dead Right on Apple," *Fortune,* June 22, 1998, 155–56.

4. B. Schlender, "Steve Jobs' Hollow Deal," *Fortune,* September 8, 1997, 93.

5. www. apple.com apple.com

6. G. R. Jones, *Organizational Theory* (Reading, MA: Addison-Wesley, 1995).

7. J. P. Campbell, "On the Nature of Organizational Effectiveness," in P. S. Goodman, J. M. Pennings, and Associates, *New Perspectives on Organizational Effectiveness* (San Francisco: Jossey-Bass, 1977).

8. L. Williams, "A Silk Blouse on the Assembly Line (Yes, the Boss's)," *New York Times,* February 5, 1995, 7.

9. H. Fayol, *General and Industrial Management* (New York: IEEE Press, 1984).

10. P. F. Drucker, *Management Tasks, Responsibilities, and Practices* (New York: Harper and Row, 1974).

11. D. McGraw, "The Kid Bytes Back," *U. S. News & World Report,* December 12, 1994, 70–71.

12. J. Kotter, *The General Managers* (New York: Free Press, 1992).

13. C. P. Hales, "What Do Managers Do? A Critical Review of the Evidence," *Journal of Management Studies* (January 1986): 88–115; A. I. Kraul, P. R. Pedigo, D. D. McKenna, and M. D. Dunnette, "The Role of the Manager: What's Really Important in Different Management Jobs," *Academy of Management Executive* (November 1989): 286–93.

14. A. K. Gupta, "Contingency Perspectives on Strategic Leadership," in D. C. Hambrick, ed., *The Executive Effect: Concepts and Methods for Studying Top Managers* (Greenwich, CT: JAI Press, 1988), 147–78.

15. D. G. Ancona, "Top Management Teams: Preparing for the Revolution," in J. S. Carroll, ed., *Applied Social Psychology and Organizational Settings* (Hillsdale, NJ: Erlbaum, 1990); D. C. Hambrick and P. A. Mason, "Upper Echelons: The Organization as a Reflection of Its Top Managers," *Academy of Management Journal* 9 (1984): 193–206.

16. T. A. Mahony, T. H. Jerdee, and S. J. Carroll, "The Jobs of Management," *Industrial Relations* 4 (1965): 97–110; L. Gomez-Mejia, J. McCann, and R. C. Page, "The Structure of Managerial Behaviors and Rewards," *Industrial Relations* 24 (1985): 147–54.

17. R. Stewart, "Middle Managers: Their Jobs and Behaviors," in J. W. Lorsch, ed., *Handbook of Organizational Behavior* (Englewood Cliffs, NJ: Prentice-Hall, 1987), 385–91.

18. K. Labich, "Making over Middle Managers," *Fortune,* May 8, 1989, 58–64.

19. B. Wysocki, "Some Companies Cut Costs Too Far, Suffer from Corporate Anorexia," *Wall Street Journal,* July 5, 1995, A1.

20. W. Cascio, "Downsizing: What Do We Know? What Have We Learned?" *Academy of Management Executive* (February 1993): 95–104.

21. S. R. Parker, T. D. Wall, and P. R. Jackson, "That's Not My Job: Developing Flexible Work Orientations," *Academy of Management Journal* 40 (1997): 899–929.

22. B. Dumaine, "The New Non-Manager," *Fortune,* February 22, 1993, 80–84.

23. K. Kelly, "The New Soul of John Deere," *Business Week,* January 31, 1994, 64–66.

24. H. Mintzberg, "The Manager's Job: Folklore and Fact," *Harvard Business Review* (July–August 1975): 56–62.

25. H. Mintzberg, *The Nature of Managerial Work* (New York: Harper and Row, 1973).

26. Ibid.

27. N. Kelleher, "Short-Term Rentals Is All Booked Up," *Boston Herald,* January 17, 1995, 26.

28. R. H. Guest, "Of Time and the Foreman," *Personnel* 32 (1955): 478–86.

29. L. Hill, *Becoming a Manager: Mastery of a New Identity* (Boston: Harvard Business School Press, 1992).

30. Ibid.

31. R. L. Katz, "Skills of an Effective Administrator," *Harvard Business Review* (September–October 1974): 90–102.

32. Ibid.

33. A. Shama, "Management Under Fire: The Transformation of Management in the Soviet Union and Eastern Europe," *Academy of Management Executive* (1993): 22–35.

34. K. Seiders and L. L. Berry, "Service Fairness: What It Is and Why It Matters," *Academy of Management Executive* 12 (1998): 8–20.

35. E. Underwood, "Levi Woos Firms: Get into Our Pants," *Brandweek,* January 30, 1995, 15–18.

36. K. Des Marteau, "Customer Manufacturers Suit Up with Technology," *Bobbin* (April 1995): 10–14.

37. C. Anderson, "Values-Based Management," *Academy of Management Executive* 11 (1997): 25–46.

38. W. H. Shaw and V. Barry, *Moral Issues in Business,* 6th ed. (Belmont, CA: Wadsworth, 1995); T. Donaldson, *Corporations and Morality* (Englewood Cliffs, NJ: Prentice-Hall, 1982).

39. A. B. Henderson, "Two Former Honda Officials Convicted of Accepting Bribes from Auto Dealers," *Wall Street Journal,* June 22, 1995, A3.

40. S. Jackson and Associates, *Diversity in the Workplace: Human Resource Initiatives* (New York: Guilford Press, 1992).

41. G. Robinson and C. S. Daus, "Building a Case for Diversity," *Academy of Management Executive* 3 (1997): 21–31.

42. D. Jamieson and J. O'Mara, *Managing Workforce 2000: Gaining a Diversity Advantage* (San Francisco: Jossey-Bass, 1991).

43. T. H. Cox and S. Blake, "Managing Cultural Diversity: Implications for Organizational Competitiveness," *Academy of Management Executive* (August 1991): 49–52.

44. D. R. Tobin, *The Knowledge Enabled Organization* (New York: AMACOM, 1998).

45. L. Grant, "Stirring It Up at Campbell," *Fortune,* May 13, 1996, 80–86.

46. G. Burns, "Crunch Time at Quaker Oats," *Business Week,* September 23, 1996, 70–73.

Chapter 2

1. H. Ford, "Progressive Manufacture," *Encyclopedia Britannica,* 13th ed. (New York: Encyclopedia Co., 1926).

2. R. Edwards, *Contested Terrain: The Transformation of the Workplace in the Twentieth Century* (New York: Basic Books, 1979).

3. A. Smith, *The Wealth of Nations* (London: Penguin, 1982).

4. Ibid., 110.

5. J. G. March and H. A. Simon, *Organizations* (New York: Wiley, 1958).

6. F. W. Taylor, *Shop Management* (New York: Harper, 1903); F. W. Taylor, *The Principles of Scientific Management* (New York: Harper, 1911).

7. L. W. Fry, "The Maligned F. W. Taylor: A Reply to His Many Critics," *Academy of Management Review* 1 (1976): 124–29.

8. J. A. Litterer, *The Emergence of Systematic Management as Shown by the Literature from 1870–1900* (New York: Garland, 1986).

9. H. R. Pollard, *Developments in Management Thought* (New York: Crane, 1974).

10. D. Wren, *The Evolution of Management Thought* (New York: Wiley, 1994), 134.

11. Edwards, *Contested Terrain.*

12. J. M. Staudenmaier, Jr., "Henry Ford's Big Flaw," *Invention and Technology* 10 (1994): 34–44.

13. H. Beynon, *Working for Ford* (London: Penguin, 1975).

14. Taylor, *Scientific Management.*

15. F. B. Gilbreth, *Primer of Scientific Management* (New York: Van Nostrand Reinhold, 1912).

16. F. B. Gilbreth, Jr., and E. G. Gilbreth, *Cheaper by the Dozen* (New York: Crowell, 1948).

17. D. Roy, "Efficiency and the Fix: Informal Intergroup Relations in a Piece Work Setting," *American Journal of Sociology* 60 (1954): 255–66.

18. M. Weber, *From Max Weber: Essays in Sociology,* ed. H. H. Gerth and C. W. Mills (New York: Oxford University Press, 1946); M. Weber, *Economy and Society,* ed. G. Roth and C. Wittich (Berkeley: University of California Press, 1978).

19. C. Perrow, *Complex Organizations,* 2d ed. (Glenview IL: Scott, Foresman, 1979).

20. Weber, *From Max Weber,* 331.

21. See Perrow, *Complex Organizations,* Ch. 1, for a detailed discussion of these issues.

22. H. Fayol, *General and Industrial Management* (New York: IEEE Press, 1984).

23. Ibid., 79.

24. T. J. Peters and R. H. Waterman, Jr., *In Search of Excellence: Lessons from America's Best-Run Companies* (New York: Harper and Row, 1982).

25. R. E. Eccles and N. Nohira, *Beyond the Hype: Rediscovering the Essence of Management* (Boston: Harvard Business School Press, 1992).

26. L. D. Parker, "Control in Organizational Life: The Contribution of Mary Parker Follett," *Academy of Management Review* 9 (1984): 736–45.

27. P. Graham, *M. P. Follett—Prophet of Management: A Celebration of Writings from the 1920s* (Boston: Harvard Business School Press, 1995).

28. M. P. Follett, *Creative Experience* (London: Longmans, 1924).

29. E. Mayo, *The Human Problems of Industrial Civilization* (New York: Macmillan, 1933); F. J. Roethlisberger and W. J. Dickson, *Management and the Worker* (Cambridge, MA: Harvard University Press, 1947).

30. D. W. Organ, "Review of Management and the Worker, by F. J. Roethlisberger and W. J. Dickson," *Academy of Management Review* 13 (1986): 460–64.

31. D. Roy, "Banana Time: Job Satisfaction and Informal Interaction," *Human Organization* 18 (1960): 158–61.

32. For an analysis of the problems in determining cause from effect in the Hawthorne studies and in social settings in general, see A. Carey, "The Hawthorne Studies: A Radical Criticism," *American Sociological Review* 33 (1967): 403–16.

33. D. McGregor, *The Human Side of Enterprise* (New York: McGraw-Hill, 1960).

34. Ibid., 48.

35. W. G. Ouchi, *Theory Z: How American Business Can Meet the Japanese Challenge* (Reading, MA: Addison-Wesley, 1981).

36. Peters and Waterman, *In Search of Excellence.*

37. J. Pitta, "It Had to Be Done and We Did It," *Forbes,* April 26, 1993, 148–52.

38. W. E. Deming, *Out of the Crisis* (Cambridge, MA: MIT Press, 1986).

39. J. D. Thompson, *Organizations in Action* (New York: McGraw-Hill, 1967).

40. D. Katz and R. L. Kahn, *The Social Psychology of Organizations* (New York: Wiley, 1966); Thompson, *Organizations in Action*.

41. T. Burns and G. M. Stalker, *The Management of Innovation* (London: Tavistock, 1961); P. R. Lawrence and J. R. Lorsch, *Organization and Environment* (Boston: Graduate School of Business Administration, Harvard University, 1967).

42. Burns and Stalker, *The Management of Innovation*.

43. J. Levine. "Philips' Big Gamble," *Business Week,* August 5, 1991, 34–36.

44. "Philips Fights the Flab," *The Economist,* April 7, 1992, 73–74.

45. C. W. L. Hill and G. R. Jones, *Strategic Management: An Integrated Approach,* 3d ed. (Boston: Houghton Mifflin, 1995).

Chapter 3

1. C. W. L. Hill, "Compaq Computer Corporation in 1994," in C. W. L. Hill and G. R. Jones, *Strategic Management: An Integrated Approach,* 3d ed. (Boston: Houghton Mifflin, 1995).

2. L. J. Bourgeois, "Strategy and Environment: A Conceptual Integration," *Academy of Management Review* 5 (1985): 25–39.

3. M. E. Porter, *Competitive Strategy* (New York: Free Press, 1980).

4. "Coca-Cola Versus Pepsi-Cola and the Soft Drink Industry," *Harvard Business School Case* #9-391-179.

5. M. E. Porter, *Competitive Advantage* (New York: Free Press, 1985).

6. P. Nulty, "1995 National Business Hall of Fame," *Fortune,* April 3, 1995, 104–14.

7. S. Weiss, *Merck & Co., Inc. (A), (B), (C), and (D)* (Business Enterprise Trust, 1991).

8. For views on barriers to entry from an economics perspective, see Porter, *Competitive Strategy.* For the sociological perspective, see J. Pfeffer and G. R. Salancik, *The External Control of Organization: A Resource Dependence Perspective* (New York: Harper and Row, 1978).

9. Porter, *Competitive Strategy;* J. E. Bain, *Barriers to New Competition* (Cambridge, MA: Harvard University Press, 1956); R. J. Gilbert, "Mobility Barriers and the Value of Incumbency," in R. Schmalensee and R. D. Willig, eds., *Handbook of Industrial Organization,* vol. 1 (Amsterdam: North Holland, 1989).

10. C. W. L. Hill, "The Computer Industry: The New Industry of Industries," in Hill and Jones, *Strategic Management.*

11. "Marks & Spencer, Ltd. (A)," *Harvard Business School Case* #9-391-089.

12. G. Klepper, "Entry into the Market for Large Transport Aircraft," *European Economic Review* 34 (1990): 775–803.

13. H. Banks, "Superjumbo," *Forbes,* October 24, 1994, 180–86.

14. "Autos–Auto Parts," *Standard & Poor's Industry Surveys,* June 24, 1993.

15. J. Schumpeter, *Capitalism, Socialism and Democracy* (London: Macmillan, 1950), 68. Also see R. R. Winter and S. G. Winter, *An Evolutionary Theory of Economic Change* (Cambridge, MA: Harvard University Press, 1982).

16. "The Coming Clash of Logic," *The Economist,* July 3, 1993, 21–23.

17. S. Sherman, "The New Computer Revolution," *Fortune,* June 14, 1993, 56–84.

18. K. West, "Boeing 2000," *Seattle Times,* October 21, 1992, A1, A10, A11.

19. A. Taylor, "Boeing–Sleepy in Seattle," *Fortune,* August 1995, 92–98.

20. N. Goodman, *An Introduction to Sociology* (New York: HarperCollins, 1991); C. Nakane, *Japanese Society* (Berkeley: University of California Press, 1970).

21. "The War Between the Sexes," *The Economist,* March 5, 1994, 80–81.

22. The Economist, *The Economist Book of Vital World Statistics* (New York: Random House, 1990).

23. For a detailed discussion of the importance of the structure of law as a factor explaining economic change and growth, see D. C. North, *Institutions, Institutional Change and Economic Performance* (Cambridge: Cambridge University Press, 1990).

24. Agis Salpukas, "Hurt in Expansion, Airlines Cut Back and May Sell Hubs," *New York Times,* April 1, 1994, A1, C8.

25. R. B. Reich, *The Work of Nations* (New York: Knopf, 1991).

26. Jagdish Bhagwati, *Protectionism* (Cambridge, MA: MIT Press, 1988).

27. "Autos–Auto Parts," *Standard & Poor's Industry Surveys,* June 24, 1993; J. Bennet, "A Stronger Yen Is Hurting Sales of Japan's Cars," *New York Times,* November 5, 1993, A1, C2; "The Price Is High," *The Economist,* August 14, 1993, 63; "Survey of the Car Industry," *The Economist,* October 17, 1992, 13–15.

28. R. B. Duncan, "Characteristics of Organization Environment and Perceived Environment," *Administrative Science Quarterly* 17 (1972): 313–27.

29. K. M. Eisenhardt and Shona L. Brown, *Competing on the Edge* (Boston: Harvard Business School Press, 1998).

30. J. S. Adams, "The Structure and Dynamics of Behavior in Boundary Spanning Roles," in M. D. Dunnette, ed., *The Handbook of Industrial and Organizational Psychology* (Chicago: Rand McNally, 1976).

31. R. H. Miles, *Macro Organizational Behavior* (Santa Monica, CA: Goodyear, 1980).

32. For a discussion of sources of organizational inertia, see M. T. Hannah and J. Freeman, "Structural Inertia and Organizational Change," *American Sociological Review* 49 (1984): pp 149–64.

33. E. A. Gargan, "For a Furniture Maker, a Taste of a Global Future," *New York Times,* March 17, 1994, C1, C3.

34. Not everyone agrees with this assessment. Some argue that organizations and individual managers have little impact on the environment. See Hannah and Freeman, "Structural Inertia and Organizational Change."

35. R. X. Cringeley, *Accidental Empires* (New York: Harper Business, 1993).

36. B. Saporito, "This Bud's for Them," *Fortune,* August 9, 1993, 12–14.

37. J. Levine, "Beer Barrel Blues," *Forbes,* June 22, 1992, 98–100.

38. P. Sellers, "How Busch Wins in a Doggy Market," *Fortune,* June 22, 1987, 100–11.

Chapter 4

1. R. Tomkins, "A Long Walk for the Shops," *Financial Times,* April 11, 1994, 13; W. Dawkins, "Revolution in Toyland," *Financial Times,* April 8, 1993, 9; L. Zinn, "The Limited: All Grown Up and Nowhere to Go?" *Business Week,* December 20, 1993, 44.

2. Zinn, "The Limited"; *Value Line* (August 1994): 1716.

3. "Limited Inc. to Open Bath & Body Stores in UK Joint Venture," *Wall Street Journal,* June 23, 1994, B3.

4. M. Pacelle, "Limited Unveils Buyback Plan of $1.62 Billion," *Wall Street Journal,* January 29, 1996, B5.

5. J. Bhagwati, *Protectionism* (Cambridge, MA: MIT Press, 1988).

6. For a summary of these theories see P. Krugman and M. Obstfeld, *International Economics: Theory and Policy* (New York: HarperCollins, 1991). Also see C. W. L. Hill, *International Business* (Homewood, IL: Irwin, 1997), Ch. 4.

7. C. A. Bartlett and S. Ghoshal, *Managing Across Borders* (Boston: Harvard Business School Press, 1989).

8. C. Arnst and G. Edmondson, "The Global Free for All," *Business Week,* September 26, 1994, 118–26.

9. W. Konrads, "Why Leslie Wexner Shops Overseas," *Business Week,* February 3, 1992, 30.

10. R. Dore, *Taking Japan Seriously: A Confusion Perspective on Leading Economic Issues* (Stanford, CA: Stanford University Press, 1987).

11. "Boeing's Worldwide Supplier Network," *Seattle Post-Intelligence,* April 9, 1994, 13.

12. I. Metthee, "Playing a Large Part," *Seattle Post-Intelligence,* April 9, 1994, 13.

13. "The Gains from Trade," *The Economist,* September 23, 1989, 25–26.

14. C. S. Tranger, "Enter the Mini-Multinational," *Northeast International Business* (March 1989): 13–14.

15. R. B. Reich, *The Work of Nations* (New York: Knopf, 1991).

16. T. Levitt, "The Globalization of Markets," *Harvard Business Review* (May–June 1983): 92–102.

17. T. Deveny et al., "McWorld?" *Business Week,* October 13, 1986, 78–86.

18. R. Wesson, *Modern Government–Democracy and Authoritarianism,* 2d ed. (Englewood Cliffs, NJ: Prentice-Hall, 1992).

19. Nobel Prize–winning economist Douglas North makes this argument. See D. C. North, *Institutions, Institutional Change, and Economic Performance* (Cambridge: Cambridge University Press, 1990).

20. For an accessible discussion of the reasons for this, see M. Friedman and R. Friedman, *Free to Choose* (London: Penguin Books, 1990).

21. P. M. Sweezy and H. Magdoff, *The Dynamics of U.S. Capitalism* (New York: Monthly Review Press, 1972).

22. The ideology is that of individualism, which dates back to Adam Smith, John Stuart Mill, and the like. See H. W. Spiegel, *The Growth of Economic Thought* (Durham, NC: Duke University Press, 1991).

23. P. Hofheinz, "Yes, You Can Win in Eastern Europe," *Fortune,* May 16, 1994, 110–12.

24. T. Walker, "Crucial Stage of the Reform Program," *Financial Times,* November 18, 1993, sec. 3, p. 1.

25. M. Magnier, "Chiquita Bets Czechoslovakia Can Produce Banana Bonanza," *Journal of Commerce,* August 29, 1991, 1, 3.

26. J. Perlez, "GE Finds Tough Going in Hungary," *New York Times,* July 25, 1994, C1, C3.

27. E. B. Tylor, *Primitive Culture* (London: Murray, 1871).

28. For details on the forces that shape culture, see Hill, *International Business,* Ch. 2.

29. G. Hofstede, B. Neuijen, D. D. Ohayv, and G. Sanders, "Measuring Organizational Cultures: A Qualitative and Quantitative Study Across Twenty Cases," *Administrative Science Quarterly* 35 (1990): 286–316.

30. R. Bellah, *Habits of the Heart: Individualism and Commitment in American Life* (Berkeley: University of California Press, 1985).

31. R. Bellah, *The Tokugawa Religion* (New York: Free Press, 1957).

32. C. Nakane, *Japanese Society* (Berkeley: University of California Press, 1970).

33. For example, see Dore, *Taking Japan Seriously.*

34. G. Hofstede, "The Cultural Relativity of Organizational Practices and Theories," *Journal of International Business Studies* (Fall 1983): 75–89.

35. Hofstede, Neuijen, Ohayv, and Sanders, "Measuring Organizational Cultures."

36. J. P. Fernandez and M. Barr, *The Diversity Advantage* (New York: Lexington Books, 1994).

37. R. E. Caves, *Multinational Enterprise and Economic Analysis* (Cambridge: Cambridge University Press, 1982).

38. B. Kogut, "Joint Ventures: Theoretical and Empirical Perspectives," *Strategic Management Journal* 9 (1988): 319–33.

39. N. Hood and S. Young, *The Economics of the Multinational Enterprise* (London: Longman, 1979).

40. P. Abrahams, "Getting Hooked on Fish and Chips in Japan," *Financial Times,* May 17, 1994, 6.

41. "Another World," *The Economist,* September 19, 1992, 15–18.

42. Bhagwati, *Protectionism.*

43. G. Smith, "NAFTA: A Green Light for Red Tape," *Business Week,* July 25, 1994, 48.

44. Free Trade or Foul," *The Economist,* June 4, 1994, 70. Also see Krugman and Obstfeld, *International Economics.*

45. A. Roddick, "Not Free Trade but Fair Trade," *Across the Board* (June 1994): 58; A. Jack and N. Buckley, "Halo Slips on the Raspberry Bubbles," *Financial Times,* August 27–28, 1994, 12.

46. A. Choi, "GM Seeds Grow Nicely in Eastern Europe," *Wall Street Journal,* April 3, 1995, A11.

Chapter 5

1. M. Galen, J. A. Byrne, T. Smart, and D. Woodruff, "Debacle at Dow Corning: How Bad Will It Get," *Business Week,* March 2, 1992, 36–38.

2. J. A. Byrne, "Here's What to Do Next, Dow Corning," *Business Week,* February 24, 1992, 33.

3. J. A. Byrne, "The Best Laid Ethics Programs . . .," *Business Week,* March 9, 1992, 67–69.

4. J. A. Pearce, "The Company Mission as a Strategic Tool," *Sloan Management Review* (Spring 1982): 15–24.

5. C. I. Barnard, *The Functions of the Executive* (Cambridge, MA: Harvard University Press, 1948).

6. R. E. Freeman, *Strategic Management: A Stakeholder Approach* (Marshfield, MA: Pitman, 1984).

7. B. Bahree, "BP Comes Back Even as Oil Prices Sink," *Wall Street Journal,* September 8, 1995, A6.

8. A. Stevens, "Boss's Brain Teaser: Accommodating Depressed Worker," *Wall Street Journal,* September 11, 1995, B1.

9. T. L. Beauchamp and N. E. Bowie, eds., *Ethical Theory and Business* (Englewood Cliffs, NJ: Prentice-Hall, 1979); A. Macintyre, *After Virtue* (South Bend, IN: University of Notre Dame Press, 1981).

10. R. E. Goodin, "How to Determine Who Should Get What," *Ethics* (July 1975): 310–21.

11. T. M. Jones, "Ethical Decision Making by Individuals in Organizations: An Issue Contingent Model," *Academy of Management Journal* 16 (1991): 366–95; G. F. Cavanaugh, D. J. Moberg, and M. Velasquez, "The Ethics of Organizational Politics," *Academy of Management Review* 6 (1981): 363–74.

12. L. K. Trevino, "Ethical Decision Making in Organizations: A Person–Situation Interactionist Model," *Academy of Management Review* 11 (1986): 601–17; W.

H. Shaw and V. Barry, *Moral Issues in Business,* 6th ed. (Belmont, CA: Wadsworth, 1995).

13. B. Carton, "Gillette Faces Wrath of Children in Testing on Rats and Rabbits," *Wall Street Journal,* September 5, 1995, A1.

14. A. S. Waterman, "On the Uses of Psychological Theory and Research in the Process of Ethical Inquiry," *Psychological Bulletin* 103, no. 3 (1988): 283–98.

15. IBM press release issued September 14, 1995.

16. B. Ziegler, "IBM Fires Three Argentine Executives Amid Investigation of Bank Contract," *Wall Street Journal,* September 15, 1995, A6.

17. M. S. Frankel, "Professional Codes: Why, How, and with What Impact?" *Ethics* 8 (1989): 109–15.

18. J. Van Maanen and S. R. Barley, "Occupational Communities: Culture and Control in Organizations," in B. Staw and L. Cummings, eds., *Research in Organizational Behavior,* vol. 6 (Greenwich, CT: JAI Press, 1984), 287–365.

19. Jones, "Ethical Decision Making by Individuals in Organizations."

20. J. R. Rest, *Moral Development: Advances in Research and Theory* (New York: Praeger, 1986).

21. B. Victor and J. B. Cullen, "The Organizational Bases of Ethical Work Climates," *Administrative Science Quarterly* 33 (1988): 101–25.

22. H. Demsetz, "Towards a Theory of Property Rights," *American Economic Review* 57 (1967):347–59.

23. B. Ortega, "Broken Rules, Conduct Codes Garner Goodwill for Retailers but Violations Go On," *Wall Street Journal,* July 3, 1995, A1, A4.

24. D. Collins, "Organizational Harm, Legal Consequences and Stakeholder Retaliation," *Journal of Business Ethics* 8 (1988): 1–13.

25. S. W. Gellerman, "Why Good Managers Make Bad Decisions," in K. R. Andrews, ed., *Ethics in Practice: Managing the Moral Corporation* (Boston: Harvard Business School Press, 1989).

26. L. K. Trevino, "Ethical Decision Making in Organizations," *Academy of Management Review* 11 (1986): 601–17.

27. M. S. Baucus and J. P. Near, "Can Illegal Corporate Behavior Be Predicted? An Event History Analysis," *Academy of Management Journal* 34 (1991): 9–36.

28. J. Flynn and C. Del Valle, "Did Sears Take Its Customers for a Ride?" *Business Week,* August 3, 1992, 24–25.

29. R. C. Soloman, *Ethics and Excellence* (New York: Oxford University Press, 1992).

30. J. Dobson, "Corporate Reputation: A Free Market Solution to Unethical Behavior," *Business and Society* 28 (1989): 1–5.

31. R. Johnson, "Ralston to Buy Beechnut, Gambling It Can Overcome Apple Juice Scandal," *Wall Street Journal,* September 18, 1989, B11.

32. E. Gatewood and A. B. Carroll, "The Anatomy of Corporate Social Response," *Business Horizons* (September–October 1981): 9–16.

33. M. Friedman, "A Friedman Doctrine: The Social Responsibility of Business Is to Increase Its Profits," *New York Times Magazine,* September 13, 1970, 33.

34. W. G. Ouchi, *Theory Z: How American Business Can Meet the Japanese Challenge* (Reading, MA: Addison-Wesley, 1981).

35. J. B. McGuire, A. Sundgren, and T. Schneewis, "Corporate Social Responsibility and Firm Financial Performance," *Academy of Management Review* 31 (1988): 854–72.

36. Friedman, "A Friedman Doctrine," 32, 33, 122, 124, 126.

37. J. B. Dozier and M. P. Miceli, "Potential Predictors of Whistleblowing: A Prosocial Perspective," *Academy of Management Review* 10 (1985): 823–36; J. P. Near and M. P. Miceli, "Retaliation Against Whistleblowers: Predictors and Effects," *Journal of Applied Psychology* 71 (1986): 137–45.

38. "The Uncommon Good," *The Economist,* August 19, 1995, 55.

39. Byrne, "The Best Laid Ethics Programs . . .," 67–69.

40. E. D. Bowman, "Corporate Social Responsibility and the Investor," *Journal of Contemporary Business* (Winter 1973): 49–58.

41. P. E. Murphy, "Implementing Business Ethics," *Journal of Business Ethics* 7 (1988): 907–15.

42. P. E. Murphy, "Creating Ethical Corporate Structure," *Sloan Management Review* (Winter 1989): 81–87.

43. G. R. Jones, *Organizational Theory: Text and Cases* (Reading, MA: Addison-Wesley, 1997).

44. D. McNerney, "The Bottom-Line Value of Diversity," *HR Focus* (May 1994): 22–23.

45. C. Lee, "The Feminization of Management," *Training* (November 1994): 25–31.

46. "Prejudice: Still on the Menu," *Business Week,* April 3, 1995, 42.

47. "Glass Ceiling Is a Heavy Barrier for Minorities, Blocking Them from Top Jobs," *Wall Street Journal,* March 14, 1995, A1.

48. R. Folger and M. A. Konovsky, "Effects of Procedural and Distributive Justice on Reactions to Pay Raise Decisions," *Academy of Management Journal* 32 (1989): 115–30; J. Greenberg, "Organizational Justice: Yesterday, Today, and Tomorrow," *Journal of Management* 16 (1990): 399–402.

49. R. Sharpe, "Women Make Strides, but Men Stay Firmly in Top Company Jobs," *Wall Street Journal,* March 29, 1994, A1, A8.

50. A. M. Jaffe, "At Texaco, the Diversity Skeleton Still Stalks the Halls," *New York Times,* December 11, 1994, sec. 3, p. 5.

51. Greenberg, "Organizational Justice."

52. W. M. Carley, "Salesman's Treatment Raises Bias Questions at Schering-Plough," *Wall Street Journal,* May 31, 1995, A1, A8.

53. G. Robinson and K. Dechant, "Building a Case for Business Diversity," *Academy of Management Executive* (1997): 3, 32–47.

54. A. Patterson, "Target 'Micromarkets' Its Way to Success; No 2 Stores Are Alike," *Wall Street Journal,* May 31, 1995, A1, A9.

55. A. Stevens, "Lawyers and Clients," *Wall Street Journal,* June 19, 1995, B7.

56. B. McMenamin, "Diversity Hucksters," *Forbes,* May 22, 1995, 174–76.

57. E. D. Pulakos and K. N. Wexley, "The Relationship Among Perceptual Similarity, Sex, and Performance Ratings in Manager–Subordinate Dyads," *Academy of Management Journal* 26 (1983): 129–39.

58. S. T. Fiske and S. E. Taylor, *Social Cognition* (Reading, MA: Addison-Wesley, 1984).

59. Ibid.

60. M. Loden and J. B. Rosener, *Workforce America! Managing Employee Diversity as a Vital Resource* (Burr Ridge, IL: Irwin, 1991).

61. B. Carton, "Muscled Out? At Jenny Craig, Men Are Ones Who Claim Sex Discrimination," *Wall Street Journal,* November 29, 1994, A1, A7.

62. A. P. Carnevale and S. C. Stone, "Diversity: Beyond the Golden Rule," *Training & Development* (October 1994): 22–39.

63. B. A. Battaglia, "Skills for Managing Multicultural Teams," *Cultural Diversity at Work* 4 (1992); Carnevale and Stone, "Diversity: Beyond the Golden Rule."

64. B. Mandell and S. Kohler-Gray, "Management Development That Values Diversity," *Personnel* (March 1990): 41–47.

65. B. Filipczak, "25 Years of Diversity at UPS," *Training* (August 1992): 42–46.

66. J. R. Dorfman and U. Gupta, "Choice Positions for Four Blacks Mask Problems," *Wall Street Journal,* February 3, 1995, B1, B2.

67. L. Copeland, "Valuing Diversity, Part 2: Pioneers and Champions of Change," *Personnel* (July 1988): 44–49.

68. "Diversity Is Up, 'Goal-Setting' Is Down in Workplace-Training Programs," *Wall Street Journal,* March 21, 1995, A1.

69. "Chevron Settles Claims of 4 Women at Unit as Part of Sex Bias Suit," *Wall Street Journal,* January 22, 1995, B12.

70. T. Segal, "Getting Serious About Sexual Harassment," *Business Week,* November 9, 1992, 78–82.

71. Carton, "Muscled Out?"

72. R. L. Paetzold and A. M. O'Leary-Kelly, "Organizational Communication and the Legal Dimensions of Hostile Work Environment Sexual Harassment," in G. L. Kreps, ed., *Sexual Harassment: Communication Implications* (Cresskill, NJ: Hampton Press, 1993).

73. M. Galen, J. Weber, and A. Z. Cuneo, "Sexual Harassment: Out of the Shadows," *Fortune,* October 28, 1991, 30–31.

74. A. M. O'Leary-Kelly, R. L. Paetzold, and R. W. Griffin, "Sexual Harassment as Aggressive Action: A Framework for Understanding Sexual Harassment" (paper presented at the annual meeting of the Academy of Management, Vancouver, August 1995).

75. S. J. Bresler and R. Thacker, "Four-Point Plan Helps Solve Harassment Problems," *HR Magazine* (May 1993): 117–24.

76. "Du Pont's Solution," *Training* (March 1992): 29.

77. J. S. Lublin, "Sexual Harassment Moves Atop Agenda in Many Executive Education Programs," *Wall Street Journal,* December 2, 1991, B1, B4.

78. "Navy is Teaching Sailors What Proper Conduct Is," *Bryan/College Station Eagle,* April 19, 1993, A2.

79. S. B. Garland, "Finally, a Corporate Tip Sheet on Sexual Harassment," *Business Week,* July 13, 1998, 39.

80. "Racial Differences Discourage Mentors," *Wall Street Journal,* October 29, 1991, B1.

81. C. Hymowitz, "How a Dedicated Mentor Gave Momentum to a Woman's Career," *Wall Street Journal,* April 24, 1995, B1, B3.

Chapter 6

1. The CSI story is based on a real incident experienced by a consulting client of one of the authors of this text. The names of the company and individuals and dates involved have been changed.

2. G. P. Huber, *Managerial Decision Making* (Glenview, IL: Scott, Foresman, 1993).

3. H. A. Simon, *The New Science of Management* (Englewood Cliffs, NJ: Prentice-Hall, 1977).

4. One should be careful not to generalize too much here, however; for as Peter Senge has shown, programmed decisions rely on the implicit assumption that the environment is in a steady state. If environmental conditions change, then sticking to a routine decision rule can produce disastrous results. See P. Senge, *The Fifth Disciple: The Art and Practice of the Learning Organization* (New York: Doubleday, 1990).

5. H. A. Simon, *Administrative Behavior* (New York: Macmillan, 1947), 79.

6. H. A. Simon, *Models of Man* (New York: Wiley, 1957).

7. K. J. Arrow, *Aspects of the Theory of Risk Bearing* (Helsinki: Yrjo Johnssonis Saatio, 1965).

8. Ibid.

9. R. L. Daft and R. H. Lengel, "Organizational Information Requirements, Media Richness and Structural Design," *Management Science* 32 (1986): 554–71.

10. R. Cyert and J. March, *Behavioral Theory of the Firm* (Englewood Cliffs, NJ: Prentice-Hall, 1963).

11. J. G. March and H. A. Simon, *Organizations* (New York: Wiley, 1958).

12. H. A. Simon, "Making Management Decisions: The Role of Intuition and Emotion," *Academy of Management Executive* 1 (1987): 57–64.

13. B. Kelley, "A Day in the Life of a Card Shark," *Journal of Business Strategy* (Spring 1994): 36–39.

14. M. H. Bazerman, *Judgment in Managerial Decision Making* (New York: Wiley, 1986). Also see Simon, *Administrative Behavior.*

15. N. J. Langowitz and S. C. Wheelright, "Sun Microsystems, Inc. (A)," *Harvard Business School Case* #686-133.

16. R. D. Hof, "How to Kick the Mainframe Habit," *Business Week,* June 26, 1995, 102–04.

17. Bazerman, *Judgment in Managerial Decision Making;* Huber, *Managerial Decision Making;* J. E. Russo and P. J. Schoemaker, *Decision Traps* (New York: Simon and Schuster, 1989).

18. M. D. Cohen, J. G. March, and J. P. Olsen, "A Garbage Can Model of Organizational Choice," *Administrative Science Quarterly* 17 (1972): 1–25.

19. Ibid.

20. Bazerman, *Judgment in Managerial Decision Making.*

21. Senge, *The Fifth Disciple.*

22. E. de Bono, *Lateral Thinking* (London: Penguin 1968); Senge, *The Fifth Disciple.*

23. Russo and Schoemaker, *Decision Traps.*

24. Bazerman, *Judgment in Managerial Decision Making.*

25. Russo and Schoemaker, *Decision Traps.*

26. F. Gulliver, "Post Project Appraisals Pay," *Harvard Business Review* (March–April 1987): 128–32.

27. D. Kahneman and A. Tversky, "Judgment Under Uncertainty: Heuristics and Biases," *Science* 185 (1974): 1124–31.

28. C. R. Schwenk, "Cognitive Simplification Processes in Strategic Decision Making," *Strategic Management Journal* 5 (1984): 111–28.

29. Kelley, "A Day in the Life of a Card Shark."

30. An interesting example of the illusion of control is Richard Roll's hubris hypothesis of takeovers. See R. Roll, "The Hubris Hypothesis of Corporate Takeovers," *Journal of Business* 59 (1986): 197–216.

31. B. M. Staw, "The Escalation of Commitment to a Course of Action," *Academy of Management Review* 6 (1981): 577–87.

32. M. J. Tang, "An Economic Perspective on Escalating Commitment," *Strategic Management Journal* 9 (1988): 79–92.

33. Russo and Schoemaker, *Decision Traps.*

34. Ibid.

35. I. L. Janis, *Groupthink: Psychological Studies of Policy Decisions and Disasters,* 2d ed. (Boston: Houghton Mifflin, 1982).

36. C. R. Schwenk, *The Essence of Strategic Decision Making* (Lexington, MA: Lexington Books, 1988).

37. See R. O. Mason, "A Dialectic Approach to Strategic Planning," *Management Science* 13 (1969): 403–14; R. A. Cosier and J. C. Aplin, "A Critical View of Dialectic Inquiry in Strategic Planning," *Strategic Management Journal* 1 (1980): 343–56; I. I. Mitroff and R. O. Mason, "Structuring III–Structured Policy Issues: Further Explorations in a Methodology for Messy Problems," *Strategic Management Journal* 1 (1980): 331–42.

38. Mason, "A Dialectic Approach to Strategic Planning."

39. D. M. Schweiger and P. A. Finger, "The Comparative Effectiveness of Dialectic Inquiry and Devil's Advocacy," *Strategic Management Journal* 5 (1984): 335–50.

40. Mary C. Gentile, *Differences That Work: Organizational Excellence Through Diversity* (Boston: Harvard Business School Press. 1994).

42. F. Rice, "How to Make Diversity Pay," *Fortune,* August 8, 1994, 78–86.

43. B. Hedberg, "How Organizations Learn and Unlearn," in W. H. Starbuck and P. C. Nystrom, eds., *Handbook of Organizational Design,* vol. 1 (New York: Oxford University Press, 1981), 1–27.

43. Senge, *The Fifth Discipline.*

44. Ibid.

45. P. M. Senge, "The Leader's New Work: Building Learning Organizations," *Sloan Management Review* (Fall 1990): 7–23.

46. Ibid.

47. R. W. Woodman, J. E. Sawyer, and R. W. Griffin, "Towards a Theory of Organizational Creativity," *Academy of Management Review* 18 (1993): 293–321.

48. T. J. Bouchard, Jr., J. Barsaloux, and G. Drauden, "Brainstorming Procedure, Group Size, and Sex as Determinants of Problem Solving Effectiveness of Individuals and Groups," *Journal of Applied Psychology* 59 (1974): 135–38.

49. M. Diehl and W. Stroebe, "Productivity Loss in Brainstorming Groups: Towards the Solution of a Riddle," *Journal of Personality and Social Psychology* 53 (1987): 497–509.

50. D. H. Gustafson, R. K. Shulka, A. Delbecq, and W. G. Walster, "A Comparative Study of Differences in Subjective Likelihood Estimates Made by Individuals, Interacting Groups, Delphi Groups, and Nominal Groups," *Organizational Behavior and Human Performance* 9 (1973): 280–91.

51. N. Dalkey, *The Delphi Method: An Experimental Study of Group Decision Making* (Santa Monica, CA: Rand Corp., 1989).

52. E. S. Browning, "Computer Chip Project Brings Rivals Together, but the Cultures Clash," *Wall Street Journal,* April 3, 1994, A1, A8.

53. "An Ex-Swordsman Ploughs into the Peace Business," *The Economist,* September 23, 1995, 59.

Chapter 7

1. B. Simon, "Upstart Cott Shakes Cola Kings," *Financial Times,* June 14, 1994, 18; "Coca-Cola Versus Pepsi-Cola and the Soft Drink Industry," *Harvard Business School Case* #9-391-179.

2. A. Chandler, *Strategy and Structure: Chapters in the History of the American Enterprise* (Cambridge, MA: MIT Press, 1962)>

3. Ibid.

4. F. J. Aguilar, "General Electric: Reg Jones and Jack Welch," in *General Managers in Action* (Oxford: Oxford University Press, 1992).

5. Aguilar, *General Managers in Action.*

6. Aguilar, "General Electric."

7. C. W. Hofer and D. Schendel, *Strategy Formulation: Analytical Concepts* (St. Paul, MN: West, 1978).

8. H. Fayol, *General and Industrial Management* (1884; New York: IEEE Press, 1984).

9. L. Iacocca, *Iacocca: An Autobiography* (New York: Bantam Books, 1984).

10. Fayol, *General and Industrial Management,* 18.

11. P. Wack, "Scenarios: Shooting the Rapids," *Harvard Business Review* (November–December, 1985): 139–50.

12. A. P. De Geus, "Planning as Learning," *Harvard Business Review* (March–April 1988): 70–74.

13. P. J. H. Schoemaker, "Multiple Scenario Development: Its Conceptual and Behavioral Foundation," *Strategic Management Journal* 14 (1993): 193–213.

14. J. A. Pearce, "The Company Mission as a Strategic Tool," *Sloan Management Review* (Spring 1992): 15–24.

15. D. F. Abell, *Defining the Business: The Starting Point of Strategic Planning* (Englewood Cliffs, NJ: Prentice-Hall, 1980).

16. The consultant was Charles Hill, one of the authors of this book.

17. G. Hamel and C. K. Prahalad, "Strategic Intent," *Harvard Business Review* (May–June 1989): 63–73.

18. E. A. Locke, G. P. Latham, and M. Erez, "The Determinants of Goal Commitment," *Academy of Management Review* 13 (1988): 23–39.

19. M. Hammer and J. Champy, *Reengineering the Corporation* (New York: Harper Business, 1993).

20. K. R. Andrews, *The Concept of Corporate Strategy* (Homewood, IL: Irwin, 1971).

21. A. Cane, "From a Caterpillar to Butterfly," *Financial Times,* May 27, 1994, 11.

22. E. Penrose, *The Theory of the Growth of the Firm* (Oxford: Oxford University Press, 1959).

23. M. E. Porter, "From Competitive Advantage to Corporate Strategy," *Harvard Business Review* 65 (1987): 43–59.

24. D. J. Teece, "Economics of Scope and the Scope of the Enterprise," *Journal of Economic Behavior and Organization* 3 (1980): 223–47.

25. M. E. Porter, *Competitive Advantage: Creating and Sustaining Superior Performance* (New York: Free Press, 1985).

26. For a review of the evidence see C. W. L. Hill and G. R. Jones, *Strategic Management: An Integrated Approach,* 3d ed. (Boston: Houghton Mifflin, 1995), ch. 10.

27. C. R. Christensen et al., *Business Policy Text and Cases* (Homewood, IL: Irwin, 1987), 778.

28. C. W. L. Hill, "Conglomerate Performance over the Economic Cycle," *Journal of Industrial Economics* 32 (1983): 197–213.

29. V. Ramanujam and P. Varadarajan, "Research on Corporate Diversification: A Synthesis," *Strategic Management Journal* 10 (1989): 523–51. Also see A. Shleifer and R. W. Vishny, "Takeovers in the 1960s and 1980s: Evidence and Implications," in R. P. Rumelt, D. E. Schendel, and D. J. Teece, *Fundamental Issues in Strategy* (Boston: Harvard Business School Press, 1994).

30. J. R. Williams, B. L. Paez, and L. Sanders, "Conglomerates Revisited," *Strategic Management Journal* 9 (1988): 403–14.

31. C. A. Bartlett and S. Ghoshal, *Managing Across Borders* (Boston: Harvard Business School Press, 1989).

32. C. K. Prahalad and Y. L. Doz, *The Multinational Mission* (New York: Free Press, 1987).

33. C. W. L. Hill, *International Business: Competing in the Global Economy* (Homewood, IL: Irwin, 1994), 490.

34. T. Hout, M. E. Porter, and E. Rudden, "How Global Companies Win Out," *Harvard Business Review* (September–October 1982): 98–108.

35. M. K. Perry, "Vertical Integration: Determinants and Effects," in R. Schmalensee and R. D. Willig, "Handbook of Industrial Organization, vol. 1 (New York: Elsevier Science Publishing, 1989).

36. T. Muris, D. Scheffman, and P. Spiller, "Strategy and Transaction Costs: The Organization of Distribution in the Carbonated Soft Drink Industry," *Journal of Economics and Management Strategy* 1 (1992): 77–97.

37. "Matsushita Electric Industrial (MEI) in 1987," *Harvard Business School Case* #388-144.

38. K. Deveny et al., "McWorld?" *Business Week,* October 13, 1986, 78–86; "Slow Food," *The Economist,* February 3, 1990, 64.

39. P. Ghemawat, *Commitment: The Dynamic of Strategy* (New York: Free Press, 1991).

40. M. E. Porter, *Competitive Strategy* (New York: Free Press, 1980).

41. C. W. L. Hill, "Differentiation Versus Low Cost or Differentiation and Low Cost: A Contingency Framework," *Academy of Management Review* 13 (1988): 401–12.

42. For details see J. P. Womack, D. T. Jones, and D. Roos, *The Machine That Changed the World* (New York: Rawson Associates, 1990).

43. Porter, *Competitive Strategy.*

44. Hill and Jones, *Strategic Management.*

45. Womack, Jones, and Roos, *The Machine That Changed the World.*

46. *See D. Garvin, "What Does Product Quality Really Mean?"* Sloan Management Review 26 (Fall 1984): 25–44; P. B. Crosby, *Quality Is Free* (New York: Mentor Books, 1980); A. Gabor, *The Man Who Discovered Quality* (New York: Times Books, 1990).

Chapter 8

1. N. Byrnes, "Kinko's Goes Corporate," *Business Week,* August 19, 1996, 58–59.

2. Z. Moutkheiber, "I'm Just a Peddler," *Fortune,* July 17, 1995, 42–43.

3. C. Rubel, "Treating Coworkers Right Is the Key to Kinko's Success," *Advertising Age,* January 29, 1996, 5.

4. G. R. Jones, *Organizational Theory: Text and Cases* (Reading, MA: Addison-Wesley, 1995).

5. J. Child, *Organization: A Guide for Managers and Administrators* (New York: Harper and Row, 1977).

6. P. R. Lawrence and J. W. Lorsch, *Organization and Environment* (Boston: Graduate School of Business Administration, Harvard University, 1967).

7. R. Duncan, "What Is the Right Organizational Design?" *Organizational Dynamics* (Winter 1979): 59–80.

8. T. Burns and G. R. Stalker, *The Management of Innovation* (London: Tavistock, 1966).

9. D. Miller, "Strategy Making and Structure: Analysis and Implications for Performance," *Academy of Management Journal* 30 (1987): 7–32.

10. A. D. Chandler, *Strategy and Structure* (Cambridge, MA: MIT Press, 1962).

11. J. Stopford and L. Wells, *Managing the Multinational Enterprise* (London: Longman, 1972).

12. C. Perrow, *Organizational Analysis: A Sociological View* (Belmont, CA: Wadsworth, 1970).

13. J. Woodward, *Management and Technology* (London: Her Majesty's Stationery Office, 1958).

14. F. W. Taylor, *The Principles of Scientific Management* (New York: Harper, 1911).

15. R. W. Griffin, *Task Design: An Integrative Approach* (Glenview, IL: Scott, Foresman 1982).

16. Ibid.

17. J. R. Hackman and G. R. Oldham, *Work Redesign* (Reading, MA: Addison-Wesley, 1980).

18. J. R. Galbraith and R. K. Kazanjian, *Strategy Implementation: Structure, System, and Process,* 2d ed. (St. Paul, MN: West, 1986).

19. Lawrence and Lorsch, *Organization and Environment.*

20. Jones, *Organizational Theory.*

21. Lawrence and Lorsch, *Organization and Environment.*

22. R. H. Hall, *Organizations: Structure and Process* (Englewood Cliffs, NJ: Prentice-Hall, 1972); R. Miles, *Macro Organizational Behavior* (Santa Monica, CA: Goodyear, 1980).

23. Chandler, *Strategy and Structure.*

24. G. R. Jones and C. W. L. Hill, "Transaction Cost Analysis of Strategy–Structure Choice," *Strategic Management Journal,* 9 (1988): 159–72.

25. W. Bounds, "Kodak Reorganizes Its Sales Force at Imaging Group," *Wall Street Journal,* January 24, 1995, B3.

26. S. M. Davis and P. R. Lawrence, *Matrix* (Reading, MA: Addison-Wesley, 1977); J. R. Galbraith, "Matrix Organization Designs: How to Combine Functional and Project Forms," *Business Horizons* 14 (1971): 29–40.

27. L. R. Burns, "Matrix Management in Hospitals: Testing Theories of Matrix Structure and Development," *Administrative Science Quarterly* 34 (1989): 349–68.

28. C. W. L. Hill, *International Business* (Homewood, IL: Irwin, 1997).

29. C. A. Bartlett and S. Ghoshal, *Transnational Management* (Homewood, IL: Irwin, 1992).

30. Jones, *Organizational Theory.*

31. "After Reengineering What's Next?" *Supervisory Management* (May 1995): 1.

32. A. Farnham, "America's Most Admired Company," *Fortune,* February 7, 1994, 50–54.

33. D. K. Denton, "Process Mapping Trims Cycle Times," *HRM Magazine* (February 1995): 56–59.

34. P. Blau, "A Formal Theory of Differentiation in Organizations," *American Sociological Review* 35 (1970): 684–95.

35. Child, *Organization.*

36. S. McCartney, "Airline Industry's Top-Ranked Woman Keeps Southwest's Small-Fry Spirit Alive," *Wall Street Journal,* November 30, 1995, B1.

37. P. M. Blau and R. A. Schoenherr, *The Structure of Organizations* (New York: Basic Books, 1971)

38. Jones, *Organizational Theory.*

39. "P&G Divides to Rule," *Marketing,* March 23, 1995, 15.

40. Lawrence and Lorsch, *Organization and Environment,* 50–55.

41. J. R. Galbraith, *Designing Complex Organizations* (Reading, MA: Addison-Wesley, 1977), ch. 1; Galbraith and Kazanjian, *Strategy Implementation,* ch. 7.

42. Lawrence and Lorsch, *Organization and Environment,* 55.

43. B. Kogut, "Joint Ventures: Theoretical and Empirical Perspectives," *Strategic Management Journal* 9 (1988): 319–32.

44. G. S. Capowski, "Designing a Corporate Identity," *Management Review* (June 1993): 37–38.

45. J. Marcia, "Just Doing It," *Distribution* (January 1995): 36–40.

46. "The Outing of Outsourcing," *The Economist,* November 25, 1995, 27.

47. © 1996, Gareth R. Jones.

48. M. Meyer, "Culture Club," *Newsweek,* July 11, 1994, 38–42.

49. C. Soloman, "Amoco to Cut More Jobs and Radically Alter Its Structure," *Wall Street Journal,* July 22, 1995, B4.

Chapter 9

1. R. L. Rose, "After Turning Around Giddings and Lewis, Fife Is Turned Out Himself," *Wall Street Journal,* June 22, 1995, A1.

2. P. J. Spain and J. R. Talbot, eds., *Hoover's Handbook of American Business* (Austin, TX: Reference Press, 1996).

3. W. G. Ouchi, "Markets, Bureaucracies, and Clans," *Administrative Science Quarterly* 25 (1980): 129–141.

4. P. Lorange, M. Morton, and S. Ghoshal, *Strategic Control* (St. Paul, MN: West, 1986).

5. H. Koontz and R. W. Bradspies, "Managing Through Feedforward Control," *Business Horizons* (June 1972): 25–36.

6. E. E. Lawler III and J. G. Rhode, *Information and Control in Organizations* (Pacific Palisades, CA: Goodyear, 1976).

7. C. W. L. Hill and G. R. Jones, *Strategic Management: An Integrated Approach,* 4th ed. (Boston: Houghton Mifflin, 1997).

8. E. Flamholtz, "Organizational Control Systems as a Management Tool," *California Management Review* (Winter 1979): 50–58.

9. W. G. Ouchi, "The Transmission of Control Through Organizational Hierarchy," *Academy of Management Journal* 21 (1978): 173–92.

10. W. G. Ouchi, "The Relationship Between Organizational Structure and Organizational Control," *Administrative Science Quarterly* 22 (1977): 95–113.

11. Ouchi, "Markets, Bureaucracies, and Clans."

12. W. H. Newman, *Constructive Control* (Englewood Cliffs, NJ: Prentice-Hall, 1975).

13. J. D. Thompson, *Organizations in Action* (New York: McGraw-Hill, 1967).

14. R. N. Anthony, *The Management Control Function* (Boston: Harvard Business School Press, 1988).

15. Ouchi, "Markets, Bureaucracies, and Clans."

16. Hill and Jones, *Strategic Management.*

17. R. Simons, "Strategic Orientation and Top Management Attention to Control Systems," *Strategic Management Journal* 12 (1991): 49–62.

18. G. Schreyogg and H. Steinmann, "Strategic Control: A New Perspective," *Academy of Management Review* 12 (1987): 91–103.

19. B. Woolridge and S. W. Floyd, "The Strategy Process, Middle Management Involvement, and Organizational Performance," *Strategic Management Journal* 11 (1990): 231–41.

20. "In Praise of the Blue Suit," *The Economist,* January 13, 1996, 59.

21. J. A. Alexander, "Adaptive Changes in Corporate Control Practices," *Academy of Management Journal* 34 (1991): 162–93.

22. J. Flynn and C. Del Valle, "Did Sears Take Other Customers for a Ride?" *Business Week,* August 3, 1992, 24–25.

23. K. Kelly and E. Schine, "How Did Sears Blow This Gasket?" *Business Week,* June 29, 1992, 38.

24. Hill and Jones, *Strategic Management.*

25. G. H. B. Ross, "Revolution in Management Control," *Management Accounting* 72 (1992): 23–27.

26. P. F. Drucker, *The Practice of Management* (New York: Harper and Row, 1954).

27. S. J. Carroll and H. L. Tosi, *Management by Objectives: Applications and Research* (New York: Macmillan, 1973).

28. R. Rodgers and J. E. Hunter, "Impact of Management by Objectives on Organizational Productivity," *Journal of Applied Psychology* 76 (1991): 322–26.

29. M. B. Gavin, S. G. Green, and G. T. Fairhurst, "Managerial Control Strategies for Poor Performance over Time and the Impact on Subordinate Reactions," *Organizational Behavior and Human Decision Processes* 63 (1995): 207–21.

30. Bureau of Business Practice, *Profiles of Malcolm Baldrige Award Winners* (Boston: Allyn and Bacon, 1992).

31. D. S. Pugh, D. J. Hickson, C. R. Hinings, and C. Turner, "Dimensions of Organizational Structure," *Administrative Science Quarterly* 13 (1968): 65–91.

32. R. Gibson, "General Mills Tries to Cook Up Fix for Restaurant Unit," *Wall Street Journal,* November 16, 1994, B4.

33. P. M. Blau, *The Dynamics of Bureaucracy* (Chicago: University of Chicago Press, 1955).

34. Ouchi, "Markets, Bureaucracies, and Clans"; M. Lebas and J. Weigenstein, "Management Control: The Roles of Rules, Markets, and Culture," *Journal of Management Studies* 23 (1986): 259–72.

35. M. Rokeach, *The Nature of Human Values* (New York: Free Press, 1973).

36. D. C. Feldman, "The Development and Enforcement of Group Norms," *Academy of Management Review* 9 (1984): 47–53.

37. G. R. Jones, *Organizational Theory: Text and Cases* (Reading, MA: Addison-Wesley, 1995).

38. H. Schein, "The Role of the Founder in Creating Organizational Culture," *Organizational Dynamics* 12 (1983): 13–28.

39. J. M. George, "Personality, Affect, and Behavior in Groups," *Journal of Applied Psychology* 75 (1990): 107–16.

40. J. Van Maanen, "Police Socialization: A Longitudinal Examination of Job Attitudes in an Urban Police Department," *Administrative Science Quarterly* 20 (1975): 207–28.

41. P. L. Berger and T. Luckman, *The Social Construction of Reality* (Garden City, NY: Anchor Books, 1967).

42. H. M. Trice and J. M. Beyer, "Studying Organizational Culture Through Rites and Ceremonials," *Academy of Management Review* 9 (1984): 653–69.

43. H. M. Trice and J. M. Beyer, *The Cultures of Work Organizations* (Englewood Cliffs, NJ: Prentice-Hall, 1993).

44. B. Ortega, "Wal-Mart's Meeting Is a Reason to Party," *Wall Street Journal,* June 3, 1994, A1.

45. Trice and Beyer, "Studying Organizational Culture…"

46. S. Mcgee, "Garish Jackets Add to Clamor of Chicago Pits," *Wall Street Journal,* July 31, 1995, C1.

47. For details of the HP Way see Chapter 5 in J. P. Kotter and J. L. Heskett, *Cor-*

porate Culture and Performance (New York: Free Press, 1992).

48. K. E. Weick, *The Social Psychology of Organization* (Reading, MA: Addison-Wesley, 1979).

49. Kotter and Heskett, *Corporate Culture and Performance.*

50. For some interesting descriptions of these phenomena see D. Miller, *The Icarus Paradox* (New York: Harper Business, 1990).

Chapter 10

1. P. J. Spain and J. R. Talbot, eds., *Hoover's Handbook of American Business* (Austin, TX: Reference Press, 1995).

2. "Apprentices Make the Grade," *Inc.* (February 1996): 98.

3. L. Bongiorno, "The Pepsi Regeneration," *Business Week,* March 11, 1996, 70–73.

4. N. Tichy and C. DeRose, "Roger Enrico's Master Class," *Fortune,* November 27, 1995, 105–06.

5. "Apprentices Make the Grade."

6. J. E. Butler, G. R. Ferris, and N. K. Napier, *Strategy and Human Resource Management* (Cincinnati, OH: Southwestern, 1991); P. M. Wright and G. C. McMahan, "Theoretical Perspectives for Strategic Human Resource Management," *Journal of Management* 18 (1992): 295–320.

7. J. B. Quinn, P. Anderson, and S. Finkelstein, "Managing Professional Intellect: Making the Most of the Best," *Harvard Business Review* (March–April 1996): 71–80.

8. Ibid.

9. C. D. Fisher, L. F. Schoenfeldt, and J. B. Shaw, *Human Resource Management* (Boston: Houghton Mifflin, 1990).

10. Wright and McMahan, "Theoretical Perspectives."

11. L. Baird and I. Meshoulam, "Managing Two Fits for Strategic Human Resource Management," *Academy of Management Review* 14 (1989): 116–28; J. Milliman, M. Von Glinow, and M. Nathan, "Organizational Life Cycles and Strategic International Human Resource Management in Multinational Companies:

Implications for Congruence Theory," *Academy of Management Review* 16 (1991): 318–39; R. S. Schuler and S. E. Jackson, "Linking Competitive Strategies with Human Resource Management Practices," *Academy of Management Executive* 1 (1987): 207–19; P. M. Wright and S. A. Snell, "Toward an Integrative View of Strategic Human Resource Management," *Human Resource Management Review* 1 (1991): 203–25.

12. Equal Employment Opportunity Commission, "Uniform Guidelines on Employee Selection Procedures," *Federal Register* 43 (1978): 38290–315.

13. R. Stogdill II, R. Mitchell, K. Thurston, and C. Del Valle, "Why AIDS Policy Must Be a Special Policy," *Business Week,* February 1, 1993, 53–54.

14. J. M. George, "AIDS/AIDS-Related Complex," in L. Peters, B. Greer, and S. Youngblood, eds., *The Blackwell Encyclopedic Dictionary of Human Resource Management* (Oxford: Blackwell, 1997).

15. Ibid.

16. J. M. George, "AIDS Awareness Training," ibid.; Stogdill, Mitchell, Thurston, and Del Valle, "Why AIDS Policy Must Be a Special Policy."

17. S. L. Rynes, "Recruitment, Job Choice, and Post-Hire Consequences: A Call for New Research Directions," in M. D. Dunnette and L. M. Hough, eds., *Handbook of Industrial and Organizational Psychology,* vol. 2 (Palo Alto, CA: Consulting Psychologists Press, 1991), 399–444.

18. D. Fenn, "When to Go Pro," *Inc. 500* (1995): 72.

19. Ibid.

20. R. L. Sullivan, "Lawyers à la Carte," *Forbes,* September 11, 1995, 44.

21. R. J. Harvey, "Job Analysis," in Dunnette and Hough, eds., *Handbook of Industrial and Organizational Psychology,* 71–163.

22. E. L. Levine, *Everything You Always Wanted to Know About Job Analysis: A Job Analysis Primer* (Tampa, FL: Mariner, 1983).

23. R. L. Mathis and J. H. Jackson, *Human Resource Management,* 7th ed. (St. Paul, MN: West, 1994).

24. E. J. McCormick, P. R. Jeanneret, and R. C. Mecham, *Position Analysis Ques-*

tionnaire (West Lafayette, IN: Occupational Research Center, Department of Psychological Sciences, Purdue University, 1969).

25. Fisher, Schoenfeldt, and Shaw, *Human Resource Management;* Mathis and Jackson, *Human Resource Management;* R. A. Noe, J. R. Hollenbeck, B. Gerhart, and P. M. Wright, *Human Resource Management: Gaining a Competitive Advantage* (Burr Ridge, IL: Irwin, 1994).

26. Fisher, Schoenfeldt, and Shaw, *Human Resource Management;* E. J. McCormick, *Job Analysis: Methods and Applications* (New York: American Management Association, 1979); E. J. McCormick and R. Jeannerette, "The Position Analysis Questionnaire," in S. Gael, ed., *The Job Analysis Handbook for Business, Industry, and Government* (New York: Wiley, 1988); Noe, Hollenbeck, Gerhart, and Wright, *Human Resource Management.*

27. Rynes, "Recruitment, Job Choice, and Post-Hire Consequences."

28. "Recruiting in Cyberspace," *Inc.* (November 1995): 93.

29. R. Narisetti, "Manufacturers Decry a Shortage of Workers While Rejecting Many," *Wall Street Journal,* September 8, 1995, A1, A4.

30. S. L. Premack and J. P. Wanous, "A Meta-Analysis of Realistic Job Preview Experiments," *Journal of Applied Psychology* 70 (1985): 706–19; J. P. Wanous, "Realistic Job Previews: Can a Procedure to Reduce Turnover Also Influence the Relationship Between Abilities and Performance?" *Personnel Psychology* 31 (1978): 249–58; J. P. Wanous, *Organizational Entry: Recruitment, Selection, and Socialization of Newcomers* (Reading, MA: Addison-Wesley, 1980).

31. R. M. Guion, "Personnel Assessment, Selection, and Placement," in Dunnette and Hough, eds., *Handbook of Industrial and Organizational Psychology,* 327–97.

32. Noe, Hollenbeck, Gerhart, and Wright, *Human Resource Management;* J. A. Wheeler and J. A. Gier, "Reliability and Validity of the Situational Interview for a Sales Position," *Journal of Applied Psychology* 2 (1987): 484–87.

33. Noe, Hollenbeck, Gerhart, and Wright, *Human Resource Management.*

34. J. Flint, "Can You Tell Applesauce from Pickles," *Forbes,* October 9, 1995, 106–08.

35. Ibid.

36. "Wanted: Middle Managers, Audition Required," *Wall Street Journal,* December 28, 1995, A1.

37. R. B. Lieber, "The Fight to Legislate Incompetence Out of the Cockpit," *Fortune,* February 5, 1996, 30.

38. J. Novack, "What If the Guy Shoots Somebody?" *Forbes,* December 4, 1995, 37.

39. Ibid.

40. Lieber, "The Fight to Legislate."

41. I. L. Goldstein, "Training in Work Organizations," in Dunnette and Hough, eds., *Handbook of Industrial and Organizational Psychology,* 507–619.

42. S. Overman, "Ethan Allen's Secret Weapon," *HRMMagazine* (May 1994): 61.

43. N. Banerjee, "For Mary Kay Sales Reps in Russia, Hottest Shade Is the Color of Money," *Wall Street Journal,* August 30, 1995, A8.

44. J. A. Byrne, "Virtual B-Schools," *Business Week,* October 23, 1995, 64–68.

45. Fisher, Schoenfeldt, and Shaw, *Human Resource Management.*

46. Ibid.; G. P. Latham and K. N. Wexley, *Increasing Productivity Through Performance Appraisal* (Reading, MA: Addison-Wesley, 1982).

47. T. A. DeCotiis, "An Analysis of the External Validity and Applied Relevance of Three Rating Formats," *Organizational Behavior and Human Performance* 19 (1977): 247–66; Fisher, Schoenfeldt, and Shaw, *Human Resource Management.*

48. J. S. Lublin, "It's Shape-Up Time for Performance Reviews," *Wall Street Journal,* October 3, 1994, B1, B2.

49. J. S. Lublin, "Turning the Tables: Underlings Evaluate Bosses," *Wall Street Journal,* October 4, 1994, B1, B14; S. Shellenbarger, "Reviews from Peers Instruct–and Sting," *Wall Street Journal,* October 4, 1994, B1, B4.

50. Lublin, "Turning the Tables."

51. Ibid.

52. Shellenbarger, "Reviews from Peers."

53. Lublin, "It's Shape-Up Time."

54. J. Flynn and F. Nayeri, "Continental Divide over Executive Pay," *Business Week,* July 3, 1995, 40–41.

55. J. A. Byrne, "How High Can CEO Pay Go?" *Business Week,* April 22, 1996, 100–06.

56. Noe, Hollenbeck, Gerhart, and Wright, *Human Resource Management.*

57. E. J. Pollock, "Workers Want More Money, but They Also Want to Control Their Own Time," *Wall Street Journal,* November 28, 1995, B1, B12.

58. Ibid.

59. S. Premack and J. E. Hunter, "Individual Unionization Decisions," *Psychological Bulletin* 103 (1988): 223–34.

60. M. B. Regan, "Shattering the AFL-CIO's Glass Ceiling," *Business Week,* November 13, 1995, 46.

61. G. P. Zachary, "Some Unions Step Up Organizing Campaigns and Get New Members," *Wall Street Journal,* September 1, 1995, A1, A2.

62. Regan, "Shattering the AFL-CIO's Glass Ceiling."

63. R. Blumenstein, "Ohio Strike That Is Crippling GM Plants Is Tied to Plan to Outsource Brake Work," *Wall Street Journal,* March 12, 1996, A3, A4.

64. J. Hannah, "GM Workers Agree to End Strike," *Bryan–College Station Eagle,* March 23, 1996, A12.

65. J. S. Lublin, "AT&T Outplacement Manager's Phone Rings Nonstop," *Wall Street Journal,* January 25, 1996, B1, B5.

66. J. J. Keller, "High Anxiety: AT&T Breakup Jolts Managers," *Wall Street Journal,* November 21, 1995, B1, B10.

67. Lublin, "AT&T Outplacement."

68. J. Cole, "Boeing Teaches Employees How to Run Small Businesses," *Wall Street Journal,* November 7, 1995, B1, B2.

Chapter 11

1. P. Sellers, "The 50 Most Powerful Women in American Business," *Fortune,* October 12, 1998, 76–98.

2. P. LaBarre, "Management Tools Must Be Managed," *Industry Week,* September

5, 1994, 78–82; G. Rifkin, "Don't Ever Judge This Consultant by Her Cover," *New York Times,* May 1, 1994, 5.

3. L. Moss, "Disney Ups Sweeney to Laybourne's Old Post," *Multichannel News,* August 24, 1998, 10; D. Petrozzello, "Sweeney Heads Disney/ABC Cable," *Broadcasting & Cable,* August 24, 1998, 47.

4. M. L. Carnevale, "Marketing and Media: FCC Would Allow Higher Charges as Cable TV Systems Add Channels," *Wall Street Journal,* October 24, 1994, B12; K. Murray, "A Cool Commander for Murdoch's Assault on Cable," *New York Times,* August 7, 1994,

5. Moss, "Disney Ups Sweeney to Laybourne's Old Post."

6. Rifkin, "Don't Ever Judge."

7. Petrozzello, "Sweeney Heads Disney/ABC Cable."

8. Moss, "Disney Ups Sweeney to Laybourne's Old Post"; Murray, "A Cool Commander"; D. Petrozzello, "Sweeney Heads Disney/ABC Cable."

9. Ibid.

10. Ibid.; Rifkin, "Don't Ever Judge."

11. C. Hymowitz and G. Stern, "At Procter & Gamble, Brands Face Pressure and So Do Executives," *Wall Street Journal,* May 10, 1993, A1, A8; Z. Schiller, "Ed Artzt's Elbow Grease Has P&G Shining," *Business Week,* October 10, 1994, 84–86.

12. J. M. Digman, "Personality Structure: Emergence of the Five-Factor Model," *Annual Review of Psychology* 41 (1990): 417–40; R. R. McCrae and P. T. Costa, "Validation of the Five-Factor Model of Personality Across Instruments and Observers," *Journal of Personality and Social Psychology* 52 (1987): 81–90; R. R. McCrae and P. T. Costa, "Discriminant Validity of NEO–PIR Facet Scales," *Educational and Psychological Measurement* 52 (1992): 229–37.

13. Ibid.

14. L. Bird, "Lazarus's IBM Coup Was All About Relationships," *Wall Street Journal,* May 26, 1994, B1, B7.

15. M. R. Barrick and M. K. Mount, "The Big Five Personality Dimensions and Job Performance: A Meta-Analysis," *Personnel Psychology* 44 (1991): 1–26.

16. Digman, "Personality Structure"; McCrae and Costa, "Validation of the Five-Factor Model"; McCrae and Costa, "Discriminant Validity."

17. Rifkin, "Don't Ever Judge."

18. J. Bamford and S. McHenry, "The Working Woman 50 Top Women Business Owners," *Working Woman* (May 1995): 37; J. Fallon, "Joan & David Debuts London Flagship, Signature Line," *Footwear News,* September 12, 1994, 5; R. C. Morais, "'If You Stand Still, You Die,'" *Forbes,* January 30, 1995, 44–45 (source of quote); "The Innovators: Designs Aside, These Are the Preeminent Minds and Personalities That Have Spearheaded the Footwear Industry," *Footwear News,* April 17, 1995, S36.

19. J. B. Rotter, "Generalized Expectancies for Internal vs. External Control of Reinforcement," *Psychological Monographs* 80 (1966): 1–28; P. Spector, "Behaviors in Organizations as a Function of Employees' Locus of Control," *Psychological Bulletin* 91 (1982): 482–97.

20. B. Dumaine, "What's So Hot About Outsiders?" *Fortune,* November 29, 1993, 63–67.

21. J. Brockner, *Self-Esteem at Work* (Lexington, MA: Lexington Books, 1988).

22. D. C. McClelland, *Human Motivation* (Glenview, IL: Scott, Foresman, 1985); D. C. McClelland, "How Motives, Skills, and Values Determine What People Do," *American Psychologist* 40 (1985): 812–25; D. C. McClelland, "Managing Motivation to Expand Human Freedom," *American Psychologist* 33 (1978): 201–10.

23. D. G. Winter, *The Power Motive* (New York: Free Press, 1973).

24. M. J. Stahl, "Achievement, Power, and Managerial Motivation: Selecting Managerial Talent with the Job Choice Exercise," *Personnel Psychology* 36 (1983): 775–89; D. C. McClelland and D. H. Burnham, "Power Is the Great Motivator," *Harvard Business Review* 54 (1976): 100–10.

25. R. J. House, W. D. Spangler, and J. Woycke, "Personality and Charisma in the U.S. Presidency: A Psychological Theory of Leader Effectiveness," *Administrative Science Quarterly* 36 (1991): 364–96.

26. G. H. Hines, "Achievement, Motivation, Occupations and Labor Turnover in New Zealand," *Journal of Applied Psychology* 58 (1973): 313–17; P. S. Hundal, "A Study of Entrepreneurial Motivation: Comparison of Fast- and Slow-Progressing Small Scale Industrial Entrepreneurs in Punjab, India," *Journal of Applied Psychology* 55 (1971): 317–23.

27. M. Rokeach, *The Nature of Human Values* (New York: Free Press, 1973).

28. Ibid.

29. Ibid.

30. L. Kraar, "The Overseas Chinese: Lessons from the World's Most Dynamic Capitalists," *Fortune,* October 31, 1994, 91–114.

31. P. Edgardio, "A New High-Tech Dynasty?" *Business Week,* August 15, 1994, 90–91; "Formosa Plastics Corp.: Company Says Pretax Profit Doubled in the First Quarter," *Wall Street Journal,* April 28, 1995, A1; Kraar, "The Overseas Chinese."

32. D. W. Organ, *Organizational Citizenship Behavior: The Good Soldier Syndrome* (Lexington, MA: Lexington Books, 1988).

33. J. M. George and A. P. Brief, "Feeling Good–Doing Good: A Conceptual Analysis of the Mood at Work–Organizational Spontaneity Relationship," *Psychological Bulletin* 112 (1992): 310–29.

34. W. H. Mobley, "Intermediate Linkages in the Relationship Between Job Satisfaction and Employee Turnover," *Journal of Applied Psychology* 62 (1977): 237–40.

35. "Managers View Workplace Changes More Positively Than Employees," *Wall Street Journal,* December 13, 1994, A1.

36. J. E. Mathieu and D. M. Zajac, "A Review and Meta-Analysis of the Antecedents, Correlates, and Consequences of Organizational Commitment," *Psychological Bulletin* 108 (1990): 171–94.

37. L. Hays, "The Outsider's New In Crowd: Five IBM Lifers," *Wall Street Journal,* January 12, 1995, B1, B8.

38. Ibid.; L. Hays, "IBM Chief Unveils Top-Level Shake-Up, Consolidating Sales Arm, Software Line," *Wall Street Journal,* January 10, 1995, B6; I. Sager and A. Cortese, "IBM: Why the Good News Isn't Good Enough," *Business Week,* January 23, 1995, 72–73.

39. E. Slate, "Tips for Negotiations in Germany and France," *HRFocus* (July 1994): 18.

40. D. Watson and A. Tellegen, "Toward a Consensual Structure of Mood," *Psychological Bulletin* 98 (1985): 219–35.

41. Ibid.

42. J. M. George, "The Role of Personality in Organizational Life: Issues and Evidence," *Journal of Management* 18 (1992): 185–213.

43. J. M. George and K. Bettenhausen, "Understanding Prosocial Behavior, Sales Performance, and Turnover: A Group Level Analysis in a Service Context," *Journal of Applied Psychology* 75 (1990): 698–709.

44. George and Brief, "Feeling Good–Doing Good"; A. M. Isen and R. A. Baron, "Positive Affect as a Factor in Organizational Behavior," in B. M. Staw and L. L. Cummings, eds., *Research in Organizational Behavior,* vol. 13 (Greenwich, CT: JAI Press, 1991), 1–53.

45. L. Berton, "It's Audit Time! Send in the Clowns," *Wall Street Journal,* January 18, 1995, B1, B6.

46. R. C. Sinclair, "Mood, Categorization Breadth, and Performance Appraisal: The Effects of Order of Information Acquisition and Affective State on Halo, Accuracy, Informational Retrieval, and Evaluations," *Organizational Behavior and Human Decision Processes* 42 (1988): 22–46.

47. H. R. Schiffmann, *Sensation and Perception: An Integrated Approach* (New York: Wiley, 1990).

48. A. E. Serwer, "McDonald's Conquers the World," *Fortune,* October 17, 1994, 103–16.

49. A. G. Greenwald and M. Banaji, "Implicit Social Cognition: Attitudes, Self-Esteem, and Stereotypes," *Psychological Review* 102 (1995): 4–27.

50. J. H. Greenhaus, *Career Management* (New York: Dryden Press, 1987).

51. M. J. Driver, "Careers: A Review of Personnel and Organizational Research," in C. L. Cooper and I. Robertson, eds.,

International Review of Industrial and Organizational Psychology (New York: Wiley, 1988).

52. *Career Path* (recruitment material provided by Dillard's Department Stores, 1994).

53. Driver, "Careers."

54. Ibid.

55. Ibid.

56. Greenhaus, *Career Management.*

57. J. L. Holland, *Making Vocational Choices: A Theory of Careers* (Englewood Cliffs, NJ: Prentice-Hall, 1973).

58. Greenhaus, Career Management.

59. Ibid.

60. W. Echikson, "Young Americans Go Abroad to Strike It Rich," *Fortune,* October 17, 1994, 185–94.

61. G. Dreher and R. Ash, "A Comparative Study of Mentoring Among Men and Women in Managerial, Professional, and Technical Positions," *Journal of Applied Psychology* 75 (1990): 525–35; T. A. Scandura, "Mentorship and Career Mobility: An Empirical Investigation," *Journal of Organizational Behavior* 13 (1992): 169–74; D. B. Turban and T. W. Dougherty, "The Role of Protégé Personality in Receipt of Mentoring and Career Success," *Academy of Management Journal* 37 (1994): 688–702; W. Whitely, T. W. Dougherty, and G. F. Dreher, "Relationship of Career Mentoring and Socioeconomic Origin to Managers' and Professionals' Early Career Success," *Academy of Management Journal* 34 (1991): 331–51.

62. T. P. Ference, J. A. F. Stoner, and E. K. Warren, "Managing the Career Plateau," *Academy of Management Review* 2 (1977): 602–12.

63. J. De Cordoba, "Mellon Heir's Labor of Love for Haitians Survives His Death," *Wall Street Journal,* January 30, 1995, A1, A8; B. Ortega, "Nearing 80, Founder of Dillard Stores Seeks to Keep on Growing," *Wall Street Journal,* May 11, 1994, A1, A5.

64. *Ernst & Young Challenges … Opportunities … No Limits* (recruiting brochure, 1994).

65. R. S. Lazarus, *Psychological Stress and Coping Processes* (New York: McGraw-Hill, 1966); R. S. Lazarus and S. Folkman, *Stress, Appraisal, and Coping* (New York: Springer, 1984); R. S. Lazarus, "Psychological Stress in the Workplace," in R. Crandall and P. L. Perrewe, *Occupational Stress: A Handbook* (Washington, DC: Taylor & Francis, 1995).

66. D. Watson and J. W. Pennebaker, "Health Complaints, Stress, and Distress: Exploring the Central Role of Negative Affectivity," *Psychological Review* 96 (1989): 234–54.

67. Watson and Tellegen, "Toward a Consensual Structure of Mood."

68. R. L. Kahn and P. Byosiere, "Stress in Organizations," in M. D. Dunnette and L. M. Hough, eds., *Handbook of Industrial and Organizational Psychology,* 2d ed., vol. 3, (Palo Alto, CA: Consulting Psychologists Press, 1992), 571–650; S. Jackson and R. Schuler, "A Meta-Analysis and Conceptual Critique of Research on Role Ambiguity and Role Conflict in Work Settings," *Organizational Behavior and Human Decision Processes* 36 (1985): 16–78.

69. J. S. Lublin, "A Career Wife Complicates the CEO's Life," *Wall Street Journal,* December 15, 1994, B1, B6.

70. Kahn and Byosiere, "Stress in Organizations."

71. W. M. Bulkeley and S. Stecklow, "Harvard's President, Citing Exhaustion, Is Going on Leave During Fund Drive," *Wall Street Journal,* November 29, 1994, B7.

72. S. Stecklow, "Chief Prerequisite for College President's Job: Stamina," *Wall Street Journal,* December 1, 1994, B1, B10; S. Stecklow, "Harvard's President, Too Slow to Delegate, Got Swamped in Detail," *Wall Street Journal,* December 9, 1994, A1, A10.

73. S. Folkman and R. S. Lazarus, "An Analysis of Coping in a Middle-Aged Community Sample," *Journal of Health and Social Behavior* 21 (1980): 219–39; S. Folkman and R. S. Lazarus, "If It Changes It Must Be a Process: Study of

Emotion and Coping During Three Stages of a College Examination," *Journal of Personality and Social Psychology* 48 (1985): 150–70; S. Folkman and R. S. Lazarus, "Coping as a Mediator of Emotion," *Journal of Personality and Social Psychology* 54 (1988): 466–75.

74. Folkman and Lazarus, "An Analysis of Coping."

75. A. Lakein, *How to Get Control of Your Time and Your Life* (New York: Wyden, 1973); J. C. Quick and J. D. Quick, *Organizational Stress and Preventive Management* (New York: McGraw-Hill, 1984).

76. Quick and Quick, ibid.

77. R. Neff, "They Fly Through the Air with the Greatest of . . . Ki?" *Business Week,* January 23, 1995, 60.

78. S. Cohen and T. A. Wills, "Stress, Social Support, and the Buffering Hypothesis," *Psychological Bulletin* 98 (1985): 310–57; I. G. Sarason, H. M. Levine, R. B. Basham, and B. R. Sarason, "Assessing Social Support: The Social Support Questionnaire," *Journal of Personality and Social Psychology* 44 (1983): 127–39.

79. D. Goleman, *Emotional Intelligence* (New York: Bantam Books, 1994); J. D. Mayer and P. Salovey, "The Intelligence of Emotional Intelligence," *Intelligence* 17 (1993): 433–42; J. D. Mayer and P. Salovey, "What Is Emotional Intelligence?" in P. Salovey and D. Sluyter, eds., *Emotional Development and Emotional Intelligence: Implications for Education* (New York: Basic Books, 1997); P. Salovey and J. D. Mayer, "Emotional Intelligence," *Imagination, Cognition, and Personality* 9 (1989–1990): 185–211.

80. S. Epstein, *Constructive Thinking* (Westport, CT: Praeger, 1998).

81. S. Begley, "The Boss Feels Your Pain," *Newsweek,* October 12, 1998, 74; D. Goleman, *Working with Emotional Intelligence* (New York): Bantam Books, 1998).

82. K. L. Alexander and S. Baker, "The New Life of O'Reilly," *Business Week,* June 13, 1994, 64–66; K. Labich, "Is Herb Kelleher America's Best CEO?" *Fortune,* May 2, 1994, 44–52; L. Smith,

"Stamina: Who Has It, Why You Need It, How You Get It," *Fortune,* November 28, 1994, 127–39.

83. Smith, "Stamina."

84. Ibid.

Chapter 12

1. W. Bounds, "Kodak's CEO Got $1.7 Million Bonus in 1994 Despite Below-Target Profit," *Wall Street Journal,* March 13, 1995, B9; C. J. Cantoni, "Manager's Journal: A Waste of Human Resources," *Wall Street Journal,* May 15, 1995, A22; M. Maremont, "Kodak's New Focus," *Business Week,* January 30, 1995, 62–68; P. Nulty, "Kodak Grabs for Growth Again," *Fortune,* May 16, 1994, 76–78; B. Saporito, "The Eclipse of Mars," *Fortune,* November 28, 1994, 82.

2. Saporito, "The Eclipse of Mars."

3. R. Kanfer, "Motivation Theory and Industrial and Organizational Psychology," in M. D. Dunnette and L. M. Hough, eds., *Handbook of Industrial and Organizational Psychology,* 2d ed., vol. 1 (Palo Alto, CA: Consulting Psychologists Press, 1990), 75–170.

4. J. P. Campbell and R. D. Pritchard, "Motivation Theory in Industrial and Organizational Psychology," in M. D. Dunnette, ed., *Handbook of Industrial and Organizational Psychology* (Chicago: Rand McNally, 1976), 63–130; T. R. Mitchell, "Expectancy-Value Models in Organizational Psychology," in N. T. Feather, ed., *Expectations and Actions: Expectancy-Value Models in Psychology* (Hillsdale, NJ: Erlbaum, 1982), 293–312; V. H. Vroom, *Work and Motivation* (New York: Wiley, 1964).

5. D. Milbank, "Long Viewed as Kaput, Many European Firms Seem to Be Reviving," *Wall Street Journal,* February 14, 1995, A1, A8.

6. J. Kaufman, "How Cambodians Came to Control California Doughnuts," *Wall Street Journal,* February 22, 1995, A1, A8.

7. M. Loeb, "Ten Commandments for Managing Creative People," *Fortune,* January 16, 1995, 135–36.

8. "Motorola Inc.: Company Is Chosen to Build Cellular System in Calcutta,"

Wall Street Journal, January 5, 1995, B4; "Motorola Inc. Plans to Increase Business with Chinese Ventures," *Wall Street Journal,* February 13, 1995, B11.

9. P. Engardio and G. DeGeorge, "Importing Enthusiasm," *Business Week/21st Century Capitalism* (1994): 122–23.

10. Ibid.

11. A. H. Maslow, *Motivation and Personality* (New York: Harper and Row, 1954); Campbell and Pritchard, "Motivation Theory in Industrial and Organizational Psychology."

12. Kanfer, "Motivation Theory and Industrial and Organizational Psychology."

13. S. Ronen, "An Underlying Structure of Motivational Need Taxonomies: A Cross-Cultural Confirmation," in H. C. Triandis, M. D. Dunnette, and L. M. Hough, eds., *Handbook of Industrial and Organizational Psychology,* vol. 4 (Palo Alto, CA: Consulting Psychologists Press, 1994), 241–69.

14. N. J. Adler, *International Dimensions of Organizational Behavior,* 2d ed. (Boston: P.W.S.-Kent, 1991); G. Hofstede, "Motivation, Leadership and Organization: Do American Theories Apply Abroad?" *Organizational Dynamics* (Summer 1980): 42–63.

15. C. P. Alderfer, "An Empirical Test of a New Theory of Human Needs," *Organizational Behavior and Human Performance* 4 (1969): 142–75; C. P. Alderfer, *Existence, Relatedness, and Growth: Human Needs in Organizational Settings* (New York: Free Press, 1972); Campbell and Pritchard, "Motivation Theory in Industrial and Organizational Psychology."

16. Kanfer, "Motivation Theory and Industrial and Organizational Psychology."

17. F. Herzberg, *Work and the Nature of Man* (Cleveland: World, 1966).

18. N. King, "Clarification and Evaluation of the Two-Factor Theory of Job Satisfaction," *Psychological Bulletin* 74 (1970): 18–31; E. A. Locke, "The Nature and Causes of Job Satisfaction," in Dunnette, ed., *Handbook of Industrial and Organizational Psychology,* 1297–1349.

19. J. S. Adams, "Toward an Understanding of Inequity," *Journal of Abnormal and Social Psychology* 67 (1963): 422–36.

20. Ibid.; J. Greenberg, "Approaching Equity and Avoiding Inequity in Groups and Organizations," in J. Greenberg and R. L. Cohen, eds., *Equity and Justice in Social Behavior* (New York: Academic Press, 1982), 389–435; J. Greenberg, "Equity and Workplace Status: A Field Experiment," *Journal of Applied Psychology* 73 (1988): 606–13; R. T. Mowday, "Equity Theory Predictions of Behavior in Organizations," in R. M. Steers and L. W. Porter, eds., *Motivation and Work Behavior* (New York: McGraw-Hill, 1987), 89–110.

21. E. A. Locke and G. P. Latham, *A Theory of Goal Setting and Task Performance* (Englewood Cliffs, NJ: Prentice-Hall, 1990).

22. Ibid.; J. J. Donovan and D. J. Radosevich, "The Moderating Role of Goal Commitment on the Goal Difficulty–Performance Relationship: A Meta-Analytic Review and Critical Analysis," *Journal of Applied Psychology* 83 (1998): 308–315; M. E. Tubbs, "Goal Setting: A Meta-Analytic Examination of the Empirical Evidence," *Journal of Applied Psychology* 71 (1986): 474–83.

23. E. A. Locke, K. N. Shaw, L. M. Saari, and G. P. Latham, "Goal Setting and Task Performance: 1969–1980," *Psychological Bulletin* 90 (1981): 125–52.

24. P. C. Earley, T. Connolly, and G. Ekegren, "Goals, Strategy Development, and Task Performance: Some Limits on the Efficacy of Goal Setting," *Journal of Applied Psychology* 74 (1989): 24–33; R. Kanfer and P. L. Ackerman, "Motivation and Cognitive Abilities: An Integrative/Aptitude–Treatment Interaction Approach to Skill Acquisition," *Journal of Applied Psychology* 74 (1989): 657–90.

25. W. C. Hamner, "Reinforcement Theory and Contingency Management in Organizational Settings," in H. Tosi and W. C. Hamner, eds., *Organizational Behavior and Management: A Contingency Approach* (Chicago: St. Clair Press, 1974).

26. B. F. Skinner, *Contingencies of Reinforcement* (New York: Appleton-Century-Crofts, 1969).

27. H. W. Weiss, "Learning Theory and Industrial and Organizational Psychology." in M. D. Dunnette and L. M. Hough, eds., *Handbook of Industrial and Organizational Psychology,* 2d ed., vol. 1 (Palo Alto, CA: Consulting Psychologists Press, 1990), 171–221.

28. J. Flynn, C. Del Valle, and R. Mitchell, "Did Sears Take Other Customers for a Ride?" *Business Week,* August 3, 1992, 24–25; K. Kelly and E. Schine, "How Did Sears Blow This Gasket?" *Business Week,* June 29, 1992, 38; G. A. Patterson, "Distressed Shoppers, Disaffected Workers Prompt Stores to Alter Sales Commissions," *Wall Street Journal,* July 1, 1992, B1, B5.

29. S. Caudron, "Master the Compensation Maze," *Personnel Journal* (June 1993): 64B–64O; J. Cusimano, "How Workers Became Trainers, Learners and Writers," *Human Resources Professional* (January–February 1995): 3–7; H. Gleckman, S. Atchison, T. Smart, and J. A. Byrne, "Bonus Pay: Buzzword or Bonanza?" *Business Week,* November 14, 1994, 62–64 (source of quote).

30. Hamner, "Reinforcement Theory and Contingency Management."

31. F. Luthans and R. Kreitner, *Organizational Behavior Modification and Beyond* (Glenview, IL: Scott, Foresman, 1985); A. D. Stajkovic and F. Luthans, "A Meta-Analysis of the Effects of Organizational Behavior Modification on Task Performance, 1975–95," *Academy of Management Journal* 40 (1997): 1122–1149.

32. A. Bandura, *Principles of Behavior Modification* (New York: Holt, Rinehart and Winston, 1969); A. Bandura, *Social Learning Theory* (Englewood Cliffs, NJ: Prentice-Hall, 1977); T. R. V. Davis and F. Luthans, "A Social Learning Approach to Organizational Behavior," *Academy of Management Review* 5 (1980): 281–90.

33. A. P. Goldstein and M. Sorcher, *Changing Supervisor Behaviors* (New York: Pergamon Press, 1974); Luthans and Kreitner, *Organizational Behavior Modification and Beyond.*

34. Bandura, *Social Learning Theory;* Davis and Luthans, "A Social Learning Approach to Organizational Behavior";

Luthans and Kreitner, *Organizational Behavior Modification and Beyond.*

35. A. Bandura, "Self-Reinforcement: Theoretical and Methodological Considerations," *Behaviorism* 4 (1976): 135–55.

36. P. Engardio, "A Hothouse of High-Tech Talent," *Business Week/21st Century Capitalism* (1994): 126.

37. A. Bandura, "Self-Efficacy Mechanism in Human Agency," *American Psychologist* 37 (1982): 122–27; M. E. Gist and T. R. Mitchell, "Self-Efficacy: A Theoretical Analysis of Its Determinants and Malleability," *Academy of Management Review* 17 (1992): 183–211.

38. E. E. Lawler III, *Pay and Organization Development* (Reading, MA: Addison-Wesley, 1981).

39. "The Risky New Bonuses," *Newsweek,* January 16, 1995, 42.

40. Lawler, *Pay and Organization Development.*

41. Ibid.

42. J. F. Lincoln, *Incentive Management* (Cleveland: Lincoln Electric Company, 1951); R. Zager, "Managing Guaranteed Employment," *Harvard Business Review* 56 (1978): 103–15.

43. Lawler, *Pay and Organization Development.*

44. M. Gendron, "Gradient Named 'Small Business of Year,' " *Boston Herald,* May 11, 1994, 35.

45. W. Zeller, R. D. Hof, R. Brandt, S. Baker, and D. Greising. "Go-Go Goliaths," *Business Week,* February 13, 1995, 64–70.

46. A. J. Michels, "Dallas Semiconductor," *Fortune,* May 16, 1994, 81.

47. M. Betts, "Big Things Come in Small Buttons," *Computerworld,* August 3, 1992, 30.

48. M. Boslet, "Metal Buttons Toted by Crop Pickers Act as Mini Databases," *Wall Street Journal,* June 1, 1994, B3.

49. C. D. Fisher, L. F. Schoenfeldt, and J. B. Shaw, *Human Resource Management* (Boston: Houghton Mifflin, 1990); B. E. Graham-Moore and T. L. Ross, *Productivity Gainsharing* (Englewood Cliffs, NJ:

Prentice-Hall, 1983); A. J. Geare, "Productivity from Scanlon Type Plans," *Academy of Management Review* 1 (1976): 99–108.

50. J. Labate, "Deal Those Workers In," *Fortune,* April 19, 1993, 26.

51. R. Jacob, "Corporate Reputations," *Fortune,* March 6, 1995, 54–64; J. R. Norman, "Choose Your Partners," *Forbes,* November 21, 1994, 88–89; S. Tully, "Why to Go for Stretch Targets," *Fortune,* November 14, 1994, 145–58.

52. Tully, ibid.

53. Ibid.

Chapter 13

1. W. M. Carley, "Engine Troubles Put GE Behind in Race to Power New 777s," Wall Street Journal, July 12, 1995, A1, A6; L. Grant, "GE: The Envelope Please," Fortune, June 26, 1995, 89–90; J. Greenwald, "Jack in the Box," Time, October 3, 1994, 56–58; M. Loeb, "Jack Welch Lets Fly on Budgets, Bonuses, and Buddy Boards," Fortune, May 29, 1995, 145–47; D. McGinn and J. Solomon, "Scratches in the Teflon," Newsweek, October 3, 1994, 50–52; J. R. Norman, "A Very Nimble Elephant," Forbes, October 10, 1994, 88–92.

2. J. Kahn, "The World's Most Admired Companies," Fortune, October 26, 1998, 207–226.

3. A. Bennett and J. S. Lublin, "Failure Doesn't Always Damage the Careers of Top Executives," Wall Street Journal, March 31, 1995, A1, A6; R. A. Melcher, D. J. Yang, and W. C. Symonds, "The Morass Engulfing Morrison Knudsen," Business Week, April 3, 1995, 54; B. O'Reilly, "Agee in Exile," Fortune, May 29, 1995, 51–74; J. Rigdon and J. Lublin, "Call to Duty: Why Morrison Board Fired Agee," Wall Street Journal, February 13, 1995, B1, B4.

4. Loeb, "Jack Welch Lets Fly."

5. O'Reilly, "Agee in Exile."

6. Ibid., 60.

7. http://www.mk.com/

8. G. Yukl, Leadership in Organizations, 2d ed. (New York: Academic Press,

1989); R. M. Stogdill, Handbook of Leadership: A Survey of the Literature (New York: Free Press, 1974).

9. R. Calori and B. Dufour, "Management European Style," Academy of Management Executive 9, no. 3 (1995): 61–70.

10. Ibid.

11. H. Mintzberg, Power in and Around Organizations (Englewood Cliffs, NJ: Prentice-Hall, 1983); J. Pfeffer, Power in Organizations (Marshfield, MA: Pitman, 1981).

12. R. P. French, Jr., and B. Raven, "The Bases of Social Power," in D. Cartwright and A. F. Zander, eds., Group Dynamics (Evanston, IL: Row, Peterson, 1960), 607–23.

13. R. L. Rose, "After Turning Around Giddings and Lewis, Fife Is Turned Out Himself," Wall Street Journal, June 22, 1993, A1.

14. J. Fierman, "Winning Ideas from Maverick Managers," Fortune, February 6, 1995, 66–80.

15. Ibid., 70.

16. J. A. Lopez, "A Better Way? Setting Your Own Pay—and Other Unusual Compensation Plans," Wall Street Journal, April 13, 1994, R6; "Maverick: The Success Story Behind the World's Most Unusual Workplace," HRMagazine (April 1994): 88–89; J. Pottinger, "Brazilian Maverick Reveals His Radical Recipe for Success," Personnel Management (September 1994): 71.

17. Fierman, "Winning Ideas from Maverick Managers."

18. A. Grove, "How Intel Makes Spending Pay Off," Fortune, February 22, 1993, 56–61.

19. Loeb, "Jack Welch Lets Fly," 146.

20. L. Bird, "Lazarus's IBM Coup Was All About Relationships," Wall Street Journal, May 26, 1994, B1, B7.

21. T. M. Burton, "Visionary's Reward: Combine 'Simple Ideas' and Some Failures; Result: Sweet Revenge," Wall Street Journal, February 3, 1995, A1, A5.

22. L. Nakarmi, "A Flying Leap Toward the 21st Century? Pressure from Competitors and Seoul May Transform the Chaebol," Business Week, March 20, 1995, 78–80.

23. B. M. Bass, Bass and Stogdill's Handbook of Leadership: Theory, Research, and Managerial Applications, 3d ed. (New York: Free Press, 1990); R. J. House and M. L. Baetz, "Leadership: Some Empirical Generalizations and New Research Directions," in B. M. Staw and L. L. Cummings, eds., Research in Organizational Behavior, vol. 1 (Greenwich, CT: JAI Press, 1979), 341–423; S. A. Kirpatrick and E. A. Locke, "Leadership: Do Traits Matter?" Academy of Management Executive 5, no. 2 (1991): 48–60; Yukl, Leadership in Organizations; G. Yukl and D. D. Van Fleet, "Theory and Research on Leadership in Organizations," in M. D. Dunnette and L. M. Hough, eds., Handbook of Industrial and Organizational Psychology, 2d ed., vol. 3 (Palo Alto, CA: Consulting Psychologists Press, 1992), 147–97.

24. E. A. Fleishman, "Performance Assessment Based on an Empirically Derived Task Taxonomy," Human Factors 9 (1967): 349–66; E. A. Fleishman, "The Description of Supervisory Behavior," Personnel Psychology 37 (1953): 1–6; A. W. Halpin and B. J. Winer, "A Factorial Study of the Leader Behavior Descriptions," in R. M. Stogdill and A. I. Coons, eds., Leader Behavior: Its Description and Measurement (Columbus _____ Bureau of Business Research, Ohio State University, 1957); D. Tscheulin, "Leader Behavior Measurement in German Industry," Journal of Applied Psychology 56 (1971): 28–31.

25. A. Taylor III, "Why GM Leads the Pack in Europe," Fortune, May 17, 1993, 83–86.

26. U. Gupta, "Starting Out; How Much? Figuring the Correct Amount of Capital for Starting a Business Can Be a Tough Balancing Act," Wall Street Journal, May 22, 1995, R7; R. Jacob, "How One Red Hot Retailer Wins Customer Loyalty," Fortune, July 10, 1995, 72–79; "Staples Taps Hanaka from Lechmere Inc. to Become Its CEO," Wall Street Journal, July 29, 1994, B2.

27. T. King, "How a Hot Ad Agency, Undone by Arrogance, Lost Its Independence," Wall Street Journal, April 11, 1995, A1, A5.

28. Ibid., A5.

29. King, "How a Hot Ad Agency."

30. E. A. Fleishman and E. F. Harris, "Patterns of Leadership Behavior Related to Employee Grievances and Turnover," Personnel Psychology 15 (1962): 43–56.

31. R. Likert, New Patterns of Management (New York: McGraw-Hill, 1961); N. C. Morse and E. Reimer, "The Experimental Change of a Major Organizational Variable," Journal of Abnormal and Social Psychology 52 (1956): 120–29.

32. R. R. Blake and J. S. Mouton, The New Managerial Grid (Houston: Gulf, 1978).

33. P. Hersey and K. Blanchard, Management of Organizational Behavior: Utilizing Human Resources (Englewood Cliffs, NJ: Prentice-Hall, 1982).

34. F. E. Fiedler, A Theory of Leadership Effectiveness (New York: McGraw-Hill, 1967); F. E. Fiedler, "The Contingency Model and the Dynamics of the Leadership Process," in L. Berkowitz, ed., Advances in Experimental Social Psychology (New York: Academic Press, 1978).

35. J. Rebello, "Radical Ways of Its CEO Are a Boon to Bank," Wall Street Journal, March 20, 1995, B1, B3.

36. Fierman, "Winning Ideas from Maverick Managers," 78.

37. Ibid.

38. M. Schuman, "Free to Be," Forbes, May 8, 1995, 78–80.

39. House and Baetz, "Leadership"; L. H. Peters, D. D. Hartke, and J. T. Pohlmann, "Fiedler's Contingency Theory of Leadership: An Application of the Meta-Analysis Procedures of Schmidt and Hunter," Psychological Bulletin 97 (1985): 274–85; C. A. Schriesheim, B. J. Tepper, and L. A. Tetrault, "Least

Preferred Co-Worker Score, Situational Control, and Leadership Effectiveness: A Meta-Analysis of Contingency Model Performance Predictions," Journal of Applied Psychology 79 (1994): 561–73.

40. M. G. Evans, "The Effects of Supervisory Behavior on the Path–goal Relationship," Organizational Behavior and Human Performance 5 (1970): 277–98; R. J. House, "A Path–Goal Theory of Leader Effectiveness," Administrative Science Quarterly 16 (1971): 321–38; J. C. Wofford and L. Z. Liska, "Path–Goal Theories of Leadership: A Meta-Analysis," Journal of Management 19 (1993): 857–76.

41. E. Norton, "Chairman of AK Steel Tries to Shake Off Tag of 'Operating Man,' " Wall Street Journal, November 25, 1994, A1, A2.

42. http://www.aksteel.com/; K. L. Alexander and S. Baker, "The Steelworkers vs. the 'Smiling Barracuda,' " Business Week, May 23, 1994, 26; M. Bensman, "Salvaging AK Steel," Institutional Investor (January 1995): 62–64; Norton, "Chairman of AK Steel."

43. S. Kerr and J. M. Jermier, "Substitutes for Leadership: Their Meaning and Measurement," Organizational Behavior and Human Performance 22 (1978): 375–403; P. M. Podsakoff, B. P. Niehoff, S. B. MacKenzie, and M. L. Williams, "Do Substitutes for Leadership Really Substitute for Leadership? An Empirical Examination of Kerr and Jermier's Situational Leadership Model," Organizational Behavior and Human Decision Processes, 54 (1993): 1–44.

44. Kerr and Jermier, "Substitutes for Leadership"; Podsakoff, Niehoff, MacKenzie, and Williams, "Do Substitutes for Leadership Really Substitute for Leadership?"

45. K. Miller, "Siemens Shapes Up," Business Week, May 1, 1995, 52–53.

46. B. M. Bass, Leadership and Performance Beyond Expectations (New York: Free Press, 1985); Bass, Bass and Stogdill's Handbook of Leadership; Yukl and Van Fleet, "Theory and Research on Leadership."

47. G. E. Schares, J. B. Levine, and P. Coy, "The New Generation at Siemens," Business Week, March 9, 1992, 46–48.

48. Miller, "Siemens Shapes Up."

49. Ibid.

50. J. A. Conger and R. N. Kanungo, "Behavioral Dimensions of Charismatic Leadership," in J. A. Conger, R. N. Kanungo, and Associates, Charismatic Leadership (San Francisco: Jossey-Bass, 1988).

51. A. L. Sprout, "Packard Bell," Fortune, June 12, 1995, 83.

52. Bass, Leadership and Performance Beyond Expectations; Bass, Bass and Stogdill's Handbook of Leadership; Yukl and Van Fleet, "Theory and Research on Leadership."

53. Ibid.

54. Miller, "Siemens Shapes Up."

55. "Combo Push from Goldstar, Zenith," Dealerscope (February 1995): 38; "L.G. Electronics Co.: South Korean Firm Raises 1995 Sales Target by 22.6%," Wall Street Journal, January 5, 1995, 10; L. Nakarmi, "Goldstar Is Burning Bright," Business Week, September 26, 1994, 129–30.

56. Nakarmi, Ibid. 129.

57. Ibid.

58. Bass, Leadership and Performance Beyond Expectations.

59. G. Rifken, "Powering the Comeback at Coopers," Forbes ASAP, October 10, 1994, 118–20.

60. Ibid.

61. A. H. Eagly and B. T. Johnson, "Gender and Leadership Style: A Meta-Analysis," Psychological Bulletin 108 (1990): 233–56.

62. Ibid.

63. Ibid.

64. Ibid.

65. Ibid.

66. A. H. Eagly, S. J. Karau, and M. G. Makhijani, "Gender and the Effectiveness of Leaders: A Meta-Analysis," Psychological Bulletin 117 (1995): 125–45.

67. Ibid.

68. P. Fritsch and C. Torres, "Mexico's Moderna to Sell Monsanto Some Seed Lines," Wall Street Journal, September 25, 1996, A14; C. Torres, "Telmex Monopoly to Face Fight from Wealthy Mexican Investor," Wall Street Journal, May 3, 1994, A10; "Upjohn Co. Is Selling Its Asgrow Seed Unit to Mexican Concern," Wall Street Journal, November 8, 1994, A2.

69. C. Torres, "Mexican Tobacco Firm Is Changing the Way Small Farmers Work," Wall Street Journal, July 26, 1995, A1, A8.

70. Ibid., A1.

71. Ibid.

Chapter 14

1. R. S. Buday, "Reengineering One Firm's Product Development and Another's Service Delivery," Planning Review (March–April 1993): 14–19; J. M. Burcke, "Hallmark's Quest for Quality Is a Job Never Done," Business Insurance, April 26, 1993, 122; M. Hammer and J. Champy, Reengineering the Corporation (New York: Harper Business, 1993); T. A. Stewart, "The Search for the Organization of Tomorrow," Fortune, May 18, 1992, 92–98.

2. Hammer and Champy, Reengineering the Corporation.

3. W. R. Coradetti, "Teamwork Takes Time and a Lot of Energy," HRMagazine (June 1994): 74–77; D. Fenn, "Service Teams That Work," Inc. (August 1995): 99; "Team Selling Catches On, but Is Sales Really a Team Sport?" Wall Street Journal, March 29, 1994, A1.

4. T. M. Mills, The Sociology of Small Groups (Englewood Cliffs, NJ: Prentice-Hall, 1967); M. E. Shaw, Group Dynamics (New York: McGraw-Hill, 1981).

5. J. Brahm, "High-Tech Tools Speed," Machine Design, January 26, 1995, 36–40; A. Farnham, "America's Most Admired Company," Fortune, February 7, 1994, 50–54; M. Loeb, "How to Grow a New Product Every Day," Fortune, November 14, 1994, 269–70; T. Stevens, "Where the Rubber Meets the Road," Industry Week, March 20, 1995, 14–18.

6. E. H. Updike, D. Woodruff, and L. Armstrong, "Honda's Civic Lesson," *Business Week,* September 18, 1995, 71–76.

7. S. Dallas, "Rock Bottom Restaurants: Brewing Up Solid Profits," *Business Week,* May 22, 1995, 74.

8. A. E. Serwer, "An Odd Couple Aims to Put Lionel on the Fast Track," *Fortune,* October 30, 1995, 21.

9. L. Armstrong and L. Holyoke, "NASA's Tiny Camera Has a Wide-Angle Future," *Business Week,* March 6, 1995, 54–55.

10. J. A. Pearce II and E. C. Ravlin, "The Design and Activation of Self-Regulating Work Groups," *Human Relations* 11 (1987): 751–82.

11. R. Henkoff, "When to Take on the Giants," *Fortune,* May 30, 1994, 111, 114.

12. B. Dumaine, "Who Needs a Boss?" *Fortune,* May 7, 1990, 52–60; Pearce and Ravlin, "The Design and Activation of Self-Regulating Work Groups."

13. Dumaine, "Who Needs a Boss"; A. R. Montebello and V. R. Buzzotta, "Work Teams That Work," *Training & Development* (March 1993): 59–64.

14. T. D. Wall, N. J. Kemp, P. R. Jackson, and C. W. Clegg, "Outcomes of Autonomous Work Groups: A Long-Term Field Experiment," *Academy of Management Journal* 29 (1986): 280–304.

15. A. Markels, "A Power Producer Is Intent on Giving Power to Its People," *Wall Street Journal,* July 3, 1995, A1, A12.

16. J. S. Lublin, "My Colleague, My Boss," *Wall Street Journal,* April 12, 1995, R4, R12.

17. W. R. Pape, "Group Insurance," *Inc. (Inc. Technology Supplement),* June 17, 1997, 29–31; A. M. Townsend, S. M. DeMarie, and A. R. Hendrickson, "Are You Ready for Virtual Teams?," *HRMagazine* (September 1996): 122–26; A. M. Townsend, S. M. DeMarie, and A. M. Hendrickson, "Virtual Teams: Technology and the Workplace of the Future," *Academy of Management Executive* 12 (3) (1998): 17–29.

18. Townsend, DeMarie, and Hendrickson, "Virtual Teams."

19. W. R. Pape, "Group Insurance,"; Townsend, DeMarie, and Hendrickson, "Are You Ready for Virtual Teams?"

20. A. Deutschman, "The Managing Wisdom of High-Tech Superstars," *Fortune,* October 17, 1994, 197–206.

21. Ibid.

22. J. D. Thompson, *Organizations in Action* (New York: McGraw-Hill, 1967).

23. Ibid.

24. Lublin, "My Colleague, My Boss."

25. R. G. LeFauve and A. C. Hax, "Managerial and Technological Innovations at Saturn Corporation," *MIT Management* (Spring 1992): 8–19.

26. B. W. Tuckman, "Developmental Sequences in Small Groups," *Psychological Bulletin* 63 (1965): 384–99; B. W. Tuckman and M. C. Jensen, "Stages of Small Group Development," *Group and Organizational Studies* 2 (1977): 419–27.

27. C. J. G. Gersick, "Time and Transition in Work Teams: Toward a New Model of Group Development," *Academy of Management Journal* 31 (1988): 9–41; C. J. G. Gersick, "Marking Time: Predictable Transitions in Task Groups," *Academy of Management Journal* 32 (1989): 274–309.

28. J. R. Hackman, "Group Influences on Individuals in Organizations," in M. D. Dunnette and L. M. Hough, eds., *Handbook of Industrial and Organizational Psychology,* 2d ed., vol. 3 (Palo Alto, CA: Consulting Psychologists Press, 1992), 199–267.

29. Ibid.

30. Ibid.

31. Lublin, "My Colleague, My Boss."

32. D. J. Yang, "Nordstrom's Gang of Four," *Business Week,* June 15, 1992, 122–23.

33. L. Festinger, "Informal Social Communication," *Psychological Review* 57 (1950): 271–82; Shaw, *Group Dynamics.*

34. Hackman, "Group Influences on Individuals in Organizations"; Shaw, *Group Dynamics.*

35. D. Cartwright, "The Nature of Group Cohesiveness," in D. Cartwright and A. Zander, eds., *Group Dynamics,* 3d ed. (New York: Harper and Row, 1968); L. Festinger, S. Schacter, and K. Black, *Social Pressures in Informal Groups* (New York: Harper and Row, 1950); Shaw, *Group Dynamics.*

36. D. A. Blackmon, "A Factory in Alabama Is the Merger in Microcosm," *Wall Street Journal,* May 5, 1998, B1, B10.

37. D. Woodruff and K. L. Miller, "Mercedes' Maverick in Alabama," *Business Week,* September 11, 1995, 64–65.

38. Blackmon, "A Factory in Alabama Is the Merger in Microcosm."

39. T. F. O'Boyle, "A Manufacturer Grows Efficient by Soliciting Ideas from Employees," *Wall Street Journal,* June 5, 1992, A1, A5.

40. Armstrong and Holyoke, "NASA's Tiny Camera."

41. Lublin, "My Colleague, My Boss."

42. H. S. Byrne, "Lifting Off," *Barron's,* March 27, 1995, 17–18; Lublin, "My Colleague, My Boss."

43. Lublin, ibid.; S. P. Talbott, "Peer Review Drives Compensation at Johnsonville," *Personnel Journal* (October 1994): 126–32.

44. Lublin, "My Colleague, My Boss."

45. P. C. Earley, "Social Loafing and Collectivism: A Comparison of the United States and the People's Republic of China," *Administrative Science Quarterly* 34 (1989): 565–81; J. M. George, "Extrinsic and Intrinsic Origins of Perceived Social Loafing in Organizations," *Academy of Management Journal* 35 (1992): 191–202; S. G. Harkins, B. Latane, and K. Williams, "Social Loafing: Allocating Effort or Taking It Easy," *Journal of Experimental Social Psychology* 16 (1980): 457–65; B. Latane, K. D. Williams, and S. Harkins, "Many Hands Make Light the Work: The Causes and Consequences of Social Loafing," *Journal of Personality and Social Psychology* 37 (1979): 822–32; J. A. Shepperd, "Productivity Loss in Performance Groups: A Motivation Analysis," *Psychological Bulletin* 113 (1993): 67–81.

46. J. M. George, "Extrinsic and Intrinsic Origins"; G. R. Jones, "Task Visibility, Free Riding, and Shirking:

Explaining the Effect of Structure and Technology on Employee Behavior," *Academy of Management Review* 9 (1984): 684–95; K. Williams, S. Harkins, and B. Latane, "Identifiability as a Deterrent to Social Loafing: Two Cheering Experiments," *Journal of Personality and Social Psychology* 40 (1981): 303–11.

47. S. Harkins and J. Jackson, "The Role of Evaluation in Eliminating Social Loafing," *Personality and Social Psychology Bulletin* 11 (1985): 457–65; N. L. Kerr and S. E. Bruun, "Ringelman Revisited: Alternative Explanations for the Social Loafing Effect," *Personality and Social Psychology Bulletin* 7 (1981): 224–31; Williams, Harkins, and Latane, "Identifiability as a Deterrent to Social Loafing."

48. M. A. Brickner, S. G. Harkins, and T. M. Ostrom, "Effects of Personal Involvement: Thought-Provoking Implications for Social Loafing," *Journal of Personality and Social Psychology* 51 (1986): 763–69; S. G. Harkins and R. E. Petty, "The Effects of Task Difficulty and Task Uniqueness on Social Loafing," *Journal of Personality and Social Psychology* 43 (1982): 1214–29.

49. B. Latane, "Responsibility and Effort in Organizations," in P. S. Goodman, ed., *Designing Effective Work Groups* (San Francisco: Jossey-Bass, 1986); Latane, Williams, and Harkins, "Many Hands Make Light the Work"; I. D. Steiner, *Group Process and Productivity* (New York: Academic Press, 1972).

50. B. Birchard, "Power to the People," *CFO* (March 1995): 38–43.

51. A. Markels, "A Power Producer Is Intent on Giving Power to Its People," *Wall Street Journal,* July 3, 1995, A1, A12.

52. Ibid.

53. Ibid.

Chapter 15

1. T. Petzinger, "Dave Hurley Gets a Lesson in Business," *Wall Street Journal,* March 14, 1997, B1.

2. Ibid.

3. G. Anders, "More Managed Health-Care Systems Use Incentive Pay to Reward 'Best' Doctors," *Wall Street Journal,* January 25, 1993, B1, B6.

4. M. Chase, "HMOs Send Doctors to School to Polish Bedside Manners," *Wall Street Journal,* April 13, 1998, B1.

5. Ibid.

6. Petzinger, "Dave Hurley Gets a Lesson in Business."

7. C. A. O'Reilly and L. R. Pondy, "Organizational Communication," in S. Kerr, ed., *Organizational Behavior* (Columbus, OH: Grid, 1979).

8. E. M. Rogers and R. Agarwala-Rogers, *Communication in Organizations* (New York: Free Press, 1976).

9. W. Nabers, "The New Corporate Uniforms," *Fortune,* November, 13, 1995, 132–56.

10. R. B. Schmitt, "Judges Try Curbing Lawyers' Body-Language Antics," *Wall Street Journal,* September 11, 1997, B1, B7.

11. D. A. Adams, P. A. Todd, and R. R. Nelson, "A Comparative Evaluation of the Impact of Electronic and Voice Mail on Organizational Communication," *Information & Management* 24 (1993): 9–21.

12. R. Winslow, "Hospitals' Weak Systems Hurt Patients, Study Says," *Wall Street Journal,* July 5, 1995, B1, B6.

13. B. Newman, "Global Chatter," *Wall Street Journal,* March 22, 1995, A1, A15.

14. "Miscommunications Plague Pilots and Air-Traffic Controllers," *Wall Street Journal,* August 22, 1995, A1.

15. R. L. Daft, R. H. Lengel, and L. K. Trevino, "Message Equivocality, Media Selection, and Manager Performance: Implications for Information Systems," *MIS Quarterly* 11 (1987): 355–66; R. L. Daft and R. H. Lengel, "Information Richness: A New Approach to Managerial Behavior and Organization Design," in B. M. Staw and L. L. Cummings, eds., *Research in Organizational Behavior* (Greenwich, CT: JAI Press, 1984).

16. R. L. Daft, *Organization Theory and Design* (St. Paul, MN: West, 1992).

17. "Lights, Camera, Meeting: Teleconferencing Becomes a Time-Saving Tool," *Wall Street Journal,* February 21, 1995, A1.

18. Daft, *Organization Theory and Design.*

19. T. J. Peters and R. H. Waterman, Jr., *In Search of Excellence* (New York: Harper and Row, 1982); T. Peters and N. Austin, *A Passion for Excellence: The Leadership Difference* (New York: Random House, 1985).

20. "Lights, Camera, Meeting."

21. B. Ziegler, "Virtual Power Lunches Will Make Passing the Salt an Impossibility," *Wall Street Journal,* June 28, 1995, B1.

22. F. A. McMorris, "Is Office Voice Mail Private? Don't Bet on It," *Wall Street Journal,* February 28, 1995, B1.

23. "E-Mail Etiquette Starts to Take Shape for Business Messaging," *Wall Street Journal,* October 12, 1995, A1.

24. "Interoffice E-Mail," *Inc.* (September 1995): 116.

25. E. Baig, "Taking Care of Business–Without Leaving the House," *Business Week,* April 17, 1995, 106–07.

26. "Life Is Good for Telecommuters, but Some Problems Persist," *Wall Street Journal,* August 3, 1995, A1.

27. "E-Mail Abuse: Workers Discover High-Tech Ways to Cause Trouble in the Office," *Wall Street Journal,* November 22, 1994, A1; "E-Mail Alert: Companies Lag in Devising Policies on How It Should Be Used," *Wall Street Journal,* December 29, 1994, A1.

28. "Employee-Newsletter Names Include the Good, the Bad, and the Boring," *Wall Street Journal,* July 18, 1995, A1.

29. O. W. Baskin and C. E. Aronoff, *Interpersonal Communication in Organizations* (Santa Monica, CA: Goodyear, 1989).

30. Magnet Media Solutions, Inc., "Internet Facts," http://www.arkansasweb.com/magnet/facts.htm.

31. P. M. Eng, "Big Business on the Net? Not Yet," *Business Week,* June 26, 1995, 100–01.

32. Ibid.; GCCGroup, "Internet Functions," http://www.gccgroup.com/netfacts.htm.

33. J. Sandberg, "Internet's Popularity in North America Appears to Be Soaring," *Wall Street Journal,* October 30, 1995, B2.

34. Magnet Media Solutions, Inc., "Internet Facts."

35. Cyberv@lley, "Internet Demographics," http://www.cybersols.com/facts.html.

36. J. W. Verity and R. Hof, "Bullet-Proofing the Net," *Business Week,* November 13, 1995, 98–99.

37. Ibid.

38. D. Jones, "On-Line Surfing Costs Firms Time and Money," *USA Today,* December 8, 1995, A1, A2.

39. M. J. Cronin, "Ford's Intranet Success," *Fortune,* March 30, 1998, 158; M. J. Cronin, "Intranets Reach the Factory Floor," *Fortune,* June 17, 1997, 122; A. L. Sprout, "The Internet Inside Your Company," *Fortune,* November 27, 1995, 161–68; J. B. White, "Chrysler's Intranet: Promise vs. Reality," *Wall Street Journal,* May 13, 1997, B1, B6.

40. Ibid.

41. Ibid.

42. G. Rifkin, "A Skeptic's Guide to Groupware," *Forbes ASAP* (1995): 76–91.

43. Ibid.

44. Ibid.

45. "Groupware Requires a Group Effort," *Business Week,* June 26, 1995, 154.

46. "On the Road," *Newsweek,* June 6, 1994, 8.

47. A. Wakizaka, "Faxes, E-Mail, Help the Deaf Get Office Jobs," *Wall Street Journal,* October 3, 1995, B1, B5.

48. L. Hays, "IBM's Helmsman Indicates That Bulk of Layoffs Is Over," *Wall Street Journal,* January 6, 1995, B3.

49. D. Tannen, "The Power of Talk," *Harvard Business Review* (September–October 1995): 138–48; D. Tannen, *Talking from 9 to 5* (New York: Avon Books, 1995).

50. Ibid.

51. Ibid.

52. Ibid.

53. Tannen, "The Power of Talk."

54. Ibid. Tannen, *Talking from 9 to 5.*

55. Ibid.

56. Tannen, "The Power of Talk," 148.

57. W. M. Bulkeley, "Will Ultimate Voice Mail Make Secretaries Obsolete?" *Wall Street Journal,* October 20, 1995, B1, B5.

58. S. H. Wildstrom, "This 'Secretary' Really Listens," *Business Week,* April 24, 1995, 19.

59. Bulkeley, "Will Ultimate Voice Mail Make Secretaries Obsolete?"

60. Ibid.

61. Wildstrom, "This 'Secretary' Really Listens."

62. Bulkeley, "Will Ultimate Voice Mail Make Secretaries Obsolete?"

63. Wildstrom, "This 'Secretary' Really Listens."

Chapter 16

1. P. M. Barrett, "How a Young Lawyer Is Making His Mark at a Washington Firm," *Wall Street Journal,* February 15, 1995, A1, A11; C. Cotts, "Starr Has Left, but K&E Is Fine," *Wall Street Journal,* August 31, 1998, A6; www.kirkland.com.

2. G. P. Zachary, "Can Unions Organize Low-Paid Workers? Watch This Woman," *Wall Street Journal,* October 23, 1995, A1, A10.

3. Barrett, "How a Young Lawyer Is Making His Mark."

4. Cotts, "Starr Has Left, but K&E Is Fine."

5. Zachary, "Can Unions Organize Low-Paid Workers?"

6. Barrett, "How a Young Lawyer Is Making His Mark."

7. Zachary, "Can Unions Organize Low-Paid Workers?"

8. Ibid.

9. J. A. Litterer, "Conflict in Organizations: A Reexamination," *Academy of Management Journal* 9 (1966): 178–86; S. M. Schmidt and T. A. Kochan, "Conflict: Towards Conceptual Clarity," *Administrative Science Quarterly* 13 (1972): 359–70; R. H. Miles, *Macro Organizational Behavior* (Santa Monica, CA: Goodyear, 1980).

10. E. Davies, "Management Style on Trial," *Fortune,* May 11, 1998, 30–32.

11. E. Davies, "Dad! Billy Keeps Suing Me!" *Fortune,* July 20, 1998, 16–18.

12. B. O'Reilly, "The Curse of the Koch Brothers," *Fortune,* February 17, 1997, 112–116.

13. Ibid.

14. E. Davies, "Dad! Billy Keeps Suing Me!"

15. S. P. Robbins, *Managing Organizational Conflict: A Nontraditional Approach* (Englewood Cliffs, NJ: Prentice-Hall, 1974); L. Coser, *The Functions of Social Conflict* (New York: Free Press, 1956).

16. L. L. Putnam and M. S. Poole, "Conflict and Negotiation," in F. M. Jablin, L. L. Putnam, K. H. Roberts, and L. W. Porter, eds., *Handbook of Organizational Communication: An Interdisciplinary Perspective* (Newbury Park, CA: Sage, 1987), 549–99.

17. J. Carlton, "Iacocca's Latest Pitch: An Indian-Run Casino in the Forests of Oregon," *Wall Street Journal,* February 14, 1995, A1, A6.

18. L. R. Pondy, "Organizational Conflict: Concepts and Models," *Administrative Science Quarterly* 2 (1967): 296–320; R. E. Walton and J. M. Dutton, "The Management of Interdepartmental Conflict: A Model and Review," *Administrative Science Quarterly* 14 (1969): 62–73.

19. G. R. Jones and J. E. Butler, "Managing Internal Corporate Entrepreneurship: An Agency Theory Perspective," *Journal of Management* 18 (1992): 733–49.

20. T. Petzinger, Jr., "All Happy Businesses Are Alike, but Heirs Bring Unique Conflicts," *Wall Street Journal,* November 17, 1995, B1.

21. J. A. Wall, Jr., "Conflict and Its Management," *Journal of Management* 21 (1995): 515–58.

22. Walton and Dutton, "The Management of Interdepartmental Conflict."

23. Pondy, "Organizational Conflict."

24. W. F. White, *Human Relations in the Restaurant Industry* (New York: McGraw-Hill, 1948).

25. K. W. Thomas, "Conflict and Negotiation Processes in Organizations," in M. D. Dunnette and L. M. Hough, eds., *Handbook of Industrial and Organizational*

Psychology, 2d ed., vol. 3 (Palo Alto, CA: Consulting Psychologists Press, 1992), 651–717.

26. E. Shapiro, J. A. Trachtenberg, and L. Landro, "Time Warner Settles Feud by Pushing Out Music Division's Fuchs," *Wall Street Journal,* November 17, 1995, A1, A6.

27. Ibid.

28. P. R. Lawrence, L. B. Barnes, and J. W. Lorsch, *Organizational Behavior and Administration* (Homewood, IL: Irwin, 1976).

29. R. Behar, "Stalked by Allstate," *Fortune,* October 2, 1995, 128–42.

30. R. J. Lewicki and J. R. Litterer, *Negotiation* (Homewood, IL: Irwin, 1985); G. B. Northcraft and M. A. Neale, *Organizational Behavior* (Fort Worth, TX: Dryden, 1994); J. Z. Rubin and B. R. Brown, *The Social Psychology of Bargaining and Negotiation* (New York: Academic Press, 1975).

31. L. Thompson and R. Hastie, "Social Perception in Negotiation," *Organizational Behavior and Human Decision Processes* 47 (1990): 98–123.

32. Thomas, "Conflict and Negotiation Processes in Organizations."

33. R. J. Lewicki, S. E. Weiss, and D. Lewin, "Models of Conflict, Negotiation and Third Party Intervention: A Review and Synthesis," *Journal of Organizational Behavior* 13 (1992): 209–52.

34. Northcraft and Neale, *Organizational Behavior.*

35. Lewicki, Weiss, and Lewin, "Models of Conflict, Negotiation and Third Party Intervention"; Northcraft and Neale, *Organizational Behavior;* D. G. Pruitt, "Integrative Agreements: Nature and Consequences," in M. H. Bazerman and R. J. Lewicki, eds., *Negotiating in Organizations* (Beverly Hills, CA: Sage, 1983).

36. R. Fischer and W. Ury, *Getting to Yes* (Boston: Houghton Mifflin, 1981); Northcraft and Neale, *Organizational Behavior.*

37. P. J. Carnevale and D. G. Pruitt, "Negotiation and Mediation," *Annual Review of Psychology* 43 (1992): 531–82.

38. A. M. Pettigrew, *The Politics of Organizational Decision Making* (London: Tavistock, 1973); Miles, *Macro Organizational Behavior.*

39. D. J. Hickson, C. R. Hinings, C. A. Lee, R. E. Schneck, and D. J. Pennings, "A Strategic Contingencies Theory of Intraorganizational Power," *Administrative Science Quarterly* 16 (1971): 216–27; C. R. Hinings, D. J. Hickson, J. M. Pennings, and R. E. Schneck, "Structural Conditions of Interorganizational Power," *Administrative Science Quarterly* 19 (1974): 22–44; J. Pfeffer, *Power in Organizations* (Boston: Pitman, 1981).

40. Pfeffer, ibid.

41. Ibid.

42. S. McCartney, "Hollywood, Silicon Valley Team Up–and Clash," *Wall Street Journal,* March 14, 1995, B1, B7.

43. M. Crozier, "Sources of Power of Lower Level Participants in Complex Organizations," *Administrative Science Quarterly* 7 (1962): 349–64; A. M. Pettigrew, "Information Control as a Power Resource," *Sociology* 6 (1972): 187–204.

44. K. Naughton and K. Kerwin, "At GM, Two Heads May Be Worse Than One," *Business Week,* August 14, 1995, 46.

45. Pfeffer, *Power in Organizations;* G. R. Salancik and J. Pfeffer, "The Bases and Uses of Power in Organizational Decision Making," *Administrative Science Quarterly* 19 (1974): 453–73; J. Pfeffer and G. R. Salancik, *The External Control of Organizations: A Resource Dependence View* (New York: Harper and Row, 1978).

46. J. S. Lublin, "Despite Poor Returns, Champion's Chairman Hangs On for 21 Years," *Wall Street Journal,* October 31, 1995, A1, A5.

47. Pfeffer, *Power in Organizations.*

48. Ibid.

49. Ibid.

50. L. Brown, "Research Action: Organizational Feedback, Understanding and Change," *Journal of Applied Behavioral Research* 8 (1972): 697–711; P. A. Clark, *Action Research and Organizational Change* (New York: Harper and Row, 1972); N.

Margulies and A. P. Raia, eds., *Conceptual Foundations of Organizational Development* (New York: McGraw-Hill, 1978).

51. W. L. French and C. H. Bell, *Organizational Development* (Englewood Cliffs, NJ: Prentice-Hall, 1990).

52. W. L. French, "A Checklist for Organizing and Implementing an OD Effort," in W. L. French, C. H. Bell, and R. A. Zawacki, eds., *Organizational Development and Transformation* (Homewood, IL: Irwin, 1994), 484–95.

Chapter 17

1. The companies are real, but their names are fictitious. Information was obtained from a personal interview with a senior manager who had experience with both companies' information systems.

2. T. A. Stewart, "Managing in a Wired Company," *Fortune,* July 11, 1994, 54.

3. N. B. Macintosh, *The Social Software of Accounting Information Systems* (New York: Wiley, 1995).

4. C. A. O'Reilly, "Variations in Decision Makers' Use of Information: The Impact of Quality and Accessibility," *Academy of Management Journal* 25 (1982): 756–71.

5. G. Stalk and T. H. Hout, *Competing Against Time* (New York: Free Press, 1990).

6. L. Uchitelle, "Airlines off Course," *San Francisco Chronicle,* September 15, 1991, 7.

7. R. Cyert and J. March, *Behavioral Theory of the Firm* (Englewood Cliffs, NJ: Prentice-Hall, 1963).

8. R. Brandt, "Agents and Artificial Life," *Business Week: The Information Revolution,* special issue (1994): 64–68.

9. E. Turban, *Decision Support and Expert Systems* (New York: Macmillan, 1988).

10. R. I. Benjamin and J. Blunt, "Critical IT Issues: The Next Ten Years," *Sloan Management Review* (Summer 1992): 7–19; W. H. Davidow and M. S. Malone, *The Virtual Corporation* (New York: Harper Business, 1992).

11. Davidow and Malone, ibid.

12. S. M. Dornbusch and W. R. Scott, *Evaluation and the Exercise of Authority* (San Francisco: Jossey-Bass, 1975).

13. J. Child, *Organization: A Guide to Problems and Practice* (London: Harper and Row, 1984).

14. C. W. L. Hill, "Airborne Express," in C. W. L. Hill and G. R. Jones, *Strategic Management: An Integrated Approach,* 2d ed. (Boston: Houghton Mifflin, 1992).

15. Macintosh, *The Social Software of Accounting Information Systems.*

16. B. Dumaine, "The Bureaucracy Busters," *Fortune,* June 17, 1991, 46.

17. P. Bradley, "Global Sourcing Takes Split-Second Timing," *Purchasing,* July 20, 1989, 52–58.

18. J. J. Donovan, *Business Re-engineering with Information Technology* (Englewood Cliffs, NJ: Prentice-Hall, 1994); C. W. L. Hill, "The Computer Industry: The New Industry of Industries," in C. W. L. Hill and G. R. Jones, *Strategic Management: An Integrated Approach,* 3d ed. (Boston: Houghton Mifflin, 1995).

19. Donovan, *Business Re-engineering with Information Technology.*

20. M. B. Gordon, "The Wireless Services Industry: True Competition Emerges," *The Red Herring* (September/October 1994): 60–62.

21. G. Bylinsky, "The Digital Factory," *Fortune,* November 14, 1994, 94.

22. E. Rich, *Artificial Intelligence* (New York: McGraw-Hill, 1983).

23. Brandt, "Agents and Artificial Life."

24. G. McWilliams, "Speech Recognition," *Business Week: The Information Revolution,* 68.

25. Benjamin and Blunt, "Critical IT Issues," 7.

26. A. D. Chandler, *The Visible Hand* (Cambridge, MA: Harvard University Press, 1977).

27. C. W. L. Hill and J. F. Pickering, "Divisionalization, Decentralization, and Performance of Large United Kingdom Companies," *Journal of Management Studies* 23 (1986): 26–50.

28. O. E. Williamson, *Markets and Hierarchies: Analysis and Anti-Trust Implications* (New York: Free Press, 1975).

29. Hill, "Airborne Express."

30. Turban, *Decision Support and Expert Systems.*

31. N. A. Nichols, "Scientific Management at Merck: An Interview with CFO Judy Lewent," *Harvard Business Review* (January–February 1994): 88–91.

32. Turban, *Decision Support and Expert Systems.*

33. Ibid., 346.

34. Rich, *Artificial Intelligence.*

35. P. P. Bonisson and H. E. Johnson, "Expert Systems for Diesel Electric Locomotive Repair," *Human Systems Management* 4 (1985): 1–25.

36. Davidow and Malone, *The Virtual Corporation.*

37. Ibid.

38. Ibid., 168.

39. Stewart, "Managing in a Wired Company," 44–56.

40. G. Rifkin, "Digital Blue Jeans Pour Data and Legs into Customized Fit," *New York Times,* November 11, 1994, A1, C4.

41. See J. R. Meredith, "The Implementation of Computer Based Systems," *Journal of Operational Management* (October 1981); Turban, *Decision Support and Expert Systems;* R. J. Thierauf, *Effective Management and Evaluation of Information Technology* (London: Quorum Books, 1994).

42. S. L. Alter, *Decision Support Systems* (Reading, MA: Addison-Wesley, 1980).

43. T. H. Davenport, R. G. Eccles, and L. Prusak, "Information Politics," *Sloan Management Review* (Fall 1992): 53–65.

44. J. Pfeffer, *Managing with Power* (Boston: Harvard Business School Press, 1992).

45. G. Dickson and J. C. Wetherby, "MIS Project Management: Myths, Opinions, and Realities," in W. McFarlin, ed., *Information Systems Administration* (New York: Holt, Rinehart, and Winston, 1993).

46. H. Mintzberg, *Mintzberg on Management: Inside Our Strange World of Organizations* (New York: Free Press, 1989).

47. From an interview conducted by C. W. L. Hill with a senior Boeing manager.

48. Stewart, "Managing in a Wired Company," 54.

49. "Woolworth Keeps Mainframes in Client/Server Push," *Chain Store Age Executive* 71 (1995): 112–14.

Chapter 18

1. Amal Kumar Naj, "Shifting Gears," *Wall Street Journal,* May 7, 1993, A1.

2. The view of quality as including reliability goes back to the work of W. Edwards Deming and Joseph Juran. See A. Gabor, *The Man Who Discovered Quality* (New York: Times Books, 1990).

3. D. F. Abell, *Defining the Business: The Starting Point of Strategic Planning* (Englewood Cliffs, NJ: Prentice-Hall, 1980).

4. For details see "Johnson & Johnson (A)," *Harvard Business School Case* #384-053.

5. M. E. Porter, *Competitive Advantage* (New York: Free Press, 1985).

6. According to Richard D'Aveni, the process of pushing price/attribute curves to the right is a characteristic of the competitive process. See R. D'Aveni, *Hypercompetition* (New York: Free Press, 1994).

7. This is a central insight of the modern manufacturing literature. See R. H. Hayes and S. C. Wheelwright, "Link Manufacturing Process and Product Life Cycles," *Harvard Business Review* (January–February 1979): 127–36; R. H. Hayes and S. C. Wheelwright, "Competing Through Manufacturing," *Harvard Business Review* (January–February 1985): 99–109.

8. L. Therrien, "Spreading the Message," *Business Week,* October 25, 1991, 60.

9. B. O'Brian, "Flying on the Cheap," *Wall Street Journal,* October 26, 1992, A1; B. O'Reilly, "Where Service Flies Right," *Fortune,* August 24, 1992, 116–17; A. Salpukas, "Hurt in Expansion, Airlines Cut Back and May Sell Hubs," *Wall Street Journal,* April 1, 1993, A1, C8.

10. K. Done, "Toyota Warns of Continuing Decline," *Financial Times,* November 23, 1993, 23.

11. The view of quality as reliability goes back to the work of Deming and Juran; see Gabor, *The Man Who Discovered Quality.*

12. See D. Garvin, "What Does Product Quality Really Mean?" *Sloan Management Review* 26 (Fall 1984): 25–44; P. B. Crosby, *Quality Is Free* (New York: Mentor, 1980); Gabor, *The Man Who Discovered Quality.*

13. N. Templin, "Toyota Is Standout Once Again," *Wall Street Journal,* May 28, 1993, B1.

14. See J. W. Dean and D. E. Bowen, "Management Theory and Total Quality: Improving Research and Practice Through Theory Development," *Academy of Management Review* 19 (1994): 392–418.

15. For general background information see J. C. Anderson, M. Rungtusanatham, and R. G. Schroeder, "A Theory of Quality Management Underlying the Deming Management Method," *Academy of Management Review* 19 (1994): 472–509; "How to Build Quality," *The Economist,* September 23, 1989, 91–92; Gabor, *The Man Who Discovered Quality;* Crosby, *Quality Is Free.*

16. W. E. Deming, "Improvement of Quality and Productivity Through Action by Management," *National Productivity Review* 1 (Winter 1981–82): 12–22.

17. D. Kearns, "Leadership Through Quality," *Academy of Management Executive* 4 (1990): 86–89; J. Sheridan, "America's Best Plants," *Industry Week,* October 15, 1990, 27–40.

18. R. Winslow, "Exercising Waste," *Wall Street Journal,* November 3, 1993, A1.

19. L. Cochrane, "Not Just Another Quality Snowjob," *Wall Street Journal,* May 24, 1993, A10.

20. J. Bowles, "Is American Management Really Committed to Quality?" *Management Review* (April 1992): 42–46.

21. O. Port and G. Smith, "Quality," *Business Week,* November 30, 1992, 66–75.

22. V. Houlder, "Two Steps Forward, One Step Back," *Financial Times,* October 31, 1994, 8.

23. Bowles, "Is American Management Really Committed to Quality?"

24. Gabor, *The Man Who Discovered Quality.*

25. Deming, "Improvement of Quality and Productivity."

26. W. E. Deming, *Out of the Crisis* (Cambridge, MA: MIT Center for Advanced Engineering Study, 1986).

27. M. A. Cusumano, *The Japanese Automobile Industry* (Cambridge, MA: Harvard University Press, 1989); Ohno Taiichi, *Toyota Production System* (Cambridge, MA: Productivity Press, 1990; Japanese edition, 1978); J. P. Womack, D. T. Jones, and D. Roos, *The Machine That Changed the World* (New York: Macmillan, 1990).

28. J. Griffiths, "Europe's Manufacturing Quality and Productivity Still Lag Far Behind Japan's," *Financial Times,* November 4, 1994, 11.

29. S. McCartney, "Compaq Borrows Wal-Mart's Idea to Boost Production," *Wall Street Journal,* June 17, 1994, B4.

30. S. C. Wheelwright and K. B. Clark, *Managing New Product and Process Development* (New York: Free Press, 1993).

31. P. Nemetz and L. Fry, "Flexible Manufacturing Organizations: Implications for Strategy Formulation," *Academy of Management Review* 13 (1988): 627–38; N. Greenwood, *Implementing Flexible Manufacturing Systems* (New York: Halstead Press, 1986).

32. M. Williams, "Back to the Past," *Wall Street Journal,* 1994, October 24, 1994, A1.

33. G. Stalk and T. M. Hout, *Competing Against Time* (New York: Free Press, 1990).

34. For an interesting discussion of some other drawbacks of JIT and other "Japanese" manufacturing techniques see S. M. Young, "A Framework for Successful

Adoption and Performance of Japanese Manufacturing Practices in the United States," *Academy of Management Review* 17 (1992): 677–701.

35. A. Kumar Naj, "Shifting Gears," *Wall Street Journal,* May 7, 1993, A1; B. Dumaine, "The Trouble with Teams," *Fortune,* September 5, 1994, 86–92.

36. Ibid.

37. See C. W. L. Hill, "Transaction Cost Economizing as a Source of National Competitive Advantage: The Case of Japan," *Organization Science* (1994); M. Aoki, *Information, Incentives, and Bargaining in the Japanese Economy* (Cambridge: Cambridge University Press, 1989).

38. J. Hoerr, "The Payoff from Teamwork," *Business Week,* July 10, 1989, 56–62.

39. M. Imai, *"Kaizen": The Key to Japan's Competitive Success* (New York: Random House, 1987).

40. R. Gourlay, "Back to Basics on the Factory Floor," *Financial Times,* January 4, 1994, 12.

41. S. M. Young, "A Framework for Successful Adoption and performance of Japanese Manufacturing Practices in the United States," *Academy of Management Review* 17 (1992): 677–700.

42. Gourlay, "Back to Basics on the Factory Floor."

43. M. Hammer and J. Champy, *Reengineering the Corporation* (New York: Harper Business, 1993), 35.

44. Ibid., 46.

45. Ibid.

46. For example, see Houlder, "Two Steps Forward, One Step Back"; Naj, "Shifting Gears"; D. Greising, "Quality: How to Make It Pay," *Business Week,* August 8, 1994, 54–59.

47. L. Helm and M. Edid, "Life on the Line: Two Auto Workers Who Are Worlds Apart," *Business Week,* September 30, 1994, 76–78.

48. J. Flint, " 'Constant Improvement' or Speedup?" *Forbes,* April 17, 1989, 94.

49. Dumaine, "The Trouble with Teams."

50. K. K. Reiste and A. Hubrich, "Work-Team Implementation," *Hospital Management Quarterly* (February 1996): 47–53.

Chapter 19

1. C. Christensen, "Quantum Corporation: Business Teams and Product Teams," in K. B. Clark and S. C. Wheelwright, *Managing New Product and Process Development* (New York: Free Press, 1993).

2. S. Tully, "The Modular Corporation," *Fortune,* February 8, 1993, 196–214.

3. Christensen, "Quantum Corporation."

4. See R. D'Aveni, *Hyper-Competition* (New York: Free Press, 1994); P. Anderson and M. L. Tushman, "Technological Discontinuities and Dominant Design: A Cyclical Model of Technological Change," *Administrative Science Quarterly* 35 (1990): 604–33.

5. J. A. Schumpeter, *Capitalism, Socialism and Democracy* (New York: Harper, 1942).

6. V. P. Buell, *Marketing Management* (New York: McGraw-Hill, 1985).

7. See M. M. J. Berry and J. H. Taggart, "Managing Technology and Innovation: A Review," *R&D Management* 24 (1994): 341–53; Clark and Wheelwright, *Managing New Product and Process Development.*

8. E. Abrahamson, "Managerial Fads and Fashions: The Diffusion and Rejection of Innovations," *Academy of Management Review* 16 (1991): 586–612.

9. See Berry and Taggart, "Managing Technology and Innovation"; M. Gort and J. Klepper, "Time Paths in the Diffusion of Product Innovations," *Economic Journal* (September 1982): 630–53. Looking at the history of 46 different products, Gort and Klepper found that the length of time before other companies entered the markets created by a few inventive companies declined from an average of 14.4 years for products introduced before 1930 to 4.9 years for those introduced after 1949—implying that product life cycles were being compressed. Also see A. Griffin, "Metrics for Measuring Product Development Cycle Time," *Journal of Production and Innovation Management* 10 (1993): 112–25.

10. Clark and Wheelwright, *Managing New Product and Process Development.* Also see G. Stalk and T. M. Hout, *Competing Against Time* (New York: Free Press, 1990).

11. C. W. L. Hill, "The New Industry of Industries?" in C. W. L. Hill and G. R. Jones, *Strategic Management: An Integrated Approach,* 2d ed. (Boston: Houghton Mifflin, 1992), 135–54.

12. See Clark and Wheelwright, *Managing New Product and Process Development;* R. E. Gomory, "From the Ladder of Science to the Product Development Cycle," *Harvard Business Review* (November–December 1989): 99–105; Stalk and Hout, *Competing Against Time.*

13. See M. R. Millson, D. P. Raj, and D. Wilemon, "A Survey of Major Approaches for Accelerating New Product Development," *Journal of Product Innovation Management* 9 (1992): 53–69, Stalk and Hout, *Competing Against Time.*

14. In the language of strategic management, the company may be able to capture a first-mover advantage. See C. W. L. Hill, M. Heeley, and J. Sakson, "Strategies for Profiting from Technological Product Innovation," *Advances in Global High Technology Management* 3 (1993): 79–95.

15. Stalk and Hout, *Competing Against Time;* B. Buell and R. D. Hof, "Hewlett-Packard Rethinks Itself," *Business Week,* April 11, 1991, 76–79.

16. See E. Mansfield, "How Economists See R&D," *Harvard Business Review* (November–December 1981): 98–106; B. Avishai and W. Taylor, "Customers Drive a Technology Driven Company," *Harvard Business Review* (November–December 1989): 107–14.

17. B. Dumaine, "Payoff from the New Management," *Fortune,* December 13, 1993, 103–10.

18. C. Power et al., "Flops: Too Many New Products Fall," *Business Week,* August 16, 1993, 76–82.

19. K. B. Clark and T. Fujimoto, "The Power of Product Integrity," *Harvard Business Review* (November–December 1990): 107–19.

20. Ibid.

21. K. B. Clark and T. Fujimoto, "Lead Time in Automobile Product Development: Explaing the Japanese Advantage," *Journal of Engineering and Technology Management* 6 (1989): 25–58.

22. B. Dumaine, "Payoff from the New Management."

23. C. W. L. Hill, "The Efficacy of the New Product Development Process," working paper, University of Washington, 1994.

24. Clark and Wheelwright, *Managing New Product and Process Development.*

25. Ibid.

26. G. K. Gill, "Motorola Inc.: Bandit Pager Project," *Harvard Business School Case* #690-043.

27. Ibid.

28. A. Griffin and J. R. Hauser, "Patterns of Communication Among Marketing, Engineering, and Manufacturing," *Management Science* 38 (1992): 360–73; R. K. Moenaert, W. E. Sounder, A. D. Meyer, and D. Deschoolmeester, "R&D–Marketing Integration Mechanisms, Communication Flows, and Innovation Success," *Journal of Production and Innovation Management* 11 (1994): 31–45.

29. See G. Barczak and D. Wileman, "Leadership Differences in New Product Development Teams," *Journal of Product Innovation Management* 6 (1989): 259–67; E. F. McDonough and G. Barczak, "Speeding Up New Product Development: The Effects of Leadership Style and Source of Technology," *Journal of Product Innovation Management* 8 (1991): 203–11; Clark and Fujimoto, "The Power of Product Integrity."

30. Clark and Wheelwright, *Managing New Product and Process Development.*

31. Clark and Fujimoto, "The Power of Product Integrity."

32. J. R. Heartly, *Concurrent Engineering* (Cambridge, MA: Productivity Press, 1992).

33. See B. Avishai and W. Taylor, "Customers Drive a Technology Driven Company," *Harvard Business Review* (November–December 1989): 107–14;

W. E. Sounder, "Managing Relations Between R&D and Marketing in New Product Development Projects," *Journal of Product Innovation Management* 5 (1988): 6–19; B. J. Zinger and M. M. Madique, "A Model of New Product Development: An Empirical Test," *Management Science* 36 (1990): 867–83.

34. C. W. L. Hill, "The Boeing Corporation: Commercial Aircraft Operations,"

in C. W. L. Hill and G. R. Jones, *Strategic Management: An Integrated Approach,* 3d ed. (Boston: Houghton Mifflin, 1995).

35. Information from remarks made by Boeing vice president Dean Cruze in a presentation to an MBA class at the University of Washington.

36. "The Mind's Eye," *The Economist,* survey of manufacturing technology; March 5, 1994, 7–11.

37. Mansfeld, "How Economists See R&D."

38. J. Keebler, "Ford Merges World Design," *Automotive News* (July 1993): 1.

39. T. Lonier, "Some Insights and Statistics on Working Solo" (www.workingsolo.com).

Photo Credits

Chapter 1

P1-1, page 3: Bernard Gotfryd/Woodfin Camp & Associates, Inc.

P1-2, page 3: AP/Wide World Photos/ Paul Sakuma.

P1-4, page 13: AP/Wide World Photos/ Jim Cooper.

P1-5, page 18: Mark Peterson/SABA.

P1-6, page 25: Michael Rosenfeld/Tony Stone Images.

P1-7, page 29: Reuters/John Hillery/Archive Photos.

Chapter 2

P2-1, page 37: CORBIS/Austrian Archives.

P2-2, page 37: Chad Ehlers/International Stock

P2-3, page 43: Corbis-Bettmann.

P2-4, page 45: 20th Century Fox (Courtesy Kobal).

P2-5, page 47: AP/Wide World Photos.

P2-7, page 58: Tom Wagner/SABA.

Chapter 3

P3-1, page 75 AP/Wid World Photos.

P3-2, page 75 Reuters/Jeff Christensen/Archive Photos.

P3-4, page 81: Corporate Archives, Merck & Co., Inc.

P3-5, page 88: Rick Maiman/SYGMA.

P3-6, page 91: Bart Bartholomew.

P3-7, page 94: Daniel Simon/Liaison Agency, Inc.

Chapter 4

P4-1, page 109: Kaku Kurita/Liaison Agency Inc.

P4-2, page 109: Frederick Charles/ Liaison Agency Inc.

P4-3, page 115: Jon Chiasson/Liaison Agency Inc.

P4-4, page 120: Fritz Hoffmann/The Image Works.

P4-5, page 125: Robert Wallis/SABA.

Chapter 5

P5-1, page 145: Roger Ressmeyer/c CORBIS.

P5-2, page 145: Brad Markel/Liaison Agency Inc.

P5-4, page 163: Courtesy McDonald's Corporation.

P5-5, page 174: Ed Quinn/SABA.

P5-6, page 177: Courtesy of United Parcel Service.

P5-7, page 177: Courtesy of United Parcel Service.

P5-8, page 181: Michael Schwarz/Liaison Agency Inc.

Chapter 6

P6-1, page 193: Charly Franklin/FPG International LLC.

P6-2, page 193: Telegraph Colour Library/FPG International LLC.

P6-3, page 196: Paul Lowe/Magnum Photos, Inc.

P6-4, page 207: Paul S. Howell/Liaison Agency Inc.

Chapter 7

P7-1, page 229: Sharon Hoogstraten.

P7-2, page 229: Sharon Hoogstraten.

P7-4, page 244: George Chan/Tony Stone Images.

P7-5, page 249: Peter Blakely/SABA.

P7-6, page 255: Doug Plummer/Photo Researchers.

Chapter 8

P8-1, page 269: © Chicago Tribune. Tribune photo by Chris Walker.

P8-2, page 269: Bart Bartholomew.

P8-3, page 274: Alain Benainous/Liaison Agency Inc.

P8-4, page 276: Bernard Boutrit/Woodfin Camp & Associates, Inc.

P8-6, page 301: Mike Yamashita/ Woodfin Camp & Associates, Inc.

Chapter 9

P9-1, page 311: Christopher Bissel/Tony Stone Images.

P9-2, page 311: Loren Santow/Tony Stone Images.

P9-3, page 313: Scala/Art Resource, NY.

P9-5, page 325: Tom Wagner/SABA.

P9-6, page 335: Courtesy of Southwest Airlines

Chapter 10

P10-1, page 347: Michael L. Abramson.

P10-2, page 347: Michael Rosenfeld/Tony Stone Images

P10-3, page 351: AP/Wide World Photos/Jeff Carlick

P10-4, page 361: AP/Wide World Photos/Town Talk, Stephen Reed.

P10-6, page 375: Richard Howard/Black Star.

Chapter 11

P11-1, page 387: c Miles Landin.

P11-2, page 387: Reuters/Rose Prouser/Archive Photos.

P11-3, page 395: AP/Wide World Photos/Susan Sterner.

P11-4, page 409: AP/Wide World Photos/Peter Cosgrove.

P11-5, page 416: William Mercer McLeod.

Chapter 12

P12-1, page 425: JamesLeynse/SABA.

P12-2, page 425: Sharon Hoogstraten.

P12-3, page 440: John Abbott.

P12-4, page 443: Cortesy of the Lincoln Electric Company, Cleveland Ohio.

P12-5, page 450: James Schnepf/Liaison Agency Inc.

Chapter 13

P13-1, page 461: Mark Peterson/SABA.

P13-2, page 461: Liason Agency Inc.

P13-3, page 465: Mark Segal/Index Stock.

P13-4, page 467: AP/Wide World Photos/Lou Krasky

P13-5, page 478: Shawn Henry/SABA.

P13-6, page : Archive Photos/Reuters/Mike Theiler.

Chapter 14

P14-1, page 497: David J. Sams/Tony Stone Images.

P14-2, page 497: Courtesy Hallmark Cards, Inc.

P14-3, page 505: c CORBIS/Neal Preston.

P14-4, page 514: Karine Weinberger/Liaison Agency Inc.

P14-5, page 522: Brian Smale.

Chapter 15

P15-1, page 535: Tom Campbell/Allstock/PNI.

P15-2, page 535: Charles Gupton/Tony Stone Images.

P15-3, page 543: Paul Chesley/Tony Stone Images.

P15-4, page 551: Courtesy of Microsoft Corporation.

P15-5a, page 563: Ellen Senisi/The Image Works.

P15-5b, page 563: Bob Krist/Tony Stone Images.

Chapter 16

P16-1, page 573: PhotoDisc, Inc.

P16-2, page 573: Jose Azel/Aurora/PNI.

P16-3, page 577: Porter Gifford/Liaison Agency Inc.

P16-4, page 588: Tom Smart/Liaison Agency Inc.

P16-5, page 588: Photofest.

Chapter 17

P17-1, page 612: Source: T.A. Stewart, "Managing in a Wired Company," *Fortune,* July 11, 1994. NETMAP Software Systems, ATLA Analytics, Inc., Dublin, OH.

P17-2, page 612: Source: T.A. Stewart, "Managing in a Wired Company," *Fortune,* July 11, 1994. NETMAP Software Systems, ATLA Analytics, Inc., Dublin, OH.

P17-3, page 616: Jeff Greenberg/The Image Works.

P17-6, page 632: Courtesy Levi Strauss & Co.

P17-7, page 632: Courtesy Levi Strauss & Co.

Chapter 18

P18-1, page 643: Peter Yates/SABA.

P18-2, page 650: PhotoDisc, Inc.

P18-3, page 650: Courtesy of Southwest Airlines.

P18-4, page 667: Courtesy Toyota Motor Manufacturing, Kentucky, Inc.

P18-5, page 668: John Chiasson/Liaison Agency Inc.

Chapter 19

P19-1, page 679: Joseph Pobereskin/Tony Stone Images.

P19-2, page 679: Peter Samuels/Tony Stone Images.

P19-3, page 682: Michael Rosenfeld/Tony Stone Images.

P19-4, page 686: Reuters/HO/Archive Photos.

P19-5, page 691: James Schnepf/Liaison Agency Inc.

P19-6, page 700: Todd Buchanan.

Index

Names

Subjects